A Reference Grammar of French

A Reference Grammar of French is a lively, wide-ranging and original handbook on the structure of the French language. It includes new information on register, pronunciation, gender, number, foreign words (Latin, Arabic, English, Spanish, Italian), adjectives and past participles used as nouns, texting, word order, frequency of occurrence of words, and usage with all geographical names. Examples come not only from France, but also from Quebec, Belgium and Switzerland. Readers will appreciate the initial passages illustrating the grammatical features of a given chapter. Also included is a user-friendly introduction to the French language, from its Latin origins to modern times. A full glossary explains any terms that might confuse the less experienced reader, and the index leads the student through the detailed labyrinth of grammatical features. This handbook will be an invaluable resource for students and teachers who want to perfect their knowledge of all aspects of French grammar.

R. E. BATCHELOR taught French and Spanish for forty years in the Department of Modern Languages at the University of Nottingham. He has published thirteen books, some on the French language, with second and third editions.

M. CHEBLI-SAADI is a senior lecturer-researcher at the Université Stendhal Grenoble 3. She has published many articles, books and dictionaries, and has a long experience in teaching French to foreign students, notably from the USA.

A Reference Grammar of
French

R. E. BATCHELOR
University of Nottingham

M. CHEBLI-SAADI
Université Stendhal Grenoble 3

CAMBRIDGE UNIVERSITY PRESS
Cambridge, New York, Melbourne, Madrid, Cape Town,
Singapore, São Paulo, Delhi, Tokyo, Mexico City

Cambridge University Press
The Edinburgh Building, Cambridge CB2 8RU, UK

Published in the United States of America by Cambridge University Press, New York

www.cambridge.org
Information on this title: www.cambridge.org/9780521145114

First published 2011

Printed in the United Kingdom at the University Press, Cambridge

A catalog record for this publication is available from the British Library

Library of Congress Cataloging in Publication data
Batchelor, R. E. (Ronald Ernest)
A reference grammar of French / R. E. Batchelor, M. Chebli-Saadi.
    p.   cm. – (Reference grammars)
Text in English and French.
Includes bibliographical references and index.
ISBN 978-0-521-19673-4 (hardback)
1. French language – Grammar.   2. French language – Textbooks for foreign speakers.
I. Chebli-Saadi, M.   II. Title.
PC2111.B35793   2011
448.2'421 – dc22   2011009498

ISBN 978-0-521-19673-4 Hardback
ISBN 978-0-521-14511-4 Paperback

Contents | Table des matières

Preface | Préface

The study of French grammar offers us a striking penetration into the national mind of France and into the French speaker's sense of cultural identity and civilization. The year 2009 witnessed a passionate, national debate, launched by President Sarkozy, on the significance of being French. An integral contribution to this debate was made by a French economist who distinguishes below one feature above all others in the pursuit of national identity and consciousness: the French language with all its anomalies of pronunciation, spelling and grammatical inconsistencies. We make no apologies for quoting in full his most lucid article on what it means to be French. The emphasis in three sentences has been added by the authors.

Le billet d'Alain Minc
Essayiste

A chacun son identité nationale

Point n'est besoin d'aller dans les préfectures pour s'interroger sur l'identité nationale. C'est un jeu auquel chacun peut, seul, se livrer. Pour ma part, je ne crois plus à la vieille ritournelle de Renan : « La nation, un plébiscite quotidien. » Quand l'Allemagne était impériale, la Grande-Bretagne aristocratique, l'Italie monarchique, le « plébiscite » sur nos valeurs égalitaires et libérales avait un sens. Aujourd'hui, les Occidentaux partagent tous les mêmes idéaux de liberté et de contrat social. Il n'y a plus, de ce point de vue, d'exception française. Qu'est-ce qui fonde la France ? Une mémoire, une culture ? Dans un univers mondialisé et bouleversé par Internet, ces traits s'estompent. *La racine de notre identité, c'est, aujourd'hui, à mes yeux, la langue. Le français est notre bien commun ; il nous différencie ; il sous-tend un esprit, une manière de penser, une façon d'être. Lui seul nous distingue des Allemands ou des Espagnols.* Mais si nous faisons nôtre cette idée, il est alors impératif de préserver la langue comme un tabernacle, de lui garantir un enseignement de qualité, de la faire évoluer sans lui porter atteinte, de conserver ses bizarreries, y compris orthographiques ou grammaticales, d'en faire notre territoire de l'esprit. Réfléchissez. Y a-t-il un autre élément qui nous réunisse avec une telle force ? Aucun.

Directsoir No. 650, mardi 24 novembre 2009, p. 2

This volume is designed to provide a clear, practical and comprehensive guide to the grammar of the French language. The principal aim of the book is to be both as complete and as straightforward as possible, avoiding much technical terminology that risks clouding the understanding of the linguistic processes of the French language. It provides a point of reference for any serious student or teacher who seeks information on the broad sweep of French grammar and its intricate detail, and who has already covered its basic structures. It hopes to provide an instrument for all those attracted by the study and mastery of French grammar by supplying close and detailed guidance on the numerous linguistic elements associated with pronunciation, alphabet, register or levels of language, gender, number, syntax, parts of speech, word order, use of verbs, and the varieties within each of these elements. Its ambition is to demonstrate that, although French is not identical in all places, any more than English retains an easy global homogeneity, it is a possible and desirable vehicle for foreign students of the language in communicating across frontiers and establishing a meaningful dialogue with numerous peoples who have inherited a fruitful and powerful method of expression.

All grammatical features are accompanied with a wealth of natural and attested examples. These examples are often presented in the feminine form. The text avoids sexist bias and reaches out to females and males alike.

Many of the chapters start with, or/and include within them, a small piece of French illustrating the function and use of the grammatical features under consideration. The relevant points are highlighted in bold. The creative skill of one of the authors (Dr. Malliga Saadi) comes into play here. Inevitably, there exists an artificial element in these pieces, but an elegant and relevant creativity is guaranteed.

It may be contended that some of the subsections in Part X, such as proper names or foreign and indigenous terms, do not correspond to grammatical structures, but it is considered that they would be of great usefulness in the articulation of these structures.

It should be emphasized that constant cross-referencing will help the reader gain a clear and more rounded picture of all the grammatical points. A few grammatical points are developed in two different chapters, so that there is here some very slight overlapping. Needless to add, treatment of the same feature is angled differently in these separate chapters.

American English takes precedence over British English. American spelling is preferred to its English counterpart but this should present no problem whatever to the non-American learner. Where there could be lexical misinterpretation, both American and British terms appear side by side.

Translations are sometimes provided for complete sentences, and occasionally for individual words, when the meaning is not clear. Otherwise, no translation appears. Furnishing a maximum amount of information on the French language had to be weighed against the systematic inclusion of translations which would have reduced the available space. As far as the vocabulary goes, modern dictionaries carry out this function more than adequately.

The book contains a general glossary which will help in understanding any semi-technical grammatical expressions that may arise. Regular use of this glossary will assist in understanding the terms appearing in the text. It is so much easier to come to grips with the grammar of a foreign language if an insight is gained into the way in which even the English language functions.

The text also has a comprehensive index designed for locating any particular point of grammar.

The book is up-to-date. For instance, it contains a section on the problems of gender now that females are working in fields once inaccessible to them. Compound nouns, once unusual in French, except for just a few, are springing up like mushrooms, and the text pays serious attention to them.

Register differences are not ignored. A regular preoccupation is the variation in colloquial or spoken language, as opposed to the written word, and a simple system of R1, R2, R3 is used, designating colloquial, standard and elevated or literary language respectively. It should be borne in mind that the present grammar does not simply offer a presentation of the standard language but, much more, it attempts to examine the state of the French language, a quite different preoccupation. In other words, we are not merely concerned with perfect grammatical accuracy promoted by the purist but also with varieties of register which any serious student will encounter at every turn. Where there are colloquial constructions that are unacceptable to many, and which could be clearly incorrect, this is indicated by the R1 assignation.

One of the authors' aims is to avoid the "dry as dust" mentality, so excoriated by Hemingway (this is his quote), that risks blighting so many grammars of whatever language, and alienating the student or teacher. Numerous references of a cultural, historical, literary, artistic, geographical, scientific and even biblical nature combine with a lighter touch involving play on words, humor, witticisms and a colorful range of expression intended to invest the work with an attractive, engaging and unique style. References are also made to other Romance languages (Italian and Spanish) to offer a more rounded, comprehensive picture. To some extent, it is grammar in context. Such an approach does not detract in any way from the intellectual rigor of the work. The aim is to combine the serious study of French grammar with an exploration of the way in which French speakers view the world and of their understanding and expression of certain values. As Alex Taylor says in his *Bouche bée tout ouïe ... ou comment tomber amoureux des langues* (2010, pp. 234–235): "Si l'on veut que les gens apprennent les langues, il faut cesser de les présenter comme une suite laborieuse de règles grammaticales... mais plutôt comme une façon de voir le monde, forgées par les expériences et les valeurs uniques de tous ceux qui les parlent."

The study of grammar is not a sterile and disaffecting pursuit. It does not exist in a vacuum. Grammatical accuracy in French will provide an entry into a splendid and admirable culture and civilization, the study of which will lead to an enrichment and flowering of one's personality. It is the hope and expectation of the authors that a firm and fluent command of French, and its grammar, will form part of a felicitous and fertile relationship between the worlds of English and French speakers.

Acknowledgments | Remerciements

An indispensable contribution to this volume was made by two French-speaking university colleagues whose willingness to be submitted to a merciless bombardment of questions is only equaled by their passion for the English language: Mme Anne-Marie Antonouris and M. Philippe Lanoë. The latter carries a splendid and unrivaled Astérix baggage.

One of the authors would also like to thank for the first time Helen Barton, commissioning editor, who has encouraged him unflaggingly over the years in his numerous ventures with Cambridge University Press. Finally, this volume has benefited immeasurably from the excellent contribution made by our copy editor, Leah Morin, whose splendid sense of accuracy and awareness of the intricacies of French grammar have provided the text with its final polish.

Brief introduction to the French language (with reference to the French of francophone countries) / Brève introduction à la langue française (avec référence au français des pays francophones)

French is the official language of twenty-nine independent states and is spoken, to a greater or lesser extent, in fifty-one or fifty-two countries.[1] Most recent calculations suggest that over 200 million use it as a first or second language. Although not as diffuse as English, but certainly more so than Spanish, since it enjoys currency on five continents and Spanish

---

[1] Henriette Walter suggests fifty-two in *Le français d'ici, de là, de là-bas* (1998, p. 135). The figure 1 beside a country indicates the authors' serious reservations about any validity over claims for *francophonie* for this country. The figure 2 beside a country indicates that French is spoken by a percentage of the population, and this could vary from country to country, who use it as a mother tongue, or as a major second language: Albanie 1, Belgique, Belgique (communauté francophone), Bénin, Brunswick 1, Bulgarie 1, Burkina Faso, Burundi 2, Cambodge 1, Canada: Nouveau, Cap-Vert 1, Centrafrique, Comores, Congo, Congo (République démocratique = RDC), Côte d'Ivoire, Djibouti, Dominique 1, Égypte 1, France, Gabon, Guinée, Guinée-Bissau 1, Guinée Équatoriale, Haïti, Laos 1, Liban 2, Luxembourg, Macédoine 1, Madagascar, Mali, Maroc 2, Maurice, Mauritanie, Moldavie 1, Niger, Pologne 1, Roumanie 1, Rwanda 2, Sainte-Lucie 2, São Tomé et Principe 1, Sénégal, Seychelles 2, Suisse 2, Tchad, Togo, Tunisie 2, Vanuatu, Viêtnam, Zaïre.

There exists some residue of French in countries like Cambodia, Vietnam and Lebanon as a result of the French presence in their colonial past. Algeria provides an interesting case, since, following independence in 1962, French was disowned and, to some extent, replaced by its rival English, with the result that, since the 1980s, numerous Algerian students have pursued their university careers in the UK, USA and Canada, and not in France. Political choices are visible here. However, French has experienced a resurgence of interest, and one may calculate that 30 percent of Algerians speak and write French.

Nevertheless, this list does not include the following, and there seems to be no understandable reason for this: Quebec, Guyana, Martinique, Guadeloupe, Monaco, Saint-Pierre and Miquelon, and Mayotte where French is an official language. This may well be because some of these countries, islands and territories form part of metropolitan France. One could also cite in this category characterized by French as an official language: the Îles Anglo-Normandes (Channel Islands), the Val d'Aoste (Aosta Valley) and Louisiana (Louisiana) in the USA.

only on three (the Americas, Europe and restricted parts of West Africa), it provides a form of expression not only for France and peripheral countries, principalities or areas such as Belgium, Switzerland, Luxembourg, Andorra and Saarland, but also for numerous countries in sub-Saharan Africa, North Africa (most frequently called the Maghreb), for Quebec where 80 percent of the population speak French as their first language, the West Indies (notably Martinique and Guadeloupe), Guyana, Madagascar, Haiti, Tahiti, Reunion, Mauritius, parts of Louisiana, and New Caledonia. It still has some lingering cultural value in Vietnam and Cambodia, which formed part of the old French Indochina Empire. A global means of communication, it is therefore a language to be reckoned with.

How did the French language acquire such a privileged and exalted position, having, like its sister Romance language Spanish, and the North European English language, both of which have challenged it over the centuries for primacy of place, set out on its universal path from relatively inauspicious beginnings? Its most distant source lies in the group of Indo-European, or Asian-European, languages which gave rise to Greek, then to Latin which splintered itself into the so-called Romance, or Neo-Latin, languages of French, Provençal, Spanish, Catalan, Italian, Portuguese and Romanian. Each of these languages, or sublanguages, like Valencian (related to Castilian Spanish and very similar to Catalan), Corsican (related to Tuscany Italian) or Galician (which is very close to Portuguese), reflects the final development of Vulgar Latin, a popular and spoken form of Classical Latin associated with Virgil, Caesar and Ovid. Vulgar Latin itself was the *lingua franca* spoken in different areas of the Roman Empire, and as this *lingua franca* slowly broke free from a central stem, it disintegrated and followed the disparate and diffuse paths of Roman administrators, colonists, soldiers and traders. All Romance languages are really the result of a kind of *créolisation* (a linguistic process involving two separate communities, one of which is European), to use the current French term.

As far as France is concerned, or Gaul as it was known in the early centuries of the Christian era, Vulgar Latin split into two main strands: *langue d'oïl* in the north and *langue d'oc* in the south. Similar to the languages of Italy and Spain, the *langue d'oc* retained much of the sound system derived from Vulgar Latin and entrenched itself to the south of a line running approximately from Bordeaux in western France to Grenoble in the east. It maintained the Latin vowels intact to a large extent, while dropping consonants. A similar phenomenon occurred in Spain and Italy, especially in the latter where the modern Italian language is distinguished by the almost total disappearance of consonants from the end of all words, whether they be verbs (*andare*), nouns (*ragazzo*) or adjectives (*inglese*).

With respect to the *langue d'oïl*, and this is our chief interest, the first text that is clearly not Latin, but still in dialect form, is the *Serments de Strasbourg* (*Strasbourg Oaths*, 842). This composition of distinctly non-Latin includes not only the first piece of so-called French, in a dialect impossible to locate, but also the first piece of German, drawn up by Charles le Chauve (Charles the Bald) on the French side and Louis le Germanique (Louis the Germanic) on the German side, both committing themselves to an alliance against Lothaire I (Lothair), the Frankish emperor. However, the first recognizable literary creation in *langue d'oïl* is *La Cantilène* or *Séquence de Sainte Eulalie* (880), which eulogizes in song the martyrdom of Saint Eulalia in Spain in approximately the year 304.

The *langue d'oïl* expanded rapidly outwards across northern France in the thirteenth century, having already started to gain ground on an international scale in the eleventh century with the successful invasion of England by William the Conqueror in 1066, and here French, with its wider administrative functions, held sway in the courts of England until 1350, with the result that two languages cohabited in England for hundreds of years: French and Anglo-Saxon. The doublets *beef* (from French *bœuf*) and *cow*, *pork* (from French *porc*) and *pig*, and *mutton* (from French *mouton*) and *sheep* are pertinent illustrations of the two parallel languages in the England of the Middle Ages. The linguistic differences reflect the social gaps: French food on the table provides a French word emanating from the ruling class while the animals tended in the fields maintain their Anglo-Saxon linguistic origin.

In the thirteenth century, while French was starting to loosen its grip in England, the opposite was happening elsewhere in Europe. In the Comté de Savoie (between France and Alpine Italy), one comes across a document written in French in 1253 (see Condeescu 1975, pp. 168–169), while in 1265 French became the official language of the realm of Naples, superseding the Toscan version of Italian, since the said realm was acquired by the counts of Anjou. Some Italian writers favored French as their mode of expression, witness Brunetto Latini who, between 1260 and 1266, drew up *Li livres dou trèsor* (*Treasure Books*), during his exile in France. The wondrous, captivating adventures of Marco Polo, of Venice provenance, found expression in the French language (*Le livre de Marco Polo*), and attracted numerous translations in Europe during the Middle Ages.

Certain watershed dates serve to highlight and explain the intense attachment the French nation feels and nurtures for its language, and it seems advantageous to recall them. The year 1539 provides a landmark in that it presided over the drawing up of the document (*ordonnance*) of Villers-Cotterêts which was not the fruit of competition between Latin and all the regional languages but rather the result of the *langue d'oïl* gaining ascendancy over all the remaining vernacular languages. Latin was no longer a choice in this case. Even before this date, in 1490, Charles VIII had decreed that all judicial inquiries and trial proceedings should take place either in French or in a regional language. Furthermore, 1512 witnesses the act of Louis XII who had pronounced a decree against the use of Latin, pointing out that such a promulgation relegated Latin to a secondary position, although it still survived most energetically in the Catholic liturgy, a tradition that still lingers to this very day in a somewhat idiosyncratic way in the activities of the late Monseigneur Lefebvre, in western France. Again, François Ier had, himself, confirmed in 1531 that all legal proceedings should take place "en vulgaire et langage du pays." Throughout all this insistence on the domination of the vernacular over Latin, the *langue d'oïl* profited at the expense of all the other regional languages, including, naturally enough, the *langue d'oc*.

The *langue d'oïl* had thus finally overcome its southern counterpart, the *langue d'oc*, by the beginning of the sixteenth century, so that the flourishing French Renaissance enjoyed an expansive, prestigious medium at the hands of Rabelais, Montaigne, Ronsard, Marot, Du Bellay and Calvin. The Renaissance period enabled the French language to acquire such a privileged status that the French nation likes to think it is unique.

Various cultural bodies have watched over the French language either to preserve its integrity against the hegemony of the latterly ubiquitous English language, or to deliberate on its development, notably lexical. These bodies include the strictly traditional Académie française, created nearly 400 years ago in 1635 by Cardinal Richelieu, and whose function was, and still is, to promote a *bon usage* or "correct" use of the French language. One of its statutes recommends: "travailler avec tout le soin et toute la diligence possibles à donner des règles certaines à notre langue et à la rendre pure, éloquente et capable de traiter les arts et les sciences." The apogee of this purifying endeavor was reached in *le grand siècle*, under Louis XIV, when the playwright Racine formulated a chasteness and immaculateness of language unrivaled to this day.

In the seventeenth century, the often weekly assemblies called *salons*, especially those of Mme de Lafayette, Mme de Rambouillet, Mme de Sévigné and Mlle de Scudéry, were most instrumental in crystallizing the *bon usage*; these were not only literary circles where the art of the novel was discussed in the form of the now less well-known *L'astrée*, *Cyrus* and *Clélie*, but also *cénacles* composed exclusively of men, like the grammarians Valentin Conrart (1603–1675) and Vaugelas (1585–1650), whose *Remarques sur la langue française* (1647) set forth the linguistic principles for *le bon usage*. Authors like the two cited aimed to "improve" the language and called upon the Académie française to preside over its destiny. Indeed, Vaugelas, according to the Père Bouhours, "devint une autorité en matière de bon usage, à la cour comme à la ville." The *salons* and the function of the Académie offered proof that France had acquired a conscience in matters artistic, and this explains why literature, art and music are regarded as topics of national concern. The influence of the Académie on the language led to a flourishing of French among English writers and artists who luxuriated in an influx of French vocabulary, particularly in the eighteenth century, similar to the reverse contemporary trend which provokes much indignation in high places of modern France. There has even been a serious governmental attempt in recent years to sanction and financially punish firms that allow the use of English in preference to the use of French. The *loi Toubon* of August 4, 1994 related to the defense of the French language made this very clear: *franglais* is not a practice to be encouraged. Italian and Spanish are suffering equally from this linguistic invasion, notwithstanding the protestation of purists.

The golden age of French literature experienced, and even rejoiced in, what writers considered the perfect linguistic tool that provided it with a beauty, harmony and rhythm that Conrart and Vaugelas promoted with their work on the minutiae of the vocabulary and grammatical constructions, preparing the austerely and highly intellectual medium in which Corneille and Racine were able to express themselves.

While the eighteenth century saw passionate debates centered on the fundamental questions of the existence of God, the reorganization of society, and the exploration of the world and universe, all encapsulated in the *Encyclopédie*, *purisme* or linguistic purity still held sway. In his *Journal de Savoie* (1817), Georges Marie Raymond (1769–1835), member of the Académie de Savoie, contributed a regular column on regional French. In this *Journal*, the author wrote less to raise awareness of the French language than to offer prescriptive rules on *le bon usage*, suggesting expressions, even Italianisms, to avoid. The French Revolution gave a new thrust to the expansion of the French language, carrying it beyond the frontiers of the *Hexagone*, in the wake of Napoleon's conquests in Italy and central Europe.

French followed in the footsteps of the colonisers and bequeathed to much of the world, from Black and North Africa (the latter known as the Maghreb in French) to Quebec, the Pacific and the Caribbean, a polished tool of linguistic identity. This explains why modern similarly crusading groups such as the Haut comité de la langue française, created by Charles de Gaulle in 1966, have arisen not just in France, but also in Belgium (Service de la langue française) and Quebec (Office québécois de la langue française). It also explains the Conseils supérieurs de la langue française de France, de Belgique et du Québec which, while offering more liberal views than the Académie française, all serve to protect and confirm the language as a unit and mode of utterance as a contribution to the world's intellectual achievement.

It must be stated at this very early stage (and we shall return to this point on numerous occasions throughout this introduction) that, with respect to the rise of French, and indeed all the Romance languages, following the fragmentation of Vulgar Latin, the lesson is very clear and unequivocal. There exists an edifying principle at stake here, and it is a principle that risks running counter to the traditional French adherence to the purity of their language. French, like Spanish and Italian, is essentially a modified, even, dare one say it, debased form of Latin. A type of expression finally considered faulty or incorrect in Latin slowly generated new patterns, culturally exciting and linguistically attractive, which ultimately resolved themselves into modern French, Spanish, Italian, Portuguese and Romanian. The tension between the spoken and written word, in the aftermath of Rome's declining empire and the conquering intrusion of Germanic tribes, both approximately in the fifth century, led to the domination of the former over the latter. What is considered a solecism or linguistic incongruity at one stage of a language's development may be construed as the standard for tomorrow. As an illustration, the colloquial and even journalistic *après qu'elle **soit** arrivée*, frequently censured by the purists, may one day oust the more written form *après qu'elle **est** arrivée*, or at least achieve a linguistic parity with it, just as *C'**est** les meilleures voitures* may one day be considered as equally acceptable as *Ce **sont** les meilleures voitures*. Similarly, one wonders how long it will take for *He came with William and I* to gain acceptability alongside *He came with William and me*, even though the pronoun *I* can only be, in a contemporary setting, the subject of a sentence.

Moreover, if the opinions of purists had prevailed in the desire to keep French in a uniform state, we would still be saying and writing "espérer *de* faire quelque chose" (see Pascal 1950, p. 84) instead of *espérer faire quelque chose*, and pronouns in the following structure would still be preceding the auxiliary verb: "je ne *te les* pourrais pas dire de bouche" (p. 84), instead of *je ne pourrais pas **te les** dire*. Similarly Voltaire, a century later, writes in *Candide*: "Comment donc! dit-il, *en* pouvez-vous douter?" instead of *pouvez-vous **en** douter?* (1988, p. 66). The colorful *Mémoires d'outre-tombe* of Chateaubriand uses this construction on every page of what is a lengthy work by any standard. In the ironic, jocular style of *Les caves du Vatican* (1914, p. 13), Gide writes: "mais pour simple qu'il désirât sa cravate,...encore *la* voulait-il choisir." French literature of the Middle Ages saw such a construction as standard, just as it is common currency in both contemporary Italian and Spanish. Furthermore, the past historic would still be in colloquial usage in French, and again just as it is common currency in both Italian and Spanish these days.

Some grammarians increasingly realize that their role, even responsibility, in the scrutiny and analysis of language consists less in prescribing and preserving norms, and, in the case of the French language, in arbitrarily imposing the Parisian variety or *francien* mode of expression, as it once was in the Île de France, on the rest of France and the numerous other French-speaking countries, than on observing its development, and actively contributing to this development. It should be added parenthetically here that, according to some commentators on the French language, notably Belgian linguists, *francien* was not the only form of French available. Resistance to change has been a mark of the *francien* variety of the French language. (A parallel resistance to change may also be viewed in the attitudes of certain, but ever diminishing numbers of, English speakers of English in relation to American speakers who often say "different than" or "different to," rather than "different from." It should be said in passing that Jane Austen, for instance in *Pride and Prejudice*, frequently resorts to "different to.")

What is undeniable is that the cultured inhabitants of a variety of French-speaking countries speak a very similar language, which makes them all intelligible to each other. Indeed, their grammatical discourses are remarkably similar. A consistent and conspicuous feature of the French language is that, although any endeavor to embrace the French of France in the same context as that of an African country, or of the Maghreb, Quebec, Martinique and so on, may appear futile, its grammar is broadly consistent everywhere. Notwithstanding the numerous and inevitable lexical differences, the French grammar of the New Caledonian Francis Carco in *L'homme traqué* or *Jésus la caille* differs little from that of the Algerian-born Albert Camus's *La peste*, or again from that of the Senegalese poet Léopold Senghor in his collections *Éthiopiques* and *Nocturnes*. The French of Marguerite Yourcenar, of Belgian descent, and the very first female to be admitted to the male bastion of the Académie française in 1981, corresponds to grammatical criteria (see *Mémoires d'Hadrien*), just as does that of Marguerite Duras who was born in French Indochina (see *Moderato cantabile* and *L'amant*), or even that of the Belgian Nobel Prize winner Maurice Maeterlinck in his plays and *Essais*, notably *La vie des abeilles*. The prolific Belgian compatriot of Maeterlinck, Michel de Ghelderode, has acquired fame in the French-speaking world with such plays as the notorious *Fastes d'enfer*, while the Algerian-born novelist Assia Djebar has followed in the footsteps of Marguerite Yourcenar by being admitted to the Académie française in 2005. Last but not least, the Senegalese novelist Abasse Ndione, who publishes regularly with the prestigious publishing house Gallimard (see the novels *Ramaka* and *Mbëkë*), contributes such articles as *Temps de disette au Sénégal* to *Libération* (August 9/10, 2008). The list is endless.

The examples of the authors cited above illustrate the worldwide diffusion of the French language which gave rise to the phenomenon known as *francophonie*, difficult to translate in one word but in a paraphrase: the French-speaking world, or a worldwide language. The term *francophonie*, born in 1880, stimulated discussions at a variety of *sommets de la francophonie*, as Henriette Walter calls them. It was given a considerable impulse by the Senegalese president Léopold Sedar Senghor, the Tunisian president Habib Bourguiba and Habib Diori who, in 1962, launched a constitution for a francophone community. The other significant landmark in the francophone universe occurred in 1986 when a large number of countries were represented at a Paris conference: Conférence des chefs d'état et de gouvernements ayant en commun l'usage du français. The fifty-two countries, referred to at the beginning of this introduction and listed at

the end, apparently subscribe to this common linguistic and even ideological ideal, if *Les correspondances du ministère des Affaires étrangères* (1998)
is to be believed. However, the imagination has to be stretched when, in
some curious manner, countries such as Albania, Bulgaria, Macedonia, Mol-
davia, Spanish-speaking Equatorial Guinea or islands like English-speaking
Dominica in the Caribbean are included in this list. Justification must lie
in the tenuous relationship between, for instance, the creole French in
Dominica and the nearby islands of Guadeloupe and Martinique. Despite
this stricture, French has survived strikingly well in many parts of the
world in the face of an ever intrusive and galloping English. An excellent
case in point is the island of Mauritius where the official language is precisely English but, paradoxically, 60 percent of the population speak French
as their mother tongue, while also speaking English, creole (a mixture of
eighteenth-century French and seamen's French, with a contribution from
parts of Africa and Madagascar) and Hindi. French and English vie with each
other on Mauritian radio and television. French has experienced a resurgence in Algeria where, after the declaration of independence from their
French colonial masters in 1962 and the concomitant rejection of French
in favor of English, it is estimated that 30 percent of Algerians now speak
French as their mother language, and 30 percent use French occasionally,
and this despite Algeria's failure to become involved in the community
of francophone countries, notwithstanding Assia Djebar's election to the
Académie française. Similar figures may be obtained for Morocco where
the novelist Tahar Ben Jelloun won the Prix Goncourt in 1987 for his *La
nuit sacrée*. One could pursue the enumeration of these statistics in relation to Black Africa, Quebec, Guyana and so on, but suffice it to refer to
the list at the beginning of this introduction to observe the full extent of
francophonie.

In all these francophone countries, it is wise to distinguish between the
French spoken by the cultured and well-educated classes, and that spoken
by the popular strata of society where formal instruction is not so evident.
Furthermore, the syntax, if not the pronunciation or vocabulary, of the
French spoken by the well-tutored social groups in, say, Algeria, Reunion,
Mauritius, Senegal, Quebec or Guyana, to take just a few countries selected
at random across the globe, is conspicuously uniform, and for this we
doubtless have to consider the centrifugal power of metropolitan France,
contested by many, and certain well-respected dictionaries such as *Le petit
Robert*, *Le petit Larousse* and the *Littré*, in tandem with the Académie française.
Such a uniformity facilitates the establishment of an all-embracing French
grammar. It should be added that, whereas the French of the *Hexagone* has
retained a high degree of homogeneity, in whichever francophone country
one finds oneself, the local language, dialect or creole differs markedly
and inevitably from one country to another, since different amorphous
linguistic, social, geographical and political forces are incessantly at work.

It should also be pointed out that, although the linguistic hegemony enjoyed by French is unrivaled in France, there do exist other languages that coexist alongside it. A quotation from Graham Robb's *The Discovery of France* proves this very point. For all the wide variation in statistics, he asserts: "the various forms of Occitan have at least two million speakers, Alsatian 1.5 million, Breton half a million, Corsican 280, 000, Basque and Flemish 80, 000 each (in France), Francoprovençal 70, 000. Figures for major dialects like Auvergnat, Norman and Picard are unavailable, though they can still be heard in daily use" (2007, p. 65). Needless to add, the speakers of these minority languages have the admirable but often unrecognized versatility to express themselves in the national tongue, although in some cases their accent seems disconcerting to speakers of "standard" French.

A shift in emphasis on the appreciation of language and its assessment in the context of the constantly evolving written and spoken word has taken place in recent years. It no longer behoves commentators of language to establish patterns and models according to which all expression is judged, or provide a code of syntax and speech, or strict linguistic analysis, so that we should all unvaryingly write and speak like the creations of Shakespeare or Cervantes or Racine. A grammar is no longer required to be prescriptive but rather to put before the public what kind of language most people agree upon. Encouraging us to speak like books is manifestly not an activity to be promoted. This still constitutes a danger for the members of the Académie française whose hidebound pronouncements persist in alienating large sections of the French-speaking public. Moreover, creative writers exhibit an increasingly restive attitude toward the Académie, to the extent that a growing number of seats remain stubbornly vacant.[2]

This explains why a language in the constant process of change, particularly with respect to pronunciation and vocabulary, should not be subject

---

[2] The state of the Académie française is parlous indeed. At the risk of appearing too critical, one may note that the average age of its members in 2008 was 79, which seems to correspond to its status as the oldest institution in France. It is woefully conservative, even obscurantist, ruling as it does with a linguistic iron fist. One may quote two examples to justify this assertion. First, when the last spelling reforms took place in 1990, the Académie initially accepted them but then withdrew them, yielding to pressure from the purists. Second, any commission seeking French equivalents of burgeoning English technical terminology must submit their proposals to the Académie.

An ever dwindling number of creative authors tend their candidature for election, for as André Gide remarked in the 1930s: "C'est comme une hérésie d'y prétendre." Philippe Sollers is quoted in the *Nouvel observateur* (March 5, 2008) as saying: "Elle est réservée aux médiocres, à ceux qui ne laisseront pas de traces durables ... Le vrai problème de l'Académie française, c'est qu'on risque d'être élu." For some, the Old Lady is *en panne*.

to such restraints that risk weakening its vitality and innovative aspirations, and it must be emphasized that most well-informed, contemporary linguists view any language, not just French, as subject to inevitable and reinventive fluctuations that reflect the vicissitudes of life. The French Académie still serves regretfully as a serious brake on the creative processes of language, maintaining its commitment to the centralizing influences of Napoleonic institutions. As against non-French speakers of French, Belgians, for instance, its members still ascribe to themselves the symbolic value of the ultimate reference for the French language, even though the Académie has not published a grammar since 1932. It exerts a restraining influence on the status of French as a world language. In an e-mail sent to one of the present authors by the Belgian linguist Daniel Blampied, one reads: "À la différence de l'Académie française, les grammairiens belges mettent au premier plan le concept d'évolution de la langue."

At the same time, the foreign learner of a language should be aware of what is meant by "correct," or "incorrect," and here there exists a fine line between the two judgments. If a native French speaker makes utterances accepted by most of his/her compatriots, these reach a degree of linguistic and even social acceptability. If, in contrast, a speaker of French, probably a foreigner, makes a statement that few native French speakers would allow, anywhere in the world, then that statement is "incorrect." One could discuss the use by a native speaker of the imperfect subjunctive in certain contexts where it might or might not be appropriate. Usually, an argument for its use may be made, however archaic a subjunctive form may sound (and a group in France meets regularly and idiosyncratically to maintain its use), but what is certain is that the possible contentious issue of the use of the imperfect subjunctive does not give rise to benchmarks of "correctness" or "incorrectness" in the same way as saying *mon femme* instead of *ma femme*, as one would hear in Reunion creole, a solecism which would provoke unmitigated condemnation if it were uttered as part of a standard French sentence. The study of French grammar requires us to adhere to what most French speakers say and write, but this does not entail a rigidity or straitjacket of language which obliges us to follow the paradigms set by some grammars that still constantly, and unhelpfully, quote classical writers like La Fontaine, Racine, Corneille or Voltaire as a means of illustrating and justifying a grammatical rule. Grevisse's *Le bon usage* is not innocent in this matter. The present volume aims to adopt a descriptive, rather than a prescriptive, approach.

From the modest, even humble status of a vulgar tongue in the Gallo-Roman period, the French language has emerged from the *langue d'oïl* most vigorously and triumphantly, shaking off the challenge of its competitor the *langue d'oc*, and has become the medium for a rich literary output, an analytical tool that can be applied to a multitude of tasks, whether in works of a didactic or scientific nature, or in public acts of government or diplomacy. It combines homogeneity and diversity, in spite of the slug-gishness of the Académie, and has thrived on a capacity for survival and innovation, developing from Latin a harmonious system of sounds, a rich seam of verb forms, a simplified case scheme, all of which favors a clear and logical manner of expression. Provided it does not return to the reac-tionary and impoverishing attitudes of the sixteenth-century Malherbe who denounced archaisms, dialectical forms, diminutives (generating so much richness and exuberance in Italian and Spanish), neologisms and foreign, borrowed terms, its future is bright indeed. Inspired by nineteenth-century Romanticism, it is slowly succeeding in throwing off the weight of its abstract and aristocratic character, the constraining dictates of grammari-ans and university professors, revolting against the artificiality and cramp-ing restrictions imposed and maintained in the name of *le bon goût*. There now exists a flourishing democratization of language where popular sen-timent nourishes and stimulates verbal representations of a higher order. The resources of the French language are limitless, corresponding as they do to our natural desire for a perfection and harmony in form and expres-sion which help to combat the forces of destruction, dissension and conflict. Language is the most fundamental form of communication which distin-guishes mankind from the animal world, conveys to us our sense of worth, dignity and courage, and provides the grasp of a human order which makes life meaningful. The study of French grammar forms part of this need to give permanence and meaning to life, imposing coherence on incoherence and a precise form on formlessness.

Part I

1

Register / Le registre

A most dominant factor in the use of language and, in the case of the present book, of grammar, is register, or variety or level of language determined by the communicative situation in which the speaker or writer finds him/herself. In other words, the level of language we resort to depends, to a very large extent, on whether we are speaking with friends, which would attract a colloquial style, writing a letter or delivering a lecture, which would involve a standard style or even a very formal register entailing an elevated type of expression that could be associated with literature or any polished written form. The levels of language may differ from informal to formal, and are determined by five factors: sex, age, status, intimacy and context or circumstances. All these factors affect, in varying degrees, the way we use language in areas of both vocabulary and grammar. Of course, the present work is concerned exclusively with grammar, the use of which will be presented in the context of register, when suitable and necessary. Register assignations as treated in this book will appear as R1 (colloquial, in French = *familier*), R2 (standard, in French = *courant*) or R3 (formal/elevated, in French = *soutenu*). These subsections may be summarized in the following manner:

extreme informality R1	R2	extreme formality R3
very informal, casual, colloquial, familiar, elliptical, grammatically unsound, repetitive, pleonastic. We are in the spoken sphere here.	standard, polite, educated, grammatically sound	formal, literary, official, language of scholars and purists, meticulously correct, reluctant to admit new grammatical structures, even archaic

It must be stressed that these subdivisions are artificial, and that the reality behind them consists of subtle, imperceptible shifts, not rigidly defined categories. We have confined these register divisions to three, as being more practicable to handle, although one could argue the case for more.

One should bear in mind that, given the more lax attitude over the tuition in French grammar, and in the grammars of many Western countries, in English, Spanish and Italian for instance, errors now occur in speech and writing in these languages, whereas once they did not. At the same time, in rural regions in particular where formal instruction has never been as available as in urban areas, the subjunctive, for example, is not respected, or at least it is used together with the indicative without the speaker or writer realizing that French grammar would require *elle vienne* after *il faut que*. In other words, among a certain percentage of the French population, *il faut que* could very easily be followed by *elle vient*, a construction that probably all well educated French speakers would find unacceptable. Whether or not such a solecism could be classed as R1 offers an unresolved difficulty since, if a French speaker utters it, it must have some validity. One could make the same kind of comments over gender "errors."

Looking toward the future, it is possible that some of what are deemed "incorrect" usages contained in R1 will become socially acceptable language. An excellent illustration of this point is the previous reluctance of British English to admit *different to* or *different than*, American importations that are now gaining credibility. Similarly, the former resistance to *après qu'elle soit sortie* in favor of *après qu'elle est sortie* has now faded. It is manifestly obvious that since the French language is spoken over vast territories, five continents in fact, it will inevitably entail grammatical diversity and even uncertainty, in light of which what is acceptable in one French-speaking country could attract censure, or at least hesitation, in another.

One does, of course, need to examine what is meant by "correctness." There are two senses in which a language is "correct." The first relates to a foreigner's manipulation of the language. If what is said is unacceptable to a native speaker or writer in any register, then it is "incorrect." The second is connected to a native speaker's attitude to her/his own language, and this is a more complex matter. In the popular and educated mind, there exists a close association between "correct" and the standard language: features of local varieties and registers which differ from "standard" usage are deemed "incorrect," even though they are used by native speakers. The Académie française was once recognized as the guardian of the "correctness" of French, but this is no longer the case (see note 2 in the introduction), for its authority is increasingly contested, by the Belgians, for instance. There are now numerous agencies over the globe offering judgments and pronouncements on the French language, and they all enjoy linguistic parity, notwithstanding any rebuke emanating from the Académie in Paris, so that the assessment of correctness has in many cases become arbitrary. Differences in use abound. The Belgians and Swiss say *septante* and *nonante* while in Romandy (Suisse romande) one hears *huitante*. In eastern France, the dialectical *septante* occurs. These cardinals are more logical and certainly more helpful for foreign speakers of French than *soixante-dix*, *quatre-vingts* and *quatre-vingt-dix*, supported as they are by the Italian (*settanta*, *ottanta*, *novanta*) and the Spanish (*setenta*, *ochenta* and *noventa*). Again, in standard French, the Belgians use the indirect object *lui* as well as the direct object *le* in: *Ça ne **lui** regarde pas* = *Ça ne **le** regarde pas*. Such usage would be more typical of dialect speech in France. *Aller **au** coiffeur/boulanger* is regarded with suspicion and even condemnation in France, where *aller **chez le** coiffeur/boulanger* reigns supreme, although this expression with *au/à la* certainly exists in France.

To note how these register categories vary, there follows a small compendium of examples illustrating how register is marked in the treatment of French grammar in the present book. The categories R1, R2 and R3 are used here by way of illustration. It should be understood that these are only rough indications, and that such divisions do not necessarily apply to all French-speaking countries. It goes without saying that many of these grammatical features with an R2 assignation may fit into R3 or R1 contexts. Many of these features will be treated more fully later in the text. See *passim*.

1. **Ellipsis**
   - **R1** Malade, lui? Impossible; **R2** Il n'est pas malade, ce n'est pas possible. / Il est impossible / Il n'est pas possible qu'il soit malade.
   - **R1** (à la) fin mai; **R2** à la fin (du mois) de mai
   - **R1** (au) début janvier; **R2** au début (du mois) de janvier
   - **R1** en fin de matinée; **R2** à la fin de la matinée
   - **R1** en début d'après-midi; **R2** au début de l'après-midi

2. **Redundancy of expression**
   - **R1** comme, par exemple; **R2** par exemple; **R3** à titre d'exemple / à l'instar de
   - **R1** mais ils ont cependant; **R2** mais ils ont / ils ont cependant
   - **R1** et puis après; **R2** et puis / après; **R1** descendre en bas; **R2** descendre; **R1** monter en haut; **R2** monter; **R1** sortir dehors (less used); **R2** sortir; **R1** prévoir à l'avance; **R2** prévoir. Note also these pleonasms in full sentences: *Avant de partir en promenade, j'ai ajouté **en plus** des vêtements chauds. En plus* is not necessary. The verb *ajouter* is sufficient. *Quand mes camarades sont sortis je les ai suivis **derrière**. Derrière* is not necessary. *Suivre* is sufficient. *Béatrice nous présente une **double** alternative. Double* is not necessary. *Alternative* already suggests a choice between two possibilities.

3. **Imperative**
   - **R1** Fermez la porte; **R2** (Vous fermez) la porte, s'il vous plaît; **R3** Je vous prie de fermer la porte; **R1** Fermez pas la porte; **R2** Ne fermez pas la porte, s'il vous plaît; **R3** Je vous prie de ne pas fermer la porte.

4. **Exclamations**

 R1 Ça alors! Elle est déjà là; **R2** Quelle surprise! Elle est déjà là; **R3** Cela m'étonne qu'elle soit déjà là. / Je m'étonne qu'elle soit déjà là; **R1** Ce qu'il a grandi! / Qu'est-ce qu'il a grandi! **R2** Comme/Qu'il a grandi!

5. **Highlighting**

 R1 L'objectif, c'est de...; **R2** L'objectif est de...; **R1** Le whisky, ça j'aime pas; **R2** Je n'aime pas le whisky.

6. **Inversion**

 R2 Il est à peine arrivé...; **R3** À peine est-il arrivé...; **R2** Elle est du moins la meilleure de la classe; **R3** Du moins est-elle la meilleure de la classe; **R2** On peut dire tout au plus que...; **R3** Tout au plus peut-on dire que...; **R2** J'ai vu une voiture qu'une dame conduisait; **R3** J'ai vu une voiture que conduisait une dame.

 Inversion is especially typical of the higher registers. It is therefore highly unlikely that the last example above would be heard in an R1 context. The subjunctive, appearing immediately below, is also more typical of the higher registers, although the first example of the subjunctive does not fit this assessment. Furthermore, some French speakers, usually in rural areas, do not use the subjunctive, or do not know how to use it.

7. **Subjunctive**

 R2 après qu'il soit venu; **R3** après qu'il est venu; **R2** le seul/premier/dernier homme que je connais; **R3** le seul/premier/dernier homme que je connaisse; **R2** la meilleure élève que je connais; **R3** la meilleure élève que je connaisse; **R1** Aucun pays permet ça; **R2** Il n'y a aucun pays qui permet cela; **R3** Il n'y a aucun pays qui permette cela; **R1** C'est pas vrai qu'elle est arrivée; **R2** Il n'est pas vrai qu'elle est arrivée; **R3** Il n'est pas vrai qu'elle soit arrivée.

8. **Tense of the subjunctive.**

 R2 le fait qu'il soit (*is/was*) le premier à partir; **R3** le fait qu'il fût le premier à partir.

9. **Past tenses**

 R2 Louis XIV a été roi de France; **R3** Louis XIV fut roi de France.

10. **Agreement with *c'est***

 R1 C'est eux; **R2** Ce sont eux; **R1** C'est les meilleures voitures; **R2** Ce sont les meilleures voitures.

11. **Agreement between pronoun + *être* and the first or third person of the following verb**

 R1 C'est moi qui l'a fait; **R2** C'est moi qui l'ai fait; **R1** C'est nous qui l'ont fait; **R2** C'est nous qui l'avons fait; **R1** C'est nous qui sont arrivés les premiers; **R3** C'est nous qui sommes arrivés les premiers.

12. **Interrogative statements**

    R1 Tu dis quoi? **R2** Qu'est-ce que tu dis? **R3** Que dis-tu? **R1** Hein/Quoi? **R2** Comment/Pardon? **R3** Plaît-il? **R1** Elle vient? **R2** Est-ce qu'elle vient? **R3** Vient-elle? **R1** Vous venez d'où? / D'où vous venez? **R2** D'où est-ce que vous venez? **R3** D'où venez-vous? **R1** Pourquoi il vient? **R2** Pourquoi est-ce qu'il vient? **R3** Pourquoi vient-il? **R1** Elle vient quand? **R2** Quand est-ce qu'elle vient? **R3** Quand vient-elle? **R1** Il le fait comment? **R2** Comment est-ce qu'il le fait? **R3** Comment le fait-il? **R1** C'était qui le premier ministre? **R2** Qui était le premier ministre? **R3** Qui fut le premier ministre?

13. ***que* versus inversion**

    R2 Peut-être qu'il viendra / Il viendra peut-être; **R3** Peut-être viendra-t-il; **R2** Sans doute qu'elle a raison. / Elle a sans doute raison; **R3** Sans doute a-t-elle raison.

14. **Pronouns**

    R1 ça; **R2** cela (celui-ci / celui-là); **R1** On est content, les éducateurs nous aident; **R2** On est content d'être aidés par les éducateurs; **R3** Nous sommes heureux que les éducateurs nous viennent en aide.

    Although one hears *on* in almost every possible context and register, there still exists the feeling that *nous* is of a slightly higher register. Native teachers of French would even now encourage their pupils/students to resort to *nous* in a *rédaction*, for instance. *On* suggests a lower register. Against this argument must be weighed the clear fact that Flaubert, stylist among stylists tormented by *les affres du style*, uses the pronoun three times in the first eight paragraphs of *L'Éducation sentimentale*. Is the Académie française at work again? Or can the creative artist kick over the traces when it comes to personal choice? This is an unresolved issue in many languages.

15. ***C'est* + adjective + *de* + infinitive as against *Il est* + adjective + *de* + infinitive**

    R1 C'est difficile de lire le roman; **R2** Il est difficile de lire le roman; **R1** Je vois la maison, c'est grand; **R2** Je vois la maison, elle est grande.

16. **Pronouns and possessive adjectives with parts of the body**

    R1 Une pierre est tombée sur ma tête;

    R2 Une pierre m'est tombée sur la tête.

    Children are especially given to this "error," and some adults, as in the R1 example. Furthermore, one would *never* say: *J'ai cassé ma jambe*, which is a pure calque on the English. One says: *Je me suis cassé la jambe*.

17. **Prepositions**

    R1 le chapeau à Marc; **R2** le chapeau de Marc; **R1** Elle y va en vélo/moto; **R2** Elle y va à vélo/moto; **R2** Dans l'église; **R3** en l'église.

One usually finds *en l'église* on formal invitations for births, weddings and deaths.

R2   près du feu; **R3** auprès du feu. *Auprès de* has a poetic connotation when used literally, as in the song of anonymous origin: "Auprès de ma blonde." These days, it is used metaphorically and here the register is standard (**R2**): Je me suis renseignée auprès du ministère des Affaires étrangères et européennes (MAEE).

18. **Negation**

   Notice how in **R1** the *ne* is lost in the first three examples (*oser, savoir, pouvoir*), is reinstated in **R2**, while in **R3** it is retained to the exclusion of *pas*: **R1** J'ose pas le faire; **R2** Je n'ose pas le faire; **R3** Je n'ose le faire; **R1** Il a pas cessé de pleuvoir; **R2** Il n'a pas cessé de pleuvoir; **R3** Il n'a cessé de pleuvoir; **R1** (Je) sais pas (moi); **R2** Je ne sais pas; **R3** Je ne sais; **R1** (Je) peux pas y aller; **R2** Je ne peux pas y aller; **R3** Je ne peux/puis y aller; **R1** Ça vaut pas le coup de le faire; **R2** Cela ne vaut pas le coup de le faire; **R1** C'est pas la peine de le faire; **R2** Ce n'est pas la peine de le faire.

19. **Partitive article with adjective before plural noun**

   R1   des belles plantes / des beaux arbres / des grosses carottes; **R2** de belles plantes / de beaux arbres / de grosses carottes.

20. **Infinitive versus *que* clause**

   R2   Demande à ta mère de venir. / Dis à ta sœur de venir; **R3** Demandez à votre mère qu'elle vienne / Dis à ta sœur qu'elle vienne.

21. **Euphony**

   R2   Si on constate que... ; **R3** Si l'on constate que...

   As has already been implied in the preceding examples, R1 speech is occasionally, and sometimes frequently, characterized by a failure to pay attention to certain grammatical requirements. One hesitates to brand such solecisms as "incorrect" if it is a native speaker who utters them. However, one can certainly speak of striking departures from the grammatical rules and norms in the following lists, which illustrate the most widespread examples of "errors," classified as R1 and characterized by deviations from the norm. R2 and R3 equivalents, as well as some explanations, are also provided.

R1	R2 + R3 equivalents
Je m'en rappelle.	Je me le/la rappelle.
(Doubtless on analogy with *Je m'en souviens*, and it is easier to say than *Je me le rappelle*.)	
du point de vue littérature	du point de vue littéraire
(*Littérature* is used here as an adjective.)	
un espèce de fou.	une espèce de fou.

R1	R2 + R3 equivalents

(That *un* agrees with *fou* and not with *espèce* is very common and one could justifiably advance the argument that it is now R2.)

vingt euros chaque	vingt euros chacun
se fâcher après	se fâcher contre
aller au dentiste/docteur	aller chez le dentiste/docteur

(*Aller au* occurs repeatedly in this context.)

Nous avons convenu de signer le contrat	Nous sommes convenus de...

(*We agreed to...*)

(*Convenir* conjugated with *avoir* may now be classified as R2, and it is even encroaching on the written language and supplanting *être* + *convenir* in R3. Most French speakers would no longer know the difference.)

Ce n'est pas de sa faute.	Ce n'est pas sa faute.
Elle fait pareil que toi.	Elle fait comme toi.
partir à Lyon	partir pour Lyon

(*À* is very common here and many R2 speakers would readily use it.)

descendre/monter sur Paris	aller / se rendre à Paris
Ce que j'ai besoin, c'est...	Ce dont j'ai besoin, c'est...

(Since *besoin* is followed by the partitive *de*, *dont* is required here: same comment for the following example.)

Ce que j'ai peur, c'est...	Ce dont j'ai peur, c'est...
lire sur le journal	lire dans le journal
une avion	un avion
une élastique	un élastique
un autoroute	une autoroute
la mode d'emploi	le mode d'emploi

(Genders can cause problems, even for French speakers.)

Revenant de voyage, notre père est venu nous chercher à la gare.	Notre père est venu nous chercher à la gare à notre retour.

(Syntactically, *revenant* relates here to *père* and not to *nous*, but this is not the meaning of the sentence.) Similarly:

Étant absent tout le week-end, ils n'ont pas pu me prévenir.	Étant absent tout le week-end, je n'ai pas pu être prévenu.

(Here, *absent* really refers to *me* but this does not fit the logic of the construction.)

Il en parle souvent (de ses amis italiens).	Il parle souvent d'eux.

(*En* is used preferably for things rather than for people.)

chez la famille Lanoë	dans la famille Lanoë
Je l'ai reconnue rien qu'à sa voix.	Je l'ai reconnue seulement en l'écoutant.

One finds with children and older people living in a rural environment
with little formal education that they "regularize" certain features
of the French language, and regularization has its logic. Children
will readily say with *intransitive* verbs that are conjugated with *être*:
J'ai tombé (instead of: *je suis tombé/e) dans les escaliers; J'ai descendu*
(instead of: *je suis descendu/e) dans la rue; J'ai monté* (instead of: *je suis
monté/e) à/dans ma chambre*.

The following few lines from the beginning of a nursery rhyme show
how common this use of *avoir* is instead of *être*: "J'ai descendu dans
mon jardin, J'ai descendu dans mon jardin (bis), Pour y cueillir
du romarin, Gentil coquelicot, Mesdames, Gentil coquelicot nouveau..." Such a "faulty" construction has its parallel in Spanish where all verbs are conjugated in the active voice with the
equivalent of *avoir* (*haber*). The same is not true of Italian which
has even more intransitive verbs conjugated with *essere* (*être*) than
French.

French-speaking children naturally meet difficulties with the conjugation of irregular verbs, and they cause them as much disquiet as
they do foreign learners of the language. A child could easily say: *Je
vais m'assir* (= *Je vais m'asseoir*), and could stumble over the present
tense of *bouillir*, saying *bouillis* instead of *bous*, or the future of *cueillir*
(= *cueillerai*), saying *cueillirai*. *Bouillir* and *cueillir* constitute obstacles
for adults too. Verbal regularization with children has its equivalent in English with, for example: *She felled down. / He caughted/catched
the ball*.

Below are three letters dealing with the same subject: asking for information on a tourist visit to the Far East. The difference lies in the
treatment and style of each letter. The first is couched in R1 colloquial or familiar style, the second in R2 standard language, and the
third in R3 elevated language. In all three cases, the particular characteristics of each register are shown in bold. It should be borne in
mind that the second letter is distinguished by a certain uniformity
or neutrality of language.

Register/R1
Mauron Frédéric

Guide des Circuits Touristiques

Agence du Grand Passage

55 Rue du Rhône

1201 Genève SUISSE

28/07/11

Salut Fredo,

Tu vas comment depuis la dernière fois ? Ça fait **un sacré bail** (*It's a helluva time ago*), **dis donc**! Tiens, donc, **avec un groupe de copains, on a décidé** de continuer à explorer le globe ... **Tu peux m'envoyer à mon adresse plus bas, dès que tu as un petit moment,** des dépliants sur les circuits touristiques en Extrême Orient ? **Ça va être hallucinant** (*great/terrific*) de découvrir cette partie du monde. **Tu peux suggérer** quelque chose **aux copains** ?

On tient à préparer **un itinéraire pour faire** le Cambodge, le Viêtnam et le Laos. **On part dans deux ans,** soit entre le 01 et le 31 août 2013.

Tu seras gentil et tu nous passes toutes les infos possibles pour bien boucler notre escapade. **Et les tarifs spéciaux, il y en a pour les jeunes** ? **Quels sont les circuits divers et variés** qui coïncident avec nos dates de vacances ?

Merci pour la doc ! Bisous

Sandrine

Sandrine Buisson, 44 Rue Maréchal Randon, 38 000 Grenoble, France

Register/R2
Sandrine Buisson, 44 Rue Maréchal Randon, 38 000 Grenoble, France, téléphone : 00 33 (0)4 76 63 08 45, e-mail : Buisson.Sandrine@free.fr

À

Mauron Frédéric

Guide des Circuits Touristiques

Agence du Grand Passage

55 Rue du Rhône

1201 Genève SUISSE

Grenoble le **28/07/11**

Mon cher ami **Fred,**

Est-ce que tu pourrais m'envoyer, dès que possible, des **informations** concernant des circuits exotiques que propose ton agence ? Je te communique ma nouvelle adresse ci-dessus. Nous avons l'intention de faire un circuit touristique en Extrême Orient.

Avec un groupe de **vieux amis, on voudrait préparer un circuit** pour faire une visite du Cambodge, du Viêtnam et du Laos. Le circuit touristique est prévu d'ici deux ans, c'est-à-dire entre le 01 et le 31 août 2013.

Je te remercie de nous faire parvenir **toute la documentation nécessaire pour bien préparer notre futur périple. Quels sont les tarifs spéciaux** pour un groupe ? **Est-ce qu'il est possible d'avoir une petite idée** de vos différents circuits en tenant compte de nos dates de vacances ?

En attendant de recevoir tes dépliants, **reçois mon très amical souvenir.**

Bien à toi,

Sandrine

Register/R3
Buisson Sandrine, 44 Rue Maréchal Randon, 38 000 Grenoble, France, téléphone : 00 33 (0)4 76 63 08 45, e-mail : Buisson.Sandrine@free.fr

À l'attention de

Mauron Frédéric

Guide des Circuits Touristiques

Agence du Grand Passage

55 Rue du Rhône

1201 Genève SUISSE

Grenoble le/ce lundi 28 juillet 2011

Objet : Demande d'informations relatives aux circuits touristiques en Extrême Orient

Monsieur,

Je **vous prie de bien vouloir me transmettre** dès que possible à mon **adresse susmentionnée** quelques brochures **relatives** à vos circuits touristiques en Extrême Orient.

Avec un petit groupe d'amis, **nous souhaiterions préparer un circuit** pour combiner une visite du Cambodge, du Viêtnam et du Laos. Ce circuit touristique **pourrait se dérouler** entre le 01 et le 31 août 2012.

Nous **vous remercions de bien vouloir nous communiquer toutes les informations nécessaires** pour préparer le voyage dans **les conditions les meilleures.** Par ailleurs, **nous vous prions de nous faire connaître** vos tarifs spéciaux pour un groupe et vos différents circuits **en fonction de** nos **dates de vacances précisées dans le paragraphe précédent.**

Dans l'attente de recevoir votre documentation, **veuillez agréer,** Monsieur Mauron, **l'expression de nos salutations distinguées.**

Buisson Sandrine

2

Alphabet, spelling, pronunciation / L'alphabet, l'orthographe, la prononciation

L'orthographe des langues est une convention dans laquelle la prononciation n'a que faire ; et la profonde erreur des grammairiens d'aujourd'hui, c'est d'avoir pris au pied de la lettre cet axiôme étourdi d'un grand écrivain : « L'orthographe est l'image de la prononciation. »

Charles Nodier (1780–1844)

If one interprets this quotation correctly, it leads to an extreme wariness of the function of spelling and its relationship with pronunciation. After all, letters merely represent a series of conventional signs which we have come to identify with certain sounds. Whether such a quotation justifies contemporary text spelling is analyzed at the end of this chapter.

It must be stressed that, if there is no other method available, by way of native French speakers, the only sure method to access truly French sounds and to reproduce them is to consult these sounds on the Internet, where a vast range of helpful sites now provide their accurate re-creation. Recommended sites to be called up are, on *Google*: *French Alphabet* or *French Pronunciation*. This much more beneficial and constructive method infinitely surpasses any value that the intricate and alienating signs of the International Phonetic Alphabet may have. Moreover, the International Phonetic Alphabet does not have the appeal it once had.

The alphabet is the same in French as it is in English. It is used to represent the sounds of French. However, French pronunciation varies from region to region, and from country to country, just as worldwide English or Spanish does. Glaswegian English differs markedly from the English heard in southern England, New York, Texas, California, Australia, New Zealand, India, Pakistan and so on. The Spanish of the Iberian Peninsula exhibits clear differences in Spain itself, from Castile to Andalusia, from Mexico to Colombia and Argentina. Similarly, French as pronounced in the north of France contrasts sharply with that of Marseilles, for instance. Indeed, the Marseilles accent is imbued with a color and vivacity that have little in common with the accent of Paris. It even has a comic resonance for the ear of the capital's inhabitants. Of a first-class engineer hailing from Marseilles appointed to an important post in Paris, a company executive is alleged to have said: "Très bien, votre ingénieur. Mais, la prochaine fois, envoyez-nous quelqu'un de sérieux. Avec son accent de Marseille, il fait rire tout le monde." Jokes sound funnier if related in a southern accent, and doubtless the legendary comedian Fernandel, among others, has reinforced this impression. One should add to this sometimes hilarious variation in accent and vocabulary the dialect of northeastern France, as exemplified by the film *Bienvenue chez les Ch'tis*, which appeared in 2008 and was directed by Dany Boon.

The making of valuable general comments upon the issues raised by pronunciation is fraught with risk. Pronunciation is the least stable, most variable of a person's speech habits, and it need not be emphasized that a single individual will not always pronounce the same word in the same way, and will be affected by a whole range of factors such as context, emotion, imitation, tiredness, pretentiousness, jocularity, desire to impress and so on. Consequently, many of the remarks in this chapter are to be treated with some reservation. Another problem is that certain tendencies of pronunciation are restricted to a particular region or regions; in such cases, disentangling accent from register is difficult. However, on the whole, as might be expected, an R1 speaker will pay less attention to her/his pronunciation than an R2 speaker, and certainly less than an R3 speaker delivering a lecture, for instance. The most obvious general characteristic of R1 pronunciation is a relative laziness in articulation, resulting in, among other things, the loss of certain sounds, and the introduction or change of others. What is undeniable is that a person reading a literary passage from a book would doubtless articulate more clearly and deliberately than a person telling a joke in a playful context to friends encouraged to laugh.

The French language contains sixteen vowels (including varieties), twenty consonants, one nasal consonant and three semi-vowels. There follows a shortened list with some of the various written accents which indicate slight differences in pronunciation. The comments that follow the list are important since they point to divergences, for many vowel sounds are composed of more than one letter, and vowels may also be lengthened, in diphthongs for instance.

2.1 Basic and single vowels

Letter	Example in words
A/a	date, chat
Â/â	pâte, tâche
E/e	le, ce, chemin, petit
É/é	pré, donné
È/è	mère, père
Ê/ê	être, hêtre
Ë/ë	Mme de Staël (of epistolary fame), aigüe

Letter	Example in words
I/i	cri, vite
Î/î	épître, gîte, maître
Ï/ï	naïf, maïs, asteroïde, glaïeul
O/o	rose, dos, chaud
Ô/ô	rôle, pôle
U/u	russe, cru
Û/û	mûr, sûr
Ü/ü	Saül, contigüe, aigüe, exigüe (once = continguë, aiguë, exiguë)
y	cycle, hypothèse

1. The â sound differs from **a** since it is pronounced higher in the mouth and corresponds approximately to the English **a** in *father*. It is sometimes stressed or elongated to sound ironic or pretentious.
2. The é (= *e accent aigu* or acute accent) is a closed sound (*e fermé*).
3. The è (= *e accent grave* or grave accent) is an open sound (*e ouvert*).
4. The ê (= *e accent circonflexe* or circumflex accent) is similar to è but is slightly longer.
5. The **i** and the **î** are the same sound, although the î could be slightly elongated.
6. The **o** and the **ô** are the same sound, although the latter could be slightly elongated. Practice of the sound(s) o/ô is offered by the quirky name of a lake in the French Pyrenees, near Bagnères-de-Luchon: Lac d'Oô which, for most French speakers, sounds like ô. Fortuitously, this is the same sound as *eau*.
7. The **u** and the **û** are the same sound, although the latter could be slightly elongated. Both sounds could be elongated if followed by an r, for instance: *mur, mûr, sûr*.
8. The letters with a *tréma* (ë, ï, ü) indicate that the preceding vowel is pronounced separately.
9. Some vowel sounds are markedly different with a southern (*méridional*) accent, for instance the **o** of *rose* or *chaud* is much more open in southern France than in the north. Likewise, the â of the Paris area is often much more pronounced and elongated than elsewhere in France.
10. The stark difference of vowel sounds arising from the north/south divide should not prevent us from considering the multitude of possibilities of other accents. Within France itself, the French accent in eastern France, notably in Alsace, differs pointedly from that of western France, to the degree that it requires considerable concentration on the part of a person from Nantes to follow local speech from, say, Guebwiller, or Riquewihr. Belgium, Switzerland, sub-Saharan Africa, North Africa, Quebec, French West Indies, Guyana, Madagascar, Reunion, Mauritius and New Caledonia all manifest distinctive characteristics that are impossible to cover in a book of this kind. An example taken

from Quebec illustrates this feature. Lengthening of vowels such as the **a** (*pâte* > *paiute*) or the **e** (*fête* > *faète*) which resolves them into diphthongs is very common, for all their censuring by teachers of the language. Such lengthening of vowels is not unusual in Belgium and Switzerland. One particular pronunciation feature that brings together all three countries, as well as Nice in southern France, is the continued distinction between the **u** of *brun* and the **i** of *brin* whereas in Paris, for example, they attract the same sound.

11.   The **e** in rapid, colloquial and sometimes affectionate speech is often lost, as in *mon p'tit gars, un p'tit bonhomme*, and **re** is also often dropped, as in *quat'* (e.g., *L'opéra de quat' sous = The Threepenny Opera*, by Kurt Weill), *à quat' pattes* (*on all fours*), *un quat' quat'* (*4x4 vehicle*).

12.   Note that the sound produced by –*ais*, as in the imperfect tense *je regardais*, is an open **e** as in **è**, but some pronounce it as a closed **e** (**é**). The difference between this **ais** sound and the **ai** sound is clear for most cultured French speakers, but some confuse it. The **ai** sound as in the past historic *je regardai* in a French dictation needs to be articulated very clearly to avoid the understanding of the imperfect tense.

13.   In the present computer age, one other vowel is to be added: ar(r)obase or @, which corresponds to the English *at* in e-mails: *orlandofurioso@btinternet.com*. Since the word *arrobase* is never seen in writing but only pronounced (the same would be the case for **w** or *double vé*), it gives rise to alternative spellings: *arrobase, arobas*. Its gender is unclear, but one must assume one says *une arrobase*, notwithstanding hesitation among informed computer professors. The origin of the word seems to be *arroba*, a Spanish unit of a measure of weight, from the Arabic, and this noun is certainly feminine.

2.2 Combinations of vowels

Letter	Example in words
eu, œu	feu, ceux, bœuf, nœud, œuf, cœur

The sound **eu/œu** is elongated when followed by certain pronounced consonants: *fleur, jeune, meule, seul, cœur, sœur*. The past participle of *avoir* (*j'ai eu*) does not correspond to this sound. The *eu* here is pronounced as **u**. Interestingly enough, a small town in northern France, inland from the port Dieppe, Eu, is pronounced as in *feu*.

2.3 Nasalized vowels (i.e., followed by **n** or **m**)

Letter	Example in words
in, ein, ain, (i)en, yn, im, aim, ym	vin, plein, main, bien, syntaxe, n'importe, faim, thym

Letter	Example in words
an, en, am, em, aon	enfant, tambour, temps, paon
on, om	mon, plomb
un, eun, um	lundi, à jeun, parfum

1. When these combinations are followed by an **e**, for instance, the previous vowel is denasalized: *bonne* (compare with *bon*), *il sonne* (compare with *son*), *panne* (compare with Pan Pan, who is Walt Disney's Thumper, and *le bon usage*). This does not always happen: *grand > grande*.

2. Loss of the nasal sound also occurs between two words when the second begins with a vowel. This feature is notably common with *plein*: *en plein air*, *en plein après-midi*, *une industrie en plein essor*, *un plein arc-en-ciel*.

2.4 Elongated nasalized vowels

Letter	Example in words
in, ein, ain, în, im	prince, ceindre, plaindre, vînmes, grimpe
an, en, am, em	danse, entre, ample, trempe
on, om	honte, nombre, compte
um	humble

2.5 Diphthongs (formed with semi-consonants)

2.5.1 With rising intonation

Letter	Example in words
ie, ia, io, iou, ien, ion, ya, yeu	chrétien, diable, pied, pierre, piano, pioche, ration, Sioux, voyage, yeux
oue, oua, oui, oi, in, ouin, way	je bois, loin, Louis, noir, ouate ouest, oui, pingouin, tramway
ue, ui, ueu	aiguille, huit, lui, lueur, muet, puits, rigueur, sueur, tueur, verdeur

2.5.2 With descending intonation

Letter	Example in words
ill	sillage
eil, ay	ensoleillé, payer
aill	travaillons
âill	bâiller
euill, œill, ueill	veuillez, œillade, cueillir

2.5.3 With descending intonation and elongation of vowel

Letter	Example in words
ille	fille, famille
eil, eill, aye	soleil, veille, paye
ail, aill	travail, travaille
âill	bâille
euil(l), œil, ueill	fauteuil, feuille, œil, orgueil, cueille

The articulation of French diphthongs is particularly difficult for English speakers, and for speakers of other European languages. The **euil(l)** type is especially awkward.

2.6 Basic consonants

Letter	Example in words
B/b	beau, bleu, bon, abbé
C/c	cire, cendre, ceinture
D/d	donner, addition, sud
F/f	feu, effet, bref
G/g	gâteau, gare, guerre, guide
H/h	habiller, heure, malheur
J/j	Jean, jouet, japonais
K/k	kiosque, karaté, képi
L/l	lait, lèvre, hôtel, table
M/m	maman, flamme, aimer
N/n	naissance, canne, âne
P/p	pain, frapper, appel
Q/q	quatre, quarante, quand
R/r	rare, marbre, rhume, marron
S/s	siffler, son, sauter
T/t	ton, table, tirer, attacher
V/v	voir, vivre, laver
W/w	Wagram, Wagner, wagon
X/x	extrême, laxatif, taxi
Z/z	zéro, zéphir, azur

1. These consonants have many other sound values. This depends almost entirely on their location in a word or group of words. Each consonant is treated in turn to consider the varieties of sounds it gives rise to.

   b   When **b** precedes an **s** or **t** it becomes a **p**: *observer, obtenir, obtus.*

   c   C sounds like an **s** when it carries a cedilla (**ç**) before **a**, **o** or **u**: *ça, leçon, maçon, Alençon, conçu.*

   When the **c** precedes **a**, **o** or **u** and does not bear a cedilla it has the sound of a **k**: *camp, coq, curé.*

   The combinations **ch/ck** also produce the sound of **k**: *bock, biftec(k), chrétien, cromlech* (neolithic stone formation), *écho.*

   Ch/a/e/o can also give the English sound **sh** as in *shoot*: *charlatan, chose, chercher.*

   C at the end of a word and following a vowel also produces a **k** sound: *lac, grec, Mauriac, tic-tac, soc.*

   C at the end of a word and following a consonant may have the sound of **k**: *parc, turc.*

C at the end of a word and following a consonant may be silent: *porc*, *marc de café* (*coffee dregs*).

C in *second/secondaire* has the value of **g**.

d   In some combinations of words, where the **d** precedes a vowel, it sounds like a **t**: *un grand homme*.

f   This letter sounds like a **v** when it precedes certain vowel combinations: *neuf heures*, *Elle a neuf ans*.

g   When **g** precedes **e** or **i**, it sounds like a **j**: *André Gide*, *gigot*, *manger*, *largeur*.

h   This letter is never pronounced. A word with an initial *h muet* is treated as if it begins with a vowel. Elision or *liaison* occurs: *l'homme*, *les hommes*, *l'histoire*, *les histoires*. An interesting case is the name of the German dictator Hitler. One would say and write *la stratégie d'Hitler* but *le nouveau Hitler* where one could expect *nouvel*. *La stratégie de Hitler* is quite possible in writing as well. Hamlet raises similar issues. One would say and write *le drame d'Hamlet* but one could easily write *le drame de Hamlet*. Last but not least, one says and writes *les épopées d'Homère*. One also writes: *L'Iliade et l'Odyssée de Homère*. Some uneasiness is felt about the juxtaposition of two vowels, which explains why the loss of the **e** in *de* in these combinations does not occur frequently in speech.

A word beginning with an *h aspiré* is treated as if it begins with a consonant, though the **h** itself is not sounded: *la harpe*, *le haut d'une colline*, *la hauteur d'un mur*, *la hotte*.

A curious anomaly occurs with the aspirate **h** of *hasard*. One says and writes *le hasard*, *à tout hasard*, *au hasard des événements* and so on, but *le bel hasard*, an R3 expression one easily finds in formal writing. One would expect the adjective *beau* here but this is not the case. Perhaps the unusual combination of the sounds **o** and **a** prevents the use of *beau*.

In a few words, **h** between vowels is treated as a *tréma*: *cahier*.

Clearly, it is not always easy for an English speaker to realize which words begin with an *h aspiré*. The following list offers the most common ones with *h aspiré*, most of which have a Germanic origin, and some an English origin. See Grevisse and Goosse (2008, p. 55) for a comprehensive picture. Cognate words are not given: *hâbleur* but not *hâblerie*, *honte* but not *honteux*, *hanche* but not *déhancher*, *hors* but not *dehors*: *hâbleur*, *hache*, *hagard*, *haie*, *haillon*, *haine*, *haïr*, *hâle*, *haler*, *haleter*, *hall*, *halle*, *hallebarde*, *hallier*, *halo*, *halte*, *hameau*, *hamac*, *hamster*, *hanche*, *hand-ball* (–*ball* pronounced as in *balle* since *hand-ball* comes from the German: *football* pronounced as in English, whence it derives), *handicap*, *hangar*, *hanneton*, *hanté*, *happer*, *hara-kiri*, *harangue*, *haras*, *harasser*, *harceler*, *hardes*, *hardi*, *harem*, *hareng, hargne, haricot, harnais, harpe, harpie, harpon, hasard, haschich, hâte, haut, hauteur, hâve, havre, havresac, hayon, heaume, hêler, hennir, hérault, here* (only heard in *pauvre here* or *poor wretch*, and causes uncertainty in French speakers with respect to *h* aspiré since one never hears *le here*), *hérisser, hernie, héron, héros* (but *l'héroïne, l'héroïsme*), *herse, hêtre, heurter, hibou, hic* (as in *Voilà le hic* or *There's the rub*, of Hamlet fame), *hideux, hippie, hisser, hobby, hobereau, hocher, hockey, holding, hold-up, homard, home, hongre* (as in *cheval hongre* or *gelded horse*), *honnir* (as in *Honni soit qui mal y pense*), *honte, hoquet, horde, hors, houblon, houille, houle, houlette, houppe, houppelande, houspiller, housse, houx, huche, huer, Huguenot, humer, hurler, hussard, hutte.*

k   This is not a true French letter. It is imported with foreign terms.

p   With the combination **ph** it sounds like an **f**, as in English: *phase, phrase, Joseph.*

q   With **u** as in *quota* (sounds like *cota*).

r   Certain adjectives ending in −**er** (closed **e**) are only pronounced, as open **e** (= **ère**) when they precede vowels: *premier acte/homme* (= sounded *première*), *dernier avion/homme* (= *dernière*).

s   This letter is not only pronounced as in *siffler* above (i.e., **s** in the English *sock*) but also like the English **z** when it occurs between two vowels: *baser, s'amuser, déphasé, laser.*
    When two **s**'s occur together the sound is as in *siffler*: *masser, tasse, casser.*
    There is some hesitation over words like *abasourdir*. Although for informed speakers the **s** here is like the **z**, the **ss** sound is not uncommon.
    In words ending −**isme**, although the standard sounds as a double **s** (*socialisme, capitalisme*), one does hear **s** as a **z**: compare *romantisme* (**ss**) and *romantisme* (**z**). Those who pronounce the **s** here as a **z** are often considered as pretentious or snobbish (sounds like *snobizme*).

t   In the combination **th**, the **t** still retains its individual sound: *théâtre, thon, théorie, thermal*. When the **t** appears at the end of a word it is not usually sounded: *petit, salit, Corot, Marat*. This does not apply, however, to *granit* where the **t** is sounded. *Granite* also exists. Although the **t** of *vingt* as an isolated word is not sounded, it is when placed with compounds: *vingt et un* (one would expect it here), *vingt-deux, vingt-trois, vingt-quatre . . . vingt-neuf.*
    T in the middle of a word is often sounded as an **ss**: *démentiel, désertion, (im)partial, ineptie, inertie, martial, national, prophétie, spartiate, spatial, station, suprématie.*

x   Has two sounds, and in one position does not sound at all. When before a vowel it sounds like **z**: *Elle a dix/deux ans/euros.*

When in isolation it sounds like ss: *"Tu en as combien ?" "Dix"* but in *deux* the **x** is not sounded.

When before a consonant, it is not sounded: *Elle a dix/deux livres sterling / dollars.*

w Like **k**, this is a letter that has arrived through borrowed words, and can vary in pronunciation between the English **w** and the French **v**: some words with the **w** sound are: *western* (i.e., a film), *whist, whisky, waterpolo, week-end, wigwam.* Some words with the **v** sound, and these are not uncommon, are: *wagon* (-*lit*), *walkyrie, Wisigoth.*

It must be added that few or no French speakers would confuse the **w** and **v** sounds in these words, although there could easily be uncertainty over a well-known French personality, now deceased, Patrick Dewaere, where the **w** is pronounced as a **v** and not as a **w**.

Although the letter **w** is imported, the actual sound it produces is not foreign to French pronunciation, witness Section 2.5 on diphthongs: *ouest, ouate, oui, oie, moi, toi, soi, loi, roi, crois, rudoyer, octroyer.*

The **w** is notably common in northeastern France, the Pas-de-Calais and Belgium, witness the name of the town Woluwe-Saint-Lambert, and especially Waterloo, scene of Napoleon's defeat at the hands of Wellington and Blücher. With respect to the **w** characteristic of this area, the following conundrum is appropriate, although not known by all French speakers: In which French department are there most women of noble descent? Answer: Pas-de-Calais, for one finds there 8,808 marchionesses or *huit mille huit cent huit marquises* (Wimille Wissant Wittes Marquise).

y Apart from being considered as a vowel, this letter also has the function of a semi-consonant: *yeux, moyen, payer, myope, pays.*

2. Consonants at the end of many French words are not pronounced. They remain silent. On the other hand, some words contain final consonants that are pronounced, and there is no sure way of separating the two groups except by resorting to dictionaries. The two lists below contain a wide range of words that function differently in these two ways. The first list includes the words where the consonant is *not* pronounced while the second list includes those that *are*. It needs to be pointed out that this list does not include conjugated verbs where, in a general way, the **s** and the **t** are not pronounced: *lis, lit, lus, lut, écris, écrit, écrivis, écrivit, cours, court, courus, courut, prends, prend, pris, prit,* and so on. The list only contains a few adjectives where the unsounded consonant in the masculine form takes an **e** for the feminine form, and here the consonant is pronounced: *gras/grasse, gros/grosse, petit/petite, grand/grande* and so on. The letters treated are: **c, d, f, l, n, p, s, t** and **x**.

c, unpronounced: *accroc, banc, blanc, broc, caoutchouc, clerc, croc, escroc, flanc, marc* (but in the given name Marc the **c** is pronounced), *porc, tabac, tronc.*

c, pronounced (as a k): *aqueduc* (as near Nîmes, southern France, or the magnificent Roman structure in Segovia, central Spain), *arc, archeduc* (as in Archduke Franz Ferdinand whose assassination by the Serb terrorist Gavrilo Princip was the fuse for World War I), *aspic* (kind of viper, but some French speakers are happy to omit the **c**), *bac, bec, bic, bouc, bric-à-brac, Cadillac, caduc, choc, clac, clic-clac, clic, couac* (*error, blunder*), *crac, cric, donc, duc, échec, fisc, flic, frac, fric, grec, hamac, hic, krack, lac, loustic, Luc, Mach* (as in *Mach 2/3*), *mastic, mastoc, mec, oléoduc* (*pipeline*), *parc, pic, plouc* (*uncouth* person, out of touch with modern activities), *pronostic, Québec, ressac, roc, sac, sec, smic, soc, stuc, suc, syndic* (*official receiver* for a failing company), *tic, tic-tac, toc, trafic, troc, truc* (*knack/thing/trick*), *turc, viaduc* (as the one designed by Norman Foster near Millau in southern France), (*en*) *vrac* (as in *en vrac = loose* / *in bulk* / *higgledy-piggledy*), *c'est ric-rac* (*it's just enough*).

Ct at the end of words is usually pronounced: *abject, contact, impact, infect, tact.* **Ct** at the end of words where it is not pronounced: *aspect,* (*in*)*distinct* (in some areas the **ct** is pronounced), *respect.*

Exact has both pronunciations, but the non-pronunciation of **ct** is more elegant.

d, unpronounced (final **d** is rarely pronounced): *badaud* (*onlooker, gawker*), *bord, crapaud, dard, échafaud, gland, lard, lord* (sometimes the **d** is pronounced, especially in the Midi), *nid, nigaud* (*stupid/dumb person*), *nœud, nord, pied, ringard, sal*(*ig*)*aud, tacaud.* However, final **d** as in *grand* is pronounced as a **t** when *liaison* occurs: *grand esprit.*

d, pronounced: *baroud* (only in *baroud d'honneur = last-ditch stand*), *bled, lad, raid* (i.e., behind enemy lines, also: long-distance endurance automobile journey), *sud.*

f, unpronounced: *cerf, clef* (follows the pronunciation of *clé*), *nerf, serf.*

f, pronounced: *bœuf* (but in the plural the **s** is not pronounced, neither is the **f**), *fief, juif, meuf* (a *verlan* word for *femme*), *nef, neuf* (adjective and figure), *œuf* (but in the plural the **s** is not pronounced, neither is the **f**), *pouf, relief.*

l, unpronounced: *cul, cul-de-sac, persil, soûl* (the **l** can be heard in the Midi), *sourcil* (but see *cil* below).

l, pronounced (final **l** is almost always pronounced): There are a great number of words ending in pronounced **al, el, il, ol, ul**, and only a few are included here as examples: *alcool, appel, austral, aval, bordel, calcul, canal, cheval, ciel, cil, col, diesel, fanal, fil* (= *thread* and the plural = *fils*: **l** pronounced here but *fils* = *son(s)* and here s is pronounced), *gel, grésil, méridional, miel, national, nombril* (see below), *occidental, oriental, péril, recel, rural, septentrional, sol, subtil, val, vol.*

The l of *nombril* is almost always pronounced, notwithstanding which, and inexplicably, four of the standard dictionaries available do not support this. Take your pick, but the choice must be for the l to be pronounced, witness Georges Brassens's delightfully scabrous "Le nombril des femmes d'agents."

n, pronounced: There are just a few words ending in **n** where this **n** is pronounced and the preceding vowel is not nazalized: *amen, dolmen* (as in Brittany), *Éden, spécimen.*

p, unpronounced: *drap, galop, loup, sirop, sparadrap, trop* (but with liaison the **p** may or may not be pronounced: *trop aimable* | *tro' aimable*).

p, pronounced: *cap, clip, stop, top.*

s, unpronounced: Final **s** is a minefield with respect to pronunciation. There is no sure way of distinguishing between this letter as pronounced or as unpronounced, except by hearing it. *Liaison* is to be reckoned with: *sans arrêt, vos amis, pas à pas* (sounds like "pazapas"). Words with an unpronounced **s** are: *abcès, abscons* (R3, *abstruse* = *un texte abscons*), *abus, amas, appus, appentis, bas, boutis* (*coverlet* for bed), *bras, brebis, brûlis, buis, cabas, cadenas, canevas, cas, cassis* (but in southern France this **s** is unquestionably pronounced), *cervelas, chas, châssis, choucas, clafoutis, clapotis, cliquetis, clos, colis, coloris, compas, compromis, courlis* (*curlew*), *cours, courtois, coutelas, croquis, cyprès, débarras, débris, décès, dessous, dessus, devis, dos, éboulis, échalas, embarras, encens, enclos, engrais, excès, exprès* (but with *express,* **ss** is sounded), *fatras* (*jumble*), *fois, fouillis, fracas, frimas, frottis* (*smear* as in: *un frottis vaginal* = *cervical smear*), *galetas, galimatias, gazouillis, glacis, glas* (as in Hemingway's *Pour qui sonne le glas*), *grès, gribouillis, gris, hachis, haras, hormis, intrus* (*intruder*), *Jésus, Judas, judas* (*spy hole* in door), *jus, lambris* (*wood paneling* on wall), *las, lilas* (as in the Porte des Lilas in Paris), *logis, Lucas, mâchicoulis* (*machicolation* = opening in fortress for despatching of missiles), *marais* (as in Le Marais, a rejuvenated district of Paris with splendid small palaces), *mas, matelas, Nicolas, nos, obtus, obus, palais, panaris, paradis, pardessus, parvis* (as in *le parvis de Notre Dame*), *pas, pavois, permis, pervers, pilotis, pis* (*udder*), *pois, pont-levis, pouls, puis, pus, radis, ramassis* (*jumble, bunch* of children), *ras, rassis, refus, remous, roulis, rubis, sans, sous, succès, sursis* (as in Sartre's *Le sursis*), *suspens, taffetas, talus, tamis, tandis que* (but the **s** can be heard), *tapis, tas, Thomas, torticolis* (*crick* in neck), *tous* (as an adjective), *tracas, vernis, vers.*

s, pronounced: *Adonis, airbus, alias, ananas* (the **s** may not be sounded here), *angélus* (as in Millet's painting *L'angélus* in the Louvre), *anus,* *arrobas, as, Atlas* (mythological giant and the mountains in North Africa), *atlas (atlas), bibliobus (book mobile / mobile library), bibus* (movable *piece of furniture* for trinkets, books, etc.), *bis, bitos, blockhaus, blocus, bonus (écologique), burnous, bus, cactus, Calmos !, cannabis, cassis* (the **s** is not sounded in northern France), *chaos, chorus, cirrus, clitoris,* Cnossos (ancient capital of Crete), *consensus, corpus, cosmos, couscous, Crésus* (as in: *riche comme Crésus), crocus, Cronos* (supreme god in Greek mythology), *cubitus* (= *ulna:* a bone in the arm; the French word is used much more than the English equivalent), *cumulus, cursus, damas* (the **s** may not be pronounced here, but the **s** of the Syrian capital is pronounced: Damas), *détritus, Dionysos, diplodocus* (a very common term in France for the prehistoric monster popularized by Spielberg's *Jurassic Park), eucalyptus, faciès, ficus, fœtus, Hélas !, herpès, hiatus, hibiscus, humérus, humus, infarctus, iris, jadis, laïus (speech), laps (de temps), lapsus, lys* (as in Balzac's *Le lys dans la vallée), malus (écologique), Mars, métis, minibus, minus* (as in *C'est un minus* = He's not very clever), *mordicus* (obstinately), *Motus !* (Don't let on! / Mum's the word!), *mucus, myosotis, nimbus, nounours (teddy bear), oasis, opus, os* (but in the plural the **s** is not pronounced, according to dictionaries and grammars, although many French speakers do pronounce it and find this acceptable), *ours, palmarès, pancréas, papyrus, Pâris* (in Greek mythology, as opposed to Paris where the **s** is not sounded), *pastis, pataquès, pathos, pénis, phallus, prospectus, pubis, radius* (the bone), *rébus, rhésus, rhinocéros, rictus, Romulus/Remus,*[1] *sens, sinus, Stradivarius, syphilis, tandis que* (but the unpronounced **s** is more elegant), *tennis, terminus, test, tétanos, thermos, tonus, tournevis,*

---

[1] Latin names are a special case in point. These names have acquired a resurgence of interest in the French population as a whole, and this is largely due to that splendid intrepid little hero Astérix, the stories of whom bedeck the shelves of most French speakers' homes. It is worthy of note that the authors, Goscinny and Uderzo, would consult the *pages roses* of the *Petit Larousse* for their Latin references. There follow a number of Latin names ending in **-us** where the **s** is invariably pronounced. Some of these names have a modern French equivalent, and these are placed in parentheses by their side: Caesar Augustus (César Auguste; incidentally, this Roman name lies at the etymological origin of the Spanish city Zaragoza which in French is Saragosse), Brutus, Caius, Cassius, Catullus (Catulle), Circus Maximus (Cirque Maxime), Gracchus, Lucilius, Lucretius (Lucrèce, not to be confused with Lutèce which was the original settlement of Paris, hence the spot called *les arènes de Lutèce*; Lutèce replaces Paris in the Astérix stories), Marcus Aurelius (Marc-Aurèle), Maximus (Maxime), Petronius (Pétrone), Plautus (Plaute), Scipio Africanus, Spartacus. Astérix's authors make great play on Latin words and especially names they often create by way of caricature: Cassius Saugrenus (*strange*), Cassius Mordicus, Tullius Mordicus. One could easily argue that with this permanent recognition of Astérix and his Roman adversaries, *les Français n'y perdent pas leur latin.*

tous (as pronoun), *typhus, us et coutumes, utérus, vasistas*[2] (from the German *Vas ist das?* or *What is that? = louver window, skylight*), *Vénus, virus, vis.*

Note that the **s** of *plus* may or may not be pronounced, and this depends on where it is in the sentence and its meaning. When it precedes a consonant it is silent: *Il y a plus de dix filles.* When it precedes a vowel, *liaison* occurs: *C'est plus amer.* When it is part of a negative, it is usually silent: *Je n'en vois plus; Je ne le ferais pas non plus.* When it suggests quantity, it is usually pronounced: *une fois de plus; trois heures de plus.* But when it is a partitive it remains silent: *Elle a plus de dix ans.*

t, unpronounced (the final **t** is generally unpronounced but there are many exceptions): *abricot, achat, adéquat, affût* (as in: *à l'affût de*), *(aux) aguets, alphabet, apostat* (as in Julien l'Apostat who abandoned his uncle's [Constantine I] recently embraced Christian creed in favor of a return to paganism), *apostolat* (*apostleship*), *apparat* (as in: *costume d'apparat = sumptuous/gorgeous dress*), *appât* (*lure/bait*), *appétit, argot, arrêt, art, artichaut, artisanat, assaut, asticot* (*maggot*), *ballet, bandit, banquet, bardot* (*small sterile mule*, not very common), *basset, benêt* (as in: *un grand benêt = a big simpleton*), *bidet, billet, biscuit, bistro(t), blet, bonnet, (un pied) bot* (*club foot*: Byron had one), *boulot, bouquet, bout, bruit, brûlot, budget, cabaret, cabinet, cabriolet, cachet, cachot, cadet, cageot, caillot, capot, carnet, cassoulet, castrat* (*castrato*), *célibat, certificat, chahut, chariot, Charlot* (*Charlie Chaplin*), *chat, chenet* (*firedog, andiron* = the metal pieces supporting logs in a fireplace), *chevet, chocolat, circuit, coffret, complot, conduit, conflit, conglomérat, constat* (*assessment / certified report*), *consulat, court, coût, crédit, creuset, criquet, crochet, culot, débat, débit, début, décrepit* (as in: *un vieux / un immeuble décrépit*), *défaut, dévot, doctorat, doigt, éclat, enduit, érudit* (*scholar*), *escargot, esprit, estaminet* (R3 = *small inn*), *fart* (skiers should know this), *fat* (the **t** can sometimes be heard), *fausset* (as in: *d'une voix de fausset = in a falsetto voice*), *feuillet, filet, flot, fort, fret, fruit, fût, gabarit, galet, gilet, goulet, goût, grenat, guilleret* (*perky/jaunty*), *habitat, hoquet, hublot, îlot, jet* (but for the airplane the **t** is pronounced), *Judas Iscariot, juillet, lacet, lauréat, lingot* (especially *lingot d'or*, and there are lots of these in Fort Knox), *lot* (see Lot in the following list), *magistrat, magnat, magot, mandat, marmot, mât, matelot, minet, moût, mulot, muscadet, muscat, noviciat* (*religious apprenticeship*, as in: *faire son noviciat*), *nuit, orphelinat, palôt, paquet, Parigot* (R1 = *Parisian*), *parquet, patronat, pavot, pet* (R1 = *fart*), *piolet, piquet, pistolet, plat, plot* (*de départ = starting block* in sport), *portrait, pot, prélat, professorat, projet, prolétariat, pugilat, quart, quolibet* (*jibe*), *rabiot, ragoût, rapiat* (*mean, skinflint*), *rat, récit, rejet, reliquat* (*remainder, rest*, after effects

[2] Originates in a question asked through a counter or office window.

of an illness), *renégat* (*renegade*), *répit* (as in: *travailler sans répit*), *ricochet, rivet, roitelet* (*pathetic little king, tin-pot king*), *rot, sabot, sachet, salut, sanglot, sanscrit, secrétariat, sénat, soldat, sort, sot, statut, subit, substitut, sujet, suppôt* (R3 = *fiend* as in: *le suppôt de Satan / du diable = Satan's henchman*), *surcroît, syndicat, tabouret, tantinet, tantôt, thermostat, ticket, tiret, tort, tôt, toupet, tout* (as adjective), *tripot* (*gambling den*), *trot, valet, vivat* (*cheering*), *wagonnet*. Note that the **st** of Christ is not pronounced in Jésus Christ, but it is when Jésus is omitted: *le Christ*.

t, pronounced: *août* (but the **t** is by no means always pronounced), *audimat* (*audience ratings*), *audit, azimut(s)* (as in: *des arrestations tous azimuts = wholesale arrests*), *bath* (*wonderful, great*, R1 but going out of fashion), *brut, compost, concept* (the **p** is pronounced as well), *correct, cricket* (the game), *dot, est, Fahrenheit, flirt, fret* (*freight*), *gadget, granit(e), huit, infect, kit, Lot* (the department), *luth, mammouth, mat* (as in: *un ton mat*; note that the **t** of *mât* above is not sounded), *maths, net, ouest, prétérit, prurit* (*intense itching, pruritus*), *rut, scout, sept, soit !* (*agreed / so be it*), *yacht, zut !*

x, unpronounced: *afflux, (c)eux, courroux* (R3 = *wrath*), *creux, doux, flux, houx, preux* (R3 as in: *Roland fut un preux chevalier =* Roland was *a valiant knight*), *reflux, roux, toux*. This category includes plurals: *canaux, chevaux, cheveux, fanaux, poux*; and names: *Des Grieux* (of *Manon Lescaut* fame), *Sioux*.

x, pronounced: *Cadix* (*Cádiz*, Spain, but here the **x** is pronounced as a **z**), *coccyx* (as −**ksis**), *codex, larynx, lynx, onyx, phénix/phœnix, pyrex, silex, sphinx* as in Ingres's *Œdipe et le Sphinx*, *Styx, thorax*.

3. There now follows a miscellaneous series of words, some referred to above, where there can be uncertainty, even for some French speakers in a few cases, over the pronunciation. This list includes comments and explanations:

abasourdi	The **s** is pronounced as a **z**. Some French speakers pronounce the **s** as **ss**, doubtless on analogy with *sourd*.
abbaye	The **aye** is fully pronounced as **ei** (like *pays*, listed later).
abrupt	The **pt** is pronounced.
acrobatie	The **t** is pronounced as an **s**. This does not apply to *acrobate*.
adéquat	The **quat** is pronounced **qwat**.
aiguille	The **ui** is pronounced **ui** but in *aguicher*, for instance, the **u** is not sounded but merely keeps the **g** as a hard sound. Similarly the **u** of *guichet* is not sounded.

aiguiser	The hard **g** is followed by an **i**. However, one cannot exclude the retention of the **u** which is not uncommon in some parts of France.
almanach	In some central and more southern regions of France, the **ch** is pronounced as a **k**. In the north, and west, it is not pronounced. Marie-Éva de Villers and *Le petit Robert* offer the latter pronunciation. The *Oxford Hachette* gives both. So take your pick.
amygdale	The **g** is not pronounced.
aoûtien	The **a** and the **oû** of *aoû* are pronounced as separate letters, as distinct from *août*. The **t** sounds like **s** (*vacationer* / *holidaymaker* in August).
appendice	The **en** is pronounced as in the French *pain*.
aquarelle	The **qua** is pronounced as **kwa**.
aquarium	The **qua** is pronounced as **kwa**.
archange	The **ch** is pronounced **k**.
aulne	The **l** is not pronounced.
automne	The **m** is not pronounced.
bacille	The **ll** is pronounced as a single **l**, as in **bal**. This differs from *faucille, Manille, bille* and so on, where the **ll** sounds like the **y** in *rayon*. However, this last **y** sound as in *rayon* is common enough and tolerated.
baptême	The **p** is not pronounced. Similarly: *baptiser* and Jean-Baptiste.
baril	The **l** may be pronounced or not pronounced.
Bengal	The **en** is pronounced as in *pain*, i.e., nazalized.
benjamin(e)	The **en** is pronounced as in *pain*, i.e., nazalized.
benzène	The **en** is pronounced as in *pain*, i.e., nazalized.
biceps	The **ps** is pronounced, as in *forceps, triceps*.
bled	The **d** is pronounced.
brasero	The **s** is pronounced as a **z**.
cerf	Generally speaking, the **f** is not pronounced. See *nerf/serf*.
charisme	The **ch** is pronounced **k**.
chef d'œuvre	The **f** is not pronounced here. In *chef* alone it is pronounced.
cheik(h)	The **ei** is pronounced **è**.
chelem	**Chel** is pronounced **chl** (*le grand chelem = the grand slam*).
chenil	The **l** may or may not be pronounced.

chœur	The **ch** is pronounced **k**.
choléra	The **ch** is pronounced **k**.
chorus	The **ch** is pronounced **k**.
cinq	The **q** is pronounced when isolated, and before a vowel or mute **h**. When before a consonant, it may be, and often is, dropped.
cliquetis	The **e** is silent. Thus: **klikti**. See *décliqueter*.
clown	The **ow** is pronounced **ou** as in *clou*.
coït	*coitus*: the **o** and the **ï** are pronounced separately. The **t** is pronounced.
credo	The **e** is closed as: **é**. See *veto*.
créer	No sound intervenes between **é** and **er**.
dam	Pronounced as in English, and only used in: *au (grand) dam de*: *Elle a abandonné ses études au (grand) dam de ses parents* (She has abandoned her studies *to the great displeasure of her parents*).
décliqueter	The second **e** is silent. This is similar to *cliquetis*.
diphtongue	The **ph** is pronounced **f**.
dompter	The **p** is not pronounced. But it is in *rédempteur/ion*.
eczéma	The **c** is pronounced as a **g**.
équateur	The **qua** is pronounced **kwa**.
équation	The **qua** is pronounced **kwa**.
équerre	The **que** is pronounced **eke** (*set square*).
équidistant	The **qui** is pronounced **cu**.
esprit humain	The **t** is not pronounced here. Similarly with Port-au-Prince in Haiti.
exempt	In the masculine form, in France, neither the **p** nor the **t** is pronounced. In the feminine form, the **t** is pronounced: *Selon le dogme catholique, la Vierge Marie était exempte de toute souillure*. For Quebec variations see *prompt* below which is a much more common adjective.
exprès	The **s** is not pronounced. This is an adverb, as in: *Il l'a fait exprès*.
express	The **ss** is pronounced **s**. This is an adjective: *un train/verdict express*.
exsangue	The ending –**gue** is pronounced as a **g**, as in *langue*. Compare with the feminine adjectives *aiguë, contiguë, exiguë* where the **u** is pronounced. The most recent spelling has *aigüe*, etc.

facétie	The **t** is pronounced as an **s**.
fait	The **t** is not pronounced in the plural. It is pronounced sometimes before a pause, and in certain expressions: au fait, en fait, de fait.
fat	Generally the **t** is not pronounced.
gageüre	The **eüre** is pronounced as the **u** in *pur*, not as in *leur*.
galop	The **p** is not pronounced, like *sirop*.
gars	The **rs** is not pronounced.
gay	= *homosexual*. The **ay** is pronounced **ai**, as in *paix* with open **e**, i.e., no diphthong as in English. Thus same as *gai*.
gentilshommes	Although all available dictionaries state unequivocally that the first **s** is pronounced, many French speakers would not pronounce it.
gong	The second **g** is generally pronounced.
grog	The second **g** is pronounced.
hall	The **h** is pronounced as a closed **o**. The **h** is aspirate: *le hall*.
hennir	The **e** is pronounced as in *reine*, or the English *pen*.
Ignace, Saint	The **gn** is pronounced as with *ni* in English *pinion*.
imbroglio	The **g** may or may not be pronounced.
import-export	The **ts** are not pronounced.
ineptie	The **t** is pronounced as an **s**.
interpeller	This verb invites confusion and hesitation among most French speakers, for a number of reasons. First, although the verb is nearly always written with two **lls**, *Le bon usage* suggests that it may be written with one (*interpeler*), but this spelling never appears in dictionaries, or any written material for that matter. Yet many French speakers think that the correct spelling is *interpeler*, on analogy with (*r*)*appeler*. Second, when written with two **lls**, dictionaries are not unanimous in the pronunciation of *interpeller*. They offer mute **e** or **é**. The logic to be followed is to accept the acute accent. But hardly any French speaker pronounces the first **e** of –**peller** with an acute **e**. They pronounce the **e** in question as a mute **e**. Third, dictionaries maintain that all tenses retain the two **lls** (*interpelle, interpellais, interpellerais, j'ai interpellé*), but in all these cases the **e** in question is not

sounded. The answer seems to be, despite the
illogicality, to keep the two **ll**s in spelling and
pronounce the **e** as mute.

Israël   The **s** is pronounced as **ss**, not as a **z**.

jonc   The **c** is not pronounced, like *banc*.

joug   The **g** is not pronounced.

klaxon   The **n** is usually pronounced, although one
              cannot exclude the nazalization of the **o**, and
              the loss of the **n**.

legs   The **g** is pronounced by just about everyone
              nowadays, but not the **s**. To be added is that,
              the sounding of the **g** was once optional,
              witness *Le petit Larousse* of 1980 and *Le petit
              Robert* of 1982.

macho   The **ch** is pronounced as in Spanish: *matcho*.

magnat   The **gn** may be pronounced separately as **g** and **n**,
              or nazalized as in *gagner*.

Michel-Ange   The **ch** is pronounced **k**.

Mickey   = Mickey Mouse. The **ey** is pronounced as an
              acute **e**: **é**.

moelle   The **moe** is pronounced **mwa**. Same for *moelleux*.

mœurs   The **s** may or may not be pronounced.

musc   The **sc** is pronounced **sk**.

nerf   The **f** is never pronounced. See *cerf/serf*.

nuptial   The **t** sounds as an **s**: *le lit nuptial*, *la marche
              nuptiale*.

orchidée   The **ch** is pronounced as **k**.

papeterie   Dictionaries offer three possible pronunciations
              of the first **e**. Mute, acute accent and grave
              accent. By far the most common is the grave
              accent, which is clearly the easiest to
              pronounce.

patriarche   The **ch** is pronounced as **sh**, as in *cracher*.

pays   The **ay** is pronounced as **ei**: see *abbaye*.

poêle   The **poê** is pronounced **pwa**.

présage   The **s** is prunuced as a **z**.

prompt   The pronunciation varies here. In France, in the
              masculine form, neither the **p** nor the **t** is
              pronounced. In the feminine form (*prompte*),
              the **t** is pronounced (*Elle est prompte*). However,
              according to Marie-Éva de Villers (Quebec), the
              p and the **t** may be pronounced in the

	masculine form. In the feminine form the **p** may or may not be pronounced but the **t** is certainly pronounced. One suspects that the Quebec possibilities are infected by the English where **p** and **t** are always sounded.
pugnacité	The **g** and the **n** are pronounced separately.
quartz	The **qua** is pronounced as **kwa**.
quatuor	The **qua** is pronounced **kwa**.
quiz	The **qui** is pronounced as **kwi**.
quota	The **quo** is pronounced **ko**.
rapt	The **pt** is pronounced.
requiem	The **qui** is pronounced with a **wi**.
respect	Neither the **c** nor the **t** is pronounced. However, when this noun is followed by *humain*, in the set expression *respect humain* (*consideration of*, or *deference towards*, others), the **c** is pronounced.
respecter	The first **e** is pronounced as in *prêt*.
responsabilité	The first **e** is pronounced as in *prêt*. Likewise: Robespierre.
responsable	The first **e** is pronounced as in *prêt*.
restaurer	The first **e** is pronounced as in *prêt*.
rhododendron	The **den** is pronounced as **ain** in *pain*.
schéma	The **sch** is pronounced **sh** as in English *shoe*.
schisme	The **sch** is pronounced **sh** as in English *shoe*.
schizophrénie	The **schi** is pronounced **ski**.
sculpter	The **p** is not pronounced.
second	The **c** is pronounced as a **g**. But *fécond* retains the **c** as in *contre*.
serf	Generally speaking the **f** is not pronounced, but this is less clear than with cerf. See *cerf/nerf*.
sirop	The **p** is not pronounced.
solennel	The **enn** is pronounced as **an**.
soûl	The **l** is or is not pronounced.
spartiate	The **ti** is pronounced as **si**.
stagnant	The two letters **gn** are pronounced separately, as in English, and not nasalized as in *cogner*. Similarly, *stagner*.
stand	The **d** is pronounced.
stop	The **p** is pronounced.
suggérer	Both **gs** are pronounced but in lax pronunciation one **g** is dropped.

supporter	Here a noun. The **er** is pronounced approximately as in English, i.e., less open than in an **ère** ending. It must be said that this English noun is being supplanted by *supporteur* which reflects the pronounciation more clearly.
tchèque	The **tch** is pronounced **ch** as in *church*.
tenace/ténacité	In the adjective, the **e** is mute but in the noun it is an acute **e: é.**
tertio	The second **t** is pronounced as an **s.**
thym	The **m** is not pronounced. Thus, rhymes with *étain.*
toast	The **s** and **t** are pronounced.
transept	The **pt** is pronounced as **pt**, not like *sept* where the **p** is silent.
varech	The **ch** is pronounced as a **k.**
veto	The **e** is pronounced as **é**, as in *donné*. See *credo.*
zénith	The **t** is pronounced.
zinc	The **c** is pronounced as a **g.**
zoo	Only one **o** is pronounced.

It is also worthy of note that the penultimate **e** of adverbs ending in –**emment**, from adjectives ending in –**ent**, is pronounced as an **a.** Here is a selection (see also Chapter 53 on adverbs, Section 53.1): *conséqu*e*mment, éloqu*e*mment, émin*e*mment, évid*e*mment, fréqu*e*mment, (im)pati*e*mment, (im)prud*e*mment, (in)consci*e*mment, (in)différ*e*mment, indol*e*mment, innoc*e*mment, néglig*e*mment, pertin*e*mment, précéd*e*mment, sci*e*mment, viol*e*mment.*

4.   Letters in French are masculine: *un/le a, un/le b, un/le e, un/le h, un/le i, un/le r, un/le s* and so on. Notice that, in general, no elision takes place: no loss of the **e** in *le* with the spelling out of letters. However, this is not a watertight rule for one does come across: *l'i, l'r, l's* and so on. It seems much safer to avoid elision since this makes the sound much clearer. One oddity from the masculine gender of letters derives from the dual way of saying *low-rent apartment / council flat / house*. One says either: **un** *HLM* or **une** *habitation à loyer modéré.*

2.7 Division of words into syllables

If possible, it is advisable to begin each syllable after a word break with a consonant: *a-ni-mal, ra-me-ner, rai-son*. For example: *un billet de cent euros qu'elle m'ordonnait d'apporter au contrô-leur.*

   Make the division between two consonants: *lais-ser, protes-tant, cin-quan-te, at-ter-rir, fil-let-te*. For example: *J'ai vu la dame aux grosses lunettes noires . . . Elle m'attendait, le chauf-feur est venu à ma rencontre… mais j'avais la sensation que nous avions tout com-pris…*

Certain combinations of consonants are never separated: **th, ch, pl, pr, bl, br, cl, cr, gl, gn, gr, tr, dr, vr** (i.e., those consonantal groups that may occur at the beginning of a word): *ca-tho-li-que, ca-cher, peu-ple, fai-ble, siè-cle, ré-gler, vien-drai, ré-gner, bor-gne.*

2.8 Stress and intonation

The tonic accent in French, or in any language for that matter, consists of a special weight or strengthening of sound given to a syllable or group of words. Those syllables or groups of words without this tonic accent are called atonic or unstressed. In all languages, stress has a great influence on sound, English, Spanish and Italian being excellent illustrations of this. Stress is not so important in French as in these other three languages quoted, for words would still be understood in French even if the stress did not coincide with normal patterns. To take one example, if one did not place the stress on the penultimate syllable in the English word *intonation*, and if one said for example *intonation* (i.e., stress on the first syllable), the meaning would not be so clear. Similarly, the Spanish *entonación* requires a heavy stress on the last syllable, and the Italian *intonazione* on the penultimate syllable, otherwise there could be a failure to understand. The French equivalent, *intonation*, with only a slight stress on the last articulated syllable, does not invite confusion in the same way.

In French words considered in isolation, the stress falls on the last syllable, or on the penultimate syllable when the last syllable is a mute **e**: *vérité, senti**ment**, indiffé**rence**, mon**tagne**, ils déses**pè**rent*. In groups of French words, the stress falls on the last articulated syllable of a group of words, not on the individual word: *Prenez votre **livre**, Je pars de**main**, Il s'y rendra cet après-**midi**, Qu'est-ce que vous en **pens**ez ?*

The definite and indefinite articles (*le/un* etc.), demonstrative or possessive adjectives (*ce, cette, mon, mes*, etc.), certain pronouns (*me, te, le*, etc.), prepositions (*par, pour, dans*, etc.) and most conjunctions (*et, mais, donc*) do not have a tonic stress and are called atonic.

It seems more helpful to call this special weight on a syllable a *stress*, rather than an *accent* since the latter term can suggest either a local or regional way of expressing oneself, or the orthographical signs placed above or underneath a letter to modify their sound. The French language has no alternative word available for *stress*, and uses *accent* for both stress and orthographical signs.

Stress on a syllable needs to be distinguished from the idea of insistence which has an impact on a syllable when it is pronounced with a special stress. This stress may be called affective or expressive and does not exclude the ordinary stress on a syllable: *Mais c'est **in**croyable !/**dé**testable !/**ex**écrable !*; *C'est é**pouv**antable ce qu'elle a fait !*; *N'oubliez pas de reven**ir** avant minuit !*

The tone with which a person expresses him/herself is also important. Tone may be defined as the degree of musicality or pitch level at which a syllable may be pronounced, such as a high tone or low tone. A sentence may be uttered with an imperious, professorial, playful, gentle or childish tone: "Soyez les bienvenus," s'exclama-t-il sur un ton impérieux/doctoral; "Mais je t'en prie," m'a-t-elle dit d'un ton badin.

The sounds one utters to form words and phrases rarely follow a uniform pattern. They entail stress, musicality, elongation of syllables, a staccato or jarring style. A rising and descending intonation invests a French sentence with two distinct parts. The first part corresponds to a rising intonation which reaches the highest point, and the second corresponds to a descending intonation which goes down to the lowest point: *Je voudrais savoir* (rising) *quand les enfants vont revenir* (descending). Interrogative sentences do not have a descending part: *Quand est-ce qu'elle viendra ?* (*Viendra* reaches the highest point of the sentence.) Exclamatory sentences usually have a descending part: *Qu'est-ce qu'il est bête/crétin/idiot/débrouillard/intelligent !*

2.9 *Liaison*

Liaison is the phenomenon which, in closely linked groups of words, causes the normally silent consonant of a word to be sounded before the initial vowel of the following word. In some circumstances, *liaison* is observed while in others it does not apply. There is a further category where *liaison* is optional. The following tables illustrate how *liaison* functions:

Liaison observed	
Circumstances	**Examples**
between qualifier and noun	*ses amis*; *deux amis*; *de grands arbres*; and in the well-known words of Jean Gabin to Michelle Morgan in *Quai des brumes* (Marcel Carné, 1938): "Tu as de beaux yeux, tu sais." The **s** or **x** in these cases sounds like a **z**. Note that an adjective ending in a nasal vowel is denasalized in *liaison* and is pronounced like the corresponding feminine form; *le prochain arrêt* for example is pronounced as though the word *prochain* had an **e** at the end.

Liaison observed (*cont.*)

Circumstances	Examples
between pronoun and verb / verb and pronoun	*elles ont*; *nous avons*; *allez-y*
between monosyllabic adverb or preposition and article, noun, pronoun, adjective or adverb	*sous une chaise*; *moins utile*; *plus important*
after the conjunction (not interrogative) *quand*	*quand il vient*
after words ending in a nasal vowel: *en*, *on*, *un*, *mon*, *ton*, *son*, *bien*, *rien*	Note that partial denasalization occurs with: *en*, *on*, *un*, *mon*, *ton*, *son*. This depends upon a variety of factors (e.g., register, place of origin): *mon ami*. With *bien* and *rien* denasalization does not occur, although even here the final **n** in both cases could be heard a little: *C'est bien arrangé, Je n'ai rien ajouté.*

Liaison does not apply

Circumstances	Examples
before numeral beginning with a vowel	*les onze de l'équipe*
after *et*	*et alors*
before *oui*	*mais oui*
between singular subject and verb	*le soldat est parti*
after words ending in a nasal vowel not specified above	*selon eux*; *bon à rien*. However, when *bon à rien* is a noun, *liaison* occurs.
before words with aspirate **h**	*un héros*; *un hibou*. Note that R1 speakers may disregard the aspirate **h** (*les handicapés, les haricots, les Hollandais*) but this feature meets with disapproval from careful R2 speakers who prefer the retention of the aspirate **h**. Uncertainty reigns with *hyène*: *l'hyène* or *la hyène*, but the latter is preferred.

There are on the other hand circumstances where *liaison* is optional. Practice may be summed up in the simple formula: the more formal the language the more possibility there is for *liaison*. The more informal the language, the fewer the *liaisons*. The dividing line may normally be situated within the R2 register: a slightly higher register is struck when *liaison* is made. Use of *liaison* is often accompanied by an element of emphasis.

Liaison optional

Circumstances	Examples	R1/2	R2/3
between plural noun and verb, adjective or adverb	*des mots impossibles à comprendre*	no *liaison* between *mots* and *impossibles*	*liaison* between s and i
	Les trains arrivent à l'heure.	no *liaison* between *trains* and *arrivent*	*liaison* between s and a
between verb and past participle, infinitive, adjective, adverb or prepositional expression	*Je suis en retard.*	no *liaison* between *suis* and *en*	*liaison* between s and e
	Elle est en retard.	no *liaison* between *est* and *en*	*liaison* between t and e
	Elle ne l'a pas obtenu.	no *liaison* between *pas* and *obtenu*	*liaison* between s and o

The application or non-application of this last group of *liaisons* may be debatable, according to speed of speech, context, age of speaker and so on. What is certain is that in some circumstances there is never *liaison*. The **t** in the following combination would not be sounded: *l'esprit humain*. However, a **t** is usually introduced to facilitate the pronunciation of two vowels, as in the unfunny "comic" film with Brigitte Bardot, *Babette s'en va-t-en guerre* (Cristian-Jacque, 1959), and the traditional song originating in the early eighteenth century: "Malbrough s'en va-t-en guerre." Likewise, an **s** is sometimes introduced to facilitate passage from one vowel to another: *Vas-y, Restes-y*.

It must be said that, although one says and writes (see above) *les onze de l'équipe* and also *le onze (number eleven) | le onzième garçon | la onzième fille*, one could easily hear in a lower register *une fille d'onze ans* instead of *une fille de onze ans*.

Whereas one would make *liaison* with the **t** in *le petit homme*, it is not made with *l'esprit humain*. With *pas encore*, *liaison* with the **s** is optional.

2.10 Elision

Elision is the loss in pronunciation of one of the final vowels **a**, **e**, **i** preceding a word beginning with a vowel or mute **h**. Elisions in pronunciation are not always marked in writing:

Pronunciation: *Elle a presqu' échoué.*   **Writing**:   *Elle a presque échoué.*

When elision takes place, the elided vowel is replaced by an apostrophe: *l'homme, l'heure, l'eau, l'église, l'or, Je l'ai vue.* Elision takes place in the following cases:

1. When an unstressed pronoun precedes the pronouns **en** and **y**, or before a verb: *Tu l'as entendue, cette voix?, Je l'y ai vue, Elle a réussi: je l'en félicite.*
2. However, when the pronoun *la* is stressed, no elision takes place: *Laisse-la entrer, Envoie-la ouvrir, Donne-la à ton frère.*
3. With unstressed pronouns, *je, me, te, se, le: j'ai, Elle m'entend, Je t'invite, Il s'avance, On l'aperçoit, Je m'en doute, Il s'y perd.*
4. However, when the pronoun *le* is stressed, elision does not take place: *Fais-le asseoir, Fais-le entrer, Donne-le à ta sœur.*
5. There is elision with the following words: *de, ne, que, jusque, lorsque, puisque, quoique: la voiture d'André, Elle n'a pas de voiture, Je veux qu'elle parte, Elle est venue jusqu'ici, lorsqu'elle est arrivée, lorsqu'en l'an deux mille, quoiqu'elle soit d'accord, avant qu'il ne parte.*
6. With the pronoun *ce* before the pronoun *en*, and initial **e** and **a** of a simple or compound form of the verb *être: c'est, c'était, ç'eût été, C'en est fait.* But this is not the case with *avoir: Ça a été difficile, Ça a fondu,* although one could not entirely exclude *Ç'a fondu . . .* A careful speaker would probably avoid the cacophony of two *as* in any case.
7. In the noun *presqu'île,* and the pronoun *quelqu'un.* But *presque* does not elide in writing in other cases: *presque entier, presque achevé, quelque autre,* although in speech it probably would.
8. When *entre* forms an initial element of the five verbs: *s'entr'aimer, entr'apercevoir, s'entr'appeler, s'entr'avertir, s'entr'égorger.*
9. The Académie no longer recommends the apostrophe after *entre* for the following verbs and nouns: *s'entraccorder, s'entraccuser, entracte, s'entradmirer, entraide, s'entraider, entrouverture, entrouvrir.*
    Entr'ouvrir has now fallen into disuse, and is replaced by *entrouvrir* so that one only sees now: *une fenêtre entrouverte.*
10. *Entre* alone is not elided in writing: *entre amis, entre eux, entre autres.*
11. When the conjunction *si* precedes *il(s),* it is elided: *S'il vient* (but *si elle vient*), *S'ils partent* (but *si elles partent*).
12. Elision does not take place before the noun *un,* or before *oui, huit, huitain, huitaine, huitième, onze, onzième* (but *l'once = ounce* as in gold weight), *yacht, yak: Le oui est nécessaire, Il m'a fait signe que oui, le un, le huit et le onze* (as in the National Lottery). Neither does it take place before proper names: *Yougoslavie, Yémen, Yucatan.*
    Although the figure *un* does not entail elision, the indefinite article does. Compare the two sentences: *L'inflation a augmenté **de** un pour cent* and *Voici le roman **d'**un auteur russe.* But one cannot exclude elision in some cases: *Je crois | Il dit qu'oui, le train d'onze heures.* There is some

hesitation here, notably in the lower registers. However, one does not make elision with: *à la une* (= on page one of a newspaper).

13. *Ouate* is an interesting case for both *la ouate* and *l'ouate* are attested.

14. With names of authors, elision occurs with *de* but one also sees the e retained, notably in writing: *Avez-vous vu les pièces d'/de Ionesco ?*, *Les poèmes d'/de Arthur Rimbaud, La Peste d'/de Albert Camus, Les chansons de France d'/de Yves Montand.* On a DVD of the film *La Môme* (life of Édith Piaf), one reads: *Un film de Olivier Dahan.* It is legitimately argued that the retention of the e here suggests insistence or emphasis, or clarity as in: *le contenu du e-mail* as against *le contenu de l'e-mail.*

2.11 Spelling

Spelling causes great difficulty for many students of French, whether they be English or French speakers. English spelling itself is notoriously demanding, given the variations of individual words over the centuries. Even the globally famous Shakespeare's name has not remained stable. Carlyle writes, for instance, *Shakspeare.* Below are a variety of features in French where spelling plays a considerable role, either because of similarity of sound to that of other words, or because of attempts to regularize words over the centuries, as is the case with American English: *color* instead of *colour, encyclopedia* instead of *encyclopaedia, z* instead of *s* and so on. (See Section 2.13 for the spelling modifications suggested by the Conseil supérieur de la langue française in 1990.) Before we embark on the various aspects of spelling, we would do well to consider for a moment the contents of an article by Olivier Faure: "Gare à l'orthogaffe" (*L'Express*, March 18, 2010). The play on words *orthographe/orthogaffe* derives from *gaffe* = blunder. The author refers to "les ravages des e-mails et des textos sur la production écrite de leur personnel." The possessive *leur* refers to companies whose "cabinets de recrutement font maintenant de l'orthographe un critère de sélection." For all the attention paid to dictations in France, French students are increasingly subject to orthographic torments, and such lacunae imperil their job prospects. Shabbily drawn-up résumés or CVs, peppered with spelling errors, alienate employers.

2.11.1 Homonyms

Pairs, groups of individual words, and groups of several words together which are identical in sound but which are different in meaning are called homonyms, and are an obvious cause of ambiguity in any language. French seems to possess an abundance of homonyms, as opposed to Spanish which has very few. There are homonyms which are differentiated by gender but have identical spelling, those that are differentiated by both gender and spelling, those that have no external distinction either in gender or in spelling, and finally those that have the same sound but are spelled in different ways. What concerns us here is the latter group which can cause uncertainty even for native speakers. The first three groups that entail gender difficulties are treated in Chapter 9.

Homonyms that differ in spelling only embrace a whole range of parts of speech, from nouns to adjectives and verbs, and in this case they are individual words. These are treated in the first list below; the second list deals with groups of words.

In the case of homonyms as single words differentiated by spelling only, the danger of ambiguity arises only if the words belong to the same word class, or closely related word classes. In other words, it is unlikely that the preposition *vers* be confused with *vert* the adjective, or *vers* meaning *worm*, or that *tends*, the second-person singular of *tendre*, be confused with *taon* the noun, whereas the identical pronunciation of *dessin* and *dessein*, or close-to-identical pronunciation of *tache* and *tâche* could provoke difficulty in understanding, although this is almost inconceivable for a native speaker. In the following list, only those examples of homonyms involving words belonging to the same word class or closely related word classes (e.g., noun and adjective) are given. See also Chapter 9, Section 9.4 for more information on this topic.

1. **Pairs of words, or three or four similar-sounding words**

bal	M	*ball* (dance)
balle	F	*ball* (for playing), *bale*, *bullet*
bar	M	*bar* (for serving drinks)
barre	F	*bar* (of wood, metal)
but[3]	M	*aim, goal* (in soccer and figurative)
butte	F	*hillock* (as in: the Butte Montmartre, the Buttes Chaumont in Paris)
censé	adjective	*supposed* (e.g. *Éléonore n'est pas censée le savoir*)
sensé	adjective	*sensible*
chair	F	*flesh*
chaire	F	*pulpit*
cher/chère	adjective	*dear* (both meanings)
capital	M	*capital, assets*
capitale	F	*capital* (city), *capital letter*
central (téléphonique)	M	*telephone exchange/switchboard*
centrale (électrique, nucléaire)	F	*(generating) station, power/nuclear plant*

[3] Generally the **t** is not pronounced here, although its pronunciation is acceptable.

chêne	M	*oak tree*
chaîne	F	*chain, television channel*
col	M	*collar, pass* (in mountain)
colle	F	*glue, paste*
coq	M	*cock(erel)*
coque	F	*shell, hull* (of boat)
cours	M	*course* (= *au cours de*), *waterway* (= *cours d'eau*), *class* (for teaching), *private school*
cour	F	*court, (court)yard*
court (de tennis/ squash, etc.)	M	*court* (sports)
fait	M	*fact*
faîte	M	*apex* (of roof)
fête	F	*festival, party*
foie	M	*liver*
foi	F	*faith*
fois	F	*time, occasion*
gène	M	*gene*
gêne	F	*discomfort*
hall[4]	M	*entrance, hall, vestibule*
halle	F	(often plural) *covered market*
maire	M	*mayor*
mer	F	*sea*
mère	F	*mother*
pair	M	*peer*
paire	F	*pair*
père	M	*father*
parti	M	*party* (political, etc.), *decision*
partie	F	*part, game* (e.g., of soccer)
pois	M	*pea*
poids	M	*weight*
poix	F	*pitch*
pot	M	*pot*
peau	F	*skin*
reine	F	*queen*
rêne	F	*rein* (for animal, child)
renne	M	*reindeer*

[4] The pronunciation of the vowel in *hall* and *halle* is different. The first sounds like a closed **o**, while the second sounds like the **a** in *balle*.

| sel | M | *salt* |
| selle | F | *saddle* |

2. **Similar-sounding groups of words or letters**

−é/−er/−ez

−é	past participle ending	*J'ai fermé le portail.*
−er	infinitive ending	*Pour fermer la porte, poussez le verrou.*
−ez	imperative ending	*Fermez la porte, s'il vous plaît.*

es/est/et/ai/aie/aies/ait/aient

es	second-person singular of *être*	*Tu es jeune.*
est	third-person singular of *être*	*Émilie est jeune.*
et	conjunction = *and*	*Lucile est intelligente et courageuse.*
ai	first-person singular of *avoir*	*J'ai dix ans.*
aie	first-person singular subjunctive of *avoir*	*Il faut que j'aie du courage.*
Similarly, *aies, ait, aient*		*Il faut que tu aies beaucoup de cran.*

a/as/à

a	third-person singular of *avoir*	*Adeline a cinq ans.*
as	second-person singular of *avoir*	*Tu as froid ?*
à	preposition	*Benjamin est à Paris.*

quel(s)/quelle(s)/qu'elle(s)

| *quel(s)/quelle(s)* | interrogative/ exclamatory adjective | *Quel courage ! | Quelle voiture ! | Quels hommes ?* |
| *qu'elle(s)* | contraction of *que* and *elle(s)* | *Voici le modèle qu'elle a choisi.* |

se (s') | ce (c') | ceux

se	third-person reflexive pronoun	*Rémi se lave les mains	s'habille.*
ce/c'	demonstrative adjective	*ce garçon	C'est à Tours que Balzac est né.*
ceux	masculine demonstrative pronoun	*Les kiwis sont ceux que je préfère.*

ces/ses/c'est/s'est/sais/sait

ces	demonstrative adjective (plural)	*ces oranges*
ses	possessive adjective (plural)	*ses parents*
c'est	auxiliary verb *être* preceded by elided demonstrative pronoun	*C'est dangereux.*
s'est	third-person reflexive pronoun with auxiliary verb *être*	*Elle s'est lavée.*
sais	first-person singular of the verb *savoir*	*Je ne sais pas.*
sait	third-person singular of the verb *savoir*	*Robin sait compter/lire/nager.*

on/ont

on	third-person singular pronoun	*On arrive demain.*
ont	third-person plural of the verb *avoir*	*Elles ont raison.*

soi/sois/soit/soient

soi	reflexive personal pronoun relating to no person in particular	*Il faut faire preuve de confiance en soi.*
sois	second-person singular of the subjunctive form of *être* / imperative of *être*	*Il faut que tu sois à l'abri / Sois tranquille !*
soit	third-person singular of the subjunctive form of the verb *être*	*Je ne crois pas qu'elle soit arrivée.* When used in isolation to suggest *agreed, of course,* the **t** is pronounced: *Je me suis trompée, soit, mais. . .* (I was wrong, very well, but. . .).
soient	third-person plural of the subjunctive form of the verb *être*	*J'ai peur qu'ils ne soient pas revenus.*

sans/sent/s'en/c'en

sans	preposition = *without*	*Céline est venue sans parapluie.*
sent	third-person singular of the verb *sentir*	*Ça sent bon.*[5]
s'en	contraction of *se + en*	*Valentin s'en aperçoit immédiatement.*
c'en	contraction of *ce + en*	*Vous faites du bruit, c'en est trop.*

dans/d'en

dans	preposition = *in*	*Laetitia est dans la cuisine.*
d'en	contraction of *de + en*	*Du pain, je viens d'en couper une tranche.*

quelque(s) | quelque | quel(s) que | quelle(s) que

quelque(s)	indefinite determinant	*Nicolas arrivera dans quelques heures.*
quelque	invariable adverb + adjective	*Quelque appétissants que soient tes gâteaux . . .*
*quel(s) que	quelle(s) que*	indefinite adjective + subordinate conjunction	*quel que soit ton projet professionnel	quelles que soient ses intentions*

la/l'a/l'as/là

la	definite article or pronoun (both cases: feminine)	*La table, je la vois.*
l'a	contraction of *le/la + a*	*L'a-t-il vu(e) ?*
l'as	contraction of *le/la + as*	*L'as-tu fini(e) ?*
là	adverb of place = *there, here*	*Sabrina est là depuis une semaine.*

sa/ça/çà

sa	possessive adjective	*Où est sa sacoche ?*
ça	demonstrative pronoun	*J'ai regardé le feuilleton mais je n'ai pas trouvé ça passionnant.*
çà	adverb of place	*On observe, çà et là, quelques affiches.*

---

[5] Note the difference in pronunciation between *pressent* (from *presser*) where –**ent** is not pronounced, and *pressent* (from *pressentir*) where –**ent** is pronounced nasally.

prêt(s)/près

prêt(s)	adjective = *ready*	*Tu es prêt ? / Vous êtes prêts ?*
près	adverb of place	*La gare est tout près.*

plus tôt / plutôt

plus tôt	adverbial expression of time	*Le boulangerie ouvre plus tôt que d'habitude.*
plutôt	adverb suggesting preference	*Ces raisins sont récoltés à la main plutôt qu'à la machine.*

quand/quant/qu'en

quand	conjunction of time	*Quand vas-tu m'appeler ?*
quant (à)	preposition = as for/to	*Quant à demain, je ne sais pas.*
qu'en	contraction of *que + en*	*Ce problème n'est simple qu'en apparence.*

ou/où

ou	coordinating conjunction	*Pour trouver la signification, consulte un dictionnaire ou (ou bien) un lexique.*
où	adverb of place, time, situation	*Où est-ce que tu habites ? / le jour où Aurélie est venue*

quoique/quoi que

quoique	conjunction = *although*	*Quoique les fenêtres soient ouvertes il faut chaud.*
quoi que	relative pronoun = *whatever*	*Quoi que tu décides, tu me préviens.*

pourquoi/pour quoi

pourquoi	adverb or conjunction = *why*	*Pourquoi l'as-tu dit ?*
pour quoi	relative pronoun = *for what*	*Cet homme, on le condamne pour quoi ?*

The following children's nursery rhyme (*comptine enfantine*) illustrates perfectly variations (four) in spelling but uniformity in sound. Foix is a town in the southwest of France: "Il était une **fois** / Une marchande de **foie** / Qui vendait du **foie** / Dans la ville de **Foix** / Elle se dit: 'Ma **foi** / C'est la dernière **fois** / Que je vends du **foie** / dans la ville de Foix.'"

In the authors' experience, one sings *une marchande de foie* but Henriette Walter suggests the masculine form: *un marchand de foie.*

Following on from this children's nursery rhyme one comes across tongue twisters (*le virelangue*), which are as plentiful in French as they are in English, or in other Romance languages for that matter. Needless to say, tongue twisters in any language do not contain too much sense or logic, relying as they do on alliteration. The reader could try the following which are common in French, and the first of which is the most frequently and universally met:

> *Les chaussettes de l'archiduchesse sont-elles sèches et archisèches ?*
> *Ton thé t'a-t-il ôté ta toux ?*
> *Tes laitues naissent-elles ? Si tes laitues naissent, mes laitues naîtront.*
> *Pauvre petit pêcheur, prends patience pour pouvoir prendre plusieurs petits poissons.*
> *Un chasseur sachant chasser sait chasser sans son chien de chasse.*
> *Le mur murant (enclosing) Paris rend Paris murmurant.*

This last tongue twister calls for an explanation. A wall was built around Paris in the nineteenth century and had various points of entry, called *péages* (*tollgates*), the same word as that used for modern expressways/motorways. Probably the most famous of tollgates in all literature and opera can be found in the third act of Puccini's *La Bohème* where the dying Mimi meets her lover Rodolfo.

A further illustration of the use of the alliterative **s** underlines the calm and fragility of the night. The poem, composed by Ipzo l'Animot, is called *Astrolâtre*. We quote the first six lines: "Une nuit sans sommeil, sans nuage et sans lune, / Sur le sable noirci au sommet d'une dune, / Sous l'espace assoupi, bercé par le silence, / Quelques grains de poussière en essaim ensemencent / L'océan et poinçonnent le ciel où s'inspirent / Les Parques dont les sombres desseins réverbèrent / L'infini . . ."

Baudelaire, in *Les Fleurs du Mal* ("À une passante"), evokes the aggressive noise of the street, again with the **s**: "La rue assourdissante autour de moi hurlait."

The onset of Oreste's madness in Racine's *Andromaque* (Act 5, scene 5) is evoked thus: "Pour qui sont ces serpents qui sifflent sur vos têtes ?" – a quotation known by any well-tutored French-speaking pupil.

The notion of alliteration explains the very common combination of verb or noun + first name, with one other personal example: *À l'aise, Blaise !*; *Allons-y, Alonzo !*; *Relax(e), Max !*; *Tu parles, Charles !*; *Courage, Gustave !*; *Ça glisse, Alice/Ulysse !*; *D'accord, Hector !*; *Fais gaffe, Olaf !*; *Cool, Raoul !*; *Pas de panique, Monique !*; *Tu déconnes, Ron !*; *Aboule, Abdul !*; and the most common left till the end: *Ça colle, Anatole !*

2.11.2 Place names

At a national level in France, there is usually agreement over the pronunciation of place names. However, one comes across, and quite frequently, alternative regional pronunciations, and even *incohérences* within a region. The following list groups together place names, and some proper names, the pronunciation of which is not always appreciated by non-native speakers of French:

Argos, Chios, Knossos, Lesbos, Paphos (many Greek names, particularly islands, end thus, and here the final **s** is pronounced).

Generally speaking, if the final **s** of a foreign place name is pronounced in the foreign language, then the French follows suit: Caracas, Indianapolis, Memphis, Phoenix, Texas, Xérès (Jerez in Spain).

Ancenis (in western France the **s** is pronounced).

Anglet (in southwestern France here the **t** is pronounced).

Auch (in southwestern France here the **ch** is pronounced as **sh** in *shoot*).

Le Wast (village in northeastern France; here the pronunciation for those outside the area would be Le Vast where both the **s** and the **t** are pronounced, but for those living in the region it is pronounced Le Wa, clearly subject to Flemish influence).

Bourg-en-Bresse (in eastern France; most French speakers, if not all, pronounce the **g** as a **k**).

Millau (in central southern France; the double **l** is pronounced as **y** as in *boy*).

Vallet and Le Pallet provide two fascinating cases. In western France, these two towns are within ten miles of each other. However, within the area, the **t** of Vallet is pronounced but the **t** of Le Pallet is not. This is what a French speaker would call an *incohérence*. Elsewhere, it is most probable that French speakers would not pronounce the **t** in either case. The **t** of Cholet in the same area is not pronounced.[6]

Saint-Mars-la-Jaille (in Brittany), unlike the planet Mars or the esplanade near the Eiffel Tower (Champ de Mars), where the **s** is sounded, keeps a silent **s**.

The **s** of Lons in Lons-le-Saunier is pronounced.

Montpellier (in the south of France) has two pronunciations, one with a mute **e** and the other with an open **e**, although the latter is less common.

Metz in eastern France is pronounced as *mess*.

The **a** of Saône (in Saône-et-Loire, for example) is not pronounced.

The **o** of Laon is not pronounced.

The **s** of Lens is pronounced.

Bruxelles and Auxerre provide endless discussion. The **x** of these two towns is heard as both **x** and **ss**. The second pronunciation is often considered more elegant or *joli*.

---

[6] Modern technology is provoking disturbances in the area of pronunciation. For instance, the French GPS (English Satnav = Satellite Navigation) provides Vallet with no **t** pronounced. This change in pronunciation must occur everywhere.

As far as Bruxelles is concerned, the **ss** sound is often heard in Belgium since this is also the Flemish sound and Brussel is the Flemish equivalent.

The **u** of Ulm as in *la Rue d'Ulm* is pronounced as in the **u** of *rue*. Ulm is a place in southern Germany, scene of one of Napoleon's victories. This Parisian street is well known since it houses the center for the Éducation nationale.

The three letters **s**, **x** and **z** in final position are sounded more the further one goes toward southern France. Chamonix and the village Saint-Jorioz (both in the Alps) illustrate this feature, although this is less true now than in former times. The **x** of Chamonix used to be sounded in the Alpine area, and the same applies to the **z** of Saint-Jorioz, but this is increasingly less so. The **z** of Saint-Tropez in the Mediterranean area would not usually be pronounced. Away from the Alps, and moving toward the Île de France and western France, and following a traditional imaginary line from Grenoble to Bordeaux, these three consonants are often dropped in pronunciation. The **s** of the small town Cassis on the French Mediterranean is pronounced or not in southern France, according to authorities in the city/town hall, and this takes us back to the drink *cassis* (see p. 35, subsection on unpronounced/pronounced words ending in **s**). Finally, a schoolchild from northern France submitted to the rigors of a French *dictée* would encounter serious difficulties if the reader of the *dictée* were from Marseilles, for instance.

2.11.3 Proper names (see also Chapter 65 on proper names)

Albert Camus (unpronounced **s**), Goth (Germanic tribe; **th** not pronounced), Mahomet (**t** is silent), Marat (**t** is silent), Clément Marot (**t** is silent), François Mauriac (**c** is pronounced as with numerous towns in the Bordeaux area where he was born: Aurillac, Bergerac, Cognac, Ribérac, Jarnac, etc.), Pâris (the Greek mythical figure; here the **s** is pronounced, unlike the capital of France, Paris), Robespierre (here the **s** is pronounced and the first **e** is open, as in **mer**), Georges Sand (here the **d** is pronounced), Christ (**st** pronounced), but in Jésus-Christ the **st** is not pronounced. The **s** of Vénus is pronounced.

2.11.4 Spelling traps

There are cases where cognate words in English and French appear identical in form. On the other hand, there are cases where slight differences exist between the two languages, for example French *juridiction* > English *jurisdiction*, French *remontrance* > English *remonstrance*. These variations often concern single/double consonants, the presence of the final **e** in French but not in English, or a difference of vowels. The divergences are often slight, but they do exist. The following selection presents some of these divergences:

abréviation	*abbreviation*	infatigable	*indefatigable*
s'acclimater	*to acclimatize*	offensant	*offensive* (adj.)
archiduc	*archduke*	inoffensif	*inoffensive*
adresse	*address*	littéral	*literal*
bagage	*baggage*	loterie	*lottery*
calme	*calm*	littérature	*literature*
caractère	*character*	littéraire	*literary*
carotte	*carrot*	livide (*deathly pale*)	*livid*
céleste	*celestial, heavenly*		
circulaire	*circular*	juridiction	*jurisdiction*
condescendance	*condescension*	provocant	*provocative*
condoléances	*condolences*	mouvement	*movement*
courrier	*courier*	(ir)responsable	*(ir)responsible*
cocon	*cocoon*	rafraîchir	*refresh*
délinquant	*delinquent*	recommander	*recommend*
développement	*development*	ressources	*resources*
dromadaire	*dromedary*	symétrie	*symmetry*
entreprise	*enterprise*	ressusciter	*resuscitate*
enveloppe	*envelope*	rime	*rhyme*
environnement	*environment*	rythme	*rhythm*
exemple	*example*	seconde	*second (of time)*
extase	*ecstasy*	sentinelle	*sentinel*
girafe	*giraffe*	solliciter	*solicit*
groupe	*group*	sollicitude	*solicitude*
(im)personnel	*(im)personal*	sycomore	*sycamore*
(in)dépendant/ce	*(in)dependent/ce*	tarif	*tariff*
liqueur	*liquor*	transfert	*transfer*
liquide	*liquid*	ustensile	*utensil*
novateur	*innovative*	végétarisme	*vegetarianism*

For American speakers note: omelette = *omlet*.

2.12 Words common to French and English

Two of the main sources of the English language are Latin and Greek, notably through the medium of one or other of the Romance languages. French also derives to a large extent from these two languages. It therefore comes as no surprise that a large number of words in English and French are very similar in form and meaning, and in some cases their form, if not their meaning, is exactly the same.

The differences in the words listed below have a certain regularity, the understanding of which will provide considerable assistance to the student of French.

2.12.1 Nouns

The following list provides the principal terminations common to both languages, embracing a very large number of words.

F	–ade	no change		*brigade, salade*
M/F	–age	no change		*équipage, personnage, cage, page, rage*
M	–al	no change		*canal, métal*
M	–alt	adds	e	*asphalte, basalte* but *cobalt*
M	–ant	no change		*éléphant, instant*
M	–arian	becomes	–aire	*centenaire, unitaire*
M	–ator	becomes	–ateur	*orateur, régulateur*
M	–ce	no change		*commerce, palace, précipice*
M	–cle	no change		*article, cercle, obstacle*
M	–ent	no change		*accident, agent, régent*
M	–ge	no change		*privilège, vestige*
M	–gen	becomes	–gène	*oxygène*
M	–graph	becomes	–graphe	*autographe, photographe*
F	–ic	becomes	–ique	*logique, musique, rhétorique*
F	–ine	no change		*discipline, doctrine, mine*
F	–ion	no change		*confusion, infusion, religion*
M	–isk	becomes	–isque	*astérisque, risque*
M	–ism	adds	e	*despotisme, romantisme, paganisme*
M/F	–ist	adds	e	*artiste, dentiste, fleuriste, pianiste*
M	–ite	no change		*granite, lignite, nitrite.* But one does see and hear *granit.* The **t** is pronounced here.
M	–ment	no change		*fragment, instrument, monument*
M	–meter	becomes	–mètre	*baromètre, kilomètre, tacomètre*
F	–mony	becomes	–monie	*cérémonie, parcimonie*
F	–nce	no change		*abondance, province, violence*
M	–oid	adds	e	*sphéroïde, stéroïde,* but *celluoïd*
M	–or	becomes	–eur	*acteur, couleur, horreur, vapeur*
M	–ose	no change		*glucose*

M	-ot	adds	e	despote, patriote
M	-phone	no change		téléphone, mégaphone, xylophone
M	-scope	no change		caméscope, microscope, téléscope
F	-sis	becomes	-se	crise, névrose, synthèse, thèse
M/F	-ter/-tre	becomes	-tre	centre, lettre
F	-tion	no change		condition, nation, tentation
F	-tude	no change		décrépitude, multitude, platitude
F	-ty	becomes	-té	éternité, société, moralité
M/F	-ule	no change		bidule, globule, module, mule, nodule
F	-ure	no change		cure, figure, (agri)culture, sinécure
M	-um	no change		aluminium, géranium, muséum (of natural history) but musée = museum
F	-y	becomes	-ie	anatomie, énergie, géographie, oncologie, technologie, zoologie, téléphonie

2.12.2 Adjectives

Only the masculine forms of the adjectives are given.

-acious	becomes	-ace	fugace, sagace, tenace
-al	no change		moral, central, fatal
-an	becomes	-ain	américain, humain
-ant	no change		abondant, dominant
-ar	becomes	-aire	circulaire, solaire
-arious	becomes	-aire	grégaire, précaire
-ary	becomes	-aire	ordinaire, contraire
-ble	no change		noble, notable, soluble
-ct	no change		compact, contact, intact
-ense	no change		dense, immense
-ent	no change		évident, prudent, effervescent
-ferrous	becomes	-fère	aurifère, carbonifère
-ic/ical	becomes	-ic/ique	pacifique, public, satirique
-id	becomes	-ide	rapide, solide, valide
-ile	no change		docile, fertile, fragile
-ine	becomes	-in	aquilin, canin, félin, léonin, masculin
-ite	becomes	-it	érudit

–ive	becomes	–if	*actif, décisif, passif*
–lent	no change		*turbulent, violent, virulent*
–nal	becomes	–urne	*diurne, nocturne*
–ocious	becomes	–oce	*atroce, féroce, précoce*
–ous	becomes	–eux	*glorieux, lumineux, monstrueux*
–tial	no change		*(im)partial*
–und	becomes	–ond	*moribond, rubicond*
–ure	becomes	–ur	*futur, (im)pur*

2.12.3 Verbs

–ate	becomes	–er	*calculer, évaluer, innover*
–fy	becomes	–fier	*amplifier, fortifier, magnifier*
–ize/ise	becomes	–iser	*civiliser, organiser, réaliser*
–e	A great number of verbs of this termination are inherited		

	from the French: *admirer, combiner, causer, continuer,*		
	determiner, imaginer, observer.		

It should be borne in mind that not all the English terminations listed above can be automatically turned into French by the changes indicated; neither should it be assumed that all words with similar or identical spellings have the same meaning.

2.13 Spelling *rectifications* as prescribed by the Conseil supérieur de la langue française in 1990 and approved by the Académie française

It must be stated at the outset that many of what are called in French *rectifications* or preferably in English "modifications" do not seem to have any weight, and the former spellings can still apply with no sanctions whatsoever. Indeed, many very literate French people pay no attention to them. One wonders why the following *rectifications* were even suggested:

1. Circumflex accents may be omitted: *apparaitre (apparaître), couter (coûter)*. In some cases of possible confusion retention is recommended: *mûr, sûr*, although where the confusion lies is open to serious conjecture. See Chapter 3 on written accents.
2. The *tréma* may change its place so that it carries out its diacritic function more clearly: *ambiguïté > ambigüité, aiguë > aigüe, contigüe > contigüe*. Otherwise, *aiguë* for instance could be pronounced **aig**. Yet even here, the pronunciation **aig** is inconceivable for a French speaker. See Chapter 3 on written accents. The *MULTI dictionnaire* of de Villers (2003) retains the old spelling, so we are no further forward here.
3. The plural of compound nouns causes a stir as well with verb + noun. The suggestion is that a plural **s** should be added: *des garde-chasses, des essuie-mains*. See the section on the plural of compound nouns in Chapter 10.

4. The past participle *laissé* followed by an infinitive remains invariable: *les arbres qu'elle a laissé pousser*. The same goes for *faire*: *les chœurs que le chef d'orchestre a fait chanter*.

5. The plural of foreign words should correspond to French practice: *des lieds* (*songs*) and not *des lieder*; *des matchs* and not des *matches*; also: *des flashs/sandwichs/sketchs*.

6. It is suggested that *allégrement* should be entirely replaced by *allègrement*, which has always existed alongside *allégrement*. There is considerable uncertainty over *événement/évènement*.

Spelling seems to provide a source of torment to the guardians of the French language. It assumes obsessive proportions, witness the passions attracted by the famous dictation of Mérimée, and the spelling championships that take place, even in Belgium. Bernard Pivot has carried these championships throughout the whole of the francophone world.

What is certain is that, notwithstanding the innumerable pitfalls lying in wait for the unsuspecting foreigner, or the uninformed native speaker, the English language does not provoke the same furore, and the English accept with equanimity the American modifications to, for instance, *colour / color*, *centre / center*, *encyclopaedia / encyclopedia* and the multifarious other changes. O that French and English spelling were as simple as that of Spanish!

2.14 Dictations

French dictations are generally taken more seriously in France than English dictations are in England, or in other English-speaking countries. They are part of the curriculum up to the age of fifteen/sixteen (*troisième*), whereas in the English-speaking world they seem to attract no national requirement at all, notwithstanding the flagrant incoherence of all English pronunciation, witness *bough*, *plough*, *through*, *though*, *thorough*, *trough*, and *Susy* and *busy*. Some of the features of a French dictation are described below.

The passage is read at normal speed in order to acquaint the pupil/student with the content. It is then read a second time, very slowly, with indications of punctuation: *point*, *virgule*, *point virgule*, *deux points*, *guillemets*, *à la ligne* (*new paragraph*), etc. Capital letters are not given, any more than accents are. You have to work out the acute, grave, circumflex, cedilla and *tréma* accents according to the precision of the sound. Small children in northern France could have problems if receiving a dictation from someone from the south. The passage is read a third time, and a further period of time is allowed for corrections. Below are two passages, written by one of the authors, that may be used as dictations. Note that, in the first passage, a *maîtresse d'école* or *institutrice* is now called a *professeure des écoles*. Note also the considerable use of capital letters, the unsounded correspondence of plural verbs with plural subject nouns, the plural **s** when often not sounded, except with *liaison*, an extra, unsounded **e** for the feminine, hyphens, the conversion of **d** into a **t** with *grand oncle*, and double **n** when one **n** is used in English: *perso**nn**alité*.

Dictation 1

This dictation narrates the experience of a very young child living her first years at Viviers-sur-Rhône, in southern France. The first paragraph contains numerous references to ecclesiastical buildings that delighted the young children at the time. The second and third paragraphs recount the initial steps on the educational ladder, as well as the most affectionate and intimate feelings generated by a happy family atmosphere, while the attractions of food formed no small part in this enjoyment. Note the following:

1. *Maîtresses* and *écoles* have unsounded final **s**'s. *Ravies* agrees with *maîtresses*, although the **es** is not heard. Note that *étaient* is plural.
2. The **C** of *Cathédrale* is a capital letter and this word ends with an unsounded **e**.
3. *Autres* has an unsounded **s** since it is plural and agrees with *monuments*.
4. *Particuliers* has an unsounded **s** and agrees with *hôtels*.
5. *Éveillent* is a plural verb form, although it could also be singular here: *éveille*.
6. *Saisissants* has an unsounded **s**, agreeing with *contrastes* which has an **e**.
7. *Inscrite* has a sounded **t**, agreeing with the preceding direct object: m' = me (feminine). *Avaient* is plural, like *connaissaient* and *cohabitaient* in the last paragraph.
8. Note the feminine agreements of the adjectives: *maternelle, aînée, donnée, reçue, laïque, ménagères, sorties*, where the ending final **e** is not sounded. Notice the dieresis (*tréma*): la*ï*que.
9. The ending **e** causes the consonants in *grande, petite* and *exquises* to be sounded but the second **s** of this last adjective is not heard.
10. Note the cedilla under the **c** of *façonné*.
11. Note the hyphen in *grand-père*.
12. Accents, acute and grave, occur frequently. The circumflex accent appears a number of times too.

Terre de lumières et de contrastes

Les maîtresses d'écoles étaient ravies de nous raconter l'histoire de Viviers-sur-Rhône dans l'Ardèche méridionale. Ce village médiéval, situé sur un rocher au bord du Rhône, affiche de nombreux symboles religieux : la Tour Saint Michel, la Cathédrale Saint Vincent, l'Église Saint Laurent, le Palais Épiscopal ou l'Ancien Évêché, le Grand Séminaire, le Couvent de Saint Roch et bien d'autres monuments et hôtels particuliers qui constituent une véritable richesse dans la région Rhône-Alpes.

Chaque coin et recoin du village éveillent en moi de merveilleux souvenirs gravés dans ma mémoire. En puisant dans mes souvenirs d'enfance, la découverte de contrastes saisissants surgit dans mon esprit. À la fin des années cinquante, mes parents m'avaient inscrite à l'école maternelle. À l'époque, ma sœur aînée avait trois ans et demi, et moi j'avais un an de moins. L'éducation donnée par mes parents et l'instruction reçue à l'école laïque ont façonné, à jamais, le caractère et la personnalité de leurs enfants.

Les Vivaroises et Vivarois se connaissaient tous et cohabitaient comme une grande famille. Papa travaillait tôt le matin, maman s'occupait de ma petite sœur, la dernière née, ainsi que des tâches ménagères à la maison. Chaque matin, mon grand-oncle paternel, que nous appelions « grand-p ère », jouait le rôle d'accompagnateur. Nous passions d'abord à la boulangerie pour acheter des brioches chaudes, sorties du four. Les odeurs exquises du pain et des pâtisseries nous donnaient l'eau à la bouche.

Dictation 2

This second dictation describes a simple form of orienteering in southern France which covers a five-kilometer circuit, designed for small children. Notice particularly the use of the preterit or past historic, the imperfect subjunctive which would certainly test young French children since it is rarely used in spoken language, except for humorous or pedantic purposes, numerous unsounded s's, as well as the sounded **s** largely through *liaison*, agreement of adjectives with feminine nouns or nouns in the plural, an aspirate **h**. The th in *cathédrale* is pronounced as a **t**. Accents occur with frequency, with a fair scattering of circumflexes. *Plein* and *pleine* are pronounced the same way in *en plein air* and *en pleine saison/campagne*.

Le jeu de piste

Sur le rocher de Châteauvieux, nous fûmes en position de surplomber l'allée du Rhône jonchée, de part et d'autre, de platanes. Nous admiri-ons avec extase les amandiers, les abricotiers, les pêchers, les cerisiers en floraison. Au fil de l'eau, des péniches traversèrent le Rhône, ce grand fleuve d'Europe. En pleine saison, nous savourions la nature et la richesse agricole de la vie rurale. Quel bonheur de se retrouver sur les hauteurs de la cité épiscopale et d'admirer la vue panoramique qui s'offrit à nos yeux d'enfants !

Le garde-champêtre nous prévint du danger pour que nous fussions prudents. Le jeudi après-midi fut réservé aux activités ludiques du patronage. Les religieuses désiraient que nous arrivassions à l'heure pile. Elles avaient agi de la sorte pour que nous eussions le temps d'examiner notre programme récréatif. Il fallait pour cela qu'elles fussent dynamiques et qu'elles aimassent animer et organiser des activités en plein air. Dès que les hirondelles annonçaient le printemps, les sœurs de Saint Roch proposaient notre jeu favori.

Le but du jeu fut de tracer un circuit pédestre, en pleine campagne, au milieu des fermes, des animaux et des arbres fruitiers. Cette activité nous donna l'occasion de travailler en équipe, de décoder des messages, de découvrir la nature. Le jeu dura tout l'après-midi sur un parcours de cinq kilomètres environ. Nous eûmes l'habitude de partir de la cathédrale, en parcourant les ruelles pavées du village médiéval, en chantant des comptines [counting/nursery rhymes], sous les applaudissements des riverains.

2.15 The language of texting (le texto = *the text*; not to be copied in formal writing)

Following the telegram which, submitted to its own constraints, created its own lapidary style, SMS (Short Message Service) or texting has also developed its characteristic language, in French as in English. SMS is also used in French.

For generational reasons, the SMS is the preferred method of communication for young people between the ages of 15 and 25. It is discrete and cheap, while its coded messages can remain indecipherable to the uninitiated, therefore to most parents. There is nothing easier to establish a sense of community and belonging than inventing a kind of dialect known only to the members of that community.

There exists also a further reason behind the popularity of texting, clearly less "social," and in the lower echelons of literary expression: to be able to send a message from a mobile phone where each key corresponds to several letters enables the user to gain time, and to avoid keying in unnecessary information. In order to communicate speedily, words are reduced to their simplest written expression, so that **qu** becomes **k**. *C'est quoi* is transformed into **cékoi** or even **ckwa**, and so on.

Abbreviations, puzzles or acronyms of all kinds are obviously welcome: **stp** = *s'il te plaît*, **raf** = *rien à faire* or, in vulgar mode, *rien à foutre*, **Ri129** = *rien de neuf*, **MDR** = *mort de rire*. Certain expressions are even more cryptic: **kézako** = *Qu'est-ce que c'est ?* The only prevailing rule in texting is precisely the absence of rules. Traditional spelling is cast to the wind, while kicking over orthographic traces is a virtue in itself. For many users, the essential is that phonetic transcription be correct and familiar or intimate: **savapa** (*Ça va pas*), **kestufé** (*Qu'est que tu fais ?*).

This new language allows the creation of a happier, livelier and more jolly sense of being: **ta ht du p1** is more acceptable than *T'as acheté du pain ?*

Je t'aiiiiiiiiiiiiiime strikes a tone of greater originality and even passion than Je *t'aime*.

There follows a simple text dictionary of terms with their full French equivalent. The full French equivalents include upper case, and other forms of orthographic signs, which highlight the differences between texting and traditonal writing. There follow five examples of texting, which even includes, not surprisingly, some use of English.

SMS vocabulary

a12c4	À un de ces quatre
a2m1	À demain
a+	À plus tard
a b1to	À bientôt !
apelré	Appellerai
asap	au plus vite (*as soon as possible*)
asv	âge, sexe, ville (ex : 33, H, Paris)
ayé	Ça y est !
bi1	Bien
B1sur	Bien sûr !
bi1to	Bientôt
Biz	Bises
Bap	Bon après-midi
bcp	Beaucoup
bjr	Bonjour !
bsr	Bonsoir !
C	C'est
C 2 labal	C'est de la balle !
Cad	C'est-à-dire ?
C b1	C'est bien !
C cho	C'est chaud !
C mal1	C'est malin !
C pa 5pa	C'est pas sympa !
C 2L8	C'est trop tard (c'est *too late*)
Dak	D'accord !
D 100	Descends !
Dsl	Désolé
fé	Fait
G1id2kdo	J'ai une idée de cadeau
G la N	J'ai la haine !
GPT lé plon	J'ai pété les plombs
Gre	Grenoble
GspR b1	J'espère bien

Gt	J'étais
GT o 6né	J'étais au ciné
J	Je
Jariveré	J'arriverai
je le sa V	Je le savais !
jenémar	J'en ai marre !
je t'M	Je t'aime !
jspr	j'espère
k	que
keske C	Qu'est-ce que c'est ?
kestudi	Qu'est-ce que tu dis ?
kestu X	Qu'est-ce que tu crois ?
kestufé, kefétu	Qu'est-ce que tu fais ? Que fais-tu ?
koi29	Quoi de neuf ?
MDR	mort de rire
Mé	mais
nvo	nouveau
num	numéro
oci	aussi
plésir	plaisir
port	portable
pr	pour
PTDR	pété de rire
Raf	rien à faire
ras	rien à signaler
rdv	rendez-vous
rép	répondu
r1	rien
savapa	Ça va pas ?
slt	Salut !
stp	s'il te plaît !
tabitou	T'habites où ?
tata KS	Tu as ta caisse (voiture) ?
tel	téléphone
ti2	T'es hideux
tjs	toujours
t ko q	T'es cocu !
tkc	T'es cassé (T'es fatigué)
t le + bo	T'es le plus beau
t oqp	T'es occupé ?
t nrv	T'es énervé ?
tré	Très
V	Vais

V1	Viens !
Vazi	Vas-y !
Ver	Vers
VrMan	Vraiment !
2	De

SMS 1

bjr Tata. C assia. il sagit du nvo num de tel port de Zinou. J V tenvoyer les 4 sms. celui ci en é 1 bon ex oci. A t bi1 to. Grosses Biz. Assia. ☺

Transcription: Bonjour Tata, c'est Assia. Il s'agit du nouveau numéro de telephone portable de Zinou. Je vais t'envoyer les quatre SMS. Celui-ci en est un bon exemple aussi. A bientôt ! Grosses bises ! Assia. ☺

This happy face allows the expression of the joy felt by the person writing the text. There exist of course all sorts of icons which point to anger, satisfaction, fear, sadness and so on.

SMS 2

Slt ca va ? Oui C tjs mon num mai gt pa a gre e jave pa mon port C pr ca. jspr k t va bi1. Gros bisous

Transcription: Salut ! Ça va ? Oui c'est toujours mon numéro mais je n'étais pas à Grenoble et je n'avais pas mon portable, c'est pour ça. J'espère que tu vas bien. Gros bisous.

SMS 3

Merci pr ton sms. dsl 2 pa avoir rep avan. ca ma fe tre plesir oci 2 te revoir. A bi1 to. Biz.

Transcription: Merci pour ton SMS. Désolée de ne pas avoir répondu avant. Ça m'a fait très plaisir aussi de te revoir. A bientôt ! Bises.

SMS 4

Ok ca marche. J fini a 12h15. J vs apelre a ce momen la. Biz a tt a lheure !

Transcription: Ok ça marche. Je finis à 12h 15. Je vous appellerai à ce moment-là. Bises, à tout à l'heure.

SMS 5

J sui reparti. J pense k jarivere a la gare ver 18h15.

Transcription: Je suis repartie. Je pense que j'arriverai à la gare vers 18h 15.

3

Written accents / Les accents écrits[1]

The passage below evokes the concept of enriching international exchanges between France and Australia, and, in this specific case, the University of Adelaide, which has a great number of attractive features to offer a student of French nationality or a professor on an exchange visit. The passage describes the delightful environment surrounding the students on the university campus. As with any French text, all the different accents are inevitably encountered, from the acute to the grave and the circumflex, to the dieresis and the hyphen. As noted in the analysis following the passage, accents also appear now on upper case letters.

Une jeunesse studieuse en Australie méridionale
Le gouvernement australien s'est fixé comme objectifs de soutenir, auprès des universités, les programmes de mobilité étudiante dans le but d'inciter un grand nombre de jeunes à participer à ces projets, d'encourager les universités étrangères à venir en Australie pour promouvoir leurs propres institutions comme destinations potentielles. Quel bonheur d'avoir pu saisir cette opportunité dans le cadre du *Australian Exchange Fair Circuit* !

Comme bon nombre de collègues d'universités étrangères, j'ai participé à cette manifestation importante en rendant visite aux universités australiennes, en découvrant leur environnement de travail, en prenant contact avec leurs étudiants, leur personnel enseignant et administratif, en faisant la promotion de l'offre de formation de mon établissement et des nombreux services offerts aux étudiants étrangers afin de les aider à s'installer et à s'intégrer plus facilement en France. Le campus verdoyant de l'université d'Adelaïde est situé à proximité du centre-ville. Il est très arboré [It is a very wooded area] et compte de magnifiques façades, de belles cours intérieures, d'anciens cloîtres [cloisters] en brique rouge et des bâtiments en pierre ocre. Des constructions modernes se combinent à l'architecture ancienne. Les étudiants organisent

---

[1] For an exhaustive study of this topic, see Louis Guéry's *Dictionnaire des règles typographiques* (2005) referred to in the bibliography.

leurs rencontres en milieu associatif grâce à un réseau dynamique de clubs sportifs, d'organisations syndicales et de nombreuses activités sociales.

Les saisons sont inversées par rapport aux nôtres. Fin mars début avril, nous avons assisté aux vendanges [grape harvest] et pris un repas dans un cadre bucolique de la célèbre vallée de Barossa, région viticole que nous avons traversée avec des températures exceptionnelles qui se situaient entre 30 et 40 degrés Celsius. La qualité de la vie à Adelaïde en fait une ville universitaire active et prête à une ouverture internationale. Les garçons et les filles passent une partie de leur bel âge à étudier et à s'épanouir dans un milieu enrichissant et stimulant. Les échanges extra-européens ont un bel avenir en perspective.

Written accents, sometimes known as orthographical signs, are signs written over or under letters (e.g., ç) which indicate the pronunciation of these letters or help differentiate between words that are written in the same way. Initially, it may be more helpful to refer to these signs as "orthographic" since the word "accent" is ambiguous. The term "accent" may point to the characteristic mode of pronunciation of a person or group, especially one that discloses social or geographical origin (compare the Parisian and Marseilles accents). "Accent" may also relate to the tonic accent, or forceful utterance associated with the particular syllable of a word, and is a strong feature of English, Spanish and Italian, whereas in French any stress falls on the last syllable of a word and is usually very slight. Our concern here is exclusively the consideration of marks that highlight often subtle differences in the pronunciation of individual letters, particularly vowels. The signs treated in this chapter are also referred to in Chapter 2 on alphabet.

There are five orthographical signs in French. These are: acute accent or *accent aigu* (é), grave accent or *accent grave* (è), circumflex accent or *accent circonflexe* (â/ê/î), dieresis or *tréma* (ë/ï/ü) and cedilla or *cédille* (ç). (The term *diérèse* exists in French but this refers to the breaking up of a diphthong and thus creating a hiatus: *trouer, fluet, oublier*). For simplicity's sake, the term "accent" is used from now on. Formerly, accents were not written over upper-case letters but this practice has changed, and all letters, upper and lower case, take an accent where necessary.

3.1 The acute accent

The acute accent is placed exclusively over the letter **e** as in: *cédille, école, regardé, série, supérieur. Jérémie est désespéré car il a perdu sa précieuse clé.* It is a clear, sharp, closed sound and is in no way diphthongized as the *e* can be in English. It sounds like the *i* in English *it.*

The vowel **e** which produces the sound **é** does not always bear an accent. There is no written acute accent if the letter **e** is followed by a double consonant or an **x**: *de***ss***in, e***ff***acer, e***ff***ort, e***rr***eur, e***ss***ence, e***x***ercice.*

There is no written accent on the **e** of the final syllable when it ends in **-d, -f, -r, -z**: *le pie**d**, la cle**f**, le boulange**r**, chante**r**, premie**r**, le ne**z**.* Interestingly enough, *la clef* is also written *la clé* and, logically, this produces the same sound.

There is no accent on the definite and indefinite articles (*les, des*) or on the possessive adjectives (*mes, tes, ses*).

The inversion of the first-person singular of certain verbs, which is high R3 register, produces an **e** acute: *aim**é**-je, puiss**é**-je.* The Conseil supérieur de la langue française recommends *aim**è**-je* and *puiss**è**-je* but the use of this grave accent is not shared by everyone. The difference in sound here between **é** and **è** is almost imperceptible and need not be a source of worry.

The acute accent is also used with capitals: *MÉDUSE (jelly fish).*

3.2 The grave accent

The grave accent is placed over the letters **e**, **a** and **u**. When it is placed over the letter **e**, it is pronounced as an open **e**, as with the *ai* in the English *pair*.

The grave accent is used when a consonant is followed by a mute **e** in a certain number of words: *le p**è**re, la m**è**re, l'**é**l**è**ve, le pi**è**ge, DEUXI**È**ME.* The third example, *élève*, illustrates perfectly the closed and open sounds of the **e**. One further example: *Cet athl**è**te poss**è**de une bonne hygi**è**ne de vie.*

The open sound of **e** also occurs in a certain number of verbs in the first group: *Je l**è**ve la main pour prendre la parole* contrasted with *Nous levons*; *Sophie ach**è**te des fruits* contrasted with *Nous achetons.*

The grave accent on the **e** is also placed over the feminine nouns and adjectives which end in **-er** and **-ier**: *le boulanger > la boulang**è**re, l'infirmier > l'infirmi**è**re, léger > lég**è**re, premier > premi**è**re.* It also occurs on a certain number of words ending in **-s**: *apr**è**s, d**è**s, exc**è**s, proc**è**s, tr**è**s.* The grave **e** used in such terms as *médi**è**viste, seizi**è**miste, dix-septi**è**miste* and *vingti**è**miste* (these terms relate to scholars of the appropriate period) should, according to the *Le petit Robert*, be an acute **e** instead: *médi**é**viste, seizi**é**miste* and so on. This confusion between **é** and **è** when they occur in unstressed positions is very common. Below are examples of words where uncertainty persists. *Le petit Robert* suggests *abr**é**gement* but *Grevisse* recommends *abr**è**gement.* Similarly, *Le petit Robert* suggests *aff**é**terie* but *Grevisse* recommends *aff**è**terie.* The following is a list where clarity is confounded. Le petit Robert precedes *Grevisse*: *all**é**gement/all**è**gement, ass**é**chement/ass**è**chement, c**é**leri/c**è**leri, cr**é**merie/cr**è**merie, cr**é**nelage/cr**è**nelage, d**é**règlementation* in both cases, *empi**é**tement/empi**è**tement, év**é**nement/év**è**nement, év**é**nementiel/év**è**nementiel* (*Grevisse* accepts both of these, while only *av**è**nement* exists), *s**é**cheresse/s**è**cheresse, s**é**cherie/s**è**cherie.*

No divergences occur with the prefixes **dé** and **pré** (*démesuré, prélever*), or with initial **é** (*échelon, écheveau, édredon, élever, émeraude, épeler, éperon*) and their cognate words (*échelonner, élevage, éperonner*).

Care needs to be taken over certain verbs in the different persons of their conjugation or corresponding nouns: *le siège / siéger / je siège*; *céder / je cède*.

When the grave accent is placed over the letter **a**, there is no phonetic difference from the **a** without it. Compare *la table* to *là* (adverb of place = *here, there*). Compare also *elle a* (verb from *avoir*) and *à* (preposition) *l'école*. Furthermore, *à* occurs in a few other words: *déjà, voilà, au-delà*.

When the grave accent is placed over the letter **u** in the word *ou > où*, it allows us to differentiate the relative pronoun and the interrogative adverb from the conjunction *ou*. There is no phonetic difference. Compare *Voici la maison **où*** (pronoun) *j'habite* / ***Où*** (adverb) *allez-vous?* and *Tu veux du thé **ou*** (conjunction) *du café?* It goes without saying that there can hardly be any confusion between *ou* and *où*.

The grave accent is also used with capitals: *Bibliothèque SAINTE–GENEVIÈVE*.

3.3 The circumflex accent

The circumflex accent (often humorously called *chapeau chinois*) is placed over all five written vowels. It marks the disappearance of a letter in modern French, and usually this letter is an **s**. In these examples, Old French precedes modern French: **as**ne > **â**ne; h**os**pital > h**ô**pital; t**es**te > t**ê**te; **is**le > **î**le; **aa**ge > **â**ge; cr**os**te > cr**oû**te. Compare these modern French words with some Spanish words (*asno, hospital, isla, costra*), some Italian words (*asino, ospedale, testa, isola, crosta*) and four English words (*ass, hospital, island, crust*).

When the circumflex occurs over an **o**, it modifies the sound by making it more closed: *notre ami / le nôtre*; *votre amie / la vôtre*.

When the circumflex occurs over the **a**, it modifies the **a** by making the sound more open and pronounced higher in the mouth: *âne, crâne, flâner/flâneur, hâbleur, mânes* as opposed to *mal(heur), sale*.

When it is placed over an **e**, the sound is open: *la fenêtre, la tête, extrême, même. Le joueur se jette tête baissée dans la mêlée.*

The circumflex accent points to certain other differences, although, as with *ou* and *où*, there is little room for confusion: *du* (partitive article) / *dû* (past participle of *devoir*); *mur* (noun) / *mûr* (adjective); *sur* (preposition) / *sûr* (adjective).

Dû loses its circumflex when in the feminine or plural form: *l'erreur due à... / les disputes dues à...*

The circumflex is also used with capitals: *MÊME*.

3.4 The dieresis

The dieresis (*tréma*) indicates that, when there are two contiguous vowels, they are pronounced separately: *le maïs* = a + i (*maize*) as opposed to *mais* (*but*), which is pronounced with an open **e**. Also: *une héroïne* as opposed to the **oine** of *pivoine* (**vwa**), for instance. Similarly, in the nouns *ambigüité* and *Sinaï*, **u + i** and **a + i** are pronounced separately. The same is true in *Hanoï* and *Shanghaï*.

When the dieresis occurs over the **u** in the syllable **güe**, it entails the pronunciation of **u**. Compare *une blague* / *une figue* and *aigüe/ambigüe* (*aiguë* and *ambiguë* are the older feminine forms but still very frequently used). The **u** in *blague* and *figue* is not pronounced.

The dieresis is also used with capitals: *Mme de STAËL*.

Here are some further words that use the *tréma*: *caïd, canoë, dalaï-lama, Dostoïevski, Haïti, Jamaïque, maoïste, Tolstoï*.

3.5 The cedilla

The term "cedilla" comes from the diminutive of the Spanish *zeta/zeda* (*z*), which disappeared from use in the eighteenth century. The cedilla appears like an upside-down **c**, and is placed beneath the consonant **c** when it is followed by an **a**, **o** or **u**. This indicates that the **c** is to be pronounced as an **ss**, and not like a **k**: *le français, nous commençons, j'ai reçu*.

The cedilla is also used with capitals: *FAÇADE NORD*.

3.6 Foreign accents

Some foreign accents are also observed, although they are not frequent. Geographical names such as Afghānistān bear an accent. Czech names are often spelled with a *háček*: Čapek (author of *The Absolute at Large*) and Hašek (of *The Good Soldier Švejk* fame, a celebrated satire of World War I).

The Spanish *tilde* (feminine in Spanish but masculine in French) is not uncommon, notably with words of Spanish origin: *cañon* (also *canyon*), *doña* (as in Doña Sol in Victor Hugo's play *Hernani*, set in the Basque Country). It should be added that, although foreigners see the *tilde* as the mark over the *n* (ñ), its true Spanish meaning refers to all written accents over Spanish words.

The above rules governing written accents apply to all writing. However, many unlettered French speakers, or people writing hastily, as in an e-mail or texting, often ignore them. This is a practice not to be copied in formal writing.

4

Punctuation, font, upper and lower case / La ponctuation, la police de caractères, les majuscules et minuscules

The passage below illustrates some of the uses of French punctuation and upper and lower cases. Notice particularly how the use of capitals (with accents), small letters (adjectives, days, months and languages, and in titles after the first substantial word, but excluding names) and inverted commas differs from English practice, although there is uncertainty in French over upper or lower case with cardinal points. Notice also the use of italics for titles of books and films, as in English. The use of upper case for *Déesse de l'Amour* (a form of personification) differs from the lower case of *dieux* and *déesses* since it is unique, just like Christians or Muslims refer to their God with a capital: *Dieu*, *Allah*.

Chypre, joyau de la Méditerranée
Cette île se situe entre l'Orient et l'Occident, un point où s'entrecroisent deux cultures. Les Grecs et les Turcs se partagent cette petite île pour des raisons géopolitiques. Cette partition se vit comme une déchirure par le peuple insulaire, d'un côté les Chypriotes grecs, de l'autre les Chypriotes turcs. La présence britannique sur l'île est caractérisée par des bases militaires qui surplombent la « Grande bleue » [the Mediterranean Sea: a common colloquial term] qui se situe au carrefour de l'Europe, de l'Afrique et de l'Asie.

Les péripéties de notre voyage nous ont conduits à Nicosie, Larnaca, Limassol puis à Paphos sur l'île de Chypre. Nous avons parcouru des paysages sublimes. La ville de Paphos force l'admiration. Elle est dotée de nombreux sites archéologiques qui remontent à la Grèce antique. Cette ville est très connue pour son temple d'Aphrodite. Des mosaïques exposent l'effigie de la Déesse de l'Amour et de la Beauté. La mythologie grecque demeure un ensemble de mythes obscurs en raison de leur complexité. Les monstres marins, les guerres intestines, les intrigues amoureuses, les héros mythiques, les dieux et les déesses gouvernent cet univers complexe. Un ouvrage en anglais intitulé *Paphos : Land of Aphrodite* brosse un tableau intéressant de ce pays légendaire.

Chypre a su préserver un environnement naturel et sauvage. L'île est séparée entre la communauté grecque et turque. Le grec et le turc sont les langues officielles. Les Chypriotes, appelés également Cypriotes, aspirent à un plan de réunification de l'île. Le 1er mai 2004, la République (grecque) de Chypre est devenue membre de l'Union européenne. Neuf autres pays ont emboîté le pas [followed suit] pour élargir l'Union européenne en passant de quinze à vingt-cinq pays membres : Estonie, Hongrie, Lettonie [Latvia], Lituanie, Malte, Pologne, République tchèque, Slovaquie, Slovénie. La Bulgarie et la Roumanie sont venues agrandir à vingt-sept membres la famille européenne. A l'heure actuelle, la procédure de réunification de l'île de Chypre semble prendre une tournure positive, en partie grâce à son adhésion à l'Europe.

4.1 Punctuation

Punctuation refers to the system of marks or points inserted in a text to clarify the meaning or signal a change in pitch or intonation, highlighting pauses or certain logical links. It is an essential element in avoiding what could be startling misunderstandings in written communication. Three examples, one in English and two in French, illustrate this possibility of hilarious misunderstanding. Lynne Truss's *Eats, Shoots and Leaves* (instead of *Eats Shoots and Leaves*) points to this feature in a highly comical and attractive manner. In this book, she quotes: "Charles the First walked and talked half an hour after his head was cut off" (2003, p. 13). Such a gruesome, yet comical, vision of Charles I makes more sense when punctuated in the following way: "Charles the First walked and talked. Half an hour after, his head was cut off." A much more straightforward, less macabre, yet equally entertaining sentence occurs in the following two French statements, the first with no semi-colon and the second with one: "Les lapins sont sortis dès qu'on [as soon as] avait ouvert la porte." "Les lapins sont sortis; des cons [idiots] avaient ouvert la porte." A third example where the comma makes all the difference: "Je l'ai rencontré à San Francisco, non, à Denver," as opposed to "Je l'ai rencontré à San Francisco, non à Denver." Clearly, care needs to be exercised over the niceties of correct punctuation.

Some punctuation marks divide discourse according to a scale of grammatical relationships. French use of punctuation marks is very similar to that of English, although there are differences. The following punctuation marks are common currency in French: the period / full stop, colon, semi-colon, inverted commas / quotation marks, suspension points / "dot dot dot" (usually three), parentheses/brackets, square brackets, interrogation point / question mark, exclamation point/mark, dash, hyphen, apostrophe, space, *alinéa* (indentation and following paragraph), asterisk, forward or backward slash. Upper and lower case are also used to help the reader navigate the text.

4.1.1 The period / full stop (.)

The period (*le point final*) indicates the completion of the largest punctuation unit, the sentence. It therefore appears at the end of the sentence and, in speech, indicates a pause where descending intonation occurs on the last word pronounced. For example: *Je voudrais aller en Mauritanie en avril. Il faut acheter du pain.* The following word is written with a capital. The period, logically, also marks the end of a paragraph.

The period appears at the end of an abbreviation and can be used in acronyms: *M.* (*Monsieur*), *ex-U.R.S.S.* (now dismantled), C.I.A., S.S. (Nazi paramilitary force). However, if the abbreviation ends with the last letter of the abbreviated word, there is no period: *Mme, Mlle.*

The period is not used to separate minutes and hours: 18h 40, 14h 30, 1h 15, 0 heure / 24 heures (*minuit*).

When the period coincides with a closing of parenthesis or inverted commas, it follows them: *C'était la première fois que Stéphanie me demandait de le faire (après un silence de dix ans). Ils m'ont dit qu'il était « impossible d'envoyer la lettre ».* However, if a grammatically complete sentence is involved, the period precedes the closing parenthesis or inverted commas: *Ils m'ont dit: « Il est impossible d'envoyer la lettre. »*

A period does not appear after a question or exclamation mark: *Quand arrive-t-elle ? Qu'est-ce qu'elle est bête !*

If the question or exclamation marks are surrounded by a parenthesis, a period is used: *Ils ne se souvenaient pas de moi (et on s'était vus la veille !).*

A period is not, quite naturally, used after suspension/ellipsis points (see more on suspension points below).

In numbers, a period is no longer recommended for numbers of a thousand or more. A space separates every set of three figures: 1 897 200 478 (see Chapter 62 on numbers). A period is not used for decimals (a comma is used instead). A period does sometimes appear, however, due to the influence of English.

Some modern writers separate a single word with a period if they wish to insist on that word. This construction does not constitute a sentence: "On avait donné dans le Nord un grand coup de pied dans la fourmilière, et les fourmis s'en allaient. Laborieusement. Sans panique. Sans espoir. Sans désespoir" (Saint-Exupéry 1953, p. 330); "Maintenant, je sais ce qu'est l'Empire. Une tenace, une constante violence. Diriger. Déterminer. Contraindre. La vie est là . . ." (Malraux 1975, p. 155). This staccato style is most reminiscent of Hemingway.

The period (= *dot*) is used in French, as in English, as part of an email address: *henricalet@wanadoo.fr* which is read as "henricalet arrobase wanadoo **point** fr."

4.1.2 The colon (:)

The colon (*les deux points*) indicates major divisions within a sentence. It points to a pause and is accompanied by descending intonation. But, in contrast to the period, it suggests that the statement is not complete. The uses of the colon are given below.

The colon precedes an explanatory enumeration: *Il existe différentes ethnies en Amérique du Nord: comanches, cheyennes, apaches, navajos, séminoles, et autres.*

It precedes textual words that are quoted: *Le dicton dit: Il ne faut pas vendre la peau de l'ours avant de l'avoir tué (Don't count your chickens).*

It is used in letters, dedications and speeches, and after the formulae *Monsieur | Chère collègue: J'ai le plaisir de vous annoncer que...*

It is used before a question or exclamation mark: *La dame me demanda: Que faites-vous ici? Les Algériens s'exclamèrent: Le président Boumédienne est mort!*

It is used after propositions such as *par exemple, à savoir: Vous pouvez le fabriquer avec bien des matériaux. Par exemple: avec du bois, du métal, du plastique...*
Des difficultés existent dans le pays. À savoir: l'inflation, le chômage, la violence urbaine, la baisse du pouvoir d'achat.

The colon is used after verbs like *affirmer, commenter, répondre, dire, écrire: Ma mère affirma/commenta/répondit/dit/écrivit: Tu ne peux pas sortir ce soir.*

It is used after words, often in an official context, such as *certifier, décréter, constater: Je, soussigné, certifie que: Monsieur Lejeune, agrégé de physique...*
Le maire décréta: Tous les jeunes de dix-huit ans doivent se présenter pour s'inscrire sur les listes électorales.
La police a constaté les infractions suivantes: excès de vitesse, non-assistance à personnes en danger, consommation excessive d'alcool, conduite en état d'ébriété.

It is used when an explanation is connected to something to be announced: *Je finis cependant par regrouper les documents suivants: deux imprimés, un manuscrit, trois lettres, un chèque libellé à l'ordre de l'agent comptable.*
C'était un mari grincheux, rouspéteur, jaloux: bref, un être insupportable.
Patrice fut un homme attentionné, compréhensif: bref, un être exceptionnel.
The reverse is also possible: *Savoir garder le silence: ça, c'est bien.*

The colon is used to exemplify something already said: *Les raisons de sa mort sont claires: drogues, délinquance, violence.*

4.1.3 The semi-colon (;)

The semi-colon (*le point-virgule*) is used to express: a connection between two clauses that are not linked grammatically. *Martin décida de partir en voyage; il avait toujours eu envie de visiter l'Asie.*

However, if one clause is short, often a comma will suffice: *Audrey l'a fait (here the main clause), mais à contre-cœur.*

The semi-colon is used in juxtaposed clauses: *L'homme positif fait toujours des progrès; les hommes aux idées négatives n'atteignent jamais leur but.*

The semi-colon is used to separate enumerations of different elements: *théâtre, roman, poésie, grammaire; porte, fenêtre, mur; canari, moineau, merle.*

The semi-colon may link grammatically complete sentences that are logically associated: "Un paysage pourra être beau, gracieux, sublime, insignifiant ou laid ; il ne sera jamais risible" (Bergson, *Le rire*, quoted in Grevisse and Goosse 2008, p. 136).

Elle se coucha tôt ; elle était fatiguée.

Sentences joined by a linking adverb are separated by a semi-colon, not by a comma: *Poitiers n'est pas une grande ville; pourtant on s'y trouve bien.*

In these cases, the intonation does not descend in front of the semi-colon as it would before a period.

4.1.4   The comma (,)

The comma (*la virgule*) marks off groups of word units that do not constitute complete sentences in themselves. Interestingly enough, the French *virgule* derives from the Latin *virgula*, as does the Italian *virgola*, as opposed to the English, the Spanish (*coma*) and the German (*komma*), which come from the Greek (*komma*). There is considerable carelessness over the omission of the comma. Its use can make all the difference in the world. Compare the two following sentences presenting casualties in World War I: *Il y eut du côté français seulement 310 000 morts et 300 000 blessés*; *Il y eut, du côté français seulement, 310 000 morts et 300 000 blessés.*

The comma is used as a pause when a speaker addresses another person, calling her/him by name (vocative case): *Valentin, viens ici.*

Papa t'a demandé, Sébastien, de ne pas sortir aujourd'hui (here both before and after Sébastien).

The comma separates analogous elements: *verbes, sustantifs, adjectifs, pronoms, phrases, propositions subordonnées*. However, if there is a linking word like *et* or *ou*, the comma is not used: *Hier, aujourd'hui, demain et toujours.*

Elle a acheté des chaussures, un sac-à-main, une robe ou un pull.

The comma is used when nouns are placed in apposition: *Rome, ville éternelle, est la capitale de l'Italie. Mexico, ville aztèque par excellence, est aujourd'hui une capitale cosmopolite. Annick, la cousine de Louis, vient d'arriver.*

The verb may disappear, and this produces an ellipsis: *Marseille, ville ouverte !*

Après Chirac, Sarkozy.

Après Castro, Raúl.

Après moi, le déluge !

The comma serves to isolate conjunctions: *Tout le monde était au courant, pourtant personne n'en parlait.*

Il a continué à pleuvoir, en conséquence, on ne pouvait sortir.

Enfin, on part demain.

When the elements linked by *mais* are brief, a comma is not necessary: *un sentiment ardent mais honorable; un intérêt bref mais intense.*

Or may or may not be followed by a comma: *Elle ne sortait jamais. Or, ce dimanche-là, elle se décida à aller à Paris.*

Jusque-là, elle avait publié seulement des romans; or elle se mit à composer des poèmes.

The comma is often used when the normal order is inverted: *Dans la cour, derrière la maison, il y a un grand vivier.*

The comma is used before contrasting conjunctions in short clauses: *C'est une dame intelligente et très belle, mais très désagréable.*

The comma is often used after adverbial phrases: *Au contraire, c'est un garçon très sympa.*

Et pourtant, elle va venir.

The comma is used after separate cities or towns from a larger entity: *Raleigh, état de la Caroline du Nord, États-Unis.*

The comma is used when the family name precedes the first name, as in administration: *Lanoë, Philippe*; *Picaud, Yves.*

The use or omission of a comma, as well as its placement, can affect meaning.

Use	*Non-use or different use*
Valérie, mange une pomme.	Valérie mange une pomme.
Vous êtes bien, sur France Musique.	Vous êtes bien sur France Musique.
Ce professeur réputé, sévère, a fini par craquer.	Ce professeur réputé sévère a fini par craquer.
L'avocat a découvert, dans ce dossier qu'on lui avait caché, de nouveaux éléments.	L'avocat a découvert dans ce dossier, qu'on lui avait caché de nouveaux éléments.
Antoine, viens avec nous.	Antoine vient avec nous.
J'aperçois Louis sur la vache, qui rit.	J'aperçois Louis sur la vache qui rit.
Adrienne me l'a dit, une fois.	Adrienne me l'a dit une fois.
Céline est partie en Angleterre avec sa fille, Amandine.	Céline est partie en Angleterre avec sa fille Amandine.

4.1.5 Inverted commas/quotation marks (« »)

Notice the difference between the English type of inverted commas (" ") and the French *guillemets.*

Inverted commas encompass the words of a speaker: Le Général de Gaulle dit : « Quand je veux savoir ce que pense la France, je m'interroge. »

They highlight a word, phrase, sentence: *Elle a obtenu sa thèse de doctorat avec «félicitations du jury et mention très honorable »* (with distinction | highest honors | summa cum laude).

Inverted commas can enclose a proverb or saying: *Selon le dicton : «Une hirondelle ne fait pas le printemps. »*

They are used to express irony: *Quand on lui a dit qu'il était le plus «intelligent », il s'est mis à rire.*

They are used in nicknames, and often with humor: *Je l'ai toujours appelé « Monsieur le Grand », même quand il était tout petit.*

They are used to highlight a proper name, institution, film, painting: *Picasso a peint le tableau « Guernica ».* (Italics are more usual here – see below.)

They are used to point to watchwords of institutions: *« LIBERTÉ, ÉGALITÉ, FRATERNITÉ », devise de la République française.*

They can be used with foreign words or phrases: *On va faire du « shopping » cet après-midi.*

They can indicate that a word or phrase belongs to colloquial language: *Ça, c'est vraiment « sensas(s) »; Qu'est-ce qu'il est « con », celui-là !*

Inverted commas can be used to show that a title is an article that forms part of a book or journal: *L'article sur « L'intelligence » m'a beaucoup plu.*

When direct speech is inserted within another quotation, the English type of quotations are often used for the words of direct speech, for clarity's sake: *« Comment peux-tu dire "Elle est bête" en sa présence ? »; « Le père a dit "C'est bien mon fils". »*

4.1.6 Suspension points (...)

Suspension points (*les points de suspension*) are a group of (usually) three dots indicating that information, perhaps understood, is withheld, or that something is held in suspense: "Il tendit l'ordre de livraison des armes. Son texte était long. Kyo le lisait : Oui, mais ... (Malraux 1976a, p. 321)
La porte s'ouvrit et...
On entendit des pas précipités...

Suspension points also express hesitation, doubt or thoughtfulness: *Je crois que..., non, il vaut mieux... eh bien, on va voir.*

They express a sudden change in subject: *Je voudrais te raconter ce qui s'est passé, mais... ça ne vaut pas la peine.*

They have the value of **etcetera** in enumerations: *D'innombrables touristes vont au Mexique: Américains, Français, Allemands...*

Question or exclamation marks come before suspension points: *Entrez !...; Qu'est-ce que vous avez fait ?...* When the word or sentence is incomplete, however, they come after: *Je déteste ce conn (ard)...!* (term to be used with care).

4.1.7 Parentheses/brackets (( ))

Parentheses or brackets (*les parenthèses*) are used to enclose a phrase by way of clarification: *Il naquit à Dakar (Sénégal).*
Les voisins (ils étaient nombreux à ne pas assister à la réunion), ont protesté contre les constants cambriolages.
Aude était un peu artiste (elle peignait à l'aquarelle), un peu rêveuse (elle se promenait souvent seule à la campagne), et même religieuse (elle allait à la messe tous les mois)...

One says, as in English: *ouvrir/fermer les parenthèses.*

Parentheses also appear in plays to mark an aside (*aparté*): *Les spectateurs ont entendu en aparté : (Mais, c'est la folie, ce qu'ils font)*

4.1.8 Square brackets ([ ])

Square brackets (*les crochets*) are similar to parentheses, but occur in special circumstances. They are used to encompass dates or clarifications within a text which is already in parentheses: *La dernière édition du dictionnaire de l'Académie française (dictionnaire général [2008]) recueille bien des néologismes.*

Square brackets are also used to encompass suspension points which indicate in the literally quoted text a word or sequence of words that are not reproduced, or to insert words that are conjectured: *Les hirondelles [. . .] reviendront.*

La religion [ou toutes les vertus chétiennes] l'obsédait.

4.1.9 The interrogation point / question mark (?)

The interrogation point (*le point d'interrogation*) appears at the end of the sentence. It naturally occurs in questions: *Où est Papa ? Qu'est-ce que tu as fait ? Qui est dans la cuisine ? Tu arrives à quelle heure ?*

It is used when one wishes to indicate credulity, doubt, irony or surprise: *Marie affirme qu'elle a quarante ans ? Tu dis qu'elle est intelligente ?*

No period is used with the question mark.

4.1.10 The exclamation point / mark (!)

The exclamation point (*point d'exclamation*) appears at the end of the sentence. It expresses emotions such as admiration, fear, anger, pain, joy: *Quel bonheur ! Quelle gentillesse ! Quelle horreur/plaie ! Que je suis contente ! Zut alors ! Pardi !*

As with the question mark, no full stop is used with the exclamation point.

4.1.11 The dash (–)

The dash (*le tiret*) indicates the beginning of a monologue/dialogue in a novel, for instance, without the need to point out who is speaking:

–   *Tu lui as montré le livre ?*
–   *Bien sûr !*
–   *Mais c'était son cadeau !*
–   *Je ne savais pas.*

4.1.12 The hyphen (-)

The hyphen (*le trait d'union*) is shorter than the dash. The hyphen is used to split words at the end of a sentence: *théâ-tre, déo-dorant, avia-teur.*

The hyphen is also used to join up components of certain compound words: *franco-espagnol, sino-américain, anglo-saxon, moi/toi-même, presse-papier, pêle-mêle.*

The hyphen can be used to indicate a continuous series of numbers: *Tu le trouveras dans les pages 25-31 du livre.*

The hyphen is used when a pronoun is attached to a verb: *Dis-le-lui maintenant. Regarde-moi droit dans les yeux.*

4.1.13 The apostrophe (')

The apostrophe (*l'apostrophe*) marks an elision, showing the disappearance of a vowel preceding another vowel: *Le mari* but *l'époux*; *Je la vois* but *Je l'ai vue*; *Si tu viens* but *S'il vient*. No elision occurs, however, in *si elle vient*.

Some elisions are not recorded in writing, yet do occur in speech: *une autre explication, presque entier* (see Chapter 2, Section 2.10 on elision).

The apostrophe is also used before names starting with a vowel: *Le vélo d'Antoine*; *la maison d'Yves*; *la voiture d'Armelle*; *La peste d'Albert Camus*; *Poèmes d'Arthur Rimbaud*. However, in the written language, one also sees: *La peste de Albert Camus*; *Poèmes de Arthur Rimbaud*.

Some authors use the apostrophe to mark the disappearance of letters and invest the writing with a colloquial element. This does not necessarily happen before a vowel: *J'vais partir*; *Elle crevait d'faim*; *mon p'tit gars*; *Je voulais êtr' marin*.

An apostrophe is not used at the very end of a line: *un défaut* | *d'attention* and not *un défaut d'* | *attention*.

4.1.14 The space

The space (*le blanc*) separates words. There is no space before or after the apostrophe. One may, on the other hand, go to the following line after a hyphen. A space is observed before and after opening and closing inverted commas, after a period and a comma, and before and after a colon, a semi-colon, and an interrogation or exclamation point. After suspension points, a space occurs: *Laurent rentra... je ne l'entendis pas.*

A space separates series of three figures: *293 141 habitants*; *9 453 621 dollars américains.*

Figures related to years, zip/postal code, pages or paragraphs of a book do not follow this rule: *en 1939*; *en (l'an) 2010*; *44000 Nantes*; *renvoi à la page 1102.*

In e-mail addresses, as in English, there are no spaces: hubertleclown@yahoo.com

4.1.15 The *alinéa*

The *alinéa* (which is masculine) points to both the passing from one paragraph to another and to the actual indentation itself. It suggests a marked pause, a real change in groups of ideas. It also indicates the different replies by people engaged in a dialogue: *Il me déclara :*

- *Mais t'es folle !*
- *Qu'est-ce que tu veux ?*
- *Maman ne me l'a pas dit.*
- *Et pourtant...*

The *alinéa* is useful for enumerating a complex series of ideas or elements: *Seront admis à la conférence:*
les proviseurs de lycées,
les professeurs agrégés,
les professeurs certifiés,

les élèves de terminale,
les parents d'élèves.

Each line of verse follows the pattern of the *alinéa*:

> *Quand vous serez bien vieille, au soir, à la chandelle,*
> *Assise aupres du feu, devidant et filant,*
> *Direz, chantant mes vers, en vous esmerveillant,*
> *« Ronsard me celebroit du temps que j'estois belle. »*
> *[...]*
> *Vous serez au fouyer une vieille accroupie,*
> *Regrettant mon amour, et vostre fier desdain*
> *Vivez, si m'en croyez, n'attendez à demain :*
> *Cueillez dès aujourd'hui les roses de la vie*

Ronsard's *Sonnets pour Hélène*, a call to the hedonism of *carpe diem*, illustrates not just the indentation of lines in poetry, but also the uncertainty of written accents up to the sixteenth century (and beyond).

4.1.16 The asterisk (∗)

The asterisk (*astérisque*, which is masculine – not to be confused with the *petit Gaulois*, Astérix) replaces a proper name that one cannot, or does not wish to, disclose: *à la sœur Louise au couvent de ***; le docteur *** qui me soigne; Son amie, la comtesse ***.*

In philological or linguistic works, the asterisk indicates an unattested or foreign word, and here it appears before the word: *Le mot* **orange** *dérive de l'espagnol* **naranja** *et s'appelait peut-être* *norange *au début de son arrivée en France.*

The asterisk, placed after a word, is frequently used to refer the reader by a *renvoi* to an explanation or further details at the bottom of the page or at the end of the chapter or book: *Steinbeck s'inspira d'un récit* indigène pour... Les ouvrages cités* par l'auteur nous invitent à penser que...*

The asterisk, or asterisks, can be used to mark a division in a text, or to separate stanzas in a poem. Several asterisks can be placed in a line or as a triangle.

4.1.17 The forward slash (/)

The forward slash (*la barre oblique*) is used elliptically: *Voilà pour la différence artisan/bourgeois; Quant aux contrastes paysan/citadin...* However, this usage can become complicated and difficult to read if it is used more than once in the same sentence: *une réflexion épistémologique qui sera le garant d'un discours bien construit à propos de/sur l'enseignement/apprentissage d'une langue.*

The formula *et/ou* highlights the simultaneous possibilities of *either/or*, or one feature *and* another: *Il y a des phrases pour la compréhension desquelles tout recours au contexte* **et/ou** *à la situation est inutile.*

The forward slash is also used in technical language: *Sur l'autoroute la vitesse est limitée à 130 k/h (= kilomètres par heure); Notre imprimante à jet d'encre donne un tirage de douze pages/minute; 24 images/seconde; 100 hab/km^2.*

The slash is used for Internet addresses: www/amazon.fr

4.2 Font

Different fonts (bold, italics, underlining or *gras, italique, soulignement/ soulignage*) are used to highlight letters, words or sentences. Ordinary (Roman) characters are described as *caractères romains* or *caractères maigres*:
Il faut écrire "curieux" en gras > **curieux**, *pas en romain.*
Pour que ce mot se détache bien, tu l'écris en italique > *parfait.*
Tu soulignes bien toute l'expression : <u>*La perfection n'est pas de ce monde*</u>.

Italics are used for titles of books and operas: *La peste* (Camus), *Crime et châtiment* (Dostoïevski), *Le paillasse* (Leoncavallo).

Generally, certain books, or sections within them, are not in italics: le Coran, la Bible, l'Apocalypse, l'Évangile, le Code civil, any more than: le Pater (Our Father), l'Ave (Hail Mary).

Italics are used for proper names given to boats, airplanes and notices: *le Reine Elizabeth*; *le Memphis belle*; *Sur l'enseigne on lisait : Coiffeuse et non Coiffeur.*

Any word or group of words which diverge from common usage can attract italics: foreign words, scientific terminology, slang, regional or dialectical terms: Je n'ai pas compris le mot *zarzuela* (Spanish dance), *querbus robur* (tree) non plus.
Le mot *pitchoune* signifie *jeune enfant*.
Je ne comprends pas la différence entre *eschatologie* et *scatologie*.
Aoûtat (moucheron) est un mot qu'on entend dans le Poitou (center of France).

4.3 Upper and lower case

4.3.1 Upper case

Whether upper case (*majuscules*) or lower case (*minuscules*) is used constitutes a linguistic minefield. Grevisse and Goosse devote some ten closely argued pages to the topic, and it must be admitted that some of their overwhelmingly copious remarks have been distilled here, and we are grateful to them for it. At the same time, other material has been consulted.

In the following cases, the upper case (capital letters) is used:

1. to start a sentence: *À ta place...* (*If I were you...*);
2. for proper names, pseudonyms, nicknames: *Jeanne, Jean-Paul Sartre, le Bien-Aimé* (nickname of Louis XV), *Voltaire* (pseudonym of François-Marie Arouet);
3. for names designating divinities: *Dieu* (considered as a single and only god), *Jésus-Christ, le Rédempteur* (Redeemer), *Vénus, Aphrodite, Bacchus, Dionysos, Priape, Titan, Prométhée, Zeus, Jupiter*;
4. for names designating lofty positions: *le Pape, le Président, le Roi, Sa Majesté, Son Éminence, Son Excellence, Sa Sainteté* but when followed by a name a lower-case letter occurs: *le pape Benoît XVI*;

5. for names of feasts: *l'Assomption, le Dimanche des Rameaux | les Rameaux (Palm Sunday), Pâques, Noël, la Semaine Sainte, l'Ascension, la Toussaint, Quasimodo (Lent), la Pentecôte, la Fête-Dieu, le Ramadan* (more a period than a festival, the end of which is the feast of Aïd), *(jour d') Actions de Grâces (Thanksgiving), Divali | Diwali;*

6. when referring to the cardinal points which have a proper character: *la phase lunaire entre l'Orient et l'Occident;*

7. when using names of stars and constellations: *la Terre* (not to confuse *Terre* and *terre* – earth and soil), *la Lune, le Soleil, la Grande | Petite Ourse, Saturne, Vénus;*

8. when referring to the state as a sovereign entity: *l'État Canadien/Colombien/Français;*

9. when speaking of government and church: *L'État et l'Église se sont prononcés contre la peine de mort;*

10. when writing abbreviations and acronyms: ONU (*Organisation des Nations Unies*), OEA (*Organisation des États Américains*), OTAN (*Organisation du Traité de l'Atlantique Nord*);

11. when using Roman numerals which indicate volume, chapter, assembly, royalty and emperor: *Charles V (Quint), chapitre X du livre, les papes Jean-Paul I/II, les rois Louis XIV, XV, XVI;*

12. on signs: COMMISSARIAT, BOULANGERIE, BUREAU DE POSTE, PTT, GENDARMERIE NATIONALE, MUSÉE DU LOUVRE. Written accents are now placed above capital letters (formerly, this was not the case);

13. for the names of religious orders: *l'Ordre du Mont Carmel* (also = *le Carmel*), *le Temple* (but individual members are in lower case: *les capucins, les templiers, les bénédictins*);

14. for prizes, distinctions and important cultural events: *le Prix Renaudot/Goncourt* (French book prizes) | *Nobel, les Oscars, la Foire du livre, le Molière* (French acting prize);

15. when a noun forms part of the title: *les Champs Élysées, l'Avenue de la Grande Armée, le Cimetière du Père Lachaise* (in Paris);

16. for nouns associated with nationalities: *les Français(es), les Argentin(e)s, les Tunisien(ne)s, les Angolais(es), les Américain(e)s, les Australien(ne)s.* This also includes the combination of *être* + nationality: *Elle est Belge/Canadienne/Américaine.* Whether *Belge, Canadienne* and so on are adjectives or nouns is not clear for many French speakers. However, informed opinion is that they are nouns;

17. for forms of address, both in letters and otherwise: *Madame Dupont, Monsieur Bernard, Mlle Saulnier, Frère Michaud, Sœur Micheline, mon Révérend Père, ma Révérende Mère* (but in these latter two the R could be lower case), *la Mère Supérieure, la Grande Muette* (= the Army);

18. for points on the compass (*les quatre points cardinaux*). Does one write *Nord* or *nord, Sud* or *sud, Est* or *est, Ouest* or *ouest* and their variants: *N/nord-E/est; N/nord-O/ouest; S/sud-O/ouest; S/sud-O/ouest*? This issue is

as complicated as it is in English. Certain features can be clarified, however. When these points are referred to as nouns they seem to attract an upper-case initial: *dans le Nord/Sud/Midi, dans l'Est/Ouest de la France, dans le Nord des États-Unis, en Italie du Nord*. When they are used as adjectives, they may take a lower-case initial: *la région sud-ouest/sud-est*, although one could say: *la région du Sud-Ouest/Sud-Est*. If a simple direction is implied, the likelihood is that the lower case is used: *se diriger vers le nord/sud d'un pays*. Some expressions do seem to be fixed: *Le Grand Nord, le Sud-Est asiatique* and, quoting *Le petit Larousse*: "Amundsen atteignit le pôle Sud en 1911," in which case one would say: *le pôle Nord*. Yet *Le petit Robert* refers to *le Pôle Sud/Nord*, using upper case for *pôle*. Grevisse and Goosse speak of this subject with unusual hesitation. *Le petit Robert* is not decisively helpful either. Clearly, there is no standard and uniform way of presenting the points of the compass. One has the impression that, apart from some fixed expressions, it is a *vraie foire d'empoigne* (*real free-for-all*).

19. frequently when a general noun is invested with a specific meaning for a group of people or a nation with respect to events: *la Création, la Genèse, la Chute, le Déluge, l'Exode, la Diaspora, la Renaissance, la Révolution (française), la Terreur, la Grande Guerre, la Résistance (française/russe), le Débarquement (Normandy landings), l'Holocauste / la Shoah, la Guerre de l'Indépendance, la Guerre de la Sécession (American Civil War)*. These nouns take a lower-case initial when used in a more general way, or when they are applied to events beyond the original one: *J'ai fait une chute; l'exode vers le Midi en été; la disapora arménienne/arabe; la renaissance de l'intérêt pour la Chine; la genèse d'un ouvrage; le déluge du 14 juillet 1987 à Montréal*.

4.3.2 Lower case

In contrast to English **lower case** (*minuscules*) is used in the following cases: days of the week (see Chapter 62 on time): *lundi, mardi, mercredi*; months of the year: *décembre, janvier, février*; seasons of the year: *printemps, été*. But upper case is used with important dates, festivals or proper names: *Printemps de Prague, Vendredi Saint*.

Adjectives relating to countries and regions, whatever their derivations, are normally in lower case: *le continent sud-américain, le Sahara algérien, les plaines canadiennes, les autorités péruviennes, le territoire afghan, le gouvernement sri-lankais, la population togolaise*.

The pronoun *je* is written in lower case, except at the beginning of a sentence. This contrasts with the English *I*.

Titles and names of dignitaries receive a lower-case initial when followed by a name: *le roi Louis XIV, le pape Jean-Paul II, le président du Brésil / de la République française*.

Lower-case letters are given to names of books, operas, songs and articles, except the initial letter and proper names: *Le nœud de vipères* (Mauriac), *Les pêcheurs de perles* (Bizet), *Le temps des cerises* (Yves Montand), *Le bon usage* (Grevisse and Goosse). It must be admitted that confusion reigns supreme here. Some authors use capitals on all the important words in a title, some just on nouns, some use lower case for the definite article, even if it is the first word. The safest method is undoubtedly the one recommended above.

The names of musical notes appear in lower case: *do, ré, mi, fa, sol, la, si*.

Proper names that apply generically take a lower-case initial: *C'est un véritable don juan, monsieur je sais tout*.

Many objects associated with inventors, discoverers, industrialists or anyone who has popularized something appear in lower case: *un zeppelin, un braille*. There is considerable hesitation here over upper and lower case. The same applies to the next three points (see also Chapter 9 on gender).

Lower case is used for objects associated with places: *un bordeaux* (wine), *un fez* (hat typical of Fez, Morocco), *C'est du limoges* (It's Limoges porcelain).

Lower case is used for objects associated with commercial makes but that are considered generic: *J'adore le martini / le vermouth sec / le pastis*.

Lower case is used for generic geographical names: *le fleuve Amazone/Niger, le lac Léman, l'île Maurice, la cordillère des Andes, la ville de Montréal, le cap Horn, le mont Blanc, les montagnes Rocheuses*. But if the generic name forms part of the proper name, upper case is used: *Val d'Isère, le Mont-Saint-Michel, le Val d'Aoste, la Sierra Madre* (Mexico), *la Sierra Nevada* (Spain).

Names of winds, unless personified in poetry or mythology, take a lower-case initial: *zéphir, borée, mistral* (cold wind in southern France), *sirocco* (hot wind blowing from the Sahara to southern Europe), *la tramontane* (northwest wind in France).

Names of religions take a lower-case initial: *brahmanisme, catholicisme, bouddhisme, islam, christianisme, protestantisme, judaïsme, mormonisme, christadelphianisme, adventisme, hindouisme, confucianisme*.

The names of tribes appear in lower case: *les* (*ethnies/tribus*) *apaches/ berbères/comanches/mayas/incas/aztèques/séminoles/sioux/touaregs*.

E-mail addresses do not normally require capital letters. Lower case seems always to suffice. If capital or lower-case are required, this would be indicated by the correspondent.

5

Agreement | L'accord

Below is a passage describing a hammam, a place of luxurious relaxation indulged in especially by females. It is an activity associated with the Arab and Turkish worlds, but is now a feature of French society. Note how important agreements are in French, as in all Romance languages. Especial attention is paid to agreement over verb endings, past tenses used with reflexive verbs, and the relationship between nouns and adjectives. Apparent also are features such as *parties*, a feminine plural describing the neuter *on*, and the varying use of plural verbs with singular nouns: *quarante-trois degrés* [. . .] *étaient/était difficile(s) à supporter; Bon nombre de femmes attendaient/attendait.* Understand also that *la plupart* would only ever take a plural verb. A deceiving point is that the masculine adjective *turc* is *turque* in the feminine while *grec* produces *grecque*. Equally confusing could be the feminine of *contigu>contigüe* where the absence of a diaresis would entail the non-pronunciation of the **u**. Many of these features are highlighted in the text. Some translations are provided. Note that the term *hammam* is well known in France.

Détente au hammam café

On est par**ties** de bo**nne** heure pour profiter au maximum de notre après-midi. Le hammam traditionnel attire surtout les femmes : mères et filles, sœurs et amies. Ce genre de loisirs **fait** beaucoup d'autr**es** adeptes désirant s'imprégner de **cette** ambiance orientale. **Cette** atmosphère délicat**e** nous invit**e** à la détente, au repos, à la méditation. **Cet** endroit est un havre pour l'esprit, un grand univers du rêve et du bien-être. Le caractère typique du lieu nous apport**e** une grand**e** sérénité. Une bo**nne** douche et un bain de vapeur ét**aient** délicieux. **Ce** cadre arab**o**-turc évoqu**e** certain**s** tableaux du miniaturiste algérien Mohamed Racim.

En franchissant le seuil de la porte, les odeurs dou**ces** de savon parfumé, les lueurs pâl**es** et vacillant**es** de bougies color**ées ont** sus-cité une profond**e** émotion. Les femmes d'un geste pudique **se sont déshabillées** puis **se sont enroulées** dans une grande serviette avant de traverser la premi**ère** petite pièce. Dans un angle [corner] de **celle-ci**, l'eau fra**îche** s'écoulait dans un bassin de pierre. Le ruissellement continu et harmonieux de l'eau nous assurait un trésor de bienfaits, de véritables moments de relaxation. **Cette** salle du hammam est consacrée aux séances de massage et aux soins de la peau. Les huiles essentielles exhalent une odeur pénétrante et très agréable de fleur d'oranger, de girofle [clove], de jasmin, de lavande, de rose ancienne, de violette et d'autres fragrances. La salle de soins corporels, qui remontent à la nuit des temps [mists of time], est contigüe à la grande salle des ablutions. Au beau milieu de **cette** dernière, une dalle [flagstone] de taille colossale occupe la place d'honneur. Nous **nous sommes allongées** pour apprécier l'effet salutaire de la dalle chaude. Des corps à demi-nus déambulaient [strolled] ou se reposaient dans le clair-obscur de la chaleur moite [moist/humid] de la pièce. La moiteur de l'air ambiant, la lumière tamisée [filtered] de **cet** endroit unique, la fraîcheur exquise de l'eau incitaient aux chuchotements et aux murmures. Bon nombre de femmes attendaient/ait avant de prendre un bain de vapeur car quarante-trois degrés de température dans l'étuve [steam room] était/étaient difficile(s) à supporter au premier abord. L'étuve humide est le dernier endroit en vase clos [in an enclosed space] où les femmes goûtaient une paix profonde et se délectaient [took delight in] dans des bains de vapeur provoquant la sudation [perspiration] et assurant une certaine détente.

Treatment of agreement appears throughout this book. For example, gender and number are analyzed in Part II, verbs and agreement of endings according to the subject receive attention in Part III, tenses according to the coincidence of main and subordinate clauses are dealt with in Part III, while agreement of adjectives with nouns is examined in Parts VI and VIII. Nevertheless, at the risk of some slight overlap between the present chapter and a variety of chapters appearing through the book, it seems helpful to deal in a general way with the concept of agreement between various grammatical accidences because it is a fundamental feature of all Romance languages, and French is no exception.

Specifically, agreement arises when a variable word (called the *receveur* in French) receives from another word in the same sentence (called the *donneur*) its particular morphological features: *La terre* **est ronde**; *Les absents* **ont** *toujours tort*; *la fleur que tu m'***avais donnée** *pour mon anniversaire*.

As opposed to English where words are modified much less frequently than in all Romance languages, many French words are subject to great variation, and change according to tense, person, function, number and gender. However, one can distinguish two main types of agreement (1 and 2):

1. Nominal agreement, which entails the coincidence of gender and number. This kind of agreement establishes the correct relationship between the noun and article or adjectives which accompany it: *la maison bleue*, **ces** *gâteaux succulents*; it also governs the relationship between a pronoun and its antecedent or subsequent feature: **les filles que** *j'ai* **vues**

> *hier*; *J'ai remis* **ton** *portable à* **ton** *mari*; it affects the way in which the subject relates to the attribute: *Son* **fils** *est* **un véritable saint**; the way the subject relates to the complement: **Annick** *se trouvait très* **fatiguée**; or the way the subject relates to a verb in the passive: *Ces* **maisons ont été construites** *en 1965*.

2. Verbal agreement, which requires coincidence of number and person (subject) with verb ending: **La** *voiture roul***ait** *trop rapidement*; **Les** *garçons cuisin***ent** *bien*.

5.1 General Rules (which are considerably developed in the appropriate chapters)

Two or more nouns or pronouns in the singular form a group which agrees with the verb, adjective or past participle in the plural: **Le** *sel et* **l'**eau **sont** *nécessaires à la vie*; *Il faut que* **les** *oignons et* **les** *carottes* **soient** *bien* **mijotés**; *Quant à l'oxygène, l'hydrogène, et le carbone, c'est l'atmosphère qui nous* **les** *fournit*.

Two or more nouns or pronouns, of different gender, are qualified by a masculine adjective or pronoun: **Lucien et Françoise** *se sont aperçu***s** *en même temps de leur erreur*; **Le chemin** *et même* **les tombes** *étaient couvert***s** *de mauvaises herbes*; *Ni* **les garçons** *ni* **les filles** *n'étaient venus à la fête du village*; **Amandine et toi**, *vous êtes blond***s** *comme vos grands-parents*.

If a noun is coordinated with the second-person pronoun (*tu*), the verb is placed in the *vous* form: **Papa et toi, vous venez** *au cinéma ?*

If one of the pronouns is in the first person, agreement is made in the first-person plural, or with **on**: *Tu t'en souviens, le jour où* **nous avons** *dansé |* **on a** *dansé, toi et moi ?*; *Ni lui ni moi n'***avons** *repéré l'erreur*.

Where there is a single determiner for various nouns, each noun is preceded by, for example, the definite article, or the possessive adjective: **La** *mère*, **la** *fille et* **son** *amie sont reparties ensemble*; **Le** *père et* **la** *belle-fille se sont revus il y a quelques jours*; *Ils ont volé* **mon** *véhicule et* **mes** *clefs*.

However, if the nouns refer to the same person, the loss of one determiner is permissible: **La** *mère et représentante de l'entreprise a dit que le chiffre d'affaires est prometteur*.

The loss of the determiner is also allowed when the nouns are preceded by an adjective: *Virginie a l'habitude de faire* **son propre** *pain et rôti*. But if, for example, the second noun were in the plural, a plural determiner would be required: *La maîtresse de maison a l'habitude de faire* **son propre** *pain et* **ses** *pizzas*.

The determiner is repeated even if the same concept is involved: *J'admire* **votre** *intérêt et* **votre** *enthousiasme*; **Les** *fenêtres et* **les** *balcons étaient fermés*.

When an adjective follows more than one noun, the preferred form for the adjective is masculine plural: *Ses cheveux et sa barbe étaient* **emmêlés**.

If the nouns are conceived as a single unit, the adjective agrees in gender and number with the nearest noun: *le tourment et la souffrance univers***elle**;

*l'influence, la volonté, le génie napoléoni**en**; les mouvements et les habitudes les plus quotidienn**es**.*

When an adjective is placed before one or more nouns, the adjective agrees with the first noun: *les **vieux** donjons et tours du château fort; Le roi détruisit son **propre** royaume et dynastie.* These constructions without the second determiner would be of a high register.

When an adjective is placed after the noun which itself is linked to another noun by the conjunction *ou*, the adjective is placed in the plural, provided that the adjective does not apply exclusively to that second noun: *Un bain ou une douche sont **bénéfiques** pour se relaxer; Un temps de repos ou du moins une pause sont **nécessaires** pour se ressourcer.*

More than one adjective in the singular can modify a plural noun when they define different parts of that noun: *les peaux **blanche** et **noire**; les langues **allemande** et **russe**; les intentions **française** et **belge**.*

Plurals in titles of books, paintings etc. attract a singular verb: ***Les dieux ont soif** de Anatole France **est** un roman extraordinaire; **Les conquérants** de Malraux **se déroule** en Asie; **Las meninas** de Velázquez m'a toujours **fasciné**;* but it is not rare to find a plural verb here: ***Les dieux ont soif sont** un ancien ouvrage de jeunesse.*

Nouns contained in titles of novels, paintings and so on do not affect adjectives which remain unchanged in the masculine singular: ***La peste** de Camus n'est pas trop **compliqué** à lire; **Suite française** d'Irène Nemirovsky est **passionnant** comme roman.*

When a cardinal functions as an ordinal, it is usually masculine: *la page numéro **un**; Trouvez la page **vingt et un**; En tennis, Venus Williams est numéro **un mondial**.*

The nouns *altesse, majesté, seigneurie* (lordship) and *excellence* attract feminine determiners and adjectives, irrespective of the sex of the person referred to: *son Altesse Royal**e**, **sa** Majesté Impérial**e**, **sa** Gracieu**se** Majesté George VI / Victoria, **sa** Gracieu**se** Excellence; Milord, **votre** Seigneurie est trop **bonne**.* However, if the adjective operates as a complement, it corresponds to the sex of the person: *Sa Majesté Impériale est parti**(e)** ce matin.* The **e** would be added if the person referred to as *Majesté* were female.

When *on* refers to persons in the plural, the adjective is placed in the plural: ***On** est content**s** de retrouver **nos** amis en Dordogne; **On** est parti**s** de bonne heure ce matin pour les rejoindre.*

Conversely, in literary style, if an author chooses to remain neutral and refers to him/herself as *nous*, then a singular adjective or past participle applies: *Nous sommes convaincu**(e)**/persuadé**(e)** que tu as pris la meilleure décision.*

If *on* refers specifically to females, corresponding adjectives or past participles are feminine: *Quand **on** est **belle** et **blonde**, on a des chances de plaire; Eh bien, petite, est-**on** toujours fâch**ée**?*

If the coordinated elements are grammatically neutral, like infinitives, the verb is in the singular: *Additionner et soustraire **est** facile; Ni ce que tu dis* *ni ce qu'elle pense n'est possible*. But, if the complement suggests a plural idea or is plural, then the verb is plural: *Informer et proposer des opinions* **sont** *deux buts pour les journalistes.*

A disjunctive or contrastive *ou* is used with either a singular or a plural verb: *Quand un individu ou un groupe d'individus s'oppose au gouvernement*; *La force ou la ruse lui permettra de l'emporter*; *Si le frère ou la sœur acceptent de venir en Suisse*; *Son père ou sa mère reviendront demain soir.* Yet logic often prevails, as in the following sentence: *Pierre ou Paul* **sera** *colonel de ce régiment* (only one colonel per regiment).

There is similarly uncertainty with the negation *ni . . . ni.* It is possible to say both: *Ni Pierre ni Paul ne viendra* and *Ni Pierre ni Paul ne viendront.*

When stating the gender of a noun, the adjective is masculine: *Tête n'est pas masculin, c'est féminin*; *Maison ne peut pas être masculin.*

When the collective noun includes the person speaking, the first- or second-person plural obtains, particularly in R1 speech: *Vous, les anciens,* **vous** *parlez toujours du passé*; *Les gens de théâtre,* **nous** *sommes tous d'accord.*

When a quantifying noun is followed by *de* + noun in the plural, in most cases the verb can be in the singular or plural. Logic requires a plural verb while grammar requires a singular verb (see also Chapter 10 on number for a full development of this issue). It must be stated that the tendency is to put the verb in the plural.

A selection of quantifiers includes: *le quart de, le tiers de, (bon) nombre de, quantité de, une douzaine/centaine de, la majorité de, une minorité de, un groupe de, la moitié de, une infinité de, une horde de, le reste de, dix pour cent de*: *Le quart de ses électeurs sont restés chez eux*; *Bon nombre d'étudiants ne vient/vien**nent** plus aux cours*; *Quantité de gens reste(**nt**) assez fortunés malgré l'inflation galopante*; *Dix pour cent de la population a/**ont** voté en faveur du parti des Verts*; *Une infinité de gens a/**ont** cru cette nouvelle*; *Le reste des spectateurs a/**ont** conspué l'arbitre*; *La cohorte d'étudiants sélectionnés a/**ont** donné satisfaction.*

The singular subject of a collective noun such as *famille, gouvernement, police, troupeau, armée* is normally followed by a singular verb, whereas in English usage is far from clear: *La famille habite au Québec depuis trente ans*; *Le gouvernement canadien ne s'est pas encore prononcé à ce sujet*; *La police le recherche toujours pour vol à main armée.*

When an adjective or past participle comes before a noun, variation occurs in the masculine and feminine form, and this depends on the context and meaning: *Veuillez trouver ci-joint des dossiers de candidature.* But: *Une fois partie, Audrey retourna directement en Martinique*; *La ministre a rendu publi**ques** ses intentions.*

Usage with numbers varies, and the verb can be influenced by the complement: *Mille euros* **était** *une coquette somme* (here the complement is singular); *Cinq minutes d'attente arrangera tout*; *Six mille dollars ne suffir**ont** pas pour rembourser la dette*; *Quarante-cinq degrés de chaleur dans le Sinaï était/**étaient*** *impossibles à supporter*; *Vingt-cinq ans de guerre leur **ont** appris la valeur de la paix.*

Past participles also agree with nouns in the following way: *Lucile a laissé la porte ouvert**e**/ferm**ée**.*

The construction *un de ceux / une de celles qui* leads to a plural verb: *J'étais un de ceux / une de celles qui **ont** nagé jusqu'à l'île d'en face*; *Un de ceux / Une de celles qui **ont** voté*; *J'étais un de ceux qui **ont** manifesté dans la rue.*

The construction *C'est moi qui* would require a first-person verb, but in colloquial R1 style, one could easily hear the verb in the third person: *C'est moi qui l'**ai** écrit*; *C'est moi qui l'**a** écrit* (R1); Similarly with *C'est nous qui*: *C'est nous qui **avons** monté la pièce de théâtre*; *C'est nous qui **ont** monté la pièce de théâtre* (R1).

With respect to the age of a person, usage over the verb in the singular and plural varies, but logic seems to dictate here: *Vingt ans **est** l'âge tendre / des folies* (here, *âge* determines the singular); *Seize ans **est** un âge où on peut se défouler* (here, *âge* determines the singular); *Chantal a trente ans accompli**s** / révolu**s** / bien sonné**s*** and *depuis l'enfance jusqu'à **ses** vingt ans.*

There is considerable hesitation over whether a singular or plural verb is used with respect to time recorded by the clock, but here again there is some logic: *Cinq heures **est** le moment où commencent les courses de taureaux* (the singular *est* is determined by *moment*); *Dix heures **sonna*** is acceptable but *Dix heures **sonnèrent*** appears more frequently: *Est-ce que onze heures **vont** bientôt sonner?*

Usage over gender and verb is uncertain with the following: *espèce, façon, genre, manière, sorte, type, putain* (R1); *un espèce de charlatan/sorcier* (R1 but now establishing itself in the written language); *C'était une espèce de balcon garn**i** de fleurs*; *une espèce de crétin qui n'a jamais pu être reç**u** au bac*; *J'arrive pas à comprendre **ce** putain de mode d'emploi!*; *Ce genre de révélations contribu**ent** à sa réputation bizarre*; *Ce genre de lunettes **fait** fureur*; *Ce n'est pas le genre de réponse qu'elle aurait fai**t** l'année dernière*; *Toute sorte de propos s'ensuivi**rent**.*

5.2 Rules over agreement with verbs, and especially the use of *être* and the past participle

Note that the rules below form part of a general introduction to agreement and that much more detailed analysis occurs in subsequent chapters.

Many French verbs are conjugated with *avoir*, but a good number are conjugated with *être*, and we concentrate precisely on these latter verbs since they offer more complications. These latter verbs are not only troublesome for foreign learners of French but also for less informed French speakers, since the variations in the past participles are frequently, and logically, not heard in speech. Compare: *Je l'ai entend**u*** and *je l'ai entend**ue*** (*I heard him/her*) or *Nous les avons v**us*** and *Nous les avons v**ues*** (*We saw them*, i.e., males/females).

There is a group of verbs that are conjugated with *être*. We list just a few here since a fuller list appears with comprehensive treatment in Chapter 14: *aller, partir, rentrer, revenir, venir.* These are all used intransitively. In other words, they do not take a direct object, except for, at least in this list, *rentrer*, which may be used transitively. When these verbs are used in the past tense (perfect, pluperfect, future in the past, etc.), the past participle varies according to gender and number. Thus: *Je suis allé* is used by a male speaker but *Je suis allée* is used by a female speaker. *Nous sommes allés* is used by a male or female speaker when referring to a mixed-gender group, while *Nous sommes allées* would be used by a female with reference to an all-female group.

The extra e/es for the feminine form highlights a difficulty that runs throughout the French language, and it is a difficulty shared by Italian, but not by Spanish, so those who study Spanish are spared this complication. The full conjugation of *aller*, as well as of other similarly conjugated verbs, is to be found in Chapter 30.

There is a large group of verbs called "reflexive" verbs, and these are all conjugated with *être* in compound tenses, when they are used reflexively. (Most of them are conjugated with *avoir* when they are used non-reflexively.) The past participles of these reflexive verbs (e.g., *s'asseoir, s'habiller, se laver, se lever*) vary with gender and number like the verb *aller* above. In other words, a male speaker would say *Je me suis assis* but a female speaker would say *Je me suis assise*. Still following the pattern illustrated above with *aller*, a male or female speaker, when referring to a mixed-gender group, would say *Nous nous sommes assis* while a female speaker, when referring exclusively to an all-female group, would say *Nous nous sommes assises*. The irregular verb *s'asseoir* is used as an example here since one can actually hear a difference in sound between the masculine, unpronounced s and the feminine, pronounced se. Had one used the example *Liliane s'est habillée*, as opposed to *Marc s'est habillé*, no difference would have been observed in sound between the two past participles.

In the sentence *Anne-Marie s'est lavée*, the reflexive pronoun is a direct object, which is why there is agreement between *Anne-Marie* and the past participle. However, if one had said *Anne-Marie s'est lavé les mains*, the direct object is no longer the reflexive *se* but the noun *mains*. In this case there is no variation in the past participle. This feature causes considerable confusion even to native French speakers.

When a pronoun precedes the verb *avoir* in compound tenses, the past participle agrees with that pronoun and, all too frequently, no difference is heard between the two following participles of the verb *voir*: *Je l'ai vu au concert/Je l'ai vue au concert* (*I saw him/her at the concert*). Similarly: *Je les ai vus* (*I saw them* [males or mixed gender]); *Je les ai vues* (*I saw them* [females alone]).

When a relative pronoun linking a main and subordinate clause refers to a noun coming before the verb, the past participle agrees in number and gender with that noun: *La voiture que j'ai conduite appartient à mon père*; *Les ami(e)s que j'ai vu(e)s hier m'ont envoyé un texto.* Needless to add, lack of difference in pronunciation in these two past participles is also a source of confusion for French speakers.

When the perfect tense involves an active agent, there is no agreement with the past participles. However, when the verb is in the passive, there is agreement. Compare the two sets of sentences:

1. *Le maçon a construit la maison* and *La maison a été construite par le maçon*;
2. *L'arbitre a expulsé deux joueurs* and *Deux joueurs ont été expulsés par l'arbitre.*

Part II

6

The definite article | L'article défini

Below is a passage commenting upon a particular film that attracted the critics' attention in France in 2008, and was a great box-office success, both in France and in Europe. It follows the comic activities of a person responsible for a mail office in the south of France who is sent to continue his work in the far northeast. The cultural, climatic and even linguistic shock, for he is faced with a dialect of French (*le ch'tis*), that he undergoes is considerable, but he survives and starts to derive great enjoyment from his stay in the north. The passage illustrates the use and variety of definite articles, from the masculine and feminine singular (*le/la*), to the elision of the **e** and **a** (*l'*), the plural form (*les/des*), as well as the combinations with the prepositions *à* and *de*.

Le succès des « *Ch'tis* »

En juin 2008, **le** meilleur film français qui ait connu une grande réussite s'intitule *Bienvenue chez les Ch'tis*. **La** comédie de Dany Boon brosse l'histoire de Philippe Abrams, responsable de **la** poste à Salon-de-Provence. **Le** fonctionnaire, contrarié par **le** mauvais caractère de son épouse Julie, triche pour obtenir sa mutation [transfer] sur **la** Côte d'Azur. L'administration découvre **la** supercherie [deception/hoax] et Philippe sera envoyé à Bergues, un village qui compte un peu plus de 4 000 habitants. Ce lieu se trouve dans **le** département **du** Nord et **la** région **du** Nord-Pas-de-Calais. Il est situé à 40 km de **la** sortie **du** Tunnel sous **la** Manche. Pour **la** famille Abrams, originaire **du** Sud de **la** France, **le** Nord est une région sinistre. Tous **les** stéréotypes y sont présents : des alcooliques, des paysans qui ne parlent pas correctement **le** français, des personnes sans éducation qui n'ont pas **le** sens de l'hygiène alimentaire et qui parlent une langue incompréhensible, **le** « *cheutimi* ». Philippe partira tout seul. Avec grand étonnement, il fait connaissance d'une équipe de travail extraordinaire, de gens sympathiques, d'une belle région. Il se lie d'amitié avec Antoine, à **la** fois **le** facteur et **le** carillonneur [bell ringer] **du** village. Lorsque Philippe rentre chez lui, son épouse n'en revient pas (is amazed / can't get over it) ! Elle refuse de croire que son époux se plaît dans **le** Nord. Julie pense même que Philippe lui raconte sciemment des histoires. Philippe fait croire à Julie qu'il est difficile

101

de vivre dans **la** petite ville **du** Nord de **la** France. Peu à peu, Philippe s'embrouille [becomes enmeshed] dans **les** mensonges qu'il raconte.

The definite article is often treated with gender, which is understandable since it is intimately linked to gender, and more specifically, to the gender of nouns. However, the ways in which the definite article is used in French differ quite considerably from those obtaining in English, and it is these different ways that are examined in this chapter, while the relationship of the definite article with the gender of nouns is treated in Chapter 9. One thing is certain: French seems to use the definite article more than English does. *Mail/Post Office* is a typical example: *la Poste*.

The definite article is the determiner of a noun with which it agrees in gender and number; it always precedes a noun. It takes three forms:

masculine singular	feminine singular	masculine/feminine plural
le	*la*	*les*

examples: ***le*** *livre* >   ***les*** *livres*
             la *table* >   ***les*** *tables*

Before a vowel or a mute **h**, there is elision, and the vowel of the definite article is lost:

le >   l': *l'arbre, l'homme, l'iris, l'ordinateur*
la >   l': *l'université, l'heure, l'eau*

The plural form always remains the same: ***les*** *arbres*, ***les*** *hommes*, ***les*** *universités*, ***les*** *eaux thermales*.

Before an aspirate **h**, there is no elision (***le*** *héros*, ***la*** *hauteur*, ***la*** *haie d'honneur*) although note that with *héroïne*, there is elision (*l'héroïne*) since, strangely enough, the **h** here is not aspirate.

There is no *liaison* either with an aspirate **h** (*les Hollandais, les haricots*) although in colloquial speech, and less elegantly, one does hear *liaison* in these two examples. Elision does not take place with following vowels in the cases below:

when *le* precedes the number *un*: *le un* (*number one*);
when *le* precedes an isolated vowel that stands by itself: *Le a n'est pas à sa place* (also: *le e/i/o/u*).

The articles *le* and *les* (not *la*) contract with the prepositions *à* and *de*:

à + le >	*au*	*Nous allons* ***au*** *cinéma /* ***au*** *stade; Je vais* ***au*** *Canada.*
à + les >	*aux*	*La professeure parle* ***aux*** *élèves /* ***aux*** *étudiantes; Audrey va* ***aux*** *États-Unis. But: Laurent parle à* ***la*** *fille; Céline va à* ***la*** *rivière.*
de + le >	*du*	*la table* ***du*** *salon*
de + les >	*des*	*les feuilles* ***des*** *arbres; la tige* ***des*** *plantes*

The article is used to denote a person or thing considered unique: *Le président de la République préside le Conseil des Ministres du mercredi*; *Le Soleil éclaire la Terre*.

When a noun has a general or abstract value, or refers to the elements or features of nature, animals or plants, of which only one can be supposed to be under consideration, the definite article is used: *L'argent ne fait pas le bonheur*; *L'envie est un péché capital*; *L'homme n'est pas immortel*; *Le soleil peut être dangereux pour la peau*; *La cigogne est un oiseau migrateur*; *Les jeunes adorent les jeux vidéo*.

The article is never immediately preceded by other determiners, except *tout*: *Tout le gouvernement s'opposa au projet*; *L'infirmière a travaillé toute la nuit*; *Ma fille va à la piscine tous les jours*.

The definite article is used in the following expressions: *Arrête de faire le mariol(le)*; *Fais pas le con !* (R1); *Il fait toujours le clown / le paillasse*; *Il fait le malin*; *Mon père fumait la pipe*; *La victime était dans le coma*.

The definite article does not always precede a noun: *le oui/non des électeurs*.

Technically, each noun is preceded by the definite article: *Elle a mis la confiture et le beurre sur la table*; *J'ai vu le scooter et la bicyclette dans le jardin*.

But if there is a close association between nouns, the second, or even third, article may disappear: *Les ministres et secrétaires d'État ont accueilli la réforme avec enthousiasme*; *Les actrices, chanteuses et danseuses ont organisé un beau spectacle*.

When a list of nouns forms a kind of enumeration, and this occurs especially in writing, the article is often left out: *Hommes, femmes, enfants, animaux, véhicules, tout a été emporté par l'ouragan*; *Professeurs, étudiants, administrateurs, ouvriers ont tous participé à la manifestation*; *Boulets, mitrailles, obus, ça explosait partout*; *Incinérateur: pour brûler feuilles, branches, papiers, mauvaises herbes en toute sécurité*; *Bâche industrielle: pour terrassement, chantier, toiture, bois, agriculture*.

The definite article has a possessive value: *Sabrina a fermé les yeux*; *Stéphanie m'a touché la main*; *On lui a marché sur le pied*; *Ce bruit me donne mal à la tête*; *Aurélien écrit de la main gauche*; *Axelle marchait le dos courbé, les mains derrière le dos*; *Diane s'est coupé le doigt*.

The definite article is used in the following superlative constructions: *les jours les plus chauds de l'été*; *les tâches les plus difficiles de la maison*. *Les* cannot be excluded from this construction.

The definite article may be used before an infinitive which is almost construed as a noun, and is especially common in *le boire et le manger*.

Both definite and indefinite article (see Chapter 7) may be omitted before a noun in apposition (i.e., when it explains a preceding noun): *Washington, capitale des États-Unis*; *Hemingway, auteur de Pour qui sonne le glas*.

The article may be omitted after the conjunction *ou*, before a noun that is merely a synonym or explanation of the preceding noun: *le vestibule ou entrée de la maison*; *Phoenix est la capitale ou ville principale de l'Arizona*.

In numerous grammatical terms suggesting the meaning "in the," *à* is joined to *le* in the following way: *au subjonctif, à l'indicatif, au passé composé/ présent/conditionnel, à l'imparfait, au pluriel/singulier/masculin/féminin*.

Peoples and languages require a preceding definite article: *les Martiniquais,* **les** *Colombiens,* **les** *Grecs,* **les** *Italiens,* **les** *Japonais;* *l'anglais américain/britannique, l'arabe, le chinois, l'hébreu, le français québécois, le turc*.

Seasons, dates and festivals similarly require the definite article: *l'hiver, le printemps, l'été, l'automne; l'appel du dix-huit juin lancé par le Général de Gaulle; le lundi premier mai (Fête du Travail); le quatre juillet (Fête de l'Indépendance Américaine); le quatorze juillet (prise de la Bastille de 1789; Fête nationale de la France), la Pentecôte, la Toussaint, le jour de l'an, l'Action de Grâces (Thanksgiving);* but *Noël* and *Pâques*.

Months and days of the week do not always require the definite article: *décembre est revenu; Ce fut pendant les derniers jours d'octobre; début avril; Viens mardi ou mercredi, cela m'est égal.* But when these nouns are qualified, they are preceded by the definite article: *le mardi suivant/précédent;* le jeudi 6 mai. Furthermore, when precision is necessary, as with opening or closing times of shops, one sees: *Fermé du samedi 1er novembre au lundi 10 novembre* and *dans la journée/matinée/soirée du dimanche.*

If a customary activity is suggested with a day of the week, *matin, jour, après-midi, soir* or *week-end,* the definite article occurs. The idea is one of *during, in the course of, at: Le dimanche, Lucile allait toujours à la messe; Le samedi, son mari allait au foot; Le matin, de bonne heure, Benjamin fait du jogging; Henri s'entraînait au basket le soir; Armelle travaille la nuit et dort le jour; L'après-midi, on se promenait sur la plage; Le week-end, on se repose.*

The definite article is used before colors: *Je préfère le bleu au gris; Le blanc me plaît plus que le vert; Le mauve est ma couleur favorite; Cet été, le rouge et le beige sont très à la mode.*

The definite article occurs before titles: *le Cardinal, le Président, la Présidente, la Reine, le maréchal Leclerc, le premier ministre, le général Legrand, le professeur Dubois, la professeure Martin, (le) Monsieur Picaud, Le Docteur Jivago* (novel by Boris Pasternak). *Madame* and *Mademoiselle* have no definite article, yet *dame* and *demoiselle* do: *la demoiselle d'Avignon* (Mireille Mathieu – celebrated singer), *Les demoiselles d'Avignon* (painting by Picasso).

The definite article occurs before family names, which remain in the singular: *les Martin, les Durand, les Lanoë, les Curie* (Pierre and Marie).

Names of families which begin with the article do not suffer a contraction of *de + le* into *du: les tableaux de Le Nain; le style (de) Le Corbusier.*

The definite article is used in colloquial style when referring to a person, and this is not in any way pejorative: *La Louise trempait le pain dans la soupe; Il n'y a pas parmi vous la Suzanne Daumaison ?; Regarde ce qu'elle a fait, la Marie-Rose.*

Following the Italian pattern, names of artists, writers and so on are often, but not always, preceded by the definite article: *l'Alighieri, le Corrège, le* Caravage, *le* Tasse, *l'*Arioste. Sometimes *le* Vinci is used, as well as *le* Dante, but this is a false Italianism and is to be discouraged.

In literary language, one comes across the definite article in the plural. This is a form of emphasis and still refers to a single writer: *Les* Corneille, *les* Racine, *les* Molière ont illustré la scène française.

Similarly (although this remark pertains to the indefinite article, it seems appropriate to make it here), the indefinite article is used in a derogatory manner when preceding names: *Il est insupportable d'être commandé par **un** Coquereau, **un** Jean-Jean, **un** Moulin, **un** Focart, **un** Bouju !; Quand **un** Lyautey arrive au Maroc, il y trouve un pays en déconfiture.*

When the title of a work or painting begins with the article, the contraction takes place with *à* and *de*: *l'auteur **du** Misanthrope; les lecteurs **des** Frères Karamazov; Je songe toujours **aux** Précieuses ridicules.*

Titles of articles in reviews and books often begin with the definite article when a particular category is being referred to: *Le livre contient plusieurs articles sur les animaux:* « *Les* chats », « *Les* chiens », « *Les* lynx »; *Tu as lu l'article* « *Les* plantes » *dans la revue Plantes et jardins?;* « *Le* saule pleureur » *est un excellent article.* Yet there does seem to be some hesitation here: *Il a évoqué le héros **du** Rouge et le noir* as against *la fin de **Le** rouge et le noir*, where contraction and non-contraction are legitimate.

The definite article occurs before measurements: *trois euros **le** kilo; cinq dollars **l'**unité; une livre **le** litre; quatre-vingts kilomètres à **l'**heure; En ce moment l'essence coûte deux dollars **le** litre.*

The definite article precedes proper names when accompanied by an adjective which characterizes a person: *le subtil Ulysse; la fidèle Rossinante* (Don Quixote's horse); *la blonde Venise; Tu as visité le vieux Québec / la Venise glorieuse ?* One may also say *Ulysse le subtil, Venise la blonde.*

The definite article is also used to give approximate figures: *Je pense qu'elle a **la** quarantaine; Une bouteille de champagne coûte dans **les** trente dollars.*

Notice the difference between *parler français/anglais* and *parler **le** français/l'anglais. Parler **le** français* suggests the ability to speak French: *Elle parle **le** chinois et **le** japonais.* It is possible to imply the same idea with *Elle parle chinois et japonais*, but this is less emphatic and elegant. Furthermore, one could not use the definite article in the following sentence: *Tout le monde parlait allemand quand je suis entrée dans la pièce.*

Both the definite and the indefinite articles may be used in the following expressions (*my* would be used in English): *Elle s'est cassé **la** jambe* (droite/gauche); *Elle s'est cassé **une** jambe.* In a general way, these two expressions amount to the same thing, but clearly the first one with *la* is more precise.

It could be argued that many prepositional expressions function adjectivally and that the definite article is therefore excluded: *un vaisseau **de** guerre; une voiture **de** sport; des tennis **de** plage; une batterie **de** cuisine.* One inconsistency: *l'armée **de** l'air* but: *l'armée **de** terre.*

There remain some distinct traces of the contracted definite article *ès* before a consonant or vowel, representing *en + les*. This is especially true of university titles: *maître **ès** arts, bachelier/licencié/docteur **ès** science / **ès** let-tres*. The legal formula *ès qualités* signifying "a person exercising a func-tion" subsists in documents: *On m'avait demandé de présider cette conférence **ès qualités***. The names of some French towns also retain this archaic expression: *Riom-**ès**-Montagnes* (in central France), *Sury-**ès**-Bois* (in the Cher department).

Numerous fixed expressions or proverbs do not include the definite arti-cle: *Noblesse oblige, Contentement passe richesse, Blanc comme neige, Donner carte blanche, Il y a anguille sous roche, Erreur ne fait pas compte, Pierre qui roule n'amasse pas mousse*.

There are many expressions of the type: verb + direct object which do not have a definite (or indefinite) article: *avoir bonne/mauvaise mine*; *avoir cours*; *avoir faim*; *avoir intérêt*; *avoir peur*; *avoir raison*; *chercher querelle*; *donner congé*; *donner cours*; *faire cause commune (avec)*; *causer/poser problème*; *garder ran-cune*; *prendre fait et cause*; *avoir/prendre rendez-vous*; *rendre justice*; *imposer (le) silence*; *perdre patience*; *tenir parole*; *demander pardon*. Similarly: *Armelle est en excellente santé, elle a très bonne mine*; *Émilie est malade ? Elle a très mau-vaise mine*; *Il y a avantage à ce que tu viennes aujourd'hui*; *Tu as intérêt à investir tout ton argent dans cette entreprise-là*; *Il y a doute dans cette affaire*; *Il y a cours aujourd'hui*; *J'ai cours à dix heures*; *La prof. a eu du mal à imposer silence aux élèves chahuteurs*; *Tais-toi, ou je perds patience*; *Il y a péril à partir sous la neige*; *J'ai eu/pris rendez-vous avec la dentiste*.

There are a great number of prepositional phrases with no article: *à cheval/gué/confesse, avec soin*; *sans gêne*; *sous clef*; *pour mémoire*; *contre nature*; *hors concours*; *à travers champs*; *d'après nature*; *avoir à cœur*; *perdre de vue*; *prêter sur gages*; *mettre sous enveloppe*; *affirmer sous serment*; *mettre à jour*; *Elle va à confesse le samedi soir* (also: *Elle vient de confesse*); *J'ai à cœur de préparer l'agrégation*; *Il faut couper à travers champs pour arriver à temps*; *Les garçons sont partis si vite que je les ai perdus de vue*; *Je passe la matinée à mettre à jour ma correspondance*; *La maison d'édition vient de mettre à jour son dictionnaire bilingue*. But *mettre au jour* is also used with the idea of publishing a book, or divulging something: *Ils ont fouillé la terre pour mettre au jour les ruines de Ninive*. To be added is the fact that some writers use both *mettre à jour* and *mettre au jour* with the idea of "publishing" a work.

The definite article is used before *un(e)*, viewed as a numeral (*one*). This is for euphony's sake, and elegance of expression, and is mainly found in the written R3 register. The Livre de Poche's publication of Camus's *La peste* reads: *L'un des grands romans de notre époque*. Yet this construction is also heard in speech: *l'un des ministres a prononcé un discours sur l'inflation*; *L'une des femmes publia un article contre le sexisme*.

Also for euphony's sake, *l'* precedes *on* in order to separate two vowels. It occurs with *que, ou, où, à qui, à quoi, si*: *Il est évident **que l'on** a envoyé la lettre* *à Robert*; *Je ne sais **où** l'on va*; *Tu sais **à qui** l'on a adressé l'enveloppe ?*; **Si l'on** *préfère agir tout de suite, il faut aller en ville.*

The definite article is frequently not used with names of streets, avenues and so on, although the use of the preposition is possible: *Je l'ai rencontrée rue Allende*; *Mes frères habitent avenue Jean Jaurès*; *On a pris rendez-vous boulevard Lecomte / passage Robin*; *Allez, on se revoit square Montcalm à sept heures*; *Mes parents demeurent impasse Leclerc*; *Ils ont un majestueux hôtel particulier place des Vosges*. Also: *Je l'ai rencontrée dans la rue Allende / sur la Place des Vosges*.

The use of the definite article, as opposed to the indefinite article, can create a kind of stress or insistence: *C'est la grande actrice* (*She really is a great actress*); *C'est la folie* or *C'est de la pure folie* (*It's sheer madness*); *C'est la belle vie !* (*It's a wonderful life!*); *C'est la belle affaire !* (*It's a fine business!*) Here, irony is implied.

The definite article is also used with geographical names (see also Chapter 64). The definite article is used with:

1. names of continents: *L'Asie est le plus vaste et le plus peuplé des continents*; *L'Amérique est divisée en Amérique du Nord, Amérique Centrale et Amérique du Sud*; *L'Europe est le plus petit des continents*;

2. names of countries (some are masculine but more are feminine; see Chapter 64 on gender): *Le Brésil/Cambodge/Canada/Danemark/Japon/ Mexique/Portugal/Québec* (as opposed to just *Québec* for the city), *les États-Unis*, *la Belgique/France/Grande-Bretagne/Suisse/Suède*, *l'Algérie/Afrique du Sud/Égypte*;

3. names of mountains: *le Caucase/Jura, l'Himalaya/Oural* (or *les Monts Oural*), *les Alpes bernoises/vaudoises*, *les* (*montagnes*) *Rocheuses*, *la Cordillère des Andes*;

4. names of oceans and seas: *l'(océan) Atlantique*, *le Pacifique* (*océan* not required here), *l'océan Indien* (*océan* required here), *la* (*mer*) *Méditerranée*, *la mer Morte*, *la mer Baltique*;

5. names of rivers: *l'Amazone/Euphrate*, *le Colorado/Danube/Jourdain/Miss- issippi/Missouri/Nil/Parana/Rhin/Rhône/Río Grande* (final *e* pronounced as *é*)/ *Tage/Tibre, la Loire/Seine/Tamise*;

6. names of lakes: *le lac de Bourget*, *le lac d'Annecy*, *le lac Constance/Huron/ Léman/Ontario/Supérieur*;

7. names of regions, departments and states within countries: *l'Ain/ Arizona/Ohio* (masculine), *le Brabant/Doubs/Labrador/Manitoba/Pas-de- Calais/Québec* (to be distinguished from *Québec*, the city)/*Yukon, l'Alberta/ Amazonie/Andalousie/Alsace/Île de France/Isère* (feminine), *la Californie/ Caroline du Nord/du Sud/Castille/Flandre Occidentale/Patagonie/Saskatchewan/ Toscane/Moravie/Sibérie/Wallonie*.

The preposition *en* is not normally used in conjunction with *le* with refer- ence to countries: *en France/Espagne/Nouvelle-Angleterre*.

The definite article is not used with *Israël*: Un conflit opposa **Israël** et les pays arabes. Neither is it used with the names of the following islands: *Bornéo, Chypre, Cuba, Haïti, Java, Madère, Madagascar, Majorque, Malte.* Thus: *les populations grecque et turque **de** Chypre*; *le régime communiste **de** Cuba*; *À Madagascar, le riz et le manioc constituent l'alimentation de la population.* However, certain islands (seen as countries) do take the definite article: *la Barbade/Grande-Bretagne/Grenade, l'Irlande/Islande, la Jamaïque/Nouvelle-Zélande/Trinité-et-Tobago*, as do some others (not seen as independent countries): *la Corse/Crète/Guadeloupe/Martinique/Réunion/Sardaigne/Sicile.* Thus: la capitale **de la** *Crète/Corse/Sardaigne/Sicile.*

Generally speaking, the preposition *de* (meaning *of* or *from*), in conjunction with *le/les* which precedes masculine countries, regions and states, leads to *du/des*: *Sabrina est revenue **du** Danemark | **des** États-Unis | **du** Canada*; *le roi **du** Maroc*; *les Incas **du** Pérou*; *les Aztèques **du** Mexique*; *Fernande est revenue **du** Québec* (but *de Québec* when referring to the city); *Quelle est la capitale **du** Brésil ?*; *J'adore les vins **du** Chili | **du** Roussillon*; *Mme de Sévigny a fait connaître les vins **du** Tricastin.*

Geographical names beginning with the article are contracted: *Les stagiaires vont **au** Caire pour suivre un stage intensif d'arabe*; *Adeline est rentrée **du** Touquet*; *Le notaire **du** Havre* (novel by Georges Duhamel).

With feminine nouns *de* or *de la* is used to signify *from* or *of*. Contrary to the rule offered by some English grammars of French, *de* and *de la* are used in this context, although *de* alone may be more common: *Laetitia est rentrée **de la/de** France*; *Mohammed vient **de l'/d'**Algérie*; *l'histoire **de la/de** Belgique*; *les vins **de la/de** Bulgarie*; *les rois **de la/de** République tchèque.*

The definite article is not used with names of cities and towns, except for some most notable exceptions: *à Berne/Bruxelles/Londres/New York/Ottawa/Paris.* Some exceptions in France where the definite article forms part of the name and is therefore in upper case are: *Les Andelys, La Baule, Le Creusot, Le Havre, L'Isle-Adam, Le Mans, Le Puy, La Rochelle.* With the prepositions *à* and *de* we have: *Aux/Des Andelys, à/de La Baule, au/du Creusot, au/du Havre, à/de La Rochelle.* Some exceptions elsewhere are: *Le Caire, La Havane, La Haye, La Mecque, La Nouvelle-Orléans.* With the prepositions *à* and *de* we have: *au/du Cap, au/du Caire, à/de La Havane, à/de La Haye, à/de La Mecque, à/de La Nouvelle-Orléans.*

It is quite obvious that the towns and cities which have the masculine definite article as part of their name lead to an inextricable problem when they are preceded by the prepositions *à* and *de*. The definite article which would be in upper case for these towns and cities becomes lower case in conjunction with these two prepositions.

There exist certain differences between usage in France and usage in Belgium, Switzerland and Quebec.

1. In Belgium one would hear: *La moitié du pays est **sous eau*** as opposed to *sous les eaux* in France; *aller à selle* (*to evacuate the bowels*) instead of *aller à la selle*; *de commun accord* instead of *d'un commun accord*; *Les frais sont **à charge du** vendeur* instead of *à la charge du vendeur*; *Il vérifia **la porte de rue*** instead of *la porte de la rue*.
2. In Switzerland one would hear: *À louer: appartement **à disposition*** instead of *disponible*.
3. In Quebec one would hear: *à matin, à soir* instead of *au matin, au soir*.

Much ink seems to have been unnecessarily spilled over the differences between use and non-use of the definite article in French. Some grammarians see a distinction between *les rois **de** France* and *les rois **de la** France*, and between *l'histoire **de** France* and *l'histoire **de la** France*. The definite article may be seen in writing but, most emphatically in speech, one only hears *les rois **de** France* / *l'histoire **de** France*, so that the definite article is disappearing in this context. An example of both in writing is offered by two books by the French Academy writer André Maurois's *Histoire **d'**Angleterre* and *Histoire **de la** France*.

For the use of the definite article with common medical terms see Chapter 8, Section 2.

7

The indefinite article / L'article indéfini

Note that, in a general way, the indefinite articles correspond to the English *a, an, some*. The forms of the indefinite article are:

Masculine singular	Feminine singular	Masculine and feminine plural
un	*une*	*des*

Do not confuse the plural of the indefinite article *des* with the contracted form of the definite article *de + les*: *Les jouets **des** enfants sont étalés sur le tapis.*
   The indefinite article is used:

1. before countable nouns (*noms comptables*, i.e., nouns that can be counted): *J'ai acheté **une** bicyclette et **des** patins à roulettes; Mon frère m'a envoyé **un** courriel de Chine; Son fiancé lui a envoyé régulièrement **des** e-mails des États-Unis;*
2. when the noun points to an unidentified person or object: ***Un** client a appelé. Il n'a pas laissé son nom | de nom* (we do not know who has called); *J'ai trouvé **des** gants par terre. Ils sont à qui ?; "J'ai **une** idée !" "Ah ! Qu'est-ce que c'est ?";*
3. when the noun is given a particular significance by an adjective: *Du haut de cette colline, on découvre **un** paysage **magnifique**;*
4. when the noun is given a particular significance by a noun complement: *Ce tableau représente **un** paysage **d'hiver**;*
5. when a relative subordinate clause is involved: *C'est **un** paysage **qui fait rêver**.*
6. in certain set expressions which do not require the indefinite article in an ordinary and non-affective context but which, when used in an emphatic or exclamatory way, attract the indefinite article and end on rising intonation: *J'ai faim/soif* but *J'avais **une** faim/soif !* Similar comparisons apply to the verb *faire*: *Il faisait froid/chaud* and *Il faisait **un** froid / **une** chaleur !* (note *chaleur* and not *chaud* here).

When the plural noun is preceded by an adjective, *des* is converted to *de*: *J'ai acheté **des** roses* but: *J'ai acheté **de** magnifiques roses; Ce jeune pianiste a fait **des** progrès* but: *Ce jeune pianiste a fait **de** grands progrès.* However, in R1 colloquial language, there is a strong tendency to keep the article *des* in the second examples above: *Ce jeune pianiste a fait **des** grands progrès*; *Rémi a eu **des** bonnes notes à l'examen*. This construction is even creeping into the written language: ***Des** vieilles chansons, **des** mauvaises gens, **des** petits trous, **des** petits cris de rats* (this last example is taken from *La peste* of Camus, a modern author singularly attached to a classical and exemplary style).

When the adjective is preceded by an adverb, often one of intensity, *de* is also used: *Elle avait **de** très jeunes enfants*. When the noun is preceded by two adjectives, the higher register leads to the use of *de*: *Imagine-toi **de** belles et rafraîchissantes jeunes filles*.

When the group adjective + noun is considered as a compound noun, *des* obtains: ***des** petits pois, **des** jeunes gens, **des** petites annonces, **des** grands magasins, **des** petites filles, **des** petites cuillères, **des** petits pains, **des** gros mots*.

The indefinite article may have a general value: ***Une** banane, c'est facile à éplucher*.

Repetition of the indefinite article occurs in cases where nouns are joined by *et* and *ou*: *Elle s'est cassé **un** bras et **un** doigt / **une** jambe et **un** bras*; *Je cherche **une** tasse et **une** soucoupe*; *Je ne sais pas si elle a **un** fils ou **une** fille*; *Tu peux l'écrire avec **un** crayon ou **un** stylo*; *Guillaume a **un** frère ou **une** sœur, je ne sais pas*.

The indefinite article also appears before a proper name, through either scorn or emphasis, in order to invest this name with the value of a common name: *On a vu **un** Néron comploter contre sa mère Agrippine*; ***Un** Alexandre, **un** César, **un** Napoléon ont bouleversé le monde*; *Ont-ils mieux mérité de l'humanité qu'**un** Pasteur, qu'**une** Marie Curie ou qu'**un** Fleming ?*

Emphasis can also be placed on numbers with *des*, and here it has, unsurprisingly, the value of *some*: *devant **des** quinzaines et **des** vingtaines de personnes*.

The indefinite plural *des* is used to evoke uncertainty of number, and here it corresponds to *quelques* or *certains*: *Son père gagne **des** cents et **des** mille*; *Ça m'a coûté trente francs suisses et **des** poussières*.

Un also has the numerical meaning of *one*, and here ellipsis does not occur: *L'inflation a augmenté **de un** pour cent*.

Cases where the indefinite article is not used in French and where an English speaker might expect it are (see also Chapter 8, Section 2 for use of medical terms):

1. when a noun is in apposition: *Sa mère, **couturière** de son état, l'a élevée toute seule*;
2. after the verbs *être, devenir, sembler, nommer, élire, croire*: *Son frère **fut général***; *Marine est **devenue docteure***; *Adeline **semblait Française** mais, plus tard, j'ai compris qu'elle **était Canadienne***; *Henriette a été **élue présidente** en juin, et tout de suite après, elle l'a **nommée ministre***; *Je la **croyais médecin** généraliste; je n'aurais jamais cru qu'elle **était chirurgienne***. However, when the noun is qualified by an adjective, or has a further complement, it is preceded by an indefinite article: *Céline était*

une brillante **professeure**; *Aude est* **une** *ingénieure* **remarquable**; *Camille était* **une** *Française* **du Canada**;

3. after quel !, quelle !, quels !, quelles ! (*What* [a]... !): *Quel dommage !, Quel écrivain astucieux !, Quel crétin !, Quels étudiants !, Quelle imbécile !, Quelle athlète incroyable !, Quelles idées !*;

4. when the direct object of the verb is preceded by *pas de*: *Je n'ai* **pas de** *dollars/***pas d'***euros; Nicolas n'a* **pas** *acheté* **de** *maison*. Nevertheless, it is perfectly normal to say *Je n'ai pas acheté* **une** *maison*: This sentence is much more emphatic than the preceding one. If a positive idea is suggested, however, *des* is used: *On ne fait pas d'omelettes sans casser* **des** *œufs; N'avez-vous pas* **des** *amis pour vous défendre ?*;

5. when the subject of the verb is preceded by *jamais*, and here the register is R3 (i.e., literary): *Jamais* **vocation** *d'écrivain ne fut plus évidente !*

6. in certain fixed expressions: (**Bon**) **nombre** *d'étudiants sont descendus dans la rue; C'est* **bon signe** | *Ce n'est pas* **bon signe** | *C'est* **mauvais signe**; *L'accusée a* **porté plainte** *contre la police; Le fermier a mis le bétail* **en lieu sûr**. Sometimes, and again in fixed expressions, *par* corresponds to the English *a/an*: *Pauline visite le Canada une fois* | *deux fois* **par** *an; Le comptable gagne sept mille euros* **par** *mois; Ça coûte cinquante dollars* **par** *personne* | **par** *tête de pipe* (R1); *Le son se propage à une vitesse de 340 mètres* **par** *seconde*. Sometimes *à* corresponds to the English *a/an*, and especially with respect to speed: *quatre-vingts kilomètres* **à** *l'heure*. The preposition *à* is sometimes omitted: *Quatre-vingts/octante; huitante kilomètres* **heure**. This corresponds to the written form 80 km/h, as in: *L'avion a franchi le mur du son en atteignant 1 500 km/h*.

7. in expressions of the kind preposition + noun (see Chapter 56 on prepositions for a full treatment of this topic): *J'ai lu votre livre* **avec intérêt** *et* **enthousiasme**; *Tu le traduis* **avec soin**, *n'est-ce pas ?; J'ai appris la nouvelle* **par hasard**; *Elle s'en est sortie* **par miracle**; **Par bonheur**, *elle est revenue saine et sauve; Je l'ai résolu* **sans problème/difficulté**. Many of these constructions may include an adjective: *Olivier a réparé la crevaison* **avec grand soin**; *Je l'ai résolu* **sans grande difficulté**. On many occasions, this type of construction does require the indefinite article when the noun is modified by an adjective: *Je l'ai trouvé* **par hasard** but: *Je l'ai trouvé* **par un hasard extraordinaire**; *Catherine a fait sa rédaction* **avec un soin minutieux**; *Le médecin s'est occupé du malade* **avec une patience exemplaire**;

8. in advertisements, where the indefinite article is often omitted: *Centre hospitalier recherche réseau de coopération*.

8

The partitive article / L'article partitif [1]

Below is a passage narrating a strenuous hike through the Sinai desert. Highlighted here are the various uses of the partitive article (*du*, *de la*, *de l'*, *des*), to be distinguished from the possessive or genitive, which has the same forms. The partitive article corresponds basically to *some* while the possessive relates to *of*. A native speaker of French is not necessarily aware of this distinction. When the partitive occurs, a (1) appears after it, while the possessive is marked by a (2). Partitive articles are also highlighted in bold.

> **Une randonnée nocturne dans le désert du Sinaï**
>
> Située à la frontière des (2) Territoires Palestiniens et d'(2)Israël, la péninsule du (2) Sinaï a captivé les quelques randonneurs et randonneuses que nous formions. Cet endroit mythique offrait le spectacle fabuleux d'(2)un plateau désertique s'étendant le long de la mer Rouge entre les stations balnéaires du (2) Sinaï : Charm el-Cheikh et Dahab. Nous avons traversé **des** (1) paysages et **de** (1) magnifiques !
>
> Notre extraordinaire expédition dans le désert nous a surpris par la diversité du (2) site : on voyait **des** (1) dunes de (2) sable, ainsi que **des** (1) plages, notamment Charm el-Cheikh (Charm el-Cheikh = *la baie du vieux* en arabe) et Dahab (= *or* en arabe). Avant de gravir les Monts, nous avons apprécié ce lieu géographique, réputé pour son *Blue Hole* (Trou Bleu) caractérisé par son grand fond sous-marin, aux eaux cristallines, qui contient un réservoir gigantesque de (2) coraux, de (2) plantes et d'(2)animaux aquatiques de (2) couleurs variées. **Des** (1) roches nous ont émerveillés, tant par leurs formes que par leurs couleurs de (2) l'arc-en-ciel : violet, indigo, bleu, vert, jaune, orange, rouge qui se dégageaient avec la luminosité. Quelle étrange fascination ! Notre promenade longue et ininterrompue s'est effectuée en présence de (2) Bédouins et de (2) leurs dromadaires. Nous ne voyions que **des** (1) dromadaires, mais pas **de** (1) chevaux. On ne voyait pas **de** (1) mules non plus. Ce circuit de (2) grande randonnée pédestre en montagne s'est fait à la nuit tombante.

---

[1] The approach in this chapter is quite broad, and includes what some might consider to be indefinite articles.

De (1) magnifiques paysages nous ont étonnés lorsqu'on gravissait le Mont Sinaï et le Mont Sainte-Catherine. Nous avons eu bien **du** (1) mal à atteindre le sommet de (2) la montagne. Le chemin caillouteux qui nous conduit aux massifs montagneux de (2) couleur rosée présentait une vue saisissante.

Après huit heures de (2) marche, on nous servit **du** (1) thé à la menthe, **d'**(1)excellents jus de (2) fruits, **de** l'(1)eau fraîche et **du** (1) pain chaud préparé par les Bédouines. En nous désaltérant, on contemplait avec admiration la lumière rougeâtre du (2) lever du (2) soleil à reflets changeants tout en écoutant un groupe de (2) touristes chanter en chœur **de** (1) splendides chants religieux à nous couper le souffle. Notre voyage fut couronné de (2) succès. Ce désert sacré serait le point de (2) rencontre des (2) trois religions : on y rencontrait **des** (1) juifs, **des** (1) chrétiens et **des** (1) musulmans. Les beautés de (2) ce haut lieu de (2) pèlerinage nous ont éblouis.

8.1 Forms and use of the partitive article

The partitive *de* combines with the articles and with adjectives to form determiners indicating a part of a whole. The English equivalent is *some*, *some of*, *any*, but the French partitive is used much more frequently then its English counterparts. The forms of the partitive article are:

Masculine singular	Feminine singular	Plural
du, de l', de	*de la, de l', de*	*des, de*

One should distinguish between the partitive *des* (= *some*) and the possessive *des* (= *of the*), which is a contraction of *de* + *les*. Compare **Des** *garçons ont chahuté le prof dans la classe* and **La plupart des** *garçons ont chahuté le prof dans la classe*.

The partitive is regularly and necessarily used, which is not the case in English or Spanish. Interestingly enough, the partitive is also used in Italian – perhaps less often than in French, although it is still quite common. All this to say that French is quite unique in its insistence on the partitive: *Nous avons pris* **du** *thé/d'un thé exquis; Donnez-moi* **de** *ce gâteau, s'il vous plaît; Donnez-nous* **de** *vos nouvelles;* **Des** *personnes malveillantes vous diront le contraire; Daniel peut emprunter* **de** *l'argent à des amis; On nous servit* **du** *bœuf rôti et* **de la** *sauce bourguignonne; Nous avons bu* **d'***excellents jus de fruits; Donnez-lui* **de** *bons conseils.*

Whereas, formerly, *du* and *de la* were reduced to *de* when an adjective preceded the noun, as in the two cases immediately above, this is no longer so. The second example below involving a singular noun is therefore archaic. Thus, French would once have had *Voilà* **de** *vraie poésie !* (modern version: *de la vraie poésie*), but standard French now has *Nous avons acheté* **du** *bon vin* and

*En voilà, **des** beaux enfants!*, although one could very easily write and hear: *En voilà **de** beaux enfants!*

The article is used when the adjective follows the noun: ***du** lait chaud*, ***des** pois secs*, ***des** filles intelligentes.*

The article is always omitted after partitive *de* before *autres*: *J'ai **d'**autres amis*; *J'en ai **d'**autres*. In archaic French one could read: *Donnez-moi **d'**autre vin, s'il vous plaît.*

The article is omitted when the adjective qualifies, or is dependent on, *en* replacing a partitive noun: *Du vin? Je peux vous en fournir: j'**en** ai **d'**excellents*; *J'**en** ai appris **des** belles sur votre compte*; *J'**en** ai vu **des** livres, et **des** beaux!*; *J'ai **du** bon fromage de chèvre dans le frigo... j'**en** ai **du** frais, j'en ai **du** camembert | **du** cantal...*

When a second adjective occurs with ellipsis of the noun, it takes or omits the article according to the construction: *Elle cueillit **des** fleurs rouges et **des** blanches* but *Dans toute école on trouve **de** bons élèves et **de** mauvais,* although one could very easily hear and see written *Dans toute école on trouve **des** bons élèves et **des** mauvais.*

A partitive noun governed by a prepositional *de* (= *of, from, by, with*, etc.) may still be preceded by *un, une* or an adjective, but not by *le, la, les*: *Nous avons pris un verre **d'un** vin exquis, **de ce** vin, **de son** vin, un verre **d'**excellent vin* but *Nous avons pris une tasse **de** thé.*

The partitive noun is governed by prepositional *de*, the partitive article being entirely omitted in three cases. It could be argued that, in these cases, the *de* indicates less a partitive article than a possessive:

1. after many nouns denoting definite or indefinite quantity: *une bouteille d'eau, un kilo **de** beurre, trois ans **de** guerre, un grand nombre | une foule **de** personnes*;
2. after a considerable number of adjectives or past participles: *une salle pleine **d'**invités, une ville privée/dépourvue **de** vivres, une expression vide **de** sens, couronné **de** succès, couvert **de** boue, rempli **de** sable*;
3. after many verbs and verbal phrases: *Il faut se munir **de** provisions*; *Les pirates étaient armés **de** coutelas*; *Il faudrait garnir **d'**arbres toutes ces avenues*; *J'avais besoin **de** combustible.*

This is also the case when *de* forms part of a compound preposition: *Près **de** maisons d'aspect misérable s'élève un magnifique hôtel.*

The negative adverbs *ne pas* and *ne point* come under 1 above, since they were originally nouns followed by prepositional de. The negative adverbs *ne plus, de guère* and *ne jamais* have, for etymological reasons, the same construction with omission of the article: *Céline n'a **pas d'**argent | **point d'**argent*; *Nous n'avons **plus d'**essence*; *Il n'y a **jamais de** musée ouvert le mardi.* However, if the negative adverb merely qualifies the verb, without intruding on the partitive noun, the partitive article stands. Compare the two following sentences: *Je ne vous donnerai **pas de** conseils* and *Je ne vous donnerai **pas des** conseils* *impossibles à suivre*. Compare also the two parts of the following sentence: *On ne peut pas faire du bien à tous, mais on peut témoigner de la bonté à tous.*

The article stands after the adverb *ne... que*, which is affirmative as regards the following noun: *On ne m'a donné **que des** conseils*; *Je ne voyais **que des** écureuils, mais pas d'oiseaux.*

The article is omitted after the adverbs of quantity *beaucoup, peu, plus, moins, tant, autant, trop, assez, combien, que!* because the following *de* was originally prepositional: ***Beaucoup de** paroles et **peu de** travail!*; *Il se trouvait **plus de** spectateurs que je ne pensais*; *Il y a **moins d'**animaux dans le bois que l'année dernière*; *Je vous donnerai **autant de** dollars que vous voudrez*; *Nous n'avons pas **assez de** café*; *Tu as compté **combien de** voitures sur le parking?*; *Le repas était excellent mais on nous a servi **trop de** viande.*

However, *beaucoup, peu* and *combien* may be followed by *des*, as illustrated by these examples: ***Beaucoup des** amies d'Adeline sont venues à l'église*; ***Beaucoup des** auditeurs ont commencé à conspuer l'orateur*; *Si les Parisiennes avaient un **peu du** génie que j'associe aux Madrilènes...*; ***De combien des** livres que tu as lus dans ton enfance te souviens-tu?* In these cases, the suggestion is: **many of the** friends, as opposed to **many** friends, **a little of the** genius, as opposed to **little genius**, or **how many of** the books, as opposed to **how many** books.

The article stands after *bien*, which is not an adverb of quantity but merely an affective expression of a superlative idea: ***Bien des** candidats se sont présentés*; *J'ai eu **bien du** mal à nager jusqu'à la plage*; *Il a fallu affronter **bien des** dangers avant d'arriver à notre destination.*

As with *bien*, so with *la plupart*, which is less an adverb and more a superlative (= *la plus grande partie*): ***La plupart de** mes amis sont arrivés à temps*; ***La plupart du temps**, Francis travaille comme quatre*. Note that *la plupart de* is followed either by a plural noun or by *temps* in the singular, but no other singular noun. For example, *la plupart* could not be followed by an uncountable noun like *beurre* or *fruit*, unless these nouns were in the plural, which is possible if one considered *beurre* or *fruit* in the context of "types of butter or fruit." Thus, one could say, in all logic, although a certain uneasiness is felt here: *la plupart des beurres* or *la plupart des fruits*.

The partitive *de* is used before adjectives and nouns after the neuter and indefinite pronouns *ceci, cela, que, quoi, ce qui, ce que, quelqu'un, quelque chose, personne, rien*: *Son cas a **ceci de** particulier que sa réputation est excellente*; ***Quoi de** neuf/nouveau?*; ***Que** sais-tu **d'**intéressant?*; *Dans tout **ce qui** m'arrive **d'**heureux ou **de** triste, je pense à ma mère*; ***Ce que** je connais **d'**intéressant, je le garde pour moi*; *Je me suis tiré d'affaire avec **ce que** je connais **de** mandarin*; *Il y a **quelqu'un de** blessé?*; *J'ai appris **quelque chose de** vraiment important.*

Personal pronouns are not preceded by *de* but by *d'entre*: *Les juges n'étaient pas d'accord*. ***Plusieurs d'entre** eux croyaient à l'innocence de l'accusé*; *Les étudiants sont entrés en coup de vent. **Trois d'entre** eux ont commencé à chahuter.* But one may say either ***l'un d'**eux* or ***l'un d'entre** eux*.

The noun is never partitive when determined by numeral or indefinite adjectives: *quatre-vingts euros*; *J'ai parlé avec plusieurs personnes*; *Attends quelques minutes.*

Joliment, a common colloquial expression, but not accepted by all, is normally followed by the full partitive form: *J'ai eu **joliment du** mal à résoudre la question.*

The partitive article is used as a complement which serves to characterize something or someone: *une table **de** marbre* (also *en* here), *un poète **de** génie*, *un adverbe **de** lieu*, *une mesure **de** longueur*. This is similar to the use of the preposition *à* which is not a partitive: *Assiette **à** soupe, boîte **à** bijoux, boîte **à** lettres* (more usually: *boîte **aux** lettres*), *coffret à bijoux/disques/CDs/DVDs, corbeille à pain/papier, panier à salade, sac à ouvrage.*

8.2 Medical terminology

Here we bring together in common medical terminology the often confusing uses of the French definite, indefinite and partitive article where there is rarely correspondence in English and where, all too frequently, the articles are not used at all. Dictionaries do not help much here.

8.2.1 Partitive article

Examples: *Elle a de l'asme* | *du diabète* | *de l'eczéma* | *de la température* | *de l'urticaire* (rash). *Elle a/fait de l'ostéoporose. Elle a/fait du rhumatisme. J'ai de la fièvre* (a temperature). *Elle a/fait de la tension* (high blood pressure). Also: *Elle a des coups de soleil* | *un coup de soleil* (sunburn) | *des crampes* | *une crampe.*

8.2.2 Definite article

Examples: *Il a l'appendicite* | *le cancer* (also: *un cancer*) | *le choléra* | *la diarrhée* | *la diphtérie* | *la dysenterie* | *la fièvre* (temperature) | *la gangrène* | *la goutte* | *la grippe* | *la lèpre* | *la leucémie* | *la maladie d'Alzheimer* | *la maladie de Parkinson* | *la maladie du sommeil* | *la maladie de la vache folle* | *la maladie du légionnaire* | *la migraine* (also *une migraine*) | *la mononucléose* (glandular fever: also *une mononucléose*) | *les oreillons* (mumps) | *le palu* (or *paludisme*, but *le palu* is much more common than the full term) | *le pied d'athlète* | *la phlébite* | *la pneumoconiose* (pneumoconiosis = miners' lung disease) | *la rage* (rabies) | *la rougeole* (measles) | *le sida* (AIDS) | *la salmonelle* | *la scarlatine* | *la syphilis* | *le tétanos* | *le torticolis* (stiff neck; also *un torticolis*) | *la tuberculose* | *la varicelle* (chicken pox) | *la petite vérole* (small pox).

La maladie is also used figuratively: *Elle a la maladie du rangement* (She's obsessively tidy). During the 1970s, Michel Sardou sang a most popular song: "Elle court, elle court, la maladie d'amour [love sickness] . . . " *La manie* occurs in a similar context: *Il a la manie de la propreté* | *de l'ordre* | *de la persécution.* Note also: *avoir le mal du pays* (homesickness) | *le mal des transports* (travel sickness) | *le mal de mer.* In a literary context, and during the Romantic period: *Musset avait le mal du siècle* (world weariness), the *Weltschmerz* we find in Goethe's *The Sorrows of Young Werther*.

8.2.3 Indefinite article

Examples: *Elle a une angine (sore throat) | une bronchite | une conjonctivite | une hépatite | une hernie | une indigestion | une insolation (sunstroke) | une méningite | une mycose (rash* and could refer to *athlete's foot) | une otite (earache) | une pneumonie | un rhume (Elle est enrhumée* is more common) *| une tendinite (tendinitis* but often *tennis elbow) | un zona (shingles). Elle fait une sinusite. Elle a fait une déprime* (R1 = *She was depressed*) is much less strong than *Elle a fait une dépression.*

8.2.4 General notes

The term *cancer* is often avoided by journalists these days, and is replaced by a euphemism: *Elle est décédée des suites d'une longue maladie. Sida* could also be replaced by *une longue maladie,* but *cancer* is the most common one here.

Elle n'a pas **le** *moral = She's a bit depressed.*

For *amygdales (tonsils),* one usually says: *Elle a les amygdales (She has tonsilitis).*

In some cases, adjectives come much more easily: *Elle est anorexique/ autiste/boulimique/épileptique/rachitique* (< *anorexie/autisme/boulimie/épilepsie/ rachitisme*).

It goes without saying that these lists only offer general guidance. See also Chapter 7 for other features where there is no correspondence with English.

9

Gender | Le genre

Exceptionally, given the length of this chapter, there are two passages of French illustrating the problems of gender in French. The first focuses on Thebes, an illustrious city in ancient Egypt, while the second describes the Saharan city of Ghardaïa.

Thebes, in Upper Egypt, is the center of an important tourist industry, given the splendor of an ancient and fascinating culture. The visit to Thebes involves Luxor and Karnac. These three ancient cities with their monuments lie along the Nile. Note that the city of Thèbes is feminine while Le Caire, Louxor and **Karnac** are masculine, a general difficulty highlighted in the body of this chapter. Note also that, together with some other towns and cities in the world, Caire is preceded by Le. Le Nil indicates that rivers are generally, but not always, masculine. There are a great number of nouns in this passage, the gender of which could be deceiving for an English speaker: *crépuscule*, *temple*, *cadre*, *musée*, *fleuve*, *mythe*, *caractère*, *hiéroglyphe*, *obélisque*, *pylône*, *vestige* and *apogée*, among other nouns, are masculine, and *nécropole*, *énigme* and *ruines* are feminine. Just a few translations are given.

Sur les traces de Thèbes

En Égypte, **la chaleur** torride du mois de juillet nous obligeait à faire nos **visites** touristiques et **culturelles** à **la tombée** de **la nuit** ou **au crépuscule du matin**. Après **un** long **voyage** nocturne depuis **Le Caire**, nous arrivâmes à **Louxor**[1] où nous étions attendus en grande pompe. Nous descendîmes à **l'hôtel central** pour nous reposer la journée avant de connaître la grandeur, la pureté et **la gloire immortelle** des **temples égyptiens**, des **palais imposants** des **anciens pharaons** de Louxor et de Karnac[2] ainsi que des **nécropoles monumentales** de **la Vallée** des **Rois** et de **la Vallée** des **Reines**.

Le **grand éclat** et **la lumière** particulière qui jaillissent de ces **hauts lieux** de **pèlerinage individuel** ou en groupe sont envoûtants. **Le cadre naturel** est absolument féerique, il s'agit **d'un véritable musée** à ciel ouvert ! De l'autre côté de **la rive**, le Nil s'écoule tranquillement au

[1] Louxor may also be written Louqsor, and means *palace* in Arabic.
[2] Karnac may also be written Karnak or Carnac, and means *fortified village* in Arabic.

rythme des **étroites felouques** [feluccas: boats typically used on the Nile]. L'**un** des plus longs **fleuves** du monde se singularise par **sa** verte **vallée** en plein milieu du désert. **Quelle magnificence** et **quel caractère** mystérieux et sacré de **ce site merveilleux** ! Les **dieux tout-puissants**, les **déesses égyptiennes**, les **héros traditionnels**, les **mythes fabuleux**, les **fameuses légendes** de la **mythologie égyptienne** sont omniprésents.

Une grande **énigme** entoure Louxor. A l'entrée **du temple**, **un obélisque** gravé de **hiéroglyphes anciens** trône avec **le** grandiose **pylône** de Ramsès II ainsi que deux **statues colossales** assises au milieu des **ruines éternelles. Un calme olympien** règne sur **la Haute-Égypte** et ses **édifices somptueux.** À chaque instant, **la splendeur** de **ces nombreux vestiges** m'émerveille. **La Thèbes** antique m'a captivée par **la beauté fascinante** de son environnement qui témoigne avec force de l'**apogée** [highest point] **lumineux** d'une civilisation millénaire [thousands of years old].

Below is a passage describing the exotic perfumes, colors and activities of Ghardaïa, an Algerian city deep in the Sahara desert where many people still either speak or understand French. Algeria remains very much a francophone country.

The gender of many nouns is indicated by definite and indefinite articles and adjectives. Adjectives often, but by no means always, can be a clue to the gender of nouns. Note that *oasis* and *coriandre* are feminine, as is *Saint-Sylvestre*, like most festivals in French. *Gingembre*, *délice* and *régime* on the other hand are masculine. Yet *délice* in the plural is feminine, as indicated below. Not all the genders are highlighted in bold, for example *la découverte*, *la richesse* and *la générosité*. Translations of some individual words or expressions are provided.

La perle **des oasis**

Notre **merveilleuse équipée** [adventure] à Ghardaïa, **une grande et belle oasis du M'zab**, a été marquée par **la célébration** de **la Saint-Sylvestre** [New Year's Eve]. La découverte de **la vie bédouine** fut **un** véritable **enchantement.** Passant par **les rues étroites** qui débouchent sur **la place du marché**, je suis attirée, comme **un aimant** [magnet], par les **odeurs alléchantes** [enticing] de toutes sortes d'épices : **l'anis étoilé, le cumin, le clou** de girofle, **la cannelle, le gingembre, la coriandre, la menthe** et bien d'autres **substances** aromatiques et **enivrantes. Quel délice** !

A ces **odeurs douces** et suaves, des **étalages** [stalls] bien **approvisionnés** en fruits et légumes s'offrent à notre regard. Ce marché est **une curiosité** inlassable. Je n'ai pas le souvenir d'avoir rencontré **une habitante**, même voilée, de Ghardaïa. Une touriste de passage me précise que depuis un mois, j'étais la première femme qu'elle rencontrait sur **cette place** où **la présence masculine** est très **forte.** La plupart du temps, **le**

burnous, **le pantalon** bouffant [baggy] et **la calotte** [skull cap] blanche caractérisent **l'habillement traditionnel du Mozabite**. Notre **journée** fut **ponctuée** par **un appel** à la prière du haut **du minaret** duquel **le muezzin** invite **les fervents fidèles** cinq fois par jour.

Fin décembre, nous avions bénéficié **d'un climat** exceptionnellement **doux**, sous **d'autres cieux cléments**. Dans le désert, **les palmeraies** [groves of palm trees] étaient **chargées** des **derniers régimes** [bunches] de **dattes gorgées** de soleil. Ghardaïa a exercé sur moi **une mystérieuse fascination**. Cette région du sud algérien est légendaire. La perle des oasis garde dans **son écrin** [jewel box] le **trésor d'une culture ances-trale** avec la richesse de **son patrimoine** historique, **la beauté** presque **irréelle** de ses caravanes de **chameaux** et de **chamelles** et la générosité de son peuple.

9.1 A note on the concept of gender

That, in French, or in most European languages (but not in Basque, Finnish, Hungarian or Turkish), the notion of gender for nouns provides the first obstacle for an English-speaking student doubtless comes as no surprise. After all, for such a speaker, the concept of gender assigned to inanimate objects strikes one as extraordinary, and lacks all logic and convincing definition. Gender applied to inanimate objects hardly exists in English. One may quote *she* for a ship, but this is the limit. However, the idea of gender in French is a presence to be reckoned with. One of the neo-Latin languages, and therefore deriving from Latin, and ultimately from Greek, French inherits the concept of gender, just like Spanish, Italian and Portuguese. One may understand masculine and feminine nouns in the context of humans (male and female) and some animals (again male and female). But that a table in French should be feminine (= *la table*), or that *tavola* (*la*) in Italian and *mesa* (*la*) in Spanish should also be feminine, while *couteau* (*le*) in French, *coltello* (*il*) in Italian and *cuchillo* (*el*) in Spanish are masculine defies rational explanation. Indeed, linguists agree that no rules may be established to justify this application of gender to nouns, save for those pointing to persons and some animals.

Furthermore, in many European languages, from Greek and Latin through to Czech, German, Polish, Russian and the Scandinavian languages, for example, one has to confront a further gender applied to nouns: neuter. In Romance languages, fortunately, this is not the case, although in Spanish, there exists the vigorous use of adjectives with a neuter value (*lo*). The imagination is stretched beyond all reasonable bounds in Old Church Russian where a fourth gender occurs with a mixture of plural masculine and feminine, the equivalent of *they*. However, for our purposes, we may safely concentrate on French masculine and feminine nouns, which have repercussions throughout the French sentence since they require agreement of adjectives and past participles.

The gender of numerous French nouns has never been stable over the centuries, which explains serious hesitation felt, at one time or another, by practically all French speakers. The same comment applies to the other Romance languages. This variability is partly due to the diverse origins of words, changes based on analogy with other words in the same language, and the constant requirements of adapting to new circumstances, as with the accession of females to what was once an exclusive male precinct. Three simple examples of the variability of genders over the centuries are the French masculine noun *miel* which is also masculine in Italian (*il miele*) but feminine in Spanish (*la miel*); *fleur* is feminine in French and Spanish (*la flor*) but masculine in Italian (*il fiore*); *opéra* is masculine in French but *ópera* is feminine in Spanish and *opera* is also feminine in Italian. Little wonder there is confusion here since *opus/operis* is neuter in Latin. In short, the study of gender is a testing minefield, and requires meticulous attention, although the restrictions of room do not allow the comprehensive treatment that the monumental *Bon usage* of Grevisse and Goosse devotes to it. In the latest edition of the said volume (2008), seventy-four pages cover the endless possibilities of gender.

Finally, in this short introduction, the common expression "discuter sur le sexe des anges" says it all. Such a discussion points to an interminable and doubtless fruitless wrangling over the sex, and therefore gender, of angels, and sex and gender are not the same thing. Whether angels can be exclusively male or female, and whether their gender in French is masculine or feminine are unresolved issues. Of course, only the latter concerns us here. Consensus of opinion suggests that *ange* is only masculine, witness the entry in the admirable Canadian *MULTI dictionnaire* of de Villers, which states unequivocally that "ange est *toujours* masculin" (our emphasis). A similar opinion is found in the Belgians Hanse and Blampain's excellent *Nouveau dictionnaire des difficultés du français moderne* (2005). Yet this trenchant assertion flies in the face of evidence adduced by *Le bon usage*, which quotes such prestigious authors as Alfred de Vigny, Gustave Flaubert, Gérard de Nerval, Antoine de Saint-Exupéry, Émile Zola, who also assign a feminine gender to the word *ange*. The simple fact is that French, as other Romance languages, finds itself inextricably involved in gender issues that remain adamantly unclear by virtue of the relationship of the nature of gender and the infinitely variable possibilities of nouns. To conclude the matter of *ange*, nearly all contemporary French speakers view it as a masculine noun. For further confusion on the sex of possible supernatural beings, *démon/démone* is merely another illustration of this labyrinth, although the feminine form is little used these days. This said, Chateaubriand uses the feminine form in his *Mémoires d'outre-tombe* (near the beginning of Chapter 12, Book 3).

9.2 Patterns of gender

Following on from the comments above, gender constitutes a basic ingredient of French grammar. It is therefore important to assign the correct gender to a particular noun. As with the other languages referred to above, rules for learning the gender of nouns would be pointless, and the only practical method is to use the definite (*le/la*) or indefinite article (*un/une*) before each noun when it is first encountered and try to remember it. At the same time, certain patterns emerge. The simplest one is the gender applied to many males and females: *le père / la mère, un oncle / une tante, le frère / la sœur, le fils / la fille, un homme / une femme, le garçon / la fille*. Beyond this most straightforward of patterns we concentrate on patterns that are not too obvious, bearing in mind that there are numerous exceptions, among which a feminine noun like *victime* applies not just to females but also to males. *Victime* is *not* preceded by *le/un* when referring to a male. Conversely, a female *witness* can only be masculine: *le témoin*, and as a blue stocking, she has to be masculine, despite the irony here: *un bas bleu*. Similarly, *bébé* can only be masculine: *Il va bien* applies to male and female babies alike, although among small children one could very easily hear *une bébé*. In the world of infancy, would a female newborn be *une fille nouveau née, une fille nouvelle née* or *une fille nouveau né*? The Belgian dictionary of Hanse and Blampain supports the use of the first of these three. Almost certainly none of these would be used in metropolitan France, and *une petite fille* would replace them.

Below is a rough, but very helpful, guide which offers a fair, but far from comprehensive, list. This presents the patterns (e.g. –**et** masculine / –**ette** feminine: *jouet/brouette*; –**s** masculine / –**sse** feminine: *bras/brasse*) that the gender follows. These patterns do have a true function, so it is worthwhile studying them.

9.2.1 Simple nouns: masculine

Names of days of the week: **le** *dimanche, lundi, mardi, samedi* (see Chapter 62 for the full list);

Names of months: *janvier, février, mars, novembre, décembre* (see Chapter 62 for the full list);

Names of seasons: *hiver, printemps, été, automne*;

Names of languages: *arabe, français, anglais américain/britannique, guarani, hébreu, náhuatl* (of the Aztecs), *russe, chinois, serbo-croate, tchèque*;

Names of trees: *acajou, balsamier, baobab, bouleau, buis, cactus, cèdre, chêne, coudrier/noisetier* (hazel tree), *cyprès, érable, eucalyptus, frêne, hêtre, houx, if* (as in Château d'If, a small island in the Mediterranean, off the coast of Marseilles), *lentisque, lilas, mélèze, mimosa, néflier, orme, palissandre, palmier, peuplier, pin, pistachier, platane* (looks feminine but isn't), *sapin, saule (pleureur), séquoia, tamarinier, teck, tilleul, tremble* (aspen). *Aubépine*, however, is feminine (if it is a tree). This masculine list includes fruit trees (*arbres fruitiers*): *abricotier, amandier, bananier, caroubier* (*carob tree*), *cerisier, châtaignier, citronnier, cocotier, dattier, ficus* (*fig tree*), *figuier, genévrier* (*juniper*), *goyavier* (*guava tree*), *grenadier* (*pomegranate tree*), *manguier* (*mangrove tree*), *marronnier, noisetier, noyer, olivier, oranger, pamplemoussier* (not very common), *poirier, pommier*. Most of the fruits of these trees are feminine (see below), as are the groves or orchards of distinctive trees (with endings **-aie**: see in the feminine-gender section below);

Names of metals: *acier, argent, bronze, cuivre, or, plomb, soufre, zinc*;

Names of human agents ending in **-eur**, **-ien**: *aiguilleur, censeur, chirurgien, couvreur* (*roofer*, a person who repairs roofs; Gervaise's husband Coupeau was a *couvreur* in Zola's *L'assommoir*), *facteur, vainqueur, sauveteur, successeur, électricien, informaticien, mécanicien, musicien, pharmacien*;

Names of volcanoes: *Etna, Popocatepetl, le Vésuve*;

Names of musical notes: *do, ré, mi, fa, sol, la, si*;

References of paintings: *un Dali/David/Diego Rivera/Goya/Picasso/Velázquez*;

Names of oceans: *l'Atlantique, le Pacifique, l'océan Indien*;

Nouns ending in **-ac**: *bric-à-brac, clic-clac, frac, fric-frac* (*break-in*, as in a robbery), *lac, ric-rac, tic-tac, trac*;

Nouns ending in **-acle**: *cénacle* (*literary/philosophical circle* = R3), *obstacle*; but *débâcle* is feminine;

Nouns ending in **-ail**: *ail, détail, éventail, soupirail, sérail*;

Nouns ending in **-ard**: *boulevard, brassard* (a soccer captain wears one), *cafard* (*cockroach*), *foulard, loubard* (*hooligan*), *lard, pétard*;

Nouns ending in **-as**: *amas, bras, coutelas, fatras, galetas, matelas, tas*;

Nouns ending in **-at**: *assassinat, forçat* (*convict*), *malfrat* (*thug*), *scélérat* (*villain* = R3), *secrétariat*;

Nouns ending in **-eau**: *anneau, bandeau, bordereau* (*form, slip, note*: used as evidence in the spurious conviction of Dreyfus in the notorious eponymous affair), *carreau, chapeau, ciseau, fourneau, gâteau, matériau, oripeau* (*faded finery* = R3), *panneau, poteau, pruneau, radeau, réseau, rideau, sceau, seau*; but *eau* and *peau* are feminine;

Nouns ending in **-ège**: *collège, cortège, florilège* (anthology of verse or any written pieces), *manège, sacrilège*;

Nouns ending in **-eil**: *soleil, sommeil*;

Nouns ending in **-ème**: *chrysanthème* (see Claude Monet's *Le vase de chrysanthèmes*), *crème, thème*;

Nouns ending in **-er**: *fer, goûter*; but *cuiller* and *mer* are feminine;

Nouns ending in **-et**: *boulet, budget, cachet, cadet, filet, fouet, galet, gilet, goulet, lacet, muret, piquet, poulet, sachet, sobriquet, tiret, tourniquet*;

Nouns ending in **-ice**: *armistice, bénéfice, calice, caprice* (as in Goya's paintings *Les caprices*), *cilice* (*hair shirt*), *sacrifice*; but *immondices* (usually plural), *justice, malice* and *police* are feminine; for usage with *délice(s)*, see Section 9.3.3 below;

Nouns ending in –**ier**: *calendrier, courrier, fermier, madrier, palier, papier, plombier, policier, serrurier, soulier*;

Nouns ending in –**in**: *poulain, requin*; but *fin* and *main* are feminine;

Nouns ending in –**isme**: *bouddhisme, capitalisme, christianisme, communisme, cubisme, dadaïsme, darwinisme, gaullisme, géocentrisme, héliocentrisme, hindouisme, positivisme, prisme, romantisme, socialisme* (and numerous other ideologies);

Nouns ending in –**ment**: *commencement, débarquement* (*unloading, landing*, as in *le Débarquement en Normandie en juin 1944*), *émolument, engagement, enterrement* (as in Courbet's *Enterrement à Ornans*), *logement, moment, monument, mouvement, paiement, serment* (as in David's *Le serment des Horaces*); but: *jument* is feminine;

Nouns ending in –**o**: *numéro, zéro*; but: *dynamo* is feminine;

Nouns ending in –**oir**: *arrosoir, boudoir, butoir, crachoir* (*spittoon*), *couloir, loir* (*doormouse; dormir comme un loir*), *lavoir, manoir, miroir, pouvoir, sarcloir* (*hoe*), *sautoir, savoir, séchoir, terroir* (as in *le goût du terroir*), *tiroir*;

Nouns ending in –**ou**: *amadou, clou, genou, hibou, manitou* (as in *le grand manitou = the boss*);

Nouns ending in –**our**: *amour* (but see Section 9.3.3), *four, tambour*; but: *cour* and *tour* (= tower) are feminine;

Nouns with two or more syllables ending in –**age**: *adage, Aréopage,*[3] *barrage* (*dam, play-off* in sport allowing a second chance to qualify), *blocage* (*locking, blocking*, as of a road), *bocage* (*hedge farmland*, as in *le bocage vendéen* or *le bocage normand* – known for the ferocious fighting during the Normandy invasion in June 1944 = *le Débarquement*), *brouillage, carrelage* (*floor tiling*), *cépage* (*grape variety*), *chauffage* (*central*), *collage, cordage, coupage, courage, covoiturage* (*car sharing*), *découpage, égrenage, élagage, élevage, étage, garage,* (*chemin de*) *halage* (*tow path*), *mage, massage, ménage, nuage, ombrage, orage, outrage, pacage, page, parrainage, pâturage, péage* (*toll*), *pelage, plumage, présage, sillage, sondage* (as in *le sondage des électeurs*), *virage* (as in *prendre un virage*); but *image* is feminine (as in *sage comme une image = good as gold*, and *image d'Épinal*, the simplistic view of French country life).

9.2.2 Simple nouns: feminine

In many of the cases below, it is evident that the final –**e** is a sign of the feminine gender, but care should still be taken. As a matter of interest, the French feminine –**e** corresponds largely to the Spanish and Italian **a** (French: *fermier* > *fermière*; *cadet* > *cadette*; Spanish: *chico* > *chica*; Italian: *ragazzo* >

---

[3] *Aréopage* (*Areopagus*) calls for some comment. The upper case refers to the supreme court in ancient Athens. According to Acts 17: 19–22, Paul addressed this tribunal in his commitment to converting the world: "Alors, ils [les Athéniens] le prirent, et le menèrent à l'Aréopage, en disant . . ." In the lower case, it refers to any august body, such as the Académie française, or the Académie des sciences.

ragazza), where it may be argued that French has developed beyond Spanish and Italian, deriving as they all do from Latin.

Names of sciences: *biologie, chimie, géologie, grammaire, informatique, mathématiques, (astro)physique, (nano) technologie*; but: *droit* is masculine;

Names of seas: *la mer Baltique, la (mer) Méditerranée, la mer Morte/Rouge*;

Names of fruits: *amande, banane, caroube (carob*, which gives food for horses), *cerise, châtaigne, datte, figue, goyave, grenade, noisette, noix de coco, orange, pamplemousse, pomme, prune*; but *abricot, citron, genièvre* (could not look more feminine), *gland* and *marron* are masculine. There is some uncertainty over *pamplemousse*, which is used increasingly in the masculine form.

Nouns ending in –**ade**: *baignade* (as in Seurat's *Une baignade, Asnières*), *bourgade, embrassade, foucade (escapade), grillade, limonade, noyade, parade, rade, salade*;

Nouns ending in –**aie**: *baie, craie, haie, plaie, raie, taie (pillowcase)*. This list includes trees as grouped together *(grove, orchard)*: *bananeraie, ceriseraie, châtaigneraie, coudraie (grove of hazel trees), futaie (grove, wood), hêtraie, noyeraie, oliveraie, orangeraie, peupleraie, pommeraie*; although feminine, *pinède* does not fit into this category;

Nouns ending in –**aille**: *broussaille(s), canaille, écaille (scale*, as of fish, and used metaphorically in *Les écailles me sont tombées des yeux), graille* (R1 = *chow/grub), grisaille (dull weather), maille, médaille, muraille* (as in *la Grande muraille de Chine), ouaille(s) (flock* of religious faithful, especially plural), *paille, taille*; but: *braille* is masculine, coming from the name Louis Braille;

Nouns ending in –**aine**: *bedaine (paunch), graine, haine, laine, marraine, migraine, plaine*;

Nouns ending in –**aise**: *aise, baise* (R*, vulgar = *a fuck*, use with great care), *braise, fadaise, falaise, foutaise** (use with care, as in *C'est de la foutaise =* It's crap), *fraise, glaise*; but: *malaise* is masculine;

Nouns ending in –**aison**: *fenaison, raison, saison, pendaison (hanging* of a criminal);

Nouns ending in –**aisse**: *baisse, bouillabaisse* (for the gourmets = *fish soup), caisse, graisse, laisse*;

Nouns ending in –**ame**: *dame, lame, rame*; but *blâme* and *amalgame* are masculine;

Nouns ending in –**ance/–anse**: *aisance, arrogance, assistance, bouffetance* (R1 = *grub), lance, manigance, outrance (exaggeration), reconnaissance, souffrance, anse, danse, transe*;

Nouns ending in –**ée**: *bouchée (mouthful* of food), *chaussée, cordée* (you would need this if you were mountain climbing), *corvée, couvée, échappée (breakaway*, as in cycle race), *équipée (prank), fessée, gorgée, (mouthful* of drink), *journée, maisonnée, mêlée, matinée, montée, soirée*[4] but: *apogée, musée, scarabée* and *trophée* are masculine;

Nouns ending in **–ence/–ense**: *cadence, carence, licence, magnificence, munificence* (R3), *défense, dépense*; but: *silence* is masculine (as in Bergman's *Le silence*);

Nouns ending in **–elle**: *aquarelle, gamelle* (*dixie, billy can* for soldiers or camping), *mamelle, marelle* (*hopscotch*, as in *jouer à la marelle*), *ombrelle, passerelle, sauterelle*;

Nouns ending in **–esse**: *allégresse, bassesse, caresse, messe* (*mass*), *mollesse, petitesse, politesse, sagesse, souplesse*;

Names of feminine agents ending in **–esse**: *comtesse, hôtesse*, (*contre*)*maîtresse*;

Names ending in **–euse/–trice**: *baigneuse* (as in Renoir's *La baigneuse*), *flasheuse* (R1, *radar speed apparatus*, not a female flasher = *une exhibitionniste*) *mitrailleuse, ouvreuse, accompagnatrice, actrice, enquêtrice, instructrice, monitrice*;

Nouns ending in **–ette**: *aigrette, allumette, baguette, bandelette, bavette, boulette, buvette, cachette, can(n)ette, carpette, casquette, cordelette, corvette, courbette, courgette* (*zucchini*), *crevette, cuvette, dette, escarpolette, espagnolette, femmelette, galette* (as in Renoir's *Moulin de la Galette* in the Louvre), *lunette(s)*, (*il y a belle*) *lurette* (*a good time ago*), *mallette, manette, mitraillette, moquette, musette, navette, pirouette, poussette, roulette, sellette, supérette, toilette(s), vachette, vedette*; but: *squelette* is masculine, however feminine it looks;

Abstract nouns ending in **–eur**: *ampleur, ardeur, grandeur, hauteur, pudeur*; but: *honneur, labeur* and *malheur* are masculine;

Nouns ending in **–ie**: *anarchie, ânerie, astronomie, bactérie* (*bacterium*), *batterie, boiserie, bonhomie, braderie, broderie, calvitie, carie, énergie, furie, galerie, gastronomie, imprimerie, industrie, minuterie, momie, ontologie, panoplie, partie, philosophie, photographie, psychologie, sanie* (R3 = *infected wound*: Camus uses this word frequently in *La peste*), *sournoiserie, stratégie, supercherie* (*hoax*), *symphonie* (as in Beethoven's *La symphonie pastorale*), *théorie* (not just *theory* but also in R3 = *procession* of people), *tromperie*, but: *génie, incendie* and *parapluie* are masculine. Many types of stores/shops have the **–ie** ending: *animalerie* (neologism: store dealing in animals, their food, etc.), *boucherie, boulangerie, brasserie, charcuterie, épicerie, hôtellerie, librairie, mercerie, pâtisserie, plomberie*;

Nouns ending in **–ière**: *bandoulière* (= *shoulder strap* as worn by Pancho Villa, for example), *bannière, barrière* (as in *La grande barrière* off the Australian coast), *brassière, carrière, chevalière* (*signet ring*), *couturière*,

---

[4] *Journée, matinée* and *soirée* refer to the length of the day: *dans la journée/matinée/soirée, toute la journée/matinée/soirée.*

croisière, fermière, filière, frontière, gibecière (game bag), lanière, matière, montgolfière (hot-air balloon from the French Montgolfier brothers in the late eighteenth century), *paupière, poudrière (powder keg), prière, rapière (rapier), ratière, salière, souricière, tabatière (snuffbox), tanière (lair), visière*; but *cimetière* is masculine;

Nouns ending in **-ille**: *bille, chenille (caterpillar), famille, grille, trille, vrille (tendril, spiral)*;

Nouns ending in **-ine**: *aspirine, colline, échine, épine, farine, latrine(s), mandoline, margarine, marine, médecine, mine, mousseline, narine, ondine (water nymph), pénicilline, praline, quinine, saline(s), statine, tartine, terrine, urine, usine*;

Nouns ending in **-ise**: *crise, entreprise, expertise, mainmise, méprise, mise, prise, reprise*;

Nouns ending in **-oire**: *armoire, bouilloire, passoire*; but: *pourboire* is masculine;

Nouns ending in **-ouille**: *andouille, bouille* (R1 = *face, mug*), *brouille, couilles* (R1 = *balls* of male), *fouille, grenouille, houille, magouille, nouille* (also used metaphorically in *C'est un plat de nouilles* = He's a weakling), *patrouille, ratatouille* (as in the film *Ratatouille*, involving a play on words with *rat*), *rouille, trouille (fear), vadrouille (stroll, wandering about*, as in the box-office film sensation *La grande vadrouille*, Gérard Oury, 1966);

Nouns ending in **-sion/-tion**: *compréhension, pension, tension, aspiration, attention, portion* (innumerable ones here); but *bastion* is masculine;

Nouns ending in **-té**: *activité, acuité, affabilité, amabilité, anxiété, beauté, bonté, brutalité, charité, cherté, cité, clarté, commodité, dureté, fatalité, fermeté, hospitalité, humidité, inanité, intensité, mentalité, morosité, netteté, obscurité, parité, probité, rapidité, rareté, rentabilité, saleté, sécurité, sensibilité, sommité, sûreté, vanité, variété, volonté, volupté*; but: *comité, comté, côté* and *été* are masculine;

Nouns ending in **-tié**: *amitié, moitié, pitié*;

Nouns ending in **-tude**: *altitude, attitude, certitude, gratitude, habitude, hébétude, incertitude, inquiétude, lassitude, latitude, longitude, mansuétude, négritude, platitude, promptitude, quiétude, rectitude, servitude, solitude, turpitude*;

Nouns ending in **-ue**: *charrue, grue, morue, mue (molting/casting off* of animal);

Nouns ending in **-ure**: *armature, bigarrure (multicolored pattern), blessure, carrure, ceinture, chaussure, clôture, enluminure (illumination, colored highlighting* of letters = R3), *fermeture, fourrure, garniture, injure, lavure, levure, marbrure (blotchiness, mottling), masure, mesure, meurtrissure, morsure, nourriture, ordure, ouverture, peinture, posture, pourriture, préfecture, serrure, salissure (dirty mark), souillure (stain, dirty mark), structure, température, tenture, tournure (turn*, i.e., of events; *tournure de phrase* = set phrase), *verdure, voiture*, and *mûre*; but *mercure, murmure* and *parjure* are masculine;

Monosyllabic nouns ending in −**age**: *cage, nage, page, plage, rage* (*anger/rabies*); but: *gage* is masculine. See also masculine *page* in Section 9.2.1 above.

9.2.3 Compound nouns

Compound nouns (unhyphenated and hyphenated, or even as separate words – it is not always clear when or why hyphens occur) are sprouting up in French like mushrooms, just as they are in Spanish and Italian, although to a lesser extent in Italian. In German, of course, the phenomenon has been a traditional and standard aspect of the language. Many of these compound nouns do not appear in recent dictionaries, so difficult is it to keep pace with them. The following analytical presentation of compound nouns is followed by a fuller, but by no means comprehensive, list:

Type of compound	Gender	Examples Masculine	Feminine
noun + noun	assigned according to gender of headword (i.e., both words are of equal importance, e.g., **un** *spectateur-auditeur*, or, if one noun qualifies the other, the noun (usually the first) which is qualified, e.g., **un** *mot-clé*, **une** *idée-choc*)	*chou-fleur* *homme-grenouille* *timbre-poste*	*loi-programme* *ville-fantôme* *porte-fenêtre*
adjective + noun or noun + adjective	assigned according to gender of noun	*coffre-fort* *rond-point*	*basse-cour* *chauve-souris* exceptions: *rouge-gorge* and *rouge-queue* (both masculine)
verb + noun	always masculine	*chauffe-eau* *pare-brise* *porte-avions* *portefeuille* *protège-tibia*	
invariable word + noun	assigned according to gender of noun, but always masculine if noun is plural	*avant-bras* *contrepoids* *haut-parleur* *deux-pièces* *mille-pattes*	*arrière-pensée* *contre-partie*

Type of compound	Gender	Examples Masculine	Feminine
verb + verb	always masculine	laissez-passer laissez-faire savoir-vivre savoir-être savoir-faire	
phrase	always masculine	sauve-qui-peut va-et-vient	

Following on from above, with further examples, a compound noun of two masculine nouns is obviously masculine: *aller-retour, appartement-témoin* (*show apartment*), *argument choc, attentat/avion-suicide, bateau-pilote, budget livres/loisirs, café-concert, café-théâtre, effet boomerang, ensemble jogging* (*jogging outfit*), *facteur-rhésus, film culte, forfait entretien* (*inclusive maintenance package*, for an automobile for instance), *gouvernement fantoche, jumbo-chèque, mot piège, frein moteur* (on a steep incline), *papier cadeau* (*gift wrapping paper*), *papier aluminium, (Le) Vaisseau fantôme* (*The Flying Dutchman*, by Wagner), *portrait-robot* (as created by the police), *prêt relais* (*bridging loan*), *prix choc* (*huge reduction*), *satellite-espion, service maximum, stylo-feutre, temps record, ticket restaurant, top secret, voyage éclair. Fleuve* is regularly used to denote an ongoing, continuous saga: *discours/procès/roman fleuve.*

A compound noun of two feminine nouns is obviously feminine: *ampoule basse consommation, année-disco/fac/lumière, auto-école, cassette-vidéo, cellule-mère, date-limite, grandeur nature* (*life-size*), *maison-mère, pochette-surprise, porte-fenêtre, reine-mère, serviette-éponge* (*terry towel*), *table-gigognes* (*nest of tables*), *voiture occasion.*

The gender of a compound noun with two different genders is determined by the gender of the first noun:

Masculine: *album-photo, avion/bateau poubelle* (*unreliable boat/airplane*), *bateau-école, bateau-mouche, bébé-éprouvette* (*test-tube baby*), *budget auto/vacances, camion-citerne, centre-ville, code-barres, coin cuisine, congé maladie* (*sick leave*), *côté éducation/température* (= with respect to . . .), *espace attente* (*waiting area*, as in a bank), *État-providence* (*welfare state*), *facteur chance/surprise, jeu vidéo, mot-clé, mot-valise* (*portmanteau word*), *niveau éducation/température* (= with respect to . . .), *ordinateur tablette* (*computer pad*), *pack sécurité* (*safety pack* for a car, for instance), *papier monnaie, plateau télé* (habit of eating a meal while watching television), *point-fidélité* (*reward point*), *programme télé, repas-étape* (restaurant where you would stop for lunch, e.g. on a highway), *rôle-clef, scénario-catastrophe, service après-vente, spot radio* (*radio commercial*), *sport automobile, stylo-bille, taxi-brousse* (taxi servicing bush country), *texte-cadre, timbre-poste, village-étape* (*village* where travelers stop overnight), *village repas* (as *repas-étape*), *vide-grenier* (*car boot sale*);

Feminine: *brasse-papillon, date-butoir* (*closing date*), *ferme modèle, guerre/visite-éclair, image choc, loi-cadre* (*framework* of a law), *machine-outil, maison-témoin* (*show house*), *nation satellite/arc-en-ciel* (*rainbow nation*, e.g. South Africa), *opération-commando, question piège, recette miracle, réponse-modèle, somme record, station-service, taxe-carbone, usine pilote, ville dortoir/champignon/fantôme/lumière/test, zone euro*.

In the case of *tensiomètre* (*blood-pressure monitor*), one would have expected a feminine gender, given *la tension*, but this compound noun is masculine.

Compound nouns formed with other parts of speech, often, but not always, with verbs, are usually masculine: *abat-jour, arc-en-ciel, arrache-clou, casse-cou, en-tête* (*heading* on note paper), *faire du/le bouche-à-bouche à un noyé* (the use of the definite article is much less common), *gobe-mouche* (*naïve person, sucker*), *grille-pain* (*toaster*), *haut-parleur, lance-flammes/roquettes/satellite, monte-plats/charges* (as in hotel), *ouvre-boîtes, qu'en dira-t-on, parapluie, paratonnerre, pique-bœuf* (bird on an animal removing its parasites, very common in the Caribbean, and not uncommon in southern France), *porte-cigarettes, porte-parole,*[5] *protège-tibia* (*shin guard*, as in soccer), *réveil-matin* (*alarm clock*), *savoir-faire, soutien-gorge* (*bra*), *tout-à-l'égout* (*drain* leading to sewer), *tout-venant, trouble-fête, trop-plein, volte-face* (this word is feminine).

The gender of compound nouns made up of *arrière* and *avant* vary according to the gender of the second noun. Thus **arrière**-*boutique/cour/cuisine/garde/pensée/saison* are feminine, while **arrière**-*goût/plan/train* are masculine. Likewise, **avant**-*garde/première/scène/veille* are feminine, while **avant**-*bras/centre/goût/propos* are masculine. *Avant-guerre* claims two genders.

For the plural of compound nouns, see Chapter 10 on number.

9.3 Difficult cases

Even native French speakers can hesitate over the gender of some nouns, such as are contained in the following list. It should be pointed out that few French speakers would make a mistake over the gender of, say, *caractère, calme* or *cadavre*. Yet masculine nouns like *antidote, astérisque* (easily confused with the Breton hero Astérix), *obélisque* (not to be confused with *Obélix*, bosom pal of Astérix), *sévices, stigmate* and *tentacule* would test some French speakers, associating as they do the −e ending with the feminine noun. Furthermore, for those who study other Romance languages, such as

---

[5] The compound nouns with the verb *porter* are too numerous to be listed here. Suffice it to point to a few: *porte-avions, porte-bagages, porte-bébé, porte-bouteilles, porte-clefs* (*key ring*), *porte-drapeau, porte-monnaie, porte-parapluie*. The list includes *portefeuille* and *portemanteau*, which are not hyphenated.

Spanish, the nouns below require serious application. (*Calma, foca, hectárea* and *uña*, quoted merely as examples, are feminine in Spanish, while their equivalents are masculine in French. Conversely, *diente, licor* and *oasis* are masculine in Spanish while their equivalents are feminine in French: *dent, liqueur, oasis*.) The lists below are as comprehensive as possible since they are naturally designed for English speakers:

Masculine: *abîme, âge, agenda, aléas, alinéa, amalgame, antidote, antre* (lair of animal), *apogée, appendice* (both senses of *appendix*: part of intestine and addition at the end of a piece of writing), *artifice, astérisque, astre, astrolabe* (Copernicus used one), *atome, autodafé, autoradio, axe* (as in *un axe routier*), *axiome, barbecue, baume, bébé* (although small children could easily use a feminine gender here), *bénédicité* (grace, said at table), *bermuda, blasphème, boom, bouge* (hovel, shack: not to be confused with feminine *bauge*), *bréviaire, bromure* (bromide), *brouhaha, buisson, cadavre, caducée,*[6] *calme, calque* (tracing paper, *calque* in linguistics), *campanile* (bell tower; also the logo of a French national chain of small hotels; not to be confused with *campanule* below), *caractère, carême* (Lent), *carrosse* (as with Cinderella), *casque, cénotaphe, châle, le Petit Chaperon Rouge* (Little Red Riding Hood; see Section 9.6 below for a discussion of this feature), *charabia* (R1 = nonsense), *charme* (as in *Je me porte comme un charme*), *chaume, chèvrefeuille, chlore* (chlorine), *chlorure* (chloride), *choix, choléra, cierge* (candle: has a religious connotation), *cilice* (hair shirt), *cloaque* (R3 = cesspit), *cobaye* (guinea pig), *Colisée* (in Rome), *comble, concile* (as in *le concile de Trente*, 1545–1563, which deliberated on the Counter-Reformation), *conciliabule, crible, crime, culte, dédale* (room for confusion here), *delta, deltaplane, dialecte, dilemme, disco* (but *discothèque* is feminine), *dithyrambe* (panegyric), *diurétique, dividende, dogme, dôme, échange* (as in *Échange n'est pas vol* = *Exchange is no robbery*), *édifice, effluve(s), élastique, éloge, emblème, épiderme, épisode, équinoxe, estuaire, exemple, exode* (as in the Bible but here = Exode), *exorde* (R3 = introduction to a piece of work), *fantoche, farniente, fascicule, faste, flegme* (as in the traditionally viewed *flegme britannique*), *fleuve, formulaire, frontispice* (title page of a book), *furoncle* (boil on body), *générique, geste, globe, globule, glucose, gouffre* (as in *les gouffres de Padeyrac*, in France), *grimoire* (book of magic, as disastrously but fascinatingly interpreted by Mickey Mouse in Paul Dukas's *L'apprenti sorcier*), *groupe, gymnase, hectare, hématome* (bruise), *hémisphère, hiéroglyphe, holocauste, humour, iguane, incendie, insecte, intermède, intermédiaire, interrogatoire, intervalle,*

---

[6] *Caducée*: emblem of the medical and pharmaceutical fraternities. Not all French speakers are aware of this term, and hardly any English speaker would know its English equivalent, *caduceus*, and this includes doctors and pharmacists.

iota (as in *sans changer un iota*), *(kilo)gramme*, *labyrinthe*, *lama* (the animal as well as the Buddhist monk), *légume*, *libelle* (R3 = lampoon), *liquide*, *lobe*, *logarithme*, *luxe*, *magma*, *manque*, *mascara*, *masque*, *mausolée*, *média(s)*, *mérite*, *miasme*, *micro-ondes*, *mime*, *minuit*, *molécule*, *monopole*, *morne* (hill, mountain, in Caribbean, Reunion, Quebec, imported by Breton sailors), *morse* (*walruss*), *moustique*, *multimédia*, *mythe* (as in Camus's *Le mythe de Sisyphe*), *obélisque*, *ongle*, *opuscule*, *orbe* (as in Copernicus's revolutionary *Révolutions des orbes célestes*), *orchestre*, *organe*, *pactole* (gold mine / nice big sum of money), *panache*, *panégyrique*, *panorama*, *parachute* (the most famous parachute in all French history is the one belonging to John Steele caught on the church steeple in Sainte-Mère-Église during the 1944 invasion of France), *parafe* (*initials*), *parapente*, *parapluie* (as in the film *Les parapluies de Cherbourg*), *parasite*, *paratonnerre* (invented by Franklin who became the first American minister to visit France and was called there "le bonhomme Richard"), *pastiche* (Marcel Proust contributed to a journal called *Pastiches et mélanges*), *pétale*, *phoque*, *pécule*, *pédiluve* (*footbath*), *pédoncule* (*stem*, of fruit), *plâtre*, *polype*, *prêche* (R3, now ousted by *sermon*, although Camus uses it in *La peste* for the two sermons delivered by Père Paneloux), *quelque chose*, *quota*, *râle*, *repaire* (lair of animal), *reproche*, *réquisitoire*, *reste*, *rêve*, *rire*, *rutabaga* (swede), *saxophone*, *scarabée*, *schéma*, *scrupule*, *service*, *sévices*, *silence*, *solstice*, *sourire*, *squelette*, *stéroïde*, *stigmate*, *suicide*, *sv/swastika*, *symptôme*, *terre-plein*, *tentacule*, *tesson*, *théorème*, *thermos* (but can be feminine), *tintamarre*, *tonnerre*, *trapèze*, *trèfle*, *trombone* (*trombone* and *paper clip*), *trophée*, *tuba* (*tuba* and *snorkel*), *uniforme*, *ustensile*, *vacarme*, *vice*, *violoncelle*, *zeste* (*peel*, of citrus fruit), *zodiaque*, *zona* (*shingles* as viral infection);

Feminine: *alcôve*, *amphore*, *ancre*, *annexe* (*annex* of a building, *appendix* of a book), *arabesque*, *artère*, *atmosphère*, *aura* (as in *une aura de mystère*), *auréole* (*halo*, both literal and metaphorical), *autoroute* (curiously for an English speaker, French speakers could easily assign a masculine gender to this noun), *bauge* (lair of wild boar), *BBC* (British Broadcasting Corporation: note that these letters can be pronounced as in English, especially among *anglicistes*), *boisson*, *boum* (*bash/hop*), *campanule* (*bluebell*), *carapace* (*shell* of an animal, tortoise for instance), *caractéristique*, *cendre*, *céphalée* (*headache*), *cible*, *cime*, *circulaire*, *CNN* (American Broadcasting Company), *contagion*, *croix*, *crypte*, *cuisson*, *cymbale*, *dent*, *dragée* (French speakers could easily consider this noun masculine), *dupe*, *dynamo*, *ecchymose* (*bruise*), *encyclique*, *énigme*, *éphéméride* (*tear-off calender*), *épigramme*, *épitaphe*, *épithète*, *équivoque*, *étoile*, *extase*, *forêt*, *fourmi*, *garden-party* (R3), *geôle* (R3), *Gestapo*, *haltère* (for the more muscular), *horreur*, *idole*, *idylle*, *java* (*party/rave*), *kalachnikov*, *libido*, *liqueur*, *mappemonde*, *meule* (as in Monet's *Série des meules de foin*), *mimique*, *mite* (*moth*), *mitre* (bishop's *miter*), *mosquée*, *moustiquaire*, *noix*, *nouba* (*North African military music/party/rave*), *oasis*, *ocre*, *ombre*, *orbite*, *orthographe*, *panacée* (*universelle* is sometimes used with this word but this is a pleonasm just as it is in English), *pantomime (theatrical mime/ridiculous attitude), pédale, pénicilline, phalange, populace, primeur (first fruit,* as in Brittany), *psyché (swivel mirror, psyche), al-Qaeda, recrue, saga, sentinelle, Shoah* (= Holocaust, becoming common these days in France; it originates in the Hebrew, where it is of the feminine gender, and signifies *destruction, catastrophe*), *sphère, spore, stalactite, stalagmite, stratosphère, strate* (R3 *stratum,* as in *une strate sociale*), *superbe (haughtiness,* R3), *toux, topaze, trêve, variable, vésicule (biliaire = gall bladder), victime, vidéo, vis, vodka.*

There are a number of masculine nouns which refer to females and males alike: *mannequin,*[7] *nu* (as in Braque's *Le grand nu*), *(top-)model,* and a number of feminine nouns which regularly refer to males: *canaille* (= *naughty person,* often used affectionately, of a child, for instance, but also *villain;* when used collectively: *rabble), coqueluche* (= *darling, idol), crapule (crook), dupe (dupe), grosse légume (big wig, top brass), ordure (foul person), recrue (recruit), sentinelle (sentry), victime (victim). Étoile* and *star,* which are feminine, apply to both male and female stars or celebrities.

When *basket* and *tennis* refer to footwear, and not types of sport, they are feminine. *Hémisphère* is masculine but *atmosphère* and *sphère* are feminine. Like *Gestapo, SS* is feminine, but this feminine form is rarely used. Instead, one hears and sees *les SS (members of the SS),* and here it is masculine. *Syllabe* is feminine but *monosyllabe* is masculine. *Sentinelle* illustrates perfectly the absurdity of applying a female gender to a male sentry. As Alex Taylor states in his hilarious analysis of the language of gender, *Bouche bée tout ouïe* (2010, p. 38): "Encore plus grotesque, lorsqu'il s'agit de décrire les allées et venues d'une sentinelle : *Elle* gravit les marches du parapet, *elle* revêtit son uniforme, et *elle* tailla ses grosses moustaches."

9.3.1 Doubtful and variable genders

It should be noted that a small number of nouns are of doubtful and variable gender and, in some cases, cause hesitation with some French speakers, witness *espace* below.

> *amour* and *délice* are masculine in the singular but feminine in the plural, although *amour* may be found as a feminine noun in R3 language, in literary texts *après-midi, pamplemousse, perce-neige* and *sandwich* have varied in gender, but are now usually masculine. However, *après-midi* in R3 written mode is often feminine. An excellent illustration of this masculine/feminine fluctuation is the word *bic,* a trade term. In the masculine (*un bic*), it means *a ball-point pen,* but in the feminine form it refers to a sailboard, made by the Bic company);
> *autoroute* is usually feminine, but is increasingly used in the masculine;

[7] Quebec French has no problem with *une mannequin* for a female, but metropolitan France does not accept this feminine form.

bidonville (*shanty town*) is now masculine;

connaisseur is usually masculine when applied to males and females: *Elle est connaisseur en vins*. But one could hear *connaisseuse* in R1 language;

enfant is masculine and feminine. It depends on the sex of the child;

espace is masculine in general use: *un espace entre deux voitures | deux tables, un espace vert*; but when used by *typographers* (typographers) it is feminine, and refers to any type of space created on the written page – here most French speakers express uncertainty, or just do not know, and this includes well-informed speakers;

espèce is feminine when meaning *kind, sort, species*, but in R1 it is masculine when followed by a masculine noun: *un espèce de poisson*. However, and increasingly, it is found in the masculine form in writing;

foudre is feminine in the meaning of *thunderbolt*. **La** *foudre est* **tombée** *sur l'église*; *Il a été frappé par* **la** *foudre*. But in certain fixed expressions it is masculine: *foudre de guerre, foudre d'éloquence, C'est un foudre de travail, Il se prenait pour un foudre d'activité*;

gens is feminine when preceded by adjectives (*des vieilles gens*), but when adjectives follow *gens*, they are masculine, resulting in an anomaly in the sentence: *De(s)* **vieilles** *gens sont arrivés ce matin*;

hymne is usually masculine: *l'hymne* **national**; *chanter un hymne* **religieux**; *L'hymne à la joie de Beethoven est très émouvant*; but in literary language it can be feminine, and this invests the noun with a certain elegance: *Ils chantaient des hymnes* **ardentes**;

holding is both masculine and feminine;

interview is both masculine and feminine, although the feminine gender seems to prevail these days;

nouveau-né may apply to male and female newborns alike, rather like *bébé*. Indeed, one is most likely to hear in all circumstances *Je vais voir le nouveau-né*, even if the baby is female. However, *la nouveau-née* does exist. *Nouvelle* would not be used here since *nouveau* is really an adverb (*nouvellement*);

œuvre is always feminine in the plural (*Les plus* **belles** *œuvres de l'industrie cinématographique*) and is usually feminine in the singular: *Une œuvre inédite d'Irène Némirovsky a connu un grand succès*. But the entire work of an author/composer/artist may be masculine, and in this sense, it is used in English: *l'œuvre* **entier** *de Beethoven*, **tout** *l'œuvre de Balzac*;

orge is feminine except in certain expressions one finds in pharmacy. *Ses grains sont plus petits que ceux de l'orge* **commune** and *orge* **mondé**/ **perl**é;

Orgue is masculine when singular but feminine when plural: **un** *orgue de Barbarie* (*barrel organ*); *les* **grandes** *orgues de Notre Dame*. When used metaphorically, it is also feminine in the plural: *les orgues* **basaltiques** (*basalt columns*). This gives rise to the name of the impressive dam in France's Massif Central: *Bort-les-Orgues*. It also explains the name of the multiple rocket launcher very common in World War II: *les orgues de Staline*;

oriflamme has an undecided gender. It can be masculine, on analogy with *drapeau* and *étendard*, but the feminine gender occurs, probably determined by *flamme*;

Pâques is treated as masculine when unaccompanied by an article: *Pâques fut **célébré** avec beaucoup de solennité*. When it is accompanied by an article or any other determiner, it is treated as feminine: *Toutes les Pâques **précédentes** ont été **fêtées** avec une grande joie; la Pâque **juive*** (Jewish Passover);

période is feminine when it refers to a point in time, and the feminine gender is far more common than its masculine counterpart: *la période quaternaire/lunaire/révolutionnaire*. But it is masculine in literary style (R3) when it means the "highest point": *le **plus haut** période; une angine de poitrine arrivée à **son dernier période***;

photocopieuse (feminine) and *photocopieur* (masculine) both exist, but the feminine form is used more;

pornographie is feminine. However, the abbreviated form, *porno*, is masculine since it has the specific meaning of a "pornographical film/book": *Allez, on va voir **un porno***;

putain, as *espèce*, is feminine when applied to a prostitute, but in colloquial R1 speech it is masculine when followed by a masculine noun: *J'en ai marre, de **ce** putain de mode d'emploi*;

réglisse is both masculine and feminine when referring to a sweet: *sucer de la réglisse / du réglisse*. As a plant, it is feminine;

SS, when applied to the notorious Nazi police/military unit, is masculine, and *SS* is most common with this meaning;

télécabine hesitates between the masculine and feminine genders, although the latter is more common.

9.4 Homonyms

The following is a list of homonyms (words which have the same sound) that have identical spellings but are of different genders:

aide	M	assistant
	F	help, female assistant
aigle	M	male eagle (also general); insignia bearing an eagle (e.g., *l'aigle blanc de la Pologne*). "General" above suggests that, if one saw an eagle, one would automatically say *un aigle*, if one were not an expert in the sex of eagles.
	F	female eagle, heraldic sign, standard surmounted by eagle (e.g. *les aigles romaines*)

aspirine	M	an aspirin tablet (R1)
	F	aspirin (medication). *Aspirine* in its masculine form is colloquial but very common and suggests the omission of *un cachet d'*, *cachet* being masculine.
basket	M	basketball
	F	trainers, sneakers
champagne	M	champagne
Champagne	F	Champagne region
chef	M	leader, boss
	F	(female) boss (R1). *Chef* used with reference to a female has a pejorative connotation: *Elle est où, la chef* ?
chose	M	thingummybob (R1). The masculine gender refers to any thing or person one cannot or does not wish to name: *Donne-moi ce . . . chose*; *Cette Madame, ce Monsieur Chose*. The masculine gender of *chose* also appears as the title of Alphonse Daudet's *Le petit chose*.
	F	thing
crêpe	M	crepe (material)
	F	pancake
critique	M	critic
	F	criticism, female critic
diesel	M	diesel (fuel)
	F	diesel (automobile)
dramatique	M	drama (i.e., what is dramatic)
	F	short play on TV
faux	M	that which is false: *distinguer le vrai du faux*; *fake* as in the paradoxal statement of a painting: *un vrai faux*
	F	scythe
faune	M	faun (mythical creature as in Debussy's *L'après-midi d'un faune*)
	F	fauna (animal kingdom)
finale	M	finale (in music)
	F	final (in soccer, rugby, etc.)
garde	M	guard, warden
	F	protection, guards, private nurse
geste	M	gesture
	F	courageous exploit (= *une chanson de geste*; as in *La chanson de Roland*). The feminine form of *geste* is slightly archaic, although it is common enough in the example provided. In the

		plural, it is frequently used in the expression: *La police l'a interrogée sur* **ses faits et gestes**.
gîte	M	resting place, lodging (R3), as in *les Gîtes de France*. The *Gîtes de France* are a popular form of "Bed and Breakfast," and this usage is common (R2).
	F	list of ship
greffe	M	record office (often for legal proceedings)
	F	graft (for plants and humans), transplant
gruyère	M	gruyère cheese
Gruyère	F	region in Switzerland
guide	M	guide (person or book). One would readily see *le Guide Michelin* (for gastronomic purposes).
	F	rein, girl guide, female guide
jet	M	jet (airplane)
	F	jet set. One does occasionally come across *jet* in the masculine form when meaning *jet set*.
livre	M	book
	F	pound (weight, money)
manche	M	handle (i.e., of broom)
	F	sleeve, round (in sport), *La Manche* (= *English Channel* and the French department: *Quel est le code postal de La Manche?*). *Une première/deuxième manche* in a game refers to the first/second game, as in tennis or table tennis.
manoeuvre	M	labourer
	F	maneuver
martyre	M	martyrdom
	F	female martyr (*martyr* means a *male martyr*)
mémoire	M	long dissertation, report; memoirs
	F	memory
merci	M	thank you (= *un grand merci*)
	F	mercy. The feminine form is largely used in the expression *à la merci de quelqu'un* (*at someone's mercy*).
mode	M	method, mood (linguistic). In the masculine form, one would see *le mode indicatif/subjonctif*.
	F	fashion
mort	M	dead person (male)
	F	death. *Morte* refers to a dead person of female sex.
moule	M	mold (for making something)
	F	mussel
mousse	M	ship's boy
	F	moss, froth (on beer, etc.), rubber foam

office	M	function, role, bureau
	F	butler's larder/pantry
ombre	M	grayling (fish)
	F	shade, shadow
page	M	page boy
	F	page (in book or newspaper)
pendule	M	pendulum
	F	clock. Clearly, the feminine form derives from *horloge à pendule*, where *horloge* is feminine.
physique	M	physique
	F	physics
poêle	M	stove
	F	frying pan
politique	M	politician
	F	politics, policy
poste	M	post, station, set (radio or television)
	F	postal service
primeur	M	seller of the early fruits of the year (*Je vais chez le primeur*)
	F	(to be the) first (to hear of something): *la primeur des nouvelles*
pub	M	(English) public house / pub (for consumption of alcohol and, now, food
	F	commercial, advertisement (R1)
pupille	M	ward (= *les pupilles de la nation*)
	F	pupil of the eye
radio	M	wireless operator
	F	radio, Xray
somme	M	siesta, snooze
	F	amount, sum
tour	M	trick, turn, journey. *C'est mon tour* = It's my turn and *À qui le tour?* = Whose turn is it? Also: *le Tour de France*
	F	tower, rook (chess)
vague	M	vagueness
	F	wave (on sea)
vapeur	M	steamer
	F	vapor, steam
vase	M	vase
	F	slime
vigile	M	night watchman, security guard
	F	vigil (on day before a feast, e.g., *la vigile de Noël* = Christmas Eve)

visa	M	visa (used with passport)
	F	Visa (credit card)
voile	M	veil (as in *le voile intégral*)
	F	sail

The following is a list of homonyms (words which have the same sound) that do *not* have identical spellings, and that have different genders:

air	M	air, draft, tune
ère	F	era (as in *ère chrétienne/tertiaire*)
aire	F	playing/rest area, threshing floor; Camus uses *aire* metaphorically in *La peste*: "l'aire sanglante de la douleur" (1962a, p. 1296). One frequently finds *une aire de repos* on the side of French highways; also *une aire récréative* = a recreational area.
haire	F	hair shirt
hère	M/F	as in *le pauvre hère* = the poor wretch; *hère* also means a *young deer*
r	M	*le r* (i.e., the letter *r*)
bal	M	ball (dance)
balle	F	ball (sport), shot, bale, bullet
bar	M	bar (for serving drinks)
barre	F	bar (of wood, metal), tiller
basilic	M	basil (herb/plant)
basilique	F	basilica
but	M	aim, goal. The **t** of *but* can be unsounded.
butte	F	hillock (as in *Les Buttes Chaumont* in Paris)
capital	M	capital, assets
capitale	F	capital city, capital letter
central	M	telephone exchange (*téléphonique*)
centrale	F	(generating) station, nuclear plant (*électrique/nucléaire*)
chêne	M	oak tree
chaîne	F	chain
col	M	collar, mountain pass
colle	F	paste, glue
coq	M	cock
coque	F	shell, hull (of ship)
cours	M	course, waterway, class (= lesson), private school
court	M	court (*de tennis/squash*, etc.)
cour	F	court (*cour royale*), yard
fait	M	fact
faîte	M	apex of roof, mountain, etc.

fête	F	festival, feast day
foie	M	liver
foi	F	faith
fois	F	time, occasion
gène	M	gene
gêne	F	discomfort, awkwardness
hall	M	entrance, vestibule, hall
halle	F	(often plural) covered market. It must be added that the **a** of *hall* is normally pronounced like a closed **o**, while the **a** of *halle* is pronounced like the **a** of *salle*, e.g., *Châtelet*/*Les Halles* (in Paris).
maire	M	mayor
mer	F	sea
mère	F	mother
pair	M	peer
père	M	father
paire	F	pair (as in *Les deux font la paire*)
parti	M	party (political, etc.), decision
partie	F	part, game (e.g., of soccer)
pois	M	pea
poids	M	weight
poix	F	pitch
pot	M	pot, luck (R1)
peau	F	skin
sel	M	salt
selle	F	saddle

The following is a list of homonyms where genders remain the same, and are differentiated by spelling only. There are two cases (*jeune*/*jeûne*, *tache*/*tâche*) where there is just a slight variation in spelling:

ancre	F	anchor
encre	F	ink
chair	F	flesh
chaire	F	pulpit, (university) chair
champ	M	field
chant	M	song
cilice	M	hair shirt (for penitence)
silice	M	silica
compte	M	account
comte	M	count, earl
conte	M	tale
cou	M	neck
coup	M	blow, knock

coût	M	cost, price
dessein	M	plan, design
dessin	M	drawing, art (as in school)
être	M	(human) being
hêtre	M	beech tree
faim	F	hunger
fin	F	end
filtre	M	filter (as for a cigarette)
philtre	M	philter, as in *philtre d'amour* = *love potion*
jeune	M (and F)	young person, youth
jeûne	M	fast(ing), as in *observer le jeûne*
mante	F	mantle, mantis, as in *mante religieuse*
menthe	F	mint, as in *thé à la menthe*
martyr	M	martyr
martyre	M	martyrdom
mess	M	mess, as in *le mess des officiers*
messe	F	mass, as in *aller à la messe* / Gounod's *La messe de Sainte Cécile*
pain	M	bread, loaf
pin	M	pine tree
saut	M	jump, leap
sceau	M	seal (as with wax)
seau	M	bucket
sot	M	fool
tache	F	stain, spot
tâche	F	task
vair	M	squirrel fur
ver	M	worm
verre	M	glass
vers	M	line of verse

There are numerous same-sounding words which may be considered as homonyms but are different parts of speech. Here is just a small sample, and only a small sample since this section deals with gender: *bas* (low) / *bas* (stocking / panty hose); *noyer* (walnut tree) / *noyer* (to drown); *prêt* (loan) / *prêt* (ready); *sur* (on) / *sur* (sharp, as of taste) / *sûr* (sure / certain). See also Chapter 2, Section 2.11.1 which has a slight overlap with this information but contains much more detail on similar-sounding groups of words.

9.5 Gender of inanimate entities

Automobiles: all names of automobiles are feminine, doubtless on analogy with the feminine form of *voiture*: *une BM(W)*, *une Buick*, *une Chrysler*, *une Ford*, *une Jaguar*, *une Rolls*, *une Toyota*. However, one does say *un break* (*station waggon / estate car*), and *un 4/4* (= un quatre/quatre = *off-road vehicle, 4x4*), the latter following the logic of *un 2, un 3, un 4*;

Boats: despite controversy among some grammarians, the masculine gender is usually assigned to boats, doubtless on analogy with the masculine form of *bateau*: *le France, le Normandie, le Reine Elizabeth*;

Vehicles: *turbo, diesel* and *turbo-diesel* are feminine when referring to the vehicle but masculine when referring to the engine. *Diesel* has no written acute accent, coming as it does from the French-born, German engineer. The gender of *semi-remorque* (*tractor trailor / articulated trailer*) is particularly controversial: the majority view is that it is feminine when it is an articulated vehicle and masculine when it is a semi-trailer. Most French speakers do not recognize the difference. Little wonder. *Le petit Robert* states it is masculine only, while the Canadian *MULTI dictionnaire* of Marie-Éva de Villers offers two genders;

Airplanes: as with names of boats, there is controversy here too. Most airplanes are masculine on analogy with the masculine gender of *avion* (*le Boeing, le Concorde, l'Airbus*) but the French airplane *Caravelle,* now out of commission, was unquestionably feminine, following the argument that the boat itself is feminine;

Watches: all names of watches are feminine since *montre* is feminine: *une Rolex, une Seiko, une Tissot*;

Companies: all names are feminine since *compagnie* is feminine: *la General Motors, la Philips, la Fiat, la BMW, la Lyonnaise des Eaux*;

Holidays and festivals: those involving saints' names, whether the saint is male or female, are feminine. Clearly the feminine *fête* determines the gender here: *à la Saint-Valentin, la Saint-Sylvestre* (= *New Year's Eve*), *la Saint-Jean* (*Midsummer Day*), *la Toussaint* (*All Saints' Day* = period of Halloween), *l'Épiphanie*; *le massacre de la Saint-Bartélemy* (marks the slaughter of Protestants in Paris in 1572);

Hotels with stars: these are masculine, on analogy with *hôtel*, which is masculine: *un trois/quatre/cinq étoiles*;

Cheeses and wines: these are masculine, following the masculine gender of *fromage* and *vin*: *du brie, du camembert, du cantal, du champagne, un côtes du Rhône, un beaujolais, un chablis, un rioja, un penedès* (Spain), *un riesling, un chianti*;

Types of grape: *un blanc, un rouge, un rosé, un cabernet sauvignon, un chardonnay*;

Students: *les première/deuxième* etc. *année* when referring to first-/second-year students, male and female, would be masculine, and would only be feminine if all the students referred to were females. Note that *première/deuxième année* is invariable for number: *Les première année sont aussi studieux que les deuxième année*;

Letters: all names of letters are masculine. The reason is that *caractère* is masculine. Strangely enough, in the Middle Ages, letters were feminine, and where and when the change took place is not clear: *le a, le b, le e, le i, le m, le x;*

Numbers: when a specific page number is referred to, the masculine form of the number is more usual, but the feminine form cannot be excluded: *Prenez vos livres à la page un/une, à la page vingt-et-un/une.* But when a collection of pages is referred to, the feminine form is used: *vingt-et-une pages.* In sporting classification, the numeral follows the noun in the masculine even if the noun is feminine: *Les États-Unis sont en poule un* (= pool 1), *le Canada en poule 2; Leur équipe est en division un;*

Names of towns: towns provide a more difficult problem. Generally speaking, they are masculine: *le tout Paris, New York est trop grand, Ottawa est très froid en hiver.* But some are feminine: *Rome la belle. Le petit Larousse* refers constantly to *Athènes* as *elle,* in the entry for this city. Logically, one would have expected all cities to be feminine, since *ville* and *cité* (old part of the city) are feminine. Uncertainty rules here: *Marseille est grand(e).* Most French people would doubtless say *le nouveau/vieux Pékin,* as in *Libération* (August 9/10, 2008), but in the same article one reads: "Pékin s'est vidée";

Names of countries (see Chapter 64 for usage with names of countries): there is not a hard and fast rule for the gender of countries. Some 60 percent of countries are feminine: *l'Argentine, la France, l'Espagne, l'Italie.* Some 40 percent of countries are masculine: *les États-Unis, le Japon, le Pérou;*

Names of rivers: names of rivers outside Europe are all masculine, doubtless on analogy with *fleuve.* At some ill-defined, probably colonial period, this masculine form imposed itself, while the feminine form for some European rivers was determined by tradition going back to the Middle Ages. Masculine: *l'Amazone/Amur/Èbre/Escaut/ Euphrate/;* *le Colorado/Danube/Gange/Limpopo/Mékong/Mississippi/Missouri/ Nil/Parana/Pô/Rhin/Rhône/Saint-Laurent/Tibre/Tigre/Tage/Yang-Tseu/Zambèze.* Feminine: *la Loire/Garonne/Saône/Tamise/Vistula/Volga;*

French *départements*: these are similarly divided over the gender issue (see Chapter 64 for usage with countries). Masculine: *l'Aveyron, le Calvados, le Doubs, le Nord, le Périgord, le Vaucluse.* Feminine: *l'Ardèche, la Charente, la Drôme, la Loire Atlantique, la Meuse;*

Administrative states and provinces in USA and Canada: some are masculine, and some are feminine. Masculine: *l'Alaska, l'Arizona, le Labrador, le Manitoba, le Nebraska, le Québec, le Yukon, le Maine, le Maryland, le Nevada, l'Indiana, l'Ohio, le Texas, le Nouveau-Mexique.* Feminine: *l'Alberta, la Californie, la Caroline du Nord/Sud, la Colombie britannique, la Floride, la Géorgie, la Louisiane, la Saskatchewan, la Virginie, la Pennsylvanie, la Nouvelle-Écosse, Terre-Neuve;*

Counties in the British Isles: all counties in England are masculine (*Je passe mes vacances dans le Hampshire / le Sussex*) save **Les** *Cornouailles;*

Regions of France and other European countries (see Chapter 64 for more on usage): these are either masculine or feminine. Masculine: *le Limousin, le Languedoc-Roussillon, le Nord-Pas-de-Calais*. Feminine: *l'Aquitaine, la Bretagne, la Franche-Comté, la Picardie, la Provence, l'Andalousie, la Castille, la Catalogne, la Galice, la Flandre, la Wallonie, la Toscane, la Bavière*.

9.6 Sex and gender[8]

This topic is a linguistic minefield, as it is in other Romance languages. As women assume new roles in Western society, roles that were denied them in the past, French, like Spanish and Italian, have had to accommodate new feminine forms, and feminists, men and women, are doing their best to establish new ways of referring to females in a constantly evolving community. As will be seen in this section, the feminine form of professional nouns is now used regularly and applies to females across the spectrum of professional activities. Quebec is in the forefront of this movement, while the Académie française is still dragging its heels. Quebec clearly does not feel the weight of tradition of metropolitan France.

9.6.1 Female professional titles

Certain nouns denoting persons change their gender according to the sex of the person denoted, and no serious disturbance is caused here: *un/une camarade, un/une complice, un/une élève, un/une enfant* (but generally *un bébé*), *un/une esclave, un/une leader, un/une pensionnaire, un/une touriste*. However, in recent years, because of the rising tide of justified female occupancy in the higher reaches of professional activities, there has been, and still is, much controversy over the feminization of professional names. A tame, and fruitless, Commission de terminologie reported on the subject in 1984, but its recommendations have not been universally accepted, let alone adopted, and practice is chaotic, partly due to male resistance, but also due to society's reluctance to admit words that sound odd or rebarbative (e.g., autrice = *female author*), or contain sexual affirmations that even some females are unhappy with, as with *autrice*. Clearly, much heated discussion has been generated over this subject, and no obvious way forward seems to have been opened up.

In some cases, it is sufficient, as with the previous group of examples, simply to change the article from the traditional masculine to the feminine to indicate that a female is being referred to. This change can be operated with no difficulty when the male word ends in an **e**, a letter one easily associates with a feminine gender: *une dentiste, une juge, une journaliste*,

---

[8] For more information on this topic, see the enlightening article in Hanse and Blampain's dictionary, "Problème de la féminisation = France, Québec, Suisse, Belgique," 2005, p. 273).

une kinésithérapeute (physiotherapist), une ministre, une pilote, une photographe, une peintre, une propriétaire. In other cases, the addition of a final e or a standard feminine form is now acceptable: *une avocate, une défenseure, une successeure, une députée (une député* is more acceptable in a higher register), *une magistrate* (given by Marie-Éva de Villers's dictionary, which describes this term as a "fonctionnaire chargé [no extra feminine e] de rendre la justice"), *une ambassadrice, une directrice, une poétesse.* Typically, however, and we take *avocate* as an example, agreement with other parts of the sentence may cause difficulty. If a collective idea is suggested, *avocat* could end up in the masculine form: *Elle est **un** des meilleurs avocats de sa génération.*

A problem can also arise when reference has been made to a female teacher (e.g., Mme Dupont): *Mme Dupont est un excellent professeur* (already uncertainty here) but afterwards does one say: *Il va malheureusement nous quitter* or ***Elle va . . .?*** Does one refer to the female Mme Dupont or *un professeur*? Logic must prevail so that *Elle* is used. The use of *Il* here would be absurd. Yet, without strict reference to Mme Dupont, a pupil would readily say *Mon professeur est absent,* although in Quebec one would hear more easily *Ma professeure est absente.* A similar difficulty arises with *le petit Chaperon Rouge (Little Red Riding Hood).* Would the sentence: *Le petit Chaperon Rouge traversa la forêt* be followed by *Il* or by *elle – Il/Elle frappa à la porte d'une chaumière? Il* would be awkward although grammatically correct while *elle* would be grammatically incorrect. One would doubtless resort to *la petite fille* to resolve the dilemma.

A number one female tennis player could be either *la tenniswoman numéro un **mondial*** or *la tenniswoman numéro un **mondiale.** Doctoresse* is normal French when speaking with a child but not among adults and especially professionally: *Allez, ma grande/puce, on va voir la doctoresse.* This does not apply to all nouns which potentially belong to this class; for example, *chercheur (research worker), éleveur (cattle breeder), professeur* (see below) and *témoin (witness)* are nearly always masculine, but feminization is occurring here: *Elle est chercheur/euse au CNRS.* Whether one uses *le* or *la* before *chercheur* leads to an unresolved debate. Certainly, *chercheuse* exists, but often only in the sense of a person who looks for something as in Rimbaud's poem: *Les chercheuses de poux.* What is incontrovertibly certain, however, is that the status of a university female teacher with research commitments is and can only be, at the time of writing, *un enseignant chercheur.* No feminine form for *proviseur* exists, so that both *Madame le proviseur* and *Madame la proviseur* occur. *Notairesse* once existed but has fallen into disuse, although Irène Némirovsky uses it in *Suite française* (1942).

In some further cases, the choice of gender is a matter of status, and this must cause dismay for some in the female community, just as the male *manager* in English is used for females with reference to a high position of authority, while the feminine *manageress* seems to offer a demeaning view of a woman. The masculine confers a high status on a female, and the feminine invests her with a much lower status. Little wonder that Hélène Carrère d'Encausse insists on her role as the *secrétaire perpétuel* of the Académie française. *Secrétaire* remains obdurately masculine when applied to a woman holding a position at the top of the organizational hierarchy. Witness also: *Madame le secrétaire du parti communiste*, although *la secrétaire* may be used here. It is quite likely that a female in this position would prefer to be known as *Madame le secrétaire*, for the obvious reason of status. The same remark applies to *conseiller*: *Mme Bernard est conseiller en économie.* French radio in 2010 refers to female inspectors and senators as *Mme l'inspecteur* and *Mme la sénateur*, again for reasons of status. *Conseillère* exists (as in *conseillère municipale*), but, quite understandably if not justifiably, is used in more lowly domains. Although *académicienne* exists, the first female of the Académie française, Marguerite Yourcenar, author of the highest literary standing, did not succeed in having the feminine form applied to her, and was known as *académicien*, although in Belgium female members of the Académie royale de Belgique are known as *académicienne*. *Procureur général* (= *attorney/director of public prosecution*) remains adamantly masculine: *Louise Arbour, procureur général, chargé de* . . . And so does Édith Cresson, who was *la première premier ministre!* In the same vein, one can say *Madame le/la maire.* Perhaps, paradoxically, the said person would prefer to be called *Madame le maire. Mairesse* also exists, and Quebec French would plead for this form, while it would not be out of place in small French towns and villages. But it would be difficult to imagine the title *Mairesse de Paris/Lyon.* Yet again, the combative leader of the French Socialist Party, Martine Aubry, is called *la Mairesse de Lille.*

Savant, with the meaning of *scientist* (*scientifique*) has traditionally only been masculine, witness examples in dictionaries. Thus one reads in *Le petit Robert*: "Marie Curie fut un grand savant." Marie-Éva de Villers states that *savant* is both masculine and feminine but it is not clear from this that *savant* has a separate feminine form: *savante*. The examples she provides are in the masculine form. However, Ève Curie, in her biography of her mother, affirms: "Elle était une très jeune savante" (1938, p. 81). In a general way, there is no reason at all why *savante* should not be used with reference to females, and this feminine form does not strike a dissonant note for the average French speaker.

Mécène (*artistic, literary benefactor*) is also a source of difficulty. All dictionaries provide only a masculine form, and *Le petit Robert* illustrates thus the use of *mécène*: "Cette riche héritière est le mécène d'un groupe d'artistes." Ève Curie states of her mother: "Elle ne trouve que trois mécènes disposés à faire un tel geste" (1938, p. 142). Probably if this term were subject to a greater diffusion, it would have enjoyed a feminine definite article: *la mécène*. Informed opinion sees no obstacle to this form.

Passé maître provides another linguistic conundrum with repect to the feminine gender. Does one say *Elle est passé maître, passé maîtresse, passée maîtresse* or *passée maître dans l'art de trouver des donateurs?* It is quite clear that the last suggestion is the only acceptable one. Just as one would only write: *Elle est passée maître dans l'art de mentir.*

One can assess the development of the French language with respect to gender by referring again to Ève Curie when she writes in the 1930s of her mother: "Professeur, chercheur et directeur de laboratoire, Mme Curie travaille…" (1938, p. 123). Nowadays one would read *professeure, chercheur et directrice de laboratoire,* but as recently as 2006 one still read of Marie Curie: "Elle assume son rôle de directeur de recherche" (Balibar 2006, p. 75). As noted above, *chercheur* wishes to remain stubbornly masculine when applied to a researcher, and in French university brochures, this is the case. Yet Marie-Ève de Villers, a Canadian, states clearly that *chercheuse* may be used for a researcher.

In numerous cases where a new form would be required, the French of France is much more reticent over admitting new gender forms. Unlike French speakers of Quebec, Belgium and Switzerland, the linguistic hierarchy resists innovation. The following terms, frequently unacceptable in France, and in some cases certainly contentious, are common currency in Quebec, where an openness and willingness to change illustrate the great divide between the Académie française and the French of Quebec. The posts available to women in the armed forces are a striking case in point. The nouns in bold below show some willingness on the part of *la France métropolitaine* to bow to the inevitable, but the very first noun in this list (*agente*), for example, meets stringent rebuttal in France. Thus, in France, a James Bond female acquaintance could be *une amante discrète* but not *une agente secrète.* Yet in Quebec she could be the latter. She could also be *une espionne* in all French-speaking countries, like Mata Hari, the Dutch dancer who extracted information from the Allies in World War I: *agente (double/immobilière/secrète/de change/de voyages/de police), aiguilleuse, annonceure/ annonceuse, armurière, aspirante, assureuse/assureure, auteure, aviatrice, banquière, barmaid, bâtonnière, boxeuse, brancadière,* **brigadière***, cadre, cadreuse, camionneuse,* **caporale***, chancelière, chauffeure/chauffeuse, chef, chercheuse, coauteure, colonelle, commandante, conférencière,* **consule***, courtière, couvreuse, croupière, diaconesse, défenseure, docteure, écrivaine, éleveuse, encadreuse, factrice, figurante, forgeronne, garde forestière (forestier* still seems to be preferred), *Garde des Sceaux,* **générale***, gérante, golfeuse, greffière, huissière, industrielle, ingénieure, intervenante, lieutenante, lieutenante-gouverneure, maçonne, maître d'hôtel, marin, matelot, médecin, militaire, motarde, officière, pasteure, patrouilleuse, policière,* **préfète***, première ministre, procureure, professeure, proviseure, rectrice, réviseuse/réviseure,* **sergente***, soldate, vainqueure.*

Comments on some of the above, with other features:

Cadre: there is some resistance in France to *une cadre,* and this depends on the working environment. A female environment would happily

accept *une cadre*. Uneasiness is felt here with many male speakers in
France. Quebec offers no resistance at all. In any case one hears *une
cadre supérieure* as much as *une cadre*;

Chef: in the English sense of *chef*, a *chef cuisinier* provokes unusual torment
in French circles. Does one refer to a female chef as *la chef* in this
context? An unresolved issue: although Quebec French sees no obstacle
in *la cheffe* (but it is not included in the *MULTI dictionnaire*) for which
there is no precedent, French *académiciens* do not find it felicitous and
reject it. The closest one comes to this novel creation is the standard
French *veuf/veuve*. It is of value to note that Switzerland uses *la cheffe* in
la cheffe des policiers in Geneva courts;

Maïeuticien is a male *sage-femme* (*midwife*). Of some currency in the 1980s,
this term is now little used. *Sage-femme* is applied to a male, but
it would be odd to say *C'est **un** sage-femme*. One regularly says now
un homme sage-femme. One could say *Il est sage-femme*, avoiding the
indefinite article, but even here uneasiness is experienced. Other
possibilities put forward: *sagehomme, sage-homme*. In Quebec, midwives
must belong to the Ordre des Sages-femmes du Québec, so that a
male midwife remains resolutely *sage-femme*. Whether one says in
Quebec **un** or **une** *sage-femme* for a male is not clear. The English
male midwife is much easier. See also *maieutique* in Chapter 10,
Section 10.5. French generally attempts to accommodate the feminization of professions with the introduction of *femme*: *une femme
auteur/écrivain/ingénieur/magistrat/médecin/officier/policier/politique/chef
d'entreprise*;

Maître d'hôtel: *maîtresse* would be unacceptable here, given its sexual connotation. This is a general problem with *maîtresse*. Similarly, *maître de
conférences/cérémonies* alone would be acceptable, as would *passé maître*
for a female. It seems clear enough that *maître* combined with *nageur*
gives *maître-nageuse* (*female lifeguard*);

Marin: *marine* already has meanings: *art of sailing, navy*;

Matelot: *matelote* already has meanings: *fish stew, hornpipe*;

Médecin: *médecine* already has an obvious meaning: *medicine*;

Coiffeur is used in the masculine in the general sense, whether reference
is made to a male or to a female: *Je vais chez le coiffeur*. But *coiffeuse* is
used specifically with respect to a female hairdresser: *Ma coiffeuse m'a
dit ce matin que . . .* ;

Otage (*un/une*) has no distinctive feminine form;

Professeur: as far as *professeur* is concerned, the following possibilities exist:
une femme professeur, Elle est mon professeur préféré or, in R1, *Elle est ma prof
préférée*;

Peintre has traditionally only been masculine. Yet there is no reason why
one should not say *une peintre*. Indeed, the Canadian Marie-Éva de Villers
is happy with this form.

On an affectionate and slightly old-fashioned note, with a literary tinge, the male refers to his female partner in the masculine form. Proust writes, for example, "Mon pauvre chéri," when the female Odette is referred to. Similarly, Colette speaks of herself and female partner: "Nous nous traitions de 'Mon vieux.'" There is some resistance to this practice, regarded as it is as a little mawkish. The converse also exists – the female using the feminine gender when referring to her male partner: *Mais, ma petite mignonne, tu as bonne figure.* This second convention is no longer apparent these days, and would create uneasiness if used.

Paria illustrates perfectly the problem of gender applied to a female. No dictionary assigns a feminine gender to it. It remains resolutely masculine. A word of Sinhalese origin, not Hindi, it refers to both males and females. There seems to be no reason why one cannot say and write: *une paria.* *Mandarin* provides an even more complicated case, since *une mandarine* refers to the mandarine orange.

Benjamin has a feminine form: *benjamine.* Surprising for an English speaker who views this name applied exclusively to the youngest male in a family or group, *benjamine* defines the youngest daughter in a family or youngest girl in a group.

Poétesse also exists, but has a pejorative resonance and has fallen into misuse. It is replaced by *poète*, which remains obdurately masculine, hence the disconcerting juxtaposition of *grande* and *grand* in François Bayrou's *Henri IV*: "Marguerite de Navarre, grande humaniste et grand poète" (1994, p. 13).

9.6.2 Names of chateaux, churches and cathedrals

The gender of these buildings can vary according to what the author or speaker has in mind, and this frequently depends on the actual name of the building. In the case of chateaux, the masculine gender is the obvious choice: *J'admire la grandeur de Versailles. Je **le** recommande*; *Blois est-il plus **grand** que Vézélay?*

In the case of churches and cathedrals, usage may vary, since Saint Peter's basilica in Rome, for instance, may be masculine or feminine, depending on whether the author has the masculine gender of Saint Pierre in mind or the feminine word *basilique*: *Saint-Pierre a été **commencé(e)** en 1134*; *Sens, Beauvais, Laon, Soissons, Amiens, Bourges sont **lumineuses** comme des halles de verre*; *Saint-Front a été **reconstruit** au XIXe siècle*. But Notre-Dame seems always to have been feminine: *Notre-Dame, **entreprise** dès 1166, n'est pas encore **achevée**.*

Grotte is always treated as a feminine noun, presumably on analogy with the feminine gender of *grotte*, although *Lascaux* is masculine: *Lascaux est **sauvé**.*

Similarly, through metonymy, numerous genders change to suit certain objects. A Dutch cheese is *du hollande* (*du fromage de Hollande* – and even notice the lower case of *hollande*); a Champagne wine is *du champagne* (*du vin de Champagne*); a Havana cigar is *un havane* (*un cigare de la Havane*); a Citroën car is *une Citroën* (*une voiture*); a camera is *un Leica*; a washing machine is *une Miele/Vedette/Whirlpool* (*une machine à laver*).

9.6.3 The world of nature (for trees see Section 9.2.1 above)

As with the often inexplicable vagaries with gender as applied to humans, gender and sex with reference to animals, birds, insects and obviously less so with flowers are fraught with difficulty. The authors make no special claims to zoological competence in the classifications below.

In a general way, the non-expert in zoology will make no distinction between the male and female *aigle*, *renard* and *renarde*, or *éléphant* and *éléphante*. Indeed, hardly any French speakers would use *renarde* and *éléphante*, and would fail to recognize them as French words. The masculine form is used in these, and other, cases. There are, however, some comforting features:

1. In many cases, there is a completely separate, and quite different, noun for males and females. In others, a feminization of the masculine noun takes place. In this initial list where the two nouns are entirely different from each other, the first noun is male/masculine and the second is female/feminine: *chameau* > *chamelle*, *cheval/étalon* > *jument*, *chevreuil* > *chevrette*, *cochon* > *truie*, *mulet* > *mule*, *taureau/bœuf* > *vache*, *daim/cerf* > *biche*, *bouc* > *chèvre*, *lièvre* > *hase*, *mouton/bélier* > *brebis*, *sanglier* > *laie*, *singe* > *guenon* (*hase* and *laie* are rare terms)

2. Feminization of the masculine noun: *âne* > *ânesse*, *chat/matou* > *chatte*, *chien* > *chienne*, *éléphant* > *éléphante*, *lion* > *lionne*, *tigre* > *tigresse*, *lapin* > *lapine*, *loup* > *louve*, *mulet* > *mule*, *ours* > *ourse*, *poulain* > *pouliche*, *rat* > *rate*, *renard* > *renarde* (*lapine*, *éléphante*, *rate* and *renarde* are rare terms)

3. There is a group of names of animals where only one gender seems to exist. In the masculine form, these are: *babouin, berger allemand, bison, buffle, chacal, chamois, chimpanzé, couguar/cougouar, coursier, coyote, dromadaire, écureuil, élan, fauve* (wild animal, big cat = lion, tiger), *gorille, guépard, hippopotame, iguane, jaguar, kangourou, lama, léopard* (as in Lampedusa's Italian novel *Le léopard* = *Il gattopardo*), *lévrier, limier, loir, mulot, orang-outan(g), orignal, panda, paresseux, poney, puma, pur-sang, putois, renne, rhinocéros, rongeur, tapir, zèbre*. Animals with only feminine genders are: *baleine, gazelle, gerbille, girafe, hyène, mangouste, marmotte, mouffette, panthère, souris, tortue*. Yet how does one deal with the male sex of a mammal with a female gender? Does one say **une** *baleine/panthère/girafe* **mâle** or **un** *baleine/panthère/girafe* (**mâle**)? Likewise and conversely, what does one say of a female mammal where only the masculine gender seems to exist – **un** *bison/écureuil/hippopotame* **femelle** or **une** *bison/écureuil/hippopotame* **femelle**? This is an inconclusive matter, and applies to all Romance languages.

Exactly the same uncertainties occur in the gender of birds where the person untutored in zoology does not and cannot distinguish between males and females. There is a small group of birds where the masculine and feminine forms exist and this causes no difficulty for most French speakers, save for *jars* and *paonne*: *canard* > *cane*, *coq* > *poule*, *dindon* > *dinde*, *faisan* > *faisane*, *jars* > *oie*, *paon* > *paonne*, *pigeon* > *pigeonne*, *sylphe* > *sylphide*, *tourtereau* > *tourterelle*.

Birds with a masculine gender include: *aigle*, *albatros*, *ara* (*macaw*), *bécasseau*, *canari*, *chardonneret*, *choucas*, *colibri*, *condor*, *corbeau*, *cormoran* (no t), *coucou*, *cygne* (swan: as in Tchaikovsky's *Le lac des cygnes*), *dodo/dronte* (now extinct), *échassier*, *épervier*, *étourneau*, *faucon*, *flamant*, *geai*, *héron*, *hibou*, *ibis*, *kestrel*, *martin-pêcheur*, *martinet*, *merle*, *milan*, *moineau*, *pélican*, *perroquet*, *pingouin*, *pique-bœuf* (tick bird, very common in the Caribbean and tropical climates where this creature removes annoying insects from cattle and therefore both derive a benefit), *pinson*, *pivert*, *pluvier*, *ptarmigan* (grouse, state bird of Alaska more known in Europe as *lagopède des Alpes*, which is also masculine), *quetzatl* (prized bird in Mexico), *ramier*, *rapace*, *roitelet*, *rossignol* (as in Stravinsky's opera *Le rossignol*), *rouge-gorge*, *sansonnet*, *vautour*.

Birds with a feminine gender include: *alouette* (as in the song *Alouette, gentille alouette . . .*), *autruche*, *bergeronnette*, *buse*, *caille*, *chauve-souris* (bat: as in Johan Strauss's *La chauve-souris*), *chouette*, *cigogne* (they fly from North Africa to Alsace in the springtime and return in the fall), *colombe*, *corneille*, *crécerelle*, *grive*, *grue*, *hirondelle*, *mouette*, *palombe*, *pie* (magpie: as in Rossini's *La pie voleuse*), *perdrix*, *pipistrelle*, *sarcelle*. As with mammals above, the man in the street, like the authors, would not recognize a male bird from a female bird when seen from a distance. If one had to distinguish, would one say: **une** hirondelle **mâle** or **un** hirondelle **mâle**? Likewise, would one say **un** geai **femelle** or **une** geai **femelle**?

There seems to be no guiding principle with respect to the gender of fish. The following is a random list of common fish and water animals classified according to gender. Masculine: *brochet*, *carrelet*, *dauphin*, *maquereau*, *marsouin*, *merlan*, *morse*, *phoque*, *ragondin*, *requin*, *rouget*, *saumon*, *thon*, *vairon*. Feminine: *anguille*, *carpe*, *dorade*, *loutre*, *morue*, *ondine*, *sardine*. Miscellaneous in this group: *crustacés* (shell fish): le crabe, la crevette, une écrevisse, le homard. Note also: *la méduse* (as in Géricault's *Le radeau de la Méduse*), *le poulpe*.

The following is a disparate group of nouns related to fauna that are not classified, except according to gender. Masculine: *alligator*, *anaconda*, *blaireau*, *boa*, *caïman*, *caméléon*, *castor* (beaver),[9] *cobra*, *crapaud*, *crocodile*, *crotale* (rattlesnake),[10] *escargot*, *faune* (a mythical creature not to be confused with

---

[9] Sartre refers picturesquely to Simone de Beauvoir, addressing her as *mon Castor* (see his *Lettres à mon Castor*).

[10] *Anaconda*, *boa*, *cobra* and *crotale* look feminine, but are unquestionably masculine, probably on account of *serpent*.

faune = fauna, which is feminine), *hérisson, lézard, opossum, papillon, porc-épic, serpent (à sonnette = rattlesnake)*. Feminine: *araignée, belette, couleuvre, grenouille, taupe, vipère* (as in Mauriac's *Le nœud de vipères*).

Insects provide difficulty as well, including the word *insecte*, which is masculine. Masculine: *bourdon, bousier (dung beetle), cafard, cloporte, coléoptère* (class of *beetles*; has a technical resonance), *colimaçon, criquet, frelon, grillon, mille-pattes, mouche (tsé-tsé), moucheron, moustique, papillon, perce-oreille, scarabée* (looks feminine but is masculine), *tsé-tsé, vers, vers luisant*. Feminine: *abeille, araignée, blatte, chenille, cigale, coccinelle, fourmi, libellule, limace, luciole, mante religieuse, mite, mouche, puce, punaise, sangsue, sauterelle, tarentule, teigne, tipule, veuve noire*.

There is no guiding principle here for the uninitiated regarding the gender of flowers and what are considered weeds. Suffice it to list the flowers according to gender. Masculine: *bégonia, bleuet, bouton d'or, cactus, camélia* (as in Alexandre Dumas fils's *La dame aux camélias*, which is less well-known than Verdi's *La traviata* that it inspired), *chardon, coucou, coqueli-cot, crocus, dahlia, forsythia, fuchsia, géranium, glaïeul, hibiscus, hortensia, iris, jacaranda, jonc, lierre, lupin, lys* (as in Balzac's *Le lys dans la vallée*), *magnolia, muguet* (bought in the streets of Belgium and France on May Day), *myoso-tis, narcisse, nénuphar* (as in Monet's *Les nénuphars*), *œillet, pavot, perce-neige, pétunia, pissenlit, pois de senteur, rhododendron, roseau, séneçon* (a very common weed = *groundsel*), *souci, tournesol* (as in *Les tournesols* by Van Gogh). Femi-nine: *anémone* (as in Claude Monet's *Anémones*), *azalée, belladone, bougainvillée* (also: *bougainvillier*, which is masculine and is increasingly used to the detriment of its feminine counterpart; this noun derives from the French eighteenth-century explorer Bougainville), *bruyère, campanule, clématite, dig-itale, églantine, gentiane, glycine, jacinthe, jonquille, marguerite* (daisy, as in the slightly old-fashioned *effeuiller la marguerite: Il/Elle m'aime, un peu, beaucoup, passionnément, à la folie, pas du tout* = She/He loves me, she/he loves me not, etc., recalling a similar activity with dandelion seeds), *orchidée, ortie, pâquerette, pensée, pervenche, pivoine, primevère, renoncule, rose* (as in Ronsard's extremely well-known poem, *Ode à Cassandre*, quoted in general conversation, but here quoted in the original: "Mignonne, allons voir si la rose qui ce matin avait déeclose . . . "), *tulipe* (recalls Alexandre Dumas's novel *La tulipe noire*), *violette*.

Heavenly bodies (*corps célestes: étoiles, planètes, constellations*) are tradition-ally masculine, and the uninformed would doubtless always opt for the masculine. Yet the word *planète* (i.e., *Mars, Vénus, Saturne* – as in Goya's *Sat-urne dévorant ses enfants* – *Pluton*, etc.) is feminine, which explains why the author/astrophysicist Jean-Pierre Luminet writes: "d'offrir à Mars un orbe plus harmonieux et plus digne d'*elle*" (2008a, p. 340). The same author is con-sistent here: "Mars la rouge" (2008b, p. 38). In keeping with this feminine idea, Grevisse quotes: "Saturne est *environnée* de dix satellites." In contrast: "*Vu* au téléscope, Jupiter montre [. . .] Mars est *enveloppé* d'une atmosphère" (2008, p. 596). However, heavenly bodies are of necessity feminine when they are preceded by the feminine article – *la Grande/Petite Ourse, l'Étoile polaire / du berger, la Voie lactée* (as in Buñuel's *La voie lactée*) – or when they were originally feminine names in Greek or Roman mythology: *Vénus, Cassiopée.* Further examples: *Jusqu'en 1930, Neptune était* **considérée** *comme la dernière planète du système solaire*; *Sirius est des millions de fois plus* **grosse** *que la Terre.*

Appendix

The following section on differing genders in French and Spanish will be of specific interest to students and professors whose study commitments take them beyond French and into Spanish. The preceding sections include the occasional reference to contrasting genders in French and Spanish, and even Italian, when there exists a close resemblance in the spelling of nouns in these different languages, and when the meaning is the same or similar. Since the study of modern languages frequently brings together the combination of French and Spanish, it seems helpful to highlight in a systematic manner the different genders in the two languages so as to avoid confusion, and experience shows that confusion there often is. As a simple example, the French *agenda* could easily be incorrectly considered a feminine noun if this same word is first seen in Spanish where it is feminine. There follow two lists. The first (1) covers French nouns of masculine gender contrasting with Spanish nouns of feminine gender. The second (2) covers French nouns of feminine gender contrasting with Spanish nouns of masculine gender. In all cases, the French noun precedes the Spanish noun, which appears in parentheses and italics. Some translations into English are provided for clarity's sake.

1. affront (*afrenta*), âge (*edad*), agenda (*agenda*), avantage (*ventaja*), bégonia (*begonia*), boa (*boa*), calme (*calma*), canoë (*canoa*), chiffre (*cifra*), cidre (*sidra*), courant (i.e., *electric current, draft = corriente*), dahlia (*dalia*), délice (*delicia*), désavantage (*desventaja*), diabète (*diabetes*), diocèse (*diócesis*), doute (*duda*), épi (*espiga*), fiel (*bile = hiel*), flegme (*flema*), gardenia (*gardenia*), gemme (*gema*), hectare (*hectárea*), javelot (*jabalina*), lait (*leche*), larynx (*laringe*), légume (*legumbre*), lièvre (*hare = liebre*), lierre (*ivy = hiedra*), lilas (*lila*), masque (*máscara*), massacre (*masacre*; this Spanish noun is just occasionally used in the masculine), mémoires (*memorias*), miel (*miel*), mimosa (*mimosa*), moral (*state of mind, morale = moral*), morse (*walruss = morsa*), ongle (*uña*), opéra (*ópera*), orchestre (*orquesta*), paradoxe (*paradoja*), pétunia (*petunia*), pharynx (*faringe*), phoque (*seal = foca*), printemps (*primavera*), ressac (*backwash = resaca*), sang (*sangre*), sel (*sal*), serpent (*serpiente*), siège (*sede*, as in *le siège épiscopal*), ulcère (*úlcera*), zèbre (*cebra*), le zona (*shingles, i.e., on the body = la zona*)
2. affection (*afecto*), ambiance (*ambiente*), analyse (*análisis*), annonce (*anuncio*), ardeur (*ardor*), archives (*archivos*), armoire (*armario*), attaque (*ataque*),

auberge (*albergue*), avance (*avance*), banque (*banco*), boxe (*boxeo*), broche (*broche*), candeur (*candor*), cartouche (*cartucho*), céréale (*cereal*), chaleur (*calor*), clameur (*clamor*), comète (*comet = cometa*), contagion (*contagio*), contrebande (*contrabando*), couleur (*color*), croisière (*cruise = crucero*), datte (*dátil*), dent (*diente*), dictée (*dictado*), digue (*dique*), douleur (*dolor*), éclipse (*eclipse*), écritoire (*writing case* containing materials for writing), emphase (*énfasis*), enclave (*enclave*), énigme (*enigma*), épaisseur (*espesor*), équipe (*equipo*), erreur (*error*), extase (*éxtasis*), faveur (*favor*), ferveur (*fervor*), figue (*higo*), fin (*fin*), fraude (*fraude*), fresque (*fresco*), frise (in architecture = *friso*), fumée (*humo*), fureur (*furor*), grosseur (*grosor*), la Guadiana (*el Guadiana*, river in Spain), horloge (*reloj*), horreur (*horror*), humeur (*mood*, and not to be confused with *humour*, which is masculine; *humor* in Spanish covers both the idea of mood and that of humor), idole (*ídolo*), idylle (*idilio*), insulte (*insulto*), jacinthe (*hyacinth = jacinto*), langueur (*langor*), lèvre (*labio*), limite (*limite*), liqueur (*licor*), mangue (*mango*), mappemonde (*mapamundi*), mer (*mar*), municipalité (*municipio*), nacre (*mother of pearl = nácar*), oasis (*oasis*), panique (*pánico*), papauté (*papado*), parenté (*family relationship = parentesco*), pensée (*pensamiento* – both the flower and the thought), planète (*planeta*), pommette (*pómulo*), pudeur (*pudor*), Pyrénées (*Pirineos*), rame (*remo*), rire (*risa*), salut (*greetings* but *salud* in Spanish = *health*), saveur (*sabor*), sentinelle (*centinela*), splendeur (*esplendor*), stupeur (*estupor*), sueur (*sudor*), terreur (*terror*), thermos (*termos*), tomate ([*jito*]*mate*), torpeur (*torpor*), torpille (*torpedo*), tulipe (*tulipán*), valeur (*valor*), vallée (*valle*), valse (*vals*), vapeur (*vapor*), vidéo (*vídeo*), vigueur (*vigor*), vodka (*vodka*)

One striking pattern emerges from this second group. The –or Spanish masculine ending corresponds to the French feminine ending –**eur**. This difference features in more than twenty nouns listed above. But there must be more. All these nouns derive from Latin masculine nouns ending in –**or**/–**oris**. How the Latin masculine *dolor*, along with all the other nouns in this group, leads to a feminine gender in French is not clear. Exceptionally in this context, the French *honneur* and the Spanish *honor* are both masculine. One further source of confusion: *labour* (*ploughing*) is masculine as is its doublet *labeur* (*work* = little used, and therefore R3) but the Spanish *labor* (*work*), is feminine. Interestingly enough, Italian nouns ending in –**ore** are masculine, which makes the French feminine ending –**eur** even more anomalous: (*l'*)*ardore*/*onore*, (*il*) *calore*/*fervore*/*furore*/*valore*/*vapore*/*vigore*, lo *splendore*, etc.

Letters are also masculine in French and feminine in Spanish. Makes of automobiles are feminine in French (on analogy with *une voiture*) and masculine in Spanish (on analogy with *un coche*). Makes of watches are feminine in French (*une montre*) and masculine in Spanish (*un reloj*).

10

Number (singular and plural) / Le nombre (singulier et pluriel)[1]

Below is a passage describing some of the attractive aspects of Paris, starting with Lutetia (the original settlement on the river Seine) and its amphitheater, moving on to some of France's illustrious painters whose names stay in the singular since they refer to paintings, and then to its buildings of social and architectural interest. Of linguistic note, and in contrast to English singular nouns, are a number of simple and compound plurals. *Information* can be plural in French, as opposed to English, where the same word is uncountable. One observes the collective noun *quarantaine* followed by a singular verb, although it could just as well, and more commonly, be followed by a plural verb: *attendent. Bourbon* could end in an **s**. *Terre-pleins* as a plural seems an oddity. At a more basic level, the singular nouns ending in **–al** assume an **–aux** ending for their plural.

Paris à mille et une facettes

Les **médias** diffusent toutes sortes d'**informations** sur la capitale politique, administrative, culturelle et intellectuelle de la France. L'ancienne Lutèce offre des contrastes saisissants que chacun devrait expérimenter. **Les Arènes** de Lutèce sont le seul amphithéâtre gallo-romain visible à Paris. Lors des mauvaises **intempéries**, nous pouvons jouir d'un bon nombre d'activités pour apprécier les **Chagall**, les **Picasso**, les **Monet**, les **Poussin** et bien d'autres peintres **géniaux** [of genius].

Les **bonnes mœurs** des Parisiens tournent autour de la fréquentation des **cafés-théâtres**, **des cafés-concerts** et des **cafés littéraires** comme le célèbre café de Flore en plein cœur de Saint-Germain-des-Prés. Plus loin, **une quarantaine** de touristes attend pour visiter le fameux Palais **Bourbon**. Ce monument historique a appartenu à la famille **des Bourbon**. À l'heure actuelle, cet édifice abrite l'Assemblée nationale où siègent les députés français. C'est au **8**[e] arrondissement que se trouvent les Champs-Élysées, la Place de l'Étoile avec son Arc de Triomphe et, aux **alentours**, la Place de la Concorde. La Tour Eiffel trône sur quatre

---

[1] This chapter treats nouns and some adjectives; see Chapter 52 for full treatment of adjectives.

terre-pleins [plinths]. Elle reçoit à ses pieds des **milliers** de touristes. Des vacanciers avec leurs légers **bagages** traversent la capitale au fil de l'eau en **bâteaux-mouches**. Bien d'autres **beaux** monuments, le Palais du Louvre, le Musée d'Orsay, les **principaux** musées, de **nombreux** hôtels particuliers, notamment sur la Place des Vosges et la Place du Tertre de la Butte Montmartre, illustrent les peintres croquant des portraits de passants ou des paysages pittoresques. L'Opéra Garnier offre des spectacles grandioses. La Cité des sciences et de l'industrie appelée « La Géode » s'étale le long du **canal** Saint-Martin.

10.1 The formation of plurals

The following comments summarize the procedure for the formation of the plural for simple (i.e., non-compound) words:

1. Words ending in **–ail** add **s**: *ails, chandails, détails, éventails, sérails*; some words, however, have the plural in **–aux**: *coraux, émaux, soupiraux, travaux, vitraux* (as in *les vitraux de la cathédrale de Chartres/Notre Dame*). The plural of **–ail** was also **aulx** but this form is now dated. *Bercail* (*sheepfold*) does not have a plural at all in normal usage. One would only see or hear the word in, for instance, *Les moutons sont rentrés au bercail*;

2. Most words ending in **–al** change to **–aux** (see Chapter 52 on adjectives for a fuller list): *amiraux, arsenaux, canaux, cérémoniaux, chenaux* (*channels*), *chevaux, fanaux* ([head]*lamp, lantern*), *fluviaux, géniaux, idéaux, illégaux, légaux, immémoriaux* (as in *depuis des temps immémoriaux*), *moraux, rivaux, royaux, signaux, sociaux, spéciaux*. But the plural of *final* is *finals* or *finaux*, although some uneasiness is felt here over both these words. Other possibilities to replace these two adjectives are: *définitifs, derniers, ultimes*. The feminine plural of adjectives ending in **–al** is **–ales**: *géniales, rivales, royales, sociales, spéciales*. Some words ending in **–al** take **–als** in the plural: *bals, banals, carnavals, chacals, étals* ([*market*] *stalls*), *fatals, festivals, navals* (as in *chantiers navals*), *récitals*; *banaux* also exists, although it is out-of-date. Certain terms like *fatals* provoke serious hesitation with French speakers, largely because they are little used, and, in the case of *fatals*, the words *mortels* or *fatidiques* come more readily to mind: *des coups mortels, des événements/jours fatidiques, l'âge fatidique*. Hesitation even occurs over adjectives like *génial* in the masculine plural since, as with many adjectives with the **–al** ending, the plural ending **–aux** simply sounds different from the singular ending. On the other hand, the feminine plural sounds the same as the singular forms (masculine and feminine). Dictionaries and grammars offer the plural of *régal* (*delight*) as *régals* but such usage is so rare it is non-existent. One would only, and regularly, see and hear it in the

singular, for example: *C'est un vrai régal; Le spectacle/repas fut un véritable régal.* Dictionaries offer the plural of arcane words such as *aval(s), cal(s), pal(s)* but such terms attract the following comments: nowadays, one only sees and hears *en aval du village* (*downstream from the village*); *donner son aval à* (*to give an endorsement to*); *cals* means *calluses* on the hands (not that this would be recognized by the average French speaker), and the standard term these days is *durillons*; *pals* means *impalements* but *empalement* has entirely replaced it, while the plural of *cal* holds little sense, and it is difficult to see even the current word in the plural. One could wonder why the expected form **–als** is often **–aux**. The development from Latin provides the answer. The **ll** in *bellus*, for instance, slowly turned into a **y** (yod), and thence into the sound **o**, as in *eau* (i.e., from what the French call *l mouillé* [*dark l*] to an **o**). This can happen in English, with *wild/world* for example;

3. Words ending in **–au/–eau** add an **x**: *beaux, berceaux, bouleaux* (*birch trees*), *bourreaux* (as in *les bourreaux de l'Inquisition*), *boyaux* (*bowels*), *bureaux, cerveaux* (as in *Copernic, Gallilée, Michel-Ange sont de grands cerveaux de la Renaissance*), *eaux, escabeaux, hameaux, louveteaux* (*cubs*, and this includes the small boys' association), *manteaux* (as in *les manteaux sont au vestiaire*), *matériaux* (as in *le bois et le fer sont des matériaux très utilisés*), *noyaux, sceaux* (*seal* as in *les sceaux du roi*), *seaux*; but *sarraus* (*smock*, once commonly used by primary school children in France) and *landaus* (the common term for *baby carriage/pram*);

4. Words ending in **–eu** add an **x**: *cheveux, feux*; but: *bleus, pneus*;

5. Words ending in **–ou** add an **s**: *clous, cous, fous, H/hindous, matous, mous, nounous, sous, trous, Z/zoulous*; but seven words take an **x** here: *bijoux, cailloux, choux, genoux, hiboux, joujoux, poux*;

6. Words ending in **–s**, **–x** or **–z** do not change: *amas, bois, cassis, gras, gris, gros, imprécis, indécis, mas, mois, paradis, précis, tas, tous, creux, index, perdrix, preux* (out-of-date and has historical and literary connotations: *un preux chevalier*), *Sioux, vitreux, croix, doux, houx, roux, nez*. The feminine plural of some adjectives ending in **–s** changes to **–sses**: *grasses, grosses*. Others end in **–ses**: *grises, indécises, précises*. The feminine plural of adjectives ending in **–x** changes to **–ses**: *creuses, douces, vitreuses*; but *roux* > *rousses*. One cannot imagine a feminine plural form of *preux* with the ending **–euses**;

7. All other nouns add an **s**: *amis, hommes, femmes, langues*. All other adjectives (masculine and feminine) end thus: *vert/verts/verte/vertes, noir/noirs/noire/noires, bleu/bleus/bleue/bleues*;

8. A very small number of words have two plural forms: *aïeul* > *aïeuls/ aïeux* = *grandparents* – *aïeuls* = (*male and female*) *ancestors* and *aïeules* = *grandmothers* or *female ancestors*; *ciel* > *cieux* = *skies, heavens* (general, collective and common term), as in "Notre Père qui êtes aux cieux..." (Lord's Prayer) or *aller vers d'autres cieux*; *ciels* is also used in meteorology

(*des ciels orageux*) and to describe the top of a four-poster bed (*baldaquin*); *œil* has the common and general plural *yeux* (*de lynx*); *œils* also exists in compounds: *œils-de-bœuf* = *small round windows*, *œils-de-chat* = *cat's eyes*, *œils-de-tigre* = *tiger's eyes*. An interesting feature of the plural *yeux* is its pronunciation in combination with *quatre*, as in the expression *entre quatre yeux* = *between us two*. The strong tendency is to add an **s**, pronounced **z**, to *quatre* and to drop the **-re** of *quatre*, for euphony's sake (*entre quat'z' yeux*). This pronunciation is difficult to avoid and occurs with most speakers. A kind of *liaison dangereuse* is in operation here. *Liaison* only occurs in the plural in the following type of expressions. Compare *le bras étendu* (no *liasion*) and *les bras étendus* (*liaison*) | *à bras ouverts* (*liaison*). Also: *un prix élevé* (no *liaison*) and *des prix élevés* (*liaison*);

9. With respect to pronunciation, some plural nouns sound quite different from their singular counterpart: *cheval/chevaux, bail/baux, fanal/fanaux, mal/maux* (see 1 above for more examples). With *bœuf* and *œuf* the **f** is sounded but in the plural the **fs** disappears in sound;

10. The pluralization of letters functions in the following way: *Il manque deux* **a/i/e/r** *à ce mot* (i.e., invariable). *Liaison* usually takes place here: *Mettre les points sur les* **i** (*liaison* usually takes place here but its omission is possible). Note also *des* **i grecs**. Foreign letters can vary: *des yods*. However, there is a tendency to make these invariable: *des delta, des gamma*;

11. The pluralization of numbers: *Il manque deux* **4/quatre** *à ce chiffre* (i.e., invariable);

12. When nouns are followed by a complement, the complement may vary: *maison de brique/briques, gelée de groseille/groseilles, lettre de condoléance/condoléances* (although according to Grevisse and Goosse the second form is the only acceptable one since 1992), *cahier de brouillon/brouillons* (the authors above prefer the first), *salle de bain/bains* (the second seeming to have won the day), *salle d'étude/études, pain d'épice/épices*;

13. Complements of the verb of the following type vary, although there is a marked preference for the singular: *Armelle bondit de rocher en rocher | de rochers en rochers; Pierre allait de porte en porte | de portes en portes; Françoise passait de boutique en boutique | de boutiques en boutiques; Le colporteur allait de maison en maison | de maisons en maisons; Sa voix changeait de moment en moment | de moments en moments*;

14. The negatives *sans* and *pas de* may be followed by a singular or a plural: *Sophie est partie sans livre/livres; Le navire naviguait sous un ciel sans nuage/nuages; La compagnie n'a pas de voiture de location | voitures de location; Les enfants ne trouvaient pas de mot/mots*;

15. As far as units of measurement are concerned, usage is as follows: *tous les lundis matin, tous les samedis soir; tous les 12 janvier, les 12 et 13 avril; cent kilomètres-heure, deux années-lumière*;

16. When several persons are involved with articles of clothing, as in for instance *They took their hats off*, the second noun is in the singular in French: *Ils ont ôté leur chapeau*; *Toutes les filles ont perdu leur sac* (*All the girls lost their bags*); *La prof a donné une casquette à bien des garçons* (*The teacher gave hats to lots of boys*). If *chapeau, sac, casquette* were in the plural, the suggestion would be that the persons involved would each have (had) two or more objects;

17. Plural of abridged forms: if the last letter of the word is retained, an **s** is added: *Mmes* (= *Mesdames*), *Mlles* (= *Mesdemoiselles*). If the last letter is not retained, no **s** is added: *200 p.* (= *pages*), *200 000 hab.* (= *habitants*);

18. In the following type of expressions characterized by metonymy, there is a mixture of singular and plural but the verb is in the plural: *Les seconde année sont partis à dix-sept heures*; *Les cinquième sont toujours au collège.*

19. Many nouns have no plural, viewed as a collective idea:
    a. Names of arts, sciences and sports: *la peinture, la littérature, la musique, la botanique, le tennis, le football. Peinture, musique* and *tennis* may be used in the plural but with different meanings: *peintures = paintings, musiques = different types of music, tennis = sneakers, trainers*;
    b. Names of materials: *or, argent, bronze, cuivre, fer*. These nouns may be used in the plural with a particular meaning: *Le forgeron façonne les fers*; *On se promenait parmi les bronzes et les marbres* (*among bronze/marble statues*);
    c. Names of specific qualities: *la solitude, la fragilité, la gentillesse*;
    d. Names of the senses: *le goût, l'odorat, l'ouïe, le toucher, la vue*;
    e. Names of the cardinal points: *le nord, le sud, l'est, l'ouest* (order as in English);
    f. Many infinitives and adjectives used in an abstract manner: *le boire et le manger, l'utile et l'agréable*;

20. *Prochain* in the sense of *fellow creature* or *one's neighbor* is singular: *Il faut aider son prochain*. However, *semblable*, with the same meaning, may be plural: *partager le sort de ses semblables*; *eux et leurs semblables*;

21. Many nouns are rarely used in the singular and are frequently used with a limited connotation: *accordailles* (R3), *affres* (R3 = torment), *agapes* (R3), *aguets, aléas* (uncertainties, as in *les aléas de la vie / du métier*), *alentours, ambages* (as in *parler sans ambages*), *annales, arabesques* (as in *des arabesques délicates*), *archives, armoiries* (as in *les armoiries des Rothschild / d'Outremont*), *arrérages, arrhes, arriérés* (arrears in payment, like *arrérages*), *auspices, babines, bajoues, basques* (R3 = flounces, as in *les basques d'une robe*), *bestiaux* (cattle; the doublet *bétail* which is only singular has a similar meaning but it covers all farm and farmyard animals, while *bestiaux* covers oxen and cows; this difference is not clear for many French speakers), *broussailles, calendes* (R3), *collatéraux* (collaterals; many French speakers do not understand this term but it is used

regularly in administrative language, referring to members who are not immediately connected to a family, e.g., uncles and aunts), *combles, comices, comics, condoléances, confins, décombres* (rubble), *dégâts* (damage, as in *Les vents violents ont causé beaucoup de dégâts*), *dépenses, ébats* (frolicking), *écrouelles* (scrofula), *émoluments* (used in administration, as in *recevoir des émoluments élevés*), *entrailles, sur ces entrefaites* (at that moment), *environs* (surrounding area), *épousailles* (R3), *étrennes* (Christmas or New Year's gift), *festivités, fiançailles, floralies* (flower show), *fredaines* (amorous adventures), *fringues* (R1 = clothes), *frusques* (R1 = clothes), *funérailles, gens, gravats* (rubble; similar to *décombres*), *hardes* (R3 = clothes, glad rags), *honoraires* (as in *L'avocat touche ses honoraires*), *ides* (R3), *instances* (insistence, entreaty, authority), *intempéries, jérémiades* (continual complaining, as in *Arrête tes jérémiades !*), *limbes* (limbo), *mânes* (R3), *matines, méandres, menées, mœurs, nippes* (R1), *obsèques* (R3 = funeral), *oripeaux* (tawdry finery = R3, as in *des oripeaux défraîchis*), *Pâques, parages* (neighborhood), *pénates* (R3), *pleurs* (R3), *prémisses, préparatifs, proches,* (*étoffe/nappe à*) *ramages* (cloth/tablecloth with a floral design), *règles* (menstrual period), *remontrances* (R3 = reprimand), *retrouvailles* (reunion), *rillettes, royalties, sévices, thermes, us et coutumes, vêpres, victuailles, viscères, vivats* (cheers uttered by a crowd, for instance).

Notes on some of the above:

Accordailles has the same meaning as *fiançailles* but is of a higher register, having an old-fashioned but elegant resonance;

Affres is used in such expressions as *les affres de la faim | mort | de la douleur | de l'humiliation*. Flaubert was acquainted with *les affres du style*, tormented as he was with stylistic perfection;

Agapes (meeting of friends, often for a meal): *des agapes somptueuses qui furent de véritables retrouvailles*. This feminine noun has a singular connotation which does not form part of the vocabulary of "Monsieur tout le monde." In its first and original sense, it referred to a communal meal enjoyed by the early Christians, doubtless recalling the Last Supper (La Cène), now of Leonardo da Vinci fame;

Aguets is usually used in: *être aux aguets*

Alentours = surrounding area. It has a similar value to *environs*. *Alentour* is used, but as an adverb: *Sur la photo aérienne, on voit la ville et la campagne alentour*;

Ambages occurs in *parler sans ambages* = to speak straight to the point;

Arrhes occurs in *verser des arrhes* = to pay a deposit;

Babines occurs in *s'essuyer | se lécher les babines* = to lick one's chops;

Bajoues exists in the dictionary as a singular but it seems only to be used in the plural: *Ce clown est drôle avec ses bajoues*;

Combles is normally used in the plural for *attic*, as in *sous les combles*. It is used metaphorically in the singular: *le comble de l'injustice | de la joie | du désespoir*;

Comices is used in the plural with the idea of *political meeting/gathering* for a specific purpose for voting (= *hustings*). See also Flaubert's *Madame Bovary*, beginning of Chapter 8 where an agricultural fair is expected: "Ils arrivèrent, en effet, ces fameux Comices !";

Ébats is only used in the plural, and has a literary connotation: *Le chien prend ses ébats dans le jardin* = *The dog is frolicking in the garden*;

Honoraires = *professional fees*, as in *les honoraires du médecin/notaire*, and it is masculine;

Ides, as in *César fut assassiné aux ides de mars* = (March 15);

Les instances, as in *Sur les instances de Philippe, je me suis ravisé* (*I changed my mind*); *les instances gouvernementales*. *Instance* has a very restricted use in the singular = *legal proceedings*. *Ils sont en instance de divorce*; *L'affaire est en instance* (pending);

Jérémiades comes from the persistent wailing of the Old Testament prophet Jeremiah;

Les intempéries is only used in the plural: *Elle était exposée aux intempéries* = *She was out in the bad weather*;

Les mânes = *household gods*, as in Roman times: *interroger/invoquer les mânes*;

Méandres, as in *les méandres d'un fleuve, d'un discours/exposé*. The singular exists but is little used;

Menées = *maneuvering, plotting*, and is always pejorative: *Elle était victime des menées de ses concurrents*;

Mœurs = *customs, traditions*. The **s** may or may not be pronounced;

Matines and *vêpres* refer to religious services in the Christian day = *matins, vespers*;

Pâques is also used in the singular: *la Pâque juive/russe* = *Passover*;

Pénates = *Roman household gods*. Used more with the humorous meaning of *home*, as in *regagner ses pénates*;

Pleurs is usually found in the expressions *être en pleurs* = *to be in tears*, *fondre en pleurs, répandre/verser des pleurs* = *to burst into tears*. *Larmes* is the more common term;

Ramages is only used in this way and has a literary connotation. Only those well versed in seventeenth-century literature will have come across *ramage* in the singular. La Fontaine's *Le corbeau et le renard* has it rhyme with *plumage*;

Remontrances is often found in the expression *faire des remontrances* (*à quelqu'un*);

Royalties is not really necessary: *droits d'auteur* is sufficient;

Thermes = *thermal baths*, and it is masculine: *les thermes de Caracalla* (in Rome), *les thermes nationaux d'Aix-les-Bains*;

Vêpres appears as *Les vêpres siciliennes* by Verdi (this is the original title);

    Viscères: abdomen area. Heard in hospitals, and only in the plural, although it exists in the singular. This noun is masculine – source of uncertainty for French speakers.

22. There is a range of nouns referring to *john/restroom/lavatory/toilet*, and these are almost entirely in the plural. Many of them are naturally of the lower register, and this is indicated: *lieux/cabinets d'aisances, latrines, commodités, privés* (R3 = rare now, as is privy in English), *goguenots/gogues* (R1), *chiottes* (R1), *feuillées* (used by soldiers) = trench dug by soldiers on a campaign and similar to *latrines, bouteilles* (used on a boat, largely by officers), *toilettes, vécés* = WC, *waters* (**w** pronounced as in English). *Le petit coin* is, of course singular. *Toilette* has a meaning in the singular, as in *faire sa toilette = to have a wash*;

23. The case of the *euro*. In 1995, considerable debate was provoked over the plural of *euro*, the monetary unit. Committees within the European Union would have preferred this noun not to take an **s** for its plural. In German, Norwegian and Italian, for example, the **s** is not a mark of the plural. The discussion took place before the admission of other countries such as the Czech Republic and Poland, where the national languages do not admit a plural **s** either. The controversy overflowed into the arena of the French language where, as *Le Bon usage* states (2008, p. 682), common sense prevailed, and the **s** is used in all contexts: *euros*.

10.2 The plural of compound words (see Chapter 9, Section 9.2.3 on the gender of compound words)

Compound words provide a source of perplexity, not just for foreign learners of French, but also for native French speakers. Hesitation abounds, and there seems to be no definitive agreement on a range of issues. What is certain is that compound nouns, once largely confined to special cases, are now burgeoning and are taking on an increasingly functional, and therefore very modern, appearance. This is very similar to the development of Spanish, and less so of Italian. Perhaps the influence of English is being felt here, since English has always been able to combine nouns, the first one performing the role of an adjective. Until the twentieth century, French, Spanish and Italian have been obliged to join two nouns with the insertion of the preposition *de*.

1. Unhyphenated words: some compound words are unhyphenated, but not very many. Terms like *arcboutants, autocars, autoroutes, bonshommes* (but *bonhommes* = R1), *entresols, platebandes, potpourris* and *portemanteaux* simply take an **s** or **x** at the end of the whole word, according to the criteria listed above. In the case of *autobus*, the plural remains the same. These words are very well established in the language. Other terms

such as *gentilshommes, mesdames, mesdemoiselles, messieurs, messeigneurs*
add an **s** within the word and at the end. At the same time, one also sees
arc-boutants, plates-bandes, pots-pourris (see section immediately below):
a perfect illustration of uncertainty in this area;

2. *Hyphenated words*: noun + noun adds an **s** or an **x** to each noun,
    but there is much uncertainty here since the second noun may
    be considered invariable if it does not really contain a plural
    idea, as in *dates-limite* and *facteurs-surprise: bars-tabac, cafés-concert(s),
    cafés-théâtre(s), chauves-souris, appartements-témoin(s), choux-fleurs, bateaux-
    mouches, dates-limite(s), facteurs-surprise(s), gardes-barrière(s), gardes-
    malades, gardes-chasse, hommes-grenouille(s), idées-clef(s)/force(s), nouveau-
    nés, prisons-modèle(s), portraits-robot(s), prix-folie, sauf-conduits, services
    après-vente, terre-pleins, villes-dortoir(s).* In the case of the element *garde*,
    if a person is alluded to, *garde* takes the plural. But if a verb is
    meant, the whole expression remains invariable: *des garde-boue. Idées-
    clef(s)/force(s)* are certainly two compound nouns where hesitation
    abounds, although Grevisse and Goosse offer, for example, only *idées-
    forces. Nouveau* does not take an **x** in *nouveau-nés* since *nouveau* is really
    an adverb = *nouvellement* (see also Chapter 9, Section 9.3.1 for the
    gender of this word).
3. Nouns neither hyphenated nor joined together: this group is ever-
    increasing, and is found notably in the area of commerce. Some trans-
    lations are given since many of these terms have only just recently
    found their way into the language, and would not be listed in any
    dictionary. Note also that the gender of these compound nouns is
    determined by the first noun: *camions poubelle (dustcarts), camping cars,
    chaises anti-fatigue, chargeurs démarreur(s), chariots garagiste, chariots porte-
    tout, coffrets plombier (plumber's tool boxes), escabeaux acier, housses cara-
    vane/fauteuil (covers for caravan/sofa), kits carrossier (kits for body-repair
    specialist, of automobile), marches pieds (small stands to reach up to
    something), pantalons treillis (overalls, dungarees), plate-formes échelle (small
    stands for reaching an object: see marches pieds above), rallonges aspira-
    teur (extension leads for vacuum cleaner), rasoirs homme, sacs cabas (shop-
    ping bags, the idea being that it can be used time and time again),
    stations service (gas/petrol stations), supports TV (TV stands), tuyaux gaz;*
4. Noun + adjective / adjective + noun adds an **s** to both parts, as
    would be expected: *basses-cours, coffres-forts, états-majors, francs-maçons,
    franc-tireurs, sages-femmes, plates-bandes.* In the case of nouns preceded
    by *grand* in the masculine form, the adjective is sometimes invari-
    able in the plural and sometimes not: *grands-mères/grand-mères, grands-
    tantes/grand-tantes* but *grands-pères, grands-oncles* are the normal forms;
5. Verb + noun may or may not change, but, logically, only the noun
    would take an **s** (see also *garde* compounds above): *garde-manger(s), perce-
    neiges(s), presse-papier(s), sèche-linge, serre-joints, vide-greniers.* In certain

cases, the singular form often involves a plural noun, and this is particularly so with the verbs *garder* and *porter*: *garde-malades* (*garde* if the idea is a verb), *garde-meubles*; uses with *porter* + plural noun: *porte-avions, porte-bagages, porte-cigarettes, porte-clés/clefs, porte-parapluies, porte-revues*. The verb *porter*, like *garder*, can involve a singular noun: and here invariability obtains: *porte-bonheur, porte-monnaie, porte-malheur, porte-parole, porte-plume, porte-serviette*. The initial noun (= *door*) of *porte-fenêtre* is not be confused with the verb *porter*: its plural is *portes-fenêtres* and note that *portefeuille(s)* is not hyphenated, and neither is *tirelire(s)*. The use of *vider* is also worthy of note: *vide-grenier* (*car boot sale*) would more easily be seen in the singular, but there is no reason why one should not see *vide-greniers*; *vide-poches* (*map compartment in car*) takes an **s**;

6. Invariable word + noun usually gives a plural **s** to the noun: *haut-parleurs, sous-marins*; but if the noun were uncountable it would remain in the singular (see the list verb + noun below);

7. Following on from above, this next list groups together *a number of compound nouns* of the verb + noun type. Indications are given with respect to the addition of an **s** for the plural. The **s** is used if the compound noun is in the singular and the noun is plural (see *tire-fesses*). If there is no indication, it may be assumed that the noun is invariable (but this is by no means clear-cut), and usually this is because the noun is uncountable. Furthermore, little logic seems to apply to, say, *casse-tête(s)* (*chinois*), where **s** is optional, and *casse-croûte* where, according to de Villers's *MULTI dictionnaire* and *Le petit Robert*, there is no **s** for the plural. Some translations are given here: **accroche**-*cœurs* = *spitkiss curl*; **appuie**-*tête(s)* = *head restraint* (in car); **attrape**-*mouche(s), attrape-nigaud(s)* = *booby trap*; **brise**-*fer/tout, brise-glace(s), brise-lames, brise-mottes, brise-vent*; **casse**-*tête(s), casse-cou(s), casse-pieds, casse-noisettes, casse-croûte*; **chasse**-*mouches, chasse-neige*; **coupe**-*légumes, coupe-cigares, coupe-circuits, coupe-feu, coupe-jambon, coupe-papier*; **couvre**-*chefs, couvre-pied(s), couvre-feu, couvre-lit(s), couvre-plats*; **essuie**-*glace(s), essuie-main(s), essuie-tout, essuie-verre(s)*; **fourre**-*tout* = *holdall, light suitcase, tote bag*; **gobe**-*mouche(s)* = *sucker*; **gratte**-*ciel* = *skyscraper*; **grippe**-*sou(s)* = *greedy person*; **lave**-*vaisselle(s)* = *dish-washer*; **lèche**-*culs* = *ass-licker*; **monte**-*plats* = *dumb waiter*; **ouvre**-*boîte(s), ouvre-huître(s)* = *tin opener, oyster opener*; **passe**-*partout* = *master key*; **pince**-*nez* = *pince-nez* (spectacles held only on the bridge of the nose); **serre**-*tête(s)/livres* = *hairband / book end*; **taille**-*crayon(s)* = *pencil sharpener*; **tire**-*bouchon(s), tire-clou(s), tire-fesses* = *ski-tow*; **trompe**-*l'œil* = *same word in English and used in art*; **trouble**-*fêtes* = *spoil sport*, as in *jouer les trouble-fêtes*;

8. The following list is a small heteroclite bunch of compound nouns that have no formal or systematic grouping. The first compound noun here (*allées et venues*) is naturally always plural: *allées et venues, allers-retours,*

branle-bas, faire-part, laisser-passer (two verbs), *pousse-pousse* (two verbs), *sous-sols, tape-à-l'œil, touche-à-tout, tout-à-l'égout, va-et-vient, qu'en dira-t-on*; but: *remettre à flot*, as opposed to *couler à flots*. Usage varies with *après-midi*: not only is its gender variable (see Chapter 9 on gender), but one also sees *des après-midi* and *des après-midis*. *Prière(s) d'insérer* (review slip used in the publication of books) takes the **s** for a plural;

9. Compound adjectives of color are invariable for both number and gender: *des robes bleu clair, des chemises jaune clair, des pantalons gris foncé, des étoffes rouge foncé, des carreaux vert jaune, des soies vert pomme, des yeux vert d'eau, des chapeaux bleu vif, des chaussettes bleu vif*. Further invariable compounds involving colors or indicating colors are: *arc-en-ciel, bleu ciel/horizon/marin/roi/turquoise/vert, café au lait, gorge de pigeon, gris acier/perle, jaune maïs, noir de jais, rouge tomate, vert amande/olive, vert-de-gris: des écharpes gris perle, des nappes bleu turquoise, une teinte rose fané*. Notice the difference with *tendre*: *des vêtements vert tendre* = soft green clothes, as against *des haricots verts très tendres* = very tender green haricot beans. There are also a great number of nouns which, when used as a color, remain invariable, both in gender and in number, and some of which occur in the list above. All these colors come from the world of nature: *abricot, acajou, agate, ambre, améthyste, ardoise, argent, aubergine, avocat, azur, bistre, bordeaux, brique, bronze, bruyère, cachou, café, canari, cannelle, caramel, carmin, carotte, cassis, chamois, cerise, champagne, chocolat, ciel, citron, clémentine, cognac, coquelicot, corail, crème, crevette, cuivre, ébène, émeraude, épinard, fraise, framboise, grenat, groseille, indigo, ivoire, jade, jonquille, kaki, lavande, lilas, magenta, marengo, marine, marron, mastic, moutarde, nacre, noisette, ocre, olive, or, orange, paille, pastel, pastèque, pêche, pervenche, pétrole, pie, pistache, platine, prune, réséda, rouille, rubis, safran, saphir, saumon, sépia, serin, soufre, souris, tabac, tango, tilleul, tomate, topaze, turquoise, vermillon; des tapis ardoise, des ombrelles jonquille, des cartes orange*, but *des soies orangées* since *orangé* functions adjectivally as a color like *bleu* or *vert*; *des cailloux argent, des chandeliers or*;

10. Numbers: 80 = *quatre-vingt**s*** (with **s**), but 81 = *quatre-vingt-**un***; 200 = *deux cent**s***, 300 = *trois cent**s***, but 201 = *deux cent un*, 301 = *trois cent un*; 2 000 = *deux mill**e*** (never **s**). Note in athletics: **le** *cent mètres*, **le** *deux cents mètres*, **le** *quatre cents mètres*. In the expression *faire les trois huit* (to work on a rota system, i.e., round the clock), the *huit* takes no **s**

10.3 The plural of foreign words (see also Chapter 66 on foreign words for a much fuller list covering numerous countries and languages)

As far as English words adopted by French are concerned, problems occur where English and French plural-forming patterns diverge. However, those who have a reasonable knowledge of English tend to use authentic English plurals; consequently, R2 users would opt for *des boxes/coaches/flashes/matches/sandwiches/smashes* (in tennis)/*sketches/ lobbies/ tories/rugbymen/tennismen* (the last two being false Anglicisms), whereas R1 users would doubtless opt for *des box/coachs/flashs/matchs/sandwichs/smashs*. Where the plural patterns are the same, no difficulty arises: *des scoops/sex-shops*. It should be noted that this distinction is masked in speech for those words ending in −(e)s, as the −(e)s is not pronounced in any case. Even so, there are still anomalous forms of English plurals created in French: *des pin-up* (without s), and both *média* and *médias* occur as plural forms. Of course, the only true Latin word here is *media* (neuter plural), so French follows a false trail with *médias*. Usually, a well-established foreign word, which may well have lost some of its foreign appearance, conforms to the French pattern by simply adding s to form the plural: *des biftecks/boléros/panoramas/référendums*. Some, on the other hand, remain invariable, and this applies especially to words of Latin origin: *des amen/forum/lapsus/veto* (pronounced é but with no written accent), although one says and writes *un agenda/des agendas*. With *addendum* and *erratum* (neuter singular), there is some confusion, or at least failure to recognize the Latin plurals: *addenda* and *errata*. One therefore reads both *addenda* and *addendas*, like *média* and *médias*: *Il y a plusieurs addenda à inclure dans le contrat*; *Un addenda a été ajouté*. As for *erratum*, one rarely sees this singular form, so that one normally comes across *faire un errata / des erratas*.

Italian has no s for the plural forms, but instead uses i or e: *des broccoli/concerti/confetti/graffiti* (also *du graffiti*) */macaroni/ravioli/spaghetti/tagliatelli*. Consequently, any verb with these nouns as subject should be in the plural, at least according to French authorities: *Ces graffiti sont obscènes*; *Les spaghetti sont cuits ?* De Villers, however, pleads for an s in order to conform to a French plural model, although this appears absurd: *Les broccolis/spaghettis/macaronis sont prêts*. These Italian plural forms are nearly always countable in French, although they are not in English: *The spaghetti is ready*. But one says and writes: *du broc(c)oli*. Both *du vermicelle* and *des vermicelles* exist at the same level of discourse, although, of course, the plural *vermicelli* is the Italian form: *J'ai pris un potage avec du vermicelle / des vermicelles*. *Prima donna* remains invariable in the plural in French, although in Italian one would say *prime donne*. Use of a foreign word is the true mark of a well-informed speaker, or is simply an affected way of expressing oneself. A person likes to show that (s)he can handle Italian plurals, and music lovers are often in this situation: *des concertos/concerti*, *des scenarios/scenarii*, *des sopranos/soprani*. (The Italian forms *soprano/soprani* are oddities in themselves, the o and i being marks of Italian masculine forms, as opposed to the feminine a and e).

10.4 The plural of proper names

Generally, proper names are invariable in the plural: *les Dupont, les Morand, les Lanoë; Les Dupont ont acheté deux Buick/Peugeot; Plusieurs Airbus sont retenus sur le tarmac* (English word) *à l'aéroport de Roissy, Charles de Gaulle; les deux*

Angleterre, la protestante et la catholique. With regard to the names of certain famous families, –s is added in the plural (but agreement as to the degree of fame necessary before such an honor is conferred upon proper names is not clear): *les Césars, les Borgias, les Médicis, les Rockefellers, les Bourbons, les Condés, les Stuarts.* Certain geographical names have –s in the plural: *les Abruzzes* (Italy), *les Açores* (in the Atlantic), *les Andes, les Ardennes* (also: *l'Ardenne* in France/Belgium), *les Asturies* (Spain), *les Amériques, les Cornouailles* (in the southwest of England), *les Émirats Arabes Unis, les Guyanes, les Flandres* (also *la Flandre*) (France/Belgium), *les États-Unis, les Canaries, les Indes* (also *l'Inde*), *les Carpates, les Baléares, les Comores, les Antilles, les Pyrénées, les Rocheuses* (Rockies), *les Vosges* (France), *les Territoires Palestiniens, les îles du Pacifique, les Philippines, les Bahamas.*

When an artist's name is applied to his/her paintings, or a film director's to a film, and so on, usage varies, but normally no –s is used: *J'ai vu bon nombre de Monet au Louvre; Jeanne a acheté trois Colette chez le bouquiniste; Deux Buñuel/Almodóvar passent à la télévision ce week-end; La soprano a chanté dans plusieurs Carmen.*

10.5 Singular/plural subjects with singular/plural verbs

According to the strict rules of grammar, subject and verb agree in number, but usage varies considerably, since frequently a singular noun implies a plural idea, just as *police* and *government* for instance do in English: *The government say/says; The police has/have released a statement.* In the following cases, logic requires a plural verb while the grammarian purist would doubtless plead for a singular. What is certain is that the singular verb indicates a high register, and a plural verb points to a standard register (R2) recognized, and used much more easily, by "Monsieur tout le monde."

A further criterion determining the singular or plural of the verb lies in the insistence or otherwise on the singular collective idea or the plurality of objects or persons. The collective singular would decide a singular verb, whereas the plurality of objects or persons would lead to a plural verb. Beyond all this discussion one simple fact stands out: grammarians like to theorize on this topic but, in reality, there is little or no difference between singular and plural verb.

Below is a list of singular nouns followed by a plural noun and the concomitant singular or plural verb; some comments are also added:

Le **tiers/quart** *des élèves est arrivé* (R3) / *sont arrivés* (R2) *trop tard.* If *la moitié* is followed by a singular verb, in a higher register, the past participle should agree here: *La* **moitié** *des élèves est arrivée trop tard* (R3). A problem arises when the noun following *les trois quarts* is feminine. This focuses on the whole problem of agreements: *Les trois quarts des voitures ont été endommagées* or *Les trois quarts des voitures ont été endommagés.* Obviously, there is no problem over a plural agreement with *les trois quarts*, since a plural noun is used. If the noun such as *moitié* or *tiers* is not followed by a plural noun, a singular verb is required. Speaking of her Jewish subjects and their persecution, Isabel the Catholic of Spain says (and this is a translation): *Un tiers se convertira, un tiers partira, un tiers périra*. A further problem of agreement in gender appears with *une/la quarantaine* if the verb agrees with *quarantaine* and not the following noun, and this of course in a higher register: *Une **quarantaine** de touristes est venue ce matin pour visiter la Tour Eiffel*; in a slightly lower register (still R2), no difficulty occurs: *Une quarantaine de touristes sont venus ce matin pour visiter la Tour Eiffel*.

*Les cinq **pour cent** des étudiantes sont Japonaises* but, in a lower, colloquial register one could hear *Le cinq pour cent des étudiantes sont Japonaises*.

Bon nombre *de professeurs ont donné* (R2) / *a donné* (R3) *des cours supplémentaires*.

Un groupe *de jeunes sont accourus* (R2) / *est accouru* (R3) / *ont accouru* / *a accouru* (R3) *vers les blessés*.

Une bonne partie *des bâtiments se sont effondrés* (R2) / *s'est effondrée* (R3). The problem of agreement is highlighted again here since, if the past participle is determined by the plural *bâtiments*, it would take an **s**, but if the past participle depends upon *une bonne partie* it would take an **e**.

Une troupe *de militaires envahit/envahirent la ville*

Cette série *d'oublis aura/auront été catastrophique(s)*.

Une ribambelle *d'enfants a/ont traversé le parc* (*ribambelle* is often used with *enfants*, doubtless because of its origin in *bambins*, from the Italian *bambini*).

Une suite/succession/série *d'événements qui l'a/ont profondément marqué*.

*Toute **une flopée** de gamins, accompagnés de leurs institutrices, est entrée* / *sont entrés chez Macdo*.

Un lot *de tableaux anciens sera proposé* / *seront proposés*.

Une kyrielle *d'informations* / *de demandes nous a/ont innondés*.

If the collective noun is not followed by a noun in the plural, the verb can easily be placed in the plural: **La moitié** / **Le tiers** *sont venu(e)s*. The following noun is understood.

La plupart + plural noun is normally followed by a plural verb, and there is agreement with the following noun: *La plupart des piscines sont fermées le lundi*. *La plupart* is only ever followed by a singular noun, at least in normal discourse, when it is followed by *temps*: *la plupart du temps*. *La plus grande partie*, in conjunction with a singular noun, is used in its place: *La plus grande partie du beurre/fromage est abîmé*.

Usage differs between French and English: sometimes a singular noun in English is conveyed by a plural in French: *les agressions* = aggression; *dans les airs* (R3) = in the air; *les aléas* (hazards); *les algues* = seaweed; *les*

applaudissements = applause; les arènes = arena (as in Les arènes de
Vérone/Béziers/Nîmes); les bagages = baggage/luggage; les buts = goal (the place);
les grandes chaleurs = period(s) of intense heat (The deadliest period of the plague
in Camus's La peste occurs understandably during les grandes chaleurs); les
grands froids = periods(s) of intense cold; les combles = attic (as in Puccini's La
Bohème); à ses côtés = at her/his side; les couverts = cutlery, placings; les crampes =
bouts of cramp; des cris = shouting; les eaux (R3) = water(s); les embruns =
spray (from water); les enchères = auction; les équipements = equipment; les
fiançailles = engagement; les Finances = the Treasury (Department, Ministry of
Finance), les floralies = flower show; les forces = strength; les funérailles =
funeral (see obsèques below); des démangeaisons = itching; les informations =
the (pieces of) information, news (on media); les intempéries = bad weather; les
intérêts = interest (financial); les labours (R3) = ploughed land; les manigances
(shady dealing); les neiges (R3) = snow; les nuisances = (environmental) nuisance;
les obsèques = funeral (see funérailles above); des pluies passagères = (patchy)
rain; les pompes funèbres (undertaker's); les précipitations = rainfall/precipitation;
faire des progrès = to make progress; avoir des remords = to feel remorse; faire
des révisions = to revise, to do revision; les rhumatismes = rheumatism; les sévices
sexuels = sexual abuse; les ténèbres (R3) = darkness; les violences = violence; les
tractations = dealings.

Une agression = a single act of aggression;

Air is perfectly common in the singular. It refers to the air we breathe:
L'air est vicié; le fond de l'air est vif. It is also used in l'armée de l'air, voyager
par air et par mer;

Applaudissements exists in the singular but it is usually figurative. Compare Sous les applaudissements du public, la diva est entrée sur scène /
Des applaudissements ont éclaté and Le livre reçut l'applaudissement de la
critique;

Arènes occurs in the singular but here it is usually figurative. Compare Les
arènes de Vérone (Italy) / d'Arles / de Nîmes and l'arène politique / descendre
dans l'arène (as a defiant gesture, for instance). Arènes occurs in the
plural form for bull fighting: les arènes de Béziers/Dax/Madrid/Mexico;

But in the singular = aim, goal, target (i.e., figurative). Used in the plural
= Pierre est défenseur et Jean est dans les buts (is the goalkeeper);

It goes without saying that chaleur has a normal equivalent (heat); similarly
froid = cold;

Comble is used regularly in the singular = the highest point: le comble du
malheur / de la joie. It is also used as an adjective: une salle comble = a
packed room;

Crampe is also used in the singular: avoir une crampe à la jambe / à l'estomac /
au mollet;

Démangeaisons is almost always used in the plural: avoir des démangeaisons;
ces démangeaisons sont insupportables. The singular exists in the dictionary but is rarely used in common discourse, even as a concept;

Eau also exists and is used more than *eaux* in daily discourse. Compare *Boire de l'eau / tomber à l'eau / une goutte d'eau / de l'eau de mer* and *les eaux de source très pures / prendre les eaux / une ville d'eaux / les eaux territoriales*;

Enchère exists in the singular: *faire une enchère* = to make a (higher) bid;

Équipements corresponds to *facilities* for a group of people, whereas *équipement* in the singular suggests *equipment used for something*, a sport, for example. Compare *les équipements portuaires/collectifs* (here for a town/village) and *l'équipement de chasse/de pêche/de ski/de tennis, l'équipement du gymnase*;

Forces is often used as in *Les forces armées du Canada*, whereas in the singular it refers to the specific strength of someone/something: *la force du boxeur/du vent/d'une entreprise*; *Ils ont employé la force*;

Les informations and *l'information* are clearly distinguished. Although they both mean *information*, which is of course uncountable in English, the plural form means *news*, as on the radio/television, and in this meaning it is often referred to in colloquial style as *les infos*. Thus one listens to *des informations politiques/sportives*, while the singular is used thus: *une information officielle* (*an official piece of information*);

Intérêt has the singular meaning of the English *interest*: *écouter avec intérêt*, as opposed to the plural: *intérêts bancaires* (*bank interest*);

Labour in the singular = *ploughing*;

Neiges is used in such expressions as *les neiges de l'hiver / les neiges éternelles*, while in the singular it occurs in daily discourse: *un bonhomme / une boule / une chute de neige*;

Précipitations is a meteorological term: *On annonce d'importantes précipitations*, while the singular = *haste*: *agir avec précipitation*;

Progrès is very common in the expression already noted above, i.e., *faire des progrès*, and in the singular it is often metaphoric: *le progrès scientifique, croire au progrès*, although it is quite possible to say *les progrès de la science*;

Remords in the singular often refers to the concept: *Je ne crois pas **au** remords*, as opposed to *le remords d'avoir offensé la mère supérieure / son supérieur*;

Révisions is often used in an examination context: *révisions d'histoire / d'anglais*. In the singular it refers to the going through, or checking over, of something like a vehicle or a policy: *la révision de la constitution / d'une doctrine politique / d'un véhicule*;

Ténèbres is only used in the plural: *les ténèbres d'un cachot / de la mort, le prince des ténèbres* (*prince of darkness* = Satan);

Tractations is often used in *tractations politiques*;

Violence also occurs in the singular, as in *La violence est partout, et surtout la nuit*, as opposed to *une flambée de violences urbaines*; *Cette femme a subi des violences*; *Les populations géorgiennes ont été victimes de violences*;

A small list of nouns that are nearly always used in the plural as opposed to their English equivalent in the singular comprises the following, all meaning *gossip*. They are all masculine: *bavardages, cancans, commérages, potins, racontars, ragots*. Of all these nouns, the last suggests more clearly malicious gossip. *Un potin/commérage* could mean a *piece of gossip*. *Bavardage* in the singular means *chattering*, as in *L'élève a été puni pour bavardage*.

Conversely, sometimes a plural in English is conveyed by a singular in French: *le bermuda = Bermuda shorts; la bouche = lips* (sometimes); *du changement = changes; le collant = tights; le dimanche = on Sundays; être dans son droit = to be within one's rights; le générique = credits* (for film, play etc.); *italique = italics; un jean = jeans; le pantalon = pants, trousers; la pince = pincers; le pyjama = pyjamas; rencontrer le regard de quelqu'un = to meet someone's eye; le sécateur = secators; le short = shorts; le slip = (under)pants; la troupe = troops*.

> *Changement: Il y eu du changement à la maison, apporter un changement à un texte, un changement de direction;*
> *Dimanche: Je ne travaille pas le dimanche = I don't work on Sundays;*
> *Italique* does have a plural form (*italiques*), but it is little used. Thus one really only sees: *Tu mets le titre de ce livre en italique;*
> *Jean* is also written *jeans*, and even *blue-jean(s)* but the first form is the most common: *Marie-Noëlle porte un jean/jeans, Elle est en jean/jeans.* Note that the **j** of this word is pronounced **dj**;
> Apart from the plural form (*Tu as des pinces pour serrer un boulon ? | saisir avec des pinces*), *pince* is commonly used in *une pince à linge = clothes peg.* Similarly: *tenailles, cisailles, ciseaux, castagnettes, coulisses, guillemets, halles.* These may be singular or plural. Obviously *castagnettes* would be used much more in the plural: *Elle chante et danse avec des castagnettes | au son des castagnettes; une paire de castagnettes.* But *perdre une castagnette* is perfectly possible. Again, *fermer/ouvrir les guillemets* is a standard expression but there is no reason why one should not say *Tu as omis le guillemet à la fin de la phrase;*
> *Ciseau* is not uncommon in the meaning of *scissors*. It is probably of a lower register in the singular, depending on context and even dialect;
> *Halles* in the plural is particularly well-know in *les Halles de Paris | de Sainte-Claire à Grenoble. Halle* in the singular = *market hall;*
> *Troupe* has the plural form *troupes* and both are commonly used: *une troupe de légionnaires, des troupes de choc/débarquement;*
> Following on from *les droits de l'homme* (*human rights*), the French say *les droits de la femme* (*women's rights*), i.e., *femme* = singular / *women* = plural.

Many apparent plurals in English have a corresponding singular term in French:

la bureautique	*office automation*	l'optique	*optics*
le diabète	*diabetes*	la physique	*physics*
la dialectique	*dialectics*	la polémique	*polemics*
la dynamique	*dynamics*	la politique	*politics*
l'économie	*economics*	la statistique	*statistics*
l'eugénique	*eugenics*	la génétique	*genetics*
la linguistique	*linguistics*	la tactique	*tactics*
la mécanique	*mechanics, engineering*	la robotique	*robotics*

La bureautique does not have a corresponding English plural;

La statistique differs from *les statistiques* in that the first term is a collective idea or a concept/discipline, as in *le Bureau de la statistique* or *la statistique descriptive/mathématique*, while the second term suggests a series, or a number: *Mme la directrice nous propose des statistiques sur les importations*;

The most important exception to this list is *les mathématiques/math(s)* (R1);

To be added to this group is the interchangeability of *moustache/moustaches*: *Le policier a une grosse moustache noire | de grosses moustaches noires*;

Noteworthy also is the didactic word *la maïeutique* (*maieutics*), which educationalists would know. A teaching technique first proposed by Socrates, appropriately son of a midwife, it suggests the drawing out of information from the student rather than offering ready-made information. See also Chapter 9, Section 9.6.1 on the term *maïeuticien*.

In French, certain words have a singular–plural duality, unlike their English equivalents:

la drogue	*drugs* (narcotics)
les drogues	*drugs* (medication)
le/un fruit	*the/a piece of fruit, some fruit*
les/des fruits	*fruit* (different types of)
un pain	*loaf* (of bread)
des pains	*loaves, different types of bread*
du pain	(some) *bread*
un raisin	(type of) *grape*
des raisins	(different types of) *grapes*
du raisin	*grapes*
un grain de raisin	(an individual) *grape*
la recherche	(practice of) *research, searching* (for)
les recherches	(detailed) *research*
une statistique	(single set of) *statistics*
des statistiques	(series of) *statistiques*
un toast	(a slice of) *toast, toast,* as in *porter un toast à quelqu'un*
des toasts	*some toast, some slices of toast*
une musique	*a piece of music*

des musiques	*pieces of music, different types of music*
de la musique	*some music*
la musique	*music* (the concept as well as the activity)

Fruit in French is not preceded by the singular partitive article *du*; this is different from *raisin = some grapes*, where one says *du raisin*;

La recherche is also used in the search for someone or something: *La recherche de l'enfant perdu*; *Jeanne est à la recherche de ses clefs*; *À la recherche du temps perdu* (Proust);

Musique: *Voici une musique qui te plaira*; *Leur fille compose de la musique*; *Mes musiques préférées sont la neuvième symphonie de Beethoven, la cinquième symphonie de Mahler et tous les opéras de Verdi*; *J'adore la musique, surtout celle de Mozart et de Berlioz.*

One or two other nouns have a different meaning in the plural in contrast to the singular: *le devoir = duty > le devoir conjugal*; *les devoirs =* usually homework but also different kinds of obligations; *l'enfer = hell > les enfers = the underworld*; *la police = the police, la police de caractères = font* (in typing) *> les polices = the police forces* (i.e., different ones), *la police des mers et des frontières.*

Compare *devoir* and *devoirs*: *Le devoir des parents est de protéger leurs enfants et le devoir du citoyen est de limiter la pollution* and *Allez, les enfants, faites vos devoirs.* Compare *enfer* and *enfers*: *Le chemin de l'enfer est pavé de bonnes intentions* and Sartre's "*L'enfer, c'est les autres*" in *Huis clos* versus *Orphée aux enfers = Orpheus in the underworld. Police* also has the meaning of *policy*, as in *une police d'assurance.*

10.6 Use of the partitive article before an adjective preceding a plural noun

With most adjectives, *de* is used, but this is tending to be associated with R3 usage: *après de longues années*; *de vieux vêtements*; *J'ai obtenu d'excellentes notes dans toutes les matières*; *Sébastien a obtenu de remarquables notes dans toutes les matières.*

However, in R2, as well as in R1 speech, and even in the written R3 registers, one comes across: *des vieux vêtements*. One would not use *des* when *excellentes* or *remarquables* precedes *notes*, however. Perhaps this is due to the length of these two adjectives, or to a slightly more elevated style.

Des is always used when the adjective and noun form an indissoluble group. This is standard practice: *des jeunes filles/gens*; *des petits pains/pois.*

Part III

11

Verbs and moods of verbs | Les verbes et les modes des verbes

This highly charged passage of figurative language narrates the total domination of a drunken man over a female partner. It remains unclear whether, at the end, an actual murder, or even suicide, occurs. The piece contains both indicative and subjunctive moods (*divorces, choisisses, pardonnes, ensuive*), together with infinitive (*engueuler, accabler, annoncer, salir, riposter, mourir*) and imperative moods (*pars*), and present participles (*gesticulant, caractérisant, sentant, dirigeant*). The passive form is also used: *est assassinée*. A range of tenses is apparent: perfect, pluperfect (*je n'avais pas lu le message*) and future (*composerai, ferai*) as well as auxiliaries like *savoir* and *pouvoir*. The verbal features are highlighted. Some translations are offered. Notice the pervasive use of the present tense, which invests the passage with a vivacity and immediacy the past tense would not necessarily suggest.

Le meurtre psychologique de la Méridionale

La Méridionale [woman from southern France] **est assassinée** à bout portant [at close range] le vendredi 21 octobre 2005 à 18h 30. Le meurtrier fou furieux, dans un état d'ébriété avancé, n'**hésite** pas à l'**engueuler** [bawl at her], à l'**accabler**, à **hurler** de toutes ses forces. Les vapeurs d'alcool **assomment** [overwhelm] la victime qui **voit** la mort s'**annoncer** à petits feux. Son agresseur **tourne** les talons. Il s'**éloigne** une dizaine de mètres plus loin en **se dirigeant** vers sa loge où il **règne** en Grand et Vénérable Maître. Il **prend** le temps de lire un message et **revient** dans une colère noire, en **gesticulant** dans tous les sens. Il **vocifère** des injures, des blasphèmes : « Oh putain ! Je **n'avais pas lu** ton message. Au nom de Dieu ! C'est la raison pour laquelle je ne **composerai** jamais avec toi. Je te **porte** au pinacle ! Haut ! Très haut ! Très très haut ! Mais il y **a** une chose que je ne **ferai** jamais, c'est de **composer** avec toi ! Il faut que tu divorces ! Il faut que tu choisisses ! Tu ne **peux** pas **être** d'un côté et de l'autre ! »

Le Grand Maître **fait** demi-tour puis **revient** quelques minutes plus tard, **peut-être pris** de remords. D'une humeur caustique, il **lance** au visage de la Méridionale qui **a** des traits physiques et une morphologie qui **caractérisent** les filles du midi : « Tu **as** de la chance d'**être** blonde aux yeux bleus ! Je te **pardonne** ! ». Tétanisée [paralyzed], se **sentant** victime d'une injustice accablante et d'une ironie mordante, la Méridionale se **rebiffe** [adopts a rebellious attitude]. Elle ne **sait** comment se **comporter** face à un alcoolique. Pourtant, elle **prend** son courage à deux mains et **rétorque** [retorts] aussitôt avec des palpitations dans la cage thoracique : « Je ne comprends pas que tu me pardonnes. C'est toi qui dois implorer mon pardon ! Il ne faut pas que tu inverses les rôles ! Je ne resterai pas dans le Temple . . . ». À lui de **riposter** du tac au tac [tit for tat] avec une violence inouïe et dans une hystérie incontrôlable: « Eh bien **pars** ! **Pars pars pars pars** maintenant ! **Pars pars pars pars** immédiatement ! **Pars pars pars pars** tout de suite ! » Il **harcèle** sa victime jusqu'à épuisement, sans se **salir** les mains et, surtout, sans aucun témoin. Le débit [outpouring] enflammé du Grand Maître **paralyse** sa victime.

Quelle violence impitoyable ! Quel traumatisme ! Quel choc émotionnel ! Il n'y **a** plus rien à **faire** si ce n'est de **partir** [apart from leaving] ! **Partir**, c'est **mourir** un peu ! Les brimades [bullying], les engueulades [violent shouting] et les mots blessants **ont fait** leur chemin jusqu'à ce que mort s'**ensuive** ! Que **reproche** le harceleur à sa victime ? Quel **a été** l'élément déclencheur de ce meurtre psychologique ? Qui **sont** les véritables complices de ce meurtre ? S'**agit**-il d'un meurtre avec préméditation ? Quel **était** le mobile du crime ? Que s'**est**-il véritablement **passé** ? À qui **profite** le crime ? Au cœur de cette triste et sombre histoire, trois éléments fondamentaux **reposent** sur la question du territoire occupé, de la domination despotique et du grand pouvoir. À cette ivresse du pouvoir se **rajoute** celle de l'alcool au pouvoir destructeur et non salvateur.

It seems helpful to offer a general and basic statement about verbs as a preface to individual characteristics which will be analyzed in much greater detail in the following chapters where, inevitably, there will be some very slight overlap.

The verb is the word par excellence which expresses judgments; for example, it expresses changes (*La plante pousse/fleurit/dépérit/meurt*); it expresses movement (*La fillette marche/court/nage*) and how we react with the phenomena of the external world (*Nous lisons/voyons/craignons/sourions*). The verb is the class of word that indicates the person and number of the subject, and the tense and mood of the clause.

Verbs are first presented in dictionaries as infinitives. Infinitives in French end in −**er**, −**re**, −**ir** and −**oir**. We call these first, second, third and fourth conjugation respectively. The verbs that do not fit easily into a specific conjugation are called irregular verbs.

Every verb has a root (technically called a lexeme), so that, when we remove the endings −**er**, −**re**, −**ir** and −**oir**, what is left usually imparts a meaning. What accompanies this root is a complex of indicators of person, tense and mood. The endings, *terminaisons*, or *désinences* as they are technically also known in French, are as follows. If we take the verb *regarder* we may split it in this way:

regard>					*er*
root or					conjugation
lexeme					

regard>	*e*	*regard>*	*es*	*regard>*	*e*
root	ending or	root	ending	root	ending
	morpheme		(present		(present
	of tense and		tense and		tense and
	person		second-		third-
	(present		person		person
	tense and		singular)		singular)
	first-person				
	singular)				

11.1 Conjugation (a full conjugation list of regular and irregular verbs appears at the end of this volume)

If we add to the root or lexeme of a verb the endings which express the different persons, number, tense and mood, we arrive at the conjugation. Generally speaking, there exist four persons in the singular (*je/tu/il/elle*). There are four plural forms (*nous/vous/ils/elles*). The plural form *vous* is also used instead of the singular *tu* form when addressing an unknown person or a person requiring an emotional or respectful distance.

Briefly, the verb expresses an action or thought completed by the subject. It also indicates the existence or state of the subject. It links the subject to its attribute, adjective or adjectival phrase (as with *être, paraître*).

11.2 Mood of the verb

Conjugations of verbs are divided into four moods: indicative, subjunctive, imperative and infinitive. The indicative mood is the mood of reality, that which is certain to have happened or will happen. The subjunctive mood expresses wish, possibility, probability, uncertainty, doubt – in short a hypothesis. The imperative is the mood of recommendation, command and request. The infinitive mood is impersonal and corresponds to the English *to* + verb. Below are the details of the four moods, the first two of which are listed in their various tenses.

11.2.1 Indicative Mood

1. Present: refers to the moment when the action takes place, or to the period when someone is speaking: *J'***envoie** *un texto* (*text message*); *Il* **fait** *du soleil ce matin; Elle* **est** *en vacances en ce moment.*

2. Perfect: formed by the auxiliary verbs *avoir* or *être* and a past participle: *J'ai vu* (*I have seen*) *la pièce*; *Sabrina a parlé* (*has spoken/spoke*) *avec son amie; Sébastien est rentré.*

3. Past historic / preterit: the past historic refers to an event that took place, often a long time ago (*passé lointain*), and at a precise point in time. The event is completely finished and has no repercussion on the present moment, whereas the perfect tense (*passé composé*) refers to happenings that encroach on the present moment. It is used almost exclusively in writing, for instance in novels and historical documents: *C'est à l'automne qu'il vint nous rendre visite; Madeleine de Verchères se battit courageusement contre les Iroquois.*

4. Imperfect: indicates a series of events or actions with no real suggestion of beginning or end. Used in narrations and descriptions. It expresses a habitual process: *Elle se promenait dans le bois; J'adorais les films avec Charlot* (*Charlie Chaplin*); *Sabrina travaillait entre 14h et 21h.*

5. Future: indicates a future event or action, although it has to compete increasingly with the present: *J'irai* (*I'll go*) *la semaine prochaine* > *J'y vais la semaine prochaine.*

6. Conditional: corresponds to the English idea of *would*: *J'aimerais revenir un jour* (*I would like to come back one day*).

7. Past anterior: formed by the past historic of *avoir* or *être* and a past participle. Little used except in narratives of novels and literary journalism: *Dès que Céline eut remis son rapport, elle se sentit en vacances* (*As soon as Céline had handed in her report, she felt as though she were on vacation*); *Aussitôt qu'Aurélie fut rentrée, nous sortîmes* (*As soon as Aurélie had come home we went out*).

8. Pluperfect: formed with the imperfect of *avoir* or *être* and a past participle. Translates the same idea as the past anterior but used much more in common discourse, spoken and written. Indicates that an event has already taken place when another occurs: *Je leur ai dit que je l'avais déjà écrit* (*I told them that I had already written it*); *Quand Adéline s'était couchée, nous avons joué aux cartes* (*When Adéline had gone to bed, we played cards*).

9. Future perfect: expresses a future action preceding another yet to come. Formed with the future of *avoir* or *être* and a past participle: *Quand tu reviendras, on aura déjà mangé* (*When you come back, we'll already have eaten*); *Après que Marcel sera rentré, on sortira* (*After Marcel has come back, we'll go out*).

10. Conditional perfect: expresses a future action in relation to a past action considered as the point of departure. Formed with the conditional of *avoir* or *être* and a past participle: *Le garage nous a informés qu'ils auraient terminé[1] la réparation lundi prochain* (*The garage informed*

---

[1] Some purists would advocate *auront terminé* here, i.e., future perfect.

us that they would have completed the repair next Monday); *Ma fille m'avait dit qu'elle **serait revenue** avant mon départ* (My daughter told me she would have come back before my departure).

11.2.2 Subjunctive mood

The subjunctive mood expresses wishes, probability, supposition, hypothesis and doubt, and is often linked to feelings. It is particularly, but not exclusively, used in subordinate clauses. It is slowly disappearing, and some less linguistically aware French speakers hardly use it at all

1. Present Subjunctive: denotes doubt, often with regard to the future: *Je ne crois pas que Cédric **vienne*** (I don't believe Cédric will come); *Daniel doute que Diane **ait** raison* (Daniel doubts Diane is right).
2. Imperfect subjunctive: as with the present subjunctive, its principal, but not exclusive, function is to denote doubt. Only the third-person singular has survived in any functional way, and even here it is reduced to a written form. The imperfect subjunctive is unquestionably an R3 phenomenon these days, although in the distant past, say the nineteenth century, most of its forms had some currency, and one would find it easily in literature of past eras. Interestingly enough, and in stark contrast, the imperfect subjunctive persists in vigorous style in Italian and Spanish. That some commentators should say that the imperfect subjunctive has disappeared in French because it is too complex or its forms too awkward to manage is belied by its permanency in these other Romance languages. In any case, it is replaced by the "easier" present subjunctive: *Personne ne croyait qu'Irène **fût** Russe* (No one believed that Irène was Russian); *Sophie aurait aimé que son ami **vînt*** (Sophie would have liked her friend to come).
3. Perfect subjunctive: as with the present subjunctive, its principal, but by no means unique, function is to express doubt. It is made up of the present subjunctive of *avoir* or *être* and a past participle: *Je doute que la neige **ait fondu*** (I doubt that the snow has melted); *La direction a déploré que les élèves **soient arrivés** en retard pour l'examen* (The head teacher regretted that the pupils/students arrived late for the exam).
4. Pluperfect subjunctive: as with the imperfect subjunctive, little remains of the pluperfect subjunctive. It is made up of the imperfect subjunctive of *avoir* or *être* and the past participle: *L'héroïne craignait que son amant ne **fût disparu*** (The heroine feared lest her lover had disappeared); *Axelle fut surprise que l'on ne l'**eût** pas **informée** personnellement* (Axelle was surprised that she had not been informed personally).

11.2.3 Imperative mood

The imperative expresses an order (positive or negative), advice, invitation, wish or desire. It has three forms, one corresponding to *tu*, the second corresponding to *vous*, and the third corresponding to *nous*. As in English, it is used without a subject. In the present imperative, the forms are: **Viens** voir cette peinture (*Come and see this painting*); **Parlez** à vos parents (*Speak to your parents*); **Reposez-vous** un peu (*Take a rest for a while*); **Nageons plus tard** (*Let's swim later*).

There is also such a construction as the perfect imperative, but it is rarely used: *Aie terminé le travail avant que je ne rentre*.

11.2.4 The infinitive

The infinitive mood expresses an idea of action or state without reference to a person or number. It is an impersonal mood. It is used both as a verb and as a noun, but almost entirely as the former: *Louise voudrait **partir** demain* (*Louise would like to go tomorrow*); *Le **déjeuner**, le **devoir** et le **rire** sont des exemples de verbes utilisés comme noms* (***Déjeuner, devoir** and **rire** are examples of verbs used as nouns*).

12

Infinitive, perfect infinitive / L'infinitif, l'infinitif passé

The infinitive is the form of the verb not inflected for grammatical categories such as person, tense and mood, and is not used with an obvious subject. In English, the infinitive nearly always consists of the word *to* followed by the verb: *to go, to run*. This construction in English is certainly unique in European languages. In French, as in the other Romance languages and beyond, the infinitive has no equivalent for the word *to*, as in *to look at*: *regarder* (in Spanish: *mirar*, in Italian: *guardare*). The infinitive of the verb is the form found at the beginning of the entry in dictionaries.

12.1 Cases where the subject of the infinitive is omitted:

1. in exclamatory, interrogative statements and maxims: *Où aller?*; *Que faire?*; *Me parler ainsi? Me reprocher ma faiblesse? Abandonner la partie? Jamais!*; *Pourquoi l'avoir avoué?*; *ménager la chèvre et le chou* (to sit on the fence); *prêcher un converti* (to preach to the converted);
2. when the subject of the infinitive and that of the main verb are identical: *Éléonore va nous rendre visite*; *Laurent est parti sans nous avertir*; *Je veux lui parler*;
3. when the infinitive is implicitly represented by a preceding possessive adjective: *Je n'oublie pas sa promesse de nous écrire*; *Sophie lui a rappelé son engagement à payer le voyage*;
4. when the infinitive has a general or indeterminate application: *C'est facile à dire*; *Il n'y a pas de quoi fouetter un chat* (It's no big deal); *Il est inutile de se fâcher*; *Prêt à porter*;
5. when certain verbs are used declaratively, an infinitive often follows, and particularly the perfect infinitive. The main verbs here are: *affirmer, annoncer, assurer, avouer, déclarer, nier*: *Les deux étudiants **affirment vouloir** assister à la cérémonie*; *Le gouvernement **annonce avoir pris** la bonne décision*; *La journaliste **assure avoir assisté** aux événements*; *Annick **avoue s'être trompée***; *L'étudiante **déclare avoir été** victime d'une agression*; *La femme **nie avoir abandonné** son enfant*. This type of construction is of a higher register (R3/2) than the subordinate clause introduced by *que*, which is a standard R2 expression: *Les deux parents **affirment qu'ils veulent***

assister à la cérémonie; *Le gouvernement* **a annoncé qu'il avait pris** *la bonne décision*; *L'étudiante* **déclare qu'elle avait été** *victime d'une agression*.

Numerous other verbs are followed by an infinitive, sometimes with a preposition: *aimer, apprendre, désirer, ignorer, promettre, renoncer, savoir, souffrir, vouloir*: *Lucile* **aime jouer** *de la guitare*; *Stéphanie* **a appris à nager**; *Émilie* **ignorait avoir commis** *une infraction*; *Philippe* **promet de venir** *demain*; *Antoine* **renonce à chercher** *son vélo*; *Élisabeth* **souffre** *toujours* **d'avoir commis** *l'erreur*. In the case of *ignorer*, the register is higher with the following (perfect) infinitive than with the subordinate clause introduced by *que*: *Émilie* **ignorait qu'elle avait commis** *une infraction*. Usage with *savoir* requires special attention. One may say, but in a higher register and with greater elegance: *Je* **savais** *le* **trouver** *là*, as opposed to *Je* **savais que je** *le* **trouverais** *là*. But when *savoir* suggests a capacity, the infinitive is needed: *Aurélien* **sait lire/nager**.

There is another small but very common group of verbs related to statements of thoughts, beliefs and recognition where a following infinitive suggests a higher register than the subordinate clause introduced by *que*: *croire, dire, penser, prétendre, reconnaître* (see Chapter 18 for a full development of this feature):

R2	R3/2
Je **croyais que je l'avais vue.**	*Je* **croyais l'avoir vue.**
Sabrina **a dit qu'elle n'avait pas composé** *le poème.*	*Sabrina* **a dit ne pas avoir composé** *le poème* / **n'avoir pas composé** *le poème.*
Océane **pensait qu'elle avait** *raison.*	*Océane* **pensait avoir** *raison.*
Jean **prétend** *(claims)* **qu'il n'est pas sorti** *ce matin.*	*Jean* **prétend ne pas être sorti** *ce matin* / **n'être pas sorti** *ce matin.*
Reconnaissez-vous que vous avez participé *au vol ?*	**Reconnaissez-vous avoir participé** *au vol ?*

12.2 Cases where the subject of the infinitive corresponds to the complement of the main verb

With numerous verbs, notably those related to perception, the subject of the infinitive may also be followed by a subordinate clause. Where an infinitive is involved, the register is higher than with a subordinate *qui* clause:

R2	R3/2
J'ai vu **ces jeunes filles qui s'approchaient** *de la ferme.*	*J'ai vu* **ces jeunes filles s'approcher** *de la ferme.*
Je **les ai entendues qui se plaignaient.**	*Je* **les ai entendues se plaindre.**

Where *will* or request are concerned, other possibilities occur. Thus the sentence *Le proviseur* **a ordonné aux élèves de quitter** le *collège* may also be expressed as *Le proviseur* **a ordonné que les élèves quittent** le *collège*. Here, a subjunctive is used. Another example of the same type: *Ma mère* **a demandé au directeur de la recevoir** versus *Ma mère* **a demandé au directeur qu'il la reçoive**.

12.3 Place of the pronoun before the infinitive (see also Chapters 45 and 46 on pronouns and Chapter 63 on word order)

The personal, reflexive or other pronoun (= *y*/*en*) is placed before the infinitive: *Je peux* **le faire/lui parler/m'en occuper/y penser**. This order is standard in both spoken and written language. However, in former times, and even into the twentieth century, the pronoun was frequently placed before the auxiliary verb, a construction found notably with such verbs as *aller*, *devoir*, *falloir*, *pouvoir*, *savoir*, *venir* and *vouloir*; less often with *croire*, *oser*, *penser*; and rarely with *compter*, *désirer*, *faillir*, *paraître*.

Hanse and Blampain (2005, p. 305) quote authors of the twentieth century: "Il *le faut croire*" (Colette), "Pour *s'aller coucher* sans attendre" (Vercors), "Ce qu'il désirait *s'allait donc se réaliser*" (Duhamel; the double reflexive here seems unusual). One could add: "J'en ai reçu des satisfactions si sensibles que *je ne te les pourrai pas dire* de bouche" (Pascal 1950, p. 84); "Ma figure était si étrange que ma mère ne *se pouvait empêcher* de rire et de s'écrier . . . " (Chateaubriand 1951, vol I, p. 440); "L'éloquence de Baraglioul *n'y pourrait rien changer*" (Gide 1961, p. 7). Such a construction, extremely common in the French of the Middle Ages, finds its echo in contemporary Italian and Spanish where the pronoun precedes the auxiliary verb as easily as it precedes the infinitive: *Lo voglio fare* (Italian) and *Lo puedo hacer* (Spanish), both meaning *I can do it*, instead of *Voglio farlo* / *Puedo hacerlo*.

The pronoun *y* cannot be separated from *avoir* in the impersonal *y avoir*: *Il* **doit y avoir** là *une erreur*. Neither can *y* be joined to *lui*: although one may say with *falloir Il* **me fallait y pénétrer** / *Il* **m'y fallait pénétrer**, one can only say *Il* **lui fallait y pénétrer**.

It happens that there is a choice of word order before the infinitive when a pronoun combines with *tout* and *rien*, and certain monosyllabic adverbs like *bien*, *mal*, *trop*, *mieux*, *tant*: *Il fallait alors* **lui tout dire** instead of *Il fallait alors* **tout lui dire**, although, admittedly, the latter construction is much more common. Likewise, with *rien* + *en* or *y*: *sans songer* **à rien en retirer** / **à en rien retirer**; *pour* **n'y rien voir** / **ne rien y voir**.

Adverbs come between the pronoun and the infinitive more frequently: *sans* **la trop serrer** (Colette), *afin de* **le mieux voir** (also Colette). However, the adverb precedes the pronoun much more in daily discourse: *sans* **trop y insister**, *pour* **bien/mieux le lire**.

When an infinitive depends upon another infinitive, a surprising number of combinations of word order with pronouns are available, witness *mieux*: *pour **mieux le lui faire avouer** | pour **le lui mieux faire avouer** | pour **le lui faire mieux avouer** | pour **le lui faire avouer mieux*** and *bien*: *pour **bien le lui entendre dire** | pour **le lui bien entendre dire***.

When a reflexive pronoun occurs, there seems to be less flexibility, in that the reflexive is usually placed before the verb: *pour **mieux se porter**, afin de **bien se raser**, pour éviter de **mal se comporter***.

Two possibilities occur with respect to word order and the reflexive verb as an infinitive, which are not without their register differences: *J'entends les enfants **se battre** (R2) | J'entends **se battre** les enfants (R3/2); J'ai vu les enfants **se laver** (R2) | J'ai vu **se laver** les enfants (R3/2)*. If the object of the complement is a pronoun, only one order is permissible: *Je les vois s'agiter; Je les entends **se** battre*.

With verbs such as *regarder*, *entendre* and *laisser*, a variety of uses exists, and this can involve the preposition *par*: *Le père **regarde dormir** les enfants* (*The father watches the children sleeping*); *Je **le laisse faire** ce qu'il veut* (*I let him do what he wants*). An alternative here with the pronoun as indirect object is possible, but this construction is less common: *Je **lui laisse faire** ce qu'il veut*. However, if the object is *chacun* or a noun, it is likely that it will be indirect: *Je **laisse faire à chacun*** (or *par chacun*) *ce qu'il veut faire*; *Je **laisse faire à Adrienne** ce qu'elle veut faire*. *Par* may be used as an alternative in the following construction: *J'ai **entendu les enfants pousser des cris** | J'ai **entendu pousser des cris par les enfants***.

Entendre is used with no direct object where one would use it in English: *Elle **entendait marcher** dans le couloir* (*She heard someone walking in the corridor*). One could resort to a subordinate *quelqu'un qui* clause here: *Elle **entendait quelqu'un qui marchait** dans le couloir*. The first of these two sentences is more elegant and of a higher register.

Given the frequency of *faire changer de*, it is worthwhile giving it detailed consideration. The constructions *faire changer d'avis | d'opinion | de place | de visage | d'humeur | de conduite | de vêtements* offer two possibilities over a direct and indirect object. Generally speaking, *faire changer de place* involves a direct object; at the same time, there is a question of word order, and here register comes into play. In the following example, it is likely that only one possibility exists: *Rémi **a changé un tableau de place** (Rémi put the painting in another place)*. But the next two examples illustrate a difference in register: *Je ne **puis changer cet enfant de place** tous les jours* (R3) (*I can't put this child in a different place every day* – remark by a teacher); *Je ne **peux changer de place cet enfant** tous les jours* (R2). Consider the above construction with the additional *faire*: *Je ne **puis faire changer cet enfant de place** tous les jours* (R3) (*I can't have this child changing places every day*); *Je ne **peux faire changer de place cet enfant** tous les jours* (R2). With a pronoun one usually hears a direct object: *Je ne **peux le faire changer de place***. But the indirect use of *le>lui* is not to be entirely excluded: *Je **l'ai fait changer d'avis*** (R2) is more common than *Je **lui ai fait changer d'avis***. With a noun, the direct object is meeting increasing competition from the indirect object, but this can depend on the place of the dative in the sentence. One says very easily: *Elle **a fait changer d'avis à son interlocutrice** (She caused the person she was speaking to to change her mind)*. The direct object would be surprising here but it would not be surprising in the following: *Elle **a fait changer son interlocutrice d'avis***.

Consider the three variations in the following:

1. *Elle **a fait changer son interlocutrice d'opinion** sur cette question.*
2. *Elle **a fait changer d'opinion son interlocutrice** sur les décisions à prendre.*
3. *Elle **a fait changer d'opinion à son interlocutrice** sur cette question.*

Similarly: *La mère **a fait changer de vêtements à l'enfant*** and *La mère **a fait changer à l'enfant les vêtements** qu'il portait*. In the first case, *enfant* could not precede *vêtements*, for the sake of balance, while in the second case an extra clause is needed for *enfant* to precede *vêtements* (*qu'il portait*), again for the sake of balance.

The verb *entendre* followed by the infinitives of *dire* and similar verbs such as *affirmer, annoncer, déclarer, expliquer, proposer, raconter* and *suggérer* requires an indirect object when the following infinitive governs a direct object. *Dire* and other verbs cannot take two direct objects here. However, this particular construction is no longer very current: *J'**ai entendu dire à mon frère** qu'il ne pouvait pas venir (I heard my brother say that he couldn't come); Nous **avons entendu annoncer au ministre que** la décision avait déjà été prise (We heard the minister announce that the decision had already been taken); Elle **a entendu proposer au comité** qu'il se réunisse plus régulièrement (She heard the committee propose that they should meet more regularly)*. In all these cases, one would now read and hear in R2 and even R3 discourse: *J'ai entendu mon frère dire que . . . | Nous avons entendu le ministre annoncer que . . . | Elle a entendu le comité annoncer que . . .*

Where two personal pronouns are involved, one of which could be a reflexive, there are several considerations.

If one pronoun is the subject of the infinitive and the second is its complement, there is no difficulty if each pronoun is placed before the appropriate verb, and this construction corresponds to the English construction: *On **le voit nous suivre** avec obstination (We see him follow us with determination); Je **le laisse se fâcher** (I let him get angry); Irène **m'envoie t'avertir** (Irène has sent me to warn you); Je **l'ai vue l'écrire** (I saw her write it)*.

Me, te, se, nous, vous precede *le, la, les*, while these last three come before *lui* and *leur* in the following types of sentences: *On **vous le voit** tenter (We/They see you attempt it); Je **te les fais** avertir (I have you warn them); Ils **me l'ont entendu** dire (They heard me say it); Je **le leur ai entendu** dire (I heard them say it); Ils **se les ont fait** envoyer (They had them sent to themselves);*

On les y a fait envoyer (*We/They have them sent there*); *Je la lui ai entendu chanter* (*I heard her sing it*); *Je le leur ai vu faire* (*I saw them do it*). But it is perfectly possible to say *On vous voit le tenter*; *Je te fais les avertir*, *Ils m'ont entendu le dire*; *Je les ai entendus le dire*; *Je l'ai entendue la chanter*; *Je les ai vus le faire*. Furthermore, for example, *On vous voit le tenter* is more common than *On vous le voit tenter*, *Je l'ai entendue la chanter* is much more common than *Je la lui ai entendu chanter*, and *Je les ai vus le faire* is much more common than *Je le leur ai vu faire*, partly in this last case because the repetitive element l can be difficult to say.

In the following combination of *vous* with *le, la, les*, however, the construction changes: *Je l'ai entendue vous parler* (*I heard her speak to you*). Here, the subject of *parler* is *la/l'*, and *vous* could not precede *entendue*.

Note the idiomatic use of *envoyer* + infinitive: *Envoie chercher le médecin* (*Send for | Go and get the physician*); *Elle l'a envoyée promener* (*She sent her off/packing*). If the subject of *promener* were a noun, it would follow the infinitive: *Elle a envoyé promener son frère, tellement il l'embêtait* (*She sent her brother packing, he was annoying her so much*).

The infinitive is regularly used on commercial labels and to indicate method of use, since it has a less authoritarian resonance: *Ne pas **exposer** à l'humidité*; *À **consommer** avant juin 2015*; ***Faire chauffer** à petit feu*; ***Remuer** la solution*; *Bien **nettoyer** la surface à peindre avant de ...*; ***Tenir** hors de portée des enfants*.

The infinitive is used to convey official orders: ***S'adresser** à la direction*; ***Rayer** la mention inutile* (*Cross out the statements that are not applicable*); *Ne pas **se pencher** au dehors* (in a train compartment).

Following on from the above, all normal instructions provided by a computer are in the infinitive: *atteindre* (*go to*), *copier coller* (*copy and paste*), *couper coller* (*cut and paste*), *envoyer* (*send*), *justifier*, *rechercher* (*find*), *remplacer* (*replace*), *répéter* (*repeat*), *sauvegarder* (*save*; the Anglicism *sauver* is common in Quebec but is frowned upon), *télécharger* (*download*; the monstrous Anglicism *downloader* is not uncommon in Quebec).

The infinitive can be the subject of a sentence: ***Lire** des romans me plaît énormément* (instead of *La lecture de romans est...*); ***Nager** est un des grands plaisirs de ma vie* (instead of *La natation est un des...*); ***Composer** des vers, **résoudre** des problèmes algébriques était pour moi un jeu* (instead of *La composition de vers, la solution de problèmes était...*).

It can also be the attribute of the subject: *Partir, c'est **mourir** un peu*; *Courir le cent mètres en neuf secondes, c'est **courir** comme une gazelle*; *Tromper, c'est **mentir***; *Voir, c'est **croire***; *Se tenir en équilibre sur une jambe n'est pas facile*.

In a narrative of R3 style an infinitive may be introduced by the preposition *de*. Such a construction invests the sentence with a vivacious quality. The sentence always begins with *Et*: *Et chacun | les invités **d'applaudir*** (*And each one | the guests applauded*); *Et elle **de dire** qu'elle avait raison* (*And she said* *she was right)*; *Et sa soeur* **de partir** *tout de suite* (*And her sister left immediately*). Hanse and Blampain (2005, p. 309) refer disapprovingly to the Quebec style characteristic of journalists where the noun follows the infinitive: *Et,* **d'ajouter le ministre** *que*...

The infinitive can easily replace the gerund or a noun in the following case: *Lire Camus aujourd'hui* (*Reading Camus today*); *Grandir avec Camus* (*Growing up with Camus*) – both these examples are taken from titles of articles in *Le magazine littéraire*, January/February 2010).

The infinitive also suggests the idea of "how to," as in educational books: *Écrire avec logique et clarté* (*How to write logically and clearly*); *Développer une idée* (*How to develop an idea*); *Trouver le mot juste* (*How to find the right word*); *Prendre la parole* (*How to speak in public*). Also, among others: *bâtir un paragraphe, choisir les prépositions adéquates, maîtriser la ponctuation, articuler/élaborer/nuancer un texte argumenté.*

13

Present tense / Le présent

The three main groups of verbs are those ending in **-er** (*chanter*), **-re** (*vendre*) and **-ir** (*finir*), although there is a smaller group, somewhat irregular, which brings together those ending in **-evoir** (*recevoir*). The only group that is truly regular is identified as that with the **-er** ending, while there are some verbs ending in **-re**, like *prendre*, some ending in **-ir**, like *venir*, and some ending in **-oir**, like *vouloir* which do not correspond to the **-re/-ir/-oir** pattern. Prefixes of *prendre*, *venir* and **-evoir** do admittedly give rise to a substantial number of similar verbs: *prendre > apprendre, comprendre, surprendre; venir > advenir, souvenir, subvenir; recevoir > décevoir* (to disappoint), *percevoir*.

Here is the present tense of the main conjugations followed by comments:

Present tense of *chanter*

je chante	I sing / am singing
tu chantes	you sing / are singing
il/elle chante	he/she/it sings / is singing
nous chantons	we sing / are singing
vous chantez	you sing / are singing
ils/elles chantent	they sing / are singing

Present tense of *vendre*

je vends	I sell / am selling
tu vends	you sell / are selling
il/elle vend	he/she/it sells / is selling
nous vendons	we sell / are selling
vous vendez	you sell / are selling
ils/elles vendent	they sell / are selling

Present tense of *finir*

je finis	I finish / am finishing
tu finis	you finish / are finishing
il/elle finit	he/she/it finishes / are finishing
nous finissons	we finish / are finishing
vous finissez	you finish / are finishing
ils/elles finissent	they finish / are finishing

Present tense of *recevoir*

je re**çois**	*I receive / am receiving*
tu re**çois**	*you receive / are receiving*
il/elle re**çoit**	*he/she/it receives / is receiving*
nous re**cevons**	*we receive / are receiving*
vous re**cevez**	*you receive / are receiving*
ils/elles re**çoivent**	*they receive / are receiving*

13.1 Verb groups

Verbs ending in **–er** constitute over 90 percent of all French verbs and run into thousands. In this sense, it could be legitimately argued that the only true regular group of verbs is the **–er** type. Furthermore, nearly all neologisms seem to be created precisely within this group, which is certainly very versatile and capable of absorbing countless new words, for example *oscariser* (*to award an Oscar*). A selection of neologisms (creations, borrowings or imitations – **calques** in French – of the past sixty or seventy years) listed below are frequently related, but by no means always, to the constantly accelerating pace of technological change: *automatiser, bureautiser, crapahuter* (*to march* over a long period / *to yomp*, of a soldier), *cybernétiser, décélérer, défolier, doper, esthétiser, faxer, flipper* (to *freak out*, to be depressed), *formater, impacter, informatiser, lifter* (*to give a facelift to*), *lock-outer, lyncher* (*to lynch* and more commonly, *to beat up*), *marginaliser, plastiquer, sécuriser, shooter, squatter, standardiser, stresser, télécopier, téléviser, tester, traumatiser, urger, verbaliser, viabiliser* (*to provide* [an area/house] *with all utilities*). Some neologisms are now, quite understandably, disappearing, like *télégraphier*, overtaken by e-mails and texting, and here one may speculate, in the year 2011, that the English *to text* (*someone*) will replace *envoyer un texto à* with *texter* (*quelqu'un*).

There are about a hundred verbs with the **–re** ending, but many of them are irregular, and they have not generated verbs with similar endings, with the result that their possibilities of alignment with other verbs may be considered defunct. There are about thirty verbs of the *vendre* type: *attendre, confondre, défendre, dépendre, descendre, distendre, entendre, épandre, étendre, fendre, fondre, mordre, pendre, perdre, pondre, prétendre, rendre, répandre, répondre, tendre, tondre, tordre*. Unusually, *rompre* (with *corrompre* and *interrompre*) diverges only marginally from this paradigm with an extra **t** in the third-person singular: *rompt*.

As with the **–re** ending type, verbs ending in **–ir**, which number about 300, are not able to engender verbs of identical conjugation, and may again be viewed as static and unable to attract contemporary additions. *Alunir* (*to land on the moon*), *atterrir* and *amerrir* seem to be the only new **–ir** verbs to have survived in any active form. Other verbs with **–ir** endings like *cueillir* and *dormir* form different subgroups. There follows a substantial list of verbs of the **-ir** type like *finir*: *abolir, aboutir, abrutir, accomplir, s'accroupir, adoucir, affaiblir, affermir, affranchir, agir, agrandir, alourdir, alunir, amerrir, aplanir, aplatir, appauvrir, applaudir, approfondir, arrondir, assainir, assombrir, s'assoupir, s'assourdir, attendrir, atterrir, avertir, bâtir, blanchir, blêmir, bleuir, (re)bondir, brandir, brunir, chérir, choisir, compatir, convertir, définir, dégourdir, démolir, démunir, désobéir, divertir, durcir, éblouir, éclaircir, élargir, embellir, endurcir, enfouir, engloutir, enlaidir, enrichir, envahir, épaissir, épanouir, établir, étourdir, s'évanouir, faiblir, finir, fleurir, fournir, fraîchir, frémir, garantir, gémir, grandir, grossir, guérir, intervertir, jaillir, jaunir, maigrir, mincir, moisir, munir, mûrir, noircir, nourrir, obéir, pâlir, périr, pourrir, punir, raccourcir, rafraîchir, raidir, rajeunir, ralentir, réagir, réfléchir, refroidir, réjouir, remplir, resplendir, rétablir, retentir, rétrécir, réunir, réussir, rosir, rougir, saisir, salir, subir, surgir, trahir, unir, verdir, vernir, vieillir, vomir.*

As for verbs with the **-evoir** ending, their forms vary greatly, and some grammarians suggest excluding them from any formal conjugation. Although *recevoir* conjugates like *percevoir, apercevoir* and *décevoir*, for instance, its forms are entirely incompatible with *vouloir, voir* and *pouvoir*.

13.2 Uses of the present tense

A most important observation to be made immediately with respect to French verbs, in certain tenses, like the present and imperfect, is that they no longer benefit from a progressive tense or gerund as in English (*I am writing/walking/reading*), Spanish (*Estoy escribiendo/caminando/leyendo*) or Italian (*Sto scrivendo/camminando/leggendo*). This is considered a serious deficiency by many linguists, including the present authors. At the same time, the irregular verb *aller* in an R3, literary context is sometimes used to perform the function of the progressive tense: *Le bruit va (en) s'apaisant* (*The noise is fading*); *Les couleurs vont (en) se dégradant* (*The colors are fading*).

Another way in which French can deal with the idea of an action continuing in the present moment is the rather long and even clumsy construction which is nevertheless in common use: *être + en train de +* infinitive. It stresses the moment when an action takes place: *Elle est en train d'envoyer un mail.* It should be added that this construction is regularly used in the imperfect tense as well.

Two similar constructions involving the present tense and referring to the immediate future are *être sur le point de* and *être en passe de* (R3): *Benjamin **est** sur le point de publier son deuxième roman* (*Benjamin is about to publish his second novel*); *Sabrina **est** en passe de remporter le trophèe* (*Sabrina is about to carry off the trophy*). The imperfect could just as well be used here: *Benjamin **était** sur le point de . . .* ; *Sabrina **était** en passe de . . .*

> The present is used for describing features obtaining at the present moment: *Les fenêtres **donnent** sur le jardin qui descend vers la rivière; Le ciel n'**est** pas dégagé aujourd'hui.*

The present tense refers to events that are happening at the present moment: *Il **fait** très froid/chaud en ce moment*; *Il **pleut/neige** à Grenoble maintenant*; *Ils **terminent** leur travail maintenant*; *Annick **lit** le journal au salon*; *Je ne **sais** que faire*.

The **historic present**, called *présent historique* or *narratif* in French, relates a past event in a striking way as though it were occurring now. Three examples illustrate this:

1. *Samuel de Champlain **fonde** Québec en 1608.*
2. *En 1789, la France était en pleine crise politique et économique. Plusieurs tentatives de réforme avaient échoué. Le 14 juillet, le peuple **s'empare** de la Bastille.*
3. *Je me promenais tranquillement dans le bois et voilà que je **rencontre** mon amie Emilie.*

    Many creative authors choose the historic present since it invests the narrative with a sense of immediacy, particularly if the narrative is cast in the first person. André Malraux's *Les conquérants* (1975, p. 6) provides a perfect illustration of this feature: "Je monte au premier étage par une sorte d'échelle. Personne. Je m'assieds, et désœuvré, regarde: une armoire européene, une table Louis Philippe [...] Par la baie arrive, avec un grésillement, [...] la forte odeur des graisses chinoises qui cuisent . . . Un bruit de socques. Entrent le propriétaire, deux autres Chinois, et un Français, Gérard, pour qui je suis ici."

Present as future: the present tense often replaces the future, and increasingly so, in daily discourse. It may be argued that this use is a result of a lack of imagination or slothfulness: *Je **rentre** demain*; *Tu **pars** la semaine prochaine ?*; *C'est décidé ! L'hiver prochain, nous **allons** au Colorado faire du ski*; *Dépêchez-vous ! Le film **commence** dans quelques minutes*.

Present as command: acts as an imperative and softens the weight of the order: *Tu **envoies** le mail maintenant, s'il te plaît*; *En partant, tu **fermes** bien la porte, s'il te plaît*.

The habitual present expresses repeated actions: *Elle **se couche** tous les jours à vingt et une heures*; *Les enfants **partent** tous les matins à 7h 30 et **reviennent** à 16h*; *Je **dors** toujours la fenêtre ouverte*.

Scientific fact: *Deux et deux **font** quatre*; *Selon Archimède, tout corps plongé dans un liquide **subit** une poussée verticale, dirigée de bas en haut, égale au poids du fluide déplacé*; *L'eau **gèle** à 0 degrés Celsius*.

The present expresses a general, eternal truth: *Le ciel **est** bleu*; *Il importe de bien maîtriser sa langue car elle **est** le véhicule de la pensée*; *L'argent ne **fait** pas le bonheur*.

An event that has just taken place may be referred to in the present tense: *La partie de foot **se termine** tout juste (has just ended)*; *Elle **arrive** à l'instant (She has just arrived)*.

The present reconstructs the text, dialogue or description of a novel or film: *Le film Babette s'en va-t-en guerre **reconstitue** en images les activités comiques d'une agente secrète au cours de la deuxième guerre mondiale; La peste de Albert Camus **décrit** les ravages d'une peste à Oran en Algérie; Le personnage principal n'**accepte** pas le cadeau et **part** tout de suite; Dans le premier chapitre, Sophie **répond** sèchement: "Impossible."*

The present is used in hypotheses with *si*, and the second part of the sentence is in the future: *Si vous **voulez** voir cette exposition, vous devrez faire la queue.*

Depuis, voilà, voici and *il y a* usually involve a present tense when in English one would expect a past tense: *Voilà/Voici/Il y a au moins deux ans que je **connais** Camille (I have known Camille for at least two years [and still know her]); Armelle **habite** à Chicago depuis six mois (Armelle has lived in Chicago for six months [and still lives there]).* But, in the negative: *Je **n'ai pas été** ici depuis dix ans (I haven't been here for ten years).*

Similarly, with *cela/ça fait*: *Cela/ça fait trois mois qu'Adrienne ne **vient** pas (That's three months that Adrienne hasn't come).*

With *la première fois*, the present tense is used where in English the perfect tense would be required: *C'est la première que je te **vois** ici (It's the first time I've seen you here); C'est la première fois que je **viens** à Québec (It's the first time I've been to Quebec).* It is worthwhile comparing the present tense in this construction with the imperfect: *C'était la première fois que je **voyais** là tous mes amis (It was the first time I had seen all my friends there).*

Venir de reflects a past idea in English: *Elle **vient** d'arriver (She has just arrived).* Note that the imperfect of *venir* in this construction is used in a similar way: *Elle **venait** d'arriver (She had just arrived).* It is to be added that a French speaker would not use *venir de* with *venir* but would doubtless use, for instance, *arriver*, as in *Elle **arrive** à l'instant.*

14

Perfect tense and agreement of the past participle / Le passé composé et l'accord du participe passé

Below is a simple dialogue concerning a female who enters a pharmacy after an accident involving a cyclist and an automobile. She herself is also slightly injured as she goes to the scene. She consults the pharmacist. The passage illustrates the uses of the perfect tense. Note especially how the past participle varies according to whether the verb is conjugated with *avoir* or *être*. Observe also how the past participle changes with reflexive verbs and may be modified according to the preceding direct object. There is agreement with *blessée*, for *me* is the direct object, but no agreement with *cassé*, for *me* is the indirect object. There is no agreement with *consacré* either. Again, the *m'(e)* is indirect, and *temps,* the preceding direct object, is masculine. Do not confuse the perfect tense with the passive voice (*la plaie est infectée*). Some translations are given.

Dialogue (à la pharmacie locale)

Pharmacienne : Bonjour, mesdames messieurs ! À qui le tour ?

Cliente : Bonjour madame, je **suis arrivée** avant le jeune homme. C'est mon tour !

Pharmacienne : Que puis-je faire pour vous ?

Cliente : **J'ai fait** du vélo ce matin et je **me suis blessée** au coude et au genou, mais je **ne me suis pas cassé** la jambe, heureusement ! Est-il possible de me donner quelque chose pour me soulager ?

Pharmacienne : Aïe aïe aïe ! Comment **avez**-vous **fait** ça ? **Avez**-vous **reçu** les premiers soins sur le lieu de l'accident ?

Cliente : Non, pas du tout, nous **avons grimpé** jusqu'au sommet de la montagne ! Là haut, je n'**ai** pas **vu** d'infirmière ou de médecin. Une voiture **a renversé** un cycliste. Je **suis allée** chercher les secours sans me préoccuper de mon cas. Je ne suis pas si douillette.

Pharmacienne : Voilà, voilà . . . j'arrive ! Asseyez-vous sur ce fauteuil ! Attendez un instant ! Nous allons voir ça de plus près. La plaie est infectée. Vous **avez eu** une profonde entaille [gash]. Je vous conseille de voir cela avec votre médecin référent [usual].

Cliente : **J'ai téléphoné** ce matin. Le carnet de rendez-vous de mon médecin traitant [usual] **a été** très **chargé**. La secrétaire médicale m'**a**

195

insérée entre deux rendez-vous. J'ai fixé ma consultation à après-demain...

Pharmacienne : Non ! Non ! Non ! Vous ne pouvez pas rester dans cet état. Voyons voir ! **J'ai procédé** à la désinfection de vos blessures. Je vais demander à mon assistante d'appliquer une crème apaisante et de vous faire un pansement avant de voir votre médecin.

Cliente : Merci beaucoup madame. Cela m'a **soulagée**.

Pharmacienne : Vous **avez été vaccinée** contre le tétanos ? L'administration de vaccin contre une maladie infectieuse comme le tétanos **est** strictement **recommandée**. Il s'agit d'une maladie grave, souvent mortelle, qu'il convient de prendre au sérieux.

Cliente : Oui j'**ai été vaccinée**, mais mes vaccins n'**ont pas été mis** à jour. J'ai la ferme intention de m'en occuper.

Pharmacienne : Vous **avez eu** des hématomes [bruises] un peu partout sur le bras et la jambe. Ne vous faites pas de souci. Tout cela rentrera dans l'ordre dans quelques semaines. À moins que votre médecin ne détecte un autre problème qu'on ne peut voir qu'en faisant une radiographie [x ray] ou une échographie [scan].

Cliente : Je vous remercie beaucoup du temps que vous m'**avez consacré**. Au revoir Madame !

Pharmacienne : À votre service ! Bonne journée. Au suivant...

As with all compound tenses in French, variations in the ending of the past participle required by agreement caused by a whole host of features leads to much dismay, not just for foreign learners of French, but also for French speakers themselves. Hanse and Blampain (2005, p. 415) quote Bescherelle, thus highlighting this perennial source of linguistic torment (our emphasis):

> Nos auteurs ont fait et font encore aujourd'hui varier ce participe dans certains cas, tandis qu'ils le laissent invariable dans d'autres. De là les difficultés assez grandes qu'offre la syntaxe de cette partie importante du discours. On a écrit sur ce sujet des traités spéciaux ; on a rempli des volumes entiers de règles, d'exceptions, d'exemples et d'applications, et, avec tout cet attirail de science, comme le dit *L'Encyclopédie moderne*, on a embrouillé une matière fort simple ; *on en a fait la torture de l'enfance, l'épouvante des jeunes personnes et le désespoir des étrangers.*

The common failure to observe agreements with the past participle leads to humorous comments, such as the following by Pierre Part, taken from *Télérama* (No. 3151, June 5–11, 2010, p. 6; the correct form is in parentheses): "Résolution : Ma décision est pris(e), et bien que douloureux(se), ne saurait être remis(e) en question. Dorénavant, comme la plupart des journalistes, présentateurs, hommes politiques, artistes, écrivains, etc. parlant sur nos médias, je n'accorderai plus les participes passés et adjectifs au féminin. Voilà, la chose est dit(e) et même écrit(e)."

Although much of this chapter is devoted to the agreement of the past participle, the initial remarks apply to the composition of the perfect tense, while, later on, there is a section on circumstances in which the perfect tense occurs.

In English, the perfect tense is made up of the auxiliary verb *to have* and a past participle: *I have spoken*. In French, the construction is similar but with one significant difference: the French perfect tense is composed of *avoir* and a past participle, but also, in numerous cases, of the auxiliary verb *être* and a past participle. We shall first deal with those verbs that are conjugated with *avoir*, and afterwards (see **2** below) with those conjugated with *être*.

14.1 The perfect tense formed with *avoir*

The four main groups of verbs are conjugated thus in the perfect tense:

-er verbs (*chanter*)		**-ir verbs** (*finir*)	
j'ai chanté	*I have sung*	j'ai fini	*I have finished*
tu as chanté	*you have sung*	tu as fini	*you have finished*
il/elle a chanté	*he/she/it has sung*	il/elle a fini	*he/she/it has finished*
nous avons chanté	*we have sung*	nous avons fini	*we have finished*
vous avez chanté	*you have sung*	vous avez fini	*you have finished*
ils/elles ont chanté	*they have sung*	ils/elles ont fini	*they have finished*

-re verbs (*vendre*)		**-oir verbs** (*recevoir*)	
j'ai vendu	*I have sold*	j'ai reçu	*I have received*
tu as vendu	*you have sold*	tu as reçu	*you have received*
il/elle a vendu	*he/she/it has sold*	il/elle a reçu	*he/she/it has received*
nous avons vendu	*we have sold*	nous avons reçu	*we have received*
vous avez vendu	*you have sold*	vous avez reçu	*you have received*
ils/elles ont vendu	*they have sold*	ils/elles ont reçu	*they have received*

It is observed that verbs with an infinitive ending in **-er** have a past participle in **-é**. Verbs with an infinitive ending in **-ir** have a past participle ending in **-i**. Most verbs with an infinitive ending in **-re** have a past participle ending in **-u**, but not always since, for instance, the past participle of *prendre* is *pris*, and the past participle of *éteindre* is *éteint*. Many verbs with an infinitive ending in **-oir** have an ending in **-u**, with the last letter of the stem being **ç**, but not always, witness *pouvoir* (*pu*) and *vouloir* (*voulu*). (See also Chapter 15 on irregular past participles.)

The past participles listed above are used in other tenses of the indicative mood: pluperfect (*j'avais chanté*), conditional (*j'aurais chanté*), future in the past (*j'aurai chanté*), past anterior (*j'eus chanté*); and in tenses of the subjunctive mood: perfect (*j'aie chanté*), pluperfect (*j'eusse chanté*).

When verbs are conjugated with *avoir*, they are considered to be transitive (see Chapter 32 on transitive and intransitive verbs). That is to say, they take a direct object: *J'ai chanté* **une chanson**; *Marie-Odile a mangé* **un sandwich**; *Lucile a envoyé* **un mail**. In these straightforward cases, the past participles do not vary.

The past participle does vary, however, when the perfect tense is in a subordinate clause and the relative pronoun (*que*) refers back to a direct object: *Antoine a chanté une chanson que j'ai déjà chantée plusieurs fois* (*Antoine sang/has sung a song that I have sung several times*). In this sentence, the subordinate clause is *que j'ai chantée*, and the relative pronoun *que* relates back to *chanson*. The past participle *chantée* must agree with what is called the preceding direct object which, in this case, is feminine. In fact, the past participle in this construction functions like an adjective. If one approached this construction in English, by way of an explanation, one could say: *The song I have sung. How do I* **have it**? *I* **have it sung**. In other words, the song *is sung*, *sung* ending up as a kind of adjective. This explanation seems involved, but an understanding of this adjectival principle is important. Furthermore, numerous native French speakers find this construction difficult to understand, so we are in good company if we fail to grasp it at the first attempt. A striking instance of this failure to make an agreement may be found in Georges Brassens's song "La première fille que j'ai pris dans mes bras". Again, if a young person says "La voiture que j'ai conduit," a well-intentioned parent could easily repeat the sentence stressing "conduite."

Further examples of this agreement with the preceding direct object:

la fille que j'ai **rencontrée** ce matin	*the girl (whom) I met this morning*
les garçons que j'ai **rencontrés** ce matin	*the boys (whom) I met this morning*
les filles que j'ai **rencontrées** ce matin	*the girls (whom) I met this morning*

In the first of these three cases, an *e* is added to *rencontré* in order to make an agreement with *fille*, a feminine singular noun. In the second case, an **s** is added to *rencontré* in order to make an agreement with *garçons*, a masculine plural noun. In the third case, an **es** is added to *rencontré* in order to make an agreement with *filles*, a feminine plural noun. It becomes clear here that the past participle of *rencontrer*, and that of all other fully functioning verbs, has four forms.

Unfortunately, the need for agreement of the past participle with a preceding direct object does not stop here. Pronouns as direct objects also have a repercussion on the past participle. This may appear difficult, but similarity with an agreement with preceding nouns is helpful. The past participle agrees with a direct-object pronoun, and it does not have to be in a subordinate clause. The following examples illustrate this feature. Speaking of a boy, one would say: *Je l'ai rencontré ce matin* (*I met him this morning*). Speaking of boys, one would say: *Je les ai rencontrés ce matin* (*I met them this morning*). Speaking of a girl, one would say: *Je l'ai rencontrée ce matin* (*I met her this morning*). Speaking of girls, one would say: *Je les ai rencontrées ce matin* (*I met them this morning*). Again, the verb *rencontrer*, as with all other fully functioning verbs, has four forms in its past participle when a preceding direct-object pronoun is involved.

One should be careful to distinguish between a direct object and an indirect object for, in the latter case, no agreement is made (see Chapter 46 on pronouns for the distinction between direct and indirect pronouns). Briefly, and this illustration merely adumbrates the full treatment of pronouns in the appropriate chapter, compare the two following sentences: *Je l'ai rencontrée ce matin* (*I met her this morning*) and *Je lui ai parlé ce matin* (*I spoke to her this morning*). In the first case, the past participle agrees with *l'* (*la*) since it is a feminine direct object; in the second case, there is no agreement since the pronoun is an indirect object, however feminine it is.

When the pronoun *en* precedes the past participle, the latter remains invariable: *J'ai cueilli des framboises et j'en ai mangé* (*I picked some strawberries and I ate some of them*). The same comment applies to the neuter pronoun *le, l'*: *La distance à parcourir est plus grande que je ne l'avais cru* (*The distance to travel is greater than I thought*). However, if the pronoun *en* is preceded by an adverb of quantity (*autant, beaucoup, combien, moins, plus*), the past participle can agree in gender and number with the preceding noun or remain invariable: *Des limonades, combien j'en ai bues/bu* (*I don't know how many lemonades I've drunk*).

Difficulties arise over agreement when quantities are involved. Does the past participle agree with the singular quantity or the plural that follows it? For instance, there is no reason why *rencontré* should agree only with *manifestants* or only with *foule*: *La foule de manifestants que j'ai rencontrée*; *La foule de manifestants que j'ai rencontrés*. Similarly, with two singular nouns but differing genders: *La moitié du travail que j'ai terminée*; *La moitié du travail que j'ai terminé*.

Special cases arise with *avoir à, donner à, laisser à, porter à* + infinitive. Does one make an agreement with *avoir/donner à* when there is a following infinitive? This depends on whether the direct object relates to *avoir* or the following infinitive. Compare the two following sentences: *les affronts que la pauvre Lucile a eu à subir* and *la peine que j'ai eue à la convaincre*. In the first case, *affronts* is the direct object of *subir*, while, in the second case, *peine* is the direct object of *avoir*. Similarly, and in the same order: *les lettres que je leur ai laissé à signer* and *les lettres que je leur ai laissées à signer*; and *la leçon que je lui ai donné à étudier* and *la leçon que je lui ai donnée à étudier*.

It is clear that, if there is an auxiliary verb preceding the infinitive, there is no agreement, a fact causing uncertainty among French speakers. The direct object in these cases depends on the infinitive, and not on the auxiliary verb: *les euros que j'ai consenti à lui donner; la tâche que j'ai pu accomplir.* But, in the following case, agreement occurs with the reflexive: *les arguments qu'elle s'est acharnée à démolir.*

Much ink has been spilt over the question of *laisser* + infinitive. Does the verb *laisser* vary according to the preceding direct object? It seems that invariability is to be recommended, just as *faire* followed by an infinitive remains invariable: *les personnes que j'ai* **fait** *venir; les élèves que la professeure a* **fait** *étudier; Je les ai* **laissé** *punir; Ils nous l'avaient* **laissé** *croire; Ils nous avaient* **laissé** *croire que...* However one does come across *Je les ai* **laissés** *dire que...* Yet again, if the verb *laisser* is reflexive, agreement would take place in *Elle s'est* **laissée** *vivre,* but not in *Elle s'est* **laissé** *conduire,* for, here, *elle* has not performed the action.

14.2 The perfect tense formed with *être*

There are many verbs that are *not* conjugated with *avoir.* As noted in the first paragraph, a large group are conjugated with *être,* and here the past participle varies, a phenomenon that also appears in Italian with the verb *essere,* but not in Spanish. In this respect, past and compound tenses in Spanish are easier to manage. French verbs conjugated with *être* fall largely into two categories: (1) intransitive verbs associated with movement or change in a particular state and (2) pronominal or reflexive verbs.

Verbs of movement include *aller, arriver, décéder, échoir* (*to fall due,* of a payment; a verb both defective and comparatively rare), *éclore* (*to bloom,* of a flower), *entrer, mourir, naître, partir, rester, retourner, sortir, tomber, venir.* This list also includes the above verbs with prefixes: *entrer* > *rentrer; naître* > *renaître; partir* > *repartir; sortir* > *ressortir; tomber* > *retomber; venir* > *advenir, devenir, revenir, parvenir, subvenir, survenir.* These verbs are conjugated in the following manner:

je suis allé(e)	*I went* (male/female)
tu es allé(e)	*you went* (male/female)
il est allé	*he/it went*
elle est allée	*she/it went*
nous somme allé(e)s	*we went* (males, males and females, females alone with extra* **e**)
vous êtes **allé(e)s**	*you went* (male, male and female, females alone with extra* **e**, single male or female when the latter has an extra* **e**)
ils sont allés	*they went* (males, males and females)
elles sont allées	*they went* (only females)

A substantial list of reflexive verbs is to be found in Chapter 33 on reflexive verbs. Suffice it therefore to offer here just a few verbs of this type since the purpose of this section is one of agreement with the verb *être*, and here are included some irregular verbs. It should be added here that most verbs used reflexively may be used non-reflexively, for instance *battre* and *cacher*: *s'en aller, se battre, se blesser, se cacher, se coiffer, s'évanouir, s'habiller, se laver, se lever, se maquiller, se passer, se quereller, se raser, se rappeler, se servir, se souvenir, se taire*. There follows a model in the perfect tense of *se cacher*:

Je **me suis caché(e)** dans le placard	*I hid in the closet/cupboard*
Tu **t'es caché(e)** dans le placard	*You hid in the closet/cupboard*
Il **s'est caché** dans le placard	*He/It hid in the closet/cupboard*
Elle **s'est cachée** dans le placard	*She/It hid in the closet/cupboard*
Nous **nous sommes caché(e)s** dans le placard	*We hid in the closet/cupboard*
Vous **vous êtes caché(e)(s)** dans le placard	*You hid in the closet/cupboard*
Ils **se sont cachés** dans le placard	*They hid in the closet/cupboard*
Elles **se sont cachées** dans le placard	*They hid in the closet/cupboard*

Comments on the above:

Cach**é**	refers to a single male
Cach**ée**	refers to a single female
Cach**é**	refers to a single male or male animal
Cach**ée**	refers to a single female or female animal
Cach**és**	refers to more than one male, or more than one male and female, and animals
Cach**ées**	refers to more than one female, and female animals
Cach**és**	refers to more than one male, or more than one male and female, and animals
Cach**ées**	refers to more than one female and animals

It is a traditional rule that certain intransitive verbs, or verbs used intransitively, are conjugated with *avoir* when they express an action, and with *être* when they convey a state resulting from a completed action. The fineness of meaning here can confuse even many native French speakers. Such verbs are: *aborder, accourir, accroître, apparaître, baisser, cesser, changer, déborder, déchoir* (R3), *dégénérer, déménager, descendre, diminuer, disparaître, embellir, empirer, grandir, monter, paraître, passer, ressusciter, vieillir*:

La factrice **est passée** à dix heures.	*The mailwoman came by at ten.*
La factrice **a passé** depuis dix minutes.	*The mailwoman has been gone ten minutes.*
J'ai téléphoné à Marine qui **a** vite **accouru**.	*I phoned Marine who came quickly.*

Marine **est accourue** pour me rassurer.	*Marine arrived quickly to reassure me.*
Depuis lors Camille **a déchu** de jour en jour.	*From then Camille lost strength every day.*
Il y a longtemps que Jean **est déchu** de ce droit.	*It's been a long time that Jean has lost this right.*
Sabrina **a disparu** subitement.	*Sabrina disappeared suddenly.*
Sabrina **est disparue** depuis quelques jours.	*Sabrina has been gone a few days.*

When certain verbs are used transitively they are conjugated with *avoir*. When they are used intransitively they are conjugated with *être*. The main ones here are: *descendre, (re)monter, rentrer, (res)sortir*. Examples with *avoir*:

Tu **as descendu** les valises?	*Have you brought the cases down?*
Virginie **a déjà monté** les verres.	*Virginie has already brought up the glasses.*
Tu **as rentré** les chaises du jardin, chéri?	*Have you brought the chairs in from the garden, darling?*
Maman **a sorti** les meilleurs couverts.	*Mum has brought out the best cutlery.*

Examples with *être*:

Armelle **est descendue** trop rapidement.	*Armelle came down too quickly.*
Rémy **est monté** comme un alpiniste.	*Rémy climbed up like a mountaineer.*
Camille, tu **es rentrée** très tard hier soir.	*Camille, you came home very late last night.*
Nous **sommes tous sortis** pour aller au cinéma.	*We all went out to go to the cinema.*

It is important to observe when verbs are used intransitively, as in the following sentence. One could, mistakenly, think that the verb *marcher* below is transitive, but this is not the case, hence no agreement: *Les trois heures que Jeanne a **marché** paraissaient très longues.* Likewise with *durer, régner* and *dormir: les années que cela a **duré**; la période que la reine a **régné**; les trois heures que j'ai **dormi**.* A conjunction like *pendant que* is implied here.

Reflexive pronouns may be direct or indirect objects, and here agreement with the past participle is to be observed, although the less well tutored French speakers have serious difficulty here. Compare the two following sentences: *Elle s'est lavée* (*She washed [herself]*); *Elle s'est lavé les mains* (*She washed her hands*). In the first case, the reflexive pronoun *se* functions as a direct object, so there is agreement with the past participle (i.e. an extra **e**). In the second case, the reflexive pronoun functions as an indirect object, so there is no agreement. A second comparison should make the difference clearer. It entails the use of the verbs *suivre* and *succéder*, which are often used in grammar classes in French-speaking countries to illustrate agreement and non-agreement in past participles: *Plusieurs rois se sont suivis rapidement* (*Several kings followed each other in quick succession*) and *Plusieurs rois se sont succédé...* (*Several kings followed each other in quick succession*). The verb *suivre* takes a direct object and therefore attracts a plural agreement with an **s** while, in contrast, *succéder* takes an indirect object (*succéder à*) so there is no agreement. An understanding of the agreement comes about with the awareness of the difference between the accusative and dative cases, or direct and indirect objects.

Impersonal verbs are conjugated with *avoir*: *Il a plu*, *Il a neigé*, *Il a tonné très fort*. When verbs are used impersonally, they follow the same pattern of conjugation with *être* and *avoir*: *Il **est arrivé** un malheur* (*A misfortune has taken place*) but *Il **a convenu** de partir* (*It was wise to leave*).

The verb *convenir* provokes some consternation in French-speaking countries, since some uncertainty reigns over the use of *être* and *avoir*. *Convenir* is conjugated with both these verbs, and the differing use depends upon the meaning intended. According to the traditional rule, when it means *to suit*, *avoir* is the "correct" form, and is used in all registers:

L'hôtel nous **a convenu**.	*The hotel suited us.*
Ces cours **ont convenu** à Luc.	*These classes suited Luc.*
Nos dispositions lui **auraient** certainement convenu.	*Our arrangements would certainly have suited him.*

When it means *to agree*, *être* is the "correct" form, and is used in R3 language. It is observed by many careful writers:

Nos enfants **sont convenus** de se réunir au parc / du prochain rendez-vous.	*Our children agreed to meet in the park / over the next meeting.*
Émilie **est convenue** de mes arguments.	*Émilie accepted my arguments.*

The second expression is often reduced to: *comme convenu*. This said, nowadays, one may use *convenir*, and without hesitation, with the auxiliary verb *avoir* in all circumstances except in the impersonal expressions *Il est convenu que / Comme il **a été convenu*** (*It was agreed that / As was agreed*).

The verb *demeurer* also causes considerable uncertainty over the choice of *être* or *avoir*. In the sense of *delaying, taking time*, *avoir* is the preferred verb:

Sa plaie **a demeuré** longtemps à guérir.	*Her wound took a long time to heal.*
L'écrivaine n'**a demeuré** qu'un mois à composer son roman.	*The writer only took a month to write the novel.*

But when it signifies *to stop* or *remain* (in a place), it is conjugated with *être*:

Stéphanie **est demeurée** muette en écoutant ces paroles.	*Stéphanie remained silent on hearing these words.*
Ma lettre **est demeurée** sans réponse.	*My letter remained without reply.*
Depuis leur départ, la maison **est demeurée** vide.	*Since their departure, the house has remained empty.*

It is sometimes unclear whether the past participles of certain verbs agree with the direct object. Such is the case with *dormir* and *vivre*: *Combien d'heures as-tu* **dormi**? (*How many hours have you slept?*). Here, the preposition *pendant* is implied, so that *heures* is not the direct object, although one could legitimately argue that it is. In the case of *vivre*, there seems to be a choice between agreement and non-agreement. Compare *les années que nous avons* **vécu** and *les heures de joie que nous avons* **vécues**.

14.3 Uses of the perfect tense (see Chapter 23 for the contrasts between the perfect, past definite and imperfect tenses)

The most dominant feature of the perfect tense is that, as a tense referring to events of the past, it conveys an openness. In other words, it expresses actions and thoughts that are often incomplete and that have repercussions on the present moment. In this sense, it resembles the English perfect tense which is less used than the French *passé composé*, since the *passé composé* frequently occurs where in English the past definite is used:

Françoise et Aurélien **ont acheté** une belle maison. Ils ont encore des travaux à faire.	*Françoise and Aurélien have bought a lovely house. They still have a lot of work to do.*
Papa **n'a pas eu** le temps de déjeuner aujourd'hui.	*Pop/Dad hasn't had / didn't have the time to eat his (midday) meal / lunch today.*

The *passé composé* is the tense used in conversation when evoking past events, even distant ones:

Tu sais que Napoléon **est né** en Corse en 1769?	*Did you know that Napoleon was born in Corsica in 1769?*
Allô, Marie! **J'ai eu** un accident de voiture hier, mais ce n'est pas grave.	*Hi, Marie! I had an automobile/car accident yesterday, but it's not serious.*

It is the tense used for informal letter writing, e-mails and texting:

Cher ami Louis,	*Dear Louis,*
J'**ai bien reçu** tes quelques mots hier. Je **n'ai pas répondu** tout de suite parce que . . .	*I certainly received your letter yesterday. I didn't reply immediately because . . .*
Votre mail **est arrivé hier** et je me dépêche de . . .	*I got your email yesterday and I hasten to . . .*
dsl 2 pa avoir rep avan (désolé de ne pas avoir répondu avant)	*Sorry not to have replied before*

The *passé composé* narrates a series of events:

À la fin du match, la journaliste **est descendue** sur le court de tennis, elle **a tendu** le micro au jeune champion et lui **a posé** beaucoup de questions. Puis, elle **a pris** des photos.	*At the end of the match, the journalist went down onto the tennis court, held the mike out to the young champion, and asked him lots of questions. Then, she took some photos.*

It is used with repetitive events:

Sophie est folle ! Elle **a vu** ce film cinq fois !	*Sophie is mad! She's seen that film five times!*

It expresses a limited duration:

Céline **a fait** son choix en un quart d'heure.	*Céline made her choice in a quarter of an hour.*
Dans la Bible, il est dit que le Déluge **a duré** pendant quarante jours et quarante nuits.	*It is said in the Bible that the Flood lasted forty days and forty nights.*
Mon père **a longtemps travaillé** à l'étranger comme conseiller militaire.	*My father worked abroad for a long time as a military advisor.*

It expresses preceding events which even have an effect on the future:

Quand on **a perdu** sa carte bancaire, il faut tout de suite le signaler à la banque.	*When you lose your bank card, you have to alert the bank straightaway.*

The perfect tense can refer to the future, particularly when a future expression of time is used:

J'**ai fini** dans un instant.   *I'll be finished in a moment.*
Si, dans une heure, Pierre **n'est**   *If Pierre isn't back in a hour, please call*
  pas revenu, tu me   *me.*
  rappelleras.

The past participle alone occurs when it follows the full perfect tense: *Je l'ai vue et remerciée; C'est un roman que j'ai lu et relu.* It can be repeated twice: *Tito a résisté au fascisme et au stalinisme, préservé la souveraineté et l'unité de son pays, et défendu l'idée du non-alignement* (Le Monde magazine, April 24, 2010).

14.4 Past participles used independently of the perfect tense

When past participles are used as adjectives, they agree with the nouns they qualify: ***Arrivée** au coin de la rue, Émilie jeta un coup d'œil en arrière;* ***Surprises** par le mauvais temps, les deux filles ont couru s'abriter sous un arbre; Des bruits **venus** de loin les ont beaucoup effrayés.*

Certain past participles, together with *étant donné*, function as prepositions: *approuvé, attendu, certifié, ci-annexé, ci-inclus, ci-joint, compris, y compris, non compris, entendu, excepté, fourni, mis à part, ôté, ouï, passé, quitté, supposé, vu.* Normally, they precede the noun and are invariable; however, a few may also follow the noun, agreeing in number and gender with it.

Past participle as preposition preceding the noun: ***Approuvé** les corrections ci-dessus;* ***Vu** les conséquences de ses actions, Adeline décida de quitter la maison; Étant **donné** la situation actuelle, la guerre ne semble pas inévitable;* **Y compris** ma tante, on sera cinq; Vous trouverez **ci-joint** la quittance; Sitôt **quitté** la ville, nous étions en pleine campagne;* ***Vu** sous cet angle, l'affaire est tout autre.*

Past participle as preposition following the noun: *Une petite minorité **exceptée**, tous les spectateurs se sont bien comportés au match; Sophie a vendu toutes ses affaires, sa voiture **comprise** (note: no y); Veuillez trouver les pièces **ci-jointes**.* The Académie française, however, admits both agreement and non-agreement with *ci-inclus: Vous trouverez **ci-inclus** une copie; Vous trouverez **ci-incluse** une lettre de votre père.*

In certain cases (*fourni, quitté, reçu, refait*), one has the impression that the auxiliary *avoir* is implied and that the direct object follows the past participle, hence its invariability: ***Repeint** la façade (i.e., J'ai repeint la façade);* ***Reçu** la somme de (i.e., J'ai reçu la somme de);* ***Quitté** la banlieue, nous avons filé à toute vitesse (i.e., Quand nous avons quitté la banlieue / Après avoir quitté la banlieue).*

Fini often agrees but may remain invariable, since the past participle may be considered elliptically: ***Finies** les vacances* but also ***Fini** les vacances (C'est fini, les vacances);* ***Fini** la journée / les manœuvres.*

Passé offers a choice when it is a question of time (i.e., the hour): **Passé** *cinq heures, les bureaux ferment*; *Il est dix heures* **passées**. But beyond this feature, it seems wiser to leave it invariable, although examples exist of variability: **Passé** *la surprise, il me restait à dire que*; **Passé** *la première maison, nous entrâmes dans le village*; **Passé** *la cinquantaine, j'ai commencé à avoir des soucis de santé*; **Passée** *la porte ouverte, je suis entrée dans la cuisine*. The verb *créer* can end up with three es: *L'entreprise/l'œuvre qu'il a cré**ée***.

A marked difference between the French use of the past participle and the English present participle: Many past participles in French associated with posture or position correspond to present participles in English. For instance: *accoudé, appuyé, juché, accroupi, assis, penché, adossé, blotti, pendu, agenouillé, couché, perché, allongé, incliné, tapi: Ils s'accroupissaient,* **adossés** *(leaning) les uns aux autres; J'ai trouvé Sophie* **agenouillée** *(kneeling) devant son fils blessé; Elle est restée* **assise** *(sitting) pendant une bonne demi-heure; J'ai trouvé le perroquet* **juché** *(perching/perched) sur son perchoir; La lampe était* **pendue** *(hanging) au plafond; La pauvre bête était* **accroupie/blottie/tapie** *(crouching) dans le fossé.*

14.5 A note on the *passé surcomposé*

The *passé surcomposé*, which is a kind of double compound tense in the past, requires some comment, however limited. It marks an event or thought that immediately precedes another event or thought expressed in the *passé composé*. It is a little-used tense. The present authors for example do not use it, since it is not really necessary, and is supplanted by the pluperfect tense. Here are two examples:

Dès que Océane **a eu prononcé** ces mots, un concert de protestations s'est élevé dans la foule.
As soon as Océane had pronounced these words, a wave of protests rose from the crowd.

À peine Axelle **a-t-elle été sortie** que la pluie s'est mise à tomber avec violence.
Hardly had Axelle gone out than the rain began to pour down.

The *passé surcomposé* has very little currency these days, and may be occasionally heard in country districts. It is not included as a tense in Marie-Éva de Villers's dictionary. The *Nouvelle grammaire du français* (Delatour 2004, p. 129) states unequivocally: "C'est un temps peu employé."

Against this must be weighed the remarks by Hanse and Blampain:

"L'usage est courant dans la langue parlée," followed by:

"Il est attesté depuis longtemps dans la langue littéraire" (2005, p. 431). Grevisse and Goosse quote Hugo, Daudet and Renan (in the nineteenth century) and Julien Green, Butor and Duras (in the twentieth), who all resort to it (2008, pp. 1040–1041).

In the passive, the *passé surcomposé* becomes most cumbersome, lacking all elegance: *Aussitôt que le paquet **a eu été envoyé*** – a construction not recommended.

A concluding remark: the *passé surcomposé* is a tense to be observed and recognized as such when it occurs, possibly idiosyncratically, in literary writing. It does not command sufficient diffusion and acceptability in France, and doubtless even less outside France, for it to justify here any extensive and detailed treatment. Notwithstanding these remarks, it should be repeated that Grevisse and Blampain both seem to suggest that it is used in spoken discourse, although the present authors have not found it in Paris, Grenoble or Nantes – a reasonable cross section of France.

15

Irregular past participles / Les participes passés irréguliers

The passage below narrates a visit paid to the enchanting monuments of ancient Rome. Composed in the perfect tense, and sent by a friend to another friend, it contains a range of irregular past participles which are highlighted and followed by their corresponding infinitive. Some translations are provided. Alice is a real Italian person living in Rome, unlike the fictitious Alice of *Alice nel paese delle meraviglie* (*Alice in Wonderland*).

Rome, la Ville éternelle

Alice nous a **accueillis** (accueillir) chez elle à Rome et nous a **convaincus** (convaincre) d'explorer les coins et les recoins de la Ville éternelle. Nous avons **reçu** (recevoir) le meilleur accueil de notre hôtesse. Nous avons **pu** (pouvoir) apprécier l'hospitalité, partager le plaisir de la table et de la convivialité des Italiens. Nous avons mangé et **bu** (boire) des spécialités italiennes aux saveurs suaves. Sur les bons conseils d'Alice, nous avons marché pendant des heures dans le dédale [labyrinth] de ruelles [small streets] de la capitale italienne.

Nous avons **parcouru** (parcourir) le Colisée de Rome et **poursuivi** (poursuivre) notre marche jusqu'à la basilique San Giovanni in Laterano. Notre chemin était parsemé [strewn] de palmiers, de cerisiers du Japon en pleine floraison, de ruines romaines, de statues et de monuments historiques. La basilique nous a **offert** (offrir) un ensemble d'œuvres qui ont été **peintes** (peindre) par d'illustres artistes. Les fresques et les mosaïques murales ont été très bien **entretenues** (entretenir). Après la visite de la basilique, nous avons **voulu** (vouloir) nous rendre au Colisée de Rome. Cette figure emblématique [iconic] de la Rome antique évoque les combats d'animaux ou de gladiateurs dans cet imposant amphithéâtre que nous avons **découvert** (découvrir). Nous y sommes restés **assis** (asseoir) une bonne demi-heure. Le Panthéon, ancien temple romain, a été **construit** (construire) avec une coupole grandiose qui a **servi** (servir) de modèle pour la basilique Saint-Pierre au Vatican. Des chefs-d'œuvre qui ont été **construits** (construire) pour l'éternité témoignent [bear witness] du génie des hommes, de l'éclat des décors et des splendeurs du temps passé. Les grandes places de Rome ont **valu** (valoir) le déplacement. Elles sont toutes ornées [adorned] de fontaines monumentales comme un bijou serti [set in] de pierres précieuses. La plus imposante, la Fontana di Trevi, est incontournable. Elle vaut le coup d'être **vue** (voir). Cette source jaillissante [gushing forth] est un chef-d'œuvre architectural unique en son genre. Elle a été bâtie au pied d'une vaste et somptueuse résidence. La Fontaine de Trevi est composée d'éléments symboliques propres à l'art baroque qui a **mis** (mettre) en scène Neptune, le dieu romain de la mer debout sur son char, entouré de délicates statues. Federico Fellini, le cinéaste et scénariste italien, a rendu cette fontaine célèbre dans la *Dolce Vita*. Nous avons **maintenu** (maintenir) le rythme de nos visites jusque sur le parvis [main square (of church)] de la Basilique Saint Pierre où le Pape Jean Paul II avait fait un discours en espagnol.

Notre expérience de l'Italie, **acquise** (acquérir) par des visites régulières, nous a **émus** (émouvoir) au souvenir des détails pittoresques et savoureux des places, des églises et d'autres monuments. Nous avons **vécu** (vivre) un séjour enchanteur et étions ravis de notre beau périple [tour]. La richesse du patrimoine historique, culturel et architectural a **conquis** (conquérir) notre cœur. Les secrets de ce pays chaleureux et vivant se dévoilent [unfolds] au fur et à mesure des visites que nous avons **faites** (faire).

It seems helpful to place all the past participles together as a unit rather than scatter them through the chapter on irregular verbs (Chapter 30), although in this chapter constant reference is made to them. Consider the comments at the end of the list as well.

Before listing the irregular past participles, we make a comment on the agreement required with the preceding direct object. Many French speakers fail to make the agreement in the following sentences, and this failure is particularly noticeable in speech, since if the final letter is a consonant it is sounded when an **e** or **es** is added to the past participle. Two lists appear here, one indicating R1 and the second R2. Asterisked past participles below refer to comments at the end of this chapter.

R1	R2
La tarte que j'ai fait est très bonne.	La tarte que j'ai faite est très bonne.
Irène va envoyer la lettre qu'elle a écrit ce matin.	Irène va envoyer la lettre qu'elle a écrite ce matin.
L'expérience que mon fils a acquis au Canada est très utile.	L'expérience que mon fils a acquise au Canada est très utile.
"Où est la voiture?" "Je l'ai mis au garage."	"Où est la voiture?" "Je l'ai mise au garage."
"Tu as trait les vaches?" "Bien sûr que je les ai trait."	"Tu as trait les vaches?" "Bien sûr que je les ai traites."

Here is a full list of irregular past participles with occasional comments, which especially point out cognate verbs that have different prefixes but that function in the same way. Highly defective verbs are not included, except if they do have a past participle which has some currency. At the end of this list are included patterns which allow us to group together quite a large number of irregular verbs, and one must question how irregular some of these groups are: *abattre* (see *battre*), *absoudre* = *absous*, *s'abstenir* (see *tenir*, but compounds tenses take *être*), *abstraire* (see *traire*), *accourir* (see *courir*, but compound tenses can take *être*), *accroire* (has no past participle, being very defective), *accroître* = *accru* (but compound tenses take both *être* and *avoir*, depending on meaning), *accueillir* (see *cueillir*), *acquérir* = *acquis*, *adjoindre* (see *craindre*), *admettre* (see *mettre*), *aller* = *allé* (this past participle is regular, notwithstanding its numerous irregularities), *apercevoir* (see *recevoir*), *apparaître* (see *paraître*), *appartenir* (see *tenir*), *apprendre* (see *prendre*), *assaillir* = *assailli*, *asseoir* = *assis*, *astreindre* (see *craindre*), *atteindre* (see *craindre*), *battre* = *battu*, *boire* = *bu*, *bouillir* = *bouilli*, *braire* = *brait* (but little used, and has no feminine or plural form), *ceindre* (see *craindre*), *circoncire* (like *suffire* in all tenses but the past participle is *circoncis*), *circonscrire* (see *écrire*), *circonvenir* (see *tenir*), *clore* (defective verb but the past participle *clos* is quite common), *combattre* (see *battre*), *commettre* (see *mettre*), *comparaître* (see *connaître*), *complaire* (see *plaire*), *comprendre* (see *prendre*), *compromettre* (see *mettre*), *conclure* = *conclu*, *concourir* (see *courir*), *conduire* = *conduit*, *connaître* = *connu*, *conquérir* (see *acquérir*), *consentir* (see *mentir*), *construire* (see *conduire*), *contenir* (see *tenir*), *contraindre* (see *craindre*), *contredire* (see *dire*), *contrefaire* (see *faire*), *contrevenir* (see *tenir*), *convaincre* (see *vaincre*), *convenir* (see *tenir*, but compound tenses take both *être* and *avoir*, depending on meaning), *coudre* = *cousu*, *courir* = *couru*, *couvrir* = *couvert*, *craindre* = *craint*, *croire* = *cru* (not to be confused with *crû*, past participle of *croître* below), *croître* = *crû* (see *cru* immediately above), *cueillir* = *cueilli*, *cuire* (see *conduire*), *débattre* (see *battre*), *décevoir* (see *recevoir*), *déchoir* = *déchu* (but compound tenses take both *être* and *avoir*, depending on meaning), *découdre* (see *coudre*), *découvrir* (see *couvrir*), *décrire* (see *écrire*), *décroître* (see *accroître*), *(se) dédire* (see *dire*, but compound tenses take *être*), *déduire* (see *conduire*), *défaillir* (see *assaillir*, but little used and parts are defective), *défaire* (see *faire*), *démentir* (see *mentir*, but it has a feminine past participle: *démentie*, unavailable for *mentir*), *démettre* (see *mettre*), *départir* (see *mentir* but the past participle has a feminine: *départie*), *dépeindre* (see *craindre*), *desservir* (see *servir*), *déteindre* (see *craindre*), *détenir* (see *tenir*), *détruire* (see *conduire*), *devenir* (see *tenir*, but compound tenses take *être*), *dévêtir* (see *vêtir*), *devoir* = *dû* (but the feminine form is *due*; the masculine form *dû* has a circumflex merely to differentiate it from the partitive article), *dire* = *dit*, *disconvenir* (see *tenir*; in compound tenses, takes *être* or *avoir*, depending on the meaning), *disjoindre* (see *craindre*), *disparaître* (see *connaître*), *dissoudre* (see *absoudre*), *distraire* (see *traire*), *dormir* = *dormi* (the feminine form *dormie* is rare but is quite possible: *trois nuits mal dormies*), *s'ébattre* (see *battre* compound tenses take *être*) échoir = échu (compound tenses take *être*), éclore = éclos (compound tenses take *être* or *avoir*, depending on meaning), éconduire (see *conduire*) écrire = écrit, élire (see *lire*), émettre (see *mettre*), émouvoir (see *mouvoir*, but the past participle has no circumflex) empreindre (see *craindre*), enceindre (see *craindre*), enclore = enclos, encourir (see *courir*), endormir (see *dormir*), enduire (see *conduire*), enfreindre (see *craindre*), s'enfuir (see *fuir*, compound tenses take *être*), enjoindre (see *craindre*), s'enquérir (see *acquérir*, compound tenses take *être*), s'ensuivre (see *suivre*; defective, only used in the infinitive and third person, and compound tenses take *être*), s'entremettre (see *mettre*; compound tenses take *être*), entreprendre (see *prendre*), entretenir (see *tenir*), entrevoir (see *voir*), entrouvrir (see *ouvrir*), envoyer = envoyé, s'éprendre (see *prendre*; compound tenses take *être*), équivaloir (see *valoir*, but *équivalu* has no feminine or plural), éteindre (see *craindre*), exclure (see *conclure*), extraire (see *traire*), faillir = failli, faire = fait, falloir = fallu, feindre (see *craindre*), férir = féru (but rarely used), forfaire = forfait, frire = frit, fuir = fui, geindre (see *craindre*), haïr = haï, inclure (see *conclure*), induire (see *conduire*), inscrire (see *écrire*), instruire (see *conduire*), interdire (see *dire*), intervenir (see *tenir*; auxiliary is *être*), introduire (see *conduire*), joindre (see *craindre*), lire = lu, luire = lui, maintenir (see *tenir*), maudire (see *dire*), méconnaître (see *connaître*), médire (see *dire*), mentir = menti (has no feminine or plural), se méprendre (see *prendre*; compound tenses take *être*), mettre = mis, moudre = moulu, mourir = mort (compound tenses take *être*), mouvoir = mû (but feminine = mue), naître = né (compound tenses take *être*), nuire = nui (has no feminine), obtenir (see *tenir*), offrir (see *couvrir*), oindre (see *craindre*), omettre (see *mettre*), ouïr = ouï, ouvrir (see *couvrir*), paître (has no past participle), paraître (see *connaître*), parcourir (see *courir*), parfaire (see *faire*), partir (see *mentir*, but has a feminine and plural), parvenir (see *tenir*), peindre (see *craindre*), permettre (see *mettre*), plaindre (see *craindre*), plaire = plu (has neither feminine nor plural form), pleuvoir = plu (has neither feminine nor plural form), poursuivre (see *suivre*), pourvoir = pourvu, pouvoir = pu, prédire (see *dire*), prendre = pris, prescrire (see *écrire*), pressentir (see *sentir*), prévaloir (see *valoir*; has neither feminine nor plural form), prévenir (see *tenir*), prévoir (see *voir*), produire (see *conduire*), promettre (see *mettre*), promouvoir (see *mouvoir*, but *promu* has no circumflex accent), proscrire (see *écrire*), provenir (see *tenir*, but compound tenses take *être*), rabattre (see *battre*), rapprendre (see *prendre*), rasseoir (see *asseoir*), réapparaître (see *connaître*), rebattre (see *battre*), reconduire (see *conduire*), reconnaître (see *connaître*), reconquérir (see *acquérir*), reconstruire (see *conduire*), recoudre (see *coudre*), recourir (see *courir*), recouvrir* (see *couvrir*), récrire (see *écrire*), recueillir (see *cueillir*), recuire (see *conduire*), redevenir (see *tenir*, but compound tenses take *être*), redire (see *dire*), réduire (see *conduire*), réélire (see *lire*), refaire (see *faire*), rejoindre (see *craindre*), relire (see *lire*), reluire (see *dormir*), renvoyer (see *envoyer*), reparaître (see *connaître*), repartir (see *partir*), repeindre (see *craindre*), se repentir (see *mentir*; compound tenses take *être*), reprendre (see *prendre*), reproduire (see *conduire*), requérir (see *acquérir*), *résoudre* = *résolu* (*résous* exists but is little used), *ressentir* (see *mentir*, but has feminine form with **e**), *resservir* (see *servir*), *ressortir** (see *mentir*, but compound tenses take *être*), *se ressouvenir* (see *tenir*, but compound tenses take *être*), *restreindre* (see *craindre*), *résulter** = *résulté*, *revenir* (see *tenir*, but compound tenses take *être*), *revêtir* (see *vêtir*), *revivre* (see *vivre*), *revoir* (see *voir*), *rire* = *ri* (has no feminine or plural form), *rompre** = *rompu*, *rouvrir* (see *couvrir*), *saillir* = *sailli*, *satisfaire* (see *faire*), *savoir* = *su*, *secourir* (see *courir*), *sentir* (see *mentir*, but compound tenses have a feminine form), *servir* = *servi*, *sortir* = *sorti*, *souffrir* (see *couvrir*), *soumettre* (see *mettre*), *sourire* (see *rire*), *souscrire* (see *écrire*), *soustraire* (see *traire*), *soutenir* (see *tenir*), *se souvenir* (see *tenir*, but compound tenses take *être*), *subvenir* (see *tenir*), *suffir* = *suffi* (but has neither feminine nor plural form), *suivre* = *suivi*, *surprendre* (see *prendre*), *surseoir* = *sursis* (feminine form is rare), *survivre* (see *vivre*), *taire* = *tu*, *teindre* (see *craindre*), *tenir* = *tenu*, *traduire* (see *conduire*), *traire* = *trait*, *transcrire* (see *écrire*), *transmettre* (see *mettre*), *transparaître* (see *connaître*), *tressaillir* (see *assaillir*), *vaincre* = *vaincu*, *valoir* = *valu*, *venir* (see *tenir*, but compound tenses take *être*), *vêtir** = *vêtu*, *vivre* = *vécu*, *voir* = *vu*, *vouloir* = *voulu*.

There is less variety, and therefore less room for confusion, if one groups together many of these irregular verbs. Indeed, one may question the term "irregular" for the groups of past participles following certain patterns, like *conduit, connu, couvert, craint, écrit, menti, mis, pris, tenu, trait*.

Note that *plu* is the irregular past participle of both *plaire* and *pleuvoir*, hence the oddity: *Il a* **plu** *qu'il ait* **plu** (*It has pleased that it has rained*, i.e., It's good that it has rained).

*It is wise to separate *recouvert* (*re-covered* [with a covering]) and *recouvré* (*recovered*, as of a sum of money, health).

*Ressorti has two meanings. *Ressortir* in the sense of *to go out again* is conjugated with *être*, and follows the *sortir* pattern, while *ressortir* in the sense of *to be the responsibility / within the competence of* is conjugated like the regular verb *finir*, and in this meaning it is conjugated with *avoir*.

*Résulter is conjugated with *avoir* indicating action and *être* indicating state. Compare *Du mal en* **a résulté** and *Il en* **est résulté** *du mal*.

*The verb *rompre* is hardly irregular at all. Its past participle, *rompu*, fits the pattern of *vendre*. Its only irregularity is the third-person singular present tense: *rompt*.

*Vêtir is rarely used except precisely in the past participle: *vêtu*.

16

Past participles used as nouns / Les participes passés considérés comme noms

The passage below describes *Aida*, one of Verdi's operas, that takes place annually in the delightful Italian city of Verona, of Romeo and Juliet fame. It illustrates the idiomatic use of past participles used as nouns. The past participles are highlighted. Some translations are provided.

Aïda dans la belle Vérone

Les arènes de Vérone sont aussi grandioses que le Colisée de Rome. Cet ancien amphithéâtre romain est très bien sauvegardé. La capacité d'accueil des arènes est énorme. Ce grand édifice circulaire peut contenir plus de 14 000 spectateurs. Le grand festival d'opéra qui se déroule chaque été dans un environnement remarquable attire bon nombre d'**invités** venant du monde entier, des visiteurs ainsi que des Véronais et des Véronaises. Les **passionnés** d'opéra fréquentent régulièrement les arènes pendant l'été.

Les représentations d'opéras célèbres comme *Aïda*, *Le Barbier de Séville*, *Carmen*, *Tosca*, *Madame Butterfly*, *Nabucco* et bien d'autres représentations font le vrai bonheur des spectateurs. En assistant à maintes reprises à la représentation de *Aïda*, l'opéra de Giuseppe Verdi, nous avons été sous le charme magique de ce chef-d'œuvre monumental dans un cadre légendaire avec des décors en trompe-l'œil [deceptive façades]. Des voix retentissantes dans la bonne acoustique des arènes, la **mise en musique** de l'œuvre accompagnée des chœurs d'opéra et de l'orchestre résonnent au plus profond de notre être. Verdi raconte une histoire d'amour entre Radamès, un commandant égyptien, et Aïda, une jeune princesse, esclave éthiopienne. La scène se déroule au palais royal en Égypte. Le peuple égyptien croyait avoir envahi l'Éthiopie, et que les **assiégés** ou les **vaincus** ne se remettaient pas de l'échec subi par leur armée. Les **condamnés** ou les **bannis**, les **exilés** ou les **expulsés**, avaient la vie dure. On comptait plusieurs **blessés** parmi eux. Radamès est appelé à combattre les Éthiopiens. En secret, il aime Aïda. Il est écartelé [torn] entre l'amour de sa **bien-aimée** et celui de sa mère patrie. Pourtant, Radamès s'est engagé avec Amneris, la fille du pharaon. Il compte la prendre pour épouse lorsqu'il sortira vainqueur de la guerre. Il ne sait pas que Aïda est de sang noble et que Amneris est amoureuse de lui. Aïda sent son cœur se déchirer. Son **bien-aimé** va faire la guerre contre le peuple éthiopien, composé de **deshérités**, commandé par son père. Radamès a reçu l'épée sacrée qui le conduira au triomphe. Amneris se prépare à fêter son retour victorieux. Elle fait croire à Aïda que Radamès a été tué et exige que son esclave assiste au retour triomphal des armées pour afficher la différence de leur rang social. Cette histoire tourne au tragique.

Nous avons savouré tous les détails poétiques du spectacle, au clair de lune, en profitant au maximum de ce moment extraordinaire d'euphorie générale. À chaque fois que l'on assiste à des représentations d'opéra, on redécouvre en grandeur nature [full-life scale] la **mise en scène** somptueuse dans une ambiance envoûtante [spell-binding]. La **mise en valeur** des costumes chatoyants [sparkling] nous imprègne [fill] de ce spectacle vivant dans la chaleur douce d'une nuit d'été.

The past participle used as a noun is a very common and vigorous practice, not only in French but also in Spanish and Italian. English has few equivalents to this phenomenon. The English equivalent is frequently higher in register (e.g., *the accused*). A further word or words like *person* or *persons* are almost always involved. Translation of such nouns deriving from past participles is often very difficult and even cumbersome, and the sentence often has to be reordered. Two strategies offer themselves: either a general statement (*abandonnés* > *the people who have been abandoned*) or, for example, a demonstrative pronoun (*les initiés* > *those initiated*). A few words correspond to an English word: *le détenu* (*the detainee*), *délégué* (*the delegate*), *accusé* (*the accused*). The nouns in many of these cases are frequently found in the plural, and in certain cases a singular past-participle noun is almost inconceivable (*les assiégés, les encerclés, les rassemblés, les réunis*). In addition to which, some singular nouns sound a little odd (*l'exterminé, l'inscrit, l'enregistré*), as opposed to their plural form. Of course, there is no reason why the feminine form in many cases should not be used as well. The singular form is given in the first list below, which is followed by a second more random list. The first list shows very clearly how a great number of verbs and their past participles lend themselves to the creation of nouns in this way, in addition to which it is surprising that English grammars of the French language do not pay attention to them, which in turn means that English speakers fail to use them in any meaningful and resourceful way. Again, this compilation would not be found in a French grammar for French speakers since, being a simple part of the language, most French speakers are not aware of this feature. It comes naturally to them.

The list contains translations for all the nouns, as well as examples. In some cases, the past participles used in this way may have a negative meaning since the past participle can entail a passive idea which, in turn, can point to a person subject to an unpleasant or painful experience:

abandonné	*person who has been abandoned: À la suite de l'invasion, les abandonnés se virent obligés de coucher à la belle étoile.*
abonné	*subscriber: Le catalogue est envoyé à tous les abonnés.*
abruti	*idiot, moron: Rémy conduit comme un abruti.*
accidenté	*injured person: Cette accidentée a été indemnisée.*
accouchée	*woman who has just given birth.*
accusé	*the accused: le banc des accusés.*
administré	*constituent: Les administrés votent ici toujours au centre.*
admis	*successful candidate* in an examination: *Les admis trouvent toujours du travail.*
affranchi	*emancipated person* (usually from slavery, but not always): *Il y avait des cas d'affranchis aux États-Unis qui voulaient garder leur statut d'esclaves; Les femmes ne jouissaient pas du statut d'affranchie au dix-neuvième siècle.*
agrégé	person who has the *agrégation* (highest competitive exam in education in France).
agressé	person attacked/mugged: *L'agressé a porté plainte en cour d'assises.*
aimé, bien/ mal	*well-loved person/disliked person: sa bien-aimée lui a offert un cadeau.*
aliéné	*insane person: Henri a été enfermé dans un asile d'aliénés.*
amputé	*amputee: En tant que médecin, Georges Duhamel décrit le drame des amputés dans ses Souvenirs de la Grande Guerre.*
angoissé	*tormented/anxious person: Il ne faut pas lui faire attention, Françoise est une angoissée perpétuelle.*
appelé	*military conscript: Les appelés ont peu de formation militaire.*
assiégés	*besieged citizens: Les assiégés de Massada se sont suicidés plutôt que de se rendre à l'armée romaine.*
assisté	*person on social benefit: La famille a une mentalité d'assistés.*
assuré	*insured person: Les non assurés affrontent de gros problèmes financiers lors des inondations.*
attaché	*attaché: Audrey est une attachée à la coopération universitaire; un attaché commercial/culturel; un attaché de presse*
banni	*a banished person: Victor Hugo fut un des grands bannis du dix-neuvième siècle.*
blessé	*injured person: L'accident a produit plusieurs blessés.*
brûlé	*burns victim: À la suite de l'accident, il y avait de nombreux brûlés.*
condamné (à mort)	*condemned person: Le condamné a été gracié par le président.*

convaincu	convinced person: *Après le discours, il y eu des quantités de convaincus.*
converti	convert: *Tu prêches un converti* (You are preaching to the converted).
convié	guest: *Les conviés ont cordialement remercié l'amphytrion (host).*
convoqué	person called (for a purpose): *Les convoqués ont tous parlé en faveur d'une hausse de salaire.*
couronné	crowned person: *Le couronné a daigné recevoir ses sujets.*
crucifié	crucified person: *Des crucifiés jalonnaient souvent La Voie Appienne de Rome à Brindisi, y compris Spartacus; le crucifié = Christ.*
débauché	debauchee: *Verlaine mena une vie de débauché.*
décédé	deceased person: *Le décédé n'a malheureusement pas laissé de testament.*
déchu	fallen person (used metaphorically): *Les déchus pourront-ils hériter du royaume de Dieu?*
décoré	decorated person: *les décorés de la Grande Guerre.*
défavorisé	ill-favored person: *Les défavorisés ont toujours du mal à monter dans l'échelle sociale.*
délaissé	abandoned person: *Les délaissés de notre société succombent souvent à la tentation d'actes criminels.*
délégué	delegate: *Tous les délégués se réunirent à Genève.*
déporté	deported person: *Les déportés ne pouvaient jamais deviner leur sort; En France il y a des quantités de Rue des déportés.*
dépossédé	dispossessed person: *On a pu loger tous les dépossédés* (i.e., those who have lost their homes).
dépravé	depraved person: *La famille a été brutalement agressée par des dépravés.*
désaxé	unbalanced person: *Un désaxé a dû mettre le feu à la maison.*
déséquilibré	unbalanced person: *Un carambolage d'automobiles a été provoqué par une déséquilibrée.*
désespéré	desperate person: *La désespérée s'est suicidée.*
déshérité	underprivileged/deprived person: *Qu'est-ce que j'admire Guillaume, il consacre tout son temps à défendre les intérêts des déshérités de la vie.*
destitué	dismissed person: *De tous les destitués, un seul officier a repris son commandement.*
détaché	seconded person: *Le détaché a regagné la France au bout de deux ans.*
détenu	detainee: *Trois des détenues ont été relâchées.*
diplômé	person with a degree/diploma, graduate: *C'est une diplômée d'une grande école.*

disparu	*person who has disappeared*: *Il y avait combien de disparus après l'avalanche?*
divorcé	*divorcee*: *Le nombre de divorcés va toujours en augmentant.*
doué	*clever/talented person*: *Elle est l'une des plus douées de la classe.*
drogué	*drug addict*: *La société doit prendre en charge le traitement des drogués.*
égaré	*person who has gone astray*: *Il a fallu plusieurs heures pour localiser les égarés.*
élu	*chosen/elected person*: *Selon certains fanatiques, il y a très peu d'élus pour le royaume des cieux*; *Les élus vont directement au sénat.*
encerclés	*people who are encircled*: *Beaucoup des encerclés dans la poche de Falaise se sont rendus* (incident in the Normandy landings); *les encerclés allemands durant la bataille de Stalingrad.*
enragé	*fanatic*: *Il va à tous les matchs. C'est un enragé du foot.*
envoyé	*correspondent, envoy*: *C'est un envoyé spécial du Monde*; *L'envoyée américaine accepta le plan de paix* : *Vous êtes l'envoyé du ciel!* (*You've come just in time!*).
évadé	*escaped prisoner*: *Il était impossible de capturer l'évadé.*
exalté	*fanatic*: *Cet attentat est le fait de quelques exaltés.*
exclu	*drop-out, outcast*: *Que faire pour les exclus s'ils ne veulent pas que l'on les aide?*; *les exclus de la croissance / du système.*
excommunié	*Kepler fut un des grands excommuniés du dix-septième siècle.*
exilé	*exiled person*: *Trotsky fut un des grands exilés du vingtième siècle.*
expatrié	*expatriate*: *Des expatriés espagnols passèrent une quarantaine d'années en France à la suite de la guerre civile en Espagne.*
expulsé	*an expelled person*: *En football, un expulsé n'a pas le droit de jouer les trois matchs suivants.*
exterminé	*people who have been exterminated*: *Comment calculer le nombre d'exterminés dans les camps de concentration?*
fiancé	*from*: (*se*) *fiancer, as in les deux fiancés*; *Les fiancés* (Italian novel by Manzoni = *I promessi sposi*).
gradé	*non-commissioned officer*: *Un gradé est moins important qu'un officier.*
habitué	*regular visitor/customer, habitué*: *les habitués de ce café se réunissent tous les samedi soirs.*
handicapé	*disabled person*: *Il faut céder la place aux handicapés.*
illuminé	*visionary, crank*: *Raspoutine, illuminé sous le règne de Nicholas II, fut assassiné par le prince Iuossoupov.*

inconnu	*stranger: J'ai croisé un inconnu dans la rue* (no infinitive).
inculpé	(*the*) *accused: le drame d'un inculpé innocent*
inédit	hitherto unpublished book/article: *un inédit de Mauriac* (no infinitive).
initié	*initiated person: une poésie ésotérique, faite pour les initiés; un délit d'initiés* (insider trading).
inscrit	*registered student/voter: Les inscrits ont déposé leur bulletin de vote dans l'urne.*
insoumis	*draft dodger, rebel: Les insoumis risquaient l'exécution pendant la première guerre mondiale; une classe d'insoumises* (no infinitive).
insurgé	*insurgent: Les insurgés se sont révoltés contre le pouvoir central; Tu as lu le roman L'insurgé de J. Vallès?*
intéressé	*interested person: Le comité a pris la décision sans consulter les intéréssés.*
interné	*interned person* as a mentally ill patient in a hospital; also a political internee as in Guantánamo Bay or the Vélodrome d'Hiver (Vél' d'Hiv) in Paris during World War II: *les internés du Vél' d'Hiv.*
interviewé	*interviewee: Après l'évènement, l'interviewé a désigné le coupable.*
intoxiqué	*person suffering from food poisoning; L'hôpital a découvert que les intoxiqués avaient mangé des champignons vénéneux.*
invité	*guest: Les invités partirent tard dans la nuit.*
laissé-pour-compte	*outcast: Les squatters ne sont que des laissés-pour-compte.*
licencié	*college graduate, person made redundant: des licenciés en droit; une licenciée de sciences; un licencié ès-sciences.*
logé	a person given accommodation: *Les logés en ville paient plus cher.*
marginalisé	*dropout: On les appelait "clochards" ou "clodos" à un certain moment mais maintenant on les appelle "marginalisés".*
marié/mariée	*bridegroom/bride: La mariée était d'une beauté éclatante.*
martyrisé	*tortured, battered, martyred: Comment compenser les martyrisés des camps de concentration?*
miraculé	*person who has made a miraculous recovery: Est-ce qu'il y a vraiment des miraculés à Lourdes?* (no infinitive).
mort	*dead person: L'accident produisit quatre morts.*
mutilé	*disabled person: Dans Les Souvenirs de la Grande Guerre, Duhamel décrit le drame des grands mutilés; un mutilé de guerre; Office national des mutilés et des réformés*
nanti	(*the*) *well-off: Ce quartier est réservé aux nantis.*

naufragé	*shipwrecked person: Le navire a découvert une cinquantaine de naufragés réfugiés sur un radeau* (no infinitive); *Delacroix peint avec un réalisme déchirant le visage tourmenté des naufragés dans son Radeau de la Méduse.*
névrosé	*neurotic person: On peut guérir plus facilement bien des maladies que les névrosés* (no infinitive).
nominé	*nominated person* (e.g., for an Oscar): *Tous les nominés étaient présents à la cérémonie de remise de prix.*
noyé	*drowned person: Le raz-de-marée a produit plusieurs noyés.*
obsédé	*obsessed person, fanatic: Le crime a été sûrement commis par un obsédé sexuel.*
oublié	*those who are ignored by society: les oubliés de la société.*
passionné	*enthusiast: Mozart et Beethoven ? Elle les adore, c'est une vraie passionnée; Norman Mailer fut un passionné de boxe, Camus un passionné de football.*
pendu	person who has just been hanged, as in Cézanne's *La maison du pendu* or Villon's *La ballade des pendus.*
persécuté	*persecuted person: L'histoire nous montre combien ont souffert les persécutés de notre société.*
perverti	*pervert: un perverti sexuel.*
pestiféré	*plague-ridden/stricken person: Il n'est pas surprenant que Camus emploie le mot "pestiférés" à d'innombrables reprises dans La peste; Tu as vu le tableau Les Pestiférés de Jaffa (1804) de Antoine Gros ?*
polycopié	sheet distributed to students, *handout: Tous les étudiants ont droit à un polycopié.*
possédé	(one) possessed: *Elle hurlait comme une possédée; Je viens de terminer Les possédés de Dostoïevski.*
privilégié	*privileged person: Je ne faisais pas partie des quelques privilégiés qui ont pu assister au concert.*
proscrit	*banned person, outlaw: Les proscrits pouvaient rarement rentrer au pays.*
rapatrié	*repatriated person: La mort de Franco a vu le retour en Espagne de milliers de rapatriés.*
rassemblés	*people gathered together: Les rassemblés votèrent la sécession.*
reclus	*recluse: Il ne sort plus, il vit en reclus, en ermite* (no infinitive).
réformé	*discharged soldier, person who has been declared unfit for military service: Les réformés ont toujours la priorité.* It is also used of members of the Protestant Church (*Église réformée* = *les réformés*). *Réformé* in these contexts is less well known these days.

refoulé	*sexually/psychologically repressed person; someone who has been forced/turned back: Selon certains psychiatres, nous sommes tous des refoulés et des hypocrites; Les refoulés à la frontière se sont trouvés sans abri.*
réfugié	*refugee: Désolation de désolation, les réfugiés n'avaient ni eau, ni nourriture, ni abri.*
réhabilité	*rehabilitated/redeemed person: Dreyfus, victime d'un anti-sémitisme endémique, fut l'un des grands réhabilités du vingtième siècle.*
repris (de justice)	*hardened criminal: Rue de Rivoli, on avait arrêté un dangereux repris de justice.*
rescapé	*survivor: les rescapés d'un naufrage / d'un incendie; Il restait peu de rescapés de Buchenwald pour raconter leur histoire* (the infinitive does not exist).
retraité	*senior citizen, pensioner: Le retraité touche une pension privée ainsi qu'une pension de l'état* (the infinitive does not exist).
réunis	*those assembled: Les réunis ont salué le vainqueur.*
révolté	*rebel: Spartacus est l'un des grands révoltés de l'histoire.*
salarié	*wage earner, salaried employee: Certains salariés ont fait appel à la grève* (the infinitive does not exist).
séquestré	*kidnapped person: La police a finalement découvert la séquestrée; Les séquestrés d'Altona est une pièce de Sartre.*
sinistré	*disaster victim: Les malheureux sinistrés attendaient avec patience sur les décombres de leur maison* (no infinitive).
sondé	*person who is polled: 60 pour cent des sondés ont enregistré leur mécontentement.*
supplicié	*torture victim: Tosca entendait son amant, le supplicié Cavaradossi, hurler de douleur.*
surdoué	*exceptionally gifted person: Chopin était un surdoué du piano* (no infinitive).
taré	*mental defective: Le nazisme a essayé d'éliminer tous les tarés.*
tiré à part	*off-print* (of an article): *Je t'enverrai un tiré à part de l'article.*
torturé	*victim of torture: Sartre a protesté au nom des torturés.*
tourmenté	*tormented person: Malraux était un des grands tourmentés du vingtième siècle.*
traumatisé	*person suffering from shock: À la suite de l'accident, les secouristes ont transporté tous les traumatisés à l'hôpital.*
tué	*person who has been killed: Après l'échauffourée, il a fallu enterrer les tués tout de suite.*

vaincu	*defeated person*: *Elle a adopté une attitude de vaincue*; *Malheur aux vaincus !*
vécu	*personal experience*: *C'est du vécu* (*It's real life*: said of a novel or a film); *le vécu quotidien* (*daily experience*)

There are other participles which are treated in dictionaries as nouns as well, but they need a *support*, as the French would say. *Venu* is one such past participle. *Les venus* has no meaning in isolation, but *les premiers/nouveaux venus* and *les premières/nouvelles venues* do have a meaning. Similarly, one would say and write *le premier arrivé / la première arrivée / les premiers arrivés / les premières arrivées, le premier servi / la première servie / les premiers servis / les premières servies, le premier sorti / la première sortie / les premiers sortis / les premières sorties*. *Parti* would function in the same way and *dernier* could replace *premier* in all these cases. A biblical reference, bringing together two entries above, may be aptly used here: "Car il y a beaucoup d'appelés et peu d'élus" ("Many are called, few are chosen," Matthew 22: 16).

Simply to show how extensive this construction is, there now follows a further random list with no translations or examples. Again, most of these past participles / nouns would appear more easily in the plural, but quite a few (e.g., *dégénéré* = degenerate person, *gazé* = gas victim, *pistonné* = someone for whom strings are pulled) occur just as easily in the singular. The following past participles / nouns are listed in the singular, except where logic or usage would require a plural. A few past participles could appear somewhat odd as nouns but there is no reason why, in a given context, they should not be used: *affecté; affolé; attablés; autorisé; branché; châtié; compensé; concerné; dégénéré; démobilisé; désemparé; mobilisé; encadré; engagé; enragé; enregistré; favorisé; guéri; indemnisé; interpellé; interrogé; promu; protégé; puni; recommandé; rejeté; relégué; sacrifié; touché; transporté*.

Although grammatically acceptable, usage would be against the exclusive use of some past participles / nouns, and *personne*, for instance would precede them: *une personne caricaturée/évoluée/hypnotisée/photographiée/politisée/trahie/traquée/violée*. Francis Carco's *L'homme traqué* is a good case in point here.

A humorous use of *allongé* is often heard: *le boulevard des allongés* = *le cimetière*.

The use of *refusé* in a particular context is most worthy of note. Traditional, bourgeois moral values in the eighteenth and nineteenth centuries required certain paintings treating unorthodox and, at that time, scandalous subjects to be consigned to the Salon des Refusés at the Boulevard des Capucines, in Paris. One such "notorious" painting was Monet's *Le déjeuner sur l'herbe*, portraying a naked woman sitting alongside two perfectly and elegantly attired men.

Two other nouns deriving from past participles merit mention. They occur in the feminine form and, as with the nouns above, they resist easy translations. The two nouns in question are *mise* and *prise*, which are followed by a preposition and then a noun. They are both feminine.

Mise suggests the idea of "placing" or "putting." No translations are given here since, generally speaking, the examples are clear enough: *mise en branle, mise en circulation, mise en état, mise en garde, mise en jeu, mise en liberté, mise en marche, mise en mouvement, mise en orbite* (also *sur*, see below), *mise en ordre, mise en place, mise en pratique, mise en scène, mise en service, mise en valeur, mise en vente, mise en vigueur, mise sur pied, mise sur orbite, mise à jour.*

Prise suggests the idea of "taking" or "assuming": *prise en charge, prise d'armes, prise d'assaut, prise de bec, prise de conscience, prise de contact, prise de contrôle, prise de décision, prise de fonctions, prise de position, prise de possession, prise de pouvoir, prise de sang, prise de son.*

Mise and *prise* give rise to *remise* and *reprise*, as in *remise en question / en valeur, reprise d'une activité / d'une pièce de théâtre, à plusieurs reprises* (*several times*).

Titles of books, novels, plays and so on sometimes involve past participles as nouns. Two are referred to above: *Les séquestrés d'Altona* (play by Sartre), *Les mal aimés* (Mauriac), *Les possédés* (translation of the title of Dostoievksy's novel = *The Devils*). Camus's *La peste* was originally entitled *Les séparés*.

17

Ablative absolute (absolute use of the past participle) / L'ablatif absolu (usage absolu du participe passé)

The following passage provides a simple description of the delights of the Tuscany region in central Italy. It recounts a visit made by tourists to the various attractions in the main towns before they arrive at their hotel where their driver appears to have mislaid the list of the group. Uses of the ablative absolute are highlighted in bold. Some translations are given.

Les splendeurs de la Toscane
Les **vacances commencées**, nous avons pris les routes qui sillonnent [go through] la Toscane. **Tout compte fait**, nous étions sous le charme et la douceur de cette région d'une beauté fascinante. La luminosité naturelle, les couleurs chaudes de la pierre rouge, jaune et ocre des monuments historiques, nous font voyager dans le temps et dans l'espace à travers les cultures du Moyen Âge et de la Renaissance, entre autres. **Le soir venu**, la campagne était de toute beauté. Avec leur végétation luxuriante, les champs étalaient généreusement leurs vignobles et leurs oliveraies [olive groves].

    Tout bien considéré, nous avons décidé de visiter Florence, Sienne, San Gimignano. Florence, ville d'art, offre de superbes panoramas sur la ville. Le Piazzale Michelangelo est une figure emblématique [iconic] de la ville. La cathédrale, le baptistère et bien d'autres édifices religieux évoquent un passé chargé d'histoire. Sienne est une magnifique petite ville avec sa fameuse Piazza del Campo, la basilique San Domenico et la chapelle de Sainte Catherine de Sienne. Les tours carrées dominent le village médiéval de San Gimignano.

    La casquette enfoncée jusqu'aux oreilles, le chauffeur nous attendait tranquillement en faisant la sieste jusqu'à notre retour. **Une fois nos visites terminées**, nous avons repris le chemin du retour en autocar. À l'hôtel, une hôtesse nous accueille avec un sourire radieux et beaucoup de gentillesses. Elle remet des cadeaux aux touristes pour fêter leur arrivée. **Les présents remis aux touristes**, l'agent d'accueil est reparti vers son bureau récupérer les clés des chambres. **Les clés des chambres récupérées**, l'hôtesse nous les distribue. Elle demande au chauffeur de lui remettre la liste du groupe mais, **les mains plongées dans les poches**, il la recherche sans succès.

L'hôtel, situé en plein cœur de la vieille ville, a été rénové. **Une fois l'hôtel rénové**, les propriétaires du lieu l'ouvrirent au public. **Une fois fortune faite**, les hôteliers s'arrêteront de travailler. **Le travail fini**, ils apprécieront les balades de gens heureux qui coulent des jours tranquilles dans cette belle Toscane.

The ablative absolute is as uncommon a structure in English as it is common in French. It is not uncommon in Spanish or Italian. It derives from the Latin construction formed by a past participle as the nucleus which has no necessary grammatical connection with the main clause, so that it is really an independent subordinate clause of circumstance. It usually contains a temporal sense of something that has already happened. The ablative absolute is normally made up of any transitive verb and an accompanying noun. The English equivalent would be "When . . . " or "As soon as . . . " The ablative absolute is particularly prevalent in the written style and would therefore be classed as R3, although there are exceptions with *une fois*, indicated in the examples below. When the structure involves a noun, the latter usually, but not always, follows the past participle which agrees with it. The main clause is separated from the noun by a comma:

Les vacances terminées, on a repris les cours.	*As soon as the vacation was over, the classes began again.*
Le paquet remis, elle est repartie.	*As soon as she handed in the package, she left.*
Sitôt arrivées les lettres, tout le monde voulait les lire.	*As soon as the letters had arrived, everyone wanted to read them.*
Sitôt les épreuves corrigées, je les renvoyai à la maison d'édition.	*As soon as I had corrected the proofs, I sent them back to the publishers.*
La messe finie, ils sont tous sortis.	*As soon as mass was over, they all went out.*
La maison vendue, ils repartirent pour l'étranger.	*When the house was sold, they set off again abroad.*
La double maison achevée (l'une pour son [Soljénitsyne] travail, l'autre pour sa famille), il se met à l'œuvre (*Libération*).	*The combined house(s) completed (one for his [Solzhenitsyn's] work, the other for his family), he gets down to work.*
Ses congénères, **toutes étiquettes confondues**, sont les meilleurs des Américains (*Libération*).	*His fellow creatures, forgetting all labels, are the best of Americans.*
À peine Jean retiré de l'affaire, son frère commença à chercher de nouveaux fonds.	*Hardly had Jean withdrawn from the business than his brother began to look for new funds.*

There are occasions where a demonstrative pronoun rather than a noun is involved, and here the register is unquestionably R3. Two examples are taken from the French historian E. Préclin:

C'est qu'il (Lincoln) voulait ménager l'État-pivot de Virginie. **Celui rallié** au Sud, le Président fit renforcer le fort Sumter (1937, p. 136).	*The fact is that he wanted to spare the pivot state of Virginia. Once the latter had rallied to the Southern cause, the President had fort Sumter reinforced.*
Aux yeux de Lincoln et de ses amis, c'est [...] que le Nord avait fait la guerre. **Celle-ci finie**, les États du Sud redevenaient en fait... (1937, p. 154)	*In the eyes of Lincoln and his friends, it was [...] that the North had waged war. Once the latter had ended, the Southern States became once again in fact...*

The ablative absolute can involve the elliptical use of *une fois* with a past participle:

Une fois rassurées, nous pourrons partir.	*Once we are reassured, we can leave.*
Il reviendra, **une fois fortune faite**.	*He'll come back once he's made his fortune.*

If the noun is accompanied by a determiner, the word order can vary considerably:

Une fois la paix signée, les deux pays ont repris des relations normales.	*Once they had signed the peace treaty, the two countries resumed normal relations.*
La paix une fois signée, les deux pays...	*Idem*
Une fois signée la paix, les deux pays...	*Idem*

Probably the most common instance of this construction is heard by a caller on the answerphone: **Une fois l'enregistrement terminé**, *vous pouvez raccrocher.*

The past participle can be left understood, and here the construction is R2. The construction often involves *une fois* and a preposition:

Une fois dans la maison, on peut préparer un repas.	*Once inside, we can get a meal ready.*
Une fois sur le toit, tu verras les dégâts.	*Once on the roof, you'll see the damage.*
Une fois à la ferme, on peut donner à manger aux animaux.	*Once at the farm, we can feed the animals.*

Although the ablative absolute is often related to time, it can be connected to manner:

Le béret enfoncé jusqu'aux oreilles, il se promenait dans le bois.	*With his beret stuffed down to his ears, he was wandering in the wood.*
Les mains plongées dans les poches, elle errait près de la rivière.	*Her hands deep in her pockets, she wandered near the river.*
Les bras enfouis dans les poches de son manteau, il avait l'air vraiment triste.	*With his arms stuffed right into the pockets of his overcoat, he looked really sad.*

It may also be conditional:

Les cheveux coupés ras, tu nagerais plus vite.	*If your hair were cut really short, you'd swim faster.*

The ablative absolute provides a number of common set phrases:

(Toute) réflexion faite, il vaut mieux...	*On reflection, it is better to...*
Toutes choses considérées, on pourra...	*All things considered, we could...*
Tout bien considéré, il convient de...	*All things well considered, it is wise to...*
Tout compte fait, on reste ici.	*Taking everything into account, we'll stay here.*
Cela dit, elle est repartie.	*Having said that, she left.*

The ablative absolute can also be used with a present participle:

Les sommes d'argent étant perçues, Papa a pu acheter la voiture.	*Once he received the sums of money, Pop was able to buy the automobile.*
Son travail étant terminé, elle regagna l'hôtel.	*Her work over, she returned to the hotel.*

It can be used in conjunction with some intransitive verbs:

Le soir venu, les invités arrivaient en masse.	*When the evening came, the guests poured in.*
Papa parti avec Maman, on a regardé un DVD sur l'Argentine.	*When Pop and Mom had gone out, we watched a DVD on Argentina.*
Je l'ai appris **par personne interposée**.	*I learned of it through someone else.*
Le soir venu, on fit une partie de canoë.	*When evening had come, we did some canoeing.*
La gloire venue, Marie Curie continua à travailler comme une forcenée.	*With the advent of glory, Marie Curie continued to work ferociously.*

If the past participle precedes the noun, no agreement is necessary: *approuvé, attendu, certifié, ci-annexé, ci-inclus, ci-joint, compris, y compris, non compris, entendu, étant donné, excepté, fourni, mis à part, ôté, ouï, passé, quitté, supposé, vu*; **Fini les pourparlers**, *le gouvernement a regagné la capitale.*

In a general way, the ablative absolute is very common in the written form, especially in prose and novel writing, witness a range of illustrations taken from Irène Némirovsky's *Suite française* (2004): **Aussitôt sortie**, *elle regagna la ferme*; **Le déjeuner fini**, *on a flâné un peu*; **Jeanne partie**, *je commençai à faire le ménage*; **Le premier détachement passé**, *un gradé s'avança à cheval*; **les meubles du grand salon enlevés**, *les rideaux décrochés, les provisions entassées dans la cabane* (here there are three); *Les gens*, **le premier instant de terreur passé**, *auraient retrouvé quelque calme*; *Florence s'était retirée chez elle, et* **sa porte verrouillée**, *elle se regardait avec consternation dans la glace*; **arrivée à la porte**, *elle se retourna.*

18

Verb + infinitive when verb + *that* + subordinate clause is used in English / Verbe + infinitif lorsqu'un verbe + *that* + proposition subordonnée s'emploie en anglais

The passage below, taken from *Le Monde* of Saturday June 27, 2009, illustrates how common the verb + infinitive construction really is. The construction is highlighted.

> **Plus du tiers des étudiants affirment avoir des difficultés à gérer leur stress**
>
> Quelque 94,8% des étudiants **assurent être** en bonne ou assez bonne santé, selon une enquête rendue publique le 22 juin par l'Union nationale des sociétés étudiantes mutualistes régionales (USEM). Toutefois, 34,5% **déclarent avoir** des difficultés à gérer leur stress, 22,6% ont des problèmes de sommeil et 8,5% **admettent avoir** eu des pensées suicidaires au cours de l'année écoulée. Quelque 11,2% des étudiants **déclarent avoir** une vision négative de l'avenir. Par ailleurs, 45,2% **estiment ne pas avoir été** suffisament **informés** sur leur choix d'orientation. 12,5% **déclarent avoir** une consommation excessive d'alcool. Le pourcentage d'étudiants ayant consulté un professionnel de santé au cours des six derniers mois est passé de 83,6% en 2007 à 80,5% en 2009. Un quart des étudiants **estiment être** peu ou mal **informés** sur les complémentaires santé [supplementary health details]. Le taux de non-adhésion est passé, entre 2007 et 2009, de 15,3% à 25%.

In a written and elegant style (R3), and this is extremely common, a verb, particularly related to the imagination or intellectual judgment, is followed by an infinitive or a perfect infinitive *when the subjects are identical*. When the direct complement (i.e., the infinitive or perfect infinitive) is replaced by *que = that* and a subordinate clause, the register is standard R2 and is more associated with the spoken language, although this construction would not be out of place in writing. However, as a general rule, it would be safe to assert that there is a clear distinction between the registers: verb + infinitive / perfect infinitive = R2/3; verb + *que* + subordinate clause = R2.

Below is a list of verbs which function in these two ways:

	R2	R2/3
admettre	Vous admettez donc que vous étiez toujours là à minuit ?	Vous admettez donc avoir été toujours là à minuit ?
affirmer	Le témoin a affirmé qu'elle avait vu l'agresseur.	Le témoin a affirmé avoir vu l'agresseur.
ajouter	Le sénateur a ajouté qu'il avait le sentiment que les élections seraient reportées à une date ultérieure.	Le sénateur a ajouté avoir le sentiment que les élections seraient reportées à une date ultérieure.
annoncer	Éléonore a annoncé qu'elle était enceinte.	Éléonore a annoncé être enceinte.
assurer	Je les ai assurés que je n'avais pas été témoin de l'accident.	Je les ai assurés ne pas avoir été témoin de l'accident.
avouer	Lucile avoue qu'elle n'avait pas vu la voiture.	Lucile avoue n'avoir pas vu la voiture.
confirmer	Les jeunes ont confirmé qu'ils étaient rentrés très tard.	Les jeunes ont confirmé être rentrés très tard.
croire	Les victimes croyaient qu'elles allaient mourir; Adeline croyait qu'elle pourrait nous aider.	Les victimes croyaient mourir; Adeline croyait pouvoir nous aider.
déclarer	Jeanne déclara qu'elle n'avait accepté aucun compromis; Robin a déclaré qu'il pouvait assister au jugement.	Jeanne déclara n'avoir accepté aucun compromis; Robin a déclaré pouvoir assister au jugement.
démentir	Mon fils dément qu'il a/ait dit cela.	Mon fils dément avoir dit cela.
dire	Julie a dit qu'elle s'était amusée toute l'après-midi.	Julie a dit s'être amusée toute l'après-midi.
espérer	Sophie espère qu'elle a réussi le portrait de sa mère.	Sophie espère avoir réussi le portrait de sa mère.
ignorer	Françoise ignorait qu'elle avait commis une erreur.	Françoise ignorait avoir commis une erreur.
s'imaginer	Dans un rêve, je m'imaginais que je volais comme un oiseau.	Dans un rêve, je m'imaginais voler comme un oiseau.
jurer	Laetitia a juré qu'elle avait rencontré l'accusé la veille.	Laetitia a juré avoir rencontré l'accusé la veille.
nier	La femme a nié qu'elle était la mère de la petite.	La femme a nié être la mère de la petite.

	R2	R2/3
penser	Diane pense qu'elle pourra jouer du piano ce soir; Mon père ne pense pas qu'il peut/puisse acheter le livre; Je ne pense pas que j'étais présente.	Diane pense pouvoir jouer du piano ce soir; Mon père ne pense pas pouvoir acheter le livre; Je ne pense pas avoir été présente.
prétendre	La fille ne prétend pas qu'elle avait reçu le chèque.	La fille ne prétend pas avoir reçu le chèque.
raconter	L'auteur raconte qu'il avait été invité à une soirée avec Debussy.	L'auteur raconte avoir été invité à une soirée avec Debussy.
se rappeler	Annick se rappelle qu'elle a rencontré ma cousine.	Annick se rappelle avoir rencontré ma cousine.
reconnaître	Marine reconnaît qu'elle avait compose la poésie pour son frère.	Marine reconnaît avoir composé la poésie pour son frère.
regretter	Louis regrette profondément qu'il ait conduit comme un fou.	Louis regrette profondément d'avoir conduit comme un fou.
rêver	J'ai rêvé que j'étais riche comme Crésus.	J'ai rêvé être riche comme Crésus.
se souvenir	Je me souviens que je l'ai dit.	Je me souviens de l'avoir dit.

However, there are circumstances, notably in elegant R3 language, where a following infinitive / perfect infinitive occurs when the subjects are not the same:

*Une actrice entra qui avait la figure et la voix qu'on m'**avait dit être** celles de Sarah Bernhard.*

*Les pieuvres qu'on **disait hanter** les profondeurs de la mer …*

*Où sont les Français que vous **dites avoir été dénoncés** par un agent double ?*

*Il faisait ce qu'il **estimait devoir être** fait.*

*Ces oiseaux que l'on **reconnaissait être** de vrais rapaces …*

*J'ai entendu une voix que les deux cousins **reconnurent pour être** celle de ma sœur.*

*Je ramenais la conversation sur des sujets que je **savais l'intéresser**.*

*J'introduisis dans le débat des idées que je **savais être** vitales.*

*J'ai vu de magnifiques flambeaux que l'on suppose **avoir été achetés** par la duchesse. elle-même.*

*L'héroïne la **croyait avoir perdu** connaissance.*

*Il **jugeait** cette récréation lui **devoir être** profitable.*

There are many verbs followed by an infinitive which suggests a future idea:

J'espère (pouvoir) venir.
Irène promet d'emmener les enfants au parc.
Élisabeth pense venir ce soir.
Yves croit pouvoir régler l'affaire dans quelques jours.

For numerous other uses of the infinitive, see Chapter 12.

19

Pluperfect tense / Le plus-que-parfait

The passage below relates a visit made by a group of young students to a well-known château at Grignan in Provence, southern France. This château was made famous by one of its seventeenth-century inhabitants, Mme de Sévigné, whose *Lettres* set down for posterity the customs, judgments and opinions of her period. Note that *Provence* is not to be confused with *province*. Provence was an old French province, among many others like Alsace, Bretagne, Limousin and Normandie.

Most of this passage is narrated in the pluperfect tense, highlighted whenever it occurs. The first two sentences, however, contain a preterit (*rentra*) and an imperfect (*gardait*), referring to what follows. The pluperfect tense, referring to what precedes, is found in both active and passive voices (*avions parcouru, avait été construit*), as well as in the reflexive (*s'était levé*).

Une petite excursion au château de Grignan
On rentra fatigués et très contents des activités d'une chaude journée au grand air. On gardait en mémoire des vues imprenables, des champs immenses, des coquelicots rouge vif [bright red poppies], la végétation luxuriante et le chant des cigales [cicadas].

Nous **avions parcouru** l'Ardèche et **avions traversé** le Rhône pour explorer et visiter le château de Grignan situé dans la Drôme provençale. Nous **étions venus** en groupe accompagné de notre professeur de français. Notre groupe **s'était levé** pour descendre de l'autocar. À peine **étions-nous arrivés**, nous **avions récupéré** les billets pour notre visite guidée. Notre professeur **avait assisté** à des programmes de visites et à des ateliers de lecture pour faire du repérage et préparer le terrain à ses élèves.

Situé à proximité de la route des vins en Provence et de « l'Enclave des Papes », le château **avait été construit** sur un immense plateau qui surplombe la campagne environnante. Cette demeure **avait été classée** monument historique. Nous **avions franchi** les portes du château pour découvrir les collections d'œuvres et d'objets d'art de cette demeure for- tifiée. À perte de vue, on apercevait de la terrasse la lavande se développer en abondance dans les terrains calcaires de la belle Provence. En été, les champs de lavande semée en zigzag déployaient toute leur richesse, leur couleur vive et fraîche. Une senteur de parfum capiteux s'élevait des fleurs bleues en épi. Les jeunes garçons et jeunes filles, de notre âge, **avaient découvert** le château à travers les lettres de Mme de Sévigné. La marquise **avait écrit** ses lettres qui **avaient remémoré** la beauté fraîche et radieuse de la Provence. Nous **nous étions imprégnés** des lieux et **avions étudié** la manière de vivre, de penser propre à une époque révolue où la vie de château **avait été** un lieu de plaisir, d'agrément et de pouvoir. Les programmes des activités théâtrales, musicales et littéraires **s'étaient vus** élaborer par des experts qui **avaient su** faire revivre la correspondance que Mme de Sévigné **avait envoyée** à sa fille, leurs échanges de lettres et leurs confidences.

Cette petite excursion **avait favorisé** la découverte de cette région riche en vignobles et en oliviers. Le charme envoûtant **avait opéré** [had exerted its effect]. Ce parcours **avait suscité** notre éveil et notre curiosité de jeunes adolescents. Le spectacle de la vie champêtre était un véritable enchantement.

The imperfect of *avoir* or *être* (see Chapter 21 for the imperfect tense) with the past participle forms the pluperfect tense. The pluperfect represents an action, event or thought as not only past but occurring before another action, event or thought which is also in the past.

Agreement in number and gender functions in exactly the same way as in the perfect tense (see Chapter 14 for the perfect tense). Suffice it therefore to offer here just three examples with respect to agreement:

Il **était déjà parti** quand je l'ai appelé. — *He had already left when I called him.*

Elle s'est rendu compte qu'on **l'avait trompée**. — *She realized they had deceived her.*

Quand je leur ai téléphoné, **ils étaient déjà sortis**. — *When I phoned them they had already gone out.*

There are a variety of usages with the pluperfect tense.

Past tense (usually the perfect tense in speech and frequently the preterit / past definite in writing) plus pluperfect tense – usage here is the same as in English:

Je lui ai dit / Je lui dis qu'il **avait écrit** la lettre / qu'elle **était venue**. — *I told her that he had written the letter / that she had come.*

La Poste a informé Céline que quelqu'un **avait déjà envoyé** le colis. — *The Post Office informed Céline that someone had already sent the parcel.*

Pluperfect tense plus perfect/preterit tense (the reverse of the above):

À peine **était-elle arrivée** qu'on l'a rappelée / qu'on la rappela.	*Hardly had she arrived when they called her back.*
Ils n'**avaient** pas encore **déjeuné** quand je suis arrivée.	*They hadn't had their lunch when I arrived.*

Pluperfect tense and conditional (see Chapter 26 for the conditional):

J'**avais cru** que la famille m'accueillerait.	*I had thought that the family would welcome me.*
David les **avait prévenus** qu'il ne pourrait (pas) partir en vacances.	*David had warned them he couldn't go on vacation.*

Pluperfect tense and present tense:

Dès cette époque, j'**avais compris** qu'il ne faut pas trop demander.	*From that time, I had understood that I mustn't expect too much.*

Pluperfect tense and a preposition + infinitive:

Stéphanie **était venue** pour vous demander de nous accompagner.	*Stéphanie had come to ask you to accompany us.*
Tu sais très bien que nous **avions acheté** les billets afin d'aller au théâtre ce soir.	*You know very well that we had bought the tickets to go to the theater this evening.*

In hypothetical clauses with the conjunction *si*, the pluperfect is used with the conditional in the past:

Si j'**avais su** le résultat, **je t'aurais offert** un cadeau.	*If I had known the result, I would have given you a present.*
Si tu **avais été** plus patiente, tu **aurais gagné** la partie.	*If you had been more patient, you would have won the game.*

In R3 literary style, the pluperfect subjunctive is still used. It is argued that such a feature is archaic, but many contemporary authors still have recourse to it in the third-person singular, and noticeably in the construction *si* in conjunction with *comme*: "Sa main quitta son veston, s'accrocha au revers de celui du pasteur, *comme s'il eût voulu* le secouer" (Malraux 1976a, p. 437); "Elle eut un mouvement de honte [. . .] comme *si elle eût craint* que ses voisins . . . " (Green 1927, p. 248); "'Plus j'y pense', continua Marie Ladouet comme si elle n'*eût rien remarqué* . . . " (Green 1927, p. 248).

In speech, *comme si* is followed by the indicative of the pluperfect:

Sabrina a poussé les hauts cris, **comme si elle était devenue** folle.	*Sabrina shouted out loud as if she had gone mad.*
Rémi s'est mis à courir rapidement, **comme s'il avait été entraîné** par le meilleur coach du monde.	*Rémi began to run fast, as if he had been trained by the world's best coach.*

As with the last example above, the pluperfect is used in the passive:

Louise **n'avait jamais été blessée**, de sorte qu'elle ne savait pas ce que c'était qu'une intense douleur.	*Louise had never been hurt, so that she did not know what intense pain was.*
Alain m'a raconté qu'ils **avaient été poursuivis** par un ours au Canada.	*Alain told me that they had been chased by a bear in Canada.*
Nous **n'avions jamais été accueillis** si chaleureusement.	*We had never been welcomed so warmly.*

The pluperfect may be used to "soften" the impact of speech:

J'étais venue pour te demander d'aller au cinéma avec moi.	*I had come to ask you to go to the cinema with me.*

Instead of:

Je suis venue pour te demander d'aller au cinéma avec moi.	*I have come to ask you to go to the cinema with me.*

Frequently, as has been observed above, the French pluperfect has an easily recognizable correspondence with its English use. However, there is one circumstance where such a correspondence does not obtain. When a conjunction of time like *quand, lorsque, aussitôt que, dès que, après que* introduces a subordinate clause which depends on a main clause in the past, a conditional in the past is used, whereas in English the pluperfect occurs. The French construction, determined by a hypothesis, seems more logical than the English pluperfect :

J'ai dit à Jeanne que je viendrais **lorsque j'aurais terminé** mon travail.	*I told Jeanne that I would come when I **had** finished my work.*
Francis a promis de réparer la crevaison **quand il aurait acheté** des rustines.	*Francis promised to repair the puncture when he **had** bought some patches.*
Le relieur m'a assurè que la thèse serait prête **quelques jours après qu'il aurait reçu** les arrhes.	*The binder assured me that the thesis would be ready a few days after he **had** received the deposit.*

The French pluperfect is sometimes equivalent to a simple past tense or perfect tense:

Je te l'**avais** bien **dit**.	*I told you so.*
Nous vous **avions parlé** du problème.	*We've already told you about the problem.*

20

Past anterior tense / Le passé antérieur

The past anterior is a purely written tense and is used only in the following situations:

tense of main/ introductory clause	subordinate clause introduced by	tense of subordinate clause
past historic	*à peine, après que, aussitôt que, dès que, lorsque, quand*	past anterior

In other words, the past anterior expresses an unrepeated event or thought which takes place in a determined or limited time before another, and this latter event or thought is expressed in the past historic. As with other compound tenses, it is conjugated with *avoir* or *être*:

Quand Valentin **fut arrivé**, je partis.	*When Valentin (had) arrived, I left.*
Dès que Marie **eut terminé** son travail, elle se leva.	*As soon as Marie finished her work, she got up.*
À peine **furent-ils sortis** qu'on les rappela.	*Hardly had they gone out than they were recalled.*

The past anterior may also be used in the following way: *Virgine* **n'eut pas** *plus tôt* **dit** *cela qu'elle le regretta* (*No sooner had Virginie said that than she regretted it*); "J'ai compris lentement qu'il était mort, au bout de quelques jours, quand l'écho de sa belle voix harmonieuse *eut fini* de sonner entre les murs" (Colette, in Grevisse and Goosse 2008, p. 1095).

The past anterior can be replaced by the *passé surcomposé*, but this is rare and carries little general conviction these days, which is why the example comes from the seventeenth century: "Aussitôt que j'ai eu envoyé mon paquet, j'ai appris une triste nouvelle" (Mme de Sévigné, in Grevisse and Goosse 2008, p. 1096). See Chapter 14, Section 14.5 for comments on the *passé surcomposé*.

21

Imperfect tense / L'imparfait

The passage below describes the traditional grape harvest in southern France that would take place during the childhood of one of the authors who would share in this activity. It is a question of fond, affectionate memories of long ago. An annual and therefore cyclical event, the grape harvest is evoked with a series of verbs in the imperfect tense which emphasizes the repetitive nature of grape harvesting. The imperfect tense is highlighted and some translations are provided.

Needless to add, wine-making is central to the way of life of many French rural communities. It explains the fortune amassed by Balzac's Père Grandet in *Eugénie Grandet*. He was a master cooper (*maître tonnelier*), and made his fortune from the production of barrels.

Une partie de vendanges dans l'Ardèche méridionale
L'Ardèche méridionale s'étend entre l'Auvergne et la Provence. Le climat naturel, l'accent des habitants, le patois ardéchois des anciens, les paysages pittoresques font de ce cadre un environnement attachant. Ce patrimoine régional **était** et reste toujours préservé. Au moment des vendanges, les péniches se **déplaçaient** tranquillement sur le bord du Rhône. Elles **descendaient** et **remontaient** ce grand fleuve, frontière naturelle arrosant plusieurs départements.

Les vendanges **étaient** annonciatrices d'une nouvelle saison. Nos voisins **possédaient** de grands vignobles en bordure du Rhône. À la fin de l'été, Hortensia et Jeannot nous **sollicitaient**, pour cueillir les raisins mûrs, le samedi et le dimanche. Une matinée de labeur **se terminait** par un Festin de Balthazar dans leur famille. L'après-midi **était ponctuée** par un goûter savoureux. La mère d'Hortensia et sa sœur Léa **préparaient** soigneusement un menu copieux et nous **demandaient** au préalable nos préférences. Jeannot **était** chansonnier [composer and singer of what are often satirical pieces] et garde-champêtre [gamekeeper] de notre village natal. Il sifflait comme un merle [blackbird]. « Le marchand de bonheur » nous **distribuait** un sécateur, un panier d'osier, une casquette, des lunettes de soleil et une bouteille d'eau minérale.

Les jeunes vendangeurs et vendangeuses **récoltaient** les fruits et **chan-taient** des chansons populaires comme « Chevalier de la table ronde », « Colchiques dans les prés »... Une joyeuse ambiance **régnait** dans les vignobles. Les couleurs chaudes et flamboyantes [bright] de l'automne **ranimaient** notre ardeur et notre enthousiasme pour remplir les cuves [vats] en bois qui **étaient rangées** sur le tracteur au bout de l'allée. Ce travail en plein air nous **ravissait** tous autant les uns que les autres.

Les vignerons **s'installaient** dans le village et **produisaient** le vin sur la place publique à proximité de notre école primaire. Lorsque les vendanges **se terminaient**, la fête villageoise **battait** son plein [was in full swing] et **attirait** beaucoup de monde, y compris ceux des villages ruraux environnants. Un char fleuri **était orné** de feuilles de vignes colorées, de raisin blanc et noir, de tonneaux [barrels] de vin. Ce char tiré par quatre chevaux **faisait** le tour du village. Un bon accordéoniste assis à côté du conducteur **jouait**, avec entrain, des morceaux de musique sous les exclamations de joie de la population.

The imperfect tense is best studied in conjunction with the perfect and preterit tenses (see Chapter 23 on the contrasts between these three tenses) since all three are frequently linked to each other. In regular verbs, the imperfect tense is obtained by adding the following endings to the stem:

	chanter	*vendre*	*finir*	*recevoir*
je	chant**ais**	vend**ais**	finiss**ais**	recev**ais**
tu	chant**ais**	vend**ais**	finiss**ais**	recev**ais**
il/elle	chant**ait**	vend**ait**	finiss**ait**	recev**ait**
nous	chant**ions**	vend**ions**	finiss**ions**	recev**ions**
vous	chant**iez**	vend**iez**	finiss**iez**	recev**iez**
ils/elles	chant**aient**	vend**aient**	finiss**aient**	recev**aient**

Note that the first- and second-persons singular of these conjugations are the same. Note also that, from the pronunciation point of view, there can be confusion over the endings –**ais**/–**ait**/–**aient** since many French speakers tend to produce a closed **e** (é), as in the past participle (*chant*é), whereas the more accepted and recommended sound is an open **e** (è). Furthermore, with respect to pronunciation, when the endings –**ions** and –**iez** are added to a verb where the root is **i** or a semi-vowel, **y** (yod), current usage does not mark the difference between the present tense (*nous oublions/sourions, nous essayons, nous travaillons*) and the imperfect (*nous oubliions/souriions, nous essayions, nous travaillions*). It is by no means incorrect to mark the double yod in pronunciation, and it could be useful for clarity's sake. At the same time, an excessive insistence on the double yod could sound pretentious. The same comment applies to the present subjunctive, first-person plural, of *oublier, sourire, essayer* and *travailler*, which is the same as the imperfect.

The fundamental value of the imperfect tense is to express continuance, as of an action prolonged either in itself or by successive repetition. It conveys what was habitual, customary, and describes qualities of persons or things, and the place or condition in which they were, in the past. It often refers to something unfinished, and therefore imperfect. *Je chantais* corresponds to the English *I was singing, used to sing, would sing*, and *sang*. In this sense, it is much simpler than the several English equivalents, which make life difficult for French speakers learning English.

21.1 Ways in which the imperfect is used

The imperfect is used to convey repeated and habitual past actions, and there are many introductory words or expressions which provide a clue to it: *tous les, chaque, autrefois, toujours, de temps à autre | en temps, d'habitude, périodiquement, parfois, quelquefois*:

Sabrina **s'habillait** à la dernière mode.	*Sabrina dressed in the latest fashion.*
À cette époque, elle **s'habillait** à la dernière mode.	*At that time, she dressed in the latest fashion.*
Chaque année toute la famille **allait** à la mer.	*Each year, the whole family would go to the seaside.*
Tous les soirs, Adeline **s'entraînait** à jouer du violon.	*Every evening, Adeline practiced on the violin.*
Autrefois, on **s'éclairait** à la chandelle.	*Once upon a time, people used candles for light.*
Autrefois, la bibliothèque **n'était** pas ouverte le dimanche.	*Formerly, the library wasn't open on Sundays.*
Le train **était** toujours à l'heure.	*The train was always on time.*
On **entendait** de temps à autre le bruissement des feuilles dans les arbres.	*We would occasionally hear the rustling of the leaves in the trees.*
D'habitude, je me **levais** à six heures du matin pour aller à la piscine.	*I usually got up at six in the morning to go to the swimming pool.*
Céline **souffrait** périodiquement des maux de tête.	*Céline suffered headaches periodically.*
Parfois, la factrice **passait** à dix heures du matin.	*Sometimes, the mailwoman would come by at ten in the morning.*
Quelquefois, l'alarme **sonnait** sans aucune explication.	*Sometimes the alarm sounded for no reason at all.*

The imperfect denotes length of time which is usually imprecise:

En juillet, toute la famille **était** en Alberta.
In July, the whole family were in Alberta.

En 2002, je **faisais** des études de médecine à Toronto.
In 2002, I was studying medicine at Toronto.

M. Legrand n'a pas pu participer à la réunion parce qu'il **était** en déplacement à l'étranger.
M. Legrand could not take part in the meeting because he was traveling abroad.

The imperfect is used in descriptions of the environment, natural or built:

Du haut de la colline, on **apercevait** un petit village dont les toits **brillaient** au soleil.
From the hilltop, we/they could see a small village, the roofs of which were shining in the sun.

La maison des étés de mon enfance **avait** des volets bleus.
The house where I spent my childhood summers had blue shutters.

Similarly in descriptions of people:

La dame **était** svelte, et d'une élégance admirable.
The lady was lissom and of an admirable elegance.

Ma mère **avait** les cheveux châtain foncé et **souriait** de façon si charmante.
My mother had dark chestnut-colored hair and smiled with such a charming smile.

Used with the conjunction *si*, the imperfect is not really a past tense but rather serves to express a hypothesis or an unreality. The other part of the sentence contains a conditional tense:

Si nous **avions** une voiture, nous pourrions visiter le Grand Canyon.
If we had an automobile, we could visit the Grand Canyon.

Si j'**héritais** d'une fortune, je me paierais un voyage en Afrique.
If I inherited a fortune, I'd treat myself to a trip to Africa.

Si mon coach m'**entraînait** comme il faut, je courrais le cent mètres en 9 secondes.
If my coach trained me correctly, I'd run the hundred meters in nine seconds.

As with the pluperfect (see Chapter 19), *comme si* is followed by the imperfect:

Elle a conduit la voiture comme si elle **conduisait** un bolide en Formule 1.
She drove the automobile as if she were driving a Formula 1 racing car.

On entendait un fracas infernal comme si la maison **allait** exploser.
We heard an appalling ruckus as if the house were going to explode.

The construction *comme si* may be followed by the imperfect subjunctive (see Chapter 44) in literary language, but this is largely restricted to the third-person singular:

"C'était comme si ce regard que le docteur avait jeté sur elle la **suivît** partout et la **contraignît** à ne penser qu'à lui" (Green 1927, p. 102).

It was as if this look the physician had cast on her followed her everywhere and forced her to only think of him.

In keeping with the hypothesis with *si* are the following:

Si j'**étais** plus jeune!
If I were younger!

Si j'**étais** vous...
If I were you...

Si on **allait** au cinéma ce soir?
What if we went to the movies this evening?

Si nous **faisions** le cours maintenant et pas demain?
Supposing we had the class now and not tomorrow?

Si jeunesse **savait**, si vieillesse **pouvait**...
If youth knew, if old people could...

Contre toute attente, elle est sortie toute souriante du bureau du chef comme si **de rien n'était**.
Against all expectancy, she came out of the boss's office all smiles, as if nothing had happened.

The hypothesis does not necessarily require a conditional in one part of the sentence:

Si elle voyait un mendiant, elle ne **manquait** pas de lui offrir de l'argent.
If she saw a beggar, she never failed to offer him some money.

Si l'on **allait** à la plage, on n'**oubliait** jamais de prendre la planche à voile.
If we went to the beach, we never forgot to take the sailboard.

Même si is followed by the imperfect:

Même si tu me **donnais** tout ton argent, je n'irais pas.
Even if you gave me all your money, I wouldn't go.

Même si j'**étais** le garçon le plus intelligent du monde, je ne me présenterais pas à l'examen.
Even if I were the cleverest boy in the world, I wouldn't sit the exam.

The *si* clause in a hypothesis is not infrequently followed by a conditional, and not the imperfect. This construction is not to be recommended, although unlettered speakers and children use it:

Si j'**aurais** de l'argent, j'achèterais   *If I had some money, I'd buy a BMW.*
une BM(W).
Si je **serais** à la plage, je ferais de   *If I were at the beach, I would so some*
la planche à voile.   *windsurfing.*

The imperfect can imply politeness or softening of a statement (*atténuation* in French) with some verbs:

Excusez-moi de vous déranger, je   *I am sorry to disturb you, I just*
voulais vous demander un   *wanted to ask you a question.*
renseignement.
Je **venais** vous prier de le recevoir.   *I have come / came to ask you to*
    receive him.
Je **pensais** que vous feriez   *I thought you would perhaps do well*
peut-être bien de lui envoyer un   *to send him an e-mail.*
courriel.

The imperfect is also used in novels, newspapers, and even television and radio documentaries when reference is made to a single event, or events in restricted time. This form is called the *imparfait narratif* or *pittoresque*, and would not be heard in normal discourse:

Staline **naissait** il y a plus de cent   *Stalin was born more than a hundred*
ans.   *years ago.*
Dans son discours, elle **évoquait**   *In her speech, she referred to the*
la crise énergétique.   *energy crisis.*
Hier soir M. Dupont **définissait**   *Yesterday evening, M. Dupont defined*
les raisons des saisies   *the reasons for house repossessions.*
immobilières.

Notwithstanding the above remark that the *imparfait narratif* would not be heard in speech, one could certainly hear in refined language:

Elle est entrée à l'hôpital le 15, et   *She went into hospital on the 15th, and*
huit jours après elle en **sortait**   *a week later she came out cured.*
guérie.

The imperfect can express a sharp and striking fact or feature following on from an imperfect, preterit or conditional tense. This applies to both writing and speech:

Il était temps; un moment après   *It was time; a moment later, she would*
elle **partait**.   *be leaving.*
Elle ouvrit la porte, et un pas de   *She opened the door, and one more*
plus, elle **était** dans le couloir.   *step, she would be in the corridor.*
J'aurais discuté, j'**obtenais** mille   *If I had argued, I would have gotten*
euros de plus.   *another thousand euros.*
Il n'avait qu'à dire une parole de   *If he had said one more word, I would*
plus et je lui **cassais** la gueule.   *have smashed his face in.*

The imperfect is also used in a hypothesis introduced by *sans*, and here the conditional occurs in English. It goes without saying that the conditional could be used in French in these examples:

Sans son aide, je **tombais**.	*But for her help, I would have fallen.*
Sans leur intervention, les pourparlers n'**aboutissaient** à rien.	*Without their intervention, the talks would have gone nowhere.*

With certain verbs (*devoir, falloir, pouvoir, valoir mieux*), the imperfect is used when followed by an infinitive:

Il ne **fallait** pas le dire.	*You should not have said it.*
Il **fallait** y penser	*You/she should have thought about it.*
Tu **devais** y penser.	*You ought to have thought about it.*
Elle **pouvait** s'en sortir.	*She could have sorted it out.*
Mieux valait m'avertir.	*It would have been better to let me know.*

Devoir, falloir, pouvoir and *valoir mieux* have the same meaning as the above in the conditional: *Il aurait fallu y penser | Tu aurais dû y penser | Elle aurait pu s'en sortir | Il aurait valu mieux m'avertir.*

The imperfect of *devoir* can also suggest a future in the past:

Ses amis le quittèrent. Il ne **devait** plus les revoir.	*His friends left him. He was not to see them any more.*
J'ai si bien réussi mon travail que l' entreprise ne **devait** plus recourir à mes services.	*I did the work so successfully that the company no longer had need of my services.*

As in English, the imperfect or present tense can follow another verb in the past when indirect speech is involved:

On a dit que Robin **était** à l'hôpital.	*They said Robin was in hospital.*
Je ne savais pas que c'**était** lui le responsable / Je ne savais pas que c'**est** lui le responsable.	*I didn't know it was he/him who was responsible.*
Je n'aurais jamais cru que c'**était** à elle qu'il fallait s'adresser / Je n'aurais jamais cru que c'**est** à elle qu'il faut s'adresser.	*I would never have believed that you had to deal with her.*

With these alternatives of imperfect or present tense, it is likely that the imperfect tense would be used, particularly if the idea in the speaker's mind sees the event as completed. This is especially true when the imperfect ending is **–ais** or **–ait**.

22

Preterit tense / Le passé simple

The following passage describes young members of a family picking figs in an orchard in southern France. It relates the conversion of these figs into jam and the enjoyment of this jam by the family the next morning. The passage also devotes a few lines to an accident narrowly avoided by one of the pickers. The whole piece is suffused with a happy tone reflecting a child's delight in the wonders of nature. The preterit or past definite is used to retell a series of events that unfold in quick succession. This tense is highlighted in every case. Some translations are offered.

La cueillette de figues

Notre plus gros figuier surplombait [overhung] un rocher et donnait dans [overlooked] la cour d'un voisin, située plusieurs centaines de mètres plus bas. Le terrain était glissant. Etant donné notre jeune âge, nous n'étions pas autorisés à nous approcher de cet arbre fruitier sans la présence d'un adulte. Ce figuier de plus de quatre mètres de haut, au tronc tortueux et aux courbes irrégulières, nous **frappa** d'étonnement. À maturité, il **donna** de délicieux fruits de couleur vert pâle et violette.

En été, nous ramassions les figues fraîches. Ce fruit charnu [fleshy] et juteux, agréable au palais, était mon dessert préféré dans sa saison. Pour cueillir plus de fruits, mon cousin **grimpa** de plus en plus haut sur le figuier. Quand soudain les branches **ployèrent** [sagged] sous le poids de cet homme. Les rameaux sur lesquels il **se redressa**, **cassèrent**. J'**eus** une grande frayeur ! Soudain, je **fis** demi-tour [I went back] pour aller chercher de l'aide à la maison. Tétanisée [Paralyzed] de peur, j'**exposai** à mes parents les faits qui s'étaient produits brusquement sous mes yeux. Quand soudain, mon cousin **se présenta** et nous **raconta** le récit de cette aventure. Je me **remis** de mes frayeurs, soulagée de savoir qu'il **s'était tiré** de l'accident sans une égratignure avec un panier rempli de fruits fraîchement cueillis. Aussitôt récoltées, les figues **se transformèrent** en confiture. La préparation de la confiture **nécessita** le savoir-faire de maman. Elle **accepta** notre aide pour la pesée [weighing] des fruits. Sous notre regard, maman **lava** rapidement les figues sous l'eau courante, les **égoutta** [drained] soigneusement, **sectionna** le pédoncule [stem] puis les **découpa** en quatre. Dans un récipient, elle **versa** délicatement le sucre en poudre. Elle **mélangea** le tout à l'aide d'une cuillère en bois, **laissa** cuire et enfin **mélangea** le tout, en écumant [skimming] régulièrement, pour éviter que le fond du chaudron de cuivre n'attache.

Le lendemain matin, mes parents se **levèrent** au chant du coq. Peu après, nous **emboîtâmes** le pas [we followed them], réveillés par le délicieux arôme de café et de chocolat. Le pain cuisant au four **cha-touilla** agréablement notre odorat. On s'en **lécha** les babines [We licked our chops] au petit-déjeuner. Une fois assis à table après avoir fait notre toilette, maman **sortit** le pain du four puis nous **servit** notre chocolat au lait et **étala** du beurre et de la confiture de figues sur des tranches de pain chaud. Ce **fut** un vrai régal [treat] !

The preterit tense is also called in English the past historic or even the past definite. In French it has two names: *passé simple* and *passé défini*. It is hardly ever used *à l'oral*, in other words in speech, but occurs frequently in writing, especially in novels and students' essays referring to historical events. One comes across it in newspapers, talks on the radio and even television which treat historical topics. It can be heard occasionally in formal speeches and lectures since it invests the style with a higher, literary tone. It therefore falls into an essentially R3 category of language. Yet it is not a tense to be ignored even if it does not appear in everyday use, for children encounter it very early: Perrault's fairy stories, like *Le chat botté* (*Puss in Boots*) or *Cendrillon* (*Cinderella*), introduce them very soon to its use and forms since it is the narrative tense par excellence. French-speaking children, like all students of the French language, need to accustom themselves to the preterit, given its pervasive appearance in novels and historical documents. They learn the models of the preterit, and the preterit of the main irregular verbs, by reciting them, just as one learns arithmetic tables. Here are the forms of the preterit in the four model verbs:

	chanter	*vendre*	*finir*	*recevoir*
je	chant**ai**	vend**is**	fin**is**	reç**us**
tu	chant**as**	vend**is**	fin**is**	reç**us**
il/elle	chant**a**	vend**it**	fin**it**	reç**ut**
nous	chant**âmes**	vend**îmes**	fin**îmes**	reç**ûmes**
vous	chant**âtes**	vend**îtes**	fin**îtes**	reç**ûtes**
ils/elles	chant**èrent**	vend**irent**	fin**irent**	reç**urent**

Only the first- and third-person singular and third-person plural forms are in current use, and even here, the first-person singular form is not too common. Since the concept of the narrative involves a recounting of what happened, what was seen, what was thought by someone, the third person is often the point of view chosen by a narrator.

It is argued that, since the forms of the past historic are difficult to handle, they have fallen into disuse. Such a reasoning holds little weight since both Italian and Spanish have constant and everyday recourse to them, and the preterit forms that exist in these two Romance languages are just as complicated as they are in French. The partial disappearance, at least in spoken discourse, of the preterit in French must remain a mystery.

As far as pronunciation is concerned, despite the circumflex accent on the first- and second-person plural forms, the vowels here are brief and sharp. Furthermore, the first-person *chantai* sounds differently from *chantais*, the preterit requiring the closed e (é), and the imperfect requiring an open e (è). This is a difference that is slowly disappearing. Despite the circumflex accents, the endings of the first- and second-person plurals sound sharp and brief, and are not lengthened in any way.

Although the preterit refers to a specific point in time, it is used when referring to any duration which has a properly defined end:

L'auteure **vécut** quarante ans au Brésil.	*The author lived forty years in Brazil.*
La guerre **dura** trente ans.	*The war lasted thirty years.*

The preterit is also used in the passive:

Lorsque les prisonniers **furent relâchés**, ils regagnèrent leur domicile.	*When the prisoners were released, they returned home.*
L'étudiant **fut encouragé** à préparer le concours.	*The student was encouraged to prepare the (competitive) examination.*
Quand son trouble **fut dissipé**, la jeune fille lui dit...	*When she regained her composure, the girl said to him/her...*

The preterit recounts in a clear-cut way an event or thought taking place in the past, usually, at a distance from the present moment. It exerts no effect on the present moment, as opposed to the perfect tense. Here are three edited examples of the use of the preterit. The first is taken from a novel, the second from a history book and the third from a children's book:

1. "Il [L'enfant] *resta* ainsi pendant de longues secondes [...] La bourrasque passée, il *se détendit* un peu, la fièvre *sembla* se retirer et l'abandonner [...] Quand le flot brûlant l'*atteignit* à nouveau pour la troisième fois et le *souleva* un peu, l'enfant se *recroquevilla*, *recula* au fond du lit [...] et *agita* follement la tête" (Camus 1962a, p. 1394).
2. "Une occasion favorable *fut* fournie au gouvernement de Washington par la rébellion canadienne de 1837. Les insurgés, réfugiés au Massachusetts et au Vermont, y *organisèrent* des associations anti-britanniques et *provoquèrent* un incident diplomatique entre Londres et le gouvernement fédéral. Aussitôt qu'il *fut* clos, les deux parties *demandèrent* la fixation d'une frontière stable entre le Maine et le Canada" (Préclin 1937, p. 110).

3. "Il était une fois un gentilhomme qui **épousa** en secondes noces une femme, la plus hautaine et la plus fière qu'on **eût** jamais vue. [...] Les noces ne **furent** pas plus tôt faites, que la belle-mère **fit** éclater sa mauvaise humeur !; elle ne **put** souffrir les bonnes qualitiés de [Cendrillon]. Elle la **chargea** des plus viles occupations de la maison" (Perrault 1983, pp. 5–6).

The preterit of *vouloir* can imply *tried*: Valentin **voulut** sortir mais en vain. *Valentin tried to get out but in vain.*

The preterit of *pouvoir* can imply *managed to*: Au bout d'une semaine difficile, Émilie **put** terminer son mémoire. *After a difficult week, Émilie managed to finish her dissertation.*

The preterit of *savoir* implies *to learn*: Après trois jours d'attente, Françoise **sut** le résultat. *After three days of waiting, Françoise learned the result.*

The mark of a cultured person is observed in the following set expressions with *fut*: Il **fut** un temps où tout le monde aspirait à une éducation universitaire. J'ai connu votre père, un digne homme **s'il en fut**. *Once upon a time, everyone aspired to a university education. I knew your father, an honorable man if ever there was one.*

C'était un garçon d'esprit **s'il en fut**. *He was a witty boy if ever there was one.*

Some authors write *fût* (imperfect subjunctive), but Grevisse and Goosse disapprove of this.

23

Contrasts between the perfect tense, preterit tense and imperfect tense / Les contrastes entre le passé composé, le passé simple et l'imparfait

Below is a passage relating a stroll along the Canal du Midi, which runs through Toulouse in southern France. The passage includes a few lines from Claude Nougaro, a well-known poet and singer who sang the delights of Toulouse, his hometown. The term *Minimes*, unknown to most modern French speakers, alludes to a recondite religious order. Reference is also made to Pierre-Paul de Riquet, a seventeenth-century engineer renowned for his creation of the canal. Toulouse is described as a *ville rose*, given the brick-colored buildings that stand out most clearly from the air. This description of Toulouse as a *ville rose* generates a resonance in the whole of France. The piece includes the three tenses: imperfect, perfect and past definite. These are referred to in the text as **(imp)**, **(p)** and **(pd)**. Note how easily they are dovetailed into each other, at least in written prose. Of course, this would not be the case in speech. Some translations are provided.

Une promenade au fil de l'eau

Pour moi, la navigation fluviale **s'est** toujours **alliée (p)** à un souvenir d'enfance. En bordure du Rhône, de nombreux bateaux de plaisance, des chaloupes de pêche [fishing boats], des chalands [barges] et des péniches [barges] **restaient (imp)** à quai le temps de nos vacances scolaires. Aussitôt **retrouvâmes**-nous **(pd)** ce cadre aux abords de Toulouse que notre regard empreint de nostalgie se **posa (pd)** sur l'embarcadère. Nous **saisîmes (pd)** immédiatement l'occasion d'une charmante promenade au fil de l'eau [stroll downstream]. La crue des eaux [rise in the waters] ne nous **permit (pd)** pas de naviguer sur la Garonne. Notre choix se **fixa (pd)** donc sur le Canal du Midi. Ce célèbre canal **a été rebaptisé (p)** le Canal des Deux Mers.

Les ouvrages construits tout au long du canal témoignent du génie de Pierre-Paul Riquet et d'une grande imagination des hommes. Le Canal du Midi est inscrit au patrimoine mondial de l'humanité. Les avenues ombragées, tout au long du canal, **ont** toujours **attiré (p)** des promeneurs. La Cité de l'Espace renferme des monuments historiques et d'imposants établissements industriels reconvertis en musées ou en universités. Ce **fut (pd)** le cas, notamment, de la Manufacture des Tabacs. La capitale de la région Midi-Pyrénées se trouve à un carrefour de l'Europe de par [by virtue of] sa situation géographique. Claude Nougaro, chanteur et poète, **naquit (pd)** à Toulouse. Il **a laissé (p)** dans les mémoires collectives sa célèbre chanson:

Ô Toulouse
Qu'il est loin mon pays, qu'il est loin
Parfois au fond de moi se raniment
L'eau verte du canal du Midi
Et la brique rouge des Minimes [...]
Ô mon pays, Ô Toulouse, Ô Toulouse.

Après une visite de la ville en passant par la Place du Capitole, nous **avons pris (p)** tranquillement, à la nuit tombante, nos billets avant de nous installer dans une ancienne péniche marchande, rénovée et aménagée pour la circonstance. Les chanceux navigateurs et propriétaires de la péniche **passaient (imp)** d'une table à l'autre pour accueillir leurs convives [guests]. Notre balade nocturne se **fit (pd)** dans la convivialité et **marqua (pd)** un événement festif.

Durant notre long circuit nous **savourions (imp)** avec un plaisir intense les spécialités du terroir tout en explorant l'ensemble des quartiers de la ville de Toulouse situés sur la rive droite et gauche du canal. Nous **tombâmes (pd)** sous le charme irrésistible de la Ville rose. Les curiosités touristiques et les mystérieuses forces de la nature **furent (pd)** une source de bien-être. L'horloge **égrenait (imp** = peeled off) ses heures. Minuit **sonna (pd)**, il **était (imp)** l'heure de regagner notre gîte. La visite de la ville nous **enchanta (pd)**. Nous **avons joui (p)** d'un séjour extraordinaire.

Since all three tenses, the perfect, past definite and imperfect, concentrate almost entirely on events in the past, it seems helpful to provide a synthesis of the way they function in relation to each other. Reference is made to the chapters on these three tenses (perfect: Chapter 14; past definite: Chapter 22; imperfect: Chapter 21) as the starting point.

23.1 Differences between the perfect and the preterit

Whereas the preterit is essentially a narrative tense, relating a series of events or thoughts in a novel or historical document, the perfect tense is one of conversation, letter writing and so on within a social context of family, friends, acquaintances and professional colleagues. Events and thoughts, however remote in time, are conveyed by this compound tense. *Elle chanta* has the resonance of a literary form and *Elle a chanté* almost automatically suggests speech and social intercourse in a quite different context from the preterit. Furthermore, the perfect tense in French often corresponds to the preterit in English, for it can refer back into distant time. *J'ai perdu connaissance* is easily used in French whereas, in English, *I have lost consciousness* has little meaning unless one has a spectacular imagination. *I lost consciousness* would be more appropriate here.

The perfect and preterit do exist comfortably side by side when a dialogue is set within a narrative recounted in the preterit, and this is normal procedure: *"Je n'ai pas reçu la lettre," s'écria-t-elle. "Mais je t'assure que je te l'ai envoyée," répondit-il / répliqua-t-il.*

23.2 Differences between the preterit and the imperfect

Whereas the imperfect tense relates to events that have no clear ending, or take place over an unspecified period of time, the preterit refers to a very sharply defined action or event but almost exclusively in the written form. The French equivalent of the English *I was reading the paper when my mother walked in* is *Je lisais le journal quand ma mère entra*. The imperfect reflects continuous time, while the preterit cuts across this continuum. Put another way, when we express two past actions, occurring at the same time, the shorter action is conveyed by the preterit while the longer one is in the imperfect. This explanation is better understood by a simple diagram:

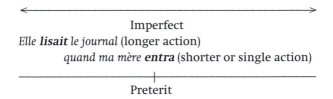

23.3 Differences between the perfect and the imperfect

Whereas the imperfect tense relates to events that have no clear ending, or take place over an unspecified period of time, the perfect refers to any event or thought occurring in the past but within a spoken context, or in letter writing and so on. The same diagram as above applies:

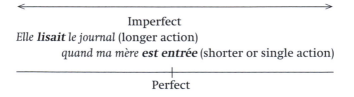

An excellent and decisive literary illustration of the differences between the three tenses is highlighted by a parallel study of two of Albert Camus's fictional works, *L'étranger* and *La peste*. The first work, which Camus calls a *roman* but which has the length of a *récit*, is written almost entirely in the perfect and imperfect tenses. The perfect tense corresponds most appropriately to the world outlook of the main character, Meursault, who narrates his past experience in the perfect tense and in the first person, with the occasional interjection of the imperfect. The openness and lack of definition implied by the perfect tense promote a sense of the uncertainty and permanent existential availability felt by Meursault, who feels a hesitation and inconclusiveness over the meaning of his presence in this world. The perfect tense, unusual in the narrative form, entails perplexity and unpredictability, not just with respect to the recent past, but also with respect to the present and even to the future. There follows a pivotal passage in the novel where Meursault describes his murder of an Arab, inconsequential from his point of view. The specific events are narrated in the perfect tense while the surrounding circumstances are conveyed by the imperfect:

> Dès qu'il m'**a vu**, il **s'est soulevé** un peu et **a mis** la main dans sa poche. Moi, naturellement, j'**ai serré** le revolver de Raymond dans mon veston. Alors, de nouveau, il **s'est laissé** aller en arrière, mais sans retirer la main de sa poche. J'**étais** assez loin de lui, à une dizaine de mètres. Je **devinais** son regard [...] Mais le plus souvent, son image **dansait** devant mes yeux, dans l'air enflammé. Le bruit des vagues **était** encore plus paresseux, plus étale qu'à midi [...] À l'horizon, un petit vapeur **est passé**, et j'en **ai deviné** la tâche noire au bord de mon regard, parce que je **n'avais pas cessé** de regarder l'Arabe [...] Mais j'**ai fait** un pas, un seul pas en avant. Et cette fois, sans se soulever, l'Arabe **a tiré** son couteau qu'il m'**a présenté** dans le soleil. La lumière **a giclé** sur l'acier, et c'**était** comme une longue lame étincelante qui m'**atteignit** au front [...] C'est alors que tout **a vacillé**. La mer **a charrié** un souffle épais et ardent. Il m'**a semblé** que le ciel **s'ouvrait** sur toute son étendue pour laisser pleuvoir du feu. Tout mon être **s'est tendu** et j'**ai crispé** ma main sur le revolver. La gâchette **a cédé**.
>
> (Camus 1962b, p. 1167)

If one compares this passage to the one taken from *La peste*, one notes immediately a difference in tone. The Zeitgeist determining the construction of *La peste* contrasts most markedly with that of *L'étranger* since the preterit set within the framework of the imperfect relates in clear, unbiased and rational detail the events of a fictitious plague that struck Oran in Algeria in the early 1940s. The preterit points to so-called factual occurrences that correspond to the certainty of the plague, and by implication to the Nazi invasion of Europe and the horrors it engendered. As Camus states early on in the narrative that he qualifies appropriately as *une chronique*:

"Ceci est arrivé." Preterit and fact support each other in a truthful account, as opposed to the perfect tense which denies any awareness of legitimate and logical reality. The passage in question tells of the narrator's discovery of a rat on the landing in his block of apartments, and his remonstrations with the janitor of the block. The rat is the undeniable first sign of the plague and, by inference, of the menace of Nazism. The preterit, couched in terms of historical fact, evokes incontrovertible evidence of the events leading to the Holocaust. In contrast, the imperfect describes the surrounding features: *elle* **constituait** *un scandale* and *il n'y* **avait** *pas de rats dans la maison.*

> Le matin du 16 avril, le docteur Bernard Rieux **sortit** de son cabinet et **buta** sur un rat mort, au milieu du palier. Sur le moment, il **écarta** la bête sans y prendre garde et **descendit** l'escalier. Mais, arrivé dans la rue, la pensée lui **vint** que ce rat n'**était** pas à sa place et il **retourna** sur ses pas pour avertir le concierge. Devant la réaction du vieux M. Michel, il **sentit** mieux ce que sa découverte **avait** d'insolite. La présence de ce rat mort lui **avait paru** seulement bizarre tandis que, pour le concierge, elle **constituait** un scandale. La position de ce dernier **était** catégorique: il n'y **avait** pas de rats dans la maison. Il **eut** beau l'assurer qu'il y en **avait** un sur le palier du premier étage, et probablement mort, la conviction de M. Michel **restait** entière. Il n'y **avait** pas de rats dans la maison. Il **fallait** donc qu'on eût apporté celui-ci du dehors. Bref, il s'**agissait** d'une farce.
>
> (Camus 1962a, p. 1223)

24

Future tense | Le futur

The future tense expresses a fact, an event or a thought which will take place at a later date in relation to the present moment. In English it is made up of the use of *will* and *shall*; in French it is formed by adding the following endings to the full infinitive of regular −er and −ir verbs, while the final **e** is dropped with −**re** verbs:

		Chanter	*Vendre*	*Finir*
je	−ai	chanter**ai**	vendr**ai**	finir**ai**
tu	−as	chanter**as**	vendr**as**	finir**as**
il/elle	−a	chanter**a**	vendr**a**	finir**a**
nous	−rons	chanter**ons**	vendr**ons**	finir**ons**
vous	−ez	chanter**ez**	vendr**ez**	finir**ez**
ils/elles	−ont	chanter**ont**	vendr**ont**	finir**ont**

Verbs ending in −**voir** function differently: *recevrai, recevras, recevra, recevrons, recevrez, recevront.*

A point of interest: these endings are related to the present tense of the verb *avoir*. Once the Latin inflexion system had died out, it was replaced by the infinitive of the verb and the Vulgar Latin *habere* that evolved into *avoir*, so that *chanterai* originally meant *I have | am to | must sing* (*cantare* + *habeo*). These comments also apply to the future tense in Spanish, Italian and Portuguese.

Although a number of irregular verbs are listed in the tables at the end of this volume, it seems appropriate to list the future tenses of the main ones here. Particularly noteworthy are the two verbs *aller* and *être*:

aller	irai, iras, ira, irons, irez, iront
avoir	aurai, auras, aura, aurons, aurez, auront
courir	courrai, courras, courra, courrons, courrez, courront
être	serai, seras, sera, serons, serez, seront
faire	ferai, feras, fera, ferons, ferez, feront
falloir	il faudra
pouvoir	pourrai, pourras, pourra, pourrons, pourrez, pourront

tenir	tiendrai, tiendras, tiendra, tiendrons, tiendrez, tiendront
venir	viendrai, viendras, viendra, viendrons, viendrez, viendront
voir	verrai, verras, verra, verrons, verrez, verront
vouloir	voudrai, voudras, voudra, voudrons, voudrez, voudront

24.1 Main functions of the future tense in French

The future expresses a fact which will be realized at some future point. It refers also to an act or thought yet to come to fruition:

| Nous **serons** en vacances fin juin. | *We'll be on vacation end of June.* |
| Adeline **arrivera** demain / la semaine prochaine. | *Adeline will come tomorrow / next week.* |

It also refers to a general truth:

| Il y **aura** toujours des gagnants et des perdants. | *There will always be winners and losers.* |
| Quoi que tu dises, la Terre **tournera** autour du Soleil tant que l'univers existera. | *Whatever you say, the Earth will go round the sun as long as the universe exists.* |

The future expresses a probable happening:

| L'été **sera** pluvieux à Halifax, je crois. | *The summer will be rainy in Halifax, I think.* |
| On **construira** des milliers de voitures l'année prochaine à Shanghaï. | *Thousands of automobiles will be built in Shanghai next year.* |

The future conveys a polite order which has the effect of an imperative but carries less weight and does not sound so authoritarian:

Tu **voudras** bien m'expliquer ce retard.	*You will kindly explain this delay to me.*
J'en ai assez, je vous **demanderai** de vous taire.	*I'm tired of this, I must ask you to keep quiet.*
Vous **voudrez** bien m'excuser, je vous prie.	*Please excuse me, I beg you.*
Je vous **demanderai** une bienveillante attention.	*I must ask for your kind attention.*

Instead of the present tense, a common and similar kind of softening of
tone in the future is heard with storekeepers, traders and so on:

Cela **fera** vingt euros.	*That'll be twenty euros.*
Ce **sera** tout?	*Is that all / Will that be all?*
Ça **ira** comme ça?	*OK like that?*

In this last case, the storekeeper could be referring to an article wrapped
up or not.

Another type of softening of expression occurs when an explanation is
offered. Again the future is a substitute for the present:

Tu **comprendras** que je ne peux pas lui faire confiance.	*You will understand that I can't trust him.*
Tu lui **feras** entendre raison ou j'abandonne mon engagement.	*Please have him see reason or I abandon my commitment.*

The future is used to convey a piece of advice or a recommendation:

Vous **prendrez** ce médicament après chaque repas.	*Take this medication after each meal.*
Tu lui **parleras** doucement parce que, autrement, elle ne fera pas attention à toi.	*Speak to her nicely or she won't pay any attention to you.*

It is not uncommon to come across a future set within the context of the
past. Such a construction is called a *futur historique*:

La bataille des Plaines d'Abraham entraîna la chute de Québec en 1759; ce **sera** la fin de la Nouvelle-France.	*The battle for the Plains of Abraham led to the fall of Quebec City; that was the end of New-France / that would be the end of New France.*
Le fanatique puritain J. Brown attaqua l'arsenal fédéral de Harper's Ferry en Virginie... Il **deviendra** le martyr de l' abolitionnisme militant.	*The Puritan fanatic J. Brown attacked the federal arsenal at Harper's Ferry in Virginia... He was to become the martyr of militant abolitionism.*

The future also expresses probability which involves a personal hypothesis or something that is likely to happen, or that has happened:

On sonne; ce **sera** mon amie.	*Someone's at the door. It's probably my friend.*
Pour qui a-t-on sonné la cloche des morts?	*Who are they ringing the death knell for?*
Mon Dieu! Ce **sera** pour Mme Legrand.	*Heavens above! It's for Mme Legrand.*
Irène est absente. Elle **aura** encore sa migraine.	*Irène is absent. She's probably gotten a migraine again.*

The future is used very often in invitations for job applications: *Août 2010, la Ville du Mans recrute un adjoint de direction: Titulaire du Certificat d'Aptitude, vous seconderez la directrice dans la gestion pédagogique. Vous accompagnerez l'élaboration du projet d'établissement et assurerez le suivi de la scolarité.*

The Ten Commandments, as in English, are conveyed in the future tense:

Tu n'**auras** pas d'autres dieux devant ma face. Tu ne te **feras** point d'image taillée. Tu ne te **prosterneras** point devant elles [images] Tu ne **prendras** point le nom de l'Éternel, ton Dieu, en vain (Exodus, 20).	*Thou shall have no other god save me. Thou shall not make any graven image. Thou shall not bow down. Thou shall not take the name of the Lord thy God in vain.*

Similarly, in biblical language: *Tu es Simon, fils de Jean; tu t'appelleras Céphas* (John 1: 42).

24.2 Use of the present as replacement for the future

An important change is taking place in contemporary French in that the future tense is slowly but surely giving way to the present tense. The present tense is easier to handle.

The present can refer to the immediate future:

Reste là. Je **descends** dans un instant.	*Stay here/there. I'll be down in a moment.*
On **part** demain/dimanche prochain.	*We go tomorrow/next Sunday.*

Increasingly, the present refers to any time in the future, near or distant:

L'été de 2014 on fait un voyage en Alaska.	*The summer of 2014 we'll go on a trip to Alaska.*

The present tense of the verb *aller* can frequently replace the future when combined with an infinitive. Again, this construction is easier than the future:

On **va faire** une partie de canotage cet après-midi.	*We'll have a boat trip this afternoon.*
Qu'est-ce que tu **vas faire** ce soir?	*What are you going to do this evening?*
Papa **va me payer** mes vacances en Floride.	*Pop's going to pay for my vacation in Florida.*

Two expressions, one more formal than the other, point to a future idea:

Adrienne **est en passe de** réussir (R3).	*Adrienne is about to succeed.*
Si Émilie gagne en demi-finale, elle **est sur le point** de remporter le trophée.	*If Émilie wins in the semi-final, she is about to win the trophy.*

25

Future perfect tense / Le futur antérieur

The future perfect suggests a degree of conjecture or possibility. This is a relatively easy concept since it corresponds well to the English equivalent, although the English remains in the perfect tense. It refers to an action regarded as completed in the future at the time of speaking. It is made up of the future tense of *avoir* in conjunction with the past participle of a verb which varies according to a preceding direct object, or the future tense of *être* with a past participle which varies according to the subject (see Chapter 14 on the perfect tense for these variations). Here are the main uses of the future perfect:

It expresses an action or thought that precedes another action or thought in the future:

Quand vous **aurez fini** vos devoirs, vous pourrez jouer dehors.	*When you have finished your homework, you can play outside.*
Aussitôt que tu **seras rentrée**, on dînera.	*As soon as you come home, we'll have our evening meal.*

Note also that the main clause, *vous pourrez jouer dehors*, cannot be expressed in the present tense as in English. In other words, *pouvez* is *not* possible in this context.

It can also express a certainty, an inevitability:

Je suis sûre qu'il **aura vite réuni** les provisions nécessaires à l'expédition.	*I am sure he will soon have gathered up the provisions necessary for the expedition.*
Il est clair que nos amies **seront arrivées** à destination à l'heure prévue.	*It is clear that our friends have arrived at their destination on time.*

It can also refer to an act or thought that is supposed to have taken place in the past. It involves a probable explanation:

Adrienne n'est pas encore là. Elle **se sera attardée** à la piscine.	*Adrienne still isn't here. She's probably held up at the swimming pool.*
Je ne trouve pas mes lunettes. Je les **aurai laissées** dans ma chambre en haut.	*I can't find my glasses. I must have left them upstairs in my bedroom.*

It can appear in a main clause where the subordinate clause is introduced by *si*. This is especially so with the verb *vouloir*:

Si les enfants sont malheureux et même malades, c'est que les parents l'**auront voulu** !	*If the children are unhappy and even sick, it's because the parents will have wanted it!*
S'il y a eu un accident, les conducteurs l'**auront voulu**, ils conduisaient comme des dingues !	*If there's been an accident, the drivers must have wanted it, driving like idiots!*

In keeping with the perfect tense, the future perfect may be used in the passive:

La maison **aura été abandonnée** il y a bien des années	*The house will have been abandoned years ago.*
Pour être la championne du monde au tennis, Venus Williams **aura été encouragée** depuis son enfance.	*To be the world tennis champion, Venus Williams was doubtless encouraged from childhood.*

26

Conditional tense | Le conditionnel

This tense corresponds to the English *would*, so it has a future idea, both in form and in usage. Its endings are added to the full infinitive, just as with the future tense, but this does not apply to the *recevoir* group. The formation of the conditional should not be difficult. The conditional was once regarded as another mood, like the subjunctive or the imperative, but not so now. It generally involves two tenses, but not always. Here are the forms of the conditional:

	chanter	*vendre*	*finir*	*recevoir*
je	chanter**ais**	vend**rais**	finir**ais**	recev**rais**
tu	chanter**ais**	vend**rais**	finir**ais**	recev**rais**
il/elle	chanter**ait**	vend**rait**	finir**ait**	recev**rait**
nous	chanter**ions**	vend**rions**	finir**ions**	recev**rions**
vous	chanter**iez**	vend**riez**	finir**iez**	recev**riez**
ils/elles	chanter**aient**	vend**raient**	finir**aient**	recev**raient**

As with the future tense (see Chapter 24), these endings are related to the imperfect tense of the Vulgar Latin verb *habere*. Once the Latin inflexion system had died out, it was replaced by the infinitive of the verb and *habere* which evolved into *avoir*, so that *chanterais* originally meant *I had | was to | must sing (cantare + habebam)*. These comments also apply to the conditional tense in Spanish, Italian and Portuguese.

Although a number of irregular verbs are listed in the tables at the end of this volume, it seems appropriate to list the conditional tenses of the main ones here. Particularly noteworthy are the two verbs *aller* and *être*:

aller	irais, irais, irait, irions, iriez, iraient
avoir	aurais, aurais, aurait, aurions, auriez, auraient
courir	courrais, courrais, courrait, courrions, courriez, courraient
être	serais, serais, serait, serions, seriez, seraient
faire	ferais, ferais, ferait, ferions, feriez, feraient
falloir	il faudrait
pouvoir	pourrais, pourrais, pourrait, pourrions, pourriez, pourraient
tenir	tiendrais, tiendrais, tiendrait, tiendrions, tiendriez, tiendraient

venir	viendrais, viendrais, viendrait, viendrions, viendriez, viendraient
voir	verrais, verrais, verrait, verrions, verriez, verraient
vouloir	voudrais, voudrais, voudrait, voudrions, voudriez, voudraient

26.1 Uses of the conditional

The conditional can express a wish or desire and, in this usage, it softens the tone of the present or future tenses:

J'**aimerais** revenir un jour.	*I'd like to come back one day.*
Axelle **voudrait** nous accompagner à La Réunion.	*Axelle would like to come with us to Réunion.*
Je vous **serais obligé** de me recevoir.	*I would be obliged if you received me.*
Je **serais** curieuse de savoir ce qu'en pense Guillaume.	*I'd be curious to know what Guillaume thinks about it.*

The conditional can express a request:

Vous **plairait-il** de fermer cette porte ?	*Would you kindly close that door?*
Verriez-vous un inconvénient à m'accompagner ?	*Would it be inconvenient to accompany me?*
Je **désirerais** un renseignement.	*I would like some information.*

It marks a refusal or doubt:

Moi, j'aurais dit cela ? Je **pourrais** lui mentir !	*Me, say that to her? I could have lied to her!*
Serais-tu malade ?	*Would you be sick?*

It marks appearance, or probability, and is often accompanied by *selon*, as in journalism:

On parle d'un accident. Il y **aurait** dix morts.	*They say there was an accident. There were probably ten dead.*
Selon certains rapports, il y **aurait** deux autres projets.	*According to some reports, there are two other projects.*

The conditional tense is used as the main clause with the conjunction *si* in a subordinate clause. If the event is presented as hypothetical, contrary to reality, the conditional is standard usage. The formula is *si* + imperfect tense + conditional tense. The corresponding English is *If you went, I would come too*. Thus:

Si Laetitia étudiait, elle **réussirait** mieux.	*If Laetitia studied, she'd do better.*
S'il venait, je lui **parlerais**.	*If he came I would speak to him.*
Si l'on m'attaquait, je me **défendrais**.	*If I were attacked, I'd defend myself.*

In the imagination of children participating in games, the distribution of roles may be expressed in the conditional:

Ça, ce **serait** la montagne, alors vous **seriez** les Indiens et Jean **arriverait** par derrière.	*That could be the mountain, so you would be the Indians and Jean would come up from behind.*

Of course, the present tense would also be appropriate here, and would be more frequent since children handle it more easily.

The conditional also occurs as a subordinate clause when the main clause is in the imperfect tense, and a relative pronoun is used. The formula is: imperfect tense + *que* + conditional tense:

Je croyais que toutes les montagnes **seraient** couvertes de neige.	*I thought that all the mountains would be covered in snow.*
Mes parents pensaient que je **serais** une brillante étudiante.	*My parents thought I would be a brilliant student.*
Tout le monde disait que ce **serait** une erreur que de partir dans la nuit.	*Everyone said it would be an error to leave in the night.*
Tout le monde a dit que ce **serait** une erreur que de partir dans la nuit.	*Idem*

In these last two cases which involve indirect speech, the conditional is used but, if direct speech occurred, the future could be used, as in English: *Tout le monde disait: "Ce sera une erreur que de partir dans la nuit."* It could be legitimately argued that, in the above second sentence with indirect speech (*Tout le monde a dit que*), the future tense is required rather than the conditional, in order that agreement of tenses be respected. Grevisse and Goosse do not seem to suggest this feature, however, and only offer examples with the conditional: *Il m'a dit qu'il reviendrait ce soir.* At the same time, since the difference in sounds between **ai** (closed **e** = **é**) and **ais** (open **e** = **è**) is slowly disappearing, the following sentence could be construed both ways:

Je lui ai dit que je le **ferai**.	*I told him I would do it.*
Je lui ai dit que je le **ferais**.	*I told him I would do it.*

If one were to distinguish between these two sentences, the first suggests more insistence and willful commitment than the second.

Grevisse and Goosse also provide examples of indirect free speech: *Elle souhaitait un fils ; il **serait** fort et beau et **s'appellerait** Georges; Les enfants partis, **déjeunerait**-elle ? Oui, elle déjeunerait.*

When a subordinate clause depends on conjunctions like *quand, lorsque* or *aussitôt*, and this clause relates to a verb in the past, the conditional is used. The formula is: past tense + *que* + conditional + conditional:

Je leur ai dit que, lorsque j'**irais** à l'université, j'étudierais la physique.	*I told them that, when I went to university, I would study physics.*
Le gouvernement a promis que, quand il **aurait** les fonds, la piscine serait gratuite.	*The government promised that, when it had the funds, the swimming pool would be free.*
Tout le monde convenait que, aussitôt que l'économie **reprendrait**, il faudrait investir plus dans les énergies renouvelables.	*Everyone agreed that, as soon as the economy picked up, it would be necessary to invest in renewable energies.*

Note this construction of very high register involving two conditional verbs referring to a hypothesis:

Elle le **jurerait** (que) je ne la **croirais** pas.	*Even if she swore on it I wouldn't believe her.*
The inclusion of the **que** raises the register even higher. Similarly with *quand même*, with the same meaning and register:	
Quand même elle le jurerait, je ne la croirais pas.	

The same high register is observed with *devoir* in the subordinate clause and the conditional in the main clause. *Devoir* is here in the imperfect subjunctive:

Dût-elle me payer une fortune, je n'**accepterais** pas l'offre.	*Were she to pay me a fortune, I would not accept the offer.*

26.2 Miscellaneous use of certain verbs

The conditional of *devoir* corresponds to the English *ought to* or *should*:

Tu **devrais** terminer le livre avant de sortir.	*You ought to finish the book before going out.*
Vous **devriez** ranger vos affaires.	*You should tidy up your things.*

The verbs *croire* and *dire*, in combination with the impersonal *on*, can have a special and very idiomatic meaning:

On **dirait** qu'elles sont fâchées.   *You would think there are angry.*
On **dirait** un fou.   *You would think he was mad.*

This conditional construction also applies to the conditional in the past (see Chapter 27).

Pouvoir in the pronominal form may be construed as *could be*:

Il **se pourrait** que je me trompe.   *It could be that I am wrong.*
Il **se pourrait** que la randonnée   *It could be that the walk be put off*
soit remise à la semaine   *till next week, if it rains.*
prochaine, s'il pleut.

In R3 language, both spoken and written, the conditional of *savoir* can have the value of the present tense of *pouvoir*. Such usage often involves the negative:

Je **ne saurais** répondre tout de   *I couldn't/can't answer that question*
suite à cette question.   *straight away.*
Qui était-ce? On **ne saurait** le dire /   *Who was it? No one can say.*
Nul **ne saurait** le dire.
Je **ne saurais** faire ce que vous me   *I couldn't do what you ask of me.*
dites.

The conditional of *savoir* may also be used with objects or even impersonally:

La pluie ne **saurait** tarder à tomber.   *It won't take long for rain to fall.*
Il **ne saurait** rien arriver de plus   *Nothing more annoying could*
fâcheux.   *happen.*

Grevisse and Goosse provide abundant examples of the conditional of *savoir* in a non-negative context, questioning this usage as either an archaism or a regionalism. At the same time, they quote modern authors in support of the use: "La mort, la destruction seule y *saurait* changer quelque chose" (Duhamel, in Grevisse and Goosse 2008, p. 1100); "Ce n'est pas parce qu'il part du local que Williams *saurait* être comparé à un régionaliste volontiers sentimental comme Carl Sandburg" (*Actualité littéraire*, in Grevisse and Goosse 2008, p. 1100).

Savoir in a full negative conditional (*ne pas savoir*) is very common in Belgium, although this example is taken from a French author: "Il arrive que la violence nous écrase, et que la force des méchants ait le dessus ; mais elles *ne sauraient pas* ébranler notre âme" (Suarès, in Grevisse and Goosse 2008, p. 1100).

27

Conditional perfect tense / Le conditionnel passé

This tense conveys an idea or an event related to the future in the past. It corresponds to the English *would have done/spoken/walked = aurait fait/parlé/marché*. Being a compound tense, it can involve the obligatory use of the verb *être* as an auxiliary, with the attendant agreement: *She would have left / They would have gone out / gotten up = Elle serait partie / Ils seraient sortis / Ils se seraient levés*.

Here are the main four conjugations:

	chanter	*vendre*	*finir*	*recevoir*
j'	aurais chanté	aurais vendu	aurais fini	aurais reçu
tu	aurais chanté	aurais vendu	aurais fini	aurais reçu
il/elle	aurait chanté	aurait vendu	aurait fini	aurait reçu
nous	aurions chanté	aurions vendu	aurions fini	aurions reçu
vous	auriez chanté	auriez vendu	auriez fini	auriez reçu
ils/elles	auraient chanté	auraient vendu	auraient fini	auraient reçu

See Chapter 14 for agreement with verbs conjugated with *être*. This includes reflexive verbs. Here is just one example of each:

Partir: je serais parti(e), tu serais parti(e), il serait parti, elle serait partie, nous serions parti(e)s, vous seriez parti(e)(s), ils seraient partis, elles seraient parties

Se lever: je me serais levé(e), tu te serais levé(e), il se serait levé, elle se serait levée, nous nous serions levé(e)s, vous vous seriez levé(e)(s), ils se seraient levés, elles se seraient levées

27.1 Uses of the conditional perfect

The most common use of the conditional perfect is in its combination with the conjunction *si* and imperfect:

Si tu étais venue, on **aurait pu** fêter ton anniversaire.	*If you had come, we could have celebrated your birthday.*
Si le chèque était arrivé plus tôt, je l'**aurais versé** sur mon compte aujourd'hui.	*If the check had arrived sooner, I would have paid it into my account today.*

Si l'on avait acheté les actions il y a quinze jours, nous **aurions gagné** des millions.	*If we had bought the shares a fortnight ago, we would have gained millions.*
Si tu l'avais appelée à sept heures, elle **se serait levée** tout de suite.	*If you had called her at seven, she would have gotten up straight away.*

In R3 language, the pluperfect subjunctive can replace the pluperfect tense. One would find this subjunctive construction these days only in the third-person singular (see Chapter 44 on the subjunctive):

Si elle **fût partie**, son mari aurait été agacé.	*If she had left, her husband would have been annoyed.*
S'il m'**eût parlé** de la sorte, je lui aurais donné une verte semonce.	*If he had spoken to me like that, I would have given him a sharp reprimand.*

A similar meaning is conveyed by the combination of two conditionals in the past, as opposed to the formula stated above. This construction is very high register, is found in literature but has little currency these days:

Lafcadio **aurait été** d'aspect farouche que peut-être Julius **aurait pris peur**.	*If Lafcadio had seemed fierce, perhaps Julius would have been afraid.*
Aurait-elle osé partir toute seule qu'elle n'aurait pas été inquiète.	*If she had dared to go alone, she would not have been worried.*

The conditional perfect can be used as part of a subordinate clause dependent on a past tense and a conditional:

Marie a dit qu'elle partirait dès que je l'**aurais appelée**.	*Marie said she would leave as soon as I called her.*
Hier soir, j'avais prévu que, lorsque l'ouragan **se serait déclenché**, tout le littoral serait inondé.	*Yesterday evening, I had predicted that, when the hurricane began, the whole coastline would be flooded.*

The conditional in the past can also depend on other factors which are not necessarily explicitly stated by a finite verb:

Un siècle plus tôt il **aurait été mis** à mort.	*A century earlier, they would have executed him.*
Arrivée dix minutes après, elle **serait tombée** dans le panneau.	*If she had arrived ten minutes later, she would have fallen into the trap.*

The statement of appearance, often introduced by *selon*, can lead to the conditional in the past dependent on an imperfect or simply an event in the past, just as a present tense can lead to the conditional. The notion is one of "*likely*" or "*probable*":

Le train a déraillé. Selon un témoin oculaire, il y **aurait eu** plusieurs morts.	*The train was derailed. According to an eyewitness, there were several dead.*
Tremblement de terre en Iran: la catastrophe **aurait fait** des milliers de morts.	*Earthquake in Iran: the catastrophe has probably caused thousands of deaths.*

27.2 Miscellaneous features with *dire, devoir, falloir, pouvoir, vouloir*

The conditional perfect of *dire* with the impersonal *on* can express the idea of appearance in relation to a past event or thought, just as the conditional expresses appearance in relation to the present:

Un orage? On **aurait dit** un ouragan!	*A storm? You would have thought it was a hurricane!*
On entendait hurler dans la rue. On **aurait dit** une bande de voyous.	*We could hear them shouting in the street. You would have thought they were a bunch of hoodlums/louts.*

In R3 literary discourse, the conditional in the past can be replaced by the pluperfect subjunctive:

Il a fait beau toute la semaine. On **eût dit** des vacances paradisiaques.	*The weather was fine all week. The vacation seemed like paradise.*
Quelques escarmouches? On **eût dit** une véritable révolution.	*Skirmishes? It looked like a real revolution.*

The conditional perfect of *devoir* expresses the idea of obligation as in the English *ought to have*:

Tu **aurais dû** appeler plus tôt.	*You ought to have called earlier.*
Vous **auriez dû** visiter les chutes du Niagara avant de quitter le Canada.	*You should have visited the Niagara Falls before leaving Canada.*

The conditional perfect of *falloir* has the same value as *devoir* in this context:

Il **aurait fallu** avertir Francis avant.	*You should have alerted Francis before.*
Je ne sais pas pourquoi tu es rentrée si tôt. Il **aurait fallu** y passer toute la journée.	*I don't know why you came back so soon. You should have spent the whole day there.*

The imperfect of *falloir* conveys the same meaning:

Audrey était malade dans la voiture. Elle a vomi. Je lui ai dit qu'il **fallait** nous le dire avant.	*Audrey was unwell in the car. She was sick. I told her she should have told us before.*
Il **fallait** impérativement faire le plein avant de quitter la côte.	*You/We should really have filled up before leaving the coast.*

The conditional perfect of *falloir* can also suggest supposition, hypothesis = *must have*:

Il **aurait fallu** être un génie pour inventer un tel procédé.	*He must have been a genius to invent such a technique.*
Il **aurait fallu** être un fou pour descendre les rapides du Saint-Laurent.	*He must have been mad to shoot the Saint Lawrence rapids.*

Interestingly enough, the perfect tense of *devoir* has the same meaning:

Elle **a dû** être drôlement intelligente pour obtenir ce résultat-là.	*She must have been really intelligent to get that result.*

The imperfect tense of *devoir* has a similar meaning in this context:

Elle **devait** être drôlement intelligente pour passer l'agrégation.	*She must have been really intelligent to pass the agrégation.*

Both *pouvoir* and *vouloir* occur very frequently in the conditional perfect:

On **aurait pu** se tirer d'affaire tout seuls.	*We could have managed by ourselves.*
Sabrina **aurait voulu** rester avec ses amies.	*Sabrina would have liked to remain with her friends.*

28

Progressive tense, present participle, gerund / Le temps progressif, le participe présent, le gérondif

It is necessary to treat these three structures together since they can easily be confused. They all express an activity in progress, an act or thought in the process of being realized. The progressive tense is the simplest one to deal with in the sense that it does not exist in modern French. However, it does attract at least one observation. Whereas all Romance languages, and English for that matter, rely quite heavily on the progressive tense, with its attendant nuances, its absence in modern French must be conceived as a radical deficiency. The French language fails to deal adequately with the English *He is reading*, which has its Italian and Spanish equivalents (Italian: *Sta leggendo*; Spanish: *Está leyendo*), and has recourse to a cumbersome but common *Il est en train de lire*, or the lame *Il lit*. Similarly, French cannot truly accommodate the past progressive tense *He was reading* (Italian: *Stava leggendo*; Spanish: *Estaba/Estuvo leyendo*), except with the help of *en train de*: *Il était en train de lire*. It may be legitimately argued that the French imperfect does perform this function moderately well (*Il lisait*), but this tense does not suggest the vigor and nuance apparent in the other languages referred to. Finally, a future progressive is inaccessible to French: *He will be reading* (Italian: *Starà leggendo*; Spanish: *Estará leyendo*).

One has to wonder whether the differences between the present participle and the gerund are so fine and even imperceptible that attempting to define distinctions leads to a cul-de-sac. It has to be underlined that an extremely high percentage of French-speaking people do not recognize the peculiarities entailed in each term. The following remarks on the values of the present participle as against the gerund are therefore to be treated with caution, although, at the same time, there are circumstances where one form would obtain, and not the other, and vice versa. The majority of French speakers would doubtless know the correctness of use without knowing how to state the rule.

As with the gerund, the actual form of the present participle is created from the root of the first-person plural of the present indicative: *chanter* > *chantant, vendre* > *vendant, finir* > *finissant, recevoir* > *recevant*. Three verbs have an irregular present participle: *être* > *étant, avoir* > *ayant, savoir* > *sachant*.

28.1 Uses of the present participle

The present participle is used as a verb and essentially restricted to writing. It relates to a noun or pronoun but it is invariable. Hence one writes *Des gens portant des pancartes défilaient dans la rue*, with no **s** attached to *portant*. The present participle has no temporal value, and assumes the tense of the main verb and main clause. It can be placed in the negative and followed by a complement:

Voulant bronzer, elle se met de la crème solaire.	*Wanting to get a tan, she puts on some suntan lotion.*
Voulant bronzer, elle s'est mis de la crème solaire.	*Wanting to get a tan, she put on some suntan lotion.*
Voulant bronzer, elle se mettra de la crème solaire.	*Wanting to get a tan, she will put on some suntan lotion.*
Voulant bronzer, elle se mit de la crème solaire.	*Wanting to get a tan, she put on some suntan lotion.*
Ne voulant pas bronzer, elle reste / est restée à l'ombre.	*Not wanting to get a tan, she stays/ stayed in the shade.*

It can have the value of a relative subordinate clause:

Les personnes **ayant (qui ont)** un ticket bleu doivent se présenter au contrôle.	*Persons having (who have/with) a blue ticket must go to the checkpoint.*
Une fillette **portant (qui portait)** un énorme bouquet s'avança vers le président.	*A girl with an enormous bouquet walked toward the president.*

It can have the value of a subordinate clause of circumstance:

Ne sachant pas (Comme je ne savais pas) te joindre, je n'ai pas pu vous prévenir de mon retour.	*Not knowing how to get hold of you, I couldn't let you know that I was coming back.*
Répondant (Quand elle a répondu) aux questions des journalistes, la ministre a confirmé qu'elle se rendrait en Russie prochainement.	*Replying to the journalists' questions, the minister confirmed that she would go to Russia in the near future.*

In standard French, the subject of the present participle is the same as the subject of the main clause, as observed above, but one does hear (and the construction is common enough) *Étant absent tout le week-end, **ils** n'ont pas pu me prévenir*, which is clearly R1 while the recommended R2 construction is *Étant absent tout le week-end, **je** n'ai pas pu être prévenu*.

In a high register, the present participle can have its own subject, particularly when the subordinate clause is at the beginning of the sentence, and separated from the main clause by a comma. A cause is usually expressed here:

La neige **n'arrêtant pas** de tomber (**Comme la neige n'arrêtait pas de tomber**), la circulation était difficile.	*As the snow did not stop falling, driving was difficult.*
Tous les hôtels du centre-ville **affichant** complet, nous avons dû en chercher un à la périphérie.	*Since all the hotels downtown were full, we had to find one outside the town center.*
Les bêtes **se fatiguant** rapidement, nous devrons faire plusieurs haltes.	*With the animals tiring quickly, we'll need to stop several times.*

Used with a determiner (*un/le/ce*, etc.), a certain number of present participles have become nouns: *un arrivant, un commerçant, un courant, un habitant, un manifestant, un montant, un partant, un passant, un tournant, à tout venant, un vivant*. Some of these are used more in the plural: *les arrivants et les partants, les vivants et les morts, à tous venants*.

The present participle can have the value of an adjective, this variation frequently producing two forms of spelling, a feature that can be confusing even for French speakers. It goes without saying that, whereas the present participle remains invariable, the adjectival form is subject to change according to gender and number. In this list, the present participle precedes the participle as adjective: *adhérant/ adhérent; coïncidant/coïncident; communiquant/communicant; convainquant/ convaincant; convergeant/convergent; détergeant/détergent; différant/différent; émergeant/émergent; équivalant/équivalent; excellant/excellent; extravaguant/ extravagant; fatiguant/fatigant; intriguant/intrigant; naviguant/navigant; négligeant/négligent; précédant/précédent; provoquant/provocant; somnolant/ somnolent; suffoquant/suffocant; zigzaguant/zigzagant*. Examples illustrating difference in usage:

Present participle	*Participle as adjective*
Convainquant ses parents de la justesse de sa cause, Marcel a pu gagner le pari.	un argument **convaincant**
Émergeant des ténèbres, l'agresseur a bondi sur la victime.	Les pays **émergents** se défendent difficilement sur le marché mondial.
Négligeant sa responsabilité, la mère a laissé ses enfants seuls toute la soirée.	C'est une employée **négligente**, elle est toujours en retard dans son travail.
Précédant tous les participants à la randonnée, Stéphanie est arrivée la première à l'auberge.	La semaine **précédente**, j'ai pu profiter d'une forte réduction.

Zigzaguant comme un gangster dans les rues de Chicago, le conducteur a fini par percuter un arbre.

Ils se sont trompés de route en suivant des cheminements **zigzagants**.

Note that the two constructions have the same form in *attaquant, subjuguant, piquant* and *trafiquant*. If the complement is indispensable to the meaning and refers to an action, a present participle is used, but if the word describes the noun, an adjective occurs. Compare the two following sentences, and note the application of commas appropriately placed: *La fillette,* **obéissant** *à sa mère, alla se coucher* and *La fillette* **obéissante** *alla se coucher*. In the first case, it is not necessary to consider that obedience is a characteristic of the girl. She could obey on this one occasion, while in the second case she is both obedient and obeys.

Brillant is another excellent illustration of the present-participle use (first expression) and the adjectival use (second expression): *des toits* **brillant** *au soleil* or *des toits* **brillants** *au soleil*. Finally, consider *pétillant*: *le champagne* **pétillant** *dans la coupe*, as opposed to *de l'orangeade* **pétillante** or *les yeux* **pétillants**.

Certain present participles have become verbal adjectives which agree in gender and number with the noun they relate to: *des livres intéressants, une rue très passante (very busy), une entrée payante, des personnes bien portantes (people in good health)*.

In a certain number of fixed expressions, the present participle is variable, performing the function of an adjective, and irregularities abound: *un café chantant* (the café does not sing, but rather the customers), *argent comptant | deniers comptants* (second expression is R3; *prompt payment in cash*), *avocat/médecin consultant, une entrée/place payante, cabinets payants* (see *café chantant* above), *couleur voyante, rue passante, un endroit commerçant, poste restante, chemin glissant, soirée dansante, un thé dansant, à la nuit tombante, une personne bien portante (healthy person) | méfiante | repentante, la partie plaignante (plaintiff), (payer) en espèces sonnantes (et trébuchantes)* (humorous expression = *cash*), *à prix coûtant (at cost price), à sept heures sonnantes/battantes/tapantes (right on seven o'clock)*, but also *à sept heures sonnant/battant/tapant, toute(s) affaire(s) cessante(s)* (R3; *straightaway/forthwith*), *tous empêchements cessants* (R3; *forthwith*), *les tenants et les aboutissants de quelque chose* (R3; *the ins and outs of something*), *les allants et venants* (people who are coming and going), *séance tenante* (R3; *in the course of the proceedings, immediately*), *les ayants droit* (R3; *legal claimants/beneficiaries*), *une maison à lui appartenante* (R3) | *à lui appartenant, une affaire pendante* (R3).

The present participle of *parler* often combines with certain adverbs which precede it: *écologiquement/économiquement/franchement/*

militairement/politiquement/socialement parlant = *ecologically/economic-ally... speaking.*

Many grammarians do not admit a present participle adjoining a noun which is the subject of a following clause. They find it clumsy, but Hanse and Blampain express satisfaction with it. An offending sentence could be *La mère a vu son mari et sa fille se dirigeant vers la maison.* But *La mère a vu son mari et sa fille qui se dirigeaient vers la maison* seems more clumsy, according to the authors quoted above. Similarly, the sentence *Il a vu des chiens courant à travers bois* would find censure with many, while it may be legitimately argued that *Il a vu des chiens qui couraient à travers bois* does not improve matters. Clearly, both constructions are equally acceptable.

28.2 Uses of the gerund

The gerund, whether accompanied by the preposition *en* or not, and it usually is, denotes action and is invariable: *On apprend en lisant; une femme charmant ses auditeurs.* The present participle denotes a state or quality; it is variable and therefore functions like an adjective: *Une femme charmante.* The gerund occurs much more frequently in the contemporary language than the present participle. In a general way, it is used in conjunction with another verb to indicate the simultaneous action performed by the same subject. It would be unusual for the subjects to be different.

The gerund performs the role of a complement of circumstance which expresses time, and this is its most common use:

En entrant dans la maison, **j'ai entendu** un drôle de bruit.	*On entering the house, I heard a strange noise.*
Mercredi, **en sortant** (**au moment où je sortais**) de la bibliothèque, j'ai rencontré deux camarades de fac.	*When I was coming out of the library on Wednesday, I met two university friends.*
Elle a été surprise **en me voyant**.	*She was surprised on seeing me.*

It is advisable not to confuse the two following sentences: *J'ai aperçu Paul sortant du métro* and *J'ai aperçu Paul en sortant du m'tro.* In the first case, *sortant* is a present participle with the meaning *Paul was coming out*, while in the second, *en sortant* is a gerund: *I was coming out.*

When one insists on the length of time suggested by the gerund, *tout* is used:

Sabrina aime travailler **tout en écoutant** de la musique.	*Sabrina likes to work while listening to music.*
Avec cette méthode, les enfants apprennent à lire **tout en jouant**.	*With this method, children learn to read while playing.*

The gerund may express cause:

Irène a pris froid **en sortant** (**parce qu'elle est sortie**) sans bonnet ni écharpe.	*Irène caught a cold because she went out without a hat or scarf.*
J'ai cassé ma montre **en la laissant** tomber (**parce que je l'ai laissée** tomber).	*I broke my watch because I dropped it.*
Je l'ai fâchée **en disant** cela.	*I made her cross by saying that.*

It also expresses manner:

Incorporez les blancs d'œuf battus en neige **en tournant** doucement la pâte.	*Beat in the egg white while stirring the mixture.*
Céline s'est mise en colère. Elle est partie **en claquant** la porte.	*Céline got angry. She left by banging the door (This is the way she expressed her anger).*
C'est **en forgeant** qu'on devient forgeron.	*Practice makes perfect.*

One could not easily use such a construction with *passer*, which requires an infinitive:

Laurent **a passé un an à apprendre** le japonais.	*Laurent spent a year learning Japanese.*

The gerund expresses condition:

En arrivant (Si vous arrivez) le premier jour des soldes, tu feras de bonnes affaires.	*If you arrive on the first day of the sales, you will get some good bargains.*

It can also be used with the suggestion of opposition:

Tout en travaillant beaucoup pour ses examens, Éléonore faisait souvent la fête.	*Even when studying hard for her exams, Éléonore often went to parties.*

Another way of expressing this idea is with *bien que/quoique: Bien qu'/ Quoiqu'elle travaille* . . .

> *En* is sometimes omitted with the gerund in certain archaisms which have a literary resonance and are not uncommon. This is notably true with the verb *aller*:

Ils **allaient criant** dans les rues.	*They went shouting through the streets.*

> A number of archaisms connected with the gerund have persisted quite vigorously to this day. One finds them more in the written form. Nevertheless, they are common enough: *chemin faisant (as we went our way / on*

our way); *tambour battant* (*quickly, briskly*), as in *Ils sont accourus tambour battant*; *ce disant* (*having said that*), *ce faisant* (*having done that*).

If there is a succession of gerunds, the *en* is generally repeated:

en entrant et en sortant	*when coming in and going out*

Although one says:

en allant et venant	*coming and going*

If the meaning is close in the two verbs, the second *en* may be omitted:

En disant et répétant que...	*While saying and repeating that...*
En expliquant et développant l'idée...	*While explaining and developing the idea...*

Aller and *s'en aller* may be followed by the present participle or the gerund with or without *en*, and here they are invariable. Used in this way, they both mark progression or continuity, and have high-register, literary associations:

Les couleurs **allaient se dégradant**.	*The colors slowly faded away.*
La maladie **va s'aggravant**.	*The sickness continues to get worse.*
Les rivalités **sont allées crescendo**.	*The rivalry continued to intensify.*

In this last case, *aller* can be replaced by *être*, notably in compound tenses:

La plupart de ces difficultés **ont été en s'aggravant**.	*Most of these difficulties have been getting / got worse.*

There are circumstances when the subjects are not the same for both verbs. It is here a question of set expressions where there is no room for ambiguity:

L'appétit vient en mangeant.	*Eating makes you hungry.*
Soit dit en passant...	*By the way / Let it be said in passing...*

When *en* has the meaning of *in the manner of*, it does not really constitute a gerund, as in: *Ils ont agi en conquérants*. Here *conquérants* is a noun. Similarly *Il a agi en despote / en jaloux*.

One very common and idiomatic use of the progressive tense is:

C'est gagnant gagnant.	*It's a win-win situation.*

29

Imperative mood | Le mode impératif

The passage below evokes the fantasy world that invades the center of New York during the festive season of Christmas. This enchanting period in the Big Apple can be bitterly cold, hence the injunctions, in the imperative form, with respect to protecting oneself against the wintry rigors. All three imperatives, including the reflexive, come into play: the second-person plural (*Visitez*, *étudiez*) exhorting people to come to New York; the second-person singular, resorted to by a friend who almost commands the author to put on extra layers before facing the glacial elements (*Couvre-toi*, *N'oublie pas*, *Met*); and finally the collective order of the first-person plural (*Procédons*, *Mettons*, *attendons*). Note the singular form of *gratte-ciel* alluded to in Chapter 10 on number, Section 10.2. Some translations are offered.

La magie de Noël à New York

La vaste conurbation de la côte nord-est des États-Unis montre des signes extérieurs de richesse et également d'extrême pauvreté. **Visitez** cette mégalopole et **étudiez**-la sous tous ses angles ! **Faites** un voyage à New York et **pénétrez** dans une société multiculturelle où plusieurs communautés cohabitent. Ainsi *Big Apple* est la ville cosmopolite par excellence. **Admirez** les monuments impressionnants et les gratte-ciel de Manhattan qui en font une ville ultramoderne où le mélange des genres se côtoie.

À l'époque, les tours jumelles [twin towers] du World Trade Center culminaient à plus de quatre cents mètres de hauteur. D'immenses gratte-ciel se dressaient dans l'île de Manhattan. Cet hiver-là était très rude. Les tempêtes de neige faisaient rage [were raging]. Une amie me conseillait la prudence : « **Couvre**-toi davantage avant de sortir ! **N'oublie** pas de mettre tes moufles de laine ! **Entoure** ton cou d'une écharpe ! **Mets** tes bottines fourrées [fur-lined bootees]. Ne **reste** pas dehors à te geler ! . . . . » Alors que d'autres amis me réprimandaient amicalement : « **Allez**, **grouille**-toi [get a move on] un peu ! On t'attend ! »

En fin d'année, le Rockefeller Center sur la Cinquième avenue s'animait la nuit de ses plus belles lumières. Des lumières extraordinaires de toutes les couleurs jaillissaient [burst forth]. La foule grouillait [milling] autour du sapin de Noël. Cet événement mettait toute la ville de New York en effervescence. **Procédons** par ordre ! **Mettons**-nous là et **attendons** notre tour ! Avant de se mêler à la foule de badauds [onlookers], **faites** attention ! **Rassemblons**-nous ! Ne nous **dispersons** pas. Le sapin [fir tree] magique trônait au beau milieu de la place publique. Les guirlandes [garlands] du sapin de Noël enroulées autour de l'arbre propageaient leur éclat étincelant en dégageant une atmosphère envoûtante [spellbinding] et féerique. Les illuminations éblouissantes des fêtes de fin d'année faisaient l'admiration des grands et des petits. **Allons** donc, **chante**, **chantons**, **chantez** la chanson traditionnelle : « Mon beau sapin, roi des forêts » en anglais et en français. Les conditions météorologiques ne nous ont pas empêchés de sortir et d'apprécier notre séjour outre-Atlantique.

L'État du New Jersey a excité notre curiosité. Les quartiers de Manhattan, de Brooklyn, de Queens, de Staten Island et du Bronx nous ont donné un aperçu de la ville de New York dans son gigantisme. Nous ressentions un froid polaire en cette fin d'année et un air glacial provenant de l'océan Atlantique. **Restons** sur une note musicale en mémoire de Frank Sinatra : « New York New York... Je veux me réveiller dans une ville qui ne dort jamais... »

The imperative has two tenses, present and perfect, although the perfect form is rarely used.

29.1 Forms of the present imperative

Apart from the verbs *avoir, être* and *savoir*, the present imperative reproduces the corresponding forms of the present indicative. The second-person singular of **–er** verbs, however, does not take **–es**, save before the pronouns *en* and *y* which are not followed by an infinitive. The present imperative has three persons: second-person singular, first-person plural and second-person plural. It has no subject pronoun.

Present imperative of **–er** verbs:

Chante ! (*Sing!*)   Chantons ! (*Let us sing!*)   Chantez ! (*Sing!*)

Present imperative of **–re** verbs:

Vends ! (*Sell!*)   Vendons ! (*Let us sell!*)   Vendez ! (*Sell!*)

Present imperative of **–ir** verbs:

Finis !   (*Finish!*)   Finissons ! (*Let us finish!*)   Finissez ! (*Finish!*)

Present imperative of **–oir** verbs:

Reçois !   (*Receive!*)   Recevons ! (*Let us receive!*)   Recevez ! (*Receive!*)

The present imperatives of *avoir, être* and *savoir* are:

Aie, Ayons, Ayez   Sois, Soyons, Soyez   Sache, sachons, sachez

Aller is a special case: *tu vas>va.*

The imperative may apply to the past, so that the construction is: imperative + past participle:

Sois rentré(e)   Soyons rentrés   Soyez rentré(e)(s)

The pronominal forms are:

Lève-toi ! (*Get up!*)	Levons-nous ! (*Let's get up!*)	Levez-vous ! (*Get up!*)
Assieds-toi ! (*Sit down!*)	Asseyons-nous ! (*Let's sit down!*)	Asseyez-vous ! (*Sit down!*)

Note the use of the hyphen between the imperative and the pronominal form.

29.2 Uses of the present imperative

It goes without saying that, as in English, there are certain verbs that do not admit the imperative form, largely because of their meaning: *pouvoir* (except in the third-person subjunctive form), *faillir, falloir, naître, valoir, pleuvoir* (except in the third-person subjunctive form). This latter remark applies to most impersonally used verbs: *geler, grêler, neiger, tonner*.

Some imperatives are hardly used: *devoir, émouvoir, défaillir, plaire* (except in the third-person subjunctive form), *suffire* (except in the third-person subjunctive form), *vêtir* (this verb is little used at all except in the infinitive and the past participle, being almost entirely replaced by *habiller*).

The present imperative is a command mood implying an order or prohibition. It is also used for offering advice or an invitation, or to express a wish or a desire. It therefore has a number of values.

The imperative as the expression of an order:

Jean, **viens** faire la vaisselle.	*Jean, come and do the dishes/washing up.*
Présentez-vous demain au bureau de la direction.	*Come tomorrow to the manager's office.*
On va être en retard. Dépêchons-nous !	*We're going to be late. Let's hurry!*

The imperative as the expression of prohibition, which usually involves a negation:

Ne **bois** pas de cette eau ! Elle n'est pas potable.	*Don't drink that water! It's not for drinking.*
Ne **sois** pas injuste !	*Don't be unfair!*
Philippe, ne **taquine** pas les filles !	*Philippe, don't tease the girls!*
Attention ! **Ne touchez pas** à ça ! C'est un produit dangereux.	*Careful! Don't touch that! It's a dangerous product.*

The imperative as an expression of advice:

Ne te **fais** pas de souci pour si peu.	*Don't worry over so little.*
Reposez-vous un peu. Vous travaillez trop.	*Rest for a while. You're working too much.*
Prends un cachet d'aspirine si tu as mal à la tête.	*Take an aspirin if you have a headache.*

The imperative as an expression of an invitation:

Viens au cinéma avec nous. Je t'offre une place.	*Come to the cinema with us. I'll buy you a ticket.*
Venez manger à la maison, ce sera à la bonne franquette !	*Come and have a meal at home, it'll be very informal.*

The imperative as a wish or desire:

Amuse-toi bien avec tes copains.	*Have a good time with your friends.*
Passez de bonnes vacances !	*Have a good vacation/holiday!*

The imperative as an expression of a request:

Mon stylo ne marche plus. **Prête**-m'en un, s'il te plaît.	*My biro isn't working any more. Lend me one, please.*
Donnez-moi des timbres, s'il vous plaît.	*Give me some stamps, please.*

The imperative can be strengthened by the addition of *donc*:

Venez donc dîner à la maison !	*Do come and have a meal with us this evening!*
Tais-toi donc !	*Do keep quiet!*
Fais donc attention !	*Pay attention, will you!*

When the imperative second-person singular of –**er** verbs is immediately followed by the pronouns *y* or *en*, it takes a hyphen and an **s**, to make pronunciation easier:

Donne**s**-en une à Pierre.	*Give one (of them) to Pierre.*
Entre**s**-y.	*Go in!*

In this last example, it would be more common to say *Entre* ! The addition of an **s** also applies to *aller*:

Vas-y, Michel !	*Go on, Michel!*

When first-person and second-person pronouns follow the imperative in the affirmative, they assume a disjunctive form corresponding to *me* and *te* (see chapter 45 on personal pronouns): *Écoute-**moi**, Dis-**moi**, Lave-**toi***. Otherwise, the direct-object pronoun remains the same as with the indicative mood:

Regarde-**les** !	*Look at them!*
Appelle-**le/la** !	*Call him/her!*
Laisse-**le/la** venir !	*Let him/her come!*
Écoutons-**la** chanter !	*Let's hear her sing!*
Regardez-**nous** !	*Look at us!*

The indirect-object pronoun also remains the same:

Donne-**lui/leur** de l'argent !	*Give him/her/them some money!*

Pronouns precede the imperative in its negative form:

Ne **te** baisse pas !	*Don't bend down!*
Ne **les** regardez pas !	*Don't look at them!*
Ne **les** laisse pas partir !	*Don't let them go!*
Ne **nous** abandonnez pas !	*Don't abandon us!*

If the pronoun is the subject or complement of an infinitive, the constructions are the same with verbs such as *écouter, entendre, faire, laisser, mener, sentir, voir*:

Faites-**le** venir !	*Have him come! / Let him come!*
Fais-**moi** appeler !	*Have me called! / Get them to call me!*
Va **la** prévenir !	*Go and tell her!*
Viens **me** voir !	*Come and see me!*
Veuillez **m**'excuser !	*Please excuse me!*

Similarly in the negative:

Ne **me** fais pas appeler !	*Don't have me called! / Don't let them call me!*
Ne **les** laisse pas venir !	*Don't let them come!*
Ne **l**'écoutes pas chanter !	*Don't listen to her sing!*

Le, la and *les* are not elided after the imperative when there is no other pronoun as complement:

Fais-**le** abattre !	*Have him struck down!*
Envoie-**la** annoncer la nouvelle.	*Send her to announce the news.*
Jette-**les** à l'égout.	*Throw them into the drain.*
Dites-**le** avec des fleurs.	*Say it with flowers.*
But: Laisse-**l**'y aller.	*Let him/her go there.*

Y and *en* are not commonly combined these days after the imperative, although they do easily combine before the verb: *Il y en a*; *J'y en ai vu*. Whereas, in principle, one could say *Mettez-y-en* or *Envoyez-y-en*, which is grammatically correct, one would turn these statements differently:

> *Mettez-y un peu de bonne volonté*; *Envoyez-en chez Philippe*; *Mettez-en dans le placard*.

En and *y* may follow a personal pronoun. There is an apostrophe in the absence of a hyphen:

Fiez-**vous-y**.	*Trust it.*
Menez-**nous-y**.	*Take us there.*
Abstenez-**vous-en**.	*Abstain from it.*
Va-**t-en** / Allez-**vous-en**.	*Go away.*
Parlez-**lui-en**.	*Speak to her/him about it.*

There is nevertheless much hesitation over the two forms *m'y* and *t'y*, which are correct but are not commonly used:

Menez-**m'y**.	*Take me there.*
Fie **t'y**.	*Trust it.*
Prends-**t'y** adroitement.	*Set about it skillfully.*
Rends-**t'y** tout de suite.	*Go there immediately.*
Rends-**t'en** compte.	*Take it into account.*

There is again some uncertainty over these constructions, which explains the "incorrect" form: *Mènes-y-moi*. In practice, other turns of phrase occur: *Veux-tu m'y mener?*; *Tu peux t'y fier*; *Tu peux t'y rendre*. If the two pronouns do not depend on the imperative, one can say very easily: *Va m'y attendre*. In principle, in R1 discourse one could hear: *Menez-moi-z-y*; *Donnez-lui-z-en*; *Abstiens-toi-z-en* (quoted by Hanse and Blampain) but, in reality, such constructions would be rare and would be turned differently: *Tu m'y mènes*; *Tu m'en donnes*; *Tu t'en abstiens*.

> Elision occurs after an affirmative imperative only before *y* and *en*. Compare *Laisse-**le** entrer* and *Laisse **l'y** aller*, *Fais-**le** entrer* and *Fais-**l'en** sortir*. But one does hear: *Envoie **le** y passer quelques jours*; *Laisse-**le** y aller*.
> If the imperative is negative, there seems to be less uncertainty or variation: *Ne **t'y** fie pas*; *Ne **l'y** mène pas*; *Ne **vous** y fiez pas*; *Ne **t'en** vante pas*.
> Two identical pronouns may occur next to each other with certain verbs followed by an infinitive:

Envoie-**le** **le/la** chercher.	*Send him to get it.*
Écoute-**la** **la** chanter.	*Listen to her sing it (= la chanson).*

29.3 Order of pronouns with an affirmative imperative

Generally speaking, the direct object precedes the indirect object, and there are two hyphens: *Donne-**le-moi***; *Rends-**la-moi***; *Tiens-**le-toi** pour dit*; *Accordez-**les-leur***; *Envoyez-**les-lui***. However, one finds in the spoken language, with the more unlettered French speakers, the reverse order, a practice not to be copied but certainly to be recognized. This is particularly true of certain very common verbs: *Donne-**moi-le**/**la***; *Dis-**moi-le***; *Rends-**moi-le**/**la**/**les***; *Coupe-**moi-le*** (of bread, for instance).

If an imperative has a complement which is the subject of a following infinitive, as well as a direct complement, the subject of the infinitive is placed first, even if it is in the dative. However, *le*, *la* and *les* precede *lui* and *leur*. Note that there is no hyphen between the two pronouns:

Regarde-**la nous** imiter.	*Look at her imitating us.*
Écoute-**les** t'applaudir.	*Listen to them applauding you.*
Écoutez-**les** m'expliquer le problème.	*Listen to them explain the problem to me.*
Laisse-**moi** t'en parler.	*Let me speak to you about it.*
Laissez-**les** le répéter.	*Let them repeat it.*

Faire followed by an infinitive needs separate treatment; *Le*, *la* and *les* are in first position:

Faites-**la-leur** envoyer.	*Have it sent to them.*
Fais-**le-moi** savoir.	*Let me know* (it).
Faites-**le-lui** comprendre.	*Make him understand* (it).

As noted above, apostrophe excludes a hyphen: *Va-t'en*; *Attache-l'y*.

When there are two imperatives, they are treated separately and the pronouns attached to them are also treated separately: *Viens me voir. Dis-moi ce que te penses > Viens me voir et dis-moi ce que tu penses*. However, in R3 literary style, if both imperatives are in the same sentence, a pronoun may precede the second imperative:

Poète, prends ton luth et **me** donne un baiser.	*Poet, take up your lyre and give me a kiss.*

Since some confusion can arise over placing of pronouns after the imperative, with concomitant and sometimes awkward hyphens and apostrophes, we have also seen in Section 29.2 above that, frequently, some constructions are avoided and replaced by a simpler statement that does not necessarily include the imperative: *Attache-l'y > Tu l'attaches au barreau / à la barre / au poteau*; *Écoute-les t'applaudir > Tu les écoutes t'applaudir*.

29.4 Features in French that perform the same function as the imperative

The infinitive often replaces the imperative in general instructions for the public, and this practice is very common, being of a polite nature:

Mettre vingt grammes de beurre dans la poêle.	*Put twenty grams of butter in the pan.*
Ne pas **dépasser** la dose indiquée.	*Do not take more than the stated dose.*
Tenir au frais.	*Keep in a cool place.*
Tenir hors de la portée des enfants.	*Keep out of the reach of children.*
Extraire la racine carrée des nombres suivants.	*Find the square root of the following numbers.*
Bien **faire** et **laisser** dire (*proverb*).	*Do right and fear no man.*
Ne pas **se pencher** à la fenêtre (*on trains*).	*Do not lean out (of) the window.*

The infinitive is also used in a colloquial way, and often in the negative:

Ne pas **toucher**! (*even:* Pas **toucher**!)	*Do not touch!*
Ne pas **s'affoler**, surtout!	*Especially, don't panic!*

Also of a polite nature is the use of the future:

Tu le **feras** demain, s'il te plaît.	*Please do it tomorrow.*
Quand vous reviendrez vous **rangerez** vos affaires.	*When you come back, please tidy up your things.*

In oral communications one hears readily:

Garçon, une bière!	*Waiter, a beer!*
Bon appétit!	*Have a good meal!*
Silence!	*Silence!*
Motus!	*Keep it under your hat / Mum's the word!*
Chut!	*Quiet!*
Pas un mot!	*Not a word!*
Feu!	*Fire!*
Paix aux hommes de bonne volonté.	*Peace to men of good will.*

On public notices one reads:

Entrée interdite	*No entry*
Défense d'entrer/d'afficher	*No entry/bills/Stick no bills*
Défense/interdiction de fumer	*No smoking*

It is possible to use the third-person conjugation preceded by *que* to create the effect of the imperative, but the form is the subjunctive (see Chapter 44 on the subjunctive). This construction has no true single equivalent in English:

Que personne ne **sorte**!	*No one go out!*
Qu'ils **entrent**!	*Let them come in!*
Si Jean ne peut faire ses devoirs aujourd'hui, qu'il les **fasse** demain!	*If Jean can't do his homework today, let him do it tomorrow!*
Dieu dit: "Que la lumière **soit**!", et la lumière fut (Genesis 1:3).	*God said: "Let there be light," and there was light.*
Qu'à cela ne **tienne**!	*Do not worry!*

There are numerous set expressions where the *que* is omitted, particularly in R3 language, and in the third person:

Dieu vous **garde**!	*May God protect/keep you!*
Dieu **soit** loué!	*God be praised! / Thanks be to God!*
Dieu **veuille** me pardonner!	*Would that God forgive me!*
Le diable m'**emporte** si j'y comprends un mot!	*The devil take me if I understand a word of it!*
Son saint Nom **soit** béni!	*May his holy Name be blessed!*
Plaise/Plût à Dieu que…	*Would to God that…*
À Dieu ne **plaise** (que…)!	*God forbid (that…)!*
Grand bien vous **fasse**!	*That'll do you a lot of good!*

The subject is sometimes repeated by a personal pronoun after the subject. R3 level of language applies here:

Dieu **puisse**-t-il m'accorder ce droit.	*May God grant me that right.*

The subject can be inverted to follow the verb. This is still R3 language.

Ainsi **soit**-il.	*So be it.*
Advienne que pourra.	*Come what may.*
Béni **soit** Dieu!	*God be blessed!*
Maudit **soit** l'importun qui me téléphone à deux heures du matin.	*Cursed be the wretch who phones me at two in the morning.*

The subjunctive of *vivre* is commonly used. It normally occurs in the singular, even if the noun is plural. The expressions here are R2:

Vive la France / la République / la Liberté!	*Long live France/the Republic/Freedom!*
Vive l'amour! **Vive** le vin!	*Long live love! Long live wine!*
Vive la mariée!	*Long live the bride!*
Vive les vacances!	*Long live the vacation/holidays!*

Much ink has been spilt over the use of the plural *vivent* with a plural noun. Does one still say *Vivent les vacances*? Probably not, although, according to Hanse and Blampain, the agreement occurs in literary texts. Grevisse and Goosse quote an example from La Fontaine, but this is going back 300 years. Hanse and Blampain argue that *Vive* is really a set formula for an acclamation, and there is no justification for a plural.

Adjectives used adverbially can also indicate the imperative idea:

Haut les mains ! (Al Capone / Robin Hood)	*Hands up!*
Haut les fusils et en avant, camarades !	*Rifles at the ready and forward, comrades!*
Bas les pattes ! (*pattes* here: R1 = hands)	*Keep your paws to yourself!*
Chapeau **bas** !	*Excellent! Well done! (Take my/your hat off)*

Often a noun is used along with the omission of the verb:

La porte !	*(Shut) The door!*
Ta **gueule** ! (R1: to be used with care)	*Shut up / Belt up!*

Certain high-register expressions are found, although they are not set expressions:

Ah ! **Vienne** vite le printemps !	*Oh, that spring would come quickly!*
Pardonnée **soit**-elle !	*May she be forgiven!*
Dieu **choisisse** !	*Let God choose!*

The verb *pouvoir*, in R3 language, is used in all persons:

Puissé-je survivre à ce supplice !	*Oh, that I may survive this punishment!*
Puisses-tu goûter un plat si délicat !	*Oh, that you may taste such a delicate dish as this!*
Puissions-nous réussir !	*Oh, that we may succeed!*
Puissiez-vous réussir !	*Oh, that you may succeed!*

Some miscellaneous expressions:

Soit (the **t** is pronounced).	*So be it. Agreed.*
À vous la parole.	*Your turn (to speak).*
Chacun son tour !	*Each one in turn!*
Écoute(z) !	*Come on!*

Although *Écoute(z)* obviously has the meaning of *Listen (to me)*, as in *Écoute(z)-moi*, it is frequently used in isolation with the idea of encouraging someone to accept an argument when that person does not reason properly. It corresponds to the English *Look here!*

Écoute, ne sois pas ridicule !	*Look here / Come on, don't be ridiculous!*
Écoute(z), le calcul est correct !	*Come on, the calculation is correct!*
Écoute, tes prévisions ne sont pas correctes.	*Look here, your forecasts are incorrect.*

The second person (singular and plural) of *savoir* does not really have its English equivalent of *know* but has to be turned some other way: *Sache(z) que...* (*Understand that...*).

Avoir is often used in the negative: *N'aie pas peur!* Similarly, the high-register injunction without the *pas*: *N'aie/ayez crainte* (*Fear not*).

Imperative forms of *vouloir* are: *veuille, veuillons, veuillez.* However, in the expression *en vouloir à quelqu'un* (*to have a grudge against someone*) which always appears in the negative, one says: *Ne m'en veux pas / ne m'en voulez pas* (*Don't hold it against me*).

The expression *Fais ce que dois* (*Do what you must*) has an R3 literary connotation.

29.5 Uses of the perfect imperative

The perfect imperative is much less frequent and is generally of a higher register than the present form. It states that an act is to be performed at a determined point in the future, with a specific indication of time:

Ayez fini tout votre travail avant samedi. — *Have all your work finished before Saturday.*

Sois partie d'ici au plus tard à midi. — *Be gone from here by midday at the latest.*

30

Irregular verbs | Les verbes irréguliers

The passage below sings the praises of the highly esteemed and sought after University of Princeton. It highlights the keen pursuit of unique intellectual attainments, for both professor and student. The university boasts numerous Nobel Prize winners. The piece contains a range of irregular verbs in a variety of tenses. Infinitives of the irregular verbs are placed in brackets after the verb. These verbs are highlighted in bold. A few translations are provided.

Le campus de Princeton

L'État du New Jersey **est né** (**naître**) sur la côte atlantique des États-Unis. Il **s'ouvre** (**ouvrir**) du nord au sud entre l'État de New York et le Delaware, et s'étend, à l'ouest, à la frontière avec la Pennsylvanie. Notre séjour sur le campus de Princeton **vaut** (**valoir**) la peine que l'on **écrive** (**écrire**) nos impressions de voyage sur cette région du monde. Il **a fallu** (**falloir**) un certain courage pour avoir **couru** (**courir**) le monde en plein cœur de l'hiver. Nous **prîmes** (**prendre**) au sérieux l'occasion qui s'**offrit** (**offrir**) à nous en acceptant l'invitation de nos amis. Nous **découvrîmes** (**découvrir**) le New Jersey dans ses dimensions éducatives, culturelles et sociales.

Cette région **faisait** (**faire**) partie des treize colonies de l'Empire britannique. Elle reste fortement influencée par l'apport culturel de ce peuple. L'université de Princeton **a acquis** (**acquérir**) une grande notoriété [celebrity]. La politique éducative vise à favoriser la formation des élites. De nombreux scientifiques en physique et en économie **ont reçu** (**recevoir**) le Prix Nobel. Princeton University **appartient** (**appartenir**) au groupe des universités prestigieuses **connu** (**connaître**) sous le terme Ivy League. Ces universités américaines **servent** (**servir**) le public étudiant en jouissant d'une très grande autonomie. Cela signifie que leur offre de formation est **promue** (**promouvoir**) en fonction du contenu des programmes d'études et de la réputation de ses professeurs évalués, en fin d'année, par les étudiants eux-mêmes. Les enseignants qui ne donnent pas satisfaction **sont démis** (**démettre**) de leur fonction [dismissed from their post]. Autrement dit, l'excellence académique, le niveau d'études et le prestige des diplômes varient d'un établissement universitaire à l'autre. Les établissements **entretiennent** (**entretenir**) ainsi une grande rivalité d'intérêts. Les droits d'inscription [registration fees] et les frais de scolarité [tuition fees] à l'université de Princeton **atteignent** (**atteindre**) des sommes exorbitantes. Les étudiants américains **interrompent** (**interrompre**) facilement leurs études pour tirer profit d'une expérience professionnelle **acquise** (**acquérir**) sur le terrain et fortement valorisée par l'institution universitaire.

Le campus universitaire **est construit** (**construire**) en dehors de la ville. Le modèle d'architecture des bâtiments anciens **plaît** (**plaire**) beaucoup aux visiteurs. Les édifices **sont conçus** (**concevoir**) autour d'un vaste parc arboré. L'étendue des bois **s'accroît** (**accroître**) aux abords du Lac Carnegie. Cette université privée **met** (**mettre**) en exergue [emphasizes] les mêmes valeurs que la plupart des universités britanniques traditionnelles. Le cadre exceptionnel de Princeton a inspiré le célèbre film intitulé *Un homme d'exception* (*A Beautiful Mind* en version originale). La série *Doctor House*, la plus **suivie** (**suivre**) au monde, **est mise** (**mettre**) en scène [is produced] dans un hôpital imaginaire de Princeton.

French irregular verbs are unquestionably more complicated than English ones, which are really relatively easy. (**S**)**asseoir** is a good case in point, and it can even be a scourge for many French speakers (e.g., the faulty *s'asseya* instead of the correct *s'assit*; the faulty *Assis-toi où tu veux t'assir* instead of *Assieds-toi où tu veux t'asseoir*).

There do seem to be a lot of irregular verbs in French. Nonetheless, many of them are quite rare, or defective, so that approximately fifty need to be learned, and several others are compounds based on shorter irregular verbs and conjugated like them. *Admettre, commettre, démettre, émettre, omettre, remettre* and so on, among a number of other similar compound verbs from *mettre*, are conjugated like *mettre*, while *venir* leads us to *contrevenir, convenir, devenir, intervenir* and so on. The prefix **re–** is notably common here. In this way, it may be argued that many French irregular verbs are far from unique, for a good number may be grouped together. A complete list of verb tables is available for reference at the end of this volume. The tables include both regular and irregular verbs of all types.

There are four main types of irregular verbs in French. They may be listed thus:

1. A group of verbs which, however they are considered, are individually unique in themselves, although these may take **re–** as a prefix to indicate repetition; examples are: *asseoir, bouillir, naître*. This group includes a small number of verbs (about fifteen). It includes the baffling *aller*, which contains a startling variety of forms deriving from three different verbs in Vulgar Latin: *ambulare* > *alare* > *allons*, *vadere* > *vais*, *ire* + *habeo* > *irai*. *Être* and *avoir* also fall into this unique category. These irregular verbs form the subject of the present chapter.

2. A second group, treated in Chapter 31, brings together verbs with ortho-graphic changes: *manger* > *mangeons*, *commencer* > *commençons*, *appeler* > *appelons*, *acheter* > *achète*, *nettoyer* > *nettoie*.
3. A third group involves those verbs which attract a large number of prefixes, like *mettre*, referred to above. These are listed below.
4. A fourth group brings together defective verbs parts of which do not exist, or used to exist but have now become defunct. These are treated separately in Chapter 35.

30.1 Forms of irregular verbs

Some of these only have slight irregularities, like *lire*. Only the more common verbs and their main irregularities are given here – complete tables are provided at the end of the book. The following are not shown here:

1. the imperfect indicative, because it is formed on the first-person plural of the present indicative;
2. the present conditional, because it is formed on the root of the future;
3. the imperfect subjunctive, because it is formed from the preterit;
4. the imperative, except when it is irregular, because it is formed from the present indicative. Verbs with prefixes are given.

Être, *avoir*, *aller* and *faire* are given separately, since they are so common, and given in full but with the exclusions indicated above:

être

Pres. ind.	je suis, tu es, il/elle est, nous sommes, vous êtes, ils/elles sont
Future	je serai, tu seras, il/elle sera, nous serons, vous serez, ils/elles seront
Preterit	je fus, tu fus, il/elle fut, nous fûmes, vous fûtes, ils/elles furent
Pres. subj.	que je sois, que tu sois, qu'il/elle soit, que nous soyons, que vous soyez, qu'ils/elles soient
Pres. part.	étant
Past part.	été

avoir

Pres. ind.	j'ai, tu as, il/elle a, nous avons, vous avez, ils/elles ont
Future	j'aurai, tu auras, il/elle aura, nous aurons, vous aurez, ils/elles auront
Preterit	j'eus, tu eus, il/elle eut, nous eûmes, vous eûtes, ils/elles eurent
Pres. subj.	que j'aie, que tu aies, qu'il/elle ait, que nous ayons, que vous ayez, qu'ils/elles aient
Pres. part.	ayant
Past part.	eu

aller

Pres. ind.	je vais, tu vas, il/elle va, nous allons, vous allez, ils/elles vont
Future	j'irai, tu iras, il/elle ira, nous irons, vous irez, ils/elles iront
Preterit	j'allai, tu allas, il/elle alla, nous allâmes, vous allâtes, ils/elles allèrent
Pres. subj.	que j'aille, que tu ailles, qu'il/elle aille, que nous allions, que vous alliez, qu'ils/elles aillent
Pres. part.	allant
Past part.	allé

faire

Pres. ind.	je fais, tu fais, il/elle fait, nous faisons, vous faites, ils/elles font
Future	je ferai, tu feras, il/elle fera, nous ferons, vous ferez, ils/elles feront
Preterit	je fis, tu fis, il/elle fit, nous fîmes, vous fîtes, ils/elles firent
Pres. subj.	que je fasse, que tu fasses, qu'il/elle fasse, que nous fassions, que vous fassiez, qu'ils/elles fassent
Pres. part.	faisant
Past part.	fait

acquérir

Pres. ind.: *j'acquiers, nous acquérons ils/elles acquièrent*; Future: *j'acquerrai*; Preterit: *j'acquis*; Pres. subj.: *que j'acquière, que nous acquerions, qu'ils acquièrent*; Pres. part.: *acquérant*; Past part.: *acquis*.
Likewise: *conquérir, requérir, s'enquérir*.

(s')asseoir

Pres. ind.: *je m'assieds/assois, nous nous asseyons/assoyons, vous vous asseyez, ils/elles s'asseyent/s'assoient*; Future: *je m'assiérai*; Preterit: *je m'assis*; Pres. subj.: *que je m'asseye/assoie, que nous nous asseyions/assoyions, qu'ils s'asseyent/assoient*; Pres. part.: *assoyant/asseyant*; Past part.: *assis*.
Likewise: *se rasseoir*.

battre

Pres. ind.: *je bats, nous battons*; Future: *je battrai*; Preterit: *je battis*; Pres. subj.: *que je batte*; Pres. part.: *battant*; Past part.: *battu*.
Likewise: *combattre, rabattre, rebattre*.

bouillir

Pres. ind.: *je bous, nous bouillons*; Future: *je bouillirai*; Preterit: *je bouillis*; Pres. subj.: *que je bouille*; Pres. part.: *bouillant*; Past part.: *bouilli*.

conclure

Pres. ind.: *je conclus*; Future: *je conclurai*; Preterit: *je conclus*; Pres. subj.: *que je conclue*; Pres. part.: *concluant*; Past part.: *conclu*.
Likewise: *exclure, inclure* (but past part.: *inclus*).

conduire

Pres. ind.: *je conduis*; Future: *je conduirai*; Preterit: *je conduisis*; Pres. subj.: *que je conduise*; Pres. part.: *conduisant*; Past part.: *conduit*.

Likewise: *construire, cuire, déduire, détruire, enduire, induire, instruire, introduire, produire, reconduire, réduire, séduire, traduire, luire* (past part.: *lui*), *nuire* (past part.: *nui*).

connaître

Pres. ind.: *je connais, nous connaissons*; Future: *je connaîtrai*; Preterit: *je connus*; Pres. subj.: *que je connaisse*; Pres. part.: *connaissant*; Past part.: *connu*.

Likewise: *apparaître, disparaître, paraître, reconnaître*.

coudre

Pres. ind.: *je couds, nous cousons*; Future: *je coudrai*; Preterit: *je cousis*; Pres. subj.: *que je couse*; Pres. part.: *cousant*; Past part.: *cousu*.

courir

Pres. ind.: *je cours, nous courons*; Future: *je courrai*; Preterit: *je courus*; Pres. subj.: *que je coure*; Pres. part.: *courant*; Past part.: *couru*.

Likewise: *accourir, concourir, recourir, secourir*.

craindre

Pres. ind.: *je crains, nous craignons*; Future: *je craindrai*; Preterit: *je craignis*; Pres. subj.: *que je craigne*; Pres. part.: *craignant*; Past part.: *craint*.

Likewise: *contraindre, plaindre*.

croire

Pres. ind.: *je crois, nous croyons, ils/elles croient*; Future: *je croirai*; Preterit: *je crus*; Pres. subj.: *que je croie*; Pres. part.: *croyant*; Past part.: *cru*.

croître

Pres. Ind: *je crois, il/elle croît, nous croissons*; Future: *je croîtrai*; Preterit: *je crus*; Pres. subj.: *que je croisse*; Pres. part.: *croissant*; Past part.: *crû, crue*.

Likewise: *accroître, décroître, recroître*.

cueillir

Pres. ind.: *je cueille*; Future: *je cueillerai*; Preterit: *je cueillis*; Pres. subj.: *que je cueille*; Pres. part.: *cueillant*; Past part.: *cueilli*.

Likewise: *accueillir, recueillir*.

devoir

Pres. ind.: *je dois, nous devons, ils/elles doivent*; Future: *je devrai*; Preterit: *je dus*; Pres. subj.: *que je doive, que nous devions*; Pres. part.: *devant*; Past part.: *dû, due, dus, dues* (note these last three where the circumflex disappears).

Likewise: *redevoir*.

dire

Pres. ind.: *je dis, nous disons*; Future: *je dirai*; Preterit: *je dis*; Pres. subj.: *que je dise*; Pres. part.: *disant*; Past part.: *dit*.

Likewise: *contredire, se dédire, interdire, médire, prédire, redire*.

dormir

Pres. ind.: *je dors, nous dormons*; Future: *je dormirai*; Preterit: *je dormis*; Pres. subj.: *que je dorme*; Pres. part.: *dormant*; Past part.: *dormi*.

Likewise: *s'endormir, se rendormir*.

écrire

Pres. ind.: *j'écris, nous écrivons*; Future: *j'écrirai*; Preterit: *j'écrivis*; Pres. subj.: *que j'écrive*; Pres. part.: *écrivant*; Past part.: *écrit*.

Likewise: *décrire, inscrire, prescrire, proscrire, réécrire, souscrire, transcrire*.

émouvoir

Pres. ind.: *j'émeus, nous émouvons, ils/elles émeuvent*; Future: *j'émouvrai*; Preterit: *j'émus*; Pres. subj.: *que j'émeuve, que nous émouvions, qu'ils/elles émeuvent*; Pres. part.: *émouvant*; Past part.: *ému*.

Likewise: *mouvoir* (past part.: *mû/mue*), *promouvoir*.

extraire

Pres. ind.: *j'extrais, nous extrayons, ils/elles extraient*; Future: *j'extrairai*; Preterit: not used; Pres. subj.: *que j'extraie, que nous extrayions, qu'ils/elles extraient*; Pres. part.: *extrayant*; Past part.: *extrait*.

Likewise: *distraire, soustraire, traire*.

falloir

Pres. ind.: *il faut*; Future: *il faudra*; Preterit: *il fallut*; Pres. subj.: *qu'il faille*; Pres. part.: not used; Past part.: *fallu*.

fuir

Pres. ind.: *je fuis, nous fuyons, ils/elles fuient*; Future: *je fuirai*; Preterit: *je fuis*; Pres. subj.: *que je fuie, que nous fuyions, qu'ils/elles fuient*; Pres. part.: *fuyant*; Past part.: *fui*.

Likewise: *s'enfuir*.

haïr

Pres. ind.: *je hais, tu hais, il/elle hait, nous haïssons, vous haïssez, ils/elles haïssent*; Future: *je haïrai*; Preterit: *je haïs, nous haïmes*; Pres. subj.: *que je haïsse, que nous haïssions, qu'ils/elles haïssent*; Pres. part.: *haïssant*; Past part.: *haï*.

joindre

Pres. ind.: *je joins, nous joignons, ils/elles joignent*; Future: *je joindrai*; Preterit: *je joignis*; Pres. subj.: *que je joigne*; Pres. part.: *joignant*; Past part.: *joint*.

Likewise: *adjoindre, disjoindre, rejoindre*.

lire

Pres. ind.: *je lis, nous lisons*; Future: *je lirai*; Preterit: *je lus*; Pres. subj.: *que je lise*; Pres. part.: *lisant*; Past part.: *lu*.

Likewise: *élire, réélire, relire*.

mettre

Pres. ind.: *je mets, nous mettons*; Future: *je mettrai*; Preterit: *je mis*; Pres. subj.: *que je mette*; Pres. part.: *mettant*; Past part.: *mis*.

Likewise: *admettre, commettre, démettre, émettre, omettre, permetttre, promettre, remettre, soumettre, transmettre.*

moudre

Pres. ind.: *je mouds, nous moulons*; Future: *je moudrai*; Preterit: *je moulus*; Pres. subj.: *que je moule*; Pres. part.: *moulant*; Past part.: *moulu.*

mourir

Pres. ind.: *je meurs, nous mourons*; Future: *je mourrai*; Preterit: *je mourus*; Pres. subj.: *que je meure*; Pres. part.: *mourant*; Past part.: *mort.*

naître

Pres. ind.: *je nais, nous naissons*; Future: *je naîtrai*; Preterit: *je naquis*; Pres. subj.: *que je naisse*; Pres. part.: *naissant*; Past part.: *né.*

Likewise: *renaître.*

ouvrir

Pres. ind.: *j'ouvre, nous ouvrons*; Future: *j'ouvrirai*; Preterit: *j'ouvris*; Pres. subj.: *que j'ouvre*; Pres. part.: *ouvrant*; Past part.: *ouvert.*

Likewise: *couvrir, découvrir, offrir, rouvrir, souffrir.*

peindre

Pres. ind.: *je peins, nous peignons*; Future: *je peindrai*; Preterit: *je peignis*; Pres. subj.: *que je peigne*; Pres. part.: *peignant*; Past part.: *peint.*

Likewise: *astreindre, atteindre, ceindre, contraindre, déteindre, enfreindre, éteindre, étreindre, feindre, geindre, restreindre, teindre.*

plaire

Pres. ind.: *je plais, il/elle plaît, nous plaisons*; Future: *je plairai*; Preterit: *je plus*; Pres. subj.: *que je plaise*; Pres. part.: *plaisant*; Past part.: *plu.*

Likewise: *déplaire, se taire* (but *tait*, i.e., no circumflex).

pleuvoir

Pres. ind.: *il pleut*; Future: *il pleuvra*; Preterit: *il plut*; Pres. subj.: *qu'il pleuve*; Pres. part.: none; Past part.: *plu.*

pouvoir

Pres. ind.: *je peux/puis, nous pouvons, ils/elles peuvent*; Future: *je pourrai*; Preterit: *je pus*; Pres. subj.: *que je puisse*; Pres. part.: *pouvant*; Past part.: *pu.*

Note: *puis* is used in R3 literary language, and also in the interrogative at a lower level: *Puis-je vous aider?*

prendre

Pres. ind.: *je prends, nous prenons, ils/elles prennent*; Future: *je prendrai*; Preterit: *je pris*; Pres. subj.: *que je prenne*; Pres. part.: *prenant*; Past part.: *pris.*

Likewise: *apprendre, comprendre, entreprendre, s'éprendre, se méprendre, reprendre, suspendre.*

résoudre

Pres. ind.: *je résous, nous résolvons, ils/elles résolvent*; Future: *je résoudrai*; Preterit: *je résolus*; Pres. subj.: *que je résolve*; Pres. part.: *résolvant*; Past part.: *résolu.*

Likewise: *dissoudre* (but past part. *dissout[e]*).

rire
Pres. ind.: *je ris, nous rions, ils/elles rient*; Future: *je rirai*; Preterit: *je ris*; Pres. subj.: *que je rie, que nous riions*; Pres. part.: *riant*; Past part.: *ri*.
Likewise: *sourire*.

savoir
Pres. ind.: *je sais, nous savons*; Future: *je saurai*; Preterit: *je sus*; Pres. subj.: *que je sache*; Pres. part.: *sachant*; Past Part.: *su*.

sentir
Pres. ind.: *je sens*; Future: *je sentirai*; Preterit: *je sentis*; Pres. subj.: *que je sente*; Pres. part.: *sentant*; Past part.: *senti*.
Likewise: *consentir, démentir, mentir, pressentir, ressentir, se repentir*.

servir
Pres. ind.: *je sers, nous servons*; Future: *je servirai*; Preterit: *je servis*; Pres. subj.: *que je serve*; Pres. part.: *servant*; Past part.: *servi*.
Likewise: *desservir, resservir*.

sortir
Pres. ind.: *je sors, nous sortons*; Future: *je sortirai*; Preterit: *je sortis*; Pres. subj.: *que je sorte*; Pres. part.: *sortant*; Past part.: *sorti*.
Likewise: *partir, ressortir*.

suffire
Pres. ind.: *je suffis, nous suffisons*; Future: *je suffirai*; Preterit: *je suffis*; Pres. subj.: *que je suffise*; Pres. part.: *suffisant*; Past part.: *suffi*.

suivre
Pres. ind.: *je suis, nous suivons*; Future: *je suivrai*; Preterit: *je suivis*; Pres. subj.: *que je suive*; Pres. part.: *suivant*; Past part.: *suivi*.
Likewise: *s'ensuivre, poursuivre*.

tenir
Pres. ind.: *je tiens, nous tenons, ils/elles tiennent*; Future: *je tiendrai*; Preterit: *je tins, nous tînmes*; Pres. subj.: *que je tienne*; Pres. part.: *tenant*; Past part.: *tenu*.
Likewise: *s'abstenir, appartenir, contenir, détenir, entretenir, maintenir, obtenir, retenir, soutenir*.

tressaillir
Pres. ind.: *je tressaille*; Future: *je tressaillirai*; Preterit: *je tressaillis*; Pres. subj.: *que je tressaille*; Pres. part.: *tressaillant*; Past part.: *tressailli*.
Likewise: *assaillir, défaillir* (but defective).

vaincre
Pres. ind.: *je vaincs*, but *il/elle vainc, nous vainquons*; Future: *je vaincrai*; Preterit: *je vainquis*; Pres. subj.: *que je vainque*; Pres. part.: *vainquant*; Past part.: *vaincu*.
Likewise: *convaincre*.

valoir

Pres. ind.: *je vaux, nous valons*; Future: *je vaudrai*; Preterit: *je valus*; Pres. subj.: *que je vaille, que nous valions, qu'ils/elles vaillent*; Pres. part.: *valant*; Past part.: *valu*.

Likewise: *révaloir*.

venir

Pres. ind.: *je viens, nous venons, ils/elles viennent*; Future: *je viendrai*; Preterit: *je vins; nous vînmes*; Pres. subj.: *que je vienne, que nous venions, qu'ils/elles viennent*; Pres. part.: *venant*; Past part.: *venu*.

Likewise: *contrevenir, convenir, devenir, intervenir, parvenir, prévenir, provenir, revenir, se souvenir, subvenir, survenir*.

vêtir

Pres. ind.: *je vêts*; Future: *je vêtirai*; Preterit: *je vêtis*; Pres. subj.: *que je vête*; Pres. part.: *vêtant*; Past part.: *vêtu*.

Likewise: *dévêtir, revêtir*.

vivre

Pres. ind.: *je vis, nous vivons*; Future: *je vivrai*; Preterit: *je vécus*; Pres. subj.: *que je vive*; Pres. part.: *vivant*; Past part.: *vécu*.

Likewise: *revivre, survivre*.

voir

Pres. ind.: *je vois, nous voyons, ils/elles voient*; Future: *je verrai*; Preterit: *je vis*; Pres. subj.: *que je voie, que nous voyions, qu'ils/elles voient*; Pres. part.: *voyant*; Past part.: *vu*.

Likewise: *entrevoir, pourvoir, prévoir, revoir*.

vouloir

Pres. ind.: *je veux, nous voulons, ils/elles veulent*; Future: *je voudrai*; Preterit: *je voulus*; Pres. subj.: *que je veuille, que nous voulions, qu'ils/elles veuillent*; Pres. part.: *voulant*; Past part.: *voulu*.

30.2 Observations

In Chapter 13, it is stated that there is only one true regular series of verbs, those ending in **–er**, an ending capable of reproducing new verbs to meet new requirements, technological, social, medical and so on. In the same chapter, categories with other endings (**–re**, **–ir** and **–evoir**) are considered as sufficiently common to justify their inclusion as forming "regular" groups: *vendre, finir* and *recevoir* (see Chapter 13). *Conduire* and *peindre* could be classed as sub-"regular" groups, if one considered the number of verbs they generate.

Irregular verbs do not cause disturbance only with foreign students of French. They also lead to an avoidance of their use with French speakers. *Émouvoir* is a good case in point. Although this verb is by no means defective, only parts of it meet approval by French speakers in the sense that they regularly and only use the past participle *ému* and the third-person singular (*Le livre m'émeut*), together with the infinitive; the other parts seem to have fallen into disuse. *Affecter, attendrir, remuer* or *toucher* often replace it, as does *émotionner* which, given its –**er** ending, is easier to handle. Similarly with *croître*, all parts of which exist, but *augmenter*, again with an –**er** ending, supersedes it. The infinitive occurs, as does the past participle *crû*: *Au cours des dernières années, les prix n'ont cessé de croître / En dix ans les arbres ont beaucoup crû*. In the first case, *augmenter* would take priority with the general French-speaking public, while in the second *pousser* or *grandir* would come more readily or easily to mind. Finally, although the list is endless, *vêtir* is almost entirely replaced by *habiller*. Only the past participle and infinitive have survived in popular usage: *Elle est bien vêtue/J'aime bien sa façon de se vêtir*. Hanse and Blampain state quite categorically: *À éviter aujourd'hui*.

> *Asseoir*: naturally enough, this verb is used very frequently. However, there are some complications since it has two forms, *assieds* and *assois*; the choice of which one to use is open to debate. By and large, the former is of a higher register than the latter, and is less frequently used, although according to Grevisse and Goosse, who are both Belgians, the *assieds* form is preferred by far in Belgium. The present authors also use this form. A consultation in three regions of France suggests that the *assois* form is much more common. *Asseoir* is also used non-reflexively (i.e., transitively): *La mère **assoit** l'enfant* (*The mother sits the child down*); *L'infirmier **assoit** le malade*. Here again, *assied* rivals with *assoit*. The conclusion must be that *assoit* is more prevalent in the transitive sense. The past participle *assis* means *sitting* in the sense of *seated*. In other words, one can only say: *Je suis assis(e), elle est assise* (*I am sitting, she is sitting*).
>
> *Bouillir*: this is an intransitive verb. In other words, one can only say *L'eau bout*; *Je fais bouillir de l'eau* (*I boil water*). *Fais* is necessary here. However, in R1 language, it is quite possible to hear *Je bous de l'eau*.
>
> *Cuire*: conjugates like *conduire*, in which group it is included. Some seem to think that this verb is only intransitive. Such is not the case. One can say *Cuire un œuf* as well as *Un poulet cuit*.
>
> *Connaître*: as with all its compounds, *croître, naître* and *plaire*, the **i** carries a circumflex before the **t**. This circumflex is no longer necessary, but is still generally inserted.
>
> *Croire* and *croître*: notice the difference between the two past participles in the masculine form: *croire > cru; croître > crû*.
>
> *Dire*: *vous dites*, but the second-person plural of all these verbs is *contredisez/interdisez/prédisez*. Some French speakers, and many children, do not observe this rule. Care should be taken over *maudire*, which has

lost all associations with *dire* save in the infinitive and the past participle. It is conjugated like *finir*.

Falloir: this verb is only used in the third-person singular and all tenses. It is included here since it is so common.

Haïr: despite all its parts being extant, it causes considerable difficulty. *Détester* often replaces it. The expression *prendre en grippe*, which is of low register, is a further substitute, as are *abhorrer* and *exécrer*, but these latter two do not find their way into common, daily discourse.

Savoir: the second-person singular and plural imperative of *savoir* occur much more frequently than the English *know*: *Sache(z) que...* > *Understand that...*

Sortir: confusion reigns with the compound *ressortir* which, in the meaning of *to go out again*, is conjugated like *sortir*, and takes *être* with compound tenses: *Elle ressort / est ressortie*. However, in the meaning of *to be the responsibility of / to be within the jurisdiction of*, *ressortir* is conjugated like *finir*, and takes the auxiliary *avoir*: *Le cas de l'accusée ne ressortit pas / n'a pas ressorti à la compétence du tribunal*. It goes without saying that many French speakers, even authors, confuse both meanings and conjugations of this verb.

Assortir (to match) promotes similar hesitation. It is conjugated like *finir* and therefore takes the auxiliary *avoir*: *Cette dame assortit ses gants à ses chaussures*. But, of course, one can say in the passive *Ces couleurs sont bien assorties*; *La règle est assortie de plusieurs exceptions, comme le verbe **assortir***; and *Le magasin est assorti d'un grand choix*.

Repartir (to set off again) and *répartir (to share)* lie at the origin of further uncertainty. The first is conjugated like *sortir* while the second is conjugated like *finir*.

repartir: *Elles repartent ce soir / sont reparties hier matin*.

répartir: *J'ai réparti les cadeaux; Je répartissais les cadeaux quand Jean est entré*. Since *(se) départir (to abandon, to lose, to swerve away from)* is only used in R3 literary style, little wonder that perplexity abounds here, and even with authors endowed with the finest style. It would appear that it is conjugated like *sortir* (auxiliary = *être*) and *finir* (auxiliary = *avoir*), and there is no clear-cut path forward here: *ce calme dont je ne me départais pas* (this calm I did not abandon); *ce calme dont je ne me départissais pas* (this calm I did not abardon).

Suivre: note merely that the first-person singular *je suis* has exactly the same form as the first-person singular of the verb *être*. Only the most schizophrenic and ontologically challenged of students of the French language would struggle with *Je suis un chien*.

Tenir and *venir* are conjugated in the same way. However, one difference emerges very clearly. *Tenir* has the auxiliary *avoir* in compound tenses while *venir* functions with *être*. The three verbs with prefixes for *venir*,

contrevenir, convenir and prévenir, do require some comment. The first
and last of these three verbs take *avoir* as the auxiliary. *Convenir* causes
bewilderment, since it takes both *être* and *avoir*, and this depends on
the meaning. See Chapter 14, Section 14.2 for a detailed explanation
of this difficulty.

Vaincre: although this verb has all operational parts, one rarely hears
vainc, just as one does not come across *convainc*. The conjugations are
too complex. The past participle does recur with frequency (*Ils sont
vaincus*), just as one would hear and write *Je suis convaincu(e) que…*
Battre, défaire, écraser or *dominer* would replace *vaincre*, while *persuader*,
déterminer and *encourager* would appeal to the speaker before *convaincre*.

Valoir has all its functional parts, but it is often avoided. The compound
verb *prévaloir* has just one difference in the present subjunctive: *que je
prévale / tu prévales*.

Vêtir see above.

30.2.1 Comments on the use of the verb *être* as a replacement for *aller*

Être can, and frequently does, replace the verb *aller* in common discourse,
but exclusively so in compound tenses: *J'ai été chercher la voiture au garage*
(*I went to get the automobile from the garage*); *Tu as été au Québec la semaine
dernière?* (*Were you in Quebec last week?*). In literary language, one finds it in
the preterit and the imperfect subjunctive, although only in the first- and
second-person singular, and the third-person plural. This is particularly
so before an infinitive: *Je fus me coucher à minuit*; "*Elle fut ensuite trouver
Madame*" (Green 1955, p. 73).

Aller used reflexively (*to go away*) also finds a substitute in *être*, but again
in R3 literary language: *Elle s'en fut le trouver = Elle s'en alla le trouver*. Charles
de Gaulle wrote in *L'unité*: "*Nous laissâmes Giraud dans sa villa et nous en
fûmes dans la nôtre*" (1956).

30.3 Appendix: poem by Raymond Devos

This poem illustrates most skillfully and humorously the torment that can
be generated by a French irregular verb. In this case, it is a question of *ouïr*,
little used these days, except for one or two forms (infinitive and past participle), and with an ironic or playful intention. Hanse and Blampain state
categorically that it is *très défectif*, while Grevisse and Goosse, together with
Marie-Éva de Villers, seem to ascribe to it all possible parts. Deriving from
audire in Vulgar Latin, it maintained a true vigor in the France of the Middle
Ages, has survived fully intact in all registers in Spanish (*oír*) and in Italian
(*udire*: although this latter verb is only used in writing these days), and may
still be heard in the town crier's invitation to listen to a proclamation (in
both France and England: *Oyez! Oyez!*). This sound, interestingly enough,
corresponds to the standard Spanish *¡Oye!* (*Listen!*).

In the humorous piece below, the French actor and comedian Raymond Devos, who is always inspired by the vagaries of language, notably play on words and nonsense rhymes, makes great play of the sounds associated with the verb *ouïr* and the name of the bird *oie* = *goose*, the screeching and inane call of which explains its metaphoric application to a stupid person. The constant repetition of the forms of the verb *ois*, *oit*, *oient* (sound: *wa*) not only recalls the pronunciation of the bird *oie*, but also fits in neatly with the barking of a dog (ouah! ouah! = woof! woof!), an onomatopoeic term occurring near the end of the poem). Not forgetting the very last word: *quoi* = (**k**)**wa**. Finally, the reading of the poem will test not only foreign students of French, but also native French speakers, given its tongue-twisting element.

Ouï-dire (Hearsay)

Il y a des verbes qui se conjuguent
très irrégulièrement.
Par exemple, le verbe **OUÏR**.
Le verbe ouïr, au présent, ça fait :
J'ois ... j'ois ...
Si, au lieu de dire « j'entends », je dis « j'ois »,
Les gens vont penser que ce que j'entends est joyeux
alors que ce que j'entends peut être
particulièrement triste.
Il faudrait préciser:
« Dieu, que ce que j'ois est triste ! »
J'ois ...
Tu ois ...
Tu ois mon chien qui aboie le soir au fond des bois ?
Il oit ...
Oyons-nous ?
Vous oyez ...
Ils oient.
C'est bête !
L'oie oit. Elle oit, l'oie !
Ce que nous oyons, l'oie l'oit-elle ?
Si au lieu de dire « l'oreille »,
on dit « l'ouïe », alors :
l'ouïe de l'oie a ouï.
Pour peu que l'oie appartienne à Louis :
« L'ouïe de l'oie de Louis a ouï. »
Ah oui ?
« Et qu'a ouï l'ouïe de l'oie de Louis ? »
« Elle a ouï ce que toute oie oit ... »
« Et qu'oit toute oie ? »

« Toute oie oit, quand mon chien aboie
le soir au fond des bois
toute oie oit :
ouah ! ouah !
Qu'elle oit, l'oie ! »
Au passé, ça fait :
J'ouïs...
J'ouïs !
Il n'y a vraiment pas de quoi !
(Devos 1989)

31

Verbs of the –er type with orthographic changes | Les verbes en –er avec modifications orthographiques

A number of groups of verbs undergo certain orthographic or spelling modifications when conjugated, largely, but not entirely, to retain the sound of the consonant as it appears in the infinitive. In other words, consistency of sound is required. As an example, if the first-person plural of *commencer* were written *commencons*, the **c** would not reproduce the sound of the **c** as it occurs in the infinitive. A cedilla is needed to avoid a **k** sound, and to keep the **s** sound before an **o**. There follows a series of verbs that are subject to spelling changes of this type in the interest of coherence of sound or ease of pronunciation.

Verbs ending in –**ger**:

When preceding an **a** or an **o**, an **e** is required: *neiger > il neigeait, nous voyageons, protegeons l'environnement, abroger, agréger, alléger, aménager, arranger, s'arroger, assiéger, bouger, changer, charger, décharger, décourager, dédommager, dégager, dégorger, déloger, démanger, déménager, départager, déranger, déroger, désagréger, diriger, échanger, égorger, émerger, encourager, endommager, engager, enrager, éponger, étager, forger, fourrager, fumiger* (R3), *fustiger* (R3), *gager, gorger, gruger, s'insurger, interroger, loger, longer, manger, mélanger, ménager, mitiger, nager, neiger, obliger, partager, patauger, plonger, propager, protéger, purger, rallonger, ranger, regorger, ronger, saccager, siéger, singer, songer, soulager, submerger, surcharger, télécharger* (to download), *voltiger, voyager.*

Verbs ending in –**cer**:

When preceding an **a** or an **o**, a cedilla is required: *avancer > avançant, nous avançons, agacer, acquiescer, amorcer, annoncer, avancer, bercer, coincer, commencer, commercer, décoincer, décontenancer, défoncer, dépecer, devancer, énoncer, s'efforcer, enfoncer, s'entrelacer, exaucer, exercer, foncer, forcer, froncer, gercer, grincer, lancer, manigancer, percer, pincer, pioncer* (R1), *placer, prononcer, rapiécer, recommencer, remplacer, renforcer, renoncer, replacer, rincer, sucer, tancer, tracer, transpercer.*

Verbs ending in –**eler**:

When, in the infinitive, an l follows a mute or unpronounced **e** (for instance *appeler*, where the first **e** is unpronounced), conjugated forms take a double consonant and the mute **e** becomes an open **e** (e.g., *j'appelle*). Otherwise, the first set of consonants would collide with the final consonant ("j'apple"), an agglutination that creates an awkward sound.

appeler

Present ind.: *j'appelle, tu appelles, il/elle appelle, nous appelons, vous appelez, ils/elles appellent*

Imperfect: *j'appelais, tu appelais,* etc.

Present subj.: as with the present, but *appelions, appeliez*

Future: *j'appellerai, tu appelleras, il/elle appellera, nous appellerons, vous appellerez, ils/elles appelleront*

Conditional: *j'appellerais, tu appellerais, il/elle appellerait, nous appellerions, vous appelleriez, ils/elles appelleraient*

Perfect: *j'ai appelé, tu as appelé,* etc.

Likewise: *amonceler, atteler, bosseler, carreler, chanceler, craqueler, dételer, ficeler, grommeler, museler, niveler, (se) pommeler, rappeler, renouveler, ruisseler*

Care needs to be taken with *interpeller*. Here, the penultimate **e** sounds as with an acute accent (but see Chapter 2, Section 2.6).

Similarly with verbs ending in **–eter**:

Jeter

Present ind.: *je jette, tu jettes, il/elle jette, nous jetons, vous jetez, ils/elles jettent*

Imperfect: *je jetais, tu jetais,* etc.

Present subj.: as with the present, but *jetions, jetiez*

Future: *je jetterai, tu jetteras, il/elle jettera, nous jetterons, vous jetterez, ils/elles jetteront*

Conditional: *je jetterais, tu jetterais, il/elle jetterait, nous jetterions, vous jetteriez, ils/elles jetteraient*

Perfect: *j'ai jeté, tu as jeté,* etc.

Likewise: *becqueter, cacheter, caqueter, colleter, déchiqueter, décolleter, dépaqueter, empaqueter, épousseter, étiqueter, feuilleter, marqueter, moucheter, projeter, souffleter, tacheter, voleter*

Verbs ending in **–eter** where the penultimate **e** takes a grave or open **e** before a mute **e**:

acheter

Present ind.: *j'achète, tu achètes, il/elle achète, nous achetons, vous achetez, ils/elles achètent*

Imperfect: *j'achetais, tu achetais,* etc.

Present subj.: as with the present, but *achetions, achetiez*

Future: *j'achèterai, tu achèteras, il/elle achètera, nous achèterons, vous achèterez, ils/elles achèteront*

Conditional: *j'achèterais, tu achèterais, il/elle achèterait, nous achèterions, vous achèteriez, ils/elles achèteraient*
Perfect: *j'ai acheté, tu as acheté,* etc.

Likewise, although *crever* here does not end in –**eter**:
breveter, crever, crocheter, haleter, racheter

> Verbs ending in –**eler**, but where, unlike *appeler*, the penultimate **e** takes a grave accent (**è**):

peler

Present ind.: *je pèle, tu pèles, il/elle pèle, nous pelons, vous pelez, ils/elles pèlent*
Imperfect: *je pelais, tu pelais,* etc.
Present subj.: as with the present, but *pelions, peliez*
Future: *je pèlerai, tu pèleras, il/elle pèlera, nous pèlerons, vous pèlerez, ils/elles pèleront*
Conditional: *je pèlerais, tu pèlerais, il/elle pèlerait, nous pèlerions, vous pèleriez, ils/elles pèleraient*
Perfect: *j'ai pelé, tu as pelé,* etc.

Likewise, although not all verbs here end in –**eler**:
amener, celer (R3), *ciseler, congeler, démanteler, emmener, geler, harceler, lever, mener, peser, ramener, relever, semer, soulever, soupeser, surgeler*

> Verbs which have an **e** acute (**é**) on the penultimate syllable take a grave **e** (**è**):

espérer

Present ind.: *j'espère, tu espères, il/elle espère, nous espérons, vous espérez, ils/elles espèrent*
Imperfect: *j'espérais, tu espérais,* etc.
Present subj.: as with the present, but *espérions, espériez*
Future: *j'espèrerai, tu espèreras, il/elle espèrera, nous espèrerons, vous espèrerez, ils/elles espèreront*
Conditional: *j'espèrerais, tu espèrerais, il/elle espèrerait, nous espèrerions, vous espèreriez, ils/elles espèreraient*
Perfect: *j'ai espéré, tu as espéré,* etc.
Likewise: *accéder, accélérer, altérer, asséner, s'avérer, céder, conférer, déblatérer* (R3), *déposséder, désaltérer, digérer, empiéter, exécrer* (R3), *fructiférer, générer, gérer, hébéter, héler, incarcérer, incinérer, s'ingérer, interpréter, lacérer, légiférer, léser, macérer, morigéner* (R3), *obséder, obtempérer* (R3), *pestiférer, péter, pondérer, posséder, préférer, proférer, se rasséréner, référer, regénérer, repérer, répéter, révéler, sidérer* (R3), *succéder, tempérer, tolérer, vénérer, vociférer* (R3)

> Verbs ending in –**oyer** change the **y** to **i** before a mute **e**:

nettoyer

Present ind.: *je nettoie, tu nettoies, il/elle nettoie, nous nettoyons, vous nettoyez, ils/elles nettoient*

Imperfect: *je nettoyais, tu nettoyais,* etc.

Present subj.: as with the present, but *nettoyions, nettoyiez*

Future: *je nettoierai, tu nettoieras, il/elle nettoiera, nous nettoierons, vous nettoierez, ils/elles nettoieront*

Conditional: *je nettoierais, tu nettoierais, il/elle nettoierait, nous nettoierions, vous nettoieriez, ils/elles nettoieraient*

Perfect: *j'ai nettoyé, tu as nettoyé,* etc.

Likewise: *atermoyer* (R3), *côtoyer, coudoyer, employer, flamboyer, se fourvoyer, guerroyer, louvoyer, noyer, ondoyer, soudoyer* (R3), *tournoyer, tutoyer, vouvoyer*

> Similarly with verbs ending in **–ayer** and **–uyer**: *appuyer, balayer, bégayer, déblayer, débrayer, défrayer, effrayer, égayer, embrayer, ennuyer, essayer, essuyer, étayer, payer, rayer, relayer, zézayer*

> Verbs ending **in –ayer** can retain the **y** before a mute **e**, but the option of **i** is more common: *je paye/paie, tu payes/paies,* etc.

> *Envoyer* has an irregular future and conditional: *j'enverrai, tu enverras,* etc.; *j'enverrais, tu enverrais,* etc.

> Note also the verb *grasseyer* (= *to pronounce the* **r** *indistinctly* with a kind of slur; a pronunciation typical of the lower social order in Paris and often frowned upon. Not many French speakers know this verb): *je grasseye, tu grasseyes,* etc., and the first- and second-person plural of the imperfect indicative and present subjunctive: *que nous grasseyions, que vous grasseyiez.*

> Note how the first-person plural of the imperfect indicative and of the present subjunctive takes an **i** in verbs of the **–ayer/–oyer** / **–uyer** type. This is, of course, standard spelling, but pronouncing the **y** next to the **i** can cause the **i** to disappear:

Imperfect ind.: nous payions, vous payiez

Present subj.: nous payions, vous payiez

The more pretentious among French speakers would doubtless insist on the spoken inclusion if the **i** to stress their knowledge of its presence.

Many of the verbs not ending in **–ger** and **–cer** cause considerable uncertainty in numerous French speakers, who are subject to confusion over the doubling of the l in *appeler* but not in *peler*. Do the verbs *amonceler, atteler* and so on take a double l or an acute accent? There is little doubt over a verb like *geler* since the French-speaking public are exposed to it during the winter months. Constant exposure to it provides a solution, just as the very frequently used *appeler* involves little hesitation. Again, does the verb *démanteler* double its l or does the **e** take a grave accent instead (see above)? Furthermore, even if this question is correctly answered, the actual pronunciation of *attelle, dételle, brevette* and so on provokes some uneasiness, since the sound does not correspond to the sound of the infinitive, and even seems awkward. The problem is most frequently avoided, both orally and in written form. Finally, the infinitive, the imperfect and the past participle of many of these verbs are generally the only three parts that are actively used: *Il faut carreler (tile) le sol de la cuisine; Tu devrais breveter (patent) ton invention; Le vent amoncelait (piled up) la neige contre la maison; Le réseau de trafiquants a été démantelé (dismantled); Le cambrioleur a crocheté (picked) la serrure; Le daim a une fourrure rousse tachetée de blanc (speckled with white); Une truite mouchetée (speckled), un cheval moucheté (dappled), une reliure en veau moucheté (flecked).*

In the *Rectifications de l'orthographe* of 1990, the Académie française suggests, but no more than that, the extension of the open **e** to a grave accent (**è**) to all verbs ending in **–eler** and **–eter**, save for the following verbs: **appeler**, **rappeler** and **jeter** and their compounds. Of course, this resolves nothing.

Grammarians do not all agree over the choice of the doubling of consonants, or one consonant or consonants followed by an accent. Grevisse and Goosse refer to Littré in this context. What is certain is that the choice makes no difference to the pronunciation.

In popular speech (R1), there is a compression of the **es**, as in: *T'achèteras* > *achèt'ras la voiture demain ?; Elle était bourrelée* > *bourlée de remords (racked with remorse).*

32

Transitive and intransitive verbs | Les verbes transitifs et intransitifs

32.1 Transitive verbs

A transitive verb has a subject –an actor who or which acts directly upon some person or thing – and an object – someone or something that suffers the action of the subject. The object is often expressed or the verb ceases to be transitive. This comment applies to both French and English. Thus in *Je vois la maison* (*I see the house*), *vois* is a transitive verb because it has an object: *maison*. Examples of other verbs used transitively, and there are innumerable verbs that may be used in this way, are:

Il lit le journal.	*He reads the newspaper.*	Je vois le film.	*I see the movie.*
Elle conduit la voiture.	*She drives the car.*	Je visite la ville.	*I visit the town.*
Il prépare le repas.	*He prepares the meal.*	Ils prennent l'avion.	*They catch the airplane.*

32.2 Intransitive verbs

If the verb does not have a direct object, it is used intransitively:

Marine court/marche tous les jours.	*Marine runs/walks every day.*
On va à Rome.	*We are going to Rome.*
On vient souvent ici.	*We come here frequently.*
Les enfants nagent dans la rivière.	*The children swim in the river.*
Le soleil brille.	*The sun shines/is shining.*
L'herbe pousse.	*The grass grows/is growing.*

As seen in the first four examples, an intransitive verb may be further extended by means of adverbial expressions of manner, time or place, but this does not amount to supplying the verb with an object.

Here is a small list of other verbs used intransitively: *bouger, dormir, éternuer, mourir, naître, pâlir, pleurer, rester, rire, rougir, sommeiller, souffrir, tousser, vivre*. Note, however, that *bouger* can be used transitively in familiar language: *Tu peux m'aider à bouger la table ?*

Most verbs of movement are used intransitively: *aller, arriver, avancer, courir, entrer, marcher, partir, reculer, rentrer, retourner, sortir, venir.*

Attention ! La voiture recule.	*Careful! The car's reversing.*
Le train est parti à dix-sept heures.	*The train left at five o'clock.*

Aller is a special case in that it is always followed by a complement of place: *Adrienne va à la banque | à la piscine | au bureau;* although this is not very apparent in *J'y vais.*

Contrary to expectation in the English-speaking world, *entrer* is also used transitively, although *inséra* may be more common in the first example:

L'infirmière **entra** l'aiguille dans la veine.	*The nurse inserted the needle in the vein.*
Les ouvriers ont entré le meuble par la fenêtre.	*The workmen put the piece of furniture through the window.*

Particularly common is its use with computers:

Tu entres les données en mémoire.	*You put the data into the memory.*

Some French grammarians argue for a further class of verbs, a kind of intermediary group. They call them indirect transitive verbs. Delatour, in the Hachette grammar, and Hanse and Blampain promote this category, referring to verbs such as *obéir* and *nuire* which attract the preposition *à* before a noun or pronoun. Grevisse and Goosse do not accept this grouping (2008, p. 321), neither do the present authors, since it engenders an unnecessary complication.

32.3 Uses of transitive or intransitive verbs

In English, most verbs may be used either transitively or intransitively. However, in French, they oscillate less frequently from one variety to the other.

If we take the use of a transitive verb in English, *The man opens the door*, we discover that the verb *to open* may be used intransitively: *The door opens.* Although the French equivalent *ouvrir* is often only used transitively (*L'homme ouvre la porte*), it cannot be used in an intransitive way unless it becomes reflexive (see Chapter 33) or refers to a repeated or customary action. However, before further analysis, one would do well to consider how the two French verbs *descendre* and *monter* may be used transitively and intransitively. By comparing the transitive and intransitive uses of *descendre* and *monter*, the differences stand out more clearly:

Transitive use	Intransitive use
Irène descend les escaliers.	Irène descend de la montagne.
Irène goes down the stairs.	*Irène goes down from the mountain.*
Descends/Monte les livres, s'il te plaît.	Les prix montent/descendent.
Bring down/up the books, please.	*Prices are going down/up.*
Céline monte les escaliers.	Céline monte au premier étage.
Céline goes up the stairs.	*Céline goes up to the first floor.*
Elle a monté les fauteuils avec une poulie.	La température monte.
She sent up the armchairs with a pulley.	*The temperature's going up.*

In the first case of transitive verbs, *descendre* has an object, *escaliers*, whereas in the first case of intransitive verbs, the noun *montagne* is not the object of *descendre* since it is preceded by a preposition, and produces an adverbial expression of place. In the second case, *livres* is the complement or direct object of *descend*, while the sentence *Les prix montent/descendent* has no direct object and stands by itself to convey a full meaning. It becomes obvious that a transitive verb usually requires an object to provide a proper meaning to the sentence, while this is not the case for intransitive verbs. Indeed, intransitive verbs do not take an object at all – otherwise, they cease to be intransitive verbs and become transitive.

Returning to the case of *ouvrir*, above, and here we include *fermer*: these verbs may be used intransitively when something occurs habitually:

Les magasins ouvrent à neuf heures.	*The shops open at nine o'clock.*
Les magasins ferment à dix-neuf heures.	*The shops close at seven.*

The reflexive form would not be used here. At the same time, one could say both: *La porte ouvre/ferme bien* and: *La porte s'ouvre/se ferme bien.*

Compare the intransitive application here to the following reflexive use (see also Chapter 33 for a fuller treatment of reflexive verbs):

Attention ! La porte **se ferme/s'ouvre** !	*Careful! The door is closing/opening!*

Se could not be omitted here, since the verb reflects something precise, imminent and active.

The concept of habitual occurrence also affects the verb *s'arrêter*:

Les cars s'arrêtent toujours ici.	*The buses/coaches always stop here.*

The non-reflexive form cannot be used here. Also:

La voiture s'est arrêtée tout d'un coup.	*The car stopped immediately* (i.e., on one occasion).

Similarly, driving an automobile, the decision to stop would involve the reflexive:

Allez, il y a une station service. Je vais m'arrêter.	*Right, there's a gas station. I'm going to stop.*

Many transitive verbs can stand freely by themselves and do not require a direct object. Such is also the case in English:

Marie va chanter.	*Marie is going to sing.*
J'ai vu que Jeanne écrivait.	*I saw that Jeanne was writing.*
"Qu'est-ce que Philippe fait?" "Il mange/boit."	*"What's Philippe doing?" "He's eating/drinking."*
J'attends/écoute/obéis.	*I am waiting/listening/obeying.*

Compare also the transitive and intransitive uses of *conduire*, and the tenses:

Le chemin nous a conduits à la fontaine.	*The path led us to the fountain* (i.e., on one occasion).
Le chemin conduisait à la fontaine.	*The path led to the fountain* (i.e., always).

As in English, certain intransitive verbs may take what is called a "cognate object": one that is allied to, or related in meaning to, the verb. In this case, they function transitively:

Sabrina pleura des larmes de joie.	*Sabrina wept tears of joy.*
Adeline pleure la mort de son père.	*Adeline weeps over the death of her father.*
Je veux vivre ma vie.	*I want to live my life.*
On a vécu des heures de joie.	*We lived joyous moments.*
Elle dort son dernier sommeil.	*She is sleeping her last sleep* (She has died).
Il joue gros jeu.	*He's betting a lot.*

Notice these expressions: *courir un danger | un risque | sa chance | la ville | les rues | le monde | les théâtres | les bals | les filles | les jupons; parler affaires | plusieurs langues | politique | chiffons (to talk fashion).*

32.4 Verbs that may be used transitively and intransitively

As stated above, some French verbs have the two values. Here is a small list of verbs that function in both ways:

	Transitive	Intransitive
blanchir	La neige blanchit les sommets.	Ses cheveux blanchissent.
	La poudre lui blanchit le visage.	Elle a blanchi de peur.
bleuir	Le froid lui bleuit le visage.	La côte bleuissait au loin.
brunir	Le soleil lui a bruni la peau.	Qu'est-ce qu'on a bruni à la mer !
grandir	Le microscope grandit les objets.	Il a grandi, le petit !
jaunir	L'automne a jauni les feuilles.	Les feuilles commencent à jaunir.
	Elle a les doigts jaunis par la nicotine.	Le papier peint a jauni.
mûrir	Pour mûrir le raisin il nous faut du soleil mais un peu de pluie aussi.	Les blés mûrissent aux champs.
	Mûrir une pensée.	Ces adolescentes ont mûri, elles sont plus raisonnables.
noircir	La fumée a noirci les murs.	La cerise mûrit, noircit et tombe.
rajeunir	Je suis maintenant grand-père, voilà qui me rajeunit.	Marie a drôlement rajeuni après l'opération.
rapetisser	La distance rapetisse les objets.	Mon pantalon a rapetissé au lavage.
ressusciter	Jésus ressuscita Lazare; Cette bonne nouvelle l'a ressuscitée.	Les morts ressuscitent (Matthew 11: 5 and Luke 7: 22).
rosir	Le froid a rosi ses joues.	Ses joues rosissent d'excitation.
verdir	Le peintre a verdi les portes du garage.	Les arbres se mettent à verdir.
vieillir	Cette coiffure la vieillit.	Les adultes aimeraient bien arrêter de vieillir.
	Je n'ai que quarante-neuf ans, vous me vieillissez d'un an !	Ce sujet n'a pas vieilli, il est toujours d'actualité.

Tomber also falls into this category. Used intransitively, it is standard R2 language (*to fall*): *La neige est tombée pendant sept heures | Les feuilles sont tombées | Elle est tombée amoureuse.* But in R1 language it can be used transitively. The first example is typical, while the second and third are less used: *Qu'est-ce qu'il fait chaud, les gars ! Allez, on tombe la veste; Il a tombé l'adversaire d'un coup de poing; Don Juan ne pensait qu'à tomber (seduce) une femme après l'autre.*

As an intransitive verb, ressusciter is conjugated with être: "Jésus est ressuscité pour notre justification" ("Jesus was raised from the dead for our justification," Romans 4: 25).

In many of these cases, whereas the French verb may be used transitively, the English equivalent cannot. This is especially true of verbs of color, like *bleuir*, *rosir* and *verdir* which require the verb *to make* or *to turn*. *Grandir*, *rapetisser* and *vieillir* also require an auxiliary verb in English to convey the transitive idea.

The converse is also true. Some English verbs, when used transitively, like *to boil*, *to enrage* and *to explode*, require the auxiliary *faire* in French: *faire bouillir/enrager/exploser*, although *bouillir* may be used transitively in a low register. Interestingly enough, *enrager* can only be used intransitively in French, whereas in English *to enrage* is only used transitively.

32.5 Transitive verbs and the passive voice

In principle, only transitive verbs may be used in a passive way. This applies to English and to all Romance languages, including French. The explanation is simple enough. The direct object of the active agent becomes the subject in the passive construction. In reality, only *avoir*, *comporter*, *pouvoir* and *valoir* have no passive application. The passive voice is composed of the verb *être*, while there is always agreement between the past participle and the subject of the verb: *La dame a ouvert la porte > La porte a été ouverte par la dame*; *On interrogea l'accusée > L'accusée fut interrogée*.

Although *obéir*, *désobéir* and *pardonner* take an indirect object introduced by *à*, and are therefore not true transitive verbs, they may all three be used in the passive voice, notably the first and the last: *Je veux être obéi | J'aime toujours me voir obéie | Votre Altesse sera obéie; Vous êtes pardonnées | La coupable a été pardonnée de ses méfaits; Ils s'attendent à être désobéis*.

33

Reflexive verbs / Les verbes pronominaux

The following passage describes the delights experienced by a group of friends who visit the Lake District in England for the first time. Lakes, mountains, sundowns and wildlife all fill the friends with admiration for an exquisite corner of the English countryside. Note the constant use of reflexive verbs, particularly when they occur in the perfect tense or the conditional perfect, since here agreement in number and gender of the past participle is imperative. The reflexive verbs are all highlighted in bold. Some translations are offered.

La région des lacs

Je **me souviens** d'un extraordinaire séjour dans la région des lacs connue en anglais sous l'appellation The Lake District. Je **ne peux m'empêcher** [I cannot help] de songer au poème de Lamartine « Le Lac ». Les plus grands poètes **se sont inspirés** des vastes étendues [expanses] des lacs et des montagnes. William Wordsworth et bien d'autres poètes **se délectaient** [reveled in] de cette région exceptionnelle. Nous avons parcouru avec un groupe d'amis cette région naturelle dans tout l'éclat de sa beauté. **Nous nous sommes réjouis** [We delighted in] à l'idée d'explorer les chemins escarpés [steep] de grandes randonnées, les massifs montagneux, la faune, la flore, les petits châteaux anciens en pleine nature surplombant [overhanging] les lacs. Nos amis **se sont bien amusés** en plein air en **se promenant** en bordure des lacs étincelants. La température ambiante était délicieuse mais pas au point de **se baigner** dans les eaux fraîches de ces lacs de montagne.

Notre excursion de plusieurs jours nous a fait découvrir l'accueil chaleureux des montagnards britanniques. Audrey, notre amie, **se levait** très tôt le matin. Elle **se lavait** pour libérer la salle de bains pour les autres convives. Elle **se fatiguait** à préparer les corvées de la journée pour le confort de ses hôtes. Audrey **s'approchait** des invités le matin pour leur servir un petit-déjeuner composé de pain grillé tout chaud, de marmelade d'oranges, de beurre onctueux sans oublier la fameuse bouillie de flocons d'avoine [porridge]. Aidés de son époux William, ils **s'asseyaient** à la table de la grande salle à manger pour achever les préparatifs de notre voyage organisé.

Le couple **se couchait** toujours très tard après une longue journée de travail. William ne **s'ennuyait** jamais. Il avait toujours à portée de main son appareil photo ou son caméscope [camcorder] pour prendre subrepticement [surrepticiously/secretly] un magnifique coucher de soleil ou un ciel chargé de nuages qui **s'amoncelaient** [piled up]. Il **s'extasiait** devant le ciel en lançant : « What a dramatic sky tonight ! » Audrey **se glissait** dans son fauteuil pour admirer, de la grande baie vitrée, le paysage qui **s'offrait** au regard. Si nous étions restés plus longtemps dans la région, **nous nous serions amusés** davantage à admirer les couchers de soleil et à partager les mêmes activités intellectuelles, manuelles et sportives. Audrey et William **se sont connus** [came to know each other] à Florence et ne **se sont jamais quittés**. Ce couple illustre parfaitement le proverbe « Birds of a feather flock together ! » c'est-à-dire : « Qui **s'assemble se ressemble** » ou encore « Les oiseaux d'un même plumage **se rassemblent** sur le même rivage ».

A transitive verb is called *reflexive* or *pronominal* when its action returns upon the actor, in other words, when the subject and object are identical. A reflexive verb is a kind of transitive verb because it does have a direct object. Although reflexive verbs exist in English, it is possible in most cases not to use them. For example, an English speaker would much more easily say *I wash this morning* than *I wash myself this morning*. However, in French, as with other Romance languages, this is not the case. If one said *Je lave ce matin*, a French speaker would wonder what was being washed – the car, clothes, sheets... If you wanted to say that you were actually washing yourself, you would need to use a reflexive pronoun with the verb *laver*. So the *me* of *me lave* is most necessary if you want to be clear about what is being washed – in this case, you. Whatever the form of the subject, and whether expressed or not, the object is always a pronoun, is always expressed, and always agrees in person and number with the verb (see Chapter 45 on personal pronouns).

The usual position of the pronominal object or pronoun object is immediately before the verb or the auxiliary verb, or attached enclitically to the positive imperative. The following pattern of the verb *se baigner* (*to have a swim*) will serve for all tenses and combinations: *je me baigne* (*I swim*), *tu te baignes* (*you swim*), *il/elle se baigne* (*he/she swims*), *nous nous baignons*, *vous vous baignez*, *ils/elles se baignent*.

Here are just a few common verbs used reflexively and non-reflexively with basically the same meaning:

Non-reflexive use		Reflexive use	
approcher	*to bring closer*	s'approcher	*to get closer*
asseoir	*to sit (someone)*	s'asseoir	*to sit (oneself) down*
coucher	*to put to bed*	se coucher	*to go to bed*

Non-reflexive use		*Reflexive use*	
crevasser	*to cause to crack*	se crevasser	*to crack, to chap*
déchirer	*to tear*	se déchirer	*to tear/get torn*
ennuyer	*to bore*	s'ennuyer	*to get bored*
fâcher	*to make cross*	se fâcher	*to get cross*
fatiguer	*to tire*	se fatiguer	*to get tired*
fendiller	*to split*	se fendiller	*to split*
fermer	*to close/shut*	se fermer	*to close/shut*
gercer	*to chap*	se gercer	*to chap*
laver	*to wash*	se laver	*to wash*
moucher	*to wipe (a nose)*	se moucher	*to wipe (one's nose)*
mouiller	*to wet*	se mouiller	*to get wet*
ouvrir	*to open*	s'ouvrir	*to open*
perdre	*to lose*	se perdre	*to get lost*
promener	*to take for a walk*	se promener	*to go for a walk*
raser	*to shave (someone)*	se raser	*to shave oneself*
réjouir	*to make happy*	se réjouir	*to cheer up*
réveiller	*to wake (someone) up*	se réveiller	*to wake up*

A great number of verbs may be used reflexively in this way, and it would serve little purpose to attempt a comprehensive list. Examples of verbs used reflexively and non-reflexively are:

Approche la chaise, s'il te plaît.	*Bring the chair closer, please.*
Je **m'approche** de la fenêtre.	*I move closer to the window.*
Cela me **fâche** de voir un tel désordre.	*It makes me angry to see this mess.*
Si tu continues je vais **me fâcher**.	*If you go on, I'll get angry.*
La mère **a mouché** la petite.	*The mother wiped the child's nose.*
Mouche-toi, petit.	*Blow your nose.*
Émilie **s'est mouchée** bruyamment.	*Émilie made a noise blowing her nose.*
J'**ai perdu** la balle.	*I lost the ball.*
On **s'est perdu** dans le bois.	*We got lost in the wood.*
Je vais **promener** le chien.	*I'm going to take the dog for a walk.*
Jeanne et son mari **se promènent**.	*Jeanne and her husband are out for a walk.*
Marie **couche/asseoit** la petite.	*Marie puts her daughter to bed/on a chair.*
Sophie **se couche** à vingt-deux heures.	*Sophie goes to bed at ten.*
Je **me suis assise** dans le fauteuil.	*I sat in the armchair.*

Some verbs may be used reflexively and non-reflexively with very little difference in meaning:

La fille **a reculé / s'est reculée** de quelques mètres.	*The girl withdrew a few yards.*
Les cours **(se) terminent** à dix-sept heures.	*Classes end at five.*
Je **(m)'imagine** que Laurent est rentré.	*I imagine Laurent's come back.*

However, there are a number of verbs the values of which change considerably when used reflexively or non-reflexively. Here is a list of very common verbs used in these two different ways, with specific comments. Generally speaking, the reflexive form carries more weight, is more specific and active and, in all cases, contains an intransitive use:

Comment	*Verb*	*Example*
unintentional	*approcher*	*Maman approche de la quarantaine.*
		L'heure du départ approche.
deliberate	*s'approcher*	*L'ennemi s'approchait de la ville.*
habitual	*fermer/ouvrir*	*Les magasins ferment à dix-huit heures.*
		Les magasins ouvrent à neuf heures.
specific	*se fermer/ s'ouvrir*	*La porte se fermait / s'ouvrait lentement.*
state	*coucher*	*Je couche à l'hôtel / à la belle étoile.*
action	*se coucher*	*Je suis crevé. Je vais me coucher.*
state	*arrêter*	*Audrey a arrêté de fumer* (for good).
action	*s'arrêter*	*Philippe s'est arrêté de fumer* (now, and for good); *Arrête ! = stop it !*
		La voiture s'est brusquement arrêtée.
state	*loger.*	*Tu loges où ? Je loge en ville.*
action	*se loger*	*Annick est arrivée et s'est logée à l'hôtel.*
abstract	*incliner*	*J'incline à penser que tout ira bien.*
concrete	*s'incliner*	*Le prêtre s'est incliné devant l'autel.*
less strong	*attaquer*	*Le conseiller a attaqué le gouvernement.*
stronger	*s'attaquer*	*Les terroristes se sont attaqués au parlement.*
		Attaquer and **s'attaquer** are interchangeable here, given the comments. The same goes for: *décider de / se décider à, refuser de / se refuser à, résoudre de / se résoudre à.*
figurative	*pencher*	*Je penche pour la seconde hypothèse.*
literal	*se pencher*	*Défense de se pencher par la portière.*
		Armelle s'est penchée sur l'eau.

Comment	Verb	Example
figurative	*reposer*	*Sa philosophie repose sur trois principes.*
		Son corps repose au cimetière du Père Lachaise.
literal	*se reposer*	*Je suis fatiguée. Je vais me reposer un peu.*

Note: *plaindre* = to pity but *se plaindre* = to complain. Also, *marier* = to marry (*someone to someone else*), whereas *se marier* = to get married:

| Le curé les maria | *The priest married them.* |
| Ils se sont mariés | *They got married.* |

One hears and reads more and more these days *se pacser* deriving from *pacte civil de solidarité* = *civil partnership*, introduced into France in 1999, and this verb applies to all types of marriage: *Elles se sont pacsées* = *They got married* (i.e., two females). Of interest is the ironic play on words with this verb accessible perhaps only to *latinistes*: *pax* (Latin for *peace*).

The following three sets of verbs illustrate the difference between the literal use of the non-reflexive verb and the figurative use of the reflexive:

Literal (non-reflexive)	Figurative (reflexive)
Sabrina a figuré dans la cérémonie.	Je me figure les choses autrement qu'elles ne sont.
Le nom de Sophie ne figure pas sur la liste	Je me le figurais couché, malade.
	Tu ne peux pas te figurer comme il est bête.
Son frère est passé cette après-midi.	Qu'est-ce qui s'est passé?
Ils sont tous sortis ce matin	J'arrive pas à m'en sortir / me sortir de cette pagaille (*get myself out of this mess*).

Some verbs only have a reflexive form, and here the reflexive pronoun adds nothing to the meaning. At the same time, the reflexive must be used: *s'absenter, s'abstenir, s'accouder, s'accroupir, s'acharner (à), s'adonner (à), s'arroger* (R3), *s'attabler, s'aventurer* (rarely non-reflexive), *se bagarrer, se blottir, se chamailler, se dédire, se délecter (à), se démener, se désister, s'écrier, s'écrouler, s'effondrer, s'efforcer, s'emparer (de), s'empresser, s'en aller, s'enquérir, s'éprendre (de), s'évader, s'évanouir, s'évertuer, s'exclamer, s'extasier, se fier, se gargariser, s'ingénier, s'insurger, se méfier (de), se méprendre* (R3), *se morfondre, se moquer (de), s'opiniâtrer à, se pâmer, se prosterner* (rarely non-reflexive), *se quereller* (rarely non-reflexive), *se raviser, se rebeller, se rebiffer, se regimber, se récrier, se réfugier, se rengorger, se repentir, se révolter, se souvenir (de), se suicider, se tapir.*

Conversely, there are many verbs that are not used reflexively, and these are by their very nature and meaning intransitive: *blêmir, brouter* (although: *Les moutons broutaient l'herbe*), *croître, décliner, demeurer, dormir, empirer* (rarely used in the reflexive), *éternuer, mourir,*[1] *naître, pacager, paître, pâlir, penser,*[2] *progresser, prospérer, renifler, rétrograder, ronfler, souffrir, tomber, tousser.* Verbs used only non-reflexively include those of color, although these may be used transitively: *blanchir, bleuir, brunir, jaunir, rosir, verdir: noircir,* however, may be reflexive: *se noircir.*

As seen above, reflexive verbs are really those verbs whose direct or indirect object refers back, via a pronoun, to the subject of the same verb. However, this is by no means always the case. A reflexive verb can also suggest actions that two or more individuals perform with respect to one another:

Les garçons se cherchaient dans les ténèbres.	*The boys looked for each other in the darkness.*
Tous les joueurs de l'équipe s'apprécient beaucoup.	*All the team players appreciate each other a great deal.*
Jean et Marie s'envoient des textos tous les jours.	*Jean and Marie send each other text messages every day.*
Ils se trompent.	*They deceive themselves / one another.*
Nous nous félicitons.	*We congratulate each other.*
Nous nous sommes longuement félicités.	*We congratulate each other at length.*
Les deux amants se sont regardés pendant quelques instants.	*The two lovers looked at each other for a few moments.*
Les sinistrés se sont aidés.	*The accident victims helped each other.*

Sometimes, a reinforcing expression is used to make the meaning clearer, and there are quite a few of these:

Aidons-nous mutuellement.	*Let us help each other.*
Les époux se détestaient mutuellement.	*Husband and wife loathed each other.*
Les amis se rendaient réciproquement de grands services.	*The friends obliged each other.*

[1] *Se mourir* is sometimes used in a literary context and clearly has an R3 flavor. It conveys the idea of "about to die."

Le roi/La reine se mourait.   *The king/queen was about to die.*

This literary application may also mean *to end, to decline:*

Le soir se mourait.   *The evening was fading away.*

This reflexive use does not allow compound tenses for obvious reasons: One is about to die or one is dead.

[2] *Croire* has a similar meaning to *penser,* but it can easily be reflexive: *Il se croit tout permis; Il se croit plus fort/intelligent.*

Les loups ne se mangent pas entre eux.	*Honor among thieves* (proverb).
Les trois femmes se sont entraidées pour repeindre la maison.	*The three women helped each other to repaint the house.*
Tous les soldats se sont regardés les uns les autres.	*All the soldiers looked at each other.*
Ils se lavent eux-mêmes.	*They wash themselves* (Here, *themselves* would suit as a translation).
Les enfants n'ont pas besoin d'aide. Ils se suffisent à eux-mêmes.	*The children don't need any help. They are self-sufficient.*

Although a plurality of individuals is logically suggested in the examples above, a singular noun or pronoun is quite possible with the same idea:

On se croisait souvent et je ne la reconnaissais pas.	*We often passed each other and I didn't recognize her.*
On s'embrasse tous les jours en France, et même plusieurs fois !	*We kiss each other every day in France, and even several times!*
Chacun se saluait sur la plage.	*Everyone greeted each other on the beach.*
Tout un chacun s'entend pour éviter d'en parler.	*Each one agrees not to speak about it.*
Dans cette communauté, tout le monde s'aime.	*In this community, everyone likes/loves each other.*
Qui se ressemble s'assemble.	*Birds of a feather flock together.*

It happens that a logically reciprocal action is presented from an individual's point of view, so that the other person appears in the complement introduced with *avec* or *contre*. Verbs here would include: *se battre, se croiser, s'entendre, se disputer, s'engueuler* (R1), *se quereller, se rencontrer, se trouver*.

Sébastien s'est battu à coups de poings avec/contre le voyou.	*Sébastien had a fist fight with the hoodlum.*
Tu t'es croisée avec mon père hier ?	*Did you pass my father yesterday?*
Pourquoi s'est-elle querellée avec son frère ?	*Why did she have a quarrel with her brother?*
Marcel s'entend bien/mal avec Louise.	*Marcel gets on well / does not get on well with Louise.*
David a encore dû s'engueuler avec la contractuelle.	*David must have had an argument again with the parking warden.*

The reflexive is also used in an impersonal way. This feature needs to be turned in English by a straight intransitive or passive verb:

Ce livre se vend comme des petits pains.	*This book sells like hot cakes.*
Ça s'achète au marché.	*You can buy that / That can be bought at the market.*
Il se prépare actuellement une nouvelle édition.	*A new edition is currently being prepared.*
Il se produit une réaction chimique.	*A chemical reaction is produced / There is a chemical reaction.*
Il ne se trouvait pas de linguiste pour traduire le document.	*You couldn't find a linguist to translate the document.*
Le clocher s'aperçoit de loin.	*The steeple can be seen from afar.*
C'est une expression qui s'entend partout.	*It's an expression heard everywhere.*
Tu sais bien que ça ne se dit pas.	*You know very well that's not said / we don't say that.*

Note also in this context the common reflexive use of the verb *agir*:

Il s'agit dans ce livre des origines de la Révolution.	*This book treats the origins of the Revolution.*
De quoi s'agissait-il ?	*What was it about?*
Il s'agira de partir dès que possible.	*It'll be a question of leaving as soon as possible.*
S'agissant de vous, nous n'insisterons pas.	*As far as you're concerned, we won't insist.*
S'agissant d'un départ imminent, elle a décidé de reporter son travail à une date ultérieure.	*Since it was a question of an imminent departure, she decided to delay her work to a later date.*

This last expression has gained much ground in the twentieth century. Grammatically it is not convincing, but one may advocate a kind of absolute meaning for it.

Certain reflexive verbs have a pronoun without any apparent logical function. The pronoun which merely reflects the subject plays no true role either as a direct or as an indirect object: *s'en aller, se douter (de), s'écrier, s'emparer (de), s'endormir, s'enfuir, s'ensuivre, s'envoler, s'évanouir, se jouer (de), se moquer (de), se mourir, se pâmer, se prévaloir (de), se repentir (de), s'en retourner, s'en revenir, se rire (de), se soucier (de), se taire*:

Irène s'est aperçue de son erreur.	*Irène realized her error.*
Henri s'est repenti de sa faute.	*Henri repented of his error.*
La malade s'est évanouie.	*The patient fainted.*

En 1453, les Turcs s'emparèrent de Constantinople.	*In 1453, the Turks took over Constantinople.*

The reflexive pronoun may be direct or indirect. Compare the two sentences:

Audrey se lave soigneusement.	*Audrey washes carefully.*
Audrey se lave soigneusement les dents.	*Audrey cleans her teeth carefully.*

In the first case, *se* is a direct object, while in the second *se* is an indirect object, since *les dents* is the direct object. Compare two further examples:

Jean s'est coupé en se rasant.	*Jean cut himself while shaving.*
Jean s'est coupé le menton en se rasant.	*Jean cut his chin while shaving.*

In the first case, the direct object is *s(e)*, and in the second, it is *le menton*, and *s(e)* becomes the indirect object.

In the present tense, this nice difference is of no real importance, but in all compound tenses (see next item below), it is fundamental since agreement of the past participle with the preceding direct object comes into play. Compare again:

Audrey s'est lavée avec soin.	*Audrey washed carefully.*
Audrey s'est lavé les mains avec soin.	*Audrey washed her hands carefully.*

Agreement in case one between *lavée* and *Audrey* is necessary, while there is no agreement in case two. Similarly:

Les deux garçons se sont giflés.	*The two boys hit each other.*
Les deux garçons se sont donné des gifles.	*The two boys gave each other blows* (or in better English: *hit each other*).

Giflés agrees in case one (*se* is direct) but not in case two where *se* is indirect.

Finally, in this context of agreement in compound tenses, *se blesser* and *se nuire* offer a striking contrast, since they both mean *to hurt oneself*. The verb *blesser* normally takes the direct object, while *nuire* takes an indirect object. A translation of *She hurt herself* could be *Elle s'est blessée* or *Elle s'est nui* (i.e., agreement in *blessée* and no agreement in *nui*).

Use of the reflexive with parts of the body involves the definite article where in English a possessive adjective would occur:

Louise s'est cassé la jambe.	*Louise broke her leg.*
Françoise s'est fait mal au genou.	*Françoise hurt her knee.*

If two verbs used reflexively follow each other, the reflexive pronoun is usually repeated:

Les deux cousins se haïssaient et se craignaient.	*The two cousins both hated and feared each other.*

But in a literary context, the pronoun may disappear:

Il se carrait et cambrait pour se préparer à la lutte.	*He tensed himself and arched his back to face the struggle.*

The use of *Je m'excuse* (*I'm sorry / Excuse me*) instead of *Excusez-moi* has caused much ink to flow. Rather than spill even more ink, suffice it to say that the reflexive use here is very idiomatic and common.

The following table illustrates how the full conjugation of a reflexive verb functions. Of particular note are the agreements in the compound tenses which are conjugated with *être* and where agreement of the subject and the past participle is of paramount importance (see also above):

infinitive	*se laver* = to wash (*oneself*)
past infinitive	*s'être lavé/lavée/lavés/lavées*
participles	present: *se lavant*; past: *lavé/lavée/lavés/lavées*
present indicative	*je me lave, tu te laves, il/elle se lave, nous nous lavons, vous vous lavez, ils/elles se lavent*
perfect indicative	*je me suis lavé(e), tu t'es lavé(e), il s'est lavé, elle s'est lavée, nous nous sommes lavé(e)s, vous vous êtes lavé(e)(s) ils se sont lavés/elles se sont lavées*
imperfect	*je me lavais, tu te lavais*, etc.
preterit	*je me lavai, tu te lavas*, etc.
future	*je me laverai, tu te laveras*, etc.
conditional	*je me laverais, tu te laverais*, etc.
conditional in past	*je me serais lavé(e), tu te serais lavé(e)*, etc.
present subjunctive	*je me lave, tu te laves*, etc.
perfect subjunctive	*je me sois lavé(e), tu te sois lavé(e)*, etc.
imperfect subjunctive	*je me lavasse, tu te lavasses*, etc.
pluperfect subjunctive	*je me fusse lavé(e), tu te fusses lavé(e)*, etc.
imperative	*lave-toi, lavons-nous, lavez-vous*

The use of reflexive verbs in Belgium, Quebec and Switzerland differs at times from usage in metropolitan France:

s'accaparer de (*to monopolize*): In both Belgium and Quebec, this verb may be reflexive with *de*, not so in metropolitan France: *Ottawa ne cherche pas à s'accaparer du plus grand nombre de compétences possibles.*

s'aider: In Switzerland, this use is commonnly used as follows: *Les classes campagnardes se ferment pour quinze jours afin que les écoliers puissent s'aider à planter des pommes de terre.*

Se glisser is also common currency in Switzerland with the meaning of *to slide*. Ramuz, the Swiss novelist, writes: *Une de ses petites sœurs était tombée en se glissant sur la glace. Se glisser* would be used in France with the idea of *to slip* (*into/under*): *Elle s'est glissée dans ses draps/sous la barrière.*

Grevisse and Goosse underline the very considerable use of what they term "superfluous reflexives" in the Midi (southern France). They quote (2008, pp. 997–998): *se languir, se penser, s'accompagner avec, se manger une salade | un morceau* (*to have a salad/bite to eat*), *se signer au nom des étudiants, s'obtenir un diplôme.*

The use of the reflexive is particularly noticeable with *manger* in the Midi, and elsewhere, although the other examples cited above come as a surprise to speakers of standard French. This does not surprise one of the authors who compares this usage to the extremely widespread and apparently superfluous application of the reflexive in Spain: *pensarse, comerse, creerse, obtenerse* and so on.

Grevisse and Goosse also quote the opposite in Belgium, and in various parts of France as well as in the Midi, i.e. non-use of the reflexive where the present authors, for instance, would normally expect and use the reflexive: *gargariser* (Belgium), *promener* (*to go for a walk*; used in the Midi), *baigner* (*to go for a swim*), *marier* (*to get married*) (both these latter in Normandy and the former in Alsace), and *dépêcher*, as in: *Dépêche(z)* ! (*Hurry up!*), which is colloquial in many parts of France, as is *Allez, grouille* ! (R1 = *Get a move on!*). The plural form *grouillez* does not seem to be used. Of these, only *promener*, *dépêcher* and *grouiller* gain real acceptance outside the regions referred to, and are certainly heard elsewhere.

34

Passive voice | La voix passive

The passage below evokes the harsh yet enchanting frozen wastes of Greenland, a Denmark possession, and commands attention by virtue of our pressing current need to protect this environment. It focuses on the animal kingdom, notably that of the penguin. The passage illustrates the use of the passive voice, including reflexive verbs, which are partially passive in idea. These reflexive verbs are marked with an asterisk. Note that, as with all Romance languages, the past participle here agrees in gender and number with the subject. No agreement exists, however, with *proposé* since the reflexive involves an indirect object: *nous*. A few translations are provided.

Vol au-dessus du Groenland

Nous **avons été transportés** dans l'Arctique au cours de notre long voyage. Nous **nous sommes laissés*** surprendre à survoler à basse altitude le Groenland. Des vues panoramiques **ont été commentées** par une voix vibrante. Nous **avons été invités** par les hôtesses à regarder par le hublot les habitants de l'arctique vêtus d'un plumage blanc et noir. Une sorte de fascination **a été exercée** par ces oiseaux marins. Les manchots [penguins] se promenaient tranquillement sur la banquise [ice floe]. Les passagers à bord de l'appareil **se sont trouvés*** dans une sorte d'extase.

Jusqu'au milieu des années soixante dix, des expéditions **ont été organisées** au Groenland par l'explorateur français Paul-Emile Victor. Les expéditions polaires françaises **ont été incarnées** par l'ethnologue qui découvrit le Groenland dans les années trente. Les gouvernements **ont été incités** à protéger l'Arctique des dommages qui **ont été subis** par la dégradation de l'environnement au niveau de la planète. Les hommes politiques **se sont proposé*** de relever le défi dans la lutte contre le changement climatique. Les partenaires européens **se sont engagés*** à sauvegarder l'environnement dans l'Arctique. Des stations d'observations polaires **ont été déployées** dans cette vaste étendue pour la recherche scientifique.

Notre aventure dans cette région polaire du nord évoque une image très forte. On ne peut s'empêcher [One cannot help] de faire un parallèle avec le film documentaire de Luc Jacquet, *La Marche de l'empereur*. Pour la survie de l'espèce, des centaines de kilomètres **sont parcourus** par le manchot empereur [Emperor penguin]. La plus belle des histoires **a été inventée** par la nature. La protection de l'environnement **a été symbolisée** par ce documentaire. Ce film est une leçon magistrale [masterly] sur le courage, la force et la solidarité d'une communauté animale dans un désert de glace et de neige qui **doit être protégée**.

De nombreux ouvrages de vulgarisation **ont été écrits** par le pionnier des expéditions polaires françaises. Son journal de bord [logbook] qui **a été rédigé** au cours de son année passée au Groenland seul parmi les Esquimaux est un récit passionnant. Ce patrimoine exceptionnel de notre planète a bien des attraits. Cette île stratégique de l'Arctique sous l'hégémonie du Danemark **est regardée** avec convoitise [jealously]. Notre courte aventure au-dessus de la banquise a réalisé un très beau rêve.

The term *voice* applies to the forms that a verb assumes to express the role of the subject in an action or thought. Voice also involves the unfolding of this action or thought. Two distinctions are possible:

Active voice: This indicates that the subject performs the action: *Le chien* ***conduit*** *l'aveugle*.

Passive voice: This indicates that the subject undergoes the action: *L'aveugle* ***est conduit*** *par le chien*.

In principle, one can turn any transitive verb into the passive if the verb can take a direct object. A second example following on from the example above shows this quite clearly: *Le juge interroge l'accusé > L'accusé est interrogé par le juge*.

It is quite clear that the French passive, as with all Romance languages, is formed in precisely the same way as the English passive: the combination of *être* and past participle therefore corresponds to *to be* and past participle (in Italian *essere/stare* + past participle; in Spanish *ser/estar* + past participle). Note that the past participle of *être > été* in compound tenses does not change, although it does in Italian (*essere = È stata ferita = She has been hurt*), but not in Spanish (*ser = Ha sido herida = She has been hurt*).

Here is an example of the verb *aimer = to like/love* used in a passive way:

Indicative mood

passive infinitive	être aimé/aimée/aimés/ aimées	*to be liked*
passive past infinitive	avoir été aimé/aimée, etc.	*to have been liked*
passive present participle	étant aimé/aimée, etc.	*being liked*
passive past participle	aimé/aimée, etc.	*(having been) liked*

passive present	je suis aimé/aimée	*I am liked*
	tu es aimé/aimée	*you are liked*
	il est aimé	*he is liked*
	elle est aimée	*she is liked*
	nous sommes aimé(e)s	*we are liked*
	vous êtes aimé(e)(s)	*you are liked*
	ils sont aimés	*they are liked*
	elles sont aimées	*they are liked*

With the remainder of the conjugation of tenses only the first-person form appears:

passive imperfect	j'étais aimé/aimée	*I was liked*
passive preterit	je fus aimé/aimée	*I was liked*
passive pluperfect	j'avais été aimé/aimée	*I had been liked*
passive past anterior	j'eus été aimé/aimée	*I had been liked*
passive future	je serai aimé/aimée	*I will be liked*
passive future perfect	j'aurai été aimé/aimée	*I will have been liked*
passive conditional	je serais aimé/aimée	*I would be liked*
passive conditional in the past	j'aurais été aimé/aimée	*I would have been liked*

Subjunctive mood

passive present	que je sois aimé/aimée	*that I may be liked*
passive perfect	que j'aie été aimé/aimée	*that I may have been liked*
passive imperfect	que je fusse aimé/aimée	*that I might be liked*
passive perfect	que j'aie été aimé/aimée	*that I may have been liked*
passive pluperfect	que j'eusse été aimé/aimée	*that I might have been liked*

Imperative mood

sois aimé/aimée	soyons aimés/aimées	soyez aimé(s)/ée(s)
be liked	*let us be liked*	*be liked*

Some of these forms are so clumsy and out-of-date (the passive imperfect and pluperfect, for instance), that one can only imagine the most punctilious of authors having recourse to them. Chateaubriand would be a good candidate in this respect.

Most commentators agree that the passive construction is less frequent in French than other forms carrying out the same role. Grevisse and Goosse (2008, p. 982) support this view, stating unequivocally that other languages use it much more. They do not say which ones, although English certainly illustrates a far greater preference for the passive than French does. However, other Romance languages would not fit into the Belgians' assertion, particularly Spanish, which avoids the passive even more than French. Interestingly enough, Grevisse and Goosse state quite clearly that, in French, "La construction passive [...] est acquise plus tard par l'enfant." Some fieldwork must have been done here but they do not say how they come to this conclusion. It is to be added that French-speaking linguists would doubtless unanimously agree that children do not use the passive very much, instructed as they often are that the passive is a "structure trop lourde." The fact that children come later to the passive construction makes an eloquent statement over the possible awkwardness of its manipulation.

However, there are certain set and common formulae which involve the passive voice. A student could easily say of the benefits of living in a *cité universitaire*: *Je suis nourri, blanchi et logé à la cité universitaire.* A soldier could use the same formula when speaking of his regiment, although he may drop the *logé* since this is understood. An advertisement for an au pair could similarly read: *Recherche une fille au pair, nourrie et blanchie.*

In support of the lack of frequency of the passive in French, one may cite the two following alternatives: *on* and the reflexive. Although some authors regard *on* as a lower-register form, it occurs at all levels of discourse with unfailing frequency. It certainly deals with a whole range of passives in English:

Examples with *on*:

On dit/pense/croit que...	*It is said/thought/believed that...*
On ne m'a pas donné le livre.	*I wasn't given the book / The book wasn't given to me.*

Examples with the reflexive:

Ça se comprend parfaitement.	*That can be understood perfectly.*
Bien sûr que ça se dit.	*Of course that's said.*
Il se vend chaque semaine plusieurs centaines d'appareils.	*Several hundred appliances are sold every week.*
Le ladin se parle encore en Suisse et en Italie du nord.	*Ladino is still spoken in Switzerland and northern Italy.*

If one compares the English passive to its French use and frequency, the difference is quite striking. An English speaker who says *I am helped in this project / to carry out this project* would rarely find the same passive in French and would hear, for instance, *On m'aide dans ce projet / à réaliser ce projet.* Similarly, *I am prevented from going out* would be turned into *On m'empêche de sortir.*

Whereas, in English, it is possible for an indirect object in an active clause to become the subject of a passive clause (e.g., *my father gave me a book* > *I was given a book by my father*), such a transformation is not permitted in French, and is to be avoided. In other words, the French active-voice sentence *La réception me plaît* has no passive equivalent, as in English: *I was pleased by the reception* (see also below). At the same time, there exists a way of dealing with this lack of the passive in these circumstances. *Voir* used reflexively (= *se voir*) is one such way, but such a construction is of a high register and would appear almost exclusively in the written language; if it were to occur in spoken French, it would have very refined associations:

Les réfugiés se sont vus offrir des cadeaux.	*The refugees were offered presents.*
Jeanne et Françoise se sont vus accorder le droit d'étudier dans la faculté des lettres.	*Jeanne and Françoise were granted the right to study in the arts faculty.*
Les Mexicains ont fait une demande de visa, mais se l'ont vu refuser.	*The Mexicans requested a visa, but were refused it.*

Other verbs of high register that function in the same manner are: *conférer*, *octroyer* (*to grant*), *attribuer*, *décerner* (*to bestow*). Similarly, *entendre* may be used with *dire* as the principal verb, but again the register is R3:

Je ne me suis jamais entendu dire que je suis si intelligente que cela.	*I have never been told that I am as intelligent as that.*

A similar construction with the reflexive applies to the use of the semi-auxiliaries *faire* and *laisser*. But there is a difference. Whereas, in the examples above, the reflexive is indirect, with these two verbs, the reflexive is direct, and the register is R2, very common currency in fact:

Il s'est fait battre par l'agresseur.	*He was beaten up by the hoodlum.*
Elle s'est fait renverser par une voiture.	*She was knocked over by a car.*
Aucun étudiant ne s'est fait coller en maths.	*No student was failed in math(s).*

Although *faire* seems to have an active meaning in these sentences, this is far from the case. It does not suggest that the subject encourages or invites something to happen to him/her. *Se faire* + infinitive is purely passive, just as the following examples are:

Elle s'est fait peindre la maison.	*She had the house painted.*
Son frère s'est laissé entraîner par une bande de voyous.	*Her brother was influenced by a bunch of hoodlums/louts.*
Ah, se laisser bercer par les vagues au bord de la mer !	*Oh, to be lulled by the waves at the seaside!*

The infinitive, the present participle and the past participle may also be used passively, and here again the register is R3. In some of these cases, the verb *être* is understood:

Élisabeth croyait être aimée de Jean.	*Élisabeth thought Jean loved her.*
Pierre, ayant été convaincu par son frère, renonça à son projet.	*Having been convinced by his brother, Pierre abandoned his plan.*
Pierre, convaincu par son frère, renonça à son projet.	*Convinced by his brother, Pierre abandoned his plan.*
Cette pratique semble observée par bien des fidèles.	*This practice seems to be observed by many of the faithful.*
On le savait respecté même par ses adversaires.	*People knew he was respected even by his adversaries.*

Two past participles, *concerné* and *moqué*, provoke considerable debate. The first finds no approval from the Académie française, whose members see in it either a straight calque from the English, and this can be sufficient to condemn it, or its persistent use. Notwithstanding this hostility, Littré expresses satisfaction with it:

Vos amis sont concernés dans cette affaire.	*Your friends are concerned by this business.*
Les intérêts concernés par cette mesure...	*The interests concerned by this measure...*

The passive use of *moquer* (*être moqué* = to be mocked) also invites uneasiness, and not only from the august body referred to, but such uneasiness is more understandable. These days, in daily discourse, one only comes across *se moquer de*. The past participle is seriously out-of-date, although it may be seen in literary texts. We quote Hanse and Blampain: "*Moquer* est aujourd'hui vieilli ou littéraire dans son emploi transitif [...] Moins rares : se faire moquer, une vertu moquée, un homme moqué par tout le monde. On dit couramment : *se moquer de* : Ils s'en sont moqués" (2005, p. 365). Of course, for an English speaker, the past participle used passively would cause no disturbance at all.

Passive transformation is not possible in the following cases:

With *avoir, comporter, pouvoir* and *valoir*.

With numerous figurative expressions: *prendre la fuite, perdre la tête, garder la tête froide, faire le fou/le malin/le mariole*; and expresssions of the type: *Cela me regarde; Elle tient de son père un caractère calme.*

When the direct object is a part of the body of the person indicated by the subject: *Adrienne baisse la tête / lève le bras.*

When the direct object is an infinitive: *Je crois me tromper; Elle aime lire; Ils commencent à rire.*

There exist other cases where the transformation is relatively rare, but not impossible: *Jérémy a trouvé une montre > Une montre a été trouvée par Jérémy.* Yet such a construction would be perfectly normal if it were in contrast, as in: *La montre a été trouvée par Jérémy, non par ma sœur.*

Although it is generally true that intransitive verbs cannot be used in the passive, it does become possible when they occur in impersonal constructions, especially in administrative language of high register (less so in literature):

Il sera sursis à toute procédure.	*All procedures will be deferred.*
Il sera statué sommairement sur le verdict.	*A pronouncement will be made on the verdict.*
Il avait été procédé à la cérémonie le plus discrètement possible.	*They proceeded most discreetly to the ceremony.*

This construction often involves *parler*:

Documents philosophiques dont il sera parlé au chapitre suivant.	*Philosophical documents which will be discussed in the next chapter.*
Dans les milieux qu'il fréquentait, il n'était parlé de la Francmaçonnerie qu'avec une extrême circonspection.	*In the circles he frequented, they spoke of Freemasonry only with extreme care.*

The passive may be followed by an infinitive when it is not a direct object. There is no difficulty in putting the following supporting verb in the passive:

L'homme fut accusé par la police d'être un terroriste.	*The man was accused by the police of being a terrorist.*
Habituée à étudier la nuit, elle dormait toute la journée.	*Accustomed to studying at night, she slept all day.*

Certain verbs expressing opinions (*présumer, reconnaître, réputer, supposer*) may be put in the passive with a following infinitive. The register here is clearly R3:

Les décisions sont présumées être l'expression de la volonté générale.	*The decisions are presumed to be the expression of the general will.*
Les dames chez qui on allait avaient été reconnues être de grandes intellectuelles.	*The ladies whom we visited were recognized as being great intellectuals.*
Sabrina était réputée dominer plusieurs langues.	*Sabrina had the reputation of mastering several languages.*

Cette théorie est supposée résoudre tous les problèmes de l'inflation.	*This theory is supposed to solve all the problems of inflation.*

Être censé is of the same category but the register is lower and occurs in daily discourse, and easily in the negative:

Je ne suis pas censée le savoir.	*I am not supposed to know.*
Elle était censée être en vacances.	*She was supposed to be on vacation.*

35

Defective verbs / Les verbes défectifs

In some ways, one hesitates to include defective verbs in the present volume since, generally speaking, they are hardly ever used, and even then, only extremely limited parts of them occur. In numerous cases, they are classed as R3, or are already on the point of exiting the language. Parts of some verbs are, of course, standard R2, like *déchu*. What is certain is that, since these verbs are defective and can vary even in usage and in form, no two French speakers necessarily agree on these features. Nevertheless, given that defective verbs form part of the French language, however tenuously, it seems appropriate to accord them treatment since some parts of certain defective verbs find themselves in current use.

Defective verbs are verbs that lack certain tenses or parts of certain tenses. They are a linguistic feature not confined to French, for one comes across them in all Romance languages (Spanish: *balbucir* = to stammer; Italian: *fervere* = to be at its height), as well as in English (*can, might, to beware*). Considerable hesitation inhibits their use, which is why they occur less and less in the contemporary language, but at the same time they make a vigorous and healthy contribution to quiz programs. One can speculate that some, if not all, the defective verbs treated below will not exist in the not-too-distant feature. Before listing the main defective verbs and their peculiarities, certain characteristics need to be pointed out.

Impersonal verbs, notably those referring to the weather, are not really defective, since they are logically only used in the third-person singular with the pronoun *il* and in the infinitive, apart from an occasional metaphoric exploitation (see Chapter 39 on impersonal verbs).

Verbs that normally only have things or animals, and not persons, as a subject do not have the full conjugation, or the full conjugation is not exploited, except figuratively: *advenir, s'amuïr, barrir, bêler, coasser, concerner, croasser, découler, dégoutter, éclore, émaner, s'ensuivre, foisonner, gazouiller, hennir, luire, pulluler, résulter, sourdre, suinter*. One could conceive of such verbs as *barrir, coasser, croasser, gazouiller* and so on being used figuratively and applied to humans. For example, a small child could have *gazouiller* applied to his/her burbling, although whether any person other than the third person would be used is another matter. *Bêler* could also apply to the silly bleating of a querulous person. But *je bêle, nous bêlons* and so on does not sound convincing.

Certain colloquial verbs such as *débequeter, se carapater, chier, engueuler, emmerder, enquiquiner* and *picoler* would hardly stand as candidates for the imperfect subjunctive or the past definite, tenses associated with high-register literary expression.

Certain verbs have survived only as past or present participles, and it is not always clear when their infinitive and their various parts ceased to function, or ever functioned at all: *carabiné, dévolu, éclopé, enneigé, éperdu, fourbu, inusité, usité* (the last two apply in daily discourse to words), *révolu, suranné, dénué* (the infinitive still exists, as does *enneiger,* and commonly, in Switzerland), *stupéfait.*

There now follows a list of defective verbs with comments and examples. As stated at the beginning of this chapter, usage can vary, and most French speakers never have recourse to them. It goes without saying that, if the verb has any currency, the infinitive is used.

Accroire is only used as an infinitive with the verbs *faire* and *laisser* = *to deceive, inveigle into (thinking)*: *Elle nous a fait/laissé accroire qu'elle avait passé son doctorat.*

Braire (to bray – of a donkey): The infinitive and third person in various tenses occur: *il brait | ils braient, il braira | ils brairont, il brairait | ils brairaient: Tu entends braire les ânes dans les champs ?* Again, as above, there is no reason why, in a figurative, Aesop | La Fontaine | Orwell satirical mode, we should not have recourse to, or invent, other persons (je/tu, etc.): *Je fus un âne, j'ai brait.*

Bruire (to rustle): Only used in the third-person singular and plural of the following tenses: present *(bruit)* and imperfect *(bruissait)* of the indicative; present subjunctive *(bruisse)*; present participle *(bruissant)*: *J'entends l'eau qui bruit; Les grands arbres bruissent/bruissaient sous le vent léger.* The very routine adjective *bruyant = noisy* comes from *bruire.*

Chaloir (to matter): Only used in the third-person singular of the present indicative, and even then only rarely used:

Peu nous en chaut.	*We are not particularly worried about it.*
Peu leur chaut mon hostilité.	*They are not much bothered by my hostility.*

Choir (to fall): Used notably in the third-person singular and plural, present indicative, and especially the infinitive after *laisser*:

Après de belles promesses, il nous a laissé choir.	*After fine promises, he dropped us.*

Clore (to close, to conclude): Used in only parts of the present tense: *je clos, tu clos, il/elle clôt.* All other parts, save the infinitive and past participle *clos*, are too arcane to be included here: *Il faut clore le débat | la discussion*; *La séance | la session est close*; *C'est une affaire close*. Camus refers to the world as a *vase clos*, a not infrequent expression signifying for him a self-contained world bereft of meaning and spiritual solution.

Déchoir (*to strip [of], to lower [oneself]*): Used in the present indicative: *je déchois, tu déchois, il/elle déchoit, nous déchoyons, vous déchoyez, ils/elles déchoient*; preterit: *je déchus*; future: *je déchoirai*; present subjunctive: *je déchoie, nous déchoyions, ils/elles déchoient*; imperfect subjunctive: *je déchusse* (we are in the realm of comedy here, so rebarbative and alien it sounds); past participle: *déchu*. The past participle still retains some frequency: *un prince déchu de son trône, un ange déchu (a fallen angel)*.

Échoir (*to fall due, to be payable*): Used in the present indicative, third person: *échoit/échoient*; imperfect: *échéait/échéaient*; preterit: *échut/échurent*; future: *échoira/échoiront*; past participle: *échu*; present participle: *échéant*. *Le cas échéant (if need be | where appropriate)* is an expression still in active use, as in *cocher le cas échéant (check | tick where appropriate)* and *Les paiements échéant le premier du mois seront retardés (Payments due the first of the month will be delayed)*. French grammars refer to the confusion arising from *échoir* and *échouer (to fail)*, the latter enjoying widespread use, but such a *mise en garde* hardly seems necessary.

Faillir (*to fail*): Used almost exclusively in the forms perfect + infinitive and past historic + infinitive: *Elle a failli s'évanouir (She almost fainted); Je faillis me noyer; Sabrina a failli à sa promesse (Sabrina did not keep her promise)*. Paradoxically, all its parts exist but they find little favor anywhere.

Férir (*to strike*): Only used in the infinitive in the expression *sans coup férir (without striking a blow)* and in the past participle: *Elle est férue d'astronomie/maths (She is keen on astronomy/math[s])*.

Frire (*to fry*): Only used in the infinitive and past participle. As an infinitive it is preceded by *faire*: *Je vais faire frire des oignons; du poisson frit*.

Gésir (*to lie, to be lying down*): Only used in the present and imperfect indicatives. Used almost entirely on tombstones, and one finds it everywhere in cemeteries: *Ci-gît (Here lies)*. The present participle has given rise to *gisant(e) (recumbent figure or effigy one finds in a church for instance)*.

Ouïr (*to hear*): Only heard in the infinitive and past participle, and even here, it has a highly literary or legal resonance. One could also hear it in the humorous: *Oyez ! Oyez !* The expression *par ouï-dire (by hearsay)* still maintains some value: *Je sais, du moins par ouï-dire, qu'elle a l'agrég(ation) (I know, at least by hearsay, that she has the agrégation)*. It is not surprising that, given the dominant position of the French language in England from 1066 for some 400 years, the town crier's invitation to pay attention to public proclamations was, and is still, preceded by *Oyez ! Oyez !*, a sound still commonly reaching Spanish ears with *¡Oye !*, part of the standard verb *oír=to hear*, again not far from the English *Oi!* (See also the end of Chapter 30).

Paître (*to graze* – of animals eating graze): Has many parts, but it is almost entirely used in the present third-person singular and plural indicative, and similarly with the imperfect. One could imagine: *je pais, tu pais, je paissais, tu paissais* and so on if Aesop et alia were describing animal activities and thoughts in the first person, but we, the readers, are very unlikely to use it as foreigners, and, from a bovine point of view, *Les vaches/moutons paissent l'herbe*. *Brouter*, a much easier and regular −**er** verb, replaces it. The circumflex in *paître* may be ignored, according to the Conseil supérieur de la langue française.

Poindre (*to appear*): Only found in the infinitive, and the third-person singular present, future and imperfect. In principle, it is conjugated like *joindre*, but there is some indecision here: *Le soleil va poindre*; *On voit poindre les bourgeons* (*buds*).

Seoir (*to suit, to fit*): Only used as a present participle and the third-person singular of the following tenses: present indicative = *sied*, imperfect = *seyait*, future = *siéra*. *Elle porte un chapeau qui sied parfaitement aux femmes*; *Ces tresses lui seyaient à ravir*. Grevisse and Goosse go on to provide subjunctive forms but only the most recondite of writings would exploit them.

Traire (*to milk* – of a cow): Not used in the preterit or the imperfect subjunctive. What on earth could these forms be? Present indicative: *Je trais, tu trais, il/elle trait, nous trayons, vous trayez, ils/elles traient*; imperfect: *je trayais*; future: *je trairai*; imperative: *traie, trayons, trayez*; present subjunctive: *je traie*; present participle: *trayant*; past participle: *trait*. *Les vaches sont traites* (*The cows are milked*). This verb once had the meaning of *to pull, to draw*, as it still does in contemporary Spanish = *traer*. To be added here is that in country regions of France, Poitou for instance, one hears and says: *Les vaches sont tirées*. Conjugated like *traire* are *abstraire, distraire, extraire, soustraire*.

Transir (*to penetrate with cold/rain*; also used of fear): Conjugated like *finir* for Grevisse and Goosse, but this is disputed by other grammarians. In any case, one need not worry since it is only used in the past participle: *Nous étions transis* (*We were soaked to the skin*); *Elles sont rentrées transies de froid* (*They came home chilled to the bone*); *En sortant de la maison hantée, ils étaient transis de peur* (*Coming out of the haunted house, they were chilled with fear*).

There do exist other defective verbs. This list contains some comments. No conjugations are provided, given their recondite and unusable nature: *adirer* (*to lose, to lack*), *apparoir* (*to appear, to be evident*), *ardre* (*to burn*; see standard R2 *arder* in Spanish), *attraire* (*to attract*; a vigorous residue of this verb is *attrayant* = *attractive*), *comparoir* (*to appear* before a magistrate in court; entirely replaced by *comparaître*), *contondre* (*to bruise*; entirely replaced by *contusionner*), *honnir* (*to shame*, only found now in *Honni soit qui mal y pense* =

Shame on him who evil thinks, expression surviving as the watchword for the British Order of the Garter); *messeoir* (*not to fit/suit*), *occire* (*to kill*; compare standard R2 Italian = *uccidere*), *quérir* (*to fetch*), *raire* (*to bellow*, as of a deer; conjugated like *traire*), *reclure* (*to confine*; past participle is still in circulation: *reclus*, as in *Elle vivait une vie recluse / en recluse*). The past participle *éclopé* still exists (*maimed, lame*), as in *un soldat éclopé*.

Two other verbs require attention: *foutre* and *ficher*. *Foutre* (*to do, to stick, to fuck*) is a very common R1 verb that should be classified with an asterisk, to be used with care. Its main conjugations are:

> Present indicative: *je fous, tu fous, il/elle fout, nous foutons, vous foutez, ils/elles foutent*
> Imperfect indicative: *je foutais*
> Preterit: *je foutis* (very rare because the preterit relates to refined language and *foutre* is anything but refined)
> Future: *je foutrai*
> Imperative: *fous, foutons, foutez*
> Present subjunctive: *foute*
> Perfect: *j'ai foutu*

This verb is used in a number of very commonplace expressions. A substantial range is provided since the verb is so flexible and widespread, and it is useful to be aware of it:

Fous/Foutez-moi la paix !	*Fuck off!*
Allez, les gars, on fout le camp.	*Right, you guys, let's fuck off.*
Qu'est-ce qu'elle a fait ? Elle a foutu la pagaille partout.	*What's she done? She's fucked up everything.*
Va te faire foutre !	*Fuck off / Bugger off!*
J'ai rien à foutre.	*I've got damn all to do with it! / I couldn't give a shit.*
Les gars n'ont rien foutu toute la journée.	*The guys have done fuck all all day long.*

Linked to this verb is *ficher*, which is entirely regular save for the past participle *fichu*, and the alternative infinitive form *fiche*. Used in the standard way, it signifies *to stick* (*into/on*), as in *ficher un pieu en terre*, but it provides a euphemistic outlet for *foutre*:

Fiche le camp !	*Clear off!*
Céline n'a rien fichu.	*Céline has done damn all.*
Va te faire fiche !	*Fuck off / Get stuffed!*
Fiche-moi la paix !	*Clear off!*

Se fiche de or *se ficher de* means *to make fun of, not to care about*:

Il s'est fichu de moi.	*He took the piss out of me.*
Elle s'en fiche complètement.	*She doesn't care at all about it.*

And *se foutre de* is its stronger expression:

Je m'en fous comme de l'an quarante.	*I couldn't care a fuck.*
Elle s'en fout, et royalement.	*She doesn't care a fuck.*
Il se fout du monde.	*He doesn't give a shit.*
Elle se fout de ma gueule.	*She thinks fuck all about me.*

36

Modal verbs / Les auxiliaires modaux

English has a relatively large number of auxiliary verbs (*will, would, may, might, shall, should, must, ought*) and verbal expressions (*to be to*: *We were to arrive at nine*; *to have to*: *We had to go*). Their main function is to express intentions or opinions (commands, possibilities, etc.). There is no straightforward match between these and their equivalents in French which, like Spanish and Italian, has a rather smaller number of auxiliary verbs (e.g., *devoir, pouvoir, vouloir*). The major differences between French and English are:

- French auxiliaries may normally be used in all tenses and moods (e.g., *Je peux/puis, j'ai pu, j'avais pu, je pus, je pourrai, j'aurai pu, j'aurais pu, je puisse, j'aie pu*), while English auxiliaries have a maximum of two (*may, might*), and sometimes only one (*must*).
- In English, the perfect auxiliary *have* is used only with the dependent infinitive (*He may have done it*), whereas in French *avoir* is used either with the dependent infinitive (*Elle a pu être vexée* = *She could have been upset*) or with the modal auxiliary (*Elle peut avoir été vexée*). There is a good deal of overlap in the values of modal auxiliaries in both French and English, but often they do not have equivalents.

36.1 Uses of the verb *devoir*

For conjugations of *devoir* in main tenses and moods, see Chapter 30, and verb tables at the end of this volume.

The most basic meaning of *devoir* is *to owe*, which determines the value of the constructions with the infinitive:

Laetitia me doit/devait cent dollars/euros.	*Laetitia owes/owed me a hundred dollars/euros.*
Antoine doit son emploi à mon intervention.	*Antoine owes his job to my intervention.*
La mauvaise qualité de la nourriture se devait aux grandes chaleurs.	*The poor quality of the food came from the intense heat.*

Devoir followed by an infinitive expresses obligation, necessity, probability or intention:

Je dois partir avant minuit.	*I have to leave before midnight.*
Vous devez respecter le code de la route.	*You must respect the rules of the road / highway code.*
Robin ne sait pas ce qu'il doit faire.	*Robin doesn't know what he has to do.*
Je l'ai quittée parce que je devais partir.	*I left her because I had to go.*
Elle a dû s'absenter.	*She had to go out / leave.*
Les garçons m'ont tellement importuné que j'ai dû les mettre à la porte.	*The boys troubled me so much that I had to show them the door.*
Jeanne devait nous accompagner mais elle en a été empêchée.	*Jeanne was to accompany us but was prevented.*
Jeanne aurait dû nous accompagner mais elle a été empêchée.	*Jeanne was to accompany us but was prevented.*

The two uses of *devoir* in the last two sentences have the same meaning.

Obligation can imply a reason for doing something:

Lucile ne sait si elle doit rire ou pleurer.	*Lucile doesn't know if she ought to laugh or cry.*

Devoir can also suggest that a person is "well placed to know."

Moi, je ne sais pas, mais lui, il doit le savoir.	*Me, I don't know, but him, he ought to know.*

Devoir can also point to what is just and reasonable:

Son succès ne m'étonne pas. Élisabeth devait réussir.	*Her success doesn't surprise me. Élisabeth was sure to succeed.*
Ça devait commencer ou finir comme ça.	*It ought to begin or end like that.*
Marie devrait être rentrée.	*Marie ought to have gone home (by now).*

Devoir often involves necessity:

Tu dois passer l'examen.	*You must take / get through the examination.*
Christophe aurait dû m'appeler.	*Christophe ought to have called me.*
Sophie a dû s'arrêter, faute d'essence.	*Sophie had to stop for she had run out of gas/petrol.*

Devoir can also evoke the idea of probability, intention or conjecture:
In the present:

Je dois le connaître.	*I ought to / must know him.*
La campagne doit être belle en ce moment.	*The countryside must be lovely at the moment.*
Vous devez être fatiguées.	*You must be tired.*

In the future:

Le colis doit arriver sous peu.	*The package must be arriving shortly.*
Il doit y avoir demain une assemblée générale.	*There has to be a general meeting tomorrow.*
Je dois le voir demain.	*I'll have to see him tomorrow.*

In this third case, the notion of likelihood is reduced, given the first-person perspective. Notice how the present tense is used in these sentences. The future of *devoir* in these examples has quite a different impact. If the three sentences immediately above changed the present tense to the future, a note of insistence or urgency would be introduced:

Le colis devra arriver sous peu.	*The package has to arrive shortly.*
Il devra y avoir demain une assemblée générale.	*There will have to be a general meeting tomorrow.*
Je devrai le voir demain.	*I'll have to see him tomorrow.*

In the past (imperfect and perfect):

Il devait être dix heures quand Jeanne s'est manifestée.	*It must have been ten o'clock when Jeanne turned up.*
Il ne devait pas être bien tard quand nos amis sont arrivés.	*It couldn't have been very late when our friends arrived.*
L'avocat doit avoir prévu ce cas.	*The lawyer must have foreseen this case.*
L'avocat a dû prévoir ce cas.	*The lawyer must have foreseen this case.*

These two sentences have exactly the same meaning, just as the two immediately below:

Stéphanie doit s'être trompée.	*Stéphanie must have made a mistake.*
Stéphanie a dû se tromper.	*Stéphanie must have made a mistake.*

Just as:

Elle doit déjà l'avoir dit.	*She must have already said it.*
Elle a dû déjà l'avoir dit.	*She must have already said it.*

Just as in the passive:

Virginie doit avoir été élue.	*Virginie must have been elected.*
Virginie a dû être élue.	*Virginie must have been elected.*

However, in certain contexts, there is a difference between the construction *a dû* + infinitive and *doit avoir/être* + past participle. In the first person, *j'ai dû partir* can only imply obligation (*I had to*), unless one were in a comatose state when one left, whereas *Il a dû partir* could suggest obligation or conjecture.

> The imperfect can also imply some future event, suggesting a kind of fatality:

Margaret Mitchell publia *Autant en emporte le vent* en 1936, mais elle devait mourir un peu plus tard dans un accident de voiture.	Margaret Mitchell published *Gone with the Wind* in 1936, but was to die a little later in an automobile accident.

The idea here is: *elle mourrait.* Similarly:

Elle quitta son mari mais devait le regretter l'année suivante. The idea here is: *elle le regretterait.*	She left her husband but was to regret it the following year.

In the future perfect:

On aura dû nettoyer la maison avant que nos parents ne reviennent.	We will have had to clean the house before our parents come home.

In the preterit (R3 here):

Le médecin dut faire l'autopsie du cadavre.	The physician had to carry out an autopsy on the body.
En plein désert, nous dûmes conserver les quelques gouttes d'eau qui nous restaient.	Deep in the desert, we had to conserve the few remaining drops of water.

In the pluperfect:

Étant donné que l'on avait dû passer la nuit en pleine jungle, on ne pouvait atteindre le fleuve avant midi.	Given that we had had to spend the night deep in the jungle, we could not reach the river before midday.

In the conditional:

Adrienne devrait terminer sa lecture.	Adrienne ought to finish her book.
Nous devrions partir maintenant si nous voulions arriver à temps.	We ought to leave now if we wanted to arrive in time.

In the conditional in the past:

Le professeur aurait dû se montrer plus indulgent.	The teacher ought to have been more indulgent.
On aurait dû conclure l'affaire ce matin.	We ought to have concluded the business this morning.

These last two examples could be turned *devrait s'être montré...* | *devrait avoir conclu...* but they are clumsy and attract the criticism that they are a calque on the English, and therefore to be avoided.

After the conjunction *si*, *devoir* underlines possibility at the same time as it points more clearly to the future. The present and imperfect occur here:

Si cela doit se reproduire, j'interviendrai.	*If that has to happen again, I'll intervene.*
Si Françoise doit revenir seulement à cinq heures, ce n'est pas la peine que nous l'attendions.	*If Françoise is to come back only at five o'clock, it's not worth waiting for her.*
Si David devait venir demain, je lui en parlerais.	*If David were to come tomorrow, I would speak to him about it.*

The use of *devoir* can combine probability with the need to tone down an affirmation:

Vous devez faire erreur.	*You must be making an error.*
Tu as dû faire erreur.	*You must have made an error.*

The construction *se devoir de* (*to be morally obliged to*), although of a high register, is in general use:

Je me dois/devais d'apporter ma contribution financière.	*I must/had to give my financial contribution.*
L'État se doit de soutenir les victimes.	*The State must / owes it to itself to support the victims.*

Devoir with the negation *ne... pas*:
The case of *devoir* in the negative can be quite complex by virtue of its several meanings. In *Je ne dois pas insister*, one denies the obligation, and the construction *ne... pas* is attached to *devoir*, just as *Cela n'a pas dû te surprendre* denies *Cela a dû te surprendre*. However, when the negation *ne... pas* is attached more to the infinitive, it implies refusal or banning, since it carries more weight and is stronger in intent. Contrast the two following sentences: *Tu ne dois pas oublier ton portefeuille* and *Tu dois ne pas oublier ton portefeuille*. The second sentence suggests a greater insistence.

Devoir in the negative can often point to probability:

Éléonore ne doit pas tarder.	*Éléonore should not be long.*
Ils n'ont pas dû s'en apercevoir.	*They couldn't have realized it.*
Jean ne doit pas être parti ce matin.	*Jean couldn't have left this morning.*
Ça ne doit pas être difficile.	That can't be difficult.

Uses of *devoir* in the subjunctive. Some of these subjunctives clearly apply to the written form alone, notably the imperfect.
Present, indicating obligation:

Je regrette que tu doives partir.	*I'm sorry you have to go.*

Present, indicating inference:

Je ne crois pas qu'elle doive travailler si dur.	*I don't think she must work so hard.*

Perfect, indicating obligation:

C'est malheureux qu'elle ait dû vendre sa voiture.	*It's unfortunate she has had to sell her car.*

Perfect, indicating inference:

Je ne crois pas qu'elle ait dû lire *Guerre et paix*.	*I don't think she could have read War and Peace.*

Imperfect, indicating obligation:

Il craignait que je dusse partir tout de suite.	*He feared that I would have to leave immediately.*

Imperfect, indicating inference:

Je ne croyais pas que Jeanne dût voyager seule.	*I did not think that Jeanne would travel alone.*

Pluperfect, indicating obligation:

Il n'était pas clair que Lucile eût dû passer toute la semaine à l'hôpital.	*It was not clear that Lucile had had to spend all week at the hospital.*

Other uses of *devoir* which are not always related to the modal concept:
As an infinitive:

Mon frère est parti sans devoir payer l'addition.	*My brother left without having to pay the bill.*
Antoine s'est rendu compte de devoir remplir ses engagements.	*Antoine realized he would have to fulfill his commitments.*

As a present participle:

Devant partir tôt le matin, on a pris le petit-déjeuner à cinq heures.	*Having to leave early in the morning, we had our breakfast at five o'clock.*

As a past infinitive:

Je regrette d'avoir dû renvoyer la bonne.	*I was sorry to have had to dismiss the maid.*

With the past participle with the idea of *what is due*:

Ce montant est dû pour le 15 avril.	*This sum is due April 15.*
les sommes dues	*the due sums*
payer son dû	*to pay one's due*

Dû also suggests cause, as in *due to*:

Cette inondation est due aux fortes pluies de juillet.	*This flood is due to the heavy July rains.*

Dû is used in the masculine singular form to distinguish it from the partitive article *du*. The other forms do not have the circumflex and there is no difference in pronunciation.

Agreement of the past participle requires care. Compare the two following sentences:

Elle lui a fait toutes les promesses qu'elle a dû (lui faire).	*She made him all the promises she had to.*
Il a toujours remboursé les sommes qu'il a dues.	*He (has) always repaid the sums he owed.*

In the first case, the preceding direct object is *promesses*, related to *faire* which is implied, and therefore there can be no agreement. In the second case, *sommes* is the preceding direct object of *devoir*, and here there is agreement.

36.2 Uses of the verb *pouvoir*

Pouvoir is an irregular verb; for conjugations, see the verb tables at the end of this volume. The uses of this verb include more than the modal values.

The infinitive is used as a noun meaning *power*:

Marcel a le pouvoir de refuser la proposition.	*Marcel has the power to refuse the proposal.*

It can also suggest *authority*:

le pouvoir législatif/exécutif	*legislative/executive power*

It also suggests influence or a mandate:

La députée recherche le pouvoir.	*The representative / member of Parliament is seeking power* (as president, for example).

Pouvoir is a true auxiliary in that it applies to a following infinitive. It corresponds to the English *to be able*, expressing physical power or prowess, often translated by the defective verb *can*:

| Élisabeth peut nager un bon kilomètre. | *Élisabeth can swim a good kilometer.* |
| Mon fils peut aller tout seul maintenant au collège. | *My son can now go to school by himself.* |

A distinction should be made here between *pouvoir* and *savoir*; the English *can / is able to* is confusing since *can* and *know how to* are possible when it is a question of *knowing how to*, where only *savoir* is possible in French. Compare the first of the two examples immediately above and the following one:

| Élisabeth sait nager / jouer du violon. | *Élisabeth knows how to swim (but not necessarily a kilometer) / knows how to play the violin (can could be used here).* |

Pouvoir also applies to permissibility:

| Les enfants peuvent jouer dans la cour. | *The children can play in the yard.* |
| On peut manger ici ? | *Can we eat here?* |

When the negative is used, *pouvoir* has two meanings, which depend on where the *ne . . . pas* is in the sentence. Compare the two sentences:

| Francis ne peut pas faire son devoir. | *Francis cannot do his homework.* |
| Francis peut ne pas faire son devoir. | *Francis does not need to do his homework.* |

Notice the use of the double negative:

| Elle ne pouvait pas ne pas hurler de douleur. | *She couldn't help screaming with pain.* |
| Jeanne ne peut pas ne pas l'avouer. | *Jeanne cannot but confess it.* |

The omission of the *pas* indicates a higher register, as with *cesser, savoir* and *oser*:

| Adrienne ne pouvait se passer de la musique classique. | *Adrienne could not do without classical music.* |
| Philippe n'a pu venir. | *Philippe hasn't been able to come.* |

The omission of the *pas* is not possible with the double-negative construction above.

As with *devoir* (see above), there is no agreement with the past participle of *pouvoir* when it is used as a modal auxiliary:

| J'ai lu tous les livres que j'ai pu pour les examens. | *I read all the books I could for the exams.* |

Pouvoir can also indicate approximation:

La dame pouvait avoir dans les quarante-cinq ans.	*The lady was probably about forty-five years old.*
Il pouvait être six heures quand j'ai entendu la bagarre.	*It was doubtless about six o'clock when I heard the row.*

Pouvoir can suggest audacity:

Comment peux-tu mettre ma parole en doute?	*How can you call my word into question?*
Comment peux-tu oser l'accuser d'un tel délit?	*How can you dare accuse her of such a crime?*

Pouvoir with *bien* can indicate opposition:

Antoine peut promettre tout ce qu'il veut mais je ne le crois pas.	*Antoine may promise all he wishes but I (still) don't believe him.*

Bien can strengthen *pouvoir*:

C'est une maladie dont il pourrait bien mourir.	*It's an illness from which he could die.*
Lucile pourrait bien s'en tirer toute seule.	*Lucile might well deal with it by herself.*

Pouvoir has some idiomatic uses, and often an infinitive is implied:

On a passé un séjour on ne peut plus agréable.	*We had a most pleasant stay.*
Cette robe lui allait on ne peut mieux.	*That dress suits her splendidly.*
Je n'en peux plus.	*I'm exhausted.*
Je n'en peux plus de fatigue.	*I'm worn out.*
Cela/Ça se peut.	*That's possible.*
Cela/Ça se pourrait bien.	*That's possible.*
Cela ne se peut pas.	*That's not possible.*

The Académie française also accepts *Cela ne se peut.*

Pouvoir does not always translate *can*, especially where perception is concerned:

On voyait au loin des colonnes de fumée.	*We could see columns of smoke far off.*
Henri avait du sable plein les yeux et ne voyait rien.	*Henri's eyes were full of sand and he could see nothing.*
J'ai entendu chanter le coq.	*I could hear the cock crow.*
Je ne sais pas ce qui se passe. Je n'entends rien.	*I don't know what is happening. I can't hear anything.*
Il sentait le parfum de ses bras.	*He could smell the perfume of her arms.*

Of course, if serious effort were suggested, *pouvoir* would be used:

> Le fermier scrutait du regard le   *The farmer peered into the valley, and*
> fond de la vallée et, finalement,   *finally, he could see the flock.*
> il put voir le troupeau.

36.3 Tenses and moods of *pouvoir* (see the verb tables at the end of this volume for the full conjugations)

Infinitive:

> Je voudrais pouvoir jouer au foot   *I would like to be able to play soccer*
> ce soir.   *this evening.*

Indicative:

Present: *je peux, je puis, tu peux*, etc.

Je peux is used much more than *je puis*, but *puis-je* replaces the other form in questions:

> Puis-je vous accompagner?   *May I accompany you?*

Perfect: *j'ai pu, tu as pu*, etc.

> Martine a pu venir avec nous.   *Martine has been able / was able to*
>   *come with us.*

Past infinitive:

> Je ne crois pas avoir pu arriver à   *I don't think I would have been able to*
> temps.   *arrive / could have arrived in time.*

Imperfect:

> Jean n'était pas assez fort. Il ne   *Jean wasn't strong enough. He*
> pouvait pas faire le trajet.   *couldn't manage the trip.*

Preterit:

> L'héroïne put sauver son amant.   *The heroine managed to save her*
>   *lover.*
>
> Nous pûmes regagner l'autre rive   *We could reach the other bank*
> sans trop de difficulté.   *without too much difficulty.*

Pûmes is less used than *put*, and *pûtes* even less so.

Pluperfect:

> On a fait tout ce que l'on avait pu   *We did all we could have to complete*
> faire pour terminer la tâche.   *the work.*

Future:

> Nous pourrons venir demain si   *We will be able to / can come*
> tu veux.   *tomorrow if you wish.*

Future in the past:

J'aurai pu préparer le repas avant ton retour.	*I'll have been able to get the meal ready before you come back.*

Conditional:

Stéphanie pourrait t'aider ce soir.	*Stéphanie would be able to / could help you this evening.*

Conditional in the past:

Guillaume aurait pu t'emmener à la gare si tu le lui avais demandé.	*Guillaume could have taken you to the station if you had asked him.*

Subjunctive:
Present:

Je ne crois pas que Philippe puisse revenir.	*I don't think Philippe can come back.*

Perfect:

Je regrette que Marie n'ait pu réussir son examen.	*I'm sorry Marie couldn't get through her examination.*

Imperfect (rarely used save in the third-person singular, and even here only in writing):

Il était douteux que le candidat fût à la hauteur.	*It was doubtful that the candidate was equal to the task.*

Gerund:
Simple:

Pouvant partir dans l'après-midi, nous avons profité de toute la matinée pour jouer aux cartes.	*Being able to leave in the afternoon, we took advantage of the whole morning to play cards.*

Compound:

Ayant pu consulter mon médecin la veille, je suis partie faire du ski au Colorado.	*Having been able to consult my physician the previous day, I left to do some skiing in Colorado.*

37

Ellipsis of verbs in main and subordinate clauses / L'ellipse du verbe dans la proposition principale et la proposition subordonnée

In a general way, ellipsis refers to the absence of words or a series of words which would be necessary for the regular construction of a sentence or the complete expression of a thought.

37.1 Ellipsis of the verb in a main clause

In several expressions, the verb of the main clause is understood through ellipsis. This usually implies the exclusion of verbs such as *être, croire, penser, assurer*:

Sûr qu'elle n'est pas pauvre.	*(I'm) sure she's not poor.*
Impossible que notre fille revienne aujourd'hui.	*Impossible that our daughter come back today.*
Sans aucun doute que tu mens.	*No doubt you are lying.*

A proposition beginning with *que* may perform the function of a subject, and this usually entails the subjunctive. This construction has the value of *the fact that* and may be seen as the shortened form of *le fait que*.

Que l'avion parte plus tard me préoccupe.	*That the airplane should leave later concerns me.*
Que nos enfants aient réussi tous les examens nous emballe.	*The fact that our children have passed their exams delights us.*
Que Pierre ait menti me fait honte.	*That Pierre should lie makes me feel ashamed.*

37.2 Ellipsis of the verb in a subordinate clause

After verbs such as *croire, penser, juger, estimer*:

Louise croit l'examen facile.	*Louise thinks the exam is easy.*
Je trouve le livre trop cher.	*I find the book too dear.*

L'athlète juge sa performance magnifique.	*The athlete judges his performance magnificent.*
J'estime sa contribution incontournable.	*I judge her contribution unavoidable.*

Que + subjunctive has a widespread use in the sense of *Let him/her, etc.* + finite verb. English has no true equivalent here, although this is a common construction in all Romance languages:

Que tout le monde s'asseye.	*Let everyone sit down.*
Si Marcel ne peut pas y aller maintenant, qu'il y aille demain.	*If Marcel can't go now, let him go tomorrow.*

Ellipsis of the finite verb in the subordinate clause is characteristic of the written style, where it is replaced by an infinitive. See Chapter 18 for a fuller treatment of this subject.

Françoise a démontré parler un japonais parfait.	*Françoise has demonstrated that she can speak perfect Japanese.*
Antoine croit toujours avoir raison.	*Antoine always thinks he is right.*

37.3 Miscellaneous applications of ellipsis

Note the loss of *il* in *il faut* in R1 language:

Faut pas venir avant midi.	*Don't come before midday.*
Faut étudier plus que ça pour réussir.	*You have to study more than that to succeed.*
Fallait pas rouler à cent quarante.	*You ought not to have driven at 140 kilometers (an hour).*

Although dates such as *le mardi 18 janvier* and *le jeudi 31 octobre* are standard these days, they are really elliptical expressions, deriving from *le dix-huitième jour du mois de janvier* and so on.

The use of *enchanté*:

"Je vous présente Mme Legrand." "Enchanté, Madame." (= Je suis enchanté de faire votre connaissance.)	*"May I introduce you to Mme Legrand?" "Delighted to meet you."*

A kind of suspension at the end of the sentence can occur in R1 style. Something is left unsaid, usually negative:

Si tu continues à m'agacer...	*If you go on annoying me...*
Tu prends un parapluie au cas où...	*Take an umbrella in case...*

Parce que can be used in a milar way:

"Pourquoi tu ne veux pas sortir avec Jean?" "Parce que..."	*"Why don't you want to go out with Jean?" "Because..."*

In dialogues, replies are often short, picking up where the first speaker leaves off:

"Où est Roland?" "Chez sa mère."	*"Where is Roland?" "At his mother's."*
"Il partira demain." "Par le train?"	*"He's going tomorrow." "By train?"*
"Annick est mécontente." "Sa mère aussi."	*"Annick is annoyed." "Her mother as well."*

Ellipsis occurs where there is coordination between two elements:

Je partirai avec ou sans votre permission.	*I'll go with or without your permission.*

In R1 language: Je partirai avec votre permission ou sans.

Ellipsis can occur when coordinated clauses have the same verb:

La plus âgée avait huit ans, la plus jeune cinq ans.	*The oldest was eight years old, the youngest five.*
Le soleil était brillant, le ciel resplendissant, la mer étincelante.	*The sun was brilliant, the sky radiant, the sea sparkling.*

While grammarians require for the same verb the same person and number, this is frequently not respected:

Tu seras le roi, et moi le comte.	*You can be the king, and me/I the count.*
Cédric retournera à New York, nous à Québec.	*Cédric will go back to New York, and we'll go back to Quebec.*
Les boutiques étaient fermées, la rue silencieuse.	*The shops were closed and the street silent.*

If the determiner applies to two nouns, it is possible to express only the second noun.

Le sentier passait entre deux ou trois fermes.	*The path went between two or three farms.*

Comme si in R1 language finds considerable favor:

Elle ne s'est aperçue de rien. Je ne puis croire qu'elle a fait comme si...	*She didn't notice anything. I can't believe that she acted as if (she didn't notice anything)...*

Tout comme has the same value:

Elle n'avait rien compris. Mais c'était tout comme.	*She understood nothing. But it was as if she had.*

When two adjectives describe the same noun, the adjective may be attached to the first or second noun:

pendant le premier et le second acte	*during the first and second acts*
entre les lignes allemande et française	*between the German and French lines*
J'adore la viande rôtie et la bouillie.	*I adore roast and boiled meat.*

If adjectives are usually placed before the noun, this noun occurs after the second adjective:

Comment distinguer entre les bons et les mauvais anges?	*How can you distinguish between good and bad angels?*
Je ne vois aucune différence entre le vrai et le faux tableau.	*I can see no difference between the authentic and false painting.*
Je n'ai pas lu l'Ancien et le Nouveau Testament.	*I haven't read the Old and New Testament.*

Ellipsis can occur even when there is no determiner:

Trente ans de vie privée et trois de publique furent le sort du Christ.	*Thirty years of private life and three public was Christ's lot.*

When two nouns are coordinated, but one expressed and the other omitted, one may see the following:

L'invasion allemande bouleversa la face de la France et du monde.	*The invasion of France overturned the whole of France and the world.*

Verbs such as *devoir, pouvoir, vouloir, dire* and *croire* are often subject to the ellipsis of the infinitive or a preposition:

Sabrina a accompli toutes les tâches qu'elle a dû.	*Sabrina fulfilled all the tasks she had to.*
Je fais tous les efforts que je peux (faire).	*I make all the efforts I can.*
Axelle m'a aidée autant qu'elle a pu.	*Axelle helped me as much as she could.*
Louis m'a fourni tous les renseignements que j'ai voulu (qu'il me donne).	*Louis gave me all the information I wanted.*

Il a vécu moins longtemps qu'il aurait cru (vivre).	*He didn't live as long as he would have believed.*
Viens quand tu peux/veux.	*Come when you can/wish.*

Faire serves as a substitute for other verbs:

Elle travaille plus que je ne fais.	*She works more than I do.*

As do disjunctive pronouns for verbs:

Il court plus rapidement que moi.	*He runs faster than I/me.*
Jeanne utilise l'ordinateur mieux que moi.	*Jeanne uses the computer better than me.*

Que can replace conjunctions *comme, quand, si* and *comme si* when these have already been used:

Comme Éléonore ne travaille pas le soir et qu'elle se lève de bon matin...	*As Éléonore doesn't work in the evening and gets up early in the morning...*
Quand Adrienne reviendra et qu'elle ne retrouvera pas sa voiture...	*When Adrienne comes back and finds her car missing...*
Si Robin peut partir de bonne heure et qu'il vienne me chercher en voiture...	*If Robin can leave early and fetch me in his car...*

Notice that with *si* the second verb can be in the subjunctive, a mark of higher register.

Below is a disparate list of words or expressions that avoid the need for repetition:

Tu restes, moi non.	*You remain, but not me.*
Elle dit que oui/non.	*She says yes/no.*
Aller en pension ? J'aime mieux pas.	*To stay in lodgings? I prefer not to.*
Mon frère a étudié toute la semaine. Moi de même.	*My brother studied all week. I did the same.*
Les feux d'artifice de Montréal auront lieu à 22h; idem ceux de Québec.	*Montreal fireworks start at 10 this evening, and the same for Quebec.*
J'ai vu dans la maison toutes sortes d'outils : des scies, des marteaux, des tournevis et cétera.	*I saw in the house all sorts of tools, saws, hammers, screwdrivers, et cetera.*
Il a cité des auteurs grecs, latins, anglais, etc.	*He quoted Greek, Latin, English authors, etc.*

Laurent a raconté tous les événements de son voyage, la perte de ses billets, l'accident à l'hôtel, la rencontre fortuite avec Pierre et patati et patata.	*Laurent related all the events of his journey, the loss of his tickets, the accident at the hotel, the fortuitous meeting with Pierre, and so on and so forth.*
Livres, bibelots, outils, paperasses et ainsi de suite, tout était là.	*Books, trinkets, tools, documents and so on, it was all there.*

"Ibid." can also be used to avoid repeating a full reference: *Camus, La peste, p. 249; ibid., p. 278.*

Notice a range of nouns with a vague meaning all evoking *thing, thingummy*: *bidule, chose, machin, truc* (all masculine, even *chose* in this context) and *histoire*, while *bazar* is not uncommon in Belgium:

Qu'est-ce que c'est ce bidule/chose/machin/truc que tu as dans ta poche ?	*What's that thing you've got in your pocket?*
C'est quoi, cette histoire-là ?	*What's that thing there?*
Le bazar a pris feu... Non, pas l'aspirateur, mais mon pantalon.	*The thing caught fire... No, not the vacuum cleaner, but my pants.*

38

Idiomatic uses of *aller, avoir, être, faire* and *prendre* | Les expressions idiomatiques concernant *aller, avoir, être, faire* et *prendre*

Below is a passage describing the delights of an autumnal Scotland, the customs associated with this country, certain activities, one of which, fox hunting, is now banned, and finally the gastronomic joys of a Scottish table. The passage includes a wide range of idiomatic expressions related to the use of verbs, and these are highlighted. Some translations are provided.

Un bel automne en Écosse

Il **est** [There are] **des souvenirs** remplis de tendresse lorsque nous évoquons notre séjour en Écosse. Les *lochs* écossais comme le Loch Ness, le Loch Lomond fascinent. De tous mes périples en Écosse, ma saison préférée reste l'automne. Un charme irrésistible s'exerce sous les brumes automnales d'Écosse, sous une pluie fine, grâce à un jeu de lumières, à un soleil radieux, ainsi qu'aux reflets de couleurs qui **vont se dégradant** [which continue to fade] au cours d'une même journée. Nous **en étions à mi-chemin** quand Irène nous **fit parvenir un texto** [had a text message sent to us] alors qu'elle **était à son travail**. Sans aucun moyen de locomotion, **on eut besoin de** prendre le train pour lui rendre visite. Nous **n'avions qu'à** l'avertir et répondre à son texto pour lui indiquer notre heure d'arrivée. Le groupe **avait trop hâte** de rencontrer Irène à la gare. Cette belle Écossaise **avait une quarantaine** d'années. Elle **s'était fait couper** les cheveux chez le coiffeur pour **se faire belle** à notre arrivée. Elle **avait les yeux noisette** [hazel-colored eyes] qui caractérisaient son regard plein de tendresse, de bonté et de générosité.

Nous décidions de **faire un tour chez** les Taylor avant **d'aller** avec Irène à un spectacle de danses écossaises. Irène était une force de la nature. Elle se plaisait à dire : « The blood is strong. » La famille d'Irène parlait la langue gaélique d'Écosse lorsque les membres de la famille se retrouvaient entre eux. Malcolm, le chef du clan, **allait sur ses soixante ans**. Il était joueur de cornemuse. Il portait souvent le kilt traditionnel, fabriqué dans un tissu de laine peignée, avant de **se rendre** au village. Le kilt lui **allait bien** ! Il faut comprendre qu'un homme portant une jupe nous **a pris au dépourvu** ! L'idée lui **avait pris** de venir nous rejoindre au spectacle. Nous adorions **prendre nos aises** dans les Highlands. Un parcours de golf situé en bordure du Loch Lomond accueille des compétitions internationales. La distillerie de whisky était très visitée. Les visiteurs appréciaient le whisky écossais fabriqué localement avec des produits du terroir comme l'orge [barley], l'avoine [oats], le seigle [rye] ou le maïs. Nous **faisions un** simple **aller-retour** pour visiter le lieu. Malcolm avait un goût prononcé pour la chasse à courre au renard et au lièvre. Heureusement que le « fox hunting » longtemps pratiqué en Écosse est désormais interdit dans cette région sous peine **d'être poursuivi en justice** [taken to court]. Plus question pour Malcolm **d'aller au sanglier, au lapin ou au chevreuil**. La préservation de la faune sauvage, de l'environnement, de ce site exceptionnel est devenue une priorité absolue.

Après notre spectacle de danse, nous **avions grand faim**. Nous **avions hâte de** manger des spécialités locales préparées par Irène. À table, son époux **faisait toujours la conversation** pendant qu'elle dressait une table magnifique en agençant avec soin les fruits de saison comme les pommes, les poires, les raisins. Nous **avions envie de** prendre un thé chaud accompagné de *scones*, de *crumpets* et de *golden syrup*. Les Écossais **avaient l'air enchanté** de recevoir dans les Highlands des visiteurs d'Outre-Manche. Même lorsque le temps **était à la pluie**, il se dégageait une atmosphère douceâtre. Il **suffisait de profiter** pleinement de ce climat de sérénité et de repartir avec des images plein la tête. Nous **allons faire de** nos souvenirs un livre. Ce voyage m'**a rendue folle** de joie. **Il y avait** vraiment **de quoi s'amuser**.

This collection of very common verbs illustrates their idiomatic uses which, generally speaking, do not correspond to the use of their English counterparts. It may be argued that this does not fall into the precinct of grammar but, in fact, most of these constructions involve grammatical difficulties. The illustrations do not contain examples which an English speaker would expect to find, and where there is a clear correspondence between English and French, for instance *Laurent va lire le journal* (*Laurent is going to read the newspaper*); *L'homme prend le train* (*The man takes the train*).

Another feature of idiom derives from the effect produced on Quebec French by the proximity to the United States, and to English-speaking Canada, which tends to supplant on occasions the traditional way of saying and writings things. What is happening in Quebec, linguistically speaking, is repeated in Mexico and much of Spanish America where calques or straightforward and literal copies and translations from the northern neighbor are provoking serious disturbances in Spanish. See the end of this chapter for some examples of this new choice of idiom in French which seems to be blighting the older and more acceptable way of expressing oneself.

38.1 Idiomatic uses of *aller*

Aller + preposition: *J'y vais à cheval / à moto / à vélo / à bicyclette* (often: *J'y vais en moto / en vélo* but this is R1); *J'y vais en bateau / en voiture / en train / en avion*; *Je vais à l'épicerie / à la boucherie / à la boulangerie*; but: *Je vais chez l'épicier / chez le boucher / chez le boulanger / chez le dentiste / chez le coiffeur / chez le garagiste / chez les Lanoë*. The preposition *à* is used for place while *chez* is used for the person who works there. In the case of *dentiste* and *coiffeur*, it is possible to say: *Je vais au dentiste / au coiffeur* but, although this expression is extremely widespread, it is considered of a lower register than its equivalent with *chez*, and some would discourage its use. For *aller* with place names, see Chapter 64 on geographical names. *Aller à* is used as a hunting term:

On va au sanglier / au lapin.   We're going to hunt wild boar / rabbits.

The expression *Comment ça va?* (*How are you?*) is used for wellbeing, as in:

Je vais très bien, merci.   *I am very well, thank you.*
Annick va mieux aujourd'hui.   *Annick is better today.*

Comment va? is also in general use, but belongs to the R1 register.

The imperatives *Vas-y!*, *Allez-y!* (*Go on / Keep it up!*) are used for encouragement.

Forms of the imperative are also used as interjections, especially in R1 style to press home a judgment, a threat or a sense of annoyance. These interjections do not accommodate translations very easily: *Crétin, va!*; *Ne t'inquiète pas, va!*; *Allons, ne t'inquiète pas!*; *Allez/Allons, viens/décidez-vous/venez ici!*; *Allons, ça recommence*; *Allons donc/Allez donc, c'est impossible.*

Aller + *en* + present participle suggests the idea of continuation and has a literary (R3) resonance. The absence of the preposition *en* no longer prevails in the current language:

Son inquiétude va en croissant.   *Her worry is growing.*

S'en aller may be used in the same way:

Cette femme s'en va mourant.   *This lady is slowly dying.*

Aller sur is used with age:

Mes grands-parents vont sur leurs   *My grandparents are coming up to*
    quatre-vingts ans.   *eighty.*

S'en aller = to go away:

Va-t-en! / Allez-vous-en!   *Go away!*
La fillette s'en est allée.   *The little girl went away.*
Je m'en suis allé.   *I went away.*

Hanse and Blampain state clearly (2005, p. 43) that *Je me suis en allé* is correct and has been common currency for a long time, but the present authors would refute it. One suspects that it is a regionalism characteristic of Belgium.

> *S'en aller* may be used as an alternative to *aller*. This is used in colloquial style and almost exclusively in the first-person singular, present tense:

Je m'en vais te le dire.	*I'm going to tell you.*

> *Aller* may be used with the idea of *to suit*:

Ce chapeau lui va bien.	*This hat suits her (well).*
La robe ne lui va pas bien.	*The dress doesn't suit her.*

If *aller* is used in compound tenses with the same meaning, the past participle *allé* can be replaced by *été*:

Cette robe ne lui va pas bien et d'ailleurs ne lui a jamais bien été.	*This dress doesn't suit her and moreover has never suited her.*

Or Cette robe ... ne lui est jamais bien allée.

> *Aller* + infinitive can have a fictitious or a metaphoric quality, as in English (*go and* + verb), and there is nearly always a negative suggestion here:

Pourvu que Jeanne n'aille pas se fâcher.	*Provided that Jeanne doesn't go and get angry.*
N'allez pas vous imaginer que je suis contente.	*Don't you go and imagine I am happy.*
Ne va pas penser que je le ferai demain.	*Don't go and think I'll do it tomorrow.*

> *Aller pour* is used in theatrical indications:

Il va pour l'embrasser mais elle le repousse.	*He makes as though to kiss her but she repels him.*
Elle va pour lui répondre, puis elle y renonce.	*She makes as though to reply to him, but she withdraws.*

> *Aller* + the infinitive of *aller* is not unusual, and is not limited to R1 usage, however pleonastic this construction may appear:

Je vais aller le voir.	*I'm going to see him / I'm going to go and see him.*

Mauriac, stylist if ever there was one, writes in his *Journal*:

Nous allons aller aux sources de la Hure (1932–1939, p. 333).	*We are going (to go) to the source of the Hure.*

One even comes across *Nous allons y aller*, with an intercalated pronoun.

Note that the verb *aller* cannot usually stand independently, as in English, if a simple direction is involved. It requires at least a pronoun like *y*:

J'y vais maintenant; On y va?; Allons-y!	*I go now; We go now?; Let's go!*

But, if the future occurs, one would say and write, omitting the *y*:

J'ai reçu un courriel de Paris. J'irai la semaine prochaine.	*I've received an email from Paris. I'll go there next week.*

Aller also serves as a noun:

un match aller et un match retour	*a first leg and a second leg*

Match aller here does not necessarily mean an *away game*, notwithstanding the apparent implication of *aller*.

J'ai pris un aller pour New York.	*I took a one-way ticket for New York.*
J'a pris deux allers pour Miami.	*I took two one-way tickets for Miami.*
J'ai pris deux allers-retours.	*I took two returns.*

One comes across *des aller et retour* and even *des aller*, but such constructions are to be discouraged.

38.2 Idiomatic uses of *avoir*

In numerous uses of *avoir*, this verb takes a noun while in English the verb *to be*, which largely corresponds to these uses, takes an adjective. If the noun is qualified in any way, one would have expected an adjective to carry out this function, as in Spanish and Italian (*Tengo mucha hambre, Ho molta fame*), but this is not the case, and there is a lack of logic here. *Très*, for example, is used: *J'ai chaud* (I am hot) | *faim* (hungry) | *froid* (cold) | *honte* (ashamed) | *peur* (frightened) | *raison* (right) | *soif* (thirsty) | *sommeil* (sleepy) | *tort* (wrong) > *J'ai très chaud/faim/froid/honte* and so on (*très* is not used with *besoin, hâte, raison, tort*). It may be added that, once upon a time, and still in certain areas, one finds *J'ai grand faim/froid* (and no *e* for *grand*). If the noun is qualified in other ways (not with *très* alone), one would have recourse to the indefinite article: *J'avais une faim de loup*; *J'avais une honte à faire rougir la fille la plus effrontée*; *J'avais une peur bleue*. This also applies to the verb *faire* below, but with *chaud* and *froid* these constructions are not possible.

These expressions may also combine with adverbs of comparison: *aussi, plus, assez, si, trop*:

J'ai aussi peur que vous.	I am as frightened as you.
Elle avait si peur qu'elle ne voulait pas partir.	She was so frightened that she wouldn't leave.
J'avais trop faim pour manger plus tard.	I was too hungry to eat later.
Le jeune homme avait très envie d'elle.	The young man really wanted her.
J'ai aussi faim que toi / si faim que...	I am as hungry as you / so hungry that...

One can also say:

| J'ai bien/fort soif. | I am very thirsty. |

Further idiomatic uses of *avoir* with no article: *avoir affaire à* (to have to deal with, to face), *avoir besoin de* (to need), *avoir envie de* (to want something, to do something), *avoir pitié de* (to pity, to take pity on), *avoir soin de* (to take care of).

In conformity with other Romance languages (Spanish = *tener*, Italian = *avere*), French requires *avoir* when referring to age, while English has the verb *to be*. This applies to *ans/années* and *âge*: *Audrey a vingt ans/une vingtaine d'années*; *Elle a quel âge, la petite?* In the first of these examples, an English-speaker could say *Audrey is twenty*, but not so in French. Yet, if *ans* has already been used, it could be omitted for the second time, when the pronoun *en* replaces it: *Daniel a dix ans, mais sa sœur en a trois.*

Avoir + noun can express a physical reaction, often in the preterit or perfect:

| Virginie a eu un geste désapprobateur. | Virginie made a disapproving gesture. |
| Marine eut un mouvement de plaisir. | Marine showed a pleasurable gesture. |

En avoir pour corresponds to the idea of time or money available, or effort required:

| "Tu peux venir maintenant?" "Non, j'en ai pour une petite heure." | "Can you come now?" "No, I've got just about an hour's work." |
| "La voiture? J'en ai pour quinze mille euros." | "The car? It'll cost me fifteen thousand euros." |

Avoir is only used in the passive with the idea of *to trick*, *to dupe*, and here it is R1 and very common:

| J'ai encore été eu(e). | I've been tricked/had again. |

Note how *avoir* may be used with the idea of having someone to a meal, or speaking to someone on the telephone:

Je les aurai demain à dîner.	*We have them for an evening meal tomorrow.*
Jeanne ? Je viens de l'avoir au téléphone.	*Jeanne? I've just spoken to her on the phone.*

Avoir de quoi + infinitive suggests having the necessary implements/tools to do something:

Tu peux le contacter. Tu as de quoi écrire.	*You can contact him. You have all you need for writing.*
J'ai crevé. Heureusement que j'ai de quoi réparer la crevaison.	*I've gotten a puncture. Fortunately, I have the tools to mend it.*

Avoir l'air + adjective = *to appear, to seem, to look*. The adjective in this case may vary in agreement, either with the subject of *avoir* or with *air*, which is masculine. Some grammarians discern a fine difference in meaning between agreement and non-agreement, but generally speaking this difference is ignored. When referring to persons, here are the two possibilities:

Cette dame a l'air douce/doux.	*This lady seems gentle.*
Les filles ont l'air heureux/heureuses.	*The girls look happy.*

But one can only say, and here there is agreement because of *la force des choses*:

Elle a l'air enceinte.	*She looks pregnant.*

A female is pregnant. An *air* cannot be pregnant.

When referring to things, both possibilities exist, but non-agreement is much more common:

Cette maison a l'air délabré(e).	*This house looks in a state of disrepair.*
Ces propositions ont l'air sérieux/sérieuses.	*These proposals look serious.*

However, if *air* itself is followed by a complement, agreement is made with *air*:

La ville avait l'air tout à la fois animé et désœuvré d'un dimanche.	*The town looked both lively and free and easy just as on a Sunday.*
Les gens avaient l'air stupide que donne la surprise.	*People looked stupid, a result of surprise.*

Similarly with the expression *trouver à quelqu'un l'air*:

Je ne lui avais pas trouvé l'air triste mais fatigué.	*I hadn't found her sad, but tired.*

Two possibilities exist in different parts of a sentence, but non-agreement is preferable:

Elle a l'air faux/fausse, mais elle est loyale.	*She looks devious, but she is honest.*

And logically:

Si je n'ai pas l'air fatigué(e), c'est que je ne suis pas fatiguée.	*If I don't seem tired, it's because I'm not tired.*

Avoir beau + infinitive suggests *to do something in vain*:

Ils ont beau se plaindre, personne ne les écoute.	*They complain as much as they like, no one listens to them.*
J'ai beau leur demander de se taire, ça continue.	*I ask them in vain to keep quiet, they go on and on.*

Avoir à + infinitive marks an obligation but carries less compulsion than *falloir* or *devoir*:

J'ai un travail à finir.	*I have some work to finish.*
J'ai une visite à faire / à faire une visite.	*I have to make a visit.*
Il a sa famille à nourrir.	*He has a family to feed.*
Tu n'as rien à répondre ?	*Have you nothing to say?*

N'avoir qu'à = *I/You/etc. only have to*:

Virginie n'a qu'à m'avertir.	*Virginie only has to let me know.*
Si tu ne peux pas lui faire visite, tu n'as qu'à lui envoyer un texto / il n'y a qu'à lui envoyer un texto.	*If you can't go and see him, you only have to send him a text message.*

In R1 language, the imperfect of *n'avoir qu'à* is the equivalent of *aurait dû*:

Tu n'avais qu'à prendre le bus.	*You ought to have caught the bus.*
Françoise n'avait qu'à faire attention.	*Françoise ought to have been more careful.*

N'avoir (pas) de cesse que de = *to be doing for evermore*. This expression is of R3 style:

Antoine n'a de cesse que de répéter la même histoire.	*Antoine is forever repeating the same story.*

This expression can take the subjunctive even if the subjects are the same:

Lucile n'aura (pas) de cesse qu'elle n'atteigne son but.	*Lucile will keep trying until she reaches her goal.*

Avoir lieu de | Il y a lieu de = to have grounds for:

David a lieu de se plaindre.	*David has grounds for complaining.*
Il y a lieu de protester.	*There are grounds for protesting.*

Avoir is often used, and more naturally, where *to be* would easily occur in English:

Stéphanie a les yeux bleus.	*Stéphanie's eyes are blue	Stéphanie has blue eyes.*
Louis a le bras cassé.	*Louis's arm is broken	Louis has a broken arm.*

If insistence were required, *être* could be used:

"Céline a les yeux noisette." "Mais non, les yeux de Céline sont bleus."	*"Céline has hazel eyes." "No, Céline's eyes are blue."*

To ask in French: *What's wrong | the matter?*, *avoir* is frequently used:

Qu'est-ce que tu as ?	*What's wrong with you?*
Qu'est-ce qu'elle avait ?	*What was the matter with her?*
Qu'est-ce qu'il y a ?	*What's wrong?*

38.3 Idiomatic uses of *être*

Fortunately for foreign students of French, there is only one verb corresponding to the verb *to be*. Life becomes much more complicated in Italian and Spanish, which offer two possibilities (It: *essere/stare*; Sp: *ser/estar*)

Être can indicate belonging:

Cettte maison est à Valentin.	*This house is Valentin's.*
À qui est ce vélo ?	*Whose bicycle is this?*
Le vélo est à moi.	*The bicycle is mine.*

Être can indicate activity or being involved in something:

Irène est à son travail.	*Irène is at work.*

Être can suggest a tendency towards something:

Le temps est à la pluie/neige.	*The weather is turning to rain/snow.*
L'heure est à l'optimisme.	*Things are becoming optimistic.*
Les prix sont à la baisse/hausse.	*Prices are going down/up.*

Être can express participation in something:

Sophie ne sera pas de la partie / de la fête.	*Sophie won't be there with us / at the party.*

Être can suggest support for or opposition to something:

Sébastien est pour l'indépendance du Québec.	*Sébastien is for Quebec independence.*
Je ne suis pas pour.	*I'm not for (it).*
Elle est contre.	*She's against (it).*

In R3 language, *il est* (*there is/are*) has an archaic resonance:

Il est des souvenirs remplis de tendresse.	*There are memories filled with tenderness.*
Il est des jours amers que je préfère oublier.	*There are bitter moments I prefer to forget.*

Il n'est que de / **Il suffit de** = *You only have to*:

Il n'est que de préciser vos raisons.	*You only have to clarify your reasons.*

N'être pas sans savoir que / **ne pas ignorer que** = *to be aware of*:

Vous n'êtes pas sans savoir que le gouvernement a déjà pris certaines mesures.	*You are certainly aware that the government has already taken certain decisions.*
Ils ne sont pas sans savoir que le résultat des élections sera publié demain.	*They must know that the result of the elections will be published tomorrow.*

A common error here is *n'être pas sans ignorer*, which is the opposite of *sans savoir*.

N'être plus / **avoir cessé d'exister** = *to be no more*. This is used in a high register and euphemistically for *to die*:

Cet âge d'or n'est plus.	*This golden age is no more.*
Mon mari n'est plus.	*My husband has died.*

A contentious issue: *c'est* or *ce sont* – *C'est des pommes vertes* or *Ce sont des pommes vertes*? Much ink has been spilled over this subject. It would be best to simplify matters by arguing that *C'est* is of a lower register than *ce sont*. Both are found in writing.

The use of the pronoun *en* with *être* suggests *to have arrived at*, or *to be at a particular point*:

Nous en sommes où (dans le chapitre)?	*Where are we (in the chapter)?*
C'en est fait de lui / de mon repos.	*It's all up with him / That's my rest done for.*
C'en est trop.	*That's just too much / That takes the biscuit.*
Il en est de ce roman comme de l'autre.	*It's the same with this novel as with the other.*
Il en est de toi comme de lui.	*It's the same for you as for him.*
J'en suis quitte pour la peur.	*I got away with just a fright.*
J'en étais pour ma peine.	*I wasted all my effort.*
Où en es-tu dans tes recherches?	*Where are you in your research?*
J'en suis à la moitié du chemin.	*I am halfway there (often used figuratively).*
Il ne sait plus où il en est.	*He doesn't know where he is (with it).*
Il n'en est rien.	*It's nowhere near the same.*

In a high register, and specifically literary language at that, *être* + *en* = *s'en aller*, and notably in the third-person singular, past historic:

Notre héroïne s'en fut au fleuve.	*Our heroine repaired to the river.*
Paul s'en fut chercher son frère.	*Paul went out to look for his brother.*

Some miscellaneous features:

Cela étant, je vous accorde un délai de deux heures	*That so, I'll grant you a limit of two hours.*
Ainsi soit-il.	*So be it / Amen (with a biblical resonance).*
On est le jeudi 9 mai.	*It's Thursday May 9.*
Toujours est-il que l'équipe n'est pas à la hauteur.	*The fact still remains that the team is not up to it.*
Elle est à court d'argent / d'idées / de souffle / de vivres.	*She's short of money / ideas / breath / food.*
C'est à moi/toi, etc. de lire la première page.	*It's for me/you, etc. to read the first page.*
Je suis d'avis qu'Aurélien s'en ira demain.	*I am of the opinion that Aurélien will go tomorrow.*
Je suis d'avis qu'Aurélien s'en aille demain.	*I am of the opinion that Aurélien should go tomorrow.*

Note that *faire*, not *être*, is used in the following:

Deux et deux font quatre.	*Two and two are four.*

38.4 Idiomatic uses of *faire*

For impersonal uses, see Chapter 39 on impersonal verbs. Fortunately, *faire* covers both *to do* and *to make* in English, two verbs that cause considerable uncertainty for foreign speakers of English.

> Although the letters **ai** produce the open **e** in almost all parts of *faire*, in (*nous*) *faisons* and *faisant* the sound is of a mute **e**.
> *Faire* can suggest *carrying out the role of, to act as*:

Adrienne faisait celle qui n'entend pas.	*Adrienne did not seem to hear.*
Le petit faisait le conducteur.	*The child pretended to be the driver.*
Arrête de faire le con (R1).	*Stop acting like an idiot.*

There are quite a few expressions here: *faire le malin* (*to show off*) | *le mariole* (*to try to be smart*) | *l'imbécile* | *le malade* | *le mort* (in all three cases = *to pretend to be*, although in the last there is the added idea of motionlessness).
Se faire = to become:

Louise s'est faite belle pour la fête.	*Louise dressed up for the party.*
Les deux frères se sont faits marins.	*The two brothers became sailors.*
Bientôt, ils se sont faits vieux/conciliants.	*They aged quickly	They soon became conciliatory.*
Il faut rentrer, il se fait tard.	*We ought to go home, it's getting late.*
Avec la crise économique, l'argent se fait rare.	*With the credit crunch, money is getting scarce.*

Se faire + *subjunctive* = *to happen* (that):

Comment se fait-il que vous soyez en retard ?	*How is it that you are late?*

Or with the indicative:

Comment se fait-il que vous êtes en retard ?	*How is it that you are late?*

Se faire à = *to get used to*.

Les étudiants se sont faits à leurs nouvelles chambres.	*The students have gotten used to their new rooms.*
Il faut s'y faire, coûte que coûte.	*You have to get used to it, at all costs.*
Les deux filles se sont faites à ce travail.	*The two girls got used to their work.*
Tu n'as qu'à te faire à l'idée et c'est simple.	*You only have to get used to the idea and it's simple.*

(Se) faire + *infinitive* = *to have* (something) *done*

Mon père va (se) faire construire une maison.	*My father is going to have a house built.*
Je ferai visiter le parc aux enfants / par les enfants.	*I'll have the children visit the park.*
J'ai fait visiter la ville à tes amis.	*I showed your friends the town.*
Il faut faire voir son intérêt à chacun.	*You have to let each one see where his interest lies.*
Mon frère a fait traverser la rue à un vieillard.	*My brother helped an old man to cross the road.*
Tu as fait manger le petit, chéri?	*Have you fed the baby, dear?*

The translations into English of the six sentences above illustrate how, very often, *faire* does not correspond to *to do/make* in the sense of *to force/oblige*. The last sentence, literally translated, would be: *Have you made the baby eat, dear?*; this would suggest *to force-feed*, which in French could be *alimenter de force*, as with a recalcitrant prisoner.

> *Se faire* + infinitive = *to get* + past participle; this construction often, but not always, has a negative sense, although this does not necessarily suggest an active idea, far from it:

Le chien s'est fait écraser.	*The dog got run over.*
Fais gaffe, tu vas te faire tuer/engueuler.	*Careful, you'll get yourself killed / you'll be told off.*
Qu'est-ce qu'il y a comme jeunes qui se font poignarder en pleine rue.	*There are lots of young people who get stabbed right in the street.*
Mon frère s'est fait arracher une dent.	*My brother had a tooth out.*
Je vais me faire couper les cheveux.	*I'm going to get my hair cut.*

Similarly with a negative connotation: *se faire agresser* (*to get mugged*), *se faire tabasser* (*to get beaten up*), *se faire gronder* (*to be scolded*), *se faire arrêter*, *se faire voler*, *se faire violer* (*to be raped*), *se faire avoir* (*to be tricked*). And with a neutral or positive connotation: *se faire opérer*, *se faire obéir*, *se faire connaître*, *se faire inviter*.

> Note the use of the preposition *de* in the following construction:

Ses parents ont fait une auberge de leur maison.	*His parents turned their house into an inn.*
Tu vas faire de tes souvenirs un livre?	*Are you going to make a book of your memories?*
Papa a fait une lanterne magique de trois ampoules.	*Pop made a magic lantern with three bulbs.*

The equivalent of *to make* + adjective requires *rendre*, not *faire*:

Le maire a rendu publics les accords entre patronat et ouvriers.	*The mayor made public the agreement between employers and the workforce.*
Les études philosophiques l'ont rendue trop sceptique.	*Philosophical studies made her too skeptical.*
Cette décision l'a rendue folle de rage.	*This decision made her mad with anger.*

As with English *to do/have*, *faire* replaces a verb that would need to be repeated:

Laétitia répondit comme les autres l'auraient fait.	*Laétitia replied as the others would have done.*
Émilie chante comme le fait une cantatrice d'opéra.	*Émilie sings as does an opera singer.*
C'est sensationnel que notre équipe l'ait emporté comme ils l'ont fait.	*It's wonderful that our team won as they did.*

But *faire* cannot replace the verbs *avoir* and *être* in the following cases:

Christophe a eu l'audace, comme tu l'as eue autrefois, de m'insulter.	*Christophe had the audacity, as you did once, to insult me.*
Aurélien est distrait comme tu l'es.	*Aurélien is absentminded like you.*

Neither can *devoir*, *falloir*, *pouvoir*, *savoir* or *vouloir* be replaced when they are preceded by *le*:

Frédéric devait lui aussi partir, comme nous le devions.	*Frédéric had to leave as well, as we had to.*
Jeanne voulait aller au théâtre, comme je le voulais.	*Jeanne wanted to go to the theater, as I wanted to.*
J'ai su régler le problème, comme ils l'ont pu.	*I was able to sort out the problem, as they could.*

There is no French equivalent when the substitute verb is stressed, as in English:

"David se défend bien aux échecs." "Oui, en effet."	*"David is good at chess." "Yes, he is."*
"Audrey nage bien." "Eh oui."	*"Audrey swims well." "She sure does."*
"Aurélien n'apprécie pas notre vin." "Mais si."	*"Aurélien doesn't appreciate our wine." "Of course he does."*

The reflexive pronoun after *faire* can be either included or excluded:

Elle l'a fait asseoir / s'asseoir.	*She sat him down.*
Je l'ai fait lever / se lever.	*I had him stand up.*

The reflexive construction suggests more courtesy and is of a higher register than the non-reflexive form. Also note the difference in meaning between *Il la fit s'arrêter* (*He made her stop*) and *Il la fit arrêter* (*He had her arrested*).

Faire with an adjective or noun can give the idea of appearance:

Ça fait très joli.	*That looks nice.*
Elle fait vieille pour son âge.	*She looks old for her age.*
Ces meubles font riche.	*This furniture gives the impression of wealth.*
Cela fait province.	*It reminds you of the provinces.*
Cela fait très vieille dame.	*She looks like a very old lady.*

Ne faire que is an ambiguous expression, and one relies on the context to interpret its meaning:

Denoting repetition or continuity:

Lucile ne fait que dire toujours la même chose.	*Lucile only ever says the same thing.*

Denoting limitation:

Pierre ne fait que répéter ce qu'on lui a dit.	*Pierre only repeats what is said to him.*
Pierre ne fait qu'obéir.	*Pierre merely obeys.*
Pierre ne fait que jouer.	*All Pierre does is play.*

Ne faire que de is used with the idea of *to have just*:

Je ne fais que d'arriver, laisse-moi réfléchir un peu.	*I have only just arrived. Let me think for a moment.*

An opposition is established with *ne pas faire que*:

Papa ne fait pas que te respecter. Il t'admire.	*Pop not only respects you. He admires you.*

Ne pouvoir faire que suggests *not to be able to bring about* (by an intervention, for instance). The subjunctive is normal here:

Je ne puis faire que Jeanne ne soit mécontente.	*I can't persuade Jeanne not to be unhappy.*
Je ne puis faire que mon fils soit heureux.	*I can't bring it about so that my son is happy* (i.e., make my son happy).

Ne faire qu'un = *to be one/united*:

Pierre et Paul / Marie et Louise ne font qu'un.	*Pierre and Paul / Marie and Louise are of the same mind.*

Faire cas de | faire grand cas de | faire peu de cas de = *to attach importance to | great | little importance to*:

Le critique fait cas du style raffiné de l'auteure.	*The critic takes into account the author's refined style.*
Philippe a fait grand cas de son avancement.	*Philippe made a big thing of his promotion.*
Ma collègue a fait peu de cas de ma participation.	*My colleague attached little importance to my participation.*

Also: *ne faire aucun cas de* = *to have no respect/esteem/etc. for*:

Mes amis ne font aucun cas de ma réussite.	*My friends showed no interest in my success.*

Ne pas s'en faire = *not to worry about*:

Il y a trop de travail, mais le directeur ne s'en fait pas.	*There is too much work, but the manager doesn't worry.*
Ne t'en fais pas, je m'en occupe.	*Don't worry, I'll deal with it.*

Faire may be used intransitively:

Laisse-moi faire (Let me do it my way); *avoir fort à faire* (to have a lot to do); *des façons de faire* (ways of acting/dealing); *Fais comme tu veux* (Do as you wish); *Je fais de mon mieux* (I do my best).

Faire en sorte que = *to act in such a way that*:

With the indicative, which points to certainty:

Je fais en sorte que j'arriverai à l'heure.	*I'll see to it that I'm on time.*

With the subjunctive:

Faites en sorte qu'on soit content de vous.	*Act in such a way that we'll be satisfied with you.*

Avoir fort à faire = *to have a lot to do*:

Tu auras fort à faire pour le convaincre.	*You will need to work hard to convince him.*

N'en faire qu'à sa tête = *to do just as you please* (without reference to others):

Tu peux lui suggérer cette solution, mais il n'en fera qu'à sa tête.	*You can suggest this solution to him, but he will only go his own way.*

Faire is used in a high register, often in a literary context, and in the third person (*he/she replied*), but this construction does not usually involve indirect objects such as *lui/leur*:

"Je viendrai," fit-il.	*"I'll come," he said.*

"Une seconde, fit-it, accordez-moi une seconde" (Green 1936, p. 246); "oh! fit-il, scandalisé" (Green 1936, p. 248).

Below is a miscellaneous collection of expressions with *faire: Faire son droit | sa médecine; faire des mathématiques | du grec | une licence | du théâtre | du sport | de l'escrime (fencing); faire de l'essence | le plein* (of gas/petrol); *faire cent kilomètres à l'heure | du cent à l'heure; faire le Canada* (to do Canada); *faire à sa guise | à sa manière* (to do as you please); *faire ses besoins* (to go to the bathroom /restroom); *Mon frère a eu une bonne note et j'en ai fait autant* (My brother had a good mark and I did the same); *Elle fait jeune* (She looks young); *faire de la température* (to have a temperature); *faire une vilaine grippe* (awful flu) | *un infarctus* (heart attack) | *une pleurésie; Ce mur fait trois mètres de haut; Cet homme fait un mètre quatre-vingt-cinq; se faire du mauvais sang | de la bile* (to get upset / to worry); *se faire fort de* (R3; to feel confident about: *Je me fais fort de la convaincre); Il faisait nuit/jour* (It was night/daytime).

Two expressions involving the present participle: *ce faisant* (R3) = having done this; *chemin faisant* = on the way.

Many expressions are constructed thus: *faire* + noun with no intervening article: *faire attention* (to take care); *faire face à* (to face up to | to be opposite); *faire gaffe* (R1 = to be careful); *faire honte à* (to make [someone] feel ashamed); *faire horreur à* (to disgust); *faire peur à* (to frighten); *faire plaisir à* (to please | give pleasure to); *faire signe à* (to beckon); *faire tort à* (to do wrong to).

38.5 Idiomatic uses of *prendre*

Some general uses of *prendre* + noun that sometimes correspond to the English *to take: On prend un objet | de l'argent | une habitude | une raclée* (a beating) | *sa température | un remède | une route | la voiture | le chemin de fer | le train | le bateau | l'avion | le départ | la relève* (to take over, i.e., from someone) | *l'initiative | le large* (to go out into the open sea) | *la porte | des nouvelles | ses aises* (to take it easy) | *de l'âge* (to get older) | *de l'embonpoint* (to get fatter | to put on weight) | *du poids | sa retraite.*

Some expressions of greater complication than immediately above: *prendre quelqu'un comme otage; prendre en otage; prendre au piège; prendre la main dans le sac* (to catch red-handed); *prendre au dépourvu* (to catch unawares); *prendre à témoin* (to call as a witness); *prendre à partie* (to accuse | to attack); *prendre sa source à tel endroit* (to have a source in a certain place: of a river); *prendre quelque chose du bon côté* (in a good-humored way | on the bright side) | *du mauvais côté* (on the bad side); *prendre en bonne/mauvaise part* (to take in good/bad part); *prendre de haut* (to take in an arrogant way); *C'est à prendre ou à laisser* (Take it or leave it); *à tout prendre* (all in all).

Prendre refers to something that happens to someone:

La fièvre l'a prise/reprise / lui a pris/repris.	The fever came over her (again).
Une faiblesse lui a pris.	He suddenly felt weak.
Qu'est-ce qui lui a pris ?	What's come over him/her?

Used impersonally:

| Il lui a pris une rage de dents. | He suddenly got toothache. |
| Il me prend une envie de voyager. | I feel like traveling. |

Prendre + infinitive:

| L'idée lui a pris de venir nous voir. | He got the idea to come to see us. |

Prendre is used of a liquid that solidifies, and here *avoir* is used for action and *être* for state:

La rivière a pris cette nuit.	The river froze last night.
Le fleuve est entièrement pris.	The river is entirely frozen.
La colle prend.	The glue is hardening.
L'huile est prise.	The oil has hardened/thickened.
La crème a pris au fond de la casserole.	The cream has thickened in the saucepan.
La glace commence à prendre : on pourra bientôt aller patiner sur le lac.	The ice has hardened: we'll soon be able to go and skate on the lake.

The same idea applies to plants which take hold in the ground:

| Les pêchers prennent mal ici. | The peach trees don't take root here (in the soil). |
| Cette bouture a pris. | This cutting has taken well. |

Similarly, used figuratively:

| Le vaccin a pris. | The vaccine has taken well / worked / is working. |
| La plaisanterie / Le mensonge a pris. | The joke/lie worked. |

Prendre is used in the sense of *taking someone to be*:

Tu me prends pour un imbécile ?	You take me for an imbecile?
Il se prend pour un poète.	He thinks he's a poet.
Pour qui se prend-il ?	Who does he think he is?

Prendre has the value of *réussir = to succeed* in some contexts:

| Ce mode de communication qu'est Internet a fini par prendre. | This method of communication that is Internet has ended up taking well. |

Prendre may be used of a fire:

Le feu a pris dans le bois.	*The fire started in the wood.*
Le feu ne prend pas. Il y a trop de vent.	*The fire's not lighting. There's too much wind.*

Se prendre à = to get caught in:

Sa robe s'est prise aux épines.	*Her dress got caught in the thorns.*
Son chapeau s'est pris à une branche.	*His hat got caught on/in a branch.*

Se prendre à = to set about (doing something):

Comment faut-il s'y prendre ?	*How do you set about (doing) it?*
Marie s'y est mal prise pour gagner la partie.	*Marie started badly to win the game.*

Se prendre à = to become interested in / attracted by:

Les trois filles se sont prises au jeu.	*The three girls got interested in the game.*

S'en prendre à = to accuse, to incriminate:

On s'en prend à moi comme si j'étais coupable.	*I am accused as if I were guilty.*
Mon père s'est pris au voisin qui fait trop de bruit.	*My father accused the neighbor who makes too much noise.*
Tu ne pourrais t'en prendre qu'à toi-même.	*You can only blame yourself.*

Prendre pour = to take as: prendre pour épouse/époux (to take as a husband/wife); prendre pour arbitre/associé; prendre une personne pour une autre.
Prendre sur soi = to assume responsibility:

Nous prendrons sur nous votre faute.	*We take the responsibility for your error.*

Prendre part à = to take part in:

Nous prendrons part à la fête.	*We'll come to the party.*

38.6 Some remarks, with examples, on the influence of English in the linguistic processes of Quebec French

The English of the United States and Canada is clearly exerting a marked effect on the French of Quebec. The linguistically aware feel outrage and see in this process a deleterious invasion of essentially foreign words and expressions that are damaging the warp and woof of the purity of the French language, especially since, in numerous ways, the French of Quebec has retained much of the flavor of former times. The French of Quebec sometimes recalls, in pronunciation and vocabulary, the eighteenth and nineteenth centuries of metropolitan France. We are witnessing a strange tension between traditionalism and the need to modernize the French language (e.g., *auteur/docteur* > *auteure/docteure*) while, at the same time, this exposure to English is provoking indignation. A language has to evolve to avoid ossification, witness the now accepted *réaliser*, which is a calque from the English in the sense of *to understand*, and even words like the noun *forcing*, a creation that has been borrowed from English but does not exist in English with this meaning. There follows a list of expressions that are currently in use in Quebec but are considered *fautives* because they are literal translations of the English. The authors do not claim to recommend any of these turns of phrase, but merely offer them for what they are. A "purer" French expression, or expressions, is/are placed alongside the Anglicism. Bear in mind that the terms in this list are merely representative of an ever-growing catalog of terms that, according to many observers, are plaguing the French language:

Faulty/incorrect expression	More acceptable expression
aller en appel	en appeler, faire appel
aller en élections	déclencher des élections
aller en grève	faire la grève
aller sous presse	mettre sous presse
faire application	postuler à un emploi / poser sa candidature
faire du sens	avoir du sens
faire sa part	apporter sa contribution / collaborer
prendre action	agir / intervenir / passer aux actes
prendre des procédures	poursuivre (en justice)
prendre la parole de quelqu'un	se fier à la parole de quelqu'un
prendre le vote	procéder au scrutin
prendre offense	se froisser / se vexer
prendre place	avoir lieu / se passer / se tenir
prendre un cours	suivre un cours / s'inscrire à un cours
prendre une chance	courir le risque / prendre le risque
prendre une marche	se promener / faire un tour

39

Impersonal verbs / Les verbes impersonnels

The following passage centers on a spring visit to Prague, capital of Bohemia and the Czech Republic. We pass from the freezing temperatures of March to the hurly-burly of downtown Prague and then on to some cultural references. Emphasis is placed on impersonal verbs, which are highlighted. Note that these verbs are introduced by *il* or *ça*, the latter being much more informal. Some translations are provided, and Czech is occasionally used for local color.

Un printemps à Prague

Nous avons apprécié la Bohème. **Il ne s'agit** ni de l'opéra en quatre actes de Puccini ni de la chanson « La Bohème » interprétée par Charles Aznavour, mais de la province de Bohème. Prague est la capitale de cette province située en Europe centrale. **Il y a** dix ans, Prague était nommée capitale européenne de la culture. Lors de notre séjour à Prague, par moments, **il soufflait un vent terrible. Il faisait un froid de canard** [It was bitterly cold]. **Il était** sur le point de neiger. Heureusement, **il n'a pas neigé** mais **il grêlait** et **il gelait. Il bruinait, il pluviotait** ou **il pleuvait à grosses gouttes. Il faisait moins de cinq degrés**, et la nuit **il faisait encore plus froid**. Comme dit le proverbe : après la pluie, le beau temps.

Il était recommandé de ne pas emprunter l'autoroute pour se rendre à Prague pendant la durée des travaux. Et les Pragois ? **Ça a roulé toute la nuit** [There was traffic all night] ! **Il faisait nuit noire ! Ça grouillait** le soir dans la ville [The city was heaving with people]. **Ça sentait bon** lorsqu'on s'approchait des restaurants. **Ça picolait** [People were drinking away] ! **Ça braillait** [People were hollering] ! **Ça bavardait ! Ça racontait** des histoires. En fait nous ne comprenions pas le tchèque. La seule chose que nous savions dire c'était *Dobrý den*, c'est-à-dire: **Bonjour ! Il n'y avait pas là de quoi fouetter un chat** [But it's no big deal]. Les Tchèques aiment recevoir et faire la fête. On chantait souvent avec entrain la fameuse comptine [nursery rhyme] : « **Il pleut, il mouille**, C'est la fête à la grenouille, **Il pleut, il fait beau temps**, C'est la fête au paysan. »

Le centre de la capitale tchèque est un lieu mémorable de l'histoire de la Bohème. La vieille ville est magnifique. **Il se passe des événements importants** dans le château de Prague (Hradčany), résidence du président de la République tchèque. Ce château royal est d'une grandeur majestueuse. Le Pont Charles (Karlův most) est le symbole emblématique [iconic] de Prague. Tout au long du pont que l'on traversait en flânant pour rejoindre la vieille ville, Staré Město, des statues baroques trônaient. Parmi les plus célèbres, je me souviens de celle du patron de la nation tchèque, Saint Venceslas. **Il est d'autres monuments** dont je pourrais recommander la visite. Le quartier juif de Prague est un endroit qu'**il vaut la peine** de visiter avec ses synagogues et son mystérieux cimetière juif. Les musées des célèbres compositeurs Bedřich Smetana et Antonín Dvořák méritent le détour. **Il en est de même** pour la maison natale de Franz Kafka. **Il suffit de** lire quelques romans de ce célèbre écrivain tchèque pour se rendre compte d'une situation kafkaïennne qui traduit une complexité extrême. **Il s'agit souvent d'une** atmosphère absurde, inquiétante et cauchemardesque. **Il ne faut pas oublier** le roman satirique de Jaroslav Hašek, *Le bon soldat Švejk,* qui tourne en dérision l'esprit militaire. La présence permanente de Jaroslav Hašek et de sa création romanesque est assurée par le restaurant Hostinec U Kalicha que l'auteur fréquentait avec ses amis, et qu'il **convient de visiter** pour se restaurer.

Impersonal verbs have neither subject nor object. Whatever they represent as being or as going on, nothing is suggested as taking any active part in it. There are some examples of such verbs in English, and French, like Spanish and Italian, has more that are either always or occasionally used. The pronoun *it* is a mere form of expression in English, but it does not represent the actor. Interestingly and helpfully, the English *it* corresponds to the French *il*. This use of *il* indicates clearly that impersonal verbs are only used in the third-person singular, and should be distinguished from verbs related to things (e.g., *consister*) or animals (e.g., *coasser*) which rarely appear outside the third-person singular and plural, unless an author has recourse to a metaphoric use. The verbs in question here are sometimes associated with weather or natural phenomena, witness the witticism displayed by Toto, the typical lad in a French elementary/primary school who plays with the ambiguity of the word *temps* (weather and tenses): "Le maître demande à Toto de lui conjuguer le verbe *savoir* à tous les temps. Toto répond: Je sais qu'il neige. Je sais qu'il pleut. Je sais qu'il gèle. Je sais qu'il tonne. Je sais qu'il vente, etc."

There follows a list of impersonal verbs related to the weather:

Il bruine/bruinait/bruinera.	*It drizzles / is drizzling / was drizzling / will drizzle.*
If floconne / floconnait / floconnera.	*It snows / is snowing / was snowing / will snow.*

Il flotte/flottait/flottera (R1).	*It rains / is raining / was raining / will rain.*
Il gèle/gelait/gèlera.	*It freezes / is freezing / was freezing / will freeze.*
Il grêle/grêlait/grêlera.	*It hails / is hailing / was hailing / will hail.*
Il dégèle/dégelait/dégèlera.	*It thaws / is thawing / was thawing / will thaw.*
Il mouille/mouillait/mouillera (R1).	*It rains / is raining / was raining / will rain.*
Il neige/neigeait/neigera.	*It snows / is snowing / was snowing / will snow.*
Il pleut/pleuvait/pleuvra.	*It rains / is raining / was raining / will rain.*
Il pleuviote/pleuviotait/ pleuviotera.	*It drizzles / is drizzling / was drizzling / will drizzle.*
Il vente/ventait/ventera.	*It is windy / was windy / will be windy.*

Three remarks flow from this:

1. In most cases, *ça* can replace *il* in R1 language. Indeed, sometimes, one would only hear *ça*: *ça bruine, ça caille* (*it's freezing*; *il* would not be used here), *ça chauffe* (*it's getting hot*; *il* would not be used here), *ça cogne* (*the sun is strong*; *il* would not be used here), *ça gèle, ça grêle, ça mouille* (*il* would not be used here), *ça pleuviote / pluviote, ça souffle* (*it's very windy*; *il* would not be used here), *ça tape* (= *ça cogne), ça tempête* (*it's blowing a gale*; *il* would not be used here). One would only say *il floconne*, however.
2. It is most unlikely that certain tenses of the above would be used. The future of *bruiner, flotter, mouiller, pleuvioter/pluvioter* fall into this category while *gèlera, grêlera* and *pleuvra* are in common use.
3. Semi-auxiliary verbs can precede these verbs of weather which then assume an infinitive form, and the construction remains essentially the same: *Il va pleuvoir*; *Il vient de pleuvoir*; *Il commence à pleuvoir*; *Il devrait pleuvoir*; *Il semblait pleuvoir*; *Il a cessé de pleuvoir*; *Il risque de pleuvoir*.

These impersonal verbs may be followed by a real subject, but the verb remains in the singular: *Il pleut de grosses gouttes*; *Il pleut des cordes / des hallebardes* (*It is pouring down*); *Il neigeait de gros flocons*; *Il neigeait de fines paillettes*; *Il soufflait un vent terrible / une bise cinglante*; *Il ne pousse rien dans le désert*; *Il tombait une neige fine*.

This construction may also be construed metaphorically, but here the style is R3 and very literary and poetic. Speaking of Napoleon who sent him into exile, Hugo writes: *Il pleut des livres et des journaux partout*; and the same author writes: *Il neige des feuilles*. A contemporary of Hugo, Musset, writes: *Il pleut des guitares et des messages secrets*.

Faire + adjective is used for the weather, where English uses *is*:

Il fait/faisait/fera beau.	*It is / was / will be fine weather.*
Il fait/faisait/fera bon.	*It is / was / will be pleasant weather.*
Il fait/faisait/fera étouffant.	*It is / was / will be stifling.*
Il fait/faisait/fera frais.	*It feels / felt / will feel fresh.*
Il fait/faisait/fera/froid.	*It is / was / will be cold.*
Il fait/faisait/fera doux.	*It is / was / will be pleasant.*
Il fait/faisait/fera chaud.	*It is / was / will be hot.*
Il fait/faisait/fera lourd.	*It is / was / will be sultry.*
Il fait/faisait/fera noir.	*It is / was / will be dark.*
Il fait/faisait/fera sombre.	*It is / was / will be gloomy.*
Il fait/faisait/fera vilain.	*The weather is / was / will be awful.*
Il fait/faisait/fera sec.	*It is / was / will be dry.*
Il fait/faisait/fera humide.	*It is / was / will be wet/damp/humid.*
Il fait 15 degrés.	*It is fifteen degrees.*

As with *avoir* (see Chapter 38), if the noun is qualified in any way, the indefinite article is required:

Il faisait une chaleur torride.	*It was desperately hot.*
Il faisait un froid de canard.	*It was intensely cold.*
Il faisait un temps splendide.	*It was splendid weather.*

In R1 language, the adjective or adjectival expression may be omitted, but with rising intonation. The effect is the same: *Il faisait une chaleur / un froid*... Note that one does not use *temps* in combination with *faire* as in English. Say: *Il fait beau*, as indicated above.

Faire + noun is also used for the weather: *Il fait du soleil / du verglas* (icy) */ du vent / de la pluie / du brouillard / de l'orage / des éclairs / un temps de chien / un temps épouvantable / clair de lune / grand soleil.*

Faire is also used for *jour* and *nuit*: *Il fait nuit / jour* = It is night / dark / day(time); *Il fait nuit noire*; *Il faisait noir comme dans un four* = It was as black as pitch.

Il est is also used for expressions of time (*c'est* is of a lower register):

To indicate a particular moment: *Il/C'est midi/minuit/tôt/tard*; *Il/C'est sept heures. Lève-toi !*

To indicate an obligation: *Il est temps de partir pour l'aéroport / Il est temps qu'on parte pour l'aéroport*; *Il est l'heure de coucher les enfants/que les enfants se couchent.*

Il y a + noun or pronoun is a common impersonal construction: *Écoute ! Il y a quelqu'un à la porte*; *Il y avait vraiment beaucoup de monde à la plage*; *Il y a du soleil aujourd'hui*; *Tu as l'air triste. Qu'est-ce qu'il y a ?*

Il y a is used for *ago* and distance: *J'ai rencontré Léa il y a dix ans au cours d'un voyage en Thaïlande*; *Il y a facilement cinq mille kilomètres entre les côtes est et ouest des USA*. In the spoken language, *il y a* can be reduced to *y a*: *Y avait rien dans l'armoire*; *Y a des poires dans la cuisine ?* The literary equivalent of *il y a* is *il est*: *Il est des parfums frais dans le jardin*; *Il est d'autres monuments dont je pourrais recommander la visite*; *Il fut un temps où les soldats voyageaient avec leurs familles*; *Il était une fois une princesse...* (*Once upon a time...*).

Il y a à + infinitive has roughly the idea of *can*, or suggests availability: *Il y a à parier que Stéphanie réussira*; *Il y a à boire et à manger*; *Il n'y a qu'à parler et on t'obéira*.

Notice also the expression *il y a de quoi* = *There are the facilities | is the wherewithal* (to do something): *Il y a de quoi manger dans le frigo*; *Il n'y a pas là de quoi fouetter un chat* (*It's no big deal*).

Il faut = *it is necessary, I/you/he/she, etc. have to* can be:

followed by an infinitive: *Il faut/fallait/faudra venir ce soir*;
followed by a noun: *Il faut un permis de conduire pour conduire une voiture*;
followed by a subordinate clause with *que* + subjunctive: *Il faut que tout soit prêt ce week-end*; *Il faudra que tu reviennes avant ce soir*.

The reflexive verb *s'agir* = *to be a question of* is very common:

to point to a subject or theme: *Dans La peste de Camus, il s'agit d'une interminable lutte contre la souffrance*;
to express advice or an obligation (= *il faut*): *Après tant de discussions, il s'agit de prendre une décision*; *Il s'agissait de savoir si tu peux réussir ton examen*; *Il s'agit que tu fasses tes devoirs tout de suite*. Although the subject can only ever be *il*, a present participle is also possible: *S'agissant de son retour, je lui ai dit que je ne serais pas à la maison*; and there is no reason why the infinitive could not be used, notwithstanding resistance from some grammarians: *Il doit s'agir d'affaires importantes dans cette réunion*; *Il va s'agir d'être prudent*; *Il semblait s'agir de brumes matinales*.

Il est + adjective is frequently used (in R1 language, one very often hears *C'est* + adjective):

Il est + adjective + *de* + infinitive: *Il est normal/important/impératif d'avoir ses papiers en règle*; *C'est difficile de répondre à cette question*; *Il est* + adjective + *que*: *Il/C'était évident que l'enfant pleurait parce qu'elle avait mal*; *Il/C'est normal que tu souffres après une telle chute*.

Verbs + *que* + indicative or subjunctive (the choice of the mood depends upon the meaning of the verb): *il importe | paraît | arrive | semble | vaut mieux | se peut | suffit* **que**:

Indicative: *Il paraît que le vin sera excellent cette année*; *Il me semble que tu as maigri*
Subjunctive with *arriver*, often with a present or future idea, but much less in the past, since uncertainty is suggested: *Il arrive qu'on puisse patiner sur le lac/que mon père parte avant moi*; *Il semble que nos amis soient déjà partis*

Il importe / *vaut mieux* / *suffit* always take a subjunctive, and not the indicative, although an infinitive is possible: *Il importe que Jean vienne ce soir* /
Peu importe que Jean vienne ce soir; *Il vaut mieux que tu le fasses maintenant* /
Il vaut mieux le faire maintenant; *Il suffit que tu lises l'introduction* / *Il suffit
de lire l'introduction*; *Il importe d'envoyer le chèque dès que possible.*
Mieux vaut may replace *il vaut mieux*: *Mieux vaut préparer le repas tout de
suite.*

Aller de soi, *convenir*, *dépendre*, *servir* and *tenir* also have impersonal possibilities, and again the indicative or subjunctive would be used according
to meaning: *Il va de soi* (It goes without saying) *que l'auteur évite cette question
brûlante*; *Il convient que tu le lui dises tout de suite*; *Il a été convenu que les ouvriers
se mettent en grève*; *Il a été convenu de se mettre en grève*; *Il n'a pas dépendu de moi
que l'affaire réussisse ou échoue*; *À quoi me sert-il que je paie tout de suite ? Il ne tient
plus qu'au capitaine de se prononcer sur l'événement* (It only remains for).

Impersonal verbs can be followed by a "real subject" (see also above
for a similar application with respect to the weather); the real subject is
the subject placed after the verb. The impersonal construction lends less
importance to the subject and insists on the verb: *Il reste quelques places dans
le train de 14 heures* (= *Quelques places restent*); *Il me manque cinq euros pour
acheter ce livre* (= *Cinq euros me manquent*); *Il suffit de quelques minutes pour faire
cuire ce plat surgelé* (= *Quelques minutes suffisent*); *En Europe il naît moins d'enfants
qu'au dix-neuvième siècle* (= *Moins d'enfants naissent*); *Il nage une pomme de terre
dans la sauce* (= *une pomme de terre nage*); *Il m'est arrivé un accident* (= *Un accident
m'est arrivé*); *Il s'y ajoutait d'autres griefs* (= *D'autres griefs s'y ajoutaient*); *Il sortait
du pus de la plaie* (= *Du pus sortait de la plaie*); *Il existait entre eux une grande
tendresse* (= *Une grande tendresse existait entre eux*); *Il se fit un bruit de bottes sur
le trottoir* (= *Un bruit de bottes se fit sur le trottoir*); *Il ne sert à rien d'essayer de la
convaincre* (= *Essayer de la convaincre ne sert à rien*).

Constructions with a verb in the passive or reflexive form are characteristic of administrative or newspaper language: *Il est rappelé qu'il est interdit
de fumer*; *Il a été décidé de limiter la vitesse sur les routes* (= *On a décidé de*); *Il
est recommandé de ne pas emprunter l'autoroute A10 pendant la durée des travaux*
(= *On recommande de*); *Il a été prouvé que le tabac cause de nombreux cancers* (=
On a prouvé que); *Il est écrit devant la barrière : "Entrée interdite* / *Défense d'entrer"*;
Selon qu'il est écrit dans la Bible, tu ne commettras pas . . . ; *Il est généralement admis
qu'une bourse est nécessaire pour l'étudiant pauvre*; *Il s'est produit une explosion
dans une usine de produits chimiques* (= *Une explosion s'est produite*); *Il se passe
des événements importants* (= *Des événements importants se passent*); *Il se faisait
un grand tapage* (= *Un grand tapage se faisait*); *Il se fait une nouvelle estimation du nombre d'habitants* (= *Une nouvelle estimation se fait*). Notice that the
impersonal form of the verb does not agree with the subject.

Many other verbs are used impersonally when preceded by *ça*: *Ça sentait
l'ail* / *la fumée* / *le feu*; *Ça brûle depuis deux jours.* This extremely widespread

and colloquial use of *ça* may be applied in two very specific ways which can overlap. It suggests intensity and/or lots of people: *Ça puait là-dedans*; *Ça schlingue* (R1 = *It stinks / pongs*); *Ça va barder!* (*It's going to be tough! / Watch out!*); *Ça a roulé toute la nuit* (*There was a lot of traffic all night*); *Ça grouillait* (*There were lots of people*; if this expression were used of insects, for instance, it would be more standard R2, *to swarm*); *Ça picolait* (*Lots of people were drinking a lot / knocking it back*). Also: *Ça braillait / bavardait/racontait des histoires*; of plants one could say: *Ça poussait partout*; of a strong sun: *Ça cogne*; of time or a person on a bike: *Ça file*; of people snoring: *Ça ronflait*; and so on. The intensity increases with the expression *Qu'est-ce que ça*, as in *Qu'est-ce que ça a roulé/picolé/bavardé/ronflé* and so on.

   C'est + noun + *de* or *que* also has an impersonal application: *C'est un outrage aux mœurs que de déféquer en pleine rue*; *C'est votre droit de vous taire*; *C'est mon devoir de parler*; *C'est un trésor que la santé*.

40

Verbs of perception + infinitive or a subordinate clause / Les verbes de perception + infinitif ou une proposition subordonnée

The first two paragraphs of the following passage describe the glories of Norwegian natural beauty, as experienced by passengers on a cruise liner (*croisiéristes*). The third concentrates on the social activities of the Norwegians. Note how verbs of perception may be followed by an infinitive or a subordinate clause introduced by *qui*. Much less common would be the use of the gerund as in English. Note also that the infinitive could follow the verb of perception immediately. The first sentence may be construed as *on ne voit pas se coucher le soleil*. Equally, the first sentence of the second paragraph could be written *aiment observer changer de couleur les eaux glaciales*. Furthermore, in the last sentence of the second paragraph, there are two consecutive infinitives following *imaginait*. The important elements are highlighted in bold. Some translations are given.

Les fjords de Norvège
Dans certaines régions de Norvège on **ne voit pas** le soleil **se coucher**. Nous **contemplions** avec étonnement le soleil de minuit **qui ne finissait pas de rayonner** dans les régions polaires. Les fjords font également partie du paysage norvégien. On **entrevoyait** [glimpsed] au loin les côtes sauvages scandinaves **qui se dessinaient** [stood out]. On **entendait** les oiseaux de mer **percer** des cris stridents et **tournoyer** [wheel around] au-dessus de nos têtes. La nature occupe une place importante dans la vie des Norvégiens.

À la belle saison, les touristes aiment **observer** les eaux glaciales **changer** de couleur, à tel moment d'un vert transparent et lumineux, à un autre moment d'un beau bleu clair. Un cadre exceptionnel et unique marque avec admiration les croisiéristes dont nous faisions partie. Nous **écoutions chanter** les oiseaux. Nous **imaginions** les fjords **qui surplombaient** [overhung] le paysage à l'époque des glaciers polaires. Les paysages norvégiens se **voient apprécier** en toute sérénité. Ils sont d'une beauté époustouflante [staggering]. Nous **voyions** avec un œil nouveau les côtes rocheuses **se profiler**. On **regardait** avec curiosité **s'animer** les villages de pêcheurs. On **imaginait entendre jouer** *Peer*

Gynt, musique de scène de Edvard Grieg qui accompagne la pièce de théâtre de Ibsen du même nom.

Nous **sentions** un délicieux arôme de café **qui chatouillait** notre odorat. Nous avions passé la soirée à savourer des spécialités norvégiennes à base de poisson frais, à **écouter** un groupe folklorique norvégien **chanter**, et à les **voir danser** dans leur costume traditionnel appelé le « bunad ». On pouvait **apercevoir** au loin les magnifiques couleurs de cette tenue traditionnelle **se mélanger** entre-elles. Les Norvégiens, lors de cérémonies, comme le baptême, le mariage ou d'autres grandes occasions, **aiment voir** leurs concitoyens **se parer** [embellish themselves] de leur costume local. Notre bain culturel en Norvège a éveillé au plus profond de nous des sensations agréables et inoubliables.

A certain number of verbs, essentially those expressing feelings or sensations, are frequently followed by an infinitive which performs the function of a direct complement. The following infinitive normally has a direct object, but not always, as would be the case of an impersonal verb. Other features to bear in mind are register (indicated in the examples below) and the possible use of a subordinate clause which can, in many instances, replace the infinitive, or modify the word order.

40.1 Verbs of seeing: *contempler, entrevoir, observer, regarder, voir*

J'ai passé le soir à contempler tournoyer les oiseaux (R3) / à contempler les oiseaux tournoyer / à contempler les oiseaux qui tournoyaient au ciel.	*I spent the evening watching the birds wheeling in the sky.*
Elle entrevit sortir l'animal de la brume (R3) / l'animal sortir de la brume / l'animal qui sortait de la brume.	*She glimpsed the animal coming out of the mist.*
Les touristes observaient dormir le lion (R3) / observaient le lion dormir / observaient le lion qui dormait.	*The tourists observed the lion sleeping.*
Elle regardait travailler les ouvriers (R3) / les ouvriers travailler / les ouvriers qui travaillaient.	*She watched the workmen working.*
Nous voyions courir les enfants (R3) / les enfants courir / les enfants qui couraient.	*We saw the children running.*

Word order is of great importance here. For instance, if an adverbial expression of place were added to, say, *Les touristes observaient dormir le lion*, one would doubtless read, for balance's sake: *Les touristes observaient le lion dormir dans la clairière. Dormir* would come after *lion*. Similarly, *Nous voyions les enfants courir dans le parc* would be preferable to *Nous voyions courir les enfants dans le parc*. Word order with verbs of perception is therefore variable.

40.2 Verbs of sound

J'entendais chanter les oiseaux / les oiseaux chanter / les oiseaux qui chantaient.	*I heard the birds singing.*
Elle écoutait babiller son bébé / son bébé babiller / son bébé qui babillait.	*She listened to her baby gurgling.*

Entendre does not necessarily have a noun or direct object as part of its complement, as in:

On entendait marcher dans le couloir / chanter dans le jardin.	*We could hear someone walking in the corridor / singing in the garden.*
J'ai entendu frapper/appeler à la porte.	*I heard someone knocking/calling at the door.*
J'ai entendu pleuvoir à verse.	*I heard it pouring down.*

40.3 Verb of smell

Je sentais monter un parfum léger de lilas / un parfum léger de lilas qui montait.	*I smelled a slight lilac perfume rising.*

It is highly unlikely that, in the first case, *monter* would follow *un parfum léger de lilas*, unless an adverbial expression of place for example were added: *Je sentais un parfum léger de lilas monter du jardin.*

40.4 Verbs of wishing

Je souhaitais entendre exprimer l'émotion de sa musique.	*I wished to hear expressed the emotion of her music.*
Nous désirions voir jouer sa meilleure pièce.	*We wanted to see his best play put on.*

41

Subordinate clauses of time /
La proposition subordonnée de temps

The following passage describes the majestic mountain scenery offered by the *route Napoléon*, from Nice to Grenoble. Of notable concern here are the various subordinate clauses introduced by conjunctions. Generally speaking, we observe a range of tenses in the indicative, with only one in the subjunctive, required by *avant que*. There is also an infinitive (*avant de s'engager*). Note how the future occurs several times in the very last sentence. The conjunctions and their concomitant verbs appear in bold. Some translations are given.

Grenoble–Nice : la route Napoléon

Si vous **souhaitez** vous rendre sur la Côte d'Azur, il convient de parcourir cette belle route pour découvrir et contempler le paysage spectaculaire en partant de Grenoble, la capitale des Alpes. **Lorsque** nous **prenons** la route Napoléon, nous suivons sur des centaines de kilomètres un circuit touristique de Grenoble à Nice. Cet itinéraire, devenu historique, fut emprunté de Nice à Grenoble par l'Empereur **quand** il **revint** de l'île d'Elbe en 1815 pour s'emparer du pouvoir **avant de s'engager** dans la funeste bataille de Waterloo en Belgique. **Depuis que** nous **avons goûté** au grand calme du paysage, nous éprouvons un plaisir intense à faire et refaire cette route. Nous avons une certaine prédilection pour ce parcours, à la belle saison, en présence d'amis. **Avant que** la neige **ne tombe**, la route est praticable pour les voitures. **Comme** nous **arrivons** à Nice, en général, le lendemain de notre départ de Grenoble, il faut réserver une nuit dans un gîte rural [bed and breakfast].

   Alors que nous **dormions** à poings fermés [deeply], la propriétaire des lieux frappa à la porte de la chambre pour nous inviter à prendre le petit-déjeuner. **Avant de manger**, nous sommes passés sous la douche. Nous arrivâmes dans la salle à manger **comme** le chef **sortait** de la cuisine. **Pendant que** nous **admirions** les chaînes de montagnes qui dominent les villes de Gap, Digne et Grasse d'où s'élevait le parfum enivrant de la lavande, une jeune fille servait les clients en apportant le café, le lait et les croissants aux amandes sur un grand plateau. Ensuite, la serveuse s'approcha de notre table pour que nous passions commande. Nos amis adorent le chocolat, **tandis que** notre famille, elle, **a** une préférence pour le thé et le café. **À mesure que** les clients du gîte **s'asseyaient** à table, la salle se remplissait. Nous appréciions cette vie montagnarde **à mesure que** nous la connaissions mieux. **Au fur et à mesure que** l'on **approchait** de Nice, nous distinguions la Grande Bleue [Mediterranean Sea].

Chaque fois que nos amis **viennent** à Grenoble, nous leur proposons de découvrir un aspect différent de la ville de Stendhal, et nous sillonnons ensemble le Dauphiné où se déroulent les premières scènes du roman *Le Rouge et le noir*. Nos amis nous rendent régulièrement visite **car** ils **adorent** la montagne. **Comme** la plupart du temps il **fait** beau, nous en profitons pour être à l'extérieur parce que c'est la meilleure manière d'apprécier la montagne. **Quand** ils **arrivent** à Grenoble, nos amis savourent [relish] la vue magnifique sur la chaîne de Belledonne. **Puisque** nos amis se **montrent** toujours satisfaits de leur séjour, nous n'hésitons pas à leur faire connaître les moindres recoins [small hidden places] de la ville et de la région. **À peine eurent-ils exploré** d'autres coins et recoins qu'ils ne regrettèrent pas leur périple [trip] parmi les Grenoblois. **Aussitôt que** les habitants de la ville **se sont échappés** pour se rendre à la montagne, Grenoble a fait place vide. **Dès que** le week-end **est arrivé**, les étudiants sont rentrés chez eux. **Quand** les grandes vacances **arriveront**, la ville se videra, et **quand** elles **se termineront** la ville se remplira.

41.1 Simultaneous action

The conjunctions *comme, lorsque, quand* and *si* indicate that two actions occur simultaneously, and the tenses do not have to be the same:

Nous sommes arrivés comme notre cousin partait.	*We arrived as our cousin was leaving.*
Comme notre héros entrait, le téléphone sonna.	*As our hero came in, the phone rang.*
Papa lisait lorsque Maman cuisinait.	*Pop read while Mom cooked.*
Sabrina rentre quand il pleut.	*Sabrina comes in when it rains.*
Sabrina sort s'il ne pleut pas.	*Sabrina goes out if it is not raining.*
Envoie-moi un texto quand tu arriveras à Prague.	*Send me a text message when you arrive in Prague.*

Alors que can indicate that the action has already started when the main clause intervenes:

Alors que je dormais, on frappa à la porte.	*While I was sleeping, someone knocked at the door.*

Pendant que indicates a notion of *durée* or length of time (=*while*):

Pendant que je travaille, va faire les courses.	*While I'm working, do the shopping.*

It is advisable to avoid confusion between *pendant que*, as in the example immediately above, and *tandis que*. The first refers specifically to time and the second suggests contrast, although they can overlap, as in the second case below:

Sophie adore le chocolat, tandis que moi j'en ai horreur.	*Sophie adores chocolate while me, I loathe it.*
Tandis que Pierre travaille, Jean se repose.	*While Pierre works, Jean takes a rest.*

A precise idea of parallel actions is evoked by *à mesure que*:

On s'aime à mesure qu'on se connaît mieux.	*We like each other as we get to know each other better/more.*
À mesure que Céline parlait / que le soir tombait la salle se vidait.	*While/As Céline was speaking / the evening was closing in, people were leaving the hall.*

Au fur et à mesure que is much more precise than *à mesure que*:

Au fur et à mesure que la soirée avançait, Louis devenait de plus en plus animé.	*As the evening wore on, Louis became more and more excited.*
Nous vendrons ces objets au fur et à mesure que croîtront nos besoins / que nous aurons besoin d'argent.	*We'll sell these objects according to how our needs grow / we need the money.*
Au fur et à mesure que l'on approchait de Cracovie, nous distinguions les toits.	*As we approached Cracow, we started to distinguish the roofs.*

Chaque fois indicates an idea of repetition:

Chaque fois que Jean enfourchait son vélo, il tombait.	*Each time Jean got on his bicycle, he would fall off.*
À chaque fois que Stéphanie ouvre la bouche, elle dit une bêtise.	*Each time Stéphanie opens her mouth, she says something stupid.*

41.2 When a secondary action precedes the main one

The secondary action can be expressed by the conjunctions *car*, *comme*, *parce que*, *puisque* and *quand*, and is often, but by no means always, followed by a compound tense:

Il m'en veut, car il ne m'a pas saluée.	*He has a grudge against me, for he did not greet me.*
Comme le train avait pris du retard, nous n'avons pas vu le début du spectacle.	*Since the train had been delayed, we didn't see the beginning of the show.*
Le chat miaule parce qu'il a faim.	*The cat is miaowing for he's hungry.*
Guillaume ne peut/pourra pas venir parce qu'il est tombé malade.	*Guillaume can't come / won't be able to come because he is sick.*
Quand Philippe a mangé, il sort.	*When Philippe has eaten, he leaves.*

The conjunctive expressions, *à peine, aussitôt que, dès que* are used to indicate an immediate succession of actions:

À peine l'eut-il dit qu'il le regretta.	*Hardly had he said it than he was sorry.*
Aussitôt que Marie m'a vue, elle m'a fait signe.	*As soon as Marie saw me, she waved.*
Dès que Pierre a téléphoné, il est sorti.	*As soon as Pierre phoned, he went out.*
Dès que sa cousine avait bu un verre, elle délirait.	*As soon as her cousin had drunk a glass, she would talk nonsense.*

41.3 When a secondary action follows the main one

The conjunctions *avant que* and *jusqu'à ce que* indicate that the secondary action of the subordinate clause follows the main one. The subjunctive is required here (see Chapter 44 on the subjunctive):

Avant que Françoise n'arrive, dis-moi ce que tu as à me dire.	*Before Françoise comes, tell me what you have to say to me.*
Avant que papa intervienne, dépêchons-nous.	*Before Pop intervenes, let's hurry.*
Insiste jusqu'à ce que Marie accepte.	*Insist until Marie accepts.*
Patientez jusqu'à ce que Maman revienne.	*Be patient until Mom comes back.*

Note that the expletive *ne* in the first example suggests a higher register than the second example.

The conjunction *depuis que* applies to a period up to the moment of speaking, and implies an idea of simultaneity. Note the use of the present tense here:

Depuis que le petit est ici, nous n'avons pas une minute de tranquillité.	*Since the boy has been here, we haven't had a moment's peace.*

41.4 Miscellaneous points

Note the use of the future with many conjunctions when a future is implied:

Quand j'irai à Québec, je t'achèterai un jouet.	*When I go to Quebec City, I'll buy you a toy.*
Pendant que tu seras en Algérie, envoie-moi un texto.	*While you are in Algeria, send me a text message.*
Dès que tu seras prête, dis-le-moi.	*As soon as you are ready, tell me.*
Aussitôt que tu arriveras à Lyon, appelle-moi.	*As soon as you are in Lyon, call me.*
Après que les enfants auront terminé leurs examens, on pourra passer une semaine en Corse.	*After the children have finished their exams, we can spend a week in Corsica.*

There is a very clear parallel between present and future, and past and conditional with conjunctions:

Je croyais que pendant que les enfants seraient au cinéma on serait tranquille.	*I thought that while the children were at the movies, we'd have some peace.*
Aurélie pensait que l'on pourrait partir en vacances quand les temps seraient meilleurs.	*Aurélie thought that we could go on vacation when times were better.*
Je lui ai promis de lui écrire quand je serais arrivé.	*I promised to write him when I arrived.*
Je me suis engagé à inviter toute la famille à m'accompagner en Alaska après qu'ils auraient fini leur travail.	*I promised to invite all the family to accompany me to Alaska after they had finished their work.*

The following construction involving a future tense when the event has already taken place is not uncommon, notably on historical topics:

Quand Napoléon mourra, toute l'Europe se réjouira.	*When Napoleon dies, the whole of Europe will rejoice.*
Quand la révolution éclatera, ce sera la fin de la monarchie.	*When the revolution broke out, it announced the end of the monarchy.*

If the subject is the same for the main and subordinate clauses, an infinitive or perfect infinitive is used in place of the subject with *avant de* and *après*, but not with the other conjunctions treated above:

Avant de manger, lave-toi les mains.	*Before eating, wash your hands.*
Après avoir mangé, ils allèrent au cinéma.	*After eating, they went to the movies.*

42

Complex verbal expressions / Les expressions verbales complexes

The following passage relates the excitement experienced by tourists enjoying a day out on a small train running through the grandiose Alpine scenery surrounding Grenoble in the department of Isère. Indicated in bold is a series of idiomatic expressions which are dealt with in this chapter and which cause uncertainty for foreign learners of French by reason of their complexity. A few translations are provided.

Le circuit de La Mure

De quoi **s'agit-il** ? **S'agit-il de** quelque chose ou de quelqu'un ? Il **s'agit de** savoir de quoi nous parlons. **Il ne s'agit pas** de la mûre [blackberry] ou du fruit noir du mûrier. **Il ne peut s'agir que de** la petite ville sur le plateau Matheysin située au cœur des Alpes à proximité de Grenoble, la capitale de cette somptueuse région montagneuse. En partant de Saint-Georges-de-Commiers, **il existe** ce qu'on appelle « le petit train de La Mure ». Pendant l'été, les wagons des années trente sont complets. Les voyageurs retrouvent le charme d'antan. Ils embarquent pour une destination faite de bons moments de détente, d'émerveillement et de plaisir. Un réel enchantement ! Un circuit magnifique surnommé « la plus belle ligne des Alpes » attire de nombreux visiteurs. **Peu s'en fallait que** je devienne machiniste [train driver] pour conduire un train !

Nous nous **attendions à ce que** l'animatrice fasse les commentaires précis sur notre visite guidée. De splendides perspectives sur le Monteynard, lac aux eaux couleur bleu turquoise, s'offraient à nos yeux. Entre le massif du Vercors et le lac de Monteynard, un itinéraire spectaculaire et contrasté s'ouvrait comme un écrin [jewel box] boisé et minéral. Nous **avions beau faire**, pour la énième fois, ce circuit pittoresque, nous étions toujours aussi émerveillés par le paysage naturel ! La ligne ferroviaire est jalonnée [full of / marked out by] de gorges, de vallées, de viaducs, de tunnels et de sommets vertigineux. Les enfants **avaient beau** crier en approchant les longs tunnels, l'animatrice n'entendait rien. Elle poursuivait ses commentaires en soulignant que nous empruntions la ligne d'un ancien train minier qui descendait le charbon de La Mure à Saint-Georges-de-Commiers. Les voyageurs **avaient l'interdiction** de fumer dans les wagons. Les enfants **avaient la défense** absolue de s'approcher des fenêtres. **Il fallait** donc **se garder de** se pencher au-dehors. Durant notre halte à la Motte d'Aveillans, nous **avions cœur à goûter et à acheter** le miel du pays. L'apicultrice **ne put se défendre** [could not help] **de sourire** aux visiteurs et clients. Elle **s'entretenait avec** un visiteur **de** la vie des abeilles. Elle nous racontait qu'elle **s'ennuyait de** ses amies qu'elle avait laissées dans la vallée.

La fin du charbon à La Mure **a défrayé la chronique de** tous les journaux régionaux. **Il n'empêche que** cette région reste très boisée et attire de nombreux touristes étrangers pendant l'été. Les sites touristiques à visiter **ne font pas défaut**. Cela nous a donné l'occasion de **faire connaissance avec** les habitants de la région qui nous ont **souhaité la bienvenue** et **nous nous en félicitons**. Notre périple [trip] touristique s'est poursuivi et **nous n'avons trouvé rien à redire** parce que la région était très accueillante. Les Murois **veillent à ce que** les touristes repartent satisfaits. Finalement, **nous n'avons pas manqué de remercier** les habitants de leur chaleureux accueil.

There exist in French, as in other Romance languages and English for that matter, numerous verbal expressions which, as a result of their apparently complicated structure, at least for foreigners, do not encourage learners to use them. This is unfortunate because such expressions often convey important shades of meaning which are difficult to express otherwise, and also because some of them recur constantly in current usage.

Note that *il s'agit de* (= *it is a question of*) is an impersonal expression, and the subject can only ever be *il*, never a noun.

De quoi s'agit-il ?	*What's it about?*
Il s'agissait de le faire correctement.	*It was a question of doing it correctly.*
Il s'agira de réécrire la lettre.	*It will be a question of rewriting the letter.*
Il ne peut s'agir que de Frédéric.	*It must have something to do with Frédéric.*

However, *s'agissant de* is permissible and, although once out of favor, it has gained a vigor among even careful writers:

S'agissant de son retour, je lui ai dit que je ne serais pas à la maison.	*With respect to her return, I told her that I would not be home.*
S'agissant de vous, nous n'insisterons pas.	*As far as you are concerned, we'll not insist.*

This contruction may also be used with the subjunctive il faut (= *you must / he must, etc.*):

Il s'agit que tu le fasses dès que possible.	*You have to do it as soon as possible.*

s'attendre à ce que + subjunctive = *to expect*

Je m'attends à ce qu'elle revienne sous peu.	*I expect she'll be back shortly.*
On s'attend à ce que la prof corrige les copies dans la semaine.	*We expect the teacher to do the marking during this week.*
Attendez-vous à des reproches.	*Expect criticism.*

As a non-reflexive verb, it can also mean *to expect*:

On attend l'arrivée du premier ministre dans la soirée.	*We are expecting the prime minister's arrival this evening.*

avoir beau faire quelque chose = *to do something in vain*

Irène a beau faire, elle n'aura pas ses examens.	*Whatever she does, Irène won't get through her examinations.*
J'ai beau crier, il n'entend rien.	*It's pointless shouting, he can't hear anything.*
A beau mentir qui vient de loin.	*He can lie as much as he likes, we can't check on him.*

avoir l'interdiction | la défense de faire quelque chose (R3) = *to be forbidden to do something*

Les élèves ont eu l'interdiction de fumer en cours.	*The pupils were forbidden to smoke in class.*
J'avais la défense absolue de quitter la ferme.	*I was strictly forbidden to leave the farm.*

avoir à cœur de faire quelque chose = *to set one's heart on doing something*

Armelle avait à cœur d'entrer au Conservatoire.	*Armelle was set on getting into the Conservatoire.*

se défendre d'être (R3) = *to refuse to admit, to deny being*

Guillaume se défend d'être anti-Européen.	*Guillaume refuses to admit he is anti-European.*
La ministre s'est toujours défendue de vouloir créer un nouveau parti politique.	*The minister has always refused to admit that she wants to create a new political party.*
Antoine ne put se défendre de sourire.	*Antoine could not help smiling.*
Je ne m'en défends pas.	*I don't deny it.*

défrayer la chronique de = to be the talk of the town

Le désastre ferroviaire / L'enlèvement des touristes a défrayé la chronique de tous les journaux.	*The rail accident / The kidnapping of the tourists has been all over the papers.*

se disputer le droit / le privilège de faire quelque chose = to argue over the right / privilege to do something

Les deux frères se sont disputé le droit de conduire la voiture.	*The two brothers argued over who would drive.*
Les athlètes se disputaient le privilège de porter le drapeau.	*The athletes argued over the privilege of carrying the flag.*

(il) n'empêche que + indicative = nevertheless

Leur équipe avait une défense très solide; (il) n'empêche qu'ils ont encaissé trois buts.	*Their team had a tough defense; they nevertheless let in three goals.*
Il m'a fait un mauvais tour ; n'empêche qu'il serait le bienvenu.	*He played a dirty trick on me; he would nevertheless be welcome.*

Note that the expression is more colloquial with the loss of the impersonal *il*.

comme si de rien n'était = as if nothing had happened

Après notre bagarre il est revenu comme si de rien n'était.	*After our fight, he came back as if nothing had happened.*
Faites comme si de rien n'était.	*Act as if nothing had happened.*

s'ennuyer de quelqu'un (R3) = to miss someone

Je m'ennuyais de mes amies que j'avais laissées au village.	*I missed my friends that I had left behind in the village.*

s'entretenir avec quelqu'un de quelque chose = to hold discussions with someone about something

Le ministre s'est entretenu avec le président de la politique agricole.	*The minister discussed the agricultural policy with the president.*

se faire faute de (R3) = to feel guilty/responsible for

Après cet accident, je me ferai toujours faute de ne pas avoir été plus prudent.	*After that accident, I'll always feel guilty over not having been more careful.*

ne pas se faire faute de (R3) = *not to fail to*

Ils ne se sont pas fait faute d'en parler.	*They did not fail to talk about it.*
Le garagiste m'a offert ses services, je ne m'en suis pas fait faute.	*The garage owner offered me his services, and I availed myself of them.*

en faire autant = *to do the same thing*

Louise a fait d'excellentes études ; je voudrais en faire autant.	*Louise studied wonderfully well; I'd like to do the same.*
Ton frère a appris à nager. Tâche d'en faire autant.	*Your brother has learned to swim; try to do the same.*

faire confiance à quelqu'un = *to place trust in someone*

Ma fille est très jeune. Si elle t'accompagne, je te fais confiance.	*My daughter is very young. If she comes with you, I trust you.*

faire connaissance avec | la connaissance de = *to come to know*

J'ai fait connaissance avec Adrienne il y a un an à Bruxelles.	*I met Adrienne for the first time a year ago in Brussels.*
Quand as-tu fait la connaissance de ma cousine ?	*When did you get to know my cousin?*

faire défaut = *to be lacking*

L'argent me fait défaut.	*I need money.*
La concision lui fait défaut.	*He lacks concision.*
Les forces m'ont fait défaut.	*I lacked the strength.*

emboîter le pas à quelqu'un = *to follow someone* (used literally and figuratively, i.e., *to take someone's lead*)

J'ai ouvert la marche et mon frère m'a emboîté le pas.	*I led the way and my brother fell in behind.*
Sabrina emboîtait toujours le pas à son frère aîné.	*Sabrina always followed suit in what her older brother did.*

faire exprès de = *to do (something) deliberately*

Sébastien fait exprès d'embêter les filles.	*Sébastien deliberately annoys the girls.*
Tu as fait exprès de cacher mon cadeau.	*You deliberately hid my present.*

avoir vite fait de faire quelque chose = *to be quick in doing something* (contains the suggestion *too quick*)

On a vite fait de juger cette personne.	*This person was judged (too) quickly.*

faire fi de quelque chose (R3) = *to scorn something*

Pourquoi fait-il fi de mon autorité / de mes conseils ?	*Why does he scorn/defy my authority/advice?*

se faire fort de = *to be confident about, to commit oneself to*

La dame s'est fait fort d'obtenir la signature de son mari.	*The lady confidently committed herself to obtaining her husband's signature.*
Elle était une brillante élève. Elle s'est fait fort d'être première au palmarès.	*She was a brilliant student. She was confident about being first in the honors list.*

Note that *fort* here is invariable.

faire honte à quelqu'un = *to make someone feel ashamed*

Le comportement impoli de mon frère me fait honte.	*My brother's discourteous behavior makes me feel ashamed.*

faire peu de cas de quelque chose = *to ignore something*

Ma cousine fait peu de cas de ce qu'on lui dit.	*My cousin ignores what is said to her.*

faire grand cas de = *to pay great attention to*

Mon fils m'obéit de façon exemplaire. Il fait toujours grand cas de mes conseils.	*My son obeys me in exemplary style. He always pays great attention to my advice.*

peu s'en faut que (R3) + subjunctive suggests the idea of *almost*

La coupable est venue s'excuser. Mais peu s'en faut que la directrice aille le dire à son père.	*The guilty girl came to apologize. But the principal/headteacher almost went to tell her father.*
Peu s'en est fallu qu'elle soit tuée dans la collision.	*She was almost killed in the collision.*

il s'en faut de beaucoup que (R3) + subjunctive = *to be far from*

Il s'en fallait de beaucoup qu'ils soient heureux.	*They were far from being happy.*

This expression also stands alone:

Pierre n'est pas si raisonnable que son frère. Il s'en faut de beaucoup.	*Pierre isn't as reasonable as his brother. Far from it.*

se féliciter de quelque chose = to express satisfaction over something

Toute la famille se félicite du mariage de leur fille.	*The whole family is happy over their daughter's marriage.*
On s'est tous félicités de l'heureuse issue de cette délicate affaire.	*We all expressed satisfaction at the happy outcome of this awkward affair.*
Notre fils a remporté un championnat d'échecs, et je m'en félicite.	*Our son has won a chess championship and I am very happy.*

se garder de = to take care not to

J'ai mes propres opinions mais je me garderais de les exprimer.	*I have my own opinions but I'll be careful not to express them.*
Maman s'est bien gardée de questionner ma sœur, autrement elles se seraient disputées.	*Mom did well not to question my sister, otherwise, they would have had an argument.*

en imposer à quelqu'un = to fill someone with respect

Avec sa carrure de boxeur, il en a imposé à l'agresseur.	*With his enormous physique, he made the mugger think twice.*
J'ai vu des gens s'inquiéter, tellement il leur en imposait.	*I saw people get worried, so much respect did he instill into them.*

intenter un procès à/contre quelqu'un (R3) = to take someone to court

La dame a intenté un procès à/contre sa voisine dont le chien laissait traîner des crottes dans son jardin.	*The lady took her neighbor to court for her dog left its mess in her yard/ garden.*

manquer à quelqu'un = to be lacking to someone, i.e., to miss

Le soleil me manque en Alaska.	*I miss the sun in Alaska.*
J'apprécie beaucoup le Canada, mais le Mexique me manque.	*I appreciate Canada very much but I do miss Mexico.*
Deux soldats manquent à l'appel.	*Two soldiers are missing the roll call.*

Note that *manquer de* contains the idea of *almost*:

Dans ma précipitation, j'ai manqué de renverser le vase.	*In my haste, I nearly knocked the vase over.*
La petite a manqué de se noyer.	*The little girl nearly drowned.*

Note also that *ne pas manquer de* means *not to fail to*:

Ne manque pas de me téléphoner en arrivant.	*Don't fail to phone me on arrival.*

mettre à même de = *to enable*

Ce système nous a mis à même de vérifier les calculs.	*This system enabled us to check the calculations.*

mettre quelqu'un en demeure de (R3) = *to oblige someone to* (has a legal connotation)

Le juge a mis l'accusé en demeure de tenir ses engagements.	*The judge placed it upon the accused to keep to his commitments.*

se passer de = *to do without*

Il est très difficile de se passer d'argent.	*It is very difficult to do without money.*
Tu te passeras de ton livre pendant ton examen.	*You will do without your book in the exam.*

passer en revue = *to review, to go through*

La reine a passé les troupes en revue.	*The queen reviewed the troops.*
L'actrice a passé en revue sa garde-robe avant de se présenter sur le plateau.	*The actress went through her wardrobe before coming out onto the set.*

porter atteinte à quelque chose (R3) = *to damage, to affect something adversely*

Cet acte ignominieux a porté atteinte à l'honneur de la députée.	*This ignominious act cast a slur on the representative's honor.*
La tradition du rationalisme consiste à porter atteinte à la religion.	*The rationalist tradition consists in attacking religion.*

s'en prendre à quelqu'un = *to criticize someone*

Les journalistes s'en sont vivement pris au gouvernement.	*The journalists launched a fierce attack on the government.*

s'en rapporter à quelque chose = to rely on something

Les parents s'en sont rapportés au bon sens des professeurs.	*The parents relied on the good sense of the teachers.*
Les créanciers s'en sont rapportés à l'arbitrage du juge.	*The creditors trusted in the judge's arbitration.*

se réclamer de quelque chose (R3) = to appeal to | to cite the authority of something

Le philosophe se réclama du marxisme pour défendre sa cause.	*The philosopher appealed to Marxism to defend his cause.*
Je me réclame de Dieu pour exiger justice.	*I appeal to God to demand justice.*
Saint Paul se réclama de César pour défendre le christianisme.	*St Paul appealed unto Caesar to defend Christianity.*

s'en remettre à quelqu'un = to rely on someone

Je m'en remets à vous pour me tirer d'affaire.	*I rely on you to get me out of this fix.*
L'accusée s'en est remise au jugement / à la décision de son avocat.	*The accused relied on her lawyer's judgment/decision.*

remonter | retaper (R1) le moral à quelqu'un = to cheer someone up

Qu'est-ce qu'il est abattu. Il faut lui remonter/retaper le moral.	*He really is depressed. We must cheer him up.*

se répercuter sur = to have repercussions on

Bien sûr, les hausses de salaire doivent se répercuter sur les prix.	*Sure enough, increased salaries must have an effect on prices.*
Les effets de la fatigue se répercutaient sur le moral.	*The effects of tiredness had repercussions on their/our morale.*

se ressentir de quelque chose = to feel the effects of something

Je me ressens toujours de l'accident.	*I still feel the effects of the accident.*
Jeanne se ressentait même hier de sa visite chez le dentiste.	*Jeanne still felt even yesterday the effects of her visit to the dentist.*

ne pas savoir à quoi s'en tenir = not to know what to believe

Puisqu'il blague toujours, je ne sais pas à quoi m'en tenir.	*Since he's always joking, I never know what to believe.*

savoir gré à quelqu'un (R3) = *to be grateful to someone*

Je lui sais gré de m'avoir avertie.	*I am thankful to him for warning me.*
Je vous saurais gré de m'accompagner jusqu'à mon domicile.	*I would be grateful to you if you could accompany me to my house.*

souhaiter la bienvenue à quelqu'un = *to welcome someone*

Elle m'a souhaité la bienvenue.	*She welcomed me.*
Vous êtes le/la/les bienvenu(e)(s).	*You are welcome.*
Soyez les bienvenus !	*Welcome!*

tenir à = *to be anxious, to be keen on*

Ma fille tenait à partir avec moi.	*My daughter was keen to come with me.*
"Ce n'est pas nécessaire de payer les billets." "Mais, j'y tiens."	*"You don't need to buy the tickets."* *"But I want to."*

tenir rigueur à quelqu'un de quelque chose = *to hold it against someone for something*

Je tiendrai toujours à cette étudiante rigueur de ne pas avoir remis son travail.	*I'll always hold it against this student for not handing in her work.*

tenir tête à = *to defy*

Les jeunes du quartier ont tenu tête aux policiers.	*The local youths defied the police.*

traiter quelqu'un de quelque chose = *to call someone something* (usually has a negative connotation)

Kafka a traité son père de tyran.	*Kafka called his father a tyrant.*
Le jeune m'a traité de tous les noms.	*The youth called me everything.*

trouver à redire à quelque chose = *to criticize*

Je ne trouve rien à redire à tout cela.	*I can't find anything wrong with that.*
Ma cousine trouve toujours à redire à/sur ce que je fais.	*My cousin always has something to criticize in what I do.*

veiller à ce que + subjunctive = *to see to it that*

Veille à ce que le travail soit terminé en temps voulu.	*See to it that the work is completed in the agreed time.*
Veille à ce que ton oncle soit content de toi.	*Make sure your uncle is happy with you.*

venir en aide à quelqu'un = to come to someone's aid

Les secouristes nous sont venus en aide à la suite de notre accident.	*The first-aid workers came to our aid following our accident.*

en vouloir à quelqu'un = to hold it against someone

Mon camarade m'en veut parce que je ne lui ai pas envoyé de texto.	*My friend is angry with me because I did not send him a text message.*
Son petit ami lui en voulait de sa froideur.	*Her boyfriend held it against her because of her coldness.*

43

Verbs of movement / Les verbes de mouvement

The following passage describes a moment of extreme danger caused by a gas leak. Firemen rush to the aid of the local people engulfed in the delirious need to escape. The final paragraph sees calm restored. Note the verbs used for movement, and the adverbs or adverbial expressions qualifying the movement. In English, the construction is often the other way round. The constructions to note are in bold. Some translations are offered.

Le tumulte de la rue

Les sapeurs-pompiers **partirent en masse** [piled out] pour effectuer leurs opérations de sauvetage. Les camions **montèrent et descendirent lourdement la rue**. Le bouchon formé par l'escorte des pompiers a obligé tous les véhicules à rouler au pas. Les gens affolés **accoururent en vitesse** [came rushing up] de toute part. Une mère de famille **monta l'escalier en courant** pour aller chercher ses enfants restés dans leur chambre. Ces derniers **rentrèrent et sortirent en coup de vent**. Le père **gagna en rampant le mur de la maison**. Il **revint en boitant** [hobbled back] du jardin. Les voisins **traversèrent la rue en courant** pour lui venir en aide. Le fils aîné **entra en trombe** dans le garage. Tous ses copains **montèrent en masse** [piled in] dans la voiture. L'un deux, affolé par le bruit, **traversa** l'Isère **à la nage**.

Un pompier portant le casque et l'uniforme déclara : « Surtout pas d'affolement ! [Don't panic]. Évacuez les lieux dans le calme et rassemblez-vous au coin de la rue. » La grand-mère, un peu dure d'oreille [hard of hearing], **descendit l'escalier sur la pointe des pieds**. Elle **avança d'un pas lent** [crept forward]. Sa petite-fille **revint à vélo**. Elle **passa comme un éclair** devant les pompiers. La jeune adolescente **suivit du regard** les pompiers et montra sa vive inquiétude. Debout dans la rue, elle **suivait des yeux** un défilé ininterrompu de pompiers, de policiers, de médecins urgentistes et de gaziers venus en renfort. Il fut impossible de **parcourir** la rue **en vitesse**. Derrière la caméra, les journalistes filmèrent l'événement. Cette situation tumultueuse trouva son explication dans une erreur humaine qui aurait pu être fatale : la fuite d'une conduite de gaz.

En fin de matinée, la rue retrouva enfin son calme. Des couples **se promenèrent le long** de l'Isère. Ils passèrent l'après-midi à **longer la rivière en flânant** [strolled along the river] et en appréciant leur balade citadine. À leur passage, les oiseaux **s'envolèrent à tire d'aile** [took to the skies] en gazouillant. Un couple s'arrêta net pour s'asseoir sur un banc de pierre. L'homme **plongea son regard** dans les yeux de sa compagne. Plus loin, d'autres promeneurs contemplèrent les cimes neigeuses de la chaîne de Belledonne. Les deux amoureux **promenèrent langoureusement leur regard** sur la montagne. Ils **fouillèrent du regard** les sapins dégageant une odeur de résine. Pour rentrer chez eux, ils **marchèrent à travers champ**.

An important difference between the French and English verbal systems concerns the way in which expressions of movement are analyzed and treated in the two languages. In French, the direction of movement is often indicated by the verb itself, and the manner of movement by a phrase, either a gerund or an adverbial expression, whereas in English the verb conveys the manner of the movement, and an adverb or prepositional expression the direction. This phenomenon in French is shared by other Romance languages such as Italian and Spanish, and is with these languages an important characteristic. The French refer neatly to this feature by way of explanation as a *chassé croisé*, a dance term meaning *set to partners* where a partner, say A, in two sets of partners, crosses over diagonally to join the partner B of the other set. For example:

Elle a traversé la rue en courant.   *She ran across the road.*

Traverser corresponds to *across* and *en courant* corresponds to *ran*.

The following list illustrates how this difference expresses itself:

French (*direction indicated by verb; manner indicated by phrase*)	**English** (*direction indicated by adverb / prepositional expression; manner indicated by verb*)
Elle a monté l'escalier en courant.	*She ran up the stairs.*
Il gagna en rampant le mur de la prison.	*He crawled toward the prison wall.*
Elle revint en boitant de la cuisine.	*She hobbled back to the kitchen.*
Il entra en coup de vent / en trombe.	*He burst in.*
Elle sortit en coup de vent / en trombe.	*She burst out.*
Byron a traversé le Tage à la nage.	*Byron swam across the Tagus.*
Elle a descendu l'escalier sur la pointe des pieds.	*She crept downstairs.*
Elle a monté l'escalier sur la pointe des pieds.	*She crept upstairs.*

Elle est revenue à vélo.	*She cycled back.*
Tous les garçons sont montés en masse dans la voiture.	*All the boys piled into the car.*
Ils sont partis en masse.	*They piled out / flooded out.*
Il est impossible de parcourir en vitesse *Guerre et paix*.	*It's impossible to race through War and Peace.*
Je ne l'ai pas entendue. Elle a dû entrer discrètement.	*I didn't hear her. She must have slipped in.*
Je l'ai vu arriver en courant.	*I saw him running up.*
Tu l'as vu passer en vitesse ?	*Did you see him whizz past/by?*
Les oiseaux s'envolèrent à tire d'aile.	*The birds flew off.*
Le Jamaïcain Bolt passa comme une foudre.	*The Jamaican Bolt flashed by.*
Les camions montaient et descendaient lourdement la rue.	*The trucks trundled up and down the road.*
Le fermier avança d'un pas lent / lentement.	*The farmer plodded along.*
On a passé l'après-midi à longer la rivière en flânant.	*We spent the afternoon dawdling along the river.*
Le bouchon a obligé tous les véhicules à rouler au pas.	*The traffic jam forced all the vehicles to crawl along.*

Despite this widespread phenomenon as illustrated above by such a variety of examples, French does on occasion follow the English pattern:

French (*direction indicated by adverb / prepositional expression; manner indicated by verb*)	**English** (*direction indicated by adverb / prepositional expression; manner indicated by verb*)
Le chien est accouru en bondissant.	*The dog came bounding up.*
Elle est passée par-dessus le mur.	*She climbed over the wall.*
Ils se sont promenés le long de la rivière.	*They walked along the river.*
Elles ont marché à travers (les) champs.	*They walked across the fields.*

Note that the singular *champ* would require *traverser* (*Elle a traversé le champ*) since *champ* is more specific, like *rue*, where *champs* is much vaguer.

Often, when the manner of movement is specified in English, it is left unclear or is completely ignored in French: a general verb occurs in French whereas English has recourse to a specific verb, although English may also use a general verb like French:

Elles ont traversé la rue.	*They crossed the road / walked across the road.*

Implicit within *traverser*, for example, is the idea of walking; if the person had run across the road, the phrase *en courant* would have been added.

A similar kind of *chassé croisé* is most apparent with a good number of verbs associated with seeing. In some cases, movement could be involved, but not always:

Le poète promenait langoureusement son regard sur la plaine.	*The poet looked languorously over the plain / cast his languorous eye over the plain.*
Les enfants, debout sur le quai, suivaient des yeux la voie ferrée.	*Standing on the platform, the children peered down the line.*
Elle fouillait du regard les coins obscurs de la chambre.	*She looked searchingly into the dark corners of the room.*
Il a scruté du regard le bois ténébreux.	*He looked carefully into the dark wood.*
Notre héros a plongé son regard / ses yeux dans les yeux de la femme.	*Our hero looked penetratingly into the eyes of the woman.*
Similarly with *examiner* and *observer*.	

Part IV

44

Subjunctive mood / Le mode du subjonctif

The following passage describes the protracted strike action adopted by French university teachers and some students during the academic year 2008–2009. At stake were the new teaching and research conditions unilaterally imposed by the Sarkozy government. The strike, which disrupted classes for close to a whole year, could only be called off by conciliatory measures offered by the French government. The passage illustrates the use of the subjunctive in various tenses – the present, the imperfect and the perfect. The subjunctive forms are highlighted in bold, as are the expressions which require the subjunctive. Some translations are provided.

> **Un long semestre de mobilisation**
>
> Les organisations syndicales **doutent que** la ministre de l'enseignement supérieur **vienne** participer à leurs débats. En effet, elle fait une communication à La Sorbonne Nouvelle. Certains pensent qu'elle va venir, d'autres **ne pensent pas qu'elle puisse venir**. J'en doute fort ! **Espérons qu'elle prenne** le temps de les rencontrer. **Encore faut-il qu'elle le veuille** ! Le mouvement de grève ne va pas s'interrompre **avant que** la ministre **ne prenne part** aux discussions. **Il faudra qu'elle vienne** pour désamorcer [to defuse] le conflit. Les syndicats étudiants doivent se concerter **avant que** la ministre **ne soit arrivée**. Madame la ministre a été attendue **jusqu'à ce que l'horloge ait sonné** midi pile. Ensuite, les cohortes d'étudiants et d'enseignants ont été obligées de partir manger au restaurant universitaire. **En attendant que** la file d'attente **s'éclaircissît**, enseignants et étudiants échangeaient des propos. **Ce sont les seuls qui aient** compris le sens de cette mobilisation.
>
> Les autorités **craignaient** que cette mobilisation enseignante et étudiante **ne servît** de prétexte pour impliquer un plus grand nombre de forces vives. **Dieu soit loué** ! Aucun affrontement sérieux ne s'est produit ! Certains étudiants lançaient : «**Vivent les enseignants et les étudiants** ! **Vive la grève** ! **Coûte que coûte**, nous resterons dans le mouvement ! **N'ayez crainte** : *El pueblo unido jamás será*

vencido![1] [Spanish expression heard during the meetings = Le peuple uni ne sera jamais vaincu !] **Advienne que pourra !**». **On eût dit que** [It looked as though] les grèves en continu [continuous] annonçaient la fin du second semestre universitaire. **Qu'il y eût** [The fact that there were] **beaucoup de** grévistes, tout le monde en est convenu. Les grévistes sont remontés à bloc. Ils décident de descendre dans la rue **quoiqu'il arrive. Quelle que soit l'intention** du gouvernement, les manifestants ne lâcheront pas prise [will not give way]. **Ne fût-ce que pour** [Even if it were only for] **une courte période**, la ministre s'est faite représenter par une médiatrice. **Que** la représentante du gouvernement **reste ou qu'elle parte**, ça leur est complètement égal.

Le mouvement de mobilisation prend de l'ampleur. **Qu'il fasse beau** les prochains jours, c'est certain. **Sachez que** « le Printemps des chaises » a été organisé. Après « le Printemps des chaises », « le Printemps des tables »[2] a emboîté le pas [followed on]. **N'en déplaise** aux autorités ! [Whether the authorities like it or not!]. À ma connaissance, cette opération a connu un grand impact. Certains étudiants refuseront à moins d'être contraints de participer à la ronde des obstinés. Ils se taisaient de crainte d'importuner leurs camarades. **Où qu'ils aillent**, les manifestants les rejoindront. Aussi longtemps qu'ils s'obstineront, ils obtiendront gain de cause [they will win their case]. **Grand bien leur fasse ! Le danger fût-il encore plus menaçant lorsque** la fin du semestre s'annonça. **Pourvu que** le semestre **soit validé** et que l'année universitaire **ne soit pas perdue** pour tous. **Viennent** les vacances [Let the vacation come], les étudiants vont faire des excursions en montagne. Tout le monde sera content.

Whereas the subjunctive mood is extremely rare in English and is by and large restricted to R3 usage, sometimes verging in fact on the positively archaic (e.g., *If I were you*; *Were you to come*; *So be it*; *Oh that it were so!*), in French the subjunctive is still a mood to be reckoned with. What is often disconcerting to the student of the French subjunctive is that, in some cases, its use seems to conform to unmistakable and well-defined rules, and in others it seems to be a matter of choice. In the following discussion, the term "black and white" subjunctive will be applied to those circumstances where the use of the subjunctive is obligatory, and the term "gray" to those where a degree of choice or discretion is permissible. It should be noted with respect to the "gray" subjunctive that its use is often determined by

[1] The Spanish song "El pueblo . . . " was composed by the Chilean Sergio Ortega in support of the Allende regime overthrown in the early 1970s. It had some currency in France during that period.

[2] The "Printemps des chaises" and the "Printemps des tables" refer to the withdrawal of chairs, and then the withdrawal of tables, in order to make tuition impossible. These expressions recall the "Printemps des poètes" that takes place yearly in certain French universities to celebrate the joys of poetry.

instinct, particularly on the part of someone who is very conscious of the way in which (s)he uses language and is seeking an elegance of expression. The notion of doubt, hypothesis or some future act is often associated with the subjunctive. In other words, if an idea is not clearly substantiated or validated, the subjunctive may well be used. Although an R2 user will attempt to use the "gray" subjunctive in accordance with traditional prescriptions, the "gray" subjunctive and even the "black and white" subjunctive may disappear in speech through inadvertence and because of the frequent breaks in continuity of structure which are characteristic of R1 speech, but also of R2 speech: *Je doute qu'elle vienne* > *Elle va venir? J'en doute*. It is considered a sign of ignorance or poor education when a person omits the subjunctive incorrectly, a common enough occurrence. It should also be noted that in some areas of the French-speaking world, notably in rural communities, the subjunctive may hardly manifest itself at all. It is consoling to realize that French speakers themselves can experience difficulty with certain forms of the subjunctive, resorting for example to *veuillons/veuillions* for the correct *voulions*, on analogy with *veuille*, and *aie* for *ait*.

44.1 Conjugation of the main types of verbs in the present, perfect, imperfect and pluperfect subjunctives

Most subjunctive forms, but by no means all, are preceded by *que je/tu*, etc. It must be admitted that one hesitates to incorporate some of these forms into the body of this book since they are rarely, if ever, seen outside grammar manuals or texts of bygone eras.

verbs ending in –er

Present	Perfect	Imperfect	Pluperfect
que je chante	aie chanté	chantasse	eusse chanté
que tu chantes	aies chanté	chantasses	eusses chanté
qu'il/elle chante	ait chanté	chantât	eût chanté
que nous chantions	ayons chanté	chantassions	eussions chanté
que vous chantiez	ayez chanté	chantassiez	eussiez chanté
qu'il/elles chantent	aient chanté	chantassent	eussent chanté

verbs ending in –re

Present	Perfect	Imperfect	Pluperfect
que je vende	aie vendu	vendisse	eusse vendu
que tu vendes	aies vendu	vendisses	eusses vendu
qu'il/elle vende	ait vendu	vendît	eût vendu
que nous vendions	ayons vendu	vendissions	eussions vendu
que vous vendiez	ayez vendu	vendissiez	eussiez vendu
qu'ils/elles vendent	aient vendu	vendissent	eussent vendu

verbs ending in –ir

Present	Perfect	Imperfect	Pluperfect
que je finisse	aie fini	finisse	eusse fini
que tu finisses	aies fini	finisses	eusses fini
qu'il/elle finisse	ait fini	finît	eût fini
que nous finissions	ayons fini	finissions	eussions fini
que vous finissiez	ayez fini	finissiez	eussiez fini
qu'ils/elles finissent	aient fini	finissent	eussent fini

verbs ending in –oir

Present	Perfect	Imperfect	Pluperfect
que je reçoive	aie reçu	reçusse	eusse reçu
que tu reçoives	aies reçu	reçusses	eusses reçu
qu'il/elle reçoive	ait reçu	reçût	eût reçu
que nous recevions	ayons reçu	reçussions	eussions reçu
que vous receviez	ayez reçu	reçussiez	eussiez reçu
qu'ils/elles reçoivent	aient reçu	reçussent	eussent reçu

For the full conjugation of the subjunctive of all verbs, including irregular and reflexive verbs, see the verb tables at the end of this book. Note that verbs conjugated with *être* are formed in the following way:

Present	Perfect	Imperfect	Pluperfect
que je vienne	sois venu(e)	vinsse	fusse venu(e)
que tu viennes	sois venu(e)	vinsses	fusses venu(e)
qu'il/elle vienne	soit venu(e)	vînt	fût venu(e)
que nous venions	soyons venu(e)s	vinssions	fussions venu(e)s
que vous veniez	soyez venu(e)(s)	vinssiez	fussiez venu(e)(s)
qu'ils/elles viennent	soient venu(e)s	vinssent	fussent venu(e)s

In a general way, not all forms of the subjunctive are observed. Many French speakers would not be aware that *regarde* in *Il faut que je le regarde* is a subjunctive form. Some of the forms of the present subjunctive of **-er** verbs are the same as those of the indicative, which is not the case in Spanish and Italian, and given that the overwhelming number of French verbs are of the **-er** ending type, it is little wonder that the French subjunctive is losing its prominence. It may be that there is a tendency for the subjunctive in the present tense to be particularly preserved with certain common verbs where the indicative and subjunctive forms are widely divergent, or the actual final sound is dissimilar. The third person of the indicative and subjunctive forms is:

verb	indicative	subjunctive
aller	va	aille
devoir	doit	doive

verb	indicative	subjunctive
dire	dit	dise
écrire	écrit	écrive
être	est	soit
faire	fait	fasse
falloir	faut	faille
mettre	met	mette
prendre	prend	prenne

44.2 Sequence of tenses with the subjunctive in subordinate clauses

As far as the sequence of tenses with the subjunctive in a subordinate clause is concerned, it is helpful to understand that R3 practice often differs from that of the other two register divisions. In broad terms, the practices may be characterized as follows:

	R3/R2/R1			R3	R2 + R1
il faut	qu'elle vienne	il fallait		qu'il vînt	qu'il vienne
il faudra	qu'elle vienne	il fallut		qu'il vînt	qu'il vienne
il a fallu	qu'elle vienne	il faudrait		qu'il vînt	qu'il vienne

	R3	R2 + R1
je dois partir	avant qu'elle (n')arrive	avant qu'elle arrive
je suis allée me coucher	avant qu'elle (ne) soit arrivée	avant qu'elle arrive
mon père était parti	avant qu'elle (n')arrivât	avant qu'elle soit arrivée
nous avions décidé de partir	avant qu'elle (ne) fût arrivée	avant qu'elle soit arrivée

From the above lists it is clear that, in the spoken language, an imperfect or conditional main clause would be followed by a present subordinate subjunctive clause: *Il fallait qu'il vienne*. Similarly, a pluperfect main clause would be followed by a perfect subordinate subjunctive: *Nous avions décidé de partir avant qu'elle soit arrivée*. Strict adherence to an imperfect subordinate subjunctive would seem odd, unless used for jocular or ironic reasons, or in literary mode, and here, these days, it would only be used in the third-person singular.

44.3 A note on the imperfect subjunctive (*subjonctif imparfait / imparfait du subjonctif*)

It is clear that the imperfect subjunctive (together with its sister conjugation the pluperfect subjunctive) is to all intents and purposes unknown in R1 and R2 discourse; if it does occur, it is usually for jocular purposes or as a parody of more elevated usage. It survives in refined R3 usage, in speeches and stories, but even in these cases it is almost exclusively the third-person singular that is met these days (*fût, fît, mît*, etc.); the other forms are avoided and are replaced by the present subjunctive and, occasionally, the perfect subjunctive. It is, in reality, in polished prose writing that the imperfect and pluperfect subjunctives most frequently occur. It seems quite legitimate therefore for foreign learners of French not to use them in speech, although they should be aware of their appropriateness in formal writing.

The imperfect and pluperfect subjunctives have lost much of their former vigor, if one goes back in time to, say, Chateaubriand (early nineteenth century) and then further back to Rabelais (sixteenth century), when we compare their current use to their ubiquitous contemporary presence in Italian and Spanish. The imperfect and pluperfect subjunctives, as well as the present and perfect subjunctives, appear with as much constancy in these two other languages as the corresponding indicative tenses. There is no problem in Spanish to say and write *que yo parase* (*that I should stop*) or, in Italian, *che io fermassi*, but there is in the French *que j'arrêtasse*. Whether this is because the sound of the *asse* in French appears rebarbative, grotesque, pejorative or just awkward is not clear (consider also *parlasse, assassinassions, caillasse, rêvasser, finasser*, for instance), but it seems quite unjustified to argue that the imperfect and pluperfect subjunctives are difficult to handle since they form a natural part of normal discourse in the other two Romance languages referred to, and we refer to all native speakers here. These two subjunctive forms cause bewilderment in many French speakers precisely because they have fallen into disuse.

In this context, two references are called upon to the French speaker's contemporary attitude to the imperfect and pluperfect subjunctives, and these references underline both, on the one hand, a serious element and, on the other, a humorous and parodic approach. First, a Comité pour la réhabilitation et l'usage (dans le langage parlé) du passé simple et de l'imparfait du subjonctif was established in the 1990s in France to defend and diffuse the use of these two tenses at a national level. The instigator of this courageous but zany move was Alain Bouissière, nicknamed Monsieur plus-que-parfait, a whimsical and unorthodox embalmer (of corpses) who must have sensed the need for resuscitation, linguistically and corporally. The said committee, now defunct it appears, enjoyed monthly meetings to discuss any current topic with enthusiastic recourse to the two forms of the subjunctive in question. Such was the resounding initial success of these meetings that Bouissière published *Le bar du subjonctif* in 1999.

The second reference illustrates, doubtless more accurately, the true status of the two subjunctive tenses in contemporary France. We enter the realm of Astérix, which, far from representing an infantile attachment to lighthearted comedy, indulges in intelligent use of language and, notably, play on words, a preoccupation greatly appreciated by an adult readership. Suffice it to quote the names of three Roman generals: Claudius Quiquilfus

Gracchus Quiquilfus (both in *Les lauriers de César*), and Encorutilfalluqueje-
lesus (in *Le tour de Gaule*). Goscinny, author of the dialogues, plays with the
endings of the subjunctive, adapting them to his burlesque aims.

The **-fus** derives from *fusse* (from *être*) which is to be interpreted as a
change from the third-person *fût*, while the **-sus** derives from *susse* (from
savoir). The **-util-** in the middle of the third concocted name recalls *eût*.
Adult readers instructed in the traditional use of the now abstruse forms
of the subjunctive are sensitive to these playful nuances.

The imperfect subjunctive[3] with the meaning of *even if* is used in conditional clauses. This is of high-register value, not really to be copied, and
recalls literary practice of the nineteenth century and further back. The
verbs *avoir, être, devoir* and *vouloir,* are most prevalent here, and inversion of
pronoun or noun is the norm:

Fussé-je devant la mort, je n'hésiterais pas.	*Were I confronted by death I would not hesitate.*
Dussé-je donner la moitié de ma fortune, je serais toujours heureux.	*Even if I had to give away half my fortune, I would still be happy.*
Eût-il seulement quinze ans il serait militaire.	*Even if he were only fifteen years of age, he would be a soldier.*
Le danger fût-il encore plus menaçant...*	*Even if the danger were more threatening...*

Likewise, the pluperfect subjunctive appears in the elevated literary
mode. Instead of: *Si elle m'avait donné l'argent, je l'aurais acheté* (*If she had
given me the money, I would have bought it*) one could read (but not hear):
Si elle m'eût donné l'argent, je l'eusse acheté. It serves little purpose to labor
over this construction since it is outmoded and is reminiscent of distant,
bygone practices. However, one does come across the third-person singular
in contemporary written style, even in newspapers: *On eût dit que les pluies
torrentielles annonçaient la fin du monde* (*It appeared that the torrential rains were
announcing the ending of the world* as a replacement for: *On aurait dit que*).

44.4 "Black and white" subjunctive

The subjunctive occurs regularly in the following circumstances:

In certain archaic or set expressions:

Advienne que pourra.	*Come what may.*
Vive le roi !	*Long live the king!*

---

[3] The use of the imperfect subjunctive is perfectly normal in all registers in Italian
and Spanish, and one wonders again over the disappearance of this construction
from common French discourse. The same observation applies to the pluperfect
subjunctive immediately below.

Vive(nt) les Québequois !	*Long live the inhabitants of Quebec!*
Puissé-je trouver le bonheur !	*Oh, that I may find happiness!*
N'ayez crainte / N'aie crainte.	*Fear not.*
Sachez que...	*Be aware that...*
Grand bien vous fasse !	*Much good may it do you!*
Ainsi soit-il.	*Amen (So be it – after a prayer)*
Coûte que coûte	*At all costs, Come what may*
N'en déplaise à...	*With all due respect to... / If you have no objection...*
Fasse le ciel que...	*Would to God that...*
Dieu te bénisse !	*God bless you!*
Dieu soit loué !	*God be praised!*
À Dieu ne plaise !	*God forbid!*

At the beginning of a sentence to indicate surprise, an order or a desire:

Que j'aille trouver un taxi ? Certainement pas !	*Me go to find a taxi? Certainly not!*
Que Marie sorte maintenant.	*Let/Make Marie go out now.*
Que Monsieur nous écrive à ce sujet.	*Ask the gentleman to write to us about it.*

To mark a hypothesis or conditional value:

Que Philippe reste ou qu'il parte, ça m'est égal.	*Whether Philippe stays or goes is the same to me.*
Ne fût-ce que pour une journée...	*If it were only for a day...*

When a noun clause introduced by *que* precedes the main clause (this usage is limited to R3 discourse):

Qu'il fasse beau demain est certain.	*That it will be fine tomorrow is certain.*
Qu'il y eût beaucoup de spectateurs tout le monde en est convenu.	*That there were many spectators everyone agreed.*

To express the pronouns *whatever, whoever*, the adjectives *however, whatever* and *wherever*:

qui que vous soyez	*whoever you are*
quoi qu'il arrive	*whatever happens*
où que tu ailles	*wherever you go*
quelle que soit votre intention	*whatever your intention is*
à quelque distance que cela paraisse	*however far that appears*

si grand soit-il (R3) / si grand qu'il *however tall he is*
  soit
pour grand qu'il soit   *however tall he is*
aussi longtemps que vous   *however long you work*
  travailliez

Note: the use of *si* for *however* + adjective is more common than *quelque/ pour* + adjective.

After the following conjunctive or adverbial expressions:

Conjunctive expression	Meaning	Comments
à condition que	*on condition that*	R2 + R3
afin que	*in order that*	R2 + R3
à moins que	*unless*	In R3 usage, an expletive *ne* is often inserted before the verb. This usage is a residue of the Latin negative idea of *ut*, e.g., *à moins qu'elle ne vienne ce soir*. See *avant que* below.
après que	*after*	Logic and tradition require an indicative tense after *après que* when referring to a past event. However, increasingly, and even prevailing usage, but contrary to grammarians' precepts, *après que* takes the subjunctive when it refers to the past (but not to the future): *après qu'elle soit arrivée, elle m'a dit. . .* There is often confusion between the past anterior and the imperfect subjunctive after *après que* in written French, e.g., *après qu'elle fût arrivée* instead of *après qu'elle fut arrivée*: this latter form is the recommended one.
à supposer que / supposé que	*supposing that*	
assez + adjective + *que*	= adjective + *enough* + *to*	*Les frères Karamazov n'est pas assez facile pour que je le lise sans l'aide de mon prof.*

Conjunctive expression	Meaning	Comments
aussi/tout/pour + adjective + que	however + adjective + verb	*Aussi/tout riche qu'il paraisse*; *Pour simple que cela paraisse*
avant que	before	In R3 usage, an expletive *ne* is often inserted before the verb, e.g., *Pourquoi lui as-tu offert le cadeau avant que l'on ne soit arrivé?* See *à moins que* above.
bien que	although	Has the same value as *quoique*: *Bien qu'il ait raison...*
de crainte que	for fear that, lest	In R3 usage, an expletive *ne* is often inserted before the verb: *J'ai envoyé le paquet il y a quinze jours de crainte qu'il n'arrive trop tard.* See also *avant que* and *à moins que*; the same reference to Latin applies here.
de façon que / à ce que	so that	It is only when *de façon que / à ce que* expresses intention that it is followed by the subjunctive mood: *Il faut revenir de façon qu'elle / à ce qu'elle te voie.* When it expresses result, the indicative mood is needed: *Elle est revenue de façon que je l'ai vue.* It appears that the newer form *de façon à ce que* is superseding the older traditional form *de façon que*, but this is far from clear. Certainly this latter form is lighter and less clumsy. *De façon à ce que* is less used when pointing to result.
de manière que / à ce que	so that	See comments on *de façon que / à ce que*.
de sorte que	so that	See comments on *de façon que / à ce que*.
en attendant que	waiting for (someone to do something)	

Conjunctive expression	Meaning	Comments
encore que	although	R3; the indicative has been possible here but does not seem to be in current use.
jusqu'à ce que	until	The standard requirement here is the subjunctive in all tenses. This is understandable with reference to the present or future but has no logic with respect to a completed event. Prevailing usage requires the subjunctive, e.g., *Attends-moi jusqu'à ce que je vienne*; but Hanse and Blampain state that the indicative is correct.
loin que	far from	R3; *Loin que je comprenne son allemand, il pourrait parler japonais et ce ne serait pas différent.*
malgré que	although	Incurs condemnation by the purists but is in vigorous current use.
moyennant que (R3)	by means of which	*Je suis preneur moyennant qu'il fasse beau demain.*
non (pas) que	not that	R3
(pour) autant que	inasmuch as	R3
pour peu que	however, if	R3; *Pour peu qu'il ait bu, il nous racontera l'histoire de sa vie* (If he's had any drink at all he will tell us his life story).
pour que	in order that	Of a slightly lower register than *afin que*.
pourvu que	provided that	
que... que	either... or	Has the same value as *soit que... soit que*: *Qu'elle vienne maintenant qu'elle vienne plus tard, ça m'est égal.*[4]

---

[4] The subjunctive also occurs in R3 usage in the second of a set of coordinated conditional clauses when *que* is used instead of *si*: *Si la pluie cesse et qu'il fasse beau demain* (*If the rain stops and it is fine tomorrow*); but not when the second clause is introduced by *si*: *Si la pluie cesse et s'il fait beau demain*.

Conjunctive expression	Meaning	Comments
quoique[5]	*although*	Has the same value as *bien que*.
sans que	*without*	*Stéphanie a fait ses devoirs sans que j'insiste* (Stéphanie did her homework without my insisting).
soit que... soit que	*either... or*	*Soit que tu le fasses maintenant soit que tu le fasses plus tard...*
sous réserve que	*with the reservation that*	R3
trop + adjective + *que*	*too* + adjective + *to*	*Michel est trop jeune pour que je lui enseigne l'arabe.*

In clauses dependent upon verbs and expressions indicating desiring, wishing, begging, ordering, forbidding, preventing: *aimer mieux, attendre, s'attendre à ce que (to expect), commander (R3), consentir (R3), crier, décréter (R3), défendre, demander (R3), désespérer (R3), désirer, dire (R3), empêcher, entendre* (R3 = with meaning of *to intend: J'entends que tu le fasses ce soir), éviter* (R3),[6] *exiger, faire attention (à ce que), implorer (R3), insister (pour que), interdire, s'opposer (à ce que), nier, ordonner, préférer, prier (R3), proposer, recommander, se réjouir (to rejoice: Je me réjouis que le résultat soit si favorable), souhaiter, supplier (R3), tenir (à ce que = to be keen that: Je tiens à ce que tu viennes tout de suite), veiller (à ce que = to see to it that), vouloir.*

To be noted also is that if the subject is the same in the main and subordinate clauses, an infinitive must be used: *J'aime mieux partir demain; Marie insiste pour préparer le repas tout de suite; Céline souhaite aller au cinéma.*

The verb *souhaiter* requires further comment. It seems to be unique in the sense that it may be followed by a subjunctive or an infinitive when the

---

[5] When the following expressions refer to a future or conditional event or idea, a future or conditional indicative may be used, particularly in the spoken language, although there is considerable uneasiness here among grammarians (this remark does not suggest a recommendation for the use of the indicative in these cases, but is merely an observation): *bien que, encore que, malgré que, quoique*, e.g., *Bien que je ne pourrai pas (puisse preferred) venir, Laurent s'en occupera; Quoique tu as (aies preferred) déjà lu le livre, il faut le relire.*

[6] The verbs *empêcher* and *éviter*, when used in R3 language, frequently lead to the expletive *ne* in the subordinate clause: *J'ai tout fait pour empêcher que les mariés ne se séparent; Tâche d'éviter qu'ils ne s'en aillent tout de suite.* However, when an interrogative or negative main clause precedes, the *ne* is hardly ever used: *Je n'ai pu éviter qu'elle parte; Leur frère ne pouvait pas empêcher que Jeanne aille directement à la banque.* The set expression *(il) n'empêche que* is always followed by the indicative: *(Il) n'empêche que Pierre a tort | que Marie serait la bienvenue.*

subject in the main and subordinate clauses is different. It makes no difference if the indirect object is a pronoun, a noun, or the name of a person: *Je
souhaite que Pierre revienne tôt*; *Je lui souhaite de revenir tôt*; *Le Président a souhaité
à tous les convives de passer une agréable soirée*; *Je souhaitais à Jean d'y réussir.*

In clauses dependent upon verbs and expressions indicating the feeling
of joy, fear, regret, unhappiness:

Verbs and expressions of feeling	Meaning	Comments
appréhender	to apprehend	In R3 usage, the expletive *ne* is sometimes inserted before the verb in the subjunctive; see also immediately above.
avoir hâte	to be anxious	
avoir peur	to be afraid	In R3 usage, the expletive *ne* is sometimes inserted before the verb in the subjunctive; see also immediately above.
craindre	to fear	In R3 usage the expletive *ne* is sometimes inserted before the verb in the subjunctive; see also immediately above.
désespérer	to despair	The expletive *ne* may appear after the negative: *Je ne désespère pas que Sophie (ne) réussisse.*
s'étonner	to be surprised	
se fâcher	to be angry	
se féliciter	to be happy/ pleased	
s'indigner	to be indignant	
se plaindre	to complain	
redouter	to dread	In R3 usage, *ne* is sometimes inserted before the verb in the subjunctive; see also immediately above.
refuser	to refuse	*Jean refuse que je lui vienne en aide.*
trembler[7]	to be terrified	In R3 usage, *ne* is sometimes inserted before the verb in the subjunctive; see also immediately above.

[7] With the verbs *appréhender, avoir peur, craindre, redouter* and *trembler*, the *ne* would
not be used if the main verb is in the negative: *Je ne crains pas qu'il parte* (*I do not fear
that he is leaving*). This expletive *ne* is not to be confused with the full negative *ne*...
pas: *Je crains qu'il ne vienne pas* (*I fear he is not coming*).

The impersonal use of some verbs like *choquer, étonner, surprendre, tarder,* and of verbal expressions like *cela me fait de la peine,* falls into this category:

Cela me choque qu'il se conduise de la sorte.	*I am shocked he behaves like that.*
Cela m'étonne qu'elle ait décroché l'agrég.	*I am surprised she's got the agrégation.*
Il me tarde que ce travail prenne fin.	*I am longing for this work to end.*
Cela me fait de la peine que Laurent soit malade.	*I am sorry Laurent is ill.*
Cela me fait plaisir que Jeanne vienne demain.	*I am delighted that Jeanne is coming tomorrow.*

With the verb *être* + adjectives expressing feeling:

Adjective	Meaning	Adjective	Meaning
choqué	*shocked*	honteux	*shameful*
content	*happy*	mécontent	*unhappy*
désolé	*sorry, disappointed*	ravi	*delighted*
étonné	*surprised*	satisfait	*contented/satisfied*
fâché	*angry*	surpris	*surprised*
heureux	*happy*	triste	*sad*
fier	*proud*		

Je suis choquée que Frédéric se soit comporté de la sorte.	*I am shocked that Frédéric should have behaved like that.*
Je suis désolé/mécontent/triste que les deux frères se soient bagarrés.	*I am sorry/unhappy/sad that the two brothers had a fight.*
Irène est étonnée/surprise que l'épreuve ait été si facile.	*Irène is surprised that the test was so easy.*
Maman est tellement fière que Jeanne ait remporté le meilleur prix.	*Mom is so proud that Jeanne has carried off the best prize.*

Similarly with the neuter *il*:

Il est honteux que les élèves aient chahuté la prof.	*It is shameful that the pupils should have played up the teacher.*
Il/C'est agaçant/embêtant qu'ils fassent tant de bruit.	*It's annoying that they make so much noise.*

One would also use the subjunctive with a whole range of adjectives expressing similar types of emotion: *Il est abasourdi/ahuri/avantageux/ déconcertant/ébahi/favorable/scandaleux/dégoûtant/immoral/stupéfait/stupéfié.*

In clauses dependent upon verbs and expressions indicating denial, doubt, evaluation, judgment, impossibility, necessity, possibility:

il y a avantage + à ce que	*there is an advantage in*
il y a intérêt / tu as intérêt + à ce que	*there is interest / you have interest in*
il y a opportunité + à ce que	*there is an opportunity in*
avoir besoin (R1)	*to need*
convenir	*to suit, to be fitting*
démentir (R3)	*to belie/deny*
c'est/il est dommage	*it's a pity*
ce n'est pas	*it is not that*
douter	*to doubt*
ignorer (R3)	*not to know*
nier	*to deny*
il faut	*I/you, etc. have to*
il importe (R3)	*it is necessary*
peu importe	*it does not matter*
il s'en faut de peu	*almost*
ce n'est pas la peine	*it is not worth*
il semble/semblerait	*it seems / would seem*

Il me semble/semblerait que (i.e. *sembler* + indirect object) is always followed by the indicative since the indirect object *me* suggests some precision, as would *il lui/leur semble*. However, the negative form, *il ne me semble pas que*, would very easily take the subjunctive, the negative implying less precision. The subjunctive would also be required with expressions such as *Il semble important/impératif que*.

supporter	*to put up with*

Note that this verb, when used in the negative, takes the subjunctive:

Je ne supporte pas que les manifestants cassent toutes ces vitres.	*I can't stand the demonstrators breaking all those windows.*

It also does when followed by certain adverbs:

Je supporte difficilement que les enfants se réveillent à quatre heures du matin.	*I have difficulty putting up with the children waking up at four.*
Je supporte facilement que l'on ne mange pas avant neuf heures du soir.	*I can easily put up with not eating before nine in the evening.*

Into this category fall a good number of adjectives preceded by *être* (*il est +* adjective + *que* + subjunctive), especially when a negative is involved: *Il est bizarre / bon / contradictoire / curieux / douteux / essentiel / exclu / extraordinaire /*

impératif | *important* | *impossible* | *improbable* | *inadmissible* | *inévitable* | *juste* |
légitime (R3) | *naturel* | *nécessaire* | *opportun* (R3) | *paradoxal* | *peu probable*[8] |
possible | *préférable* | *rare* | *remarquable* | *significatif* | *temps* (here a noun). *Il
est inadmissible que le proviseur l'ait puni pour une telle erreur*; *Il est rare que
Lucile revienne tard*; *Il est remarquable que tous se soient trompés*; *Il est significatif
qu'ils ne vous aient pas attendus*; *Il n'est pas vraisemblable que Sébastien s'en soit
aperçu.*

In clauses dependent upon a superlative formed with *plus* or *moins*:

C'est le livre le plus comique que j'aie jamais lu.	*It's the funniest book I've ever read.*
C'est le garçon le plus intelligent que je connaisse.	*He's the most intelligent boy I know.*
C'est le moins que je puisse dire.	*That's the least I can say.*

In speech and even in writing, the subjunctive is not always observed
in this construction. A good percentage of French speakers would easily
use *ai* instead of *aie* and *connais* instead of *connaisse*. This would be R1
style.

In clauses dependent upon verbs and expressions indicating chance:

risquer	*to risk*
il arrive que	*it happens that*
il est fréquent que	*it often happens that*
il n'y a aucune chance que / pour que	*there is no chance that*
il y a de grandes/fortes chances que / pour que	*it is very likely that*
c'est une chance que	*there is a chance that*
il y a le danger que	*there is the danger that*
c'est un hasard que	*there is the chance that*
Michel risque que son nom soit oublié au moment des récompenses.	*There is a risk that Michel's name be forgotten when rewards are given out.*
Il arrive assez souvent qu'elle soit en retard.	*It happens quite often that she is late.*

But with an indirect object:

Il lui arrive d'être en retard.	*She is sometimes late.*
C'est une chance que Marie soit là.	*There is a chance that Marie be there.*

[8] In most cases, *il est probable* is followed by the indicative, given the increased
certainty it suggests.

When *faire* is used with a subordinate clause that is *non-validé* or non-substantiated, a subjunctive is required. A quotation from the Romantic writer Senancour's *Obermann* (1904, letter 90), illustrates this:

"L'homme est périssable. Il se
peut ; mais périssons en
résistant, et si le néant nous
est réservé, ne faisons pas que
ce soit une justice."

Man is perishable. That is possible,
but let us resist this perishable
possibility, and if nothingness
awaits us, let us not act in such a
way that it will be an injustice.

However, when the subordinate clause is *validé* or substantiated, an indicative is needed:

Jean a raté le train, ce qui fait
qu'il est rentré très tard.

Jean missed the train, which meant
that he arrived home late.

44.5 "Gray" subjunctive

As stated on more than one occasion, the use of the subjunctive frequently corresponds to a higher register of language, particularly when there is a choice between the subjunctive and the indicative. R3 users may introduce subtle shades of meaning and a touch of elegance into their French by a discreet balancing and contrasting of indicatives and subjunctives, the latter being used to imply a subjective attitude to what is being said, the former to convey concrete facts. An R2/R1 speaker could easily say and write in a soccer context:

C'est la dernière partie de foot
que j'ai vue.

It's the last soccer game I've seen.

A theatergoer or student of a play would say and write in more sophisticated language:

C'est la dernière pièce de
Tchechov que j'aie vue / j'aie á
étudier.

It's the last Chekov play I've see seen /
I have to study now.

It goes without saying that the pronunciation of *ai* and *aie* is the same.

It is often what precedes the verb followed by the subordinate clause that determines the use of the subjunctive. In the following cases, an element of doubt is present, which triggers the subjunctive for R3 users:

Je ne puis m'imaginer que Sophie
ait tenu sa promesse.

I can't imagine that Sophie has kept
her promise.

Je suis loin d'espérer que Céline
revienne.

I am far from hoping Céline will come
back.

Je n'ai pas l'impression que Pierre soit convaincu.	*I don't have the impression Pierre is convinced.*
Je refuse de croire que l'accusée soit coupable.	*I refuse to believe the accused is guilty.*
J'ai du mal à croire qu'elle soit Anglaise.	*I have difficulty believing she is English.*

In clauses dependent upon a superlative and similar expressions (e.g., *dernier, premier, seul, ne . . . que, unique* – these latter expressions may be considered as superlatives since they express uniqueness), the subjunctive use points to an elegance of style which is often the mark of the subjunctive where discretion is available:

R1 + R2	R2 + R3
C'est la première/dernière athlète qui a couru le cent mètres en 10,7 (dix secondes virgule sept).	C'est la dernière athlète qui ait couru le cent mètres en 10,7.
C'est le meilleur/pire élève que je connais.	C'est le meilleur/pire élève que je connaisse.
Il n'y a que mon père qui le fait.	Il n'ya que mon père qui le fasse.

A play on words with the commercial for Maille mustard produces the following: *Il n'y a que Maille qui m'aille* (*Only Maille mustard suits me*).

C'est le seul de mes collègues avec qui je me suis vraiment lié d'amitié.	C'est le seul de mes collègues avec qui je me sois vraiment lié d'amitié.

Françoise Giroud translates Einstein's eulogy of Marie Curie in the following way: "La seule personne que la gloire n'ait pas corrompue" (1981, p. 7). This group would also include the adjective *rare*, which similarly highlights uniqueness, as in:

R1 + R2	R2 + R3
C'est un des rares aventuriers qui ont traversé ce désert.	C'est un des rares aventuriers qui aient traversé ce désert.

Note that after expressions involving *fois* (*première/dernière/seule fois*), the indicative is used with the present or imperfect tense:

C'est la première fois que je te vois ici.	*It's the first time I've seen you here.*
C'était la première fois que je la voyais là.	*It was the first time I'd seen her there.*

The subjuctive can occur in clauses dependent upon a negative or indefinite antecedent:

R1 + R2	R2 + R3
Il n'y a personne qui peut réparer ma radio.	Il n'y a personne qui puisse réparer ma radio.
Il n'y a rien qui est plus difficile que les maths.	Il n'y a rien qui soit plus diffcile que les maths.
Il n'y a aucune matière que Françoise ne comprend pas.	Il n'y a aucune matière que Françoise ne comprenne pas.
Ce n'est pas un homme qui te prend au sérieux.	Ce n'est pas un homme qui te prenne au sérieux.
Il faut quelqu'un qui est à la hauteur.	Il faut quelqu'un qui soit à la hauteur.
Je préfère/préférais quelque chose qui est/était plus sucré.	Je préfère quelque chose qui soit plus sucré.
J'ai besoin d'un homme qui peut garantir le succès.	J'ai besoin d'un homme qui puisse garantir le succès.
Pierre désire une situation qui lui plaît.	Pierre désire une situation qui lui plaise.
Trouve-moi l'adresse d'une infirmière qui sait faire la piqûre.	Trouve-moi l'adresse d'une infirmière qui sache faire la piqûre.

It goes without saying that if, in the last example, the definite article were used, a subjunctive would not occur, given the precise nature of the knowledge, so that only *Trouve-moi le médecin qui sait* would apply.

The subjunctive can occur in clauses dependent upon expressions denying and questioning probability and certainty:

R1 + R2	R2 + R3
Il n'est pas certain que Sébastien viendra.	Il n'est pas certain que Sébastien vienne.
Est-il certain que Sébastien viendra?	Est-il certain que Sébastien vienne?
Il n'est pas sûr que Jeanne est rentrée.	Il n'est pas sûr que Jeanne soit rentrée.
Il n'est pas clair que Philippe a réussi.	Il n'est pas clair que Philippe ait réussi.
Est-il clair que Philippe a réussi?	Est-il clair que Philippe ait réussi?

Similarly with the adjectives *évident, exact, incertain, improbable, probable, sûr, vrai, vraisemblable* and even, in very high register, *incontestable, indéniable, indiscutable, inévitable, infaillible*. Note that the above subordinate clauses are introduced by the conjunction *que*. When the subordinate clause is introduced by the conjunction *si*, only the indicative occurs: *Il n'est pas sûr si Pierre est rentré*. Under this heading are the expressions related to doubt, even if this doubt is negated in some way. In other words, even if there is no doubt whatsoever, the mere use of *doute* implies the subjunctive: *Il n'y a pas de doute que | Il ne fait pas de doute que | Il n'est pas douteux que*. Some would plead, however, for the possibility of the indicative here, including Hanse and Blampain.

The subjunctive can occur in clauses dependent upon verbs of thinking and declaring in the interrogative and/or negative: *accepter, admettre, affirmer, assurer, comprendre, concevoir, convaincre, croire, déclarer, dire, envisager, expliquer, garantir, insister, penser, prétendre*. Elegance of style is very conspicuous here:

Je n'accepte pas que l'avocat le défende.	*I do not accept that the lawyer defend him.*
Je ne comprends pas que Laurent ait commis une telle erreur.	*I can't understand that Laurent should have made such an error.*
Pierre ne dit pas que son frère ait raison.	*Pierre does not say his brother is right.*
Comment peux-tu prétendre que ce soit le résultat voulu?	*How can you claim this is the desired result?*

In R3 language many of these verbs may be used positively, with no sense of doubt through negation or questioning:

J'admets que tu aies raison.	*I admit you are right.*
Je comprends que tu veuilles partir.	*I understand that you wish to leave.*

The subjunctive can occur in clauses dependent upon expressions of the following type, often involving nouns. These expressions are very frequently connected to verbs that appear earlier in this chapter:

Le but / le dessein / l'intention est que...	*The aim/intention is that...*
Il se fait que / ce qui fait que...	*It happens that / which means that...*
L'idée que...	*The idea that...*
Il se trouve que...	*It happens that...*
espérer (R1)	*to hope*
prévoir	*to foresee*
Le fait que cette étudiante soit plus intelligente n'est pas surprenant.	*The fact that this student is more intelligent is not surprising.*
L'idée qu'ils aillent au cinéma à minuit me paraît folle.	*The idea that they should go to the movies at midnight seems mad to me.*
Le tableau est très sombre, ce qui fait que le public s'y soit moins intéressé.	*The painting is very dark, which meant that the public is less interested in it.*

| Le gouvernement prévoit que l'économie fasse un bond en avant. | *The government intends that the economy will leap forward.* |

In all these cases, the indicative would be quite acceptable. Some uncertainty exists over usage with *espérer*. *Espérer* used affirmatively requires the indicative in standard French but, in colloquial language, one can come across the subjunctive: *J'espère qu'elle vienne*. At the same time, the negative form of this verb could easily lead to the subjunctive in R3 style:

| Je n'espère nullement que mes collègues lui fassent confiance. | *In no way do I expect my colleagues to place their trust in her/*him. |

Other forms of *espérer* could also lead to the subjunctive:

| J'aurais espéré que ma mère ait les billets. | *I would have hoped that my mother had the tickets.* |
| Il faut / est à espérer que les statistiques soient correctes. | *We must hope / It is to be hoped that the statistics are correct.* |

When *prévoir = foresee*, the indicative is normal:

| J'ai prévu que mon amie reviendrait. | *I foresaw my friend would return.* |

When it means *to intend/mean*, however, the subjunctive is very common.

Note how *venir* may be used in the higher register, and this subjunctive recalls an English subjunctive. This construction refers to time, replacing *quand* with the future:

Vienne la fin de l'année, tout le monde sera content.	*Come the end of the year, everyone will be happy.*
Vienne une invasion, on sera écrasé.	*Come an invasion, we'll be crushed.*
Viennent les vacances / les beaux jours, on va faire des excursions en montagne.	*Come the vacation / happy days, and we'll go off to the mountains.*

Because of uncertainty over the appropriateness of the subjunctive, particularly with respect to gray areas, the possibilities of avoiding the subjunctive do exist. This may easily be done in certain circumstances, although we do not always suggest that avoiding the subjunctive is a pattern to observe. However, if the subject of the main clause and the subordinate clause is the same, one would expect the infinitive, and not the subjunctive, as with the following prepositional phases:

Preposition	To replace
à condition de	à condition que
afin de	afin que
à moins de	à moins que

Preposition	To replace
avant de	avant que
(de) crainte de / par crainte de	craindre / de crainte que
de façon à	de façon que / à ce que, de sorte que
de manière à	de manière que / à ce que, de sorte que
de peur de	avoir peur que / de peur que
sans	sans que

For instance:

Laetitia refusera à moins d'y être contrainte.	*Laetitia will refuse unless she is forced (to accept, etc.).*
Tu fais un brouillon avant de rédiger la version définitive.	*You do a draft copy before drawing up the final version.*
Il se taisait (de) crainte de les importuner	*He remained quiet for fear of troubling them.*

Certain prepositional phrases are available to replace clauses with a subjunctive:

Prepositional phrases	To replace
avant mon départ	avant que je (ne) parte
après mon départ	après que je sois parti (*I have left*)
à mon insu	sans que je le sache
à ma connaissance	à ce que/autant que je sache

Jusqu'à ce que / avant que and *en attendant que* + subjunctive may very easily be replaced in the following way:

Je l'ai attendue jusqu'au moment où l'horloge a sonné sept heures.	*I waited for her until the moment when the clock sounded seven o'clock.*
J'ai été obligée de partir avant le moment où elle a dû rentrer.	*I had to leave before the moment when she must have come back / had to come back.*
En attendant le moment où le train arrivait en gare, je me suis payé un pot.	*Waiting for the moment when the train would arrive in the station, I had a drink.*

The expressions above do not necessarily lead to a subjunctive or indicative subordinate clause, which may be neatly and elegantly avoided in the following way: *à* + infinitive or perfect infinitive:

C'est le seul à avoir visité le Congo.	*He's the only one to have visited Congo.*

Elle est la première/dernière femme à courir le 200 mètres en 20,9 secondes (vingt virgule neuf secondes).	*She's the first/last woman to run the two hundred meters in 20.9 seconds.*
C'est une des rares femmes à faire le tour du monde seule en bateau.	*She's one of the rare women to have circumnavigated the world alone in a boat.*

Part V

45

Personal pronouns and pronouns as objects / Les pronoms personnels, les pronoms comme objets[1]

The following passage concerns a sixteenth-century house in Viviers in the Ardèche, in southern France. Age and neglect had caused it to lose some of its attractiveness but its facade still retained an element of style. Twenty years ago, a group of Americans tried unsuccessfully to buy the facade. The husband and wife in the passage had spent their youth there and wanted to buy it, but since it was a listed building, the mayor intervened to prevent the sale. Clearly, he wanted the house to remain part of Viviers's heritage. The passage contains a great number of highlighted personal pronouns, in the subject case (*il/elle/nous/vous/ils/on*), in the object case (*le/la/les/nous/vous*) and as indirect objects (*lui/leur*). Also are to be found a number of reflexive pronouns (*se/nous*). Disjunctive pronouns are common too: *moi, toi-même, eux-mêmes, soi*. Notice the agreement of pronouns with the past participle when they precede it: *C'est moi qui l'ai remarquée*. Notice also, in a number of cases, the noun repeated and therefore highlighted by the pronoun (*la > façade*). Some translations are provided.

La Maison des Chevaliers

Félix et son épouse **s'**arrêtent devant la Maison des Chevaliers et **la** contemplent avec un regard attendri. C'est **moi** qui l'ai remarquée avant les autres. C'est la maison de leur jeunesse ! Nous **la** regardons tous, cette belle façade style renaissance, richement sculptée de frises [friezes], de colonnades antiques, de médaillons, de bustes en relief et d'une chevauchée de cavaliers. Regardez-**la** donc, cette magnifique façade et cette architecture si délicate. Cette bâtisse [building] est devenue un véritable monument historique.

Le maire du village passe dans les parages [in the vicinity]. **Il s'**arrête pour saluer la foule. Il y **en** a, des spectateurs ! **Il se** dirige vers Félix et son épouse en **leur** disant : « Pardon, excusez-**moi**, Félix, mais **nous** ne vendons pas cette maison. **Vous** finirez par accepter les choses. **Vous** recevrez un dédommagement [compensation] pour cela ! »

---

[1] For agreement of pronouns with the past participle, see Chapter 14 on the perfect tense; for reflexive pronouns, see Chapter 33 on reflexive verbs; for pronouns with the infinitive, see Chapter 12; for pronouns with the imperative, see Chapter 29.

Félix, furieux, fixe [stares at] le premier magistrat de la bourgade et **lui** lance : «**Vous m**'avez dépossédé de mes biens ! **On** a beau être citoyens, **on** n'est pas toujours égaux ! Comme **vous** voudrez. **Ils** peuvent être fiers d'**eux**-mêmes. Regardez-**les** ! **Je nous** vois contraints de **nous** défendre.»

Le maire tente d'apaiser son interlocuteur et son épouse en **leur** indiquant : «Cette maison-ci, **je l**'ai vue dans un état délabré [dilapidated] ! **Je le** dis et **je le** répète, cette maison doit être réhabilitée [renovated]. **Elle** fait l'objet d'études dans le cadre de la réhabilitation et de la préservation du patrimoine vivarois. Allez ! **On se** dit « tu », Félix ? Regarde-**moi** cette tête ! Allez donc, **on** prend un verre ?»

Enfin le trio **se** rend au café du coin. **On** s'amusait et **se** défoulait [chilled out] à l'intérieur. Qu'est-ce qu'**on** va boire cet après-midi ? Félix ouvrit la lettre du maire, **la** lut puis **la** jeta au panier. **Tu t'en** occupes **toi**-même, de ce relogement et de ce dédommagement. **Nous** comptons sur **toi** ! Le maire **se** leva, paya le tenancier [bartender] du bar, car **il** devait partir pour un rendez-vous au conseil municipal. **Je vous** admire et **je vous** félicite, mes chers concitoyens ! L'épouse de Félix s'entête et s'acharne [insists and insists]. **Elle** ne boit ni ne mange. **Elle** passe son temps à rêver de souvenirs lointains de cette maison. Son époux **lui** a fait un beau sermon. Prends garde à **toi**, chérie ! Je l'ai échappé belle [I had a narrow miss]. Alors, **on** ne pense qu'à **soi**. **On** s'émeut et **on se** passionne pour cette Maison des Chevaliers.

There are two types of pronouns: conjunctive and disjunctive. The first conjoins or connects the pronoun to the verb: *Je l'ai vu = I saw him*; the second separates or isolates the pronoun from the verb, and often introduces the notion of stress: *C'est moi qui l'ai dit = It's me/I who said it*. Apart from the first- and second-person plurals (*nous, vous*), conjunctive and disjunctive pronouns are different in appearance.

45.1 Conjunctive pronouns

45.1.1 Personal pronoun as subject

The following personal pronouns are consistently used as the subject of a sentence:

je	*I*	nous	*we*
tu	*you* (one person)	vous	*you*
il	*he*	ils	*they* (male)
elle	*she*	elles	*they* (female)

As opposed to Italian and Spanish, which continue the Latin tradition, French subject pronouns are used very regularly, largely to avoid ambiguity. This becomes clear if we conjugate an **–er** verb:

je regarde la maison	*I look at the house*
tu regardes la maison	*you look at the house*
il regarde la maison	*he looks at the house*
elle regarde la maison	*she looks at the house*
nous regardons la maison	*we look at the house*
vous regardez la maison	*you look at the house*
ils regardent la maison	*they look at the house* (males / males and females)
elles regardent la maison	*they look at the house* (females)

In this present-tense conjugation, the only forms that differ in sound from the rest are *regardons* and *regardez*. A summary glance at the other main conjugations reveals a similar but not identical uniformity of sound: *vendre > vends, vends, vend, vendons, vendez, vendent; finir > finis, finis, finit, finissons, finissez, finissent; recevoir > reçois, reçois, reçoit, recevons, recevez, reçoivent.* Furthermore, there is a similarity of sounds with the subjunctive and the indicative. The singular subjunctive forms of the present tense of the verb *recevoir* are *reçoive(s)* and the third-person plural is *reçoivent*, a sound recalling the third-person plural indicative. The use of the subject pronouns is therefore most important.

Note that *nous* refers to all males, all females or a mixture; *vous* refers to one single person not of intimate acquaintance, to all males, all females or a mixture; *ils* refers to all males or a mixture of males and females. As with *nous* and *vous*, even if there is only one male in a large group of females, *ils* still holds sway. *Nous* and *vous* by themselves are not concerned with male and female distinctions but if there are agreements this would become significant.

The following table shows broadly the situation in which the second-person pronouns *tu* (and allied terms: *toi, te, t', ton, ta, tes*) and *vous* (and allied terms: *votre, vos*) are used as modes of address in the singular:

Tu	*Vous*
used when speaking to:	used when speaking to:
young children	a much older person one does not know
parents	sometimes a distant relative
near relatives	a professional contact one does not know well
domestic animals	
an assumed higher being	a priest or any minister of religion
	any person one comes across in the street
	a politician
	a superior in the military

Tu	Vous
used between:	used between:
friends, workmates	professional contacts, depending
soldiers in the same unit and	on frequency of communication
usually of the same class	
children in the same school	
students (but not always)	

It goes without saying that this table is merely a helpful guide, and that actual usage is far more complicated than it would suggest. Recourse to *tu* and *vous* is affected by a large number of factors such as age, personal attitudes, social circumstances, relationships within a hierarchy and so on.

For obvious sociological reasons, there has been a general movement from *vous* to *tu*, a residue of the deep social disturbances of the events of 1968 caused by the convulsions of a breakdown in social order and an attack on the social hierarchy. Yet, whereas *tu* seemed to be replacing *vous* in many unsuspected circumstances following the 1968 troubles, the old order of the *tu/vous* divide has largely reasserted itself. Intriguingly enough, this is not so much the case in Italian (*tu*) and Spanish (*tú*) where these two pronouns have assumed a greater role in modern discourse since about the 1980s. Life has become less formal.

Whereas, once, probably all teachers used *vous* when addressing older pupils (say from the age of fifteen onwards), a good number no longer observe this practice; similarly with the priest. However, *tu* is discouraged across military ranks for conspicuous reasons of discipline. The appropriateness of *tu* or *vous* can often be obscured if, for instance, a child's age is not known. Indeed, a genuine awkwardness may ensue if a child's age is unknown, and the situation might arise where an older person would find it necessary to ask a younger person's permission to *tutoyer* him/her if the age is unclear. The age of 14 or 15 would, initially at any rate, require the respectful *vous*, but if this young person were in the company of others whom the older person knew and addressed as *tu*, *tu* could be used straightaway.

Catholics now follow the well-established Protestant example of using *tu* to address God (no assumption of God's existence is implied here). At the same time, in certain aristocratic families, or in any family of high social status, as with some lawyers, parents even now use *tu* to address their children, while the latter address their parents as *vous*. This *vous-Régence* is particularly applicable to the higher echelons of government. It is often parodied in French films and plays: use of inappropriate pronouns in some contexts – switching from distance (use of *vous*) to intimacy or humiliation (use of *tu*) – can generate comic, odd or disarming effects. In play, children may easily mimic members of high society or simply adults by using the *vous* form. *Tu* is used with pets, but *vous* in such circumstances could sound really comic if done deliberately.

The feature to remember is that the use of *tu* and *vous*, and the passage from the one to the other, contains subtleties capable of expressing strong feelings, likes and dislikes, a sense of distance, superiority, indifference, in fact the whole spectrum of attitudes and emotions. Thus, a driver, on observing poor driving by an unknown motorist could very easily say, or think: "T'as eu ton permis de conduire dans une pochette-surprise?" (a child's present with a surprise item). This intimate form invests the speaker with a sense of superiority, and he puts the guilty driver in his/her place. Since English no longer possesses two second-person pronouns, although it once did (*thou* and *you*; Voltaire refers to this in his *Lettres philosophiques*), the subtleties, social tactics and jokes available in French cannot be effectively conveyed in translation from French into English. When François Mitterrand, leader of the Socialist party, assumed the mantle of French president, and heard a left-wing colleague say "Allez! On se dit tu," he is alleged to have replied icily: "Comme vous voudrez." In a similar way, movement up or down the social hierarchy can create embarrassment: if two people have been on close terms and have been in the habit of addressing each other as *tu*, even for years, and if their contact is broken because one of them rises up the social, professional or academic ladder, on a subsequent meeting, there could easily be a problem as to which pronoun to use. A convenient stratagem could be recourse to the third person *on*: "On prend une cannette?" Another difficulty arises when one meets for the first time the partner of a friend with whom one is naturally on *tu* terms; this is all the more acute if partners are present: does one use the respectful *vous* because one does not know the partner or *tu* by virtue of the association with the friend? *Tu* and *vous* can even be used between two people at different times of the day! Two colleagues who run a hairdressing business in Paris use *vous* on the premises and *tu* when away from their work. The pronoun *tu* would not suit their formal approach to their profession. A well-known example of the sexual exploitation of the different values of the two pronouns occurs in a song made famous by Juliette Greco, which elicits the following comment: "*Déshabillez-moi* est bien plus érotique que *Déshabille-moi*": recourse to *vous* rather than to *tu* adds a connotation of exciting suggestiveness (distance in intimacy) to the *liaison*.

The most awkward moment can occur in the actual transition from *vous* to *tu*, that is passing from the stage of distance and respect to that of friendliness and so on. This is felt especially acutely between the sexes where movement from *vous* to *tu* marks a step toward intimacy and confidence. If a speaker inadvertently addresses a stranger as *tu*, an apology could be felt to be required on the part of the speaker ("Pardon, excusez-moi!"). On the other hand, were it done deliberately, an insult could ensue.

Finally, if A is addressed in the *tu* form by B, A should not automatically use the *tu* form in return, and certainly this could be the case if an adult speaks to a much younger person as *tu*. Again, a safe solution is to use *on* as a provisional expedient.

45.1.2 Personal pronoun as direct object

elle me regarde	*she looks at me* (male or female)
elle te regarde	*she looks at you* (singular male or female)
elle le regarde	*she looks at him/it*
elle la regarde	*she looks at her/it*
elle nous regarde	*she looks at us* (males and/or females)
elle vous regarde	*she looks at you* (one male/female; males and/or females)
elle les regarde	*she looks at them* (males and/or females)

Le (masculine) and *la* (feminine) also refer to objects: *Je le regarde* = I look at it (*le livre*); *Je la regarde* = I look at it (*la maison*). These two pronouns also refer to fauna: *Je le regarde* = I look at it (*le lapin*); *Je la regarde* = I look at it (*la bête*).

As observed in the examples above, pronouns precede an affirmative verb. They also precede the infinitive: *Je veux le voir* = I wish to see him. This is a different practice from Italian (*Voglio vederlo*) and Spanish (*Quiero verlo*), where the pronoun is attached to the infinitive.

Pronouns precede a verb in the negative: *Je ne le touche pas* = I don't touch it; *Je ne veux pas le voir* = I do not wish to see him.

They do not precede the verb in the affirmative imperative: *Regarde-moi* = Look at me; *Regardez-les* = Look at them.

They do precede the verb when the imperative is in the negative: *Ne me regarde pas* = Don't look at me; *Ne les regardez pas* = Don't look at them.

Me/te/le/la are elided before a vowel: *Elle m'/t'/l'a vu(e)* = She saw me/you/him/her.

45.1.3 Personal pronoun as indirect object

il me parle	*he speaks to me* (male or female)
il te parle	*he speaks to you* (singular male or female)
il lui parle	*he speaks to him/her/it*
il nous parle	*he speaks to us* (males and/or females)
il vous parle	*he speaks to you* (one male/female, males and/or females)
il leur parle	*he speaks to them* (males and/or females)

45.1.4 Personal pronouns and word order

The order of unstressed pronouns excluding subject pronouns with respect to the verb is as follows. It is really a question of where the direct and indirect objects appear in relation to each other:

With *me/te/nous/vous/se* as indirect objects:

me			
te	le		
nous	la	y	en
vous	les		
se			

With *lui/leur* as indirect objects:

le	lui		
la	leur	y	en
les			

This order is respected in all tenses and moods of verbs, except the positive imperative. The most important feature in this order is that, when *me/te/nous/vous/se* are used as indirect objects, they precede the direct object. On the other hand, the indirect objects *lui* and *leur* follow the direct object. Highlighted in the examples are the indirect objects.

elle **me** le donne	*she gives it to me*
elle **te** le donne	*she gives it to you*
elle le **lui** donne	*she gives it to him/her*
elle **nous** le donne	*she gives it to us*
elle **vous** le donne	*she gives it to you*
elle le **leur** donne	*she gives it to them*
j'**y en** ai vu	*I saw some there*
il **y en** a	*there are some*

Verbs that follow this pattern are:

1. verbs of saying: *affirmer, annoncer, apprendre, assurer, avouer, communiquer, confirmer, conseiller, déclarer, demander, dire, expliquer, informer, notifier, raconter, réciter, recommander, signifier, solliciter, suggérer, transmettre; Jeanne m'a appris son intention de partir; Je lui ai expliqué ma théorie; Stéphanie m'a raconté son histoire;*

2. verbs of giving: *accorder, attribuer, conférer, décerner, donner, filer* (R1), *remettre, octroyer, payer, verser; Louis m'a accordé une faveur; ma compagnie m'a octroyé une prime exceptionnelle; Adrienne a remis sa traduction à son professeur; As-tu versé la somme au fisc (treasury department / tax office)?*

Many of the verbs of saying may take an indirect object and a subordinate clause: *Je lui ai dit que je viendrai; Irène lui a affirmé que son père était absent; Le gouvernement a annoncé au public qu'il y aura des élections; Je lui ai assuré qu'il s'agissait de racontars; Je lui ai suggéré que nous prenions une pause.*

Some verbs may take a direct object and a subordinate clause: *avertir, aviser, convaincre, informer, persuader, prévenir; Marie a averti son mari qu'elle allait sortir; Irène a convaincu ma mère que j'avais l'agrégation; Pourquoi as-tu informé Jean que j'avais d'excellentes notes ?; J'ai persuadé mon frère que cette solution est la bonne; Tu as prévenu Sophie qu'on part ?*

The corollary of this construction is that these verbs may be used in the passive, as opposed to *dire, donner*, for instance (in English, this is also possible: *I was told that . . . I was given a book*): *Aseline est convaincue/persuadée que son frère finira par réussir; Je dois informer Pierre qu'une décision a été prise.*

The two pronouns *je* and *nous* may be juxtaposed, as in English:

Je ne nous vois pas faire cela.	*I can't see us doing that.*
Je nous vois contraints de nous défendre.	*I see us obliged to defend ourselves.*

A schoolchild's trick for remembering the *y/en* order is: **Y** before **en** as the donkey knows. In other words, **y** + **en** could be construed as the ono-matopoeic sound for the snorting of a donkey.

It is not acceptable before the verb to combine the direct objects *me*, *te*, *nous*, *vous*, *se* with the indirect objects. The indirect object comes after the verb: *Mon père m'a présenté à elle*; *Je ne me fie pas à eux*; *La question qui se pose à nous*. . .

Pronouns follow the imperative in this order: *assieds-toi*; *asseyez-vous*; *asseyons-nous*; *donne(z)-le(s)-moi/nous*; *donne(z)-la-lui/leur*; *donne(z)-les-lui/leur*; *donne(z)-lui/leur-en*; *donnons-le/la/les-lui/leur*; *mets-y-en*; *mettez-y-en*; *donnons-leur-en*. Some combinations cause hesitation: *Donne-lui-en*; and in R1 spoken language, one could very easily hear *Donne-luis-en* (with *liaison*). See the following chapter for separate treatment of *y* and *en*.

Pronouns precede the imperative when it is negated: *ne te lève pas*; *ne nous levons pas*; *ne vous levez pas*; *ne me/le donne(z) pas*; *ne nous les donne(z) pas*; *ne la/le-lui/leur donnons pas*; *ne lui/leur en donnons pas*.

45.1.5 Repetition

The repetition of nouns in the form of pronouns in French is very common. Reference can be made to a noun before it or after it. This feature also occurs in both Spanish and Italian. It is not so much a question of stress, although this must be a factor, as one of linguistic habit:

Ce roman-là, je l'ai lu et relu.	*I've read and reread that novel.*
Cette maison-ci, je l'ai vue dans un état délabré.	*I saw this house in a dilapidated state.*

Such a repetition is reminiscent of spoken registers, as are the following involving prepositions or implying their presence:

À son frère, elle ne lui rend jamais visite.	*She never visits her brother.*
J'en ai, des œufs.	*I have some eggs.*
Il y en a, des spectateurs.	*There are (many) spectators.*
À Bruxelles, j'y vais rarement.	*I rarely go to Brussels.*

The first of the four examples is not heard so much, as the prepositional phrase seems awkward.

Repetition of a different sort is also common, with respect to both the subject and the object:

Je le dis et je le répète.	*I say it and I repeat it.*
Je vous admire et je vous félicite.	*I admire you and congratulate you.*

In the first example, the second *je* may be omitted, but not the *le*. Similarly in the second one, the *je* may be omitted, but not so for the *vous*. One can also say in compound tenses both *Je l'ai dit et je l'ai répété* and *Je l'ai dit et répété*.

The reflexive pronoun *se* is repeated in simple tenses:

Ils se voient et s'écrivent.	*They see and write to each other.*
Elle s'entête et s'acharne.	*She is stubborn and persistent.*

Repetition of the subject pronoun does not occur with *ni... ni*:

Elle ne boit ni ne mange.	*She neither drinks nor eats.*
Je ne joue du piano ni ne parle chinois.	*I neither play the piano nor speak Chinese.*

To convey a rapid succession of events, exclusion of pronouns is common:

César est venu, a vu, a vaincu.	*Caesar came, saw and conquered.*
J'ouvris la lettre, la lus, la jetai au panier.	*I opened the letter, read it, and threw it into the trash bin.*
Elle frappa, entra, et s'assit.	*She knocked, went in and sat down.*

But, if an explanation is required, a pronoun could be repeated, after its exclusion:

Enfin il se leva, paya, il devait partir.	*Finally, he got up, paid, for he had to go.*

A subordinate conjunction requires the repetition of a personal pronoun if it is itself repeated:

Il vous excusera parce qu'il vous connaît et parce qu'il vous fait confiance.	*He will excuse you because he knows you and because he trusts you.*

One could, of course, say and write: *Il vous excusera parce qu'il vous connaît et vous fait confiance.*

Verbs used impersonally usually need the repetition of *il*:

Il pleut et il vente.	*It is raining and is windy.*
Il grêle et il neige.	*It is hailing and snowing.*

This also applies to *on*:

On s'émeut et on se passionne.	*We are moved and get excited.*
On s'amusait et se défoulait.	*We enjoyed ourselves and let off steam.*

45.1.6 Uses of *on* (*one*)

One can be translated in a variety of ways and can replace all the subject pronouns although, in reality, it is only sometimes a substitute for *tu* and *vous*. It can sometimes be used as stratagem to avoid the difficulty of whether to address a person with one or the other. It is surprisingly flexible and corresponds largely to the impersonal *se* in Spanish.

On is usually treated as a masculine singular subject pronoun:

Quand on n'a rien à faire, on s'ennuie.	*When you have nothing to do, you get bored.*
Qu'est-ce qu'on va voir cet après-midi?	*What are we going to see this afternoon?*

However, it may also be used with reference to feminine or plural subjects, and entails appropiate agreements of adjectives. *On* always takes the third-personal singular verb:

Quand on est mère, on est fière de ses enfants.	*As a mother one is always proud of one's children.*
On a beau être citoyens, on n'est pas toujours égaux.	*It's fine being a citizen but you are not always equal.*
On a été sages aujourd'hui?	*Have you been well-behaved today?* (mother speaking to children)
On est venus aussi vite que possible.	*We came as quickly as we could.* (two or more people speaking)

On functions only as a subject; when it is required to express a direct object or other complement, other forms are used:

Complements of on		*Examples*
reflexive	*se*	*On se lève, on se lave.*
	soi (R3 only)	*On doit aider les plus infortunés que soi.*
	soi-même (oneself)	*De temps en temps, on doit prendre une décision soi-même.*
non-reflexive	*nous* (including speaker)	*On voit bien ses cheveux gris quand elle est près de nous/vous.*

It is not uncommon for *nous* to be used in apposition to *on*:

Nous autres Norvégiens, on ne le fait pas comme ça.	*We Norwegians don't do it like that.*

The possessive adjective associated in a general way with *on* is *son/sa/ses*:

On entre, on enlève son chapeau et ses gants...	*You go in, you take off your hat and gloves...*

Tu may be used in a similar way here:

Tu entres, tu achètes ton billet, tu t'assieds...	*You go in, you buy your ticket, you sit down...*

But, if a plural idea is suggested with *on* (= *nous*), and a specific instance is pointed to, the possessive adjective must be *notre/nos*:

On est entré, on a enlevé nos   *We went in, took off our clothes and*
   vêtements et nos chaussures.   *shoes.*

If one used *ses* here, one would wonder if the *vêtements* and *chaussures* were *à lui* or *à elle* and not *à nous*. A second example will make this feature clearer:

On vient de renouveler nos   *We've just renewed our passports.*
   passeports.

    Often in R3 usage, but in spoken language as well, and for the sake of euphony, the form *l'on* is preferred: *L'on préfère rester à Paris*; *Il est clair que l'on doit acheter les billets ce soir.*

    Since *on* is such a flexible pronoun (and it is used much more frequently than *one* in English), attitudes to its use vary. In writing, it can attract censure, associated as it is with a looseness and informality of style (but see the reference to Flaubert in Chapter 1 on register, which discounts this argument). Consequently, *nous* is recommended in preference, yet tolerance of the use of *on* is creeping in more and more.

    Nous can also stand as a substitute for *je* in the same way, functioning as a singular pronoun, with reference to a male in the first example, and a female in the second (and therefore requiring agreement of the past participle): *Nous sommes tentés de suggérer que. . .* ; *Nous nous sommes efforcée de décrire. . .*

45.1.7   Neuter *le*

In addition to its function as referring to persons (*Je le vois* = I see him), *le* can provide a link between what is being said and what has just been said. There is not always an equivalent in English:

Elle me l'a dit.   *She told me (so).*

In R1 language, the *le* is omitted but such an omission is not to be encouraged:

Il voulait être grand, et il l'est.   *He wanted to be tall, and he is.*
Pauvre, il risque de l'être.   *He's in danger of being poor.*
Elle est plus grande que je ne le   *She's taller than I thought.*
   pensais.
Cela va mieux que je ne le   *It's better than I thought.*
   pensais.
"Mademoiselle, êtes-vous   *"Are you a nurse?" "Yes, I am."*
   infirmière ?" "Oui, je le suis."

This neuter pronoun *le* forms an integral part of certain verbal expressions:

Je l'ai échappé belle.	*I had a narrow escape.*
C'est le skieur canadien qui l'a emporté sur ses adversaires.	*The Canadian skier defeated his competitors.*
On lui a offert un cadeau mais il l'a vraiment pris de haut.	*We gave him a present but he looked down his nose at it.*

By contrast, the English *it* has no equivalent in the following construction: *Je considère/estime/juge/trouve + difficile/impossible/inutile/nécessaire/ possible/prudent de + infinitive*:

Nous considérons impératif/nécessaire de couvrir les frais.	*We consider it imperative/necessary to cover the costs.*
Je juge inutile de prendre le train de 15 heures.	*I find it pointless to take the three o'clock train.*

45.1.8 *Il* or *ce*?

In French constructions equivalent to the English *It's nice to meet you*, it is sometimes difficult to decide whether to use *il est* or *c'est*, and *à* or *de*. The following table illustrating the possible usages shows that it is a matter of what the pronoun refers to, and at times a matter of register as well:

Introducing a new idea or statement		Examples
R2 + R3	*Il est* + adjective + *de* + infinitive	Il est difficile de réparer le vélo.
R1	*C'est* + adjective + *de* + infinitive	C'est difficile de réparer le vélo.

With reference to a preceding idea or statement		Example
R1/R2/R3	*C'est* + adjective + *à* + infinitive	L'athlète a couru le cent mètres en moins de dix secondes : c'est difficile à faire.

45.2 Disjunctive pronouns and pronouns with prepositions

The disjunctive pronouns are, preceded by a preposition:

moi	*I/me*	(male or female)	nous	*we/us* (males and/or one/some female[s])
toi	*you*	(male or female)	vous	*you* (one male, males and/or females)
lui	*he/him*		eux	*they/them* (males)
elle	*she/her*		elles	*they/them* (females)

These disjunctive pronouns are joined to *même*, which can be a way of highlighting a feature:

moi-même	*myself*	nous-mêmes	*ourselves*
toi-même	*yourself*	vous-même	*yourself*
		vous-mêmes	*yourselves*
lui-même	*himself/itself*	eux-mêmes	*themselves*
elle-même	*herself/itself*	elles-mêmes	*themselves*

For instance:

Tu t'en occupes toi-même.	*You deal with it yourself.*
Laisse les filles jouer elles-mêmes.	*Let the girls play themselves.*
Tu mets le lait dans le bol et Minet se sert lui-même.	*You put the milk in the bowl and Minet (the cat) helps himself.*
L'oiseau prend les miettes lui-même dans le plateau.	*The bird takes the crumbs itself from the tray.*

The use of disjunctive pronouns is determined by a number of conditions (notice how repetition, i.e., subject pronoun + disjunctive pronoun, can become a feature):

The notion of emphasis (not always easily translated):

Je ne peux pas le faire, moi / Moi, je ne peux pas le faire.	*I can't do it.*
Qu'est-ce qu'il est bête, lui !	*What an idiot he is!*

Contrast:

Tu restes là, lui il part.	*You stay here, he can go.*
Il est intelligent, mais elle, elle est une grosse tête.	*He's intelligent, but her, she's a genius.*
Eux ? Je les admire énormément.	*Them? I admire them enormously.*

The repetition in the disjunctive pronoun requires the preposition *à* when an indirect object occurs:

Me reprocher ça à moi ?	*Reproach me with that?*
Pourquoi lui offrir le cadeau à lui ?	*Why give **him** the present?*
Ne le donne pas à eux, mais à elles.	*Don't give it to them (males), but to them (females).*

The disjunctive pronouns *nous* and *vous* can combine with *autres* by way of further emphasis:

Nous autres Canadiens, on ne parle pas comme ça.	*We Canadians do not talk like that.*
Oui, mais vous autres universitaires, vous êtes trop intelligents pour moi.	*Yes, but you university types are too intelligent for me.*

In the following type of construction, the conjunctive pronoun may be used for emphasis but this is the only difference:

Lucile et moi (nous) allons au Mexique.	*Lucile and I are going to Mexico.*
Martine et toi (vous) alliez arriver demain, non ?	*Were you and Martine going to arrive tomorrow?*
Leur mère et lui (ils) achètent une nouvelle maison.	*He and their mother are buying a new house.*

But if the sentence entails inversion, the conjunctive pronoun is required:

Antoine et toi voulez-vous m'accompagner ?	*Do you and Antoine want to come with me?*

This also applies to adverbial phrases:

Sans doute les deux filles et eux partiront-ils ensemble ?	*Will they and the two girls leave together?*

But *sans doute* followed by *que* would not function in the same way, since there would be no inversion:

Sans doute que les deux filles et eux partiront ensemble.	*The two girls and they will doubtless leave together.*

It must be added that this is a clumsy, inelegant kind of construction, and that would be advised to say, for instance : *Sans doute les deux filles partiront-elles avec eux*

Use of *être* with:

C'est moi qui l'ai fait.	*It's I who have done it.*
C'était lui qui l'a écrit.	*It was he who wrote it.*
C'est nous qui l'avons envoyé.	*It is we who sent it.*

The agreement of the following verb is with the disjunctive pronoun, but in R1 discourse, one will readily come across *C'est moi qui l'a fait*/*C'est nous qui l'ont fait*; these constructions are considered incorrect.

With prepositions:

Je suis partie avec eux/elles.	*I left with them.*
Mon frère l'a écrit pour moi.	*My brother wrote it for me.*
Quant à toi, tu n'as rien à faire.	*As for you, you don't have to do anything.*

Similarly, *sans moi/nous*, etc.; *de lui/nous*, etc; *par toi/eux*, etc.

After the construction *ne … que = only*:

| Je ne peux emmener que toi, ou lui. | *I can only take you or him.* |
| Il n'y a qu'eux qui ont accepté l'invitation. | *Only they have accepted the invitation.* |

Disjunctive pronouns can stand alone when a verb is implied because already used:

"Qui a cassé la vitre?"	*"Who broke the window?"*
"Moi/lui/elle, etc."	*"Me/him/her, etc."*
"Qui s'en occupe?"	*"Who's dealing with it?" "Me/us/them,*
"Moi/nous/eux, etc."	*etc."*

Following the comparative construction *plus intelligent/petit* etc. *que*:

| Philippe n'est pas plus intelligent que moi/lui/elle. | *Philippe is not more intelligent than me/him/her.* |

As the subject of an infinitive in exclamations:

| Moi/Toi/Lui, etc. partir maintenant? | *Me/You/Him go now?* |

45.2.1 The reflexive disjunctive pronoun *soi*

It is not used as widely as its associated pronoun *se*. It generally relates to an indeterminate and vague subject: *Chacun pour soi* (*Each one for himself*); *Alors, on ne pense qu'à soi* (*So, we only think of ourselves*); *Ne travailler que pour soi n'est pas admissible* (*Only working for yourself/oneself is not acceptable*). After *chacun/aucun*, *lui/elle*, *lui/elle-même* are equally valid:

| Aucun d'eux ne pense qu'à lui-même. | *None of them only thinks of himself.* |

It would be abnormal to use *soi*, or even *soi-même*, to refer to a plural subject like *ceux qui*: *ceux qui ne pensent qu'à eux/qu'à eux-mêmes.*

In certain expressions *soi* can refer to a subject that is not indeterminate in any way:

| Un bienfait porte sa récompense avec soi. | *A good deed brings its own reward.* |

With prepositions *soi* is common enough:

Cela va de soi.	*It goes without saying.*
Ce sont des choses qui vont de soi.	*They are things that don't need saying.*
Cette attitude en soi est défendable.	*This attitude in itself can be defended.*

And *à part soi* is not uncommon:

| faire des réflexions à part soi | *to think inwardly about something* |

Sartre, the philosopher, establishes the opposition *l'en-soi* (one's inner being) and *le pour-soi* (what comes from the outside).

Although *soi* usually suggests something indeterminate, some authors are quite happy to use it in the specific context of a person, but this is R3 style, and could even appear archaic and incorrect to many:

Elle leva la tête et regarda autour de soi.	*She raised her head and looked around.*

Autour d'elle(-même) is strongly recommended here.

Soi is usually replaced in R2 discourse by *soi-même* when there is no clear antecedent:

Il faut l'écrire soi-même.	*You have to write it yourself.*
aimer son prochain comme soi-même	*to love one's neighbor as oneself*

There are some noun phrases which involve *soi*: *le chez-soi* = home; *la confiance en soi* = self-confidence; *le contentement de soi* = self-satisfaction; *le respect de soi* = self-respect.

45.2.2 Uses of the disjunctive pronoun

The disjunctive pronoun is used with *être* to show possession:

Ce vélo est à moi, pas à toi/lui.	*This bike is mine, not yours/his.*

It is used with verbs indicating motion:

Francis a couru vers moi.	*Francis ran to me.*
Jeanne est venue à nous, et pas nous à elle.	*Jeanne came to us, and not us to her.*

With reflexive verbs, the disjunctive pronoun is used after the verb:

Pour l'existentialiste, le destin ne s'impose pas à lui. Il l'assume.	*For the existentialist, destiny does not impose itself upon him. He assumes it.*
J'ai vu la directrice et me suis présenté à elle.	*I saw the principal and introduced myself to her.*
Elle s'est confiée à eux.	*She trusted them.*

The two indirect pronouns are not possible before the verb here.

Similarly with such verbs as *penser, réfléchir, songer* and *rêver*:

Le jeune homme pensait/songeait à elle sans cesse.	*The young man thought constantly of her.*
Elle passait ses moments de loisir à rêver aux pays lointains.	*She spent her leisure moments dreaming of distant countries* (the suggestion = thinking).
Je n'ai fait que rêver de toi toute la nuit.	*All I did was dream of you all night.*

Note that *rêver à* indicates imagining while *rêver de* indicates actual dreaming.

Some verbs which take a preposition in French, and not necessarily in English, are logically followed by a disjunctive pronoun: *en appeler à, recourir à, renoncer à, avoir affaire à, prendre garde à*. The most well-known historical example for *en appeler à* recalls Saint Paul who states to Festus in Palestine: "J'en appelle à César" ("I appeal unto Caesar") to which Festus replies: "Tu en as appelé à César ; tu iras devant César" (Acts 25: 12).

Other examples:

Elle a renoncé à lui.	*She has given him up.*
Prends garde à toi ! (as Carmen sings to Don José in Bizet's *Carmen*).	*Watch out!*

Pronouns, both conjunctive and disjunctive, can express personal interest:

Regarde-moi cette tête !	*Look at that person's face!*
Il lui a fait un beau sermon.	*He gave him a right telling off.*

46

The pronouns *en* and *y* / Les pronoms *en* et *y*

The first paragraph of the following passage describes Bénédicte's return from a vacation in the Azores with her mother, after a stay with some of her family who live there. The second and third paragraphs center on apple picking and preparations for a birthday party for Bénédicte's niece, Marion. There are joyous moments when the children sing nursery rhymes. The passage uses repeatedly the pronouns *y* and *en* which are highlighted in bold. *En* as a pronoun is marked out from *en* as a preposition – the latter appears in italics a number of times in the second paragraph. *En* as a pronoun is also to be distinguished from *en* which precedes a gerund, as with *en profitant* in the first paragraph. Some translations are given.

Un événement festif

Bénédicte et sa mère se rendent régulièrement aux Açores. Elles **en** reviennent le plus souvent détendues [relaxed]. Elles passent leurs vacances sur les îles en profitant au maximum de leur séjour, de la beauté des paysages, de l'air marin et des membres de leur famille qui y vivent. Elles **en** viennent tout juste d'ailleurs. Le voyage a été très long. Elles sont enfin arrivées. Elles **en** sont ravies. Elles **en** ont fini avec les vacances d'été. Une autre saison pointe déjà le bout de son nez. Au début, Bénédicte n'avait pas voulu **y** aller, mais sa mère l'**y** avait encouragée. Elle l'**y** avait poussée pour faire la véritable coupure de l'année.

À leur retour, Bénédicte prend contact avec des amis. Ils vont joyeusement à la cueillette des pommes. Ils ont cueilli pas mal de pommes [quite a few apples] mais il **en** reste les trois quarts. Il va falloir les écouler [sell] d'une façon ou d'une autre. Coûte que coûte, elle **y** réussira. C'est la spécialiste de la tarte aux pommes et du clafoutis [fruit dessert cooked in batter]. Il **y en** avait tellement qu'elle **en** a vu de toutes les couleurs. Elle organise une petite fête à l'occasion de l'anniversaire de sa nièce Marion. Elle **en** profite pour inviter tous les petits copains et copines de Marion, pas plus haut que trois pommes [not even knee-high to a grasshopper], dont l'esprit est toujours en éveil. Bénédicte, aidée de ses amis, passe beaucoup de temps à éplucher les fruits. Elle orchestre dans les règles de l'art cet événement festif. Toutes les occasions sont bonnes pour fredonner [hum] des mélodies. Tous en chœur,

452

ils se mettent à chanter la comptine [nursery rhyme] préférée de Marion: « Pomme de reinette [rennet apple] et pomme d'api [small apple]. Tapis, tapis rouge. Pomme de reinette et pomme d'api. Tapis, tapis gris… ». Comme par enchantement, les fruits ronds et parfumés se transforment *en* appétissantes tartes aux pommes, *en* alléchant [appetizing] clafoutis et *en* succulent jus de pomme destinés aux enfants et aux accompagnateurs. Le maître de cérémonie [compere] s'occupe des préparatifs pour être prêt à recevoir les petits artistes *en* herbe [burgeonning].

Les nombreux convives [guests] commencent à se présenter, accompagnés d'adultes en tendant des cadeaux et des pochettes-surprises [child's novelty of several small presents in a cone] pour Marion. Il s'**en** est présenté bien d'autres. Par moment, Bénédicte n'**en** revenait pas [couldn't get over it]. Elle n'**y** voyait plus très clair. Elle ne se souvenait pas forcément de tous les invités. Elle n'hésitait pas à dire aux enfants : « Quel est ton prénom ? Je ne m'**en** souviens plus. Je vous **en** prie, avancez vers la salle de jeu et installez-vous. Je vous **en** supplie ! » Les discussions n'**en** sont qu'à leur début. Les petits ogres ont faim. Un enfant lance: « Il y a des assiettes ici. On peut s'**en** servir ? » La fête bat son plein [is in full swing] au rythme des rires et des chansons enfantines de toujours.

46.1 Uses of *en*

It is helpful to distinguish between *en* as a preposition and *en* as a pronoun. *En* as a preposition is treated in Chapter 56. Its origin lies in the Latin *in*. *En* as a pronoun comes from *inde* in Latin. It is purely coincidental that these two Latin words end up as the same word in French. It should be added that *en* as a pronoun has its equivalent in Italian (*ne*) and functions very much in the same way. Strangely, the two letters in *en* are inverted. *En* also has the value of an adverb of place. It indicates coming from or out of: *Je sors de la maison > J'en sors*; *Elle vient de Paris > Elle en vient*.

46.1.1 *En* as a pronoun

As a pronoun, *en* is a very versatile word and has a number of different values, ranging from reference to specific objects to an extremely indeterminate use, merely providing a weak link with what has been said previously. This use often has no equivalent in English and is not always easily translatable. Some of the following examples, graded according to the degree of explicitness of reference of *en*, contain fixed expressions:

Voici une fourchette. Servez-vous-en.	*Here is a fork. Use it.*
Je n'ai pas de pommes. Achètes-en demain.	*I haven't any apples. Buy some tomorrow.*
Il y a des pinceaux ici. Je peux m'en servir ?	*There are some paintbrushes here. May I use them?*

Quel est son prénom ? Je ne m'en souviens pas.	*What's her/his first name? I can't remember it.*
"T'as fini tes devoirs ?" "J'en ai fait les deux tiers."	*"Have you done your homework?" "I've done two thirds of it."*
J'ai cueilli pas mal de pommes mais il en reste les trois quarts.	*I picked quite a few apples but there still remain three quarters of them.*
"Voici un cadeau pour ta fille." "Je t'en remercie."	*"Here's a present for your daughter." "Thank you."*
J'ai congédié le premier. Il s'en est présenté un deuxième.	*I dismissed the first one. A second one came in.*
C'est une histoire fascinante. On devrait en faire un film.	*It's a fascinating story. They ought to make a movie of it.*
Je suis enfin arrivé. J'en suis content/heureux.	*I have finally arrived. I am happy.*
Adrienne a échoué aux examens. Elle en est fâchée/désolée.	*Adrienne has failed her exams. She is angry/upset.*
Francis ne peut que s'en prendre à lui-même.	*Francis only has himself to blame.*
Nous devons nous en rapporter au verdict du juge.	*We have to rely on the judge's verdict.*
Émilie s'en est remise à la discrétion de son petit ami.	*Émilie put her trust in her boyfriend's discretion.*
Elle m'en veut de ce que j'ai fait.	*She holds it against me for what I did.*
J'en passe, et des meilleurs.	*That's the least of it. I could go on and on (after listing things).*
Ma mère en a vu de toutes les couleurs.	*My mother has seen the lot (had lots of experiences).*
Il faut les en/l'en empêcher.	*You'll have to prevent them/him/her.*
Je vous en prie.	*Don't mention it.*
Je t'en supplie.	*I beg you.*
Philippe ne veut pas en démordre.	*Philippe won't give up.*
Il risque d'en découdre avec son frère.	*He's in danger of having a fight with his brother.*
L'entraînement au foot ? On en a bavé.	*Soccer training? It was tough.*
J'en appelle au juge / à votre bon sens / à votre générosité.	*I appeal to the judge / your good sense / your generosity.*
Comment en est-elle arrivée là ?	*How did she get into that state?*
Vingt sur vingt ? Je n'en reviens pas.	*Twenty out of twenty (Full marks)? I can't get over it.*
Le sort en est jeté.	*The die is cast.*
Il en est des collèges comme dans certains lycées.	*It's the same with some collèges as with certain lycées.*

Le cinéaste a fait un film comme on en voit trop peu.	*The director has made a film the likes of which you see too few.*
Les discussions n'en sont qu'à leur début.	*The discussions are just beginning.*
J'en ai fini avec des vacances en janvier.	*I've had enough of vacations in January.*
C'étaient des débats à n'en plus finir.	*They were endless debates.*
Annick n'en est pas à sa première défaite.	*This isn't Annick's first defeat.*
Ce genre d'erreur en dit long sur l'éducation de nos jours.	*This type of mistake says a lot about education nowadays.*
Je n'en crains pas moins son retour.	*I nonetheless fear her/his return.*
C'en est fait de lui.	*He's done for.*
C'en est fait de mon repos.	*That's put an end to my rest.*
C'en est trop.	*That's too much.*
J'en suis là.	*That's where I am.*
J'en suis quitte pour la peur.	*I got away with just a fright.*
Ils en sont venus aux mains.	*They came to blows.*
J'en reste là.	*That's where I stop.*
Un train peut en cacher un autre.	*One train can conceal another.*

46.1.2 Agreement with the past participle

No agreement is made between *en* and the past participle in compound tenses conjugated with *avoir* since *en* is not a direct object:

Stéphanie a des robes comme j'en ai eu.	*Stéphanie has some dresses like the ones I had.*
C'est le type de jeune fille comme j'en ai connu par le passé.	*She's the sort of girl I knew in the past.*

But Grevisse and Goosse quote Proust (2008, p. 1171):

"Mais les fleurs, il n'en avait jamais vues."	"*But flowers like that, he had never seen them.*"

Despite the unassailable authority of Proust, it seems wiser not to make the agreement.

46.1.3 *En* as an intensifier

On en parlera longtemps de ce coup-là.	*They'll talk a long time about that.*
Il en faut du courage pour un tel sacrifice.	*You certainly need courage for such a sacrifice.*
Des précautions, on n'en prend jamais assez.	*You can never take enough precautions.*

Du papier, j'en ai trouvé.	*I've found some paper.*
J'en ai assez de ces manières.	*I've had enough of this behavior.*

It is perfectly legitimate to say: *On parlera de ce coup-là | Il faut du courage pour un tel sacrifice | On ne prend jamais assez de précautions | J'ai trouvé du papier.* In these cases, there is less stress on the following noun. Yet in the case of the expression *en avoir assez*, the *en* must be retained, however pleonastic this may appear, just as one must say: *J'en ai assez de ces erreurs/histoires*, etc. The same applies to *en avoir marre | en avoir ras-le-bol*, both R1 expressions: *J'en ai marre | ras-le-bol de ses conneries* = (*I am fed up with his bullshit | his stupid behavior*).

Two other expressions that often take, but by no means always, the pleonastic *en* are: *Je m'en fous de son opinion | Je m'en fiche de son opinion* = (*I don't care a damn about his opinion*). Both of these (*se foutre de | se ficher de*) are in very common use and may be classed as R1. However, *foutre* in other contexts (e.g., *Va te faire foutre!* = *Fuck off!*) should be avoided by learners of the French language. Interestingly enough, one would have expected this verb to lose some of its highly offensive weight when used in certain ways, so frequently is it used, but this is not the case.

46.1.4 Miscellaneous points

Strictly speaking, *en* is not used with reference to people. Compare the two examples:

On devrait en faire un brevet.	*You ought to make a patent from it.*
Ses tournées font de lui l'artiste le mieux payé des États-Unis.	*His tours make him the best-paid artist in the United States.*

However, such examples as the following are normal despite the censure of the purists:

Il y en a des médecins dans le coin?	*Any physicians around here?*
Le président en a fait sa première ministre.	*The president made her his prime minister.*
Elle ne sort plus avec cette amie, elle en est jalouse.	*She doesn't go out with that friend any more. She is jealous of her.*

With a verb in the passive which expresses a feeling, *en* is very common:

Ce roi aime son peuple et il en est aimé.	*This king loves his people and he is loved by them.*

Note also the translation of Margaret Mitchell's *Gone with the Wind: Autant en emporte le vent*. The use of *en* refers to the destruction of the old South.

En can be used with *voici* and *voilà* which are prepositions, although they carry out the function of verbs:

| Tu veux le lire ? En voici le texte. | *You want to read it? Here's the text.* |
| Tu en veux ? En voilà. | *Do you want some? There you are.* |

46.1.5. Choice between *en* and a possessive determiner

There is some hesitation between the use of the possessive determiner (*son/sa/ses*, *leur*, etc.). In some cases, the use of *en* is repudiated as a sign of poor and inelegant style or even lack of clarity. Here are some guiding principles:

> The possessive is needed if the possessor is in the same clause as what is possessed:

| Je distinguais la maison et sa cour. | *I made out the house and its courtyard.* |

Je is the possessor here and *cour* is possessed.

> The possessive is needed if the noun of what is possessed is preceded by a preposition:

| J'aime ce parc, j'aime la régularité de ses lignes, je ne ne me lasse pas de ses ombrages. | *I like this park, I like the harmony of its lines, and do not tire of its shady corners.* |

En is frequently used with the verb *être*:

| Ne réponds pas à cette lettre ; le ton en est impertinent. | *Don't answer this letter; its tone is impertinent.* |
| Le terroriste a fomenté ce complot ; il en est l'inspirateur. | *The terrorist organized this plot; he is its instigator.* |

Likewise:

| Le train ne peut partir que les portes fermées : ne pas en gêner la fermeture. | *The train can't leave with the doors open; do not obstruct the closing doors.* |

In all these three cases, *en* must be used.

> The possessive is used if sentences are separated:

| Ils ont planté un saule au cimetière. J'aime son feuillage / son ombre. | *They planted a willow in the cemetery. I love its foliage/shade.* |

If the idea of belonging cannot really be conceived, *en* must be used:

| J'ai vu ce monument, j'en ai même vu une photo. | *I have seen this monument, I have even seen a photo of it.* |

Cette maison tombe en ruine ; un arrêté vient d'en prescrire la démolition.	*This house is falling into ruins; a decree has just ordered its demolition.*
Ce métier me pèse. J'en supporte mal l'ennui.	*This job is weighing on me. I am having difficulty with the boredom.*

46.1.6. *En or no* en?

With many adjectives, past participles and nouns, there is a choice between the use or non-use of *en*. Consider these sets of two sentences:

Je suis sûr. / J'en suis sûr. } *I am sure.*

Je suis certaine. / J'en suis certaine. } *I am certain.*

Je suis persuadé. / J'en suis persuadé. } *I am convinced.*

Je suis convaincu. / J'en suis convaincu. } *I am convinced.*

One has the feeling, but attitudes are mixed over this assertion, that the addition of *en* in these sentences invests them with more precision and raises the register somewhat. In any case, both are possible. However, one can only say and write:

J'en ai la certitude.   *I am certain.*

Both exclusion and inclusion of *en* are possible with *remercier*:

Je te remercie / Je t'en remercie.   *I thank you.*

46.2. Uses of *y*

Like *en*, *y* functions both as an adverb and as a pronoun.

Y as an adverb:

Je vais à la fac : j'y vais.	*I'm off to college: I'm off.*
"T'es arrivé ?" "Oui, j'y suis arrivé."	*"Have you arrived?" "Yes."*
J'y suis, j'y reste.	*Here I am and here I stay.*

Y as a pronoun does not have the same range of values as *en*. Basically, it means *there* or *to there* but it can be construed otherwise in English, as with *encourager* below:

Je pense à ce que tu as dit : j'y pense.	*I am thinking of what you said: I'm thinking about it.*
"Est-elle décidée à se présenter ?" "Oui, elle y est décidée."	*"Has she decided to go?" "Yes, she has."*

Sa mère l'y a encouragée.	*Her mother encouraged her to do it.*
Je ne voulais pas y aller, mais elle m'y a poussé.	*I didn't want to go, but she pushed me into it/going.*
Coûte que coûte, j'y réussirai.	*Come what may, I'll succeed.*
Je n'y vois pas clair.	*I can't see clearly / I don't quite understand.*

One does need to distinguish between *y* and the indirect pronouns *lui* and *à eux/elles*, when used with verbs. *Lui, eux* and *elles* refer to persons and domesticated animals while *y* refers to inanimate objects, and non-personalized animals:

| Je ne me fie pas à lui/eux/elles. | *I don't trust him/her/them.* |
| Minou a faim. Je vais lui donner à manger. | *Pussy is hungry. I'll give him/her something to eat.* |

But:

| Ce chien est méchant. Il ne faut pas s'y fier. | *This dog is dangerous. You mustn't trust it.* |

As with *le* and *en*, *y* forms part of verbal expressions:

| Il y va de ma vie. | *It's a question of life or death.* |
| Je n'y peux rien. | *I can't do anything about it.* |

When a future or conditional tense is used and the idea is (*to*) *there*, the *y* disappears to avoid a hiatus, in the interests of euphony:

| J'irai. J'irais volontiers avec toi. | *I'll go. I'd willingly go with you.* |

But one would easily say:

| Je m'y installerai. | *I'll settle down there.* |

47

Possessive adjectives and possessive pronouns / Les adjectifs possessifs et les pronoms possessifs

The following passage evokes the traumas suffered by the Cambodian people at the hands of the notoriously brutal Khmer Rouge regime. The torments undergone by the Cambodians find their expression in an exhibition in Grenoble. Given the colonial heritage that links Cambodia to France, it was logical that an exhibition of this kind should take place in France and especially in Grenoble, whose inhabitants welcomed a persecuted people. The passage makes considerable use of the varied forms of possessive adjectives and pronouns which are highlighted in bold. Note particularly that the possessive adjective differs from the possessive pronoun in that the latter is preceded by the definite article: *notre/les nôtres, leur/le leur*. Some translations are given.

Une exposition temporaire marquante
Notre Musée de la Résistance et de la Déportation à Grenoble organise des expositions temporaires sur des thématiques [groups of subjects] qui nous touchent tous. La ville de Grenoble se vide pendant l'été. Les Grenoblois regagnent **leur** ville à la fin du mois d'août. Certains profitent de l'ouverture de **leurs** musées pour s'informer, s'enrichir et se cultiver. Une exposition temporaire marquante et très émouvante concerne le génocide des Cambodgiens. Celle-ci brosse un tableau sinistre des crimes perpétrés par les Khmers rouges au milieu des années soixante-dix. Tout au long de cette exposition, on découvre les atrocités de ce génocide, la chute des Khmers rouges et la fin de **leur** dictature en 1979. Le Cambodge livré à lui-même en plein désastre doit se reconstruire. L'ampleur des dégâts [devastation] dépasse **notre** entendement, et certainement **le mien**.

De nombreux Cambodgiens ayant perdu **leur** femme, **leurs** enfants, **leurs** frères et sœurs ont choisi de s'exiler en France comme terre d'asile et, plus précisément, à Grenoble. Un long parcours du combattant pour ces refugiés s'annonce. Ils sont accueillis dans des centres d'hébergement du Secours catholique. D'autres associations départementales d'entraide s'organisent pour leur prêter assistance. Tous ces réfugiés du sud-est asiatique ont besoin d'être soutenus dans

460

leurs démarches administratives, dans **leur** intégration sociale et professionnelle. Un jeune cambodgien qui a pu venir avec **ses** père et mère, **ses** frères et sœurs est heureux d'apprendre le français et d'étudier pour **son** avenir. Il manifeste **sa** passion pour les études. Ces richesses sont **siennes**. **Leur** long voyage ne leur fait pas oublier **leurs** us et coutumes [their ways and customs]. Au cours de toute **sa** vie, ce jeune et bien d'autres s'en souviendront.

Cette exposition temporaire marque les mémoires, et notamment **les nôtres** à Grenoble. Elle souligne les témoignages de Cambodgiens après ce traumatisme affectif, psychologique et psychique. Les victimes prendront le temps de reconstruire, de **leur** mieux, **leur** nouvelle vie. Ils y ont mis chacun **du sien**. Ceux qui sont restés au pays doivent s'atteler [contribute] à **sa** reconstruction. La France joue un rôle prépondérant au Cambodge, compte tenu de **ses** liens établis par le protectorat. Au sein de l'Union européenne, la France demeure l'interlocuteur de ce pays. En effet, une importante diaspora cambodgienne est installée dans l'Hexagone [France]. Grand nombre de Cambodgiens et **leurs** élites possèdent la double citoyenneté. Une nouvelle génération d'Isérois [inhabitants of the Isère department] d'origine cambodgienne est née. Ils n'ont jamais eu l'occasion de retourner au pays de **leurs** feus [late = deceased] oncles, tantes et grands-parents. Un jour viendra où ils rassembleront **leurs** souvenirs et évoqueront chacun **les leurs**.

Like English and all Romance languages, French has two series of words which indicate possession. Possessive adjectives, often called possessive determiners, since for some it is a more precise term, precede the noun, defining it with respect to possession. Their English counterparts are *my*, *your*, *his*, etc. Possessive pronouns replace nouns while still indicating possession. Their English counterparts are *mine*, *yours*, *his*, etc.

47.1 Possessive adjectives

In keeping with all Romance languages, the most important feature in French possessive adjectives is that they agree with the thing possessed and not with the possessor: the possessive adjective varies according to the gender and number of the person or object it refers to.

Here are the possessive adjectives:

Masculine singular	Feminine singular	Masculine and feminine plural
mon = *my*	ma = *my*	mes = *my*
ton = *your*	ta = *your*	tes = *your*
son = *his/her/its*	sa = *his/her/its*	ses = *his/her/its*
notre = *our*	notre = *our*	nos = *our*
votre = *your*	votre = *your*	vos = *your*
leur = *their*	leur = *their*	leurs = *their*

For example:

> *mon fils/livre; ma voiture, ma maison; mes amis = my...*
> *ton ami/jardin; ta chaise/table; tes amies = your...*
> *son ordinateur/tableau; sa fleur/robe; ses lunettes = his/her...*
> *notre e-mail/texto/chambre/fille; nos enfants = our...*
> *votre message/peinture/cousin(e) = your...*
> *vos pieds/jambes = your...*
> *leur voyage/appartement/tante; leurs parents = their...*

These possessive adjectives also come before adjectives defining nouns: *mon petit fils, ta belle maison, nos excellents résultats, vos merveilleuses fleurs.*

Before a noun beginning with a vowel or mute **h**, the masculine singular form *mon/ton/son* is used when the noun is feminine, for the sake of euphony: *mon amie, mon escorte, mon ombre, son héroïne, mon histoire.*

It goes without saying that the *ton/ta/tes* forms correspond to *tu* and the *votre/vos* forms correspond to *vous.*

Note that *tout* and *feu* are the only adjectives that precede a possessive adjective: *pendant tout son examen; au cours de toute sa vie; J'ai regardé tous ses résultats.* With the little-used, high-register *feu* (= *late*, i.e., *deceased*) the order can be: *feu mes oncles* or *tes feus oncles.* In other words, before the possessive determiner, there is no agreement, but after the determiner there is. Other examples with *feu: feu ma mère | feu Madame | feu mes tantes* but *mes feux parents | tes feues grands-mères.* One can only speculate that few French speakers would be able to apply this rule correctly.

The possessive adjective is usually repeated before each noun if the nouns refer to different people: *ma sœur et mon frère; ma femme et mon beau-père.* But, if the nouns refer to the same person, it is more than likely that the possessive would disappear: *mon amie et collègue Mme Lanoë; mon cousin et grand ami Philippe; leur propriété ou terrain en Normandie.* However, there are numerous phrases, and others that may be considered so, where the second possessive adjective is omitted: *à ses pertes et profits; leurs us et coutumes; ses frais et honoraires; ses dommages et intérêts; ses allées et venues; à ses risques et périls; ses avantages et inconvénients; leurs exportations et importations; ses attaques et contre-attaques, ses responsabilités et privilèges.* One can come across in R1 discourse: *ses père et mère, ses frère et sœur,* particularly the latter which would surprise no one. Of course, in these last two cases, the purist would plead for *son père et sa mère, son frère et sa sœur.* Into this category would also fall: *vos nom, prénom et qualité (occupation)* when filling out a form.

When emphasis is required, the disjunctive pronoun occurs: *mon vélo à moi, pas à lui; notre chambre à nous.* Similarly when some distinction needs to be made between the different values of *son*, *sa* and *ses* (e.g., *his/her*): *Sa voiture à elle est plus vieille que sa voiture à lui*; and with *leur*: *Leur maison à eux est plus grande que leur maison à elles*. Of course, it would be very rare to come across this second example.

In R1 discourse, the **r** of *notre* and *votre* can very easily disappear when preceding a consonant: *not'/vot' frère/père/voiture/maison*, as with *à quat' pattes* indicated in Chapter 2 on pronunciation, Section 2.1

In old French the elision of *ma*, *ta*, *sa* took place: *t'enfance* (*ton enfance*), *s'amie* (*son amie*), *t'espee* (*ton épée*). One comes across a residue of this elision in the literature of more recent past centuries (*m'amie*, *m'amour*), but this practice has completely died out. One even meets, through some faulty analysis, *ma mie*, which in modern French could only mean *my crumb*! However, a folk song by Georges Brassens is entitled "À l'ombre du cœur de ma mie." Furthermore, one would associate *ma mie* with folk songs in general.

In writing, a sense of intimacy can be conveyed by the use of *notre*, not alien to an English style: *Notre héros Julien rebroussa chemin* (*Our hero Julien retraced his steps*).

The possessive adjectives with members of a family are very common. They express deference and respect, affection or a touch of aggression: *Oui, mon père / mon fils / ma mère / ma fille*. One regularly hears *Allez, mes enfants*, just as husband and wife would say to each other: *mon chéri / ma chérie, mon amour*. Note also *mon petit bonhomme* (used when addressing a small child) and *Je vous y prends, mon gaillard !* (when addressing a male who has done something reprehensible).

Military ranks vary. When addressing a captain and so on, *mon* is usually required: *mon adjudant/capitaine/lieutenant*. But one says *Monsieur le Maréchal* (Foch for instance) and simply *Amiral* in the navy. When someone of a higher rank is addressing someone of a lower rank, no possessive determiner is used: *Colonel/Major*.

Usage with priests and nuns: *Mon père/Père, ma mère/Mère, ma sœur/Sœur*; and in confession: *"Votre repentir est sincère ?" "Oui, mon Père."* Given the secular tendency of all churches, one wonders whether the first name of the priest will one day dominate.

The use of the possessive determiner is also used in a kind of "third-person" way, so that the verb appears in the third person:

Votre Majesté est-elle satisfaite ?	*Is your Majesty satisfied?*
Leurs Majestés sont-elles satisfaites ?	*Are your Majesties satisfied?*

The possessive adjectives *mon/ma/mes* occur in *monsieur* (originally: *my lord*), *madame*, *mademoiselle* and their plurals *messieurs*, *mesdames*, *mesdemoiselles*. The expression *Messieurs dames !* is frequent in R1 speech, on entering a room, a restaurant, for example. The preferred and more polite form to be recommended is *Mesdames, messieurs*.

The English third persons *of it, of them* can be replaced by *its* and *their*. Likewise, in French, *en* can and, sometimes must, stand in place of *son/sa/ses/leur/leurs*. See Chapter 46, Section 46.1.5 for an analysis of this question.

There can sometimes be serious hesitation between the singular and plural of the thing possessed. When there is more than one person possessing one single object, difficulties arise, notably in the third person. Ambiguities or even awkwardness spring from the following: *Ils se promenaient avec leur femme* (one single wife accompanying all of them?) or *Ils se promenaient avec leurs femmes* (a wife for each one). It must be argued here that both are possible but, if any serious doubt were engendered in this sentence, one could add *chacun*: *Ils se promenaient chacun avec sa femme*. Similarly, does one say *Les cavaliers, penchés sur leurs chevaux, galopaient* or *Les cavaliers, penchés sur leur cheval, galopaient*? *Chacun* seems to be the clearest option here although riding on a plurality of horses could seem a spectacular circus feat. More possible is the following sentence where several possessors could own several objects: *Ils ont ouvert leurs parapluies*, although for all practical purposes one would expect *Ils ont ouvert leur parapluie*. However, the plural for *parapluie* could simply refer to all the umbrellas.

When a plurality of objects is possessed by each possessor, there can be no hesitation: *Les ouvriers mangeaient leurs portions*. But what if one added *litre*, for instance: *Les ouvriers mangeaient leurs portions et buvaient leur litre de vin*? There is no reason to suppose that workmen stopped at one liter of wine . . . In all the following sentences, with singular and plural possibilities indicated, pure linguistic logic cannot solve the difficulty, but common sense can: *Ils sont sortis avec leur(s) fiancée(s)*; *Tous regardaient leur(s) montre(s)*; *Tous les garçons ont enfourché leur(s) bicyclette(s)*. Both are possible, although there is clearly a preference for the singular form. When the thing possessed only has plural form, no ambiguity is created: *Ils ont cassé leurs lunettes*; *Ils ont ri à vos dépens* (*They laughed at your expense*); *Les poules étaient suivies de leurs poussins*.

When it is a question of reciprocity, the plural is required: *Ils ont échangé leurs cartes de visite / plusieurs lettres*. When a singular form is the only one, no difficulty arises: *Vous étudiez pour votre avenir*; *Nous gagnons notre vie*; *Les Parisiens regagnent leur ville à la fin du mois d'août*. When reciprocity obtains, a plural is required: *Nous avons échangé nos cartes / nos textos*. When a part of the body, which takes a singular noun, is involved, only a singular is possible: *Ils étaient assis sur le derrière*. Similarly, an abstract notion nearly always attracts a singular noun: *Ils manifestent leur haine de l'hypocrisie / leur passion de l'Espagne / leur intérêt pour la musique*.

47.2 Possessive pronouns

These are:

Masculine singular	Feminine singular	Masculine plural	Feminine plural	
le mien	la mienne	les miens	les miennes	*mine*
le tien	la tienne	les tiens	les tiennes	*yours*
le sien	la sienne	les siens	les siennes	*his/hers/its*
le nôtre	la nôtre	les nôtres	les nôtres	*ours*
le vôtre	la vôtre	les vôtres	les vôtres	*yours*
le leur	la leur	les leurs	les leurs	*theirs*

The possessive pronoun varies according to the gender and number of the noun it represents. Since each possessive pronoun takes four forms, these pronouns are certainly more complicated than the English all-purpose single word. Examples:

ta femme et la mienne	ma femme et la tienne
your wife and mine	*my wife and yours*
leur frère et le sien	leur sœur et la sienne
their brother and his/hers	*their sister and his/hers*
mon père et le vôtre	leurs cousins et les vôtres
my father and yours	*their cousins and yours*

The possessive pronouns are not used with the verb *être*, except to indicate contrast, and are replaced by *à* + disjunctive pronoun. Compare these two sentences:

Cet USB est à moi/lui/vous/eux.	*This memory stick is mine/his/yours/theirs.*
Ces USB sont les tiens ; les miens sont dans le coffret.	*These memory sticks are yours; mine are in the box.*

Possessive pronouns can combine with numbers:

tes enfants et les deux miens	*your children and my two*

Theoretically, there exists a distinction between *vôtre* and *le vôtre*. Compare the two sentences:

Aimez cette enfant comme vôtre.	*Love this child as if she were yours.*
Aimez cette enfant comme la vôtre.	*Love this child as you do your own.*

Les vôtres / les siens can refer to the members of a family:

Mes meilleurs vœux pour vous et les vôtres.	*My best wishes for you and yours.*
Malheureusement, je ne puis être des vôtres à Noël.	*Unfortunately, I can't be with all of you this Christmas.*
La mère adore les siens.	*The mother adores her family.*

Use of possessive pronouns with *chacun*:

Rassemblons nos souvenirs ; nous évoquerons chacun les nôtres.	*Let's bring our memories together, we'll each of us call upon our own.*
Nous y mettrons chacun du nôtre.	*Each of us will contribute our own.*
Ils y ont mis chacun du sien.	*Each of them contributed his own* (in preference to *du leur*).

Miscellaneous uses of possessive pronouns:

Referring to a letter, *la vôtre* is used:

J'espère que vous avez reçu ma lettre. La vôtre m'est parvenue aujourd'hui même.	*I hope you have received my letter. Yours reached me precisely today.*

Faire des siennes = to be up to one's old tricks:

Le voilà encore qui fait des siennes.	*There he is again up to his old tricks.*

In answering a toast, one says:

"À votre santé !" "À la vôtre !"	*"To your health!" "Cheers!"*

Faire sien = to make one's own

les opinions de Jean qu'elle a faites siennes	*Jean's opinions that she has made her own / has adopted*

The definite article may be omitted as with the verb *être*. The possessive pronoun operates here like an adjective:
Ces richesses sont siennes. *This wealth is his/hers.*

48

Possessive adjectives, definite articles and usage with parts of the body and with clothes / Les adjectifs possessifs, les articles définis et l'usage concernant les parties du corps et les vêtements

The following passage narrates the suffering of the people of Haiti subject to the appalling earthquake of January 2010. The brief narrative points to both the physical and moral torment of the victims and the frantic activities of doctors, nurses and the entire rescue operation. Highlighted are the numerous uses of the definite article related to the human body as opposed to the possessive adjectives that would appear in English.

The name *Haïti* does not begin with an aspirate h, witness *l'île d'Haïti* in the first paragraph. However, there is some uncertainty over this (see Marie-Éva de Villers's *MULTI dictionnaire*). Doubtless the Haitians themselves have the last word as seen in the notice: "Police Nationale d'Haïti."

Le séisme dévastateur en Haïti

Depuis quatre jours, toutes les chaînes de télévision françaises et étrangères passent en boucle [in a continual loop / continuously] des images insoutenables [unbearable] du séisme ravageur dans l'île d'Haïti. Les victimes haïtiennes se comptent par dizaines de milliers et les secours affluent du monde entier. Les premiers secours s'organisent. L'ampleur des dégâts est effroyable.

Les immeubles effondrés donnent une image apocalyptique, et les secouristes tentent d'extraire délicatement les survivants avec les moyens dont ils disposent. Une femme a été extraite du fond d'un amas d'immeubles avec **les** vêtements déchirés, **les** jambes allongées sur une civière [stretcher]. **La tête lui** tournait [Her head was swimming]. Elle avait **mal au dos** et **au ventre**. **Les yeux lui** piquaient [stinging] et **les** oreilles bourdonnaient [buzzing]. Son cœur battait et son front brûlait. Son frère a levé **le bras** en signe de reconnaissance. Un secouriste allonge **les jambes** de la victime sur un coussin et lui demande de **plier le bras** gauche. Une autre victime s'appuya sur une jambe, hocha [nodded] **la** tête et plia **les bras**.

Une autre femme a été repérée [spotted] dans un bâtiment en ruines. Elle s'est cassé **la jambe** et saignait abondamment. Elle s'est fait panser **la plaie**. De plus, elle avait mal **aux reins** [her back was hurting her]. En sortant la victime, un sauveteur s'est cogné **la tête** contre la paroi [wall] de l'immeuble, s'est tordu **le poignet**, s'est cogné **la hanche** et s'est égratigné [scratched] **le genou**. Certaines victimes se sont fait amputer **les jambes** ou **les bras** de peur de développer la gangrène due à l'infection des blessures très graves. Les victimes soignent leurs maux en désespoir de cause. Les structures sanitaires pour traiter les blessés ont été anéanties [annihilated]. L'eau, le gaz et l'électricité manquent cruellement. Le cœur de la capitale haïtienne connaît des scènes de violence et de pillages depuis les dégâts dus au séisme.

Les aides humanitaires aux sinistrés [victims] tardent à venir. Il semble que des problèmes de logistique et de coordination se posent et freinent les efforts des sauveteurs. Un grand élan [surge] de solidarité internationale et de soutien politique, militaire, financier et moral est apporté aux habitants de l'île sinistrée. Un grand défi [challenge] de reconstruction de l'ensemble du pays se pose à la communauté internationale.

48.1 Parts of the body

In French, as in all Romance languages, there is frequently, but not always, a choice between the use of the possessive adjective or determiner and the definite article. As a simple example, whereas in English one would say *I raised my arm*, in French one would probably say *J'ai levé le bras*. However, practice can be more complicated than this. Furthermore, reference to clothes follows a similar pattern (see below). First we note the simpler pattern:

Sabrina allongea les jambes.	*Sabrina stretched out her legs.*
Pierre croisa les mains derrière le dos.	*Pierre folded his hands behind his back.*

Similarly: *Adrienne haussa (shrugged) les épaules | étendit le bras vers la fenêtre | plia les bras | cogna (banged) la tête contre la porte | ferma les yeux | ferma la bouche | secoua la tête | posa les jambes sur un coussin | s'appuya sur une jambe.*

When a reflexive is used (i.e., when you do something to yourself), the formula is usually *me/te/se*, etc. + verb + definite article:

Françoise s'est coupé les ongles.	*Françoise cut her nails.*
Les garçons se sont tous lavé les mains.	*All the boys washed their hands.*
Je me suis tordu le poignet.	*I twisted my wrist.*

Similarly: *Jeanne s'est couvert la tête | s'est mordu le doigt | s'est teint (dyed) les cheveux | s'est cogné la hanche | s'est égratigné (scratched) le genou | s'est cassé la jambe | s'est rouvert la plaie (opened up her wound again) | s'est gratté (scratched) la tête.*

There is no agreement between the reflexive pronoun and the past participle because, in this construction, the reflexive is indirect.

Some verbs allow two possibilities. Compare the two following sentences:

Sophie s'est blessée/brûlée au pied.	*Sophie hurt/burned her foot.*
Sophie s'est blessé/brûlé le pied.	*Sophie hurt/burned her foot.*

Agreement is with Sophie in the first case (*se* = direct object) but not in the second (*se* = indirect).

Other expressions to be noted here are:

Louise avait mal aux dents / au pied / au doigt / aux yeux / à la gorge / à la tête / au dos / aux reins / au ventre.	*Louise had toothache	a sore foot	a sore finger	sore eyes	a sore throat	headache	backache	stomachache.*

Moreover, one can just as easily say: *J'ai un mal de tête | un mal de ventre*; *Le ventre me fait mal*; *J'ai les dents qui me font mal | le dos qui me fait mal | les yeux qui me piquent | les oreilles qui me tintent* (ringing in my ears) and, following on from this last expression: *Les oreilles ont dû te tinter* = Your ears must have been ringing (i.e., *Someone's been talking about you*).

If the noun is qualified, it is more than likely that the possessive adjective would be used:

Elle leva ses bras chargés de bracelets.	*She raised her arms laden with bracelets.*
Robin resta là planté sur ses pieds écartés.	*Robin remained there, with his feet wide apart.*
Céline releva la tête et tourna ses beaux yeux vers son amant.	*Céline raised her head and turned her lovely eyes toward her beloved.*

However, if the adjective is more than a simple epithet, and forms an integral part of a noun, the article is used:

Emmanuelle avait les yeux bleus/bruns.	*Emmanuelle had blue/brown eyes.*
Elle gardait les yeux ouverts.	*She kept her eyes open.*
J'ai reçu un coup sur l'œil droit.	*I received a blow over my right eye.*
Pliez le bras droit.	*Bend your right arm.*

If insistence is needed, the possessive adjective could be used: *Écoute, plie ton bras droit, et pas ton bras gauche*; *Ouvre tes yeux, voyons, il ne faut pas les garder fermés*. A doctor would say to her patient with the same idea of insistence or precision *Donnez-moi votre bras*, just as the possessive adjective would reinforce *dents* in the following: *Il montra ses dents*; *Montrez-moi vos dents* (this second would be used by a dentist).

Usage is not always constant however. It is quite possible to read and say:

Il s'assit, se carra sur le siège et allongea ses jambes.	*He sat down, settled into the chair, and stretched out his legs.*
Ce petit garçon qui traînait ses pieds...	*This little boy who was dragging his feet...*
Il est parti, les mains dans ses poches.	*He left, with his hands in his pockets.*

Equally valid are: *traîner les pieds / les mains dans les poches* and *Essuyez vos pieds / Essuyez-vous les pieds*.

If reference is to a characteristic of a person, a possessive adjective may well be used: *J'ai ma migraine*; *J'ai encore mal à ma jambe*; *Il me répondit de son air doux*; *Elle a avancé vers lui, avec son regard pénétrant*. If the definite, or preferably in most cases here, indefinite article were used, reference to the habitual characteristic would be lost: *J'ai une migraine*; *Il me répondit d'un air doux*; *avec un regard pénétrant*.

When the subject is a part of the body, the possessive determiner is often used:

Sa tête tournait, son cœur battait.	*Her head was spinning, her heart beating.*
Son front brûlait.	*His forehead was burning.*

In spoken language, *la tête lui tournait* is certainly more common but this alternative would not apply to *son cœur battait*; *son front brûlait*.

Note the formula *faire* + infinitive + part of the body. The definite article is used:

Je me suis fait couper les cheveux.	*I had my hair cut.*
Je me suis fait couper les ongles.	*I had my nails cut.*
Elle s'est fait panser/soigner la plaie.	*She had her wound dressed/bandaged.*

But one would only say:

Je soigne mon rhume.	*I am looking after / taking care of my cold.*

48.2 Parts of clothing

Generally speaking, clothes are preceded by possessive determiners:

Elle se leva, secoua sa robe.	*She got up and shook her dress.*
Louise s'essuya les mains à son tablier.	*Louise wiped her hands on her apron.*

In the first case one would say: *secoua **la** tête.*

Beyond this generality, one could say both *Elle a déchiré sa jupe* and *Elle s'est déchiré la jupe* (i.e., non-reflexive verb + possessive determiner or reflexive verb + definite article). Similarly, as indicated above: *Il a (met) les mains dans ses poches / dans les poches* and even *Il a ses mains dans ses poches.*

49

Relative pronouns / Les pronoms relatifs

The following passage centers on an exhibition that took place in Grenoble recalling the Spanish Civil War (1936–1939) and its aftermath involving refugees seeking protection in Grenoble and the surrounding area of the department of Isère. Some references are made to authors of international stature who expressed a deep commitment to the Republican cause. The passage illustrates the use of relative pronouns which are highlighted in bold.

Évocation de la guerre civile espagnole

Une exposition temporaire, **dont** la thématique était d'une époque trouble, regroupant les documents iconographiques, photographiques ainsi que les témoignages de républicains espagnols, a suscité toute notre curiosité. Nous aimons beaucoup fréquenter les expositions et les musées **qui** apportent un tout autre point de vue de la résistance à l'oppression. Le Musée de la Résistance et de la Déportation donne le plus souvent un éclairage précieux des faits et des chiffres **que** peu de gens connaissent au sujet des réfugiés politiques espagnols **qui** ont fui la péninsule ibérique.

L'exposition intitulée « Le train s'est arrêté à Grenoble... » décrit l'arrivée des exilés espagnols dans le département de l'Isère en 1937 et en 1939. Comment les événements se sont-ils déroulés ? Pendant la guerre civile espagnole, de nombreux volontaires **qui** combattirent aux côtés des républicains espagnols portent un témoignage sur les conditions épouvantables **dans lesquelles** ils vécurent. Cette exposition attire beaucoup de visiteurs et en particulier les descendants de ceux **qui** ont dû faire un choix difficile. Partir ou rester ? **Lequel** des deux choisir ? **Lequel** est préférable ? Bien entendu, beaucoup ont préféré l'exil plutôt que de vivre sous la dictature de Franco. L'époque **où** le fascisme envahit toute l'Europe a beaucoup inspiré des auteurs comme Ernest Hemingway **qui** publia, en 1940, *For Whom the Bell Tolls*, son roman **qui** a été traduit en français par *Pour qui sonne le glas*, **dont** le romancier américain évoque ce **qu'**il a déjà connu en tant que journaliste pendant la guerre civile espagnole. George Orwell, écrivain britannique, fait paraître en 1938 *Hommage à la Catalogne*, et en 1945 *Animal Farm* (traduit en français par *La Ferme des animaux*), une ferme **dans laquelle** les animaux s'emparent du pouvoir et chassent les êtres humains. L'auteur écrivit cette œuvre suite à des expériences **qu'**il avait vécues **dont** celle durant la guerre d'Espagne. C'était pendant cette période-là **que** Jean-Paul Sartre a publié *L'être et le néant*. Antoine de Saint-Exupéry s'engage également aux côtés de ceux qui combattent le franquisme et préparent la résistance. Inutile d'ajouter **que** l'un des grands combattants français **qui** défendirent la cause républicaine fut André Malraux **dont** le roman *L'espoir* chante l'héroïsme des membres de la brigade internationale.

Malgré l'accueil peu chaleureux des Isérois en raison d'un contexte difficile **qui** annonçait la veille de la seconde guerre mondiale, les exilés se sont installés dans Grenoble et sa région. La façon **dont** les familles espagnoles se sont tirées d'affaire est remarquable. **Que** sont-elles devenues ? *La ley de memoria histórica* ou *Loi sur la mémoire historique* adoptée par le parlement espagnol met en œuvre des moyens pour aider ceux **qui** ont souffert de persécution, de violence et de l'exil. À la sortie de l'exposition, les Espagnols parmi **lesquels** nous avons passé toute l'après-midi, se présentaient les vœux de la nouvelle année dans leur langue maternelle : *Feliz Año Nuevo! Amor, Salud y Dinero* . . .

Relative pronouns relate a subordinate clause to a main clause. In general terms, in English, the subject of the subordinate clause relating back to the main clause is *that/who* while the object of the subordinate clause is *that/whom* (this latter is less and less used):

The lady who sings speaks Chinese.
The lady who(m) I see speaks Chinese.

In the first case, *who* is the subject of the subordinate clause, while in the second, *whom* is its object. French operates in a similar way but with differences:

La dame qui chante parle chinois.
La dame que je vois parle chinois.

Qui refers to *la dame* and is the subject of the subordinate clause (*chante*), while *que* refers to *la dame* but is the direct object of the subordinate clause since *je* is its subject. Generally speaking, French relative pronouns are the same whether they refer to persons or things, but this is not always the case. Here, in tabulated form, are the French relative pronouns:

	Referring to people	Referring to things	Referring to neuter pronouns
subject	*qui*	*qui*	*qui*
direct object	*que*	*que*	*que*
genitive or possessive	*dont, de qui*	*dont, duquel,* etc.	*dont, duquel,* etc.
after prepositions	*qui, lequel*	*lequel,* etc.	*quoi*

Note that *que* is not used after prepositions. To say *the person to whom I speak* one says in French: *La personne à qui je parle. Dont* always comes at the beginning of a clause but this is not the case of *duquel*, which follows a noun, for instance.

After prepositions, the forms of relative pronouns are:

Referring to people:

after *de*	(generally) *dont*
after *à*	*à qui*
after other prepositions	*pour qui, avec qui, par qui*

Referring to things:

	Masculine singular	Feminine singular	Masculine plural	Feminine plural
after *de*	*duquel*	*de laquelle*	*desquels*	*desquelles*
after *à*	*auquel*	*à laquelle*	*auxquels*	*auxquelles*
after other prepositions	*lequel*	*laquelle*	*lesquels*	*lesquelles*

Lequel and so on can be used instead of *qui* when referring to persons, but *qui* is much more common. Indeed, *lequel* is largely an R3 written form, and many French speakers would not use it at all. Nearly all French speakers would say *Les hommes à qui je parle*; few would say *Les hommes auxquels je parle*. At the same time, *parmi* requires the *lequel* forms: *Les gens parmi lesquels j'ai passé toute l'après-midi. Qui* is not possible here.

The direct-object pronoun *que* cannot be omitted, as frequently happens with *that/which*: *La fille que j'ai vue hier = The girl I saw yesterday.*

Prepositions cannot be tacked onto the end of clauses as they can in English. They need to precede the relative pronoun or form a unit with it:

le monsieur à qui j'ai donné le document	*the gentleman I gave the document to*
le monument dont j'ai fait le tour	*the monument I walked round*
Où est la voiture où t'as laissé mon portable ?	*Where is the car you left my cellphone in?*
Je ne trouve pas l'enveloppe dans laquelle tu as mis les euros.	*I can't find the envelope you put the euros in.*

The possessive idea of *whose* does not have a French equivalent. Rearranging the sentence in French is called for, in a variety of ways. The formula is largely: main clause + *dont* + noun of subordinate clause + verb of subordinate clause:

| Je te présente un ami dont l'épouse t'a appelée la semaine dernière. | *May I introduce you to the friend whose wife phoned you last week.* |

Voilà la maison dont le propriétaire vient de décéder	*There's the house whose owner (the owner of which* is preferable here in English) *has just died.*
Ce roman, dont l'auteure a déjà écrit des recueils de poèmes...	*This novel, the author of which has already written collections of poems...*
Mon père dont on dit qu'il a d'énormes connaissances en physique...	*My father, of whom it is said that he has enormous knowledge in physics...*
Le directeur dont je sais que vous avez suivi les conseils...	*The director whose advice I know you have followed...*
C'est ce jeune homme dont je t'ai dit qu'il avait perdu sa mère.	*It's this young man who I told you had lost his mother.*

The last three examples which have the insertion *on dit/je sais/je t'ai dit* are of an R3 style and very literary, and in common speech one would probably intercalate a short statement as follows: *Mon père qui a, selon les gens, d'énormes... ; Le directeur dont vous avez suivi les conseils, à ce que je sache... ; Je t'ai parlé de ce jeune homme qui avait perdu sa mère...*

Where the preposition *de* is involved, *dont* would be needed:

le malheur dont je suis menacée	*the misfortune that threatens me*
la façon dont elle s'est tirée d'affaire	*the way she dealt with the difficulty*
la manière dont mon frère manie son épée	*the way in which my brother handles his sword*
C'est ce dont je me souviens.	*That is what I remember.*
On ne l'a pas reconnu, ce dont il s'est ému.	*He was not recognized, which upset him.*
les soucis dont vous êtes accablé	*the troubles which overwhelm you*

Dont can be the complement of a numeral:

Prenez soin de ces livres dont deux sont rares.	*Take care of these books, of which two are rare.*
J'ai retenu quelques faits dont je citerai quelques-uns.	*I've kept a few facts of which I'll quote a few.*
Je vous envoie deux bagues, dont il y a une pour toi.	*I am sending you two rings, one of which is for you.*

The repetition of *dont* by *en* was quite common in past eras but is now not recommended:

Deux écrivains l'ont vivement critiqué, dont j'en citerai deux.	*Two writers criticized him sharply, two of whom I shall quote.*
On a publié deux pamplets dont j'en ai deux.	*Two pamphlets have been published of which I have two.*

A pleonastic construction of a similar type is much more common these days. It involves *dont* and a personal pronoun. Needless to say, pleonasms are not to be imitated even if well-considered writers indulge in them. The first sentence is preferred to the second:

les enfants que leurs parents ont bien élevés	the children whose parents have brought them up well
Les enfants dont les parents les ont bien élevés	

Likewise, for the same reason the first is preferred to the second:

l'enfant pour qui son père s'est sacrifié	the child for whom the father sacrificed himself
l'enfant dont le père s'est sacrifié pour lui	

A further pleonasm involves *de* and *dont*. The first sentence is acceptable, the second invites censure: *C'est de lui que je parle; C'est de lui dont je parle.*

Dont may be used without a verb, a turn of phrase not found in English:

J'ai entendu dire par mon ami, dont voici les propres paroles...	I heard my friend say, and here are his very words...
Ils ont cinq enfants, dont trois filles.	They have five children, three of whom are girls.
Trois personnes, dont moi, ont protesté.	Three people, including me, protested.
J'ai emprunté quatre magazines à Irène, dont deux en arabe.	I borrowed four magazines from Irène, two of which are in Arabic.

Dont and *d'où*: with verbs such as *venir, sortir, partir, descendre, résulter, conclure* (i.e., verbs suggesting *away from, whence*), a distinction needs to be made.

D'où applies to things to indicate moving away from a departure point: *la ville d'où tu viens; un appartement d'où la vue est fort belle; un fait d'où je conclus que.../ D'où je conclus que...* In R3 style, usually literary, one sees: *Le pays dont elle sort* (also: *d'où elle sort*).

Dont is used of people, family, race: *Le sang* (or *La famille*) *dont il sort.* *D'où* could not be excluded here: *Le sang d'où elle sort.*

Whose does not have a straight parallel when the noun is governed by a preposition. *Dont* cannot be used in the following sentences and is replaced by *qui*, or *duquel / de laquelle*:

l'homme sur les pieds de qui j'ai marché	the man on whose feet I walked
la femme aux intérêts de qui j'ai nui	the woman whose interests I damaged

la colline du haut de laquelle on
   voit la ville

the hill from the top of which you can
   see the city

49.1 Uses of *lequel, laquelle,* etc.

Qui is replaced by *lequel* and so on after prepositions, when things, abstract ideas or animals are involved:

le lit sur lequel elle s'est allongée

les tables sur lesquelles les
   serveurs ont mis les couverts

une complicité sans l'aide de
   laquelle elle n'aurait pas réussi
le chien dans le poil duquel le
   maître trouvait des puces

the bed on which she stretched out
the tables on which the waiters put
   the cutlery
complicity without the help of which
   she would not have succeeded
the dog in whose hair the master
   would find fleas

When persons are referred to, *qui* or *lequel* are used, although *qui* is much more common (see above):

des complices sans l'aide
   desquels / de qui ils ne se
   seraient pas tirés d'affaire

accomplices without whose help they
   would not have managed

However, *lequel*, *laquelle* and so on could be preferable to avoid ambiguity, since this can express gender and number:

Le fils de ma cousine, lequel
   prépare l'agrégation, est au
   Brésil.

My cousin's son who is studying for
   the agrégation is in Brazil.

If *qui* were used here, it could refer to the *cousine*. Of course, grammatically, there could be confusion, but context and other language features such as adjectives would clear up any doubt.

Instead of *qui*, *lequel* can represent the subject in the higher registers, in literature and legal language, but only after a comma. It has the effect of stress:

Un homme se leva au milieu de
   cette assemblée, lequel parla
   de...
J'ai rencontré M. Durand, lequel
   m'a dit que...

A man stood up in the middle of this
   meeting, and spoke of...

I met M. Durand who said to me
   that...

Lequel as an interrogative pronoun implies a choice or a specific opinion between persons or things:

Parmi ces étoffes / ces amies,
   laquelle est la plus belle ?

Among these materials/friends,
   which/who is the most attractive?

Laquelle choisis-tu?	*Which/whom do you choose?*
"Je vais te poser une question."	*"I'm going to ask you a question."*
"Laquelle?"	*"Which one?"*
Tu as deux vélos. Duquel des deux veux-tu te défaire?	*You have two cycles. Which of the two do you want to get rid of?*

Lequel can be used as an indirect question:

Choisis lequel d'entre nous tu veux pour compagnon.	*Choose which of us you want as a companion.*

Lequel can be used as a neuter pronoun:

Lequel des deux est le plus agréable? Partir ou rester?	*Which of the two is the most pleasant? Go or stay?*

Also *Lequel est préférable? | Lequel préfères-tu?* Or even: *Que préfères-tu?*
Lequel can be used as a relative adjective:

Plusieurs personnes ont vu l'accident, lesquels témoins disent que...	*Several people saw the accident. As witnesses, they say that...*
Je te donne cinquante euros, laquelle somme je te dois depuis un mois.	*I give you fifty euros, which sum I have owed you for a month.*

The most common construction here is *auquel cas*:

Ils vous avertiront, auquel cas, vous me préviendrez.	*They'll let you know, in which case, you'll tell me.*

Note that one says: *La raison pour laquelle* (not: *pourquoi*) elle vient / il le fait.

49.2 Uses of *quoi*

As a relative pronoun, *quoi* has a neuter value that refers to something indeterminate. It can represent an idea that has just been expressed. In this case, it is preceded by a preposition:

Ce pour quoi je lutte, c'est...	*What I am struggling for is...*
C'est en quoi tu te trompes.	*It's what you are mistaken over.*
Ce sont des choses à quoi tu ne prends pas garde.	*They are things you don't bother about.*
Il y a quelque chose à quoi je pense.	*There's something I'm thinking about.*
Elle fit semblant de ne pas me voir, à quoi je fus très sensible.	*She pretended not to see me, at which I felt very sensitive.*
À quoi cela sert-il?	*What's that for?*

En quoi cela peut-il t'intéresser ?	*In which way can that interest you?*
De quoi as-tu besoin ? / Tu as besoin de quoi ?	*What do you need?*
Sur quoi comptez-vous ? / Vous comptez sur quoi ?	*What are you counting on?*

Quoi can be used without an antecedent, especially before an infinitive, and at various registers which are indicated:

Il y a de quoi nous contenter (R2).	*That's enough to satisfy us.*
Nous avons de quoi nous tirer d'affaire.	*We have enough to manage.*
Nous avons de quoi vivre.	*We have enough to live on.*
Il n'y a pas de quoi être fier.	*That's nothing to be proud about.*
C'est une femme qui a de quoi (R1).	*She is a woman with all she needs.*
Il n'y a pas de quoi (me remercier) (R1).	*You're welcome / Don't mention it.*
Il s'est trompé, comme quoi personne n'est infaillible.	*He made a mistake, which proves that no one is infallible.*
L'avocat a produit un certificat comme quoi on était présent.	*The lawyer produced a certificate showing we were present.*

Quoi can be a subject in elliptical sentences or expressions:

| Quoi d'étonnant / de plus en vogue / de mieux ? | *How surprising / What is more in vogue? / What better?* |

Quoi may stand as an attribute before *devenir* (in the first example *que* is more common):

Quoi devenir ?	*What am I / are we, etc. to become?*
Tu seras quoi ?	*What will you be?*
Tu deviendras quoi ?	*What will you become?*

Quoi may stand as a direct complement before certain infinitives: *dire, faire, manger, répondre, voir*:

| Mais quoi répondre ? | *But what can I / we reply?* |
| Quoi faire ? | *But what do I / we do?* |

Que would be more common in these two cases}.
    Quoi may stand after certain verbs:

| Tu disais quoi ? | *You said what?* |
| Antoine voulait que j'avoue, mais avouer quoi ? | *Antoine wanted me to confess, but confess what?* |

Que may not replace *quoi* in these constructions.
Quoi may stand alone

Quoi! Tu as l'audace de l'insulter?	*What! You have the audacity to insult her?*

To have something repeated, *quoi* is used but care is needed here since, as an interjection, it can sound abrupt and impolite:

Quoi?	*What (did you say)?*

Much more acceptable are: *Plaît-il?* (R3), *Pardon?*, *Comment?*, *Vous dites?*, *Comment dites-vous?*
Quoi as an interjection can indicate surprise, indignation:

Quoi, tu l'excuses?	*What, you excuse him?*

This can be reinforced by: *Hé quoi | En bien quoi!*
To complete an explanation, or an enumeration:

Elle lit n'importe quoi, ouvre et ferme son poste, elle s'ennuie, quoi!	*She reads anything, turns on her television, then turns it off, she just gets bored, you know!*

Quoi may be used as a relative pronoun after a demonstrative adjective, but, although grammatically correct, it seems clumsy and awkward, doubtless partly by virtue of the proximity of vowels:

Ce à quoi je pense, c'est ton examen.	*What I am thinking of is your exam.*
Ce avec quoi j'envoie le message, c'est mon portable.	*What I am sending the message with is my laptop.*

But see *ce pour quoi* above where there is no juxtaposition of vowels.
One does observe the use of *quoi* instead of *lequel* etc. when the antecedent is a noun referring to a thing or things. Yet, since *quoi* evokes a neuter idea, this is a practice not to be recommended, and would only be found in some writers:

Les louvoiements sournois à quoi cette fausse situation l'obligeait (Gide).	*The cunning maneuvering this awkward situation forced him into.*

(*Auxquels* is suggested here as an alternative, notwithstanding the authority of Gide.)

Il n'était pas de sacrifice à quoi tu n'aurais pas consenti (Mauriac).	*There was no sacrifice to which you would not have consented.*

(*Auquel* is suggested here as an alternative.)

Note the very common use of *je ne sais quoi*, which stands independently of an infinitive:

Il y avait là je ne sais quoi.	*There was something there I can't describe.*
On entendait dans son ton un je ne sais quoi d'arrogant.	*You could hear in her tone something arrogant.*

49.3 Uses of *ce qui, ce que, ce dont, ce à quoi, ce avec quoi* etc. (see also above for these last two items)

These constructions refer either to a general statement that has come before (corresponding to the English [*that*] *which, what*) or to a following statement. Their forms and values are:

subject	*ce qui*
direct object	*ce que*
that of which	*ce dont*
with other prepositions	*ce à quoi, ce avec quoi*
Ils sont tous tombés d'accord, ce qui m'a consolée.	*They were all in agreement, which consoled me.*

Ce qui is the subject referring to the whole sentence/clause: *Ils sont tous*. Compare with:

Ils n'étaient pas d'accord, ce que je ne suis pas arrivé à comprendre.	*They were not in agreement, which I couldn't understand.*

Ce que is the direct object, referring to *Ils n'étaient pas d'accord*; the subject is *je*.

Ce qui me passionne, c'est l'architecture aztèque.	*What excites me is Aztec architecture.*
Ce que tu as fait me paraît impressionnant.	*What you've done seems impressive to me.*

There is no reason why the *c'est* in the first sentence could not be plural, as in: *Ce qui me passionne, ce sont les coutumes aztèques*. Note also the formula *ce qui* + verb + *c'est* + infinitive or noun. Here, even French speakers can be confused, given the closeness in sound between the i in *ce qui importe* and that in *ce qu'il importe*.

Ce qui importe, c'est partir au plus tôt.	*What is important is to leave as soon as possible.*
Ce qu'il importe, c'est partir au plus tôt.	

In the first case, *ce qui* is the subject, while in the second, *il* is the subject, and *ce que* is the direct object.

Likewise:

Jean avait prévu ce qui allait arriver.	Jean had foreseen what was going to happen.
Jean avait prévu ce qu'il allait arriver.	

Ce qui and *ce que* can correspond to *what* in the following way:

Sophie a pris sur la table ce qui / ce qu'il lui restait de papier.	Sophie took from the table what remained of the paper.
Avec ce que Louise avait d'euros, elle se tira d'affaire.	With what Louise had by way of euros, she managed.

Use of *ce dont* (see also above):

Ce dont tu parles ne m'intéresse nullement.	What you are speaking about doesn't interest me at all.
Voilà ce dont je voudrais te parler.	That's what I'd like to talk to you about.

Note how some expressions (with *qui* replacing *ce qui*) are still in current use:

qui mieux est	what is better
qui pis est	what is worse
qui plus est	what is more

And particularly with *voilà*:

Voilà qui m'étonne/emballe.	That really is surprising/thrilling.
Voilà qui est louche/bien.	That looks odd/fine.
Voilà qui vaut mieux.	That looks better.

Also note the survival of archaic expressions:

Fais ce que bon te semblera.	Do what you think fit.
Advienne que pourra.	Come what may.
Coûte que coûte.	At all costs.
Vaille que vaille.	For what it is worth.

49.4 Uses of *où*

Où has the basic meaning of *where* but usage means these terms do not always correspond. In the following sentence, there is very clear correspondence:

Londres est la ville où j'ai fait sa connaissance.	London is the city where I met her.

la chambre où j'ai mis ton portable	the room where I put your cellphone

With respect to time, English uses *when?* but not always so in French:

le jour / le moment / la minute / la semaine où mon oncle est arrivé	*the day/moment/minute/week when my uncle arrived*
l'instant précis où j'appelais Jean	*the precise moment I was phoning Jean*
l'époque où Napoléon envahit toute l'Europe	*the period when Napoleon invaded all Europe*
du/au temps où on faisait de la planche à voile	*at the time when we did windsurfing*
à partir du moment où je l'ai vue	*from the moment I saw her*

Que sometimes replaces *où* in these sentences/phrases, but *où* is preferable by far, and it could be argued that the use of *que* is of lower register: *au temps qu'on faisait de la planche à voile* and *à partir du moment que je l'ai vue*.

Quand/lorsque would be used in:

C'était ce jour en janvier quand il faisait très froid.	*It was that day in January when it was very cold.*
C'était pendant cette période-là, quand les feuilles tombaient des arbres...	*It was during that period, when the leaves were falling from the trees...*

Note that *quand/lorsque* are not relatives but conjunctions.

Although the definite article + *jour* and so on is followed by *où*, the indefinite article requires *que*:

Un beau jour que je me promenais au parc...	*One fine day when I was walking in the park...*

Où can easily be preceded by a preposition, especially *de* and *par*:

la rue d'où Sabrina sortait	*the street Sabrina was coming out from*
le bois par où tu es passé	*the wood you went through*

49.5 Multiple use of *qui*

Last and least is the double or multiple use of the relative pronoun *qui* but in special R3 context, meaning *some... others*. Probably never heard in spoken French, it is limited to a very literary style: *Tout le monde somnolait, qui dans la cabine, qui sur le pont; Les enfants étaient tous déguisés, qui en indien, qui en pirate, qui en prince, qui en médecin.*

50

Interrogative pronouns, adjectives and adverbs / Les pronoms, les adjectifs et les adverbes interrogatifs

The following passage narrates some of the pleasant experiences enjoyed by an American student at the university of Grenoble. Kaycee obviously derives great pleasure from her contact with French people, and notably with her host family. The surrounding lofty mountains are a sheer delight for her. This piece highlights some of the uses of interrogative pronouns, adjectives and adverbs which stand out in bold. Some translations are provided.

L'expérience de Kaycee au cœur des Alpes

Qui est Américain dans ce groupe? Une grande majorité d'étudiants lèvent le doigt. **Qui** accepterait de faire un bilan [make a report] de son séjour en France? Il conviendrait de répondre aux questions suivantes : **Quelle** a été la première impression à votre arrivée ? **Qui** avez-vous rencontré? **Quels** étaient les moments difficiles que vous avez connus ? **Quel** est le quartier de la ville que vous préférez ? **Quelles** sont les leçons que vous tirez de votre expérience en tant qu'étudiants étrangers dans la capitale des Alpes?

Qui lève la main le premier? Kaycee lève la main spontanément et se présente. **Qui** est-elle, Kaycee? Il s'agit d'une jeune étudiante américaine, dont les parents habitent la Floride, qui découvre, au fil du temps [with the passing time], la vie universitaire sur le grand campus de Grenoble. **Où** loge-t-elle? Chez l'habitant, plus exactement, une famille d'accueil qu'elle considère comme la sienne. La jeune Américaine n'hésite pas à dire : « Ma famille d'accueil est adorable. Trois membres de la famille sont venus m'attendre à l'aéroport. C'est une famille française formidable... » Dites-moi **qui** vous êtes? Cela a été la première question de la charmante personne qui est venue accueillir Kaycee. **Où** est donc la voiture? Voilà, nous y sommes! **Quels** sont ces deux enfants? C'est un chien à **qui** elle fait mille et une caresses lorsqu'elle monte dans la petite voiture qui l'attend sur le parking de l'aéroport international. Sur le siège arrière du véhicule de marque française, Kaycee trouve des clefs. Ces clefs sont à **qui**? **Qui** parmi vous a laissé les clefs dans la voiture? **Pourquoi** sont-elles là? Elle se demande aussi **qui** a ouvert la vitre. Pour **qui** connaît [For anyone who knows] Kaycee, elle est d'une douceur d'ange. Çà et là, l'étudiante donne ses premières impressions. Elle pose quelques questions : « **Combien** êtes-vous dans la famille ? **Quand est-ce que** nous allons arriver à destination ? »

Qu'est-ce qu'elle pense de la France et des Français, la jeune fille ? **Qu'est-ce qui** lui plaît à Grenoble ? **Que** pense-t-elle des transports publics qui sont particulièrement efficaces, du moins pour un Français ? Elle ne porte que des jugements favorables. Mais, un véritable choc culturel l'attend : les Français passent leur temps à se faire des bisous, souligne-t-elle. **Qui d'autre** [Who else] dans le monde passerait son temps à faire la bise à tout le monde, et jusqu'à quatre fois ! **En quoi** les différences culturelles se font-elles sentir tout au long du séjour ? Les connaissances des Français sur le monde, les rapports familiaux et sociaux sont foncièrement différents des préoccupations de l'Américain moyen. **Quel** est l'attrait des montagnes que Kaycee adore ? Elle se complaît à se promener en montagne avec qui que ce soit [anyone], indique-t-elle, parce que ces montagnes font la beauté de la ville. Quoi de plus impressionnant que ces ruelles [alleyways] caractéristiques et historiques ainsi que ces cafés typiquement français. La rue Jean-Jacques Rousseau évoque bien des événements d'une grande portée historique Il faut avouer que le paysage est magnifique, **n'est-ce pas** ? C'est l'une des grandes préoccupations de la municipalité grenobloise que de protéger l'environnement. Le climat est relativement doux, sauf au cœur de l'hiver. Les routes sont bien conçues. Quoi de plus beau que le style d'architecture de certains bâtiments et leur esthétique qui sont très harmonieux ? **Lequel** des endroits est le plus attirant de la ville de Grenoble ? La Belledonne (italien = *belles dames*), qui domine majestueusement la vallée où elle se trouve encaissée.

See the very important observations near the end of this chapter regarding the use of inversion and its natural avoidance. See also Chapter 51 on inversion.

All the interrogative terms above involve asking questions. The pronouns and adjectives are really the same form, although there are differences, as with *lequel* and so on which only exist as pronouns. In English their equivalents are: *which?, what?, who?, whom?, whose?* They occur in direct and indirect questions: *Which/Who is the most intelligent boy?; Let me know which/who is the most intelligent boy.*

50.1 Interrogative pronouns and adjectives

The forms of the interrogative adjectives are:

Masculine	Masculine plural	Feminine	Feminine plural
quel	quels	quelle	quelles

Examples:

Quel est le meilleur film ?	*What's the best movie?*
Quels étaient les moments difficiles ?	*What were the difficult moments?*

Quelle est la couleur que tu préfères?	*Which is the color you prefer?*
Quelles sont les routes à éviter?	*What are the roads to avoid?*

The words corresponding to *who* and *whom* are as follows. These forms are used in direct question (i.e., when a straight question is asked: *How are you?*) as well as in indirect questions (i.e., where a question is implied: *she asked him how he was*).

Subject	Direct object	With *de* (whose?)	With *à* (whose?)
qui	qui	de qui	à qui

Qui is used after other prepositions as well as with *à* Note that *qui* is, happily, an all-purpose pronoun. It stands for all the variations in gender and number, but in a straight direct question, as with the verb *être* or *avoir*, it can only ever be followed by a singular third person when it represents the subject, and there is no complement:

Qui est Américain dans ce groupe?	*Who is American in this group?*
Qui avait la clef de la porte?	*Who had the door key?*

But when there is a complement, a plural verb is possible:

Qui sont ces enfants?	*Who are these children?*
Qui sont ces dames?	*Who are these ladies?*

Qui as direct object:

Qui as-tu vu ce matin? / Tu as vu qui ce matin? (R1)	*Who(m) did you see this morning?*
T'as battu qui au tennis?	*Who did you beat at tennis?*

Qui can be used in conjunction with *de*. Such a construction is awkward and forced, although grammatically sound:

De qui a-t-elle obtenu l'autorisation?	*Whose authorization did she get?*

Qui with *à* indicating possession:

À qui est cet ordinateur?	*Whose computer is this?*
Ces clefs sont à qui? (R1)	*Whose keys are these?*

An English speaker could be forgiven for thinking that possession in French should be indicated with *de*, and not with *à*. Certainly this is the case in Italian (*di*) and Spanish (*de*).

Qui with *à* not indicating possession:

Tu as donné ton USB à qui? (R1)	*Who did you give your USB/memory stick to?*
Sophie a emprunté le vélo à qui? (R1)	*Who(m) did Sophie borrow the bike from?*
À qui as-tu prêté ton cahier?	*Who(m) did you lend your exercise book to?*

Qui with other prepositions:

T'as joué au tennis avec qui ce matin ? (R1)	*Who did you play tennis with this morning?*
Pour qui ont-ils voté ?	*Whom did they vote for?*
De tous ces politiciens, en qui as-tu confiance ?	*Of all these politicians, whom do you trust?*

Qui corresponds to the subject and the direct object of a subordinate clause. It also follows prepositions as in the following cases:

Subject:

Je voudrais savoir qui va venir.	*I'd like to know who's coming.*
Dites-moi qui vous êtes.	*Tell me who you are.*
Je me demande qui a ouvert la fenêtre.	*I wonder who opened the window.*
On ne sait plus qui est qui.	*We don't know who is who.*

Direct object:

J'ignore qui on choisira.	*I don't know who(m) they'll choose.*
Je me demande qui je préfère.	*I wonder who(m) I prefer.*

With prepositions:

À qui parlais-tu ?	*Who were you speaking to?*
Nous ne savons à qui nous adresser.	*We don't know who(m) to ask.*
Par qui a-t-elle été nommée ?	*Who was she nominated by?*
Tu as collaboré avec qui ?	*Who did you collaborate with?*
Tu habites chez qui en ce moment ?	*Who are you living with at the moment?*

Note also the following type of construction where a choice occurs between individuals:

Qui de nous le fera ?	*Who among us will do it?*
Qui d'entre nous oserait ?	*Who among us would dare?*
Qui parmi vous a passé le bac ?	*Who among you has got through the bac (French state competitive exam for school leavers)?*
Qui des deux viendra ?	*Who of the two will come?*
Qui de vous trois va m'accompagner ?	*Who of you three will come with me?*
Qui de ton frère ou de ta sœur peut me donner un coup de main ?	*Of your brother or sister, who can give me a hand?*

Miscellaneous uses of *qui*:

Qui may be used with domestic animals and pets:

C'est un chien à qui elle fait mille caresses.	*It's a dog she strokes time and again.*
Regarde-moi tous ces chats pour qui il sacrifie tout son argent.	*Look at all those cats he sacrifices all his money for.*

À qui can suggest the idea of rivalry or "going beyond the next person":

C'est à qui applaudira le plus fort.	*Let's see who applauds the loudest.*
C'est à qui gagne le plus de points en une heure qui remporte le titre.	*It's the person who collects the most points in an hour who takes the title.*

Qui d'autre = who else

Qui d'autre s'en souviendra ?	*Who else will remember?*
À qui d'autre le dirais-tu ?	*Who else would you say it to?*

Note that some expressions with *qui* do not need an antecedent:

Je le dirais à qui de droit.	*I would say it to the right/appropriate person.*

The expression: *À qui de droit* is quite commonly used at the head of a letter of reference supporting a job application for instance (= *To whom it may concern*). Also:

Elle se montre aimable envers qui elle veut.	*She's friendly with anyone she likes.*
Pour qui la connaît, elle est la douceur même.	*For anyone who knows her, she is sweetness itself.*
Tu ne peux pas employer cette expression avec qui que ce soit.	*You can't use that expression with anyone you like.*
Tout vient à qui sait attendre.	*Everything comes to him who waits; Patience is a virtue.*
Qui diable a dit ça ?	*Who the devil said that?*

Qui diantre... ? (euphemism for the expression above) was once used but has disappeared from modern currency, even in ironic mode.

There is a series of expressions used in direct questions only which correspond to *qui = who*:

Subject	Direct object	After prepositions
qui est-ce qui	qui est-ce que	à qui est-ce que

Subject:

Qui est-ce qui est là ?	*Who's there?*
Qui est-ce qui a fait ça ?	*Who did that?*

Direct object:

Qui est-ce que t'as vu ?	*Who did you see?*
Qui est-ce qu'elle a rencontré ?	*Who did she meet?*

After prepositions:

Pour qui est-ce qu'il a voté ?	*Who did he vote for?*
Avec qui est-ce qu'elle a fait le voyage ?	*Who did she travel with?*
À qui est-ce qu'il s'est adressé ?	*Who did he approach?*

The forms for *what* are, in direct questions:

Subject	Direct object	After any preposition
qu'est-ce qui	que/qu'est-ce que	quoi

Subject:

Qu'est-ce qui t'embête ?	*What's troubling you?*
Qu'est-ce qui m'arrive ?	*What's happening to me?*
Qu'est-ce qui fait cette fumée-là ?	*What's making that smoke?*

Direct object:

Qu'est-ce que tu veux ? / Que veux-tu ?	*What do you want?*
Qu'est-ce qu'elle chante ?	*What's she singing?*

After prepositions:

De quoi as-tu besoin ?	*What do you need?*
Sur quoi comptez-vous ?	*What are you counting on?*
À quoi penses-tu ?	*What are you thinking about?*

Qu'est-ce que and *que* also stand as a complement with the verbs *être* and *devenir*:

Que serons-nous ?	*What will we be?*
Qu'est-ce que c'était ?	*What was it?*
Qu'est-elle devenue ?	*What became of her?*
Qu'est-ce que nous deviendrons ?	*What will become of us?*

Qu'est-ce que and *Qu'est-ce que c'est que* (this latter in R1 discourse) are the equivalent of *What is / What are*:

Qu'est-ce que la beauté ?	*What is beauty?*
Qu'est-ce que c'est qu'une céphalée ?	*What's a céphalée?*
Qu'est-ce que c'est que cette tache ?	*What's that stain?*

This last expression occurs commonly in exclamations:

Qu'est-ce que c'est que cette robe-là ?	*What in heaven's name is that dress?*

Qu'est-ce que has an exclamatory value as well:

Qu'est-ce qu'il est bête !	*He is really dumb!*

Quoi can stand as a direct object:

To stress something already said, often with rising intonation:

Tu seras quoi ?	*You'll be what?*
Elle deviendra quoi ?	*She'll become what?*

With the infinitive of verbs like *dire, faire, manger, répondre, voir*:

Quoi dire/faire/répondre ?	*What can we say/do/reply?*

In these cases, *que* is much more usual: *Que dire/faire/répondre?*

With the preposition *pour*:

"Tu viens avec moi?" "Pour quoi faire?"	"Are you coming with me?" "What for?"

Pour quoi needs to be distinguished from the single word *pourquoi* = why. *Quoi* can be used independently:

"Tu peux répéter ça?" "Quoi?"	"Can you repeat that?" "What?"
Quoi de neuf/nouveau?	Any news?
"J'en ai assez." "De quoi?"	"I'm fed up with it." "With what?"
"Même si..." "Même si quoi?"	"Even if..." "Even if what?"
"Je voudrais bien, mais..." "Mais quoi?"	"I would really like to but..." "But what?"
Quoi de plus facile?	What could be easier?

The forms for *what* in indirect questions are:

Subject	Direct object	After prepositions
ce qui	ce que	quoi

These expressions cannot obviously be used for persons or for specific objects or things. They have a neuter value. They refer to something general = *what/that which*.

Subject:

T'as compris ce qui le gêne?	Have you understood what troubles him?
Je ne sais pas ce qui l'intéresse.	I don't know what interests her.

Direct object:

Il faut leur demander ce qu'ils vont faire.	You have to ask them what they're going to do.
Ce qu'il convient de faire, c'est appeler tout de suite.	What it is sensible to do is phone immediately.

After prepositions:

Je ne comprends pas de quoi ils parlent.	I don't understand what they're talking about.
Je lui ai demandé avec quoi elle allait réparer le vélo.	I asked her what she was going to fix the bike with.

Note the use of *que de* in the following construction which entails at least one infinitive:

C'est se tromper que de croire cela.	That's fooling yourself thinking that.
C'est rendre un mauvais service à la famille que de lui rendre l'enfant malade.	It's doing a disservice to the family to return the sick child to them.
Voilà ce que c'est que de désobéir.	See what happens when you disobey.

As the object of an infinitive in indirect questions, *que* is used, not *ce que*:

Je ne sais toujours pas que lui dire.	*I still don't know what to say to her.*
Ne t'en fais pas. Nous savons que lui répondre.	*Don't worry. We know what to reply to him.*

It is worth noting the variation in *que* and *quoi* with the verb *savoir*: In written, literary discourse, *savoir* in the negative can lose its *pas*: *Je ne sais où il est.* This holds true when *savoir* with this partial negative is followed by an indirect-object pronoun: *Je ne sais que dire/faire.* But, when the full negative (*ne... pas*) is used, *quoi* nearly always replaces *que*: *Je ne sais pas quoi dire.*

The forms for *which* as a pronoun in direct and indirect questions are:

	Masculine singular	Feminine singular	Masculine plural	Feminine plural
subject + direct object	lequel	laquelle	lesquels	lesquelles
+ de	duquel	de laquelle	desquels	desquelles
+ à	auquel	à laquelle	auxquels	auxquelles

The only separation occurs with the feminine singular form + *de/à*:

Parmi ces bâtiments lequel est le plus beau?	*Which is the finest of these buildings?*
"J'ai vu ton copain hier." "Lequel?"	*"I saw your friend yesterday." "Which one?"*
Je ne me souviens plus dans lequel de ces livres j'ai trouvé la solution.	*I no longer remember in which of these books I found the solution.*
Sais-tu auquel de ses amis elle a donné mon adresse?	*Do you know to which of his friends he has given my address?*

50.2 Interrogative adverbs

There are a number of adverbs used in questions, both direct and indirect. These are:

combien (de)	*how many*	quand	*when*
comment	*how*	où	*where*
pourquoi	*why*		

Direct questions:

Combien êtes-vous?	*How many are you?*
Combien de dollars as-tu?	*How many dollars have you got?*
Comment Sophie travaille-t-elle?	*How does Sophie work?*
Pourquoi ne se couche-t-elle pas?	*Why does she not go to bed?*
Quand saura-t-on le résultat?	*When will we know the result?*
Où vont-ils au cinéma?	*Where are they going to the movies?*

Indirect questions:

Je leur ai demandé combien ils étaient à venir.	*I asked them how many of them were coming.*
Je ne sais pas comment ils se sont tirés d'affaire.	*I don't know how they managed it.*
Philippe m'a demandé pourquoi je voulais partir.	*Philippe asked me why I wanted to leave.*
Éléonore nous a demandé quand/ où on ira en Espagne.	*Éléonore asked us when we were going to Spain / where we were going to in Spain.*

50.3 Observations on interrogative pronouns, adjectives and adverbs with respect to inversion (see also Chapter 1 on register)

Asking questions in French may be approached in a variety of ways. By far the most elegant, and the way to be recommended in writing, entails inversion. This is the least common, and it can be the most difficult to handle, particularly in compound tenses (this applies to French speakers as well). It is a question of register.

Examples of inversion: *Quand viendra-t-elle ?* / *Quand viendra ton fils ?* / *Quand viendra Irène ?*; *Quand t'a-t-il parlé ?*; *Combien as-tu d'euros ?* / *Combien de beurre y a-t-il dans le frigidaire ?*; *Pourquoi tiennent-ils à payer le voyage ?*; *Pourquoi ne se sont-ils pas présentés ?*; *Où est la voiture ?*

In spoken discourse, and notably in R1 speech, inversion becomes less common, or almost non-existent. It is easier to say: *Il vient quand ?* than *Quand vient-il ?*; *Tu en as combien ?* than *Combien en as-tu ?*; *Ils vont où ?* than *Où vont-ils ?* The first sentence in these three cases is easier to manipulate because the construction follows the affirmative pattern: *Il vient quand il veut* / *Ils vont où ils veulent*. Similarly it is easier to say *Pourquoi ils ne se sont pas présentés ?* than *Pourquoi ne se sont-ils pas présentés ?* Rising intonation forms part of this R1 construction.

The fact that the straightforward affirmative construction is so easy explains, paradoxically, the use of the formula *Est-ce que* and the consequent lengthening of the sentence – paradoxically, because there is a strong tendency to shorten sentences so as to simplify them. We are clearly now in the R1 territory of spoken discourse: *Comment est-ce que t'as fait ça ?*; *Pourquoi est-ce qu'elle (ne) vient pas ?*; *Où est-ce qu'ils vont passer leurs vacances ?*; *Quand est-ce que le train arrive ?*

There is considerable debate among linguists over the ubiquitous use of the formula *est-ce que*. Purists regard it as a lower form of expression. Hanse and Blampain accept it without reservation and take to task some grammarians (2005, p. 236) who regard it as a negligent way of speaking. It is doubtless true that writers of the French classical tradition such as Stendhal, Flaubert, Julien Green and Camus would eschew it in their compositions.

Finally the use of the adverb *n'est-ce pas?* is not as common as it is made out to be. It has its equivalents in the much more common Spanish (*¿verdad?*) and in Italian (*non è vero? / nevvero?*), and is translated in a multiplicity of ways in English: *didn't I/you?*; *wouldn't you?*; *can't we?*; *do you?*; *can we?*; *have they?* It may follow an affirmative or negative statement. However, *n'est-ce pas* is less used than the question tags in English, and is certainly of a higher register.

Ils viennent ce soir, n'est-ce pas?	*They're coming this evening, aren't they?*
Les enfants n'ont pas de congé, n'est-ce pas?	*The children don't have a holiday, do they?*

The younger generation would doubtless use *hein?* instead of *n'est-ce pas?*

Tu ne m'en veux pas, hein?	*You're not mad at me, are you?*
On joue au foot ce soir, hein?	*We'll play soccer this evening, won't we?*

51

Inversion / L'inversion

The following passage, an anecdote taken from a real event of some fifty years ago, narrates the tale of the death of a budgerigar that the little girl Esmeralda had offered to Blanche, an elderly woman. In this mock tragedy, Blanche comes to see Esmeralda's parents to announce the budgerigar's death. The small bird is buried in some kind of strange religious ceremony. The passage illustrates the extensive use of inversion, notably in the written mode. The inversions are set in bold, as well as the expressions leading to the inversions. Some translations are provided.

La perruche d'Esmeralda

Pourquoi Esmeralda **adorait-elle** les animaux domestiques ? Sa mère avait de magnifiques perruches en cage. **Pourquoi** les gens du voisinage **appréciaient-ils** tellement ces oiseaux de petite taille ? Ils avaient un plumage éclatant de couleur verte, rose, bleue et jaune. **Que faisaient-ils** tous les matins, ces oiseaux grimpeurs ? Du haut de leur perchoir, ils chantaient en réveillant les riverains [neighbors] de la rue Saint Laurent.

À **peine** Esmeralda **est-elle** hors de son lit qu'elle entend une voisine ronchonner [complaining/grumbling]. « **Quelle heure est-il** ? **Que se passe-t-il** ? » La femme **qu'a vue Esmeralda** par la fenêtre de sa chambre semble bouleversée [deeply shaken]. « Ton père **est-il** là ? » « Non ! Papa et maman sont allés s'occuper du jardin à l'allée du Rhône. Est-ce que je peux vous aider, Blanche ? **Puis-je** vous aider ? » **continua Esmeralda**. La vieille dame insiste : « **Quand** tes parents **rentreront-ils** ? Tes petits frères **sont-ils** au jardin avec eux ? J'ai perdu la perruche jaune que tu m'as offerte ! **Ai-je raison** d'aller les voir ? **Dois-je** le faire ? » À l'annonce de la mauvaise nouvelle, Esmeralda était tout en pleurs. Blanche tentait de consoler la petite fille dans ses malheurs. Rien ne put la consoler. « **Comme dit le proverbe biblique** : À chaque jour **suffit sa peine**. [Sufficient unto the day is the evil thereof.] À **quoi sert-il** de gémir et de se plaindre ? » **s'exclama la voisine**. « Est-ce que je sors ? Je voudrais voir ma perruche. C'est triste qu'elle soit morte. **Penses-tu** que je pourrai organiser l'enterrement [burial] de ma perruche adorée ? **Est-ce possible** ? **N'est-ce pas** ? » Esmeralda prit Blanche au dépourvu [caught Blanche unexpectedly]. **Aime-t-elle** autant cet oiseau que la petite ?

Va-t-elle convaincre les parents de l'enfant de s'occuper de la cérémonie ? **Dira-t-elle** comment s'y prendre ?

Ennuyé par les bavardages [gossip], un riverain est à peine sorti de son lit qu'il lança : « Faites taire ces deux perruches ! » Esmeralda et Blanche **se sont-elles tues** à cette remarque ? Bien sûr ! Ensuite, elles allèrent voir le curé du village. Elles montèrent par les chemins tortueux, puis par les escaliers jusqu'à la cathédrale. **Arriveraient-elles** à la cure [presbytery = the priest's house] que le prêtre ne s'en serait pas étonné [If they had arrived at the presbytery, the priest would not have been surprised]. « Qui est-ce qui est venu me rendre visite ? Quelle agréable surprise ! **Que se passe-t-il ? Quelle heure est-il ?** » **s'écria** le curé de la paroisse. Du haut de ses huit ans, la petite fille raconta sa tristesse et son chagrin. « **Comment s'appelle-t-il**, l'oiseau dont tu me parles ? Oui, mon enfant, **reprit le curé**. Pauvre petite bête ! Cela **dût-il** m'être reproché je te donnerai tous les conseils de la sagesse [If I were reproached for it, I would give you all the advice that wisdom can offer]. Tout **a-t-il été prévu** pour accompagner ta perruche dans sa dernière demeure [abode] ? **As-tu envoyé** un mot à tes camarades de classe ? » « C'est vrai, **répliqua-t-elle**. Je vais annoncer la nouvelle à mes camarades », **confia Esmeralda**. « Quel plaisir **m'a fait votre visite** ! » fit le curé.

Esmeralda, avec l'approbation de ses parents, décida d'enterrer sa perruche au pied de la statue de la vierge qui se situe au sommet de la colline de La Joanade. Cette tombe domine les hauteurs du village. Le sentier qui y monte était difficile pour les enfants de notre école primaire. Une fois montées, nous avions une vue imprenable [magnificent/unassailable] sur la cathédrale, la Tour, le séminaire et le Palais épiscopal [bishop's palace]. Esmeralda inscrivit sur la tombe : « **Ci-gît** [Here lies] **la reine** des perruches à tout jamais. »

The French word *inversion*, used in a grammatical context, occurs much more frequently than its English counterpart. Doubtless many English-speaking people would wonder what it means even in English grammar, while it is part of the grammatical stock-in-trade for French students dealing with their own language. Inversion, put simply, describes the reversal of the normal order of words where the subject comes after the verb: *You go to the movies > Do you go to the movies?* These sentences in French would be, literally translated: *Tu vas au cinéma > Vas-tu au cinéma ?*

51.1 How to form the inversion of the subject and the verb in direct questions

There are essentially three kinds of inversion in French:

1. The subject as pronoun comes after the verb. This is a simple inversion (*inversion simple*):

Où travaille-t-il ?	*Where does he work?*
Vient-elle ?	*Is she coming?*
Part-on ?	*Are we going?*

2. The subject as noun follows the verb. This is also a simple inversion:

Où travaille ton frère ?	*Where does your brother work?*

3. The simple inversion of noun and verb is possible in relative clauses, which produces two possibilities. Compare the two sentences below:

La femme que ton frère a vue...
La femme qu'a vue ton frère... } *The woman that your brother saw...*

The difference in these two sentences resides in the elegance of the second sentence. Already, we notice that inversion can, and often is, a sign of a more refined and literary style.

When the noun as subject remains before the verb, it is recalled, as it were, by a pronoun. This is what the French call a *pronom de rappel* which can be more complex (*inversion complexe*), and it is a construction worth bearing in mind throughout this chapter:

Votre frère est-il là ?	*Is your brother there?*
Les petits sont-ils au jardin ?	*Are the children in the garden?*
Aussi ma sœur lui a-t-elle écrit.	*So my sister wrote him/her.*

In compound tenses, the noun comes after the past participle, while the personal pronoun or *ce/on* comes after the auxiliary verb:

Où a travaillé ton père ?	*Where did your father work?*
Où a-t-elle travaillé ?	*Where did she work?*
Où a-t-on mis la voiture ?	*Where have we put the car?*

Directly before the subject pronouns *il*, *elle* and *on*, a **t** is placed between two hyphens after an **a** or an **e** of the third person. This is clearly for euphony's sake: *Aime-t-il/elle ?*; *Va-t-il/elle ?*; *Dira-t-il/elle ?* This also happens after *vainc* and *convainc*: *Convainc-t-il quelqu'un ?* Such a construction with these two verbs would be extremely rare, however.

In the present indicative, the inversion of *je* is hardly ever made, especially after monosyllables, save after *ai*, *dis*, *dois*, *fais*, *puis*, *sais*, *vais*, *veux*, *vois* (but not all these are in frequent use with *je*):

Ai-je raison ?; *Dois-je le faire ?*; *Puis-je vous aider ?* It would be unthinkable for *je* to follow *cours*, *pars*, *sors*, unless for a jocular purpose. There is always the possibility of using *est-ce que* with a straightforward pronoun + verb: *Est-ce que je cours/pars/sors ?*

If the first person of a verb ends in an **e**, which is most frequent, the inversion of *je* is theoretically possible, but exceptional, and here the mute **e** would change to an acute **e**: **é**. But this is an exaggerated form of pedantry.

Est-ce que is always on hand. Thus, instead of *Hésité-je ?* one would use *Est-ce que j'hésite ?*; instead of *Pensé-je* one would say *Est-ce que je pense ?*

Inversion of *ce* with most forms is not used at all, for instance *furent-ce*, *fussent-ce*. But some forms are entirely acceptable: *sont-ce*, *fut-ce* and so on.

51.2 When to use inversion

In a general way, inversion is characteristic of a higher form of expression, and is often associated with the written R3 style, while its avoidance in speech is perfectly normal, either with *est-ce que* or with some other subterfuge, such as rising intonation. It is as well to point out this feature as a mark of varying register. Thus, *Viennent-ils ?* in writing or careful speech could be considered R3, *Est-ce qu'ils viennent ?* could be considered standard R2, and *Ils viennent ?* with rising intonation would suggest a colloquial but very common style (R1). Below is a list of circumstances in which inversion occurs:

In direct questions with simple inversion and personal pronoun, *ce* or *on*: *Vient-elle ?*; *Part-on ?*; *Est-ce possible ?*; *N'est-ce pas ?*; *Vous a-t-on répondu ?*; *Lui a-t-on envoyé un mot ?*

If there is a noun or another pronoun, a recall of the noun occurs: *Ton père vient-il avec nous ?*; *Chacun en est-il persuadé ?*; *Tout a-t-il été prévu ?*

When an interrogative word begins a sentence, and this can be preceded by *car*, *et*, *mais*: *Qui l'a dit ?*; *Mais qui s'en plaint ?*; *Combien de gens l'ont vu ?*; *Lequel de ces romans te paraît le meilleur ?*; *Quel témoin a vu l'accusé ?*; *Qui est-ce qui est venu ?*; *Et qui est-ce qui a cassé la vitre ?*

With *combien . . . ne pas* inversion with a recall by the pronoun is normal: *Combien d'entre vous ne l'ont-ils pas fait ?* But with *combien* in the positive both use and absence of the recall pronoun are possible: *Combien d'entre vous l'ont fait / l'ont-ils fait ?*

If the verb is impersonal, the pronoun *il* follows the verb: *Que faut-il ?*; *Que se passe-t-il ?*; *Quelle heure est-il ?*; *Que vous semble-t-il de cette affaire ?*; *À quoi sert-il de se plaindre ?* It seems appropriate to be reminded that the formula *Qu'est-ce que* may replace some of these expressions in a lower but still acceptable register: *Qu'est-ce qu'il faut ?*; *Qu'est-ce qui se passe ?*; or the straightforward sentence with no inversion but with rising intonation: *Il est quelle heure ?*; *Ça sert à quoi de se plaindre ?*

After *que*, a simple inversion is necessary: *Que disent-ils ?*; *Que veulent ces gens ?*; *Que prouve cette lettre ?*

After *qu'est-ce que*, the subject can precede or follow the verb, but this excludes a personal pronoun, *ce* and *on*: *Qu'est-ce que prouve cette lettre ?*; *Qu'est-ce que cette lettre prouve ?* (The first sentence, with inversion, is more elegant than the second.)

After *qui*, simple inversion is necessary if the subject is a personal pronoun or *on*: *Qui aime-t-elle ?*; *Qui a-t-on consulté ?*

But if the subject is another pronoun or a noun, there are two possibilities: *Qui concerne cela ? | Qui cela concerne-t-il ?*; *Qui désignera le sort ? | Qui le sort désignera-t-il ?*

After *quel* followed by a noun, there is simple inversion: *Quel livre as-tu lu ?*; *Quel livre a lu ton fils ?*

If the subject is neither a personal pronoun nor *on*, a recall by the pronoun is possible: *Quel livre ton fils a-t-il lu ?*; *Quel ami votre frère soupçonne-t-il ?*

With reflexive verbs, and in a higher register, there is usually inversion and a recall by the pronoun, as with *se* in *Quand les Français se sont-ils établis en Louisiane ?* Although this is the only possibility with this sentence, there is more than one with the following: *Comment s'appelle l'homme dont tu parles ? | Comment l'homme dont tu parles s'appelle-t-il ?* Here again the more colloquial register would be: *Il s'appelle comment, l'homme dont tu parles ? | L'homme dont tu parles s'appelle comment ? | L'homme dont tu parles, il s'appelle comment ?*

Usage with semi-auxiliary verbs like *aller*, *devoir*, *pouvoir* and *vouloir*, does not allow a noun to be placed between them and the infinitive when there is inversion: *Où ton frère doit-il se rendre ?*; *Où doit se rendre ton frère ?*; but *Quand va-t-il arriver ?*

51.3 How to form the inversion of the subject and the verb in indirect questions

If the subject is a personal pronoun, *ce* or *on*, there is no inversion: *Je ne sais (pas) où elle est | qui c'est | pour quand c'est*; *Qui c'est, je l'ignore.*

In indirect questions, there is no recall by a pronoun. One can only say *Je me demande pourquoi cette enfant a échoué.*

If the subject is not a personal pronoun, *ce* or *on*, recourse to simple inversion is possible: *Je me demande souvent ce que m'a dit mon frère*; *Je ne sais où s'est rendu chacun d'eux.* These inversions are of a slightly higher register than *Je me demande souvent ce que mon frère a dit*; *Je ne sais où chacun d'eux s'est rendu.*

Inversion also occurs after *qui* and *quel*: *Je me demande qui est cet individu*; *Je ne sais pas quel est ton avantage.* This construction explains why French, and indeed Spanish, speakers say in English: *I wonder who is that individual.*

When there is a choice between inversion and non-inversion, as above, it can be a question of the stylistic balance of a sentence, especially when the verb is shorter than the subject: *Je ne sais pas où est l'employé*; *Je me demande quand viendra le docteur.*

There is never inversion after *si* (often the case in Spanish: *No sé si vendrá el médico*): *Je ne sais pas si le médecin viendra.*

Inversion would be avoided if there were possibility of confusion. Compare: *Je ne sais pas qui a rencontré mon frère* and *Je ne sais pas qui mon frère a rencontré*. In the first case, *frère* is the object, while in the second case, *frère* is the subject.

51.4 Other circumstances in which inversion occurs

With exclamatory statements, inversion can occur: *Est-elle stupide !*; *Quel plaisir m'a fait sa visite !* One can also say, in a lower register: *Qu'est-ce qu'elle est stupide !* But one would prefer *Ah ! Combien j'en ai vu qui... !* to *Combien en ai-je vu qui... !* A similar preference would be for *Combien de pays il a visités !* instead of *Combien de pays a-t-il visités !* or even *Combien a-t-il visité de pays !* (all of which are correct).

In certain expressions associated with wishes one comes across inversion: *Puisse-t-elle arriver à temps !*; *Puisse mon amie être reçue à son examen !*; *Puisse le ministre l'écouter !* (All = *Oh that... !*)

Similarly with a hypothesis or a future idea:

Vienne l'hiver, nous retournons en ville.	*If/when the winter comes, we'll go back to the town.*

This construction is of the R3 type corresponding in English to *Oh! that she may...*

After certain adverbs, inversion is used: *aussi* (= *so, thus*), *aussi bien, à peine, au moins, à tout le moins, du moins, encore, mais encore, à plus forte raison, en vain, vainement, peut-être, tout au plus, sans doute*: *Aussi ne l'ai-je pas écoutée*; *Aussi sa colère est-elle vite tombée*; *Aussi bien ne m'écouterait-il pas*; *À peine est-il hors de son lit qu'il entendit une explosion*; *Du moins donnait-il cette raison*; *Au moins convient-il qu'elle s'explique*; *Encore vaut-il mieux s'abstenir*; *Encore cette affaire n'a-t-elle réussi qu'à moitié*; *Peut-être concluront-ils l'affaire demain*. When some of these expressions are not used at the beginning of a sentence, inversion would not occur, and the register would be lower: *Il est à peine sorti de son lit que...*; *Ils concluront peut-être l'affaire demain*. *Ainsi* (*in this way*) is often followed by inversion: *Ainsi parlait mon père*; *Ainsi ferons-nous*.

After certain proverbs and set expressions, inversion occurs: *Tant va la cruche à l'eau qu'à la fin elle se casse* (*That's what comes from taking too much for granted*); *Autant en emporte le vent* (*Gone with the Wind*: title of Margaret Mitchell's bestseller); *Si grand soit-il*; *Si grand que soit cet homme*; *Ainsi soit-il* (*So be it*); *Ici repose...* (*Here lies...*; as in a cemetery); *Ci-gît...* (*Here lies...*; as in a cemetery); *À chaque jour suffit sa peine* (biblical saying: *Sufficient unto the day is the evil thereof*).

After statements made by a person or character in a novel, inversion occurs with verbs like: *affirmer, annoncer, assurer, avouer, continuer, crier, déclarer, demander, dire, s'écrier, expliquer, murmurer, proférer, protester, raconter, reprendre, souffler, soupirer*. This construction is frequently found in the preterit, including *faire* with the same value: "C'est vrai, dit-elle"; "Elle a tort, affirma-t-elle"; "Reviens, s'écria-t-elle"; "Je viendrai ce soir, annonça-t-il"; "Je ne savais que répondre, dit-il"; "Alors, fit-elle en ôtant de sa manche un fil imaginaire"; "Je vais l'appeler, dit Marie Ladouet"; "Oui, mon enfant, reprit Monsieur Agnel" (Green 1936).

In vivacious style, both written and spoken, inversion occurs when stress falls less on the verb than on the noun:

Reste à fixer le jour de notre prochaine séance.	*There remains to fix the day for our next session.*
Suivit une bagarre dans le café.	*There followed a fight in the café.*
Suivit une explication de son comportement.	*There followed an explanation of her behavior.*
Voilà que tout d'un coup revient notre ami.	*And there suddenly our friend comes back.*
À ce moment se manifeste l'enfant égaré.	*And then the lost child appears.*

In R3 language, inversion is used with conditional constructions and pronouns:

Arriverait-elle que je ne m'en serais pas étonné.	*If she arrived I would not be surprised.*
Elle pourrait, le voudrait-elle, se souvenir, mais sa volonté est d'abolir tout cela.	*If she wanted, she could remember, but her will could be to abolish it all.*

But with nouns this is not the case:

Pierre / Le directeur arriverait, que je ne me serais pas étonné.	*If Pierre / the manager arrived I would not be surprised.*

In R3 and very literary language, the first clause of a hypothesis in the subjunctive or conditional (less common) may be found with inversion:

Le voulût-il, il ne le pourrait pas.	*Even if he wanted to, he couldn't.*
Le voudrait-elle, elle ne le pourrait pas.	*Even if she wanted to, she couldn't.*
Fussent-elles pénibles, il était prêt à accepter toutes les conditions.	*Even if they were painful, he was ready to accept all the conditions.*
Il fait tout ce qu'on lui demande, fût-ce avec beaucoup d'effort.	*He does all that is asked of him, even if it means a great deal of effort.*

When a noun is the subject in these constructions, recall by a pronoun occurs:

Pierre le voulût-il, il ne le pourrait pas.	*Even if Pierre wanted to, he couldn't.*
Tout eût été tenté, il ne faut pas se décourager.	*Even if everything has been tried, we must not be discouraged.*

Again in high register, the imperfect subjunctive of *devoir* appears in inversion:

Dussé-je être blâmé, je vous soutiendrais.	*Even if I had to be accused, I would support you.*
Cela dût-il m'être reproché, je te donnerais tous les bénéfices.	*Even if I had to be blamed for it, I would give you all the profits.*

Part VI

52

Adjectives | Les adjectifs

The following text offers us a description of Venice with its tourist delights of canals, gondolas, shops and attractive streets lined with unique residences of wealthy Venetians. The passage highlights in bold the most varied use of adjectives, from agreement according to the gender of the noun, to agreement of adjectives according to the position of masculine and feminine nouns when they are together, and to non-agreement where invariability is required. As far as the latter is concerned, of special note are: *chic*, *cher* (here used as an adverb), *art nouveau*, *nu-pieds*, *bleu-violet*. Translations are offered in some cases. The expression *bon chic bon genre* in the second paragraph describes a stylish person with a conservative touch.

Promenades vénitiennes

Les **exquises** promenades **vénitiennes**, à pied, en gondole ou en bateau à vapeur nous donnent un **bel** aperçu [glimpse] de la ville sous d'**agréables et multiples** facettes. La beauté **exceptionnelle** du **vieux** Venise, des chemins **tortueux**, des passages **voûtés** [arched passageways], des culs de sac **peu éclairés**, des **petites** rues **étroites** où nous nous adossons [lean against] au mur pour laisser passer en face la personne **flâneuse** [strolling].

Les boutiques **chic** dont les vêtements B. C. B. G. (bon chic bon genre) coûtent extrêmement **cher** présentent des couleurs **variées** et des peintures **art nouveau**. Les **petits** jardins sont **fleuris** et **colorés** à la **belle** saison. Les **riches** Vénitiens, qui ont l'air **décontractés** [look relaxed] sur leur balcon **fleuri**, regardent les touristes **étrangers**, les juillettistes et les aoûtiens [July and August vacationers], errer sous une chaleur **torride**, dans un dédale [labyrinth] de ruelles. Les **grands** canaux **sombres**, et le **grand** canal de Venise des **quinzième et seizième** siècles, sont parcourus par les gondoles **traditionnelles**. À Venise, les **braves** gondoliers **musclés** aux bras **nus** proposent aux visiteurs de faire une promenade sur une barque **vénitienne** pour se diriger vers le Pont des Soupirs [Ponte dei Sospiri] qui relie le **splendide** Palais des Doges aux prisons. Les ponts **miniatures** attirent le regard **curieux** des passants, ainsi que les **jeunes** garçons qui courent **nu-pieds** çà et là.

Les vacanciers nourrissent les pigeons qui se dandinent [waddle] à droite et à gauche sur la Piazza San Marco. Cette **élégante** place **publique** est bordée de monuments **historiques** et de **magnifiques** arcades. Les dames à chapeaux **orange** s'attardent [linger] devant la terrasse du **célèbre** Café Florian où joue un orchestre **symphonique**. **Certains** visiteurs dégustent des biscuits **secs** aux amandes avec les **fameuses** glaces **italiennes** [gelati]. D'**autres** savourent un cappuccino ou un expresso ou encore un *tiramisu*, un **succulent** dessert **italien** à base de fromage **lombard** [mascarpone], d'œufs, de biscuits imbibés de café, le tout saupoudré [sprinkled with] de cacao. La **stricte** interdiction des véhicules à moteur dans la ville donne aux visiteurs la possibilité d'investir tous les quartiers où se concentrent de **superbes** résidences, de **somptueux** palais comme le Palais des Doges. La luminosité **naturelle** du ciel offre un paysage qui baigne dans la lagune **bleu-violet** sous des reflets **changeants** et de teintes **légères**.

Nous sommes convaincus que cette ville **ancestrale** continuera à attirer des gens **avides** [keen to] de connaître la vie des **chers** Vénitiens et Vénitiennes. Les histoires **ancienne et moderne** développent une énergie et un caractère **particuliers**. Une facilité et un charme **délicieux** de rencontrer les Vénitiens s'en dégagent. La Cité des Doges a inspiré beaucoup d'auteurs et de cinéastes, voire [nay] Shakespeare qui écrivit avec une habileté **incomparable** *Le marchand de Venise* (*The Merchant of Venice*) qui traite d'un usurier **retors** [cunning] et **impitoyable**.

For the position of adjectives in a sentence, see Chapter 63 on word order. As with all Romance languages, the agreement of adjectives in French forms an integral part of the language. Generally speaking, adjectives agree in a distinctive way in gender and number with the noun or pronoun they describe or are attached to. The agreement of adjectives with nouns and pronouns creates a range of anomalies and uncertainties which lead to much debate, particularly where more than one noun or pronoun are involved, or even the type of adjective. For example, is it more acceptable to say *Chers Philippe et Martine* or *Cher Philippe et chère Martine*? It could be argued that the second is more grammatically sound but it seems unnecessarily awkward. The first sentence is easier, less complicated and quicker, and since the adjective stands next to the masculine *Philippe*, no disturbance is provoked, and the construction is entirely acceptable. Yet a feminist on a rising tide of female affirmation might advocate *Chère Martine et cher Philippe*; and a male chauvinist could plead for *Chers Martine et Philippe*. Doubtless *Chère Martine et Philippe* is going too far. But, in speech, all these possibilities of *cher*, however outrageous or "incorrect" one or two may appear, sound the same. Such is the perplexing nature of adjectives in French, a perplexity shared by all its Romance neighbors.

52.1 **General rules on gender** (but there are many exceptions, and these rules are only guidelines)

To form the feminine, an **e** is added to the masculine adjective: *grand* > *grande*: *un grand garçon / une grande fille*; *un grand bâtiment / une grande maison; petit* > *petite*: *un petit champ / une petite maison*; also, among a multitude of others: *absolu(e), carré(e), civil(e), direct(e), dur(e), espagnol(e), général(e), poli(e)*. When the **e** is added to a consonant, the consonant is voiced: *droite, grande, maladroite, petite, plate*. This is particularly true of adjectives ending in **t**.

Numerous adjectives do not add an **e** to form the feminine since the masculine already ends in **-e**. Here is a brief selection: *brave, calme, deuxième (troisième, etc.), drôle, catholique, celte, écarlate, facile, gauche, jeune, lisse, mauve, moderne, morne, orthodoxe, pâle, pauvre, propre, rare, riche, rouge, russe, sage, sale, scandinave, suisse, tchèque, tendre, terne, tranquille: une femme sage; une église catholique/orthodoxe/moderne; une pauvre dame; une famille riche.*

Some adjectives not only add an **e** to create their feminine form but also double the final consonant: *algérien* > *algérienne, ancien* > *ancienne, bon* > *bonne, brésilien* > *brésilienne, égyptien* > *égyptienne, exceptionnel* > *exceptionnelle, européen* > *européenne, iranien* > *iranienne, mignon* > *mignonne, nul* > *nulle, pareil* > *pareille, net* > *nette, opérationnel* > *opérationnelle, paysan* > *paysanne, traditionnel* > *traditionnelle, tunisien* > *tunisienne.* But: *lapone, lettone, mormone, nipone;* although the double consonant does exist with these adjectives (laponne, etc.). The sound remains the same with the adjectives ending in **-el** and one or two in **-et**, but not so with the endings **-en/-an/-on**. In the case of *algérien,* for instance, the final syllable loses its nasal sound.

This loss of the nasal sound is very common when an **e** is added for the feminine form: *américain* > *américaine, argentin* > *argentine, brun* > *brune, catalan* > *catalane, commun* > *commune, fin* > *fine, partisan* > *partisane, plein* > *pleine, prochain* > *prochaine.*

Adjectives ending in **-er** have their feminine form in **-ère**: *étranger* > *étrangère, premier* > *première, dernier* > *dernière.* The sound of the **e** goes from closed to open.

Adjectives ending in **-s** take an **e** for their feminine form: *anglais* > *anglaise, chinois* > *chinoise, divers* > *diverse, français* > *française, gris* > *grise.* The **s** then sounds like a **z**. But: *tiers* > *tierce.*

Some adjectives ending in **-s** take an extra **s** before the **e** for their feminine form: *bas* > *basse, épais* > *épaisse, gras* > *grasse, gros* > *grosse, las* > *lasse.*

Some adjectives ending in **-et** form their feminine in **-ète**: *complet* > *complète, concret* > *concrète, désuet* > *désuette, (in)discret* > *(in)discrète, incomplet* > *incomplète, inquiet* > *inquiète, replet* > *replète, secret* > *secrète* (the sound changes from closed to open **e**). But: *coquet* > *coquette, muet* > *muette* (the sound is from closed to open **e**).

There are a number of cases where the consonant or syllable is modified for the feminine form:

f > ve	neuf > neuve, bref > brève, négatif > négative, positif > positive
eux > euse	affreux > affreuse, moelleux > moelleuse, nerveux > nerveuse, rugueux > rugueuse (But: vieux > vieille)
c > che	blanc > blanche, franc > franche, sec > sèche
(t)eur > (t)euse	chasseur > chasseuse, flatteur > flatteuse, menteur > menteuse, moqueur > moqueuse
teur > trice	détecteur > détectrice, éditeur > éditrice, émetteur > émettrice, exécuteur > exécutrice, interrogateur > interrogatrice, observateur > observatrice, persécuteur > persécutrice, protecteur > protectrice
eur > eresse	chasseur > chasseresse (as in, almost exclusively: Diane la Chasseresse), enchanteur > enchanteresse, vengeur > vengeresse
eau > elle	beau > belle, jumeau > jumelle, nouveau > nouvelle
ou > olle	fou > folle, mou > molle
aître > aîtresse	maître > maîtresse, traître > traîtresse: un coup maître; une pièce maîtresse; un coup traître; une âme traîtresse

Traîtresse is particularly literary and is often replaced by the masculine form: *une pieuvre traître; la vengeance traître*. Also note that the adjectives *beau, nouveau, vieux* have two forms for their masculine singular:

Before a consonant	Before a vowel or mute **h**
un nouveau manteau	un nouvel appartement
un beau tableau	un bel homme
un vieux chien	un vieil ami

The *nouvel, bel, vieil* forms are for euphony's sake: *nouveau* before *appartement* and *beau* before *homme* would sound awkward, although *vieux* before *ami* would not sound awkward at all. Compare the plural: *nouveaux appartements*. However, with names of towns, both in France and elsewhere, there is some tendency, disputed by certain French speakers, to retain the masculine form *vieux* when these towns begin with the vowels **a** or **o**, and with a non-aspirate **h** + **a** or **o**. Here is a brief list of towns in France where this phenomenon obtains: *le vieux Agen/Alençon/Amiens/Angoulême/Annecy/Arles/Arras/Avignon/Orléans*. Elsewhere: *le vieux Alger | Amsterdam | Annaba* (Algeria) *| Anvers* (Antwerp) *| Atlanta | Albacète | Alicante | Almería* (all three in Spain) *| Hambourg | Hanovre* (both in Germany) *| Odessa* (Ukraine) *| Ottawa*. A certain percentage of French speakers would avoid this use of *vieux* but numerous cultured French speakers see no obstacle in its use. One wonders whether *le vieux Avignon* is really an elliptical form of *le vieux quartier d'Avignon*. Some would even argue that the use of *vieux* here may be found in the written form (for instance in tourist guides), and less so in the spoken language. In the highest register, when *vieux* precedes *et*, for instance, it reverts to *vieil*: *son vieil et grincheux oncle*. In normal language, however, one would easily hear *son oncle vieux et grincheux*; *un vieux et rustique bâton*. *Beau* always becomes *bel* in the set expression *bel et bien*: *C'était bel et bien une attaque contre sa politique* (*It really was...*).

N > **gn** occurs in two cases: *bénin* > *bénigne*, *malin* > *maligne*.

C > **qu** occurs in *caduc* > *caduque*, *public* > *publique*, *turc* > *turque*; but *grec* > *grecque*.

52.2 General rules on plural adjectives

An **s** is added to the singular adjective to form the plural: *grand* > *grands*: *les grands garçons*. When a noun is both feminine and plural, an **e** and an **s** are added: *les grandes maisons* / *les grandes filles, des jupes longues*.

Adjectives ending in **–s** or **–x** do not change in the masculine plural: *un mur bas* > *des murs bas*, *un sourire doux* > *des sourires doux*.

Masculine adjectives ending in **–eau** take an **x**: *un film nouveau* > *des films nouveaux*, *un frère jumeau* > *des frères jumeaux*.

Masculine adjectives ending in **–al** change to **–aux** (see also Chapter 10 on number): *un problème national* > *des problèmes nationaux*, *un organisme régional* > *des organismes régionaux*. Likewise: *ancestraux*, *animaux* (as in: *instincts animaux*), *architecturaux* (as in: *des concours architecturaux*), *artisanaux* (as in: *des produits artisanaux*), *astraux* (as in: *des signes astraux*), *auguraux* (as in: *les arts auguraux*), *automnaux*, *colossaux*, *conjugaux* (as in: *les devoirs conjugaux*), *doctoraux* (as in: *tons doctoraux*), *ducaux* (as in: *des palais ducaux*), *égaux* (as in: *Ils sont égaux*), *estivaux* (as in: *des souvenirs estivaux*), *filiaux*, *frugaux* (as in: *des repas frugaux*), *géniaux*, *gutturaux* (as in: *des sons gutturaux*), *impériaux* (as in: *des conseillers impériaux*), *initiaux*, *joviaux*, *libéraux* (as in: *les arts libéraux*), *locaux* (as in: *usages locaux*), *machinaux* (as in: *des gestes machinaux*), *magistraux* (as in: *des cours magistraux*), *martiaux* (as in: *les arts martiaux*), *matinaux* (as in: *Ils sont matinaux, ces gens-là*), *matrimoniaux* (as in: *régimes matrimoniaux*), *médicaux* (as in: *soins/experts médicaux*), *médicinaux* (as in: *arbustes médicinaux*), *méridionaux* (as in: *des accents méridionaux*), *monumentaux* (as in: *des immeubles monumentaux*), *occidentaux* (as in: *les pays occidentaux*), *orientaux* (as in: *les pays orientaux*), *pastoraux* (as in: *les devoirs pastoraux d'un curé*), *picturaux* (as in: *des effets picturaux*), *principaux* (as in: *les points/éléments principaux*), *professoraux* (as in: *des tons professoraux*), *provinciaux* (as in: *des comités provinciaux*), *royaux*, *septentrionaux* (as in: *les pays septentrionaux*), *spéciaux*, *sidéraux* (as in: *les mouvements sidéraux*), *théâtraux* (as in: *des gestes théâtraux*), *tribaux* (as in: *des usages tribaux*), *triomphaux*, *végétaux* (as in: *aliments végétaux*), *viscéraux* (as in: *troubles/spasmes viscéraux*), *zodiacaux* (as in: *les signes zodiacaux*).

In masculine adjectives, –al becomes –**als**: *australs, bancals* (as in: *des meubles/systèmes bancals*), *banals, boréals* (R3, as in: *les pays/hivers boréals*), *causals, cérémonials* (as in: *des rites cérémonials*), *chorals, glacials, facials, fatals, finals, idéals, marials* (of the Virgin Mary: *les cultes marials*), *nasals, natals* (as in: *leurs pays natals*), *navals* (as in: *les chantiers navals*), *pascals* (as in: *des festins pascals*), *tonals*. But considerable variation is felt here. A poll carried out among French speakers over the plural of the following would reveal uncertainty, largely because some of these adjectives are not used very much and are not necessarily even recognized: *austraux, banaux, bancaux, boréaux, choraux* (but rare), *glaciaux, faciaux, finaux* (but rare), *idéaux* (same status as *idéals*), *mariaux, pascaux* (as in: *des cierges pascaux* = Easter *candles*).

52.3 Singular versus plural

Adjectives qualifying more than one masculine noun or pronoun are masculine plural: *le gouvernement et le parlement américains.* When both nouns or pronouns are feminine the adjective is feminine plural: *la marine et l'aviation françaises.*

If the nouns or pronouns are of different genders, the masculine plural form applies: *Nombreux sont les garçons et les filles*; *Le garçon et la fille sont intelligents*; *Lui et sa sœur sont doués/saufs*; *Sa sœur et lui* (less common) *sont doués.*

But if the adjective immediately follows the noun a certain uneasiness is felt with *un garçon et une fille intelligents*: this phrase is grammatically correct but *intelligents* juxtaposed to *fille* sounds odd for many French speakers. One would expect to hear a feminine e at the end of *intelligent*. One would doubtless change the order to: *une fille et un garçon intelligents.* However, if one said *un dictionnaire et une grammaire tchèques*, there would be no uneasiness since *tchèques* does not have a distinctly masculine or feminine sound although, in writing, it could be avoided by changing the order of *dictionnaire* and *grammaire*. At the same time, one could say and write *un dictionnaire et une grammaire tchèque*, but this could only mean a *Czech grammar and* (any) *dictionary*. Other variations and examples: *avec un élan et une verve naturelle*; *un caractère et une énergie particuliers* (but more easily: *une énergie et un caractère particuliers*); *une facilité et un charme délicieux*; *un charme et une félicité vraiment délicieux*; *Il a soulevé l'indignation et la colère générale(s)*; *l'esprit et le caractère national*; *le drame et la comédie humaine.*

Past participles function like adjectives when qualifying nouns: *un portefeuille perdu / une occasion perdue*; *des tables et des chaises cassées*; *des vitres et des volets cassés.*

Where an adjective qualifies a plural noun but this noun contains two singular ideas, the adjective stays in the singular, masculine or feminine: *dans plusieurs secteurs des fronts méridional et occidental*; *les églises catholique et orthodoxe/réformée*; *les armées française et allemande.* This applies particularly to: *les douzième et treizième siècles* / *les seizième et dix-septième siècles* or *le douzième et le treizième siècle(s)*. Also: *du douzième au quatorzième siècle* (here *siècle* is singular). Other examples: *L'ancien et le nouveau maire étaient là*; *la première et la troisième déclinaison latines* (considerable linguistic gymnastics are visible here). A choice occurs between: *les codes civil et pénal* / *le code civil et le code pénal*; *les histoires ancienne et moderne* / *l'histoire ancienne et l'histoire moderne*. One can see the complications of agreement in both gender and number with the following: *Les massifs coraliens donnent aux eaux leurs couleurs bleue et émeraude transparentes*.

If the nouns are synonymous, and suggest some form of gradation, the adjective agrees with the nearest noun: *Nous trouvons singulier son étonnement, sa mauvaise foi*. Yet here there are certain fixed expressions: *un certificat de bonne vie et mœurs*; *en pleine liberté et indépendance*; *mon cher collègue et ami* (since there is only one person).

Where two nouns are joined by *et, ou, ni...ni*, a choice is available: *le véhicule et le passager étranger(s)*; *Elle a lu tous les livres et journaux tchèques*; *Le foie gras ou le pâté périgordin(s)*; *Je n'ai trouvé ni un journal ni un magazine italien(s)*. Again, if it is not clear that one or the other is described, a singular or plural adjective applies: *Elle en sortira avec une côte ou un bras cassé(s)*. However, if it is entirely clear that the adjective applies to both nouns, a plural applies: *On demande un homme ou une femme âgés*; *de la viande ou du poisson grillés*.

Adjectives used with *des plus, des moins, des mieux* agree in gender and number when these are implied: *Cette femme est des plus loyales*; *Ces toiles sont des mieux réussies*. But if a neuter pronoun is used, a singular occurs: *Cela est des plus immoral*. Note also the construction where a singular subject is used: *La situation était des plus embarrassante*. But a similar construction with a plural subject would require a plural adjective: *Ils étaient des plus sages*.

Notice the agreement with *des meilleurs, des moindres, des pires, des plus mal*: *La réponse n'est pas des meilleures*; *Mon souci n'est pas des moindres*; *Sa performance est certainement des pires*; *Ce couple est des plus mal assortis*. Similarly: *une des conséquences les plus inattendues* but *la conséquence la plus inattendue* (in the first case, the adjective agrees with the plural noun, while in the second it can only agree with the one noun available).

An adjective is singular when nouns are joined by *ainsi que, aussi bien que, autant que, comme, de même que, plus que*: *L'autruche a la tête, ainsi que le cou, garnie de duvet*; but *L'élève a remis une rédaction ainsi qu'une dictée remplies de fautes*. The presence or absence of commas is of striking value in these two similar sentences. *Aussi bien que, autant que, comme, de même que, plus que* could also be construed in the same way.

Avoir l'air seems to have no logic. It allows agreement both with *air* and with the subject: *Elle avait l'air heureux* / *Elle avait l'air heureuse*. However, as far as frequency is concerned, the agreement with the subject (*heureuse*) is by far more common. One could suggest that it is a difference of register.

Agreement with the subject would be R2 language while agreement with *air* would be of a higher register (R3), characteristic of the written style. It may also be argued that *avoir l'air* + agreement of adjective with the subject functions on analogy with *sembler/paraître*: *Elle semblait/paraissait heureuse.*

Although *on* is an indefinite pronoun with a kind of neuter value, it has now asserted itself much more and its use has spread over to replace the other pronouns (*je, tu, nous, vous, ils*, etc.). This is especially the case of *nous* (see also the use of *on* in Chapter 1 on register). *On* therefore attracts agreement in both number and gender, yet the verb of which it is the subject remains in the singular. For the Hispanists, it corresponds very frequently to the impersonal use of *se* (the *pasiva refleja*). For example: *On n'a plus rien à se dire*; *On va au théâtre*; *On est voisins*; *On est bien contents tous.* Even *nous* mingles with *on*: *Nous, on veut bien*; *On part ce soir, nous.* As far as gender is concerned, there is no difficulty in construing *on* as feminine: *On n'est pas toujours jeune et belle.* No difficulty either in using *on* with the plural *des*: *On n'est pas des esclaves, nous!*; *On n'est pas des crétins!*

Nu preceding a noun and attached to it by a hyphen is invariable: *Elle est sortie nu-tête sous la pluie*; *Il ne faut pas marcher nu-pieds sur la plage*; *Tu vas attraper froid nu-jambes comme ça*; *Couvre-toi, sortir nu-bras n'est pas à conseiller.* When *nu* follows the noun, it agrees: *Il préfère courir les pieds nus*; *C'est dangereux de se promener sous le soleil la tête nue | la tête et le torse nus.*

Possible offers no problem over agreement in the following: *toutes les erreurs possibles.* Here *possibles* applies rigorously to *erreurs* and therefore agrees. Likewise, it can agree when it follows a superlative (*le plus | le moins | le meilleur*) and a plural noun. To quote Leibniz taken up by Voltaire's Pangloss in *Candide* (1988, Chapters 1 and 6): "Tout est pour le mieux dans le meilleur des mondes possibles." Yet, if the superlative precedes the noun, *possible* is invariable: *Faites le moins possible d'erreurs*; *Il eut le moins de contacts possible avec son frère.* There is certainly some confusion here. Nevertheless, in most cases, invariability seems to prevail: *Faites le plus de distinctions possible*; *les plus grands malheurs possible*; *des limites aussi nettes que possible.* The difficulty resides in the fact that the same sound is heard for the singular and plural forms of *possible.*

Strangely enough, an adjective preceding *gens* is feminine but, when it follows *gens*, it is masculine. See Chapter 9 on gender, Section 9.3.1.

When *demi* precedes a noun and is attached by a hyphen, it is invariable: *une demi-douzaine*; *une demi-heure*; *des gaufres demi-cuites.* But when it follows, it agrees: *une heure et demie*; *Une pomme et demie me suffit*; *midi et demi*; *minuit et demi.* However, one finds with some authors: *midi et demie*; *minuit et demie.* Note also: *Cette pendule sonne les demies*; *la demie de trois heures.* The adverbial expression *à demi* is of course invariable: *une bouteille à demi pleine*; *des malheureuses à demi mortes de faim.*

Mi is feminine in the following construction: *à la mi-juin/septembre* (*in the middle of June/September*). It is also feminine in the following, although one neither sees the feminine nor hears it: *jusqu'à mi-jambes*; *à mi-voix*; *à mi-hauteur*; *à mi-côte*.

52.4 Agreement with past participles

With *on*, the past participle agrees in gender and number, despite the fact that the verb remains in the singular: *Est-on toujours fâchée?* (talking to a small girl); *On est montés ensemble*; *On s'est quittés de bons amis*; *On est partis ce matin*; *On s'est vus ce matin*; *On n'a pas été bien reçus*; *On n'a pas la chance d'être nées à Paris*. If uncertainty is experienced over the use of *tu* or *vous* with respect to someone being addressed, *on* can be most convenient. *Tu* could be too intimate while *vous* could be too indifferent or distant, *on* provides the solution: *On se retrouve ce soir?*; *On prend un pot?*

When *approuvé, attendu, (y) compris, entendu, excepté, fourni, mis à part, ôté, ouï, passé, quitté, refait, supposé, venu* and *vu* (among others), precede the noun, they function as prepositions: *approuvé les corrections ci-dessus*; *ouï les témoins* (R3); *excepté eux*; *Sitôt quitté la ville, nous étions en pleine campagne*; *y compris les vieilles personnes*. However, if the past participle is carried over and agrees with a noun of a following clause, usually the main clause, agreement obtains: *Déjà comprises au compte précédent, ces sommes n'ont pas dû figurer ici*; *Vue sous cet angle, l'affaire est tout autre*; *Approuvée par tous, cette mesure s'est facilement imposée*; *Tous se sont trompés, cinq ou six exceptés*. When the past participles remain invariable before the noun, as in the following cases, one has the impression that the verb *avoir* has been omitted, and a kind of ellipsis obtains: *Repeint la façade*; *Reçu la somme de mille euros*; *Fourni deux sacs de ciment*; *Quitté la banlieue, nous avons filé à toute vitesse* (= *Après avoir quitté la banlieue*...). In the case of *fini*, both *Fini les vacances* and *Finies les vacances* seem acceptable.

With *passé*, there is considerable uncertainty. The general pattern seems to conform to non-agreement before the noun and agreement after, as with *heure*: *passé dix heures / six heures passées*; *passé la première phase / la première phase passée*; but the following examples show that this is by no means decisive: *passée la porte ouverte / la porte ouverte passée*; *passée la dernière maison / la dernière maison passée*. It does appear that when the idea of *passé* is figurative it is invariable, and when it is literal it agrees. However, Hanse and Blampain plead for invariability. This is unquestionably an unresolved issue.

Likewise, there seems to be a choice over *étant donné*: *étant donné les circonstances familiales / étant données les circonstances familiales*; *étant donné(e) sa stupidité*.

It would appear that when *ci-joint, ci-inclus* and *ci-annexé* appear before the noun, there is no agreement, particularly if they stand at the beginning of the sentence: *Ci-joint la quittance / les quittances*; *Ci-joint les pièces demandées*; *Ci-annexé les formulaires à remplir*. Likewise near the beginning of the sentence:

Vous trouverez ci-joint | ci-inclus copie du contrat. But when they follow there is usually agreement: *les documents ci-joints.* Yet one does come across: *Vous trouverez ci-incluse la copie que vous avez demandée*; and even *La lettre dont vous trouvez la copie ci-inclus* (i.e., no agreement after the noun). The most convincing argument for no agreement before the noun is that these expressions function as adverbs. After the noun, they function as adjectives and therefore agreement applies.

52.5 Adjectives functioning as nouns

Many adjectives function as nouns. This category includes colors:

le beau	*the beautiful, that which is beautiful*
le blanc	*the white* (of an egg, of the eye)
un bleu	*a bruise*
le noir	*the dark*
le large	*the high	open sea*

Le blanc, le bleu, le jaune, le noir and all the other colors may be used in pointing to one of a series:

Je prends le blanc / le bleu / le jaune / le noir.	*I'll have the white/blue/yellow/black one.*

If the objects were feminine, one would say *Je prends la blanche | la bleue. Un blanc | une blanche* (a male/female White person), *un noir | une noire* (a male/female Black person) are also common enough. Also *la traite des blanches* (the White female slave trade), *la traite des noirs* (the Black slave trade). *Nègre*, like *peau rouge*, is now best avoided. Other examples: *On fait la belle* = *We'll play a decider* (in sport); *Elle travaille avec beaucoup de sérieux.*

Some adjectives derive from a noun + adjective combination where the noun is dropped, largely for brevity's sake: *Je prends du bleu* (*du fromage bleu*); *Je prends un noir* (*un café noir*); *Je prends du rouge* (*du vin rouge*); *Je me suis payé un complet* (*un costume complet* = a suit); *la capitale* (*la ville capitale*); *la majuscule* (*la lettre majuscule* = capital letter); *la minuscule* (*la lettre minuscule* = lower-case letter), *la (répétition) générale* (dress rehearsal in theater); *la (l'étoile) nébuleuse* (nebula, amorphous grouping); *C'est combien, la douloureuse* (bill in restaurant; probably a contraction from *addition*)?

The disappearance of the noun *journée* is apparent in the historic expression relating to the July 1830 revolution that provoked the fall of Charles X: *les Trois Glorieuses* (July 27, 28 and 29). This expression is picked up in the current, common reference to the rapid industrialization of postwar France: *les Trente (Années) Glorieuses* (approximately 1945 to 1975).

With respect to humans, adjectives replace nouns with no difficulty – a common occurrence in Romance languages. English often has to resort to an adjective + noun here when the noun is singular, but not necessarily with a plural noun: *les aveugles* (*the blind*), *les muets* (*the dumb*), *les pauvres* (*the poor*), *les sourds* (*the deaf*), *les sourds-muets*. But: *un(e) aveugle* (*a blind person*), *un(e) pauvre* (*a poor person*), *un(e) sourd(e)* (*a deaf person*). Other examples: *un aliéné / une aliénée*; *un cérébral / une cérébrale* (R3 = *an intellectual*); *un fâcheux / une fâcheuse* (*an awkward person*), *un fou / une folle*; *un handicapé / une handicapée / des handicapés / des handicapées*; *un incapable / une incapable*; *un insolent / une insolente*; *un intellectuel / une intellectuelle* (also: *un/une intello* = R1); *un/une lâche*; *un malheureux / une malheureuse / des malheureux / des malheureuses*; *un mécontent / une mécontente / des mécontents / des mécontentes*; *un/une misérable*; *un original / une originale* (*oddball, weirdo*); *un(e) universitaire* (*university professor/teacher*); *un vaniteux / une vaniteuse*. As with *handicapé*, a past participle functions like a noun (see Chapter 16 for a full discussion of this topic.)

Increasingly in French, as in Spanish, the reverse is happening and nouns are starting to function like adjectives. This is, of course, standard practice in English where almost any noun can qualify another noun: *paper handkerchief, newspaper reporter*. In the past, this was not the case in French, and one had to resort to the combination of noun + *à/de/en* + noun, as in *scie à métaux* (*metal saw*), *papier de soie* (*tissue paper*), *rideaux de la chambre* (*bedroom curtains*). This is still the case in many instances but the practice is changing, notably for new creations: *appartement-témoin* (*showroom*), *café-théâtre, homme-grenouille*. In these more traditional examples a hyphen is frequently used, but in the most recent combinations this is not so: *camion poubelle, rasoir homme*. For a much fuller list see Chapter 10 on number.

When nouns are used as pure adjectives, and suggest a certain characteristic, they are invariable: *un style Second Empire*; *les formules les plus Régence*; *les néologismes bidon* (*false*), *une excuse/histoire bidon* (*a deceptive/false excuse/story*); *des fruits nature*; *des familles de valeurs très tendance*; *les maisons les plus collet monté* (*poshest*); *des livres bon marché / meilleur marché*; *des peintures art nouveau*. This noun + noun construction is gaining ground in daily discourse: *une assurance automobile/vie/maladie/santé* (*car/life/health insurance*), *une journée lessive* (*wash day*), *une journée shopping* (*shopping day*), *une journée jeunesse* (*day devoted to youth*).

52.6 Adjectives and color

Color can be indicated by one or several adjectives or one or several nouns. Adjectives always agree with the noun: *une robe verte/bleue*; *des jupes blanches*. Only *kaki* and *auburn* are invariable: *des uniformes kaki*; *des tenues auburn*. Some adjectives deriving from nouns are recognized as adjectives and agree with the noun: *écarlate, mauve, pourpre, rose*; *des étoffes pourpres/roses*. (For a complete list of invariable colors deriving from nouns and their function see Chapter 10 on number, Section 10.2) *Châtain* was once invariable. Once one said *une femme châtain*, but now *une femme châtaine* is common enough.

When a color is indicated by a noun or two coordinated nouns, invariability is required, despite hesitation over some nouns: *des gants paille, des yeux marron, des gants crème, des rubans orange, des chevaux pie*. But one says *des rouges, des émeraudes* (these are actually nouns and names of colors).

When *couleur* + noun is used, invariability occurs: *des bas couleur de chair, des bas couleur chair*, but *des écharpes de couleur brune | de couleur bleu foncé*.

If the name of the color is qualified by an adjective, the adjective varies: *un brun foncé, des jaunes pâles, des roses clairs*. If the name of the color is qualified by a noun, invariability obtains: *des jaunes paille, des roses chair, des roses bonbon*.

If two colors are joined to qualify a noun (i.e., one color qualifies another), there is no agreement: *des cheveux châtain clair | d'un châtain clair, des étoffes jaune paille, des yeux bleu clair, une robe gris bleu | de couleur bleu foncé, une tenue bleu horizon, des foulards vert bouteille, des cheveux noir de jais, des robes jaune doré, une robe bleu vif*. Haute couture indulges in the following: *des robes noir bronze | vert pomme | rouge colère | bleu pétrole | rose bonheur | gris ardoise mouillée | jaune citron*.

When two color adjectives are joined by *et*, agreement occurs since each adjective is independent: *une écharpe bleue et grise, de grands yeux verts et bleus*. However, one could come across *des drapeaux blanc et jaune*. Here one flag is white and the other yellow.

Further combinations: *une blouse à petites rayures blanche et bleu ciel, des étoffes rayées blanc et noir, des tons vert et or, le pavillon à trois bandes, orangée, blanche et bleue, un grand papillon bleu et noir, un gilet à raies alternativement jaunes et puce*. What seems to be indefensible is *une marinière (smock) blanc et bleue* (quoted by Hanse and Blampain 2005, p. 30, from J.-L. Curtis), which should read *blanche et bleue* or *blanc et bleu* (preferably the former). Or is this a spelling mistake?

The use of *grand* with a further adjective leads to agreement: *les yeux grands ouverts, une porte grande ouverte*.

52.7 Adjectives functioning as adverbs

A considerable number of adjectives function as adverbs and are therefore invariable: *bas, bon, cher, clair, court, creux, doux, droit, dru, faux, ferme, fin, fort, franc, grand, gros, haut, jeune, juste, long, lourd, mauvais, net, profond, raide, ras, sec, serré, vrai*; *Cet avion vole très bas*; *Parle plus bas*; *Ça sent bon*; *Ça coûte cher*; *Elle a coupé court au débat*; *s'arrêter court*; *demeurer court*; *des cheveux coupés court*; *ces boîtes sonnent creux* (hollow, because empty); *filer doux* (to be docile); *se la couler douce* (to take it easy); *aller droit au but*; *les yeux fixés droit devant elle*; *marcher tout droit*; *La pluie tombe dru* (It is raining heavily); *Elle travaille dur*; *Ils frappent dur*; *sonner/jouer/chanter faux*; *frapper/lancer/serrer fort*; *Ces vêtements coûtent cher mais ils font jeune* (These clothes are expensive but they make you look younger); *Ils ont parlé franc et net*; *Ils l'ont dit tout franc*; *Il faut viser plus grand*; *Il faut manger moins gras, moins salé, moins sucré*; *Elles jouent gros et risquent gros* (They play high stakes and risk a lot); *Il faut jouer très fin* (You have to play cleverly); *Elle l'a dit bien haut*; *Haut les mains !* (says the robber); *penser tout haut*; *Elle est haut placée* (She is well placed); *Cela en dit long sur son état d'esprit*; *Elle a voyagé incognito*; *creuser profond*. *Juste* is used in a whole range of expressions: *Il avait juste neuf ans*; *Ces horloges vont juste*; *Ces attaques ont touché juste*; *arriver juste*; *calculer juste*; *compter juste*; *deviner juste*; *Ces sandales me chaussent un peu juste*; *La clé entre juste*; *Elle raisonne juste*. More examples: *Ces boîtes ne pèsent pas lourd*; *Ça sent mauvais*; *Elle a été tuée net*; *La voiture s'est arrêtée net*; *casser/parler/trancher net*; *L'herbe a été tondue très ras* (The grass has been cut very low); *La voiture a démarré sec* (The car pulled away speedily); *Ils jouent serré* (They are playing a tight game); *Elle a calculé serré* (She calculated things carefully); *Tu peux lui faire confiance, il parle toujours vrai, sans détour* (He always speaks plainly); *Son discours sonne vrai* (Her speech has the ring of truth); *La formule tient toujours bon* (The formula always hold good); *Elle est tombée raide morte* (She collapsed and died on the spot). The literary language has carried this use of an adjective as an adverb much further: *flamber rouge*; *penser universel*; *sourire vilain*.

Conversely, *bien* is an adverb that can function like an adjective. It is the equivalent of *decent* or *correct*, *comme il faut* as the French say: *une fille bien*; *une femme très bien*; *des gens bien*; *Il fait des choses bien*; *Ce spectacle est bien*; *C'est bien, Aujourd'hui*; *le malade est bien*; *C'est quelqu'un de bien*.

52.8 Use of compound adjectives

If both adjectives qualify the same noun, they vary: *Des filles sourdes-muettes*; *des paroles aigre-douces*; *les listes sociales-chrétiennes*; *des revues suisses-allemandes*; *les doctrines nationales-socialistes*; *des attitudes libres-penseuses*. Similarly, if the adjectives are used as nouns: *les sociaux-démocrates*. *Mort* is invariable in *mort-né* and *nouveau-né*: *des enfants morts-nés / nouveaux-nés*.

If there is an abbreviation as with the final element of the first adjective, this adjective remains invariable: *les guerres franco-allemandes*; *les rapports franco-britanniques/algériens/tunisiens*; *une danse latino-américaine*; *des poèmes héroï-comiques*.

The first element remains invariable if it is an invariable word, as with a preposition or adverb: *des attaques sous-marines*; *une fillette court-vêtue*; *de soi-disant docteurs*; *une soi-disant marquise*; *les soi-disant héritiers*. As far as *soi-disant* goes, some French speakers apply it to things, but such practice has little logic (the use of *dire* for things), and has acquired little approval: *de soi-disant faveurs*; *une théorie soi-disant irréfutable*.

In keeping with a certain traditional usage, the first element does agree in some cases: *des fleurs fraîches écloses / fraîches cueillies*; *des fenêtres grandes / larges ouvertes*; *les enfants premier- / derniers-nés*. But *grand*, *large* and *frais* can remain invariable, acting like adverbs: *une fenêtre grand ouverte*; *des portes large ouvertes*; *des fleurs frais cueillies*.

Franc in *franc-comtois* (of Franche-Comté) and in *franc-maçon(nique)* is invariable, but can be followed by a plural adjective: *des notables franc-comtois*; *des horloges franc-comtoises*; *les journaux franc-maçons*; *les loges franc-maçonnes*. There is some uncertainty over collectives, but agreement has its logic. In *Ce groupe de touristes est Canadien*, both *est* and *Canadien* are singular, but one could say both *Une majorité des élèves sont Américains* and *Une majorité des élèves est Américaine*.

52.9 Miscellaneous

Avant-coureur has no true feminine form, only a masculine: *des signes avant-coureurs*.

Chic: This adjective was once invariable and still has no specific feminine form: *un homme chic*; *une femme chic*; *des femmes chic*. Agreement in number, however, is becoming common: *les gens chics; les femmes chics*.

Note the ever-decreasing use of *feu* (= *deceased*). For obvious reasons, it hardly exists in the plural. It does or does not agree with a feminine noun according to where the article or demonstrative adjective falls. What is certain is that *feu* always comes before the noun: *la feue reine*; *feu la reine* (both = *the late queen*); *ma feue mère*; *feu ma mère* (both = *my late mother*). Other examples: *les feus rois*; *feu mes parents*; *feu Madame*; *feu Mathilde Dupont*. *Feu* has almost entirely been replaced by *défunt* (*sa défunte mère*; *mes amis défunts*) or euphemisms like *pauvre* (*ma pauvre mère*) or even *regretté* (*la regrettée Martine Lefèbvre*).

Usage with *bot*: This adjective is only used in the masculine singular form: *un pied bot* = *a club foot*.

Bredouille varies, although once it formed part of an adverbial expression (*en bredouille*): *Elles sont revenues bredouilles*.

Costaud is invariable in spoken French. There is some uncertainty here over the feminine form, *costaude*, which is rarely used.

Extra seems to have no other form: *des dîners extra*; *quelques étrangers pas extra* (*not particularly interesting foreigners*); but *ultra* can vary: *des revanchards ultra*; *des sentiments ultras*; *des opinions ultras*.

Grand is invariable in a good number of compound nouns when joined by a hyphen: *grand-croix*, *grand-maman*, *grand-mère*, *grand-messe*, *grand-rue*, *grand-route*, *grand-tante*, *pas grand-chose*, *à grand-peine*, *avoir grand-faim*, *avoir grand-soif*, *grand-peur*, *grand'place*. One also comes across compounds with an apostrophe, but these expressions are more literary: *grand'nef*, *grand'lune*, *grand'porte*, *grand'hâte*.

Junior and *senior* are invariable: *une équipe junior/senior*; but as nouns they change: *des juniors/seniors*.

Laïc and *laïque* (*male/female layperson*) are distinguished as nouns. The feminine form has taken over from the masculine form when used as an adjective: *un saint laïque*; *en habit laïque*.

Latino = *Hispanic* (i.e., with reference to Latin Americans in the United States) is invariable: *la communauté latino*.

Usage with *maximum, minimum, optimum*: One comes across the Latin feminine forms *maxima, minima, optima, extrema*: *la peine maxima*; *une réforme orthographique maxima*; *des températures maxima/minima*. *Maximal, minimal, optimal* and *extremal* are now the recommended forms: *un prix maximal, des températures maximales/minimales*.

Pantois (= *flabbergasted*) now has a feminine form: *Elle en est restée pantoise*.

Plastique once provoked uncertainty. Now, one can happily say: *des matières/sacs plastiques*.

Plein is invariable when it is placed before a noun and its article. Compare: *Adrienne a les poches toutes pleines d'argent* and *Elle a des billets pleins les poches*. Compare also: *Il a les poches toutes pleines d'argent* and *Il a de l'argent tout plein les poches*; *Il a les cheveux tout pleins de flocons* and *Il a des flocons tout plein les cheveux*; *Le petit a la truffe* (R1 = *nose*) *pleine de chocolat* and *Le petit a du chocolat plein la truffe*. The invariable R1 colloquial use of *plein* in the sense of *many/much* is very idiomatic: *J'ai reçu (tout) plein de cadeaux*; *Elle a tout plein d'amies*; *Je l'aime déjà tout plein*; *Il est mignon tout plein*; *C'est mignon tout plein chez vous*.

Radar and *laser* vary as adjectives: *des stations/écrans/échos radars*; *des faisceaux lasers*. But one does see *des lecteurs laser*; *des échos radar*.

Relax occasionally takes an **e**, both for the masculine and for the feminine forms: *Il/Elle est relax(e)*.

Snob has a plural form but no feminine: *des magazines snobs*; *des jeunes femmes snobs*.

Standard has no feminine but has a plural form: *une prononciation standard*; *des thèmes standards*.

Sexy is invariable: *une bouche sexy*; *des attitudes sexy*.

Superbe as an adjective is standard R2 = *superb*: *une superbe robe*; *un jardin/palais superbe*. But as a noun (*haughtiness*) it is distinctly R3: *Elle faisait étalage d'une superbe insupportable*.

Sterling is invariable: *des livres sterling*.

Tabou can take the whole range of possibilities: *taboue/tabous/taboues*: *un sujet tabou*; *des mots tabous*; *des institutions taboues*. But it can also be invariable: *des questions tabou*.

Vainqueur has no feminine, but help is at hand with *victorieuse*.

Vidéo seems only to have a singular as an adjective: *des films/cassettes vidéo*.

Adjectives suggesting ethnic characteristics can vary: *une femme bengali(e)*, *coutumes bantou(es)*, *épopée zoulou*, *cuisine tandouri*, *des villes maya*, *enfants tutsi et hutu*, *les Républiques boers*, *les autorités sikhs*.

When adjectives are shortened, and stand by themselves, they are usually invariable: *des produits bio*; *des agriculteurs bio*; *chanter des tubes rétro* (*hit song of a former period*).

The following adjectives, of colloquial R1 style, are invariable: *baba* (*flabbergasted*); *cracra/crado* (*filthy*); *flagada* (*exhausted*); *gaga*; *paf* (*drunk*); *raplapla* (*worn out*); *toc-toc* (*stupid, dumb*); *zinzin* (*stupid, nutty*); *zozo* (*idiot*). But both *porno* and *sympa* have a masculine plural form: *des films/cartes postales pornos*; *des amis vraiment sympas*.

Compound nouns beginning with *anti* do not vary in gender, but they do in number: *la loi anticasseur* (recent law forbidding antisocial behavior, i.e., breaking things); *un phare antibrouillard*; *des phares antibrouillards*; *un canon antichar*; *des canons antichars*.

Soi-disant: This compound adjective is invariable, and originally referred to persons alone since, logically, persons only could attribute qualities to themselves: *de soi-disant docteurs*; *une soi-disant marquise*; *les soi-disant héritiers*. However, a break with logic occurs with this expression, although it is absurd that a thing or an error should ascribe *soi-disant* to itself, but this is the case, which explains why the extension of the use of this adjective is contested. One now readily says: *une soi-disant expérience*; *une soi-disant escroquerie*; *un soi-disant défaut*; *de soi-disant faveurs*. *Soi-disant* may also qualify a further adjective: *une théorie soi-disant irréfutable*; *des plaisirs soi-disant innocents*. It may even be used as an adverb: *des vers soi-disant traduits de l'allemand*.

There is a case where adjectives applying to nationalities do not correspond in English and French. Whereas, in English, one says *the English team* to describe both the national team and a club team, in French the distinction is clear: *l'équipe française/américaine* refers to any team from France, notably a club side, while *l'équipe de France/des États-Unis* refers specifically and uniquely to the national side.

Some adjectives, such as *clair, fort, gros, profond*, join with the superlative *le plus* in the following way:

Je passai le plus clair de la traversée dans la cabine.	*I spent most of the crossing in the cabin.*
Le plus gros de la classe a voté "oui."	*Most of the class voted "yes."*
Le chef fut blessé au plus fort de la bataille.	*The leader was wounded in the fiercest part of the battle.*
Audrey souffrait au plus profond de son être.	*Audrey suffered deep down in her being.*

Lambda (*average, usual*) is an increasingly used adjective which is invariable: *Proust est trop difficile pour les lecteurs lambda*; *Les citoyens lambda n'ont jamais protesté*. Needing to solve the problem of "élèves perturbateurs," President Sarkozy wishes to see them in schools with "élèves lambda" (*Le Monde*, May 5, 2010). There is, however, some hesitation over the invariability of this adjective. This adjective is also used thus: *M./Mme Lambda = Mr/Mrs So-and-So*.

Use of *nous* as an expression of modesty or discretion. *Nous* can designate one person to avoid self-importance. This is very much a literary convention. The past participle retains the masculine form, even if the speaker/writer is female: *Nous avons été consulté; Nous sommes convaincu que* . . .

53

Adverbs | Les adverbes

The following passage evokes the memory of Albert Camus who, in all his works, denounces the scandal of the injustice inherent in our human condition. The fiftieth anniversary of his sudden death in a road accident provides the occasion for a national homage paid to an author of colossal moral status. The passage has recourse to a number of adverbs and adverbial phrases, all of which are highlighted in bold. Only one translation is provided.

Reference is made to the Panthéon where France honors her eminent children by receiving their mortal remains in the form of ashes. Exceptionally, a quotation taken from Camus's *La chute* forms the middle paragraph. It expresses the irony of the vilifying of a person in life being transformed into the unrestrained eulogizing of that same person in death.

Vibrant hommage à Camus

Actuellement en France, toutes les radios et les télévisions passent **rapidement** en revue des documents sonores ou iconographiques sur l'écrivain Albert Camus qui disparut **brutalement** le 4 janvier 1960 dans un absurde accident de voiture. Pourquoi absurde? Parce que Camus, **précisément** le philosophe de l'absurde, mourut **de façon violente et complètement imprévue**.

Ce début d'année 2010 a marqué **de manière indélébile** le cinquantième anniversaire de la mort de cet écrivain qui fut **assurément** un grand homme, **voire** [nay] la conscience de l'Europe de l'après-guerre, selon bien des critiques. Certains détracteurs présentent **décidément** un personnage à multiples facettes, sous différents angles, **parfois** même contradictoires. **D'une part**, Albert Camus, originaire d'Algérie, avait protesté **avec véhémence** contre le colonialisme. **D'autre part**, l'écrivain n'avait pas exprimé **assez clairement** sa position politique pendant la guerre d'Algérie. Ce cinquantième anniversaire de la mort de Camus permet de rendre hommage **publiquement** au mérite et au talent de l'auteur de *L'étranger*, *La peste*, *La chute*, *Le mythe de Sisyphe* et **bien d'**autres œuvres littéraires.

Laissons l'auteur de *La chute* répondre **laconiquement**: «Peut-être n'aimons-nous pas **assez** la vie? Avez-vous remarqué que la mort seule

réveille nos sentiments? Comme nous aimons les amis qui viennent de
nous quitter, **n'est-ce pas**? Comme nous admirons ceux de nos maîtres
qui ne parlent plus, la bouche pleine de terre! L'hommage vient alors
tout naturellement, cet hommage que, **peut-être**, ils avaient attendu
de nous toute leur vie. Mais savez-vous pourquoi nous sommes toujours
plus justes et plus généreux avec les morts? La raison est simple! Avec
eux, il n'y a pas d'obligation. Ils nous laissent libres, nous pouvons
prendre notre temps, caser l'hommage entre le cocktail et une gentille
maîtresse, **à temps perdu, en somme**. S'ils nous obligeaient à quelque
chose, ce serait à la mémoire, et nous avons la mémoire courte. Non,
c'est le mort frais que nous aimons chez nos amis, le mort douloureux,
notre émotion, nous-mêmes **enfin** !» (1962c, p. 1492).

Ironiquement, ce passage prévoit **de façon insolite, étonnante,
voire déconcertante** la volte-face adoptée par Sartre qui, s'inspirant
d'un athéisme **violemment** ressenti, avait refusé **catégoriquement**
l'humanisme de Camus.

Cet événement commémoratif a été l'occasion de faire **mieux**
connaître les œuvres du romancier et philosophe qui creusent **profondément** dans la nature d'une humanité souffrante. **Évidemment**,
l'auteur a fait couler **beaucoup** d'encre. Une grande polémique à propos
du transfert des cendres d'Albert Camus au Panthéon a **immédiatement**
provoqué de grands remous. Ces vives réactions **farouchement** hostiles
trouvent leur explication dans la crainte de récupération politique. À
tort ou à raison, Jean Camus, le fils d'Albert Camus, est **totalement**
opposé à l'idée de faire entrer son père au Panthéon. Catherine, la fille
de l'auteur qui administre l'œuvre de son père n'a pas **franchement**
rejeté ce projet du gouvernement, **contrairement** à son frère Jean. Le
Prix Nobel de littérature occupe **curieusement** le devant de la scène
politique.

For the position of adverbs in a sentence, see Chapter 63 on word order; a
substantial number of adjectives function as adverbs. See also Chapter 52,
Section 52.7 on adjectives functioning as adverbs. An adverb is an invariable
word that accompanies a verb, an adjective or another adverb to modify
their meaning. In English, adverbs are often made up of an adjective with a
−**ly** ending: *quick* > *quickly*, *lazy* > *lazily*. In French, adverbs are often composed of an adjective in the feminine form with the ending −**ment**: *rapide*
> *rapidement*, *lent* > *lentement*. This type of French adverb is explained by the
ablative form of the feminine Latin word *mens/mentis* (*mind, spirit, disposition*),
mente, which can mean *with a spirit/mind*. An adverb in French is explained
therefore in the following way. The sentence *Elle bouge lentement* really
means *She moves with a slow spirit*, that is: *She moves slowly*. This formation of
many French adverbs from adjective + **ment** reflects the common root for
adverbs in all Romance languages. In Spanish we have: *La chica se mueve lentamente* = *The girl moves slowly*. In Italian we have: *La ragazza si muove lentamente*.

There are a few adverbs formed from adjectives in French which do not easily correspond to their English counterparts: *intérieurement, longuement, précédemment; J'ai longuement parlé avec elle; Il s'est dit intérieurement que . . . ; Le locataire a été prévenu précédemment de la fin du bail (The tenant was previously advised of the end of the lease)*. On the other hand *court* does not have a fully recognizable adverbial ending as does *shortly* in English; it remains *court*.

There are eight kinds of adverbs in French. They may be classified in the following way:

1. adverbs of manner (generally characterized by the ending **–ly** in English and **–ment** in French);
2. adverbs of quantity or intensity;
3. adverbs of time;
4. adverbs of place;
5. adverbs of affirmation;
6. adverbs of negation (see Chapter 61 on negation);
7. adverbs of doubt or approximation;
8. interrogative adverbs (see Chapter 50 on interrogative pronouns, adjectives and adverbs).

53.1 Adverbs of manner

Here is a selection of adverbs of manner with the common **–ment** ending, indicating the process of adjectives moving from the masculine form to the feminine form to the adverb: *Beau > belle > bellement* (now out-of-date), *clair > claire > clairement, complet > complète > complètement, dernier > dernière > dernièrement, doux > douce > doucement, fort > forte > fortement, fou > folle > follement, grand > grande > grandement, nouveau > nouvelle > nouvellement, premier > première > premièrement, présent > présente > présentement* (= *now*, common in Quebec, but less so in France), *public > publique > publiquement, soigneux > soigneuse > soigneusement, tendre > tendre > tendrement, utile > utile > utilement, vif > vive > vivement*. Examples: *David parle clairement; La tâche est complètement terminée; Dernièrement (Recently), j'ai beaucoup travaillé; Parle doucement; Il était follement amoureux; L'infirmière lui a soigneusement pansé la plaie.*

A number of adjectives ending in **–e** form their adverbs with the ending **–ément**, doubtless for the sake of euphony: *aveugle > aveuglément* (not to be confused with *aveuglement* = *moral blindness*), *commode > commodément, conforme > conformément, énorme > énormément, immense > immensément, incommode > incommodément, intense > intensément, passionnément, uniforme > uniformément; Ils suivent aveuglément ses conseils; La banquette arrière se replie commodément pour le transport des vélos; Ils travaillent intensément pour finir à temps; conformément à notre entente (in keeping with our agreement); Elle l'aimait* *passionnément; Il s'accrochait passionnément à cette idée.* But note: *extrêmement, inversement, opiniâtrement (stubbornly).*

Adverbs from the following adjectives which have no ending in −**e** in their masculine form take **é** before −**ment**, again doubtless for the sake of euphony: *commun > commune > communément, confus > confuse > confusément, diffus > diffuse > diffusément, exquis > exquise > exquisément, exprès > expresse > expressément, importun > importune > importunément, obscur > obscure > obscurément, opportun > opportune > opportunément, précis > précise > précisément, profond > profonde > profondément, profus > profuse > pro-fusément; Cet outil, communément nommé marteau; Benjamin nous avait promis expressément d'être présent; Lucile est venue nous saluer opportunément; Christophe allait précisément sortir quand le téléphone sonna.*

A note on the adverb dependent on *possible: possiblement* is in very current and vigorous use in Quebec (e.g., *Il sera possiblement là*), but nowhere else where French is spoken, except perhaps in a literary text. It may be that this adverb in Quebec has been influenced by the English *possibly*. Its absence elsewhere in standard French is all the more striking since *possibilmente* is common currency in Italian, as is *posiblemente* in Spanish. The French of France, Switzerland and Belgium would opt instead for *peut-être* or *vraisemblablement*.

The adverbs *bien* and *mal* correspond to the adjectives *bon* and *mauvais: Marcel a bien travaillé ce soir; J'ai mal compris ce qu'a dit Irène. Bon* does have an adverb = *bonnement*, but only in the expression *tout bonnement*:

Je lui ai dit tout bonnement qu'on n'allait pas l'inviter.	*I told her quite simply that we were not going to invite her.*

Although the feminine of *bref* is *brève*, the adverb is *brièvement*:

Veuillez nous exposer la situation le plus brièvement possible.	*Kindly explain the situation to us as briefly as possible.*

Other adverbs of manner are: *ainsi, comme, comment, debout, ensemble, exprès, franco, gratis, impunément, incognito, mieux, pis, plutôt, presque, quasi, vite, volontiers*:

À s'amuser ainsi, ils ont oublié l'heure.	*They forgot the time enjoying themselves like that.*
"Il l'a fait exprès" dit son petit frère.	*"He did it deliberately," his little brother said.*
des colis franco de port et d'emballage	*parcels with no payment for post and packaging*
La rivière était un obstacle quasi infranchissable.	*The river was an obstacle that we could hardly cross.*
Il ne pourra détourner des fonds impunément.	*He won't be able to embezzle funds with impunity / and go unpunished.*

Notes on *comme*:

Comme is used in set expressions with the meaning of *as* + adjective + *as*: *fort comme un bœuf* (*as strong as an ox*); *Elle est devenue blanche comme un linge* (*She went white as a sheet*); *Il est malin comme un singe* (*He really is a little monkey*).

Comme also corresponds to *like* in the following: *Elle parle comme elle écrit*; *ce jeune homme se conduit comme un enfant*; *Elle court comme une gazelle*; *Il travaille comme quatre / un forçat* (*galley slave*; now any prisoner committed to hard labor).

Comme is also used with the idea of *How!*: *Comme elle chante bien*; *Comme elle est intelligente/belle* !

This usage with *comme* is often replaced in R1 style by *Ce que*... :

Ce qu'ils sont solides comme équipe !	*How tough they are as a team!*
Ce qu'ils travaillent dur !	*How hard they work!*

Comment has the value of *What!* Maupassant is alleged to have said that marriage would not have suited him. To get up the next morning and be confronted by his newlywed wife would have alarmed him thus: *Comment! Tu es toujours là!*

The adverb corresponding to *gentil* is *gentiment*, although the feminine adjective is *gentille*. Likewise, *traître* > *traîtresse*, but the adverb is *traîtreusement*: *Le terroriste a livré traîtreusement leur secret.*

Most adjectives ending in −**ai**, −**é**, −**i** and the adjective **dû** add −**ment** to the masculine form: *aisé* > *aisément*, *délibéré* > *délibérément*, *dû* > *dûment*, *poli* > *poliment*, *vrai* > *vraiment*:

Philippe a aisément gagné la première manche.	*Philippe easily won the first round.*
Camille m'a envoyé un chèque dûment libellé.	*Camille sent me a check duly made out.*

Most adjectives ending in −**ant** and −**ent** take −**amment** or −**emment** as their ending: *abondant* > *abondamment*, *brillant* > *brillamment*, *constant* > *constamment*, *courant* > *couramment*, *vaillant* > *vaillamment*, *différent* > *différemment*, *évident* > *évidemment*, *fréquent* > *fréquemment*, *prudent* > *prudemment*, *récent* > *récemment*, *suffisant* > *suffisamment*, *violent* > *violemment*. *Instamment* (*urgently*) comes from the adjective *instant*, which is rarely used as an adjective these days and mostly used as a noun. When the adjectives ending in −**ent** provide the adverbial form, the −**emment** ending is pronounced **amment**. (See Chapter 2, on pronunciation, Section 2.6 for a substantial list.) Exceptions with adjectives ending in −**ent**: *lent* > *lente* > *lentement*, *présent* > *présente* > *présentement*, *véhément* > *véhémente* > *véhémentement*.

Some adverbs have no corresponding adjective: *journellement* (*daily*, but less used than *quotidennement*), *notamment*, *nuitamment* (R3 and rarely used = *at night*), *précipitamment* (*hurriedly*), *sciemment* (*knowingly*; first **e** pronounced as an **a**). *Grièvement* falls into this category, being a doublet of *gravement*, which comes from *grave*.

Two expressions where grammarians hesitate a great deal are (*tout*) *battant neuf* and (*tout*) *flambant neuf* (both expressions = *brand new*). *Battant, flambant* and even *neuf* can either remain invariable or agree. Invariability seems to be the best option: *des vêtements flambant neuf*; *une façade battant neuf*; *des affiches flambant neuf*; *une villa flambant neuf*. *Neuf, battant* and *flambant*, being invariable here, may be considered adverbs, since they all function as adverbs. Examples of (partial) agreement are: *des vêtements flambant neufs*; *une maison toute flambante neuve* (this latter example is exceptional). A thesis could be written on this topic without a satisfactory conclusion.

There is some lack of logic in the creation of some adjectives ending in **–i** and **–u**. The Académie française would do well to rationalize the irregularities that follow. According to this august body, one should write *gaiement*. Other dictionaries suggest this form and *gaîment*. But why not write *gaiment* like *vraiment*? The Académie insists on *absolument*, *ambigument*, *éperdument*, *ingénument*, *irrésolument* and *résolument*, but retains *assidûment*, *congrûment*, *continûment*, *crûment*, *dûment*, *goulûment*, *incongrûment*, *indûment* and *nûment*. There is no reason to retain the circumflex accent in these adverbs. The only reason for *dû* to take a circumflex accent is to distinguish it from the partitive *du*.

There are numerous adverbial expressions of manner made up of prepositions or other constructions (see Chapter 56 on prepositions for a much fuller list).

With *à*: *à l'envi* (not **–ie**; R3), *à qui mieux mieux*, *à dessein*, *à raison*, *à tort*, *à tort et à travers*, *à propos*, *à la manière/façon de*, *à cheval/pied*, *à la dérobée*:

Les dames imitaient à l'envi l'impératrice Eugénie.	The ladies rivaled each other in their imitation of the empress Eugénie.
Les étudiants ont chanté à qui mieux mieux.	The students tried to sing better than each other.
J'ai choisi cette bicyclette à dessein parce qu'elle est plus robuste.	I chose this cycle deliberately because it is tougher.
La police l'a accusé à tort / à raison.	The police accused him wrongly / with reason.
Son épouse dépense à tort et à travers.	His wife spends without rhyme or reason.
Ils sont arrivés tambour battant.	They came running up.
Elle a accompli sa tâche à la manière d'une experte.	She carried out her task in the style of an expert.

With *de*:

d'une voix heureuse/triste, d'un ton triste	*with a happy/sad voice*
Mon frère a envoyé le texto de manière/façon discrète.	*My brother sent the text message discreetly.*
de toute(s) façon(s)	*at any rate*
Je l'ai approuvé de bon cœur / de tout mon cœur.	*I approved it wholeheartedly.*
d'une main tremblante	*with a trembling hand*

With *en*: dormir en paix, rester en silence, en catimini (R3) / en sourdine (*secretly*), voyager en avion / en voiture / en train.

53.2 Adverbs of quantity or intensity

Adverbs of quantity or intensity point to amounts of something. Among this type of English adverbs are: *enough, as, so, too, much, more, less, fewer; enough beer, too much wine, fewer cars*. It is helpful to realize from the outset that in French, in many cases, the noun is preceded by *de: J'ai bu trop de vin / de bière; Il y a moins de voitures ce soir; beaucoup d'élèves*.

The main adverbs of quantity and intensity are: *à demi, à moitié, à peine, assez, aussi, autant, beaucoup, bien* (+ *du / de la / des*, not *de*), *combien, comme, comment, davantage, environ, fort, guère, moins, moitié, par* (*trop*), *pas mal, peu, plus, presque, quasi, que, quelque, si, tant, tout, tout à fait, tellement, très, trop, voire* (R3); *Le travail est à demi / à moité terminé* (*half finished*); *C'était un sentier à peine tracé* (*It was a barely visible path*); *assez de farine / d'argent / de fleurs*; *Pierre vient et Jean aussi; Tu le veux et moi aussi; Un homme aussi sage, aussi estimé que lui, qui parle aussi bien que personne; Il y a autant d'hommes que de femmes* (*as many men as women*); *Il a autant de courage que toi* (*He has as much courage as you*); *Il s'entraîne autant que son frère; Le petit mange autant que son grand frère; Je t'aiderai autant que je pourrai* (*I will help you as much as I can*); *Elle est aussi sportive que son cousin; beaucoup de messages / d'amis; Il y a bien des années que je l'ai vue / que je ne l'ai pas vue* (same meaning = *I haven't seen her for years*); *Il y a combien de touristes ?; Je prendrai davantage de framboises* (*I will take more raspberries*); *J'ai environ deux cents dollars* (*I have about two hundred dollars*); *Le pichet est à moitié vide/plein* (*The pitcher/jug is half empty/full*); *J'ai vu pas mal de lapins* (*I have seen quite a few rabbits*); *Le stade était presque vide; Les spectateurs étaient presque* (no elision) *en colère; un obstacle quasi infranchissable; la quasi-totalité/-certitude; Elle était si/tellement fatiguée que . . . ; Il y a trop d'eau sur le plancher; Il me faut plus de temps pour achever ma rédaction* (*I need more time to complete my essay*); *Ils étaient quelque* (no **s**) *dix mille spectateurs; une femme si sage, si estimée qui parle si bien; Elle a tant de courage* (*She has so much courage*); *Cette précaution est inutile, voire dangereuse* (*This precaution is unnecessary, indeed dangerous*); *Je l'ai trouvée difficile, voire insolente* (*I found her difficult, nay insolent*).

Note that *voire* may also be considered a conjunction (see Hanse and Blampain 2005, p. 615). It occurs in an elegant (and usually written) form, to reinforce an assertion or idea: *Ce remède est inutile, voire dangereux* (*nay dangerous*); *J'y ai passé de longs mois, voire des années.* A pleonastic, and therefore criticized, *même* is frequently added: *Ce plat est bon, voire même succulent.*

The combination *avoir assez/trop de* + noun can be replaced by *en avoir assez/trop*, as in:

"Tu as du pain ?" "Oui, j'en ai assez."	*"Do you have some bread?" "Yes, I have enough."*
"Tu as beaucoup de travail." "En effet, j'en ai trop."	*"You have too much work." "Sure enough, I have too much."*

Assez and *trop* may also be used with adjectives and other adverbs, and the order does not always correspond to the English:

C'est assez facile.	*It's easy enough.*
Céline court assez rapidement.	*Céline runs quite quickly.*
Françoise nous rend visite assez souvent.	*Françoise visits us quite frequently.*

With certain adverbs of the quantity type, *pour* is used in the following way:

Nous avons assez d'argent pour aller au cinéma.	*We have enough money to go to the movies.*
J'ai trop de travail pour pouvoir sortir.	*I've too much work to go out.*

And the same goes for adjectives:

Les élèves sont assez intelligents pour obtenir le bac.	*The pupils/students are intelligent enough to pass the bac (= le baccalauréat).*
Le boxeur est trop fort pour son adversaire.	*The boxer is too strong for his opponent.*

There is the occasional alternative to *aussi* + adjective + *que* + adjective in adjective + *autant que* + adjective: *Ce plat est aussi succulent que nourrissant / Ce plat est succulent autant que nourrissant* = *This dish is as tasty as it is nourishing.*

In negative sentences, one finds both *tant de* and *autant de* with no difference in meaning: *Jean n'a pas tant/autant d'énergie que toi* = *Jean doesn't have as much energy as you*; *Tu y tiens tant/autant que ça ?* = *You are as keen on it as that?*

Tant can have an indeterminate value: *Cette employée gagne tant par jour* (*This worker earns so much a day*). *Autant* could not be used here.

In negative sentences, *non plus* is used instead of *aussi*:

Tu ne veux pas y aller? Moi non plus.

You don't want to go? Neither do I.

Remarks on *beaucoup*:

Beaucoup is used a great deal in French, rather like *much* and *many* in English, *mucho/a/os/as* in Spanish or *molto/a/i/e* in Italian. It is so overworked that one could consider recourse to many possibilities to replace it, particularly in writing: *bien du | de la | de l' | des* (see also below), *quantités de, d'innombrables, maint* (R3; see also below), *force* (R3; see also below), *bon nombre (de), de nombreux, énormément de* (R1; see also below) are just a few synonyms for *beaucoup (de)*. Further examples with the meaning of *much, many, a lot*:

Elle a beaucoup de courage/joyaux.

She has a lot of courage | many jewels.

"Avez-vous des cousins?" "Oui. J'en ai beaucoup."

"Do you have any cousins?" "Yes. I have a lot."

"Il y a du beurre là?" "Oui, il y en a beaucoup."

"Is there any butter?" "Yes, there's a lot."

J'ai beaucoup étudié ces jours-ci.

I have studied a lot these days.

Beaucoup is also used with *plus* and *moins*:

Elle est beaucoup plus/moins discrète que sa nièce.

She is much more/less discreet than her niece.

Beaucoup may also be used when preceded by *de* to express a comparative:

Émilie est de beaucoup plus douée que moi.

Émilie is cleverer by far than me.

Le climat est de beaucoup plus humide au Congo.

The climate is much wetter by far in Congo.

Jean est plus calé que son frère, et de beaucoup.

Jean is smarter than his brother, and by far.

And to express a superlative:

Émilie est de beaucoup la plus douée de la classe.

Émilie is by far the cleverest in the class.

Beaucoup may also precede *trop*:

Ils étaient beaucoup trop fatigués pour faire le voyage de retour.

They were too tired by far to do the return journey.

It cannot be preceded by *très* as *very many* in English.

The expressions *bien du | bien de la | bien de l'* (*much*), *bien des* (*many*) carry greater feeling than *beaucoup de* which is much blander. They evoke satisfaction, surprise or disapproval:

J'ai eu bien du mal à faire ce calcul.	*I had real difficulty doing that calculation.*
Marcel a bien du courage pour faire ça.	*Marcel's got a lot a courage to do that.*
Bien des gens ont fait la remarque.	*Many people made the remark.*

Bien du differs from *beaucoup de* in that it is rarely used in the singular for concrete nouns – one would more easily say *J'ai mangé beaucoup de pain*. *Bien du* would sound odd here.

In the past, *bien des* would lose its **s** before an adjective, but this is no longer the case. Furthermore, an expression like *Il y avait bien des/de belles églises* is rarely heard these days. *Beaucoup de*, or other synonyms, would replace it.

However, *bien d'autres* is common enough: *J'ai reçu bien d'autres plaintes* (*I received a lot of other complaints*); *Bien d'autres se sont plaints* (*Several others complained*).

Maint (an adjective) has four forms: *maint* (masculine singular), *maints* (masculine plural), *mainte* (feminine singular), *maintes* (feminine plural). They are all of a high register (R3). All these forms are used before a noun: *En maint endroit* (in many a place); *maintes fois* (many a time); *à maintes reprises* (many a time | time and again); *à mainte et mainte occasion*; *à maintes et maintes reprises*.

Force as an adverb has the meaning of *several*. As with *maint*, it is of high register and would be found in writing: *après force recommandations*; *On s'est séparé avec force poignées de main* (*We separated after many handshakes*).

Énormément de is very common in popular discourse:

Il me faut énormément d'argent pour me tirer d'affaire.	*I need a lot of money to get out of this difficulty.*
Il y avait énormément de spectateurs dans le stade.	*There was an enormous number of spectators in the stadium.*

It is best to see *peu (de)* as *not much*, rather than *little* (i.e., as an adverb as opposed to an adjective):

Ils vivaient de peu.	*They lived on little.*
On était content de peu.	*We were satisfied with little.*
Philippe a peu apprécié cette plaisanterie.	*Philippe didn't appreciate this joke very much.*
Ils ont peu travaillé.	*They didn't work very much.*

Il est peu intelligent.	*He's not very intelligent.*
Je l'ai rencontrée il y a peu.	*I met her a little time ago.*
C'est un raisonnement peu clair.	*It's not very clear reasoning.*

Peu is also used with other adverbs: *Elle lit assez peu* | *bien peu* | *fort peu* | *quelque peu* | *très peu* | *trop peu*; also: *peu après, peu avant, peu auparavant, peu souvent.*

Peu is used after some prepositions, such as *avant peu, après peu, sous peu*:

Nous recevrons les colis sous peu.	*We'll receive the parcels shortly.*

Peu à peu = slowly, little by little: *On y arrivera peu à peu* (*We'll get there little by little*). *À peu près* = about, approximately: *J'ai à peu près fini* (*I've just about finished*); *J'en étais à peu près sûre* (*I was pretty sure*); *C'est à peu près ça* (*That's about it*).

Très corresponds well to the English *very* when qualifying adjectives and adverbs: *C'est très difficile/facile*; *Elle marche très lentement/rapidement*. It is also used with past participles and adverbial expressions where the English would doubtless have recourse to another adverb (e.g., *most, highly*): *Ce banquet a été très apprécié*; *Elle est très aimée par ses parents*; *La minijupe était très à la mode dans les années 60*; *Papa était très en colère*; *Je ne suis pas très au courant* (*I'm not really with it*); *Ça, c'est très vieux jeu* (*That's a bit old hat*).

Très is used elliptically in R1 discourse: *"Est-il intelligent ?" "Pas très."* It can be used before certain nouns: *Il est encore très enfant*; *Elle est très femme*; *Il reste très bébé*; *Il est très ami du directeur*. *Très* in combination with *avoir* and *faire* is now standard French: *J'ai très faim/soif/froid/chaud*; *Il fait très froid/chaud*. Some purists would plead, unsuccessfully, for *grand(e)* in these cases, since an adverb does not really qualify a noun. In French, in both speech and writing, *grand* is now entirely out-of-date with these expressions and only *très* is valid, although one does hear on occasion *J'ai grand faim*. The use of *grand* here invests the sensation with a certain stress.

Other expressions with *très* are: *faire très attention* | *très peur*. Synonyms of *très* are *bien* and *fort*. They are used less often than *très* and, precisely because of this, they are found in higher registers, notably *fort*: *C'est bien mauvais*; *Elle est bien jeune/contente*; *C'est bien dommage*. Some would argue that *fort* as an adverb is archaic or certainly very literary. This is not really the case in France. Furthermore, Hanse and Blampain state unequivocally that its use as an adverb is common in Belgium: *C'est fort difficile*; *Elle est fort intelligente/malheureuse*; *Cela me déplaît fort/très fort*; *J'en doute fort/très fort*; *Elle crie fort*; *Je la soupçonne fort de m'avoir menti*; *Cela lui tient fort à cœur*. As far as register values are concerned, one could classify these three adverbs in the following way: *Elle est très contente de te voir* (R2); *Elle est bien contente de te voir* (R2/R3); *Elle est fort contente de te voir* (R3, excluding Belgium where *fort* as an adverb is certainly R2).

53.3 Adverbs of time

The main adverbs of time are: *actuellement* (not *actually* = *en réalité*), *alors*, *antérieurement* (R3), *après*, *aujourd'hui*, *au lendemain*, *auparavant*, *au préalable* (R3), *autrefois*, *avant*, *avant-hier*, *bientôt*, *brièvement*, *de bonne heure*, *déjà*, *demain*, *depuis*, *dernièrement*, *dorénavant*, *désormais*, *donc*, *encore*, *enfin*, *ensuite*, *en retard*, *hier*, *immédiatement*, *jadis* (R3), *jamais*, *longtemps*, *lors de*, *naguère* (R3), *parfois*, *maintenant*, *or*, *postérieurement*, *précédemment*, *puis*, *quelquefois*, *soudain*, *soudainement*, *sous peu*, *souvent*, *subitement*, *au surlendemain*, *tantôt* (much more common in Belgium than in France = *tout à l'heure*), *tard*, *tôt*, *toujours*, *tout d'un coup*, *tout à coup*, *tout à l'heure*, *tout de suite*, *ultérieurement* (R3); *Elle est absente actuellement* (She's not here at the moment); *Ils avaient alors une jolie maison à la campagne* (They had a pretty house in the country at that time); *La ville de Québec a été fondée antérieurement* (before) *à celle de Montréal*; *Au lendemain de son arrivée dans la capitale...* (On the day following her arrival in the capital...); *Si tu veux t'absenter, previens-moi auparavant* (If you want to go out, let me know beforehand); *Tu dois partir, mais mange un peu au préalable* (You need to leave, but eat a bit before you go); *Autrefois, il n'y avait pas d'autoroutes* (Once upon a time, there were no highways); *Je la connais depuis dix ans* (I've known her for ten years); *Je l'ai vu dernièrement* (I saw him recently); *Dorénavant/Désormais cette épicerie sera ouverte le dimanche* (From now on, this grocery will be open on Sundays); *Jadis, les hommes vivaient dans des cavernes* (One upon a time, men lived in caves); *Naguère, on tapait les lettres à la machine, maintenant; on emploie un ordinateur* (Not too long ago, letters were typed on a typewriter; nowadays, we use a computer); *Parfois/Quelquefois, je travaille jusqu'à minuit* (Sometimes I work until midnight); *C'est un projet de loi qui a été voté postérieurement à celui-ci* (That bill was voted on after this one); *Le locataire a été prévenu précédemment de la fin du bail* (The tenant was warned previously of the termination of the lease); *Il faut le faire immédiatement/tout de suite; Et voilà qu'il a fait irruption subitement / soudain / soudainement / tout d'un coup / tout à coup dans la salle* (And then he suddenly burst into the room); *Il vint la voir au surlendemain de son arrivée* (He came to see her two days after his arrival); *Je reviendrai tantôt / tout à l'heure* (I'll return shortly); *Nous verrons ultérieurement ce qu'il faut faire* (We'll see later what we have to do).

Dorénavant and *désormais* both mean *henceforth, from now on*. The first is of a very high register (R3), and would only be used in writing. The second is also of a high register, but less so than *dorénavant*, and could be heard in careful speech.

Five of the adverbs of time, *alors*, *puis*, *ensuite*, *donc*, *lors*, may be translated by *then*, but they do not easily correspond to each other. Here are their main uses and differences:

Alors
   Alors = *at that time*
   On avait alors une grosse voiture.   *We had a big car at that time.*

Alors = *so, therefore*

Alors, qu'est-ce que tu décides ?   *So what are you deciding to do?*

"Elle est très douée." "Elle   *"She's very clever." "So she's studying*
    prépare l'agrég(ation) alors ?"   *for the agrégation?"*

Alors is extremely common as a filler, allowing the speaker time to think. It is the exact high-frequency equivalent of the Italian *allora*. In Spanish, this would be *pues*.

Puis and ensuite

Puis and *ensuite* both mean *next, afterwards*:

On a visité les Chutes du Niagara,   *We visited the Niagara Falls, and*
    puis/ensuite les Grands Lacs.   *then the Great Lakes.*

It goes without saying that a common spoken combination of these two adverbs produces a pleonasm, and one would do well to avoid it, as with other combinations: (*et*) *puis ensuite* / (*et*) *puis après, puis alors*.

Donc

Donc = *therefore, so*

Je pense, donc je suis (Descartes).   *I think, therefore I am.*

Variations on this usage:

Donc, la proposition est acceptée.   *So, the proposal is accepted.*
Il rit, donc il va bien.   *He's laughing, so he's OK.*
Qu'elle était donc gentille !   *How pleasant she was then!*

Donc is used to resume an interrupted speech:

Nous disions / Je disais donc   *We were / I was saying that...*
    que...

Donc can be used to pick up what another person is saying:

"Ils sont venus tous ensemble."   *"They all came together." "So, they*
    "Donc, c'était la fête, quoi."   *had a good time, then?"*

Donc can express surprise or irritation:

Tu y es allée toute seule donc ?   *So you went on your own?*
Qu'as-tu donc ?   *What's up then?*
Allons donc !   *Come on! (You're talking nonsense.)*

Lors

Lors in the sense of *alors* = *then* is no longer in use by itself, but is common enough in set expressions:

Elle a fait la connaissance d'Alec   *She has come to know Alec, et since*
    et, depuis lors, ne parle que de   *then, she only talks about him.*
    lui.

Dès lors que nous serons en
vacances, nous partirons à la
campagne.

As soon as we're on vacation, we'll leave for the countryside.

Lors de notre première rencontre,
tu portais un chandail rouge.

When we first met, you were wearing a red sweater.

Encore has five meanings:
Encore = still:

Elle est encore là.

She is still there.

Il est 20h et il fait encore clair.

It's 8 o'clock and still light.

Toujours has this meaning:

Antoine travaille toujours.

Antoine is still working.

Antoine ne travaille toujours pas.

Antoine still isn't working.

This use of *toujours* does not have the same meaning when its position changes:

Antoine ne travaille pas toujours.

Antoine does not always work.

Encore = yet:

Je ne l'ai pas encore fait.

I haven't done it yet.

Encore = again:

Tu as encore fait la même erreur.

You've made the same error again.

Je voudrais y retourner encore.

I'd like to return there again.

Je prendrais encore de la glace
aux pistaches.

I'd like pistachio ice cream again.

Encore = even:

Elle est encore plus rapide que
son frère.

She's even faster than her brother.

Encore = but:

Il est agréable de voyager; encore
faut-il disposer d'assez de temps.

It's pleasant to travel, but you need to have enough time.

Encore une fois stresses *encore*:

La petite Canadienne a battu le
record encore une fois.

The little Canadian girl/woman has broken the record again.

Ensuite is really a composition of two words: *en* + *suite* (from *suivre* = to follow). *Suite* gives rise to a number of other adverbial and prepositional phrases: *à la suite, à la suite de, et ainsi de suite, comme suite à, dans la suite, de suite, par la suite, par suite, par suite de, tout de suite*:

La directrice parlera à la suite du
président.

The manager will speak after the president.

À la suite de cette décision injuste,
elle décida de démissionner.

As a result of this unjust decision, she decided to resign.

Comme suite à votre demande du 15 avril, nous vous faisons parvenir le document ci-inclus.	*In reply to your request of April 15, we send you the enclosed document.*
Ils ont déménagé, et dans la suite je les ai revus à quelques reprises.	*They moved house, and afterwards I saw them again a few times.*
Vous parlez trop bas, et par suite, je ne vous comprends pas.	*You are speaking too softly, and in consequence, I can't understand you.*
Par la suite, ils s'excusèrent.	*They apologized afterwards.*

(Notice the difference between *par suite* [*in consequence*] and *par la suite* [*afterwards*].

Viens tout de suite.	*Come immediately.*

Jamais = ever. This adverb occurs notably in direct and indirect questions, after comparisons, and after *si* (*if*):

la plus jolie musique que j'aie jamais entendue	*the loveliest music I've ever heard*
Je me rends au travail à pied, jamais à vélo.	*I walk to work, and never go on a bike.*
Si jamais tu envoies un texto à Luc, dis-lui que je suis d'accord.	*If ever you send a text message to Luc, tell him I agree.*

Jamais also appears in set expressions: *Cette famille est partie à tout jamais (for ever)*; *Je ne le verrai pas, au grand jamais (never ever)*; *C'est maintenant ou jamais (now or never)*; *Gagner huit médailles d'or aux Jeux olympiques, c'est du jamais-vu (that's never happened)*; *Je ne lui donnerai pas l'argent, jamais de la vie (never in your life)*.

Tard and *en retard* both mean *late*, but they are not used in the same circumstances. *Tard* refers generally to *late*, but *en retard* suggests after a specific, agreed or intended time. Compare the two sentences:

Irène s'est couchée très tard.	*Irène went to bed late.*
Antoine est arrivé en retard; il a raté le train.	*Antoine arrived late, he missed the train.*

Similarly:

Comment se fait-il que notre fils rentre toujours tard?	*How is it that our son always comes home late?*
Mariette est en retard, comme d'habitude. On commence la discussion sans elle?	*Mariette is late as usual. Shall we begin the discussion without her?*

Note also the adverbial expressions: *Votre demande doit nous parvenir le 29 du mois au plus tard (at the latest)*; *Marcel s'est mis à l'informatique sur le tard (at an* advanced age); *Nous y arriverons tôt ou tard* (*sooner or later*). The opposite of *tard* / *en retard* is *de bonne heure*: *Jeanne est levée de bonne heure* (*Jeanne is up early*).

> *Tôt* (*early*) needs to be differentiated from *bientôt* (*soon*). Compare *arriver/partir tôt*; *Ne venez pas tôt* (*Don't come early*); *Elle se lève tôt* (*She gets up early*); and *Elle va se lever bientôt* (*She'll get up soon*); *À bientôt!* (*See you soon!*). It is wise not to confuse *bien tôt* (*really early*) and *bientôt*. *Tôt* can also be qualified by other adverbs: *Elle est arrivée assez tôt* / *très tôt* / *plus tôt que de coutume*. Note also the use of *au plus tôt = at the earliest*: *Je ne peux pas venir à dix-huit heures : au plus tôt à vingt heures* (*eight o'clock at the earliest*). (*Au*) *plus tôt* and *plutôt = rather, quite* should also be distinguished: *Je préfère venir plutôt à vingt et une heures* (*I'd rather come at nine o'clock*). The other compounds of *tôt* are: *aussitôt* (*immediately*), *sitôt* (*as soon as*) (not to be confused with *si tôt = so soon*), *tantôt* (*presently, a bit later*), *tantôt... tantôt* (*sometimes... sometimes*):

Sophie m'a répondu aussitôt.	*Sophie answered me immediately.*
Elle s'est manifestée aussitôt qu'elle pouvait.	*She came as soon as she could.*
Sitôt levé, il se met au travail.	*As soon as he's up, he's working.*
Ils sont arrivés si tôt que je n'avais même pas pris mon petit-déjeuner.	*They arrived so early I hadn't even had time to have my breakfast.*
Elle était tantôt triste tantôt heureuse.	*She was sometimes sad and sometimes happy.*

Tantôt can have the meaning of *this afternoon*, especially in the Paris area, but Parisians like to think it is an expression from the provinces. This meaning is also associated with Belgium. In reality, some confusion arises over the ambiguity of *tantôt = later* or *this afternoon*. It seems wiser to use *tout à l'heure* for *a bit later*.

Aussitôt and *sitôt* are used as past participles. See the example above for *sitôt*. As for *aussitôt*: *Aussitôt rentré, il se coucha* (*As soon as he came home, he went to bed*). See also Chapter 17 on the ablative absolute for a fuller discussion of this topic.

53.4 Adverbs and adverbial expressions of place

Common adverbs of place are: *à droite, à gauche, ailleurs, alentour, au-dedans, au-dehors, au-delà, au-dessous, au-dessus, au-devant, autour, dedans, dehors, derrière, dessous, dessus, devant, en arrière, en avant, en bas, en dedans, en dehors, en dessous, en dessus, endroit, haut, ici, là, là-bas, loin, par-derrière, par-devant, (un peu) partout, près, quelque part, tout droit*; *La France et les États-Unis roulent à droite tandis que les Anglais et toutes les ex-colonies britanniques roulent à gauche*; *Allez faire du bruit ailleurs* (*Go and make a noise somewhere else*); *Ils sont venus d'ailleurs* (*They have come from elsewhere*); *Il pleut, les enfants peuvent jouer au-dedans* (It's raining; the children can play *inside*); *Il fait du soleil, les enfants peuvent jouer au-dehors* (It's sunny; the children can play *outside*); *Ils font du bruit au-dessous ou au-dessus ?* (Are they making noise *below or above*?); *Le prix est inscrit dessous* (*The price is written underneath*); *les documents de dessus* (*the documents on top*); *Regarde en arrière* (*Look behind*); *Viens ici* (*Come here*); *Es-tu déjà allée là ?* (*Have you already been there?*); *Ils habitent là-bas, dans la vallée* (They live there, *over there in the valley*); *L'ennemi a attaqué par-derrière* (The enemy attacked *from behind*); *Il y a des fourmis* (*un peu*) *partout* (*There are ants everywhere*); *Tu vas tout droit, et après, c'est à droite* (*You go straight on and then it's to the right*).

Ici and *là*: *Ici* corresponds to the first person *je/nous*. It is closest to the person(s) speaking or writing (= *here*) and, in a sense, it is more specific and precise. *Là* corresponds to the places where a person is not (= *there*): *C'est ici que je travaille*; *Viens ici*; *Ici, c'est l'hiver tandis que chez vous, là où vous êtes, les jonquilles sont déjà en fleur* (would say a person in Canada to a person in Virginia). However, *ici* = *here* and *là* = *there* are synonymous in many cases, particularly in spoken French. *Là* is frequently used for *ici*. Indeed, it is used more frequently: *Tu es là depuis quand ?* (*How long have you been here?*); *Viens donc par là !* (*Come here!*). At the same time, a dog would be called to heel only with *Ici ! Au pied !* It would appear that when one says "*Viens ici*," the *ici* refers to where the speaker is, but when one say "*Viens là*" (still the same meaning) one is referring to where the addressee is.

53.5 Adverbs and adverbial expressions of affirmation

The main ones are: *absolument, à la vérité, après tout, assurément, bien sûr, certainement, certes, d'accord, effectivement, en fait, en vérité, évidemment, exactement, justement, oui, parfaitement, pour sûr, précisément, probablement, sans doute, si, sûr, volontiers, vraiment, vraisemblablement*; *Il faut y aller absolument* (You really must go); *Je suis, à la vérité / en vérité, fort loin de penser que le mariage est une mauvaise institution* (I am, in truth, very far from thinking that marriage is a bad institution); *On a annoncé de la grêle et, effectivement, il a grêlé* (They said it would hail and, sure enough, it hailed); *C'est justement ce qu'il fallait écrire* (That is precisely what you had to write); *Il compte précisément*; "*Ils ne vont pas participer à la fête ?*" "*Si, ils viendront*" ("Will they come to the party?" "Yes they'll come"); *Je prendrais volontiers un jus bien frais* (I'd willingly have a nice fresh juice); *Elle le croit volontiers* (She believes it quite easily).

Si, with the meaning of *yes*, occurs in the affirmation over against a denial/negation. *Oui* would not be suitable in these contexts, as in this example: "*Elle n'est pas assez intelligente pour obtenir sa licence.*" "*Mais si*" (Of course she is).

53.6 Adverbs of doubt or approximation

The main adverbs of doubt are: *à peu près, approximativement, apparemment, environ, éventuellement* (not *eventually*), *par hasard, peut-être, probablement, selon toute probabilité, sans doute, possiblement* (only in Canada), *selon toute vraisemblance*:

Adrienne habite à la Nouvelle Orléans depuis dix ans à peu près.	*Adrienne has been living in New Orleans for about ten years.*
Cela fait approximativement 5 pour cent du total.	*That makes approximately 5 percent of the total.*
Apparemment, il fera beau pour le week-end.	*Apparently it'll be fine for the weekend.*
Le pont se situe à un kilomètre environ / à environ un kilomètre.	*The bridge is about a kilometer from here.*
Ces documents pourront servir éventuellement.	*These documents will possibly be of use later on.*
Tu n'as pas par hasard vingt euros ?	*You don't have twenty euros by chance?*
Nos amis viendront sans doute demain.	*Our friends will doubtless come tomorrow.*
Selon toute vraisemblance/ probabilité, ils sont déjà partis.	*In all probability, they have already left.*
Elle gagnera peut-être le premier prix.	*Perhaps she will win the first prize.*
Sans doute acceptera-t-elle de parrainer la recommandation.	*She will doubtless accept to sponsor the recommendation.*

54

Comparative adjectives, adverbs and nouns / Les adjectifs, les adverbes et les noms comparatifs

The following passage treats the burning question of the partial or total covering up of the female form in the Muslim world. Understandably enough, different countries follow various ideological routes to deal with this question. France seems to be moving toward a position of intransigence while the United Kingdom and the USA are following a more cautious line. Highlighted are the various uses of adjectives, adverbs and nouns as they would appear in comparative contexts. Some translations are given. Explanations of the terms *burqa*, *hijab* and *niqab* are provided in the last paragraph. Of interest are the alternative spellings *burka* and *burqa*, which are both masculine and feminine.

La polémique autour du voile intégral
En France, la mission parlementaire sur la question du voile intégral, de la burqa et du niqab, propose d'interdire **aussi rapidement que possible** le port de cette tenue vestimentaire dans les lieux publics (établissements scolaires, hôpitaux, transports en commun). Cette tenue est **autant désirable** pour certaines femmes **que repoussante** pour d'autres. La mission, de beaucoup la plus importante jusqu'à nos jours, a été confiée à des représentants de tous bords politiques (Union pour un Mouvement Populaire [UMP], Parti Socialiste [PS], Parti Radical de Gauche (PRG), Nouveau Centre (NC), Parti Communiste Français [PCF] et les Verts). Les membres de cette assemblée ont travaillé **de plus en plus** pour parvenir à un consensus. Un débat, de loin le plus houleux [stormy] ces jours-ci, s'est engagé sur une question qui est **aussi essentielle** pour les uns **que dérisoire** pour les autres. Selon certaines organisations, il s'agit d'un épiphénomène [epiphenomenon = secondary or additonal phenomenon] si on tient compte des statistiques publiées par le ministère de l'Intérieur. Pourtant, la polémique fait rage, **plus même que l'on n'aurait jamais pensé**. La meilleure ou la pire solution n'est pas encore perceptible. La situation va **de mal en pis** [is deteriorating].
   Les femmes musulmanes portent **de plus en plus** le voile intégral, **autant** dans les milieux intellectuels **qu'**ailleurs. Il semblerait que cette nouvelle tendance n'ait rien de traditionnel et qu'elle s'inspire **moins du** Coran **que** d'une simple évolution des mœurs. Shirin Ebadi, avocate

iranienne, Prix Nobel de la paix 2003, considère que le voile intégral porté au nom de l'Islam est **beaucoup moins** « musulman » **qu'on ne** le pensait. Elle préconise l'interdiction du voile intégral. Le port du voile résulte d'un choix **plus** personnel qu'imposé de l'extérieur. Mais chaque cas est un cas particulier. Certaines femmes se plient à la pression d'un père, d'un frère ou d'un mari ou même d'un groupe social ou religieux. La pression est **encore plus** grande lorsqu'il s'agit d'un groupe. **Faute de mieux**, certaines musulmanes acceptent d'être soumises [to remain submissive]. L'exploitation et l'amalgame sur le port du voile intégral et l'identité nationale attisent [fan the flames of] **aussi bien** la haine **que** la discorde, la querelle et la peur. Les chaînes de radio jouent un rôle **moindre que** la télévision hertzienne ou câblée. **Plus** le débat s'étendra, **plus** on risquera de heurter [strike up against] des intérêts cachés ou des susceptibilités.

En Allemagne par exemple, le port du voile intégral occupe une place **beaucoup plus** marginale et, en conséquence, **moins** contestée. Aucune loi interdisant le port du voile intégral n'a été votée. Suite à l'actuel débat dans l'Hexagone [France], le Royaume-Uni s'oppose fermement à une interdiction du voile intégral. La burqa (voile intégral qui cache les yeux derrière un tissu grillagé), le hijab (appelé foulard islamique), le niqab (masque qui dissimule le visage sauf les yeux) sont admis partout de l'autre côté de la Manche [on the other side of the English Channel]. D'ailleurs, **de plus en plus de** femmes musulmanes se voilent et, **qui plus est**, occupent des postes de responsabilité dans les entreprises en Grande-Bretagne. Certaines femmes s'investissent [take on important roles] **autant que** les hommes et ont fait leurs études dans les mêmes universités prestigieuses. Les États-Unis, la Grande-Bretagne ou les pays scandinaves n'ont pas la **même** approche politique **que** la France sur cette question épineuse [thorny] qui risque de provoquer des prises de position **non seulement** inébranlables **mais aussi** dangereuses. Certains pays offrent **plus de** choix **que** d'autres et n'hésitent pas à permettre aux femmes de se voiler la face.

54.1 Adjectives

When we compare, we establish a relationship between people, things or facts. There are three types of comparison:

1. A relationship of resemblance or difference:

Mon fils Augustin est aussi grand que son père.	*My son Augustin is as tall as his father.*
Jean est plus grand que Jeanne.	*Jean is taller than Jeanne.*

2. A relationship of identity:

Patrick a fait ses études dans la même université que moi.	*Patrick studied in the same university as me.*

3. A relationship of proportion:

Plus tu liras, plus tu enrichiras ton vocabulaire.	*The more you read the more you will enrich your vocabulary.*

Notice how the comparison is used with *de* in measurements:

Elle est plus grande que toi de plusieurs centimètres.	*She is several centimeters taller than you.*
L'estuaire de l'Amazone est de beaucoup plus large que celui du Mississippi.	*The Amazon estuary is wider by far than that of the Mississippi.*

The formula for comparison with *better* (*supériorité*), *sameness* (*égalité*) and *worse* (*infériorité*) is:

1. better: *plus* + adjective + *que*;
2. sameness: *aussi* + adjective + *que*;
3. worse: *moins* + adjective + *que*.

This formula is more or less the same as in Italian (*più ... di*), and Spanish (*más ... que*). The *que* element usually stands alone, like *than* and *as* in English. In other words, *que* is not followed by a verb, although in some circumstances it would be:

Ce documentaire est plus/moins intéressant que l'autre.	*This documentary is more/less interesting than the other one.*
Cette secrétaire est aussi compétente que ma sœur.	*This secretary is as competent as my sister.*

Circumstances where a verb would follow *que*:

Ce film est plus intéressant que je (ne) le pensais.	*This film is more interesting than I thought.*
Ta voiture est moins coûteuse que je (ne) le pensais.	*Your car is less costly than I thought.*

This type of construction ending in *que je (ne) le pensais* requires comment with respect to register. The first of the three sentences below would be of the written style R3, with the extra, and unnecessary, **ne**, or expletive as it is often known. The second is slightly less formal, suitable for both written and spoken R2. The third is most informal R1:

Ta voiture est moins coûteuse que je ne le pensais.
Ta voiture est moins coûteuse que je le pensais.
Ta voiture est moins coûteuse que je pensais.

After a negation or a question, *aussi* may be replaced by *si*, and there is no difference in register or meaning:

Elle n'est pas aussi/si docile que son frère.	*She's not as docile as her brother.*

Some adjectives which have a very strong meaning or are close to a superlative idea are not used in comparatives: *affreux, délicieux, excellent, essentiel, magnifique, splendide, superbe, suprême*. One would not replace *beau* in the following sentence by *magnifique*, for example:

Ce tableau est plus beau que les autres.	*This painting is finer than the others.*

There are some irregular comparatives: bon(s) / bonne(s) = *good*; meilleur(s) / meilleure(s) = *better*; pire = *worse*:

La baguette de pain d'un artisan-boulanger est meilleure qu'une baguette du supermarché.	*A master baker's baguette is better than one from the supermarket.*
Il est de pire humeur qu'hier.	*He is in a worse temper than yesterday.*

Meilleur and *pire* can be strengthened by *bien*:

Ces gâteaux sont bien meilleurs que chez nous.	*These cakes are much better than where we live.*
La neige ? C'est bien pire.	*Snow? It's much worse.*

Meilleure can follow the noun, and here it is of a slightly higher register: *la meilleure solution = la solution la meilleure* (*better/best solution*).

Two adjectives, *petit* and *mauvais*, require considerable comment. *Petit* takes *plus* in the literal way to indicate size and measurement:

Ma valise est plus petite que la tienne.	*My suitcase is smaller than yours.*

However, when *petit* is used in a figurative way, it is replaced by *moindre*:

Dans la vie politique, la radio joue un rôle moindre que la télévision.	*In political life, radio plays a lesser role than television.*

One could just as well say *un moindre rôle que*. *Mauvais* can take the form *plus mauvais* in most cases, but *pire* expresses an extra insistence:

On annonce à la radio que demain le temps sera plus mauvais qu'aujourd'hui.	*They forecast on the radio that the weather tomorrow will be worse than today.*
Quel mauvais devoir ! Il est pire que le précédent.	*What awful homework! It's worse than the last one.*

Plus mauvais and *pire* are sometimes interchangeable, as in: *Sommes-nous devenus meilleurs ou plus mauvais/pires ?*; *Cette excuse est plus mauvaise/pire que la précédente*; *Il est de pire/plus mauvaise humeur qu'hier*. But when the noun itself evokes something wrong or evil (an illness, etc.), only *pire* would suit:

chagrin, désagrément, détresse, difficulté, douleur, ennui, erreur, faute, fléau, mal, misère, tristesse; *La dernière faute est pire que la première*; *Je ne connais pas de pire détresse/misère que l'isolement*. When a defect or imperfection is referred to, however, *plus mauvais* seems to be preferred: *Sa vue est plus mauvaise que la mienne*; *Cette machine est plus mauvaise que je ne croyais*.

54.2 Adverbs

The comparative of adverbs follows the same pattern as adjectives. The formula for b*etter (superiorité), sameness (égalité)* and *worse (infériorité)* is therefore:

1. better: *plus* + adverb + *que*;
2. sameness: *aussi* + adverb + *que*;
3. worse: *moins* + adverb + *que*:

Gabriel conduit plus vite que toi.	*Gabriel drives more quickly than you do.*
Marcel travaille aussi efficacement que son frère.	*Marcel works as efficiently as his brother.*
Aurélie marche moins rapidement que moi.	*Aurélie walks less quickly than I do.*
Aurélie ne marche pas aussi/si rapidement que moi.	*Aurélie does not walk as quickly as I do.*

Mieux is the corresponding comparative adverb to *bon*:

Sarah comprend mieux les maths que sa cousine.	*Sarah understands math(s) better than her cousin.*

The order *Sarah comprend les maths mieux que sa cousine* is of a lower register than the order above.

Other expressions with the adverb *mieux*: *Je vais mieux (I am better,* i.e., in health); *Ça va mieux ? (Better?*; usually in health); *Elle est mieux portante (She's better,* i.e., in health); *Les deux garçons ont dessiné à qui mieux mieux (The two boys tried to beat each other at drawing); tant mieux (so much the better / that's better*).

Mieux can be used as an adjective: *La fièvre l'a quittée, elle est mieux (The fever has gone, she's better); Je l'ai trouvé mieux (I found him better,* i.e., in health); *Il est venu, et qui mieux est, il était le premier (He came and, even better, he was the first*).

Mieux can also be used as a noun: *Je m'attendais à mieux; J'espérais mieux; Il y a mieux; Faute de mieux (For lack of anything better); Je ne demande pas mieux qu'elle s'en aille (I ask nothing more than she go); Le mieux est de partir maintenant (The best thing is to leave now); Le mieux se maintient (Progress is being maintained); Il y a un mieux (There's something better); Elle fait toujours de son mieux (She always does her best); Sa maman agit toujours pour le mieux (Her mother always acts for the best*); *C'est le mieux que je puisse faire* (*It's the best I can do* – note the subjunctive here).

The comparative of *mauvais* as an adverb is always *plus mauvais*: *Ça sent plus mauvais* (*That smells worse*). *Pire* cannot be an adverb, although there is some uncertainty here (see Hanse and Blampain 2005, p. 444). The corresponding adverb to *mauvais* is *pis*, but its use is limited to some expressions: *aller de mal en pis | de pis en pis* (*to go from bad to worse | to get worse and worse*); *un pis-aller* (*a lesser evil*); *tant pis* (*That's just too bad*).

54.3 Nouns

Comparatives are also used in the context of nouns. The references in English are: *more/less* + noun + *than* and *as much as | as many as*. The French formulae here are: *plus de* + noun + *que*, *autant de* + noun + *que* and *moins de* + noun + *que*:

Ce grand magasin d'informatique offre plus de choix que tous les autres.	*This computer shop offers more choice than all the others.*
Elle a parlé plus d'une heure.	*She spoke more than an hour.*
Il a plus de dollars que moi.	*He has more dollars than I have.*
Adrienne a autant d'intelligence que moi.	*Adrienne has as much intelligence as me.*
Irène a acheté autant de robes que sa sœur.	*Irène has bought as many dresses as her sister.*
On dit qu'en France il y a autant de fromages que de jours dans l'année.	*They say that in France there are as many cheeses as days in the year.*
Avec la crise économique, il y a moins de travail qu'avant.	*With the credit crunch, there is less work than before.*
Mon frère a moins de trophées que notre neveu.	*My brother has fewer trophies than our nephew.*

Beaucoup may combine with *plus* and *moins*: *Mon frère a beaucoup plus de courage/livres que moi*. Note the formula with numbers: *J'ai deux ans de plus que ma sœur et trois ans de moins que mon frère*. Also note the formula verb + *plus/autant/moins* + *que*:

Christophe a mûri: il réfléchit plus qu'avant quand il doit prendre une décision.	*Christophe has developed: he thinks more than before when taking a decision.*
À l'époque de l'audiovisuel, est-ce qu'on lit autant qu'avant ?	*In the audiovisual era, do people read as much as before?*
Je ne travaille pas moins qu'avant.	*I don't work less than before.*

54.4 Miscellaneous

Note these formulae in compound tenses, and especially variants in word order:

Il a moins neigé qu'hier.	*It has snowed less than yesterday.*
Il a neigé plus qu'hier.	*It has snowed more than yesterday.*
Cette année mon fils a mieux travaillé que l'année dernière.	*This year, my son has worked better than last year.*
Ils ont mieux joué qu'hier.	*They played better than yesterday.*

In the first sentence, *moins* could easily follow *neigé*. In the second sentence, *plus* could not easily precede *neigé*. In the third and fourth cases, *mieux* could follow *travaillé* and *joué* but it is preferred before.

The idea of progression is as follows: *de plus en plus/de moins en moins*:

With a verb:

La population canadienne vit de plus en plus dans les villes.	*The Canadian population lives increasingly in the cities.*
On lit de moins en moins de nos jours.	*People read less and less these days.*

With a noun:

De plus en plus de femmes occupent des postes de responsabilité dans les entreprises.	*More and more women occupy posts of responsibility in companies.*
De moins en moins de journaux se vendent face à la télévision.	*Fewer and fewer newspapers are sold because of television.*

With an adverb:

"Tu joues encore du saxophone ?"	*"Do you still play the saxophone?"*
"Non, j'en joue de moins en moins souvent."	*"No, I play less and less often."*

With an adjective:

Dans les pays riches, la durée de la vie humaine est de plus en plus longue.	*In rich countries, the life span is longer and longer.*

Notice the French equivalent of *the more . . . the more/the less . . . the less*:

Plus je travaille, plus je m'enthousiasme.	*The more I work the more I get enthusiastic.*
Plus ils gagnent d'argent, plus ils sont contents.	*The more money they earn, the happier they are.*
Moins je dors moins je suis fatiguée.	*The less I sleep, the less tired I am.*

A general observation on the pronunciation of *plus*:

1. Before an adjective or adverb beginning with a consonant, the **s** is not pronounced: *plus grand, plus petit, plus vite, plus rapidement.*
2. Before a vowel, the *liaison* occurs: *plus agréable, plus heureux, plus intéressant, plus agréablement, plus harmonieusement.*
3. In all other cases, the **s** is pronounced: *Il a plus de travail que moi; Elle travaille plus que moi; Ils ont travaillé de plus en plus.*

55

Superlative adjectives, adverbs and nouns / Les adjectifs, les adverbes et les noms superlatifs

The following passage describes the Winter Olympics that took place in Canada in 2010. It evokes the great enthusiasm and passion generated by this four-yearly event. Much of the action depends on the snow which, in recent years, has not proved so reliable. This almost proved the case in Vancouver, but the weather came to the rescue as the games were about to start. The piece illustrates the use of superlatives which are highlighted in bold. A few translations are provided. Some further comments: The Latin *in fine* has a didactic connotation with the meaning provided in the text. The expression *planète bleue* means the Earth, doubtless as it appears blue from outer space, as opposed to *planète rouge* which signifies Mars.

Les Jeux olympiques de Vancouver

Dans la Grèce antique, les Jeux olympiques étaient organisés tous les quatre ans près de la ville d'Olympie. Les **pays extrêmement** puissants ont développé des trésors d'imagination pour célébrer des rencontres sportives au niveau international. Les **meilleurs** athlètes de la planète bleue s'entraînent régulièrement pour battre le record mondial et décrocher la médaille d'or dans leur spécialité. En février 2010, les Jeux olympiques de Vancouver offrent un **spectacle des plus exaltants** et dégagent des **émotions on ne peut plus intenses**. Les sportifs de haut niveau entrent dans une vive compétition qui suscite **les passions et les ardeurs les plus folles. Les plus chevronnés** [seasoned/experienced] montent sur le podium pour afficher leur victoire.

En général, les mois de janvier et de février sont les mois où il neige **le plus** au Canada. Cette **année** reste **exceptionnelle**. Il a beaucoup moins neigé que les années précédentes. En raison des **conditions météorologiques les plus mauvaises** et des **difficultés les plus désagréables**, l'organisation s'est trouvée dans une **situation des plus critiques**. Pourtant, les organisateurs ont été attentifs aux **moindres détails**. Il est **rarissime** d'avoir à utiliser les canons à neige en pareil cas. In fine [In short], les circonstances atmosphériques ont été plus clémentes et la neige est tombée à nouveau. Le **moment le plus réussi**

548

et **le plus émouvant** du spectacle reste la remise des médailles [award-ing of medals]. Les habitants de Vancouver garderont le **meilleur des souvenirs** de ces olympiades. Les chaînes de télévision sont celles qui fix-ent **le plus longtemps possible** cet événement en direct. Le **plus grand intérêt** des visiteurs consiste à participer à cet événement **exceptionnel** de l'année et à découvrir la ville. Les **analystes canadiens les plus pas-sionnés** mettent en relief les répercussions positives de ces Jeux sur la société canadienne, sur l'économie et sur l'environnement. Le **bénéfice le plus frappant** de ces retombées se fera sentir à plus ou moins long terme. La flamme olympique attise [stokes up / releases] généralement le patriotisme et, dans certains cas, un chauvinisme **ultra-fanatique**. Le pays hôte se lance l'un **des plus grands défis** qui est celui d'être le **suprême vainqueur** des Jeux olympiques d'hiver. Quels sont les sports dans lesquels on compte le **moins de femmes**? On constate que le saut à ski ne compte, pour l'instant, aucune femme. Il s'agit de la **discipline la plus masculine** des Jeux de cette année 2010. C'est une **question des plus délicates**. En effet, cette discipline devrait compter autant d'hommes que de femmes.

This chapter deals specifically with relative superlatives as opposed to absolute superlatives. Relative superlatives treat the highest degree of a quality or deficiency in the context of a comparison while absolute superla-tives do not imply any degree of comparison. It would be helpful to dis-cuss briefly absolute superlatives which can be formed in four different ways:

1. Absolute superlatives are often formed by certain adverbs preced-ing an adjective. These are in the main: *absolument, bien, entièrement, fort, extrêmement, infiniment, totalement, très; Marie est extrêmement/fort/très savante (Marie is extremely/very knowledgeable)*.
2. They are sometimes marked by prefixes: *archifou/ennuyeux, extra-fin, surfin, superfin, ultra-comique; des petits pois extra-fins; la performance ultra-comique d'un clown; du chocolat superfin*.
3. They are occasionally marked by the suffix *–issime* which relates to etiquette, deriving from the Latin *issimus*, which appears much more frequently and in a general way in Spanish (*excelentísimo, hermosísimo, riquísimo*), and in Italian (*eccellentissimo, cortesissimo, bellissimo*). They may also be used in a jocular manner, by virtue of their inflated idea: *excellentissime, importantissime, illustrissime, éminentissime; excellen-tissimes seigneurs; son illustrissime cardinal Benedetto*. This jocular touch may also surface in colloquial language: *Grandissime, rarissime, richissime* (although there is nothing jocular about *gravissime: Le cas du malade est gravissime*); *Ces pierres sont rarissimes et, par là, très précieuses; un avocat richissime*. One also comes across in historical documents *la Sérénissme* (*république de Venise*).

4. The absolute superlative is also formed with noun + *des plus* + plural adjective which can be feminine:

un choix des plus délicats	*a most delicate choice*
une affaire des plus épineuses	*a most awkward business*
une expérience des plus pénibles	*a most difficult experience*
un spectacle des plus exaltants	*a most uplifting spectacle*

55.1 Relative superlatives of adjectives

The relative superlative expresses, by way of comparison, a quality or a weakness:

Monsieur Dupont, c'est la personne la plus agréable / la plus désagréable de notre immeuble.	*Monsieur Dupont is the most pleasant/unpleasant person in our apartment block.*

The formula to create the relative superlative is: *le/la/les plus* + adjective or *le/la/les moins* + adjective:

Le Louvre est le plus grand musée de France.	*The Louvre is the biggest museum in France.*
Voici l'ordinateur portable le plus léger et le plus performant que nous ayons.	*Here is the lightest and most capable portable computer we have.*
Les exercices 1 à 5 sont les moins difficiles de ce chapitre.	*Exercises 1 to 5 are the least difficult in this chapter.*

The place of the superlative is determined by the place of the adjective. One can always place the superlative after the noun, but the article needs to be repeated:

Élise est la plus jolie fille de la classe.	*Élise is the best-looking girl in the class.*
Élise est la fille la plus jolie de la classe.	

It goes without saying that, if the adjective normally follows the noun, only one possibility exists:

C'est le sommet le plus élevé d'Amérique du Nord.	*It is the highest peak in North America.*

Other determiners like possessive adjectives follow the pattern of the definite article:

| Mon plus grand intérêt consiste à lire Dostoïevski. | *My greatest interest consists in reading Dostoievsky.* |
| Leur plus jeune enfant va déjà au collège. | *Their youngest child already goes to school.* |

As with the comparative, the superlative of *bon(ne)* is *meilleur(e)*:

| On a élu la meilleure actrice de l'année. | *The finest actress of the year has been elected.* |
| Les astuces les plus courtes sont les meilleures. | *The shortest jokes are the best.* |

As with the comparative, the superlative of *petit* offers two possibilities. *Le plus petit* refers to physical size:

| C'est le plus petit appareil photo numérique (APN) qui existe. | *It's the smallest digital camera available.* |
| Irène est la plus petite fille de la classe. | *Irène is the smallest girl in the class.* |

Although *petit* by itself, like a number of other adjectives, precedes the noun, with a superlative it can follow just as easily: *Irène est la fille la plus petite de la classe.*

Moindre refers mainly to something of little value or importance:

| Il faut faire attention aux moindres détails. | *You have to attend to the tiniest details.* |
| Jeanne dort mal. Elle se réveille au moindre bruit. | *Jeanne doesn't sleep well. She wakes up at the slightest noise.* |

Whereas *moindre* could rarely, if ever, replace *le plus petit* in the literal sense, the reverse is quite possible: *Il faut faire attention aux plus petits détails / aux détails les plus petits.* Such a change would not be possible with *au moindre bruit*.

In the negative form, *moindre* strengthens the negation:

| On voulait faire du surf, mais il n'y avait pas la moindre vague ni le moindre vent. | *We wanted to do some (wind)surfing but there was not the slightest wave or the slightest wind.* |
| "Où sont-ils partis en vacances ?" "Je n'en ai pas la moindre idée." | *"Where have they gone for their vacation?" "I haven't the faintest idea."* |

Other expressions with *moindre*:

| le dernier mais pas le moindre | *last but not least* |
| la loi du moindre effort | *the law of least effort* |

As with the comparative, the adjective *mauvais* has two superlatives. The difference between *le plus mauvais* and *le pire* is that the latter points to a form of insistence, and is stronger in its application:

Pour ce spectacle, il ne restait que les plus mauvaises places ; je n'ai donc pas pris de billets.	*There only remained the poorest seats for the show so I didn't take any tickets.*
Mon accident de voiture a été le pire moment de ma vie et mon plus mauvais souvenir.	*My car accident was the worst moment of my life and my worst memory.*

The complement of the superlative is introduced by the preposition *de*, rarely by other prepositions:

La plus jeune de la famille, c'est ma fille Charlotte.	*My daughter Charlotte is the youngest in the family.*
Le Nil est le plus long fleuve du monde.	*The Nile is the longest river in the world.*
Ce poème est un des plus connus de la littérature mexicaine.	*This poem is one of the most well-known in Mexican literature.*

As opposed to English, where the superlative needs a noun (often *thing*), an adjective in the superlative can stand freely in French, as in:

Le plus simple c'est de partir maintenant.	*The easiest thing is to leave now.*
Faire le calcul en cinq minutes, c'est ça le plus difficile.	*To do the calculation in five minutes, that's the most difficult thing.*

Plus needs to be repeated if it precedes two adjectives. We quote from Marie-Éva de Villers' dictionary: "la description la plus fidèle et la plus juste du bon usage d'aujourd'hui" (2003).

The subjunctive normally follows a superlative adjective:

C'est la fille la plus douée que je connaisse.	*She's the most gifted girl I know.*

For a discussion of this construction, see Chapter 44 on the subjunctive, Section 44.4.

55.2 Relative superlatives of adverbs

The relative superlative form of adverbs is *le* + *plus/moins* + adverb:

Prenez ces fleurs. Ce sont celles qui durent le plus longtemps possible.	*Take these flowers. They are the ones that last the longest.*
Monsieur Legrand est timide. C'est lui qui prend la parole le moins souvent dans les réunions.	*Monsieur Legrand is shy. He speaks the least often in meetings.*

| les victimes les plus grièvement blessées | *the most seriously injured victims* |
| les villes les moins sérieusement touchées | *the least seriously affected cities* |

Since adverbs are invariable, they do not agree with nouns, pronouns and so on:

| Parmi toutes les étudiantes, c'est Adrienne qui vient le plus souvent / travaille le plus diligemment. | *Among all the students, Adrienne comes most often / works the most diligently.* |

Le plus and *le moins* may be used by themselves as superlative adverbs:

Les prépositions *à* et *de* sont celles qui s'emploient le plus en français.	*The prepositions *à* and *de* are those that are used the most in French.*
En général, les mois de janvier et de février sont les mois où il neige le plus en Alberta.	*In general, the months of January and February are the months when it snows the most in Alberta.*
En Italie, juillet et août sont les mois où il pleut le moins.	*In Italy, July and August are the months when it rains least.*

The adverb *bien* has the superlative equivalent *mieux*:

| En cas de grippe, le mieux est de rester au chaud et de boire beaucoup. | *When you have flu, it is best to remain in the warm and drink a lot.* |

Pis as a superlative adverb is not used these days, and there seems no point in discussing it at length.

The R3 expression *on ne peut plus* equates to *as... can be*. Rarely heard, it is reasonably common in writing: *La traversée était on ne peut plus calme; Les élèves sont on ne peut plus sages.*

55.3 The superlative with a noun

Note the construction *le plus de / le moins de* + noun:

| C'est le samedi qu'il y a le plus de monde dans les magasins. | *It's on Saturdays that there are most people in the shops.* |
| Quelles sont les professions dans lesquelles on trouve le moins d'hommes? | *Which are the professions where you find least men?* |

Part VII

Part III

56

Prepositions / Les prépositions

Given the broad range of prepositions in French, two passages are offered in this chapter. The first treats specifically prepositions as a single word, while the second deals with compound prepositions.

The first passage below analyzes the speedy and even unrestrained development of the Internet over the past two decades. The passage, of great topical importance, emphasizes its multiple and various uses, stressing not only its undoubted commercial and social benefits, its staggering communicative capacity, but also its dangers associated with, for instance, financial scams, pedophilia and even medical perils. The passage exploits the multifarious applications of prepositions. It is quite evident that *de* and *à* dominate the prepositional scene, notwithstanding the wide variety of prepositions that exist in French. One needs to differentiate between the preposition *de(s)* and the partitive article *de(s)*, which is dealt with in Chapter 8, and the uses of which, logically, are not emphasized. Note that the French term **Internet** takes a capital letter and that it is not preceded by the definite article as in English. Some translations are provided.

Les enjeux de la Toile [Issues related to the Web]
Avec le développement ahurissant [staggering] **des** technologies **de** l'information, Internet a bouleversé le comportement **des** individus en créant **de** nouveaux horizons **dans** tous les domaines. L'information circule **de** manière extrêmement rapide. L'usage **de** l'ordinateur ou **du** téléphone portable permet **d'**accéder **à** des dizaines **de** milliers **de** sites **parmi** lesquels des sites commerciaux, administratifs, sociaux, ou des pages personnelles appelées blogs. Des achats **en** ligne se développent **d'**année **en** année et transforment les règles **de** la concurrence [competition] **avec** le commerce traditionnel. Des produits et des services sont proposés **à** des prix défiant toute concurrence [unbeatable].

Le volume **du** commerce **en** ligne représente désormais plusieurs milliards [billions] **d'**euros et les distributeurs traditionnels ont été obligés **de** créer leurs propres sites commerciaux et **de** vendre **par** Internet. On y vend toute sorte **de** choses comme, par exemple, des sacs **à** main, des cannes **à** pommeau sculpté [walking sticks with sculptured knobs], des pommes **de** terre, des voitures neuves et **d'**occasion, des

logements, et différents autres objets insolites. **De** plus, Internet permet **de** voir le produit, **de** parler **avec** le vendeur, **de** lui faire part **de**
propositions **de** prix, et **de** finir **par** une décision rapide d'achat **de** ce
produit.

Des sites sociaux ont pris une ampleur stupéfiante **en** un temps
record et se sont imposés à la fois **dans** le paysage politique et **dans**
le paysage économique. **Parmi** ces sites, les plus connus sont *Facebook*,
MySpace et *Twitter*, et chacun compte environ 150 millions d'adhérents
représentant un enjeu primordial, tant d'un point **de** vue commercial
en termes **de** consommateur cible [targeted consumers] que d'un point
de vue politique **en** termes **de** destinataires d'un message politique.
Les sites sociaux véhiculent [convey] tous les problèmes **de** la société,
et chaque adhérent raconte tous les détails **de** sa vie personnelle et
même ceux **de** ses amis ou **de** ses ennemis. Les sites sociaux consistent également à rechercher des amis d'enfance, d'école ou même une
personne disparue.

Chaque adhérent s'évertue [strives to] à montrer son visage **sur** Internet et prend plaisir à raconter **par** le menu détail les événements qu'il
juge nécessaires. Il contribue à satisfaire la curiosité **des** autres internautes mais il s'expose aussi à des critiques si les détails qu'il fournit
ne correspondent pas à la réalité ou s'il s'ingénie à montrer une image
idyllique **de** sa personne. **En** outre, **devant** l'expansion débordante [over-
whelming] d'Internet, des problèmes juridiques graves se posent **au**
niveau **de** la protection **des** personnes (protection **des** mineurs, usurpa-
tion d'identité, droits d'auteurs, fraudes à la carte bancaire, etc.). **Par**
conséquent, des équipes spécialisées **de** la police se consacrent à tra-
quer les fraudeurs et s'efforcent à les empêcher **de** nuire. Ces équipes
s'acharnent [strive to] à détecter les réseaux **de** pédophiles, à repérer
les sites bancaires fictifs destinés à hameçonner [trap] les victimes, et
à attraper ceux qui s'adonnent **de** façon illégale **au** téléchargement
[downloading] **des** chansons, **des** films ou **des** ouvrages **au** détriment **de**
leurs auteurs.

Pour conclure, les internautes doivent s'abstenir **de** toute action
illégale et **de** prendre garde à ne pas tomber **dans** une arnaque [scam].
En effet, **sur** Internet, il est possible **de** tout acheter et on peut se presser
de commander un produit sans se soucier **de** son origine réelle et être
victime d'une contrefaçon [counterfeit]. Le cas est plus grave lorsque
l'on envisage d'acheter un médicament qui peut avoir de sérieuses
répercussions **pour** la santé parce que la composition **du** médicament
ne répond pas à toutes les exigences [requirements] et **aux** normes
sanitaires.

The second passage provides a straightforward overview of the violent
disturbances caused by the sharp changes in the world's weather patterns.
It also reveals the need to combat these changes, and to create governmental
organizations so that global measures may be taken collectively in the hope

of diminishing the effects of these changes on the world's more vulnerable populations. The passage includes a number of compound prepositions that are listed toward the end of this chapter. These compound prepositions are highlighted in bold in the text. A few translations are given, although the text is self-explanatory and easily accessible to non-native speakers of French.

Les perturbations climatiques

Durant les trente dernières années, les conditions climatiques ont beaucoup changé, et elles semblent résulter principalement des activités de plus en plus polluantes de l'homme. **D'après** les spécialistes du Groupe Intergouvernemental sur l'Évolution du Climat (GIEC), le réchauffement [warming] de la planète est dû à la pollution atmosphérique qui émane des gaz d'échappement [exhaust fumes] des voitures, des activités polluantes des usines et des chauffages domestiques. **À force de** polluer, le climat se dégrade, et la couche d'ozone rétrécit [is getting thinner] dangereusement selon les écologistes.

Au sujet du climat, on constate que les étés sont plus chauds et les hivers sont plus rudes que les années précédentes. **Quant aux** étés, la température augmente continuellement et se situe très souvent **au-dessus de** la moyenne saisonnière [seasonal average]. Par contre, en hiver, le froid atteint des niveaux très bas. Ces bouleversements climatiques touchent à la fois les pays du nord et les pays du sud. En Afrique, par exemple, la zone désertique s'étend davantage à une vitesse plus rapide, et les précipitations deviennent plus rares. Dans les pays européens, il fait beaucoup plus chaud qu'avant.

Par ailleurs, les catastrophes naturelles se multiplient d'une année sur l'autre. Les tempêtes sont plus violentes et causent des dégâts [damage] de grande ampleur avec des vents violents et de très fortes précipitations provoquant des inondations, des pertes humaines et des milliers de blessés **à travers** le globe terrestre. Généralement, les ménages souscrivent une assurance mais cela ne suffit pas puisque le gouvernement doit d'abord déclarer l'état de catastrophe naturelle pour que les intéressés soient indemnisés [compensated] sous cette condition. **En dehors de** cette situation, les victimes des dommages occasionnés ne peuvent pas prétendre [claim] à une quelconque indemnisation.

À propos de lutte contre le réchauffement climatique, d'importantes initiatives ont été prises **à travers** le monde, notamment l'accord ou le protocole de Kyoto qui a été signé par de nombreux pays acceptant de limiter leur taux de pollution par des mesures coercitives [coercive/compulsory] telles que la taxe carbone. Cependant, les deux grands pollueurs mondiaux, les États-Unis et la Chine, n'ont pas encore signé d'accord et refusent de prendre des mesures anti-pollution dans leur pays, craignant de heurter les intérêts de leurs entreprises et de bloquer leur croissance économique.

Competent and accurate handling of prepositions is as sure a mark as any of a speaker's ease in a foreign language. The main problem for an English speaker speaking French, or Spanish or Italian for that matter, is knowing when to use the same preposition as in English, when to use a different one, and whether to use one at all.

Reduced to its most basic function, a preposition is a linking word which may express a relationship between what precedes and what follows it. The relationship may be one of place, time, aim, means, manner, possession, quantity, measurement, cause, purpose, accompaniment, support/opposition, concession, exception or reference. It is well-known that there is not a one-to-one correspondence between relationship and preposition. Certain prepositions have a constant value in themselves, for instance *avec*, *devant*, *environ* and *parmi*, whereas others in isolation have a more indeterminate value, which may become defined to a certain extent by the meaning of the construction or context in which they occur, for instance *à*, *de*, *en*. This latter series may lose their identity altogether and become integrated into compound words. Compare for example: *une pomme de terre* and *la pomme de Jeanne* with *un sac à main* and *une canne à pommeau sculpté*.

Prepositions may link different categories of words:

adjective/noun to noun   adjective/noun to infinitive
verb to infinitive   adverb to noun
verb to noun

These groups of words function in a variety of ways, principally to introduce:

an adverbial expression: *agir par jalousie*
an indirect object: *donner à quelqu'un*
a complement of a verb: *mordu par un chien*
an adjectival expression: *la voiture de mon père*
an expression with an infinitive: *j'ai fini par me coucher*
a prepositional phrase: *à cause de mon mal de tête*

Now, which preposition to use, since there is no one-to-one correspondence between English and French? The most obvious illustration of this is the simple problem of knowing which preposition to use to link a verb and an infinitive in French. In English, the solution is straightforward: verb + *to* + infinitive (except of modal verbs *can*, *must*, *ought*, etc.), but in French the possibilities are wider: verb + *à* / *de* / *par* / *pour* / no preposition (...) + infinitive. The ellipsis within parentheses (...) is used to indicate that no preposition is required to link the infinitive (or noun or pronoun) to the verb.

The following sections offer a systematic analysis of the use of French prepositions. Note that, although for some, it is necessary in formal French to repeat a preposition before coordinated nouns and pronouns which are not closely related in sense, this does not hold true for most French speakers: *J'ai parlé avec ma mère et la directrice du collège; J'ai parlé avec sa mère et son père; J'ai fait part de l'événement à ses amis et connaissances.* Repetition of prepositions would become heavy and clumsy in these cases. Only if real insistence were required would one commonly read or hear: *"Tu as vu sa mère seulement?" "J'ai parlé avec sa mère et avec son père."* With the construction verb + preposition + infinitive, the preposition is normally repeated: *J'ai commencé à lire le journal et à faire les mots croisés; J'ai fini de préparer le repas et de faire la vaisselle.*

See Section 56.8 for a feature on varying prepositions which indicates circumstances in which the same verb may be followed by a different preposition according to meaning and register.

56.1 Verb + preposition + infinitive

The various constructions are: verb + *à* + infinitive; verb + *de* + infinitive; verb + *par* + infinitive; verb + *pour* + infinitive; verb (...) + infinitive.

56.1.1 Verb + **à** + infinitive

Elle s'est abaissée à fréquenter des gens misérables.	*She stooped low to frequent socially inferior people.*
J'ai demandé à voir le proviseur.	*I asked to see the principal.*
Il s'acharne à terminer la tâche ce soir.	*He strives to complete the task this evening.*
Ils tardent à venir.	*They are taking a long time in coming.*
On est parvenu à régler l'affaire.	*We succeeded in concluding the business.*
Elle a hésité à répondre à la question.	*She hesitated to answer the question.*
Je tenais à voir toute la famille.	*I was keen to see the whole family.*

This construction with *à* functions in the same way with all the following verbs: *s'abaisser à, aboutir à, s'accorder à, s'acharner à, s'adonner à, aimer à* (also with no preposition), *s'amuser à, s'animer à, s'appliquer à, apprendre à, s'apprêter à, aspirer à, s'assujettir à* (R3), *s'astreindre à* (R3 = to strive to), *s'attacher à, s'attendre à, s'avilir à* (R3), *avoir à, se borner à, se buter à* (to be obstinate over), *chercher à, commencer à, se complaire à* (R3), *concourir à, se consacrer à, consentir à, consister à, conspirer à, se consumer à* (R3), *continuer à, contribuer à, se décider à, demander à, se déterminer à, se dévouer à* (R3), *se disposer à, se divertir à, s'efforcer à, s'employer à, s'engager à, s'enhardir à* (R3), *s'ennuyer à, s'entraîner à, équivaloir à, s'essayer à* (R3), *s'évertuer à* (R3), *exceller à* (R3), *s'exposer à, se fatiguer à, s'habituer à, se hasarder à, hésiter à, incliner à* (R3), *s'ingénier à* (to contrive to), *insister à, s'intéresser à, se mettre à* (to begin to), *s'obstiner à, s'occuper à, s'offrir à, s'opiniâtrer à* (R3 = to insist on), *parvenir à, passer son temps à, peiner à, perdre son temps à, persévérer à, persister à, se plaire à, se plier à* (R3 = to submit to), *se prendre à*

(R3 = *to find oneself doing*), *prendre plaisir à, se préparer à, se refuser à, renoncer à, répugner à* (R3 = *to be reluctant to*), *se résigner à, se résoudre à, réussir à, revenir à, servir à, songer à, tarder à, tenir à, travailler à, veiller à* (R3 = *to be careful to*), *venir à.*

56.1.2 Verb + *de* + infinitive

Sophie s'est abstenue de commenter le cas.	*Sophie abstained from commenting on the case.*
Henri s'est avisé de partir tout de suite.	*Henri took it into his head to leave straightaway.*
L'armée menaçait de franchir la frontière.	*The army threatened to cross the frontier.*
Tu mérites de recevoir une médaille.	*You deserve to receive a medal.*
Vous avez eu raison de venir.	*You were right to come.*
Il suffit de lui envoyer un texto.	*You only have to send her a text message.*

This construction with *de* functions in the same way with all the following verbs: *s'abstenir de, accepter de, accuser de, achever de* (to finish doing), *affecter de* (R3 = *to pretend*), *s'affliger de* (R3), *ambitionner de* (R3 = *to aim to*), *s'applaudir de* (R3 = *to congratulate oneself on*), *s'arrêter de, attendre de, s'aviser de, avoir peur de, brûler de, cesser de, se charger de* (to take responsibility for), *choisir de, commencer de* (less common than *commencer à*), *comploter de, continuer de, convenir de, craindre de, décider de, dédaigner de, se dépêcher de, désespérer de, se devoir de* (R3 = *to owe it to oneself to*), *discontinuer de* (R3), *disconvenir de* (R3 = *to deny having; used mainly in the negative*), *se disculper de* (R3 = *to apologize for*), *s'efforcer de, s'empêcher de, s'empresser de, s'ennuyer de, entreprendre de, envisager de, espérer de* (R3 with *de*), *essayer de, s'étonner de, éviter de, s'excuser de, exulter de* (R3), *bien faire de, faire semblant de* (to pretend to), *se féliciter de* (to congratulate oneself on), *finir de, se flatter de, être forcé de, se garder de* (R3 = *to take care not to*), *se glorifier de* (R3), *se hâter de, s'indigner de, jurer de* (to swear to), *manquer de* (to almost do), *en avoir marre de* (R1 = *to be fed up with*), *méditer de, se mêler de, menacer de, mériter de, négliger de, être obligé de, s'occuper de, offrir de, omettre de, oublier de, parler de, se piquer de* (to pretend / to like to make out), *prendre garde de* (R3 = *to take care to*), *se presser de, prévoir de, projeter de* (to plan to), *promettre de, se proposer de, avoir raison de, redouter de* (to dread to), *refuser de, regretter de, se repentir de, résoudre de, se retenir de* (to refrain from), *risquer de, rougir de* (to blush at), *simuler de* (to pretend to), *souhaiter de, se souvenir de, suffire de, supporter de, tâcher de, tenter de, avoir tort de, se vanter de* (to boast about), *venir de* (to have just).

56.1.3 Verb + *par* + infinitive

J'ai commencé par relire le contrat.	*I began by reading the contract.*
Audrey a fini par crier comme une énergumène.	*Audrey ended up screaming like a mad person.*
Céline finira bien par gagner.	*Céline will really end up winning.*

56.1.4 Verb + *pour* + infinitive

J'ai hésité pour lui dire que...	*I hesitated to say to him that...*
Jeanne insista pour venir.	*Jeanne insisted on coming.*
Il suffisait de dix minutes pour la convaincre.	*Only ten minutes were needed to convince her.*

56.1.5 No preposition between the verb and the infinitive

J'aime le faire / y aller.	*I like to do it / to go (there).*
Tu peux partir si tu veux.	*You can go if you wish.*
On pensait lui envoyer un texto.	*We thought about sending him a text message.*
On a beau insister, il ne voulait pas venir.	*We insisted in vain, he didn't want to come.*

This construction with verb + infinitive functions in the same way with all the following verbs: *adorer, aimer, aimer mieux, aller, avoir beau, compter, daigner, détester, devoir, entendre* (R3 = to intend), *entrer, espérer, faillir, falloir, manquer, oser, penser, pouvoir, préférer, savoir, souhaiter, valoir mieux, venir, vouloir.*

56.1.6 Usage with *faire, entendre, laisser* and *voir* + infinitive group

In this group, the infinitive may have a subject and an object (which may be a *que* clause) of its own:

J'ai vu une jeune fille sortir de la salle.	*I saw a girl coming out of the room.*

Here, *jeune fille* is the subject of the infinitive *sortir*. In the following case, *jeune fille* is the subject of the infinitive while *chansons* is the object:

J'ai entendu une jeune fille chanter des chansons.	*I heard a girl singing songs.*

The following table illustrates the various constructions:

Structure	Notes	Examples
faire + infinitive with pronoun subject only	If the subject is a noun, it precedes the infinitive; if it is a pronoun, the pronoun precedes the finite verb.	Elle a entendu son père arriver; Elle l'a entendu crier.
faire, etc. + infinitive with object only	If the object is a noun, it follows the infinitive; if it is a pronoun, it precedes the finite verb.	Elle a fait réparer la voiture; J'ai entendu dire que...; J'ai entendu chanter des chansons; Elle l'a fait réparer.

Structure	Notes	Examples
faire, etc. + infinitive with subject and object	The subject figures as an indirect object; *faire* + following verb has a variety of values = *to make, to force, to get to, to have*	Elle lui fit lire le journal; Il a fait admettre à sa mère que... = *He had his mother admit that...*; Je lui ai fait voir la ville = *I took her round the town*; Je lui ai fait comprendre que... = *I let him understand that...*
entendre, laisser, voir + infinitive with noun subject only	The subject may precede or follow the infinitive. There is no difference in meaning.	Elle a entendu son père crier; Elle a entendu crier son père; Il a laissé son fils partir; Il a laissé partir son fils.
entendre, laisser, voir + infinitive with subject and object	verb + subject + infinitive + object	Nous avons entendu des garçons chanter des cantiques; J'ai vu plusieurs ouvriers construire la maison.

56.2 Verb + preposition + noun/pronoun

The various constructions are: verb + *à* + noun/pronoun; verb + *de* + noun/pronoun; verb + *avec | dans | sur* + noun/pronoun.

Whereas in English it is possible for an indirect object in an active clause to become the subject of a passive-voice clause (e.g., *My father gave me a book* > *I was given a book by my father*), in French such a transformation is not permitted in any way. In other words, French *La réception me plaît* has no passive equivalent, whereas in English *I was pleased by the reception* is normal enough. A second example: the English *The enemy was resisted* has to be approached in another way in French since *résister* takes an indirect object (i.e., *résister à*): *Ils ont résisté à l'ennemi.* This is a general characteristic of Romance languages. However, one may say: *Ils sont interdits de séjour* (*They were not allowed entry*); *Les archéologues demeuraient interdits de recherches dans le pays* (*The archaeologists were not allowed to carry out research in the country*).

56.2.1 Verb + *à* + noun/pronoun

Je me suis attendu à son arrivée.	*I expected her arrival.*
Cette arrogance lui a nui.	*This arrogance harmed him.*
Elle peut remédier à ces absences.	*She can correct these absences.*
Qui a succédé au Tsar Alexandre III ?	*Who succeeded Czar Alexander III?*
Quand tu lui as téléphoné ?	*When did you phone her?*

These constructions with *à* function in the same way with all the following verbs: *assister à, s'attendre à, se confier à, être confronté à, consentir à, convenir à, croire à, déplaire à, désobéir* (can be used in the passive voice, although not common: *L'ordre ne sera pas désobéi; Je ne serai pas désobéi*), *échapper à, faillir à, faxer à, se fier à, insulter à* (R3, although R2 when taking a direct object), *manquer à, se mêler à, nuire à, obéir à* (as with *désobéir* but more common in the passive: *se faire obéir, Elle est obéie, Mon ordre sera obéi*), *pardonner à* (also used in the passive voice: *Tu es pardonnée*), *parer à* (to parry), *participer à, penser à, plaire à, prendre part à, profiter à* (to be profitable to; *Cela profite à l'investisseur*), *remédier à, renoncer à, répondre à, répugner à* (R3; *Cela lui répugne =* He finds that repugnant), *résister à, ressembler à, ressortir à* (R3 = to be under the jurisdiction of), *réussir à, satisfaire à* (but only with things: *satisfaire à ses devoirs | à ses engagements | à la demande*; when used transitively, i.e., with no *à*, it is used of persons), *servir à, songer à, subvenir* (often in *subvenir aux besoins de quelqu'un =* to meet someone's needs), *succéder à, suffire à, surseoir à* (R3 = to delay, to defer), *survivre à, téléphoner à, toucher à* (as in *toucher à sa fin*), *vaquer à* (to attend to; *vaquer à ses affaires | ses obligations*).

56.2.2 Verb + *de* + noun/pronoun

Elle a accouché de trois enfants.	*She gave birth to three children.*
Sa famille s'accommode d'une petite voiture.	*Her family is happy with a small car.*
Sa conversation s'alimente d'astuces et de calembours.	*Her conversation thrives on jokes and play on words.*
Je conviens de mon erreur.	*I agree over my error.*
Il faut s'en méfier.	*You must be careful about him/her/it.*

This construction with *de* functions in the same way with all the following verbs: *abuser de, s'accommoder de, accoucher de, s'aider de, s'alimenter de, s'alourdir de, s'apercevoir de, (s') approcher de, s'armer de, avoir besoin/honte/peur de, changer de, se charger de, convenir de, se défier de* (R3 = to mistrust), *se démettre de* (R3 = to resign), *démissionner de, dépendre de, se dorer de* (R3 = to turn to gold), *se douter de* (to suspect), *s'échapper de, écoper de* (R1; *écoper d'une amende =* to get a fine), *s'embellir de, s'émerveiller de, s'emparer de* (to take hold of), *s'ennuyer de, s'enrichir de, s'entourer de, s'envelopper de, s'évader de, s'excuser de, s'indigner de, s'inquiéter de, s'inspirer de, se jouer de* (R3 = to make fun of), *jouir de, manquer de, médire de* (to curse), *se méfier de, se mêler de, se moquer de, s'occuper de, s'offenser de, s'offusquer de* (to be offended by), *s'orner de* (R3 = to be adorned by), *se parer de* (R3 = to be adorned with), *partir de, se passer de* (to do without), *penser de* (to have an opinion about), *profiter de, répondre de* (to be responsible for), *rire de* (R3), *se saisir de, sortir de, se souvenir de, se targuer de* (R3 = to boast), *témoigner de, triompher de, se tromper de, user de* (R3), *se vanter de, vivre de.*

56.2.3 Verb + *avec* / *dans* / *sur* + noun/pronoun

Le verbe s'accorde avec le sujet.	*The verb agrees with the subject.*
Il faut se familiariser avec cette nouvelle méthode.	*You must familiarize yourself with this new method.*

Il a toujours rivalisé avec son cousin pour arriver le premier.	*He has always emulated his cousin to be in first place.*
Les ingénieurs se sont solidarisés avec les ouvriers au cours de la grève.	*The engineers expressed solidarity with the workers during the strike.*
Pourquoi s'embarquer dans une affaire si louche ?	*Why embark on such a shady venture?*
Les deux associés se sont accordés sur la meilleure méthode à adopter.	*The two associates agreed on the best method to adopt.*
Ils se sont branchés sur Radio-Canada.	*They connected up to Radio-Canada.*
J'insiste sur mes droits.	*I insist on my rights.*
Renseigne-toi sur l'horaire.	*Get the information on the times.*

There is sometimes the possibility of choice of preposition with certain verbs:

Le Sénat a débattu / a discuté (de) la question.	*The Senate debated/discussed the question.*
Il n'est pas facile de juger (de) la hauteur de cet arbre.	*It's not easy to judge the height of this tree.*
Qu'est-ce qu'on fait avec/de la voiture ? On la met au garage ?	*What do we do with the car? Put it in the garage?*

Here are some other verbs that offer two possibilities, bearing in mind that no preposition is also a possibility, indicated thus (. . .): *anticiper* + (. . .) / *sur, débattre* + (. . .) / *de, délibérer* (R3) + (. . .) / *de, discuter* + (. . .) / *de, faire* + *avec/de, s'identifier* + *à/avec, informer* + *de/sur, inscrire* + *dans/sur, s'intégrer* + *à/dans, juger* + (. . .) / *de* (= *to estimate*), *juger* + *par/sur* (*to judge by*), *méditer* + (. . .) / *sur, se passionner* + *de/pour, présider* + (. . .) / *à, réfléchir* + *à/sur, rêver* + *à/sur* (more common than *à*), *sauver la vie* + *à/de quelqu'un, traiter* (. . .) / *de.*

56.3 Verb + direct object + preposition + infinitive

56.3.1 Verb + direct object + *à* + infinitive

Le comité m'a autorisée à partir.	*The committee authorized me to go.*
Cette idée m'amène à dire que…	*This idea brings me to say that…*
La défaite les a condamnés à souffrir bien des années sous le joug étranger.	*The defeat condemned them to suffer many years under the foreign yoke.*
Cela ne vous engage pas à travailler toute la semaine.	*That does not commit you to working all week.*

This construction with *à* functions in the same way with all the following verbs: *aider à, amener à, appeler à, autoriser à, condamner à, conduire à, contraindre à* (R3), *convier à, décider à, déterminer à, encourager à, entraîner à, exhorter à* (R3), *forcer à, inviter à, pousser à.*

56.3.2 Verb + direct object + *de* + infinitive

La police l'a accusée d'avoir commis le crime.	*The police accused her of committing the crime.*
Le maire m'a empêché de voter.	*The mayor prevented me from voting.*
Je te prie de me fournir tous les détails.	*I beg you to let me have all the details.*
Je tiens à te remercier de m'avoir aidée.	*I am keen to thank you for helping me.*

This construction with *de* functions in the same way with all the following verbs: *accuser de, avertir de, conjurer de* (R3 = to beg), *contraindre de* (R3), *décourager de, défier de* (to challenge), *dissuader de, empêcher de, féliciter de, implorer de* (R3), *intéresser de* (but used impersonally), *menacer de, persuader de, prier de, remercier de, sommer de* (R3 = to command / to summon), *soupçonner de, supplier de* (R3 = to beg).

56.4 Verb + preposition + noun/pronoun + preposition + infinitive

56.4.1 Verb + *à* + noun/pronoun + *de* + infinitive

Il m'appartenait/incombait de signer le contrat tout de suite.	*It was incumbent upon me to sign the contract immediately.*
Il a (dé)conseillé à son épouse d'y aller.	*He dissuaded/advised his wife from going / not to go.*
Je lui ai demandé/dit de venir.	*I asked/told him to come.*
Elle savait gré à son père de l'aider.	*She was grateful to her father for helping her.*
Il pardonne à son amie de l'avoir omis.	*He excused his friend for omitting him.*
Il lui tardait de la revoir.	*He longed to see her again.*

This construction with *à... de* functions in the same way with all the following verbs, bearing in mind that the active–passive transformation, so common in English, is not possible (*My father gave me the book* > *I was given the book by my father*): *appartenir* (impersonal) *à... de, arriver* (impersonal) *à... de, commander à... de, conseiller à... de, déconseiller à... de, défendre à... de, demander à... de, dire à... de, imposer à... de, être impossible à... de, incomber* (R3; impersonal) *à... de, interdire à... de, ordonner à... de, pardonner à... de, permettre à... de, peser* (R3; impersonal) *à... de, plaire* (impersonal) *à... de, proposer à... de, reprocher à... de, répugner* (R3; impersonal) *à... de, savoir gré à... de, faire signe à... de, souhaiter à ... de, suggérer à... de, tarder* (impersonal) *à... de, en vouloir à... de.*

56.4.2 Verb + *à* + noun/pronoun + *à* + infinitive, only with *apprendre*

La professeure lui a appris à lire l'arabe.	*The teacher taught him to read Arabic.*
Le père a appris à sa fille à étudier le chinois.	*The father taught his daughter to study Chinese.*

(*Enseigner* does not function in this way: only *enseigner quelque chose à quelqu'un*.)

54.4.3 Verb + *de* + noun/pronoun + *pour* + infinitive, only with *s'inspirer*

L'étudiante s'est inspirée de Goya pour peindre de beaux tableaux.	*The student was inspired by Goya to create fine paintings.*

56.5 Verb + direct object + preposition + noun/pronoun

56.5.1 Verb + direct object + *à* + noun/pronoun

Note that the preposition is most frequently *à* in French and *from* in English, for instance:

Ce refus lui aliène toutes les sympathies.	*This refusal removed all interest in him.*
La sœur a caché le cadeau à son frère.	*The sister hid the present from her brother.*
La voiture a coûté vingt mille euros à mon père.	*The car cost my father twenty thousand euros.*
J'ai évité à mon fils la tâche d'envoyer le texto.	*I removed the need for my son to send the text message.*
Le capitaine imposa le silence à ses hommes.	*The captain demanded silence from his men.*
J'ai acheté le micro-ondes à mon cousin.	*I bought the microwave from my cousin.*

Note that *acheter quelque chose à quelqu'un* is ambiguous: *to buy something from/for someone*. The context is necessary to understand the meaning. This construction with *à* functions in the same way with all the following verbs: *accommoder à* (R3), *accorder à, acheter à, aliéner à, apprendre à, arracher à, assigner à, associer à, cacher à, chercher à, commander à, communiquer à, comparer à, conférer à, confier à, coûter à, décerner à* (R3 = to bestow), *défendre à, demander à, dérober à, devoir à, dissimuler à, donner à, emprunter à, enlever à, enseigner à, envier à, envoyer . . . à, épargner . . . à, éviter . . . à, exprimer . . . à, extorquer . . . à, fournir à, garantir à, imposer à, imprimer à, inspirer à, interdire à, intéresser à, manifester à, montrer à, octroyer à* (R3 = to grant), *ôter à, pardonner à, payer à, permettre à, prêcher à, prendre à, préparer à, présenter à, prodiguer à* (R3 = to lavish), *rappeler à, réclamer à, recommander à, refuser à, reprendre à, reprocher à, réserver à, restituer à* (to restore), *retirer à, retrancher à* (to take away, to cut out), *souhaiter à, soustraire à (to subtract, to take away), substituer à, transmettre à, voler à.*

56.5.2 Verb + direct object + *de* + noun/pronoun

On l'a accusée de vol.	*She was accused of theft.*
J'ai débarrassé la pièce de toutes les babioles.	*I cleared all the trinkets from the room.*
Il m'a excusée de l'erreur.	*He excused me of the error.*
Jeanne m'a félicité de ma victoire.	*Jeanne congratulated me on my victory.*
Préviens-moi de ton arrivée.	*Let me know when you come / are coming.*

This construction with *de* functions in the same way with all the following verbs: *absoudre de* (R3 = to absolve), *accabler de* (overwhelm), *accuser de*, *approcher de*, *arracher de*, *assurer de*, *avertir de*, *aviser de*, *bombarder de*, *charger de*, *complimenter de*, *débarrasser de*, *décharger de*, *dégoûter de*, *délivrer de*, *détourner de* (to divert), *dispenser de* (to give, to hand out), *écarter de*, *éloigner de*, *enlever de*, *excuser de*, *exempter de*, *féliciter de*, *frapper de*, *informer de*, *libérer de*, *menacer de*, *ôter de*, *persuader de*, *prévenir de*, *remercier de*, *traiter de*.

56.5.3 Verb + direct object + **avec/dans/par** + noun/pronoun

J'ai comparé le tableau avec un Monet.	*I compared the painting with a Monet.*
Audrey a glané les informations dans l'encyclopédie.	*Audrey gleaned the information from the encyclopedia.*
Notre héroïne a pris les documents dans le tiroir.	*Our heroine took the documents from the drawer.*
Lucile puisa (R3) des confetti dans son sac.	*Lucile drew confetti from her bag.*
Adeline a puisé ses idées dans un dictionnaire.	*Adeline culled her ideas from a dictionary.*
Mon père a remplacé sa BM par une Ferrari.	*My father replaced his BMW with a Ferrari.*

56.6 Noun + preposition + infinitive

56.6.1 Noun + *à* + infinitive

Son acharnement à compléter le travail m'étonna.	*Her endeavor in completing the work surprised me.*
Il avait une extraordinaire habileté à défendre la cause de la victime.	*He had an extraordinary skill in defending the victim's cause.*
Quelle ardeur à lutter pour la vérité !	*What ardor in struggling for the truth!*

This construction with *à* functions in the same way with all the following nouns: *acharnement à, aisance à, aptitude à, avidité à, détermination à, difficulté à, facilité à, habileté à, hésitation à, impuissance à, insistance à, intérêt à, persistance à, regret à, répugnance à, retard à*. Note: *un homme à craindre = a man to be feared; un homme à tout faire = a handy man*

56.6.2 Noun + *de* + infinitive

Je me suis trouvé dans l'impossibilité de partir.	*I found myself unable to go.*
Sa volonté de gagner me bouleversa.	*Her will to win staggered me.*
Ma mère a saisi l'opportunité de consulter un spécialiste.	*My mother seized the chance to see a consultant.*
J'ai demandé la permission de m'y rendre.	*I asked for permission to go (there).*
Irène avait la rage de réussir.	*Irène was passionate about succeeding.*

This construction with *de* functions in the same way with all the following nouns: *autorisation de, besoin de, capacité de, désir de, honte de, impossibilité de, incapacité de, nécessité de, obligation de, occasion de, plaisir de*. Note the use of *de* + infinitive with: *avoir honte/les moyens/peur/raison/le temps/tort, faire semblant*:

J'avais honte de parler de mon erreur.	*I was ashamed to speak of my error.*
Tu as raison/tort de partir maintenant.	*You are right/wrong to go now.*

Raison is normally followed by *de*, not *pour*, with a noun or pronoun: *Je ne me suis pas expliqué la raison de son refus*. However, one says *la raison pour laquelle* + relative clause: *la raison pour laquelle elle envoya le message* (*pourquoi* = *why* could not be used here).

56.7 Adjective + preposition + infinitive

56.7.1 Adjective + *à* + infinitive

Qu'est-ce qu'elle est lente à raisonner !	*Isn't she slow in reasoning!*
Ils étaient assis à lire les journaux quand...	*They were sitting reading the newspapers when...*
Marie est encline à se taire.	*Marie is inclined to remain silent.*
Il faut créer un barrage, quitte à inonder des fermes.	*We have to create a dam, at the risk of flooding some farms.*

This construction with *à* functions in the same way with all the following adjectives: *apte à, décidé à, déterminé à, disposé à, fondé à, habile à, long à, préparé* à, prêt à, prompt à, propre à (calculated to), résolu à, réticent à (R3), unanime à (also pour). Note: *C'est lourd à porter* = It's heavy to carry; *C'est facile à faire*; *C'est agréable à entendre*; *Il est le premier/seul/deuxième/dernier à arriver.*

56.7.2 Adjective + *de* + infinitive

"Je suis bien curieux de connaître Caloub" (Gide 1925, p. 499).	"I really am curious to know Caloub."
Vous êtes libres de partir.	*You are free to go.*
On est heureux de faire de la planche à voile.	*We are happy to do some windsurfing.*
Je suis ravie de faire sa connaissance.	*I am delighted to know him.*

This construction with *de* functions in the same way with all the following adjectives: *avide de* (**d** is pronounced twice here), *capable de, certain de, content de, désireux de* (R3), *libre de, mécontent de, reconnaissant de, responsable de, satisfait de, sûr de*. Note: *être content / heureux de quelque chose* but *être content/heureux avec quelqu'un*: *J'étais heureuse de sa réponse / de partir le lendemain* and *Je suis heureuse avec mon mari*.

Note also the use of *de* with many past participles of an abstract and passive nature: *adoré de, aimé de, apprécié de, connu de, couronné de, détesté de, épris de* (in love with), *estimé de, haï de, honoré de, méconnu de, méprisé de, mésestimé de; C'est une actrice aimée/adorée/appréciée de tout le monde; Un romancier estimé de tous les critiques / couronné de succès / connu du grand public*. When the agent is active, *par* is frequently used: *Jean a été mordu par son chien; Mon père a été frappé par le voleur. Accompagné* and *suivi* offer a choice: *accompagnée/suivie par un / d'un chien. Pour* must be used after *trop* and *assez*:

Marie est assez/trop grande pour le faire.	*Marie is tall enough / too tall to do it.*

56.8 Varying prepositions

In certain cases, depending on meaning, register, euphony, context or construction, the preposition following a verb or related expression varies. It goes without saying that one should fit the right preposition with the right set of circumstances. The following list provides an attempt to highlight the most important verbs and expressions involved in these prepositional variations:

abuser

Il abuse (R3) le public.	*He deceives the public.*
Elle abuse de la bonté de son amie.	*She takes advantage of her friend's good nature.*
Le père a abusé de sa fille.	*The father abused his daughter.*

accommoder

Il accommode (R3) sa conduite à toutes les circonstances.	*He adapts his behavior to all circumstances.*
Je m'accommoderai de ce logement modeste.	*I'll accept this modest accommodation.*

s'accorder

Tout le monde s'accorde à reconnaître que c'est le meilleur violoniste.	*Everyone agrees in recognizing he's the best violinist.*
Le verbe s'accorde avec le nom.	*The verb agrees with the noun.*
Ils se sont accordés sur le traité de paix.	*They agreed over the peace treaty.*

achever

Il acheva de se ruiner.	*He ended up ruining himself.*
Elle commença par rire, acheva par pleurer.	*She began by laughing, ended up crying.*

aimer

J'aime à croire (R3) qu'ils ont raison.	*I like to think they are right.*
Sophie aime jouer de la guitare.	*Sophie likes playing the guitar.*
J'aime mieux travailler que de jouer.	*I prefer working to playing.*

Note the *de* here.

arracher

Il arracha la chemise à son frère.	*He tore the shirt from his brother.*
Il arracha le coussin du fauteuil.	*He tore the cushion from the armchair.*

Note the use of *à* with persons and *de* with things, although *à* is also possible with things. The same comment applies to *enlever*.

assurer

Je lui ai assuré qu'il n'y avait rien à craindre.	*I assured her there was nothing to fear.*
Assure-le de mon respect.	*Assure him of my respect.*

The first sentence above suggests affirmation, the second guarantee.

attendre

Stéphanie attendait pour/de (R3) partir.	*Stéphanie waited to go.*
Francis ne s'attendait pas à cette insulte.	*Francis didn't expect this insult.*

Louise s'attend à ce qu'il revienne.	*Louise expects him to come back.*
J'attendais le bateau.	*I was waiting for the boat.*

se battre

David s'est battu avec son frère.	*Davis fought his brother/with his brother.*

This is ambiguous: the sentence above could mean either *against* or *on the same side*.

Ils se sont battus contre l'ennemi.	*They fought the enemy.*

changer

Il faut changer l'ordinateur.	*You must change the computer.*
Je change de vêtements.	*I am changing clothes.*
Je vais me changer.	*I'm going to change clothes.*

In the first case: changing one set of clothes for another, even in a shop; in the second, merely to change for a purpose.

Aurélie a changé ses meubles contre des tableaux.	*Aurélie exchanged her furniture for paintings.*
Cédric a changé d'avis.	*Cédric changed his mind.*
L'alchimiste a changé le fer en or.	*The alchimist changed iron into gold.*
J'ai changé quelques dollars en euros.	*I changed some dollars into euros.*

commencer

Mon père a commencé par dire que...	*My father began by saying that...*
Christophe a commencé sa conférence en disant que...	*Christophe began his talk by saying that...*
Françoise a commencé à/d'avoir des regrets.	*Françoise began to have regrets.*

Note that *de* may replace *à* in R3 language to avoid the awkwardness of two contiguous vowels. See *continuer*.

comparer

La prof a comparé les résultats des deux classes.	*The teacher compared the results of the two classes.*
J'aime toujours comparer le printemps à la jeunesse.	*I always love to compare spring to youth.*

La banque a comparé ma signature avec celle consignée au dossier.	*The bank compared my signature with the one deposited in my record.*

The authors make no claim to establish a difference between *à* and *avec* in the second and third sentences above. It is true that the two examples for the two prepositions fit very well.

compter

Annick comptait partir demain.	*Annick was counting on leaving tomorrow.*
Il faut compter avec Axelle.	*You have to take Axelle into consideration.*
Attention ! Je compte sur toi.	*Careful! I'm relying on you.*

Note that *escompter* takes no preposition: *escompter un résultat*.

(se) confier

Marcel se confie à moi.	*Marcel trusts me.*
En mon absence, je te confie ma maison.	*In my absence, I leave my house in your hands.*
Je te fais confiance.	*I trust you.*

connaître / se connaître

Marine s'y connaît.	*Marine is an expert (on the subject).*
Pierre se connaît en tableaux.	*Pierre is an expert on painting.*
J'ai connu mon épouse à Rome.	*I came to know my wife in Rome.*
J'ai fait la connaissance de ma femme à Mexico.	*I met my wife in Mexico City.*
Il a fait connaissance avec elle l'an dernier.	*He met her last year.*

consentir

Les deux pays limitrophes ont consenti un traité.	*The two neighboring countries authorized a treaty.*
J'ai consenti à son séjour à l'étranger.	*I consented to his stay abroad.*

construire

une maison construite de pierre	*a stone-built house*
une maison construite en pierre	*a house built in stone*

Much play has been made of *de* and *en* here. The consensus is that *en* highlights the material more.

continuer

À and *de* are equally common with *continuer*:

Elle continue à chanter.	*She continues to sing.*
Elle continue d'aimer la musique.	*She continues to love music.*

The second example shows how *de* avoids the awkwardness of the hiatus. See *commencer*.

contraindre

Adrienne s'est vue contrainte de donner son accord.	*Adrienne was constrained to give her agreement.*
Ils m'ont contraint à partir.	*They constrained me to go.*

As with *obliger* and *forcer*, the past participle is followed by *de* while the active form is followed by *à*.

convenir

Cet arrangement n'a pas convenu à Jean.	*This arrangement did not suit Jean.*
Ils sont convenus de venir.	*They agreed to come.*
Nous sommes convenus d'une rencontre en juin.	*We agreed on a June meeting.*

Note that when *convenir* means *to suit*, it is conjugated with *avoir*. When it means *to agree*, it is conjugated with *être*. This difference is not observed by many French speakers. The use of *être* here is R3. *Avoir* is commonly used in all circumstances.

courir

Le petit passe son temps à courir dans le jardin.	*The child spends his time running in the garden.*
Courir le cent mètres en 9, 5 (9 virgule 5), c'est battre le record du Jamaïquain Bolt.	*Running the hundred meters in 9 point five is to beat the Jamaican Bolt's record.*
Il court (après) les filles tous les week-ends.	*He's chasing skirts every weekend.*
Adeline court les facultés pour trouver un cursus qui lui convient.	*Adeline is visiting all the universities to find a suitable program.*

croire

Elle croit sincèrement à la médecine.	*She sincerely believes in medicine (i.e. that medicine is a valid discipline).*
Tu crois en Dieu, toi?	*Do you believe in God?*

Moi, je crois en l'homme, comme Camus.	*Me, I believe in mankind, like Camus.*
Ce qui est certain, c'est que je ne crois pas au diable, aux fantômes non plus.	*What's certain is I don't believe in the devil, or in ghosts.*
Je crois devoir te préciser que...	*I think I must point out to you that...*

décider

Ce raisonnement m'a décidée à partir.	*This reasoning persuaded me to leave.*
C'est à toi de décider de mon avenir.	*It is for you to decide on my future.*
J'ai décidé d'y aller.	*I decided to go.*
Elle s'est décidée à abandonner les études.	*She decided to abandon her studies.*

Note that *décider de* suggests quickly while *se décider à* suggests careful deliberation.

Marie s'est décidée pour le Parti Socialiste.	*Marie opted for the Socialist Party.*

demander

J'ai demandé à partir.	*I asked to leave.*
Ils lui ont demandé de partir.	*He was asked to leave.*

devoir

Sophie doit faire ses devoirs.	*Sophie must do her homework.*
Tu lui dois cent dollars.	*You owe him a hundred dollars.*
Tu te dois à (R3) toi-même de bien travailler.	*You owe it to yourself to work hard.*

dire

Je lui ai dit de partir.	*I told him to go.*
J'ai dit avoir lu le livre.	*I said I had read the book.*
Il se dit notre allié mais je ne le crois pas.	*He claims to be our ally but I don't believe him.*
Ça se dit pas en français.	*You don't say that in French.*

divorcer

Ils ont divorcé.	*They divorced / got a divorce.*
Il a divorcé avec / d'avec / de sa femme l'an dernier.	*He divorced his wife last year.*
Je suis divorcé.	*I am divorced.*

douter

Je ne doute pas de son honnêteté.	*I don't doubt her honesty.*
La petite ne se doute pas du tout de la fête qui a été organisée.	*The little girl doesn't suspect the party that has been organized.*
Je m'en doutais.	*That's what I suspected.*

Note: douter = *to doubt*; se douter de = *to suspect*.

avoir le / être en droit

J'ai gagné, donc j'ai droit à un prix.	*I've won so I have a right to a prize.*
Tu as le droit de choisir.	*You have the right to choose.*
Les parents ne sont plus en droit de punir leurs enfants.	*Parents no longer have the right to punish their children.*

échapper

Le voleur a échappé à la police.	*The thief avoided the police.*
Personne n'échappe à la mort.	*No one escapes death.*
Ils se sont échappés de l'ambuscade.	*They got clear from the ambush.*
Deux hommes se sont échappés de la prison.	*Two men escaped from prison.*
Je l'ai échappée belle.	*I had a narrow escape.*

Note that *s'échapper d'une prison* is possible in writing but rarely, if ever, heard. In speech, one uses *s'evader d'une prison. Échapper à la prison* is normal = *to escape (going to) prison.*

s'efforcer

Les deux étudiants se sont efforcés d'atteindre l'objectif.	*The two students strove to reach their objective.*
Ils s'efforcèrent à l'entraîner hors de la maison.	*They struggled to drag her from the house.*
Les deux dames s'efforcèrent à la politesse.	*The two ladies made great efforts to be polite.*

By far the more usual construction is with *de*. À is R3 and has literary resonances.

enlever

See *arracher* above.

ennuyer

Je m'ennuyais à/d'attendre.	*I was bored waiting.*
Marie s'ennuie de son petit ami.	*Marie misses her boyfriend.*

Il m'ennuie d'être si longtemps
séparé de toi.

I miss you so long away from me (here
used impersonally).

entendre

J'entendis un bruit singulier.

I heard a strange noise.

Mon fils s'entend à la peinture /
en peinture (R3).

My son is an expert on painting.

Je m'entends (bien) avec elle.

I get on well with her.

Ils s'entendent comme larrons
en foire.

They are as thick as thieves.

Ils ne s'entendent pas.

They don't get on well.

Entendons-nous bien. . .

Let's get this straight. . .

entrer

La petite est entrée au collège en
septembre dernier.

*The little girl started school last
September.*

Je t'ai vu entrer dans le bâtiment.

I saw you go into the building.

The first sentence suggests entering for the first time, and therefore has a
metaphoric application while the second is much more literal. *Entrer* is also
used transitively: *entrer un code dans l'ordinateur*; *L'infirmière entra l'aiguille
dans la veine*; *Elle entra la clé dans la serrure*.

espérer

J'espère venir.

I hope to come.

Je ne puis espérer de (R3) recevoir
la réponse.

I cannot hope to receive a reply.

The use of *de* would be common in past centuries, in Chateaubriand and
Flaubert for instance.

se fâcher

Pourquoi tu te fâches avec ton
frangin ?

*Why do you get angry with your
brother?*

Ils se sont fâchés contre ces
importuns.

*They got angry with these awkward
people.*

faillir (only a few parts of this verb are used)

J'ai failli glisser.

I almost slipped.

Le héros faillit à sa promesse (R3).

The hero broke his promise.

faire

Qu'est-ce que t'as fait avec/de
mon USB ?

*What have you done with my memory
stick?*

Il a fait son devoir de/par lui-même.	*He did his homework by himself.*
Sophie ne fait que d'entrer / que d'arriver / que de s'éveiller.	*Sophie has just come in / arrived / woken up.*
Je viens de faire construire un garage.	*I've just had a garage built.*

se familiariser avec

Il faut se familiariser avec les nouvelles méthodes.	*You must get used to the new methods.*
Je suis familière avec/de plusieurs langues.	*I am familiar with several languages.*

se fier / (se) / confier / défier / se méfier

Je me fie à mon ami.	*I trust my friend.*
Jeanne m'a confié son secret.	*Jeanne confided in me with her secret.*
Il faut se défier/méfier de cette bande-là.	*Be careful of that bunch.*

Note: *se défier* = R3.

Quelle dévergondée ! Elle défie même la police.	*What a brazen hussy! She even defies the police.*

finir

La conférencière a fini par dire que...	*The speaker ended by saying that...*
Elle a fini sa conférence en disant que...	*She finished her talk saying that...*
J'ai fini d'écrire mon dossier attaché.	*I've finished writing my attachment.*

forcer

Ses parents ne le forcent pas à étudier.	*His parents don't make him study.*
Je ne suis pas forcée d'étudier.	*I am not obliged to study.*

The active voice uses *à* while the passive voice uses *de*; see also *contraindre* and *obliger*.

habituer

Il faut s'habituer à parler en public.	*You must get used to speaking in public.*
Sabrina a l'habitude de se coucher tôt.	*Sabrina usually goes to bed early.*

hésiter

Elle n'a pas hésité à/pour répondre.	*She didn't hesitate in replying.*
Notre héroïne hésitait entre le vice et la vertu.	*Our heroine hesitated between vice and virtue.*
J'hésite toujours sur le choix d'une profession.	*I am still hesitating over the choice of a profession.*

insister

J'insiste à/pour t'accompagner.	*I insist on going with you.*
Pourquoi tu insistes pour que j'y aille ?	*Why do you insist on my going?*
Papa insiste sur le fait que le voyage est nécessaire.	*Pa insists that the journey is necessary.*
Ce qui m'étonne, c'est son insistance à ne lire que du Tolstoï.	*What surprises me is his insistence on just reading Tolstoy.*

insulter

La mari a insulté sa femme.	*The husband insulted his wife.*
Le luxe insulte à (R3) la misère publique.	*Luxury is an insult to public poverty.*

intéresser

Je m'intéresse à partir pour l'Alaska.	*I am interested in leaving for Alaska.*
Tu as intérêt à faire des économies.	*It is of interest for you to save.*
Il y a intérêt à payer maintenant.	*You have an interest in paying now.*
Je suis intéressé par tes propos.	*I am interested in your remarks.*
Elle est inintéressée / peu intéressée par tes idées.	*She is uninterested / little interested in your ideas.*
Cela m'intéresse de composer une symphonie.	*It interests me to compose a symphony.*
Un intérêt pour l'histoire, ça c'est bien.	*An interest in history, that's good.*
Il est intéressant de voir comment vivent ces gens-là.	*It's interesting to see how those people live.*
Pourquoi tu te désintéresses de mes propos ?	*Why aren't you interested in my remarks?*

jouer

Sarah Bernhardt est une grande tragédienne qui joue tous les grands rôles.	*Sarah Bernhardt is a great tragedy actress who plays all the great roles.*

Il a joué Hamlet / King Lear / Macbeth.	He has played Hamlet / King Lear / Macbeth.
Je voudrais jouer du Chopin au violon.	I'd like to play Chopin on the violin.
Jouer du piano, voilà mon rêve !	To play the piano, that's my dream.
On joue au foot cet après-midi ?	A game of soccer this afternoon?

Note that *jouer de* is used for an instrument; *jouer au* is used for sport.

Cette sonate se joue en duo.	This sonata is played as a duet.
Mon copain m'a joué un mauvais tour.	My friend played a dirty trick on me.
Ils se sont joués de (R3) leur directeur.	They made fun of their principal.

manquer

Deux livres manquent. Où sont-ils ?	Two books are missing. Where are they?
La famille manque de pain.	The family lacks bread.
Le pain manque à la famille.	The family lacks bread.
Il ne faut pas manquer une bonne occasion de se taire.	Don't miss a good chance to keep quiet.
Tu risques de manquer ton avion / ton train.	You risk missing your airplane/train.

Also here: *manquer l'école / un cours / la messe.*

Ils se sont manqués de quelques minutes seulement.	They missed each other just by a few minutes.
Ma patrie me manque.	I miss my homeland.
L'épouse dit au mari : "Tu m'as beaucoup manqué."	The wife said to the husband: "I missed you a lot."
Le mari dit à son épouse : "Je t'ai beaucoup manqué."	The husband said to his wife: "You have missed me a lot."

The use of *manquer* in these last two sentences has exactly the same meaning. French speakers in Quebec have serious problems over this use, diverted as they are by the use of the English *to miss*, which occurs in an opposite meaning. A French speaker in Quebec could easily say *Je vous ai manqué* instead of *Vous nous avez manqué = I missed you*. There is also considerable uncertainty over agreement with *manquer* and the past participle. Does the husband say *Je t'ai manqué* or *manquée* to his wife? In other words, is the pronoun *te* direct or indirect? If it is indirect, as with *manquer* in the sense of *to be lacking to* (*Le pain leur a manqué*), then there is no agreement. Note, however, that in the sentence above (*Ils se sont manqués de quelques minutes*) there is agreement with the past participle since the meaning is different: *to fail to see (someone)*. Also:

Ne manque pas de venir.   *Don't fail to come.*

Note: *manquer de* does not mean *to fail to*. It suggests the idea of "almost": *J'ai manqué (de) tomber = I almost fell.* Notice also the indirect use: *manquer à un engagement | à un devoir | à une promesse.*

marier

Le prêtre les a mariés.	*The priest married them.*
Elle s'est mariée avec le fils du maire.	*She married the mayor's son.*
Il est marié à/avec une Péruvienne.	*He's married to a Peruvian.*
Elle a marié sa fille à/avec un ingénieur.	*She married her daughter to an engineer.*

mêler

Se mêlant à la foule, il disparut.	*Mingling with the crowd, he disappeared.*
Pourquoi tu te mêles de la politique ?	*Why do you meddle in politics?*
Voilà qu'elle se mêle de nous donner des conseils.	*See her giving us advice.*

obliger

See *forcer* above.

occuper

Maman, tu t'occupes de la petite ?	*Mom, can you deal with the baby?*
J'étais toujours occupée à envoyer des mails.	*I was always busy sending e-mails.*
La députée s'occupait à/d'envoyer des tracts.	*The parlementarian was busy sending tracts.*

ôter

See *arracher* above.

participer

Ma femme participait à ma joie.	*My wife shared in my joy.*
Le mulet participe de (R3) l'âne et du cheval.	*The mule is part donkey and part horse.*
Sa participation au/dans le débat me surprit.	*Her participation in the debate surprised me.*

passionner

Mon fils se passionne pour le foot.	*My son is passionate about soccer.*
Ma fille est passionnée de natation.	*My daughter is mad about swimming.*
Elle éprouvait une profonde passion pour lui.	*She felt a deep passion for him.*
J'ai la passion du Mexique.	*I have a passion for Mexico.*

payer

J'ai payé le livre à Amazon.fr.	*I paid for the book through Amazon.*
J'ai payé trente euros à mon ami.	*I paid my friend thirty euros.*
J'ai payé vingt dollars le livre au libraire.	*I paid the bookseller twenty dollars for the book.*

pénétrer

Louise pénétra dans le jardin.	*Louise went into the garden.*
Comment pénétrer ce mystère / le marché?	*How can you understand this mystery / penetrate the market?*

Dans is used more literally; the construction with no preposition applies to figurative usage.

penser

Je pense souvent à ma mère décédée.	*I often think of my mother who has passed away.*
Que penses-tu de Hemingway?	*What do you think of Hemingway?*
La famille pense partir en vacances pour Noël.	*The family is thinking of going on holiday for Christmas.*

prendre

J'ai pris le jouet à ma sœur.	*I took the toy from my sister.*
Elle a pris le portefeuille dans le tiroir.	*She took the billfold/wallet from the drawer.*
Laurent a pris le livre sur la table.	*Laurent took the book from the table.*

If *sortir* were used in the second case, the wording would be *sortir du tiroir*. If *enlever/ôter* were used in the third case, the wording would be *enlever/ôter de la table.*

prévoir

Le mariage était prévu pour mai.	*The wedding was planned for May.*
J'avais prévu de partir demain.	*I had planned to leave tomorrow.*

profiter

Il faut profiter de l'occasion.	*You have to take advantage of the chance.*
Qu'est-ce que cela profite à l'homme s'il gagne des millions ?	*What does it profit the man if he wins millions?*

rappeler

J'ai rappelé l'incident à mon père.	*I reminded my father of the incident.*
Tu te rappelles l'événement ?	*Can you remember the event?*

Note the very common usage of *Tu te rappelles de l'événement ?* on analogy with *Tu te souviens de l'événement ?* This construction is censured but is gaining ground.

refuser

Je refuse d'y aller.	*I refuse to go.*
Sophie se refuse à me payer l'entrée.	*Sophie refuses to pay for my entry.*
Pourquoi tu refuses à ton collègue le droit de nous accompagner ?	*Why do you deny your colleague the right to go with us?*

répondre

Réponds à ma question.	*Answer my question.*
Tu dois répondre de tes actes.	*You must take responsibility for your actions.*

répugner

Le personnage répugna (R3) à s'y engager.	*The character was reluctant to commit himself.*
Cet homme répugne à mon père (R3).	*My father finds that man repugnant.*
Cela lui répugne de contacter la police.	*He is reluctant to contact the police.*

résoudre

Tu as résolu la question ?	*Have you solved the question?*

résoudre de | se résoudre à

See *décider* above.

ressortir

Elle est entrée dans la maison pour en ressortir tout de suite après.	*She entered the house and came out again immediately afterwards.*
Cette affaire ressortit (R3) au juge de paix.	*This business is to be decided by the Justice of the Peace.*

Note that *il ressort = he goes out*; *cela ressortit de = that is the responsibilty of*. In this latter meaning, *ressortir* is conjugated like *finir*. Such a difference is not observed by many French people.

réussir

Émilie a réussi un grand exploit.	*Émilie pulled off a great feat.*
On a réussi à terminer la tâche.	*We succeeded in finishing the job.*
Tout lui réussit.	*He's successful in everything.*

satisfaire

L'élève satisfait son maître.	*The pupil satisfies his master.*
Comment satisfaire à cette promesse / à cette obligation / à ce besoin ?	*How can I meet this promise / this obligation / this need?*
Je suis satisfaite de ton travail.	*I am satisfied with your work.*

servir

Maman, je peux me servir ?	*Mom, can I help myself?*
Le moteur peut encore servir.	*The engine is still fit for use.*
La lecture sert à la formation des étudiants.	*Reading helps in training students.*
Le moteur sert à faire marcher une voiture.	*The engine enables the car to move.*
Cela ne sert à rien d'envoyer le texto ce matin.	*It is of no use to send the text this morning.*
Que sert-il à un homme de gagner tout le monde, s'il perd son âme ?	*What does it profit a man to gain the whole world, if he loses his soul?*
Ces serviettes servent de couvertures.	*These towels serve as blankets.*
Tu peux te servir de mon ordinateur.	*You can use my computer.*

souhaiter

J'ai tant souhaité (de) le voir. Usage with or without *de* is acceptable.	*I so wished to see him.*

Je te souhaite d'être en bonne santé.	*I wish you good health.*
On lui a souhaité la bienvenue.	*We welcomed him/her.*

souscrire

J'ai souscrit une assurance / un plan d'épargnement / un abonnement.	*I subscribed to an insurance policy / savings plan; I took out a subscription.*
Sophie a souscrit au journal *Libération* / à une œuvre (charitable).	*Sophie subscribed to the newspaper Libération / to a charity.*
Je ne souscris pas à cette opinion-là.	*I do not subscribe to that opinion.*

suffire

Dix minutes ont suffi pour terminer la tâche.	*Ten minutes were enough to end the job.*
Cinq jours ont suffi à l'écrivaine pour composer son roman	*Five days were enough for the author to create her novel.*
Écrivaine is the Swiss and Quebec form.	
Il suffit de le faire tout de suite.	*It's good enough to do it right now.*

tarder

Qu'est-ce qu'elle tarde à venir !	*She's a long time in coming!*
Il lui tardait de revoir ses parents.	*He longed to see his parents again (impersonal).*

tenir

Mon fils tient à ses livres.	*My son values his books.*
J'y tiens / Je tiens à le faire.	*I am keen on it / to do it.*
Elle tient de sa mère.	*She takes after her mother.*

(se) tromper

Elle m'a trompé.	*She deceived me.*
Je me suis trompé d'adresse.	*I got the address wrong.*

user

Tu vas user tes chaussures comme ça.	*You're going to wear your shoes out like that.*
Mauriac use d'un style classique (R3).	*Mauriac uses a classical style.*

venir

Je viens te dire que...	*I have come to tell you that...*
Elle vient de lui envoyer un texto.	*She's just sent him a text message.*

The combination *venir de* and *revenir* would sound odd and non-French. Instead, say *Elle est revenue à l'instant*.

Une voiture vint à passer (R3).	*A car happened to pass by.*

viser

Pour vendre ce livre, il faut viser un grand marché.	*To sell this book, you must aim for a big market.*
La compagnie vise à créer un nouveau système.	*The company aims to create a new system.*

vivre

J'ai vécu dix ans à Québec.	*I lived for ten years in Quebec City.*
Le retraité vit de sa pension.	*The pensioner lives off his pension.*

56.9 Prepositional expressions

It is in this section that the differences between patterns in English and French appear most markedly. It is quite impossible to legislate on the translation of prepositional expressions from one language to another, and this applies to Spanish and Italian as well. Very few clear tendencies emerge. This is why it seems advisable to compare and contrast as many examples as possible for as many prepositions as possible. A consistent attempt has been made, where appropriate, to classify the examples according to the relationships expressed between the preposition and the noun.

à expressing position

à l'équateur (see *sous*)	*at/on the equator*
au pôle nord/sud	*at the North/South Pole*
aux Tropiques (see *sous*)	*at the Tropics*
à l'horizon	*on the horizon*
à Oran (Algérie)	*in Oran*
à la maison	*at home* (could be in the garden)
à l'hôtel	*at the hotel*
à la faculté / à la fac (R1; see *en*)	*at university*
des tableaux pendus au mur	*paintings hanging on the wall*
au tableau noir/blanc (see *sur*)	*on the blackboard/whiteboard*
travailler à la mine	*to work in the mines*
à la campagne (see *en*)	*in the countryside*
à la montagne (see *dans/en*)	*in the mountains*

travailler aux champs / à un ranch	*to work in the fields / on a ranch*
au jardin	*in the garden*
au salon	*in the living room*
à la cuisine	*in the kitchen*
une mouche au plafond	*a fly on the ceiling*
à la ferme (see *dans*)	*on the farm*
Papa parle au téléphone.	*Pop's on the phone.*
Moi, au paradis? Jamais!	*Me, in paradise? Never!*
entrer au paradis	*to go to paradise*
Ne reste pas au soleil.	*Don't stay in the sun.*
Reste plutôt à l'ombre (see *dans*).	*Remain rather in the shade.*
tomber à terre (see *par*)	*to fall to the ground*
tomber à l'eau (see *dans*)	*to fall into the water, to fail (of plan)*
au contact de l'eau	*in contact with water*
à bord d'une voiture / d'un avion / d'un train	*in a car/plane/train*
être à bicyclette/vélo (see *en/sur*)	*to be on a bicycle*
Elle est blessée au bras.	*She has hurt her arm.*
tomber aux mains de quelqu'un (see *dans*)	*to fall into someone's hands*
Il avait la cigarette/pipe à la bouche.	*He had a cigarette/pipe in his mouth.*
Elle tenait un livre à la main.	*She had a book in her hand.*
J'ai une épine au pied.	*I have a thorn in my foot.*
à la première page	*on the first page*
(Point)... à la ligne	*Period ... new paragraph*
à la place de / au lieu de	*in place of / instead of*
Je suis allé à sa rencontre.	*I went to meet him/her.*

à expressing time

à l'heure actuelle	*at the present time*
à notre époque	*in our time*
à l'époque	*at that time*
au vingt et unième siècle	*in the twenty-first century*
au printemps	*in the spring*
à l'été prochain (but *en été* = *in the summer*)	*next summer*
à l'automne (see *en*)	*in the fall*
à la mi-avril/juin	*in mid-April/June*
à la Saint-Sylvestre / à la Toussaint (the feminine *fête* is implied here)	*New Year's Eve / All Saints' Day*
au bout d'un mois	*at the end of a month*
au début de l'après-midi (see *en*)	*at the beginning of the afternoon*

à la fin de la séance (see *en*)	*at the end of the session/meeting*
à la mi-temps	*at half-time* (as in a soccer game)
à mon arrivée/retour	*on my arrival/return*
au temps des Aztèques	*at the time of the Aztecs*
la date à laquelle elle a envoyé. . .	*the date when she sent. . .*
Ils sont arrivés à temps.	*They arrived in time.*
arriver à l'avance (see *de/par*) (only: *Je l'ai fait bien à l'avance*)	*to arrive in advance*

à: figurative usage

à ce que je vois	*from what I can see*
à ce que je sache	*from what I know*
à ce que j'ai entendu	*from what I have heard*
Je ne comprends rien à ce qu'il dit.	*I understand nothing of what he says.*
Il ne comprend rien au problème.	*He understands nothing of the problem.*
à son avis	*in his opinion*
à mon point de vue	*from my point of view*
à ce point de vue-là	*from that point de of view*
Je l'ai reconnue à sa voix.	*I recognized her from her voice.*
rouler à bicyclette/vélo (see *en/sur*)	*to ride a bicycle*
aller à moto (see *en*)	*to travel by motorbike*
aller à cheval	*to travel on horseback*
aller à dos de chameau	*to travel by camel*
Je l'ai entendu à la radio.	*I heard it on the radio.*
Je l'ai vu à la télé.	*I saw it on TV.*
Tu écris toujours à l'encre, toi ?	*Do you still write in ink?*
Non, mais j'écris au crayon.	*No, but I write with a pencil.*
lire à la lumière d'une lampe	*to read by the light of a lamp*
un instrument à cordes / à cuivre / à vent	*a string/brass/wind instrument*
à partir de cette idée	*from this idea*
au nom du président	*in the name of the president*
Ce livre vient de paraître aux Éditions Gallimard.	*This book has just come out with Gallimard.*
le gouvernement au pouvoir	*the government in power*
Ils l'ont abattu à coups de poing/bâton/hâche/revolver/ couteau.	*They punched him till he fell to the ground	They hit him with sticks	an axe	a revolver	a knife until he fell to the ground.*
Elle l'a emporté à coups de pédale.	*She pedaled off with it.*

Il le fait à sa manière (see *de*).	*He does it in his (own) way.*
à pas lents / feutrés / de géant / de loup	*slowly / silently / with giant strides*
Elle est sortie à la dérobée.	*She crept out.*
Tu peux avancer à reculons, toi ?	*Can you go forward walking backwards?*
Je vous informe à regret que...	*I regretfully inform you that...*
À la rigueur elle peut venir.	*If need be, she can come.*
Au secours ! / Voleur !	*Help! / Stop thief!*
Elle est où, la boîte à/aux lettres ?	*Where's the mailbox?*
Il faut le classer dans la boîte à archives.	*It needs to be classified in the file box.*
un pot à beurre / à eau / à fleurs	*a butter dish / water pitcher / jug / flower pot*

If *de* were used here, the container would have butter/water/flowers in it. *À* suggests that the container is used for a specific purpose, but it does not necessarily contain anything. Similarly with:

un verre à bière / à vin	*a beer/wine glass*
Ils marchaient côte à côte.	*They walked side by side.*
Il faut me suivre mot à mot.	*You must follow me word by word.*
Doucement, et pas à pas.	*Carefully, and step by step.*
Les animaux ne sont pas entrés un à un dans l'arche de Noë, ils y sont entrés deux à deux.	*The animals did not go into Noah's arc one by one, they went in two by two.*
Mon père travaille aux PTT (see *dans*).	*My father works for the mail service / Post Office.*
Oui, mais avant, il travaillait aux chemins de fer ?	*Yes, but before, didn't he work on the railroads/railways?*
Je ne voudrais pas être au chômage (see *en*).	*I wouldn't like to be out of work.*
Il a fait une drôle de remarque à mon propos / à mon égard / à mon sujet.	*He made an odd remark about me.*
Tu recules au moins dix mètres.	*You go back at least ten meters.*
Sophie a au moins le mérite de parler anglais, russe et chinois.	*Sophie at least has the merit of speaking English, Russian and Chinese.*
mariage à l'indienne/italienne	*marriage Indian/Italian style*

à expressing measurement

à une vitesse de cent kilomètres à l'heure	*at a speed of sixty miles an hour*

Pas possible ! Lire à raison de
40 pages à l'heure ? Et c'est du
Dostoïveski par-dessus le
marché.

*Not possible! Reading at the rate of
40 pages an hour? And Dostoievsky
at that.*

Ils louent à l'heure la planche à
voile.

They hire the windsurfer by the hour.

Ça se vend au litre / au mètre.

It's sold by the liter/meter.

au-dessous de expressing position

Le petit jeta la balle au-dessous
de la table (see *en dessous de*).

The child threw the ball under the table.

au-dessous de: figurative usage

Mon collègue a trouvé un poste
au-dessous de ses compétences.

*My colleague found a job beneath his
qualifications.*

au-dessus de expressing position

L'église était située au-dessus du
village.

*The church was situated above the
village.*

Une enseigne se trouvait
au-dessus de nos têtes.

There was a sign above our heads.

L'oiseau vola au-dessus du mur
(see *par-dessus*).

The bird flew along/over the wall.

au-dessus de: figurative usage

Elle a épousé au-dessus d'elle.

She married above her station.

chez expressing position

Tu dînes chez nous ce soir ?

Eat with us this evening?

Chez elle on s'amuse.

We have a good time at her home.

On va chez le docteur ?

Are we going to the physician's?

Also: *aller chez l'épicier | le
boulanger* and so on. One would
not say *au | à la* in this context.

chez: figurative usage

Chez les Argentins il y a cette
coutume.

*Among the Argentinians, there is this
custom.*

Ce livre vient de paraître chez
Hachette.

*This book has just come out with
Hachette.*

contre expressing position

Elle a appuyé l'échelle contre le
mur.

She leaned the ladder against the wall.

contre: figurative usage

J'ai échangé ma Rolls contre une Lamborghini.	*I exchanged my Rolls for a Lamborghini.*
Pourquoi tu t'es fâchée contre moi ? (also *avec* here)	*Why did you get angry with me?*

dans expressing position

s'élever dans l'air / dans les airs (R3; see *en*)	*to rise up in the air*
L'astronaute se promena dans l'espace (see *en*).	*The astronaut walked in space.*
Tu vas dans les Alpes pour faire du ski ?	*You're going to the Alps to ski?*
J'adore l'air pur dans la montagne (see *à/en*).	*I love the mountain air.*
Tu habites dans la région parisienne ? (see *en*)	*You live in the Paris area?*
Le président arrive dans la capitale.	*The president is arriving in the capital.*
J'habite dans le 19e arrondissement.	*I live in the 19th district (of Paris).*
J'ai trouvé un billet de cinquante dollars dans la rue.	*I found a fifty-dollar bill in the street.*
Il y a des quantités de piétons dans l'avenue / dans le boulevard (see *sur*).	*There are lots of people in the avenue / on the boulevard.*
J'ai trouvé une montre dans l'allée.	*I found a watch on the path.*
On se réunit dans le square.	*We get together in the square (small public square with garden).*

But: **sur** *la place* (e.g. *de la Concorde*).

Attention ! Tu tombes dans l'eau (see *à*).	*Careful! You're falling in the water.*
On a passé la nuit dans une tente (see *sous*).	*We spent the night in a tent.*
Papa est dans la maison ?	*Is Pop in the house?*
Note that with *à la maison*, Pop could be anywhere in/around the house.	
Il y avait bien des spectateurs dans le stade (see *sur*).	*There were lots of spectators in the stadium (not on the field of play).*

C'est casse-pieds ! Le goal passe tout son temps dans les buts.	*It's boring! The goalkeeper spends all his time in goal.*
Il y a une vache dans la ferme !	*There's a cow in the farmhouse!*

Note that à *la ferme* = *on the farm*, so no surprise here.

Qu'est-ce qu'on poireaute dans l'aéroport !	*How we waste our time in the airport (buildings)!*
Il n'y a pas de place dans le parking (see *sur*).	*There's no room in the parking lot / car park (here it is enclosed and multi-storied).*
Mon père travaillait dans la mine à côté.	*My father worked in the mine near here.*
dans la campagne / les champs / le jardin	*in the countryside/fields/garden*
dans le salon / la cuisine	*in the living room / kitchen*
dans la chambre	*in the bedroom*

Note that only *dans* is possible here.

dans les coulisses	*in the wings* (literal and figurative)
dans l'escalier	*on the stairs*
dans le train	*on the train*

Only in Westerns are they **sur le train** = *on the top of the train.*

Il est dans la voiture de son père.	*He's in his father's car.*

Dans is used when *voiture* is qualified but *en voiture* = *in a car.*

monter dans un avion	*to get into an airplane*
Je vais l'inscrire dans mon carnet (see *sur*).	*I'll put it in my notebook.*
Je l'ai lu dans le journal (see *sur*).	*I read it in the newspaper*
J'étais assise dans le fauteuil.	*I was sitting in the armchair.*
J'ai une mouche dans mon assiette.	*I have a fly on my plate.*
Il buvait dans un verre / une tasse quand...	*He was drinking from a glass/cup when...*
Son image se reflétait dans le soleil.	*His image was reflected in the sun.*
Je préfère rester dans l'ombre (see *à*).	*I prefer to stay in the shade.*
dans l'espace de dix mètres (see *en* for time)	*in the space of ten meters*

dans expressing time

dans le même temps (see *en*)	*at the same time*
dans la semaine (see *en*)	*in the week*

dans l'après-midi / la matinée / soirée	*in the afternoon/morning/evening*
Je le ferai dans dix jours.	*I'll do it in ten days* (in ten days' time).

But: *Je l'ai fait en dix jours.*

Dans le temps, je ne le faisais pas ainsi.	*A long time ago, I didn't do it like that.*
On est dans les temps.	*We're on time / on schedule.*
dans les prochains jours / les trois jours	*in the next days / the next three days* (from this point in time)

dans: figurative usage

dans une forme littéraire (see *sous*)	*in a literary form*
dans la situation actuelle	*in the present situation*
dans le secret/privé (see *en*)	*in secret/private*
travailler dans les chemins de fer (see *à*)	*to work on the railroads*
travailler dans les PTT (see *à*)	*to work for the mail service*
Les enfants morts sans baptême sont dans les limbes ? Ça n'a pas de sens.	*Children who die unbaptized are in Limbo? That's crazy.*
Mon fils est souvent dans la lune (see *sur*).	*My son is often on the clouds.*
être/rester dans l'expectative	*to wait and see*

de expressing position

Le chemin de la gare, s'il vous plaît ?	*The way to the station, please?*

Note that the above could also mean *from the station*: ambiguity here.

le train de Washington	*the Washington train* (ambiguity again)
de Mexico à Miami	*from Mexico City to Miami*
aller de ville en ville	*to go from town to town*
Le colporteur va de porte en porte.	*The peddler goes from door to door.*
une rue de Lyon	*a street in Lyon*
J'ai regardé le paysage du haut du balcon / des remparts.	*I looked at the countryside from the balcony/ramparts* (suggesting height).
On les voit de ce côté.	*You can see them from this side.*

Tu les vois de l'autre côté.	You can see them from the other side.
du côté de la gare	in the direction of the station
Je l'ai vue de dos / de face / de profil / de derrière / de côté.	I saw her from the back / face on / in profile / from the back / from the side.

de expressing usage with materials

Note that *de* is less concrete than *en* in the following expressions; *en* stresses the material (see *en*).

Les Troyens construisirent un cheval de bois, selon Homère.	The Trojans built a wooden horse, according to Homer.
Il fait chaud, mets une chemise de coton	It's hot, put on a cotton shirt.
Une barrière de métal, ça (se) rouille.	A metal gate, that goes rusty.

de expressing time

de notre temps / de nos jours	in our time
Je vais au cinéma de temps en temps.	I go to the movies from time to time.
d'heure/année en heure/année	from hour/year to hour/year
Je dors de dix heures à midi!	I sleep from ten to twelve!
du temps des Pharaons (see *à*)	in the time of the Pharaohs
Il faut différer/remettre/reporter notre rendez-vous de dix jours.	We'll have to put off our meeting for ten days.
C'était une jeune fille de 15 à 16 ans.	She was a girl of 15 or 16.
d'avance (see *à* and *par*)	in advance

Prévoir d'avance is very common, but is a pleonasm.

| Je l'ai vu la semaine d'avant / d'après. | I saw him the week before/after. |

de: figurative usage

Sophie parlait d'une voix triste/heureuse.	Sophie spoke in a sad/happy voice.
Philippe s'exprima d'un ton heureux/triste/enjoué (see *sur*).	Philippe spoke in a happy/sad/lively tone.
Marcel se comporta d'une manière/façon étrange (see *à*).	Marcel behaved in a strange way.
De l'avis de Jean, Roland est doué.	In Jean's opinion, Roland is clever.
Je te salue de la part de Henri.	I greet you on Henri's behalf.
Dites-le-lui de ma part.	Tell him on my behalf.

Je la connais de vue.	*I know her by sight.*
un pot de beurre/lait/fleurs (see *à*)	*a pot of butter/milk/flowers*
un verre de bière/vin (see *à*)	*a glass of beer/wine*
Je suis inquiet de (R3) lui (see *pour*).	*I am worried about him.*
Il est de mon côté.	*He's on my side.*
de toutes façons/manières	*at any rate*
de l'autre côté	*on the other hand/side*
Il y a une volonté de dialogue de part et d'autre.	*Both sides are willing to talk.*
Je t'avoue de tout mon cœur que...	*I confess to you with all my heart that...*
Mon frère agit toujours de bon cœur.	*My brother always acts sincerely.*
Il était très généreux de son vivant.	*He was very generous while he was alive.*

Also: *de leur vivant = while they were alive*

Je travaille de toutes mes forces.	*I work with all my strength.*
Elle l'a touché d'une main tremblante.	*She touched him with a trembling hand.*
Le public a battu des mains.	*The spectators clapped hands.*
Le voyou m'a frappé du pied.	*The hoodlum/lout kicked me.*
Cédric cligna des yeux à cause du soleil.	*Cédric screwed up his eyes because of the sun.*

Also: *cligner les yeux*

La chaudière ne marche pas. Mais j'ai un chauffage d'appoint.	*The boiler's not working. But I have an extra heating appliance.*
C'est un livre d'emprunt. Il n'est pas à moi.	*It's a borrowed book. It's not mine.*
Autant en emporte le vent: un film d'exception.	*Gone with the Wind: an exceptional movie.*
Tu choisis un avocat / un expert d'office.	*You choose an official lawyer/expert.*
C'est la pièce d'origine (not *originale*).	*It's the original part (of a car, machine, etc.).*
d'après le roman de Émile Zola	*after the novel by Émile Zola*
Il n'est pas bête du moins.	*At least, he's not dumb.*

de expressing measurement

On avance le départ de dix jours.	*We're bringing the departure forward by ten days.*

Ils ont augmenté/majoré le prix de l'essence de cinquante centimes.	*They've put up the price of gas by fifty cents.*
Ils ont réduit le prix de l'essence de quarante centimes.	*They've reduced the price of gas by forty cents.*
Bolt a battu son adversaire de cinq mètres.	*Bolt beat his opponent by five meters.*
Marie est plus intelligente de beaucoup.	*Marie is by far the smartest.*
La durée de la traversée est de 7 heures.	*The crossing lasts 7 hours.*
Le prix est de dix dollars.	*The price is ten dollars.*
La distance est de dix kilomètres.	*The distance is ten kilometers.*
Il gagne 300 euros de l'heure.	*He earns 300 euros an hour.*

de expressing passive agent in passive voice

Elle est morte d'un cancer.	*She died of cancer.*
Mon ami souffre d'une bronchite.	*My friend is suffering from bronchitis.*
Le maître est toujours suivi de son chien (see *par*).	*The master is always followed by his dog.*

Note that a subtle register distinction may occur when *de* precedes the indefinite article or a name beginning with a mute **h**, or before the plural indefinite article in book titles and so on:

R2	R2/R3
le règne d'Henri quatre	le règne de Henri quatre
augmenter d'un pour cent	augmenter de un pour cent
la dictature d'Hitler	la dictature de Hitler
Steinbeck, auteur des *Raisins de la colère*	Steinbeck, auteur de *Les raisins de la colère*

durant expressing time

| trois heures / des journées durant (R3) | *for three hours / for days* |
| J'ai creusé durant trois heures. | *I dug for three hours.* |

Note that when *durant* follows the noun, the register is higher.

en expressing position

En is becoming increasingly common as a preposition (doubtless because it is an economical way of avoiding longer constructions of the type *dans le/ la, au/à la,* etc.):

On peut acheter ce roman en librarie (instead of *dans une*).
Je l'ai rencontrée en Gare du Nord (instead of *à la*).
Lire en page 6 (instead of *à la*).
rouler en Renault
En has a more general value than *à* and *dans*: *L'ouvrage peut s'acheter
en librairie dès demain* as opposed to *L'ouvrage peut s'acheter dans cette
librairie-là* and *Mon père travaille en faculté* (regular work) as opposed
to *Mon père travaille à la faculté* (today).

En is used in the following expressions: *en l'air* (see *dans*), *en République
française*, *en Avignon/Arles* (used of southern towns to avoid hiatus, but not
of northern towns, e.g., *à Arles, en région parisienne*; see *dans*), *en métropole*
(in the capital, i.e., Paris, in France, see *dans*), *en banlieue, en périphérie
nantaise/newyorkaise, en montagne* (see *à* and *dans*), *en car* (*by long distance bus*),
en couverture (*on the cover*, i.e., of a book or magazine), *en rade de la Nouvelle
Orléans* (*in the harbor*), *en serre* (*in a greenhouse*), *en mer* (*at sea*; see *sur*), *mettre en
orbite basse* (see *sur*), *aller en paradis* (R3; see *au*), *aller en enfer/en purgatoire, aller
en classe, regarder en coulisses* (used figuratively = *to look at secretly*; see *dans*),
en lycée, en faculté (R1 = see *à*), *aller en expédition, aller en ville, en campagne* (see
à), *en pleine campagne* (*right in the countryside | in the midst of a campaign*), *en
pleine rue, en brousse* (*in the bush*, as in Africa), *en usine* (*in the factory*).

Note all the expressions with *en milieu* (*in . . . environment*): *en milieu agricole/
domestique/hospitalier/pédagogique/scolaire/sportif/universitaire; en conseil des
ministres, en bibliothèque/librairie/pharmacie, en résidence surveillée* (*under house
arrest*), *en grande surface* (*in a supermarket*; but *au supermarché*), *tennis en salle*
(*indoor tennis*), *en pleine salle* (*in the middle of the room*), *en centre sportif/nautique,
en document/dossier attaché* or *en pièce jointe* (as an attachment; this latter
expression is the most common), *en ligue des champions* (in the Champions'
league = European soccer), *en pole position, en salle d'opération | d'examen, en
studio, en zone occupée, en amont de* (*upstream from*), *en aval de* (*downstream from*),
en plein vol (*in full flight*, of airplane/bird), *en plein soleil* (*right in the sun*), *Le
drapeau est en berne* (*The flag is at half-mast*), *Il m'a cogné en pleine figure* (*He
smashed me right in the face*), *avoir une idée en tête, en ballon/mongolfière* (*in a hot-
air balloon*), *monter en avion* (see *dans* = *to go up in a plane*), *voyager en avion* (see
par), *filer en vélo* (R1; see *à, sur*), *aller en moto* (R1; see *à*), *voyager en scooter | en
Vespa, rouler en deux roues* (*to ride a bicycle/motorbike*), *voyager en voiture | en auto*
(see *dans; en auto* is now old-fashioned), *rouler en BM, voyager en train* (see *par*),
voyager en bateau (see *par*), *en radeau* (*on a raft*), *être en selle* (*in a saddle*, as with
a horse), *en première page* (see *à*), *en piscine* (also *à la*), *en terrasse* (also *sur la*), as
in a restaurant: *Vous voulez manger en terrasse ?, Le journal s'achète en kiosque.*

en expressing materials

un cheval en bois, une chemise en coton, une barrière en métal (see
de)

en expressing time

En même temps (see *dans*), *en (l'an) 1950, en été | en hiver, en automne* (se
à), *en avril/juin/septembre, Je travaille toujours en semaine* (as opposed to
the week-end), *en début d'après-midi* (see *à*), *en fin de séance* (at the end of
the meeting), *en fin de parcours* (at the end of the trail/trip, etc.), *en l'espace
de trois semaines* (see *dans*), *Je l'ai fait en dix jours* (I did it in ten days), *en
première/deuxième mi-temps* (in the first/second half of a game), *en
période électorale, en période de sécheresse* (in a period of drought), *un match
en nocturne* (evening game), *On va partir en week-end, l'expérience | l'année
en cours* (the present/current experience/year), *Irène est en cours* (Irène has a
class), *la dernière publication en date* (the last publication to date), *en milieu
de journée, en ce temps-là* (at that time), *Elle est arrivée en retard* (She
arrived late, i.e., after a specific time, whereas *arriver tard* is simply to
arrive late with no implication of commitment), *La correspondante est
en communication* (The line is engaged, i.e., on the telephone).

en: figurative usage

se changer / se transformer en simple spectateur	*to change	be transformed into a mere spectator*
se déguiser en prêtre	*to disguise oneself as a priest*
se comporter en invité	*to behave like a guest*

Also: *un assassin en série* (a serial killer), *une femme en cheveux* (R3 = a
woman without a hat), *Je me suis trouvé en danger, Elle dort en paix, rester
assis en silence, Ils se sont retirés en catamini* (R3 = They slipped out), *Ils
sont sortis en cachette | en sourdine* (They left quietly/discreetly), *En clair, cela
veut dire qu'il refuse* (To put it clearly, this means he is refusing), *Elle était en
string sur la plage* (She was in a G string on the beach), *être en uniforme | en
civil* (to be in a uniform | plain clothes), *être en maillot de bain* (to be in a
swimming costume) *| en bikini, être en pagne* (to be in a loincloth), *être en
smoking | tenue de soirée* (to be in a dinner jacket | evening dress), *en secret |
en privé* (in secret | in private), *en état de guerre/siège/crise* (in a state of
war/siege/crisis), *Les rockers sont partis en tournée* (The rock musicans went
on tour), *Je suis partie en mission d'enquête/information* (I went on an
enquiry mission), *Les professeurs sont en réunion* (The teachers are in a
meeting), *une édition en livre de poche* (a paperback edition), *L'équipe de
France est en poule 2* (The French national team are in pool 2), *Le petit est en
âge d'aller à l'école, être en chômage* (see *à*), *rester en course* (to stay in the
race), *un film en version originale | en VO* (in the original, of a movie), *en
récital* (in concert), *Ils sont entrés/sortis en masse* (They piled in/out), *L'avion
est descendu en catastrophe* (The airplane crash-landed), *La voiture est en
mal de vitesse* (The car is losing speed), *L'évadé est en cavale* (The fugitive is
on the run), *Ces articles sont en promotion* (These items are on special offer),
en quête de (in search of; *Six personnages en quête d'auteur* de Pirandello),

un ciel d'azur et des rochers ocres immortalisés en mémoire, en cure de désintoxication (on a drying-out course), en moyenne (on average), en première lecture, Je suis en ligne (I am online, as with the Internet), *avoir un livre en chantier (to be preparing a book), Le soldat était en permission* (The soldier was on leave), *des valeurs cotées en Bourse* (shares quoted on the Stock Exchange), *en la situation actuelle* (R3; see *dans*), *en ma faveur* (in my favor), *en l'honneur de la championne, en l'occurrence, il a décroché trois médailles* (As it turned out, he landed three medals), *en mon nom* (in my name; see *à*), *en l'absence de* (in the absence of), but: *en présence de, L'équipe a gagné trois deux en finale* (The team won 3–2 in the final), *Ils l'ont transmis en direct* (They broadcast it live), *Ils l'ont transmis en différé* (It was a recording), *Il y avait une fortune en jeu* (There was a fortune at stake), *en tout cas* (in any case).

en dessous de expressing position

Elle jeta la balle en dessous de la table (see *au-dessous de*).	*She threw the ball under the table.*

entre expressing position

entre les maisons	*between the houses*
Il est tombé entre les mains de l'ennemi.	*He fell into the hands of the enemy.*

entre: figurative usage

entre parenthèses (see *par* with no final **s**)	*in parenthesis*

hors de expressing position

Il fait froid hors de la maison.	*It's cold outside the house.*

hors de: figurative usage

hors de danger	*out of danger*
hors d'haleine	*out of breath*
C'est hors de doute.	*It's beyond doubt.*

jusqu'à expressing time

J'ai attendu jusqu'à sept heures.	*I waited until seven.*

jusqu'à expressing position

Michel m'a accompagnée jusque chez moi.	*Michel accompanied me home.*
Marine m'a accompagné jusqu'au village.	*Marine accompanied me as far as the village.*

jusqu'à: figurative usage

Les manifestants ont incendié jusqu'aux voitures.	*The demonstrators even burned the cars.*

par expressing position

On se promène par les champs ?	*Go for a walk over the fields?*
Elle est tombée par terre.	*She fell down.*
par-ci, par là	*here and there*
Viens par ici.	*Come over here.*
Est-ce qu'il a neigé par là ?	*Has it snowed there?*

par expressing time

par un temps pareil	*in such weather*
par le temps qui court	*at the moment*
par mauvais temps	*in bad weather*
par un jour froid d'hiver	*on a cold winter's day*
deux fois par semaine	*twice a week*
Je réserve toujours par avance (see *à/de*).	*I always book in advance.*

par: figurative usage

J'ai obtenu un prêt par l'intermédiaire/entremise de...	*I obtained a loan through...*
par une tierce personne	*by a third party*
On voyage par chemin de fer.	*We travel by train.*
On voyage par le train (see *en*).	*We travel by train.*
On voyage par avion (see *en*).	*We travel by plane.*
On voyage par bateau (see *en*).	*We travel by boat.*
Je le contacterai par écrit.	*I'll contact him in writing.*
par parenthèse (see *entre*)	*in parenthesis*
J'ai agi par compassion/amitié/ ignorance/amour/prudence/ inadvertence.	*I acted out of compassion/friendship/ ignorance/love/prudence/carelessness.*

par expressing active agent in passive voice

Il a été mordu par un chien.	*He has been / was bitten by a dog.*

par-dessus expressing position

Il regarda par-dessus le mur.	*He looked over the wall.*

par: figurative usage

Il a gagné cent dollars, et un cadeau par-dessus le marché.	*He won a hundred dollars, and a present into the bargain.*

pendant expressing time

pendant la journée	*during the day*
Aurélie a travaillé pendant trois heures.	*Aurélie worked for three hours.*

pendant expressing space

Elle était triste pendant bien des kilomètres.	*She was sad for many kilometers.*

pour expressing time

Laurent sera à Poitiers pour quinze jours.	*Laurent will be in Poitiers for a fortnight.*
Elles sont ici pour trois jours.	*They're here for three days.*
J'ai assez de travail pour un mois.	*I've enough work for a month.*

pour: figurative usage

Il est bon/gentil pour moi.	*He's good to me.*
Je suis inquiète pour lui (see *de*).	*I'm worried about him.*
J'ai échangé ma maison pour un palais (see *contre*).	*I exchanged my house for a palace.*

près expressing position

La boulangerie est près de l'église.	*The baker's is near the church.*
les villages près de la rivière	*the villages near the river*
le village le plus près (R1; *proche* would be R2 since it is the required adjective)	

Difference between *près de* and *auprès de*: The first means *near* (in space): *près de la maison*; the second means *with*, *to* with the idea of speaking to someone: *Je me suis enseignée auprès de Marie. Auprès de* can mean *near* but in a high register, as in Brassens's songs: "Auprès de ma blonde," "Auprès de mon arbre."

sous expressing position

Sous l'équateur (see *à*), *sous les Tropiques* (see *à*), *Il est passé sous le balcon, sous une tente, Le chien est sous l'arbre, On a marché sous la neige/pluie* (not *dans*, although *dans la neige* is possible if the snow were lying), *J'ai le texte sous les yeux.*

sous expressing time

Sous le règne de Henri IV (in the reign of Henri IV), *Je te téléphone sous peu* (*I'll phone you shortly*).

sous: figurative usage

sous une forme littéraire (see *dans*), *sous un jour favorable*, *sous tous les rapports* (*in all respects*), sous peine d'amende (*on pain of a fine*), J'ai ton message sous la main (*I have your message at hand*), *sous l'emprise | l'empire* (R3) | *l'influence | le coup de* (*under the influence of*), *Il est sous antibiotique/ hypnose/morphine/perfusion/traitement/ventilation* (*on antibiotics | under hypnosis | on morphine | on a drip | under treatment | on oxygen*), *sous l'égide* (R3) *de | les auspices de* (*under the auspices of*), *Le chef a la situation sous contrôle, La compagnie | L'étudiant | L'équipe était sous pression* (*The company/student/team was under pressure*), *La réunion s'est déroulée sous la présidence de...* (*The meeting took place with ... in the chair*).

sur expressing position

Sur la lune (see *dans*), *Les astronautes vont sur la lune, lancer sur une orbite basse* (*to launch into a low orbit*), *mettre une navette sur orbite* (*to put a space shuttle into orbit*), *Il y a peu de voitures sur le parking* (*There are few cars in the parking lot;* see *dans*), *Tu vois le bateau sur la mer?* (see *en*), *sur l'aéroport* (*at the airport*, but on the runway/tarmac, see *à/dans*), *sur le chantier* (*in the workyard*), *sur les docks, sur l'hippodrome | le champ de course* (*at the racecourse*), *sur la place* (*in the square*, but *dans le square* = square meaning small square, with garden in the center), *sur le stade* (*in the stadium* as a competitor, see *dans*), *sur le ring* (*in the ring*), *Les spectateurs s'étalaient sur bien des kilomètres* (*The spectators stretched out over several kilometers*), *Je l'ai vu sur l'avenue | sur le boulevard* (*I saw him in the avenue/boulevard;* see *dans*), *Le piéton renversé est resté sur la chaussée* (*The pedestrian who was knocked down remained in the road*), *On marchait sur la route* (*We walked on the road* but *dans la rue*), *Notre appartement donne sur la rue* (*Our appartment looks on the sea*), *sur le trottoir* (*on the sidewalk*), *Il n'y avait aucun acteur sur (la) scène* (*There were no actors on the stage*), *sur le tableau noir* (see *à*), *La clef est sur la porte, Elle était assise sur un canapé/divan/sofa, Un couvreur* (*roofer*) *grimpe sur le toit* (as in Zola's *L'assommoir* where Gervaise's husband works on roofs), *Je suis sur mon/le vélo* (see *à/en*), *sur la selle* (*on the saddle*, i.e., of a bicycle), *Je l'ai inscrit sur mon carnet* (*I have written it in my notebook;* see *dans*), *Je l'ai lu sur le journal* (see *dans*), *Elle est revenue sur ses pas* (*She retraced her steps*).

sur expressing time

Ça peut durer sur plusieurs jours.	*That could last several days.*
Il s'est marié / a commencé ses études sur le tard.	*He married	began his studies late on.*
Elle m'a dit sur le tard que...	*She told me a bit late that...*

sur: figurative usage

Un livre sur la mode, Je suis inquiet sur son sort (I'm worried about his fate), naviguer/surfer sur le Net, Tu trouves tout sur Internet, Je l'ai découvert sur la Toile/sur le Web (I discovered it on the Web), Le gérant m'a convoqué et je me suis trouvé sur la sellette (The manager called me in and I found myself in the hot seat), Je le crois sur parole (I believe his word), Marie va sur ses dix ans (Marie will soon be ten years old), Vous recevrez le cadeau sur simple demande (you will receive the gift simply by applying), Elle m'a dit sur un ton triste/heureux (see de), Dix-huit sur vingt pour toi, dix-neuf pour moi et vingt pour le bon Dieu (Eighteen out of twenty for you, nineteen for me and twenty for the Lord).

vers expressing position

Ils se dirigeaient vers la ville.	*They went toward the town.*

vers: figurative usage

Je viens vers midi.	*I'll come about midday.*

The following prepositions have a specific and restricted value. Many of these are compound prepositions, made up of more than one word:

à cause de	*because of*	au travers de	*across*
à force de	*by*	avant	*before*
à même	*from*	avec	*with*
à propos de	*about*	concernant	*about*
à travers	*across*	d'après	*according to*
au dehors de	*outside*	devant	*before*
au moyen de	*by*	durant	*during*
au sujet de	*about*	en dehors de	*outside*
en raison de	*because of*	près de	*near*
en travers de	*across*	quant à	*as for*
envers	*to, toward*	sans	*without*
environ	*about*	selon	*according to*
moyennant	*by (means of)*	suivant	*following*
parmi	*among*		

Note that *sans* + infinitive = *without* + past participle: *Elles sont parties sans parler.* Although *parmi* is usually used with plural nouns, it may also accompany a singular collective noun: *parmi la foule.*

For example: *Elle n'est pas sortie à cause de son rhume; Il a terminé la tâche à force de travailler toute la nuit; Prends un verre ; pourquoi tu bois à même la bouteille ?; À propos du voyage demain . . . ; Les enfants jouent au-dehors (R3) / en dehors de la maison; La mesure a été acceptée moyennant / au moyen d'un référendum; Je me suis expliqué au sujet de mon refus; En raison du mauvais temps, on a reporté le départ au lendemain*; *Leur attitude envers moi fut désagréable*; *Ils sont arrivés à dix heures environ*; *Viens avant onze heures*; *Viens avec lui*; *Tu mets toujours du lait avec* (*with it*: this construction is considered faulty by some, since it is felt that *avec* requires a noun or pronoun); *Concernant sa maladie, je dois dire que...* ; *D'après le psychologue...* ; *La maison est trop près de la rivière*; *Quant à sa performance au cent mètres...* ; *Quant à aller à la piscine demain...* ; *Selon la radio | mon père...* ; *Suivant les propos du maire...* (*According to the mayor's remarks...*).

Usage for *à*/*au travers* and *au-dessus*/*par-dessus*: *Elle traversa le pré en courant* (*She ran across the meadow*); *Ils franchirent/traversèrent le pont* (*They crossed the bridge*). Verbs of motion cannot normally be used with *à travers* when the space crossed is narrow, or limited like a road, a river, a stream, a yard, a field, a garden. However, one can say: *Elle a couru/marché à travers les champs | les près | le bois | la forêt* when distance is implied. Similarly: *ses voyages à travers le monde*.

Au travers de is used in the following way: *Il étudia le marxisme au travers des écrits de Marx*. *À travers* is also possible here. Although they are largely synonymous in their abstract meaning, *au travers de* is of a higher register than *à travers*. Note that in the sentence *L'arbre est tombé en travers de la route*, neither *au travers de* nor *à travers* are possible.

Par dessus and *au-dessus* are used in the following way: *Il regarda par-dessus* (*over*) *le mur*; *L'oiseau vola par-dessus* (*over*) *le mur* (i.e., to the other side); *L'oiseau vola au-dessus du mur* (*along/above the wall*). *Par-dessus* implies a more rapid movement to the other side, while *au-dessus* implies high above or along. *Au-dessus* can imply a static idea: *Le ballon est/vole au-dessus de la ville* (*above* rather than *over*).

The prepositional expression *à même* is used in the following way: *André a bu à même la bouteille* (André drank *straight from* the bottle); *Les scouts ont couché à même le sol* (The scouts slept *right on* the ground); *Philippe a écrit à même le bois de la table* (Philippe wrote *straight on to the wood of the table*)

56.10 Different constructions in French and English.

It happens that where French uses a verb + direct object, English uses a verb + preposition + direct object: *Céline affectionne* (*is fond of*) *cet endroit | cette activité*; *J'approuve* (*I approve of*) *ta suggestion*; *Je t'attends ici* (*I wait for you here*); *J'ai commenté* (*I commented on*) *cette mesure en disant...* ; *J'ai compensé* (*I compensated for*) *leur perte par un beau cadeau*; *C'est une entreprise qui nous concurrence* (*compete with*) *dangereusement*; *Je demande* (*I ask for*) *ton approbation*; *Toutes nos factures sont domiciliées* (*All our bills are paid by credit transfer | by direct billing | by banker's order*); *Tu m'écoutes?* (*Are you listening to me?*); *Sophie a hâte d'étrenner ses patins* (*Sophie is longing to use her skates for the first time*); *Le physicien a expérimenté* (*experimented with*) *un nouveau procédé*; *Un pyromane a dû incendier* (*must have set fire to*) *la forêt*; *La députée a officialisé* (*The representative | member of parliament made official*) *la création d'un nouveau centre nautique*; *Elle* s'est fait opérer de l'appendicite (She had an appendix operation); Tu paies (paying for) le billet tout de suite?; Les Français plébiscitèrent (voted in favor of) Louis-Napoléon Bonaparte; Les deux gouvernements ont plébiscité la partition; Didon pleura le départ d'Énée (Dido wept over the departure of Aeneas, in Virgil's Aeneid); postuler un poste (also with à); Ça ne sert à rien de prêcher les mécréants (It serves no purpose to preach to the miscreants), but: prêcher l'Évangile (to preach the Gospel); J'ai présidé (presided over) la réunion; Ça sert à quelque chose de prier le bon Dieu / la Vierge Marie?; Je privilégie (give preference to) cette interprétation-là; Impossible de le raisonner (Impossible to make him see reason); Je cherche mon stylo; La compagnie recherche (is looking for) un expert en comptabilité; Pourquoi tu me regardes comme ça?; Comment responsabiliser les élèves (How do you make the pupils feel responsible?); Il faut sécuriser les citoyens (We must give a sense of security to the public); Ces marginalisés n'ont pas le droit de squatter (to take over) ce logement; L'avion a survolé (flew over) la région; Tu veilles (watch over) la petite si je sors?; Le voyou m'a volé (The thug/hoodlum stole from me); On a voté (voted for) la mesure, but: voter pour un candidat.

The reverse is also true in some cases. French verb + preposition + noun/pronoun = English verb + direct object: Stéphanie a hérité (inherited) d'un appartement / d'un beau tapis; Dostoïevski a certainement influé sur (influenced) les romans modernes (but influencer + direct object); Notre fils s'est marié avec (married) une princesse (but épouser quelqu'un); Tu as téléphoné à Papa?

Note that comme used as a preposition occurs with the meaning of as when one is spelling out a word or name the hearer cannot follow. This happens frequently on the telephone: Picot: P comme Paris, I comme Inde, C comme Colombie, O comme Oslo, T comme Texas.

Part VIII

57

Demonstrative adjectives / Les adjectifs démonstratifs

The following passage treats the deliberations of a world body whose aim is to abolish the death penalty. The conference, made up of various activities, took place in Geneva in early 2010. The second paragraph points to several countries where the death penalty is still practiced, while the third and fourth exhibit the passionate concerns expressed by a number of thinkers of European stature. The passage illustrates the several uses of French demonstrative adjectives, applied to both singular and plural nouns. These adjectives are highlighted in bold. Some translations are offered.

Congrès mondial contre la peine de mort
La Suisse a réuni, **ces** jours-**ci**, un grand nombre de participants au quatrième congrès mondial contre la peine de mort. **Ce** congrès mondial s'est tenu à Genève du 24 au 26 février 2010. Une bonne centaine de pays étaient représentés lors de **cet** événement marquant [outstanding]. Les associations organisatrices de **ce** congrès international s'efforcent d'atteindre l'abolition universelle de **cette** peine capitale. Tous **ces** congressistes ont pris part à des réunions faisant l'objet de sessions plénières, de tables rondes et d'ateliers. L'ouverture officielle de **ces** débats s'est déroulée [took place] dans **ce** fameux Palais des Nations et, plus précisément, dans la Salle des Droits de l'Homme. Le choix de **ce** lieu n'est pas tout à fait fortuit. **Cet** endroit chargé d'histoire accueille **ces** hauts dirigeants qui font de **ce** sujet brûlant une véritable lutte politique.

    Cette excellente initiative vise à plaider en faveur d'une justice qui ne débouche pas [end in] sur **cette** mort relevant d'un acte de barbarie. Certains pays, comme les États-Unis, la Chine, l'Arabie Saoudite, l'Algérie, la Tunisie, l'Iran, le Pakistan et bien d'autres encore, enregistrent un trop grand nombre d'exécutions capitales par électrocution, par pendaison [hanging], par décapitation, par fusillade [by a firing squad] ou par injection létale. **Ces** modes d'exécution ne sont pas acceptables au XXI siècle.

Le processus de la démocratisation du monde occidental a mené logiquement à l'appel à **cette** suppression de la peine capitale. Le Canton de Genève est partisan de l'abolitionnisme depuis 1871, soit une dizaine d'années après que Victor Hugo ordonna expressément aux Genevois de renoncer à **cet** atroce supplice de la guillotine. À **cette** époque-**là**, **ce** grand écrivain se prononça farouchement contre la peine de mort. Deux de ses œuvres magistrales, *Les Châtiments* et *Les Misérables*, témoignent notamment de son engagement poétique, littéraire et politique.

Si l'on continue dans **cette** veine littéraire, l'écrivain russe Dostoïevski exprime son admiration pour Hugo dans la mesure où celui-**ci** s'élève énergiquement contre **ce** supplice suprême (voir le *Journal d'un écrivain* de Dostoïevski où il loue, à d'innombrables reprises, *Le dernier jour d'un condamné* de Hugo). **Ce** même romancier russe évoque dans *L'idiot* la terrifiante image du condamné à mort qui contemple sa brutale exécution sur un échafaud à Lyon, en l'occurrence près de Genève. **Cette** liste de penseurs qui protestent contre **cette** pratique barbare ne connaît pas de limites. Qu'il suffise de citer deux autres auteurs, Koestler et Camus, qui ont collaboré à écrire *Réflexions sur la peine capitale*. Plus récemment encore, Robert Badinter, Garde des Sceaux et ministre de la Justice dans le gouvernement de François Mitterrand, a été l'initiateur de l'abolition de la peine de mort en 1981. L'exécution capitale a été abolie à **cette** date-**là** en France.

Quels sont les enjeux de **ce** quatrième congrès ? S'agit-il d'enjeux politiques ou économiques ou encore du respect des droits de l'homme ? Tous **ces** nombreux ministres européens et **ces** représentants gouvernementaux ainsi que **ces** organisations mondiales prônent [plead for] l'abolition de la peine de mort dans tous les pays du monde. **Cette** idée-**là** nous paraît lumineuse. Le chef du gouvernement espagnol, José Luis Rodríguez Zapatero, a souligné, **ce** mois-**ci**, la mise en place d'une commission internationale sur la peine de mort pour obtenir un moratoire d'ici à 2015. Il est grand temps de mettre fin à **ce** « châtiment suprême ». **Ce** jour-**là**, on célébrera **cette** pierre angulaire [cornerstone] des sociétés civilisées.

Demonstrative adjectives, or demonstrative determiners as some like to call them, allow us to point specifically to a person or object, abstract or concrete. English has: *this, that, these, those*. The French equivalents are:

singular		*plural*
masculine	*feminine*	*masculine/feminine*
ce, cet	cette	ces

The form *cet* occurs before a masculine noun beginning with a vowel or mute **h**:

ce magazine (*this magazine*), *ce garçon* (*this boy*), *ce livre* (*this book*) *cette maison* (this house), *cette jeune fille* (this girl), *cette cuisine* (this kitchen)

ces lits (these beds), *ces films* (these films), *ces jardins* (these gardens) – all masculine

ces forêts (these forests), *ces chaises* (these chairs), *ces chaussures* (these shoes) – all feminine

cet endroit (this place), *cet arbre* (this tree), *cet hôtel* (this hotel), *cet hôpital* (this hospital)

The form *cet* also occurs before a masculine adjective beginning with a vowel or mute **h**:

cet admirable paysage (this admirable countryside), *cet excellent roman* (this excellent novel)

The masculine *ce* is used before an aspirate **h**:

ce héros (this hero), *ce haut-parleur* (this loudspeaker)

Usage in sentences points to a person or object: *Cette dame, c'est la directrice de l'école* (This lady is the school's headteacher); *Tu vois cet autobus, il va à la gare de Lyon* (You see this bus, it's going to the gare de Lyon).

The demonstrative adjective also refers back to something already mentioned: *J'ai une petite Toyota; cette voiture consomme très peu* (this car uses little gas).

The demonstrative adjective can have an emphatic value: *Rouler à 180 km/h – il est fou, ce type !*

French demonstrative adjectives are often followed by two adverbs of place which are attached to them with a hyphen. *Ce/cette* and so on are sometimes insufficient in themselves since they do not indicate nearness or distance as in the English *this/that*. In consequence, to point to proximity, and provide the idea of *this*, as opposed to *that*, French has recourse to *ci*. To indicate distance or apartness, French uses *là*:

Uses of *ci* indicating nearness:
  In time:

Il y a beaucoup de vent ces jours-ci.	There's a lot of wind these days.
Ce mois-ci, je dois faire de nombreux déplacements à l'étranger.	This month, I have to travel abroad a lot.

In space (less frequently used for space than it is for time, it nevertheless has its place): *ce couteau-ci* (this knife), *cette fourchette-ci* (this fork), *ces outils-ci* (these tools).

Uses of *là* indicating distance:
  In time:

Au XVIIe siècle, les voyages étaient très lents. À cette époque-là...	*In the seventeenth century, journeys were very slow. At that time...*
Venez tous à la maison le 25 juin. Ce jour-là, on fêtera mon anniversaire.	*All come to our house on June 25. On that day, we'll celebrate my birthday.*

  In space:

Cet arbre-là, au fond du jardin, a plus de deux cents ans.	*That tree, at the end of the yard, is more than two hundred years old.*
Tu vois ces immeubles. Il y a dix ans, à cet endroit-là, c'était la campagne.	*You see those apartment blocks. Ten years ago, that was the countryside.*

Ci and *là* differentiate between two nouns:

Qu'est-ce tu préfères ? Cette photo-ci en noir et blanc ou cette photo-là en couleur ?	*What do you prefer? This photo in black and white or that color photo?*

Curiously enough, in spoken language, *là* replaces *ci* in many circumstances:

Cette idée-là me paraît bonne.	*This/That idea seems good to me.*
Cet enfant a sept ans ; à cet âge-là, il devrait savoir lire.	*This child is seven. At this/that age he ought to be able to read.*
Ce bus-là part bientôt ?	*Does this bus leave soon?*

As with the definite article and the possessive adjective (*mon/ma*, etc.), demonstrative adjectives are repeated before each noun: *cette chaise et ce fauteuil, ces dames et ces messieurs*; but one hears regularly: *Ces messieurs-dames*, and even *Ces étudiants et étudiantes*.

The formula *tout* + demonstrative adjective is common: *tout ce pain, toute cette pagaille* (*all this mess*), *tous ces spectateurs*.

58

Demonstrative pronouns / Les pronoms démonstratifs

The passage below deals with the need for the recognition of women's rights, which have been so long ignored in our civilized society. It refers to the yearly International Women's Day, the role of which is to draw attention to the persistent prejudice women have been subjected to from time immemorial. It briefly covers their achievements in the world of politics and science, and in the general area of professional endeavor. Domestic cruelty toward women is not neglected. The passage illustrates the use of demonstrative pronouns in their different masculine, feminine and neuter forms. These pronouns are highlighted in bold. Some translations are provided although the text does not indulge in recondite language.

Le statut social de la femme
Chaque année, des milliers de manifestations à travers le monde célèbrent la journée internationale de la femme lancée le 8 mars 1910 à Copenhague pour promouvoir le vote des femmes. **Cela** démontre que le statut de la femme ne se situe pas au même niveau que **celui** des hommes. En effet, le vote des femmes n'existait pas dans tous les pays. Le premier pays au monde à accorder le vote aux femmes est la Nouvelle-Zélande en 1893. En réalité, le droit de vote accordé aux femmes est relativement récent. En France, ce droit existe seulement depuis la fin de la deuxième guerre mondiale. En Suisse, **celui-ci** n'a été applicable qu'à partir de 1972, au Koweït à partir de 2005 et aux Émirats-Arabes-Unis à partir de 2006.

Même dans les pays développés, le statut de la femme est parfois en retard par rapport à [compared to] **celui** que l'on retrouve dans certains pays en développement. **Cela** peut se vérifier lorsque l'on compare la parité hommes–femmes dans les parlements français et rwandais où, dans ce dernier, la proportion de femmes est supérieure à **celle** qui existe dans le parlement français. **Ce qu'il** est important d'observer c'est que le statut dont bénéficie la femme n'est pas le même que **celui** de l'homme en matière de responsabilité politique. Cependant, il existe bien quelques exceptions qui confirment la règle. Certaines femmes ont marqué la vie politique de leur pays et ont même accédé à un statut international. Mais **celles-ci** se comptent sur les doigts d'une main, et **ceci** n'est pas applicable à toutes les femmes. Moins connue est sans doute l'héroïne Olympe de Gouges qui défendit les droits de la femme lors de la Révolution française, paya de sa personne et fut guillotinée. Dans la foulée de [Following on from] **celle-ci**, on peut citer les notoriétés de Indira Gandhi, Evita Perón, Margaret Thatcher, Bénazir Bhutto et bien d'autres.

Dans le milieu professionnel et scientifique, le nombre de femmes exerçant des responsabilités se situe plutôt à un niveau faible. **Celles** qui réussissent à un niveau élevé également sont rares. **Celle** qu'il conviendrait de citer en matière scientifique est Marie Curie qui, au sommet de la gloire intellectuelle et morale féminine, fut la première femme à recevoir deux Prix Nobel, en physique et en chimie, exploit ahurissant. **Cela** traduit l'exceptionnelle capacité de ces femmes à se hisser [raise themselves] à des niveaux qui dépassent parfois **ceux** des hommes. **Ceci** ne doit pas être compris comme une rivalité historique entre les hommes et les femmes mais simplement un droit naturel de la femme à être l'égale de l'homme. Tous les droits de la femme ne sont pas bafoués [scorned] mais **ceux** concernant son statut dans le domaine politique et professionnel sont les plus visibles.

Un autre domaine dans lequel la situation de la femme ou de l'homme est dramatique est **celui** de la vie de couple où des milliers de femmes et hommes sont battu(e)s. S'il y a bien un problème urgent à régler, c'est bien **celui-là**. On ne peut tolérer qu'une femme soit battue à mort, et aucun motif ne peut justifier **cela**. **Celles** qui en souffrent doivent saisir la justice ou prendre contact avec une association de défense des femmes battues. Il faut espérer que le statut de la femme va évoluer très favorablement dans tous les pays, et **cela** très rapidement.

Demonstrative pronouns, as opposed to demonstrative adjectives (see Chapter 57), actually replace nouns, and they agree in gender and number with the noun/nouns they replace. They correspond to the English: *this one, that one, these ones, those ones*. Here are their forms:

		singular	*plural*
masculine	**simple form**	celui *the one*	ceux *the ones*
	compound form	celui-ci *this one*	ceux-ci *these ones*
		celui-là *that one*	ceux-là *those ones*
feminine	**simple form**	celle *the one*	celles *the ones*
	compound form	celle-ci *this one*	celles-ci *these ones*
		celle-là *that one*	celles-là *those ones*
neuter		ce/ceci *this*	
		ça/cela *that*	

Generally speaking, demonstrative pronouns refer to a noun already mentioned, and help avoid repetition or allow the establishment of a difference.

58.1 Compound and simple forms

Uses of compound forms:

"C'est bien ce disque que tu veux?" "Oui, c'est celui-là."	*"This is the disk you really want?" "Yes, it's that one (over there)."*
"Tu veux cette chaise?" "Non, je veux celle-ci."	*"Do you want that chair?" "No, I want this one (here)."*
Tu préfères quelles fleurs? Celles-ci ou celles-là?	*Which flowers do you prefer? These or those?*

The simple forms are followed by the preposition *de* or by a relative pronoun:

L'ascenseur de gauche est en panne. Prenez celui de droite.	*The elevator/lift on the left has broken down. Take the one on the right.*
Les prévisions de la météo d'hier étaient mauvaises. Celles d'aujourd'hui sont meilleures.	*The weather forecast yesterday was bad. Today's is better.*
J'avais plusieurs possibilités de me connecter à Internet; j'ai choisi celle que propose le réseau X.	*I had several possibilities to connect up to the Internet; I chose the one offered by company X.*
Il y a deux chemins qui mènent au village ; celui qui passe par le bois est plus court.	*There are two paths leading to the village; the one through the wood is shorter.*

The pronoun may also be followed by a past participle or a preposition other than *de*:

Il y a trop d'accidents sur les routes ; ceux causés par l'alcool sont les plus fréquents.	*There are too many accidents on the roads; those caused by drink are the most frequent.*
Les émissions sur la science m'intéressent plus que celles sur le sport.	*Programs on science interest me more than those on sport.*

58.2 Uses of the neuter pronoun

The neuter pronoun has three forms in current use: *ce, cela, ça*. This last one is the colloquial form of *cela*.

58.2.1 The pronoun *ce*

The pronoun *ce* is used with the verb *être*:

"Qui a téléphoné?" "C'est Monsieur Lepetit."	*"Who called?" "It was Monsieur Lepetit."*
"Qu'est-ce que c'est que cette bestiole-là?" "C'est un frelon."	*"What's that insect?" "It's a hornet."*

Ce refers to a sentence or group of words:

Il y avait beaucoup de monde à la fête. C'était très sympa.	*There were a lot of people at the party. It was very nice.*
Être maire d'une grande ville, c'est une lourde responsabilité.	*Being mayor of a big city is a heavy responsibility.*
La tarte aux pommes, c'est mon dessert préféré.	*Apple tart, that's my favorite dessert.*

In R1 colloquial usage, *c'* + *est* replaces *il est* in impersonal constructions:

C'est très utile de savoir conduire.	*It's very useful to know how to drive.*
C'est dommage que nous habitions loin de la mer.	*It's a pity we live far from the sea.*

Ce may also be followed by a relative pronoun which refers to an imprecise idea of object:

Choisis ce que tu veux comme entrée.	*Chose what you like for the entrée.*
Pierre m'a raconté tout ce qui s'était passé.	*Pierre told me all that had happened.*

Ce refers to a proposition, and in this sense it functions with a relative pronoun:

Il s'est mis à pleuvoir, ce qui nous a obligés à rentrer.	*It started raining, which made us go home.*
Bien des magasins sont ouverts le dimanche, ce que les clients trouvent très pratique.	*Lots of shops stay open on Sundays, which customers find very useful.*

In the first of these sentences, *ce qui* is the subject of *a obligés*, while in the second *ce que* is the object of *trouvent*.

58.2.2 The pronoun *cela*

Cela (frequently *ça* in speech) is used as a subject before a verb other than *être*. Compare *C'est intéressant de lire la biographie d'un romancier célèbre* and *Cela/Ça m'intéresse de lire la biographie d'un romancier célèbre*. Compare also *C'est étonnant qu'elle ne soit pas encore là* and *Cela/Ça m'étonne qu'elle ne soit pas encore là*.

58.2.3 The pronoun *ça*

Ça refers more easily than *cela* to a group of words or a sentence:

Adrienne est partie ? Qui t'a dit ça ?	*Adrienne's gone? Who told you that?*
Quelle pagaille ! Il faut que tu ranges tout ça.	*What a mess! You must clear all that up.*
Jeanne m'a posé des questions sur ma vie privée. Ça m'a énervé et je lui ai dit que ça ne la regardait pas.	*Jeanne asked me questions on my private life. That annoyed me so I told her it was none of her business.*

Ça is very commonly used in set expressions: *Comment ça va ? (How are you?); Qu'est-ce que c'est que ça ? (What's that?); Arrête ! Ça suffit comme ça ! (Stop it! That's enough!); Regarde-moi ça (Just look at that); Écoute-moi ça (Just listen to that); Tu fais de la gymnastique tous les jours ? C'est bien, ça (You do gymnastics every day? That's really good, that is); "T'as fini ?" "Oui, ça y est" ("Have you finished?" "Yes, that's it").*

Ça can replace a pronoun (*le, la, les*) when the noun has a general value:

"Tu aimes le thé à la menthe ?" "Non, j'aime pas ça."	*"Do you like mint tea?" "No, I don't like that/it."*
Les films avec Juliette Binoche, j'adore ça.	*Movies with Juliette Binoche – I adore that/them.*

59

Indefinite pronouns and adjectives, and *tout* as an adverb | Les pronoms et les adjectifs indéfinis, et *tout* comme adverbe

The following passage outlines the medical community's approach to diseases in the context of genetically modified organisms. The aim is to find ways of combating serious, life-threatening illnesses through biotechnological research. The third paragraph treats agricultural methods inspired by laboratory research into food production, and the possible dangers this scientific interference may engender. Intellectual property and vested interest foil any agriculturalist's attempt to remain independent. The passage shows how indefinite pronouns and adjectives are articulated. They are shown in bold. Some translations are given, as is, in one case, an explanation of *maladie orpheline*.

> ### Les organismes génétiquement modifiés (OGM)
> La recherche en biotechnologie a fait des progrès inouïs, surtout depuis le séquençage [sequencing = determining of the order in which the components of a molecule appear] du génome à la fois humain et végétal. **On** se retrouve alors dans un monde nouveau qui **nous** effraie parce que la science n'a pas révélé **tous** les tenants et les aboutissants [the ins and outs] de cette recherche biotechnologique. Pour le séquençage du génome humain, **diverses** personnes ont participé à un protocole [procedure] en utilisant des ordinateurs qui ont fonctionné, au même moment, à travers le monde entier. En ce qui concerne la recherche dans le domaine végétal, **plusieurs** entreprises privées ont investi le secteur parce que les enjeux [stakes] représentent **quelque** centaines de milliards de dollars.
> Si **on** raisonne au niveau médical, ce progrès technologique peut rendre de grands services à **quiconque** souffre de maladies graves et que les médecins traitent difficilement pour le moment. Par exemple, **n'importe qui** souffrant d'une maladie orpheline[1] peut garder l'espoir

---

[1] The expression *maladie orpheline* is part of the French-speaking person's linguistic stock-in-trade. It signifies a rare disease which has no real treatment. The words are not confined to the medical community in France. Its English equivalent, *orphan*

de guérir grâce à la biotechnologie. En effet, les médecins tentent **quelque chose, chaque** fois qu'ils en ont l'occasion, pour **quelqu'un** qui souffre d'une maladie que la médecine traditionnelle n'a pas réussi à éradiquer. **Rien ne** peut être négligé pour venir en aide aux patients. **Quelques-uns** parmi eux sont très heureux d'avoir échappé au cancer, grâce à la recherche génétique.

L'**autre** domaine concerné par la biotechnologie touche **chacun** d'entre **nous** dans notre vie quotidienne parce qu'il relève de notre alimentation essentiellement en produits végétaux et produits dérivés. **Tout le monde** est inquiet des suites de la consommation de ces produits dont **personne ne** connaît réellement les effets secondaires [side effects]. **Tout** secteur agricole a été la proie d'entreprises privées qui se sont empressées d'enregistrer des droits de propriété intellectuelle sur des propriétés génomiques de produits de la nature qui, normalement, doivent appartenir à l'humanité.

Or, ces propriétés de la nature ont été enregistrées comme propriétés intellectuelles appartenant à une entreprise privée, et **nul ne** peut les utiliser sans en payer une redevance [license fee]. Par exemple, l'entreprise américaine Monsanto détient 80 pour cent des droits de propriété intellectuelle de **différents** produits de la nature comme le maïs, ou **d'autres** produits agricoles. Lorsque le maïs OGM est vendu à une **autre** entreprise ou un pays, la semence [seed] n'est valable que pour une année parce que le maïs récolté n'est pas reproductible. **Toute** maladie qui toucherait ce maïs ne trouverait de remède que chez l'entreprise qui l'a vendu.

Les cultures OGM sont souvent autorisées sans que la recherche scientifique n'ait examiné précisément l'impact sur **quiconque**, sur l'environnement et sur les cultures traditionnelles. Pour l'instant, **aucune** recherche poussée n'a été réalisée sur **autrui** pour déterminer exactement l'impact, à long terme, des cultures OGM sur l'homme et son environnement.

Indefinite pronouns and adjectives express shades of meaning related to identity and quantity. As the term "indefinite" suggests, they do not refer to specific persons or objects.

59.1 Indefinite pronouns

Indefinite adjectives could be treated alongside indefinite pronouns but it is wise to treat them separately and later in this chapter.

disease, is anything but common in the English-speaking world, and does not form part of the medical vocabulary of English-speaking doctors either. An English speaker would instead resort to *rare*, for instance.

On: is a very common singular pronoun and much more frequent than the English *one*. It can represent one or several persons. It is usually but not always, masculine, and it has several applications:

It refers to people in general: *Au Canada on fait beaucoup de canoë; En Algérie, on prend le thé à la menthe. En Louisiane on parle toujours le français;*

It refers to one or several indeterminate persons: *On a sonné à la porte. Pierre, va ouvrir, s'il te plaît; Maman, on a laissé un colis (package) sur la véranda;*

It replaces *nous* in many circumstances. This use is censured by purists but it is common and finds its way into literary expression, even with Flaubert: *Si tu veux, on ira au théâtre après le dîner; On part la semaine prochaine pour la Suisse?* The use of *on* instead of *nous* can produce a mismatch with the agreement of adjectives or past participles: *On sera plus tranquilles (We'll be more peaceful) si les enfants se couchent maintenant; Quand on s'est séparés (When we separated), ma femme a pleuré; On n'est pas toujours jeune et belle; Allez, ma petite, on est toujours malheureuse* (in both these latter cases, *on* refers to females); *Pierre et moi, on était fatigué(s) et on est resté(s) à la maison* (the past participle may or may not agree here);

For euphony's sake, after *si, que* and *où, l'* may precede *on*. It is argued that this is a higher form of expression found largely in literature, but such is not the case in practice for *l'on* occurs not uncommonly in speech. It is of course true that *si l'on*, for instance, is more elegant than *si on*, and it is easier to say: *Si l'on part maintenant?; La Suisse est un des pays où l'on parle quatre langues.*

Quelqu'un = someone points to a single indeterminate person: *Quelqu'un a oublié une écharpe au vestiaire; Mon amie parle avec quelqu'un que je ne connais pas; J'ai rencontré quelqu'un d'extraordinaire* (notice the extra *de* here); *Tu connais quelqu'un qui puisse donner des cours de maths à mon fils?*

Personne = nobody is usually accompanied by *ne*. Originally, in French classical times, *personne* was a feminine noun as in *une personne = a person*. In former times, but *only* in former times, one could come across *Personne n'était plus belle que Cléopâtre*, but in this negative sense of *nobody*, *personne* no longer has a feminine application. One would say and write now: *Aucune femme n'était plus belle que Cléopâtre. Personne* can also be used with the negative forms: *ne … plus, ne … encore, ne … jamais. Personne* is the negation of *quelqu'un, on* and *tout le monde: Personne ne peut entrer dans le laboratoire sans autorisation* (No one can enter the lab without permission); *Personne d'autre que la directrice ne peut prendre cette décision* (No one other than the principal can make this decision); *"Quelqu'un a téléphoné?" "Non, personne"; Il n'y a personne de blessé* (There is no one hurt; notice the use of *de*); *Je ne connais personne de si heureux que cette femme.* Although *personne* has a negative meaning, there are occasions when it can be used in a positive way, as in interrogative constructions or statements implying doubt. This applies also to sentences where the main clause is in the negative, after *que* following a comparative or after *avant que, sans, sans que, pour que, assez pour que, plus que, trop pour que*: *Y a-t-il personne d'assez courageux?* (*Is there no one | anyone courageous enough?*); *Ne t'imagine pas que tu choques personne* (*Don't imagine you will surprise anyone*); *Il ne veut pas que personne ne soit lésé* (*He does not want anyone to be hurt*); *Adrienne est venue sans personne avec elle*; *Philippe a parlé deux heures sans que personne intervienne*; *Mon père est meilleur juge que personne*; *Avant d'accuser personne...* ; *Mon ami est incapable de tromper personne*. *Personne* is also used after *comme*: *Elle travaille comme personne*. The *ne* is frequently omitted in colloquial R1 style: *Je vois personne* (*I can't see anyone*).

Quelque chose = something refers to an object or an indeterminate idea: *Attention! T'as laissé tomber quelque chose* (*Careful! You've dropped something*); *J'ai quelque chose d'important à te dire* (notice the use of *de*).

Rien = nothing is a singular which is used with *ne* but again with the caveat that in colloquial style this *ne* can very easily be dropped: *Je vois rien* (*I can't see anything*); *J'ai rien dit* (*I didn't say anything*). *Rien* occurs in combination with: *ne...plus, ne...encore* and *ne...jamais*. It is the negation of *quelque chose* and *tout*: *Quel enfant difficile! Rien ne lui plaît*; *Il n'y a plus rien dans le réfrigérateur*; *Parle un peu plus fort, je n'ai rien entendu*; *"Qu'est-ce que tu fais dimanche?" "Rien de spécial"*; *Je n'ai jamais rien compris à ce que dit Sophie*.

Summary of the order of the pronouns *personne* and *rien*:

simple tenses	compound tenses	with an infinitive
Je ne vois personne.	Je n'ai vu personne.	Je ne vais voir personne.
(*I can see no one.*)	(*I saw no one.*)	(*I'm going to see no one.*)
Je ne dis rien.	Je n'ai rien dit.	Je ne vais rien dire.
(*I'm not saying anything.*)	(*I said nothing.*)	(*I am going to say nothing.*)

Summary of the use of *quelqu'un, personne, quelque chose* and *rien* with an adjective. These pronouns can be followed by a masculine singular adjective preceded by the preposition *de*: *quelqu'un | personne | quelque chose | rien + de + masculine adjective*. As noted at various points above, *de* is essential in these constructions: *C'est quelqu'un de très gentil qui m'a renseigné* (*It's someone very nice who gave me the information*); *À la réunion, il y avait M. Lagarde, M. Dubois et moi-même. Personne d'autre n'est venu*; *J'ai quelque chose de très amusant à te raconter* (*I've something very funny to tell you*); *"Vous avez reçu des informations sur cette affaire?" "Non, rien de nouveau."* *Quelques-uns/quelques-unes = some people*. These pronouns, the second of which is the feminine form, refer to a preceding noun. They function in the following way: *"Tu connais des chansons napolitaines?" "Oui, j'en connais quelques-unes"* (*yes, I know some [of them]*); *Notre prof nous a donné des exercices à remettre pour demain. Il y en a quelques-uns de très compliqués* (There are some which are very complicated).

Plusieurs = several has the same form in the masculine and feminine: *J'ai acheté plusieurs fruits; J'avais pris plusieurs photos mais plusieurs sont ratées.*

Certains/certaines = some / certain ones (the second form is the feminine): *Parmi les salariés de cette entreprise, certains sont employés à mi-temps, d'autres à plein temps* (Some of the employees of this company are employed part-time, others are employed full-time); *Ces étudiantes sont intelligentes, et certaines sont super-douées.*

Aucun/aucune, pas un (seul) / pas une (seule) = None, not one. These pronouns can be used with *ne ... plus, ne ... encore* and *ne ... jamais: Pour le mariage de ma sœur, j'ai essayé plusieurs chapeaux. Aucun ne me plaisait* (I didn't like any of them); *"Tu as des nouvelles de Jacques?" "Non, aucune"; "Est-ce qu'il y a encore des visiteurs dans le musée?" "Non, il n'y en a plus un seul."* D'aucuns in R3 language, literary and slightly old-fashioned, has a positive connotation, and means *some people: D'aucuns le croiront* (Some will believe it); *D'aucuns s'imaginent que ce métier est facile.*

Some of these pronouns take *de* + adjective: *L'hôtel compte trente chambres, il y en a quelques-unes/plusieurs/certaines de libres; L'hôtel compte trente chambres, il n'y en a aucune / pas une de libre.*

Chacun/chacune = each one. These are singular pronouns: *Cet artisan fabrique de très jolies poteries. Chacune est décorée d'un motif particulier. Elles coûtent moins de cinquante euros chacune* (Each one costs less than fifty euros); *L'hôtesse a appelé les passagers et a remis à chacun sa carte d'embarquement* (The air hostess called the passengers and handed to each one his/her boarding card).

The pronouns *quelques-un(e)s, certain(e)s, plusieurs, chacun(e), aucun(e)* and *pas un(e)* may be followed by a noun which itself is preceded by *de*. The formula is therefore: pronoun + *de* + noun: *En raison d'une tempête de neige, quelques-uns de nos amis* (some of our friends) *n'ont pas pu venir au réveillon du premier janvier* (New Year's party); These pronouns may also be followed by a pronoun preceded by the preposition *d'entre*. The formula is: pronoun + *d'entre* + pronoun: *Pour la fête de l'école, plusieurs d'entre nous ont apporté* (several of us brought) *une boisson ou un gâteau.*

Nul = no one is used in literary or administrative style, and is followed by *ne: Nul n'est censé ignorer la loi* (No one is supposed not to know the law); *Nul d'entre nous ne l'a dit* (No one among us said it).

Autre(s) = another, others. In the plural only, *d'autres* exists in the sense of some: *Certains enfants marchent à dix mois tandis que d'autres marchent plus tard* (others walk later); *Une seule baguette de pain, ce n'est pas assez, prends-en une autre* (take another); *Je te prête ce stylo, car j'en ai d'autres; Il n'y a que dix étudiants dans la classe, où sont les autres?*

L'un(e) ... l'autre, les un(e)s ... les autres = the one ... the other, some ... the others: *Ce pianiste donnera plusieurs concerts: l'un le 13 mai, les autres en* septembre; *On va examiner les questions l'une après l'autre; Dans la vie, il faut se rendre service les uns aux autres* (we have to do each other favors).

Autre chose = something else. A neuter pronoun which can suggest both something else and something different: *Ce modèle ne me plaÎt pas. Auriez-vous autre chose à me proposer?* (Have you anything else to show me? = something different); *Attends, j'ai autre chose à te dire* (I've something else to say to you = something else/extra).

Autrui = others / other people. Used in formal style: *les biens d'autrui* (other people's property); *sans l'aide d'autrui* (without other people's help); *Il faut respecter la liberté d'autrui* (other people's freedom).

Le même, la même, les mêmes = the same ones: *J'adore ce genre de veste. J'ai presque la même en vert* (I've almost the same one in green); *Pierre et moi, on a des goûts communs en musique mais pas du tout les mêmes en peinture* (but not the same ones at all in painting). When *même* occurs after a noun, it points to insistence: *J'ai trouvé un appartement le jour même de mon arrivée à Londres* (the very day of my arrival in London); *"Allô! Je voudrais parler avec le docteur Lenoir." "C'est lui-même"* (Speaking).

N'importe qui / n'importe quoi = anyone/anything. These are singular pronouns: *La porte n'est jamais fermée: n'importe qui peut entrer* (anyone can come in); *Je n'ai jamais mal à l'estomac. Je peux manger n'importe quoi* (I can eat anything). *N'importe* may combine with *où, quand* and *comment*: *J'irai n'importe où pour trouver le soleil; Je suis chez moi, tu peux passer n'importe quand* (you can come any when); *C'est très simple, tu peux le faire n'importe comment* (any how).

Quiconque = whoever (R3): *David a pris la décision sans consulter quiconque* (without consulting anyone); *Sophie défie quiconque voudrait la contredire* (defies anyone who would contradict her); *Il est nécessaire à quiconque de connaÎtre la loi* (for everyone to know the law).

Tous, toutes = all. As a pronoun the **s** is pronounced. Contrast with the adjective below: *Les verbes sont compliqués. Tous ne sont pas réguliers / Ils ne sont pas tous réguliers; Nous devons tous faire des efforts pour respecter l'environnement; Mes sœurs n'aiment pas la vie parisienne. Elles vivent toutes en province.* In compound tenses, *tous* and *toutes* fall between the auxiliary and the past participle: *Leurs enfants ont tous fait des études scientifiques; J'ai pris d'innombrables photos mais elles ne sont pas toutes réussies. Tous* and *toutes* are also used with the direct object *les*: *Goûtez nos glaces. Nous les préparons toutes avec des fruits frais* (We prepare them all with fresh fruit); *Lucile avait bien des disques des années quatre-vingt, mais elle les a tous vendus.*

Tout le monde = everyone: *Aline est très sympa et jolie. Tout le monde l'aime; Ce film peut être vu par tout le monde; Tout le monde n'a pas la chance de voyager.*

Tout = everything, all. This is a neuter pronoun: *Dans mon studio, tout est blanc; Pas de problèmes! Tout va bien!; Le tremblement de terre a tout détruit; Quand on conduit une voiture, il faut tout contrôler.*

Tous and *toutes* are used with *les* + numerals: *Pierre et Jean sont venus tous les deux*; *Nos cousines sont venues toutes les trois*.

The order in which *tout* occurs varies according to a simple finite verb, an infinitive, or a compound tense: *Nous comprenons tout*; *Nous ne comprenons pas tout*; *Nous allons tout comprendre*; *Nous n'allons pas tout comprendre*; *Nous avons tout compris*; *Nous n'avons pas tout compris*.

59.2 Indefinite adjectives

Quelques = *some* (this is the masculine and plural form): *J'ai acheté quelques tomates*; *Il reste encore quelques feuilles sur les arbres*; *Il n'y avait personne dans la rue sauf quelques personnes qui prenaient des photos*. In R3 language, *quelques* may be preceded by *les*: *Les quelques conseils que tu m'as donnés m'ont beaucoup aidée*. Also in R3 language, *quelque* may be used before an abstract noun: *On gardait quelque espoir de* (We/They had some hope of) *mettre fin au conflit*.

Quelque may be used as an adverb (thus invariable), suggesting *about/approximately*:

Il y avait quelque cinq cents personnes dans la salle (There were some five hundred people in the room).

Plusieurs = *several* (this is the masculine and feminine form): *J'ai acheté plusieurs posters pour décorer ma chambre*; *J'y suis retourné plusieurs fois*.

Certains/certaines = *some/certain*: *Certains vins, comme le Beaujolais nouveau, ne se conservent pas longtemps*; *Certaines personnes sont allergiques à l'aspirine*. In the singular, *certain* is preceded by the indefinite article: *C'est un homme d'un certain âge* (i.e., about middle age); *Ce tableau a une certaine valeur*; *Tu as lu Un certain sourire de Françoise Sagan ?*

Ne . . . aucun/aucune = *not one/none*: *Je n'ai aucun ami à qui demander conseil sur cette question*; *Malheureusement, elle n'a aucune expérience professionnelle*. *Aucun(e)* can reinforce a negation: *Notre déménagement* (removal) *s'est fait sans aucun problème*.

Chaque = *each*: *Lors d'un championnat, chaque skieur porte un casque et un dossard* (each skier wears a helmet and a number); *Chaque matin, je pars vers sept heures*; *Chaque fois que j'ai congé il pleut*; *La facteur passe chaque jour*. *Chaque* may only be followed by a singular noun. In the plural, one would use *tous/toutes les*. Compare *J'y vais chaque dimanche* and *J'y vais tous les dimanches*.

Nul/nulle = *none / not one* (used in administrative or elevated language): *Nul mineur ne sera admis au film*; *Je suis athée. Je n'éprouve nulle crainte devant la mort*.

Autre = *another/other*: *Je passe te voir un autre jour*; *J'ai une autre cousine qui est médecin*. The plural of *autre* in the sense of *some* is *d'autres*: *J'ai un autre livre* > *J'ai d'autres livres*; *Je vois une autre mangouste* (mangoose) > *Je vois d'autres mangoustes*.

Le même | les mêmes = the same: *Ils habitent le même quartier que nous* (They live in the same district as us; note the construction *que nous*); *Carole et sa sœur jumelle ne portent jamais les mêmes vêtements.*

Tel(s), telles(s) = such. When used with an indefinite article: *Comment veux-tu réussir avec de telles méthodes de travail?* (with such working methods); *On n'a jamais vu une telle chaleur au mois de mai.* When used without an article: *Je t'envoie un courriel disant que j'arriverai tel ou tel jour* (such and such a day); *Que tu prennes telle ou telle lessive* (such and such a washing powder), *ton linge sera bien lavé.*

N'importe quel(s)/quelle(s) = any: *Viens chez nous n'importe quel jour* (any day); *Envoie-moi n'importe quels vêtements, ils seront toujours utiles*; *Viens me voir n'importe quelle heure demain.*

Différents/différentes, divers/diverses = different, various. These adjectives are not preceded by *des/de*: *Je connais différents auteurs qui ont écrit sur le sujet*; *Différentes personnes se sont opposées à cette mesure*; *Au cours de la réunion, divers points de vue ont été exprimés.* *Différents* before and after a noun has a different meaning. Compare *Différentes* (Several) *personnes ont été entendues* and *Des personnes très différentes* (Very different people) *se sont présentées.*

Quelconque = any: *Cette soirée m'ennuie ; je trouverai un prétexte quelconque* (any pretext) *pour ne pas y aller.* *Quelconque* also has the nuance of *mediocre*: *C'est un restaurant tout à fait quelconque* (It's only an average sort of restaurant).

Tout, toute, tous, toutes = all, every. When *tous* is used as an adjective, the **s** is unpronounced. Contrast the adjective with the pronoun above: *Tu dois finir tout ce travail avant demain*; *Le vent a soufflé toute la nuit*; *Tous les produits | Tous ces produits proviennent de l'agriculture biologique* (organic); *Nous avons examiné toutes les candidatures.* *Tout* expresses a habit or frequency: *Je fais du kayak tous les dimanches*; *Prends ce médicament toutes les six heures*; *Pourquoi ont-ils planté des arbres tous les dix mètres ?*

Tout may be used without an article, notably in maxims, laws and rules: *Tout homme doit obéir à la loi*; *Entrée interdite à toute personne étrangère au service.*

Tout is used in many expressions: *J'ai filé à toute vitesse | à toute allure*; *La piscine est toujours ouverte, tu peux y aller à toute heure*; *Le mérite de la natation, c'est qu'on peut faire de l'exercice à tout âge*; *Je fais du vélo en toute saison*; *Il faut gagner à tout prix* (come what may).

Tout as an adverb = *entirely, quite.* Even as an adverb, it can sometimes vary.

Before a masculine adjective, either singular or plural, it remains invariable: *Je me suis payé un tout petit téléphone portable*; *Les enfants jouent tout seul dans le jardin*

Before a feminine adjective, either singular or plural, and beginning with a consonant, *tout* agrees with the adjective: *C'est une salle de cinéma toute neuve*; *Lave-toi les mains ! Elles sont toutes sales.*

Before a feminine adjective, either singular or plural, and beginning with a vowel or mute **h**, agreement or non-agreement is possible: *Elle était tout/toute étonnée de son succès; Elles étaient tout/toutes heureuses de se revoir.* The agreement/non-agreement here leads to unresolved debate. Some grammarians would plead for no agreement. After all, *tout* here is used adverbially.

Other uses of *tout*:

Before a preposition or adverb: *Le parking est tout près du supermarché; Parlez tout doucement, le bébé dort.*

Before a gerund: *Nous bavardions tout en nous promenant (while walking); Tout en souriant, il enrageait (While yet smiling, he was furious).*

In a great number of adverbial expressions: *tout de suite, tout à fait, tout à l'heure, tout à coup, tout de même.*

Part IX

60

Conjunctions / Les conjonctions

The passage below details some of the advantages derived from the Erasmus scheme, which encourages European students to spend a whole university year in another country so that they benefit from the acquisition of a deepening expression in another language, and also develop a new strength of personality. The Erasmus scheme attracts highly motivated students whose year abroad is counted as an integral part of their studies. This year stands as a full year were it spent in the home university. It places heavy demands on the student but its advantages far outweigh any disadvantages. The students' intellectual growth enables them to confront the task of finding employment with conviction and confidence. The passage below illustrates the use of conjunctions in French. The conjunctions, which are sometimes difficult to separate from adverbs or adverbial phrases, are highlighted in bold. Some translations are included.

La mobilité étudiante

Dans le cadre des échanges ERASMUS, **par exemple**, des milliers d'étudiants se déplacent d'une université à l'autre pour valoriser [to invest with greater value / to promote] leurs études **et** obtenir un diplôme permettant de trouver facilement un emploi. **Pendant que** leurs camarades poursuivent leurs études dans leur université d'origine, certains étudiants choisissent de poser leur candidature à une université étrangère **et** suivre des cours dans une autre langue. Ils obtiennent **à la fois** une véritable chance de partir à l'étranger, **et** ils se perfectionnent dans la langue du pays **et** développent leurs compétences linguistiques.

Effectivement [Sure enough], **pour** être en mesure de suivre des cours en langue étrangère, il faut **en même temps** faire des efforts en langues. **Or**, l'étudiant qui n'est pas capable de comprendre le cours dans une autre langue **que** sa langue maternelle **ne** pourra **ni** suivre convenablement ses études dans un pays étranger **ni** réussir aux examens. **Par conséquent**, il doit progresser **en même temps que** ses camarades pour garder toutes les chances d'obtenir son diplôme à la fin de l'année. **Cependant**, les étudiants qui sont candidats aux échanges avec des universités étrangères sont généralement plus motivés **mais** ils doivent

quand même travailler davantage **puisqu**'ils envisagent de poursuivre leurs études dans une langue étrangère.

Toutefois, des étudiants étrangers peuvent parfois se trouver dans une situation difficile **lorsque** les résultats ne sont pas très bons. **Aussi**, ils doivent redoubler d'efforts pour se remettre au niveau et passer leurs examens avec succès. **En somme**, la réussite aux examens signifie pour eux de longues journées ou de longues nuits de travail, **ou** parfois les deux, **car** on ne peut pas être diplômé sans effort. **Cependant**, **lorsqu**'un étudiant travaille régulièrement, il se donne alors toutes les chances de réussir aux examens.

Par la suite, **lorsqu**'il aura obtenu son diplôme, l'étudiant peut chercher un emploi **soit** [either] dans un pays étranger **soit** [or] dans son pays d'origine. **Si** la recherche d'emploi se déroule [takes place] dans un pays étranger, l'étudiant entamera [set in motion] alors les démarches [measures/steps] pour une autorisation de travail qui, **toutefois**, peut lui être refusée **s**'il ne réunit pas toutes les conditions requises. **En admettant qu**'il trouve du travail, il lui faudra aussi chercher rapidement un logement décent pour s'établir durablement dans le pays en question. La recherche de logement est souvent difficile pour un étranger, **à moins qu**'il ne soit logé provisoirement chez des amis **et qu**'il réside près de son lieu de travail.

S'il décide de regagner son pays d'origine **et qu** [and if] 'il y cherche un emploi, il devra prendre toutes les mesures nécessaires pour être embauché [taken on / given work] le plus rapidement possible **car** le taux de chômage [unemployment rate] est plutôt élevé **et** la concurrence [competition] entre diplômés [graduates] est farouche. Ensuite, il devra également rechercher un logement **en supposant qu**'il ait déjà obtenu un travail **et que** son salaire lui permette de payer le loyer exigé par le propriétaire du logement. **Par conséquent**, l'étudiant est passé de l'étape des études à celle du travail **et** se retrouve ainsi confronté aux problèmes courants de la vie ordinaire.

A conjunction is any word or group of words, other than a relative pronoun (*who/which/that = qui/que*), that connects words, phrases or clauses, for instance *and/while = et/pendant que*). They may be split into two categories: coordinating conjunctions (see below for a comprehensive list) and subordinating conjunctions.

Before analyzing the use of conjunctions, it is worthwhile making the comment that there is sometimes difficulty in distinguishing between some conjunctions and adverbs. *Effectivement, en somme, ensuite, toutefois, cependant, du reste, néanmoins, par la suite* are cases in point. Adverbs (or adverbial expressions) of time, like adverbs of manner, also carry out the function of joining up different parts of a sentence.

60.1 Coordinating conjunctions

Coordinating conjunctions link two parts of a sentence which have much in common. *Et* is a good example of this. *Et* can link verbs: *J'ai fait mon devoir et je vais me coucher.* It can link nouns: *les garçons et les filles.* It can link adjectives: *La maison est noire et blanche.* It can bring together adverbs: *Elle écrit clairement et correctement.*

Apart from *et*, there are *ou* and *ni* which can be repeated, corresponding to *both...and, either...or, neither...nor*: *Les étudiants viennent de Paris et de Madrid; Ça m'est égal, le froid ou la chaleur; Tu veux du café ou du lait?; Ou tu acceptes ou tu cèdes* (Either you accept or you give in); *Ils sont ou Espagnols ou Mexicains; Je ne fais ni la natation ni la planche à voile* (I do neither swimming nor windsurfing).

Variety is always useful. Thus *et*, for instance, can be replaced by *en même temps que* (at the same time as) and *à la fois* (at the same time): *Ne parle pas en même temps que tu manges; Sophie est à la fois belle et intelligente.*

Mais, like its English equivalent *but*, can indicate a restriction, an objection or a contrary idea. It is often preceded by a comma: *Le candidat a une bonne formation, mais il n'a pas l'expérience voulue* (The candidate has good training, but not the desired experience); *Marcel n'a pas pu étudier, mais il tient à passer l'examen* (Marcel hasn't been able to study, but he is anxious to take the exam). *Mais* can also introduce the first clause: *Mais ils sont déjà partis* (here there would be no comma).

Car (for/because) cannot introduce the first clause, explaining as it does the meaning of the main clause: *L'enfant n'ira pas à l'école demain, car il a la rougeole* (since he has measles).

Puisque carries out the function of *since* at the beginning of a sentence: Puisque mon collègue est absente, on me demande de la remplacer

Or (now) is sometimes considered to be an adverb, but it is equally considered to be a coordinating conjunction. It serves to introduce a new idea and is usually followed by a comma: *On l'attendait jeudi; or, il n'arriva que le samedi.* It also links the terms in a reasoned argument, as with a syllogism: *Les poissons vivent dans l'eau; or, le saumon est un poisson; donc, le saumon vit dans l'eau.*

The following list offers both simple and compound coordinating conjunctions:

conjunctions suggesting alternatives: *ou, au contraire, ou bien* (or else), *soit... soit* (either... or), *tantôt... tantôt* (sometimes... sometimes);
conjunctions suggesting cause: *car, en effet, effectivement;*
conjunctions suggesting consequence: *ainsi* (so, thus), *alors, aussi, c'est pourquoi, donc, d'où* (whence), *en conséquence, par conséquent, par la suite* (as a result);
conjunctions suggesting explanation: *à savoir* (that is to say), *c'est-à-dire, par exemple, soit* (that is);

conjunctions suggesting linking (*liaison*): *alors, aussi* (thus), *comme* (as/since), *de plus* (what is more), *en outre* (moreover), *ensuite* (next), *et, mais aussi, même* (even), *ni, puis*;

conjunctions suggesting restriction: *cependant* (however), *du moins* (at least), *du reste* (moreover), *mais, néanmoins* (nonetheless), *or, pourtant* (however), *toutefois* (however);

conjunctions suggesting a following idea or statement: *alors, enfin, ensuite, puis*;

conjunctions suggesting transition: *après tout, bref, d'ailleurs* (besides), *en somme, or, peut-être*: *Tantôt il adore la musique, tantôt il la déteste; On annonçait de la grêle, et effectivement* (sure enough), *il a grêlé; Ses résultats ne sont pas très bons. Aussi (So) a-t-elle jugé raisonnable de poursuivre son travail; Il a plu toute la journée, par conséquent / en conséquence on n'a pas pu sortir; David a perdu son portefeuille, d'où la nécessité de m'appeler à la maison; Les élèves ont terminé leurs devoirs, ont-ils cependant étudié leurs leçons ?; Elle a été injuste envers moi, néanmoins je lui pardonne; Cette voiture est très rapide, toutefois elle consomme beaucoup d'essence; Henri était toujours en retard, alors la directrice a dû le réprimander; En premier, il y avait une girafe, ensuite un éléphant; Bref, passons (In short, let's keep going).*

60.2 Subordinating conjunctions used with the indicative mood

Subordinating conjunctions can consist of one or several words. Most subordinating conjunctions indicating cause, clear consequence, comparison and time are followed by verbs in the indicative mood and the conditional, whereas others indicating concession, intention, condition and time express uncertainty and entail the subjunctive mood. The difference between the indicative and the subjunctive moods is brought into sharp relief with *de façon que* and *de sorte que*. They are used with the indicative when suggesting consequence or result: *Les athlètes ont réussi d'excellentes performances de façon/sorte que deux records ont été battus* (indicative); *Bolt a couru le deux cents mètres de façon/sorte que personne ne puisse le rattraper* (subjunctive).

A range of subordinating conjunctions is listed below:

subordinating conjunctions indicating cause: *attendu que* (since), *comme* (as/since), *du fait que* (given the fact that), *étant donné que* (given that), *parce que, puisque* (since), *sous prétexte que, vu que* (seeing that;

subordinating conjunctions indicating consequence: *à tel point que, au point que, de façon que, de sorte que, si bien que, tellement que*;

subordinating conjunctions indicating comparison: *ainsi que, comme, de même que* (just as), *moins que, plus que*;

subordinating conjunctions indicating time: *alors que, à mesure que* (while, according as), *après que, au moment où, aussitôt que* (as soon as);

subordinating conjunctions indicating condition: *au cas où* (*in case*), *même si* (*even if*), *si, si ce n'est* (*except*);

subordinating conjunctions indicating concession: *alors que, en dépit du fait que, pendant que, tandis que: Attendu que | Comme | Étant donné que | Vu que la décision est prise . . .* (*Given that the decision has been taken . . .*); *Ils ont marché au point que | à tel point qu'ils ont eu des ampoules aux pieds* (*They walked to the point that they had blisters on their feet*); *Paul, ainsi que Pierre, est gentil; Germaine, de même que ma cousine, sera de la fête; Si tu viens, je t'attendrai; Marcel est très compétent tandis que sa collègue est inexpérimentée; Je ne l'ai jamais vue, si ce n'est de loin* (*I've never seen her, save at a distance*).

60.3 Subordinating conjunctions used with the subjunctive mood

A much fuller treatment, with examples, of these conjunctions may be studied in Chapter 44 on the subjunctive. The list below records some of the most common conjunctions that are used with the subjunctive:

subordinating conjunctions indicating intention: *afin que* (*so that*), *de façon que, de manière que, pour que, de crainte que* (*for fear that*), *de peur que* (*for fear that*);

subordinating conjunctions indicating concession: *en admettant que, bien que, quoique, encore que* (*although*), *malgré que* (disputed by some grammarians: *despite the fact that*);

subordinating conjunctions indicating condition: *à supposer que, en admettant que, pourvu que*;

subordinating conjunctions indicating time: *avant que, après que, en attendant que, jusqu'à ce que*.

60.4. *Que* as a subordinating conjunction

When the *que* clause is the subject, the verb is usually in the subjunctive: *Qu'il vienne demain ne me surprendrait pas* (*That he should come tomorrow would not surprise me*); *Que tu le fasses ou que tu ne le fasses pas, ça m'est égal.*

When the *que* clause is the object, the verb is in the indicative or in the subjunctive: *On dit qu'il va* (indicative) *neiger demain; Je doute que Émilie vienne* (subjunctive); *Je ne pense pas qu'ils aient* (subjunctive) *raison.*

When *que* is repeated in alternative clauses, the subjunctive occurs: *Que notre équipe les batte ou qu'elle perde, je ne vais pas pleurer; Que tu restes ou que tu partes . . .* (*Whether you remain or go . . .*).

Que in conditional constructions is of the R3 variety and is found largely in writing and particularly literature. It expresses hypothesis: *Vous me le refuseriez que je n'en serais pas étonnée* (*Even if you refused me I would not be surprised*); *Il me le dirait une dizaine de fois que je ne le croirais pas* (*Even if he told me ten times I would not believe him*).

Que can be used as the equivalent of other conjunctions. If the notion of a conjunction is repeated, *que* frequently replaces the second occurrence: *puisque Marie sort ce soir et que je dois rester* (since Marie is going out this evening and I must stay); *comme il faisait tard et que nous n'avions plus de lumière* (as it was getting late and we had no more light); *quand ils sont partis et que j'ai pu nettoyer la cuisine* (when they left and I was able to clean the kitchen); *bien qu'il fasse beau et que nous ayons le temps* (although it is fine and we have the time).

Que may replace *si* in R3 language as the second *si*, and a subjunctive would then be in order: *si Jean appelle et qu'il te dise qu'il peut venir; si le danger est réel et que nous courions le risque d'être inondés; s'il vient me voir et qu'il se plaigne.* The indicative may also occur here. This use is considered faulty by many but Blampain states unequivocally that it is acceptable: *si Jean revient et qu'il te dit que.* Blampain quotes from literary sources as well: "Ils continuaient à se parler de profil comme si le chanteur ne s'était pas tu et qu'un invisible spectacle se déroulait dans le salon" (Françoise Sagan, in Hanse and Blampain 2005, p. 480). Two *si*'s are of course also possible: *si Anne-Marie prépare le repas et si nous nettoyons le salon.*

With the meaning of *alors que, quand* and so on, *que* may be used to express simultaneity of action or an action immediately following: *Il parlait encore que je lui avais déjà tourné le dos* (He was still talking when I had already turned my back on him); *Adrienne avait à peine dit cela que la porte s'ouvrit.*

Que explains a previous statement in the following way: *Tu l'avais donc prévenu, qu'il a devancé mes objections ?* (You had warned him, so that he was aware of my objections?);

In **R1** language, *que* may replace *tant / tellement que: Il souffre que cela fait peine à voir* (He suffers so much that it is painful to see).

After an imperative, *que* may replace *pour que, afin que: Viens me voir, que nous réglions cela* (Come and see me so that we can sort it out); *Couvre le petit, qu'il ne prenne pas froid; Ferme la porte, qu'on ne nous entende pas.*

In R3 style, after a negative main clause, *que* may replace *avant que* and *sans que: Jean n'avait pas voulu partir que tout ne fût réglé* (Jean had not wanted to leave before everything was sorted out); *Il ne levait jamais les yeux que son regard ne croisât celui de Joseph* (He never lifted his gaze without his eyes meeting those of Joseph).

Que may replace *parce que* after *c'est* following on a main clause: *Si je te le dis, c'est que je le pense* (If I say that, it's because I think it).

Notice how *que* may follow an adjective: *Il ne nous regardait plus, fier qu'il était de son nouveau titre* (He no longer looked at us, proud that he was of his new title); *Ils ne nous accorderont qu'un instant, occupés qu'ils sont par leur travail* (They will only give us a moment, busy as they are with their work).

61

Negation | La négation

The following passage describes the dangers of cigarette smoking. It points to some of the methods used by the appropriate authorities to combat smoking. Young people are attracted by it and it risks damaging their lives and leading to a premature death. Yet, whatever measures are taken, our youth still continue to indulge in this activity which has the result of filling the coffers of the state. The passage exploits the various negative expressions in French which are highlighted in bold. Notice how full negative expressions precede the infinitive. Some translations are provided.

La lutte anti-tabac

Depuis quelques années, le tabac est interdit dans les lieux publics, les restaurants, les hôtels et tout autre endroit accueillant du public. Cette interdiction de fumer est appliquée dans de nombreux pays européens et aux États-Unis. **Aucun ne** peut fumer dans ces lieux avec des indications « Espace **non fumeur** [Non-smoking area] » ou « **Non fumeur** » sous peine de forte amende [with a risk of a heavy fine]. La fumée est nocive [harmful] pour la santé et pour les **non-fumeurs** qui inhalent la fumée malgré eux. Les affiches et pancartes signalent qu'il **ne faut jamais** fumer dans ces lieux.

En effet, le tabac tue chaque année des dizaines de milliers de personnes qui meurent en raison du cancer que cela engendre. Les fumeurs **ne se rendent pas compte** qu'ils risquent de contracter le cancer du poumon ou de l'œsophage [throat cancer / cancer of the oesophagus] en continuant de fumer. Dans certaines familles, il se peut qu'il **n'y ait aucun** membre qui fume mais dans d'autres, il arrive que tout le monde fume par imitation, du plus jeune au plus âgé. Les ravages de la cigarette devraient convaincre les fumeurs de **ne plus jamais fumer**. Mais leur addiction à la nicotine rend très difficile de **ne plus être tenté** par la cigarette.

Aussi, les personnes qui prennent la décision de **ne plus fumer** utilisent d'abord la méthode douce telle que celle des patches ou des pastilles. Mais cette méthode **n'est pas** toujours efficace, et le fumeur **ne peut parfois s'empêcher** de fumer à nouveau. Alors, pour **ne plus toucher** à la cigarette, le fumeur doit parfois solliciter l'aide d'un médecin spécialisé qui doit **non pas le convaincre** d'arrêter de fumer, mais lui expliquer comment il **peut ne plus dépendre** de la cigarette. Pour cela, le médecin spécialiste établit un protocole [procedure] pour un arrêt définitif de la consommation de la cigarette.

La cigarette fait des dégâts considérables parmi les jeunes qui commencent à fumer dès l'âge de 10 à 12 ans. Dans les collèges et les lycées, les jeunes fument des cigarettes pour ressembler aux adultes et, par imitation, le nombre de fumeurs augmente très rapidement. Les campagnes publicitaires, les messages imposés [printed] sur les paquets de cigarettes **n'ont que** peu d'impact sur ces jeunes. **Rien n'y fait** [They don't do any good]. Pourtant, on **ne doit pas baisser** les bras parce les jeunes fumeurs d'aujourd'hui sont les grands fumeurs et les victimes potentielles du cancer de demain. De plus, les dépenses de santé pour traiter les symptômes de la cigarette **ne peuvent se compter qu'**en centaines de millions d'euros.

La lutte contre le tabagisme [tobacco addiction/smoking] est une lutte de longue haleine [a long, drawn-out struggle] et **rien ne doit être négligé**. Les pouvoirs publics sont partie prenante [are favorably inclined] des campagnes **anti**-tabac parceque la vente des tabacs **ne peut se réaliser qu'**avec l'autorisation de l'État qui prélève des taxes importantes. Pour éradiquer le nombre de fumeurs, il **n'y a que** les pouvoirs qui puissent mettre en œuvre [apply] tous les moyens, avec l'aide des associations, pour convaincre les fumeurs de **ne plus fumer**.

61.1 Negative words and expressions

The word *non* is not used with *ne*, whereas *aucun, jamais, ni . . . ni, pas, personne, plus, que* and *rien* are used with *ne*. *Non* is used in the following ways:

as a negative reply to a question: *"Elle est là ?" "Non" | "Je crois que non" | "Tu peux être sûr que non"; "Tu le feras?" "Peut-être que non";*
to negate any part of speech, save a verb:
  noun: *C'est sa cousine, non sa sœur;*
  past participle / adjective: *une chambre non meublée (unfurnished);*
  prepositional phrase: *Lucile est entrée non sans hésitation; Ils habitent non loin de Philadelphie.*

Non may be combined with other negative words:

non pas: Elle a des flatteurs, non pas des amis; J'ai essayé, non pas de la convaincre, mais de lui expliquer mon opinion;
non pas que: This expression is used with the subjunctive: *Je ne veux pas y aller avec lui, non pas que je veuille le vexer | non pas que je n'aie pas le temps;*
non plus: meaning *neither: "Je ne savais pas que Céline avait réussi son examen." "Je ne savais pas non plus" (I didn't know either); "Je ne le savais pas." "Ni moi non plus."*

Note that *si* is always used to contradict a negative question or suggestion: *"Tu ne veux pas venir avec nous ?"* *"Si, je viens"*; *"Il n'y a aucun Argentin dans la salle."* *"Mais si."* *Oui* may be used like *non* after *que*: *Je crois que oui*; *Peut-être que oui*.

Pas combines with *ne* to provide the straightforward negative *not*: *Je ne viens pas*; *Je ne veux pas*; *Je ne veux pas y aller*. In indirect questions introduced by *si*, *ne... pas* is sometimes used to stress doubt in the speaker's mind, and this usage often occurs with the verb *demander*. Compare the two following sentences: *Je leur ai demandé s'ils ne voulaient pas m'accompagner* and *Je leur ai demandé s'ils voulaient m'accompagner*. Compare also *Aurélie se demande s'il n'y a pas de solution* and *Aurélie se demande s'il y a une solution*.

In the following example, unlike the equivalent English sentence, *ne... (pas)* directs the listener's attention to the period of time which has elapsed since the last sighting of the person in question: *Voilà / Il y a deux jours que je ne l'ai pas vue* (*It's two days since I saw her*). In a similar way, the French use a negative in the following example, where in English a positive means of expression would be used: *Quelle n'a pas été ma surprise / ma stupéfaction quand elle s'est manifestée* (*Imagine my surprise when she turned up*).

Point appears in a literary context and is infrequent these days. It has no greater emphasis than *pas*: *Il n'y a point de vent aujourd'hui*.

Mot is used only with verbs of speaking in R3 usage: *Elle ne dit mot* (*She remained completely silent*).

Goutte is used only with *voir* in R1 speech: *Je n'y vois goutte* (*I can't see a thing*).

Que dalle is a slang term used only in R1 speech: *Je ne pige que dalle* (*I don't understand a thing*).

Pas de has the meaning of *not any*. Note that *des / du / de la* becomes *de / d'* when *pas de* is used: *Je vois des oiseaux* > *Je ne vois pas d'oiseaux*. *Pas de* is used with nouns in negative sentences: *Je n'ai pas de livres / d'argent*; *Je ne trouve pas de solution / de banque*.

Pas un is more emphatic than *pas de*. It suggests *not a single one*: *Je n'ai pas un dollar* (*I haven't got a single dollar*); *Il n'y a pas une maison à dix kilomètres à la ronde* (*There's not a single house within ten kilometers*); *Pas une des filles n'a répondu*; *J'ai pas un radis* (R1 = *I haven't got a dime/penny*).

Omission of **ne** with **pas**: This construction occurs in very similar circumstances to those in which **non** is used, but in a less formal register. *Pas* is used to negate any part of speech except a verb:

noun: *J'ai vu son frère mais pas sa sœur*;

past participle / adjective: *Elle est jolie, pas belle*;

prepositional phrase: *J'ai assez de pommes, pas assez de poires*;

in informal, often elliptical speech situations: *"Tu viens ce soir ?"* *"Pourquoi pas ?"*; *"Elle vient de mettre au monde des triplés."* *"Pas possible !* *Je ne savais pas qu'elle était enceinte."*

Uses of *plus*:

ne . . . plus = *no longer/no more* refers to both time and quantity: *Je suis
retourné chercher mon parapluie ; il n'y était plus* (*it was no longer there*);
Mon père ne travaille plus aux PTT (my father *no longer works for the postal
service*); *"Encore des cerises " "Non, merci, je n'en veux plus | je ne veux plus
de cerises."*

Plus by itself may have a negative value but refers only to quantity (*no
more*): *Allez, plus d'histoires ! (Come on, no more nonsense!); Quel bonheur !
Plus d'impôts ! (No more taxes!); Son mari n'est plus* (R3 = my husband
has died). Care needs to taken over the negative and positive aspects
of this construction. The context is important here and so is the
pronunciation. The **s** is pronounced when *plus* has the meaning *more*,
but not when it means *no more*: *Quel bonheur ! Plus de congés ! (More
holidays!); Quel malheur ! Plus d'impôts ! (More taxes!).* This rule is not
absolute, however, and the **s** is sometimes pronounced as a **z**: *Plus on
est de fous, plus on rit (The more the merrier).*

Jamais = *never*: *Jeanne ne quitte jamais son travail avant six heures (Jeanne
never leaves her work before six).* In more formal language, *jamais* may
introduce a sentence. This inversion has the value of emphasizing a
statement: *Jamais elle ne vient me voir avant sept heures du soir. Jamais* used
by itself has a negative value: *"Tu es allé au zoo ?" "Jamais."* But it is also
used quite frequently without *ne*, meaning *ever*: *L'avez-vous jamais fait ?;
Je l'ai écouté toute la journée sans jamais comprendre; Si jamais mon fils me
téléphone, dis-lui que. . . (If ever my son calls, tell him . . .).*

Que is placed immediately before the element of a sentence which is being
qualified: *Diane n'est revenue qu'hier soir (Diane only came back yesterday
evening); Ce n'était que ce matin que j'ai appris la nouvelle (It was only this
morning that I learned the news); L'absence du chef ne fait que rendre le choix
plus difficile (The boss's absence only makes the choice even more difficult). Que*
can be a long way from the negative *ne*, and this can be confusing
for non-native speakers of French: *Je ne voudrais lui parler aujourd'hui ou
demain, ou même après demain, qu'en présence de son père (I should only like to
speak to him, today, tomorrow or even the day after tomorrow, in his father's
presence).* This separation of the *ne* and the *que* can be illustrated by a
series of five sentences, where these two elements move further and
further away from each other:
Je ne l'ai vue qu'une seule fois.
Je ne l'ai vue à Paris qu'une seule fois.
Je ne l'ai vue à Paris, et brièvement, qu'une seule fois.
Je ne l'ai vue à Paris, et là encore très brièvement, qu'une seule fois.
Je ne l'ai vue à Paris, et là encore très brièvement, le 30 avril, qu'une seule fois.

One could speculate that the psychological meanderings of a Proustian
style could stretch the gap between *ne* and *que* a lot further, over many
lines of prose.

Rien que = *merely*: *Rien qu'à lire le journal, je suis pris de panique* (*Merely by reading the newspaper, I am in a panic*).

When *ne . . . que* combines with *pas* it means *not only*: *Tu ne vois pas que des Italiens. Il y a aussi des Suisses* (*You not only see Italians. There are also Swiss*); *Il n'y avait pas que des planches à voile, il y avait aussi des pédalos* (*There were not only windsurfers, there were also pedal boats*). In speech, *que* may stand by itself with the meaning of *only*: *"Ça m'a coûté trente euros." "Que trente euros ?"* (*"It cost me thirty euros." "Only thirty euros?"*); *"Nos amis sont rentrés hier." "Que hier?"* (*"Only yesterday?"*); *Le camping, c'est que du bonheur !*

Ni . . . ni (*neither. . . nor*): *Je ne comprends ni le japonais ni le chinois* (*I understand neither Japanese nor Chinese*). When qualifying the subject of a sentence, *ni. . . ni* can entail a singular or a plural verb: *Ni l'un ni l'autre n'est venu | ne sont venus* (*Neither the one nor the other came*); *Ni le chauffage ni la lumière n'a | n'ont fonctionné* (*Neither the heating nor the lighting worked*). *Ni. . . ni* may combine with any part of speech except finite verbs, when only one *ni* is required: *Adeline n'a vu ni elle ni moi* (*Adeline saw neither her nor me*); *Cet outil n'est ni bon ni utile*; *Je ne veux ni peux y aller* (*I neither want to nor can go*); *Cela n'est permis ni par la loi ni par la morale* (*That is allowed neither by the law nor by moral standards*). *Ni. . . ni* is used with infinitives introduced by *sans*: *Sans parler ni à sa mère ni à son frère, il est parti* (*Without speaking to his mother or brother, he left*). R1 speakers generally avoid the *ni. . . ni* construction, and prefer to attach *non plus* at the end of a sentence: *J'aime pas le prof, le collège non plus*, instead of *Je n'aime ni le professeur ni le collège*. Similarly: *Je bois pas le café, le thé non plus*, instead of *Je ne bois ni le café ni le thé*.

Personne, *rien* and *aucun* have negative values in themselves when used without a verb: *Je n'ai vu personne* (*I saw no one*); *"Qui a frappé à la porte ?" "Personne"* (*"No one"*); *Je n'ai rien fait* (*I did nothing*); *"Qu'est-ce que tu as fait ?" "Rien"* (*"Nothing"*); *Je n'ai aucun désir de visiter le musée* (*I have no desire to visit the museum*); *"Il te reste combien d'euros ?" "Aucun."*

61.2 Combination of negative words

When combined, negative words are ordered in the following way:

1	2	3	examples
jamais	plus	personne	Je n'y comprends plus rien.
		rien	Il ne m'a jamais rien donné.
		que	Il n'y a plus personne.
		ni . . . ni	Il n'a jamais ni portable ni télévision.
			Je ne pourrais jamais plus étudier.

Aucun may also be used with *jamais*, where English would use *any*: *Je n'ai jamais lu aucun roman de Sartre* (*I've never read a single novel by Sartre*). This construction is more forceful than *Je n'ai jamais lu un/de roman de Sartre*.

61.3 The negation of infinitives

The various elements are ordered in the following way:

	examples
ne pas	Mon père me recommande de ne pas y aller.
ne jamais	Ma mère m'a demandé de ne jamais sortir après vingt heures.
ne rien	Ma cousine m'a encouragée à ne rien acheter.
ne plus	Notre amie s'est engagée à ne plus jamais revenir.

Notice the order with *ne/sans* + infinitive + *personne / nulle part*: *Ils sont partis sans voir personne / sans parler à personne* (*They left without seeing anyone / without speaking to anyone*); *Mon frère m'a demandé de n'aller nulle part sans lui.*

Notice how the position of the negative or the number of negatives can affect meaning:

Je ne peux pas le faire.	*I can't do it.*
Je peux ne pas le faire.	*I can not do it* (i.e., I can refuse to do it).
Je ne peux pas ne pas le faire	*I can't not do it* (i.e., I can't avoid doing it).

The following examples show how more complex constructions involving the negation of infinitives work, and are influenced by considerations of register:

R2: Je lui reproche de ne pas être honnête / de ne pas avoir été honnête.

R2 + **R3**: Il me reproche de ne l'avoir jamais compris; Il me reproche de n'avoir rien fait; Il me reproche de n'avoir plus rien fait.

R3: Je lui reproche ne d'être pas honnête; Je lui reproche de n'avoir pas été honnête.

Il me reproche de ne l'avoir jamais compris; Il me reproche de ne rien avoir fait.

61.4 Negation and register

The impact of register considerations upon negation causes the following adjustments to the normal *ne...pas*: R1 users, and to a lesser extent R2 users, can very easily drop the *ne*, whereas R3 users, and sometimes R2 users, prefer the *ne* without the *pas* with some verbs:

no *ne* (**R1**, sometimes **R2**): *(Je) crois pas; C'est pas juste/vrai; David Lanoë? Connais pas; Ça fait rien.*

no *pas* (**R3**):

with *cesser, oser, pouvoir, savoir*: *Il ne cesse de pleuvoir; Je n'ose le faire; Je ne sais le prononcer; Je ne saurais l'expliquer; Elle ne pouvait s'en passer* (*She couldn't do without it*). *Bouger* and *daigner* used to appear in past centuries without the **pas** but they no longer do;

     in rhetorical questions introduced by *qui* or *que*: *Qui ne l'aurait compris ?*
     (*Who would have understood it?*); *Qui ne viendrait dans de telles circon-*
     stances ?; *Que ne ferait-elle pour vous plaire ? Quel adversaire ne lui rendrait*
     justice ? (*Which adversary would dispense justice for him?*);

     in certain set expressions, often in the higher registers: *Qu'à Dieu ne*
     plaise (*Would to God* [R3 = that it should not happen]); *Qu'à cela ne*
     tienne (*certainly*); *Je n'ai que faire de vos excuses* (*I am not interested in your*
     excuses); *N'aie* / *N'ayez crainte* (R3 = Fear not); *n'avoir cure de* (R3 = not
     to worry about): *David n'avait cure de tondre sa pelouse*; *ne dire mot* (*not to*
     say a word): *Elle ne disait mot*; *ne souffler mot* (*not to say a word*); *n'y avoir*
     âme qui vive (*there not to be a living soul*): *Il n'y avait âme qui vive*; *ne voir*
     âme qui vive (*not to see a living soul*);

     in certain conditional clauses (**R3**; sometimes **R2**): *si je ne me trompe* (*if*
     I'm not mistaken); *si je ne m'abuse* (*if I'm not mistaken*); *S'il n'était venu*
     à mon secours, je me noyais (*If he hadn't come to rescue me I would have*
     drowned); *si ce n'est* (*except*): *Je n'ai jamais visité la ville, si ce n'est de passage*
     (*I've never visited the town, except in passing*);

     n'importe (**R2** = never mind): *n'importe comment/qui/pourquoi/quand/quoi*:
     Il ne faut pas le faire n'importe comment/quand; *Tu peux le demander à*
     n'importe qui; *David ne dit que des âneries, il dit n'importe quoi* (*David only*
     says stupid things, he says anything that comes into his head).

By contrast, in certain types of subordinate clauses, a superfluous *ne*,
sometimes known as an expletive *ne*, occurs in **R3** usage, sometimes in **R2**
usage, but never in **R1**, save perhaps for jocular reasons. The explanation is
simple enough: within the verb lies the feeling or desire that an event or
circumstance should not take place:

     with verbs and expressions of fearing (the subjunctive is required here):
     avoir crainte/peur, craindre, de crainte/peur, redouter, trembler, appréhender:
     Je n'ose pas partir de crainte qu'elle ne vienne pendant ce temps; *Je crains qu'elle*
     ne puisse venir; *Ils redoutent que leurs adversaires ne soient mieux préparés*
     qu'eux; *Elle appréhende qu'il ne se mette à pleuvoir*. If these constructions
     were followed by the *pas*, the meaning would be quite different, and
     the register would be R2. Compare the sentences *Je crains qu'elle ne vienne*
     (*I fear lest she will come*) and *Je crains qu'elle ne vienne pas* (*I fear lest she will*
     not come);

     with verbs expressing avoiding or preventing: *empêcher, éviter, prendre*
     garde: *Il faut empêcher qu'elle ne parte* (*We must prevent her from leaving*);
     Tâche d'éviter qu'ils ne s'en aillent (*Try to stop them from going*); *Prenez garde*
     qu'on ne vous surprenne (*Take care that someone will not catch you*);

     with *s'en falloir de peu*: *Il s'en est fallu de peu qu'elle vienne* (*She almost came*);
     Peu s'en est fallu qu'il ne tombe;

with expressions of doubt in the negative: *ne pas douter, nul doute, ne pas nier: Je ne doute pas qu'il n'ait raison* (I don't doubt if he is right); *Nul doute qu'elle n'ait raison*;

with *à moins que* and *avant que: à moins qu'il ne vienne le premier* (unless he comes first); *Avant qu'elle ne sorte, elle doit prendre son repas*;

in comparisons: *Émilie est plus/moins intelligente que je ne le pensais*; *Audrey a accompli la tâche mieux que je ne le croyais*. It is preferable to use *ne le* rather than *ne* in these cases.

61.5 Miscellaneous features

When there is ellipsis of the verb, the omission of *ne* is necessary: *Pas de gros mots !* (No swear words!); *Pas d'histoires !* (No messing around!); *un soldat pas très courageux*; *pas un souffle* (not a breath of air).

Pas is not used in the following expressions: *Je ne le reverrai de ma vie* (I'll never see him again); *Je ne le reverrai de longtemps / de sitôt* (I'll not see him for a long time / so soon); but it is included in *Je n'ai pas dormi de la nuit* (I haven't slept all night long).

Pas plus que requires a negative: *Pas plus que je n'ai besoin de lui, pas plus il n'a besoin de moi* (No more than I need him does he need me); *Je n'ai pas besoin de lui pas plus qu'il n'a besoin de moi* (I don't need him any more than he needs me).

The prefix *anti* may also be considered as a negative expression when combined with both adjectives and nouns, and these come in a plentiful supply. Of course, some of these expressions may communicate a positive expression. Here are just a few: *un appareil antibruit, un liquide antigel, un mouvement anti-Québec, un produit anticancéreux/antidépressif, une attitude anticléricale, un dispositif antidémarrage, une opinion antifasciste/antisémite, un produit anti-inflammatoire*.

In- or **im-** may also be used as prefixes with the idea of negating: *commode > incommode, connu > inconnu, égal > inégal, élégant > inélégant, exact > inexact, fidèle > infidèle, pénitent > impénitent, précis > imprécis* (and there are many more).

Peu almost accomplishes the same effect: *peu aimable, peu clair, peu délicat, peu intéressant, peu pratique, peu inquiet, peu nombreux, peu recommandable, peu souvent*.

Non preceding an adjective or noun also has the effect of a negation, and here it may conjure up a euphemistic sense. Generally speaking, *non* + adjective does not entail a hyphen, while with a noun it does: *un pacte de non-agression* (as with the Russian–German pact of 1939–1941), *un pays non aligné, la non-assistance* (à une personne en danger), *non belligérent, la non-belligérence, une unité non combattante, un non-conformiste, les non-croyants, la non-discrimination, la non-violence, les objets volants non identifiés (ovni), un non-fumeur* (can be used of person or place, e.g., railroad carriage), *une politique de non-ingérence, une politique de non-intervention, un non lieu (no case, dismissal of a charge*, as in law), *un non chrétien/musulman, non-paiement du loyer, un non-résident, un non-sens, un vol quotidien non-stop entre Paris et Los Angeles* (a very common Anglicism), *un*[1] *non-voyant, un point de non-retour, les non-dits* (the things that are implied but are not expressed), *une quantité non négligeable, un peintre non figuratif* (and there are many more such terms).

Non ? replaces *n'est-ce pas ?* which is not as common as non-native speakers think it is: *T'as vu le film, non ?; Vous êtes allés avec eux, non ?; Maman, je peux les accompagner, non ?*

Non may be used to balance a previous statement: *Pierre veut jouer au tennis, les autres non; J'adore le chocolat, mais les bonbons non.*

Non may also be used as a noun: *Elle m'a répondu par un "non" catégorique; Il faut venir et je n'accepte pas un "non."*

Défense and *interdit* are commonly used with the idea of refusal or negating, and these usually appear on public signs: *Défense d'afficher, Défense d'entrer, Défense de fumer, Défense de manger dans la bibliothèque, Entrée interdite, Passage interdit, Sens interdit, Stationnement interdit, Toute reproduction interdite* (in publishing).

---

[1] As opposed to this term, which means a *blind person*, a *malvoyant* is a *visually impaired person*. On the same theme, a *malentendant* means a person who is hard of hearing. There seems to be no equivalent here for *non-voyant*. These are euphemistic words, just as they are in English.

62

Numbers, time, measurements | Les nombres, le temps, les mesures

The following passage describes betting on games of chance. Several types of gambling are detailed, from television programs where enormous sums can be won, to casinos controlled by strict rules, and to betting shops. Many expressions of number and measurement appear in the passage. They are highlighted in bold. Notice the twenty-four hour system for time in the French-speaking world. Notice also how, in similar constructions, verbs can be in the singular or plural, although the main noun is only in the singular. Compare the second sentence in the first paragraph ("Le nombre de joueurs se compte") and the first sentence of the last paragraph (un bon nombre de joueurs engloutissent"). Notice also that there is no elision of *de* with the number 1 in "de 1 à 150 000 euros," as opposed to the use of the indefinite article "un."

Les jeux de hasard

Depuis le **début des années 1980 (années 80 / années quatre-vingt)**, les jeux de hasard **se sont multipliés** au fur et à mesure de l'aggravation de la crise économique. Le **nombre de joueurs se compte** par **dizaines de millions** à travers le monde. En France, tous les jours, les joueurs doivent valider leurs jeux de tirage [gambling] avant **19 heures**, sinon ceux-ci ne seront pris en compte. En jouant aux jeux de hasard, les joueurs espèrent gagner **plusieurs millions**, sinon plusieurs **milliers d'euros**, et mener enfin une vie de rentier [a life of leisure]. Par contre, les jeux sont interdits aux mineurs, c'est-à-dire aux **moins de 18 ans**.

Aussi, les mises [bets] des joueurs représentent chaque semaine des **dizaines de milliards d'euros** dont un **quart** est prélevé [deducted] par l'État sous forme de taxes diverses, **la moitié** revient à la société émettrice du jeu et le **dernier quart** est distribué aux gagnants. En fonction de son **revenu**, le joueur moyen **mise de 2 à 50 euros** sur chaque jeu. Généralement, on observe **deux** types de jeux : les jeux de tirage [draw] et les jeux de grattage [scratch card]. Le **premier** jeu est basé sur un tirage de **numéros** qui se fait à la télévision sous le contrôle d'un huissier. Les jeux de tirage les plus connus sont le **Loto** et l'**Euromillion** qui se déroulent consécutivement dans **neuf** pays européens. Le Loto invite le joueur à choisir **cinq numéros**, plus un **numéro** complémentaire. **L'Euromillion** consiste à identifier **cinq numéros**, plus **deux numéros** complémentaires. Le **lot** des jeux de tirage comme celui de **l'Euromillion**, par exemple, peut dépasser **cent millions d'euros** à partager avec les joueurs de **premier** rang. Le **deuxième** jeu permet au joueur d'acheter **une** ou **plusieurs** cartes de jeux sur lesquelles il doit gratter des cases [boxes/squares] grises révélant tout de suite les **gains** qui vont de **1 à 150 000 euros**.

Il existe des jeux avec un tirage **par semaine** comme celui de l'Euromillion, **trois tirages par semaine** comme celui du Loto mais également des jeux avec **deux** tirages **par jour** dont le **premier** doit être inscrit [registered] avant **12h 45** et le **second** avant **21h**. Ce **dernier** jeu s'appelle le Kéno. Les joueurs doivent respecter les **dates limites**, sinon leurs jeux sont invalidés. **Certains** joueurs acquièrent généralement des mécanismes et évitent d'arriver trop tard chez le buraliste [newsdealer/ agent] qui valide leurs jeux. En outre, on **compte** également les joueurs qui fréquentent les casinos où se trouvent des **dizaines** de machines à **sous** [bandits manchots = one-arm bandits], **trois ou quatre** tables de poker et de black jack. Pour les machines à **sous**, les joueurs doivent introduire un jeton acheté chez le caissier du casino et tourner une manette [handle] pour espérer gagner le **gros lot** [jackpot] lorsque les **trois 7** sont alignés. En ce qui concerne les tables de poker et de black jack, les joueurs investissent parfois **plusieurs milliers d'euros**, mettant en danger leur propre patrimoine. Dans **certaines** circonstances, des joueurs qui sont accros [fanatics] aux jeux demandent paradoxalement au service de sécurité du casino de leur interdire l'entrée au casino.

En espérant gagner une **fortune** et arrêter de travailler, un **bon nombre** de joueurs engloutissent, chaque mois, près de **20%** de leur salaire sans s'en rendre compte, et font face à des **découverts** [overdrafts] bancaires avec des **agios** [bank charges] **de 17%**. Aussi, il convient de ne pas trop céder à la tentation de **miser gros** [play high stakes] en rêvant de gagner des **millions**. Les films américains qui affichent Las Vegas ou encore la « Sin City » font tourner la tête à des **millions** de spectateurs. Ce paradis des jeux de hasard peut se transformer en véritable cauchemar [nightmare] pour ceux qui perdent leurs **fortunes**.

62.1 Numbers

62.1.1 Cardinal numbers and their spoken equivalents[1]

zéro	0	cinq	5	dix	10
un/une	1	six	6	onze	11
deux	2	sept	7	douze	12
trois	3	huit	8	treize	13
quatre	4	neuf	9	quatorze	14

[1] The figures here are Arabic. Roman numerals are treated at the end of this section.

quinze	15	soixante	60	. . .	
seize	16	soixante et un	61	quatre-vingt-dix	90
dix-sept	17	soixante-deux		quatre-vingt-onze	91
dix-huit	18	. . .		. . .	
dix-neuf	19	soixante-dix	70	quatre-vingt-dix-sept	97
vingt	20	soixante et onze	71	quatre-vingt-dix-huit	98
vingt et un	21	soixante-douze	72	quatre-vingt-dix-neuf	99
vingt-deux	22	soixante-treize	73	cent	100
vingt-trois	23	soixante-quatorze	74	cent un	101
vingt-quatre	24	soixante-quinze	75	cent deux	102
vingt-cinq	25	soixante-seize	76	. . .	
vingt-six	26	soixante-dix-sept	77	deux cents	200
vingt-sept	27	soixante-dix-huit	78	deux cent un	201
vingt-huit	28	soixante-dix-neuf	79	. . .	
vingt-neuf	29	quatre-vingts	80	neuf cent quatre-vingt-dix-neuf	999
trente	30	quatre-vingt-un	81	mille	1 000
trente et un	31	quatre-vingt-deux	82	mille un	1 001
trente-deux	32			. . .	
trente-trois	33			dix mille	10 000
. . .				dix mille un	10 001
quarante	40			. . .	
quarante et un	41			cent mille	100 000
quarante-deux	42			deux millions	2 000 000
. . .				trois milliards	3 000 000 000
cinquante	50				
cinquante et un	51				
cinquante-deux	52				
. . .					

Note that thousands are separated by a space, decimals by a comma: *Elle court le cent mètres en 10,9 (dix secondes virgule neuf)*; *Bolt a couru le cent mètres en 9,7 (neuf secondes virgule sept)*. The word *millions* is written in letters to avoid a confusing series of zeros: 50 millions / 500 millions / 500 000 millions.

In all general use (scientific, administrative, financial and so on), the Arabic system of figures is used: *La fête aura lieu à 15h 30*; *La distance entre Montréal et Québec est de 253 km*. However, in literary, poetic texts, the figures are frequently written out in letters (*en toutes lettres*). This also applies to checks, or any official document where fraud is possible: *25$ = vingt-cinq dollars*. The main cases where letters are used are:

express duration: age, number of years/months/days/hours/minutes/seconds: *La traversée est de sept heures*; *Philippe a quinze ans et demi*;

Fractions of hours following *midi* and *minuit* (see also Section 62.2.2 on time and the clock): *midi et quart, minuit et demi*. If the hour is noted in figures, the fractions cannot appear in letters: *Il viendra à 12h 45*;

Counting from 10, numbers are generally written in figures: *La collection comporte 13 titres*;

At the beginning of a sentence, numbers are written in letters: *Quatorze chercheurs ont recueilli des données dans dix pays*;

In legal statements, letters are used: *Pour la somme de vingt-cinq mille dollars* (*25 000$*);

When numbers are written as nouns, they appear as letters: *J'ai misé sur le neuf de cœur* (I bet on the nine of hearts); *voyager en première* (*classe*); *manger les trois quarts d'une tarte*; *passer un mauvais quart d'heure* (to have a bad time);

Letters are used when they form part of a compound noun: *Le boulevard des Quatre-Bourgeois, la ville de Trois-Rivières* (both in Canada); *un deux-mâts*.

Agreement with numbers: *Un* can take a feminine form: *J'ai mangé une pomme, pas deux*; *trente et une voitures*. Note the use of *cent*: *Il y en avait trois cents* / *trois cent deux*; *J'ai lu sept cents pages*; *trois cents ans/euros*; but one writes *tous les cent ans*; *la page deux cent*. One also writes: *pendant les années quatre-vingt*.

Use of fractions: *le millième, le centième, le dixième, le quart, le tiers, la moitié, les trois quarts*: *Nous n'avons même pas terminé le centième* / *le dixième du travail*; *On a fait le quart* / *la moitié* / *les trois quarts du travail*.

Agreement with fractions: When the fraction is clearly plural, the verb is in the plural: *Les trois dixièmes* / *Les deux tiers* / *Les trois quarts des étudiants ont réussi*; *Deux tiers des maisons ont été détruites/détruits* (both past participles are possible). When the fraction is clearly singular, the verb is in the singular: *Un tiers de la région a été ravagé/ravagée* (both past participles are possible); *Un bon quart du fromage était pourri*. If the fraction is in the singular and the following noun is in the plural, a choice is available. Compare *La moitié des députés a voté pour et l'autre contre* and *La moitié des gens sont partis plus tôt*. It could legitimately be argued that the first sentence with a singular verb is more grammatically sound since *a voté* is governed by a singular noun.

The odd case of *zéro* followed by a noun: When *zéro* precedes a noun and functions like an adjective, the noun remains in the singular: *J'ai fait zéro faute*. This is different from the English. If, however, one might have expected to find several of the items in question, the plural is acceptable: *Il y avait zéro livres dans la bibliothèque*; *Il y a zéro voitures en ville*. This singular nevertheless remains the most logical form to use.

Cardinal numbers are nouns, singular and masculine: *Son dossard portait un neuf (The number on his back was a nine)*; *Deux cent deux a gagné le prix.*

Million and *milliard* are nouns and are followed by *de* if a noun follows: *trois cent millions de dollars*; *deux millions et demi d'habitants*; *Des milliards d'euros ont été convertis en dollars.*

Demi is invariable when used as part of a number: *quatre et demi*; or Fellini's film *Huit et demi.* As for time, see Section 62.2.

Mi is a reduced form of *demi* and is used thus: *La maison de Pierre est à mi-chemin (halfway) du port et du village*; *Le héros a ébauché un sourire mi-figue mi-raisin (ambiguous smile)*; *une réponse mi-figue mi-raisin (uncertain)*; *à la mi-mai/juin (mid-May/June).*

Septante (70) and *nonante* (90) are standard in Belgium and Switzerland. Much easier for foreign speakers than *soixante-dix* and *quatre-vingt-dix*. *Huitante* (80) can be heard in dialect form. These forms fit logically with the Spanish (*setenta/ochenta/noventa*) and the Italian (*settanta/ottanta/novanta*).

62.1.2 Percentages

Pour cent is abridged to *p.c., p. cent* or *p.100*, or has the symbol %, as in many languages. The preposition *de* is used to denote increase or decrease: *L'inflation a augmenté/diminué de deux pour cent.*

If the percentage is followed by a singular noun, a singular verb is used and the adjective or past participle agrees with the noun: *Vingt pour cent de la classe est d'accord et se montre enchantée de la décision.* If the percentage is followed by a plural noun, the verb takes a plural form: *Soixante-cinq pour cent des personnes interrogées ont été retenues (were kept on).*

When a complement is understood and not made explicit over gender, there are two choices with respect to gender. Compare *En ce qui a trait au budget publicitaire, 13% seront affectés au lancement de notre nouveau produit* and *Relativement aux dépenses, 5% sont liées à la formation du personnel.*

62.1.3 Pronunciation of numbers

Un has a feminine form: *une*, as in *une (one page* or *a page).* But in enumerations one can say: *Cherchez la page un/une, la page vingt et un/une* and so on.

When *un* has specifically the meaning of *one*, no elision takes place in writing: *L'inflation a augmenté de un pour cent.* Yet, in speech, both *de un pour cent* and *d'un pour cent* (this second form for the sake of speed) are used, although one may argue for no elision in all cases.

With *six*, like with *dix*, the x is pronounced in a number of ways, depending upon its position with respect to the following word, if there is one. Before a noun beginning with a consonant the x is not sounded: *six/dix maisons.* Before a vowel or mute h, it has the sound of z: *six/dix animaux, six/dix hommes* Standing by itself or with no noun following, it has the sound of ss: "*Il y avait combien de passagers?*" "*Il y en avait six/dix/soixante-six.*"

The t of *huit* is sounded in isolation, or before a mute h: "*Tu as combien de dollars?*" "*Huit*"; *huit hommes.* If it precedes a consonant, it is not sounded: *huit tables.*

Preceding a consonant or standing in isolation the **f** of *neuf* is pronounced: "*Tu as vu combien de vaches dans la rue?*" "*Neuf*"; *J'ai vu neuf chevaux*. But when preceding a vowel or a mute **h**, it sounds like a **v**: *neuf étoiles, neuf hommes*. Elision does not take place with *onze*: *le onze novembre*.

The **t** of *vingt* is not pronounced in isolation or before a consonant: "*Il y en avait combien?*" "*Vingt*"; *J'en ai vingt*; *J'ai trouvé vingt dollars dans la rue*. From *vingt et un* to *vingt-neuf* the **t** is pronounced.

Liaison with the **t** of *cent* is not clear. One pronounces the **t** in *cent ans*. However, the **t** in *cent étudiants* or *cent élèves* is open to discussion. The authors recommend no pronunciation of the **t** in these two cases.

62.1.4 Ordinal numbers (i.e., first, second, third, etc.)

The forms for these are: *premier/première, deuxième/second(e), troisième* (as in *le Troisième Reich*), *quatrième... septième* (as in Bergman's *Le septième sceau*), *dixième, onzième... vingtième, vingt et unième, vingt-deuxième... trentième, quarantième, cinquantième, soixantième, soixante-dixième, quatre-vingtième, centième, cent unième, millième, dix millième, cent millième, millionième, dernier/dernière*.

Ordinal numbers function like adjectives and therefore agree in number. Only *premier, second* and *dernier* have a feminine form: *le premier garçon* / *la première fille*, *Elle est arrivée en troisième/dernière position*.

Ordinal numbers can function like nouns: *Ils sont les premiers à breveter cette invention* (*They are the first to patent this invention*); "*Messieurs les Anglais, tirez les premiers*" (writes Pierre Daninos in *Les carnets du Major Thomson*); *Ils habitent au deuxième* (étage); *Je vais au sixième* (in an elevator/lift).

Second (the **c** is pronounced as a **g**) replaces *deuxième* in some cases, and it is argued that *second* really signifies the second of two elements, as in *la seconde guerre mondiale*. But this is not always the case and one hears: *la deuxième guerre mondiale*. Theoreticians would like to establish a difference between these two words. It is true that one only says: *les causes secondes* (*secondary causes*); *le Second Empire*; *C'est une seconde Marie Curie*; *Il faut espérer que Barack Obama soit un second Abraham Lincoln*; *le second avènement* (*second coming* [of Christ]); *apprendre une nouvelle de seconde main*. However, beyond these fixed expressions, one comes across: *C'est leur deuxième/second fils*. The second term could sound odd to some. At the same time, one would only hear: *les étudiants de premier, deuxième et troisième cycle; le deuxième bureau* (*information service*); also Simone de Beauvoir's *Le deuxième sexe* (1949).

Kings or popes are referred to in the following way: *Guillaume premier, Guillaume deux/trois, Louis quatorze/seize; Benoît premier/deux/trois/seize* (Pope Benedict XVI). See also Section 62.1.6 on Roman numerals.

Word order with ordinals functions in the following way: *les deux premiers rois* (*the first two kings*), *les trois dernières reines* (*the last three queens*). This is the reverse order of the English. Notice also: *Je te dis pour la énième fois qu'il ne faut pas sortir* (*I tell you for the nth time that you mustn't go out*).

In sports competitions, progress beyond the group stage is recorded thus: *Ils sont en huitième de finale (in the last sixteen) | en quart de finale | en demi-finale | en finale.*

62.1.5 Telephone numbers

One could discuss ad infinitum the various postal codes and their uses in different francophone countries. They all have a national code which precedes the local number, which makes telephone contacts relatively easy. To some extent, what is said about France could apply to Belgium, Switzerland, Quebec, North Africa and so on. France is therefore taken as a general pattern for all French-speaking countries.

France is divided into five zones. For phone calls made within France, each number consists of five sets of two digits (10 digits in all). A person living in Nantes, for instance, could have the following number: 02 (code for Nantes) 40 25 69 83 (*zéro deux, quarante, vingt-cinq, soixante-neuf, quatre-vingt-trois*). To phone Nantes from outside France, for instance from the United States or United Kingdom, the initial 0 is dropped and 00 33 is added so that the number above would be come: 00 33 240 25 69 83 (*zéro zéro, trente-trois, deux cent quarante, vingt-cinq, soixante-neuf, quatre-vingt-trois*). To phone a number in the United Kingdom from France, again the initial 0 is dropped, and 00 44 is added; consequently a number in Nottingham phoned from Grenoble might be: 00 44 1159 259 381. It serves no purpose to list the codes for different countries or their localities. These appear in any telephone directory (*annuaire*). A free number in French is *un numéro vert*.

62.1.6 Roman numerals

Although English speakers, whether in the United States, Canada, United Kingdom or elsewhere, do not learn the system of Roman numerals in elementary/primary school, it has traditionally formed part of the curriculum of French-speaking children, and that of Spanish and Italian speakers as well. Roman numerals may not appear important to English speakers, but for French speakers they are important and some attention should be paid to them.

Roman numerals[2] are based on seven letters of the Latin alphabet: I = 1, V = 5, X = 10, L = 50, C = 100, D = 500, M = 1000. Although in old texts lower case is sometimes used, only upper case is used now: *le Vème siècle (the fifth century), les pages XIX–XXIII (pages 19–23).*

---

[2] The notion of zero (0) was unknown in the Greek and Roman worlds. It made its appearance in India in the ninth century AD, whence it was conveyed westwards via Arab mathematicians, Al-Farazi and the Spanish–Arab astronomer/physicist Averroës (1126–1198) for instance. We use the Hindu–Arabic numerical system today, doubtless because the Roman formulae were far too limited, clumsy and unmanageable. How Romans and Greeks would have coped with millions and billions leaves much scope for the imagination.

The same letter is not repeated more than three times. Thus: CCCXXXIII = 333 but CDXLIV = 444. A letter is never repeated if another letter has the same value. VV could *not* be written instead of X. When a letter is followed by another letter of the same or lower value, they are added together: VI = 6, XV = 15, XXVII = 27. When a letter is followed by a letter of a higher value, the value of the first is taken from that of the second, and precedes it: IV = 4, IX = 9, XL = 40, XC = 90, CD = 400, CM = 900, MCMXCIX = 1999, MM = 2000. It goes without saying that, in speech, Roman numerals are not apparent.

Roman numerals are mainly used for:

centuries and millenia: *au VIème siècle a.v. J.-C. (in the sixth century BC), le XVIème siècle (the sixteenth century), le IIème millénaire;*

names of sovereigns and dynasties: *sous le règne de Louis XIV (in the reign of Louis XIV), Napoléon III, les Pharaons de la IIIème dynastie (the Pharoahs of the third dynasty);*

names of popes: *Alexandre VI (Alexander VI), Jean XXIII (John XXIII), Benoît XVI (Benedict XVI);*

names of Olympiads and other important periodic events: *les XXIIIèmes Jeux olympiques, la VIIème Internationale, la XXIIème Foire internationale du livre;*

divisions of a text: *tome IV (volume 4), volume III, fascicule IX (booklet/part 9), avant-propos, p. IV (introduction, p. 4);*

inscriptions on monuments and tombstones: *MCMXC = 1990; Jean Garnier décédé le 9 décembre MCMXXX (Jean Garnier, passed away on December 9, 1930);*

film credits: *Autant en emporte le vent ... MCMXXXVIII (Gone with the Wind ... 1938).*

62.2 Time

62.2.1 Days of the week, months, seasons

In civil life, the week starts on a Monday, but from the traditional and religious point of view it starts on a Sunday. All days of the week are masculine and are written in lower case: *lundi (Monday), mardi, mercredi, jeudi, vendredi, samedi (Saturday and Sabbath), dimanche.* (Oddly enough, although most days in Romance languages are masculine, *Sunday* in Italian is feminine: *domenica.*) A specific day close in time is referred to thus, with no article: *jeudi prochain/dernier.* A general day is referred to thus in the singular: *Je vais toujours au théâtre le vendredi (soir).*

Months of the year are all masculine and are written in lower case: *janvier (January), février, mars, avril, mai, juin, juillet, août, septembre, octobre, novembre, décembre.* The preposition *en* is used in most cases: *Je fais du ski en janvier/ mars.*

The seasons of the year usually take the following prepositions: *au printemps (spring), en été, à l'automne / en automne, en hiver.*

62.2.2 Time and the clock

Time is told in the following way: *Il est une heure (It is one o'clock) | deux heures | trois heures*; *Il est midi (midday) | minuit (midnight)*; *Il est deux heures cinq (five past two) | trois heures vingt-cinq (twenty-five past three) | quatre heures et demie* (note the extra **e** on *demie = half past four*), *dix heures moins vingt (twenty to ten) | onze heures moins le quart (a quarter to eleven) | onze heures moins cinq (five to eleven)*. *C'est midi* is of a lower register.

French speakers do not have the English *a.m.* and *p.m.* division of time. They use the twenty-four hour system, and not just on timetables, in administration and so on: *Le train arrive à vingt heures*; *L'avion part à treize heures quarante-cinq | à dix-sept heures trente*. The twenty-four hour system occurs frequently in daily discourse: *On se verra à dix-sept heures (We'll see each other at five)*; *Le cours commence à quinze heures (The class begins at three o'clock)*.

Note also the following expressions connected with time: *avant-hier (day before yesterday)*, *hier (yesterday)*, *aujourd'hui (today)*, *demain (tomorrow)*, *après-demain (the day after tomorrow)*, *la semaine prochaine/dernière (next/last week)*, *le lendemain (on the following day)*, *le surlendemain (two days after)*, *la semaine | l'année prochaine (next week/year)*; *la prochaine fois (next time)*, *l'heure de pointe (commute/rush hour)*, *arriver à temps (to arrive in time)*, *l'horaire (schedule/timetable)*, *changer de fuseau horaire (to change time zone)*; *Bonjour (Good morning/day)*, *Bonsoir (Good evening)*, *Bonne nuit (Good night)*. Note that the expressions *Bonne matinée | journée | après-midi* are perfectly normal when you wish someone to have a good day; *J'y ai passé quinze jours | une quinzaine (a fortnight)*; *une décennie (a decade)*, but *une décade (period* of ten days: can signify *decade* but this is emphatically R3 and, generally speaking, *décade* is little used); *av. J.-C. (BC), ap. J.-C. (AD)*.

62.2.3 Further divisions of time

temps: time in its widest and most general sense, but not with specific reference to the clock, which is *heure*. It is also used in science and philosophy: *perdre/gagner du temps*; *J'ai assez de temps pour terminer mon travail*; *Einstein a consacré des études sur le temps et l'espace*. Lamartine invokes time in the following way in his poem *Le lac*: "Ô temps, suspend ton vol !" Note that *temps* for *time* and *temps* for *weather* are not to be mixed up. If ever one needs to separate the two phenomena, one could say *temps durée (time)* and *le temps qu'il fait (weather)*;

actuel: present moment, not *actual*; *à l'heure actuelle*; *les actualités (current affairs)*;

âge: l'âge adulte; *le troisième âge*; *l'âge d'or | d'airain (bronze) | de fer*. André Malraux's Shade in *L'espoir* recalls metaphorically Madrid in flames during the Spanish Civil War: "Un crépuscule sinistre se levait sur l'Âge du Feu" (1976b, p. 891).

courant: present; *l'année courante = l'année en cours*. As a noun: *dans le courant de l'année | de la semaine | du mois*;

délai: time taken/allowed. Does not mean *delay*, which is *retard*. *Il faut remettre le travail dans un délai de trois jours*;

époque: much more used than *epoch* in English; *Je l'ai vue à la même époque l'année dernière*; *l'époque des grandes invasions*; *le meilleur roman de notre époque*; *la Belle Époque* (around the year 1900);

ère: less used than *era* in English; *l'ère chrétienne/primaire/tertiaire*;

fois: Note how this noun is used with the present and the imperfect tenses: *C'est la première fois que je te vois* (have seen) *ici*; *C'était la première fois que je la voyais au restaurant* (had seen);

lustre: period of five years (R3); *mes douze lustres* = *mes soixante ans*;

millénaire: *les dynasties égyptiennes du deuxième millénaire avant Jésus-Christ*;

passé: *past*; *Il est midi passé*. As a noun: *Le romancier est l'historien du présent, l'historien est le romancier du passé*;

période: *la période classique/électorale/révolutionnaire*;

présent: present moment = *maintenant* (now). *Il faut vivre dans le présent*. As an adjective: *le moment présent*;

prochainement: soon; *Je reviendrai prochainement*. Slightly more elegant than *bientôt*;

siècle: century; *le vingt et unième siècle*; Victor Hugo's autobiographical poem points to the beginning of the nineteenth century: "Ce siècle avait deux ans ! Rome remplaçait Sparte; déjà Napoléon perçait sous Bonaparte" (1949, p. 29, *Ce siècle avait deux ans*). Two adjectives derive from *siècle*, and are not easily distinguished by most French speakers: *séculaire* and *séculier*. The first refers to a period of one hundred years: *un cèdre du Liban séculaire*. The second means *lay* or *secular*, as opposed to *religious*, *ecclesiastic*: *La France est un état séculier ou laïque*;

veille: previous day; *la veille de mon départ*; *l'avant-veille*. *Le jour précédent* is also used but is less frequent.

The terms in the following doublets have slightly different meanings (the first in each case is masculine and the second is feminine): *matin/matinée*, *jour/journée*, *soir/soirée*. The masculine nouns are more precise than their feminine counterparts: *Je l'ai vu ce matin/soir*; *Je travaille le matin/soir*. The feminine nouns relate to duration, length of time or process: *On se verra dans la matinée/journée/soirée*; *Je suis là pour toute la matinée/journée/soirée*.

Après-midi is both masculine and feminine. In the latter form, it is of a higher register, and usually found in literature. The idea of gender and duration does not apply, as with *jour/journée*: *Elle est venue cet(te) après-midi*; *J'ai travaillé tout(e) l'après-midi*.

Note how *que* and *où* are used with *jour*: *le jour où ils sont venus | un jour que je me promenais dans le bois*. Note also: *l'heure à laquelle ils sont partis*; *date à laquelle il faut expédier la paquet*. *Quand* is not possible here.

In constant use are the expressions: *en début/fin de matinée/journée/soirée*. These expressions are more common than *au début | à la fin de la matinée* and so on. Also worthy of attention are the expressions *le jour d'après / d'avant*.

62.3 Measurements (any world records listed below are subject to change)

Metrication has a long history in France, its use having become legal in 1795, and compulsory from 1840, driven forward by the Napoleonic desire for uniformity and even logic. In the English-speaking world, however, two systems of weights and measures, metric and imperial, coexist in certain domains, while in others either metric or imperial has the upper hand. The result of this is not only hesitation in the minds of English speakers using their own language, but also, on many occasions, different standards in different countries. In the series of tables that follow, accepted approximations for the two systems are stated (exact equivalents are generally not necessary in speech), certain norms are mentioned and "records" are provided to ease comparison. It is, of course, important when undertaking specialized translations from English to French and vice versa to change carefully from one system to the other.

62.3.1 Distance

metric	imperial	metric	imperial
10 centimètres	4 inches	100 mètres	100 yards
50 centimètres	$1\frac{1}{2}$ feet	1 kilomètre	$\frac{1}{2}$ mile
1 mètre	1 yard	2 kilomètres	1 mile

62.3.2 Height

un enfant de quatre-vingt-dix centimètres	*a three-foot-tall child*
un homme d'un mètre quatre-vingts	*a man six-foot-tall*
un homme de deux mètres	*a six-foot-six-tall man*

France's highest mountain is the Mont Blanc: 4 807 *mètres = 15,782 feet*; Mount McKinley in Alaska: 6 190 *mètres = 20,320 feet*; Mount Everest: 8 880 *mètres = 29,002 feet*; world-record high jump: 2,40 *mètres = 7 feet 9 inches*.

62.3.3 Length

Length: world-record long jump: 8,95 *mètres = 29 feet 5 inches*. The French-speaking world uses the term *mille* only in *un mille marin = nautical mile* (1 852 *mètres = 2,027 yards*).

62.3.4 Speed

Speed: *100 kilomètres/heure = 60 mph*; speed of light: *300 000 kilomètres/seconde = 186,000 miles per second*; speed of gravity: *981 centimètres/seconde carrée = 32.2 feet/second squared*; world record for a car: *1 232 kilomètres/heure = 770 mph*; world record for an airplane: *3 529 kilomètres/heure = 2,113 mph*.

Measurements of length, height, depth and width are expressed in the following ways:

    long: un mur long de deux mètres; un mur de deux mètres de long; Ce mur a/fait deux mètres de long; Ce mur est long de deux mètres;

    haut: un poteau haut de trois mètres; Le poteau a/fait trois mètres de haut; Le poteau est haut de trois mètres;

    profond: un trou profond de deux mètres; Le trou a deux mètres de profondeur; Le trou est profond de deux mètres;

    large: une route large de quatre mètres; Cette route a/fait quatre mètres de large / de largeur; Cette route est large de quatre mètres.

62.3.5 Weight

metric	*imperial*
un quart de kilogramme / kilo / 250 grammes / une demi-livre	$^1/_2$ pound
un demi kilo / cinq cents grammes	1 pound
un kilo(gramme)	2 pounds
un homme de soixante kilos	a ten-stone man
un homme de quatre-vingts kilos	a thirteen-stone man

62.3.6 Area

metric	*imperial*
6 centimètres carrés	1 square inch
1 mètre carré	1 square yard
1 000 mètres carrés	a quarter of an acre
1 hectare / 10 000 mètres carrés	$2^1/_2$ acres
50 hectares	125 acres
250 hectares / 2,5 kilomètres carrés	1 square mile
une ferme de quarante hectares	a 100-acre farm

The surface of a house in France is calculated according to its *mètres carrés habitables*. *Habitables* indicates the living space or area (first/ground floor, second/first floor, bedrooms, bathroom, etc.) and does not include a garage or a garden. An average property in France would have *120 (cent vingt) mètres carrés habitables*. A comfortably sized house would have *cent cinquante mètres carrés habitables*.

62.3.7 Volume

metric	*imperial*
1 litre	2 pints
4 litres	1 gallon
16 litres	4 gallons
24 litres	6 gallons

Ma voiture fait six litres aux cent = *My car does fifty miles to the gallon; Ma voiture fait onze litres aux cent* = *My car does twenty-five to the gallon; un demi de bière* = *a pint of beer.* It goes without saying that the use of *gallon* as a strict measurement is slowly fading.

62.3.8 Temperature

centigrade	Fahrenheit
0	32
10	50
20	68
30	86

The following formulae convert the temperature scales: centigrade/Celsius > Fahrenheit: C × 9 ÷ 5 + 32 = F; Fahrenheit > centigrade/Celsius: F − 32 × 5 ÷ 9 = C.

Body temperature is *37 degrés Celsius = 98.4 degrees Fahrenheit*. One should consult a doctor when one's temperature rises above 40 degrees Celsius or 104 Fahrenheit. In France and other French-speaking countries, degrees Celsius are used in most circumstances. The term *Centigrade* is slowly disappearing. It is possible that the term *Celsius* evokes a higher register than *Centigrade*. The Quebec *MULTI dictionnaire* states clearly that *Celsius* has replaced *Centigrade*.

62.3.9 Age

Age is expressed with the verb *avoir* + *âge/ans*: "*Tu as quel âge?*" "*J'ai quinze ans.*"

62.3.10 Currency

France, and most of her European partners, adopted the euro on 1 January 1999. It is used in all areas of financial transactions, from the daily running of a house to the stock exchange. In January 2011, 1 euro = 1 pound = 1.56 dollar. The euro circulates in notes of 5, 10, 50, 100, 200 and 500. Coins (*pièces*) have eight different values: 1, 2, 5, 10, 20 and 50 cents, and 1 and 2 euros. The French coins are distinguished from those of other countries in that they bear the initials RF (*République française*) on the national side. Some older people still have some difficulty adjusting to the change from the franc to the euro. This also applies to Belgium.

62.3.11 Clothing sizes: some examples of equivalents

dress sizes	France	38 40 42 44	*shoe sizes*	France	37 38 39 40 41 42 43 44 45
	US	8 10 12 14		US	3 4 5 5½ 6 7 8 9 10

shirt collar sizes	France	30 33 35 38 41 43 46
	US	12 13 14 15 16 17 18

62.3.12 Numerals

Presentation of numerals, thousands and millions is different in the French-speaking world from that of the English-speaking world. For decimals, a comma, *virgule*, is used instead of the *point. Courir le cent mètres en 9,9 (neuf virgule neuf); Elle court le quatre cents mètres en 49,5 (quarante-neuf, cinq).*

For thousands and millions, instead of punctuation marks, numerals are spaced out thus: 4 320 = *quatre mille, trois cent vingt*; 7 654 321 = *sept millions six cent cinquante-quatre mille trois cent vingt et un*.

62.3.13 Mathematical expressions and signs

These are:

+	plus
−	moins
^{2}	au carré
:	divisé par
×	multiplié par
%	pour cent

Note that the Anglo-American division sign ÷ is not used in the French-speaking world. Note also the following terms: *l'addition/additionner, la soustraction/soustraire, la multiplication/multiplier, la division/diviser*: $9 + 5 = 14$ (*neuf plus cinq font quatorze*); $15 - 6 = 9$ (*quinze moins six font neuf*); $16 = 4^2$ (*seize sont quatre au carré*); *Le taux d'intérêt est de 5%* (*cinq pour cent*).

62.3.14 Collective numbers

There are a number of French nouns that correspond to the English *about*: *une douzaine | une quinzaine | une vingtaine | une trentaine* (only up to *une soixantaine*); *une centaine, un millier*. With reference to the agreement of verbs and collective numbers, see point Chapter 5 on agreement, Section 5.1.

63

Word order / L'ordre des mots

The passage below offers us a moving tribute to one of the most memorable of contemporary artists/singers, most appreciated and lauded for his traditional French folk style. Born in a persecuted family, he appealed to his Jewish roots. His love of humanity was only equaled by his passion for nature, and he composed and sang his compositions to express these attachments in equal measure. The passage stresses particularly the order in which certain adjectives may precede or follow the noun, the way in which past participles come after the noun, and the order in which adverbs or adverbial expressions often appear between the subject of the verb and the past participle (e.g., in the third paragraph: *longtemps*, *clairement*, *quelquefois*, *également*). The beginning of the fourth paragraph contains the negative construction *ne . . . que*, and here it is worthwhile noting how separated these two elements are (see also Chapter 61 on negation, Section 61.1, for a development of this point). All the features on word order are highlighted in bold. Some translations are given.

Inoubliable Jean Ferrat

Un chanteur d'une **grande** et **majestueuse** renommée en France et tout autant apprécié dans les pays **francophones** vient de s'éteindre [has just died] à l'âge de 79 ans en **plein** cœur de l'Ardèche. Ces chansons sont très appréciées par le public parce qu'elles véhiculent [convey] une générosité **débordante** et une **grande** humanité. Il chantait pour la paix dans le monde. On peut dire que c'était un **grand** homme qui a mené une vie **simple** en chantant les valeurs **humaines** et en fuyant les mondanités et le tumulte de la célébrité. Pour les personnes engagées politiquement, Jean Ferrat les conforte [strengthens] dans leur **véritable** engagement [commitment] **politique** en faveur des gens **pauvres**. C'était un homme de gauche, d'une **grande** gentillesse, très proche du parti **communiste** mais non membre de ce parti.

Marqué par la mort de son père, qui pendant la guerre fut déporté par les nazis, Jean Ferrat a quitté très tôt Paris pour aller vivre dans un **petit** village de l'Ardèche **méridionale** dont les **magnifiques** montagnes lui ont inspiré la **fameuse** chanson « La montagne » qui a connu un succès **immense**. Cet artiste **incontesté** a préféré se retirer dans un havre de paix [haven of peace] plutôt que de vivre dans les Hauts de Seine où il est né. Dans cet **humble** village **ardéchois** qui l'a **tout de suite** adopté, il a **beaucoup** apprécié sa vie de **simple** citoyen et s'est engagé comme adjoint au maire pendant des années. Antraïgues et tous ses habitants gardent de lui un souvenir **unanime** très **émouvant** qui témoigne de sa simplicité **légendaire** et de son **inégalable** sincérité. Les chansons de Jean Ferrat portent sur l'amour mais également sur les problèmes **politiques**, ainsi que sur la nature.

Concernant les chansons d'amour, il a mis en musique les **grands** poèmes d'Aragon en lui consacrant deux **magistraux** albums exprimant notamment l'amour **fou** d'Aragon pour Elsa Triolet, *Les yeux d'Elsa*. Ces chansons d'amour sont d'une **belle** sensibilité et touchent un très **large** public. Elles ne peuvent laisser **insensible** aucun auditeur. Son engagement **politique** lui a fait composer les chansons bien **connues** de *Potemkine* qui a été **longtemps** censuré et celles de *Nuit et brouillard*, ainsi que *Camarade*. Il a **clairement** affiché [displayed] son engagement à gauche en faveur de la classe **ouvrière** et a **quelquefois** participé aux **éclatantes** manifestations **politiques** à Paris. Il s'est **également** insurgé contre la **puissante** industrie du disque qui, selon lui, est **dangereuse** pour la liberté de création. Jean Ferrat a obtenu le **grand** prix de la chanson de la SACEM en 1994. Il s'est tenu à l'écart des feux de la rampe [footlights] pendant de **longues** années.

Jean Ferrat n'était sorti d'un **long** silence **qu'en** 2003 que pour apparaître dans une émission de télévision durant laquelle il a confirmé son **indéfectible** passion pour la chanson et la politique. Cette émission est à marquer d'une pierre **blanche** car elle a mis en lumière le **suprême** artiste qu'il était et qu'il restera toujours. La France vient de perdre l'**inoubliable** Jean Ferrat dont les **poignantes** idées donnent chaud au cœur. C'était un chanteur poète et un **magnanime et courageux** idéaliste. Il était de la **même** trempe que Jacques Brel, Léo Ferré et Georges Brassens. On gardera de lui un souvenir **ému** de son visage **sympathique** avec ses **longs** cheveux **blancs** et sa **grosse** moustache ainsi que ses refrains **mémorables**.

The position which a word occupies in a sentence in French, as in many languages for that matter, and this includes English, is very often related to style, personal preference and register. Speakers or writers sometimes deliberately use unconventional or unexpected sequences of words in their speech or writing, in order to create a certain effect. They may carefully balance one part of a sentence against another, striving for symmetry or asymmetry; they may wish to introduce a certain rhythm, harmony or euphony into what they say or write, or they may wish to emphasize a certain word or phrase by placing it in a prominent position in a sentence or paragraph. There exists, therefore, a certain degree of flexibility as far as word order is concerned, but this flexibility is subject to a minimum of grammar to safeguard intelligibility. On the other hand, certain word orders are fixed and may not be altered. In this section, it is less style than grammatical constraints and usages which are treated, although it is not always possible to dissociate style and grammar (see also Chapter 40 on verbs of perception).

63.1 Adjectives and word order

The position of an adjective in relation to the noun it qualifies is one of the most subtle aspects of French, a not unusual phenomenon in Romance languages. The following subsections indicate the major considerations to be borne in mind in this connection.

The following table illustrates "normal" usage for the positioning of adjectives with respect to the noun they qualify. Normal usage means language unaffected by particular or idiosyncratic considerations of style, emphasis and so on.

Types of adjectives which normally precede the noun	Types of adjectives which normally follow the noun
short, very common adjectives:	color: *un livre noir, une maison blanche*
bon: un bon élève, une bonne intention	nationality: *une voiture japonaise*
gentil: un gentil garçon, une gentille dame	arts and sciences: *une étude littéraire*
grand: un grand homme, une grande dame	religion: *un pays musulman/ bouddhiste*
gros: un gros ballon, une grosse fortune	the quality denoted by the adjective is stressed: *une maison solide, une serviette inutile*
long: un long chemin, une longue route	long adjectives and past participles used as adjectives: *un paysage pittoresque, un homme fatigué*
mauvais: un mauvais citoyen, de mauvaise humeur	
méchant: un méchant livre	
petit: un petit garçon, une petite fille	
vieux: un vieux jardin, un vieil ordinateur, une vieille voiture	
vilain: un vilain temps, de vilaines dents	
adjectives forming a unit with the noun: *une jeune fille, un petit pain, un grand garçon*	

Note that *bon, grand, mauvais* and *méchant* have different meanings when they follow the noun (see below).

63.1.1 Adjectives which change their meaning according to their position

The meaning of certain adjectives changes according to their position with respect to the noun they qualify, often becoming more specialized. In some cases, the meaning of the adjective is conditioned in part by the meaning of the noun, and will only be used in a certain position with a limited number of nouns (e.g., *bon, faux*). In a general way, the adjective following the noun is more literal and has a solidity about it. *Jeune, pur* and *sale* are good examples of this, although *sacré* only partially corresponds to this judgment.

before noun	after noun	before noun	after noun
former	*old*	*good, nice*	*kind, thoughtful*
un ancien prisonnier	une coutume ancienne	un bon homme	un homme bon
obliging, honest	*courageous*	*certain (indefinite)*	*definite, clear*
un brave homme	un homme brave	un certain temps	un fait certain
dear, beloved	*expensive*	*last of series*	*last, preceding*
mon cher Jean	une voiture chère	le dernier mois de l'année	le mois dernier
various	*different*	*various*	*diverse, distinct*
différentes maisons	des maisons différentes	diverses opinions	des opinions diverses
false, not genuine	*untrustworthy*	*well-mannered*	*attentive to women*
la fausse monnaie	un homme faux	un galant homme	un homme galant
great	*tall*	*high, open* (of sea)	*high* (of tide)
un grand homme	un homme grand	la haute mer	la mer haute
of good breeding	*honest, honorable*	*young*	*youthful*
un honnête homme	un homme honnête	un jeune homme	un homme jeune
slight activity (figurative)	*light* (of weight)	*bad*	*evil*
une légère reprise/baisse (i.e., in economic activity)	une armoire légère	une mauvaise réputation	avoir l'air mauvais (*to look evil*)
disagreeable	*spiteful, naughty*	*same*	*very, even*
une méchante affaire	un chien/enfant méchant	le même nom	les enfants mêmes

before noun	after noun	before noun	after noun
poor (pitiful)	*poor* (no money)	*the one in question*	*present* (in time)
un pauvre homme	un homme pauvre	le présent ouvrage/auteur	le moment présent
own, very	*clean, appropriate*	*simple, plain*	*pure, free from impurity*
ses propres paroles	le linge propre; le mot propre	la pure vérité	l'or pur
intensifying adjective (R1)	*sacred, holy*	*nasty*	*dirty*
sacré nom de Dieu	le nom sacré de Dieu	un sale chien; un sale type	un chien sale; avoir les mains sales
only, single, sole	*lonely, alone*	*ordinary, only*	*simple, unsophisticated*
un seul[1] homme; La seule France (*only France*) est capable de...	une femme seule; L'Allemagne seule (*Germany alone*) n'est pas capable...	une simple question de temps	un plaisir simple; un billet simple (*a single ticket*)
inauspicious, dull	*sad*	*determined, large* (used figuratively)	*stout, strong*
un triste visage	un visage triste	une forte femme; une forte somme	une femme forte; un château fort; un vent fort
strange, odd	*curious, inquisitive*		
un curieux enfant	un enfant curieux		

Word order with *chaud* requires care. Compare the two following sentences: *Ce sera un week-end chaud* (It'll be a hot weekend [for weather]) and *Il a passé un chaud week-end avec sa copine* (He spent a randy weekend with his girlfriend). This second meaning of *chaud* occurs with the following: *Tout comme Henri IV de France, Henri VIII d'Angleterre fut un chaud lapin* (a randy guy).

Following on the use of *sacré* just above, there are two other past participles that function like adjectives, and may be considered as colloquial (R1): *fichu, foutu*. Their meaning varies according to whether they precede or

---

[1] Further examples with *seul*: *Le film Titanic a rapporté des milliards d'euros sur le seul marché américain* (on just the American market); *pour la seule (et même) raison que...* (for the one and only reason that...).

follow the noun. When *fichu* precedes the noun, it has the meaning of *foul, hopeless*: *Il a un fichu caractère; un fichu temps/métier; Ce fichu gamin ne veut rien apprendre.* When it follows the noun, it is much stronger: *C'est une chaudière fichue, elle ne fonctionne plus.* Similarly, *foutu* can precede the noun: *Elle tombe toujours en panne, cette foutue (fucking/bloody) voiture; Je ne l'aime pas, il a un foutu (awful) caractère; Elle n'est pas bien, elle est dans un foutu (hopeless) état.* Or it can follow the noun: *C'est un micro-onde foutu (finished), il faut le remplacer; Il a le genou foutu (His knee is fucked/buggered up), il ne peut plus jouer au foot.*

63.1.2 Adjectives whose position does not affect meaning

Certain adjectives may be placed before or after the noun with little change in meaning: *de bas nuages / des nuages bas; un bref entretien / un entretien bref; un charmant tableau / un tableau charmant; une courte histoire / une histoire courte; un double programme / un programme double; un énorme lion / un lion énorme; une excellente performance / une performance excellente; un faible esprit / un esprit faible; une forte économie / une économie forte; les futures générations / les générations futures; un gros homme / un homme gros; d'innombrables livres / des livres innombrables; Elle a de longs cheveux / Elle a les cheveux longs; une magnifique voiture / une voiture magnifique; une modeste somme / une somme modeste; la principale ville / la ville principale; un rapide coup d'œil / un coup d'œil rapide; un terrible accident / un accident terrible.*

On the other hand, usage fixes certain expressions:

bas: *un bâtiment bas, un coup bas* (a dirty trick, low blow [in boxing]), *une table basse*;

charmant: *un livre/film charmant*;

chaud: *un point chaud* (*dangerous place* [in town, country], *stall* selling quickly prepared hot food), *un chaud lapin* (*sexy guy*: often applied to Henri IV – see above);

double: *un mot à double entente, faire coup double* (to kill two birds with one stone), *un agent double*;

droit: *le chemin droit* (in metaphoric sense), *la/en ligne droite* (in literal sense);

faux: *une fausse déclaration, un faux billet* (counterfeit), *un faux départ* (false start in swimming, athletics), *un homme faux* (untrustworthy), *un faux mouvement* (an awkward movement which could damage a muscle);

fort: *de fortes chances pour que* (a strong chance that), *un homme fort, une femme forte* (a stout woman);

franc: *un homme franc, une zone franche* (area free from taxes), *une franche canaille* (a real villain);

futur: *ma future épouse, ma future maison, le futur président, les futures publications*;

gros: *une grosse tête* (a very intelligent person, a whizz kid);

léger: *un poids léger, un léger rhume*;

libre: *la libre entreprise, l'école libre* (private school);

long: *une longue journée, une longue rue, une jupe longue*;

lourd: *une lourde responsabilité, un poids lourd* (*a truck/lorry*), *l'industrie lourde*;

modeste: *un logement/salaire modeste, une femme modeste*;

moyen: *un cours moyen* (*a medium-level class*), *un avion moyen courrier, le Moyen Âge*;

premier: *le premier chapitre, le premier homme et la première femme* (Adam and Eve), *les matières premières* (*commodities / raw materials*);

saint: *un saint homme, les Écritures saintes* (*Holy Scriptures*), *la Terre sainte* (*Holy Land*);

second: *seconde nature, second souffle* (*second wind*).

Other composite set expressions: *Bonne* (*et heureuse*) *année !* (*Happy New Year!*); *avec la meilleure volonté du monde* (*with the best will in the world*).

63.1.3 Register and usage

There is an increasing tendency to place adjectives which normally follow the noun before it. This tendency is noticeable in the media: newspapers, advertising, television and radio. Placing an adjective before a noun in these circumstances focuses attention it on because it is unusual and arresting, and therefore lends extra weight to what is being said. Register level is also involved: register level is raised if an adjective which is traditionally placed after the noun instead precedes it. The following two examples illustrate this phenomenon:

"Et l'on y suit une longue et finalement très cohérente existence... jusqu'à l'extrême mais toujours lucide vieillesse d'un monstre sacré de la littérature" (*Les échos*, August 18, 1998) and "La belle, la sombre, la mélancolique, la mystérieuse, l'inaccessible Élizabeth" (Luminet 2008b, p. 183).

R2 noun + adjective	R3 adjective + noun	R2 noun + adjective	R3 adjective + noun
des parents anxieux	d'anxieux parents	un geste brusque	un brusque geste
un produit dangereux	un dangereux produit	les années difficiles de la guerre	les difficiles années de la guerre
une journée dure	une dure journée	un risque éventuel	un éventuel risque
ce drame horrible	cet horrible drame	la protection mutuelle	la mutuelle protection
un accord possible	un possible accord	une bataille rude	une rude bataille
une idéologie stupide	une stupide idéologie	des images sublimes	de sublimes images

Premier, dernier and *meilleur* come before the noun in R2 discourse, but in R3 the situation is reversed: *le premier chapitre* (R2); *le chapitre premier* (R3); *ces derniers jours* (R2); *ces jours derniers* (R3); *le meilleur film* (R2); *le film le meilleur*

(R3). *Durant* may be included here, although *durant* is not an adjective, but a preposition: *Jean a creusé durant trois heures* (R2); *Jean a creusé trois heures durant* (R3).

63.1.4 Miscellaneous matters

Word position is also sometimes dictated by consideration of what is known as *cadence majeure*; that is, in French there is a preference for phrases to be constructed with words which increase in length, and a reluctance to form phrases with a long adjective preceding a short noun: *une vue magnifique*, as opposed to *une magnifique vue*. However, it is also true to say, in light of Section 63.1.3, that the register in the latter case is higher than in the former: *une magnifique vue* (R3/2) | *une vue magnifique* (R2); *un excellent film* (R3/2) | *un film excellent* (R2).

When two adjectives follow a noun, the adjective immediately after the noun relates to it more intimately than the second adjective (unless the adjectives are linked by *et*, in which case they both apply equally): *la littérature québécoise contemporaine, l'opinion politique populaire; les partis républicain et démocrate, l'idéologie marxiste et capitaliste.*

If three adjectives attach to a noun, one could precede the noun and two follow, although this formula is not watertight: *le Saint empire romain germanique*. In this particular case, *Saint empire romain* is a set phrase and *germanique* could not intervene within it, but must needs follow it.

Because of the desire for *cadence majeure*, as defined above, when a series of adjectives follows a noun, it is preferable for the longest to be placed at the end: *des murs gris et délabrés* is preferred to *des murs délabrés et gris*. Notice the order of two adjectives following a noun, the second carrying greater weight: *la politique économique américaine; le système monétaire européen.* The same criterion applies to three adjectives following a noun, and here *naturelle* acquires most importance: *des bains de pied d'eau chaude, minérale et naturelle*. When a numeral is combined with an adjective preceding the noun, the order is: numeral + adjective + noun: *les six derniers films que j'ai vus, les quatre premiers cours.*

Usage with *demi* and *nu* is as follows: when they precede the noun, they remain invariable: *une demi-heure, nu-pieds*; when they follow they agree: *une heure et demie, les pieds nus.*

The presentation of dates differs from that of the English: *le samedi 2 janvier, le mardi 21 septembre*, and Goya's two paintings *Le deux mai* (*El dos de mayo* and *Le trois mai* (*El tres de mayo*).

Tel/tels/telle/telles may vary in position: *Les enfants faisaient un tel bruit que je n'ai rien entendu | Les enfants faisaient un bruit tel que je n'ai rien entendu. Tel* following the noun raises the register a little, but if the noun qualified by *tel* ends the sentence, *tel* would precede: *Je n'ai jamais eu une telle peur* but *J'ai eu une peur telle que je me suis enfui.*

Note the oddities of the following pairs in spoken French (distinguished in writing by their spelling): *un pied bot* (*club foot*) | *un beau pied; une belle sale | une sale belle (a dirty good-looking girl* – unlikely but possible); *une enceinte romaine (a surrounding wall | enclosure of Roman origin) | une Romaine enceinte (a pregnant Roman woman).*

63.2 Adverbs and word order

In a sentence consisting of a subject, verb, object and adverb, the adverb normally precedes the object. However, when it is stressed, the adverb follows the object. Usage with adverbs of time and place is somewhat different. Adverbial phrases (rather than simple adverbs) follow the object, whatever the circumstances, because they are longer than the object. (Here again, authors have their distinctive preferences to convey a particular effect, and these preferences do not always correspond to the norm.)

normal order (other than adverbs of time and place)	subject + simple tense of verb + simple adverb + object	J'aime beaucoup le cidre; Il attend patiemment le train.
	subject + compound tense of verb + auxiliary verb + simple adverb + past participle + object	J'ai longuement regardé le paysage; Elle a soigneusement nettoyé la chambre.
	subject + verb + object + adverbial phrase	J'ai lu le livre encore une fois.
order with stress on adverb	subject + verb + object + adverb	Il attend la voiture patiemment; Elle a nettoyé la chambre soigneusement
normal order with adverbs of time and place	subject + verb + object + adverb	Je suis allée à la librairie hier; J'ai vu un film de Bergman hier; Il fera son travail demain; Il achète son journal ici/là.
order with stress on adverb of time	adverb + subject + verb + object	Aujourd'hui je suis allée à la librairie; Hier, j'ai vu un film de Bergman; Demain je ferai mon travail.
order with stress on *là*	subject + verb + *là* + object	Elle fait là son travail.

The position of common short adverbs such as *bien*, *mal* and *mieux*, as well as *tout* as a direct object, is flexible in relation to an infinitive preceded by an unstressed object pronoun:

adverb tout	normal order	less frequently found order
bien	pour bien me comprendre	pour me bien comprendre
		pour me comprendre bien
mieux	pour mieux le faire	pour le faire mieux
		pour le mieux faire
trop	sans trop en prendre	sans en prendre trop
tout	Je vais tout vous dire.	Je vais vous dire tout.

The addition of an adverb like *bien* or *mal* to an expression like *parler français* has certain repercussions on the form of the expression as can be seen by the following examples: *parler français > parler bien le français | parler français extrêmement bien*; *parler espagnol > parler mal l'espagnol | parler espagnol extrêmement mal*. When *bien* combines with *vouloir*, the varying order sometimes reflects a contrast in register:

structures	example	register
bien + finite form of *vouloir*	Je veux bien t'aider.	all registers
	Il a bien voulu me prêter de l'argent.	all registers
bien + infinitive of *vouloir*	Je vous demande de bien vouloir m'excuser.	R2 + R1
	Je vous demande de vouloir bien m'excuser.	R3

The position of adverbs in conjunction with a negative expression also requires comment. Certain adverbs precede the negative particle *pas* rather than follow it: *Il ne pleut donc/même/toujours pas; Je ne l'ai donc/même/toujours pas fait*. With *encore* and a simple tense, the norm is: *Il ne pleut pas encore*. But with a compound tense, there are two possibilities: *Je ne l'ai encore pas fait | Je ne l'ai pas encore fait* (more usual).

For word order with personal pronouns see Chapter 45, Section 45.1.4. For word order with inversion see Chapter 51.

63.3 Interrogatives and word order

French interrogative sentences are of two types:

1. those that involve an interrogative word and require a detailed reply: *qui, que, quoi, comment*;
2. those that do not involve an interrogative word and that invite a yes/no answer.

Questions may be expressed in the following ways. Register considerations are important.

type of question	form of question	register	examples
questions without interrogative word	inversion of subject + verb	R2/R3	Allez-vous manger ici? Ma mère, t'a-t-elle appelé?
	use of *est-ce que* + direct order	R2	Est-ce que tu y vas maintenant? Est-ce que mon père vient?
	addition of *n'est-ce pas* at end of direct order	R2	Tu vas manger maintenant, n'est-ce pas? Mon père vient, n'est-ce pas?
	direct order + rising intonation	R1	Tu vas manger maintenant? Mon père vient?
questions with interrogative word (*combien, où, quand, comment, lequel, pourquoi, qui, que, quoi*)	interrogative word + inversion	R2, R3	Pourquoi êtes-vous sortis? Pourquoi ton père est-il sorti? Quand vas-tu partir? Pourquoi ne dort-il pas? Que fais-tu dans ce trou?
	interrogative word + *est-ce que* + direct order; *qui est-ce qui* in the case of *qui* subject	R2	Pourquoi est-ce que vous êtes sortis?; Pourquoi est-ce que votre père est sorti?; Qui est-ce qui vient ce soir?; Qui est-ce que tu as invité?
	direct order with interrogative word placed at end of sentence	R1	Tu sors quand?; Papa sort quand?; Philippe est allé où?
	interrogative word + direct order	R1	Où tu vas?; Comment tu fais ça?

type of question	form of question	register	examples
	interrogative word + c'est que	R1	Quand c'est que tu sors?
	highlighting by placing noun or stressed form of pronoun before interrogative word or at end of question in direct order	R1	Papa, pourquoi il est sorti?; Elle, pourquoi elle est sortie?; Pourquoi Papa il est sorti?; Pourquoi il est sorti, lui?

Si and not *oui* is used for an affirmative reply to a negative question or suggestion: *"Tu ne manges pas tout de suite, n'est-ce pas?" "Si!"* The use of *n'est-ce pas* implies agreement with the statement contained in the question.

Qui alone is more common than *qui est-ce qui*. On the other hand, the long forms of the other interrogative pronouns are more frequently used than the short forms: *Qui est-ce que vous voyez?* rather than *Qui voyez-vous?* and *Qu'est-ce que tu fais?* rather than *Que fais-tu?*

63.4 Exclamations and word order

form of exclamation	register	examples
inversion of subject pronoun	R3	Est-elle jolie!
inversion of subject pronoun with repetition by pronoun	R3	Est-elle jolie, cette fille!
comme/que + direct order with pronoun and highlighting of noun	R2/R3	Comme elle est jolie! Qu'elle est jolie, cette fille!
ce que / qu'est-ce que + direct order and highlighting	R1	Ce que / Qu'est-ce que c'est bête, ce film!

63.5 Highlighting

Highlighting is the means whereby a certain element of a sentence is brought into prominence and has attention focused upon it. It is naturally a very common process in daily discourse when it is essential for the person addressed to appreciate immediately what is the most significant point in what is being said. Highlighting is achieved by adjusting "normal" word order.

The element highlighted is called a focal element. Elements of a sentence may be highlighted in the following way:

means of highlighting	*examples*
by isolating the focal element in front of the sentence and, if appropriate, repeating it by a pronoun	Lui, il a écrit ce livre; Ce livre, il l'a écrit; Penser aux vacances, j'ose pas / je ne l'ose pas; Paris, j'en rêve souvent.
by isolating the focal element after the sentence, and, if appropriate, heralding it by a pronoun	Il a écrit ce livre, lui; Il l'a écrit, ce livre; J'en rêve souvent, de Paris; Il y en a, des voitures.
by using *c'est…qui/que*	C'est elle qui a écrit ce livre; C'est ce livre-ci qu'elle a écrit; C'est à Paris que je pense souvent; C'est demain que je vais chez le médecin.
by using the passive voice, if appropriate	Ce livre a été écrit par Camus.
double focus may be achieved by combining different means of highlighting	Ce livre, c'est lui qui l'a écrit.

In *si* clauses, in speech as well as in writing, an object may become the focal element without repetition of a pronoun; the register is higher than for the unhighlighted order: *Si accord il y a…*; *Si harmonie tu vois en tout cela…*; *Si indifférence ils montrent…*

63.6 Word order and set phrases

Certain set phrases allow the following noun to be used in the middle of, or after, the complete expression. Compare the following sets of two sentences:

Elle n'a pas pris ma décision au sérieux / Elle n'a pas pris au sérieux ma décision;
L'ennemi a pris la ville d'assaut / L'ennemi a pris d'assaut la ville;
Je n'arrive pas à mettre la théorie en pratique / Je n'arrive pas à mettre en pratique la théorie;
Le mécanicien a mis le moteur au point / Le mécanicien a mis au point le moteur;
Il faut prendre sa maladie en compte / Il faut prendre en compte sa maladie;
La maison d'édition a mis le dictionnaire à jour / La maison d'édition a mis à jour le dictionnaire;
L'auteur a mené son ouvrage à terme / L'auteur a mené à terme son ouvrage;
Elle a mené sa tâche à bien / Elle a mené à bien sa tâche.

Here is a further list of expressions that function in a similar way:

Connaître de vue: *Je connaissais de vue sa sœur* | *Je connaissais sa sœur de vue*;

Désigner du doigt: *Laurent désigna du doigt le coupable* | *Laurent désigna le coupable du doigt*;

Mettre (de l'argent) de côté, mettre (en lumière) les faits, mettre (un système) en place, mettre (des stocks) en réserve, mettre (un système) sur pied, mettre (une pièce) en scène, mettre (une fortune) en jeu, mettre (ses compétences) en doute, mettre (sa vie) en danger, mettre (sa bonne foi) en cause; *Les policiers ont mis en garde à vue l'accusé* | *Les policiers ont mis l'accusé en garde à vue* (The police placed the accused under arrest); *mettre (une idée) à exécution*; *remettre (sa bonne foi) en question*;

Parcourir du regard /des yeux: *Elle a parcouru le salon du regard* | *des yeux* | *Elle a parcouru du regard* | *des yeux le salon*;

Perdre de vue: *J'ai perdu le bateau de vue* | *J'ai perdu de vue le bateau*;

Prendre en amitié | *en aversion* | *en grippe* | *en haine* | *en pitié* | *en photo* (all these referring to people); *Prendre à témoin*: *J'ai pris mon frère à témoin* | *J'ai pris à témoin mon frère*; *Il ne faut pas prendre ces résultats au tragique* | *Il ne faut pas prendre au tragique ces résultats*; *Il a pris le mendiant en pitié* | *Il a pris en pitié le mendiant*; *L'officier a pris le commandement en main* | *L'officier a pris en main le commandement*;

Revoir en esprit: *Elle a revu en esprit l'accident* | *Elle a revu l'accident en esprit*;

Suivre du regard | *des yeux*: *Elle a suivi les nuages du regard* | *des yeux*; *Elle a suivi du regard* | *des yeux les nuages*;

Tenir (sa collègue) en estime.

The important feature to remember in these sentences is that, if the noun is qualified in any way, it will doubtless come at the end, for the sake of balance: *La maison d'édition a mis à jour un grand dictionnaire français – arabe*; *Le PDG a mené à bien le développement de la compagnie*; *Il faut prendre en compte sa maladie qui l'a foudroyée*; *J'ai pris en photo toute la famille qui était drôlement nombreuse*; *Les policiers ont mis en garde à vue l'accusé qui clamait haut et fort son innocence.*

There are numerous set phrases in French which respect a particular order of words, just as there are in English. For instance, one usually writes and says in English: *black and white, knife and fork, bits and pieces*. Reversing *black and white, knife and fork*, and *bits and pieces* would seem odd. The following list of expressions, mainly of nouns, illustrates some of the most common set phrases in French: *télévision (en) noir et blanc*; *chambre et petit-déjeuner*, *cuillers et fourchettes* (nothing for *couteaux*); *du pain beurre*; *Ils s'entendent comme chien et chat*; *Mesdames Messieurs*; *papa et maman*; *père et fils*; *mère et fille*; *garçons et filles*; *les riches et les pauvres*; *princes et princesses*; *les rois et les reines de la France*; *chevaucher par monts et par vaux* (like Roland and his paladin friends in *La chanson de Roland*); *programmes pour radio et télévision*; *des orages et des éclairs (thunder and lightning); poivre et sel; poissons frites; viande et légumes; du papier et un crayon; être en costume cravate; un drapeau bleu blanc rouge; les hauts et les bas de la vie; ingénieur des ponts et chaussées (civil engineer); J'étais nourri, blanchi et logé à la cité universitaire (I had full/half board, with laundry included on campus); Tu appliques la pommade matin et soir.*

Part X

64

Names of continents, countries, regions, states, provinces, rivers, mountains, volcanoes and their uses | Les noms de continents, pays, régions, états, provinces, fleuves, montagnes, volcans et leur usage (for names of towns see following chapter)

The following passage offers a cursory glance at contemporary events in the Americas and Asia. It concentrates notably on the economic and political processes in the countries of these two continents. In quick succession, we read of a considerable number of countries confronted by financial worries, and of just a few that have escaped the worst of the economic downturn. The passage illustrates the variation in genders of different countries as well as the way in which the prepositions *à* and *de* precede these countries. The passage is quite straightforward, so translations are reduced to a minimum.

Voyage À travers le monde

L'Amérique du Sud compte une dizaine de grands pays. **L'Argentine** va célébrer ses 200 ans d'indépendance fin mai 2010. **La Bolivie** risque de faire face à des difficultés économiques. **Au Brésil** se préparent de nouvelles élections. **Au Chili**, les Chiliens sortent peu à peu de la crise économique qui a touché un grand nombre de pays. Vu que **l'Afrique** est considérée comme une région sensible, le $32^{\text{ème}}$ rallye Dakar se déroule désormais sur les hauts plateaux **des Andes** entre **le Chili** et **l'Argentine**. **La Colombie** est un pays multiethnique. **À Cuba**, les responsables politiques s'efforceront de normaliser leurs relations avec **les États-Unis**. **En Équateur**, les autorités développent un programme aérien et comptent ouvrir le nouvel aéroport de Quito courant 2010. **Au Paraguay**, le gouvernement se fixe pour objectif d'avoir un budget excédentaire. **Au Pérou**, les leaders politiques préparent les élections de 2011 au milieu de tensions entre les communautés amérindiennes. **En Uruguay**, la préoccupation majeure consiste avant tout à rééquilibrer le budget. **Au Venezuela**, la population s'enlise [is slipping] dans la récession, et connaîtra sans doute de violentes protestations.

L'**Asie** fait couler beaucoup d'encre à l'heure actuelle. Ce grand continent affiche un dynamisme sans précédent. L'**Australie** semble être l'un des rares pays à avoir évité la récession en 2009. Les responsables **de la Chine** connaissent une période d'expansion économique, grâce à leurs clients avides de consommation parmi lesquels les **Américains** et les **Européens**. **En Corée du Sud**, on enregistre une reprise économique modeste. **Hong Kong** rencontre les mêmes problèmes économiques que les pays développés. On a paradoxalement enregistré un accroissement économique **del' Inde** lors de la crise mondiale. Les Jeux **du Commonwealth** pourraient se dérouler [take place] **en Inde** sous certaines conditions garantissant la sécurité à 71 pays participant à ces jeux. L'**Indonésie** se trouve dans une situation comparable à celle de l'Inde, du point de vue économique. Le pouvoir politique **du Japon**, pays du soleil levant, renforcera ses liens avec **la Chine**. **Au Kazakhstan**, le peuple bénéficiera de la hausse des cours de matières premières [commodities / raw materials], notamment dans le secteur du pétrole [oil]. **La Malaisie** entretient une atmosphère politique des plus conflictuelles. **Les Néo-Zélandais** auront tendance à épargner plutôt qu'à consommer. **En Ouzbékistan**, les Ouzbeks enregistreront une croissance économique non négligeable. Les forces de l'ordre **du Pakistan** seront toujours confrontées au problème de sécurité nationale. **Aux Philippines** se préparent les élections de 2010. **À Singapour**, la cité-État, s'organise, à l'occasion de la RoboCup, un tournoi international de robotique et d'intelligence artificielle. La sécurité nationale **du Sri Lanka** a toujours du mal à contenir les attentats [terrorist attacks] et les tensions entre les ethnies [ethnic groups]. Des élections législatives sont attendues prochainement. **Taïwan** observera une période de redressement économique, et le gouvernement en place devrait regagner le soutien populaire. **La Thaïlande** sera confrontée à un déficit budgétaire. Des élections pourraient y avoir lieu en 2010. **Au Vietnam**, les Vietnamiens vont devoir s'endetter [take on debts] pour assurer la croissance économique. Ce pays se tourne vers **la Chine** pour développer ses relations extérieures, et marquera 35 années de relations diplomatiques avec l'**Allemagne**.

The following table illustrates the usage of prepositions with respect to names of countries:

	masculine names beginning with a consonant	*masculine names beginning with a vowel*	*feminine names*
position:	au: Elle est au Brésil.	en: Il est en Iran.	en: Il est en France.
movement toward:	au: Elle va au Portugal	en: Elle va en Irak.	en: Elle va en Espagne.

	masculine names beginning with a consonant	masculine names beginning with a vowel	feminine names
movement away from:	du: Elle vient du Danemark.	d': Elle vient d'Iran.	de:[1] Il vient de Belgique.

When the country is qualified by an adjective or any other expression, the following usage is observed: *dans l'Algérie contemporaine, dans le Canada d'aujourd'hui*; *dans le Japon moderne*; *dans la Russie du dix-huitième siècle*.

When referring to cardinal points (*points cardinaux*) of a country, one says: *Elle est dans le nord | le sud | l'est | l'ouest de la France*. Less common would be: *Il est dans la France du nord*. One comes across: *Elle est en Italie du nord | du sud*; *Elle est dans le nord/sud de l'Italie*. Note also the use of capital letters in French. If a cardinal point is used as part of the name of a country, it is in upper case: *l'Amérique du Nord/Sud, le Grand Nord, le Nord canadien, le pôle Nord, l'Afrique du Sud, l'Europe de l'Est, l'Ouest canadien*.

64.1 Usage with place names in France

Most regions in France are feminine. One says: *Il est/va en Alsace, en Aquitaine, en Bourgogne, en Bretagne, en Normandie, en Picardie, en Provence, en Lorraine (du Sud), dans les Cévennes, en région parisienne, en Île-de-France*. Note that *métropole* is viewed as a national entity with respect to her overseas territories or former colonies. Thus one says: *travailler en métropole*. Some regions are masculine: *dans le Poitou, dans le pays basque* but also *en Anjou, en Limousin, en pays basque*. Note also: *sur la Côte d'Azur* (French Riviera), *sur la Riviéra* (Italian Riviera).

Departments are either masculine or feminine. There are ninety-five departments (any administrative map of France provides the complete list, but without genders – the *Petit Larousse* provides these). The *masculine* departments include: *Il est/va dans l'Ain, dans le Doubs, dans le Finistère, dans le Gard, dans le Gers, dans le Jura, dans le Loir et Cher, dans le Lot, en Maine-et-Loire, dans le Tarn, dans le Var, dans le Vaucluse*. There is one masculine plural: *dans les Hauts-de-Seine*. The feminine departments include: *Elle est/va dans la/en Charente, dans la Creuse, dans la/en Gironde, dans la/en Loire Atlantique, dans la Meuse, dans la/en Seine-et-Marne*. One normally hears: *en Corse (du Sud), en Côte d'Or, en Saône-et-Loire, en Vendée*. Feminine plurals include: *dans les Alpes Maritimes, dans les Ardennes, dans les Bouches-du-Rhône, dans les Hautes-Pyrénées, dans les Landes, dans les Pyrénées-Orientales, dans les Yvelines*. With respect to the use of *en* or *dans le/la*, there is some elasticity. Sometimes, it is a question of habit, personal choice or where one lives.

---

[1] *de la* is no longer used in this context. One could plead for: *Elle vient de l'Inde* but this expression, like *Elle vient d'Inde*, sounds odd and would be avoided.

Mountain areas are treated as follows: *Il est/va dans les Alpes (du Nord / du Sud), dans les Pyrénées, dans les Vosges, dans le Massif Central.*

With names of towns beginning with a definite article, the article combines with *à* and *de*, as in normal circumstances: *Il va au Creusot, au Havre, au Mans, à La Rochelle; Elle vient du Creusot, du Havre, du Mans, de La Rochelle.* The same applies to express movement away from regions, departments and mountain areas: *Elle vient du Jura, de Normandie, de Vendée, des Alpes Maritimes.*

Contrary to English, names of inhabitants of regions and towns in France (*gentilés*) are very common. This practice corresponds to usage in Italian and Spanish. Bear in mind that the inhabitant takes an upper-case initial, while the adjective takes a lower-case initial (see below).

Regions: Alsace > *Alsacien*, Auvergne > *Auvergnat* (as in Brassens's a "Chanson pour l'Auvergnat"), *Bretagne* > *Breton* (as in *un Breton bretonnant*), *Franche-Comté* > *Franc-comtois* (but *comté* is masculine), *Normandie* > *Normand, Picardie* > *Picard, Poitou* > *Poitevin, Provence* > *Provençal*;

Towns: apart from the usual *Parisien* (in jocular language = *Parigot*), *Marseillais, Lyonnais, Toulousain, Nantais* and *Strasbourgeois*, here is a small selection of a vast number of less easily recognizable names. Note that all French towns and villages have a name for their inhabitants, and this applies to other francophone countries as well. The name of the inhabitant is very frequently determined by a Latin root: *Angers* > *Angevin, Bayeux* > *Bayeusain, Besançon* > *Bisontin, Bordeaux* > *Bordelais, Évreux* > *Ébroïcien, Île de France* > *Francilien, Lisieux* > *Lexovien, Pont-Saint-Esprit* > *Spiripontain, Saint-Étienne* > *Stéphanois, Saint-Jean-de-Luz* > *Luzien, Saint-Malo* > *Malouin* (gives rise to *Les Malouines* [The Falklands] originally inhabited by the *Malouins*).

Usage with names of inhabitants: *Elle est Québécoise/New-Yorkaise/Brésilienne. C'est une Québécoise | une New-Yorkaise | une Brésilienne.* But *une ville canadienne/américaine.* In the case of *Il/Elle est* + inhabitant, much uncertainty exists over the use of upper- and lower-case initials. However, informed opinion is clear enough, and upper case should prevail: *Elle est Québécoise/Française/Américaine.* With names of languages, a lower-case initial is used: Elle parle très bien le portugais / le chinois / le russe / l'arabe.

64.2 Usage with place names in Europe (*Europe*), and their inhabitants

The formulae are: *il est/va; elle vient; il/elle* + *est* + adjective: *Il est/va en Albanie, Elle vient d'Albanie, Albanais.* Likewise: *en Allemagne, d'Allemagne, Allemand* (the term *nazi* is now preferred, as it is in English, when referring to the Hitlerian years), *en Prusse | Rhénanie (Rhineland) | Bavière | Basse Saxe | Saxe; en Andorre, d'Andorre* (note: *à Andorre* = Andorra the capital); *en Angleterre, d'Angleterre, Anglais; en Autriche, d'Autriche, Autrichien; aux Baléares (à Majorque, à Minorque), des Baléares (de Majorque, de Minorque), Majorquin, Minorquin, Espagnol; en Belgique, de Belgique, Belge, en Biélorussie, de Biélorussie, Biélorusse; en Bosnie, de Bosnie, Bosniaque; en Bulgarie, de Bulgarie, Bulgare; à Chypre, de Chypre, Cypriote/Chypriote; en Corse, de Corse, Corse/Français; en Crète, de Crète, Crétois/Grec; en Croatie, de Croatie, Croate; au Danemark, du Danemark, Danois; en Écosse, d'Écosse, Écossais; en Eire/République d'Irlande, d'Eire, de la République d'Irlande, Irlandais; en Espagne, d'Espagne, Espagnol* (note: *au pays basque | en pays basque), Basquais; en Andalousie; d'Andalousie, Andalou/Andalouse; en Catalogne, de Catalogne, Catalan; en Galice, de Galice, Galicien; en Estonie, d'Estonie, Estonien; en Finlande, de Finlande, Finlandais* (but the language is *finnois,* although the uninformed could easily say *finlandais); au Pays de Galles, du Pays de Galles, Gallois; en Flandre, dans les Flandres, de Flandre, des Flandres, Flamand; en Grande-Bretagne, de Grande-Bretagne, Britannique* (French speakers often confuse *Britannique* and *Anglais;* the same applies to *Angleterre, la Grande-Bretagne* and *le Royaume-Uni), dans les Îles britanniques, dans le Hampshire, dans le Kent, dans le Yorkshire, du Hampshire, du Kent, du Yorkshire,* but uniquely *en/de Cornouailles.* The French equivalent of the Battle of Britian is *la bataille d'Angletere* – a reference to the aerial battles in 1940 between English, Polish and Czech pilots and the German Luftwaffe. The noun/adjective *Anglo-Saxon* is commonly used for the English but in fact includes North Americans, Canadians, Australians, New Zealanders – all the "White" countries where English is spoken. This would obviously not include India, Pakistan, the West Indies, Africa and so on.

A note on *Albion*: This term is used by well informed French speakers in the set expression *la perfide Albion,* a reflection of the taut, treacherous relationship between France and England over the centuries, but often used now in a lighthearted way. The word *Albion* (same word in English) comes from the white cliffs of Dover, first seen by the Roman military as they approached those same white (*albus* in Latin) cliffs.

En Arménie, d'Arménie, Arménien; en Grèce, de Grèce, Grec (feminine *Grecque;* compare *Turc/Turque); au Grœnland, du Grœnland, Grœnlandais/Danois, en Hollande/aux Pays-Bas, de Hollande | des Pays Bas, Hollandais/Néerlandais* (there is considerable confusion over *Hollande* and *Pays-Bas;* Holland is the main province of the Netherlands and not the country); *en Hongrie, de Hongrie, Hongrois; en Irlande du Nord | en Ulster, d'Irlande du Nord | d'Ulster, Britannique, Irlandais; en Italie, d'Italie, Italien (au/du Vatican, à San Marino/Saint-Marin), en Toscane/Vénétie (Veneto* = region around Venice); *en Laponie, de Laponie, Lapon; en Lettonie (Latvia), de Lettonie, Lette/Letton; en Lit(h)uanie, de Lit(h)uanie, Lit(h)uanien; au Luxembourg, du Luxembourg, Luxembourgeois (à Luxembourg = Luxemburg town); en Macédoine, de Macédoine, Macédonien; à Malte, de Malte, Maltais; à Monténégro, de Monténégro, Monténégrin; en Norvège, de Norvège, Norvégien; en Pologne, de Pologne, Polonais; au Portugal, du Portugal, Portugais; en Prusse, de Prusse, Prussien; en Roumanie, de Roumanie, Roumain; au Royaume-Uni, du Royaume-Uni, Britannique* (note that le *Commonwealth* is masculine); *en Russie*

/ *en ex-Union soviétique* / *en URSS* (*Union des Républiques socialistes soviétiques*); *Sardaigne, de Sardaigne, Sarde*; *en Serbie* / *en Grande Serbie, de Serbie, Serbe*; *au Kosovo, du Kosovo, Kosovien*; *en Sicile, de Sicile, Sicilien/Italien*; *en Slovaquie, de Slovaquie, Slovaque*; *en Slovénie, de Slovénie, Slovène*; *en Suède, de Suède, Suédois*; *en Suisse, de Suisse, Suisse* (*une Suissesse*), also *helvète* (R3) as in *la justice helvète* = Swiss justice, although *helvétique* is more common, as in *la Confédération helvétique* (these terms come from *les Helvètes*, which was eastern Gaul, roughly modern Switzerland); *en République tchèque* / *Tchéquie* (this latter term is gaining ground although it is not the official one), *de la République tchèque* / *de Tchéquie, Tchèque* (*Prague* > *un Pragois*), *en Bohême/Moravie*; *dans les Sudètes* (in Sudetenland: was German-speaking and annexed by Nazi Germany in 1938 in its expansionist drive), *en Turquie* / *Turquie, Turc* (feminine *Turque*; compare *Grecque*); *en Ukraine, d'Ukraine, Ukrainien*; *en ex-Yougoslavie, d'ex-Yougoslavie, Yougoslave*. Note the following compound nouns and adjectives: *Anglo-Français, Franco-Anglais, Franco-Britannique, Franco-Espagnol, Hispano-Français, Germano-Russe, Russo-Allemand*. One also says *les pays baltes* but: *les régions baltiques*.

64.3 Usage with place names in Africa (*Afrique*)

Il est/va en Afrique du Sud, Elle vient d'Afrique du Sud, Sud-Africain; *en Algérie, d'Algérie, Algérien*; *en Angola, d'Angola, Angolais*; *aux Açores, des Açores, Portugais*; *au Bénin, du Bénin, Béninois*; *au Botswana, du Botswana, Botswanais*; *au Burkina Faso* (was *la Haute Volta*), *du Burkina Faso, Burkinabé/ Burkinais* (was *Voltaïque*); *au Burundi, du Burundi, Burundais*; *au Cameroun, du Cameroun, Camerounais*; *en Côte d'Ivoire, de la Côte d'Ivoire, Ivoirien*; *en Égypte, d'Égypte, Égyptien, du Caire* (*aller au Caire*) / *Cairote*; *en Éthiopie, d'Éthiopie, Éthiopien*; *au Gabon, du Gabon, Gabonais*; *au Ghana, du Ghana, Ghanéen*; *en Guinée, de Guinée, Guinéen*; *au Kenya, du Kenya, Kenyien/Kenyen*; *au Libéria, du Libéria, Libérien*; *en Lybie, de Lybie, Libyen*; *à Madagascar, de Madagascar, Malgache*; *au Malawi, du Malawi, Malawi*; *au Mali, du Mali, Malien*; *au Maroc, du Maroc, Marocain*; *à l'Île Maurice, de l'Île Maurice, Mauricien*; *en Mauritanie, de Mauritanie, Mauritanien*; *au Mozambique, du Mozambique, Mozambiquais*; *en Namibie, de Namibie, Namibien*; *au Niger, du Niger, Nigérien*; *au Nigéria, du Nigéria, Nigérian*; *en Ouganda, d'Ouganda, Ougandais*; *en République Centrafricaine, de la République Centrafricaine, Centrafricain*; *en République Congolaise, de la République Congolaise, Congolais*; *à La Réunion, de La Réunion, Réunionnais*; *au Ruanda, du Ruanda, Ruandais*; *au Sénégal, du Sénégal, Sénégalais*; *en Sierra Leone, de Sierra Leone, Sierra-Leonien*; *en Somalie, de Somalie, Somalien*; *au Soudan, du Soudan, Soudanais*; *en Tanzanie, de Tanzanie, Tanzanien*; *au Tchad, du Tchad, Tchadien*; *au Togo, du Togo, Togolais*; *en Tunisie, de Tunisie, Tunisien*; *en Zambie, de Zambie, Zambien*; *au Zimbabwe, du Zimbabwe, Zimbabwéen*. Note: *l'Afrique du Nord* refers to *le Maghreb*: *le Maroc, la Tunisie* and *l'Algérie*. Its southern equivalent is *l'Afrique Australe* (*Southern Africa*) – not to be confused with *l'Afrique du Sud* (*South Africa*). The following compounds are also available: *Afro-Asiatique, Égypto-Israélien, Israélo-Égyptien*.

64.4 Usage with place names in Asia and Australasia
(*Asie et Australasie*)

Il est/va en Afghanistan, il vient d'Afghanistan, Afghan; en Australie, d'Australie, Australien; en Azerbaïdjan, d'Azerbaïdjan, Azéri; au Bangladesh, du Bangladesh, Bangladais; en Birmanie, de Birmanie, Birman; au Cambodge, du Cambodge, Cambodgien; au Kampuchéa, du Kampuchéa; en Chine, de Chine, Chinois (note *sino* in compounds: *Sino-Américain, Sino-Japonais, Sino-Vietnamien*), *Pékin* > *Pékinois; en Corée du Sud | du Nord, de Corée du Sud | du Nord, Sud-Coréen/Nord-Coréen; en Inde* (note that *aux Indes* still exists, but is not used as a political expression and it has a historical resonance), *Hindou/Indien* (*Hindou* really refers to the Hindu religion but is used as much as *Indien*).

The use of *Inde* with *de | de la* is rare and sounds odd (it is best avoided). *En Indonésie, d'Indonésie, Indonésien; au Japon, du Japon, Japonais* (*Nippon* exists but is less used than *Japonais*); *au Laos, du Laos, Laotien; en Malaisie, de Malaisie, Malaisien; au Népal, du Népal, Népalais; en Nouvelle-Calédonie, de Nouvelle-Calédonie, Néo-Calédonien* (of original inhabitants: *Kanak, Canaque, Caldoche*); *en Nouvelle-Zélande, de Nouvelle-Zélande, Néo-Zélandais; au Pakistan, du Pakistan, Pakistanais; aux Philippines, des Philippines, Philippin; à Singapour, de Singapour, Singapourien; au Sri Lanka, du Sri Lanka, Sri Lankais; en Tasmanie, de Tasmanie, Tasmanien; en Thaïlande, de Thaïlande, Thaïlandais; au Tibet, du Tibet, Tibétain; au Vietnam, du Vietnam, Vietnamien.* Note also: *Je vais en Extrême-Orient, en Asie du Sud-Est; J'ai visité le pourtour pacifique* (the Pacific Rim).

64.5 Usage with place names in the Middle East (*le Moyen-Orient*)

Il est/va en Arabie Séoudite, Il vient d'Arabie Séoudite, Séoudien (*Saoudite* is just as common but is refuted by purists); *dans la Bande de Gaza; à Bahreïn; en Cisjordanie* (West Bank), *de Cisjordanie, Cisjordanien; en Irak, d'Irak, Irakien; en Iran, d'Iran, Iranien; en Israël, d'Israël, Israélien. Israël* is not preceded by the definite article: *le premier ministre d'Israël; Israël est un petit pays.* It would be preceded by the indefinite article if qualified: *dans un Israël ravagé par la guerre.* The adjective *israélite* also exists. It is applied to the Israelites of ancient biblical times, but it does occasionally creep in and replace *Israélien. Hébreu* applies to the Hebrew people: *le peuple hébreu, le département d'hébreu* (as in a university). It has no feminine form and is replaced by *hébraïque*, as in: *études hébraïques, Université hébraïque de Jérusalem.* Dictionaries give the example *la langue hébraïque*, but this does not fit current usage and *l'hébreu* suffices. Note also the compound adjectives: *israélo-arabe/turc. En Jordanie, de Jordanie, Jordanien; à Koweït; au Kurdistan, du Kurdistan, Kurdistanais; au Liban | Liban-Sud, du Liban, Libanais; au Qatar; en Syrie, de Syrie, Syrien; au Yémen, du Yémen, Yéménite.* Note also: *Elle est au Proche-Orient | au Moyen-Orient; Elle vient du Proche-Orient | du Moyen-Orient.*

64.6 Usage with place names in North America (*Amérique du Nord*)

A little-known fact among English speakers: Amerigo Vespucci from Florence, Italy, is the origin of the name "America." A German geographer, Martin Waldseemüller, decided in 1507 on the application of *Amerigo* > *America* without consulting Vespucci.

Elle est/va au Canada, Elle vient du Canada, Canadien. Likewise: *aux États-Unis* (in speech often *aux USA*), *des États-Unis, Nord-Américain*; *au Mexique, du Mexique, Mexicain* (note *Aztèque, Maya*; also, geographically speaking, Mexico is part of North America); *au Québec, du Québec, Québecois*. It is worthwhile pointing out that the inhabitants of Quebec in Northern Canada like to be called *Inuits* and not *Esquimau*, which they consider a pejorative term. *Amérindiens*, as opposed to *Indiens/Peaux Rouges*, is used for the same reason. European speakers of French do not see the nuance with reference to *Inuits* but they do with reference to *Amérindiens*. Canada also refers to these indigenous groups as *les Premières nations*. The English terms are similar: *Inuits, Amerindians, First Nations*.

With respect to individual states in the United States, the usage is: *dans l'* before a vowel or mute **h**; *au* before masculine noun beginning with a consonant; *en* before a feminine noun beginning with a consonant: *dans l'Ohio, dans l'Utah*; *au Nevada, au Texas*; *en Californie, en Caroline du Nord | du Sud, en Alaska*. Other states with distinctive French forms: *Dakota du Nord | du Sud, Floride, Georgie* (note different pronunciation from *Géorgie*, the independent state to the south of Russia; the *Petit Larousse* offers *Géorgie* as well for the North American state but this no longer seems valid), *Louisiane* (feminine), *Nouveau Mexique* (masculine), *Pennsylvanie* (feminine), *Virginie Occidentale* (feminine). Some of the states that make up *Nouvelle-Angleterre*, which is feminine, are: *Maine, New Hampshire, Vermont, Massachusetts, Rhode Island, Connecticut*. These are all masculine but some uncertainty attaches to the gender of these latter states, particularly for French speakers from Europe.

As far as Canadian provinces are concerned, here is a list: *Il est/va en Nouvelle-Écosse (Novia Scotia), Elle vient de la Nouvelle-Écosse; au Nouveau Brunswick, du Nouveau-Brunswick; au Manitoba, du Manitoba. Alberta, Colombie britannique, Saskatchewan* and *Terre-Neuve (Newfoundland)* are feminine. *Québec, Ontario* and *Yukon* are masculine. For a French speaker in France, many of the above genders are unclear, although, understandably, for a French speaker in North America, and notably Quebec, no hesitation exists. An inhabitant of *Montréal* is a *Montréalais*; one of *Trois Rivières* is a *Trifluvien*.

Note that, for a French speaker, *Américain/américain* means a North American (from the USA, not Canada), although, strictly speaking, the term refers to all the Americas. The neologisms (adjective and noun) *étatsunien/Étatsunien* are frequently found in the written form but have been subject to some discussion. Some speakers still feel uneasy about them.

64.7 Usage with place names in Central America (*Amérique Centrale*)

Elle est aux Antilles (West Indies), *Elle vient des Antilles, Antillais; aux Bahamas, des Bahamas, Bahamien; à la Barbade* (from the Spanish *barba* = beard, which bears a resemblance to the hanging threads of typical trees on the island), *de la Barbade, Barbadien; aux Bermudes, des Bermudes, Bermudien; aux Camaïans, des Camaïans; aux Caraïbes, des Caraïbes, Caraïbe* (*les Caraïbes* refers either to the Caribbean Sea or to the islands); *au Costa Rica, du Costa Rica, Costaricain; à Cuba, de Cuba, Cubain; à la Dominique, de la Dominique, Dominicais; à la / en Guadeloupe, de la Guadeloupe, Guadeloupéen; à/en Haïti,[2] d'Haïti, Haïtien* (*de Haïti* also exists but is less common); *à la / en Martinique, de la Martinique, Martiniquais* (in these three last cases, *en* is now more common than *à* [*la*]); *au Guatémala, du Guatémala, Guatémaltèque; au Honduras, du Honduras, Hondurien; à la Jamaïque, de la Jamaïque, Jamaïquain; au Nicaragua, du Nicaragua, Nicaraguayen; au Panama, du Panama, Panaméen* (note that *à Panama* refers to the capital, Panama City, and is not to be confused with *Paname*, a popular term for Paris); *à Porto Rico, de Porto Rico, Portoriquain; en République Dominicaine, de la République Dominicaine, Dominicain; au Salvador, du Salvador, Salvadorien* (note: *à San Salvador* = in San Salvador – the capital).

64.8 Usage with place names in South America (*Amérique du Sud*)

Elles sont/vont en Argentine (this name comes from the exploitation of silver = *argent* in French), *Elles viennent d'Argentine, Argentin; en Bolivie* (from Simón Bolívar), *de Bolivie, Bolivien; au Brésil, du Brésil, Brésilien; au Chili, du Chili, Chilien; en Colombie, de Colombie, Colombien* (from Christophe Colomb), *Carthagène; en Équateur* (Equador), *d'Équateur, Équatorien; en Guyane, de Guyane, Guyanais; aux Malouines* (Falklands), *des Malouines, Malouin* (see Section 64.1); *au Paraguay, du Paraguay, Paraguayen; au Pérou, du Pérou, Péruvien* (note: Inca); *au Surinam, du Surinam, Surinamais; en Uruguay, d'Uruguay, Uruguayen; au Venezuela, du Venezuela, Vénézuélien* (an idiosyncrasy of language: all dictionaries write *Venezuela* with no written accents, notwithstanding which the *gentilé* and adjective do contain written accents: *Vénézuélien*). One says and writes: *Ils vont/sont en Amérique du Nord / du Sud, en Amérique Centrale; Ils viennent d'Amérique du Nord / du Sud, d'Amérique Centrale*. A common compound adjective also worthy of note is: *latino-américain*.

---

[2] Whereas once one heard and wrote *à Haïti*, the awkward pronunciation of the contiguous a's has led to *en Haïti*. But this pronunciation has generated uncertainty: Does one nasalize the *en* and separate the sound of this preposition from the noun, or does one proceed to a *liaison* and partially drop the nasal sound? Both seem to be possible.

64.9 Pejorative terms

There are a number of nouns in French that are sometimes used with reference to a person's nationality. Generally speaking, these terms are pejorative. The terms in the list marked with * are *extremely offensive* and are *not* to be used under any circumstances. They are included merely by way of information and recognition. One or two comments defining these nouns also appear. The precarious status of these nouns makes it unclear whether the initial letter should, in some cases, take upper or lower case:

amerloque/ricain	*North American*
*bicot/bougnoule/ crouille/melon/ raton	*North African*
beur (masculine) / beurette (feminine)	*North African* (does not have a very pejorative connotation)
boche/fritz	*German, kraut* (still used, but for a non-native speaker care is recommended)
British	*British* (has a touch of humor, like *rosbif* below). There could even be a slight sense of condescension too: *T'as vu ce British, comme il est fringué* (dressed)?
*chinetoque	*Chinese* (very pejorative)
espingouin	*Spaniard* (becoming out-of-date)
macaroni	*Italian* (has a humorous connotation)
nipon	*Japanese*
polaque	*Pole* (This slightly pejorative term recalls the standard Italian *Polacco* and the Spanish *Polaco*, which proves only too well that words in themselves are neutral, and that it is their emotional or belligerent charge which makes them offensive).
rastaquouère/ rasta	*person from Central or South America* (used more now to indicate a flashy foreigner)
rital	*Italian*
rom	*immigrant* from Eastern Europe (not very pejorative)
rosbif	*English person* (has a humorous connotation and is not pejorative)
*youpin	*Jew*

64.10 Usage and gender with names of seas, oceans, rivers, mountains, volcanoes and other topographical phenomena

Seas: *dans la | en mer du Nord, dans la | en mer Noire/Rouge, dans la | en mer Caspienne, dans la | en mer Égée (Aegean Sea), dans la | en mer de Chine,* dans la / en mer du Japon, dans la / en Manche (English Channel), dans la / en Méditerranée, dans la (mer) Baltique, dans le golfe de Californie / du Mexique;

Oceans: dans l'(Océan) Atlantique, dans l'(Océan) Pacifique, but only dans l'Océan Indien;

Rivers: masculine: l'Amazone, le Colorado, le Danube (as in Strauss's waltz Le Danube bleu), le Duero, l'Èbre, l'Escaut (Scheldt, runs through France, Belgium and the Netherlands), l'Euphrate, le Guadalquivir, le Guadiana (these latter two in Spain), le Jourdain, le Mékong (in Indo-China), le Mississippi, le Missouri, le Nil, l'Orénoque (Orinoco), le Pô, le Rhin (Rhine), le Rhône, le Saint-Laurent (Saint Lawrence), le Tibre (Tiber), le Tigre (Tigris), Yang-tseu (Yangste), le Yukon, le Zambèze (Zambezi); feminine: la Dordogne, la Garonne, la Loire, la Ruhr, la Seine, la Tamise, la Vistule, la Vltava (runs through Prague and was immortalized in Smetana's second of four symphonic poems making up Má Vlast = Ma patrie), la Volga;

Mountains: masculine: dans les Appalaches, dans le Caucase, dans l'Himalaya, dans l'Oural, dans le Tyrol (Austria), le Mont Blanc (in the Alps); feminine: dans la Cordillère des Andes, dans les Andes, dans les Alpes, dans les Pyrénées, dans les (Montagnes) Rocheuses. Note also la Jungfrau (peak in the Swiss Alps; this mountain is feminine, given its meaning of virgin/maiden in German);

Volcanoes: Etna, le Vésuve (le is part of the name; destroyed Pompei and Herculaneum), le Mount McKinley (highest peak in North America), le Perbuatan (Krakatao), le Popocatepetl, Stromboli (in the Mediterranean);

Deserts: l'Atacama (Chile), le Gobi, le Sahara (le Sahel = sub-Sahara), la dépression de Qattara (Egypt).

Estuaire is masculine; Oasis is feminine. Also: les Grandes Plaines, le Grand Canyon/Cañon of the USA and les Prairies of Canada.

64.11 Miscellaneous

Use of outre = beyond: outre-Atlantique, outre-Rhin, outre-Manche, outre-mer. As in: les pays d'outre-mer, la politique d'outre-Atlantique / d'outre-Manche;

Note: sous les tropiques / aux Tropiques, à l'équateur (at the Equator), sous la ligne du Cancer / du Capricorne, au pôle Nord/Sud;

One says: en Orient (in the East) / en Extrême Orient, en Occident (in the West);

The adjective for Nations-Unies, at least in writing, is onusien: dans le cadre onusien.

65

Proper names / Les noms propres

The following passage involves a sketch of various European countries, underlining the distinctive economic, political and cultural features, as well as their geographical relationships with each other. The names of these countries, together with those of some of their capitals, and their genders, are highlighted in bold. Notice how the gender varies with different countries, although this is not always obvious when the vowel of the definite article is elided. It may appear infantile that an alphabetical list of countries should appear in the last paragraph. The reason is simple enough. As opposed to Italian and Spanish, countries are nearly always preceded by the definite article in French. This is a useful way for a nonnative speaker of French to see and retain the gender. A few translations are given.

> **Tour d'horizon de quelques pays et villes d'Europe**
> L'Europe est un vieux continent qui compte un grand nombre de pays. **L'Allemagne** apporte un fort dynamisme économique au sein de l'**Union européenne** avec, à la tête du pays, Angela Merkel. Des villes comme **Berlin**, la capitale, **Francfort** et **Ratisbonne** [Regensburg] sont des sièges [centers] culturels, économiques et financiers.
>
> **L'Autriche** semble connaître un déficit budgétaire comme bien d'autres pays en raison de la conjoncture économique. Pourtant, **Vienne**, la capitale de l'**Autriche**, attire beaucoup de visiteurs pour ses monuments architecturaux, ses manifestations culturelles et son beau Danube bleu.
>
> **La Belgique** abrite la plupart des institutions européennes à **Bruxelles**. Les communautés **flamande** et **wallonne** cohabitent. **Anvers** [Antwerp] appelé « **le diamant des Flandres** » et **Gand** [Ghent] sont de grandes villes industrielles et commerciales. Elles affichent une dimension internationale.
>
> **La Bulgarie**, devenue membre de l'UE en 2007, entre dans un processus pour lutter contre la corruption et le crime organisé. Ce pays a des relations normalisées avec ses voisins. **Sofia**, la capitale, représente également le centre universitaire le plus prestigieux avec son ancienne université « Saint Clément d'Ohrid ».

La Croatie se situe au carrefour de la **Méditerranée** et de l'**Europe centrale**. Cette ancienne république de l'**ex-Yougoslavie** est pleinement souveraine depuis 1998, quand une guerre meurtrière [deadly] s'est soldée [ended] par le départ de la minorité serbe. **Zagreb** reprend sa place de capitale. Les touristes commencent à s'intéresser à cette destination.

Le Danemark est une monarchie constitutionnelle. Au Conseil européen de **Copenhague**, la capitale danoise, le pays a conclu des négociations d'adhésion avec une dizaine de pays. **Elseneur**, situé face à **la Suède**, est célèbre pour son ancienne forteresse de Kronborg. Il faut ajouter par parenthèse que la plupart des scènes de *Hamlet* s'y déroulent. La forte croissance économique fait **du Danemark** l'un des plus riches pays d'**Europe**.

L'Espagne traverse une période difficile. Elle connaît la crise du crédit, un taux de chômage [unemployment rate] élevé et un déficit budgétaire. Néanmoins, les touristes continuent à affluer à **Barcelone**, **Cordoue**, **La Corogne**, **Madrid**, **Saint-Sébastien**, **Salamanque**, **Saragosse**, **Séville**, **Tarragone**, **Tolède**, **Valence** et bien d'autres agréables villes.

L'Estonie a conquis son indépendance en 1991. Ce pays est passé d'une économie centralisée à une économie de marché [market economy]. **L'Estonie** se distingue en particulier dans le secteur de l'Internet [vote en ligne = online voting], Skype et carte d'identité électronique multifonctionnelle.

La Finlande, le pays des Aurores Boréales, est située entre **la Russie** à l'est, **la Norvège** au nord et **la Suède** à l'ouest. Le finnois et le suédois sont les langues officielles du pays. **Helsinki** est une ville cosmopolite. La capitale enregistre la plus forte communauté immigrée de tout le pays.

D'autres pays méritent un grand détour. Visitons, par ordre alphabétique, **la France**, **la Grèce**, **la Hongrie**, **l'Irlande**, **l'Italie**, **la Lettonie**, **la Lituanie**, **la Norvège**, **les Pays-Bas**, **la Pologne**, **le Portugal**, **la République tchèque**, **la Roumanie**, **le Royaume-Uni**, **la Russie**, **la Slovaquie**, **la Slovénie**, **la Suède**, **la Suisse**, **la Turquie**, **l'Ukraine**. Tous ces pays offrent de multiples facettes politiques, économiques, linguistiques, culturelles et touristiques.

65.1 Names of towns

Many towns, particularly in Europe, have a peculiarly French form. Below is a list of the most common ones. Towns that have the same name in English are generally not included. Europe has a strikingly large number of towns with a French form, given their development over time:

North America: *États-Unis: la Nouvelle-Orléans* (*Elle est à La Nouvelle-Orléans*), *Philadelphie*; *Canada: Montréal, Québec* (*Je suis à Québec*: the city, to be distinguished from *au Québec*: the province);

Central America: *Mexique: Mexico (Mexico City); Cuba: La Havane (Nous sommes à La Havane)*;

Europe: *Allemagne: Berlin, Dresde, Francfort* (the **c** is pronounced), *Ratisbonne (Regensburg); Autriche: Vienne; Belgique: Anvers (Antwerp), Bruxelles, Gand (Ghent); Chypre: Nicosie; Danemark: Copenhague, Elseneur* (of Shakespeare's Hamlet fame); *Espagne: Barcelone, Cordoue, La Corogne (Corunna), Saint-Sébastien, Salamanque, Saragosse* (< Cæsarea Augusta < Cæsar Augusto), *Séville, Tarragone, Tolède* (of El Greco fame), *Valence; Grande-Bretagne: Cantorbéry, Douvres, Édimbourg, Londres; Grèce: Athènes* (as in Raphaël's *L'école d'Athènes*), *Thessalonique; Italie: Bologne, Catane, Ferrare, Gênes* (Genoa = birthplace of Christopher Columbus*), Livourne (Leghorn* but this English equivalent is now out-of-date), *Mantoue* (birthplace of Virgil), *Messine, Padoue* (Galileo spent much time here), *Palerme, Pise* (Galileo was born here and is associated with the gravity experiment at the Leaning Tower = *Tour penchée), Ravenne, Rome (la Ville éternelle)*,[1] *Salerne, Sienne* (of Catherine of Siena fame), *Tarente, Venise* (also known in high register as *La Sérénissime), Vérone* (location of Shakespeare's *Romeo and Juliet), Vicence; Malte: La Valette (Elle est à La Valette); Pays-Bas (Netherlands* – frequently confused with *Hollande*, which is a major province of the Netherlands): *La Haye; Pologne: Cracovie* (Copernicus studied and taught here), *Varsovie; Portugal: Lisbonne; République tchèque: Prague* (Kepler spent most of his life here, not to mention Kafka), *Russie: Moscou, St Pétersbourg; Suisse: Bâle, Genève, Berne*;

Africa: *Afrique du Sud: Le Cap (Elle est au Cap); Algérie: Alger* (inhabitant: *Algérois); Égypte: Alexandrie, Le Caire (Ils sont au Caire;* inhabitant: *Cairote); Éthiopie: Addis-Abéba; Ghana: Khoumassi; Maroc: Tanger, Marrakech; Tunisie: Bizerte*;

Asia: *Afghanistan: Kaboul/Kabul; Chine: Chang-haï, Pékin; Corée du Sud: Séoul; Malaisie: Singapour; Népal: Katmandou; Philippines: Manille; Tibet: Lhasa*;

Australasia: *Nouvelle-Calédonie: Nouméa*;

Middle East: *Arabie Séoudite: La Mecque (Ils sont à La Mecque), Médine; Iran: Téhéran; Liban: Beyrouth; Israël: Bethléem, Jérusalem; Syrie: Alepp, Damas*.

65.2 Personal names and some place names of ancient times

Although there are French equivalents for a number of English personal names (Peter = *Pierre*, Stephen = *Étienne*, Joan = *Jeanne*, Mary = *Marie*), the names of individuals are not translated from one language to another. John Smith remains John Smith in French, and likewise Pierre Dupont remains Pierre Dupont in English.

---

[1] Note also that Paris may be referred to in literary language as *la Ville Lumière*, and Marseille as *la vieille cité phocéenne*.

Famous or notorious historical figures, however, do often have a distinctive French name. Although this does not apply to English names, Latin, Greek and Italian names are especially affected. There are also particular French forms for modern-day Russian names, as well as historical ones.

Greek, including mythological names: *Achille* > *le tendon d'Achille, Alexandre* (*le Grand*), *l'Amazone, Aphrodite* (Roman *Vénus*), *Apollon, Archimède* (who exclaimed *Eurêka! Eurêka!* = *J'ai trouvé ! J'ai trouvé !*), *Aristote, Athéna* (Roman *Minerve; une minerve* in contemporary French means *a neck brace / surgical collar*, doubtless on the probable assumption that Minerva wore a collar as an embellishment, but this is by no means cogently attested. It must be added that, for all the copious and lengthy consultations of dictionaries and learned people of all kinds, from Latin scholars to the medical fraternity, there is no clear answer to this conundrum), *Atlas, Cassandre* (prophetess everyone ignored at their peril), *le Centaure, Cerbère* (*Cerberus*: a dog, the guardian of Hell ruled over by Hades = *Hadès* in French; strangely enough, there is a small town in France near the Spanish border called Cerbère. Surely Spain could not have been regarded as hell?), *Cnossos* (original capital of Crete), *Crésus, Cronos* (in mythology, guilty of the most monstrous crimes), *Dédale* (which gives rise to *le dédale* = *labyrinth*), *Diane la Chasseresse* (the common word for *huntress* in French is *chasseuse*), *Diogène, Éole* (windsurfers rely on him), *Eschyle, Ésope, Euclide* (the most famous of Greek mathematicians), *Euripide, Galien* (the most famous of Greek physicians but rivaled by Hippocrate in this respect, given his *serment d'Hippocrate* = *Hippocratic oath*), *Hélène* (*de Troie*), *Héraclès* (*Hercules*, one of whose labors was the cleaning of the Augean stables = *les écuries d'Augias; Hercule* is the Roman equivalent), *Homère, l'Hydre, Icare, Junon, Léandre, Œdipe* (as in *le complexe d'Œdipe*), *Mont Olympe, Morphée* (*Morpheus*, which gives rise to the common expression *les bras de Morphée* = *sleep*, and the drug morphine), *Narcisse* (fell in love with his water reflection and was turned into a narcissus), *Orphée, Pan* (origin of the word *panique* = *panic*), *Périclès* (Byron liked to dress up like him as a warrior), *Phèdre, Platon, Plaute, Prométhée* (who stole fire from the gods for the comfort of mankind, and was consequently punished), *Pythagore, Sisyphe* (whose stoicism is celebrated by Camus in *Le mythe de Sisyphe*), *Socrate, Sophocle, Thésée, la Licorne, l'Unicorne, Zénon, Zeus* (the **z** is pronounced as **dz**, and the **eu** is pronounced as in *nœud*). Note that the final **s** in *Pâris* is pronounced – he precipitated the siege of Troy, through his elopement with Helen, wife of Menelaus (*Ménélas*). Also *Ulysse,* as in Du Bellay's well-known and oft-recited poem *Heureux qui, comme Ulysse*: "Heureux qui, comme Ulysse, a fait un beau voyage, ou comme cestuy-là [celui-là], conquit la toison [*fleece*]." Not forgetting the ill-fated *Maison des Atrides* (*House of Atreus*), to which belonged the doomed *Clytemnestre, Égiste, Électre* and

Oreste in Sophocles's tragedies. The Greek language has given rise to two names of planets in the solar system: *Uranus* and *Pluton* (the most recently discovered, which is probably why they have Greek names, although it is not clear why their discoverers should have abandoned the tradition of Roman names). The rest are precisely Roman names: *Mercure, Vénus, Terre, Mars, Jupiter, Saturne, Neptune*. Some Greek place names: *les champs Élysées* (origin of *les Champs-Élysées* of Paris fame and paradise for the Greeks) and *le Styx*;

Roman names: *Auguste, Caton, Jules César, Cicéron, Cléopatre, Lavinie, Marc-Antoine, Marc-Aurèle, Néron, Ovide, Priape, Scipion, Tibère, Vénus, Virgile*;

Biblical names: *Barthélemy* (Bartholomew), *Bethsabée* (Bathsheba), *Élie* (Elijah), *Ésaïe* (Isaiah), *Esdras* (Ezra), *Goliath* (the **t** is pronounced), *Jérémie, Josué, Moïse* (*moïse* = bassinet / Moses basket), *Hérode, Jean-Baptiste, Josué* (Joshua), *Judas* (the **s** is not pronounced), *Lazare, Noë* (as in *l'arche de Noë*), *la Reine de Saba* (Queen of Sheba), *Salomon, Zachée* (Zachaeus). *Jésus Christ* is the same as in English, apart from the written accent, although the second **s** of *Jésus* and the **st** of *Christ* are not pronounced. On the other hand, the **st** of *Christ* in isolation, referred to as *le Christ*, is pronounced. *Antéchrist* (note the **é**, not **i** as in English). The Old Testament character Saul becomes *Saül* in French, while the New Testament Saul, before his conversion, is called **Saul**. After his conversion, he is known as *Paul de Tarse*. Also *Mahomet/Muhammad*. Some of Christ's disciples and other figures: *André, Mathieu, Marc, Luc, Jean, Pierre, Jean-Baptiste, Jacques* (James), *Hérode, Ponce Pilate* (whence the metaphoric expression *s'en laver les mains*). *Yavhé, la géhenne* (gehenna/hell in the Bible: the **g** is pronounced as a **j**), *le paradis, le purgatoire*;

Italian names: Sometimes, the names of Italian artists and writers are preceded by *le*, and this corresponds to the Italian *il*: *l'Arioste, Boccace, le Caravage, Christophe Colomb* (Christopher Columbus), *le Corrège, Farnèse, Galilée, Léonard de Vinci, Lucrèce Borgia, Machiavel, Médicis, Michel-Ange, le Pérugin, Pétrarque, Raphaël, Savonarole, le Tasse, le Tintoret, le Titien, Véronèse* (because born in Verona). Note that when names that include *le* are preceded by *de*, *le* and *de* combine to form *du*: *les toiles du Caravage / du Titien, les bâtiments du Corbusier*. This does not apply to the politician *Le Pen*. Note also *le Duce* (Mussolini), as in *le lynchage du Duce en 1945 à Milan*. *Duce* is pronounced as in Italian: *doutché*;

Russian names: *Borodine, Cholokhov, Dostoïevski, Elstine, Poutine, Lénine, Raspoutine, Soljenitsyne, Staline, Tchaïkovski, Tchékhov, Tolstoï, Tourgueniev, Boris Godounov, Ivan le Terrible, Pierre le Grand, Frédéric le Grand / l'Unique*. Catherine the Great is usually translated as *la Grande Catherine*;

Other names: *Ramsès* (Egyptian dynasty; the second **s** is pronounced), *Schéhérazade, Cléopâtre, Boadicée, Erik le Rouge* (a Norwegian who was probably the first European to go to North America), *Charlemagne le Grand, Richard Cœur de Lion, Guillaume le Conquérant, Le Cid, Robin des Bois* (consensus argues that the translation of *Hood* by *Bois* arises from the French misunderstanding of the meaning of *Hood*, which is really *capuchon*, through the confusion of *hood* with *wood*). The Spanish painter El Greco is called *Le Greco* (*les peintures du Greco*). Also *Alphonse le Sage de Castille*. The emperor Charles V is known as *Charles Quint*, clearly on analogy with the Spanish *Carlos Quinto*. *Isabelle et Ferdinand, Philippe II, Fernand de Magellan, François Pizarre, Hernán Cortés* (same in Spanish), *Sainte Thérèse d'Avila, Saint Jean de la Croix, Copernic* (*Copernicus*, as in *rue Copernic*, in the sixteenth *arrondissement* in Paris), *Tycho Brahé* (Danish astronomer), *Érasme, Comenius* (Europe's greatest pedagogue of the Renaissance), *Saint Ignace de Loyola*.

There are also numerous nicknames in French, called *diminutifs*, which express affection. Sometimes, these are composed of a repetitive element from the original names: *Albert > Débert, Alexandre > Alex, André > Dédé, Antoine > Tonio, Bernard > Nanart, Charles > Charlot = Charlie Chaplin, Christophe > Totof, Florent > Floflo, Françoise > Fanfan* (which provides the film title *Fanfan la tulipe* with Gérard Philippe), *Frédéric > Frédo, Gérard > Gégé, Gilles > Gillou, Henri > Riton, Jacques > Jacquot, Jean > Jeannot, Joseph > Jojo, Marc > Marco, Marie-Thérèse > Marie-Thé/Nénette, Philippe > Fifi/Phiphi, Pierre > Pierrot, Thomas > T(h)om*.

Some proper names invite comment. For example, the name Mégane provoked a serious disturbance when it was used for the model of a Renault car. Parents of children named Mégane expressed unhappiness over this association. Breton names were outlawed during the 1960s because of the Breton independence movement. Despite the splendid early nineteenth-century novel by Benjamin Constant, *Adolphe*, this name was eschewed from the World War II onwards for obvious reasons, and has not reappeared.

There exist in French not only *diminutifs*, but also *surnoms* or *sobriquets*, which are also translated as *nicknames*. These two nouns are very similar in meaning. Some *surnoms* characterize people in a very positive way: *Richard Cœur de Lion, Guillaume le Conquérant*. Sartre referred to his partner Simone de Beauvoir as *le Castor* (*beaver*). But most sobriquets contain a mocking or pejorative tone, suggesting, for example, hypocrisy, cunning, some degree of criminality or even a physical defect: *Henri le rusé, Jean le renard, Philippe le mafioso, Pierre le moine*. In a rural area, a child suffering from a leg deformation could be called *la p'tite patte*, without reference to his/her proper name. For alliteration involving first names, see Chapter 2, end of Section 2.11.1.

66

Foreign words and borrowings | Les mots d'origine étrangère et les mots d'emprunt

The following passage covers some foreign words of very different provenance associated with the culinary arts, and other foreign practices such as smoking and sport where English plays an important role. It illustrates how receptive the French palate is to foreign tastes and how easily foreign culinary terms are absorbed into the French language. The terms extend from Latin to Arabic, to Vietnamese, to Italian, to Spanish, to English and so on. Of interest here is that the passage contains some Anglicisms but also false Anglicisms – words that have been modified and do not exist in English with certain meanings: *baskets* (*sneakers/trainers*), *foot* (*soccer/football*), *footing* (*jogging*), *jogging* (*track suit* in this context). It is abundantly clear that globalization has introduced numerous foreign terms into the French language, just as it has into the English language, or Spanish or Italian. It may be that some of these words cause difficulty of understanding for the foreign speaker but the lists below will assist in the interpretation. Some translations are given. Notice the play on words with *cum grano salis*. The word *nems* is singular or plural.

Saveurs culinaires

Dans tous les pays du monde, la cuisine représente, **grosso modo**, l'endroit où se préparent, **a priori**, les mets [delicate dish[les plus délicats agrémentés [embellished[de saveurs locales. Dans chaque pays, il existe des plats nationaux qui exigent de respecter, **a fortiori**, les ingrédients qui entrent dans la préparation de ces plats. Les spécialités les plus connues sont **la pizza**, **le hamburger**, **le couscous**, **le chicken tika masala**, **le chili con carne**, **les tacos**, etc.

Par exemple, pour préparer un **couscous**, il faut une bonne semoule, des légumes frais et un beau et bon morceau de viande d'agneau et/ou un mélange de poulet. Le cordon bleu doit **primo** préparer la semoule en l'imbibant [soaking] d'eau et **secundo** en la mettant à la vapeur dans un couscoussier. Ensuite, il doit laver et éplucher les légumes avant de les mettre dans la marmite accompagnés de toutes sortes d'épices et de viande. On peut constater **de visu** toutes les couleurs que peut offrir la préparation du **couscous**. Lorsque la graine de couscous est bien passée à la vapeur, on la verse **illico** dans un ustensile afin de l'humecter [moisten] d'eau à nouveau et la faire repasser une deuxième fois à la vapeur. Si le couscous n'est pas assez salé, le cuisinier peut ajouter, **in extremis**, **cum grano salis**. Un couscous passé à la vapeur trois fois accompagné de légumes tendres et d'une viande d'agneau bien cuite, c'est le **nec plus ultra**. Parfois, il ne faut pas appliquer **in extenso** la recette que l'on trouve dans les livres de cuisine parce que les mesures conseillées ne sont pas toujours adaptées aux nombres de personnes invitées.

On peut toujours trouver un **alibi** pour aller manger un bon plat et faire son **mea culpa** par la suite. En effet, lorsque le ventre est creux [empty], tous les moyens sont bons pour aller **ipso facto** avec sa **smala** trouver un restaurant et déguster un bon **steak-frites** ou des **spaghetti** à la bolognaise. Mais il ne faut pas trop abuser de la fourchette parce que des ennuis de santé peuvent se produire et on peut faire appel au **toubib** parce qu'on a mal au ventre. Cependant, on peut avoir comme devise **Carpe diem**, surtout lorsqu'on a des invités et qu'il faut respecter leur **desirata**. Parfois, lors de visites touristiques dans différents pays, on cède à la tentation de goûter des **churros** en Espagne, un **mezze** au Liban entouré de fumeurs de **narguilé**, un **kebab** en Turquie juste après avoir profité du **hammam**, ou des **nems** au Vietnam ou n'importe quel autre pays d'Asie. La condition **sine qua non** pour réussir son voyage est d'abord de consulter son médecin et de se faire vacciner afin d'éviter de tomber malade à l'étranger. Ensuite, on peut mener la **dolce vita** et pratiquer le **farniente** tous les jours. Certaines **stars** cherchent à s'isoler pendant leurs vacances, comme dans les îles Galapagos par exemple, pour éviter d'être photographié par des **paparazzi**.

Lorsqu'on est en vacances, on a tendance à s'habiller en **blue-jean**, **teeshirt** et *baskets*. Les sites touristiques proposent plusieurs sortes de sport tels que le **tennis**, le **golf**, le **badminton**, le **trekking**, le **basket-ball**, le **baseball**, le **foot**, etc. Ils mettent également à la disposition des touristes des parcours de *footing* en *jogging* ou des circuits où les touristes peuvent faire du **camping**. En tout cas, la période des vacances offre l'occasion de vivre en **dilettante**.

It could be argued that the lexical aspects of a language should not be considered in a book on its grammatical functions. The first relates more to semantics, or the pursuit of meaning, while the second illustrates how a language is organized. However, it does seem appropriate to offer a chapter on what constitutes, after all, an integral part of any language. The grammar cannot operate meaningfully without the semantic values of the words that function with it. This chapter concentrates, therefore, and at varying lengths, on foreign terms: Latinisms, Arabic terms, Anglicisms, Italianisms and Hispanisms.

Generally speaking, noun borrowings from Latin, Arabic, Spanish and Italian retain the original gender, but not always, *opéra* being a good case in point. The reasons for gender assignation for nouns (i.e., definite articles for masculine, feminine, neuter) taken from English are not always clear since the notion of gender of nouns does not exist here. The terms of these different groups are not treated in the same way.

66.1 Latin expressions

Educated French speakers will occasionally use Latin expressions in their fairly formal R3 discourse. They may also, but less frequently, introduce certain ones into more relaxed R2 speech. *Etc.* (*et cetera, et caetera*), *illico, ex aequo* and *grosso modo* are probably the only Latin expressions to find their way into the most informal register. There follows a list of the more common expressions, with their meanings and, where they exist, their French-language counterparts. Expressions marked with an asterisk are also used in English. The formula is: Latin > French equivalent > meaning in English. In a few cases, there is no French equivalent since the Latin word is standard. The expressions are presented within register categories:

R3: *ad hoc** > *destiné expressément* / *à cet effet* > *arranged for this purpose; un addendum** / *addenda** > *notes ajoutées à un ouvrage; a fortiori** > *à plus forte raison* > *with all the more reason; a posteriori* > *par la suite* > *after the event; une alma mater** > *université où l'on a fait ses études; un alter ego** > *un autre moi-même; carpe diem** > *mets à profit le jour présent; cum grano salis* > *avec une pincée de sel* > *with a pinch of salt; une desiderata** > *ce qui est nécessaire; de visu* > *pour l'avoir vu* > *as an eye witness, at first hand; ex cathedra** > *officiellement, d'un ton doctoral* > *with the highest authority; un errata** (*erratum* exists but is very rare) > *liste d'erreurs dans un texte; un ex-voto** > *vœu* > *offering made in pursuit of a vow; in* (when referring to an article in a magazine or journal; one could see, for example, La création artistique chez Albert Camus *in La revue des deux mondes*); *in medias res* > *au milieu des choses* > *right in the middle* (e.g., of a plot); *in situ** > *dans l'endroit même* > *in the very place; ipso facto** > *par le fait même* > *by the very fact; un modus vivendi** > *arrangement* > *working agreement; (le) nec plus ultra* > *le meilleur* > *the best; une persona non grata** > *(personne) indésirable* > *unwelcome person; une rara avis** > *(ce) qui est extraordinaire; (une condition) sine qua non** > *indispensable; urbi et orbi** > *à la ville et à l'univers* (accompanies the pope's blessing);

R3/R2: *idem** > *de même* > *idem, ibid, the same; in extremis** > *à l'extrême limite* > *in the last extremity, if pushed; in vitro** > *en milieu artificiel, en laboratoire; manu militari* > *par la force des armes* > *by force of arms; primo/secundo/tertio* > *premièrement/deuxièmement/troisièmement* > *in the first/second/third place; le summum* > *le plus haut point* (used figuratively: Les frères Karamazov de Dostoïevski est *le summum de la littérature européenne*) > *the apogee;*

R2: *un alias* > autrement appelé; un alibi* > prétexte; a priori* > avant/ auparavant > beforehand; une mea culpa* > C'est ma faute > It's my fault; un curriculum vitae > CV > résumé; un mémorandum > note administrative; un quiproquo > malentendu > mistake, misunderstanding* (not the English use = *an exchange); un référendum > vote direct; un réquiem*; un statu quo** (note spelling) > *dans l'état actuel des choses; un ultimatum*; un ultra > un extrémiste > extremist; via* > au moyen de; vice versa* > inversement;*

R2/R1: *ex aequo* (e.g., *Elle était deuxième ex aequo = She was equal second*) > *à égalité > equal; grosso modo > en gros > in broad detail; illico > immédiatement > immediately.*

Note that in the following combination *ès* is a survival from the Old French (*ès = en les*): *docteur-ès-lettres, licencié ès sciences.* Also from Old French is *nonobstant* (R3) = *despite.*

66.2 Arabic terms

The French language has borrowed a large number of Arabic words. Those that come immediately to the French tongue were brought over to France during the period of colonization. These have a slipshod resonance, associated with the lower registers. Such terms that fall into the R1 category are: *un bled = village, un clebs = dog, le flouse/flouze = cash, un gourbi = hut, maboul = mad/stupid, toubib = doctor/doc, smala = family/tribe.*

French acquired a number of Arabic words via Spain, following the Muslim conquest of the Iberian Peninsula. The extremely active intellectual surge that marked Cordoba in the eight and ninth centuries bequeathed to much of the Western world substantial works that had disappeared from the Greek classical period. Greek terms that arrived via the Arabic and have a permanent place in the French language are: *un alambic = still* (in chemistry), *un élixir, l'estragon* (feminine), *une guitare.* It is only too well known that Arab mathematicians counted among their number outstanding minds, with the result that the agility of Arabic numerals soon superseded clumsy Roman numerals. Here are other Arabic terms: *un abricot = apricot, l'alcool* (masculine); *une alcôve; un alezan = (horse) chestnut; un amiral > admiral; un artichaut = artichoke; un assassin; azimut = azimuth* (but these days = *total/wholesale); l'algèbre* (feminine) = *algebra; l'azur* (masculine) = *azur, blue; bakchich = sweetener, backhander; la burka = burka; la Casbah = old part of a town, especially Algiers; cadors = expert, skilled person; la charia; le chiffre = number/figure; le djihad; un fakir; la fatwa; une gazelle; une gerboise = gerbil; une girafe; le hammam = a kind of Turkish bath,* frequented especially by females and small children; *un harem; le hasard = chance; l'hégire* (marks the date 622 when Mohammed fled from Mecca to Medina; this noun is feminine); *jasmin; un magasin = store/shop; un moudjahidin; un nénuphar = water lily, un niqab = burka; une noria = water wheel; orange* (feminine); *le sirop = syrup; le sorbet; le souk; le zénith; le zéro* (introduced into Europe with the Muslim invasion of Spain in 711).

Inevitably, important personages and their functions were imported into French: *caïd = boss, big shot,* and in this sense R1, more specifically = *Muslim magistrate; calife; califat; chérif; émir; sultan; vizir.* Note also *c'est du kif-kif = It's all the same.*

66.3 Italianisms

French cultural relations with Italy were of the closest during the Renaissance period, with the result that Italian has bequeathed to the French language many popular terms which are hardly recognized these days as Italian, so embedded are they now in the French language. Here is a brief list: *agrume, air, ambassade, antichambre, appartement, aquarelle, arcade, arpège, artisan, babiole, bagatelle, bagne, baguette, balcon, baldaquin, ballerine, bambin, banderole, bandit, banque, banqueroute, banquet, barcarolle, bataillon, bicoque, bilan, biscotte, bizarre, bosquet, bouffon, bravade, bravo, bravoure, brigade, brigand, brio, burlesque, cabriole, calepin, calque, campanile, canaille, canon, cantate, cantine, caprice, carnaval, cartouche, casino, cavalcade, cavalerie, citadelle, concert, confetti, contrebande, cortège, courtisan, crédit, dégrader, dilettante, disgrâce, la dolce vita, dôme, duo, escapade, escarpin, escorte, esquisse, façade, faillite, fanal, fantassin, le farniente (laziness), le fascisme, fiasco, fioriture, fugue, fumerole, galbe, ghetto* (from the Jewish ghetto in Venice), *gigolo, gondole, gouache, graffiti, grandiose, granit, grotesque, improviste, incartade, lagune, lampion, lavande, loto, macarroni, malaria (= bad air), manège, maquette, nonce, numéro, pantalon, partisan, pastel, perruque, piédestal, pistache, politesse, radis, rafale, reflet, régate, ristourne, ritournelle, salon, saltimbanque, semoule, soldat, sourdine, soutane, store, tarentelle, trafic, vedette, veste, volte-face, voltiger.*

Italy has left an imprint on musical terminology, understanding and appreciation in France, just as in the whole of Europe. Here is a small list which excludes the technical aspects of Italian musical terms. The Italianisms speak for themselves, except in one or two cases. The French adaptation is given: *bel canto, crescendo, la diva, le livret (libretto), opéra, piano, la prima donna, le solfège, la sérénade, la sonate, la soprano, sottovoce* (R3), *le ténor, le trille, le violon, le violoncelle, virtuose.*

There is considerable confusion over the singular and plural of most of the nouns in this list. Italian masculine plurals, nouns and adjectives end in −i or −e, never in −s (*ragazzi = boys, donne = women*). This explains, for example, the use of the French singular *les/des* for *some spaghetti: les/des spaghetti.* The French have similar difficulty with *paparazzo,* which is the Italian singular while *paparazzi* is the plural. (See Walter 1997, pp. 167–181 for a most informative and comprehensive list.)

66.4 Spanish terms

The first meaningful contacts between the French and Spanish languages occur in the eleventh century, during the period of Sancho, king of Castile. The pilgrimages from Paris to Santiago de Compostella served to strengthen immeasurably this linguistic osmosis. The demise of Arab domination and its concomitant cultural withdrawal opened the way for French penetration into Spain. Over the centuries, a whole flood of Hispanisms invaded France. Many of these terms are not always identified as of Spanish provenance these days since they are deeply set in the French language. Such terms are: *la baie, la bourrique, le/la camarade, le canari, le casque, la cédille, le gitan, la jonquille, la mantille, le moustique, le mousse* = ship's boy, *la pastille, la peccadille, la sieste, la vanille.* Some words are clearly identified as Spanish for any French speaker: *aficionado, chorizo, conquistador, gambas, gazpacho, guérillero, macho, matador, paella, picador.*

It is also worth remembering that Spain bequeathed to the French language a wide variety of terms the Spanish conquistadors came across themselves in Spanish America: *un avocat* = avocado, *la cacahuète* = peanut, *le caoutchouc* = rubber, *le chocolat, le coyote, le maïs, un ocelot, le tabac, la tomate.* Interestingly enough, all these words ending in −t or −te caused considerable discomfiture for the Spanish invaders since the Náhautl language of the Aztecs contains numerous terms (even the term *Náhautl* itself) ending in −tl, carried over into Spanish as −te since this ending was more easily accommodated in speech.

66.5 English terms

Given the technological advances and financial domination associated with the United States, English has inevitably invaded the French language in an almost merciless way. Franglais has almost become a term of abuse. Canadian French is particularly vulnerable to the intrusive behavior of English, given Canada's proximity to the United States (see end of this chapter for outrageous examples).

Modern French has therefore numerous borrowings from English. Although some of these borrowings may prove to be only fleeting additions to the French lexicon, others appear to be firmly entrenched in the language, and are not necessarily to be avoided, despite the strictures of purists. Many writers, especially journalists, like to use Anglicisms, either to attract attention or to flaunt their knowledge, and this certainly applies to the realms of sport and technology. A number of Anglicisms do not correspond exactly in meaning to the original English words. There has been some coinage of pseudo-English words, especially those ending in −ing: *brushing* (blow dry), *footing* (jogging), *forcing* (pressure in the figurative sense), *pressing* (dry cleaning). It is also worth noting that neologisms that are carried

A Reference Grammar of French

over from the English and end up as verbs have an **-er** ending: *crasher* and *stopper* are two excellent illustrations of this feature.

It could be argued that the influence of English is not restricted to single words, since, in English, nouns can be used freely as adjectives, and French, like its sister language Spanish, is increasingly following suit (for what amounts to compound nouns, see Chapters 9 and 10 on gender and number). There follows a list of Anglicisms that provoke indignation in some quarters of the defenders of the French language. Gender, plural forms and translations are provided where it is deemed necessary. As far as gender is concerned, there seems little guiding logic in choice of masculine or feminine. Most nouns seem to be masculine. There are also false Anglicisms. *Un bungalow*, for instance, is not a *bungalow* (= *plain-pied*). It evokes for a French speaker some kind of rudimentary structure for a weekend, a *cabanon* as one would say in the Midi: *aluminium, auburn, baby-boom, baby-sitter, bacon, badminton, bar, barman/barmen, baseball, basket-ball, best-seller, bifteck, blazer, blue-jeans, bluff, bluffer, une BM(W), bobsleigh, booster* = *to boost* (*redynamiser* would be more than adequate here), *bowling, le box* = *lock-up garage/stall* for a horse, *boycott, le boom, break* (*pause* or *repos* are more than adequate here), *bridge* (game), *bulldozer, bungalow, le caddie* = *trolley* for superstore, *camping-car* = *camper van, camping* = *campsite* (*faire du camping*) *campus, cardigan, chips* (feminine) = *potato chips, crisps*), *la City* = *the City* (financial center of London), *le clone, club, clown, coach* = *trainer, manager in sport, cocktail, cow-boy, crasher* (of airplane), *le crawl* (swimming stroke), *customiser, dealer* = big-time *drug dealer, design* (very common in commerce), *doping, e-mail* (also *mail* and increasingly *mél*), *fair-play, fan* (e.g., of music groups), *fast food, fax, faxer, ferry/ferries, film, fitness, flash, flash-back, flirt, footing, freezer* = *freezer* part of a fridge, *fuel* = *heating oil, folklore, foot*(*ball*), *gang, gangster, la garden party* (for socialites, and especially applied to the Elysées celebration on Bastille Day, 14 July), *gay, gentleman, geyser, gin, golf, hall, handicap, hippy, hobby, hockey, holding, hold-up, hooligan, une interview, jazz, la jeep, jockey, jogging* (also: *track suit*), *joker, junior* (sport), *le kilt, le kit* (for building something), *kitchenette, knock-out, laser, leader, lifting* = *face-lift, lock-out, look, lunch, mailing, mixer, manager* (in sport and music), *marketing, master* = *master's degree, le match* (game), *miss* (as in *Miss Univers*), *music-hall, non-stop* (as in *un vol quotidien non-stop entre Paris et New York*), *nylon, no man's land, nominer* (*un Oscar*), *un outsider, un overbooking, une overdose, un pack* (e.g., *de bières*), *le palace* = *elegant house, panel* (for adjudication), *le pedigree, le penalty* (in sport), *people* = *celebrity* (as in *les couples people*), *la performance* (in sport), *une pin-up, le ping-pong, un pique-nique, le plaid, le planning* = *schedule, le poker, la pop music, une pop star, un poster* (decorative), *un pub* (*une pub* = *commercial*), *le punch, le puzzle* (constituting a game), *le quota, radar, le raglan, le raid* = *raid* (attack carried out behind enemy lines; long-distance automobile drive testing endurance), *le rail, le rallye* = *automobile rally, record* (in sport), *reporter* (of news), *revolver, rhum, sandwich, scotch, scout, short* = *pair of short pants, senior* (in sport, with no written accent), *le scanner, le scooter, un scoop, sexy, le self-control, le self-service* (in a shop – although this use has faded – or restaurant/canteen; very common in R1 as *le self*), *un sex-shop, shampooing, shérif, shocking, slip* = *underpants, le sketch* = *small play, slogan, smash* (in tennis), *smoking* = *dinner jacket, snob, le soda, un speech* = *short speech, speaker* = *newscaster* (for media), *spot publicitaire, spray* (for perfume, etc.), *sprinter, le square* = *small square* with garden, *stand* (in exhibition), *standard, standing* = category (*un immeuble de grand standing*), *steak, stop, stopper, stock, star* (always feminine), *stress, stressant, stresser, le striptease, le studio, le suspense, le tank, tartan, le tee-shirt, le tennis* (but *la tennis* = *sneaker, trainer*), *test, ticket, tie-break, c'est le top* = *the best, topless, un top-model* (masculine), *top secret, tour operator, tramway* (*streetcar, tram*), *transistor, volley-ball, wagon, un walkie-talkie* / *un talkie-walkie, un walkman, water-polo, les waters* (masculine) = *john, toilet, le Web* = world-wide *web*), *week-end, western* (movie), *le whisky, zapping, le zoom*.

Several false Anglicisms ending in –**ing** are treated with gleeful ingenuity by Alex Taylor (2010, p. 128): "Considérez le cas de ce monsieur, qui, après son footing dans le camping, va chercher son smoking dans le pressing avant de consulter dans le parking le planning pour faire son lifting."

Anglicisms imported into Quebec fall into four main categories:

1. useful borrowings, in other words terms that have no true French equivalent, as in many sports and technologies originating in the English-speaking world: *baseball, e-mail, football, golf, soccer, steak, stock, tennis*;
2. pointless or groundless borrowings where the French has a perfectly acceptable term: *bumper/fender* = *pare-chocs, computer* = *ordinateur, discount* = *rabais, opener* = *ouvre-bouteille, refill* = *recharge, software* = *logiciel*;
3. *faux-amis*, where a French word similar to the English changes its meaning according to the English meaning: *agressif* = *dynamique, balance* = *solde, batterie* = *pile, breuvage* = *boisson, juridiction* = *compétence, quitter* = *démissionner, sanctuaire* = *réserve (naturelle), voûte* = *chambre forte* (as in a bank). There exist also misleading similarities where words that appear the same have a different meaning. For a comprehensive list in the world of *francophonie*, see Batchelor and Offord (2006, pp. 31–37);
4. syntactic calque or imitation. This is doubtless the one truly reprehensible area for aping English since it damages the actual fabric of the French language. It carries over the entire syntactic construction from English into French: *à date*, calque for *up-to-date* instead of *jusqu'à maintenant, à ce jour; aller en grève* for *to go on strike* instead of *faire la grève; hors d'ordre* for *out of order* instead of *en panne; passé dû* for *past due* instead of *échu; prendre pour acquis* for *to take for granted* instead of *tenir pour acquis; prime de séparation* for *severance pay* instead of *indemnité de départ; siéger sur un comité* for *to sit on a board/committee* instead of *siéger à un comité; retourner un appel* for *to return a call* instead of *rappeler; temps supplémentaire* for *overtime* instead of *heures supplémentaires*.

67

Differences in frequency of similar words in the two languages / La différence en fréquence d'usage dans les deux langues

The following passage describes the great benefits of evening walks. Young people, guided by their teacher, learn a great deal about their surroundings when visiting monuments and any other kind of urban attraction of a historical character. When monuments are lit up, the imagination is fired so that young people enjoy their surroundings with an extra impetus. History comes alive as a study case is placed before the students. A reading of the passage displays the high frequency of some French words, as opposed to their relatively infrequent use in English. The French words in question are highlighted in bold. Some translations are provided.

Promenade nocturne

Dans certaines villes du monde, une promenade **nocturne** est très **agréable** parce que la **luminosité** des sites touristiques est **impressionnante**. Pour **accéder** à ces sites exceptionnels, des points **lumineux** jalonnent le parcours avant d'arriver à destination et de bénéficier de l'**apothéose** des monuments historiques mis en lumière. Mais on peut également traverser certains quartiers **périphériques** avec des passages **lugubres** où l'on risque de se faire **assassiner**, et il serait **aberrant** de s'y **hasarder** sans prendre les précautions nécessaires.

Les visites touristiques ont toujours une vertu **pédagogique**, surtout pour les enfants qui peuvent **interroger** le guide pour obtenir tous les détails des sites visités. Elles s'**inscrivent** dans le cadre d'un programme scolaire pendant lequel des élèves doivent présenter à leurs camarades le compte-rendu [report] de leur visite et l'**intégrer** [insert] dans le cours d'histoire qu'ils poursuivent en classe. Ces jeunes garçons et jeunes filles commencent d'abord par présenter les **divers** [several] aspects du pays concerné et par décrire ensuite la **zone** géographique précise où se trouve le monument historique avec ses multiples facettes. L'ensemble de la classe peut être **sollicité** [encouraged] pour **émettre** des questions relatives à l'histoire du pays et du site historique. Chaque élève peut présenter son opinion du travail accompli et, **éventuellement** [possibly], saluer le travail de ses **compagnons** de route.

En fait, ce type de travail **pédagogique** est très utile parce qu'il permet aux enfants de bien assimiler des éléments importants de l'histoire à travers une étude de cas. Il s'agit de **transmettre** un savoir [knowledge] grâce à l'implication directe des jeunes et d'un travail approprié *in situ* [on the spot]. Les apprenants [learners] peuvent donc **évoluer** [develop] sur le terrain, trouver des **interlocuteurs** locaux et les **interroger** pour obtenir toutes les **précisions** utiles à leur exposé à présenter à l'oral en classe. Ils ne doivent pas **renoncer** devant les difficultés rencontrées et doivent poursuivre leur travail en parfaite **autonomie** par rapport à leur **professeur**. Cela démontrera qu'ils ont été capables d'accomplir une tâche sur le terrain en faisant appel à leur intelligence et aux connaissances acquises en classe.

Une promenade **nocturne** procure des sensations magiques, parfois jusqu'à l'**euphorie** parce que la mise en scène [presentation] par des lumières de différentes couleurs des sites à visiter **transporte** le visiteur dans un monde imaginaire et fait déborder son imagination. Les sentiments recueillis peuvent être très denses grâce à la mise en valeur [highlighting] du site concerné. Il ne faut donc pas **renoncer** à se rendre, en pleine nuit, à des sites qui paraissent difficiles d'accès mais dont la **luminosité** exerce une force attractive et une curiosité que l'on ne peut pas contenir. Ces sites **manifestent** un intérêt indéniable qui se vérifie sur le terrain.

Very often, words that are cognates in English and French, that is words that bear a strong resemblance to each other, both in form and in meaning, are used in largely the same way in both languages. In other words, they appear in identical contexts and with similar frequency. For example, the French word *machine* occurs just as frequently in French as the English *machine*, *pilote* as *pilot*, *illustrer* as *to illustrate*. However, there are also cases where frequency of use can vary between the two languages, and it is important for the non-native learner of French to be aware of such differences. Words in one language can apply to literal and metaphorical contexts whereas in the other they have a reduced application, either literal or metaphorical. The French word *supérieur* is a good case in point. It has a literal application (*l'étage supérieur*) and a metaphorical one (*un être supérieur* = God, *une intelligence supérieure*), and to quote De Gaulle in one of his wartime speeches from London: "Il faut protéger l'intérêt supérieur de la patrie." In English, *superior* is reduced to this latter metaphorical meaning alone, and even then it is not used a lot. In the De Gaulle quotation, English would doubtless require *higher*. Again, *zone* in English often has an administrative or military connotation, but in French it is much more general: *une zone tropicale/littorale/militaire/de libre-échange/d'activité*. Historically, during World War II, France was divided into two areas and here it has a specific reference: *zone libre / zone occupée = unoccupied France / occupied France*. In English, the word *region* or *area* would often be used in these contexts.

There is a danger of a word being overused and therefore used inappropriately in the second language simply because its cognate is common in the first language. This would appear odd to a native speaker of the second language. In the following cases, the French word appears much more often than the English cognate. The French word appears first: *aberrant = aberrant, accéder = to accede, annuler = to annul, antérieur = anterior, apothéose = apotheosis, assassiner = to murder | to assassinate, austral = austral, autonomie = autonomy, camarade = comrade, commencer = to commence, compagnon = companion, se désister = to desist, divers =diverse, émettre = to emit, épiderme = epidermis, époque = epoch, euphorie = euphoria, évoluer = to evolve, inférieur = inferior, inscrire = to inscribe, intégrer = to integrate, interlocuteur = interlocutor, interroger = to interrogate, juriste = jurist, lugubre = lugubrious, lumineux = luminous, luminosité = brightness/luminosity, maladie cutanée = skin complaint, manifester = to manifest* (oneself, i.e., to appear), *méridional = meridional, multiple = multiple, nocturne = nocturnal, occidental = occidental, pédagogique = pedagogic(al), périphérie = periphery, postérieur = posterior, proposer = to propose, réintégrer = to reintegrate, renoncer = to renounce, saluer = to salute, solliciter = to solicit, supérieur = superior, transmettre = to transmit, transporter = to take | to drive* (someone) *| to transport, urticaire = urticaria* (rash), *vérifier = to verify, zone = zone.*

This situation also functions in reverse. The following is a brief list of English words that occur more frequently than their French counterparts: *area = aire, appropriate = approprié, to blame = blâmer, dense = dense, disadvantage = désavantage, disappointment = désappointement, erratic = erratique, fragrant =fragrant, magnitude = magnitude, substantial = substantiel.*

A corollary of the above is that very often a more frequently used English word appears instead of the cognate term: *dans un but pédagogique = with an educational objective; Il faut vérifier les pneus = We/You have to check the tires; émettre une opinion = to express an opinion.*

68

Miscellaneous: truncation, interjections, fillers, transition words, forms of address, figures of speech, doublets, informal / colloquial language and slang, backslang / Divers : la troncation, les interjections, les formules de remplissage, les mots de transition, les formules de politesse, les figures de rhétorique, les doublets, le langage familier / populaire et l'argot, le verlan

The following passage relates the experience of a young man who returns to his native France and tells his friend how things went in a prestigious multinational. He obviously had a good time, although work proved very demanding, and he was sometimes anxious over how his performance would appear, particularly with respect to his presentation. Naturally enough, his boss caused him the greatest apprehension. In order not to get too stressed, he would go to discos and mingle with a wide range of guys. It is clear he enjoyed his year abroad for he regretted leaving all his colleagues. The passage uses a number of abbreviated words which appear in bold, while there are also some transition words which are underlined, together with a balancing statement (*d'une part . . . d'autre part*). Some translations are given.

Récit d'une expérience de stage

L'année 2010 représente le quarantième anniversaire de la francophonie qui réunit des dizaines de pays à travers le monde et près de 200 millions de francophones. Le français a beaucoup évolué avec le temps. <u>Alors que</u> le français écrit a subi peu de transformation, le français parlé s'est beaucoup livré à la facilité du langage oral. <u>En conséquence</u>, on peut imaginer un jeune âgé de 25 ans environ qui raconte à son copain le stage qu'il vient de passer à l'étranger dans une multinationale:

«J'étais super content d'avoir obtenu un stage auprès d'une boîte [company] archi-connue à l'étranger. À mon arrivée, j'ai été accueilli, à 10h du **mat**, par le **dirlo** qui m'a offert un **apéro** avec des amuse-gueules. Il m'a ensuite montré mon bureau où il n'y avait aucune **déco**. Dans l'**aprem**, la secrétaire m'a accompagné pour m'installer dans mon **appart** qui était équipé de la **clim** et d'un grand **frigo**. En soirée, j'ai proposé à la secrétaire d'aller au **ciné** ou dans une **disco** mais, malheureusement, elle n'était pas **dispo**. Le lendemain, j'ai pris mon **petit-dej** dans le bistrot près de chez moi.

Pour aller au boulot, j'ai dû acheter un vélo **d'occas**. Mon premier jour de boulot consistait à consulter la **doc** de l'entreprise pour prendre connaissance de toutes les **infos** nécessaires. J'ai fait de mon mieux et je me suis donné à **max**. Quant au **boss**, il m'a demandé de faire une **expo** sur la francophonie, avec des **diapos**, qui serait suivie par une **conf** d'un autre collègue. La **rédac** de l'**expo** m'a pris un **max** de temps. D'une part, j'ai dû utiliser pas mal de **dicos**, et d'autre part, il ne fallait surtout pas employer des **textos** [text messages]. Je craignais **la cata**. Au contraire, c'était **sensas** et tous les collègues ont trouvé mon **expo sympa**. À la fin de la **conf**, du **champ** a été servi à tout le monde.

Par la suite, j'ai eu d'autres missions à accomplir avec un **max** de boulot mais j'ai fait attention de ne pas être trop stressé et **maso** parce que j'avais peur d'attraper une **dep**. Il fallait pas que ça me gave [overwhelm] ni que ça me prenne trop la tête. Aussi, j'allais tous les soirs me défouler [chill out] dans les **discos** de la région avec des potes [guys] qui étaient **mécanos**, **métallos**, flics, etc. Parfois, un mec bourré [plastered] n'arrêtait pas de me bousculer [pushed me about] dans la **disco**. Alors, je lui ai dit casse-toi, tu me gonfles [you're getting on my nerves], lâche-moi les baskets [give us a break], sinon tu vas prendre une beigne [wallop] ou une châtaigne [clout]. Au bout de quelques secondes, il s'est barré [cleared off]. Par contre, tu y trouves des mecs hyper **sympas** qui ont de la classe et vraiment **tip top**. Il m'est arrivé de faire un tour en **hélico** avec un mec que j'ai connu dans la **disco** et c'était mega cool. Le paysage vu du ciel était d'enfer [terrific]. C'était trop bien.

À la fin de mon stage, j'avais vraiment la **déprime** [was depressed] parce que j'allais quitter des potes formidables qui assuraient. De plus, à la sortie de mon **appart**, je me suis foulé la cheville [sprained my ankle] et j'ai dû aller faire une **radio** au **labo** et suivre des séances de **kiné** [physio]. Heureusement, c'était pas trop grave et j'ai pu dire au revoir à tous mes potes avec qui j'ai passé des moments mega top. Depuis que je suis rentré, on communique avec des **textos**.»

These miscellaneous features of the French language have, to varying degrees, an effect upon its grammatical functions. They are also connected to register values.

68.1 Truncation

Truncation is the process whereby a word is shortened by one or more syllables, or simply one or two sounds. Since these are unestablished words, there is uncertainty around the spelling of some of them. Truncation has become a dominant aspect of the current spoken language, and with a few exceptions, most of the truncated forms fall into the R1 category. Exceptions which have become part of the standard (R2) language are: *métro*, *photo*, *topo* (*talk*), *vélo*.

Others are also of long standing but have not been raised to R2 status; most are formed by young people: *auto*(*mobile*), *bac*(*calauréat*), *dac* (*d'accord*), *diapo*(*sitive*) = *slide* for viewing, *dico* (*dictionnaire*), *disserte* (*dissertation*),*fac*(*ulté*), *maths* (*mathématiques*), *philo*(*sophie*), *prof*(*esseur*), *rab*(*iot*) = *extra food*, as in canteen, *rédac*(*tion*), *sympa*(*thique*).

The following list presents some more recent creations and illustrates the wide-ranging nature of the phenomenon: *un accro*(*ché*) = *fanatic*: *les accrocs des textos*; *l'amphi* (*théâtre*) = *lecture theater*: *la conf*(*érence*) *aura lieu en amphi 1*; *un anar*(*chiste*); *un apéro* (*apéritif*); *un appart*(*ement*); *cet aprem* (*après-midi*); *un aristo*(*crate*); *le béné*(*fice*): *faire du béné* = *to make profit*; *une bio*(*graphie*); *le calva*(*dos*): *Tu prends du calva ?*; *la cata*(*strophe*): *C'est la cata !*; *catho*(*lique*): *le public catho*; *le champ*(*agne*): *Tu prends du champ ?* (**p** is pronounced); *le ciné*(*ma*); *la clim* (*climatisation*) = *air conditioning*: *Il fait trop chaud, on met la clim*; *un collabo*(*rateur*); *une compo*(*sition*); *une conf*(*érence*); *un croco*(*dile*); *D un/deux* (*division un/deux*, in sport): *C'est une excellente équipe, ils sont en D 1 depuis vingt ans*; *Ils ne sont pas très solides, ils sont en D 2*; *comme d'hab*(*itude*); *la dactylo*(*graphe/graphie*); *sans déc*(*onner*) = *no kidding*; *les arts déco*(*ratifs*); *la déco*(*ration*); *le petit-déj*(*euner*); *la dém*(*ission*); *la dép*(*ression*); *un dino*(*saure*); *le dirlo* (*directeur*, of school, business): *on a une réunion avec le dirlo*; *une disco*(*thèque*): *de la musique disco*; *un docu*(*mentaire*): *Ils passent un docu à la télé ce soir*; *un édito*(*rial*); *un expat*(*rié*); *une expo*(*sition*); *un fana*(*tique*); *le foot*(*ball*); *un frigo* (*frigidaire*); *le gaspi*(*llage*); *la chasse au gaspi*; *la géo*(*graphie*); *un hebdo*(*madaire*); *un hélico*(*ptère*); *un imper*(*méable*); *les infos* (*informations*); *un intello* (*intellectual*); *une interro*(*gation*) = *short test* (in school); *la Place d'It*(*alie*) (Paris); *le kiné*(*sithérapeuthe*); *le labo*(*ratoire*); *Libé*(*ration*) (French daily newspaper); *une manif*(*estation*); *maso*(*chiste*); *le max*(*imum*), *un mécano* (*mécanicien*); *faire du mélo*(*drame*): *C'est du pur mélo* = *It's a real tear jerker*; *un mémo*(*randum*); *un métallo* (*métallurgiste*); *une mob*(*ylette*); *Le nouvel obs*(*ervateur*) (French news magazine); *l'occas*(*ion*): *Il faut profiter de l'occas*; *ordi*(*nateur*): *Allez, les gars, on va jouer à l'ordi*; *otorino* (*oto-rhino-laryngologiste*) = *ears, nose and throat specialist*; *parano*(*iaque*); *un pédé*(*raste*); *une perf*(*ormance*): *réaliser une belle perf*; *le périf* (*périphérique*) = *beltway, ringroad*, *la perm*(*ission*) = (soldier's) *leave*; *une photocop*(*ie*); *les Sciences Po*(*litiques*); *la polio*(*miélite*); *un polycop*(*ié*) = *handout* (for a talk, for students); *un porno* (*un film pornographique*); *la porno*(*graphie*); *la prépa* (*classe préparatoire*) for the *Grandes Écoles*; *un projo* (*projecteur*); *les prolos* (*prolétaires*) = *the plebs*; *une promo*(*tion*): *plusieurs produits en* *promo; les pros (professionnels, as in sport); la psycho(logie); la pub(licité)* = *commercial, advert* (not to be confused with *le pub* = *pub*, as in England); *un pull(over)* = *sweater; le pyj(ama); la radio(graphie)* = *xray: J'ai passé une radio des poumons; rapido (rapidement): Fais-le et rapido; un Rasta(farian;* there seems to be no full accredited French form); *réac(tionnaire): les gens réac; réglo (réglementaire): Il est réglo* = *He's straight; restau-U (restaurant universitaire): On va au restau-U à quelle heure ?; rétro(spective); la mode rétro; un rhino(céros); les rollers* = *roller skates; sado (sadique); la Sécu (Sécurité Sociale); sensass (sensationnel): C'est sensass; un sous-off(icier)* = *non-commissioned officer; une chaîne stéréo(phonique; une chaîne* is also used by itself); *les Stups: la Brigade des Stupéfiants* = *Drugs Squad; sup(plémentaire): Elle fait des heures sup; un survêt(ement)* = *track suit; tel (téléphone,* only in writing); *la télé(vision); un toxico(mane)* = *drug addict; un travelo (transvesti)* = *transvestite.*

68.2 Interjections

In the measured, self-conscious speech of R3, interjections are by definition rare. On the other hand, at the opposite end of the formality–informality scale, in the more spontaneous speech of R1, interjections (similar to slang and colloquialisms) occur frequently, as involuntary, emotional reflexes. R2 speech, lying between R3 and R1, also contains a certain number of interjections, but is more selective in their use. In this section, an attempt has been made to grade the interjections according to intensity and decency; that is to say, the interjections are placed on a continuum, one end of which is termed "respectable usage" and covers the R2 expressions and to a lesser extent the first two R1 expressions, and the other end of which is termed "indecent usage" and covers the expressions in the last series. It is accepted that "respectable" and "indecent" are relative terms; attitudes toward indecency and swearing are highly subjective, and age and movement of the times have much to do with this. It is stressed that the use of interjections by non-native speakers needs to be exercised with caution, as an inappropriate usage may cause deep offense at the worst, or, at the very least, embarrassment. It may be wiser for the learner to avoid many R1 interjections altogether. It suffices to appreciate their force without necessarily using them oneself.

Interjections of surprise and annoyance are often interchangeable, the emotion expressed depending entirely on intonation and the attitude of the speaker. Popular speech and slang, including interjections, are often subject to the whim of fashion, and there is a constant gain and loss of expressions, while persistent use of what were once offensive terms, like *foutre*, can soften their impact. *Foutre* no longer invites the same censuring as it once did, not that it is suggested that it should be used, and it depends upon the context. The expressions below, which are often preceded by *C'est*

(*C'est le top*) and followed by an exclamation point or question mark when written, are all in contemporary use. R1* indicates indecent usage.

Admiration
R2 (respectable usage, accepted in most circles): *excellent*; *formidable*; *parfait*; *parfaitement*

R1: *Ça assure, Ma, la bombe* (of a girl); *C'est de la bonne* (of a girl); *Ça, c'est la classe*; *clean*; *cool*; *Eh bien*; *dis donc*; *d'enfer*; *génial*; *hyper cool*; *méga trop cool*; *l'panard*; *le pied*; *Ça roule*; *tip top*; *top*; *top méga top*; *Ça tope*; *trop bon*

R1*: *bandant, enculé, hyper bien foutu, jouissif*

Agreement
R2: *d'accord*; *C'est clair*; *entendu*; *impeccable*

R1: *d'acc*; *ben oui*; *Ça boom*; *Ça colle* (Anatole); *et comment*; *cool ton plan*; *Mais ne te gêne pas*; *impec*; *OK*; *OK et pas d'embrouille*; *Y a pas photo, pourquoi pas ?*; *va* (occurs after a statement: *Je t'aime, va !*), *Ça va*; *Vas-y, fais comme chez toi*; *Si tu veux, ma poule*

Annoyance
R2: *bigre*; *fichtre*

R1: *Casse-toi*; *Elle* (subject) *m'empoisonne*; *espèce d'idiot*; *flûte*; *Tu vas prendre une beigne, Tu me prends la tête !*; *punaise*; *Ça me gave/gonfle*; *Lâche-moi les baskets*; *mince alors*; *nom d'un chien*; *sacré nom de Dieu*; *la purée*; *bon sang*; *Va te faire shampooiner*; *zut (alors)*

R1*: *berk* (expressing disgust); *bordel*; *bordel de merde*; *Il me fait caguer/chier*; *Ha*; *tu fais chier*; *Va chier*; *espèce de con*; *quel con/connard*; *quelle conne* (**very strong**); *couillon*; *Je t'emmerde*; *Va te faire enculer/foutre*; *putain (de merde)*; *résidu de capote*; *salaud*; *saligaud*

Disbelief
R2: *sans blague*

R1: *Arrête de bourrer*; *Arrête ton char/charre* (Ben Hur); *Je n'y crois pas*; *C'est dingue*; *mais alors*; *mon œil*; *pas possible*; *T'as vu la vierge ?*; *C'est pas vrai*

R1*: *Tu déconnes, sans déc/déconner*; *rien à foutre*; *putain pas possible*; *putain tu rigoles*

Joy
R2: *chic alors*

R1: *Ça baigne*; *bath*; *C'est la bombe*; *bon Dieu de bon Dieu*; *chouette alors*; *C'est l'extase*; *C'est giga*; *Ça fait hyper du bien*; *C'est méga*; *le pied*; *Roule ma poule*; *sensas(s)*; *super*; *super bien*; *super génial*; *c'est trop*; *top clean*; *top cool*

R1*: *Je pète le feu | la forme*

Objection
R2: *mais tout de même*

R1: *et après?*; *ben quoi ?*; *cacahuète camembert*; *Qu'est-ce que tu embrouilles, toi ?*; *Tu te fous de moi ?*; *n'importe quoi*; *tu rêves ?*; *tu rigoles*; *et ta sœur ?*; *Tu tapes dans les boîtes ou quoi ?*; *(et) toc*; *Ça va pas la tête ?*; *Ça va pas ou quoi ?*

R1*: *bordel*; *merde*; *putain*; *putain de bordel de merde*

Relief
   R2: *ouf*
Surprise
   R2: *grands dieux; ma foi; parbleu; (mille) tonnere(s) de Dieu*. Note that *pardi*
    and *ma foi* could fall into an R2 category
   R1: *ça alors; eh ben ça alors; ah non alors; eh ben; bondieu; quel con; cool;*
    délire; eh ben dis/dites; j'hallucine; ouf; pas possible; tu rigoles; non je suis
    vert
   R1*: *tu déconnes; sans déc/déconner*
Warning
   R2: *attention*. Note that *prends garde* could easily be classified as R3
   R1: *défie-toi mec; faire gaffe; fais gaffe; gare/gare-gare; Tu vas t'en prendre une;*
    Je te préviens ça va pas le faire; Je suis vert
   R1*: *Va te faire foutre; J'vais te tuer; Vire ton cul*

68.3 Fillers

In informal speech, where hesitation is common and the right word can be
slow in coming, sentences are rarely completely formed, and fillers such as
the following are called upon to bridge the gap. Similarly, in English, *well*
all too frequently precedes a statement made by a person who is asked a
question.

allez	Allez, tu dis ça pour me faire rire.
allons donc	Allons donc, tu plaisantes.
alors	Alors, raconte, qu'est-ce qui s'est passé ?: Alors, tu viens ?; Il parlait tout le temps, alors je lui ai dit de se taire; Et alors, qu'est-ce que tu veux que je fasse ?
ben	Ben, je sais pas.
bof	"Tu penses que cette cravate va avec ton costume ?" "Bof, pourquoi pas ?"
bon	Allons bon, il pleut; Vous voulez connaître la vérité ? Bon je vais tout vous dire; Bon, ne te fâche pas.
bref (passons)	J'ai passé la journée à courir d'un magasin à l'autre. Bref, je suis épuisée.
c'est-à-dire	Tu es sûr de l'avoir vue ? C'est-à-dire, tout le monde peut se tromper; Je ne peux pas t'aider. C'est-à-dire, je n'en ai pas le droit.
déjà	C'est combien, déjà ?
disons	Disons, je ne me rappelle plus.
écoute(z)	Oh, écoute, il faut pas le faire comme ça; "Qu'est-ce tu penses du film?" "Oh écoute, il n'est pas passionnant."

eh bien	"Comment vas-tu?" "Ça va mieux." "Eh bien, c'est parfait."
enfin	Ce meuble est très cher, mais enfin, je peux peut-être l'acheter; Je vous ai dit ce que je pensais. Enfin, c'est à toi de décider.
euh	La rue Victor Hugo? Euh, je crois que c'est la première à gauche.
ma foi	Cette maison est bien située, et, ma foi, je pense qu'elle vous plaira.
un peu	Tu as des nouvelles, un peu?; Dis-moi un peu, tu as des nouvelles?
quoi	Allons, quoi, faut pas te décourager.
remarque	Remarque, tu peux mettre le bouquin sur le rayon.
tu vois / vois-tu	C'est quelqu'un de très bien, tu vois / vois-tu.
vous voyez / voyez-vous	C'est un monsieur très important, vous voyez / voyez-vous; Vous voyez / Voyez-vous, il ne faut jamais désespérer.

68.4 Transition words

In R3 speech and writing, where careful organization of structure is important, particularly when a discussion is taking place, transition words, marking the points of an argument, are very common. They also occur quite frequently in R2 language:

alors que	Il a plu tout l'été, alors que cet hiver on n'a pas eu une goutte d'eau.
au contraire	Elle a dit que ce problème de maths était très simple. Moi, au contraire, je l'ai trouvé très difficile.
aussi	J'ai raté le train. Aussi a-t-il fallu que je prenne l'autocar.
car	Il n'a pas pu se baigner car il a trop mangé.
en conséquence / par conséquent	Adrienne n'a pas gagné beaucoup d'argent. En conséquence / Par conséquent, elle n'a pu partir en vacances.
en effet	Ils ont prévu que votre équipe allait gagner. En effet, c'est ce qui s'est passé.
en fait / en réalité	On a cru que Dupont était un bon sculpteur. En fait / En réalité, il est plutôt peintre.
en résumé	Les règles de la grammaire italienne sont très nombreuses. En résumé, ce manuel peut t'aider.

en revanche /	On n'a pas pu visiter le château. En revanche / Par
par contre	contre, nous sommes allés au musée
or	Les restrictions budgétaires devraient réduire
	l'inflation. Or, celle-ci continue à monter.
partant (R3)	Les études littéraires sur l'œuvre de Sartre sont de
	plus en plus nombreuses. Partant, l'intérêt du
	lecteur s'est considérablement accru.
quant à	Quant à la dame d'en face, je dirais que...
voire (R3)	Nous pourrons peut-être étudier les romans de
	Butor, voire même ceux de Pinget.

In addition to transition words, there are also balancing words or phrases favoring contrasts and comparisons:

d'un côté...	La critique contemporaine se divise en deux clans.
de l'autre	D'un côté les traditionalistes, de l'autre (côté) les
(côté)	modernistes.
d'une part...	Dans un travail de rédaction, il faut faire attention
d'autre part	d'une part au contenu et d'autre part à la forme.

In a carefully reasoned argument, the following series of terms are available: *premièrement... deuxièment... troisièmement; primo... secundo... tertio; en premier lieu... en second lieu... en troisième lieu.*

68.5 Forms of address

When meeting someone, or when writing a letter/e-mail to some one, it is important from the very beginning of the encounter to strike the right chord on the register scale: First words create first impressions, and will therefore affect the subsequent attitude of the addressee. Consequently, a gambit or opening comment should ensure a favorable hearing thereafter. The following expressions illustrate the various formulae that are available in contemporary French.

In speech and on meeting
  R1: *Salut, tu vas bien ?; Vous allez bien ?; (comment) ça va ?; ça marche ?; ça boum ?; ça gaze ?; Ça fait un bail / une paie qu'on ne s'est pas vu; quoi de neuf/nouveau ?*
  R2: *Bonjour, Monsieur / Madame / Mademoiselle / jeune homme, Comment vas-tu ?; Comment allez-vous ?*
  R3: *Monsieur/Madame se porte bien ? À qui ai-je l'honneur ?* (on meeting for the first time someone you do not know)
In speech and on leave-taking
  R1: *salut; ciao; tchao; à la revoyure*
  R2: *au revoir; au plaisir (de vous/te revoir); à bientôt; à tout de suite; à la semaine prochaine; bonne journée/matinée/soirée; bon retour; bon voyage;*

bonne route; *bonne chance*; *bonne continuation de vacances | de travail* (or whatever the other person is doing)

R3: *adieu*

In a letter: introduction

R1: *salut Jean*

R2: *Cher Monsieur*; *Chère madame*; *Chère Mademoiselle*

R3: *Madame/Mademoiselle/Monsieur*; *Monsieur le Directeur | Madame la Directrice*; *Monsieur le Président*

In a letter: conclusion

R1: *à bientôt*; *grosses bises*; *bisous*; *salut*

R2: *grosses bises*; *bisous*; *affectueusement*; *amitiés*; *bien à toi/vous*; *amicalement*; *toutes mes amitiés à tes parents*

R3: *Je vous prie | Veuillez agréer (l'expression de) mes salutations distinguées | mes respectueuses salutations | mes sentiments distingués | respectueux | les meilleurs*

There exists one other form of address which is a cross between the formal and the informal, and this formula does not occur in English. On speaking to someone, the formula *Monsieur/Madame/Mademoiselle* with the first name contains a gentle, humorous and even intimate tone, suggesting as it does a sense of fun. It suggests nothing unpleasant: *Alors, Monsieur Philippe | Madame Martine, tu vas bien ?*; *Mademoiselle Adrienne, tu sors ce soir ?* The *vous* form is also possible here: *Bonjour Madame Sophie, vous allez bien ?* Referring to a person in the third person, one may also say: *Tu dis à Monsieur Christophe que j'ai appelé.* This statement avoids the stiffness and starchiness of, say, *Monsieur Dupont.*

68.6 Figures of speech

Figures of speech really represent a transfer of ideas from one sphere to another, usually from concrete images to abstract, and vice versa. They are common in numerous languages, and are intimately connected to grammatical functions. Their appreciation is essential in the understanding of literary discourse. The following is a list of such figures as they exist in French.

Simile: Similes involve words like *comme, ainsi que, de même que*: *Ce cheval est rapide comme l'éclair*; *Un enfant blond comme les blés*; *Elle s'élança telle une gazelle*; *Ainsi qu'un jeune chien, elle gambadait*; "Et c'était comme quatre coups brefs que je frappais sur la porte du malheur" (Camus 1962b, p. 1168).

Metaphor: This is a kind of simile but is much more direct, replacing one image for another: *La neige a recouvert la campagne d'un blanc manteau*; *Il faut s'attaquer à la racine du mal*; "les cymbales du soleil" (Camus 1962b, p. 1168). Metaphors can also be sustained (*métaphore filée*), as in this example from Lamartine's poem *Le lac*: "Ne pourrons-nous jamais sur l'océan des âges / Jeter l'ancre un seul jour ?"

Hyperbole: Deliberate exaggeration to stress an experience: *Je meurs de faim; Merci mille fois; C'était un géant (un homme de haute taille); C'était un pygmée (un petit homme).*

Litotes: *Elle n'est pas bête (Elle est intelligente); Je ne le déteste pas (Il me plaît).* Camus's *La peste* is a perfect example of the art of litotes.

Euphemism: Softening of sharp or brutal words: *Ton chien est au paradis (Il est mort); Les aînés / les seniors (les personnes âgées).*

Allegory: Expression of an idea by an image, a painting or a human being; Delacroix's *La liberté guidant le peuple* is an allegory; Camus's *La peste* is a striking allegory representing the suffering of mankind.

Synecdoque: Expression of a part for the whole: *Ils sont sans toit (Ils n'ont pas de maison); le cultivateur (les cultivateurs).*

Metonymy: The substitution of a word referring to an attribute for the thing that is meant: *la couronne (le roi / la reine); Mange ton assiette (Mange ton repas); Elle est née sous une bonne étoile.*

68.7 Doublets

French, like several other languages, derives largely from Latin. It is interesting to observe that the same Latin word gives two French words, differing in form and in use or meaning, and even in gender: *chaîne* (feminine) / *cadenas* (masculine), *poison* (masculine) / *potion* (feminine). These pairs of words are called doublets (*doublets* in French). Thus, the words *parole* and *parabole* come from the Latin word *parabola*. *Parole* was subject to the usual phonetic development while *parabole* was borrowed directly from Latin, bypassing centuries of morphological change. There now follows a series of doublets, the first being the popular form and the second a straightforward borrowing: *aigre/âcre, évier/aquarium, écouter/ausculter, chaîne/cadenas, chaire/cathédrale, chose/cause, cheville/clavicule, cailler/coaguler, cueillette/collecte, combler/cumuler, dessiner/désigner, frêle/fragile, hôtel/hôpital, entier/intègre, livrer/libérer, mâcher/mastiquer, métier/ministère, nager/naviguer, œuvrer/opérer, œuf/ovule, parole/parabole, poison/potion, porche/portique, recouvrer/récupérer, raide/rigide, serment/sacrement, sûreté/sécurité, sevrer/séparer, sembler/simuler, étroit/strict, soupçon/suspicion, vœu/vote.*

68.8 Informal/colloquial language and slang

The small section above on truncation already refers to an informal level of discourse. However, a more general statement needs to be made on the subject of informal French which corresponds to lax and slipshod grammar.

As far as *argot* or slang is concerned, this term originally signifies, in its most precise meaning, the language of *le milieu* or the criminal underworld. This language hardly ever reaches the wider elements of society. We are therefore concerned with *argot* in its general application to society as a whole.

Informal language could be separated from colloquial language but these terms lead to such an overlap that it is wiser and simpler to treat them as one category: R1. The vulgar variety of slang is classified as R1*, to be treated with great care, and, it is suggested, to be avoided until a firm awareness of the French language is mastered. This R1* section is really for information only, since its content is usually of a sexual nature, centered on bodily functions, or of a sexist and racist character which most people would find repellent. It is therefore much shorter than the one devoted to informal and colloquial French. It would not be appropriate to include a lengthy presentation of vulgar French in the present book.

There now follows a brief, and only brief, list of common colloquial expressions of the R1 category, which leads on to a second list of the vulgar variety. Equivalent translations do not appear. Translations are usually of the neutral type. Bear in mind that these are core words, and that others are often associated with them, for instance *engueuler* > *engueulade* (feminine; *reprimand, row*); *marrant* > *se marrer* (*to laugh*).

R1: *aboule ta viande* (*come here*); *amocher* (*to smash, to beat up*); *quelle andouille !* (*what an idiot!*); *arnaque* (feminine: *trick, scam*); *Arrête ton char, Ben Hur !* (*You must be joking!*); *Il s'est fait avoir* (*He was tricked*); *bagnole* (feminine: *automobile, jalopy*); *balancer* (*to throw, to chuck, to dismiss*); *en baver* (*to have a hard time of it*); *bidule* (masculine: *thing, whatdoyoucall it?*; also *machin* and *truc*, both masculine); *bizutage* (masculine: *hazing/ragging* of a new student); *buerk !* (*yuk!*); *beurré* (*drunk*); *binette* (feminine: *face, mug*); *bordel* (masculine: *mess, disorder*); *bouffer* (*to eat*); *bourré* (*drunk*); *caboche* (feminine: *head*); *C'est pas très catholique* (*It's not right | It looks suspicious*); *champignon* (masculine: *accelerator* in car); *chiader* (*to study*); *la chose* (*sex*), *cochonnerie* (*dirtiness, filth, trash*); *crevant* (*tiring, hilarious*); *crevé* (*exhausted*); *cuistot* (*cook*), *système D* (masculine: *getting by/through, wrangling*), *débile* (*weak, pathetic*); *se débrouiller* (*to manage, to get by*); *déconner* (*to talk nonsense, to act in a foolish manner*); *se défouler* (*to let your hair down*); *se dégonfler* (*to lose confidence, to get cold feet*); *dégueulasse* (*foul*); *draguer* (*to look for boys/girls, to pull*); *en écraser* (*to sleep*); *engueuler* (*to insult, to bawl at*); *emballer* (*to please, to turn on*); *ficher le camp* (*to go away*); *flancher* (*to weaken*); *flanquer* (*to give, to chuck, to kick out*); *fabriquer* (*to be up to: Qu'est-ce que tu fabriques là ?*); *flemme* (feminine: *laziness: J'ai la flemme d'étudier = I don't feel like studying*); *flinguer* (*to shoot [dead]*); *foirer* (*to go wrong, to flop*); *fourrer* (*to put, to stick, to shove*); *fric* (masculine: *cash*); *fringues* (feminine plural: *clothes*); *Fais gaffe !* (*Careful!*); *gamberger* (*to think hard, to worry*); *gars* (masculine: *guy*); *glandouiller* (*to hang around, to waste time*); *godasse* (feminine: *shoe*); *gogues* (feminine plural: *bathroom, toilet*); *se gourer* (*to blunder, to make a* *mistake); se grouiller (to get a move on); gueuler (to bawl, to holler); histoire* (feminine: *Qu'est-ce que c'est que cette histoire ? = What's going on?); jean-foutre* (masculine: *worthless person, layabout); C'est du kif-kif (It's all the same); faire la java/nouba (to party); lèche-cul* (masculine: *ass-licker); lolo* (masculine: *milk); loubard* (masculine: *hoodlum, yobbo); se magner (to hurry up); magouille* (feminine: *underhand scheme, wangle), malade (stupid, dumb); marrant (funny); en avoir marre (to be fed up); mec* (masculine: *guy, fellow); mémé* (feminine: *grandmother); mirettes* (feminine plural: *eyes); nana/nénette* (feminine: *girl, woman, chick); être bien nippé (to be well dressed); patate* (feminine: *potato); paumé (bewildered, psychologically disturbed); pécu* (masculine: *toilet paper); pépé* (masculine: *grandfather); avoir la pétoche (to be frightened); picoler (to drink, i.e., alcohol); pif* (masculine: *nose, hooter); piger (to understand); faire pipi (to urinate, to pee); piquer (to steal); piston* (masculine: *influence); pognon* (masculine: *cash); être à poil (to be naked); poulet* (masculine: *policeman); plaquer (to jilt), rigoler (to laugh); roi des cons* (masculine: *roidec = prize idiot); schlasse (drunk); schlinger (to stink); tordant (funny); virer (to throw, to chuck, to dismiss); Va te faire voir ! (Clear off !); zigouiller (to kill).*

R1*: *baiser (to have sexual intercourse with); avoir la main baladeuse (to be a groper); (Il) y a du monde au balcon (She's well-upholstered); bandant (sexually desirable, wonderful); bite* (feminine: *penis, dick); branleur* (masculine: *lazy person, wanker); chier (to crap: Il me fait chier = He annoys me); les chiottes* (feminine plural: *bathroom, toilet); con* (masculine: *vagina*; however, when this noun is used as an adjective, it can lose some of its offensive character and means *dumb, stupid,* and could be classified as R1. The same may be said of *connerie = mistake, blunder* and *déconner*). On the other hand, *connard* [masculine: *motherfucker*] and *connasse/conne* [feminine: *bitch*] are extremely repellent); *Couilles* (feminine plural: *male genitals, balls); couillon* (as an adjective: *stupid, dumb*; as a masculine noun: *stupid person, dickhead); couillonner (to swindle); cul* (as a masculine noun: *ass*; as an adjective: *sexually attractive); se démerder (to cope, to manage); emmerder (to annoy); emmerdeur* (masculine: *annoying person); fesse* (feminine: *woman* as a sexual object; *Il y aura de la fesse = Some chicks will be there.* However, when this noun, often in the plural, is used for *buttocks/ass*, it would be classified as R1); *Foutez-moi la paix ! (Clear off !); Ta gueule ! (Shut up !), putain* (feminine: *prostitute*; can be used in a masculine way: *Ce putain de temps me fait chier = This fucking weather gets on my tits); pute* (feminine: stronger than *putain); fils de pute/salaud/saligaud* (masculine: *son of a bitch); saloperie* (feminine: *dirty trick, nasty remark, trash), zob* (masculine: *penis, dick*).

Some of the above terms may be used in a friendly way, if the relationship allows it. A person could say to a friend *Mais t'es con,* and, as noted above, this is less offensive than *Quel gros con !* when this is said of someone you do not know, who has done something stupid in a car, for instance. The same may be said of *couillon* and *emmerdeur* – *Le voilà, l'emmerdeur.* It all depends on the context and intonation.

68.9 Backslang

The term *verlan* suggests a coded language which consists of inverting syllables of certain words and expressions. The word *verlan* is precisely an inversion of *envers = the other way round, the wrong way*. It is associated with certain districts, and few uninitiated people understand it. Here are some examples: *Africain > Cainfri, Arabe > Beur, branché > chébran, chaud > auch* (in the sense of *dangerous*), *femme > meuf, fou > ouf, juif > feuj, mec > keum, mère > rem, père > rep, métro > tromé.*

Part XI

Verb tables / Tableaux des conjugaisons

Much information on verbs and their structures is found in Part III. How-ever, here are in a condensed form the four model regular verbs (–er, –re, –ir and –oir), followed by all the main irregular verbs, verbs with spelling changes and one reflexive verb (*se laver*: note that here compound tenses are conjugated with *être*, not *avoir*).

The four model regular verbs

Chanter (*to sing*)

Indicative (simple tenses)

Present	*Imperfect*	*Preterit*	*Future*	*Conditional*
Je chante	Je chantais	Je chantai	Je chanterai	Je chanterais
Tu chantes	Tu chantais	Tu chantas	Tu chanteras	Tu chanterais
Il/Elle chante	Il/Elle chantait	Il/Elle chanta	Il/Elle chantera	Il/Elle chanterait
Nous chantons	Nous chantions	Nous chantâmes	Nous chanterons	Nous chanterions
Vous chantez	Vous chantiez	Vous chantâtes	Vous chanterez	Vous chanteriez
Ils/Elles chantent	Ils/Elles chantaient	Ils/Elles chantèrent	Ils/Elles chanteront	Ils/Elles chanteraient

Indicative (compound tenses)

Perfect	*Pluperfect*	*Past Anterior*	*Future in the Past*	*Conditional in the Past*
J'ai chanté	J'avais chanté	J'eus chanté	J'aurai chanté	J'aurais chanté
Tu as chanté	Tu avais chanté	Tu eus chanté	Tu auras chanté	Tu aurais chanté
Il/Elle a chanté	Il/Elle avait chanté	Il/Elle eut chanté	Il/Elle aura chanté	Il/Elle aurait chanté
Nous avons chanté	Nous avions chanté	Nous eûmes chanté	Nous aurons chanté	Nous aurions chanté
Vous avez chanté	Vous aviez chanté	Vous eûtes chanté	Vous aurez chanté	Vous auriez chanté
Ils/Elles ont chanté	Ils/Elles avaient chanté	Ils/Elles eurent chanté	Ils/Elles auront chanté	Ils/Elles auraient chanté

Subjunctive (simple tenses)

Present	*Imperfect*
Je chante	Je chantasse
Tu chantes	Tu chantasses
Il/Elle chante	Il/Elle chantât

Subjunctive (simple tenses) (*cont.*)

Present	*Imperfect*
Nous chantions	Nous chantassions
Vous chantiez	Vous chantassiez
Ils/Elles chantent	Ils/Elles chantassent

Subjunctive (compound tenses)

Perfect	*Pluperfect*
J'aie chanté	J'eusse chanté
Tu aies chanté	Tu eusses chanté
Il/Elle ait chanté	Il/Elle eût chanté
Nous ayons chanté	Nous eussions chanté
Vous ayez chanté	Vous eussiez chanté
Ils/Elles aient chanté	Ils/Elles eussent chanté

Imperative: Chante, chantons, chantez
Non-personal forms

Infinitive			Gerund	
Simple	*Compound*	*Past participle*	*Simple*	*Compound*
Chanter	Avoir chanté	Chanté	Chantant	Ayant chanté

Vendre (*to sell*)
Indicative (simple tenses)

Present	*Imperfect*	*Preterit*	*Future*	*Conditional*
Je vends	Je vendais	Je vendis	Je vendrai	Je vendrais
Tu vends	Tu vendais	Tu vendis	Tu vendras	Tu vendrais
Il/Elle vend	Il/Elle vendait	Il/Elle vendit	Il/Elle vendra	Il/Elle vendrait
Nous vendons	Nous vendions	Nous vendîmes	Nous vendrons	Nous vendrions
Vous vendez	Vous vendiez	Vous vendîtes	Vous vendrez	Vous vendriez
Ils/Elles vendent	Ils/Elles vendaient	Ils/Elles vendirent	Ils/Elles vendront	Ils/Elles vendraient

Indicative (compound tenses)

Perfect	*Pluperfect*	*Past Anterior*	*Future in the Past*	*Conditional in the Past*
J'ai vendu	J'avais vendu	J'eus vendu	J'aurai vendu	J'aurais vendu
Tu as vendu	Tu avais vendu	Tu eus vendu	Tu auras vendu	Tu aurais vendu
Il/Elle a vendu	Il/Elle avait vendu	Il/Elle eut vendu	Il/Elle aura vendu	Il/Elle aurait vendu
Nous avons vendu	Nous avions vendu	Nous eûmes vendu	Nous aurons vendu	Nous aurions vendu
Vous avez vendu	Vous aviez vendu	Vous eûtes vendu	Vous aurez vendu	Vous auriez vendu
Ils/Elles ont vendu	Ils/Elles avaient vendu	Ils/Elles eurent vendu	Ils/Elles auront vendu	Ils/Elles auraient vendu

Subjunctive (simple tenses)

Present	*Imperfect*
Je vende	Je vendisse
Tu vendes	Tu vendisses
Il/Elle vende	Il/Elle vendît
Nous vendions	Nous vendissions
Vous vendiez	Vous vendissiez
Ils/Elles vendent	Ils/Elles vendissent

Subjunctive (compound tenses)

Perfect	*Pluperfect*
J'aie vendu	J'eusse vendu
Tu aies vendu	Tu eusses vendu
Il/Elle ait vendu	Il/Elle eût vendu
Nous ayons vendu	Nous eussions vendu
Vous ayez vendu	Vous eussiez vendu
Ils/Elles aient vendu	Ils/Elles eussent vendu

Imperative: Vends, vendons, vendez
Non-personal forms

Infinitive			Gerund	
Simple	*Compound*	*Past participle*	*Simple*	*Compound*
Vendre	Avoir vendu	Vendu	Vendant	Ayant vendu

Finir (*to finish*)
Indicative (simple tenses)

Present	*Imperfect*	*Preterit*	*Future*	*Conditional*
Je finis	Je finissais	Je finis	Je finirai	Je finirais
Tu finis	Tu finissais	Tu finis	Tu finiras	Tu finirais
Il/Elle finit	Il/Elle finissait	Il/Elle finit	Il/Elle finira	Il/Elle finirait
Nous finissons	Nous finissions	Nous finîmes	Nous finirons	Nous finirions
Vous finissez	Vous finissiez	Vous finîtes	Vous finirez	Vous finiriez
Ils/Elles finissent	Ils/Elles finissaient	Ils/Elles finirent	Ils/Elles finiront	Ils/Elles finiraient

Indicative (compound tenses)

Perfect	*Pluperfect*	*Past Anterior*	*Future in the Past*	*Conditional in the Past*
J'ai fini	J'avais fini	J'eus fini	J'aurai fini	J'aurais fini
Tu as fini	Tu avais fini	Tu eus fini	Tu auras fini	Tu aurais fini
Il/Elle a fini	Il/Elle avait fini	Il/Elle eut fini	Il/Elle aura fini	Il/Elle aurait fini
Nous avons fini	Nous avions fini	Nous eûmes fini	Nous aurons fini	Nous aurions fini
Vous avez fini	Vous aviez fini	Vous eûtes fini	Vous aurez fini	Vous auriez fini
Ils/Elles ont fini	Ils/Elles avaient fini	Ils/Elles eurent fini	Ils/Elles auront fini	Ils/Elles auraient fini

Subjunctive (simple tenses)

Present	*Imperfect*
Je finisse	Je finisse
Tu finisses	Tu finisses
Il/Elle finisse	Il/Elle finît
Nous finissions	Nous finissions
Vous finissiez	Vous finissiez
Ils/Elles finissent	Ils/Elles finissent

Subjunctive (compound tenses)

Perfect	*Pluperfect*
J'aie fini	J'eusse fini
Tu aies fini	Tu eusses fini
Il/Elle ait fini	Il/Elle eût fini

Subjunctive (compound tenses) (*cont.*)

Perfect	*Pluperfect*
Nous ayons fini	Nous eussions fini
Vous ayez fini	Vous eussiez fini
Ils/Elles aient fini	Ils/Elles eussent fini

Imperative: Finis, finissons, finissez
Non-personal forms

Infinitive			Gerund	
Simple	*Compound*	*Past participle*	*Simple*	*Compound*
Finir	Avoir fini	Fini	Finissant	Ayant fini

Recevoir (*to receive*)
Indicative (simple tenses)

Present	*Imperfect*	*Preterit*	*Future*	*Conditional*
Je reçois	Je recevais	Je reçus	Je recevrai	Je recevrais
Tu reçois	Tu recevais	Tu reçus	Tu recevras	Tu recevrais
Il/Elle reçoit	Il/Elle recevait	Il/Elle reçut	Il/Elle recevra	Il/Elle recevrait
Nous recevons	Nous recevions	Nous reçûmes	Nous recevrons	Nous recevrions
Vous recevez	Vous receviez	Vous reçûtes	Vous recevrez	Vous recevriez
Ils/Elles reçoivent	Ils/Elles recevaient	Ils/Elles reçurent	Ils/Elles recevront	Ils/Elles recevraient

Indicative (compound tenses)

Perfect	*Pluperfect*	*Past Anterior*	*Future in the Past*	*Conditional in the Past*
J'ai reçu	J'avais reçu	J'eus reçu	J'aurai reçu	J'aurais reçu
Tu as reçu	Tu avais reçu	Tu eus reçu	Tu auras reçu	Tu aurais reçu
Il/Elle a reçu	Il/Elle avait reçu	Il/Elle eut reçu	Il/Elle aura reçu	Il/Elle aurait reçu
Nous avons reçu	Nous avions reçu	Nous eûmes reçu	Nous aurons reçu	Nous aurions reçu
Vous avez reçu	Vous aviez reçu	Vous eûtes reçu	Vous aurez reçu	Vous auriez reçu
Ils/Elles ont reçu	Ils/Elles avaient reçu	Ils/Elles eurent reçu	Ils/Elles auront reçu	Ils/Elles auraient reçu

Subjunctive (simple tenses)

Present	*Imperfect*
Je reçoive	Je reçusse
Tu reçoives	Tu reçusses
Il/Elle reçoive	Il/Elle reçût
Nous recevions	Nous reçussions
Vous receviez	Vous reçussiez
Ils/Elles reçoivent	Ils/Elles reçussent

Subjunctive (compound tenses)

Perfect	*Pluperfect*
J'aie reçu	J'eusse reçu
Tu aies reçu	Tu eusses reçu
Il/Elle ait reçu	Il/Elle eût reçu
Nous ayons reçu	Nous eussions reçu
Vous ayez reçu	Vous eussiez reçu
Ils/Elles aient reçu	Ils/Elles eussent reçu

Imperative: Reçois, recevons, recevez

Non-personal forms

Infinitive			Gerund	
Simple	*Compound*	*Past participle*	*Simple*	*Compound*
Recevoir	Avoir reçu	Reçu	Recevant	Ayant reçu

Main irregular verbs

Être (*to be*)

Indicative (simple tenses)

Present	*Imperfect*	*Preterit*	*Future*	*Conditional*
Je suis	J'étais	Je fus	Je serai	Je serais
Tu es	Tu étais	Tu fus	Tu seras	Tu serais
Il/Elle est	Il/Elle était	Il/Elle fut	Il/Elle sera	Il/Elle serait
Nous sommes	Nous étions	Nous fûmes	Nous serons	Nous serions
Vous êtes	Vous étiez	Vous fûtes	Vous serez	Vous seriez
Ils/Elles sont	Ils/Elles étaient	Ils/Elles furent	Ils/Elles seront	Ils/Elles seraient

Indicative (compound tenses)

Perfect	*Pluperfect*	*Past Anterior*	*Future in the Past*	*Conditional in the Past*
J'ai été	J'avais été	J'eus été	J'aurai été	J'aurais été
Tu as été	Tu avais été	Tu eus été	Tu auras été	Tu aurais été
Il/Elle a été	Il/Elle avait été	Il/Elle eut été	Il/Elle aura été	Il/Elle aurait été
Nous avons été	Nous avions été	Nous eûmes été	Nous aurons été	Nous aurions été
Vous avez été	Vous aviez été	Vous eûtes été	Vous aurez été	Vous auriez été
Ils/Elles ont été	Ils/Elles avaient été	Ils/Elles eurent été	Ils/Elles auront été	Ils/Elles auraient été

Subjunctive (simple tenses)

Present	*Imperfect*
Je sois	Je fusse
Tu sois	Tu fusses
Il/Elle soit	Il/Elle fût
Nous soyons	Nous fussions
Vous soyez	Vous fussiez
Ils/Elles soient	Ils/Elles fussent

Subjunctive (compound tenses)

Perfect	*Pluperfect*
J'aie été	J'eusse été
Tu aies été	Tu eusses été
Il/Elle ait été	Il/Elle eût été
Nous ayons été	Nous eussions été
Vous ayez été	Vous eussiez été
Ils/Elles aient été	Ils/Elles eussent été

Imperative: Sois, soyons, soyez

Non-personal forms

Infinitive			Gerund	
Simple	*Compound*	*Past participle*	*Simple*	*Compound*
Être	Avoir été	Été	Étant	Ayant été

Avoir (*to have*)
Indicative (simple tenses)

Present	Imperfect	Preterit	Future	Conditional
J'ai	J'avais	J'eus	J'aurai	J'aurais
Tu as	Tu avais	Tu eus	Tu auras	Tu aurais
Il/Elle a	Il/Elle avait	Il/Elle eut	Il/Elle aura	Il/Elle aurait
Nous avons	Nous avions	Nous eûmes	Nous aurons	Nous aurions
Vous avez	Vous aviez	Vous eûtes	Vous aurez	Vous auriez
Ils/Elles ont	Ils/Elles avaient	Ils/Elles eurent	Ils/Elles auront	Ils/Elles auraient

Indicative (compound tenses)

Perfect	Pluperfect	Past Anterior	Future in the Past	Conditional in the Past
J'ai eu	J'avais eu	J'eus eu	J'aurai eu	J'aurais eu
Tu as eu	Tu avais eu	Tu eus eu	Tu auras eu	Tu aurais eu
Il/Elle a eu	Il/Elle avait eu	Il/Elle eut eu	Il/Elle aura eu	Il/Elle aurait eu
Nous avons eu	Nous avions eu	Nous eûmes eu	Nous aurons eu	Nous aurions eu
Vous avez eu	Vous aviez eu	Vous eûtes eu	Vous aurez eu	Vous auriez eu
Ils/Elles ont eu	Ils/Elles avaient eu	Ils/Elles eurent eu	Ils/Elles auront eu	Ils/Elles auraient eu

Subjunctive (simple tenses)

Present	Imperfect
J'aie	J'eusse
Tu aies	Tu eusses
Il/Elle ait	Il/Elle eût
Nous ayons	Nous eussions
Vous ayez	Vous eussiez
Ils/Elles aient	Ils/Elles eussent

Subjunctive (compound tenses)

Perfect	Pluperfect
J'aie eu	J'eusse eu
Tu aies eu	Tu eusses eu
Il/Elle ait eu	Il/Elle eût eu
Nous ayons eu	Nous eussions eu
Vous ayez eu	Vous eussiez eu
Ils/Elles aient eu	Ils/Elles eussent eu

Imperative: Aie, ayons, ayez
Non-personal forms

Infinitive		Past participle	Gerund	
Simple	Compound		Simple	Compound
Avoir	Avoir été	Eu	Ayant	Ayant eu

Acquérir (*to acquire*)
Indicative (simple tenses)

Present	Imperfect	Preterit	Future	Conditional
J'acquiers	J'acquérais	J'acquis	J'acquerrai	J'acquerrais
Tu acquiers	Tu acquérais	Tu acquis	Tu acquerras	Tu acquerrais
Il/Elle acquiert	Il/Elle acquérait	Il/Elle acquit	Il/Elle acquerra	Il/Elle acquerrait
Nous acquérons	Nous acquérions	Nous acquîmes	Nous acquerrons	Nous acquerrions

Indicative (simple tenses) (*cont.*)

Present	Imperfect	Preterit	Future	Conditional
Vous acquérez	Vous acquériez	Vous acquîtes	Vous acquerrez	Vous acquerriez
Ils/Elles acquièrent	Ils/Elles acquéraient	Ils/Elles acquirent	Ils/Elles acquerront	Ils/Elles acquerraient

Indicative (compound tenses)

Perfect	Pluperfect	Past Anterior	Future in the Past	Conditional in the Past
J'ai acquis	J'avais acquis	J'eus acquis	J'aurai acquis	J'aurais acquis
Tu as acquis	Tu avais acquis	Tu eus acquis	Tu auras acquis	Tu aurais acquis
Il/Elle a acquis	Il/Elle avait acquis	Il/Elle eut acquis	Il/Elle aura acquis	Il/Elle aurait acquis
Nous avons acquis	Nous avions acquis	Nous eûmes acquis	Nous aurons acquis	Nous aurions acquis
Vous avez acquis	Vous aviez acquis	Vous eûtes acquis	Vous aurez acquis	Vous auriez acquis
Ils/Elles ont acquis	Ils/Elles avaient acquis	Ils/Elles eurent acquis	Ils/Elles auront acquis	Ils/Elles auraient acquis

Subjunctive (simple tenses)

Present	Imperfect
J'acquière	J'acquisse
Tu acquières	Tu acquisses
Il/Elle acquière	Il/Elle acquît
Nous acquiérions	Nous acquissions
Vous acquiériez	Vous acquissiez
Ils/Elles acquièrent	Ils/Elles acquissent

Subjunctive (compound tenses)

Perfect	Pluperfect
J'aie acquis	J'eusse acquis
Tu aies acquis	Tu eusses acquis
Il/Elle ait acquis	Il/Elle eût acquis
Nous ayons acquis	Nous eussions acquis
Vous ayez acquis	Vous eussiez acquis
Ils/Elles aient acquis	Ils/Elles eussent acquis

Imperative: Acquiers, acquérons, acquérez
Non-personal forms

Infinitive			Gerund	
Simple	Compound	Past participle	Simple	Compound
Acquérir	Avoir acquis	Acquis	Acquiérant	Ayant acquis

Aller (*to go*)
Indicative (simple tenses)

Present	Imperfect	Preterit	Future	Conditional
Je vais	J'allais	J'allai	J'irai	J'irais
Tu vas	Tu allais	Tu allas	Tu iras	Tu irais
Il/Elle va	Il/Elle allait	Il/Elle alla	Il/Elle ira	Il/Elle irait
Nous allons	Nous allions	Nous allâmes	Nous irons	Nous irions
Vous allez	Vous alliez	Vous allâtes	Vous irez	Vous iriez
Ils/Elles vont	Ils/Elles allaient	Ils/Elles allèrent	Ils/Elles iront	Ils/Elles iraient

Indicative (compound tenses)

Perfect	Pluperfect	Past Anterior	Future in the Past	Conditional in the Past
Je suis allé(e)	J'étais allé(e)	Je fus allé(e)	Je serais allé(e)	Je serais allé(e)
Tu es allé(e)	Tu étais allé(e)	Tu fus allé(e)	Tu seras allé(e)	Tu serais allé(e)
Il/Elle est allé(e)	Il/Elle était allé(e)	Il/Elle fut allé(e)	Il/Elle sera allé(e)	Il/Elle serait allé(e)
Nous sommes allé(e)s	Nous étions allé(e)s	Nous fûmes allé(e)s	Nous serons allé(e)s	Nous serions allé(e)s
Vous êtes allé(e)(s)	Vous étiez allé(e)(s)	Vous fûtes allé(e)(s)	Vous serez allé(e)(s)	Vous seriez allé(e)(s)
Ils/Elles sont allé(e)s	Ils/Elles étaient allé(e)s	Ils/Elles furent allé(e)s	Ils/Elles seront allé(e)s	Ils/Elles seraient allé(e)s

Subjunctive (simple tenses)

Present	Imperfect
J'aille	J'allasse
Tu ailles	Tu allasses
Il/Elle aille	Il/Elle allât
Nous allions	Nous allassions
Vous alliez	Vous allassiez
Ils/Elles aillent	Ils/Elles allassent

Subjunctive (compound tenses)

Perfect	Pluperfect
Je sois allé(e)	Je fusse allé(e)
Tu sois allé(e)	Tu fusses allé(e)
Il/Elle soit allé(e)	Il/Elle fût allé(e)
Nous soyons allé(e)s	Nous fussions allé(e)s
Vous soyez allé(e)(s)	Vous fussiez allé(e)(s)
Ils/Elles soient allé(e)s	Ils/Elles fussent allé(e)s

Imperative: Va, allons, allez
Non-personal forms

Infinitive			Gerund	
Simple	Compound	Past participle	Simple	Compound
Aller	Être allé	Allé	Allant	Étant allé

Battre (*to beat*)
Indicative (simple tenses)

Present	Imperfect	Preterit	Future	Conditional
Je bats	Je battais	Je battis	Je battrai	Je battrais
Tu bats	Tu battais	Tu battis	Tu battras	Tu battrais
Il/Elle bat	Il/Elle battait	Il/Elle battit	Il/Elle battra	Il/Elle battrait
Nous battons	Nous battions	Nous battîmes	Nous battrons	Nous battrions
Vous battez	Vous battiez	Vous battîtes	Vous battrez	Vous battriez
Ils/Elles battent	Ils/Elles battaient	Ils/Elles battirent	Ils/Elles battront	Ils/Elles battraient

Indicative (compound tenses)

Perfect	Pluperfect	Past Anterior	Future in the Past	Conditional in the Past
J'ai battu	J'avais battu	J'eus battu	J'aurai battu	J'aurais battu
Tu as battu	Tu avais battu	Tu eus battu	Tu auras battu	Tu aurais battu
Il/Elle a battu	Il/Elle avait battu	Il/Elle eut battu	Il/Elle aura battu	Il/Elle aurait battu

Indicative (compound tenses) *(cont.)*

Perfect	Pluperfect	Past Anterior	Future in the Past	Conditional in the Past
Nous avons battu	Nous avions battu	Nous eûmes battu	Nous aurons battu	Nous aurions battu
Vous avez battu	Vous aviez battu	Vous eûtes battu	Vous aurez battu	Vous auriez battu
Ils/Elles ont battu	Ils/Elles avaient battu	Ils/Elles eurent battu	Ils/Elles auront battu	Ils/Elles auraient battu

Subjunctive (simple tenses)

Present	Imperfect
Je batte	Je battisse
Tu battes	Tu battisses
Il/Elle batte	Il/Elle battît
Nous battions	Nous battissions
Vous battiez	Vous battissiez
Ils/Elles battent	Ils/Elles battissent

Subjunctive (compound tenses)

Perfect	Pluperfect
J'aie battu	J'eusse battu
Tu aies battu	Tu eusses battu
Il/Elle ait battu	Il/Elle eût battu
Nous ayons battu	Nous eussions battu
Vous ayez battu	Vous eussiez battu
Ils/Elles aient battu	Ils/Elles eussent battu

Imperative: Bats, battons, battez

Non-personal forms

Infinitive			Gerund	
Simple	Compound	Past participle	Simple	Compound
Battre	Avoir battu	Battu	Battant	Ayant battu

Bouillir (*to boil*)
Indicative (simple tenses)

Present	Imperfect	Preterit	Future	Conditional
Je bous	Je bouillais	Je bouillis	Je bouillirai	Je bouillirais
Tu bous	Tu bouillais	Tu bouillis	Tu bouilliras	Tu bouillirais
Il/Elle bout	Il/Elle bouillait	Il/Elle bouillit	Il/Elle bouillira	Il/Elle bouillirait
Nous bouillons	Nous bouillions	Nous bouillîmes	Nous bouillirons	Nous bouillirions
Vous bouillez	Vous bouilliez	Vous bouillîtes	Vous bouillirez	Vous bouilliriez
Ils/Elles bouillent	Ils/Elles bouillaient	Ils/Elles bouillirent	Ils/Elles bouilliront	Ils/Elles bouilliraient

Indicative (compound tenses)

Perfect	Pluperfect	Past Anterior	Future in the Past	Conditional in the Past
J'ai bouilli	J'avais bouilli	J'eus bouilli	J'aurai bouilli	J'aurais bouilli
Tu as bouilli	Tu avais bouilli	Tu eus bouilli	Tu auras bouilli	Tu aurais bouilli
Il/Elle a bouilli	Il/Elle avait bouilli	Il/Elle eut bouilli	Il/Elle aura bouilli	Il/Elle aurait bouilli
Nous avons bouilli	Nous avions bouilli	Nous eûmes bouilli	Nous aurons bouilli	Nous aurions bouilli

Indicative (compound tenses) (*cont.*)

Perfect	Pluperfect	Past Anterior	Future in the Past	Conditional in the Past
Vous avez bouilli	Vous aviez bouilli	Vous eûtes bouilli	Vous aurez bouilli	Vous auriez bouilli
Ils/Elles ont bouilli	Ils/Elles avaient bouilli	Ils/Elles eurent bouilli	Ils/Elles auront bouilli	Ils/Elles auraient bouilli

Subjunctive (simple tenses)

Present	Imperfect
Je bouille	Je bouillisse
Tu bouilles	Tu bouillisses
Il/Elle bouille	Il/Elle bouillît
Nous bouillions	Nous bouillissions
Vous bouilliez	Vous bouillissiez
Ils/Elles bouillent	Ils/Elles bouillissent

Subjunctive (compound tenses)

Perfect	Pluperfect
J'aie bouilli	J'eusse bouilli
Tu aies bouilli	Tu eusses bouilli
Il/Elle ait bouilli	Il/Elle eût bouilli
Nous ayons bouilli	Nous eussions bouilli
Vous ayez bouilli	Vous eussiez bouilli
Ils/Elles aient bouilli	Ils/Elles eussent bouilli

Imperative: Bous, bouillons, bouillez
Non-personal forms

Infinitive			Gerund	
Simple	Compound	Past participle	Simple	Compound
Bouillir	Avoir bouilli	Bouilli	Bouillant	Ayant bouilli

Conclure (*to conclude*)
Indicative (simple tenses)

Present	Imperfect	Preterit	Future	Conditional
Je conclus	Je concluais	Je conclus	Je conclurai	Je conclurais
Tu conclus	Tu concluais	Tu conclus	Tu concluras	Tu conclurais
Il/Elle conclut	Il/Elle concluait	Il/Elle conclut	Il/Elle conclura	Il/Elle conclurait
Nous concluons	Nous concluions	Nous conclûmes	Nous conclurons	Nous conclurions
Vous concluez	Vous concluiez	Vous conclûtes	Vous conclurez	Vous concluriez
Ils/Elles concluent	Ils/Elles concluaient	Ils/Elles conclurent	Ils/Elles concluront	Ils/Elles concluraient

Indicative (compound tenses)

Perfect	Pluperfect	Past Anterior	Future in the Past	Conditional in the Past
J'ai conclu	J'avais conclu	J'eus conclu	J'aurai conclu	J'aurais conclu
Tu as conclu	Tu avais conclu	Tu eus conclu	Tu auras conclu	Tu aurais conclu
Il/Elle a conclu	Il/Elle avait conclu	Il/Elle eut conclu	Il/Elle aura conclu	Il/Elle aurait conclu
Nous avons conclu	Nous avions conclu	Nous eûmes conclu	Nous aurons conclu	Nous aurions conclu

Indicative (compound tenses) *(cont.)*

Perfect	Pluperfect	Past Anterior	Future in the Past	Conditional in the Past
Vous avez conclu	Vous aviez conclu	Vous eûtes conclu	Vous aurez conclu	Vous auriez conclu
Ils/Elles ont conclu	Ils/Elles avaient conclu	Ils/Elles eurent conclu	Ils/Elles auront conclu	Ils/Elles auraient conclu

Subjunctive (simple tenses)

Present	Imperfect
Je conclue	Je conclusse
Tu conclues	Tu conclusses
Il/Elle conclue	Il/Elle conclût
Nous concluions	Nous conclussions
Vous concluiez	Vous conclussiez
Ils/Elles concluent	Ils/Elles conclussent

Subjunctive (compound tenses)

Perfect	Pluperfect
J'aie conclu	J'eusse conclu
Tu aies conclu	Tu eusses conclu
Il/Elle ait conclu	Il/Elle eût conclu
Nous ayons conclu	Nous eussions conclu
Vous ayez conclu	Vous eussiez conclu
Ils/Elles aient conclu	Ils/Elles eussent conclu

Imperative: Conclus, concluons, concluez
Non-personal forms

Infinitive			Gerund	
Simple	Compound	Past participle	Simple	Compound
Conclure	Avoir conclu	Conclu	Concluant	Ayant conclu

Connaître (*to know*)
Indicative (simple tenses)

Present	Imperfect	Preterit	Future	Conditional
Je connais	Je connaissais	Je connus	Je connaîtrai	Je connaîtrais
Tu connais	Tu connaissais	Tu connus	Tu connaîtras	Tu connaîtrais
Il/Elle connaît	Il/Elle connaissait	Il/Elle connut	Il/Elle connaîtra	Il/Elle connaîtrait
Nous connaissons	Nous connaissions	Nous connûmes	Nous connaîtrons	Nous connaîtrions
Vous connaissez	Vous connaissiez	Vous connûtes	Vous connaîtrez	Vous connaîtriez
Ils/Elles connaissent	Ils/Elles connaissaient	Ils/Elles connurent	Ils/Elles connaîtront	Ils/Elles connaîtraient

Indicative (compound tenses)

Perfect	Pluperfect	Past Anterior	Future in the Past	Conditional in the Past
J'ai connu	J'avais connu	J'eus connu	J'aurai connu	J'aurais connu
Tu as connu	Tu avais connu	Tu eus connu	Tu auras connu	Tu aurais connu
Il/Elle a connu	Il/Elle avait connu	Il/Elle eut connu	Il/Elle aura connu	Il/Elle aurait connu
Nous avons connu	Nous avions connu	Nous eûmes connu	Nous aurons connu	Nous aurions connu

Indicative (compound tenses) *(cont.)*

Perfect	Pluperfect	Past Anterior	Future in the Past	Conditional in the Past
Vous avez connu	Vous aviez connu	Vous eûtes connu	Vous aurez connu	Vous auriez connu
Ils/Elles ont connu	Ils/Elles avaient connu	Ils/Elles eurent connu	Ils/Elles auront connu	Ils/Elles auraient connu

Subjunctive (simple tenses)

Present	Imperfect
Je connaisse	Je connusse
Tu connaisses	Tu connusses
Il/Elle connaisse	Il/Elle connût
Nous connaissions	Nous connussions
Vous connaissiez	Vous connussiez
Ils/Elles connaissent	Ils/Elles connussent

Subjunctive (compound tenses)

Perfect	Pluperfect
J'aie connu	J'eusse connu
Tu aies connu	Tu eusses connu
Il/Elle ait connu	Il/Elle eût connu
Nous ayons connu	Nous eussions connu
Vous ayez connu	Vous eussiez connu
Ils/Elles aient connu	Ils/Elles eussent connu

Imperative: Connais, connaissons, connaissez
Non-personal forms

Infinitive			Gerund	
Simple	Compound	Past participle	Simple	Compound
Connaître	Avoir connu	Connu	Connaissant	Ayant connu

Courir (*to run*)
Indicative (simple tenses)

Present	Imperfect	Preterit	Future	Conditional
Je cours	Je courais	Je courus	Je courrai	Je courrais
Tu cours	Tu courais	Tu courus	Tu courras	Tu courrais
Il/Elle court	Il/Elle courait	Il/Elle courut	Il/Elle courra	Il/Elle courrait
Nous courons	Nous courions	Nous courûmes	Nous courrons	Nous courrions
Vous courez	Vous couriez	Vous courûtes	Vous courrez	Vous courriez
Ils/Elles courent	Ils/Elles couraient	Ils/Elles coururent	Ils/Elles courront	Ils/Elles courraient

Indicative (compound tenses)

Perfect	Pluperfect	Past Anterior	Future in the Past	Conditional in the Past
J'ai couru	J'avais couru	J'eus couru	J'aurai couru	J'aurais couru
Tu as couru	Tu avais couru	Tu eus couru	Tu auras couru	Tu aurais couru
Il/Elle a couru	Il/Elle avait couru	Il/Elle eut couru	Il/Elle aura couru	Il/Elle aurait couru
Nous avons couru	Nous avions couru	Nous eûmes couru	Nous aurons couru	Nous aurions couru

Indicative (compound tenses) (*cont.*)

Perfect	Pluperfect	Past Anterior	Future in the Past	Conditional in the Past
Vous avez couru	Vous aviez couru	Vous eûtes couru	Vous aurez couru	Vous auriez couru
Ils/Elles ont couru	Ils/Elles avaient couru	Ils/Elles eurent couru	Ils/Elles auront couru	Ils/Elles auraient couru

Subjunctive (simple tenses)

Present	Imperfect
Je coure	Je courusse
Tu coures	Tu courusses
Il/Elle coure	Il/Elle courût
Nous courions	Nous courussions
Vous couriez	Vous courussiez
Ils/Elles courent	Ils/Elles courussent

Subjunctive (compound tenses)

Perfect	Pluperfect
J'aie couru	J'eusse couru
Tu aies couru	Tu eusses couru
Il/Elle ait couru	Il/Elle eût couru
Nous ayons couru	Nous eussions couru
Vous ayez couru	Vous eussiez couru
Ils/Elles aient couru	Ils/Elles eussent couru

Imperative: Cours, courons, courez
Non-personal forms

Infinitive			Gerund	
Simple	Compound	Past participle	Simple	Compound
Courir	Avoir couru	Couru	Courant	Ayant couru

Craindre (*to fear*)
Indicative (simple tenses)

Present	Imperfect	Preterit	Future	Conditional
Je crains	Je craignais	Je craignis	Je craindrai	Je craindrais
Tu crains	Tu craignais	Tu craignis	Tu craindras	Tu craindrais
Il/Elle craint	Il/Elle craignait	Il/Elle craignit	Il/Elle craindra	Il/Elle craindrait
Nous craignons	Nous craignions	Nous craignîmes	Nous craindrons	Nous craindrions
Vous craignez	Vous craigniez	Vous craignîtes	Vous craindrez	Vous craindriez
Ils/Elles craignent	Ils/Elles craignaient	Ils/Elles craignirent	Ils/Elles craindront	Ils/Elles craindraient

Indicative (compound tenses)

Perfect	Pluperfect	Past Anterior	Future in the Past	Conditional in the Past
J'ai craint	J'avais craint	J'eus craint	J'aurai craint	J'aurais craint
Tu as craint	Tu avais craint	Tu eus craint	Tu auras craint	Tu aurais craint
Il/Elle a craint	Il/Elle avait craint	Il/Elle eut craint	Il/Elle aura craint	Il/Elle aurait craint
Nous avons craint	Nous avions craint	Nous eûmes craint	Nous aurons craint	Nous aurions craint

Indicative (compound tenses) (*cont.*)

Perfect	Pluperfect	Past Anterior	Future in the Past	Conditional in the Past
Vous avez craint	Vous aviez craint	Vous eûtes craint	Vous aurez craint	Vous auriez craint
Ils/Elles ont craint	Ils/Elles avaient craint	Ils/Elles eurent craint	Ils/Elles auront craint	Ils/Elles auraient craint

Subjunctive (simple tenses)

Present	Imperfect
Je craigne	Je craignisse
Tu craignes	Tu craignisses
Il/Elle craigne	Il/Elle craignît
Nous craignions	Nous craignissions
Vous craigniez	Vous craignissiez
Ils/Elles craignent	Ils/Elles craignissent

Subjunctive (compound tenses)

Perfect	Pluperfect
J'aie craint	J'eusse craint
Tu aies craint	Tu eusses craint
Il/Elle ait craint	Il/Elle eût craint
Nous ayons craint	Nous eussions craint
Vous ayez craint	Vous eussiez craint
Ils/Elles aient craint	Ils/Elles eussent craint

Imperative: Crains, craignons, craignez

Non-personal forms

Infinitive			Gerund	
Simple	Compound	Past participle	Simple	Compound
Craindre	Avoir craint	Craint	Craignant	Ayant craint

Croire (*to believe*)
Indicative (simple tenses)

Present	Imperfect	Preterit	Future	Conditional
Je crois	Je croyais	Je crus	Je croirai	Je croirais
Tu crois	Tu croyais	Tu crus	Tu croiras	Tu croirais
Il/Elle croit	Il/Elle croyait	Il/Elle crut	Il/Elle croira	Il/Elle croirait
Nous croyons	Nous croyions	Nous crûmes	Nous croirons	Nous croirions
Vous croyez	Vous croyiez	Vous crûtes	Vous croirez	Vous croiriez
Ils/Elles croient	Ils/Elles croyaient	Ils/Elles crurent	Ils/Elles croiront	Ils/Elles croiraient

Indicative (compound tenses)

Perfect	Pluperfect	Past Anterior	Future in the Past	Conditional in the Past
J'ai cru	J'avais cru	J'eus cru	J'aurai cru	J'aurais cru
Tu as cru	Tu avais cru	Tu eus cru	Tu auras cru	Tu aurais cru
Il/Elle a cru	Il/Elle avait cru	Il/Elle eut cru	Il/Elle aura cru	Il/Elle aurait cru
Nous avons cru	Nous avions cru	Nous eûmes cru	Nous aurons cru	Nous aurions cru
Vous avez cru	Vous aviez cru	Vous eûtes cru	Vous aurez cru	Vous auriez cru
Ils/Elles ont cru	Ils/Elles avaient cru	Ils/Elles eurent cru	Ils/Elles auront cru	Ils/Elles auraient cru

Subjunctive (simple tenses)

Present	*Imperfect*
Je croie	Je crusse
Tu croies	Tu crusses
Il/Elle croie	Il/Elle crût
Nous croyions	Nous crussions
Vous croyiez	Vous crussiez
Ils/Elles croient	Ils/Elles crussent

Subjunctive (compound tenses)

Perfect	*Pluperfect*
J'aie cru	J'eusse cru
Tu aies cru	Tu eusses cru
Il/Elle ait cru	Il/Elle eût cru
Nous ayons cru	Nous eussions cru
Vous ayez cru	Vous eussiez cru
Ils/Elles aient cru	Ils/Elles eussent cru

Imperative: Crois, croyons, croyez
Non-personal forms

Infinitive		Gerund	
Simple	*Compound*	*Past participle*	*Simple*	*Compound*
Croire	Avoir cru	Cru	Croyant	Ayant cru

Cueillir (*to pick*)
Indicative (simple tenses)

Present	*Imperfect*	*Preterit*	*Future*	*Conditional*
Je cueille	Je cueillais	Je cueillis	Je cueillerai	Je cueillerais
Tu cueilles	Tu cueillais	Tu cueillis	Tu cueilleras	Tu cueillerais
Il/Elle cueille	Il/Elle cueillait	Il/Elle cueillit	Il/Elle cueillera	Il/Elle cueillerait
Nous cueillons	Nous cueillions	Nous cueillîmes	Nous cueillerons	Nous cueillerions
Vous cueillez	Vous cueilliez	Vous cueillîtes	Vous cueillerez	Vous cueilleriez
Ils/Elles cueillent	Ils/Elles cueillaient	Ils/Elles cueillirent	Ils/Elles cueilleront	Ils/Elles cueilleraient

Indicative (compound tenses)

Perfect	*Pluperfect*	*Past Anterior*	*Future in the Past*	*Conditional in the Past*
J'ai cueilli	J'avais cueilli	J'eus cueilli	J'aurai cueilli	J'aurais cueilli
Tu as cueilli	Tu avais cueilli	Tu eus cueilli	Tu auras cueilli	Tu aurais cueilli
Il/Elle a cueilli	Il/Elle avait cueilli	Il/Elle eut cueilli	Il/Elle aura cueilli	Il/Elle aurait cueilli
Nous avons cueilli	Nous avions cueilli	Nous eûmes cueilli	Nous aurons cueilli	Nous aurions cueilli
Vous avez cueilli	Vous aviez cueilli	Vous eûtes cueilli	Vous aurez cueilli	Vous auriez cueilli
Ils/Elles ont cueilli	Ils/Elles avaient cueilli	Ils/Elles eurent cueilli	Ils/Elles auront cueilli	Ils/Elles auraient cueilli

Subjunctive (simple tenses)

Present	*Imperfect*
Je cueille	Je cueillisse
Tu cueilles	Tu cueillisses
Il/Elle cueille	Il/Elle cueillît
Nous cueillions	Nous cueillissions
Vous cueilliez	Vous cueillissiez
Ils/Elles cueillent	Ils/Elles cueillissent

Subjunctive (compound tenses)

Perfect	*Pluperfect*
J'aie cueilli	J'eusse cueilli
Tu aies cueilli	Tu eusses cueilli
Il/Elle ait cueilli	Il/Elle eût cueilli
Nous ayons cueilli	Nous eussions cueilli
Vous ayez cueilli	Vous eussiez cueilli
Ils/Elles aient cueilli	Ils/Elles eussent cueilli

Imperative: Cueille, cueillons, cueillez

Non-personal forms

Infinitive			Gerund	
Simple	*Compound*	*Past participle*	*Simple*	*Compound*
Cueillir	Avoir cueilli	Cueilli	Cueillant	Ayant cueilli

Devoir (*must, ought to, to have to, to owe*)
Indicative (simple tenses)

Present	*Imperfect*	*Preterit*	*Future*	*Conditional*
Je dois	Je devais	Je dus	Je devrai	Je devrais
Tu dois	Tu devais	Tu dus	Tu devras	Tu devrais
Il/Elle doit	Il/Elle devait	Il/Elle dut	Il/Elle devra	Il/Elle devrait
Nous devons	Nous devions	Nous dûmes	Nous devrons	Nous devrions
Vous devez	Vous deviez	Vous dûtes	Vous devrez	Vous devriez
Ils/Elles doivent	Ils/Elles devaient	Ils/Elles durent	Ils/Elles devront	Ils/Elles devraient

Indicative (compound tenses)

Perfect	*Pluperfect*	*Past Anterior*	*Future in the Past*	*Conditional in the Past*
J'ai dû	J'avais dû	J'eus dû	J'aurai dû	J'aurais dû
Tu as dû	Tu avais dû	Tu eus dû	Tu auras dû	Tu aurais dû
Il/Elle a dû	Il/Elle avait dû	Il/Elle eut dû	Il/Elle aura dû	Il/Elle aurait dû
Nous avons dû	Nous avions dû	Nous eûmes dû	Nous aurons dû	Nous aurions dû
Vous avez dû	Vous aviez dû	Vous eûtes dû	Vous aurez dû	Vous auriez dû
Ils/Elles ont dû	Ils/Elles avaient dû	Ils/Elles eurent dû	Ils/Elles auront dû	Ils/Elles auraient dû

Subjunctive (simple tenses)

Present	*Imperfect*
Je doive	Je dusse
Tu doives	Tu dusses
Il/Elle doive	Il/Elle dût
Nous devions	Nous dussions
Vous deviez	Vous dussiez
Ils/Elles doivent	Ils/Elles dussent

Subjunctive (compound tenses)

Perfect	Pluperfect
J'aie dû	J'eusse dû
Tu aies dû	Tu eusses dû
Il/Elle ait dû	Il/Elle eût dû
Nous ayons dû	Nous eussions dû
Vous ayez dû	Vous eussiez dû
Ils/Elles aient dû	Ils/Elles eussent dû

Imperative: Dois, devons, devez (little used)

Non-personal forms

Infinitive		Past participle	Gerund	
Simple	Compound		Simple	Compound
Devoir	Avoir dû	Dû	Devant	Ayant dû

Dire (*to say*)
Indicative (simple tenses)

Present	Imperfect	Preterit	Future	Conditional
Je dis	Je disais	Je dis	Je dirai	Je dirais
Tu dis	Tu disais	Tu dis	Tu diras	Tu dirais
Il/Elle dit	Il/Elle disait	Il/Elle dit	Il/Elle dira	Il/Elle dirait
Nous disons	Nous disions	Nous dîmes	Nous dirons	Nous dirions
Vous dites	Vous disiez	Vous dîtes	Vous direz	Vous diriez
Ils/Elles disent	Ils/Elles disaient	Ils/Elles dirent	Ils/Elles diront	Ils/Elles diraient

Indicative (compound tenses)

Perfect	Pluperfect	Past Anterior	Future in the Past	Conditional in the Past
J'ai dit	J'avais dit	J'eus dit	J'aurai dit	J'aurais dit
Tu as dit	Tu avais dit	Tu eus dit	Tu auras dit	Tu aurais dit
Il/Elle a dit	Il/Elle avait dit	Il/Elle eut dit	Il/Elle aura dit	Il/Elle aurait dit
Nous avons dit	Nous avions dit	Nous eûmes dit	Nous aurons dit	Nous aurions dit
Vous avez dit	Vous aviez dit	Vous eûtes dit	Vous aurez dit	Vous auriez dit
Ils/Elles ont dit	Ils/Elles avaient dit	Ils/Elles eurent dit	Ils/Elles auront dit	Ils/Elles auraient dit

Subjunctive (simple tenses)

Present	Imperfect
Je dise	Je disse
Tu dises	Tu disses
Il/Elle dise	Il/Elle dît
Nous disions	Nous dissions
Vous disiez	Vous dissiez
Ils/Elles disent	Ils/Elles dissent

Subjunctive (compound tenses)

Perfect	Pluperfect
J'aie dit	J'eusse dit
Tu aies dit	Tu eusses dit
Il/Elle ait dit	Il/Elle eût dit
Nous ayons dit	Nous eussions dit
Vous ayez dit	Vous eussiez dit
Ils/Elles aient dit	Ils/Elles eussent dit

Imperative: Dis, disons, dites
Non-personal forms

Infinitive		Past participle	Gerund	
Simple	*Compound*	*Past participle*	*Simple*	*Compound*
Dire	Avoir dit	Dit	Disant	Ayant dit

Écrire (*to write*)
Indicative (simple tenses)

Present	*Imperfect*	*Preterit*	*Future*	*Conditional*
J'écris	J'écrivais	J'écrivis	J'écrirai	J'écrirais
Tu écris	Tu écrivais	Tu écrivis	Tu écriras	Tu écrirais
Il/Elle écrit	Il/Elle écrivait	Il/Elle écrivit	Il/Elle écrira	Il/Elle écrirait
Nous écrivons	Nous écrivions	Nous écrivîmes	Nous écrirons	Nous écririons
Vous écrivez	Vous écriviez	Vous écrivîtes	Vous écrirez	Vous écririez
Ils/Elles écrivent	Ils/Elles écrivaient	Ils/Elles écrivirent	Ils/Elles écriront	Ils/Elles écriraient

Indicative (compound tenses)

Perfect	*Pluperfect*	*Past Anterior*	*Future in the Past*	*Conditional in the Past*
J'ai écrit	J'avais écrit	J'eus écrit	J'aurai écrit	J'aurais écrit
Tu as écrit	Tu avais écrit	Tu eus écrit	Tu auras écrit	Tu aurais écrit
Il/Elle a écrit	Il/Elle avait écrit	Il/Elle eut écrit	Il/Elle aura écrit	Il/Elle aurait écrit
Nous avons écrit	Nous avions écrit	Nous eûmes écrit	Nous aurons écrit	Nous aurions écrit
Vous avez écrit	Vous aviez écrit	Vous eûtes écrit	Vous aurez écrit	Vous auriez écrit
Ils/Elles ont écrit	Ils/Elles avaient écrit	Ils/Elles eurent écrit	Ils/Elles auront écrit	Ils/Elles auraient écrit

Subjunctive (simple tenses)

Present	*Imperfect*
J'écrive	J'écrivisse
Tu écrives	Tu écrivisses
Il/Elle écrive	Il/Elle écrivît
Nous écrivions	Nous écrivissions
Vous écriviez	Vous écrivissiez
Ils/Elles écrivent	Ils/Elles écrivissent

Subjunctive (compound tenses)

Perfect	*Pluperfect*
J'aie écrit	J'eusse écrit
Tu aies écrit	Tu eusses écrit
Il/Elle ait écrit	Il/Elle eût écrit
Nous ayons écrit	Nous eussions écrit
Vous ayez écrit	Vous eussiez écrit
Ils/Elles aient écrit	Ils/Elles eussent écrit

Imperative: Écris, écrivons, écrivez
Non-personal forms

Infinitive		Past participle	Gerund	
Simple	*Compound*	*Past participle*	*Simple*	*Compound*
Écrire	Avoir écrit	Écrit	Écrivant	Ayant écrit

Envoyer (*to send*)
Indicative (simple tenses)

Present	Imperfect	Preterit	Future	Conditional
J'envoie	J'envoyais	J'envoyai	J'enverrai	J'enverrais
Tu envoies	Tu envoyais	Tu envoyas	Tu enverras	Tu enverrais
Il/Elle envoie	Il/Elle envoyait	Il/Elle envoya	Il/Elle enverra	Il/Elle enverrait
Nous envoyons	Nous envoyions	Nous envoyâmes	Nous enverrons	Nous enverrions
Vous envoyez	Vous envoyiez	Vous envoyâtes	Vous enverrez	Vous enverriez
Ils/Elles envoient	Ils/Elles envoyaient	Ils/Elles envoyèrent	Ils/Elles enverront	Ils/Elles enverraient

Indicative (compound tenses)

Perfect	Pluperfect	Past Anterior	Future in the Past	Conditional in the Past
J'ai envoyé	J'avais envoyé	J'eus envoyé	J'aurai envoyé	J'aurais envoyé
Tu as envoyé	Tu avais envoyé	Tu eus envoyé	Tu auras envoyé	Tu aurais envoyé
Il/Elle a envoyé	Il/Elle avait envoyé	Il/Elle eut envoyé	Il/Elle aura envoyé	Il/Elle aurait envoyé
Nous avons envoyé	Nous avions envoyé	Nous eûmes envoyé	Nous aurons envoyé	Nous aurions envoyé
Vous avez envoyé	Vous aviez envoyé	Vous eûtes envoyé	Vous aurez envoyé	Vous auriez envoyé
Ils/Elles ont envoyé	Ils/Elles avaient envoyé	Ils/Elles eurent envoyé	Ils/Elles auront envoyé	Ils/Elles auraient envoyé

Subjunctive (simple tenses)

Present	Imperfect
J'envoie	J'envoyasse
Tu envoies	Tu envoyasses
Il/Elle envoie	Il/Elle envoyât
Nous envoyions	Nous envoyassions
Vous envoyiez	Vous envoyassiez
Ils/Elles envoient	Ils/Elles envoyassent

Subjunctive (compound tenses)

Perfect	Pluperfect
J'aie envoyé	J'eusse envoyé
Tu aies envoyé	Tu eusses envoyé
Il/Elle ait envoyé	Il/Elle eût envoyé
Nous ayons envoyé	Nous eussions envoyé
Vous ayez envoyé	Vous eussiez envoyé
Ils/Elles aient envoyé	Ils/Elles eussent envoyé

Imperative: Envoie, envoyons, envoyez
Non-personal forms

Infinitive			Gerund	
Simple	Compound	Past participle	Simple	Compound
Envoyer	Avoir envoyé	Envoyé	Envoyant	Ayant envoyé

Faire (*to do, to make*)
Indicative (simple tenses)

Present	Imperfect	Preterit	Future	Conditional
Je fais	Je faisais	Je fis	Je ferai	Je ferais
Tu fais	Tu faisais	Tu fis	Tu feras	Tu ferais
Il/Elle fait	Il/Elle faisait	Il/Elle fit	Il/Elle fera	Il/Elle ferait
Nous faisons	Nous faisions	Nous fîmes	Nous ferons	Nous ferions
Vous faites	Vous faisiez	Vous fîtes	Vous ferez	Vous feriez
Ils/Elles font	Ils/Elles faisaient	Ils/Elles firent	Ils/Elles feront	Ils/Elles feraient

Indicative (compound tenses)

Perfect	Pluperfect	Past Anterior	Future in the Past	Conditional in the Past
J'ai fait	J'avais fait	J'eus fait	J'aurai fait	J'aurais fait
Tu as fait	Tu avais fait	Tu eus fait	Tu auras fait	Tu aurais fait
Il/Elle a fait	Il/Elle avait fait	Il/Elle eut fait	Il/Elle aura fait	Il/Elle aurait fait
Nous avons fait	Nous avions fait	Nous eûmes fait	Nous aurons fait	Nous aurions fait
Vous avez fait	Vous aviez fait	Vous eûtes fait	Vous aurez fait	Vous auriez fait
Ils/Elles ont fait	Ils/Elles avaient fait	Ils/Elles eurent fait	Ils/Elles auront fait	Ils/Elles auraient fait

Subjunctive (simple tenses)

Present	Imperfect
Je fasse	Je fisse
Tu fasses	Tu fisses
Il/Elle fasse	Il/Elle fît
Nous fassions	Nous fissions
Vous fassiez	Vous fissiez
Ils/Elles fassent	Ils/Elles fissent

Subjunctive (compound tenses)

Perfect	Pluperfect
J'aie fait	J'eusse fait
Tu aies fait	Tu eusses fait
Il/Elle ait fait	Il/Elle eût fait
Nous ayons fait	Nous eussions fait
Vous ayez fait	Vous eussiez fait
Ils/Elles aient fait	Ils/Elles eussent fait

Imperative: Fais, faisons, faites
Non-personal forms

Infinitive			Gerund	
Simple	Compound	Past participle	Simple	Compound
Faire	Avoir fait	Fait	Faisant	Ayant fait

Mettre (*to put*)
Indicative (simple tenses)

Present	Imperfect	Preterit	Future	Conditional
Je mets	Je mettais	Je mis	Je mettrai	Je mettrais
Tu mets	Tu mettais	Tu mis	Tu mettras	Tu mettrais
Il/Elle met	Il/Elle mettait	Il/Elle mit	Il/Elle mettra	Il/Elle mettrait

Indicative (simple tenses) (*cont.*)

Present	Imperfect	Preterit	Future	Conditional
Nous mettons	Nous mettions	Nous mîmes	Nous mettrons	Nous mettrions
Vous mettez	Vous mettiez	Vous mîtes	Vous mettrez	Vous mettriez
Ils/Elles mettent	Ils/Elles mettaient	Ils/Elles mirent	Ils/Elles mettront	Ils/Elles mettraient

Indicative (compound tenses)

Perfect	Pluperfect	Past Anterior	Future in the Past	Conditional in the Past
J'ai mis	J'avais mis	J'eus mis	J'aurai mis	J'aurais mis
Tu as mis	Tu avais mis	Tu eus mis	Tu auras mis	Tu aurais mis
Il/Elle a mis	Il/Elle avait mis	Il/Elle eut mis	Il/Elle aura mis	Il/Elle aurait mis
Nous avons mis	Nous avions mis	Nous eûmes mis	Nous aurons mis	Nous aurions mis
Vous avez mis	Vous aviez mis	Vous eûtes mis	Vous aurez mis	Vous auriez mis
Ils/Elles ont mis	Ils/Elles avaient mis	Ils/Elles eurent mis	Ils/Elles auront mis	Ils/Elles auraient mis

Subjunctive (simple tenses)

Present	Imperfect
Je mette	Je misse
Tu mettes	Tu misses
Il/Elle mette	Il/Elle mît
Nous mettions	Nous missions
Vous mettiez	Vous missiez
Ils/Elles mettent	Ils/Elles missent

Subjunctive (compound tenses)

Perfect	Pluperfect
J'aie mis	J'eusse mis
Tu aies mis	Tu eusses mis
Il/Elle ait mis	Il/Elle eût mis
Nous ayons mis	Nous eussions mis
Vous ayez mis	Vous eussiez mis
Ils/Elles aient mis	Ils/Elles eussent mis

Imperative: Mets, mettons, mettez
Non-personal forms

Infinitive			Gerund	
Simple	Compound	Past participle	Simple	Compound
Mettre	Avoir mis	Mis	Mettant	Ayant mis

Moudre (*to grind*)
Indicative (simple tenses)

Present	Imperfect	Preterit	Future	Conditional
Je mouds	Je moulais	Je moulus	Je moudrai	Je moudrais
Tu mouds	Tu moulais	Tu moulus	Tu moudras	Tu moudrais
Il/Elle moud	Il/Elle moulait	Il/Elle moulut	Il/Elle moudra	Il/Elle moudrait
Nous moulons	Nous moulions	Nous moulûmes	Nous moudrons	Nous moudrions
Vous moulez	Vous mouliez	Vous moulûtes	Vous moudrez	Vous moudriez
Ils/Elles moulent	Ils/Elles moulaient	Ils/Elles moulurent	Ils/Elles moudront	Ils/Elles moudraient

Indicative (compound tenses)

Perfect	Pluperfect	Past Anterior	Future in the Past	Conditional in the Past
J'ai moulu	J'avais moulu	J'eus moulu	J'aurai moulu	J'aurais moulu
Tu as moulu	Tu avais moulu	Tu eus moulu	Tu auras moulu	Tu aurais moulu
Il/Elle a moulu	Il/Elle avait moulu	Il/Elle eut moulu	Il/Elle aura moulu	Il/Elle aurait moulu
Nous avons moulu	Nous avions moulu	Nous eûmes moulu	Nous aurons moulu	Nous aurions moulu
Vous avez moulu	Vous aviez moulu	Vous eûtes moulu	Vous aurez moulu	Vous auriez moulu
Ils/Elles ont moulu	Ils/Elles avaient moulu	Ils/Elles eurent moulu	Ils/Elles auront moulu	Ils/Elles auraient moulu

Subjunctive (simple tenses)

Present	Imperfect
Je moule	Je moulusse
Tu moules	Tu moulusses
Il/Elle moule	Il/Elle moulût
Nous moulions	Nous moulussions
Vous mouliez	Vous moulussiez
Ils/Elles moulent	Ils/Elles moulussent

Subjunctive (compound tenses)

Perfect	Pluperfect
J'aie moulu	J'eusse moulu
Tu aies moulu	Tu eusses moulu
Il/Elle ait moulu	Il/Elle eût moulu
Nous ayons moulu	Nous eussions moulu
Vous ayez moulu	Vous eussiez moulu
Ils/Elles aient moulu	Ils/Elles eussent moulu

Imperative: Mouds, moulons, moulez
Non-personal forms

Infinitive			Gerund	
Simple	Compound	Past participle	Simple	Compound
Moudre	Avoir moulu	Moulu	Moulant	Ayant moulu

Mourir (*to die*)
Indicative (simple tenses)

Present	Imperfect	Preterit	Future	Conditional
Je meurs	Je mourais	Je mourus	Je mourrai	Je mourrais
Tu meurs	Tu mourais	Tu mourus	Tu mourras	Tu mourrais
Il/Elle meurt	Il/Elle mourait	Il/Elle mourut	Il/Elle mourra	Il/Elle mourrait
Nous mourons	Nous mourions	Nous mourûmes	Nous mourrons	Nous mourrions
Vous mourez	Vous mouriez	Vous mourûtes	Vous mourrez	Vous mourriez
Ils/Elles meurent	Ils/Elles mouraient	Ils/Elles moururent	Ils/Elles mourront	Ils/Elles mourraient

Indicative (compound tenses)

Perfect	Pluperfect	Past Anterior	Future in the Past	Conditional in the Past
Je suis mort(e)	J'étais mort(e)	Je fus mort(e)	Je serais mort(e)	Je serais mort(e)
Tu es mort(e)	Tu étais mort(e)	Tu feus mort(e)	Tu seras mort(e)	Tu serais mort(e)
Il/Elle est mort(e)	Il/Elle était mort(e)	Il/Elle fut mort(e)	Il/Elle sera mort(e)	Il/Elle serait mort(e)
Nous sommes mort(e)s	Nous étions mort(e)s	Nous fûmes mort(e)s	Nous serons mort(e)s	Nous serions mort(e)s
Vous êtes mort(e)(s)	Vous étiez mort(e)(s)	Vous fûtes mort(e)(s)	Vous serez mort(e)(s)	Vous seriez mort(e)(s)
Ils/Elles sont mort(e)s	Ils/Elles étaient mort(e)s	Ils/Elles furent mort(e)s	Ils/Elles seront mort(e)s	Ils/Elles seraient mort(e)s

Subjunctive (simple tenses)

Present	Imperfect
Je meure	Je mourusse
Tu meures	Tu mourusses
Il/Elle meure	Il/Elle mourût
Nous mourions	Nous mourûmes
Vous mouriez	Vous mourûtes
Ils/Elles meurent	Ils/Elles mourussent

Subjunctive (compound tenses)

Perfect	Pluperfect
Je sois mort(e)	Je fusse mort(e)
Tu sois mort(e)	Tu fusses mort(e)
Il/Elle soit mort(e)	Il/Elle fût mort(e)
Nous soyons mort(e)s	Nous fussions mort(e)s
Vous soyez mort(e)(s)	Vous fussiez mort(e)(s)
Ils/Elles soient mort(e)s	Ils/Elles fussent mort(e)s

Imperative: Meurs, mourons, mourez
Non-personal forms

Infinitive		Past participle	Gerund	
Simple	Compound		Simple	Compound
Mourir	Être mort(e)	Mort(e)	Mourant	Étant mort(e)

Ouvrir (*to open*)
Indicative (simple tenses)

Present	Imperfect	Preterit	Future	Conditional
J'ouvre	J'ouvrais	J'ouvris	J'ouvrirai	J'ouvrirais
Tu ouvres	Tu ouvrais	Tu ouvris	Tu ouvriras	Tu ouvrirais
Il/Elle ouvre	Il/Elle ouvrait	Il/Elle ouvrit	Il/Elle ouvrira	Il/Elle ouvrirait
Nous ouvrons	Nous ouvrions	Nous ouvrîmes	Nous ouvrirons	Nous ouvririons
Vous ouvrez	Vous ouvriez	Vous ouvrîtes	Vous ouvrirez	Vous ouvririez
Ils/Elles ouvrent	Ils/Elles ouvraient	Ils/Elles ouvrirent	Ils/Elles ouvriront	Ils/Elles ouvriraient

Indicative (compound tenses)

Perfect	Pluperfect	Past Anterior	Future in the Past	Conditional in the Past
J'ai ouvert	J'avais ouvert	J'eus ouvert	J'aurai ouvert	J'aurais ouvert
Tu as ouvert	Tu avais ouvert	Tu eus ouvert	Tu auras ouvert	Tu aurais ouvert
Il/Elle a ouvert	Il/Elle avait ouvert	Il/Elle eut ouvert	Il/Elle aura ouvert	Il/Elle aurait ouvert
Nous avons ouvert	Nous avions ouvert	Nous eûmes ouvert	Nous aurons ouvert	Nous aurions ouvert
Vous avez ouvert	Vous aviez ouvert	Vous eûtes ouvert	Vous aurez ouvert	Vous auriez ouvert
Ils/Elles ont ouvert	Ils/Elles avaient ouvert	Ils/Elles eurent ouvert	Ils/Elles auront ouvert	Ils/Elles auraient ouvert

Subjunctive (simple tenses)

Present	Imperfect
J'ouvre	J'ouvrisse
Tu ouvres	Tu ouvrisses
Il/Elle ouvre	Il/Elle ouvrît
Nous ouvrions	Nous ouvrissions
Vous ouvriez	Vous ouvrissiez
Ils/Elles ouvrent	Ils/Elles ouvrissent

Subjunctive (compound tenses)

Perfect	Pluperfect
J'aie ouvert	J'eusse ouvert
Tu aies ouvert	Tu eusses ouvert
Il/Elle ait ouvert	Il/Elle eût ouvert
Nous ayons ouvert	Nous eussions ouvert
Vous ayez ouvert	Vous eussiez ouvert
Ils/Elles aient ouvert	Ils/Elles eussent ouvert

Imperative: Ouvre, ouvrons, ouvrez
Non-personal forms

Infinitive			Gerund	
Simple	Compound	Past participle	Simple	Compound
Ouvrir	Avoir ouvert	Ouvert	Ouvrant	Ayant ouvert

Peindre (*to paint*)
Indicative (simple tenses)

Present	Imperfect	Preterit	Future	Conditional
Je peins	Je peignais	Je peignis	Je peindrai	Je peindrais
Tu peins	Tu peignais	Tu peignis	Tu peindras	Tu peindrais
Il/Elle peint	Il/Elle peignait	Il/Elle peignit	Il/Elle peindra	Il/Elle peindrait
Nous peignons	Nous peignions	Nous peignîmes	Nous peindrons	Nous peindrions
Vous peignez	Vous peigniez	Vous peignîtes	Vous peindrez	Vous peindriez
Ils/Elles peignent	Ils/Elles peignaient	Ils/Elles peignirent	Ils/Elles peindront	Ils/Elles peindraient

Indicative (compound tenses)

Perfect	Pluperfect	Past Anterior	Future in the Past	Conditional in the Past
J'ai peint	J'avais peint	J'eus peint	J'aurai peint	J'aurais peint
Tu as peint	Tu avais peint	Tu eus peint	Tu auras peint	Tu aurais peint
Il/Elle a peint	Il/Elle avait peint	Il/Elle eut peint	Il/Elle aura peint	Il/Elle aurait peint
Nous avons peint	Nous avions peint	Nous eûmes peint	Nous aurons peint	Nous aurions peint
Vous avez peint	Vous aviez peint	Vous eûtes peint	Vous aurez peint	Vous auriez peint
Ils/Elles ont peint	Ils/Elles avaient peint	Ils/Elles eurent peint	Ils/Elles auront peint	Ils/Elles auraient peint

Subjunctive (simple tenses)

Present	Imperfect
Je peigne	Je peignisse
Tu peignes	Tu peignisses
Il/Elle peigne	Il/Elle peignît
Nous peignions	Nous peignissions
Vous peigniez	Vous peignissiez
Ils/Elles peignent	Ils/Elles peignissent

Subjunctive (compound tenses)

Perfect	Pluperfect
J'aie peint	J'eusse peint
Tu aies peint	Tu eusses peint
Il/Elle ait peint	Il/Elle eût peint
Nous ayons peint	Nous eussions peint
Vous ayez peint	Vous eussiez peint
Ils/Elles aient peint	Ils/Elles eussent peint

Imperative: Peins, peignons, peignez

Non-personal forms

Infinitive			Gerund	
Simple	Compound	Past participle	Simple	Compound
Peindre	Avoir peint	Peint	Peignant	Ayant peint

Pouvoir (*can, to be able*)
Indicative (simple tenses)

Present	Imperfect	Preterit	Future	Conditional
Je peux / je puis	Je pouvais	Je pus	Je pourrai	Je pourrais
Tu peux	Tu pouvais	Tu pus	Tu pourras	Tu pourrais
Il/Elle peut	Il/Elle pouvait	Il/Elle put	Il/Elle pourra	Il/Elle pourrait
Nous pouvons	Nous pouvions	Nous pûmes	Nous pourrons	Nous pourrions
Vous pouvez	Vous pouviez	Vous pûtes	Vous pourrez	Vous pourriez
Ils/Elles peuvent	Ils/Elles pouvaient	Ils/Elles purent	Ils/Elles pourront	Ils/Elles pourraient

Indicative (compound tenses)

Perfect	Pluperfect	Past Anterior	Future in the Past	Conditional in the Past
J'ai pu	J'avais pu	J'eus pu	J'aurai pu	J'aurais pu
Tu as pu	Tu avais pu	Tu eus pu	Tu auras pu	Tu aurais pu
Il/Elle a pu	Il/Elle avait pu	Il/Elle eut pu	Il/Elle aura pu	Il/Elle aurait pu

Indicative (compound tenses) (*cont.*)

Perfect	Pluperfect	Past Anterior	Future in the Past	Conditional in the Past
Nous avons pu	Nous avions pu	Nous eûmes pu	Nous aurons pu	Nous aurions pu
Vous avez pu	Vous aviez pu	Vous eûtes pu	Vous aurez pu	Vous auriez pu
Ils/Elles ont pu	Ils/Elles avaient pu	Ils/Elles eurent pu	Ils/Elles auront pu	Ils/Elles auraient pu

Subjunctive (simple tenses)

Present	Imperfect
Je puisse	Je pusse
Tu puisses	Tu pusses
Il/Elle puisse	Il/Elle pût
Nous puissions	Nous pussions
Vous puissiez	Vous pussiez
Ils/Elles puissent	Ils/Elles pussent

Subjunctive (compound tenses)

Perfect	Pluperfect
J'aie pu	J'eusse pu
Tu aies pu	Tu eusses pu
Il/Elle ait pu	Il/Elle eût pu
Nous ayons pu	Nous eussions pu
Vous ayez pu	Vous eussiez pu
Ils/Elles aient pu	Ils/Elles eussent pu

Imperative: not used
Non-personal forms

Infinitive			Gerund	
Simple	Compound	Past participle	Simple	Compound
Pouvoir	Avoir pu	Pu	Pouvant	Ayant pu

Résoudre (*to solve, to resolve*)
Indicative (simple tenses)

Present	Imperfect	Preterit	Future	Conditional
Je résous	Je résolvais	Je résolus	Je résoudrai	Je résoudrais
Tu résous	Tu résolvais	Tu résolus	Tu résoudras	Tu résoudrais
Il/Elle résout	Il/Elle résolvait	Il/Elle résolut	Il/Elle résoudra	Il/Elle résoudrait
Nous résolvons	Nous résolvions	Nous résolûmes	Nous résoudrons	Nous résoudrions
Vous résolvez	Vous résolviez	Vous résolûtes	Vous résoudrez	Vous résoudriez
Ils/Elles résolvent	Ils/Elles résolvaient	Ils/Elles résolurent	Ils/Elles résoudront	Ils/Elles résoudraient

Indicative (compound tenses)

Perfect	Pluperfect	Past Anterior	Future in the Past	Conditional in the Past
J'ai résolu/résous	J'avais résolu/résous	J'eus résolu/résous	J'aurai résolu/résous	J'aurais résolu/résous
Tu as résolu/résous	Tu avais résolu/résous	Tu eus résolu/résous	Tu auras résolu/résous	Tu aurais résolu/résous
Il/Elle a résolu/résous	Il/Elle avait résolu/résous	Il/Elle eut résolu/résous	Il/Elle aura résolu/résous	Il/Elle aurait résolu/résous

Indicative (compound tenses) (*cont.*)

Perfect	Pluperfect	Past Anterior	Future in the Past	Conditional in the Past
Nous avons résolu/résous	Nous avions résolu/résous	Nous eûmes résolu/résous	Nous aurons résolu/résous	Nous aurions résolu/résous
Vous avez résolu/résous	Vous aviez résolu/résous	Vous eûtes résolu/résous	Vous aurez résolu/résous	Vous auriez résolu/résous
Ils/Elles ont résolu/résous	Ils/Elles avaient résolu/résous	Ils/Elles eurent résolu/résous	Ils/Elles auront résolu/résous	Ils/Elles auraient résolu/résous

Subjunctive (simple tenses)

Present	Imperfect
Je résolve	Je résolusse
Tu résolves	Tu résolusses
Il/Elle résolve	Il/Elle résolût
Nous résolvions	Nous résolussions
Vous résolviez	Vous résolussiez
Ils/Elles résolvent	Ils/Elles résolussent

Subjunctive (compound tenses)

Perfect	Pluperfect
J'aie résolu/résous	J'eusse résolu/résous
Tu aies résolu/résous	Tu eusses résolu/résous
Il/Elle ait résolu/résous	Il/Elle eût résolu/résous
Nous ayons résolu/résous	Nous eussions résolu/résous
Vous ayez résolu/résous	Vous eussiez résolu/résous
Ils/Elles aient résolu/résous	Ils/Elles eussent résolu/résous

Imperative: Résous, résolvons, résolvez

Non-personal forms

Infinitive		Gerund	
Simple	Compound	Past participle	Simple	Compound
Résoudre	Avoir résolu/résous	Résolu/Résous	Résolvant	Ayant résolu/résous

Savoir (*to know*)

Indicative (simple tenses)

Present	Imperfect	Preterit	Future	Conditional
Je sais	Je savais	Je sus	Je saurai	Je saurais
Tu sais	Tu savais	Tu sus	Tu sauras	Tu saurais
Il/Elle sait	Il/Elle savait	Il/Elle sut	Il/Elle saura	Il/Elle saurait
Nous savons	Nous savions	Nous sûmes	Nous saurons	Nous saurions
Vous savez	Vous saviez	Vous sûtes	Vous saurez	Vous sauriez
Ils/Elles savent	Ils/Elles savaient	Ils/Elles surent	Ils/Elles sauront	Ils/Elles sauraient

Indicative (compound tenses)

Perfect	Pluperfect	Past Anterior	Future in the Past	Conditional in the Past
J'ai su	J'avais su	J'eus su	J'aurai su	J'aurais su
Tu as su	Tu avais su	Tu eus su	Tu auras su	Tu aurais su
Il/Elle a su	Il/Elle avait su	Il/Elle eut su	Il/Elle aura su	Il/Elle aurait su
Nous avons su	Nous avions su	Nous eûmes su	Nous aurons su	Nous aurions su
Vous avez su	Vous aviez su	Vous eûtes su	Vous aurez su	Vous auriez su
Ils/Elles ont su	Ils/Elles avaient su	Ils/Elles eurent su	Ils/Elles auront su	Ils/Elles auraient su

Subjunctive (simple tenses)

Present	*Imperfect*
Je sache	Je susse
Tu saches	Tu susses
Il/Elle sache	Il/Elle sût
Nous sachions	Nous sussions
Vous sachiez	Vous sussiez
Ils/Elles sachent	Ils/Elles sussent

Subjunctive (compound tenses)

Perfect	*Pluperfect*
J'aie su	J'eusse su
Tu aies su	Tu eusses su
Il/Elle ait su	Il/Elle eût su
Nous ayons su	Nous eussions su
Vous ayez su	Vous eussiez su
Ils/Elles aient su	Ils/Elles eussent su

Imperative: Sache, sachons, sachez

Non-personal forms

Infinitive			Gerund	
Simple	*Compound*	*Past participle*	*Simple*	*Compound*
Savoir	Avoir su	Su	Sachant	Ayant su

Sentir (*to smell, to feel*)
Indicative (simple tenses)

Present	*Imperfect*	*Preterit*	*Future*	*Conditional*
Je sens	Je sentais	Je sentis	Je sentirai	Je sentirais
Tu sens	Tu sentais	Tu sentis	Tu sentiras	Tu sentirais
Il/Elle sent	Il/Elle sentait	Il/Elle sentit	Il/Elle sentira	Il/Elle sentirait
Nous sentons	Nous sentions	Nous sentîmes	Nous sentirons	Nous sentirions
Vous sentez	Vous sentiez	Vous sentîtes	Vous sentirez	Vous sentiriez
Ils/Elles sentent	Ils/Elles sentaient	Ils/Elles sentirent	Ils/Elles sentiront	Ils/Elles sentiraient

Indicative (compound tenses)

Perfect	*Pluperfect*	*Past Anterior*	*Future in the Past*	*Conditional in the Past*
J'ai senti	J'avais senti	J'eus senti	J'aurai senti	J'aurais senti
Tu as senti	Tu avais senti	Tu eus senti	Tu auras senti	Tu aurais senti
Il/Elle a senti	Il/Elle avait senti	Il/Elle eut senti	Il/Elle aura senti	Il/Elle aurait senti
Nous avons senti	Nous avions senti	Nous eûmes senti	Nous aurons senti	Nous aurions senti
Vous avez senti	Vous aviez senti	Vous eûtes senti	Vous aurez senti	Vous auriez senti
Ils/Elles ont senti	Ils/Elles avaient senti	Ils/Elles eurent senti	Ils/Elles auront senti	Ils/Elles auraient senti

Subjunctive (simple tenses)

Present	*Imperfect*
Je sente	Je sentisse
Tu sentes	Tu sentisses
Il/Elle sente	Il/Elle sentît

Subjunctive (simple tenses) (*cont.*)

Present	Imperfect
Nous sentions	Nous sentissions
Vous sentiez	Vous sentissiez
Ils/Elles sentent	Ils/Elles sentissent

Subjunctive (compound tenses)

Perfect	Pluperfect
J'aie senti	J'eusse senti
Tu aies senti	Tu eusses senti
Il/Elle ait senti	Il/Elle eût senti
Nous ayons senti	Nous eussions senti
Vous ayez senti	Vous eussiez senti
Ils/Elles aient senti	Ils/Elles eussent senti

Imperative: Sens, sentons, sentez

Non-personal forms

Infinitive		Past participle	Gerund	
Simple	Compound		Simple	Compound
Sentir	Avoir senti	Senti	Sentant	Ayant senti

Servir (*to serve*)

Indicative (simple tenses)

Present	Imperfect	Preterit	Future	Conditional
Je sers	Je servais	Je servis	Je servirai	Je servirais
Tu sers	Tu servais	Tu servis	Tu serviras	Tu servirais
Il/Elle sert	Il/Elle servait	Il/Elle servit	Il/Elle servira	Il/Elle servirait
Nous servons	Nous servions	Nous servîmes	Nous servirons	Nous servirions
Vous servez	Vous serviez	Vous servîtes	Vous servirez	Vous serviriez
Ils/Elles servent	Ils/Elles servaient	Ils/Elles servirent	Ils/Elles serviront	Ils/Elles serviraient

Indicative (compound tenses)

Perfect	Pluperfect	Past Anterior	Future in the Past	Conditional in the Past
J'ai servi	J'avais servi	J'eus servi	J'aurai servi	J'aurais servi
Tu as servi	Tu avais servi	Tu eus servi	Tu auras servi	Tu aurais servi
Il/Elle a servi	Il/Elle avait servi	Il/Elle eut servi	Il/Elle aura servi	Il/Elle aurait servi
Nous avons servi	Nous avions servi	Nous eûmes servi	Nous aurons servi	Nous aurions servi
Vous avez servi	Vous aviez servi	Vous eûtes servi	Vous aurez servi	Vous auriez servi
Ils/Elles ont servi	Ils/Elles avaient servi	Ils/Elles eurent servi	Ils/Elles auront servi	Ils/Elles auraient servi

Subjunctive (simple tenses)

Present	Imperfect
Je serve	Je servisse
Tu serves	Tu servisses
Il/Elle serve	Il/Elle servît
Nous servions	Nous servissions
Vous serviez	Vous servissiez
Ils/Elles servent	Ils/Elles servissent

Subjunctive (compound tenses)

Perfect	*Pluperfect*
J'aie servi	J'eusse servi
Tu aies servi	Tu eusses servi
Il/Elle ait servi	Il/Elle eût servi
Nous ayons servi	Nous eussions servi
Vous ayez servi	Vous eussiez servi
Ils/Elles aient servi	Ils/Elles eussent servi

Imperative: Sers, servons, servez

Non-personal forms

Infinitive			Gerund	
Simple	*Compound*	*Past participle*	*Simple*	*Compound*
Servir	Avoir servi	Servi	Servant	Ayant servi

Suivre (*to follow*)

Indicative (simple tenses)

Present	*Imperfect*	*Preterit*	*Future*	*Conditional*
Je suis	Je suivais	Je suivis	Je suivrai	Je suivrais
Tu suis	Tu suivais	Tu suivis	Tu suivras	Tu suivrais
Il/Elle suit	Il/Elle suivait	Il/Elle suivit	Il/Elle suivra	Il/Elle suivrait
Nous suivons	Nous suivions	Nous suivîmes	Nous suivrons	Nous suivrions
Vous suivez	Vous suiviez	Vous suivîtes	Vous suivrez	Vous suivriez
Ils/Elles suivent	Ils/Elles suivaient	Ils/Elles suivirent	Ils/Elles suivront	Ils/Elles suivraient

Indicative (compound tenses)

Perfect	*Pluperfect*	*Past Anterior*	*Future in the Past*	*Conditional in the Past*
J'ai suivi	J'avais suivi	J'eus suivi	J'aurai suivi	J'aurais suivi
Tu as suivi	Tu avais suivi	Tu eus suivi	Tu auras suivi	Tu aurais suivi
Il/Elle a suivi	Il/Elle avait suivi	Il/Elle eut suivi	Il/Elle aura suivi	Il/Elle aurait suivi
Nous avons suivi	Nous avions suivi	Nous eûmes suivi	Nous aurons suivi	Nous aurions suivi
Vous avez suivi	Vous aviez suivi	Vous eûtes suivi	Vous aurez suivi	Vous auriez suivi
Ils/Elles ont suivi	Ils/Elles avaient suivi	Ils/Elles eurent suivi	Ils/Elles auront suivi	Ils/Elles auraient suivi

Subjunctive (simple tenses)

Present	*Imperfect*
Je suive	Je suivisse
Tu suives	Tu suivisses
Il/Elle suive	Il/Elle suivît
Nous suivions	Nous suivissions
Vous suiviez	Vous suivissiez
Ils/Elles suivent	Ils/Elles suivissent

Subjunctive (compound tenses)

Perfect	*Pluperfect*
J'aie suivi	J'eusse suivi
Tu aies suivi	Tu eusses suivi
Il/Elle ait suivi	Il/Elle eût suivi
Nous ayons suivi	Nous eussions suivi
Vous ayez suivi	Vous eussiez suivi
Ils/Elles aient suivi	Ils/Elles eussent suivi

Imperative: Suis, suivons, suivez
Non-personal forms

Infinitive			Gerund	
Simple	*Compound*	*Past participle*	*Simple*	*Compound*
Suivre	Avoir suivi	Suivi	Suivant	Ayant suivi

Tenir (*to hold*)
Indicative (simple tenses)

Present	*Imperfect*	*Preterit*	*Future*	*Conditional*
Je tiens	Je tenais	Je tins	Je tiendrai	Je tiendrais
Tu tiens	Tu tenais	Tu tins	Tu tiendras	Tu tiendrais
Il/Elle tient	Il/Elle tenait	Il/Elle tint	Il/Elle tiendra	Il/Elle tiendrait
Nous tenons	Nous tenions	Nous tînmes	Nous tiendrons	Nous tiendrions
Vous tenez	Vous teniez	Vous tîntes	Vous tiendrez	Vous tiendriez
Ils/Elles tiennent	Ils/Elles tenaient	Ils/Elles tinrent	Ils/Elles tiendront	Ils/Elles tiendraient

Indicative (compound tenses)

Perfect	*Pluperfect*	*Past Anterior*	*Future in the Past*	*Conditional in the Past*
J'ai tenu	J'avais tenu	J'eus tenu	J'aurai tenu	J'aurais tenu
Tu as tenu	Tu avais tenu	Tu eus tenu	Tu auras tenu	Tu aurais tenu
Il/Elle a tenu	Il/Elle avait tenu	Il/Elle eut tenu	Il/Elle aura tenu	Il/Elle aurait tenu
Nous avons tenu	Nous avions tenu	Nous eûmes tenu	Nous aurons tenu	Nous aurions tenu
Vous avez tenu	Vous aviez tenu	Vous eûtes tenu	Vous aurez tenu	Vous auriez tenu
Ils/Elles ont tenu	Ils/Elles avaient tenu	Ils/Elles eurent tenu	Ils/Elles auront tenu	Ils/Elles auraient tenu

Subjunctive (simple tenses)

Present	*Imperfect*
Je tienne	Je tinsse
Tu tiennes	Tu tinsses
Il/Elle tienne	Il/Elle tînt
Nous tenions	Nous tinssions
Vous teniez	Vous tinssiez
Ils/Elles tiennent	Ils/Elles tinssent

Subjunctive (compound censes)

Perfect	*Pluperfect*
J'aie tenu	J'eusse tenu
Tu aies tenu	Tu eusses tenu
Il/Elle ait tenu	Il/Elle eût tenu
Nous ayons tenu	Nous eussions tenu
Vous ayez tenu	Vous eussiez tenu
Ils/Elles aient tenu	Ils/Elles eussent tenu

Imperative: Tiens, tenons, tenez
Non-personal forms

Infinitive			Gerund	
Simple	*Compound*	*Past participle*	*Simple*	*Compound*
Tenir	Avoir tenu	Tenu	Tenant	Ayant tenu

Vaincre (*to win*)
Indicative (simple tenses)

Present	Imperfect	Preterit	Future	Conditional
Je vaincs	Je vainquais	Je vainquis	Je vaincrai	Je vaincrais
Tu vaincs	Tu vainquais	Tu vainquis	Tu vaincras	Tu vaincrais
Il/Elle vainc	Il/Elle vainquait	Il/Elle vainquit	Il/Elle vaincra	Il/Elle vaincrait
Nous vainquons	Nous vainquions	Nous vainquîmes	Nous vaincrons	Nous vaincrons
Vous vainquez	Vous vainquiez	Vous vainquîtes	Vous vaincrez	Vous vaincrez
Ils/Elles vainquent	Ils/Elles vainquaient	Ils/Elles vainquirent	Ils/Elles vaincront	Ils/Elles vaincraient

Indicative (compound tenses)

Perfect	Pluperfect	Past Anterior	Future in the Past	Conditional in the Past
J'ai vaincu	J'avais vaincu	J'eus vaincu	J'aurai vaincu	J'aurais vaincu
Tu as vaincu	Tu avais vaincu	Tu eus vaincu	Tu auras vaincu	Tu aurais vaincu
Il/Elle a vaincu	Il/Elle avait vaincu	Il/Elle eut vaincu	Il/Elle aura vaincu	Il/Elle aurait vaincu
Nous avons vaincu	Nous avions vaincu	Nous eûmes vaincu	Nous aurons vaincu	Nous aurions vaincu
Vous avez vaincu	Vous aviez vaincu	Vous eûtes vaincu	Vous aurez vaincu	Vous auriez vaincu
Ils/Elles ont vaincu	Ils/Elles avaient vaincu	Ils/Elles eurent vaincu	Ils/Elles auront vaincu	Ils/Elles auraient vaincu

Subjunctive (simple tenses)

Present	Imperfect
Je vainque	Je vainquisse
Tu vainques	Tu vainquisses
Il/Elle vainque	Il/Elle vainquît
Nous vainquions	Nous vainquissions
Vous vainquiez	Vous vainquissiez
Ils/Elles vainquent	Ils/Elles vainquissent

Subjunctive (compound tenses)

Perfect	Pluperfect
J'aie vaincu	J'eusse vaincu
Tu aies vaincu	Tu eusses vaincu
Il/Elle ait vaincu	Il/Elle eût vaincu
Nous ayons vaincu	Nous eussions vaincu
Vous ayez vaincu	Vous eussiez vaincu
Ils/Elles aient vaincu	Ils/Elles eussent vaincu

Imperative: Vaincs, vainquons, vainquez
Non-personal forms

Infinitive		Past participle	Gerund	
Simple	Compound		Simple	Compound
Vaincre	Avoir vaincu	Vaincu	Vainquant	Ayant vaincu

Venir (*to come*)
Indicative (simple tenses)

Present	Imperfect	Preterit	Future	Conditional
Je viens	Je venais	Je vins	Je viendrai	Je viendrais
Tu viens	Tu venais	Tu vins	Tu viendras	Tu viendrais
Il/Elle vient	Il/Elle venait	Il/Elle vint	Il/Elle viendra	Il/Elle viendrait
Nous venons	Nous venions	Nous vînmes	Nous viendrons	Nous viendrions
Vous venez	Vous veniez	Vous vîntes	Vous viendrez	Vous viendriez
Ils/Elles viennent	Ils/Elles venaient	Ils/Elles vinrent	Ils/Elles viendront	Ils/Elles viendraient

Indicative (compound tenses)

Perfect	Pluperfect	Past Anterior	Future in the Past	Conditional in the Past
Je suis venu(e)	J'étais venu(e)	Je fus venu(e)	Je serai venu(e)	Je serais venu(e)
Tu es venu(e)	Tu étais venu(e)	Tu fus venu(e)	Tu seras venu(e)	Tu serais venu(e)
Il/Elle est venu(e)	Il/Elle était venu(e)	Il/Elle fut venu(e)	Il/Elle sera venu(e)	Il/Elle serait venu(e)
Nous sommes venu(e)s	Nous étions venu(e)s	Nous fûmes venu(e)s	Nous serons venu(e)s	Nous serions venu(e)s
Vous êtes venu(e)(s)	Vous étiez venu(e)(s)	Vous fûtes venu(e)(s)	Vous serez venu(e)(s)	Vous seriez venu(e)(s)
Ils/Elles sont venu(e)s	Ils/Elles étaient venu(e)s	Ils/Elles furent venu(e)s	Ils/Elles seront venu(e)s	Ils/Elles seraient venu(e)s

Subjunctive (simple tenses)

Present	Imperfect
Je vienne	Je vinsse
Tu viennes	Tu vinsses
Il/Elle vienne	Il/Elle vînt
Nous venions	Nous vinssions
Vous veniez	Vous vinssiez
Ils/Elles viennent	Ils/Elles vinssent

Subjunctive (compound tenses)

Perfect	Pluperfect
Je sois venu(e)	Je fusse venu(e)
Tu sois venu(e)	Tu fusses venu(e)
Il/Elle soit venu(e)	Il/Elle fût venu (e)
Nous soyons venu(e)s	Nous fussions venu(e)s
Vous soyez venu(e)(s)	Vous fussiez venu(e)(s)
Ils/Elles soient venu(e)s	Ils/Elles fussent venu(e)s

Imperative: Viens, venons, venez
Non-personal forms

Infinitive		Past participle	Gerund	
Simple	Compound		Simple	Compound
Venir	Être venu(e)(s)	Venu(e)	Venant	Étant venu(e)(s)

Vivre (*to live*)
Indicative (simple tenses)

Present	*Imperfect*	*Preterit*	*Future*	*Conditional*
Je vis	Je vivais	Je vécus	Je vivrai	Je vivrais
Tu vis	Tu vivais	Tu vécus	Tu vivras	Tu vivrais
Il/Elle vit	Il/Elle vivait	Il/Elle vécut	Il/Elle vivra	Il/Elle vivrait
Nous vivons	Nous vivions	Nous vécûmes	Nous vivrons	Nous vivrions
Vous vivez	Vous viviez	Vous vécûtes	Vous vivrez	Vous vivriez
Ils/Elles vivent	Ils/Elles vivaient	Ils/Elles vécurent	Ils/Elles vivront	Ils/Elles vivraient

Indicative (compound tenses)

Perfect	*Pluperfect*	*Past Anterior*	*Future in the Past*	*Conditional in the Past*
J'ai vécu	J'avais vécu	J'eus vécu	J'aurai vécu	J'aurais vécu
Tu as vécu	Tu avais vécu	Tu eus vécu	Tu auras vécu	Tu aurais vécu
Il/Elle a vécu	Il/Elle avait vécu	Il/Elle eut vécu	Il/Elle aura vécu	Il/Elle aurait vécu
Nous avons vécu	Nous avions vécu	Nous eûmes vécu	Nous aurons vécu	Nous aurions vécu
Vous avez vécu	Vous aviez vécu	Vous eûtes vécu	Vous aurez vécu	Vous auriez vécu
Ils/Elles ont vécu	Ils/Elles avaient vécu	Ils/Elles eurent vécu	Ils/Elles auront vécu	Ils/Elles auraient vécu

Subjunctive (simple tenses)

Present	*Imperfect*
Je vive	Je vécusse
Tu vives	Tu vécusses
Il/Elle vive	Il/Elle vécût
Nous vivions	Nous vécussions
Vous viviez	Vous vécussiez
Ils/Elles vivent	Ils/Elles vécussent

Subjunctive (compound tenses)

Perfect	*Pluperfect*
J'aie vécu	J'eusse vécu
Tu aies vécu	Tu eusses vécu
Il/Elle ait vécu	Il/Elle eût vécu
Nous ayons vécu	Nous eussions vécu
Vous ayez vécu	Vous eussiez vécu
Ils/Elles aient vécu	Ils/Elles eussent vécu

Imperative: Vis, vivons, vivez
Non-personal forms

Infinitive			Gerund	
Simple	*Compound*	*Past participle*	*Simple*	*Compound*
Vivre	Avoir vécu	Vécu	Vivant	Ayant vécu

Voir (*to see*)
Indicative (simple tenses)

Present	*Imperfect*	*Preterit*	*Future*	*Conditional*
Je vois	Je voyais	Je vis	Je verrai	Je verrais
Tu vois	Tu voyais	Tu vis	Tu verras	Tu verrais
Il/Elle voit	Il/Elle voyait	Il/Elle vit	Il/Elle verra	Il/Elle verrait

Indicative (simple tenses) (*cont.*)

Present	Imperfect	Preterit	Future	Conditional
Nous voyons	Nous voyions	Nous vîmes	Nous verrons	Nous verrions
Vous voyez	Vous voyiez	Vous vîtes	Vous verrez	Vous verriez
Ils/Elles voient	Ils/Elles voyaient	Ils/Elles virent	Ils/Elles verront	Ils/Elles verraient

Indicative (compound tenses)

Perfect	Pluperfect	Past Anterior	Future in the Past	Conditional in the Past
J'ai vu	J'avais vu	J'eus vu	J'aurai vu	J'aurais vu
Tu as vu	Tu avais vu	Tu eus vu	Tu auras vu	Tu aurais vu
Il/Elle a vu	Il/Elle avait vu	Il/Elle eut vu	Il/Elle aura vu	Il/Elle aurait vu
Nous avons vu	Nous avions vu	Nous eûmes vu	Nous aurons vu	Nous aurions vu
Vous avez vu	Vous aviez vu	Vous eûtes vu	Vous aurez vu	Vous auriez vu
Ils/Elles ont vu	Ils/Elles avaient vu	Ils/Elles eurent vu	Ils/Elles auront vu	Ils/Elles auraient vu

Subjunctive (simple tenses)

Present	Imperfect
Je voie	Je visse
Tu voies	Tu visses
Il/Elle voie	Il/Elle vît
Nous voyions	Nous vissions
Vous voyiez	Vous vissiez
Ils/Elles voient	Ils/Elles vissent

Subjunctive (compound tenses)

Perfect	Pluperfect
J'aie vu	J'eusse vu
Tu aies vu	Tu eusses vu
Il/Elle ait vu	Il/Elle eût vu
Nous ayons vu	Nous eussions vu
Vous ayez vu	Vous eussiez vu
Ils/Elles aient vu	Ils/Elles eussent vu

Imperative: Vois, voyons, voyez
Non-personal forms

Infinitive		Past participle	Gerund	
Simple	Compound		Simple	Compound
Voir	Avoir vu	Vu	Voyant	Ayant vu

Vouloir (*to want*)
Indicative (simple tenses)

Present	Imperfect	Preterit	Future	Conditional
Je veux	Je voulais	Je voulus	Je voudrai	Je voudrais
Tu veux	Tu voulais	Tu voulus	Tu voudras	Tu voudrais
Il/Elle veut	Il/Elle voulait	Il/Elle voulut	Il/Elle voudra	Il/Elle voudrait
Nous voulons	Nous voulions	Nous voulûmes	Nous voudrons	Nous voudrions
Vous voulez	Vous vouliez	Vous voulûtes	Vous voudrez	Vous voudriez
Ils/Elles veulent	Ils/Elles voulaient	Ils/Elles voulurent	Ils/Elles voudront	Ils/Elles voudraient

Indicative (compound tenses)

Perfect	Pluperfect	Past Anterior	Future in the Past	Conditional in the Past
J'ai voulu	J'avais voulu	J'eus voulu	J'aurai voulu	J'aurais voulu
Tu as voulu	Tu avais voulu	Tu eus voulu	Tu auras voulu	Tu aurais voulu
Il/Elle a voulu	Il/Elle avait voulu	Il/Elle eut voulu	Il/Elle aura voulu	Il/Elle aurait voulu
Nous avons voulu	Nous avions voulu	Nous eûmes voulu	Nous aurons voulu	Nous aurions voulu
Vous avez voulu	Vous aviez voulu	Vous eûtes voulu	Vous aurez voulu	Vous auriez voulu
Ils/Elles ont voulu	Ils/Elles avaient voulu	Ils/Elles eurent voulu	Ils/Elles auront voulu	Ils/Elles auraient voulu

Subjunctive (simple tenses)

Present	Imperfect
Je veuille	Je voulusse
Tu veuilles	Tu voulusses
Il/Elle veuille	Il/Elle voulût
Nous voulions	Nous voulussions
Vous vouliez	Vous voulussiez
Ils/Elles veuillent	Ils/Elles voulussent

Subjunctive (compound tenses)

Perfect	Pluperfect
J'aie voulu	J'eusse voulu
Tu aies voulu	Tu eusses voulu
Il/Elle ait voulu	Il/Elle eût voulu
Nous ayons voulu	Nous eussions voulu
Vous ayez voulu	Vous eussiez voulu
Ils/Elles aient voulu	Ils/Elles eussent voulu

Imperative: Veuille/veux, voulons, veuillez/voulez
Non-personal forms

Infinitive			Gerund	
Simple	Compound	Past participle	Simple	Compound
Vouloir	Avoir voulu	Voulu	Voulant	Ayant voulu

Verbs with spelling changes

Appeler (*to call*)
Indicative (simple tenses)

Present	Imperfect	Preterit	Future	Conditional
J'appelle	J'appelais	J'appelai	J'appellerai	J'appellerais
Tu appelles	Tu appelais	Tu appelas	Tu appelleras	Tu appellerais
Il/Elle appelle	Il/Elle appelait	Il/Elle appela	Il/Elle appellera	Il/Elle appellerait
Nous appelons	Nous appelions	Nous appelâmes	Nous appellerons	Nous appellerions
Vous appelez	Vous appeliez	Vous appelâtes	Vous appellerez	Vous appelleriez
Ils/Elles appellent	Ils/Elles appelaient	Ils/Elles appelèrent	Ils/Elles appelleront	Ils/Elles appelleraient

Indicative (compound tenses)

Perfect	Pluperfect	Past Anterior	Future in the Past	Conditional in the Past
J'ai appelé	J'avais appelé	J'eus appelé	J'aurai appelé	J'aurais appelé
Tu as appelé	Tu avais appelé	Tu eus appelé	Tu auras appelé	Tu aurais appelé
Il/Elle a appelé	Il/Elle avait appelé	Il/Elle eut appelé	Il/Elle aura appelé	Il/Elle aurait appelé
Nous avons appelé	Nous avions appelé	Nous eûmes appelé	Nous aurons appelé	Nous aurions appelé
Vous avez appelé	Vous aviez appelé	Vous eûtes appelé	Vous aurez appelé	Vous auriez appelé
Ils/Elles ont appelé	Ils/Elles avaient appelé	Ils/Elles eurent appelé	Ils/Elles auront appelé	Ils/Elles auraient appelé

Subjunctive (simple tenses)

Present	Imperfect
J'appelle	J'appelasse
Tu appelles	Tu appelasses
Il/Elle appelle	Il/Elle appelât
Nous appelions	Nous appelassions
Vous appeliez	Vous appelassiez
Ils/Elles appellent	Ils/Elles appelassent

Subjunctive (compound tenses)

Perfect	Pluperfect
J'aie appelé	J'eusse appelé
Tu aies appelé	Tu eusses appelé
Il/Elle ait appelé	Il/Elle eût appelé
Nous ayons appelé	Nous eussions appelé
Vous ayez appelé	Vous eussiez appelé
Ils/Elles aient appelé	Ils/Elles eussent appelé

Imperative: Appelle, appelons, appelez
Non-personal forms

Infinitive			Gerund	
Simple	Compound	Past participle	Simple	Compound
Appeler	Avoir appelé	Appelé	Appelant	Ayant appelé

Commencer (*to begin*)
Indicative (simple tenses)

Present	Imperfect	Preterit	Future	Conditional
Je commence	Je commençais	Je commençai	Je commencerai	Je commencerais
Tu commences	Tu commençais	Tu commenças	Tu commenceras	Tu commencerais
Il/Elle commence	Il/Elle commençait	Il/Elle commença	Il/Elle commencera	Il/Elle commencerait
Nous commençons	Nous commencions	Nous commençâmes	Nous commencerons	Nous commencerions
Vous commencez	Vous commenciez	Vous commençâtes	Vous commencerez	Vous commenceriez
Ils/Elles commencent	Ils/Elles commençaient	Ils/Elles commencèrent	Ils/Elles commenceront	Ils/Elles commenceraient

Indicative (compound tenses)

Perfect	Pluperfect	Past Anterior	Future in the Past	Conditional in the Past
J'ai commencé	J'avais commencé	J'eus commencé	J'aurai commencé	J'aurais commencé
Tu as commencé	Tu avais commencé	Tu eus commencé	Tu auras commencé	Tu aurais commencé
Il/Elle a commencé	Il/Elle avait commencé	Il/Elle eut commencé	Il/Elle aura commencé	Il/Elle aurait commencé
Nous avons commencé	Nous avions commencé	Nous eûmes commencé	Nous aurons commencé	Nous aurions commencé
Vous avez commencé	Vous aviez commencé	Vous eûtes commencé	Vous aurez commencé	Vous auriez commencé
Ils/Elles ont commencé	Ils/Elles avaient commencé	Ils/Elles eurent commencé	Ils/Elles auront commencé	Ils/Elles auraient commencé

Subjunctive (simple tenses)

Present	Imperfect
Je commence	Je commençasse
Tu commences	Tu commençasses
Il/Elle commence	Il/Elle commençât
Nous commencions	Nous commençassions
Vous commenciez	Vous commençassiez
Ils/Elles commencent	Ils/Elles commençassent

Subjunctive (compound tenses)

Perfect	Pluperfect
J'aie commencé	J'eusse commencé
Tu aies commencé	Tu eusses commencé
Il/Elle ait commencé	Il/Elle eût commencé
Nous ayons commencé	Nous eussions commencé
Vous ayez commencé	Vous eussiez commencé
Ils/Elles aient commencé	Ils/Elles eussent commencé

Imperative: Commence, commençons, commencez

Non-personal forms

Infinitive		Past participle	Gerund	
Simple	Compound		Simple	Compound
Commencer	Avoir commencé	Commencé	Commençant	Ayant commencé

Jeter (*to throw*)
Indicative (simple tenses)

Present	Imperfect	Preterit	Future	Conditional
Je jette	Je jetais	Je jetai	Je jetterai	Je jetterais
Tu jettes	Tu jetais	Tu jetas	Tu jetteras	Tu jetterais
Il/Elle jette	Il/Elle jetait	Il/Elle jeta	Il/Elle jettera	Il/Elle jetterait
Nous jetons	Nous jetions	Nous jetâmes	Nous jetterons	Nous jetterions
Vous jetez	Vous jetiez	Vous jetâtes	Vous jetterez	Vous jetteriez
Ils/Elles jettent	Ils/Elles jetaient	Ils/Elles jetèrent	Ils/Elles jetteront	Ils/Elles jetteraient

Indicative (compound tenses)

Perfect	Pluperfect	Past Anterior	Future in the Past	Conditional in the Past
J'ai jeté	J'avais jeté	J'eus jeté	J'aurai jeté	J'aurais jeté
Tu as jeté	Tu avais jeté	Tu eus jeté	Tu auras jeté	Tu aurais jeté
Il/Elle a jeté	Il/Elle avait jeté	Il/Elle eut jeté	Il/Elle aura jeté	Il/Elle aurait jeté
Nous avons jeté	Nous avions jeté	Nous eûmes jeté	Nous aurons jeté	Nous aurions jeté
Vous avez jeté	Vous aviez jeté	Vous eûtes jeté	Vous aurez jeté	Vous auriez jeté
Ils/Elles ont jeté	Ils/Elles avaient jeté	Ils/Elles eurent jeté	Ils/Elles auront jeté	Ils/Elles auraient jeté

Subjunctive (simple tenses)

Present	Imperfect
Je jette	Je jetasse
Tu jettes	Tu jetasses
Il/Elle jette	Il/Elle jetât
Nous jetions	Nous jetassions
Vous jetiez	Vous jetassiez
Ils/Elles jettent	Ils/Elles jetassent

Subjunctive (compound tenses)

Perfect	Pluperfect
J'aie jeté	J'eusse jeté
Tu aies jeté	Tu eusses jeté
Il/Elle ait jeté	Il/Elle eût jeté
Nous ayons jeté	Nous eussions jeté
Vous ayez jeté	Vous eussiez jeté
Ils/Elles aient jeté	Ils/Elles eussent jeté

Imperative: Jette, jetons, jetez
Non-personal forms

Infinitive		Past participle	Gerund	
Simple	Compound		Simple	Compound
Jeter	Avoir jeté	Jeté	Jetant	Ayant jeté

Manger (*to eat*)
Indicative (simple tenses)

Present	Imperfect	Preterit	Future	Conditional
Je mange	Je mangeais	Je mangeai	Je mangerai	Je mangerais
Tu manges	Tu mangeais	Tu mangeas	Tu mangeras	Tu mangerais
Il/Elle mange	Il/Elle mangeait	Il/Elle mangea	Il/Elle mangera	Il/Elle mangerait
Nous mangeons	Nous mangions	Nous mangeâmes	Nous mangerons	Nous mangerions
Vous mangez	Vous mangiez	Vous mangeâtes	Vous mangerez	Vous mangeriez
Ils/Elles mangent	Ils/Elles mangeaient	Ils/Elles mangèrent	Ils/Elles mangeront	Ils/Elles mangeraient

Indicative (compound tenses)

Perfect	Pluperfect	Past Anterior	Future in the Past	Conditional in the Past
J'ai mangé	J'avais mangé	J'eus mangé	J'aurai mangé	J'aurais mangé
Tu as mangé	Tu avais mangé	Tu eus mangé	Tu auras mangé	Tu aurais mangé

Indicative (compound tenses) (*cont.*)

Perfect	Pluperfect	Past Anterior	Future in the Past	Conditional in the Past
Il/Elle a mangé	Il/Elle avait mangé	Il/Elle eut mangé	Il/Elle aura mangé	Il/Elle aurait mangé
Nous avons mangé	Nous avions mangé	Nous eûmes mangé	Nous aurons mangé	Nous aurions mangé
Vous avez mangé	Vous aviez mangé	Vous eûtes mangé	Vous aurez mangé	Vous auriez mangé
Ils/Elles ont mangé	Ils/Elles avaient mangé	Ils/Elles eurent mangé	Ils/Elles auront mangé	Ils/Elles auraient mangé

Subjunctive (simple tenses)

Present	Imperfect
Je mange	Je mangeasse
Tu manges	Tu mangeasses
Il/Elle mange	Il/Elle mangeât
Nous mangions	Nous mangeassions
Vous mangiez	Vous mangeassiez
Ils/Elles mangent	Ils/Elles mangeassent

Subjunctive (compound tenses)

Perfect	Pluperfect
J'aie mangé	J'eusse mangé
Tu aies mangé	Tu eusses mangé
Il/Elle ait mangé	Il/Elle eût mangé
Nous ayons mangé	Nous eussions mangé
Vous ayez mangé	Vous eussiez mangé
Ils/Elles aient mangé	Ils/Elles eussent mangé

Imperative: Mange, mangeons, mangez
Non-personal forms

Infinitive			Gerund	
Simple	Compound	Past participle	Simple	Compound
Manger	Avoir mangé	Mangé	Mangeant	Ayant mangé

One model reflexive verb

Se laver (*to wash oneself*)
Indicative (simple tenses)

Present	Imperfect	Preterit	Future	Conditional
Je me lave	Je me lavais	Je me lavai	Je me laverai	Je me laverais
Tu te laves	Tu te lavais	Tu te lavas	Tu te laveras	Tu te laverais
Il/Elle se lave	Il/Elle se lavait	Il/Elle se lava	Il/Elle se lavera	Il/Elle se laverait
Nous nous lavons	Nous nous lavions	Nous nous lavâmes	Nous nous laverons	Nous nous laverions
Vous vous lavez	Vous vous laviez	Vous vous lavâtes	Vous vous laverez	Vous vous laveriez
Ils/Elles se lavent	Ils/Elles se lavèrent	Ils/Elles se lavèrent	Ils/Elles se laveront	Ils/Elles se laveraient

Indicative (compound tenses)

Perfect	Pluperfect	Past Anterior	Future in the Past	Conditional in the Past
Je me suis lavé(e)	Je m'étais lavé(e)	Je me fus lavé(e)	Je me serai lavé(e)	Je me serais lavé(e)
Tu t'es lavé(e)	Tu t'étais lavé(e)	Tu te fus lavé(e)	Tu te seras lavé(e)	Tu te serais lavé(e)
Il/Elle s'est lavé(e)	Il/Elle s'était lavé(e)	Il/Elle se fut lavé(e)	Il/Elle se sera lavé(e)	Il/Elle se serait lavé(e)
Nous nous sommes lavé(e)s	Nous nous étions lavé(e)s	Nous nous fûmes lavé(e)s	Nous nous serons lavé(e)s	Nous nous serions lavé(e)s
Vous vous êtes lavé(e)(s)	Vous vous étiez lavé(e)(s)	Vous vous fûtes lavé(e)(s)	Vous vous serez lavé(e)(s)	Vous vous seriez lavé(e)(s)
Ils/Elles se sont lavé(e)s	Ils/Elles s'étaient lavé(e)s	Ils/Elles se furent lavé(e)s	Ils/Elles se seront lavé(e)s	Ils/Elles se seraient lavé(e)s

Subjunctive (simple tenses)

Present	Imperfect
Je me lave	Je me lavasse
Tu te laves	Tu te lavasses
Il/Elle se lave	Il/Elle se lavât
Nous nous lavions	Nous nous lavassions
Vous vous laviez	Vous vous lavassiez
Ils/Elles se lavent	Ils/Elles se lavassent

Subjunctive (compound tenses)

Perfect	Pluperfect
Je me sois lavé(e)	Je me fusse lavé(e)
Tu te sois lavé(e)	Tu te fusses lavé(e)
Il/Elle se soit lavé(e)	Il/Elle se fût lavé(e)
Nous nous soyons lavé(e)s	Nous nous fussions lavé(e)s
Vous vous soyez lavé(e)(s)	Vous vous fussiez lavé(e)(s)
Ils/Elles se soient lavé(e)s	Ils/Elles fussent lavé(e)s

Imperative: Lave-toi, lavons-nous, lavez-vous

Non-personal forms

Infinitive			Gerund	
Simple	Compound	Past participle	Simple	Compound
Se laver	S'être lavé(e)(s)	Lavé(e)(s)	Se lavant	S'étant lavé(e)(s)

Glossary | Glossaire

Many of the words glossed here are treated in much greater depth in the relevant chapters (e.g., accent, gerund).

Accent, circumflex, grave, acute / *accent circonflexe, grave, aigu*; for **cedilla**, see below	Sign written over a letter, usually a vowel (*a, e, i, o*, and *u*), at least in French.
	The circumflex accent marks the loss of an **s** in Old French. The spelling requires this circumflex. Examples of ô: *hôpital, côte, diplôme, le nôtre, le vôtre, les nôtres, les vôtres*; â: *crâne, théâtre, âpre*; ê: *blême, hêtre, fête*; î: *paraître, connaître, accroître*; û: *jeûne, moût*. The circumflex also occurs over the third person singular of the imperfect subjunctive: *qu'il voulût, qu'il dût*.
	The grave accent distinguishes between certain words: *la/là, ça/çà*. The grave accent over the **e** > **è** indicates an open **e**: *père, mère*. The grave accent over the **u** > **ù** distinguishes between the relative pronoun *où* (*where*), and the coordinating conjunction *ou* (*or*).
	The acute accent is placed over the **e** to indicate a closed sound: *café, fermé, aimé, événement/ évènement, allégement/allègement*. In the last two cases the acute accent is recommended.
	Observation: The decree of December 28, 1976 and the modifications of 1990 allow for the grave accent to be placed over the **e** if it is pronounced as an open **e**.
	See also *dieresis*. Accent is often confused with *stress* – see *stress*.
Accidence / *morphologie*	The part of grammar concerned with changes in the form of words for the expression of tense, person, case, number and so on. Gender is one of the accidences of a **noun**.

Adjective / *adjectif*	A word that defines a **noun**. It agrees with the noun it qualifies. For example: *une **belle** maison, des nuages **gris**, un **grand** garçon* (*a lovely house, gray clouds, a tall boy*).
Adjective, demonstrative / *adjectif démonstratif*	An **adjective** that points to something, e.g., ***cet** homme, **cette** femme, **cette** maison, **ces** rues* (*this man, that woman, that house, those streets*).
Adverb / *adverbe*	A word (or group of words) that modifies a **verb**, **adjective** or another **adverb**, e.g., *Je peux le faire **facilement*** (*I can do it easily*); *Ce pain est **très** bon* (*This bread is very good*).
Agent / *agent*	The person or thing performing the action indicated by the **verb**, e.g., *Le **chat** a attaqué le chien* (*The cat attacked the dog*). Here the agent is the cat, as in the following example: *Le chien a été attaqué par le **chat*** (*The dog was attacked by the cat*).
Agreement / *accord*	There are three kinds of agreement in French: Agreement in number: **Adjectives, verbs** and **articles** agree with the **nouns** and **pronouns** they relate to, e.g., *La fille intelligente **fait ses devoirs**.* Gender agreement: **Adjectives** agree with the **noun** they qualify, e.g., *Un **grand** garçon, une **belle** fille.* Agreement of tense: A correspondence of **tenses** is required in French, e.g., *Je **voulais** que mon frère m'**aide**/m'**aidât*** (R3) (*I wanted my brother to help me*); *Je lui **ai dit** que j'**irai** au cinéma* (*I have told him/her that I will go to the pictures*). See also **verbs**.
Antecedent / *(antécédent*	A word or phrase to which a **pronoun** refers. The word or phrase always precedes the pronoun, e.g., *The boy who lives down the road is a genius. Boy* is the antecedent of *who*. When the antecedent is unclear or indeterminate, the following **verb** is very often in the **subjunctive mood**.
Apocopation / *apocope*	Shortening of some **nouns**, e.g., *télé* for *télévision*, *mat* for *matin*, *radio* for *radioscopie*.
Apposition / *apposition*	Two words placed side by side, so that the second word modifies the first, e.g., *Paris, capitale de la France*. It may be said that *capitale* is in apposition to *Paris*.

Article, definite / *article défini*	Word which, when placed in front of a **noun**, determines it by giving it **gender** and **number**, e.g., *le* père, *la* mère, *les* parents, *les* mères. The English equivalent is the easier, all-purpose *the*.
Article, indefinite / *article indéfini*	Determines a **noun** when placed in front of it, but less precise than the definite article. It indicates gender and number, e.g., *un* disque dur, *une* clé USB, *des* portables/ordinateurs, *des* écrans plats. The English equivalent is *a/some*.
Asterisk / *astérisque*	Orthographical sign in the form of a star (∗) which can indicate a note or a point requiring the reader's attention.
Atonic/unstressed vowel / *voyelle ou syllabe atone*	A vowel, syllable or word which does not bear any stress. These are usually short words: *Le est une syllabe atone* (The word *le* is an unstressed word).
Augmentative / *augmentatif*	Affix (suffix or prefix) that may be added to a word to express *big* or *great*. Augmentatives are very common in Italian (*librone* = *big book*) and Spanish (*librote* = *big book*) but are really quite sparse in French: *archicélèbre, archiconnu, archifaux, archiriche, archiplein, hyperstressé, richissime*. The suffix −**asse** usually has a pejorative implication: *paperasse(s), fadasse*. See also **diminutive**.
Cedilla / *cédille*	The letter **ç**, or *c cédille*. The c cedilla is followed by the vowels **a**, **o** or **u**, and indicates that the **c** is to be pronounced as an **s** – *façade, garçon* – and not like a **c** as in *cas*.
Clause / *proposition*	Words forming part of a sentence containing a **finite verb**. In the sentence *Je pense qu'Irène va venir, Irène va venir* is a (subordinate) clause.
Clause, main / *proposition principale*	A clause on which depends a secondary clause, or more than one secondary clause. In the sentence *Si tu y vas maintenant et si tu vois ton père, on pourra partir cet après-midi, on pourra partir cet après-midi* is the main clause. A main clause can also stand alone as a sentence, e.g., *J'ai descendu les escaliers* (I went down the stairs), or even *Je parle*.
Clause, subordinate / *proposition de subordination*	A **clause** in a sentence that depends on a **main clause** to make sense, e.g., *Je suis allé(e) au marché avant que mon frère n'arrive* (I went to

the market before my brother arrived). *Je suis allé(e) au marché* is the main clause, while *avant que mon frère n'arrive* is the subordinate clause.

Comparison / *comparatif*	Applies to **adjectives** and **adverbs** that are modified to convey greater or lesser intensity, e.g., *meilleur, pire, moins / plus intelligent* (*better, worse, less intelligent / more intelligent*).
Complement / *complément*	Word, **phrase** or **clause** that completes the meaning of a sentence. *A genius* is the complement in the senence *She is a genius. He would be early* is the complement in *I hoped he would be early.*
Conjugation / *conjugaison*	Model followed by **verb** forms. There are three regular **conjugations** in French: 1st group: *parler, danser, aimer, manger*; 2nd group: *finir, choisir, établir*; 3rd group: *répondre, vendre.* There are numerous **irregular verbs**, which can confuse even French speakers, especially children.
Conjunction / *conjonction*	Any word or group of words, but not a **relative pronoun**, that connects words or **phrases**, e.g., *J'ai eu l'entrée et le plat principal mais pas le dessert* (I had the first course **and** the second but not the dessert).
Consonant / *consonne*	A speech sound or letter other than a **vowel**, e.g., **b, c, d**: *les vingt consonnes de l'alphabet français.*
Determiner / *déterminant*	A word such as a number, article or personal pronoun that determines or limits the meaning of a noun phrase: *l'article, l'adjectif possessif, le numéral et le démonstratif sont des déterminants. Son* is a determiner in *son chat noir.*
Dieresis/diaeresis / *tréma*	Orthographical sign placed above **e** > **ë**, **i** > **ï** or **u** > **ü** in the syllables *aigüe, contigüe, haïr, naïf, Noël.* This produces a pronunciation of two syllables of two distinct vowel sounds where normally there is a diphthong, e.g., *pied, lien.*
Diminutive / *diminutif*	Letters added to the end of a word (**suffix**) to indicate the meaning of *small*. This often conveys an affectionate tone, and is often used with children. The French do have some diminutives but nowhere near as many as Spanish or Italian speakers: *mignon > mignonnet, table > tablette, jupe > jupon,*

	Pierre > *Pierrot, Jean* > *Jeannot*. The opposite of the diminutive is the **augmentative** (see above), as in *caisse* > *caisson*, but there are not many of these in French, although in Spanish and Italian they are very numerous.
Enclitic / *enclitique*	Relates to a monosyllabic and unaccentuated word or form that is treated as a **suffix** of the preceding word. The French enclitic is more common than the English equivalent since many pronouns are attached to verbs under certain conditions, e.g., *ce* > *qu'est-ce*. Examples of unaccentuated pronouns placed after the verb: *Conseille-**moi**, Donne-**le-moi**.*
Figure of speech / *figure de style ou de rhéthorique*	Expression of language, such as a metaphor, by which the literal meaning of the word is not used, e.g., *une source de chagrin, un monument de bêtise* are metaphors.
Gender / *genre*	Gender what distinguishes **nouns** and **pronouns**. All nouns and pronouns have a gender, not just male and female human beings and animals, e.g., *le garçon* (the boy), *la fille* (the girl), *le soleil* (the sun), *la lune* (the moon), *Je le vois* (I see him), *Je la vois* (I see her). Agreement must be made between the noun and **adjective** or **past participle**, as used to form the **perfect tenses**, with **avoir**: *une maison blanche, Je l'ai vue* (I saw her).
Interjection / *interjection*	Words that express an exclamation and denote any strong emotion, e.g., *Grand/Bon dieu !, Doux Jésus !* (Wow!, Jeez!, Geez!).
Language, figurative / *sens figuré*	Language that uses a figure of speech, e.g., *Elle a lutté **comme un lion*** (She fought like a lion); *brandir **le drapeau de la liberté*** (to raise the standard of freedom); *Ses projets commencent à **se dessiner*** (Her plans are starting to take shape).
Morpheme / *morphème*	Speech element having a meaning or grammatical function that cannot be divided into further such elements, e.g., *morphème lexical (lexème) / grammatical / discontinu*. The smallest unit of meaning: *Il/Elle va/parle*.
Noun / *nom/substantif*	A word used to name a person, thing or concept. Nouns can be concrete – *homme, voiture* – or abstract – *joie* (joy), *malaise* (uneasiness). There is no difference between *nom* and *substantif*.

Number, cardinal / *nombre cardinal*	A cardinal number enables us to count: *un, deux, trois...*
Number, ordinal / *nombre ordinal*	A number indicating order in which things appear: *premier, second, troisième... (first, second, third...).*
Orthography / *orthographe*	Correct way of spelling words and punctuating sentences. The more usual term in English is *spelling,* but *orthographe* is the normal word in French. *Orthographe d'usage* or *orthographe d'accord* indicates the usual spelling of words according to their function in a sentence or expression.
Phoneme / *phonème*	One of the set of speech sounds that serves to distinguish one word from another, e.g., *entre* "*pain,*" "*vin*" *et* "*rein*" (between *pain, vin* and *rein* there is only one change of phoneme. In French one can speak of *phonème vocalique, consonantique, oral, nasal, sourd, sonore.* French has thirty-six phonemes (sixteen vowels and twenty consonants).
Phrase / *locution*	A meaningful group of words in a sentence that does not contain a finite **verb**, e.g., *dans le jardin (in the garden), dans la rue (down the street).* Not to be confused with the French *phrase,* which means both *sentence* and *phrase.*
Prefix / *préfixe*	**Syllable(s)** attached to the front of a word. There are many prefixes in French, e.g., **anti**raciste, **anti**constitutionnel, **contre**-attaquer, **entre**tenir, **més**estimer, **pré**établir, **re**mettre.
Preposition / *préposition*	A word that usually comes before a **noun**. It expresses the relation of things to each other in respect of time and place, e.g., **Avec** mon ami, je vais **au** Mexique; **à** six heures; **à** la messe; **sur** la chaise; **sous** l'arbre; Il vient **de** l'Arizona.
Preposition, compound/*préposition / mot composé*	Juxtaposition of two or even more prepositions, e.g., *Elle n'a pas réussi à son examen* **à cause de** *son rhume; Il a sauté* **par-dessus** *le mur.*
Pronoun, demonstrative / *pronom démonstratif*	Pronoun that indicates something, e.g., **Celle-ci** *est bonne,* **celle-là** *est mauvaise (This one is good, that one is bad).*
Pronoun, interrogative / *pronom interrogatif*	Pronoun involving a question, e.g., *Qui a gagné le prix ? (Who has won the prize?).* Other interrogative pronouns are: *que ? (what?) quoi ? (what?), lequel ? / laquelle ? (which?), combien ? (how many/much?).*

Pronoun, personal / *pronom personnel*	A word that replaces a noun. There are four kinds of personal pronouns: subject, direct- and indirect-object pronouns, and disjunctive pronouns, e.g., *je, tu, il, elle, nous, vous, ils, elles,* (*I, you, he* etc.) are subject pronouns. *Me, te, se, nous, vous* and *les* (*me, you, him, her, us, you, them*) are direct-object pronouns while *à moi/toi/lui/elle/nous/vous/eux* and *elles* (*to me/you/him/her/us/you/them*) are disjunctive pronouns: *Viens avec* **moi**; *J'y vais avec* **toi**; *Je suis tombé sur* **lui**.
Pronoun, possessive / *pronom possessif*	A pronoun indicating possession, e.g., *le mien/la mienne, le tien/la tienne, le sien/la sienne, le nôtre/la nôtre, le vôtre/la vôtre, le leur/la leur* (*mine, yours, etc.*). *Où est la mienne/le mien ?* (*Where's mine?*)
Quantifier / *indicateur de quantification*	A word or phrase, such as *quelques* (*some*), *tous* (*all*) or *aucun/aucune* (*none*), which expresses quantity.
Question, direct / *question, style direct*	A **sentence** asking a straight question, e.g., *Où vas-tu ? Où allez-vous ?* (*Where are you going?*).
Question, indirect / *question, style indirect*	Question included in a **subordinate clause**, e.g., *Elle m'a demandé où j'allais* (*She asked me where I was going*).
Relative pronoun / *pronom relatif*	Links a relative clause to what precedes it, e.g., *J'ai vu le garçon* **qui** *est venu hier* (*I saw the boy who came yesterday*). Other relative pronouns are *celui qui, que, lequel*.
Singular/plural / *singulier/pluriel*	A singular **noun** refers to one object while a plural noun refers to more than one, e.g., *l'arbre/les arbres* (*the tree / the trees*).
Stem / *racine*	Root form of a word, e.g., *achat* is the stem of the verb *acheter* and the noun *acheteur*.
Stress / stressed syllable / *accent tonique / accentuation*	The syllable of a word spoken most forcibly or loudly. Stress is less important in French than it is in English, Spanish or Italian since the weight of the accent usually falls on the last sounded syllable of a word or sentence. In normal French, speech is more uniform than in the other languages quoted above. In *appeler*, the stress falls on **er**, in *appel*, the stress falls on **el**, in *courage* the stress falls on *age*, while in *chien* the stress falls on *en*. Of course, if one were to introduce any kind of emotion into the expression, the stress could change. In the sentence *Mais c'est* **im**possible *!* the stress could easily fall on **im**. Another example: *C'est* **for**midable *!*

Suffix / *suffixe*	**Syllable(s)** attached to the end of a word. These are sometimes **augmentatives** and **diminutives**, e.g., *caisson, jardinet, tablette*. Many pronouns are suffixes used **enclitically**.
Superlative / *superlatif*	Applies to **adjectives** and **adverbs** that are modified to the greatest or least intensity, e.g., *c'est le **meilleur** / le plus mauvais étudiant*.
Syllable / *syllabe*	A combination or set of units of sound. It always contains a **vowel**. *Va* contains one syllable, *allons* contains two syllables and *partiront* contains three syllables.
Verb / *verbe*	A verb is a word that indicates the occurrence or performance of an action or the existence of a state. A sentence cannot usually be called a "sentence" if it is deprived of a verb. It is the dominant feature of a sentence. The **infinitive** of the verb is the headword in a dictionary. Examples in French with their English counterparts: *courir (to run), faire (to do, to make), frapper (to hit), aimer (to like, to love), croire (to believe), penser (to think).*
Vowel / *voyelle*	Letter that represents a speech sound characterized by an absence of obstruction in its emission. A, **e**, **i**, **o** and **u** are vowels.

Verbs / *verbes*

Agreement / *accord*	Correspondence between masculine and feminine **nouns** and parts of the verb, and between the plural of nouns and verb endings: *Elle est assise (She is sitting down)*; *Les garçons jouent dans la rue (The boys are playing in the street).*
Auxiliary verb / *verbe auxiliaire*	An auxiliary verb helps to form a compound tense or precedes an **infinitive**. In the sentence *Je vais voir un film, vais* is the auxiliary verb.
Compound tense / *temps composé*	Tense made up of the verbs *avoir/être* and a *past participle*, e.g., *Elle est partie; Il avait/aurait marché/parlé/écrit.*
Conditional / *conditionnel*, Conditional in the past / *passé du conditionnel*	Includes a condition and a result, e.g., *Si tu me **donnais** l'argent, **j'achèterais** le pain (If you gave me the money, I'd buy the bread). Si tu m'**avais donné** l'argent, j' **aurais acheté** le pain (If you had given me the money I would have bought the bread).*

Double compound perfect / *passé surcomposé*	Compound tense that replaces in speech, less in writing, the **pluperfect tense**. Not used by any means by all French speakers and not recognized by many. A tense that merely requires comment but is not necessary for foreign speakers of French: *Je suis partie quand j'ai eu terminé* (*I left when I had finished*).
Finite verb / *verbe conjugué*	The form of a verb which is not the **infinitive**, e.g., *il* **court** (*he runs*), *je* **lis** (*I read*), *nous* **parlons** (*we speak*).
Future perfect / *futur antérieur*	**Tense** that refers to a future event that will have happened before a given moment, e.g., *Nous* **aurions dû** *arriver avant qu'elle ne sorte/sortît* (R3) (*We ought to have arrived before she left*).
Future tense / *futur*	**Tense** referring to the future, e.g., *j'irai* (*I'll go*).
Gerund / *gérondif*	French verb form ending in –**ant**, like *ing* in English, e.g., *marchant* (*walking*), *courant* (*running*), *allant* (going), *lisant* (*reading*).
Historic present / *présent de narration*	Present tense used to invest a description or narration with a greater vividness. The tense moves from the past to the present: *Je me* **promenais** *tranquillement sur la plage et, voilà que je* **tombe** *sur mon grand ami qui me* **raconte** *l'histoire de son frère* (*I was wandering peacefully along the beach, when I bump into my great friend who tells me the story of his brother*).
Imperative mood / *mode impératif*	Part of the verb which conveys a command, e.g., *Parle !* (*speak!*), *Va-t'en !* (*go away!*), *Mangez !* (*eat!*).
Imperfect / *imparfait*	**Tense** indicating a continuous or repeated action in the past, e.g., *Je jouais au golf* (*I used to play / was playing / would play / played golf*). The French imperfect tense is much simpler and less varied than the imperfect in English
Infinitive / *infinitif*	Part of a **verb** which does not change, and which you always find in dictionaries, e.g., *vivre* (*to live*), *marcher* (*to walk*), *voir* (*to see*).
Intransitive / *intransitif*	A **verb** that does not have a direct object or complement. *Aller* (*to go*) and *venir* (*to come*) are intransitive verbs. See **transitive**.
Irregular verb / *verbe irrégulier*	A **verb** that does not conform to a pattern. Very inconvenient for foreigner learners and French-speaking children. *Aller* and *être* are such verbs. Interestingly and understandably enough, just as they do in English, many

French-speaking children try to "regularize" irregular verbs. For example, they may say *bouillis* instead of *bous* or *cueillirai* instead of *cueillerai*, and even *Je vais m'assir* instead of *Je vais m'asseoir* (of course, this practice is not to be copied).

Mood, indicative / *mode indicatif*	Part of a verb which makes a clear statement, e.g., *Il est prêt* (He's ready); *J'aime le chocolat* (I like chocolate).
Mood, subjunctive / *mode subjonctif*	Part of a **verb** which indicates emotion, pleasure, fear, uncertainty, doubt. It is often, but not always, used in a subordinate clause. Has nearly disappeared in English (e.g., *It is possible he **be** right*), but very common in all **tenses** in Spanish and Italian, becoming less common in French where the imperfect subjunctive is very infrequent, and is only found nowadays in writing and the third-person singular, although it was very common in all persons in literature of past centuries, e.g., *Il est possible que Georges **ait*** (present subjunctive) *raison* (*Georges may be right*); *Elle avait peur que son frère ne **sortît*** (imperfect subjunctive) *trop tard* (*She was afraid her brother would go out too late*).
Past anterior / *passé antérieur*	Tense made up of the **preterit** / **past historic** of *avoir* / *être* and a **past participle**, e.g., *Quand Marie **fut arrivée**, nous sortîmes en ville* (*When Marie [had] arrived, we went to town*); *Dès qu'il **eut fini**, il se leva* (*As soon as he [had] finished, he got up*). This **tense** is only used in elevated language, for instance in novels. The **tense** in common discourse is the **pluperfect**, or, in the speech of some French speakers, the **double compound perfect** which does not find favor with many, and is not even recognized.
Past participle / *participe passé*	Part of the **verb** which, in conjunction with the verb *avoir* or *être*, makes up the perfect tense, e.g., *j'ai **marché**; elle est **partie*** (*I have walked; she has gone*).
Perfect tense / *passé composé*	**Compound tense** made up of *avoir* or *être* and **past participle**, e.g., *J'ai **vu*** (*I have seen*); *Elles **sont revenues*** (*They've come back*).
Pluperfect / *plus-que-parfait*	**Tense** formed by **imperfect** of *avoir* (*avais*, etc.) or *être* (*étais*, etc.), and the **past participle**, e.g.,

	*Quand nous **avions dîné**, nous sommes allés au cinéma* (*When we had eaten we went to the movies*); *Aussitôt qu'elles **étaient parties**, on s'est couché* (*As soon as they had gone, we went to bed*).
Present participle / *gérondif*	Name given to the –ing part of the verb in English and to the –ant ending in French, e.g., parl**ant** (*speaking*), *mangeant* (*eating*), lis**ant** (*reading*).
Preterit / past historic/ *passé simple*	Simple past tense. Refers to a specific action in the past. The British English spelling is **preterite**. Almost entirely replaced by the **passé composé** in speech, but in vigorous use in literature, although less so in journalism. French children learn it very early on since it is a very common ingredient of fairy tales, Walt Disney tales and so on. Again very common in narrating distant events in the past and associated with historical events: *Le théâtre principal des opérations **fut** la frontière entre le Mexique et le Texas* (*The main theater of operations was the frontier between Mexico and Texas*).
Pronominal verb / *verbe pronominal*	A **verb** that is conjugated in all its forms with the **pronouns** *me, te, se, nous, vous*. This means that the subject and the reflexive pronoun refer to the same person, e.g., *Je **me** vois dans la glace* (*I see myself in the mirror*); *Je **me** rase tous les jours* (*I shave every day*). Pronominal verbs are a common characteristic of all Romance languages.
Reflexive verb / *verbe réfléchi*	A **verb** conveying an action done by a person or thing to himselfitself, e.g., *Je **me** lave* (*I wash* [*myself*]); *Le soleil **se cache** derrière les nuages* (*The sun hides behind the clouds*). The English does not have a reflexive form in the second case but it is necessary in French. Otherwise, you would be wondering what the sun was hiding. There are many **verbs** that behave non-reflexively and reflexively in French. In effect, this is the same phenomenon as a **pronominal verb**.
Regular verb / *verbe régulier*	A **verb** that conforms to a pattern. Very convenient for foreign learners, and French-speaking children. *Parler, finir* and *vendre* are regular verbs.

Tense | *temps*   Part of the **verb** which indicates the moment
                                     when an action or thought takes place, e.g.,
                                     nage is the present tense of the verb *nager*.
                                     Nageais is the imperfect tense of the verb
                                     nager.

Tonic accent | *accent*   An accent in which an emphatic syllable stands
   tonique   out from the other syllables in a word, but no
                                     written marker indicates this, as in Spanish.
                                     The tonic accent is very common in English,
                                     Spanish and Italian, but less so in French,
                                     which is why less critical importance is given
                                     to it in French. Any stress that falls on a
                                     French word is at the end, and this is uniform:
                                     Elle laissa tomber son chapeau.

Transitive | *transitif*   A verb that takes a **direct object**, e.g., *Je vois* la
                                     porte (*I can see the door*). See **intransitive**.

Voice, active/passive | The active voice relates to the subject of the
   voix active | passive   sentence performing the action. The sentence
                                     The boy broke the window is in the active voice,
                                     whereas *The window was broken by the boy* is in
                                     the passive voice. A **verb** in the active voice
                                     can be **transitive** or **intransitive** but a verb in
                                     the passive voice can only be transitive.

Latin terms

These are still used by French speakers in language appreciation. Greek
and Latin are still studied in France so it is worthwhile including the terms
below. They also occur in all-French grammars and dictionaries.

Nominative case | *cas*   Denotes a case of nouns and pronouns in
   nominatif   inflected languages that is used especially to
                                     identify the subject of a finite verb, e.g., **La**
                                     fille *parle avec son père* (*The girl speaks with her*
                                     father). **Fille** is in the nominative case.

Vocative case | *cas*   Denotes a case of nouns in inflected languages
   vocatif   when the referent of the noun is being
                                     addressed, e.g., **Ô Dieu**, *aide-moi !* (*Oh God, help*
                                     me!). *Dieu* is in the vocative case.

Accusative case | *cas*   Denotes a case of nouns, pronouns and
   accusatif   adjectives in inflected languages that is used
                                     to identify the direct object of a finite verb,
                                     e.g., *Je touche* **la table** (*I touch the table*). *Table* is
                                     in the accusative case.

Genitive case / *cas génitif*	Denotes a case of nouns and pronouns in inflected languages used to indicate a relation of possession or ownership, e.g., *La maison de Philippe* (*Philippe's house*). *Philippe* is in the genitive case. The expression *cas génitif* is, in fact, little used, but is included for completion's sake.
Dative case / *cas datif*	Denotes a case of nouns and pronouns in inflected languages used to express the indirect object, e.g., *Je donne le livre à Pierre* (*I give the book to Pierre*). *Pierre* is in the dative case.
Ablative case / *cas ablatif*	Denotes a case of nouns or pronouns indicating the agent, instrument or manner of the action, e.g., *Le chien a été frappé par le garçon* (*The dog was hit by the boy*). *Garçon* is in the ablative case.
Ablative absolute / *ablatif absolu*	Grammatical construction in which a past participle stands by itself with, for example, a noun, and replaces a finite verb, e.g., *Fini les pourparlers, les délégations se sont dispersées* (*Once the talks were over, the delegations dispersed*); *Une fois transmis le message, elle est repartie* (*As soon as she had communicated the message, she went away*). This type of construction is not uncommon, and is used more in writing than in speech. Note that *fini*, preceding as it does *pourparlers*, does not agree with this plural noun.

Bibliography | Bibliographie

The following annotated list includes not only grammars on the French language, but also volumes on usage and dictionaries.

Grammars

Ball, R., 2000. *Colloquial French Grammar*. Oxford, Blackwell. Excellent and entertaining coverage of the lower registers of spoken French grammar.

Bled, É., and Bled, O., 2007. *Orthographe, grammaire*. Paris, Hachette. This grammar is used and recommended in French schools.

Delatour, Y., 2004. *Nouvelle grammaire du français*. Paris, Hachette. Excellent grammar written with foreign students in mind.

Grevisse, M., 2005. *Le petit Grevisse: Grammaire française*. Bruxelles, de Boeck and Larcier. A précis of the monumental work below and very clear and helpful.

Grevisse, M., and Goosse, A., 2008. *Le bon usage*. Bruxelles, Duculot, de Boeck and Larcier. A giant of a grammar. Has everything you want to know. Two drawbacks: finding a particular point and discovering that too many examples are taken from literary sources of bygone eras. Some illustrations no longer suit the modern world.

Guéry, L., 2005. *Dictionnaire des règles typographiques*. Paris, Victoires Éditions. All you want to know about punctuation, accents, lower case, upper case and so on.

L'Huillier, M., 1999. *Advanced French Grammar*. Cambridge, Cambridge University Press. Very complete for the advanced student.

Price, G., 2007. *A Comprehensive French Grammar*, 5th edn. Oxford, Blackwell. Full coverage of French grammar; has been highly praised.

Spelling (exclusively)

Bescherelle, 2000. *L'orthographe pour tous*. Paris, Hatier.

Bled, É., 1999. *Orthographe*, Collection Éducation. Paris, Hachette.

Jouette, A., 2002. *Dictionnaire de l'orthographe*, Collection les usuels poche. Paris, Éditions Le Robert.

Usage and grammar

Batchelor, R. E., and Offord, M., 2006. *A Guide to Contemporary French Usage*, 3rd edn. Cambridge, Cambridge University Press.

Bernet, C., and Rézeau, P., 1989. *Dictionnaire du français parlé*. Paris, Seuil.

Blampain, D., *et al.*, 1997. *Le français en Belgique*. Bruxelles, Duculot. Excellent coverage, not just of Belgium but of Belgium's former colonies, written with thirty-two collaborators.

Brunet, F., 1996. *Dictionnaire bilingue de l'argot d'aujourd'hui: Français–Anglais/ French–English*. Paris, Pocket.

de Villers, M.-É., 2003. *MULTI dictionnaire de la langue française*, 4th edn. Montréal, Québec Amérique. A splendid work, again of a hybrid nature, treating grammar and vocabulary in the same context. The treatment is French-Canadian and numerous examples are from North America, notably Canada. A sheer joy to browse through.

Hanse, J., and Blampain, D., 2005. *Nouveau dictionnaire des difficultés du français moderne*, 5th edn. Bruxelles, de Boeck. Refreshing view of the hybrid nature of the French language, seen both lexically and grammatically. A new way of considering grammar in general and presented from a Belgian point of view. Cannot be praised enough.

Hawkins, R., and Towell, R., 1990. *French Grammar and Usage*, 2nd edn. London, Arnold.

Hérail, R., and Lovatt, E., 1987. *Dictionary of Modern Colloquial French*. London, Routledge. For those who wish to indulge their most spirited attraction for the French language.

Peeters, B., *et al.*, 2000. *Tu parles ! ?, Le français dans tous ses états*. Paris, Flammarion. A very modern and even iconoclastic view of the state of modern French. Exhilarating.

Pratt, Fletcher. 1939. *Secret and Urgent: The Story of Codes and Ciphers*. London, Ribbon Books. For those interested in the frequency of French letters. The most frequently occurring letter in the French language is incontestably the e with its accented partners: é, è, ê, ë. A, à, â and ä come in second place.

Vandel, P., 1993. *Le DICO français/français*. Paris, J.-C. Lattès.

Walter, H., 1997. *L'aventure des mots français venus d'ailleurs*. Paris, Laffont. A magnificent work that burrows deep down into the etymology of words coming into the French language from far and wide.

  1998. *Le français d'ici, de là, de là-bas*. Paris, Éditions J.-C. Lattès. Most adventurous and enthralling study of the worldwide phenomenon of the French language. Combines the most serious scholarship and humor. To be applauded.

Miscellaneous

Balibar, Françoise, 2006. *Marie Curie*. Paris, Gallimard.

Bayrou, François, 1994. *Henri IV*. Paris, Flammarion.

Camus, Albert, 1962a. *La peste*. Paris, Gallimard.

    1962b. *L'étranger*. Paris, Gallimard.

    1962c. *La chute*. Paris, Gallimard.

Chateaubriand, François-René de, 1951. *Mémoires d'outre-tombe*, 2 vols. Paris, Gallimard.

Condeescu, N. N., 1975. *Traité d'histoire de la langue française*. Bucarest, Editura didactica si pedagogica.

Curie, Ève, 1938. *Marie Curie*. Paris, Gallimard.

de Gaulle, Charles, 1956. *Mémoires de guerre*, vol. II: *L'unité : 1942–1944*. Paris, Plon.

Devos, Raymond, 1989. *À plus d'un titre : sketches inédits*. Paris, Éditions Olivier Orban.

Gide, André, 1925. *Les faux-monnayeurs*. Paris, Gallimard.

    1961. *Les caves du Vatican*. Paris, Gallimard.

Giroud, Françoise, 1981. *Une femme honorable*. Paris, Fayard.

Green, Julien, 1927. *Adrienne Mesurat*. Paris, Plon.

    1936. *Minuit*. Paris, Plon.

    1955. *Le malfaiteur*. Paris, Plon.

Hugo, Victor, 1949. *Choix de poésies lyriques*. Paris, Larousse.

Luminet, Jean-Pierre, 2008a. *Le secret de Copernic*. Paris, LGF.

    2008b. *La discorde céleste*. Paris, J.-C. Lattès.

Malraux, André, 1975. *Les conquérants*. Paris, Gallimard.

    1976a. *La condition humaine*. Paris, Gallimard.

    1976b. *L'espoir*. Paris, Gallimard.

Mauriac, François, 1932–1939. *Journal*. Paris, La table ronde.

Némirovsky, Irène, 2004. *Suite française*. Paris, Éditions Denoël.

Pascal, Blaise, 1950. *Pensées*. Paris, Hachette.

Perrault, Charles, 1983. *Cendrillons : édition illustrée en couleurs*. Lisbon, Erres e Esses.

Préclin, E., 1937. *Histoire des États-Unis*. Paris, Armand Colin.

Robb, Graham, 2007. *The Discovery of France*. London, Picador.

Saint-Exupéry, Antoine de, 1953. *Pilote de guerre*. Paris, Gallimard.

Senancour, Étienne Pivert de, 1904. *Obermann*. London, William Ryder and Son Ltd.

Taylor, Alex, 2010. *Bouche bée tout ouïe . . . ou comment tomber amoureux des langues*. Paris, J.-C. Lattès.

Truss, Lynne, 2003. *Eats, Shoots and Leaves*. London, Profile.

Voltaire, 1988. *Candide*. London, Hodder and Stoughton.

Walter, Henriette, 1998. *Le français d'ici, de là, de là-bas*. Paris, J.-C. Lattès.

General index / Index général

This is a general index for grammatical structures. It does not contain all the lexical elements, as this would make it unmanageable. The subjunctive has a separate index (see below). (Abbreviations: adj. = adjective; adv. = adverb; fut. = future; imp. = imperfect; imper. = imperative; ind. = indicative; inf. = infinitive; perf. = perfect; plup. = pluperfect; prep. = preposition; pp = past participle; pres. = present; pres. part. = present participle; subj. = subjunctive)

à, 587
à la fois, 631
à + le = au, 102
à + les = aux, 102
à même, 605
à mesure que, 388, 632
à peine, 389
à peine + pp, 225
à savoir, 631
à tel point que, 632
a(n), 110
à/au travers, 605
able, to be, 345
abuser, 571
accommoder, 572
accorder, with passive, 329
(s')accorder, 572
accourir + avoir/être, 201
accroire, 334
achever, 572
acute accent, 72
adj., singular versus plural, 510
adj. as adverb, 516
adj. + gender, 507
adj. + no comparative, 543
adj. of color, 515
adj. + prep. + inf., 570
adj. used as noun, 519
adv., no English equivalent, 524
adv. of affirmation, 538
adv. of doubt, 538
adv. of manner, 524

adv. of place, 537
adv. of quantity/intensity, 528
adv. of time, 333
agir, s', 321, 380, 392
ago, 379
agreement with pp, 513
aimer, 572
ainsi que, 632
alinéa, 84
aller, idiomatic uses of, 358
aller de soi, 381
alors, 533, 631
alors que, 387, 632
anti + adj., 520, 642
anti + noun, 642
apostrophe, 84
apprendre, 568
(s')approcher, 317
après que, 390, 632
arracher, 572
(s')arrêter, 310, 317
asseoir, 298
assortir, 299
assurer, 572
asterisk, 85
(s')attaquer, 317
attendre, 572
attendre à ce que, s', 393
attendre que, 632
attribuer with passive, 329
aucun, 622, 632
au-dessous de, 591

Subjunctive index / Index du mode subjonctif

This index includes much vocabulary necessary for the handling of the subjunctive. All the entries pertain to Chapter 44.